HOUGHTON MIFFLIN SOCIAL STUDIES

Across the Centuries

TEACHER'S EDITION

Beverly J. Armento

Jacqueline M. Córdova

J. Jorge Klor de Alva

Gary B. Nash

Franklin Ng

Christopher L. Salter

Louis E. Wilson

Karen K. Wixson

Houghton Mifflin Company • Boston
Atlanta • Dallas • Geneva, Illinois • Princeton, New Jersey • Palo Alto

Houghton Mifflin Social Studies
Consultants and Reviewers

Photo Credits: **T3** (t) © John Henley/The Stock Market; (m) © Mugshots/The Stock Market; (b) © Jose L. Pelaez/The Stock Market; **T10** © Gabe Palmer/The Stock Market; **T17** Ira Garber; **T19** © Gary Landsman/The Stock Market; **T26** (t) E. Curtis, University of Washington Libraries (detail): (b) J.G. Heron/ Stock Boston; **T27** (l) Museum of American Political Life, University of Hartford, photo by Sally Andersen-Bruce: (m) Henry Moore. *Family Group.* 1948-49. Bronze (cast 1950). 59 1/4 x 461/2", at base 45 x 29 7/8". Museum of Modern Art, New York. A. Conger Goodyear Fund: (r) Scala/Art Resource, NY

Printed in U.S.A.

ISBN: 0-395-93071-5

123456789-VH-04 03 02 01 00 99 98

Welcome to
Across the Centuries

The goal of Houghton Mifflin Social Studies is the development of literate citizens—individuals with the knowledge, skills, and civic values they need to become active and reflective participants in the world of the twenty-first century. Our program weaves together knowledge, skills, and citizenship to form an integrated program. And because we focus on depth rather than breadth, our program helps you take the time to truly captivate, develop, question, and stretch your students. Take a moment and discover some of the ideas and people that make this program a powerful classroom tool.

HOUGHTON MIFFLIN SOCIAL STUDIES
Table of Contents

Meet Your Authors

Dr. Beverly Armento

"The overall goal of a sound social studies program is the development of an informed, active, caring decision maker who draws on meaningful knowledge, who has well-developed skills, who has a sense of what's important and what's not, and who is then able to take all of that and apply it to social issues."

*Professor of
Social Studies Education
Department of
Middle/Secondary Education
and Instructional Technology
Georgia State University,
Atlanta, GA*

Dr. J. Jorge Klor de Alva

"First all boys and girls need to see people like themselves in their textbooks. Then students will be ready to respect others who are different from themselves."

*President
University of Phoenix,
Phoenix, AZ*

**Dr. Jacqueline
M. K. Córdova**

"LEP students may be able to share with classmates related cultural or historical information based on their prior life experiences and academic exposure. Inviting their participation is one of the most significant ways to build self-esteem, to actively engage them in the lesson, and to stimulate prior knowledge of the topic."

*Professor of Spanish
and TESOL
Department of Foreign
Languages and Literatures
California State University,
Fullerton*

Dr. Gary B. Nash

"Instruction in social studies should be based on the belief that an accurate portrayal of historical figures will inspire more admiration of them among students, not less. It may also help young people to recognize more of the hero in themselves, instead of viewing heroism as a trait reserved for superhuman men and women."

*Professor of History
University of California,
Los Angeles*

Dr. Franklin Ng

"History opens up new vistas and panoramas. Explored with creativity and imagination, it socializes us into the human community. We learn about diverse lifeways and the many paths to the contemporary world in which we live."

Franklin Ng

*Professor of Anthropology
California State University,
Fresno*

Dr. Christopher L. Salter

"An understanding of the needs and costs of land transformation is of vital concern in the study of geography and of growing importance in our finite world."

Christopher L. Salter

*Professor and Chair
Department of Geography
University of Missouri,
Columbia, MO*

Dr. Louis Wilson

"A mature understanding of history and culture is empathetic as well as intellectual. As students learn to identify with the feelings and aspirations of those around them, you can extend this identification to people in other times and places."

*Associate Professor/Chair
African American
Studies Department
Smith College,
Northampton, MA*

Dr. Karen K. Wixson

"No matter how full the narrative or engaging the biography, if the instructional design doesn't facilitate the learning process, and if students aren't challenged to extend their knowledge by applying the information, the lessons and insights of a social studies education will be lost."

Karen Wixson

*Professor of Education
University of Michigan,
Ann Arbor, MI*

Across the Centuries
Program Components

The **Geography Kit** engages students with basic concepts of geography. The portfolio-sized kit includes:

- Desk maps
- Map Masters
- Overhead Transparencies
- Wall map

Each chapter in the **Student Text** opens with strong visuals and captions that help students focus. In addition to lesson pages and special features, the text includes an array of appendices:

- Minipedia
- Atlas
- Geographic Glossary
- Gazetteer
- Biographical Dictionary
- Glossary

www.eduplace.com

Houghton Mifflin Education Place provides a free on-line site for **The Social Studies Center,** which continually updates information and activities that support Houghton Mifflin Social Studies.

The Teacher's Edition provides instructional strategies and activities in the form of interleaf pages and point-of-use notes, with these additional features:

- A Professional Handbook
- An extensive bibliography including technical resources for each chapter
- A unit- appropriate Geography Project and notes on a unit-appropriate literary selection in Bookshelf II

Reading Support Resources

The **Workbook** and resource package are designed to support and develop the skills needed by all students for reading content.

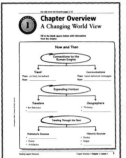

Chapter Overview

Lesson Preview

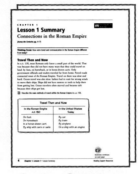

Lesson Summary
available in:
- English
- Spanish
- Chinese
- Hmong
- Khmer
- Vietnamese

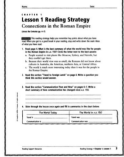

Reading Strategy

Lesson Review

Lesson Summaries
available on audiotapes.

Lesson Support/Transition

Activities for SDAIE: **S**pecially **D**esigned **A**cademic **I**nstruction in **E**nglish

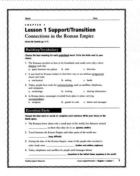

Ultimate Reader

This CD-ROM provides students complete access to the pupil text by enabling them to hear the text read aloud by computer-generated voicing.

These ancillaries will help you assess and enrich your students, social studies experience:

- **Citizenship Simulations**
- **Research Handbook**
- **Lesson Planner**
- **Assessment Options**
- **Study Guides**
- **Study Prints**
- **Posters**
- **Home and Community Involvement**
  with letters to parents in English, Spanish, Chinese, Hmong, Khmer, and Vietnamese

Bookshelf II

The Bookshelf II offers seven or eight fiction and nonfiction paperbacks that entertain as well as raise student awareness of how people behaved during some of the major moments in history. The Bookshelf II Teacher's Resources help to connect titles with the unit contents.

Reading Support for Social Studies Content

Helping students develop and perfect their reading skills is one of the most important goals of elementary and middle school education. Much class time is spent teaching strategies for decoding and comprehending literature, and teachers who instill a love of reading in their students can rightly consider themselves successful.

Nonfiction is an important part of reading instruction, but students often do not get enough opportunity to apply language arts strategies and skills to informational text, particularly textbooks. As they move through the intermediate elementary and middle school grades, students must comprehend content and concepts from increasingly complex textbooks. All too often, teachers and students are frustrated by the difficulty in accessing this content, not realizing that there are particular strategies and skills that can be applied to make this possible.

The reading support provided by Houghton Mifflin Social Studies not only allows comprehension of the rich content of the program, but has as its goal the development of the student's ability to access informational text whatever it may be. Such ability is not only essential to students' success as they advance in their formal education, but is a vital life skill as well.

Building Background

Students' lack of prior knowledge is one of the main reasons they have difficulties understanding informational text. Researchers have found that the brain learns by sifting through new information looking for data that connects to ideas with which it is already familiar. These connections build knowledge; totally foreign information, on the other hand, is easily lost. Since the subject of history is often particularly foreign to the young student, it is unlikely he or she can retain the content without considerable assistance. Thus it is essential for teachers to build background and activate prior knowledge before the student begins to read.

Previewing the Chapter

Houghton Mifflin Social Studies provides a variety of prereading support toward this end.

- In the pupil edition, each chapter begins with a timeline preview of information, and a collage of visuals with captions that announce the content covered in the chapter.

- The Teacher's Edition presents a strong "Preview" strategy.

- *Reading Support Resources* uses a similar prereading approach. With the one-page Chapter Overview, students will become familiar with the key ideas and the organizational framework of the chapter before beginning to read. When appropriate to the lesson content, *When Where* and *Who* labels assist students' grasp of key concepts. Most important for students struggling for language proficiency, each Chapter Overview provides a graphic organizer that clearly depicts the key information presented in the chapter. Students must complete the graphic organizer as they preview the chapter.

Previewing the Lesson

Lesson previewing is another strong prereading strategy.

- In the pupil edition, the opening page of each lesson lists the Key Terms covered in the lesson.

- In the Teacher's Edition, an "Introduce" strategy at the start of each lesson includes preteaching these Key Terms, while a "Develop" strategy suggests how best to present an accompanying graphic organizer to students.

- The identical graphic organizer followed by two questions appears in the Lesson Preview in *Reading Support Resources*. Here, the focus of both questions is to engage students in previewing the lesson and thinking about what they will learn.

Graphic Organizers

Graphic organizers have proven especially effective for those students with diverse languages, reading abilities, and learning styles, as well as for others who may lack the skills necessary for success in content-area classes. The graphic organizer can help you use an interactive approach to show your students connections among the key ideas in each chapter and lesson. Teachers have found that students become more actively engaged in the previewing strategy as they work with this visual tool.

In each lesson, *Reading Support Resources* employs a graphic organizer best suited to the lesson content and to the instructional objectives. Among the types students will work with are:

- **hierarchical organizers** that present main ideas and supporting details,
- **comparative organizers** that show similarities and differences within key concepts,
- **cluster organizers** that emphasize relationships among sets of ideas,
- **sequential organizers** that illustrate a series of steps or events showing chronological order or emphasizing cause and effect.

Reading Support Resources presents, furthermore, carefully designed graphic overviews with similar supporting facts side-by-side in similarly shaped cells and, whenever appropriate, with similar wording. This format makes it easier for students to remember key facts and concepts.

Applying Reading Strategies

Many students who have already spent years learning reading strategies and skills may be unsure how they relate to their textbooks. Students who are still struggling with these strategies are truly at a loss. Houghton Mifflin Social Studies provides students with ample opportunities to apply the following strategies to their reading of informational text:

- Predict/Infer
- Self-question
- Find the Main idea
- Summarize
- Evaluate
- Think About Words
- Use the Visuals
- Cause and Effect
- Compare and Contrast
- Sequence

In the pupil edition, the "Thinking Focus" question at the start of each lesson should guide students' reading, directing them to look for the most essential information in the lesson. The red square question at the end of each section of the lesson is support for comprehension. If students can answer that question, they can identify the important concepts.

The Reading Strategy page in *Reading Support Resources* provides additional practice. Students can use the Reading Strategy page to guide their reading of the pupil edition page. The Reading Strategy page sequences questions from easy to more difficult, frequently with an activity modeling the strategy first, then a question requiring more critical thinking and, finally, asking for a student response.

Lesson Summaries

For some students, particularly non-native speakers of English and very poor readers, facing a textbook can feel overwhelming. They need even more background and alternative avenues to the content. Visuals, such as those provided in the Posters and Study Prints are powerful aids. In *Reading*

Continued on next page

HOUGHTON MIFFLIN SOCIAL STUDIES

Reading Support

Many students in today's diverse classrooms need material that is easier to read than the pupil edition for their grade level. Houghton Mifflin Social Studies provides the *Reading Support Resources* for non-native speakers of English and for other students you think need extra support. The materials will accommodate students with:

- diverse languages,
- diverse reading skills,
- and diverse learning styles.

Reading Support Resources:
You will find a Chapter Overview and six pages of support materials for each lesson in the pupil edition.

- Lesson Preview (1 page)
- Reading Strategy (1 page)
- Lesson Summary (2 pages)
- Lesson Review (1 page)
- Lesson Support/ Transition (1 page)

Reading Support for
Social Studies Content *(continued)*

Support Resources, two-page Lesson Summaries written with simplified vocabulary to assist comprehension include a graphic that also helps to deliver the content. Furthermore, these Lesson Summaries have been translated into five languages besides English and are available on audiotape: Spanish, Chinese, Hmong, Khmer, and Vietnamese.

Each Lesson Summary presents the Thinking Focus question from the pupil edition. The Key Terms are used in context as well as defined in the margins. The Summary clearly and succinctly develops all of the main ideas included under each major lesson head, and the red square questions are repeated, ensuring that students comprehend those same key concepts covered in the pupil edition. Since these are translated, the teacher has a way of assessing student mastery of the content in all six languages.

Post Reading Activities

Building background, applying reading strategies, and using graphic organizers and lesson summaries are all methods that will enable students to develop their ability to access content from informational text. Post reading activities, however, are critical to helping them incorporate that content into their knowledge base. Individual, group, and whole class activities such as those found in the pupil edition's Chapter Review and in the Teacher's Edition offer many opportunities for students to take ownership of the concepts and information. Encourage students to raise their own questions while reading, and later in discussions with the whole class or small groups.

You may wish to check for understanding before or after these discussions. In *Reading Support Resources,* the Lesson Review page uses the Stanford 9 Test format to provide a check that permits you to assess students' understanding of the lesson. This review page is based on the

Lesson Summary, not on the pupil edition; consequently, students who have read only the Lesson Summary should be able to answer all Lesson Review questions. ■

For Further Reading

Feathers, Karen M. Infotext *Reading and Learning.* Ontario: Pippen, 1993.

Moore, David W. *Prereading Activities for Content Area Reading and Learning.* No. 233-961, International Reading Association.

Simpson, Anne. "Critical Questions: Whose Questions." *The Reading Teacher.* Vol. 50, No. 2, October, 1996.

Thomas, Ellen Lamar and H. Alan Robinson. *Improving Reading in Every Class, A Sourcebook for Teachers.* (3rd ed.), Boston: Allyn and Bacon, 1982.

Chapter Overview

(1 page)

Purpose

To familiarize students with the organization and the key ideas in the chapter before they begin to read the pupil edition

- *When Where* and *Who* labels assist students' grasp of key concepts.
- A graphic organizer depicts key facts, concepts and relationships in the chapter.

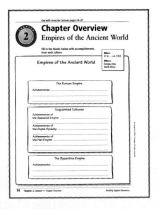

Lesson Preview

(1 page)

Purpose

To help students become familiar with the organization and key ideas in the lesson before they begin to read

- A graphic organizer from the Teacher's Edition presents key facts, concepts and relationships in the lesson.
- Questions direct students to study the graphic organizer and look at heads, maps and other visuals in the pupil edition.

Reading Strategy

(1 page)

Purpose

To help students apply ten reading strategies

- Concise directions define the strategy.
- Questions sequenced by level of difficulty reinforce the reading strategy.
- A variety of formats require simple responses easy to grade.

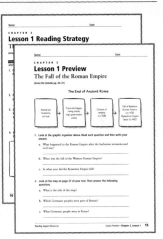

Lesson Summary

(2 pages)

Purpose

To provide reading support for non-native speakers and those needing extra support

- Summaries of key facts and ideas under each B head in the pupil edition use Key Terms introduced in the lesson.

- A variety of visuals, such as maps, timelines or other illustrations serve as memory enhancers.
- Simplified vocabulary assists comprehension.
- Translations in 5 languages: Chinese, Hmong, Khmer, Spanish, Vietnamese

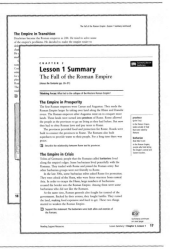

Summaries also available on audiotape.

Lesson Review

(1 page)

Purpose

To assess students' understanding of the lesson

- Students can answer the Lesson Review's sequenced questions by reading the Lesson Summary only.
- This page uses the Stanford 9 Test format.

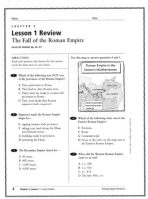

Access to Social Studies for Limited English Proficient Students

Because of rapid demographic changes nationwide, many school districts now enroll a significant number of students whose first language is not English. Language diversity in a social studies classroom poses new challenges to students and teachers alike. Not the least among these challenges is helping students acquire a new language at the same time that they are learning new subject content.

Social studies presents special challenges to learners. Because the content has many abstract and difficult concepts, social studies is very heavily language dependent. Finally, there is the demanding challenge of building self-esteem so that students can feel successful even in the most frustrating of circumstances.

In most cases, the Limited English Proficient (LEP) students in a school have widely different educational backgrounds and function at a broad range of achievement levels, depending on their prior academic experiences and level of proficiency in their own language(s). Almost invariably, well-prepared LEP students make the transition to studying completely in English more rapidly and efficiently than do those who, for whatever reason, have poor native language ability and less developed academic skills.

Students who are completely non-English speaking may need to access social studies through their first language while acquiring English. Or, students may be placed in classrooms where sheltered methodologies that employ English as a Second Language (ESL) techniques and strategies are used to teach social studies and other subject content areas. As students reach intermediate-level fluency in English, they usually can take in basic content taught in the new language when teachers make effective use of context clues such as visuals, realia (relief maps, models, real objects), interactive study guides, and role plays. Nevertheless, the complex and demanding language of social studies may necessitate further help for LEP students. For that reason, they also benefit greatly from those activities that highlight the significant vocabulary of each lesson and those that enable them to focus on the most relevant factual matter and the most important ideas.

Access Features of Houghton Mifflin Social Studies

Houghton Mifflin Social Studies has been designed to facilitate maximum access to social studies concepts for students from a wide variety of cultural and linguistic backgrounds. The unique Visual Learning strand and prominent instructional visuals throughout the program provide a channel of access for LEP students. Additional LEP-appropriate activities clearly identified for you in the Planning at a Glance chart preceding each chapter are:

- Reading Support and Review Pages
- SDAIE Lesson Support/Transition Pages
- Access Strategies and Activities
- Diverse Learning Strategies

Strategies for Accessible Instruction

Teachers can implement a number of techniques and strategies in order to enable LEP students to be more successful in the social studies. The following suggestions outline the most helpful.

Use language-sensitive techniques.

Some techniques that lower the language barrier for LEP students of intermediate fluency are:

- **Modifying speech.** Effective strategies include articulating clearly, pausing frequently so that information can be absorbed, using shorter phrases and sentences, avoiding idiomatic speech, defining new vocabulary through words students already know and use, and clarifying contracted forms such as *won't, shouldn't,* and *I'll.*

- **Using TPR (Total Physical Response).** This strategy allows students to demonstrate comprehension through actions such as pantomime, pointing, and drawing, even when they are not yet fluent in the language or feel uncomfortable producing oral language in the classroom.

- **Using gestures and facial expressions.** Bear in mind that these may not be universal, and can, on occasion, cause miscommunication. It is frequently beneficial, when students seem not to understand gestures and other kinesthetic language, to clarify your meaning in order to prevent confusion.

- **Modeling the desired performance, whether in oral or written language.** Students from other backgrounds particularly benefit from such modeling since they may have little experience with making oral presentations, questioning the teacher, or applying information in creative ways.

- **Using visuals and realia.** While visuals are helpful, research shows that students who have never seen a certain object or scene profit more from seeing the real thing, whenever possible.

- **Showing a sample of the finished product.** Some LEP students will at first tend to produce replicas of what you show them. Nevertheless, this first step will provide them with some of the skills necessary to create their own products later.

- **Breaking down complicated tasks into subtasks.** This technique allows students to proceed sequentially and to focus on each step.

- **Checking frequently for understanding.** Asking students to repeat or paraphrase

what you have just said or to share what they understand with classmates enables their fluency and builds confidence.

Build background knowledge.
You can help students unlock key concepts in the lesson by using the TE Access Strategy and by discussing the Study Prints, Posters, and Overhead Transparencies. Students who are from other backgrounds may have a great deal of knowledge about their countries of origin, but may not have the specific information required to fully comprehend lessons in Houghton Mifflin Social Studies.

Tap prior knowledge.
Have students brainstorm what they already know about the topic, do quick-writes, and use Venn diagrams to show similarities and differences among ideas or events. *(See page T36.)* LEP students may be able to share with classmates related cultural or historical information based on their prior life experiences or academic exposure. Inviting their participation is one of the most significant ways to build self-esteem, to actively engage them in the lesson, and to stimulate their prior knowledge of the topic.

Preteach essential vocabulary.
Remember, however, that for English language learners a seemingly innocuous word may be confusing and may delay access to the targeted concept, especially since when reading or listening to a new language, it is difficult to know which are the key words. Where possible, introduce families of words in context with interactive activities. *(See pages T36–T37.)* Encourage students from European language backgrounds to seek similarities in such cognate words as *history, historical, geography, geographical, circumnavigate, immigrate,* and so on. If possible, show pictorial representations of new vocabulary as well as the written or oral forms of the new concepts. Use Bingo and/or Flash Card games of the most

Continued on next page

Access to Social Studies for Limited English Proficient Students *(continued)*

important concepts in a unit to provide needed practice, repetition, and visualization of the new vocabulary needed for successful comprehension of the major ideas of the unit.

Use lesson summaries.

Introducing a lesson with a summary serves LEP students well, especially those who are most limited in English language proficiency. The summaries, found in *Reading Support Resources* provide an excellent synthesis of the lesson content using simplified vocabulary, and enable students to focus on the most important points prior to reading the dense material of each lesson.

Utilize collaborative learning.

These activities enable pairs and small groups of students to read selected sections of text together. *(See T34–T35.)* Research indicates that peer tutoring in which students with more proficient English skills are paired with less proficient speakers produces outstanding results. These strategies are also productive with written assignments and with the preparation of oral presentations.

Use oral and visual language.

Talk through the Graphic Overview and Thinking Focus for each new lesson to help LEP students focus on key concepts.

Assign the specially designed activities for LEP students.

The Lesson Support/Transition pages in *Reading Support Resources* are best used at appropriate times during the lesson or chapter. These activities focus on essential vocabulary and/or concepts. Since language, and especially vocabulary, is the key mode of access to the content of social studies, these activities will greatly facilitate student success.

Social Studies and the Overall LEP Program

There is no simple way to eliminate completely the language barrier to social studies for LEP students. Recent research indicates that it may take as long as seven years before the average second language learner is able to perform at the median on standardized tests! There are exceptions in both directions: those who are well prepared in language and concept development can make the transition more rapidly than those who require additional time and modification of instruction. However, there are many avenues that can be used to help students make a more rapid and successful transition to mainstream instruction.

In the majority of cases, LEP youngsters are most successful when they have a program that enables them to achieve functional fluency in both oral and written English quickly. Such a program begins with intensive ESL lessons designed to teach the basics of English. Introductory ESL may be followed by an advanced program known as ELD (English Language Development), in which students learn social studies and other content area vocabulary and build conceptual development. In some schools, students receive instruction called SDAIE (Specially Designed Academic Instruction in English), which is a compendium of techniques and strategies to modify instruction—without lowering expectations for comprehension and production of difficult subject content area. In all cases, these programs enable students to derive maximum benefit from the Houghton Mifflin Social Studies.

In addition to a sequential English language development program, students who are in the initial phases of acquiring English may need primary language support to comprehend fully the key concepts in the program. This may be provided by a bilingual classroom setting, the help of a bilingual aide (when possible), or by the use of peer tutors who speak the same language. To benefit all students, Houghton Mifflin Social Studies has been designed to facilitate access to grade-level social studies through instructional strategies that are grounded in language and learning theory as well as in good teaching. ■

For Further Reading

Brinton, D., M.A. Snow, and M.B. Wesche. *Content-Based Second Language Instruction.* New York: Newbury House Publishers, 1989.

Córdova, J. M. and B. Segal. *Linking the ESL and the "At Risk" Student to the Mainstream: A Resource Handbook.* Brea, CA: Berty Segal, Inc., 1994.

Cantoni-Harvey, G. *Content-Area Language Instruction: Approaches and Strategies.* Reading, MA: Addison-Wesley, 1987.

Crandall, I. A., D. Christian, and D.J. Short. *How to Integrate Language and Content Instruction: A Training Manual.* Berkeley, CA: Center for Language, Education and Research, University of California, 1989.

Diamond, B.J. and M.A. Moore. *Multicultural Literacy: Mirroring the Reality of the Classroom.* White Plains, NY: Longman, 1995.

Peitzman, F. and G. Gadda. *With Different Eyes: Insights into Teaching Language Minority Students Across the Disciplines.* Reading, MA: Addison Wesley Publishing Company, 1994.

Richard-Amato, P.A. *Making it Happen: Instruction in the Second Language Classroom, from Theory to Practice.* New York: Longman, 1988.

Access Features

Diverse Learning Strategies
listed in the Planning at a Glance chart in the Teacher's Edition before each chapter facilitate maximum access to social studies content for students from a variety of cultural and linguistic backgrounds.

Teacher's Edition Features
Both the Access Strategy and Access Activity at the beginning of each lesson in the Teacher's Edition tap students' prior knowledge and emphasize essential vocabulary and, thus, promote access to unlocking key concepts.

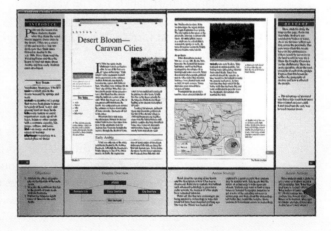

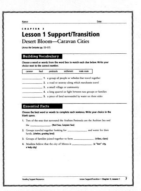

Lesson Support/Transition
pages for students receiving SDAIE instruction are featured in *Reading Support Resources* and focus on essential vocabulary and/or concepts.

Individualizing Instruction in the Social Studies

Houghton Mifflin Social Studies has built into its program many opportunities for individualizing instruction, opportunities designed to help meet the needs of a widely diverse student population. These opportunities are contained in editorial features in the student text, suggested where applicable throughout the Teacher's Edition, and embodied in additional ancillary features in the program.

In the Teacher's Edition at the beginning of each chapter in the Planning at a Glance chart, labels for the various approaches are provided as a means of tracking the variety of teaching strategies in any lesson.

Diverse Learning Strategies

The listing in this article outlines the types of strategies to be found and the labels that identify these. The first three labels *(visual, kinesthetic,* and *auditory)* describe various types of intelligence, or learning styles; the last four categories *(GATE, extra support, SDAIE, and multi-age)* refer to academic, social, and/or behavioral differences.

Boundaries between and among these categories are exceedingly fluid. In actual classroom practice, one category seldom, if ever, stands in isolation. Usually more than one strategy can be used to reach a particular student, and a particular approach may be very effective with students of various types. For example, instruction appealing to the visual domain is effective not only with students identified as visual learners but also with most SDAIE students, given the universal language of images. A learner who thrives on instruction that focuses on the kinesthetic domain may also respond very well to visual stimulus. Further, those learners who don't immediately show themselves to be strong in, for example, the logic/mathematical domain can nonetheless be guided through these types of activities in order to foster or strengthen that area.

In like manner, no appealing activity should be reserved for only those students who immediately show a facility for it. While GATE students as a group tend to excel in drama, if given the chance, so too do many of those learners who need extra support. These labels provide easy reference during advance planning for the most appropriate individual and group instruction for the students in your class.

Visual

These activities use illustrations and other images to appeal to those students whose learning process is strongly visual. Of course, activities so labeled are also essential in strengthening visual awareness in all learners. Photographs, reproductions of paintings, facsimiles of historical documents, maps, and other artifacts are provided so that all students might construct meaning from what they observe. In addition, and where appropriate throughout the text, are activities that allow teachers to guide students in the creation and use of their own visuals such as graphic organizers, illustrations of various events or ideas, original maps, and posters.

Kinesthetic

Activities in this realm are specifically designed for students who learn best through physical action and hands-on experience. In addition, they serve all students well because they get members of the class out of their seats and moving about in a purposeful manner. Pantomimes, constructing models to scale or actual size, rearranging classroom furniture to create a particular environment, and making three-dimensional maps are only some of the activities found in the lessons.

Auditory

Activities with this label are designed to reach those students who respond better to the spoken word than to written text. However, they also hold universal appeal of the sort that has throughout history lent the bard, or storyteller, a fabled role in society. (Current educational research attests to the beneficial effect of reading aloud up to and throughout high school.) Activities suggested include this reading aloud, sharing information with a small group or a partner, role-playing, interviewing and reporting back, and presenting oral reports.

Gifted and Talented (GATE)

These activities work well with students classified as gifted and talented who require additional stimulation and challenge. Such suggestions include writing projects, in-depth research, and sharing results with classmates. Since lack of skill in English does not equate with lack of ability, teachers would do well to remember that there are gifted Limited English Proficient (LEP) students who would also enjoy the challenge of these activities.

Extra Support

Activities bearing this label are designed to help students having difficulty reading, comprehending, and making meaning from the written word. Tapping prior knowledge and connecting new ideas to students' lives, previewing, questioning, and predicting are only some of the strategies included that have proven helpful.

Specially Designed Academic Instruction in English (SDAIE)

Ever-increasing numbers of students whose first language is not English are being taught in English-only classrooms. These SDAIE activities focus on vocabulary development and help the teacher move these students through the stages of developing English proficiency. Since most of these activities rely on few words, they may be similar to visual and kinesthetic activities. Other activities facilitate learning for LEP students through the use of modified speech, choice of less demanding vocabulary, and help in identifying key words and concepts. They also draw on abilities found in the mixed class by suggesting pairing or grouping these students with others with greater English proficiency.

Multi-Age

Activities with this label contain suggestions for approaches to students in the classroom that contains several grade levels or in the ungraded, multi-age setting. These activities can be easily modified and individualized or used with less mature as well as more mature learners.

Ancillary support for even more effective individualizing is provided in the Reading Support and Review pages and the Lesson Support/Transition pages for SDAIE students found in *Reading Support Resources*, as well as through the multi-language lesson summaries in Spanish, Chinese, Hmong, Khmer, and Vietnamese with accompanying audiotapes. Taken together, these tools in Houghton Mifflin Social Studies provide a kaleidoscope of access strategies that will help practitioners reach all students in today's diverse classrooms. ■

For Further Reading

Armstrong, T. *Multiple Intelligences in the Classroom.* Association for Supervision and Curriculum Development (Alexandria, VA), 1994.

Gardner, Howard. *Frames of Mind: The Theory of Multiple Intelligences.* Basic Books, 1985.

Joyce, B., et al. *Models of Teaching.* Allyn and Bacon, 1994.

Planning at a Glance
Planning at a Glance charts in the Teacher's Edition before each chapter list the variety of teaching strategies in each lesson.

Graphic Organizers
Highly visual graphic organizers that show connections among key concepts in chapters and lessons appear in every lesson in the Teacher's Edition, and in every Chapter Overview and Lesson Preview in *Reading Support Resources.*

Using Technology in the Social Studies Classroom

The power of technology has transformed the classroom. New tools help teachers enrich and extend major topics while providing effective support to students with diverse learning styles. Through multimedia such as sound, video, music, or simulations, students can experience another culture, or a particular historical period. With widespread Internet access, students can reach beyond the classroom to a variety of additional content sources and educational experiences.

When teams of students and teachers utilize new technology tools, learners become interactive with ideas, information and with other learners in a new way. Technology challenges students to assume greater responsibility for their own learning as they seek information from a variety of sources to build knowledge. Major trends include a shift from whole-class to small group instruction, from a competitive to cooperative classroom structure, and from the primacy of verbal thinking to the integration of visual and verbal thinking.

Teachers' roles are also changing. Beyond instructing, teachers have become mentors and facilitators in a collaborative learning environment, as well as coaches as they circulate among students to encourage and give direction and assistance to those working on computers.

Technology has also allowed teachers to present material in a variety of formats. Utilizing CD-ROMs, video, and Internet access, social studies instructors can

- build background information, primary sources, and other data on a social studies topic or concept.

- enhance and enrich major topics by finding new data.

- provide a venue for learning and applying real-life information literacy and research skills.

- offer opportunities for collaborative and cooperative learning as students conduct research.

- assess and foster critical thinking and problem-solving skills.

- provide access to content for diverse learning styles.

Educational Value

Current learning theories focus on the process of knowledge construction. Many educators feel that learning goals can be achieved if students become active, self-directed learners. Utilizing authentic learning experiences and real-world problem-solving tasks, students gather information from many sources and many perspectives, formulate tentative conclusions, and then test those conclusions in relevant situations. This process of knowledge building mirrors the way children actually develop. One of the favorite aphorisms of famed child psychologist Jean Piaget was: "To understand is to invent."

Since multimedia programs invite interaction, students become active seekers of knowledge, rather than passive recipients of information. Multimedia packages can offer inquiry-based learning, where students construct and demonstrate solutions in a variety of simulated environments. Multimedia can also provide individualized learning paths so students can progress at their own pace—a critical issue for students of all abilities. Because children are so fond of computers and video, they are generally more highly motivated to use these tools.

Types of Technology

Technology offers learning opportunities through simulations, educational games,

research and data collection, and direct video viewing. Primary classroom technologies include CD-ROMs, video, and the Internet.

CD-ROM

CD-ROMs can store enormous amounts of graphics, images, and sounds. They support an open-ended, discovery approach to learning and allow students to direct their own learning based on their individual abilities and interests. Unlike traditional materials, a CD-ROM can give immediate feedback at point of use, and is self-paced. Most CD-ROMs allow teachers to monitor student progress through printouts, on-screen journals, or built-in management systems.

Computer-based simulation programs place students into lifelike situations in which they must solve problems and make real-world decisions. Simulations can also build in primary resources and research materials, so that students can further their investigations.

Video

Videotapes and videodiscs effectively provide background information for major topics, enrich major topics and concepts, and reinforce prior learning. Videodiscs offer high-quality sound and picture, and quick access to information. With a remote control or barcode reader, a teacher or student using a videodisc can instantly go to any frame or video segment. Videodiscs can contain more than two hours of film clips, still images, maps, music, and narration, and often provide a separate audio channel for a second language.

Internet

The Internet can provide almost infinite resources and learning opportunities to teachers and students. By effectively utilizing the Internet, students first learn how to find useful information quickly and judge its accuracy, and then improve their research skills by learning how to seek reliable content and verify sources. Such information literacy helps students deal with the excessive amount of information encountered in daily life. Online cross-curricular projects offer students indispensable opportunities to build knowledge, connect and utilize ideas, and integrate multiple disciplines. Virtual field trips can take students all over the globe. Internet access can also provide teachers with useful classroom resources, like printable lesson plans, blackline masters, and theme extensions.

Houghton Mifflin Education Place™ (www.eduplace.com) provides integrated program support for Houghton Mifflin Social Studies. Online support aligned to the student textbook and Teacher's Edition provides an integrated, purposeful program with thematic coherence. *Education Place* Discussion Forums give teachers the opportunity to share ideas and discuss important topics in social studies instruction. *Education Place* also provides access to professional resources to help teachers apply technology effectively in the classroom and to extend the curriculum. ■

For Further Reading

Grabe, Mark and Cindy. *Integrating Technology for Meaningful Learning*. Boston, Massachusetts: Houghton Mifflin Company, 1996.

Braun, Joseph A. *Technology Tools in the Social Studies Classroom*. Wilsonville, Oregon: Franklin, Beedle & Associates, 1998.

HOUGHTON MIFFLIN
SOCIAL STUDIES
Technology

Social Studies Center at Education Place (www.eduplace.com/ss/hmss/index.html) provides online overviews and outlines of every textbook lesson, student activities, monthly current events features, and teacher's discussion forums.

Rescue Geo 1 ® is an interactive CD-ROM with 600 questions and over 1,400 maps that reinforce major geography concepts.

Discoveries™ offers students a video and animation-filled exploration of information hot spots, a reference library, and an online journal.

We the People videotapes provide students with a compelling visual experience of history, geography, and culture, through photography, art, and maps.

Assessment in Social Studies

Assessment is the process of gathering information to aid in the evaluation of students' academic progress. That evaluation can be useful for both individual and collective decision-making.

Assessment today usually means balanced assessment, which includes and *values* a teacher's informal, day-to-day appraisal as well as more formal documentation of student performance. Thus it allows students to demonstrate their progress in a variety of ways. In social studies, this means measuring not just a student's ability to recall particular facts, but also their understanding of concepts, repertoire of skills, and insight into civic values and responsibilities.

Balanced assessment, then, becomes both a learning and teaching opportunity. It allows you to tailor your instruction to individual needs. It also involves students in the process, encouraging them to set goals and make decisions about their own learning and, ultimately, to become more reflective, critical learners.

Informal Assessment

Informal assessment utilizes the ongoing observations you make on a daily basis and focuses on the processes that students use as well as the products they create.

Any of the following may become elements in your informal assessment process: anecdotal notes, checklists and forms, oral presentations, performances assessment, conferences, interviews, conversations, journal entries, learning logs. The Assessment Multiple-Use Masters in the Test booklet will also provide opportunities for informal assessment. Keep in mind that not all assessment activities need to be done for all students at all times.

Informal assessment also involves students in the evaluation of their own learning

process. While teachers are informally assessing students, students are assessing themselves as learners and can contribute insights that may help shape your instructional plans.

Formal Assessment

Formal assessment provides a "snapshot" of each student at a given time and often includes pencil-and-paper assessment instruments such as chapter tests. In a balanced assessment program, formal test results are one important component of the total assessment picture. Indeed, you may want to "test" the test results of your students against what you see in your observations and in their portfolios, presentations, and group work. While pencil-and-paper tests continue to be a traditional format for formal assessment, current formal assessment instruments are including more assessment *activities* that reflect instructional activities—for example, real-world writing activities such as letters, newspaper editorials, and speeches.

In today's education setting, formal assessment—especially standardized tests—play an increasingly prominent role. For that reason, a balanced assessment program will include exercises that familiarize students with the format and content of common standardized tests. Such assessment options provide one means to sharpen classroom focus on core content and key issues in social studies.

Self-Assessment

Involving students in the assessment and evaluation process is an essential part of balanced assessment. When students become partners in the learning process, they gain a better sense of themselves as learners and thinkers. As students reflect on what they have learned and how they learn it, they develop the tools to become more effective learners. As they examine their work, they can think about what they do well and in which areas they still need help. If you provide students with criteria or target behaviors, they will have the framework they may need for successful self-examination.

Portfolio Assessment

Portfolio assessment is a long-term approach to ongoing assessment that offers opportunities to monitor students' changing progress throughout the year. The collection of student products in a portfolio provide an overview of students' intellectual capabilities and academic experiences. Portfolios can help you focus on the growth of the individual over time rather than on how the student's performance compares to that of his or her peers.

Portfolios can be highly personalized, such as when an artist creates his or her own portfolio and makes all the decisions about content and presentation. On the other hand, they can be quite standardized, if a standard format is required by an individual teacher, school, district, or state. The intended purpose of the portfolio will determine its contents and the kind of assessment tool it will become. You may want to work with other teachers to develop evaluation criteria of portfolios.

As you revisit portfolio entries with your students, you may want to encourage them to continue a work-in-progress, revise or improve a draft, expand or extend a brief assignment, or look at a product as a basis of comparison for a similar piece of work. Portfolios also give you an opportunity to share an overview of a student's work with families, with other teachers, or with school administrators.

In all, a balanced assessment program with a variety of approaches best evaluates students' ability to relate ideas and concepts, to apply skills, and to think critically. ■

For Further Reading

Grant Wiggins, *Educative Assessment: Designing Assessments to Inform and Improve Students' Performance.* Jossey-Bass, San Francisco, 1998.

Student Text Features

Houghton Mifflin Social Studies has built into its Student Text many instructional features that can also serve an assessment function. These features are found within lessons, special feature pages, and the Chapter Review.

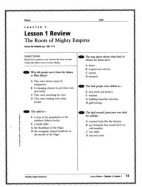

Lesson Reviews in *Reading Support Resources*

These one-page reviews follow the Stanford 9 test in both form and content. They can be used by students to review the lesson's text or by you to test students' understanding of each lesson.

Chapter Tests

A four-page test in blackline master form is provided for each chapter. These tests assess each of the three strands and are structured as follows:

- Part I consists of a variety of short-answer formats.
- Part II consists of free-response questions, including at least one longer "essay" question.

Multiple-Use Masters

In the test booklet you will find a series of black-line master pages that offer options for self-assessment, open-ended questioning, and performance assessment.

Teacher's Edition Features

You may also use for assessment purposes many of the activities and strategies provided in the Planning at a Glance pages and lesson notes in the Teacher's Edition.

Integrating the Social Studies Strands

Social studies is the study of people in their social world. When you study people, you have to look at how they live, work, worship, and play together. You have to consider how they govern themselves, how they make a living, and how they make important decisions.

Developing Meaningful Knowledge

Knowledge of the social world should be holistic and interrelated; it should be representative of all the elements of life. Thus, the content of a social studies program should maintain an interdisciplinary balance that draws from history, geography, economics, culture, ethics and belief systems, and social and political systems. The Houghton Mifflin Social Studies program draws on the vast knowledge of the world, of United States history, and of the various social sciences to build a curriculum that is integrated and interesting, thematic yet thorough, and chronologically conceptual. How is this achieved?

History, geography, and culture form the major threads of this curriculum, with content and conceptual ideas from these and the other social science disciplines woven carefully through these major areas of study. History, geography, and culture are selected as the center of the curriculum, in part because of their inherently interdisciplinary nature. Historians study the lives of people at a particular time and in a particular place; they investigate the beliefs and social systems of the people, the ways they organize to govern themselves, and the ways they earn a living and produce goods and services. In addition, historians focus on the causes of events, and the ways different groups see and understand events and phenomena; they look at the lives of the people and see how events are influenced by different groups, and how the events affect different individuals and groups.

History

The study of history forms the center of this curriculum; yet, all the other areas of the social sciences are easily integrated into the study of the past and the present. The social studies curriculum has been compared to a symphony: sometimes all the instruments play together to form an integrated whole (resembling an interdisciplinary approach), and sometimes individual elements of the symphony are highlighted for a deeper look at one aspect. In such cases, for example, students may focus on learning particular geographic knowledge and skills so that later they can apply these to the content knowledge in the next unit of study. Both solo and integrated approaches to curriculum are used in Houghton Mifflin Social Studies, for both are needed to build a sound curriculum for young learners.

It is critical that history is made more accessible and relevant to students. Lively, honest accounts of the lives of historical characters can stimulate a student's interest in and empathy with that time in history and can provide an entry point for understanding the factual material. In addition, students should appreciate that the most important historical movements were the result of particular decisions and actions made by men and women of all classes, colors, and conditions. This emphasis in the study of history provides a strong basis for democratic citizenship.

Geography

Geography helps us see the links between the landscape of life and the unfolding of human development and history. The pupil editions in Houghton Mifflin Social Studies begin with a fifteen-page Map and Globe Handbook, each section reviewing a specific geographic skill. While the focus of the geography instruction throughout the program centers around the five themes of location, place, human/environment interaction, movement, and region, the Geography Projects located in the Teacher's Edition at the beginning of each unit also address the more comprehensive instructional Six Essential Elements and the Eighteen Geography Standards published in *Geography for Life: National Geography Standards 1994.* The Geography Education Standards Project resulted from the Goals 2000: Educate America Act, which mandated the inclusion of geography as a core subject in curricula nationwide. In Houghton Mifflin Social Studies, the instructional approaches that work with both themes and standards provide an ample framework for student inquiry into the role that geography plays in human history. They also help students realize a critical understanding of the world around them, both now and in the past. Such knowledge is fundamental to sound social studies instruction and will lead to informed judgment and better citizenship not only in matters of resources and the environment, but in life overall.

Economics
How people use the resources of the environment and of their abilities forms the basis of the study of economics. In the elementary and middle grades, it is important for students to recognize the choices people make and how these economic choices form patterns of different economic and ideological systems across the world. With trade and rapid communications, most countries of the world today are highly interdependent, and this economic reality brings benefits as well as introduces new issues.

Culture
Culture, or the total way of life of a people, including their beliefs and traditions, is a central concept in any sound social studies curriculum. In Houghton Mifflin Social Studies, students learn about the cultural similiarities and differences that exist among societies of different times and places. People often express their beliefs and heritage in their arts, literature, architecture, and legends; these human creations play a major role in helping students learn about the inner life of a people and their struggles and joys.

Through a culture's literature, art, and other documents and artifacts, students will recognize that all societies have ideals and standards of behavior. In addition, students will see the role and importance of religion in human society and will reflect on how people in different societies over time have struggled with ethical and moral issues.

An interdisciplinary balance in the social studies curriculum brings a new vitality and relevance to the study of people. By promoting the "big picture" and bringing all elements of life together, an integrated social studies instills in students a greater appreciation for their own culture. Furthermore, an integrated social studies provides students with a three-dimensional view of the world and a practical understanding of the ideas and issues that will influence their daily lives.

Civic Understanding and Values
In a democratic society, it is vital that all citizens are active, informed participants and that they understand and appreciate the kind of behavior necessary for the smooth functioning and maintenance of a democracy. In part, this means that students should understand the essence of democratic ideas and should realize that people create a national identity to reflect the essential beliefs of the nation. In addition, civic understanding implies developing a respect for human rights and for the rational settlement of disputes.

Continued on next page

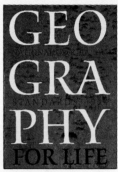

Both themes and standards provide an ample instructional framework for geography as a core subject.

Each section of the 15-page Map and Globe Handbook covers a specific geographic skill.

Students see how historical documents often reflect a society's ideals and standards of behavior.

Integrating the Social Studies Strands *(continued)*

Civic understanding and the development of values are goals of education; however, the social studies curriculum plays an important role in this area. Since social studies essentially is the study of people and their societies, it also is the study that undergirds one's perspective on one's own life. That is, social studies should enable students to better comprehend their own ways of life, the values that guide their nation and other cultures, and the issues that face their nation and community.

Skills

Study skills, visual learning skills, map and globe skills, critical thinking skills, and social participation skills are essential components of any effective social studies program. These skills play a major role in Houghton Mifflin Social Studies, for without these, knowledge cannot be meaningful, and civic understanding cannot become action. *Skills are best learned in the context of content knowledge, and are best applied to closely related content.* This principle of learning is maintained throughout the Houghton Mifflin Social Studies program. The Understanding Skills and Making Decision features are integrally related with knowledge developed in the unit of study, and the skill development within a grade level and across the program closely parallels our knowledge of child development and learning.

Since the study of the social world implies gathering a wide range of data, portrayed in a variety of forms (charts, tables, graphs, diagrams, maps, primary source documents, photographs, symbols, artifacts, and more), it is important that students learn how to "read" these data sources accurately and with a sense of purpose. These skills should be purposefully taught to students, for they are complex and critical to meaningful learning. Throughout the Houghton Mifflin Social Studies program, students are engaged in direct instruction in the necessary skills; in subsequent lessons, these skills are then actively applied.

In the same way that history and the social sciences provide a basis for an integrated and interdisciplinary knowledge base for the curriculum, the three major aspects of the Houghton Mifflin Social Studies program provide the foundation for a holistic approach to the study of the social world. Knowledge, civic understanding and values, and skills are all essential parts of a sound, powerful social studies program. Such a program should enable students to truly understand the "facts" as well as the issues. It should engage students in true inquiry and active involvement in the social world; it should help students see the complex interrelationships among beliefs and human choices; and it should enable the student to be a powerful citizen in the contemporary social world. ■

For Further Reading

Braun, Joseph A. *Technology Tools in the Social Studies Classroom*. Wilsonville, Oregon: Franklin, Beedle & Associates, 1998.

Carretero, Mario and James F. Voss, Editors. *Cognitive and Instructional Processes in History and the Social Sciences*. Hillsdale, NJ: Lawrence Erlbaum Associates, 1994.

Darling-Hammond, Linda, Jacqueline Ancess, and Beverly Falk. *Authentic Assessment in Action: Studies of Schools and Students at Work*. New York: Columbia University Press, 1995.

Leinhardt, Gaea, Isabel L. Beck, and Catherine Stainton, Editors. *Teaching and Learning in History*. Hillsdale, NJ: Lawrence Erlbaum Associates, 1994.

Houghton Mifflin Social Studies
Scope and Sequence

This Scope and Sequence has been designed to provide students with the comprehensive knowledge, civic values, and intellectual skill they will need to meet the challenge of citizenship in the 21st Century. The three strands of the program have been tightly integrated at all levels, so that skills are always taught in the context of the lesson content, and knowledge is enhanced by the application of sound values.

The three integrated strands are:

- **Knowledge and Understanding**
- ▲ **Civic Understanding and Values**
- ■ **Skills**

HOUGHTON MIFFLIN SOCIAL STUDIES
The Integrated Strands

The goals of each strand are listed on the following two pages. References in the Teacher's Edition key all learning objectives to these goals. Typically the student is introduced to a subject or skill at an early level, taught to actively use it at an intermediate level, and encouraged to analyze and critique it at an advanced level.

● Knowledge and Understanding	▲ Civic Understanding and Values	■ Skills
History	National Identity	Study Skills
Geography	Constitutional Heritage	Visual Learning
Economics	Citizenship	Map and Globe Skills
Culture		Critical Thinking
Ethics and Belief Systems		Social Participation
Social and Political Systems		

● KNOWLEDGE AND UNDERSTANDING

HISTORY

1. Develop an understanding of the reasons for studying history and of the relationships between the past and the present
2. Develop an awareness of the ways in which we learn about the past and the methods and tools of the historian
3. Create a sense of empathy for the past
4. Understand the meaning of time and chronology
5. Analyze the sometimes complex cause-and-effect relationships of ideas and events, recognizing also the effects of the accidental and irrational on history
6. Understand the reasons for both continuity and change
7. Recognize the interrelatedness of geography, economics, culture, belief systems, and political systems within history
8. Comprehend the history of women, minorities, and the full range of social classes, not just the history of the elite or the notable individual

GEOGRAPHY

1. Develop locational skills and understanding
2. Develop an awareness of place
3. Understand human and environmental interaction
4. Understand movement of people, goods, and ideas
5. Understand world regions and their historical, cultural, economic, and political characteristics

ECONOMICS

1. Identify and apply basic concepts of economics (basic wants and needs, scarcity, choices, decision making, opportunity costs, resources, production, distribution, consumption, markets, labor, capital)
2. Develop an awareness of past and present exchange systems
3. Recognize and analyze the economic systems of various societies, including the United States, and their responses to the three basic economic questions: what to produce (value), how and how much to produce (allocation), and how to distribute (distribution)
4. Recognize the economic global interdependence of societies
5. Recognize the impact of technology on economics

▲ CIVIC UNDERSTANDING AND VALUES

NATIONAL IDENTITY

1. Develop an appreciation for the multicultural, pluralistic nature of U.S. society
2. Understand the basic principles of democracy
3. Understand and appreciate American ideals, as expressed in historical documents, speeches, songs, art, and symbolic representations and activities
4. Recognize that the American patriotic ideals are not yet fully realized and that to be protected they must constantly be reaffirmed

CONSTITUTIONAL HERITAGE

1. Develop an appreciation for the balance of power established by the Constitution between majority and minority, the individual and the state, and government by and for the people
2. Understand the historical origins of the Constitution and how it has been amended and changed over time
3. Recognize the Constitution as an expression of democratic ideals that is reinterpreted from time to time

CITIZENSHIP

1. Recognize the reciprocal relationship between the individual and the state in a democracy
2. Understand and appreciate the kind of behavior necessary for the functioning and maintenance of our democratic society
3. Learn the duties and method of selection of our leaders
4. Develop a respect for human rights, including those of individuals and of minorities
5. Develop an understanding and appreciation for the rational settlement of disputes and for compromise
6. Recognize the special strategies required to allow the different elements within our pluralistic society to live together amicably
7. Develop an understanding of the processes that have led to the fall of democracies

■ SKILLS

STUDY SKILLS

1. Locate, select, and collect information by interviewing or by using appropriate reference materials
2. Organize information from reference sources to address issues or problems
3. Present information convincingly in spoken or written forms

VISUAL LEARNING

1. Develop careful and directed observation of images, objects, and the environment
2. Understand, use, and create graphic information (timelines, charts, tables, other graphic organizers, graphs, diagrams)
3. Interpret and respond to photographs, paintings, cartoons, and other illustrative materials
4. Understand and use symbols
5. Express meaning through sensory forms of representation

MAP & GLOBE SKILLS

1. Identify and use map and globe symbols; identify and use different map projections
2. Understand and use locational terms; locate places and positions on a map or globe
3. Interpret and use directional terms and symbols on a map or globe
4. Understand and use terms to describe relative size and distance; identify and use map scales
5. Construct and use maps and geographic models

CULTURE

1. Understand that culture encompasses all aspects of a human society that are learned, not inherited, and know how culture is transmitted
2. Develop an appreciation for the rich complexity of a society's culture and an understanding of how the parts of a culture interrelate
3. Recognize and appreciate the multicultural and multiethnic dimensions of our society and the contributions made by various groups
4. Appreciate the cultural similarities and differences that exist among societies of different times and places
5. Recognize the roles everyday customs and beliefs, along with rituals, literature, and the arts play in reflecting the ideals of a people and in projecting a people's image of themselves to the world
6. Learn about the beliefs, legends, and myths, along with the heroes and heroines, of cultures from different times and places

ETHICS & BELIEF SYSTEMS

1. Recognize that all societies have ideals and standards of behavior
2. Understand that the ideas people profess affect their actions
3. Recognize the importance of religion in human society and its influence on history
4. Become familiar with the basic ideas of major religions and ethical traditions of other times and places
5. Develop an understanding of how different societies have tried to resolve ethical issues when conflicts occur between individuals, groups, and societies

SOCIAL & POLITICAL SYSTEMS

1. Develop an awareness of the reciprocal relationship between the individual and various social and political groups: family, community, and nation
2. Understand the role of law and its relationship to social and political systems
3. Develop an appreciation for the tension between opposing ideals in human affairs
4. Develop an awareness of the structure of social classes and the changes in status of women and racial and ethnic minorities in U.S. society and other societies
5. Understand comparative political systems, past and present
6. Understand the complex relationship and interdependence that exists among the world's nations

CRITICAL THINKING

1. Define and clarify problems, issues, and ideas
2. Evaluate and judge information related to a problem, an issue, or an idea
3. Solve problems and draw conclusions related to an issue or idea*

*Critical thinking is taught both in a problem-solving and in a decision-making context.

SOCIAL PARTICIPATION

1. Develop interpersonal skills
2. Work successfully in groups

Early Farming Societies → Improved farming methods → Surplus → Permanent settlements → Cities

Population growth

Specialization

Teaching About Religion in Public Schools *Charles C. Haynes*

Growing numbers of educators throughout the United States recognize that study about religion in social studies, literature, art, and music is an essential part of a complete public school education. States and school districts are issuing new mandates and guidelines for the inclusion of teaching about religion in the curriculum. As a result, textbooks are expanding discussions of religion's role in history and culture, and many new supplementary materials concerning religion in history are being developed.

In light of this national trend to include more about religion in the curriculum, the question for teachers is no longer "Should I teach about religion?" but rather, "What should I teach, and how should I do it?" This publication is designed to provide the civic and academic framework for answering the questions of "what" and "how." The aim of the guidelines and suggestions that follow is to help classroom teachers meet the challenges of teaching about religion in ways that are constitutionally permissible, educationally sound, and sensitive to the beliefs of students and parents.

Why Study about Religion is Important

Teaching about religion is important and necessary if public schools are to provide students with a complete education. Much of history, art, music, literature, and contemporary life is unintelligible without an understanding of the major religious ideas and influences that have shaped history and culture throughout the world. Even teaching religious liberty, the civic foundation that sustains the United States as one nation of many faiths, requires teaching about the role of religion in history and culture. A recent report by the Association for Supervision and Curriculum Development described the place of religion in the curriculum:

> The proper role of religion in the school is the study of religion for its educational value. The task is to teach about religions and their impact in history, literature, art, music, and morality. It seems natural that the art curriculum, for example, must pay attention to the impact of Christianity on the work of Michelangelo, just as a history class focusing on the colonization of America must pay attention to the religious upheaval in sixteenth-century Europe that fueled that colonization. [1]

Understanding the role religion plays in history and culture is of special importance in our increasingly diverse society. Expanding religious pluralism in the United States confronts our schools and our nation with unprecedented challenges. The United States has shifted from the largely Protestant pluralism of the eighteenth century to a pluralism that now includes people of all faiths and a growing number of people who indicate no religious preference. New populations of Muslims, Buddhists, and many other religious and ethnic groups are entering schools throughout the nation.

If we are to live with our differences, we must attempt through education to replace stereotypes and prejudices with understanding and respect. Students need to recognize that religious and philosophical beliefs and practices are of deep significance to much of our citizenry. Omission of discussion about the religious and philosophical roots of developments in history can give students

[1] An excerpt from *Religion in the Curriculum*, Alexandria, Virginia: Association for Supervision and Curriculum Development, 1987.

the false impression that the religious and ethical traditions of humankind are insignificant or unimportant.

A Civic Framework for Teaching about Religion

Congress shall make no law respecting an establishment of religion, or prohibiting the free exercise thereof. . . .

The Religious Liberty clauses of the First Amendment to the Constitution provide the civic framework for teaching about religion in the public schools. The United States Supreme Court has interpreted the First Amendment to mean that public schools may neither promote nor inhibit religious belief or non-belief. The public school curriculum may not, therefore, include religious indoctrination in any form (including hostility to religions or religion in general). Such teaching would constitute state sponsorship of religion and would violate the freedom of conscience protected by the First Amendment.

Religious indoctrination, however, is not the same as teaching about religion. In the 1960s school prayer cases (which ruled against state-sponsored school prayer and devotional Bible-reading), the Supreme Court indicated that public school education may include teaching about religion. In *Abington v. Schempp* (1963), the court stated:

[I]t might well be said that one's education is not complete without a study of comparative religion or the history of religion and its relationship to the advancement of civilization. It certainly may be said that the Bible is worthy of study for its literary and historic qualities. Nothing we have said here indicates that such study of the Bible or of religion, when presented objectively as part of a secular program of education, may not be effected consistently with the First Amendment.

All public school teachers must have a clear understanding of the crucial difference

between the teaching of religion (religious education) and teaching about religion. In 1988, a broad coalition of seventeen religious and educational organizations published guidelines that distinguish between teaching about religion and religious indoctrination. The guidelines state, in part:

- The school's approach to religion is *academic*, not devotional.

- The school strives for student *awareness* of religions, but does not press for student *acceptance* of any one religion.

- The school sponsors *study* about religion, not the *practice* of religion.

- The school *exposes* students to a diversity of religious views; it does not *impose* any particular view.

- The school *educates* about all religions; it does not *promote* or *denigrate* any religion.

- The school *informs* students about various beliefs; it does not seek to conform students to any particular belief.

In addition to these baseline distinctions, the Religious Liberty clauses provide guiding principles for how teaching about religion may best be carried out in the classroom. These principles are the civic values at the heart of American citizenship. They are so fundamental and enduring that they may be called the three Rs of religious liberty:

- **Rights:** Religious liberty, or freedom of conscience, is a basic and inalienable right founded on the inviolable dignity of the person. In a society as religiously diverse as the United States, it is essential that schools emphasize that the rights guaranteed by the Constitution are for citizens of all faiths and none.

- **Responsibilities:** Religious liberty is not only a universal right, but it also depends upon a universal responsibility to respect that right for others, treating others as we ourselves desire to be treated. Students must recognize the inseparable link between the preservation of

Continued on next page

Charles C. Haynes

Charles C. Haynes is Senior Scholar for Religious Freedom at the Freedom Forum First Amendment Center in Arlington, Virginia. He presently serves on the Board of Directors of the Character Education Partnership. Dr. Haynes was one of the principal organizers and drafters of "Religious Liberty, Public Education, and the Future of American Democracy: A Statement of Principles," sponsored by more than twenty major educational and religious organizations. He also co-chaired the coalitions that produced a series of consensus guidelines on "Religion in the Public School Curriculum," and "Religious Holidays in the Public Schools." Dr. Haynes holds a master's degree in religion and education from Harvard Divinity School and a Ph.D. in theological studies from Emory University. He formerly taught world religions at Randolph-Macon College and social studies in both public and private secondary schools.

Teaching About Religion in Public Schools *(continued)*

their own constitutional rights and their responsibility as citizens to defend those rights for all others. This is what may be called the golden rule for civic life.

- **Respect:** Debate and disagreement are vital to classroom discussion and a key element of preparation for citizenship in a democracy. Yet, if we are to live with our differences, particularly our religious differences, how we debate, and not only what we debate, is critical. At the heart of good citizenship is a strong commitment to the civic values that enable people with diverse religious and philosophical perspectives to treat one another with respect and civility.

Rights, responsibilities, and respect, then, are the civic ground rules for teaching about religion in the public schools just as they are the ground rules of American citizenship. When we teach about the many cultures and religions of our nation and the world, we must simultaneously teach our common ground—the civic values and responsibilities that we share as American citizens. If this is done, teaching about religion becomes an excellent opportunity to teach respect for the universal rights and mutual responsibilities, within which the deep differences of belief can be negotiated.

Approaches to Teaching about Religion

Teachers need to make clear to students (and their parents) that teaching about religion is an important part of the curriculum in such subjects as social studies, literature, music, and art. Make them aware that all study about religion will be within the civic framework provided by the Constitution and will serve the educational goals of the academic program.

Natural Inclusion

Study about religion should take place within a historical and cultural context. Courses in history, literature, art, and music on the elementary and secondary levels as well as discussions of community and instruction about religious festivals and cultures offer natural opportunities to include discussion about religious influences and themes.

Keep in mind, however, that these discussions are not courses in religion or theology. What is taught about the religion or religions of a particular historical period or present-day culture should be only what is essential to understanding the events or peoples under consideration. Decisions concerning how much to discuss religion and which religions to include in the discussion should be determined by the academic requirements of the course being taught.

Students should be told that their study of religious traditions as a part of their study of history and culture is necessarily limited. Make clear why certain religious influences and themes have been selected for study. Remind students that there is much more to learn about the complexity and richness of each faith. Alert them to the fact that there is a wide diversity of opinion about religious events and ideas not only among the various religions, but also within the traditions themselves.

Fairness and Balance

Classroom discussions concerning religious traditions in history, literature, or other courses must be conducted in an environment that is free of advocacy on the part of the teacher. While various perspectives should be presented, no religious or anti-religious point of view should be advocated by the teacher. When discussing religious beliefs, teachers can avoid injecting personal religious beliefs by teaching through attribution (e.g., by reporting that "most Buddhists believe . . .").

Fair and balanced study about religion includes critical thinking about historical events involving religious traditions. Religious beliefs have had a part in some of the best and some of the worst developments in history. The full historical record (and various interpretations of it) must be available for analysis and discussion.

Teachers should use primary sources where possible so that students can work directly with the historical record.

Please note, however, that consideration of destructive or oppressive acts carried out in the name of a religious belief is not an opportunity to attack the integrity of the religion itself. All religious traditions can point to tragic chapters in their story and historical incidents where the ideals of the faith were not fully lived. This part of the record can be taught without condemning a particular religion or religion in general. Teaching that includes attacks on religion or on the theology or practice of any faith does not belong in a public school classroom.

Avoid asking qualitative comparisons between religions (e.g. religion A supercedes or is superior to religion B). Structural parallels, on the other hand, such as pointing out that most religious traditions have scriptures and community worship, may be a helpful way to organize the class discussion. It is also appropriate to compare and contrast the different perspectives religious groups might have on historical or current events.

Respect for Differences

When teaching about the major faiths of humankind in history, teachers must take great care not to present religious truth claims as relative or to reduce all religions to a common denominator.

Sometimes, in an effort to sound "tolerant" or "neutral," people speak of all religions as "all the same" underneath their differences. A Peanuts poster of some years ago parodied this approach by saying: "It doesn't matter what you believe as long as you are sincere." For many religious people, however, such "toleration" from others distorts their faith and is anything but neutral. It matters very much to a Christian or to a Jew or to a Muslim, for example, what one takes to be ultimately true. These faith communities, and many others, subscribe to absolute truths derived from the sources of revelation and authority in their tradi-

tions. The view that all faiths are ultimately the same may be compatible with some world views, but this is itself a philosophical position. For a teacher to advocate this view is a form of indoctrination.

Equally problematic are attempts by a teacher to "explain away" religious faith as merely social or psychological phenomena. Such teaching often leaves the impression that truth is relative and that there are no absolutes. It is permissible to present various theories of religion and to introduce students to the social, economic, and cultural context in which religions have formed and changed. However, it is first and foremost essential to report how people of faith interpret their own practices and beliefs, and how these beliefs have affected their lives historically as well as how they affect people's lives today.

Remember, public school teachers are required to teach about the various approaches to religious truth without advocating one religious or philosophical position over another. Teaching respect for differences is a key part of understanding the beliefs of the world's religious traditions. By taking care not to portray as relative or to reduce the truth claims of religions, the teacher allows the student to learn how each faith understands itself.

Use of Religious Scriptures

Study of history or literature would be incomplete without exposure to the scriptures of the world's major religious traditions. Some knowledge of biblical literature, for example, is necessary to comprehend much in the history, law, art, and literature of Western civilization, just as exposure to the Qur'an is important for understanding Islamic civilization. In this sense, the classical religious texts are part of our study of history and culture.

At the same time, students need to recognize that while scriptures tell us much about the history and cultures of humankind, they are considered sacred accounts

Continued on next page

Students need to recognize that religious and philosophical beliefs and practices are of deep significance to much of our citizenry.

Teaching About Religion in Public Schools *(continued)*

Understood properly, and carried out with sensitivity, the challenge of teaching about religion in public schools is an exciting opportunity for enriching the curriculum. Teaching about religion within the civic framework of religious liberty can do much to prepare citizens for living and working together in a pluralistic society.

by adherents to their respective traditions. Religious documents give students of history the opportunity to examine directly how religious traditions understand divine revelation and human values.

In a history class, selections from these accounts should always be treated with respect and used only in the appropriate historical and cultural context. Alert students to the fact that there are a variety of interpretations of scripture within each religious tradition.

Role Playing

Recreating religious practices or ceremonies through role playing activities should not take place in a public school classroom. Such activities, no matter how carefully planned or well-intentioned, risk undermining the integrity of the faith involved. Religious ceremonies are sacred to those who practice them. Recreations may unwittingly mock or, at the very least, oversimplify the religious meaning or intent of the ritual.

Role playing religious practices may also violate the conscience of students who are asked to participate. Use audio-visual resources and primary-source documents to introduce students to ceremonies and rituals of the world's religions.

Guest Speakers

When teaching about religion in history, it may be helpful to invite a guest speaker for a more comprehensive presentation of the religious tradition under study. Care should be taken to invite someone with the academic background necessary for an objective and scholarly discussion of the historical period and the religion being considered.

Faculty from local colleges and universities often make excellent guest speakers, or can make recommendations of others who might be appropriate for working with students in a public school setting. Religious leaders or clergy in the community can also be a valuable resource. Remember, however, that they have commitments to their own faith. Be certain that any guest speaker

understands the First Amendment guidelines for teaching about religion in public education, and is clear about the nature of their assignment. When the goals of the course are clearly communicated and the task specific, religious leaders can be helpful.

The Beliefs of Teachers and Students

Teachers

We have already seen that teaching about religion in public schools must never be used by teachers as an opportunity to proselytize or to impose religious or anti-religious views on the students.

What should the response be, however, when students ask the teacher to reveal his or her own religious beliefs? Some teachers prefer not to answer the question, stating that it is inappropriate for a teacher to inject personal beliefs into the discussion. Teachers of very young children, in particular, sometimes find this to be the most satisfactory response.

Many other teachers, however, do not wish to leave students guessing about their personal views. In the interest of establishing an open and honest classroom environment, these teachers answer the question straightforwardly and succinctly.

The teacher who decides to answer the question by telling the students his or her religious background should probably not do so at the beginning of the course. Such questions are best answered once the teacher has had an opportunity to demonstrate how various religious and non-religious perspectives may be taught about with sensitivity and objectivity.

When answering the question, teachers may take the opportunity to say something like: "These are my personal beliefs, but my role here is to present with fairness and sensitivity a variety of beliefs as we study the history of the world's great cultures." Answering the question briefly, with little elaboration or discussion, can be a good lesson in civic values. Students learn that people with deep convictions can teach and learn about the convictions of others in ways that are fair and balanced.

Students

Teachers should not solicit information about the religious affiliations or beliefs of students. Nor should students be requested to explain their faith or religious practices to the class. Such requests put undue pressure on students who may not wish to act as spokespersons for their tradition. Keep in mind also that students may not be qualified or prepared to represent their tradition accurately.

Students may choose on their own to express their religious views during a class discussion or as part of a writing project or art activity. This is appropriate as long as it is relevant to the subject under consideration and meets the requirements of the assignment.

At the beginning of the course, especially in the social studies, students should consider the civic values that will be the ground rules for class discussion. Teachers may wish to introduce the first principles of rights, responsibilities, and respect that flow from the First Amendment. By teaching within this framework, they help students learn to respect religious distinctiveness while affirming our constitutional guarantees.

When civic values and responsibilities are in place, the classroom environment is conducive to exploring a broad range of beliefs and practices, of ideas and views, in a way that is non-judgmental and non-threatening. Students learn that differences, even our deepest differences, can be discussed with civility and respect, and that ridicule and prejudice have no place in our society.

Meeting the Challenge

The United States is fortunate to have many talented and dedicated teachers. Given proper educational and administrative support, and working with sound materials, teachers will meet the challenge of study about religion in the core curriculum of the public schools. As schools go forward with teaching about religion, it is important that teachers:

- Take advantage of educational opportunities offered by national institutes and local continuing education courses to learn more about the world's great religious traditions and about the role of religion and religious liberty in United States and world history.

- Encourage school districts to offer pre-service and in-service education for all teachers faced with the responsibility of teaching about religion. Such programs should focus on how to teach about religion in ways that are constitutionally permissible, educationally sound, and culturally sensitive.

- Be familiar with state and local guidelines for teaching about religion in the curriculum.

- Have clear educational objectives for the inclusion of study about religion in courses where such study may be appropriate.

- Make certain that administrators, students, and parents understand how and when study about religion will take place in the classroom (have guidelines available to help answer questions).

- Use textbooks and supplementary materials that discuss the role of religion in history and culture, and do so in a way that is fair and balanced.

Understood properly, and carried out with sensitivity, the challenge of teaching about religion in public schools is an exciting opportunity for enriching the curriculum. Teaching about religion within the civic framework of religious liberty can do much to prepare citizens for living and working together in a pluralistic society. Through education and commitment to civic values, public schools can and must ensure that our diversity remains a source of national strength. ▪

For More Information

The Freedom Forum First Amendment Center is a non-profit, educational foundation that provides legal and educational guidelines on the constitutional role of religion in public education. The Center also offers seminars for teachers and suggests supplementary resources for teaching about religions in the classroom. For more information contact:

Charles C. Haynes, Ph.D.
The Freedom Forum First Amendment Center
1101 Wilson Blvd.
Arlington, VA 22209
(703) 528-0800

or

Marcia Beauchamp
First Amendment Center
Pacific Coast Center
1 Market St.
Steuart Tower, 21st Floor
San Francisco, CA 94105
(415) 281-0900

Web site
www.freedomforum.org

Using Collaborative Learning in Social Studies

Collaborative learning is a strategy or structure for learning that can be adapted to many lessons and activities. There are many models or approaches to collaborative learning (or cooperative learning), but all of these models share certain basic characteristics:

- Students work together to achieve a common goal.
- Students work face-to-face in heterogeneous groups.
- Each member of the group has a clearly defined role and is individually accountable for tasks.
- Each member makes an important contribution to the success of the group's effort ("positive interdependence").

Working together in collaborative groups is an excellent way to develop students' skills of social participation, always a key goal of the social studies curriculum. Furthermore, since interdependence is a hallmark of many cultures, collaborative learning techniques are especially useful with limited English proficient students (LEP). However, these students, and many fluent English speakers as well, do need special help with procedures when they have specifically assigned tasks they must carry out. Since they are not as likely to be able to divide up tasks, teachers need to demonstrate and have students practice grouping strategies, assigning individual responsibilities, and other group techniques such as reaching consensus.

Your Role as Teacher

It is important to bear in mind that collaborative learning supplements direct instruction—it does not replace it. As always, the teacher provides the solid instruction that is the basis for learning. Simply putting students in groups and giving them an interesting assignment does not lead to successful collaborative learning. Instead, you as teacher play the key role of providing structure, guidance, and feedback. In a very real sense, your role becomes that of coach or facilitator.

An important ingredient in the success of collaborative groups is effective use of interpersonal skills. As facilitator, you can help groups identify ahead of time the kinds of interpersonal skills that will be important to the task they are undertaking. These skills may range from something as simple as speaking quietly to a more complex skill such as giving constructive criticism. Modeling these skills for students and helping students practice them are important parts of your role.

Another area in which student groups need support is in learning to manage the process of group interaction. It is usually easier for students to divide up tasks such as research and writing than it is for them to make sure that someone keeps the group on target and monitors their progress. Supporting and guiding students in these process tasks can help assure the success of the group's efforts.

Practical Tips

1. It takes time for group members to become comfortable with one another and work together effectively. You may want to begin by having groups engage in some simple brainstorming activities just to become acquainted and begin to develop trust. For the same reason, it is usually best to keep groups together for at least several weeks before regrouping.

2. Try to build in time for groups to evaluate their performance after completing an activity. How well did they do not only with the academic task but with their interpersonal and group processes? What lessons can they apply to future collaborative efforts? The Multiple Use Master in the Assessment Options booklet that comes with the program can be used to assess groupwork.

Strategies

The following strategies can be adapted to many lessons and activities in Houghton Mifflin Social Studies.

Three-Step Interview

Procedures: Students work in pairs to interview each other about an assigned topic.

1. One student interviews the other about the topic.
2. The students switch roles as interviewer and interviewee.
3. Each student shares with the group what he or she learned during the interview.

Uses: The Three-Step Interview can be used effectively to build background knowledge in conjunction with the Introduce part of the Teacher's Edition lesson. You can use the notes under Introduce to formulate a question for the interview such as, "What do you know about [topic of lesson]?" As an option for the Close part of the lesson, occasionally you might also have students do a Three-Step Interview on a question such as, "What's the most important thing you learned about [topic of lesson]?" or "What else would you like know about [topic]?"

Benefits: Promotes participation, listening skills, divergent thinking

Jigsaw

Procedures: In the Jigsaw strategy, each member of the team becomes "expert" about a particular topic related to a larger team project. Team members then share information to prepare a presentation or solve a problem. Following are the main steps:

1. Identify several manageable topics related to a larger topic or concept.
2. Set up an "expert" group for each topic made up of one member from each team.
3. Have expert groups work together to research their topic.

4. Experts return to their original teams and share what they have learned.
5. You as teacher may assign or let teams select a particular format for presenting their findings.

Uses: The Jigsaw approach can be used with many of the Collaborative Learning activities in the Chapter Reviews. It is particularly effective in helping students prepare for informed debate or to acquire and present new information.

Benefits: Promotes interdependence, helps students discover connections among concepts and bodies of information

Group Investigation

Procedures: Students work in teams to prepare a presentation or project to share with the class. Students form teams and divide the work so that each student on a team has a definite task to perform.

Uses: This strategy helps students to synthesize information from several sources. Many Chapter Review activities lend themselves to this approach.

Benefits: Promotes organizational and presentation skills; helps students direct their own learning.

Pair Debate

Procedures: Students debate an issue in pairs. First, each student defends one side of the issue; then pairs switch partners, and each student must defend the other side of the same issue.

Uses: Pair Debate can be used as an effective Close, especially for lessons that deal with conflict or controversy in history.

Benefits: Promotes role-playing, knowing, and respecting different points of view. ■

For Further Reading

Slavin, R.E. *Cooperative Learning: Theory, Research and Practice.* Englewood Cliffs, NJ: Prentice Hall, 1990.

Stahl, Robert J. *Cooperative Learning in Social Studies: A Handbook for Teachers.* Menlo Park, CA: Addison-Wesley, 1994.

HOUGHTON MIFFLIN SOCIAL STUDIES
Collaborative Learning

Chapter Review
In each Chapter Review, the Preparing for Citizenship feature has a Collaborative Learning activity.

Teacher's Edition
Frequent stimulating Collaborative Learning and Social Participation activities at point of use provide practice in interpersonal skills.

Developing Concepts and Vocabulary

Vocabulary instruction plays an important role in social studies, as it does in all content area reading. But teaching students a social studies term usually does not mean teaching them a new label for a concept they already have. In most cases, it means teaching students an unfamiliar concept.

Houghton Mifflin Social Studies integrates vocabulary instruction with the teaching of other concepts and knowledge. Always the emphasis is on starting with what students already know and linking that prior knowledge to new concepts and information or by building background before they start reading. This approach is solidly grounded in research that shows that knowledge is not just unrelated facts but sets of relationships. We learn new information by relating it to what we already know.

Many features of this program will assist you in helping your students activate their prior knowledge and link new concepts. In the Teacher's Edition, the Unit Previews, the Chapter Overviews, and the Introduce portion of each lesson provide useful strategies. The Graphic Overviews— which are also presented to the student in the Lesson Preview pages in *Reading Support Resources*—can help you show your students connections among the key ideas in each lesson. The Lesson Support/ Transition pages in the SDAIE portion of *Reading Support Resources* reinforce student understanding of essential vocabulary. In the students' own books, the Connect question in each lesson review helps students link what they have learned in that lesson to previous learning. The Key Terms taught in the lesson relate to important ideas in that lesson and, furthermore, are terms that students will encounter frequently in their social studies reading.

Vocabulary Strategies

The strategies that follow present useful options for preteaching and reviewing vocabulary for any lesson.

Semantic Feature Analysis

This strategy is particularly effective in helping students identify connections among related concepts. For this reason, it works best with terms that are closely related in meaning. A Venn diagram can be used effectively for semantic feature analysis. Borrowed from the field of mathematics, a Venn diagram is a pictorial representation that uses intersecting circles to show features shared by two or more concepts and features peculiar to each concept.

Example:

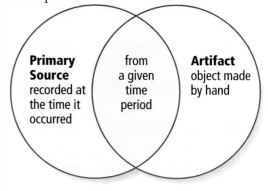

Primary Source recorded at the time it occurred | from a given time period | **Artifact** object made by hand

Contextual Redefinition

The strategy called contextual redefinition explicitly teaches students to use context as a clue to meaning. Because all Key Terms in Houghton Mifflin Social Studies are clearly defined in context, this strategy can be easily used with any lesson.

1. Present the words in isolation. Write each Key Term on the board or an overhead, and ask students to supply a meaning for each word. Students should defend their suggestions and come to consensus on the best definition.

2. Have students read the sentence from the lesson in which the term appears in boldface (dark type). Then ask students again to suggest definitions and defend

their suggestions. In this way, more skilled readers model for other students the thinking processes involved in formulating a definition from context.

3. Have students consult the Glossary, if appropriate, to confirm the definition.

Games

Research shows that students not only have fun, but are highly motivated by playing games. Games provide opportunities for learner-centered instruction, and can be used as cooperative learning activities. The games described below can be used to review Key Terms from a lesson or chapter.

Social Studies Bingo

Organization: Individual players

Length: 10-15 minutes

Preparation: Have students create a bingo board of five rows and five columns, writing a different Key Term in each empty space on the grid. Have students cut up paper into nine small pieces that can cover the spaces on the grid.

Rules of Play:

1. At random, read aloud a definition of a Key Term (definitions appear in the Teacher's Edition at the start of each lesson).

2. If students find the correct Key Term on their board, they should cover the space.

3. Continue reading aloud definitions. The first student to fill in a row or column (or the entire grid, if that is the goal) should shout "social studies," and wins if he or she identified the Key Terms correctly.

Olympic Password

Organization: Teams of two students.

Length: 10-15 minutes.

Preparation: Draw a tree like the one shown to keep track of how teams are doing, and have students fill it in as the game progresses.

Game Design for Olympic Password

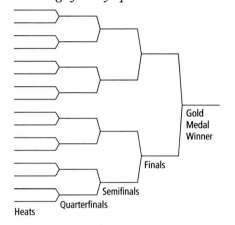

Gold Medal Winner

Finals

Semifinals

Quarterfinals

Heats

Rules of Play:

1. Have two competing teams sit with teammates facing each other. Give one player on each team a paper with the same Key Term on it, making sure that their teammates cannot see the term.

2. The player on the first team holding the term gives a one-word clue to his or her teammate, who has a chance to guess the term. If he or she guesses correctly, the team gets the point. If not, the person on the other team with the term gives a one-word clue. Teams take turns giving clues until the term is guessed.

3. Give the next term to the two players who guessed during the first round, and repeat the rules of play from above. Have the players take turns giving clues until all the Key Terms have been guessed.

4. The team with the most points wins the heat and continues to the quarterfinals. Teams can progress up the "tree" until the class has gold, silver, and bronze medalists. ■

For Further Reading

Bromley, Karen, Linda Irwin-De Vitis, and Marcia Modlo. *Graphic Organizers, Visual Strategies for Active Learning.* New York: Scholastic Professional Books, 1995.

Nagy, William E. *Teaching Vocabulary to Improve Reading Comprehension.* Urbana, IL: ERIC Clearninghouse on Reading and Communication Skills, 1988.

Student Edition
The opening page of the lesson lists the Key Terms covered in the lesson.

Chapter Review
Activities in Reviewing Key Terms in each Chapter Review enable students to use key terms in context.

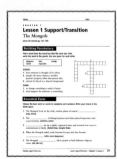

Reading Support Resources
The Lesson Support/ Transition pages reinforce students' understanding of essential vocabulary.

Character Education and Social Studies

Good citizenship in a democratic society such as ours implies active participation in the community, respecting and working together with other citizens to address common problems, and finding better ways to live in the community and in the world. Such activity suggests attitudes of respect for individuals and for the diversity amongst individuals and cultures, attitudes of caring for others and the environment, and attitudes of respect for human dignity.

In addition, young citizens must have a sense of responsibility, a belief that they themselves are responsible for the improvement of the society and the community, and that they must bring information and thoughtfulness to local, national, and international problems.

In Houghton Mifflin Social Studies, students examine historical time periods for evidence of civic behavior and civic values. They analyze the choices that individuals have made in certain circumstances, and assess the consequences of these actions. Students examine the personal and social qualities that contribute to a moral society within the context of the historical and cultural examples under investigation.

Proponents of character education urge that learners evaluate people from all of human history in light of those qualities that we consider admirable. They encourage educators to help students recognize and appreciate positive character traits and attitudes like those listed above. Qualities like these when taken together form the backbone of good citizenship. When most citizens aspire to these behaviors, the resulting society is the better for it. If students examine these qualities within their various historical contexts and determine whether and why such qualities are desirable, they will have taken the first step toward becoming civic-minded citizens. Houghton Mifflin Social Studies builds opportunity for this sort of examination.

Note how students first look closely at the period they are studying for evidence of civic virtue. From such concrete examples, they move to apply their knowledge to a larger context. Then they may be urged to actually take part in some civic project in their own community.

Because suggestions for character education are presented as natural outgrowths of the material under consideration, students won't feel they are being lectured or preached to. As with other elements of Houghton Mifflin Social Studies, character education is woven seamlessly into the general context. ■

For Further Reading

Boyer, Ernest L. "The Commitment to Character: A Basic Priority for Every School," *Update on Law Related Education* (vol. 20, no. 4) 1996

Character Education (Journal of the California Council for the Social Studies), vol. 37, no. 1, California Council for the Social Studies, 1997.

Haynes C.C. and L. James. *Fostering Civic Virtue: Character Education in the Social Studies,* National Council for the Social Studies, 1996.

Quigley, C.N., et al., *National Standards for Civics and Government,* Center for Civic Education (Calabasas, CA), 1994.

School-to-Career and Social Studies

In the closing years of the twentieth century, national attention becomes increasingly focused on the need for an alliance between the schools and the business world in order to prepare students for life outside the classroom.

With this attention comes the realization that the social studies already lends itself to and assumes responsibility for a large share of this preparation even as it seeks to find suitable channels to do more.

What Is

To speak of rapidly changing technology has become a cliché even as technology speeds ever faster toward the millennium. Employers in a world of work that moves so rapidly will seek applicants not with a particular field of technical expertise but rather with the skills necessary to approach and acquire new knowledge, and to adjust to an ever-changing workplace.

Ability to do this has been and is being fostered in the social studies classroom. Through methods that require formation and use of higher level thinking skills, of teamwork and cooperation, of respect for diversity and what can be learned from one's peers, the social studies classroom is indeed creating an atmosphere that provides learners the kind of liberal education necessary for the workplace of the future. In this workplace, the independent thinkers possessing effective social approaches to problem solving will reap the rewards.

What Is to Come

In addition to developing skills needed in the workplace, Houghton Mifflin Social Studies also offers means for students to deepen understanding of the human heritage connected with work. Note the School-to-Career feature, which appears on the Planning at a Glance pages before every chapter. In the feature, the discussion and suggested activities point out the world of work in a specific time and place and its continued importance in modern life. When appropriate, students trace the evolution of particular jobs up to the present day and may even get a chance to do some field work.

Too often today, with images of multi-million-dollar pro sports contracts and lives of the super models foremost in their minds, young people fail to appreciate—or at times even notice—those who perform and produce essential but less glamorous goods and services. Consistent reference to this School-to-Career feature in the course of instruction can lay realistic foundations and foster growth of respect for honest labor and for the full range of jobs available in the modern society.

Through their inquiry, students can begin to build a work ethic. All of us owe respect and a show of decency to those who perform less glamorous but completely essential jobs. Furthermore, those who prosper in any field will do a better day's work if they have a sense and sympathy for those forebears who dug coal, built roads, or sold trinkets from a pushcart to make a better life for those who followed them.

As stronger links between the schools and the workplace are forged, we can expect these to find reflections in the social studies. Even as this happens, students in today's social studies classroom continue to build strong foundations for the future as they make ready for the one thing they can be sure of—the inevitability of change. ▪

For Further Reading

Bonstingl, John J., *Learning for the Future: Building Core Competencies for the 21st Century Through Quality Principles and Practices*, Association for Supervision and Curriculum Development, 1998.

Service Learning, (*Social Studies Review* vol. 32, no. 2), California Council for the Social Studies, 1997.

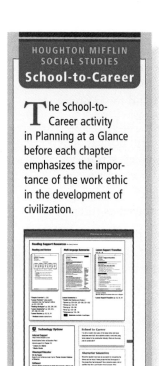

HOUGHTON MIFFLIN
SOCIAL STUDIES
School-to-Career

The School-to-Career activity in Planning at a Glance before each chapter emphasizes the importance of the work ethic in the development of civilization.

Teaching Multicultural Perspectives

Three important changes in the United States during the last 30 years have profoundly affected the content and methods of social studies education.

First, Asians and Latin Americans are now the largest immigrant groups. Newcomers from these and other parts of the world have dramatically altered the demographic composition of most classrooms.

Second, more than ever before, scholars have focused on the historical and social reality of gender, ethnic and racial groups. This research has resulted in the reevaluation of the roles these groups have played in the making of the United States.

Third, the momentous social and political changes resulting from the civil rights movement and the more recent affirmation of cultural distinctions have led to widespread concern with ethnic and racial identity. Expressions of this concern have ranged from celebration to censure.

Instructional Goals

With today's heightened awareness of cultural diversity, we must address our differences with respect and common sense. Houghton Mifflin Social Studies assists you in fulfilling that task. The multicultural perspectives employed throughout the series promote three important goals.

1. Facilitating readiness to learn in the classroom: Students who find people like themselves in their textbooks will be more at ease in the school setting and will gain the sense of belonging that prepares them to learn. The variety of foreign-born students in today's classroom makes inclusive representation more difficult. Houghton Mifflin Social Studies achieves inclusiveness through empathetic descriptions of the aspirations and achievements of all groups.

2. Providing a more accurate representation of historical events and the world today: To achieve the second goal, the program incorporates the most recent applicable scholarship in history, geography, anthropology, and the other social sciences. The aim is to represent factually the relevant groups and individuals—mainstream or minority—that have contributed to the making of the United States and other nations, while avoiding the suggestion that all cultures have been equally prominent in all times and places. Instructional materials make use of primary sources and quotations to present the positions of the affected actors in their own words. And multiple perspectives provide a stage for students to explore, debate, and make informed judgments regarding contrasting interpretations of human events.

3. Encouraging respect for ethnic, cultural, and social differences: The third goal requires balanced descriptions of ethnic, racial, and religious groups. Group or individual descriptions are scrutinized to avoid language that might appear patronizing, stereotypical, or demeaning. This commitment to accuracy allows exploration of the barriers that have restricted choices for racial and ethnic groups and for women.

Houghton Mifflin Social Studies includes a discussion of religious and ethical beliefs in contexts where such beliefs strongly influence the culture or history of a group. Care is taken that no belief system is ridiculed, trivialized, or portrayed as inferior.

What students read about people from other historical periods and other cultural backgrounds profoundly affects the students' attitudes. The goal of Houghton Mifflin Social Studies is to help students understand and respect all peoples as equals. ■

For Further Reading

Banks, James. *Teaching Strategies for Ethnic Studies.* Boston: Allyn and Bacon, 1991.

Nash Gary. *A Teacher's Guide to Multicultural Perspectives in Social Studies.* Boston: Houghton Mifflin Company, 1991.

Teaching Controversial Issues

In Jesse Stuart's classic American short story, "Split Cherry Tree," a father, angry about the way his son is treated by a teacher and even more so by a curriculum he does not understand, confronts that teacher, demanding some answers.

During the visit—and because the teacher is especially sensitive—the father appreciates what his son is learning and stops fearing the changes that have occurred in the classroom since his own youth.

Would that all problems like this were so beautifully resolved.

Today, with increasing frequency and vehemence, various segments of the public take to task schools and teachers for a variety of issues concerning both what is taught and how this knowledge is imparted. Educators often feel tugged in several directions at once as groups and individuals with varying beliefs insist that theirs is the one true way.

The controversial issue might be one of pedagogy. For example, a parent may demand to know why his or her child should be expected to help the less capable in a cooperative learning situation.

More often, the trigger for such conflict grows directly from course content. A student reacts strongly and emotionally to learning about the Nazi death camps; another is morally outraged to learn that white settlers in the Americas were less than tolerant of the native population. And both talk about their feelings at the dinner table.

The uproar that can result in situations like those just described might be said to be based on a "sin of commission" viewpoint that teachers have opened doors most often left closed and "put ideas in my child's head." At the same time, the profession is vulnerable to accusations of "sins of omission" from another wrathful camp that thinks the instruction is shying away from the upsetting details of human existence that form a less-than-rosy picture.

Addressing the Issues

Although there is no way to guarantee that a social studies program will not evoke some controversy, Houghton Mifflin Social Studies has taken a thoughtful and consistent approach to the problem. While the program does treat potentially controversial issues in a direct manner, it does so within the historical context in which these occur.

Furthermore, during the writing of the textbooks, every effort has been made to examine all issues of content and pedagogy —controversial and otherwise—from differing points of view, thus encouraging learners to develop an awareness of complexity and allowing them to exercise their own judgments once they have the data and experience to do so. Teachers have the comfort of knowing that a wide range of specialists have contributed to the makeup of the text and, in effect, stand with them if they are called upon to defend course content.

Teachers themselves play a role equal in its importance to that of the text. Knowledge of the local community, its political, sociological, racial, national, and ethnic makeup, can go a long way to stop problems before they start.

Whether teachers view controversy as a learning tool or wish to keep distracting controversy at a minimum, Houghton Mifflin Social Studies and the teachers' own good judgment and knowledge of their communities can work together at the task at hand, the education of our young. ■

For Further Reading

Nash, Gary, Charlotte Crabtree, and Ross E. Dunn, *History on Trial: Culture Wars and the Teaching of the Past*, Knopf, 1997.

The Role of Primary Sources and Literature

Primary source material and authentic literature represent the voices of the people of a particular time and place. What better way to study a culture or an event or historical issue than to read about it from the perspective of those living then and there!

In a well-designed social studies curriculum, students come face to face with a full range of human experience in many times and places. To convey the richness of this experience, a textbook must employ a variety of modes of presentation: exposition, narration, description, and visual presentation. The inclusion of literature and primary sources can enhance the effectiveness of all these modes of presentation.

Houghton Mifflin Social Studies integrates literature and primary sources throughout the program. Every unit includes at least one full-length literature selection. In addition, many lessons include shorter excerpts from literature. Most chapters make extensive use of primary sources, such as letters, speeches, diaries, and newspaper accounts as well as official documents. In most grades, the Time/Space Databank also includes a collection of important primary sources. The inclusion of these materials provides students the opportunity to learn how to synthesize information across various sources.

The major function of the literature in Houghton Mifflin Social Studies is to help students develop empathy for the experiences of people in other times and places. Through reading stories, legends, and poems, students can gain insight into the thoughts, feelings, and experiences of people who lived the history they are studying.

Using Literature

The major literature selections in Houghton Mifflin Social Studies are found before or after lessons at their most appropriate point of use. Sometimes literature provides an engaging point of entry for students into a new topic or period. Other times it expands on or exemplifies ideas of events that students have studied in a previous lesson. In either case, the goal is not to have students analyze the literature but rather to have them respond to it in ways that help them

- enrich their understanding of other times and places,
- promote their development of historical empathy,
- broaden their perspectives on historical events, and
- deepen their appreciation of the ways in which events and ideas affect people's daily lives.

The Teacher's Edition notes with each literature selection provide suggested activities and strategies for student response.

In addition, each unit opener spread in the Teacher's Edition lists the titles from the Houghton Mifflin Social Studies Bookshelf II that relate to that unit. Furthermore, on Teacher's Edition pages 43–49, you will find an extensive bibliography that includes other literature appropriate for use with the unit.

Using Primary Sources

Diaries, letters, newspaper accounts, photographs, and other primary documents also let people of the past speak directly to students. Reading these sources exposes students to opposing opinions, alternative points of view, and accounts of how events affected people in various walks of life. In this way, students also begin to develop familiarity with many of the kinds of evidence that historians use and interpret. ■

For More Information

A valuable source of information on recently published literature is the annual bibliography of outstanding children's trade books in the field of social studies that appears in the April/May issue of *Social Education*, published by the National Council for the Social Studies.

Bibliography for Teachers and Students

Bibliography Updates

Each year, new titles are correlated with *Across the Centuries* and posted on the HMSS web site on Houghton Mifflin's Education Place: **www.eduplace.com**.

UNIT 1
Links to the Ancient World

Independent Reading

Easy Books

The Roman News
by Andrew Langley and Philip De Souza
Candlewick, 1996 (32p)

The authors depict life in ancient Rome through the form of a newspaper with news stories, lively articles on daily life, and letters to the editor.

Fossil Detective
by Joyce Pope
Troll, 1994 (32p)

Students learn about the nature and origin of fossils and what's involved in the collection and study of them.

Writing and Arithmetic: Ancient Civilizations (3500 B.C.–A.D. 1)
by Paul Russell
Tambourine, 1994 (48p)

The author explains how people wrote and computed in ancient civilizations of Asia, Africa, Europe, and the Americas.

Average Books

How We Know About the Romans
by Louise James
Bedrick, 1997 (32p)

The author explains how historical knowledge is gleaned from the work of archaeologists and anthropologists.

Street Smart!
Cities of the Ancient World
by Lerner Geography Department
Runestone, 1994 (80p)

The authors explain how ancient cities in Rome, Greece, and Egypt were built and what functions they had in their cultures.

India's Gupta Dynasty
by Kathryn Hinds
Benchmark, 1995 (80p)

Maps, reproductions, and photographs illustrate this book about the Gupta dynasty, which includes a section on what young people experienced in everyday life then.

The Byzantine Empire
by James A. Corrick
Lucent, 1997

The author provides an overview of the Byzantine Empire and its cultural and historical legacy.

Challenging Books

Ancient India: Land of Mystery
by Time-Life Editors
Time-Life, 1994 (228p)

The finds of archaeologists clarify what life was like in ancient India.

The Emperor's Winding Sheet
by Jill Paton Walsh
Farrar, 1992 (288p) paper

In this historical novel, a shipwrecked English boy finds his way to the court of Constantine.

The Eagle's Daughter
by Judith Tarr
Forge, 1996 (224p)

This historical novel recounts how the Empress Theophano finds herself in a major war of succession when Otto II dies suddenly and leaves his empire to his four-year-old son.

Books to Read Aloud
Heroes, Gods, and Emperors from Roman Mythology
by Kerry Usher
Bedrick, 1992 (132p)

Black-and-white and color illustrations enchance this collection of stories from Roman mythology.

Demons, Gods, & Holy Men from Indian Myths and Legends
by Shahrukh Husain
Bedrick, 1995 (132p)

This collection contains Hindu as well as other myths and legends from India.

Books for Teachers
The Age of Augustus
by Don Nardo
Lucent, 1996 (112p)

The author details the prosperous reign of Augustus Caesar and includes lengthy quotations from primary and secondary sources.

What Life Was Like When Rome Ruled the World: The Roman Empire, 100 B.C.–A.D. 200
by Time-Life Editors
Time-Life, 1997 (192p)

This volume concentrates on the accomplishments of the Roman Empire from the reign of Julius Caesar to the death of Hadrian.

 **Multimedia Resources**

Videocassettes

Latitude and Longitude 22 min.
National Geographic, 1994

Every Stone Has a Story 20 min.
National Geographic, 1995

Ancient Rome 15 min.
Encyclopaedia Britannica, 1993

Software

Ancient World 2000
(Computer-Interactive Videodisc)
Decision Development, 1995

Ancient Civilizations (CD-ROM)
ENTREX Software, 1995

World Geo Graph II (Floppy Disk)
Learning Company, 1993

Picture Atlas of the World
(CD-ROM)
Now What Software, 1995

Bibliography for Teachers and Students

Independent Reading

Easy Books

Ramadan
by Suhaib Hamid Ghazi
Holiday, 1996 (32p)

Young Hakeem joins his family in fasting and feasting to celebrate Ramadan, the ninth month of the Muslim lunar year.

What Do We Know About Islam?
by Shahrukh Husain
Bedrick, 1996 (44p)

The author asks basic questions about the beliefs, practices, sacred places, and books of Islam and provides clear answers.

Id-ul-Fitr
by Rosalind Kerven
Raintree, 1996 (31p)

From the *World of Holidays* series, this book looks at the observance of Id-ul-Fitr.

The Storytellers
by Ted Lewin
Lothrop, 1998 (32p)

In Fez, Morocco, Abdul and his grandfather stop by an old gate, where Grandfather performs as a storyteller and crowds gather.

Average Books

The Rise of Islam
by John Child
Bedrick, 1995 (64p)

The author takes a historical look at Islam, discussing its early years.

Mecca
by Shahrukh Husain
Dillon, 1993 (48p)

From the Holy Cities series, the author explores Mecca, the spiritual center of Islam.

Challenging Books

The Spread of Islam
by John Dunn
Lucent, 1996 (128p)

Islam has spread to many lands, and today many millions practice it.

Muhammad: His Life Based on the Earliest Sources
by Martin Lings
Inner Traditions Ltd., 1987 paper

This engaging narrative tells of the life of the prophet Muhammad, based on the biography by Ibn Hisham.

Books to Read Aloud

Anthology of Islamic Literature: From the Rise of Islam to Modern Times
by James Kritzeck
New American Library, 1989 paper

The author provides a useful compendium of literature, poetry, tales, historical treatises, and other genres of writing.

Books for Teachers

The Adventures of Ibn Battuta: A Muslim Traveller of the 14th Century
by Ross E. Dunn
U. of California, 1990

This is an account of Ibn Battuta's twenty years of travel ranging from Morocco to China.

The Hajj: The Muslim Pilgrimage to Mecca and the Holy Places
by F. E. Peters
Princeton U., 1994 (399p)

Included here are firsthand accounts of travelers who have made the pilgrimage to Mecca.

Multimedia Resources

Videocassettes

Middle East: History and Culture 20 min.
Barr Films, 1993

Software

Non-European World History
(Computer-Interactive Videodisc)
Instructional Resources, 1996

Independent Reading

Easy Books

Ashanti to Zulu: African Traditions
by Margaret Musgrove
Puffin, 1992 (32p) paper

This award-winning book combines beautiful illustrations with factual information about African peoples, their history, and culture.

African Beginnings
by Jim Haskins and Kathleen Benson
Lothrop, 1998 (48p)

In this first volume of a planned seven-part series, the authors present overviews of several ancient African kingdoms, including Nubia, Ghana, Mali, Songhay, and Kongo.

Sundiata: Lion King of Mali
by David Wisniewski
Clarion, 1992 (32p)

In the thirteenth century, Sundiata overcame physical handicaps, social disgrace, and strong opposition to rule the West African trading empire of Mali.

Mufaro's Beautiful Daughters
by John Steptoe
Lothrop, 1987 (32p)

This award-winning, beautifully illustrated book retells a Zimbabwean Cinderella story.

Average Books

Songhay: The Empire Builders
by Philip Koslow
Chelsea, 1995 (64p) paper

Students learn about the trading state of Songhay, which reached its peak in the 1400s and 1500s.

Mali: Crossroads to Africa
by Philip Koslow
Chelsea, 1995 (64p) also paper

The author tells the history of the West African empire that flourished from 1240 to 1500.

Bibliography for Teachers and Students

Centuries of Greatness: The West African Kingdoms 750–1900
by Philip Koslow
Chelsea, 1994 (64p) also paper

Beginning with Ghana, Koslow traces early African kingdoms.

Kongo, Ndongo: West Central Africa
by Kenny Mann
Dillon, 1996 (105p)

The author uses legends, oral histories, and recorded events to trace the histories of these African kingdoms.

Challenging Books

From Afar to Zulu: A Dictionary of African Cultures
by Jim Haskins and Joan Biondi
Walker, 1995 (212p)

With maps, illustrations, and photos, the authors introduce thirty African peoples from pre-Islamic times through the present.

African Folktales: Traditional Stories of the Black World
edited by Roger D. Abrahams
Pantheon, 1983

This collection contains almost one hundred tales of universal themes that also evoke unique African culture and traditions.

The Eye, The Ear, and the Arm
by Nancy Farmer
Orchard, 1994 (311p) also paper

In this popular fantasy, set in Zimbabwe of the past and the future, the children of the chief of security are kidnapped.

Books to Read Aloud

Kings, Gods, and Spirits from African Mythology
by Jan Knappert
Bedrick, 1993 (88p)

This collection of colorful tales proves again the universal appeal of myth across the cultures of the world.

Tokoloshi: African Folktales Retold
by Diana Pitcher
Tricycle, 1993 (64p)

These seventeen folktales are primarily Bantu, set against a background of Zulu life and customs.

Books for Teachers

Africa's Glorious Legacy
by Time-Life Editors
Time-Life, 1995 (168p)

This richly illustrated book focuses on the life and customs of people in ancient Nubia and the kingdoms of Mali, Ghana, Benin, and Zimbabwe.

African Art: An Introduction
by Frank Willett
Thames & Hudson, 1993 (288p)

In this revised edition of Willett's book, the author discusses many facets of African art.

 Multimedia Resources

Videocassettes
Crossing the Ancient Desert
11 min.
Stanton Films, 1995

Africa: Land and People 24 min.
Africa Series
Barr Films, 1990

Software
STV: World Geography; Africa and Europe
(Computer-Interactive Videodisc)
National Geographic, 1994

Africa Trail (CD-ROM)
The Learning Company, 1995

UNIT 4
Asian Civilizations

Independent Reading

Easy Books

The Mongols
by Robert Nicholson
Chelsea, 1994 (32p)

Daily life, religion, clothing, and food are a few of the points discussed.

The Silk Route: 7,000 Miles of History
by John S. Major
Harper, 1995 (32p) also paper

This handsomely illustrated book tracks goods on a journey from China to Byzantium via the Silk Route in 700 B.C.

The Song of Mulan
by Jeanne M. Lee
Front Street, 1995

Mulan disguises herself as a boy to join the Khan's soldiers in fighting the invading Tartars. In English and Chinese.

What Do We Know About Buddhism?
by Anita Ganeri
Bedrick, 1997 (44p)

The author explains the origins and practices of Buddhism.

Average Books

Silk and Spice Routes
by Paul Strathern and Struan Reid
Silver, 1994 (48p)

Trade between East and West is explored in the four books in this series: *Exploration by Land, Exploration by Sea, Inventions and Trade,* and *Cultures and Civilizations.*

Oracle Bones, Stars, and the Wheelbarrows: Ancient Chinese Science and Technology
by Frank Ross
Houghton Mifflin, 1982 (192p) also paper

Covers the achievements of the ancient Chinese in astronomy, medicine, botany, and engineering, as well as Chinese inventions including gunpowder, the compass, and printing.

Inside a Samurai Castle
by Fiona Macdonald
Bedrick, 1995 (48p)

An overview of the education and training of samurai and their role in feudal Japan.

Challenging Books

Den of the White Fox
by Lensey Namioka
Browndeer, 1997 (216p)

The masterless samurai warriors Zenta and Matsuzo find danger and intrigue as they wander through medieval Japan.

Bibliography for Teachers and Students

The Samurai's Tale
by Eric Haugaard
Houghton Mifflin, 1984 (256p) also paper

This classic story, set in sixteenth-century Japan, is about the orphaned Taro, who becomes a samurai.

Books to Read Aloud
Maples in the Mist: Children's Poems from the Tang Dynasty
translated by Minfong Ho
Lothrop, 1996 (32p)

Illustrated with Chinese brush paintings, the poems represent the larger repertoire usually taught to children in China.

Dragons, Gods & Spirits from Chinese Mythology
by Tao Tao Liu Sanders
Bedrick, 1994 (132p)

This lavishly illustrated edition is a comprehensive collection of Chinese mythology.

Mysterious Tales of Japan
by Rafe Martin
Putnam, 1996 (80p)

Martin retells ten Japanese folktales, including "The Boy Who Drew Cats."

Books for Teachers
The Cambridge History of Ancient China
edited by Edward L. Shaughnessy and Michael Loewe
Cambridge U., 1998

All aspects of ancient China are covered in this volume.

The Japanese Today
by Edwin O. Reischauer
Harvard U., 1995 (459p)

The author presents a comprehensive view of Japan.

Multimedia Resources

Videocassettes

Asia 25 min.
Physical Geography of the
Continents Series
National Geographic, 1991

India: The Empire of the Spirit
60 min.
Origins of a Civilization Series
Ambrose Video, 1992

China: Sichuan Province 25 min.
National Geographic, 1988

Japan 25 min.
Window to the World: Asia Series
IVN Communications, 1995

Buddhism: The Middle Way of Compassion 20 min.
United Learning, 1993

Software

Non-European World History
(Computer-Interactive Videodisc)
Instructional Resources, 1996

STV: World Geography
Asia and Australia (Computer-Interactive
Videodisc)
National Geographic, 1994

Battles of the World (CD-ROM)
Compton's NewMedia, 1996

UNIT 5
Medieval Societies

Independent Reading

Easy Books

Breaking Into Print: Before and After the Invention of the Printing Press
by Stephen Krensky
Little, 1996 (32p)

The author explains how books were produced before Gutenberg's invention and the later impact of his printing press.

First Facts About the Vikings
by Fiona Macdonald
Bedrick, 1996 (32p)

Illustrations, side bars, and maps help tell the story of the Vikings and their explorations.

Medieval Castle
by Jim Pipe
Millbrook, 1996 (32p) paper

Using mazes and puzzles to solve a mystery, students learn about daily life in a castle.

Average Books

The World of the Medieval Knight
by Christopher Gravett
Bedrick, 1997 (64p)

The author looks at the life of a knight, from armor and weapons, to jousting and feasting.

A Day With a Noblewoman
by Régine Pernoud
Runestone, 1997 (48p)

This book first presents an overview of the life of a French noblewoman and then looks at the life of one particular noblewoman. Also in the *A Day With* series, see *A Miller, A Stonecutter,* and *A Troubadour.*

A Proud Taste for Scarlet and Miniver
by E. L. Konigsburg
Atheneum, 1973 (201p) paper

In this critically acclaimed biography of Eleanor of Aquitaine, she and three people who knew her recall the events of her life.

Catherine, Called Birdy
by Karen Cushman
Clarion, 1994 (224p) also paper

Catherine, a spirited and inquisitive young woman of good family, narrates the story of her fourteenth year—in 1290.

Challenging Books

The Age of Feudalism
by Timothy L. Biel
Lucent, 1994 (128p)

This account of feudalism contains numerous primary source quotations.

There Will Be Wolves
by Karleen Bradford
Lodestar, 1996 (208p) also paper

In this historical novel, Ursula joins thousands of other pilgrims in the People's Crusade in 1096, an arduous journey filled with danger.

Bibliography for Teachers and Students

His Majesty's Elephant
by Judith Tarr
Harcourt, 1993 (193p)

Set in Germany during the reign of Charlemagne, this novel centers on Rowan, the emperor's daughter, who finds herself in danger.

Books to Read Aloud
Favorite Medieval Tales
Retold by Mary Pope Osborne
Scholastic, 1998 (96p)

Retold here are nine stories from medieval Europe, about King Arthur, Beowulf, Roland, Robin Hood, and Sir Gawain.

Of Swords and Sorcerers: The Adventures of King Arthur and His Knights
by Margaret Hodges and Margery Evernden
Simon, 1993 (112p)

This retelling of the Arthurian legend includes stories about the boy Arthur, Merlin, Sir Lancelot and Elaine, and Sir Galahad.

I Am Mordred: A Tale from Camelot
by Nancy Springer
Philomel, 1998 (192p)

Springer tells the story of King Arthur's son.

Books for Teachers
The Voice of the Middle Ages: In Personal Letters 1100–1500
by Catherine Moriarty
Bedrick, 1991 (352p) paper

Letters from persons such as Dante, Thomas à Becket, and Dürer, as well as from those less well-known, reflect on all facets of life during the Middle Ages.

In the Age of Chivalry: Medieval Europe A.D. 800–1500
by Time-Life Editors
Time-Life

The editors focus on the daily life and customs in medieval Europe during the time of the plague.

Multimedia Resources

Software
Knights and Kings (CD-ROM)
ENTREX Software, 1992

In the Holy Land
(Computer-Interactive Videodisc)
Understanding Our World Series
Optical Data, 1989

Pathways Through Jerusalem
(CD-ROM)
The Learning Company, 1995

UNIT 6
Europe: 1300–1600

Independent Reading

Easy Books

A Renaissance Town
by Jacqueline Morley
Bedrick, 1997 (48p)

Detailed illustrations provide a glimpse into fifteenth-century Florence.

Renaissance People
by Susan Howarth
Millbrook, 1992

The author provides a look at people in the various reaches of Renaissance society. By the same author, see also *Renaissance Places*.

Leonardo da Vinci
by Diane Stanley
Morrow, 1996 (48p)

Stanley gives an excellent overview of Leonardo's life and work.

Antonio's Apprenticeship: Painting a Fresco in Renaissance Italy
by Taylor Morrison
Holiday, 1996

Young Antonio learns a lot about painting frescoes.

Average Books

The Starry Messenger
by Peter Sís
Farrar, 1996 (32p)

Galileo's life and ideas, sometimes in his own words, are beautifully presented in this creative book that also relates other events in the rest of the world.

Waiting for Filippo: The Life of Renaissance Architect Filippo Brunelleschi
by Michael Bender
Chronicle, 1995 (10p)

This intricate pop-up book reveals the works of Filippo, who designed and built the Cathedral of Florence.

Breaking Into Print: Before and After the Invention of the Printing Press
by Stephen Krensky
Little, 1996 (32p)

The author explains how books were produced before Gutenberg's invention and the later impact of his printing press.

Martin Luther
by Sally Stepanek
Chelsea, 1986 (128p)

Stepanek explores the life of the German monk who led the Protestant Reformation.

Challenging Books

The Italian Renaissance
by Karen Osman
Lucent, 1996 (112p)

Osman enlivens the history and achievements of the Italian Renaissance with carefully selected details and special emphasis on Florence and Rome.

Leonardo da Vinci: Artist, Inventor, and Scientist of the Renaissance
by Francesca Romei
Bedrick, 1994 (64p)

The oversized format of this book allows for the wonderful reproductions of Leonardo's work that accompany this story of his life.

Bibliography for Teachers and Students

The Black Death
by Phyllis Corzine
Lucent, 1997

The author discusses the causes and effects of the deadly plague that killed millions of Europeans during the fourteenth century.

Books to Read Aloud

The Second Mrs. Giaconda
by E. L. Konigsburg
Aladdin, 1998 (160p) paper

In this novel, the author offers an intriguing answer to the questions about Leonardo's painting of the Mona Lisa.

Alberic the Wise
by Norton Juster
Simon, 1992

This deceptive, simple, ironic fable about the farmer Alberic contains important messages about failure and success.

Books for Teachers

From the Closed World to the Infinite Universe
by Alexandre Koyré
Johns Hopkins U., 1994 paper

The ideas of Copernicus, Galileo, More, Newton, and other thinkers are expressed in their own words.

The Italian Renaissance: Culture and Society in Italy
by Peter Burke
Princeton U., 1987

The author looks at the parallels among the art, music, architecture, and literature of the Italian Renaissance.

Multimedia Resources

Videocassettes

Treasure Hunt 28 min.
Origins: A History of North America Series
Journal Films, 1989

Beginnings of Exploration: Why Did Europe "Discover" America in 1492? 11 min.
Age of Exploration Series
Encyclopaedia Britannica, 1990

Software

Leonardo the Inventor (CD-ROM)
The Learning Company, 1994

Western Civilization (CD-ROM)
Instructional Resources, 1996

Where in Time is Carmen Sandiego? (Floppy Disk)
Broderbund Software, 1990

Discover: The Age of Exploration (CD-ROM)
ENTREX Software, 1994

UNIT 7
Civilizations of the Americas

Independent Reading

Easy Books

What Do We Know About the Aztecs?
by Joanna Defrates
Bedrick, 1993 (44p)

Discussed here are the history, customs, and religion of the Aztecs and speculation about their eventual fate.

Rain Player
by David Wisniewski
Clarion, 1991 (32p)

In this original tale based on Mayan beliefs, a boy must defeat the rain god in a ball game to save his people from disaster.

Aztec, Inca, and Maya
by Elizabeth Baquedano
Knopf, 1993 (64p)

Color photos enhance this discussion of three of the great civilizations of the West.

Maya's Children: The Story of La Llorona
by Rudolfo Anaya
Hyperion, 1997 (32p)

Anaya tells his version of the Latin American legend of La Llorona, known as "the crying woman."

Average Books

The Aztec News
by Philip Steele, et al
Candlewick, 1997 (32p)

In newspaper format, this fact-filled introduction to Aztec life and times includes information on sports, politics, and religion.

Discovering the Ice Maiden
by Johan Reinhard
National Geo., 1998 (48p)

Anthropologist Reinhard tells of his discovery of a mummified Inca female on the summit of Ampato. Photos, maps, and timeline included.

The Secret of the Andes
by Ann Nolan Clark
Puffin, 1976 (136p) paper

In this award-winning story, a modern Incan boy lives in the mountains of Peru and trains in the traditions and customs of his ancestors.

The Corn Grows Ripe
by Dorothy Rhoads
Puffin, 1993 (96p)

When his father is injured, Tigre must assume the responsibility for planting the corn the family needs to survive and to appease the Mayan gods.

Challenging Books

The Monkey's Haircut and Other Stories Told by the Mayans
edited by John Bierhorst
Morrow, 1986 (160p)

Into a discussion of Mayan culture, the author weaves twenty-two myths and folktales.

The Captive
by Scott O'Dell
Houghton Mifflin, 1979 (224p)

A Jesuit seminarian is changed forever when he witnesses the enslavement and exploitation of the Maya by the Spanish.

Bibliography for Teachers and Students

The Feathered Serpent
by Scott O'Dell
Houghton Mifflin, 1981 (224p)

A man the Mayas believe is the god Kukulcan sees the coming of Cortés and the capture of the Aztec city Tenochtitlán.

Daily Life in the Inca Empire
by Michael A. Malpass
Greenwood, 1996 (80p)

Anthropologist Malpass presents in alternating chapters a day in the life of a ruling family and of a conquered family.

Books to Read Aloud
The Mythology of Mexico and Central America
edited by John Bierhorst
Morrow, 1990 (256p)

Bierhorst introduces the gods, heroes, and mythology from the Aztec and Maya civilizations and of Indian groups living today.

The Quetzal: Sacred Bird of the Forest
by Dorothy Hinshaw Patent
Morrow, 1996 (40p)

The author tells the story of this endangered bird and its significance to the people of Mexico and Central America.

The Tree Is Older Than You Are
by Naomi Shihab Nye
Simon, 1995 (112p)

This collection of poems and stories from Mexico is in English and Spanish and illustrated by Mexican artists.

Books for Teachers
Aztecs: Reign of Blood and Splendor
edited by Charlotte Anker, et al.
Time-Life, 1992 (168p)

Accompanying this close look at Aztec life are colorful illustrations of Aztec art and architecture.

The Blood of Kings: Dynasty and Ritual in Maya Art
by Linda Schele and Mary Ellen Miller
George Braziller, 1986 (355p)

The authors offer detailed information about the rise and fall of the Maya before the arrival of the Spanish.

Multimedia Resources

Videocassettes
Mayan: Apocalypse Then 27 min.
Centre Communications, 1988

Lost Empire of Tiwanaku 17 min.
National Geographic, 1993

The Second Voyage of the Mimi
12 videocassettes each 30 min.
Sunburst Communications, 1988

Suemi's Story: My Modern Mayan Home 25 min.
United Learning, 1991

Software
South America and Antarctica
(Computer-Interactive Videodisc)

STV: World Geography
National Geographic, 1994

Exploring the Lost Maya (CD-ROM)
Sumeria, 1996

Legends of the Americas (CD-ROM)
Troll Associates, 1995

UNIT 8
Europe: 1600–1789

Independent Reading

Easy Books

King's Day: Louis XIV of France
by Aliki
Harper, 1989

This look at Louis XIV focuses on the elaborate ceremonies that accompanied everything he did, from dressing and eating to conducting affairs of state.

Average Books

Helen Williams and the French Revolution
edited by Jane Shuter
Raintree, 1966 (48p)

This informative book is based on letters written by a British woman living in Paris at the time of the Reign of Terror.

The Glorious Revolution
by Clarice Swisher
Lucent, 1996 (112p)

The author describes the events leading to the bloodless overthrow of the English monarchy in 1688.

Challenging Books

Life in the Elizabethan Theater
by Diane Yancey
Lucent, 1996 (112p)

The author describes the lives of those involved in Elizabethan theater and how the theater reflected the social and political concerns of the time.

Black Swan
by Farrukh Dhondy
Houghton Mifflin, 1993 (208p)

While visiting in present-day London, Rose suddenly finds herself in the world of Elizabethan theater and in a mystery about the true authorship of Shakespeare's plays.

Books to Read Aloud
Shakespeare's Stories: Tragedies
retold by Beverly Birch
Bedrick, 1990

Birch's retellings provide a good introduction to Shakespeare's plays. By the same author, see also *Shakespeare's Stories: Histories* and *Shakespeare's Stories: Comedies*.

The Three Musketeers
by Alexandre Dumas
Puffin, 1995 (224p)

Dumas' swashbuckling adventure set in sixteenth-century France has been abridged. Other editions available.

Books for Teachers

The First Elizabeth
by Carolly Erickson
St. Martin's, 1997 (448p)

All facets of the life of the diplomatic ruler of England are brought to life.

*W*e have not journeyed all this way **across the centuries,** *across the oceans, across the mountains, across the prairies, because we are made of sugar candy.*

Winston Churchill

Jacqueline M. Córdova
J. Jorge Klor de Alva
Gary B. Nash
Franklin Ng
Christopher L. Salter
Louis E. Wilson
Karen K. Wixson

Across the Centuries

Houghton Mifflin Company • Boston

Atlanta • Dallas • Geneva, Illinois • Princeton, New Jersey • Palo Alto

ISBN: 0-395-93066-9
23456-VH-04 03 02 01 00 99 98

Developed by Ligature, Inc.

Consultants

Sandra Alfonsi
Academic Advisory Board
Hadassah
Queens, New York

Charmarie Blaisdell
Department of History
Northeastern University
Boston, Massachusetts

Richard Griswold del Castillo
Department of Mexican American Studies
San Diego State University
San Diego, California

Ross Dunn
Department of History
San Diego State University
San Diego, California

Benjamin Elman
Director, Center for Chinese Studies
University of California, Los Angeles
Los Angeles, California

Stephen Fugita
Department of Psychology
Santa Clara University
Santa Clara, California

Erich Gruen
Department of Classics and History
University of California, Berkeley
Berkeley, California

Charles Haynes
Senior Scholar for Religious Freedom
Freedom Forum First Amendment Center
Arlington, Virginia

Lidwien Kapteijns
Department of History
Wellesley College
Wellesley, Massachusetts

Shabbir Mansuri
Founding Director
Council on Islamic Education
Fountain Valley, California

Michelle Maskiell
Department of History
University of Montana
Missoula, Montana

Doug Monroy
Department of Southwest Studies
The Colorado College
Colorado Springs, Colorado

Forrest Turpin
Christian Educators Association
  International
Pasadena, California

Skirball Institute
Los Angeles, California

Rabbi Alfred Wolf
Founding Director
Skirball Institute
Los Angeles, California

Elliot N. Dorff
Rector
University of Judaism
Los Angeles, California

Robert Ellwood
School of Religion
University of Southern California
Los Angeles, California

B. Srinivasa Murthy
Department of Religious Studies (retired)
California State University, Long Beach
Long Beach, California

Ven. Dr. Havanpola Ratanasara
Buddhist Sangha Council of Southern
  California
Los Angeles, California

Rev. Thomas P. Rausch, S.J.
Rector, Jesuit Community
Loyola Marymount University
Los Angeles, California

Acknowledgments

Grateful acknowledgment is made
for the use of the material listed below.
The material in the Minipedia is
reprinted from *The World Book*
Encyclopedia with the expressed permission of the publisher. © 1998 by World
Book, Inc.

–Continued on page 557.

From Your Authors

*W*omen gad about in the market place. . . . They go out visiting, to see their relatives, and proceed there by starlight or carrying torches, night after night; they take a large suite with them, setting the street ablaze . . . maids, messengers, clerks, and footmen."

So begins an account of real events in China's history. The ladies were having too much fun for the writer of this account. He was more worried about the nomadic horsemen who were attacking the northern frontier. In Chapter 8 of this book, you will read more about Chinese life and the problems of keeping such a large empire together.

Most of the people you will meet in this book lived long ago in places that may seem very far away from home. But they all had feelings just like yours and faced many of the same challenges you will face in your life. And whether they were great leaders or ordinary people, their decisions and actions helped shape the world you live in.

As you read about these people, places, and events, we hope you will ask many questions. Some questions may be about history: "What caused these people to make the decisions they did?" or "How do we know about these events?" Other questions may be about geography: "What are the land and weather like in that place?" or "Why did people choose to settle there?" Still other questions may be about economics: "How did people meet their needs for food and shelter?" or "How did people work out ways for using scarce resources?"

Most of all, we hope you catch the excitement of thinking, questioning, and discovering answers about your world—now and in the 21st century.

Beverly J. Armento
Professor of Social Studies Education
Department of Middle/ Secondary Education and Instructional Technology
Georgia State University

Jacqueline M.K. Córdova
Professor of Spanish and TESOL
Department of Foreign Languages and Literatures
California State University, Fullerton

J. Jorge Klor de Alva
President
University of Phoenix

Gary B. Nash
Professor of History
University of California, Los Angeles

Franklin Ng
Professor of Anthropology
California State University, Fresno

Christopher L. Salter
Professor and Chair
Department of Geography
University of Missouri

Louis E. Wilson
Associate Professor and Chair
Department of African American Studies
Smith College

Karen K. Wixson
Professor of Education
University of Michigan

Contents

Understanding Skills

Each "Understanding Skills" feature gives you the opportunity to learn and practice a skill related to the topic you are studying.

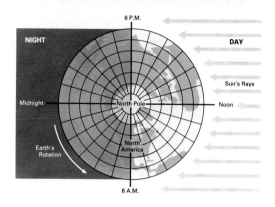

Exploring

The story of the past is hidden all around you in a world of the present. "Exploring" pages tell you the secrets of how to find it.

Understanding Concepts

Each "Understanding Concepts" feature gives you more information about a concept that is important to the lesson you are reading.

Making Decisions

Much of history is made of people's decisions. These pages take you step-by-step through fascinating problems from history and today. What will you decide?

Literature

Throughout history people have expressed their deepest feelings and beliefs through literature. Reading these stories, legends, poems, and shorter passages that appear in the lessons will help you experience what life was like for people of other times and places.

Primary Sources

Reading the exact words of the people who made and lived history is the best way to get a sense of how they saw themselves and the times in which they lived. You will find more than 50 primary sources throughout this book including the following:

A Closer Look

Take a closer look at the objects and pictures spread out on these special pages. With the clues you see, you'll become a historical detective.

A Moment in Time

Someone or something from the past is frozen at an exciting moment. You'll get to know these people or things by reading about where they are and the objects around them.

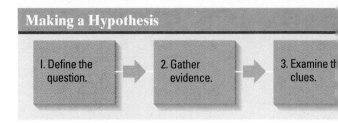

Making a Hypothesis

1. Define the question. → 2. Gather evidence. → 3. Examine the clues.

Charts, Diagrams, and Timelines

These visual presentations of information help give you a clearer picture of the people, places, and events you are studying.

Maps

The events of history have been shaped by the places in which they occurred. Each map tells its own story.

Starting Out

What makes this textbook so much more interesting than others you've used? In this book, the people of the past speak directly to you, through their actual words and the objects they used. You'll walk inside their houses and look inside their cooking pots. You'll follow them as they go to school, build cities, fight wars, work out settlements for peace.

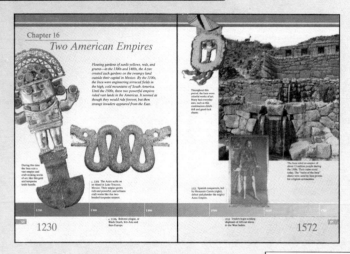

From unit to chapter to lesson— each step lets you see history in closer detail. The photos show you where events happened. The art introduces you to the people.

The titles outline the lesson. The red titles tell you the main topics discussed in the lesson on the Maya.

When and where? The timeline at the beginning of each lesson tells you when these events took place. The lesson title tells you what the lesson is about.

Right from the beginning the lesson opener pulls you into the sights, sounds, and the smells of historical investigation.

Like a road sign, the question that always appears here tells you what to think about while you read the lesson.

Look for these key terms. They are listed here so you can watch for them. The first time they appear in the lesson they are shown in heavy black print and defined. Key terms are also defined in the Glossary.

B.C. A.D.

2000   1000   1500
1800   900

L E S S O N   3

The Maya

I t is impossible to describe the interest with which I explored these ruins. The ground was entirely new. . . . We could not see ten yards before us, and never knew what we should stumble upon next. The beauty of the sculpture, the solemn stillness of the woods, disturbed only by the scrambling of monkeys and the chattering of parrots, the desolation of the city, and the mystery that hung over it, all created an interest higher, if possible, than I had ever felt among the ruins of the Old World.

THINKING
FOCUS

In what ways were the Maya an advanced civilization?

Key Terms

• stele
• codex

➤ *The seven-inch-tall ceramic ballplayer at top right is part of the religious art of the Maya. Real players on the losing side sometimes became sacrifices to the gods. The large Mayan temple, on the right, was built between A.D. 600 and 800. Artist Frederick Catherwood, who accompanied explorer Stephens, painted this view of the Mayan temple.*

ball court watched over by six enormous stone parrots. And he found heavy stone columns carved with images of jaguars, birds, serpents, and men in fabulous feathered headdresses. Stephens had no idea who the builders of this city were, but he was sure he had found evidence of a magnificent civilization.

With these words, John Lloyd Stephens described his discovery in 1839 of a ruined city in the jungles of Central America. Among the ruins and tangled vines, he found a temple with a broad stairway that was inscribed with thousands of strange symbols. He also found a

A Growing Civilization

Stephens had discovered the ruins of Copan, an ancient Mayan city. Like the Olmec, the Maya settled in a fertile region. Notice on the map on page 405 that this region stretched south along an extended finger of land that is surrounded by water.

The 125,000 square miles that the Maya occupied contained both highlands and lowlands. The highlands in the south ran along a mountain range that included active volcanoes. A long rainy season and deep, fertile soil made this area good for farming.

The lowlands
the central and no
the region. Some
covered with den
with fertile soil. O
rough, dry grass w
not good for farmi
were rich in the 1
Maya needed for
the flint they used

Archaeologist
may have begun
tile areas of the lo
as 1800 B.C. Betw
500 B.C., the May
small farming vill
ered food from th
also raised crops.
and A.D. 200, som
grew into cities w
palaces and pyran
sans carved huge
pillars to adorn th

During the he
civilization, betwe
900, about three n
lived in Mayan ci
through the regio
map at the above
major cities.

Mayan cities
religious centers.

Take a closer look, in this case at the Mayan calendar. Look at the diagram to see how it works.

Charts and graphs help you understand difficult information— in this case the Mayan number system.

The Mayan Calendar

Why do people have good days and bad days? Why do crops grow well one year and poorly the next? The Maya believed it was because different gods ruled each day. By consulting their two calendars and using the right mathematics, Mayan priests knew which gods ruled which days. Then the priests had to figure out what influence the gods would have.

On the 260-day religious calendar, each day was given a name and a number. The name *Imix* meant "water lily," and represented the ocean. *Ik* was named for the wind, and *Akbal* was named for the darkness of night.

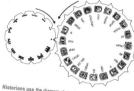

Historians use the diagram above to explain the 260-day religious calendar. Each name and each number was a divine being—two gods for every day. When you turn the wheels, you discover that the same name and the same number only fall together once every 260 days. Then the cycle starts all over again.

1 Imix—the New Year's day of the Mayan 260-day year

Dates were skillfully carved in Mayan hieroglyphs like these

The other Mayan calendar was based on the earth's orbit around the sun and had 365 days like ours. Each of these days had a god, too. This calendar had 18 months of 20 days each, plus 5 extra days. It was considered bad luck to do anything on those 5 days, so people did very little. They didn't even eat!

to record information about astronomical events. The detailed astronomical charts and tables that they made using this system are quite accurate. Their system was based on the number 20 instead of 10, which is the basis for our decimal system. As you can see at the top of this page, they used dots and dashes to represent numbers and even had a symbol for zero.

To record important dates and events in the lives of their rulers, the Maya developed hieroglyphs. Each hieroglyph represents a sound. When the pictures are put together, they can make up part of a word or a whole word. Some hieroglyphs represent ideas, such as "life" or "happiness." Others represent objects like "corn" or "water."

The Mayan priest-kings used hieroglyphs to write record books, each of which was known as a **codex.** Archaeologists have studied the three existing codices and deciphered part of them to learn about religious ceremonies, astronomy, and Mayan calendars.

The codices reveal that the Maya had two calendars. They used them to determine the best time to plant crops, hunt, and perform religious ceremonies. The Mayan priest-kings developed the

calendars from their close observations of the movements of the sun, moon, and stars.

Mayan cultural achievements also included the magnificent architecture of their cities and beautiful works of decorative art. For example, Mayan artisans made jewelry out of jade, gold, and shells. King Pacal, in his tomb at Palenque, was found wearing a life-size mosaic mask made from jade. He also wore jewelry of jade and mother-of-pearl. The Maya were also accomplished weavers, and they communicated nonverbally through their weaving designs. (See Exploring Nonverbal Communication on pages 410–411.)

These are only some of the achievements of the ancient Mayan civilization. The Mayan culture has survived, however, unlike many other early American cultures. Today, Mayan people live in Guatemala, Belize, and parts of Mexico. ■

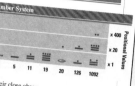

The Mayan Number System

								Positional Values
							••	x 400
		••••					••••	x 20
	•		•••••				•••••	x 1
0	1	4	5	11	19	20	126	1092

▲ *In the Mayan number system, symbols represented basic numerical values. Find the bar above that equals 5. Vertical positions also indicated that the basic value was multiplied by a certain number (1, 20, 400, and so on). Thus, the representation above for 1,092 translates into this equation: $12 + (14 \times 20) + (2 \times 400) = 1,092$. Translate the representation for 126 into a numerical equation.*

■ *Describe the Mayan writing and number systems.*

1. **FOCUS** In what ways were the Maya an advanced civilization?
2. **CONNECT** What agricultural techniques made Mayan farming more efficient than Olmec farming?
3. **BELIEF SYSTEMS** What did the Maya worship? What important role did the priest-kings play in the Mayan religion?
4. **CULTURE** How have archaeologists learned so much about King Pacal?
5. **CRITICAL THINKING** Why was the invention of a number system important in Mayan society?
6. **WRITING ACTIVITY** Write a message for a classmate using your own hieroglyphs. First, write out the message you want to send. Then create simple pictures for each sound, word, or idea you want to get across. Remember, when someone looks at your picture, they will need to be able to guess the sound, word, or idea it represents. Trade messages, and decipher them.

409

Early American Civilizations

Every map tells a story. The maps in this book tell the story of the rise and fall of cities, states, and trade routes.

A.D. 300–900

NORTHERN AREA

YUCATAN PENINSULA

Caribbean Sea

CENTRAL AREA

▲ *Find Copan on the map. Look at the Copan ball court below. Guess the size of the buildings by comparing them with the car in the background.*

■ *What were Mayan cities like?*

ually built tall hat were surn plazas. At ds they built priest-kings ceremonies at

Frozen at a moment in time, the European mapmaker extends your knowledge of the world. You learn all about him through his equipment, his clothes, and the place he's working.

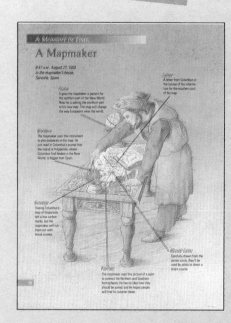

Continuing On

As you get to know the people of the past, you'll want ways of understanding and remembering them better. This book gives you some tools to use in learning about people and places and remembering what you've learned.

Giving you the inside story is the purpose of two special paragraphs. Across Time & Space connects what you're reading to things that happened centuries ago or continents away. Its companion, How Do We Know?, tells you where information about the past comes from. (See page 414 for an example.)

Across Time & Space

The Inca built many rope bridges that spanned steep-cliffed canyons and crossed over fast-flowing rivers. Today, many Inca descendants still rely on rope bridges. They often spin as much as 20,000 to 30,000 feet of rope from grass to build or repair their bridges.

■ *What methods did the Inca use to control their empire?*

▼ *The llama was very important to the Inca. Its wool, shown here, was spun into thread, which was used to make beautiful fabrics like the weaving below. These fabrics were used by all levels of society.*

length of the empire. Roads were built in the highlands and along the coast. When necessary, the roads included tunnels, causeways, and stone or even rope bridges. Built to quickly move the Inca army, the highways also helped transport crops and other goods throughout the empire. Scholars estimate that the Inca built nearly 10,000 miles of roads.

Under Inca rule, the commoners had few individual freedoms. They weren't allowed to travel without government approval. The government also decided when and whom they married. Marriage was encouraged, because only married couples were assigned plots of land from which goods for tribute could be raised. ■

Working the Land

Though they enjoyed little freedom, Inca subjects rarely went hungry. The Inca's clever farming techniques allowed them to make full use of their varied lands. In addition, their strong organizational skills made them efficient producers and distributors of food.

Once the Inca conquered a region, they took total control of the land. They sent administrators, who were members of the nobility, to evaluate the geographic resources of the region. Then they divided the region's farmland into three parts. The commoners harvested one part of the farmland for government workers, one part to support Inca religious leaders, and one part for themselves.

The farmland varied greatly from region to region because the Inca Empire lay in and around the Andes. Some valleys lie as high as 8,000 feet above sea level. Others are only a few hundred feet above sea level.

Because soil, temperature, and other conditions change as altitude increases, only certain crops could be grown in certain areas. In the low valleys, farmers grew maize (corn), beans, and squash. In the mountains, they raised llamas and alpacas for wool and meat. This growing of crops according to the height of the land is called a **vertical economy.**

The Inca were able to grow surplus amounts of food by using very productive farming techniques. One of these techniques was **terrace farming.** The soil on the mountain slopes in the highlands was thin and didn't receive enough rainfall. The Inca carried topsoil and gravel from the more fertile lowlands to the hillsides. There, they packed it into narrow farming terraces like the ones pictured above. To protect against drought, the Inca constructed elaborate canal systems for irrigation.

The government built huge warehouses to store surplus food in case of emergencies such as crop failure or war. The quipu recorded how much food was stored and where it was stored. Because the government distributed food and goods to the people, free trade and huge markets like those the Aztec enjoyed did not exist in the Inca Empire. ■

▲ *Inca terraces were such an effective farming technique that they are still used in modern-day Peru.*

■ *Why was Inca agriculture so productive?*

Praying to the Ancestors

Not all of the commoners worked to produce food for the empire. Some commoners helped to build massive cities. To learn more about an Inca city, see A Closer Look on page 434.

Other commoners paid their tribute by making pieces of art and

433

Two American Empires

You're in charge of your reading. See the red square at the end of the text? Now find the red square over in the margin. If you can answer the question there, then you probably understand what you just read. If you can't, perhaps you'd better go back and read that part of the lesson again.

A picture is worth a thousand words. But just a few words in a caption can help you understand a picture, a photograph, a map, or in this case, how past and present are related.

Every age has its great storytellers. Many chapters include short examples of fine writing from or about the period. The literature is printed on a tan background with a blue initial letter and a multicolored bar.

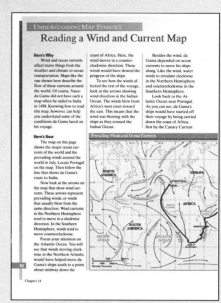

A special kind of Understanding page looks at concepts—the big ideas that help put all the pieces together. This section helps you understand ideas like Civilization, Conquest, or Reform.

Some tools you'll always use. The Understanding pages walk you through skills that you will use again and again, as a student and later on in life.

The things people make and use tells a great deal about them. In this book you'll find lots of photographs of the paintings people made, the tools and weapons they used, and the gold they wore.

Letters, diaries, books—short passages from these primary sources let people from the past speak to you. When you see a tan background, a red initial letter, and a gray bar, you know that the quotation is a primary source.

After you read the lesson, stop and review what you've read. The first question is the same one you started out with. The second question connects the lesson to what you've studied earlier. Other questions and an activity help you think about the lesson you've read. Chapter Review questions help you tie the lesson together. (See pages 418 and 419 for an example.)

Also Featuring

Some special pages show up only once in every unit, not in every lesson in the book. These features continue the story by letting you explore an idea or activity, or read a story about another time and place. The Time/Space Databank in the back of the book brings together resources you will use again and again.

School isn't the only place where you can learn social studies. This feature gives you a chance to explore history and geography outside the classroom—at home or in your own neighborhood.

EXPLORING

Nonverbal Communication

Or do people need special knowledge in order to understand them, as they would for the signals of the basketball referee?

◄ *Its beacon flashing in the night, this lighthouse transmits information to incoming sailors about conditions close to shore.*

Move Ahead

Display your sketches of nonverbal messages on the bulletin board. Try to "read" the messages your classmates drew. Can they "read" yours?

Did you find any nonverbal

MAKING DECISIONS

The Great Wall

H ad the Great Wall not already existed, Yangdi [the second Sui emperor] would certainly have conceived it. As it was, he had to be content with rebuilding it.

Robert Silverberg, 20th-century historian

► *The Great Wall still snakes for thousands of miles across modern China. However, the wall that is still standing is not Shihuangdi's wall, but a later version, built during the Ming Dynasty.*

Background

Records show that Yangdi's rebuilding of the Great Wall in 607 required more than a million workers. Over half of them died of overwork or fled the harsh conditions.

The original building of the Great Wall, begun in 221 B.C., also involved a huge work force. Shihuangdi, the Chinese emperor who conceived of this project, connected shorter walls that had been built along China's northern border centuries before. He also extended the wall for hundreds of miles. The resulting fortified wall was and still is the longest structure on earth.

► *These coins, which were issued by Shihuangdi, were the standard currency throughout the empire at the time when the Great Wall was being built.*

Before embarking on any massive work, such as the building of the Great Wall of China, a wise decision maker will try to weigh the benefits and the costs of the project. We can look at historical events to try to compare the benefits and the costs of building the Great Wall of China.

Benefits and Costs of the Great Wall

The most obvious benefit of building the Great Wall was protection. The wall helped prevent nomadic horsemen from invading China's farms along the northern border. Also, it kept farmers living along the border from joining the nomads.

Building the Great Wall enabled Shihuangdi to get rid of his

enemies. He ordered them to work on distant parts of the wall. He also sent soldiers to work on the wall. As a result, the soldiers could not band together and rise up against the emperor.

However, building Shihuangdi's wall is estimated to have required more than 300,000 workers, most of whom were drafted against their will. Thousands of farmers and merchants were required to supply the workers with food, clothing, tools, and shelter. Most of these supplies never made it

to the work sites; bandits roaming the countryside robbed the supply caravans.

The work of constructing the wall was so difficult and living conditions were so harsh that thousands of workers died. Often they were buried in the wall itself. Thus, the Great Wall of China gained the gruesome title of "the world's longest cemetery."

▼ *Sturdy horses, like the one at the left, carried nomads who raided China's northern border. In response, the Great Wall was built, using labor-intensive construction methods as shown. Study the chart for a comparison of the Great Wall's long-range benefits and short-term costs.*

**Decision
Build Great Wall**

Outcomes

• People are safer
• More farmers stay on farms
• Fewer threats to emperor arise

• Many laborers die
• People become poorer
• Supply caravans often attacked

Decision Point

1. What were the benefits of constructing the Great Wall of China? What were the costs?
2. Do you think these were the only benefits and costs of the Great Wall? Where would you look to find more information about the role of the Great Wall in Chinese history?
3. Based on the information on these pages and any other information you have found,

do you think the benefits and costs of building the Great Wall balanced out? Explain.

4. Collect information from newspapers and magazines about upcoming plans for large government projects in the United States. Discuss the projected benefits and costs of each project. Decide which projects you would support and which you would oppose.

China

199

Chapter 8

► *Using a traditional back-strap loom, this Mayan woman weaves patterns used in her village for generations. For the Mayan weaver, snakes symbolize the earth, toads symbolize saints, and eagles symbolize life and death.*

Chapter 15

What would you do? The Making Decisions pages show you an important decision from the past. Then you practice the steps that will help you to make a good choice.

Stories have always been important parts of people's lives. Each unit in the book has at least one story about the time and place you're studying. In this case, it's a re-creation of Columbus's audience with King Ferdinand and Queen Isabella.

LITERATURE

The Audience

C. Walter Hodges

In Lesson 3 you learned about Columbus's appeal to Ferdinand and Isabella. Here is an imaginative recreation of his second appearance before that King and Queen.

As you have learned in this chapter, the dream of wealth and the of riches drove Columbus and other explorers like him. They undertook of unknown dangers and uncertain outcomes to pursue that dream. But they needed financial support. As you read this story, play the role of the audience— the King or Queen. Would you support Columbus? Why or why not?

T he town was taken, the Moors were driven out, the wars were at an end. Now, now at last there must be time to hear Columbus. Now at last the victorious Sovereigns would give him ships to sail in quest of his new horizon.

He went to his friend Alonzo de Quintanilla and implored him to obtain audience for him soon. The Accountant-General promised to do so, and on the following day Columbus was summoned into the presence of Their Majesties.

Father Juan Perez, Luiz de Santangel and I went with him to the audience. The antechamber was full of people, little groups talking in low voices. Court officials, men and women with petitions to present. Presently an usher call...

and he w...

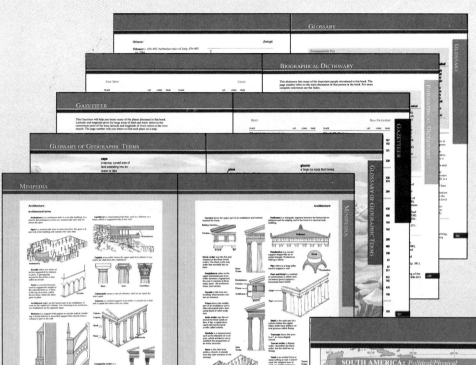

The Time/Space Databank is like a reference section of a library at your fingertips. It's the place to go for more information about the places, people, and key terms you meet in this book.

What's a minipedia? It's a small version of an encyclopedia, one that you don't have to go to your library to use. It's bound right into the back of your book so you can quickly look up its articles, charts, and graphs.

The Atlas maps out the world. Special maps tell you about the languages, religions, climates, and resources of the world. Historical maps let you compare what was going on at the same time in different places.

Map and Globe Handbook

*Y*ou are about to begin an exciting journey across the centuries. In this handbook, you'll explore roads built by the Inca almost 500 years ago, learn how people built dikes and dams to reclaim land in the Netherlands, and travel to a mountaintop in Indonesia. In addition, you'll visit empires that existed almost 4,000 years ago, and learn about the battle that ended the American Revolution.

Since all journeys require maps, your adventure starts right here. This handbook will help you unlock the secrets of maps and globes. Turn to page G1, and let your journey begin.

Contents

Bibliography

Books for Students

Bell, Neill. *The Book of Where: Or, How to Be Naturally Geographic.* Boston: Little Brown & Co., 1982. This book contains activities to use in studying maps and globes and other basic concepts of geography.

Blandford, Percy W. *The New Explorer's Guide to Using Maps and Compasses.* Blue Ridge Summit, PA: TAB Books, 1992. This guide will bring out the explorer in students.

Atlas of World History. Chicago: Rand McNally, 1995. Themes in world history are organized around maps.

Books for Teachers

Geography Education Standards Project. *Geography for Life: National Geography Standards.* Washington, DC: National Geographic Research & Exploration, 1994. This guide sets forth nationally recognized geography standards.

Snyder, John P. *Flattening the Earth: Two Thousand Years of Map Projections.* Chicago: University of Chicago Press, 1997. This history of map projections summarizes over 200 different projections.

 An Odyssey of Discovery™: Continent Explorer II (CD-ROM) Pierian Spring, 1998.

Understanding Our Planet

A map is a representation of a part of the earth drawn on a flat surface. Study the satellite image and the map below. The image shows what South America looks like from miles above the earth. Mapmakers sometimes use these images to help draw maps. Now look at the map of roads that the Inca built almost 500 years ago in the Andes of South America. Notice how the shape of the coastline in the image matches the shape of the map. The locator map in the top right-hand corner helps you find where this region is located on earth.

Satellites collect information in space and send it back to earth. The information can then be turned into images that look like photographs. The colors on this satellite image show different geographical features of South America.

This map shows the roads that the Inca built almost 500 years ago. Look at the size of the empire. How do you think having a systems of roads helped strengthen the Inca Empire?

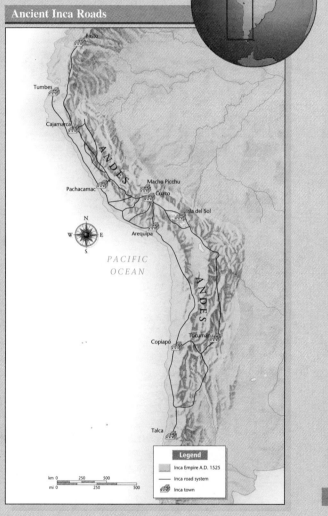

Ancient Inca Roads

Pasto
Tumbes
Cajamarca
ANDES
Machu Picchu
Pachacamac
Cuzco
Isla del Sol
Arequipa

PACIFIC
OCEAN

ANDES

Copiapó
Tucumán

Talca

Legend
Inca Empire A.D. 1525
Inca road system
Inca town

km 0   250   500
mi 0   250   500

G1

Ask students how maps help us understand the earth. Discuss what our lives—and the world—might be like without maps. Draw their attention to the satellite image of South America and the map of ancient Inca roads on the page. Also display a globe, and have a volunteer locate Peru. What similarities and differences do students see among the three different representations? List them on the board. Ask students what the map shows that the satellite image can't. *(compass, scale, legend, Inca towns and roads from 500 years ago)* How do satellite images help mapmakers? *(such images help confirm shapes of landmasses and islands, distances, and physical features)*

GEOGRAPHY
Visual Learning

Challenge students to create their own maps from memory. Their maps should show a 10-block area that includes their school. Allow time for students to discuss and compare maps.

▶ *Roads allowed for faster communication and transportation; easier to move animals.*

Mathematics Connection

Tell students that they have been appointed by the Inca ruler to survey the empire. Have pairs of students plan trips along the Inca roads that will allow them to visit each town at least once. Have them use the map scale to determine the number of miles between each town and the total number of miles for the entire trip.

Objectives

1. Compare images, maps, and globes to understand that maps are visual representations of real places. (Visual Learning 1)
2. Understand that maps may represent places as they were in the past. (Visual Learning 1)

CLASS ACTIVITY

Remind students that although there are many different kinds of maps, all maps are created with common characteristics to allow them to be easily read. Examples of this are the compass rose, latitude and longitude, scale line, and legend or key. After discussing each of these characteristics, call on volunteers to use each to read the map of Australia. For instance, you might ask someone to use the scale to find the distance across Tasmania or to use the compass rose to describe the location of Perth in relation to Sydney.

GEOGRAPHY

Map and Globe Skills

Divide the class into small groups. Using the map of Australia, have students develop a set of five questions based on the map characteristics discussed above. Then direct groups to switch sets of questions and answer them.

Objective

Interpret and use basic map-reading characteristics common to most maps. (Map & Globe Skills 1–4)

Understanding a Map

Take a few minutes to look quickly at the maps in this handbook. You'll notice that there are maps of different sizes, featuring different places. Most of the maps show a portion of the world, and a few represent the entire world. Depending on the type of map, you can find out about a place's climate, population density, migration patterns, elevation, time zones, or people.

All maps share certain characteristics. Every part of a map contains important information. To understand the whole map, you need to know how to read each part of it. Look at the map below. It shows the continent of Australia.

The **compass rose** points out directions. The tips of this compass rose point to north (**N**), south (**S**), east (**E**), and west (**W**), as well as intermediate, or in-between, directions.

An **inset** is related to the larger map. This inset map is a **locator inset,** which helps you to find what part of the earth is shown on the larger map.

Latitude and **longitude** are imaginary lines that form a **grid** over the earth. A grid is a pattern of lines that cross one another. You can use the grid to locate places on the map.

The **scale line** shows how much smaller the map is than the actual area it represents.

The **legend,** or **key,** explains what the symbols on the map mean. The legend identifies state, territorial, and national capitals.

Modern Australia

Legend
- ⊛ National capital
- ★ State or territorial capital

Research

Show students a map of the world and point out where Australia is located in relation to other great landmasses. Remind students that Australia is one of the seven continents, but that it is the smallest. Ask whether it could also be considered an island. Have students research to find a list of the largest islands in the world to check their answer, and consult a dictionary or encyclopedia for definitions of *continent* and *island.*

Using the Legend and Grid

Maps can help you make connections between different events and cultures. The map below shows four different civilizations that settled in or near the eastern Mediterranean in the 600s B.C. By seeing how close some of these cultures were to each other, you can begin to think about the influences they may have had on each other.

A grid helps you to locate places on the map. Look up Corsica in the map's index, and read the letter and number beside the name, *A1*. Find the letter A on the map, and then find the number 1. Is Corsica located within the square formed by the grid lines?

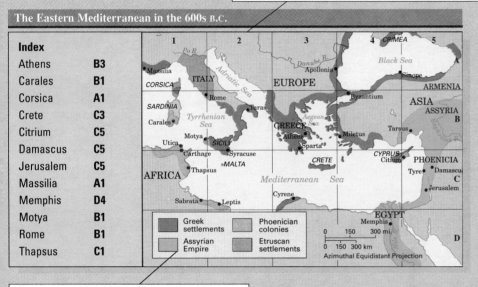

The Eastern Mediterranean in the 600s B.C.

Index

Athens	B3
Carales	B1
Corsica	A1
Crete	C3
Citrium	C5
Damascus	C5
Jerusalem	C5
Massilia	A1
Memphis	D4
Motya	B1
Rome	B1
Thapsus	C1

Legend:
- Greek settlements
- Phoenician colonies
- Assyrian Empire
- Etruscan settlements

0   150   300 mi.
0   150 300 km
Azimuthal Equidistant Projection

The legend uses different colors to indicate where people were settled in the eastern Mediterranean during the 600s B.C. In Corsica, Etruscan settlements surrounded Greek settlements.

MAP SKILLS

1. **REVIEW** In which grid square is the island of Crete located? Who lived in Crete in the 600s B.C.?

2. **REVIEW** Name at least two cities in grid C5.

3. **THINK ABOUT IT** What appears to be the significance of major rivers and coastlines on the map?

4. **TRY IT** Add four more cities to the map index.

G3

CLASS ACTIVITY

Begin with a discussion of the legend. Ask students how the use of different colors helps them in reading the map. Encourage them to describe where each culture seems to be concentrated. Display a variety of atlases. Show students the indexes at the back of the atlases. Have a volunteer locate the island of Crete in one atlas without using the index. Then let another volunteer locate the island of Sardinia in an atlas, this time using the index. How do their efforts compare? Also, ask the volunteer who used the index whether he or she used a grid to help locate Sardinia. If so, have the student demonstrate how they did it for the class.

▶ *Yes. Corsica falls within A1.*

Geography Theme: Movement

Point out to students that Greek culture is concentrated in the peninsula labeled *Greece* on the map, but that it is also found along the shores of Asia Minor, the Black Sea, southern Italy, and elsewhere. Challenge students to explain why Greek culture would be found in so many places other than Greece. (*The Greeks had set up colonies.*)

G3

CLASS ACTIVITY

Use a large globe to review the basics of latitude and longitude. Call on a volunteer to point out latitude lines. Tell students that these lines are sometimes called parallels and ask a volunteer to explain why. Have another volunteer show the lines of longitude and explain where they begin and end. Then talk about how the Equator divides the Northern and Southern Hemispheres. Finally, point out the prime meridian and say that it (along with the 180th line of longitude on the opposite side of the world) separates the Western and Eastern Hemispheres.

Geography Theme: Location

Ask students how they would tell another person about the location of a place. One way to give the location is by relating it to the location of another place (e.g., Greenland is north and east of Canada's maritime provinces). Location can also be described using reference systems such as latitude and longitude. Have students describe the location of Washington, D.C., in terms of latitude and longitude. Ask them to explain why this is known as "absolute location."

G4

Understanding Hemispheres, Latitude, and Longitude

When you study a map or a globe, you'll see a grid of lines composed latitude and longitude. These imaginary lines are used to locate places on map or globe. This imaginary grid of lines also helps to divide the earth in four hemispheres—northern, southern, western, and eastern. The word hemisphere is from Greek and translates as "half a sphere."

Northern Hemisphere

Southern Hemisphere

Western Hemisphere

Eastern Hemisphere

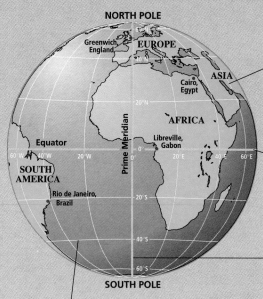

Longitude is the number of degrees east or west the prime meridian. Line of longitude meet at the North and the South Poles.

The **Equator** is 0° latitude. It separates the Northern and Southern Hemispheres.

The **prime meridian** is 0° longitude and goes through Greenwich, England. The prime meridian and the longitude line opposite it at 180° separate the earth into the Eastern and Western Hemispheres.

Lines of **latitude** run east and west across the globe. Latitude is the number of degrees north or south of the equator. Lines of latitude never meet.

MAP SKILLS

1. **REVIEW** In which two hemispheres would you find the United States?
2. **REVIEW** What is the approximate latitude and longitude for Cairo, Egypt and Rio De Janeiro, Brazil?
3. **THINK ABOUT IT** Why do you need both the latitude and longitude to locate a place on a map? What would happen if you only had of the measurements?
4. **TRY IT** Look at the map of China on page 1? At what latitude and longitude is Chengdu located?

•G4

Objectives

1. Determine in which hemisphere(s) a country is located. (Map and Globe Skills 2)
2. Practice finding the latitude and longitude of specific places. (Map and Globe Skills 2)

Answers for Map & Globe Skills

1. Northern and Western Hemispheres
2. Cairo—30°N, 31°E; Rio de Janeiro—23°S, 43°W
3. There are many places at the same latitude, or at the same longitude, so you need both to get the exact location. If you had only one measurement, you would get the location of a line rather than a point.
4. 30°N, 97°E

Collaborative Learning

Divide the class into groups of 3 or 4. Have each group find out the significance of one of the following: Tropics of Cancer and Capricorn, Arctic Circle, Antarctic Circle. *(The Tropics of Cancer and Capricorn mark the most northerly and southerly latitudes at which the sun will be directly overhead at some point during the year; the Arctic and Antarctic circles mark the latitudes beyond which the land will have at least one day each year when the sun doesn't set, and one day each year when the sun doesn't rise.)*

Drawing Inferences from Maps

You know from reading that authors don't always spell out every detail. As a reader, you have to rely on your own experience and clues in the text to figure out information about a plot. When you do this, you're making inferences.

You can also make inferences from maps. A map's scale, legend, and details will give you clues. This map shows the canals, dams, and waterways of the Netherlands today. How do you think these natural and human-made features have affected people's lives?

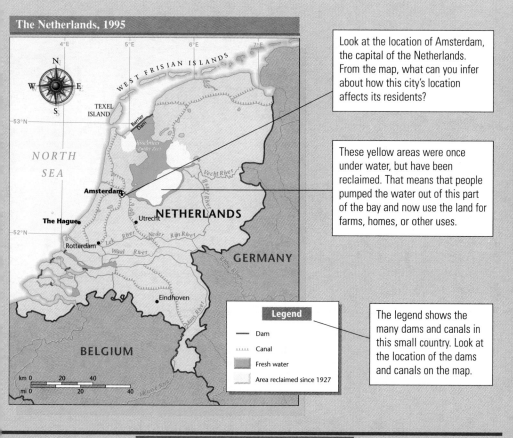

The Netherlands, 1995

Look at the location of Amsterdam, the capital of the Netherlands. From the map, what can you infer about how this city's location affects its residents?

These yellow areas were once under water, but have been reclaimed. That means that people pumped the water out of this part of the bay and now use the land for farms, homes, or other uses.

The legend shows the many dams and canals in this small country. Look at the location of the dams and canals on the map.

Legend
— Dam
⋯⋯ Canal
▓ Fresh water
▒ Area reclaimed since 1927

MAP SKILLS

REVIEW Look at the location of Rotterdam. What can you infer about the kinds of jobs that people in Rotterdam might have?

THINK ABOUT IT What natural disasters do you think people in the Netherlands worry about? Why?

3. **TRY IT** Look at northern South America on the map of world climates on page 530. Based on its climate pattern, what can you infer about land use there? Now look at the world land use map on page 531 to see if you were correct. Try this for other regions of the world.

G5

CLASS ACTIVITY

Demonstrate inferences by having students look at the World Vegetation map on p. 530. The purple areas are tundra. Remind students that the purple area in central Asia is where the Himalayas are. If you didn't know what tundra was, you could infer that it is the characteristic vegetation of very cold areas, since it is found in the far north and at high altitudes. Then direct students' attention to the legend of the map on p. G5. Ask what inference they can make about the Netherlands based on the legend. *(Controlling water is important.)*

► *Amsterdammers might have water-related jobs, such as transportation or fishing; might use water for recreation; climate might be affected by the water.*

HISTORY
Map and Globe Skills

Beginning in the Middle Ages, the Dutch began to reclaim land from the sea. Today, the reclaimed areas, called polders, amount to about 965 square miles. Along the west coast, a series of dams known as the Delta Project was completed in 1986. Have students locate the series of dams on the map and ask them how the dams protect the Netherlands. *(prevent the North Sea from overwhelming coastal lowlands)*

G5

Objectives

1. Determine how location affects people. (Map and Globe Skills 2/ Visual Learning 1)
2. Draw conclusions based on information shown on a map. (Critical Thinking 1)

CLASS ACTIVITY

To prepare for a discussion on map projections, bring in several tennis balls or oranges. Also make several individual copies of each of the projections shown on pages G6 and G7, or any of the smaller world maps in the Atlas on pages 529–533. Ask what shape the earth has. *(sphere)* Challenge students to cut out the world maps and then form cones and cylinders. Also have them shape the maps to the balls. Talk about the results and the need for projections.

GEOGRAPHY

Map and Globe Skills

The textbook contains more types of map projections. Tell students to find another type of projection and compare it to the four projections shown in this Handbook.

➤ *South America looks longer, thinner, and much larger on the Peters Projection than on the Mercator Projection.*

Understanding Projections

Suppose you have a map of the world and a sphere. You want to cover the sphere with the map to make a globe. Since the map is flat and the sphere is round, you won't ever have a perfect fit. Cartographers still wrestle with the problem of representing the round earth on a flat map. They use projections, or ways of transferring the curved surface of the earth onto a flat map. All projections have some distortion of distance, direction, size, or shape.

In 1569 the German cartographer (mapmaker) Gerhardus Mercator first published this projection. A Mercator Projection maintains the shapes of the continents but distorts their sizes, especially near the poles. Look at the size of Greenland on this projection. In reality, it's about the same size as Mexico!

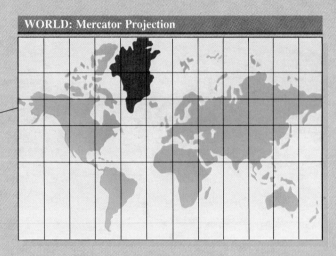

WORLD: Mercator Projection

In 1974, Arno Peters, a West German cartographer, created the Peters Projection. The sizes of the continents in relation to each other are accurate, but their shapes are distorted. Look at South America on the Peters Projection map. How does its size and shape compare to that of South America on the Mercator Projection?

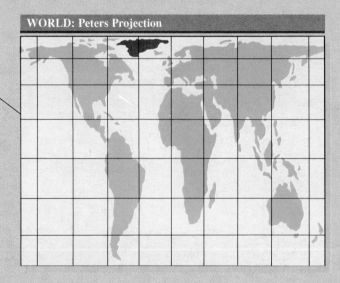

WORLD: Peters Projection

G6

Objectives

1. Understand how the shape of the earth affects maps. (Critical Thinking 1/Visual Learning 1)
2. Compare map projections of the world. (Map and Globe Skills 1 and 5)

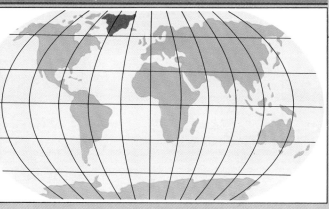

RLD: Goode Projection

Paul Goode, a cartographer from the University of Chicago, combined elements of two other projections to create the Goode Projection in 1923. Notice how the projection divides the world into sections. These divisions help make the projection of continents more accurate in terms of size and shape, but distances are difficult to measure.

RLD: Robinson Projection

In 1963, American cartographer Arthur Robinson created this projection. The Robinson Projection shows the sizes, shapes, and distances between the continents fairly accurately. Most of the world maps in this book use the Robinson Projection as their base.

MAP SKILLS

IEW On which projection does Africa k the largest? On which projection does ok the smallest?

IEW Which projection would you use to out the correct size of Greenland? the rtest route between South America and stralia? the shape of Antarctica? the shape Africa?

3. **THINK ABOUT IT** Look at South America on the Goode and on the Mercator Projections. Why do they look similar while Greenland and other areas near the poles look so different? Use a globe to answer the question.

4. **TRY IT** Choose a map in this book. Which projection does it use? Explain the advantages of using that particular projection.

G7

G7

Answers to Map Skills

1. Africa looks largest on the Peters Projection. It looks smallest on the Mercator Projection.
2. Peters; Robinson; Robinson; Mercator
3. Because the Mercator distorts sizes so much more as you get closer to the poles, Greenland and the other areas near the poles look larger than South America and other places near the Equator.
4. Specific maps that students choose will vary. The advantages will be either correct size, correct shape, ease of measuring distance, or some combination of these.

CLASS ACTIVITY

To illustrate the way flow arrows are used on maps, start by drawing a simple arrow on the chalkboard and have students acknowledge that the arrow indicates direction. Then at the base of the arrow draw a symbol that suggests goods of some kind, perhaps something that is locally produced. Ask students what they think the two symbols—the arrow and the symbol at its base—mean together. Then draw another arrow leading away from the product symbol, but make it much heavier than the first and leading in a different direction. Ask again to interpret the meaning of the arrows.

▶ *More Africans were sent to the West Indies than to Central America.*

Geography Theme: Movement

With the movement of people, there is also the movement of ideas. How did the flow of enslaved Africans affect the cultures of North, Central, and South America? Encourage students to think about language, arts, food, religion, and clothing.

G8

Interpreting Flow Lines

Maps can show the movements of people, ideas, and goods by using flow lines. Flow lines are arrows on maps that show where something came from and where it went. Because they vary in thickness, graduated flow lines also show the quantity of what has moved. The map below shows the number of Africans who were enslaved and sent to the Americas.

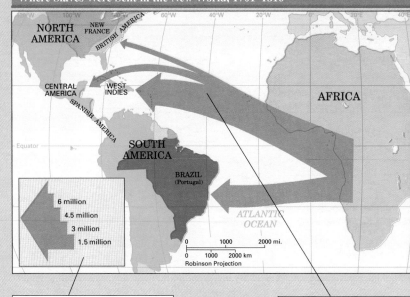

Where Slaves Were Sent in the New World, 1701–1810

The legend shows how the thickness of the arrows relates to the number of Africans who were sent to the Americas.

Graduated flow lines let you compare amounts quickly. Based the map, were more Africans s to Central America or the West Indies?

MAP SKILLS

1. **REVIEW** About how many Africans were sent to Brazil as slaves?
2. **REVIEW** Name the four places on the map where Africans were sent. Rank them from where the most Africans went to where the fewest went.
3. **THINK ABOUT IT** What else might you show with flow lines on a map?
4. **TRY IT** Make or obtain a map of your community. Use arrows to mark the flow of your class members as you travel from school to home.

Objective

1. Understand that a map can show the movement of people, goods, and ideas. (Map and Globe Skills 1 and 3)

Answers to Map Skills

1. About 2 million.
2. West Indies, Brazil, Central America, British America
3. Answers will vary, but could include immigration information or data about types and amount of products traded.
4. Answers will vary but should reflect an understanding of how flow lines work on maps.

Homework Options

The map on pages 36–37 shows invasions in Europe, North Africa, and Asia at the time of the fall of Rome. Have students write descriptions of the invasions based on the map's flow lines. Encourage them to depict the action in the form of newspaper headlines or as television or radio news bulletins.

Reading Different
Kinds of Maps

As you've already seen, maps can show more than the shape of land. They can show details about historical places; how people have changed their land; and the flow of people, goods, or ideas. In this section, you'll learn to use several different kinds of maps.

A Relief Map with a Vertical Profile

A relief map shows the topography, which means the natural surface features of the land. It does this by showing the land's elevation, or height above sea level. A vertical profile is a diagram on a physical map that presents a side view of an elevation line (also called a profile line) drawn across the map. This map shows the topography of the island of Sumatra, in Indonesia, along an elevation line.

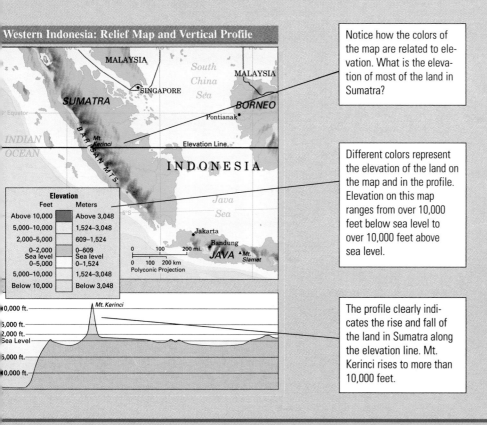

Western Indonesia: Relief Map and Vertical Profile

Elevation	
Feet	Meters
Above 10,000	Above 3,048
5,000–10,000	1,524–3,048
2,000–5,000	609–1,524
0–2,000 Sea level	0–609 Sea level
0–5,000	0–1,524
5,000–10,000	1,524–3,048
Below 10,000	Below 3,048

0   100   200 mi.
0   100   200 km
Polyconic Projection

Notice how the colors of the map are related to elevation. What is the elevation of most of the land in Sumatra?

Different colors represent the elevation of the land on the map and in the profile. Elevation on this map ranges from over 10,000 feet below sea level to over 10,000 feet above sea level.

The profile clearly indicates the rise and fall of the land in Sumatra along the elevation line. Mt. Kerinci rises to more than 10,000 feet.

Making a Map with a Profile

Obtain topographical maps of your area. Students can use these maps to create different vertical profiles.

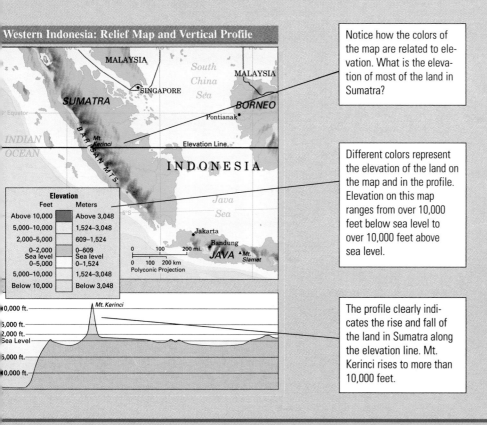

Lead the class in a review of the different kinds of maps they have encountered so far in the Handbook and the kinds of information each one carries. Explain that in the next section the Handbook will introduce maps that carry information on relief (topography) and other geographic features.

➤ *Most of Sumatra is between 0 and 2,000 feet above sea level.*

A Relief Map with a Vertical Profile

The map on this page shows the topography, or the natural surface features, of the island of Sumatra. In addition to a color-coded legend that represents elevation, the map includes a vertical profile of Sumatra. You may also want to display a globe or a world map that gives some sense of where Sumatra is in relation to India, China, and Australia. Note for students that Sumatra is a part of Indonesia.

Looking Forward

The Skills Feature in Chapter 16, page 436, goes into greater detail on analyzing elevation.

Objectives

1. Determine the elevation of a country. (Geography 1/Visual Learning 1, 4/Map and Globe Skills 1, 4)
2. Understand what a vertical profile is. (Map and Globe Skills 1, 4)

CLASS ACTIVITY

As you narrate the action in the Battle of Yorktown, have students follow the events on the map. Then go back and dissect each of the five events on the map. After each event, ask questions such as these: (after event 2) If you were Cornwallis, what would you have done after the British Navy withdrew? What might have happened if the British Navy had forced the French to withdraw?

Geography Theme: Place

Provide physical maps of Yorktown and the Chesapeake Bay area. Ask students what kinds of physical features might affect a battle here, apart from peninsulas? How would students allow for geography in their battle plans?

A Battle Map

A battle map illustrates the events of a particular battle or series of battles. Since the outcome of a battle is often affected by the land on which it occurs, maps are a good way to show battles. The map below uses symbols to show the positions and movements of troops during the Battle of Yorktown that took place during the American Revolution.

The green arrows stand for American troops, the red arrow and shapes stand for British troops, and the blue arrows stand for French forces. The direction of the arrows shows the movement of the forces.

The map shows that Cornwallis's British troops became trapped at Yorktown, because it was on a peninsula. Once Washington's American troops and Rochambeau's French troops moved in, the British troops had nowhere to go to escape. Cornwallis was forced to surrender.

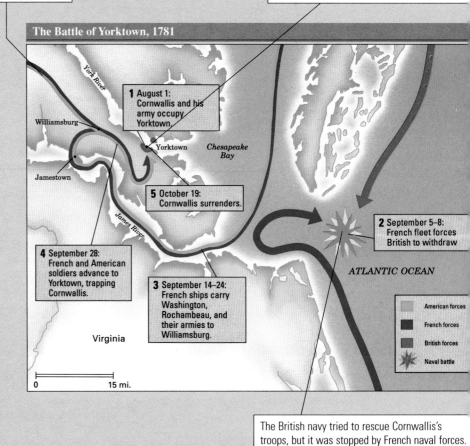

The Battle of Yorktown, 1781

York River

Williamsburg

Jamestown

James River

Yorktown

Chesapeake Bay

1 August 1: Cornwallis and his army occupy Yorktown.

5 October 19: Cornwallis surrenders.

4 September 28: French and American soldiers advance to Yorktown, trapping Cornwallis.

3 September 14–24: French ships carry Washington, Rochambeau, and their armies to Williamsburg.

2 September 5–8: French fleet forces British to withdraw

ATLANTIC OCEAN

Virginia

0   15 mi.

American forces
French forces
British forces
Naval battle

The British navy tried to rescue Cornwallis's troops, but it was stopped by French naval forces.

Objective

Understand how geography can affect specific historical events and how this interaction can be portrayed on maps. (Geography 3/Map and Globe Skills 2, 3/Visual Learning 1)

Access Strategy

Review the geographic term *peninsula* with students. Explain that a peninsula is a piece of land that juts out into water. Peninsulas are normally surrounded on three sides by water. Show several different maps that contain examples of peninsulas. Then let students write and illustrate their own definitions of peninsula as it might appear in the Glossary of Geographic Terms on pages 534–535.

Language Connection

How do students think Cornwallis felt about peninsulas before and after the Battle of Yorktown? Invite them to step into his shoes and describe the advantages of his location before the battle and the disadvantages after the battle.

Comparing Maps

Maps can contain many different kinds of information. Look at the two maps of South Africa below. The top map shows the economic resources the country and the bottom map shows its population. By comparing the two maps, you can learn how economic use and population are related in South Africa.

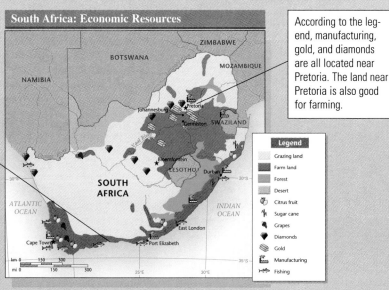

South Africa: Economic Resources

According to the legend, manufacturing, gold, and diamonds are all located near Pretoria. The land near Pretoria is also good for farming.

There are fewer economic resources along the coast of South Africa between Cape Town and Port Elizabeth. What are they?

Legend
- Grazing land
- Farm land
- Forest
- Desert
- Citrus fruit
- Sugar cane
- Grapes
- Diamonds
- Gold
- Manufacturing
- Fishing

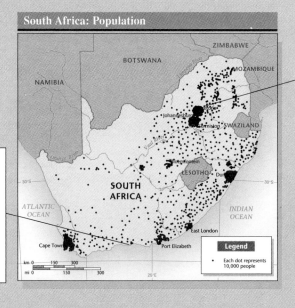

South Africa: Population

The many red dots near Pretoria show that the city and the region around it are densely populated.

What is the population of the coast between Cape Town and Port Elizabeth? Based on these two maps, what conclusions can you draw about a region's economic resources and its population?

Legend
- Each dot represents 10,000 people

Writing

Obtain population and economic resources information about your community from the local chamber of commerce or government. Let students study the material. Then have them write brochures highlighting the relationship between resources and population. The brochures should be geared toward people or new businesses interested in relocating to the community.

Open the discussion by asking students to list the economic resources that are essential to their community. Talk about what kinds of businesses and industry the community has, and what kinds of occupations parents have. How would students characterize their community—urban, rural, suburban, or a combination? Can they make generalizations about population concentrations within the community? Discuss with students how they might represent this information on a map.

► *Fishing and manufacturing.*

► *Bottom left caption: The population appears moderate—less than in the largest cities, more than in parts of the country's interior. From these maps, one can conclude that regions with the most economic resources tend to have the greatest population.*

Looking Forward

The Skills feature on China on pp. 216–217 compares two maps of China, topographic and land use, to learn how physical features affect land use.

Geography Theme: Human and Environments

Using the two maps on this page, find out where students would choose to live in South Africa and why.

Objective

Compare information on resource and population maps to draw conclusions about how resources affect population. (Map and Globe Skills 1, Geography 3, Critical Thinking 3)

CLASS ACTIVITY

This map offers a single view of one region, but at the same time shows how that region changed over time. Talk about the way the map shows this. *(by labeling and dating the empires that existed in the region between 2350 and 1750 B.C.)* Then have students write descriptions of each empire based on the map. Encourage them to include natural features and the relationship of the empires' locations to each other.

► *Assyria was a little more than half the size of Babylonia.*

Looking Forward

This textbook offers many opportunities for students to study a variety of historical maps. For instance, the map on page 311 shows how the Great Plague spread throughout Europe between 1346 and 1353.

Geography Theme: Regions

As the map shows, regions change over time. Timelines are one way to show that change. Challenge students to create a timeline for the map on page 171 to show the expansion of the Ottoman Empire.

► *Rivers allowed people to grow crops and to travel more easily.*

G12

A Historical Map and a Timeline

Many of the maps in this handbook are historical maps. Cartographers toda can draw historical maps based on historical records and writings and archaeolo cal discoveries. This historical map shows three empires that existed in the part the world known as Mesopotamia between 2350 and 1750 B.C. The two rivers i this region, the Tigris River and the Euphrates River, were important for some the earth's earliest known civilizations.

The red line marks the approximate boundaries of th early empire of Assyria. How did its size compare with the size of Babylonia?

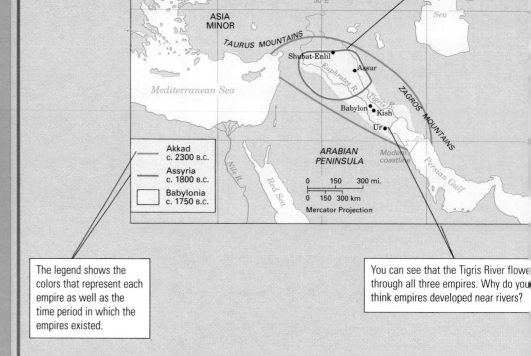

Early Empires: Akkad, Assyria, Babylonia, 2350–1750 B.C.

The legend shows the colors that represent each empire as well as the time period in which the empires existed.

You can see that the Tigris River flowe through all three empires. Why do you think empires developed near rivers?

G12

Objective

Interpret the way maps can present historical information about particular regions. (Geography 5/Map and Globe Skills 1, 2, 4)

Role Playing

Divide the class into groups of three students. Each student will take the role of one of the rulers of each empire (see the timeline on p. G13) and explain where he or she wants to expand the empire and why.

Timelines record events that occurred in the past. They present the ...nts in order so you can see and understand the sequence of different ...nts. This timeline gives a sequence of some events that occurred in the ...adian, Assyrian, and Babylonian empires shown on the map on page .... It also shows some other events that occurred in this region.

...e timeline is broken into intervals of ...0 years. The numbers on this timeline ...crease as you move to the right, because ...e dates are B.C., which stands for Before ...rist. This means the dates refer to the ...mber of years before Jesus was born, so ...e numbers decrease as you move closer ...Jesus' birth. After Jesus' birth the num- ...s increase.

The timeline identifies two rulers whose empires were not shown on the map. Based on the information here, can you add those empires to the map? Why or why not?

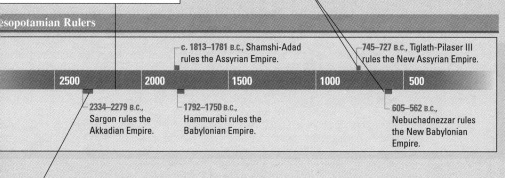

...esopotamian Rulers

c. 1813–1781 B.C., Shamshi-Adad rules the Assyrian Empire.

745–727 B.C., Tiglath-Pilaser III rules the New Assyrian Empire.

| 2500 | 2000 | 1500 | 1000 | 500 |

2334–2279 B.C., Sargon rules the Akkadian Empire.

1792–1750 B.C., Hammurabi rules the Babylonian Empire.

605–562 B.C., Nebuchadnezzar rules the New Babylonian Empire.

This area of the timeline shows the reign of Sargon, who created the world's first empire, Akkad. How long did Sargon rule Akkad?

How is the information that you learn from the map on the left page similar to the infor- mation on this timeline? How is the informa- tion different?

G13

Prepare index cards that tell the history of your community. Each card should contain a date (year) and an event, and each student should receive a card. Whenever possible the card should also contain some geo- graphic information about the event described. Draw a time- line on the board. The yearly increments will depend upon the age of your community and the range of events. Ask stu- dents to enter their events, in order, on the timeline.

➤ *You could not add the two additional empires to the map, because the timeline only gi es their dates, not locations.*

HISTORY
Visual Learning

To reinforce the concept of timelines, have students create timelines of their own lives.

➤ *55 years*

➤ *Similar: The timeline and the map show the dates of rulers. Different: The timeline makes it easier to quickly see which rulers came first and for how long they ruled. The map shows the locations of the empires.*

G13

Objective

Interpret events on a timeline. (Geography 5/Visual Learning 2)

CLASS ACTIVITY

Before discussing cartograms, get students' first reactions to the map on this page. Then talk about how the cartogram is similar to other kinds of maps they have studied. *(It has a legend, and the countries are shown in proper relationship to each other.)*

GEOGRAPHY

Map and Globe Skills

Have students use the cartogram to list the four largest economies in order from largest to smallest, based on their GNP.

Looking Forward

On p. 531, the Atlas features a cartogram representing the world's population.

A Cartogram

You already know that maps can show physical features, like land a water. But they can also show statistics, almost like a graph. These kind maps are called cartograms. Cartograms look very different from physi maps. The cartogram below shows the gross national product (GNP) fo countries of the world. The GNP is the total value of all the goods and vices produced by a country in a single year.

On a physical map, Canada would appear larger than the United States. On this cartogram, it is much smaller. That means that Canada's GNP is considerably smaller than that of the United States. Cartograms often distort the size and shapes of countries.

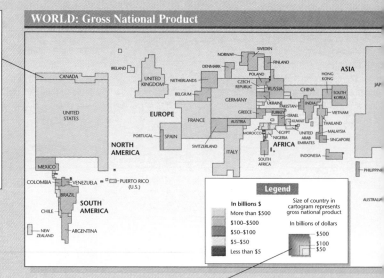

WORLD: Gross National Product

Like physical or political maps, cartograms have scales or legends. Scales on cartograms, however, don't measure distance. This scale explains that the size of each country reflects the size of its gross national product.

MAP SKILLS

1. **REVIEW** How did the geography of the land help defeat the British in the Battle of Yorktown?

2. **REVIEW** Which ruler in Mesopotamia controlled the city of Ur and ruled until 1750 B.C.?

3. **REVIEW** Name three countries whose GNPs are equal to or larger than France's.

4. **THINK ABOUT IT** How would changing the vation line on the map on page G9 chang the profile you see?

5. **TRY IT** Compare two different types of ma of your state. Make a table to compare v the maps tell you about your state.

Objective

Interpret the information on a cartogram. (Map and Globe Skills 1/ Visual Learning 1)

Answers to Map Skills

1. Geography hurt the British because Cornwallis became trapped on a peninsula, and the American and French controlled the seas around it. When Washington's troops approached Cornwallis's troops, the British had nowhere to go.

2. Hammurabi

3. Answers will vary. Possible answers: United States, Japan, Germany, Great Britain

4. Changing the elevation line would mean you need to create an entirely new profile. If the profile did not contain Mt. Kerinci, it would be flatter.

5. Answers will vary but should demonstrate a solid grasp of the varied kinds of information a map can carry.

Using Geographic References

What is a cataract? Where is Flanders located? Which languages are spoken in Africa? The Time/Space Databank on pages 503–548 will help you answer these and other geography questions.

The **Atlas,** pages 518–533, includes many types of maps, such as physical, political, historical, climate, land use, and resources. The map on page 529 shows where specific languages are spoken. This portion of the map shows Africa. African, Semitic, Malayo-Polynesian, and Indo-European languages are all spoken in Africa.

The **Glossary of Geographic Terms,** pages 534–535, illustrates and defines key geographic terms, such as cataract. From the description, you can tell that Niagara Falls is a major cataract.

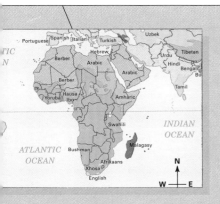

cataract
a large, powerful waterfall

F			
ernando Póo (island off W. Africa)	4°N	9°E	465
anders (region noted for woolen trade; France, Belgium)	51 N	3°E	330
orence (cultural center of Renaissance Italy)	44°N	11°E	317
ustat (Cairo; capital of Fatamid caliphate; Egypt)	30°N	31°E	80

The **Gazetteer,** pages 536–537, lists locations, accompanied by brief descriptions, latitude and longitude, and where to find that location in this book. Flanders is a region in Europe. It is at 51° North, and 3° East, and is shown on a map on page 330.

MAP SKILLS

REVIEW You want to find the location of the Great Rift Valley. In which part of the Time/Space Databank would you look?

THINK ABOUT IT What is the relationship between a savanna, a sahel, and a desert?

Where would you look in the Time/Space Databank to find the answer?

3. **TRY IT** Choose any two terms from the Glossary of Geographic Terms. Find examples of these features in the Atlas.

G15

G15

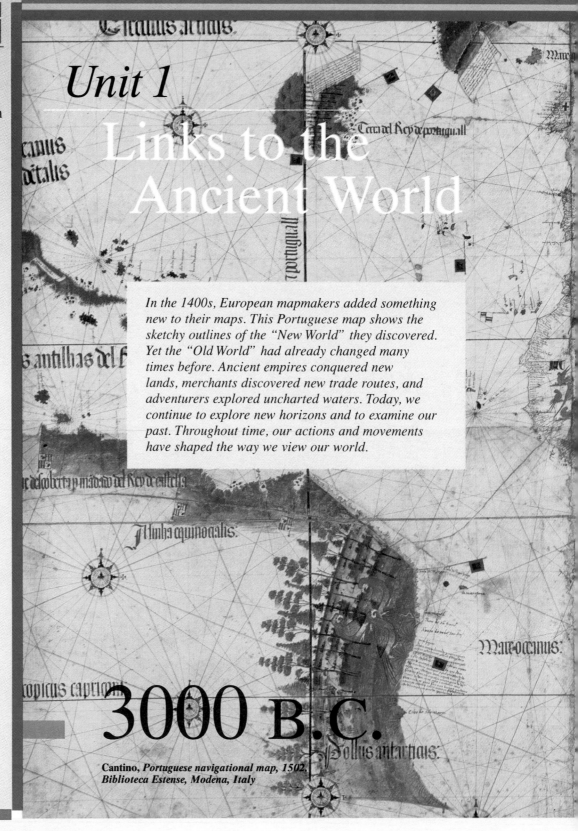

UNIT
OVERVIEW

Write the unit title on the chalkboard and discuss with students what links they might have with the past. *(They are linked by their families to earlier generations and to the places where their ancestors lived; they are linked by objects they have that were made in earlier times; they are linked by what they learn about the past.)* Then have students read the narrative and study the map. Ask them how our world view has changed since the map was made. *(We have a more exact view of the New World; our horizons now extend into space.)*

Looking Forward

Tell students that in the next two chapters they will learn basic concepts that will aid their study of history:

Chapter 1 *A Changing World View*
Chapter 2 *Empires of the Ancient World*

Unit 1
Links to the Ancient World

In the 1400s, European mapmakers added something new to their maps. This Portuguese map shows the sketchy outlines of the "New World" they discovered. Yet the "Old World" had already changed many times before. Ancient empires conquered new lands, merchants discovered new trade routes, and adventurers explored uncharted waters. Today, we continue to explore new horizons and to examine our past. Throughout time, our actions and movements have shaped the way we view our world.

3000 B.C.

Cantino, *Portuguese navigational map, 1502*,
Biblioteca Estense, Modena, Italy

GEOGRAPHY PROJECT

Imperial Visit

Geography Skill Make a Route Map
Students use the skills of Acquiring and Organizing geographic information.

Geography Themes Regions/Movement

Geography Standards 5, 10 interpreting earth's complexity; characteristics and distributions of cultures

Activity *Create a Speech*
Materials note cards, pencils or pens
Management Individual

Students travel back in time to an empire mentioned in this unit and write two speeches: one for the leader of the empire describing the student's homeland, and one to be given upon returning home describing the culture and geography of the visited empire.

Have students:

- write notes for two speeches and/or make a gift representing their homeland and another gift that represents the empire they visit.
- include a map to show the route traveled and the location of the empires.
- practice presenting the speeches, using appropriate voice and gesture.

Today

Understanding the Map

The map is one of the first ever made showing the lands of the New World. It is named for Alberto Cantino, an agent for an Italian duke who commissioned the map. Ask students what they notice about the map. *(The representations of Europe and Africa are quite accurate, but the New World is not as accurate because explorers still did not know much about it.)*

Understanding Chronology

This unit presents an overview of basic concepts about history. It also reviews the fall of the Roman Empire and sets the stage for studying the world events that occurred after the fall of Rome. Remind students of the meanings of B.C. and A.D.—"before Christ" and "*anno Domini*," "in the year of our Lord." Some scholars prefer B.C.E. and C.E.— "before common era" and "common era"—since they do not reflect a religious connotation. However, B.C. and A.D. are the terms students are more likely to encounter in daily life.

For research support activities, see the *Research Handbook.*

For simulations correlated to this unit, see *Citizenship Simulations*, p. vii.

1

HOUGHTON MIFFLIN SOCIAL STUDIES

Bookshelf II

Citymaze!

by Wendy Madgwick

This colorful, pictorial book uses maps as mazes for cities around the world and poses problems based on these mazes.

Motivate Read aloud pp. 22– 23, Istanbul, showing the illustration as you read. Have volunteers try to follow the route described in the book. Ask students to find Istanbul on a world map and to explain why it has been a bustling port since ancient times. Explain that cities like Istanbul, or Constantinople, are present-day links to ancient times. Have students look at pp. 2–3 and 24–25 and predict what this unit will be about.

To connect this book with the unit content, use the planning guide and student activity blackline masters beginning on p. iv of the *Bookshelf II Teacher's Resources.*

For additional books that are Easy, Average, and Challenging, see the Unit Bibliography on p. T43. See bibliography updates at www.eduplace.com/ss/hmss.

Planning at a Glance
A Changing World View

	Objectives	Reading Support *and* Other Resources	Diverse Learning Strategies
Lesson 1 **Connections in the Roman Empire** *pp. 4–7* 2–3 days	• Compare and contrast modes of travel in A.D. 150 with those in use today. • Assess the impact of modern technology on communication.	• **Workbook** or **Reading Support:** pp. 2–5 Review p. 1 Lesson Support/Transition p. 1 Multi-lang. Sum. pp. 1–2 • **Other Resources:** Geography Kit, Poster 4, Study Guide p. 1	Access Strat. **(Extra Support)** TE p. 5 Access Act. **(SDAIE)** TE p. 5 Map and Globe Skills **(Visual)** TE p. 5 Speaking and Listening **(Auditory)** TE p. 6 Audiotapes of Multi-language Lesson Summaries **(Auditory)**
Skill: Using Time Zones *pp. 8–9* 1 day	• Read and use a time zone map and explain how the rotation of the earth affects time of day.	• **Other Resources:** Study Guide p. 2	Making a Bulletin Board **(Visual)** TE p. 8
Lesson 2 **The Expanding Horizon** *pp. 10–15* 2–3 days	• List the major reasons for long-distance travel in the years between A.D. 150 and 1500. • Describe the early inventions that made traveling by land and sea easier. • Assess the influence of early travelers. • Summarize the limitations of early mapmaking.	• **Workbook** or **Reading Support:** pp. 6–9 Review p. 2 Lesson Support/Transition p. 2 Multi-lang. Sum. pp. 3–4 • **Other Resources:** Geography Kit, Study Guide p. 3, Study Print 1	Access Act. **(SDAIE)** TE p. 11 Visual Learning **(Kinesthetic)** TE p. 12 Writing **(GATE)** TE p. 13 Mapmaking **(Visual)** TE p. 14 Audiotapes of Multi-language Lesson Summaries **(Auditory)**
Lesson 3 **Traveling Through the Past** *pp. 16–19* 2–3 days	• Describe the sources of information historians use to learn about the past. • Explain how point of view affects our interpretation of historical sources.	• **Workbook** or **Reading Support:** pp. 10–13 Review p. 3 Lesson Support/Transition p. 3 Multi-lang. Sum. pp. 5–6 • **Other Resources:** Study Guide p. 4	Access Strat. **(Extra Support)** TE p. 17 Collaborative Act. **(Extra Support)** TE p. 18 Homework Options **(Auditory)** TE p. 19 Audiotapes of Multi-language Lesson Summaries **(Auditory)**
Exploring Archaeology: Clues and Connections *pp. 20–21*	• Analyze everyday items for clues to the lives of the people who used them.		Activity **(Kinesthetic)** TE p. 20 Visual Learning **(Extra Support)** TE p. 20
Chapter Review *pp. 22–23* 1 day		Chapter 1 Test pp. 1–4 *(See facsimiles on TE p. 559.)*	Assessment Multiple-Use Masters pp. 73–80

Reading Support Resources *for Every Lesson*

Reading and Review

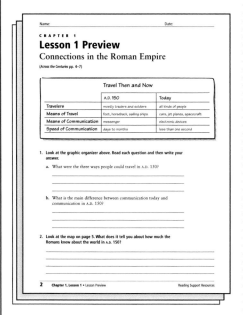

Multi-language Summaries

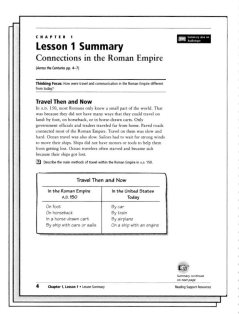

Lesson Support /Transition
S D A I E

Activities for SDAIE
Specially **D**esigned **A**cademic **I**nstruction in **E**nglish

- **Chapter Overview*** p. 1
- **Lesson Previews*** using graphic organizers from the Teacher's Edition pp. 2, 6, 10
- **Reading Strategies*** pp. 3, 7, 11
- **Lesson Summaries*** pp. 4–5, 8–9, 12–13
- **Lesson Reviews** pp. 1, 2, 3

  * **Workbook** includes starred items.

- **Lesson Summaries** in:
  - English (See Reading and Review.)
  - Spanish pp. 4–5, 8–9, 12–13
  - Chinese pp. 1–6
  - Hmong pp. 1–6
  - Khmer pp. 1–6
  - Vietnamese pp. 1–6

  Summaries available on audiotapes

- **Lesson Support/Transition** pp. 1, 2, 3

Technology Options

Internet Support
http://www.eduplace.com

Social Studies Center at Education Place
Internet support for Chapter 1:
- *Lesson at a Glance*
- *A Mapmaker*

Software
Student Writing Center (CD-ROM) (Macintosh® or Windows®)
An Odyssey of Discovery™: Continent Explorer II (CD-ROM)

School to Career

Historians analyze the past by studying documents and artifacts. Divide students into small groups. Ask each group to research a specific part of their community's or school's history. How did the events and people of the past shape how the community or school is today?

Character Education

Things people never thought were possible are now taken for granted. An active imagination can help individuals picture a better, safer, cleaner world. Have students write a short story about what they believe the ideal world of tomorrow would be like.

1B

Chapter 1
A Changing World View

Roman traders who journeyed to the Far East 2,000 years ago measured distance not in miles but in how far they traveled by camel in an hour. As they approached their destination, they neared the edge of their known world. How the world has changed since then! Today, we travel far into space. We also look back, learning about our past. Our world view expands as we explore distant horizons and the evidence of past worlds.

c. 1000 B.C. We travel back in time by examining the objects ancient people left behind. The writing in this bronze dish tells of a border dispute settled by two rival groups in China.

3000	2000	1000

2

3000 B.C.

c. 500 B.C. North African people settle in present-day Nigeria and begin making iron tools.

Traveling Through the World

Before the advent of satellite photography, electronic communications, and the like, the only way to learn about an unknown place was to go there. For thousands of years people pieced together a world view that was often based as much on imagination and fear as on knowledge and experience.

Although travel was the chief means of learning about the world, most early travelers were motivated by commercial, political, or religious concerns rather than by the quest for knowledge. Nevertheless, merchants, soldiers, and pilgrims contributed information that helped mapmakers change the shape of the known world. And as the technology of travel improved, the pace of exploration quickened.

Traveling Through the Past

Today, we benefit from another kind of travel: travel to our past. Historians, archaeologists, linguists, and other scholars are constantly finding new evidence to help us understand how and why we got to where we are today. Sometimes the information they

During the 1400s, explorers and traders set sail from Lisbon, Portugal, for the far reaches of the world they knew—Europe, Africa, and Asia. This illustration of Lisbon, drawn about 1590, helps us see what life in the past was like.

c. 1450 Antoine de La Salle includes the discoveries of the Portuguese explorers in his map of the world. Even so, it is far from accurate. Today, radar allows travelers to plot courses across seas, over continents, and into space.

MAREANTIPODES PTINCOGNITVM

B.C.	A.D.		1000		Today

c. 100 B.C. Merchants use camels to transport goods in the arid regions of Asia and the Middle East.

Today

Understanding the Visuals

The bronze dish (p. 2) has 357 archaic Chinese characters inscribed in it.

The painting (center) shows explorers in the process of leaving on an expedition. In the bottom right corner, the explorer (far right) meets with the man who is paying for the expedition. The scene was painted in 1590 by Theodore DeBry.

The map (bottom, p. 3) was printed in 1522 in Paris. De La Salle's original from the mid-1400s is lost. Note the large blob lying on the equator; this is Africa.

For a geography activity, ask students to imagine they are in an entirely unknown wilderness region. After they have an image in their minds of what this place looks like, have them draw maps of their regions. Ask students to write a few sentences about what it felt like to map an unknown region.

Understanding Chronology

Refer the students to the timeline. Point out that the entries show how travel affected life in different parts of the world at different times in history.

uncover causes us to change our view of the past or present, or to modify our plans for the future.

For instance, by 1986, the Windover Archaeological Research Project, directed by Florida State University, had uncovered more than 100 well-preserved skeletons in a peat bog in central Florida. The remains are those of hunter-gatherers who lived in the region 7,000 to 8,000 years ago. The most startling discovery was that some of the skulls still contained brains, and the brains still contained the genetic coding molecule, DNA.

Although scientists are unable to learn much from the DNA now, future technology may allow them to revisit the past by examining human genes. Protein preserved in the bones may reveal new information about diseases this population suffered. In order to ensure that the better-equipped historians of the future will have the opportunity to learn more from this evidence, scientists have left part of the site unexcavated.

Meanwhile, bits of cloth buried with the bones have already shown that these people had developed more sophisticated weaving

techniques than any known in the Americas from that time period. In effect, these bits of cloth changed our view of the past.

INTRODUCE

Briefly review key points about the Roman Empire with students, such as location, time period, size, and type of government. Point out the lesson title and ask students what is meant by "connections." Then have students read the Thinking Focus and predict how people traveled and communicated in the Roman Empire. Have them read to confirm or reject their predictions.

Key Terms

Vocabulary Strategies: T36–T37
electronic communication— communication devices, such as fax, Internet, the telephone, television, and computer, that have reduced the time necessary for transmitting information
satellite—a manufactured object orbiting the earth, often used to transmit information

➤ *Sample answers: Tokyo is in Japan, Moscow is in Russia, the Eiffel Tower is in Paris, France; from books, magazine articles, school, and television programs.*

	B.C.	A.D.		
3000	2000	1000		
			150	TODAY

L E S S O N   1

Connections in the Roman Empire

THINKING FOCUS

How were travel and communication in the Roman Empire different from today?

Key Terms

• electronic communication
• satellite

➤ *What do you know about any of the places on these brochures? How do you know about them?*

Paris, Alexandria, Athens. Would you like to visit these cities? What about Sydney, Nairobi, or Moscow? Which of these names is most familiar to you?

You have probably heard of some, if not all, of these places. Even Sydney, Australia, across the vast Pacific Ocean, is now part of the world view of most Americans.

If you had lived in Rome in A.D. 150, your world view would have been quite different. Paris

(then called "Lutetia"), in Gaul; Alexandria, in Africa; and Athens, in Greece, were all part of the Roman Empire. As a merchant or soldier, you might have traveled to these cities.

Sydney? Nairobi? Moscow? These cities did not exist in A.D. 150. More important, the Romans were unaware of cultures in Australia, the Americas, central Africa, and northern Asia. Their limited world view made the world smaller than the one we know today.

4

Chapter 1

Objectives

1. Compare and contrast modes of travel in A.D. 150 with those in use today.
2. Assess the impact of modern technology on communication.

Graphic Overview

	A.D. 150	Today
Travelers	mostly traders and soldiers	all kinds of people
Means of Travel	foot, horseback, sailing ships	cars, jet planes, spacecraft
Means of Communication	messenger	electronic devices
Speed of Communication	days to months	less than one second

The World the Romans Knew or Knew About, A.D. 150

Travel Then and Now

The Romans of A.D. 150 knew of only a small part of the earth's surface, as you can see on the map above. Yet distances within their known world—for example, from Rome to Lutetia—seemed greater to them than they seem to us. That is because the ways we look at and experience the world have changed greatly since Roman times.

If you had to walk three miles uphill to school, would it seem near or far to you? How about if you took an express train and arrived in two minutes? The longer we must travel to get someplace, the farther away it seems to be.

Travel Within the Empire

In A.D. 150, most people in the Roman Empire knew very little about the world away from home. In fact, peasants and members of the lower classes rarely traveled beyond their village.

Those people who did travel went on foot, on horseback, or in horse-drawn carts. More than 50,000 miles of paved highways connected all parts of the empire to Rome. But travel was slow. The public wagons averaged only 60 miles a day, a distance we can now travel in one hour by car!

Roman merchants and government officials sailed in ships to imperial provinces in Spain, North Africa, or the Middle East. Speed varied, of course, with the winds. The voyage from Sicily, at the southern tip of Italy, to Alexandria in North Africa took six days with good winds. Today, many diesel-powered transport ships follow that same route in less than one-third the time.

A Compare your known world with the world known to the Romans in A.D. 150 (shown in purple). How are they different?

How Do We Know?

ECONOMICS *Large numbers of Roman coins found in India show that India and Rome carried on extensive trade. Several Roman coins struck in the late A.D. 100s have been found in a port city in modern Cambodia, and 16 Roman coins have been found in the Chinese city of Shansi.*

A Changing World View

5

D E V E L O P

Point out that this lesson compares and contrasts transportation and communications in A.D. 150 with those of today. Draw the Graphic Overview from p. 4 on the chalkboard but omit the entries. Discuss with the class the entries that belong in the Today column, and fill in their responses on the chart. Tell them to copy the chart from the board and complete it as they read the lesson.

GEOGRAPHY

Map and Globe Skills

Have students use a modern world map to locate the places shown on the travel posters on p. 4. Ask them by what means they could travel to those places. Tell students to use the map on p. 5 to list five regions Roman citizens could have visited in A.D. 150. (*Western Europe, North Africa, Greece, Arabia, Asia Minor.*) Ask them by what means the Romans could have traveled there. (*Foot, horseback, horse-drawn cart, ship.*)

5

Access Strategy

Ask students to identify current methods of transportation. List their suggestions on one side of the chalkboard. Then ask them to identify current methods of communication, and list those on the other side of the chalkboard. Finally, ask students to identify five adult occupations (*for example, cashier, day-care worker, secretary, senator, factory worker*), and list those in the middle of the board. Discuss with students the ways in which people in each occupation use or are affected by the listed methods of transportation and communication. (*Examples: A cashier might drive or take a bus to work and use an electronic cash register at work; a senator uses the telephone frequently and uses television to campaign for office.*) Connect the side columns to the middle column with lines to indicate usage. Then ask students how those jobs would change if modern transportation and communication methods were eliminated.

Access Activity

Have students keep track for three to five days of the number of times they do the following activities: ride in a car, bus, or train; walk one mile or more; talk on the telephone; read a newspaper; write or receive a letter; use a TV or radio; ride a horse; visit another town or city. Ask them to predict how their daily lives would be different if they lived 1,800 years ago.

GEOGRAPHY
Critical Thinking

Have students compare and contrast the two ships pictured on p. 6 with respect to speed, capacity, navigation, control, number of passengers, provisions, purpose of voyage. Ask them which ship they would like to travel on and why.

■ *Most people walked or rode on horseback or in horse-drawn carts. Merchants and others who needed to cross the sea sailed on ships.*

▲ *Compare the sizes of a modern ocean liner, the* Queen Elizabeth II, *and a Roman sailing vessel from about* A.D. *100. The modern ship measures 963 feet long and the ancient one 120 feet. Hulls of reinforced steel have replaced wooden ones. And with powerful turbine engines, today's captains need not rely on rowers or the wind.*

■ *Describe the main methods of travel within the Roman Empire in* A.D. *150.*

Travel to Foreign Lands

Roman merchants in A.D. 150 traded gold, textiles, glassware, wine, and papyrus for spices, gems, silk, cotton, and fabric dyes from China, India, and Southeast Asia. Routes to the east, whether by land or sea, were long, difficult, and dangerous.

The overland route from Antioch, on the eastern Mediterranean shore, to Luoyang, capital of China, was over 4,000 miles long. Hardly anyone ever traveled the whole way. Goods changed hands in the great trading cities along the route.

Merchants with goods bound for India shipped their merchandise up the Nile to Coptos, where it was transferred to camel caravans for the trip to the ports of the Red Sea. Other goods were shipped from the Persian Gulf. Traders loaded their cargo onto ships for the two-month voyage to India.

Sea travel was hazardous and often delayed. Captains of sailing ships required favorable winds to reach their desired ports. Also, sailors had no navigational charts or instruments, such as the magnetic compass, to help them find their way. Once at sea, travelers commonly fell victim to, and some even died from, storms, sickness, malnutrition, starvation, and dehydration.

Because of the great distances, discomforts, and dangers involved, very few people ever traveled beyond the boundaries of the empire. Most of those who did sought to trade with or invade foreign lands.

Today, all kinds of people travel all over the world for business and for pleasure. Jet planes, cars, trains, and cruise ships carry travelers in comfort and safety where once only brave soldiers and traders dared to go. ■

Communication Then and Now

Just as travel has become easier and faster, communication has improved. At the time of the Roman Empire, messages could be sent only one way—they were hand carried. Messengers crisscrossed the empire carrying correspondence. Often, people asked travelers to deliver letters to faraway places.

Chapter 1

Study Skills

Divide the class into small groups to research the effects recent inventions have had on transportation and communication. Members of each group should also summarize the impact the invention has had or will have on their own lives. You might suggest topics such as the cathode ray tube, optical fiber cable, fax machine, laser, or silicon chip.

Speaking and Listening

Have each student interview an older relative or friend to find out what inventions in the fields of transportation and communication were created during his or her lifetime. Students should ask what life was like before those inventions and whether the person thinks these inventions are useful or harmful. Students should summarize their information in a written or oral report.

Research

Suggest that students research the inventions mentioned in their interview for the Speaking and Listening activity. Students should find out information such as who invented it, when, how, and why; why the invention is important; whether the invention is in use today; and how it has changed since its earliest form. If the resources are available, have students photocopy or quote from newspaper or magazine articles written when the invention was introduced.

Communication was only as fast as the messenger's transportation. Messengers on foot could cover only about 25 miles a day. The official Roman postal service, which used horses or horse-drawn carriages day and night, covered an average of 100 miles a day. Carried over land and sea, a letter that was sent from a general in Rome could take more than 30 days to reach a legion outpost in Britain.

Today, we can contact people in other parts of the world without anyone having to make a journey.

Electronic communication, which includes such inventions as the fax machine, Internet, radio, television, computers, and the telephone, has revolutionized the way we communicate. Communication **satellites** orbit the earth transmitting telephone and television signals. In less than a second, they can relay signals and messages to almost anywhere on earth. Space probes now explore and send back information about our universe.

Through these many scientific developments, our world view has expanded. At the same time, the earth seems to be much smaller than it seemed to the Romans. Today, our frontiers lie in space rather than beyond a distant ocean or unknown continent. ■

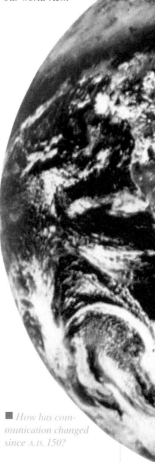

◄ *In A.D. 150, the Appian Way (lower left) led Romans to known destinations. Today, communication satellites have greatly expanded our world view.*

■ *How has communication changed since A.D. 150?*

7

R E V I E W

1. **FOCUS** How were travel and communication in the Roman Empire different from today?
2. **GEOGRAPHY** How do you think a merchant from Lutetia (Paris) would have reached the North African city of Alexandria in A.D. 150?
3. **CRITICAL THINKING** How is space travel today like taking an ocean voyage in A.D. 150?
4. **CRITICAL THINKING** Why would silk clothing have been a sign of wealth in the Roman Empire?
5. **CRITICAL THINKING** Explain this statement: The world shrank on the day when communication no longer depended on transportation.
6. **ACTIVITY** Imagine that you are standing in a major transportation center 1,500 years in the future. Draw a sketch or write a description of the scene. Be sure to include what the destinations might be. Show or describe new methods of travel that you think might exist.

A Changing World View

Ask students to explain what the Roman road and the satellite on p. 7 have in common. (*Both are modes of communication.*) Ask them to summarize how they are different. (*Speed, ease, cost, efficiency, reliability, maintenance.*)

■ *Communication in A.D. 150 was much slower because messages had to be delivered by hand. Today electronic communication devices can send messages almost anywhere in seconds.*

C L O S E

Discuss with students their completed Graphic Overview charts and compile their entries on the chalkboard. Then divide the class into groups and have each group use the information from their charts to create a new chart illustrating the relationship between transportation and communications and world view. Finally, have the groups share their charts with the class.

Answers to Review Questions

1. In the Roman Empire travel was very slow, uncomfortable and dangerous by today's standards. Communications then were linked to transportation. Today we can send or receive messages almost instantaneously, without depending on transportation.
2. The merchant might have gone by horse or cart from Lutetia to an Italian seaport. From there he would sail across the Mediterranean Sea to Alexandria.
3. Both require courage to explore the unknown and to face hardships and possibly even death. Both are also means for obtaining information about what exists around us.
4. Because the silk had to travel a long and difficult route and changed hands many times, it was expensive in Rome.
5. The world seemed smaller because distant places seemed closer when people could contact them faster and more easily.

Homework Options

Have students do research to learn about one of the famous Roman roads, such as the Appian Way, the Aurelian Way, or the Flaminian Way.

Study Guide: p. 1

UNDERSTANDING
LOCATION

This skills feature teaches students how to read and use a world time zone map and explains how the rotation of the earth affects time of day.

GEOGRAPHY
Map and Globe Skills

Have students read the first paragraph in Here's How. Then review the diagram on p. 9. You may want to use a flashlight and globe to demonstrate how half of the earth is always receiving light from the sun. Then explain that the earth rotates about 15 degrees each hour, making a complete rotation in 24 hours. Be sure students can relate our experience of day and night to the earth's rotation.

Ask students to look at the time zone map on pp. 8 and 9 and locate the 24 time zones, the Prime Meridian, and the International Date Line.

8

Using Time Zones

Here's Why

Just as there are standard systems that help people around the world communicate about weights and distances, there is also a world standard system to help establish time differences. A time zone map shows the time differences between locations on earth. Because people and information can quickly travel long distances, knowing how to use a time zone map can be a valuable skill.

Here's How

The diagram on page 9 shows that half of the earth's surface is always receiving light from the sun. As the earth rotates on its axis, the part of its surface that receives that light changes. This change provides us with a way to measure time.

The exact time at any place on earth is measured from noon, when the sun is directly overhead. When it is noon for you, the time east of you is a little later, and the time west is a little earlier.

This small difference in time was not very important when people and information traveled slowly. Today, however, people need to communicate immediately with others in distant places. A system of standard time zones was established in

1884, within 10 years of the invention of the telephone.

The earth was divided into 24 time zones, one for each hour of a day, as shown on the map below. Each zone covers about 15 degrees of longitude, the number of degrees the earth rotates in one hour. In some places zone lines are crooked to account for political borders.

The starting point is an imaginary line called the prime meridian, which goes

through Greenwich, England. The time there is called Greenwich mean time or GMT. The time one time zone east of the GMT is one hour later, and the time one time zone west is one hour earlier.

The time that divides days is midnight. When it is noon in Greenwich, it is midnight at the International Date Line, which is halfway around the world at the 180th meridian. When you cross the International Date

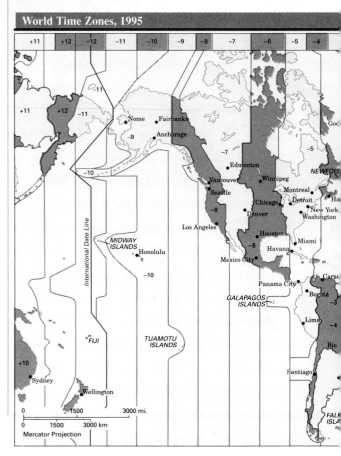

World Time Zones, 1995

Objective

Read and use a time zone map and explain how the rotation of the earth affects time of day. (Map and Globe Skills 2)

Making a Bulletin Board

Have a group of students make a bulletin-board display showing the time of day in other parts of the world. Students should pick a number of cities to highlight on a world map and calculate the time in those cities when it is noon in their city.

Writing

Ask students to imagine that their job requires them to know the time in time zones different than their own. (Travel agent, airline flight attendant, banker, international businessperson, journalist.) Have students write paragraphs explaining how time differences affect their work.

Line going west, you add a day. Going east you subtract a day.

Find Anchorage, Alaska, on the map below, east of the International Date Line. Suppose you are leaving Anchorage at 6 P.M. to fly to Washington, D.C., and you want to set your watch to the correct Washington time. You can see from the map that you will enter four time zones on the trip. To find out what time it is in Washington

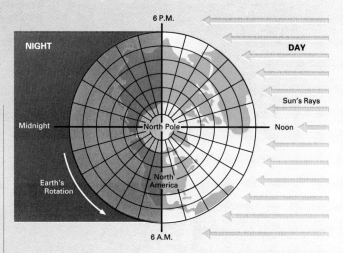

NIGHT

DAY

Sun's Rays

6 P.M.

Midnight

North Pole

Noon

Earth's Rotation

North America

6 A.M.

when you are leaving Anchorage, add one hour to the Anchorage time for each time zone you enter. To have the correct Washington time,

you should set your watch to 10 P.M.

If you fly west from Washington, D.C., to Denver, Colorado, subtract one hour for each time zone you enter. When it is 8 A.M. in Washington, it is 6 A.M. in Denver.

If you fly south from Washington, to Lima, Peru, you do not need to change your watch. Although in different hemispheres, both are in the same time zone.

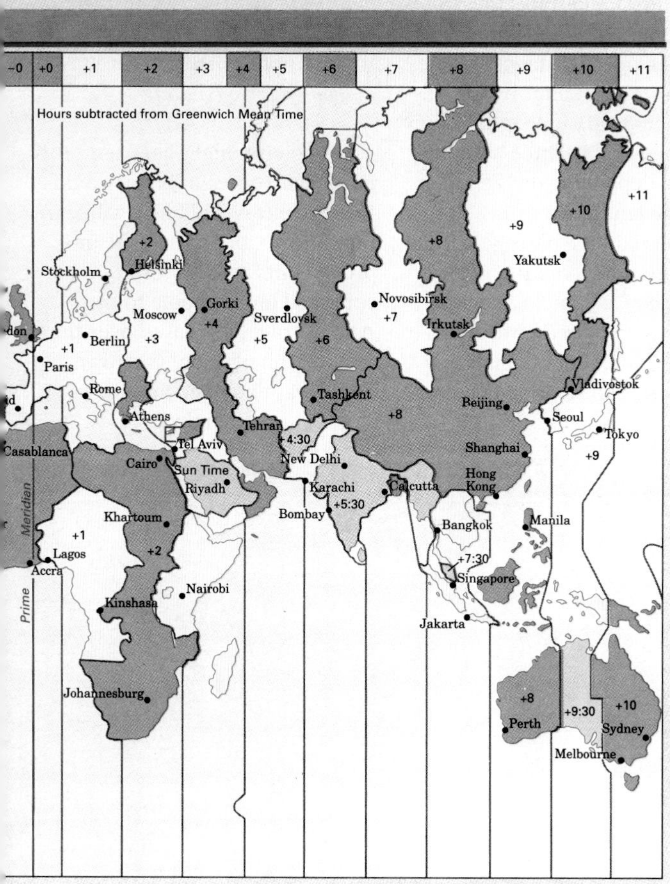

Try It

Use the time zone map to see what time it is in Montreal, Canada, when it is 8 P.M. in Los Angeles, California. What time is it then in Rio de Janeiro, Brazil? How much earlier is it in Stockholm, Sweden, than in Perth, Australia?

Apply It

Suppose you have friends in New York and in San Diego and you want to call them both on your birthday. If you call at 6 P.M., what time is it in each city?

A Changing World View

Time zone map labels:

−0 +0 +1 +2 +3 +4 +5 +6 +7 +8 +9 +10 +11

Hours subtracted from Greenwich Mean Time

Stockholm, Helsinki, Moscow +4, Gorki, Sverdlovsk +5, Novosibirsk +7, Irkutsk, Yakutsk +9, +10, +11, +8, +9, Berlin +1, Paris, Rome, Athens, Tashkent, Beijing, Vladivostok, Seoul, Tokyo +9, Casablanca, Cairo, Tel Aviv Sun Time, Tehran +4:30, New Delhi, Shanghai, Karachi +5:30, Calcutta, Hong Kong, Khartoum, Bombay, Bangkok, Manila, +1, Lagos +2, Accra, Kinshasa, Nairobi, +7:30, Singapore, Jakarta, Johannesburg, +8 Perth, +9:30, +10 Sydney, Melbourne, Moscow +3, Riyadh, London, Prime Meridian

9

9

Ask students to discuss why time zones were not developed until 1884. *(It was not until 1884 that there was a need— in this case to make railroad schedules—to communicate about time to so many people over such great areas.)* A good way to open discussion is to ask students about what it would be like if everyone used a system of local time. *(The time would be different from place to place, even over a small geographic area.)*

Discuss other reasons why time zones are useful. Have students use the map on pp. 8 and 9 to determine the time in other places around the world.

Answers to Try It

1. 11:00 P.M.
2. 1:00 A.M.
3. 7 hours.

Answers to Apply It

Answers depend on the location of the caller's home relative to New York and San Diego.

Map and Globe Skills

Use the time zone map to answer the following: When it is 8:00 A.M. in Chicago, what time is it in Hong Kong? *(10:00 P.M.)* In Rio de Janeiro? *(11:00 A.M.)* What is the difference in time between Washington and Moscow? *(8 hours.)* Moscow and Beijing? *(5 hours.)* Johannesburg and Stockholm? *(1 hour.)*

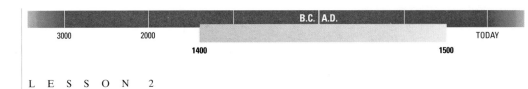
INTRODUCE

Have students define the word *horizon*. Ask what the lesson title suggests in relation to the chapter title. Have students read the Thinking Focus and recall who traveled and why in A.D. 150 in the Roman Empire (Lesson 1). Point out that this lesson covers people in other times and regions as well. Ask students to predict how travel changed by A.D. 1500 and to look for details in the lesson to support their predictions.

Key Terms

Vocabulary Strategies: T36–T37
caravan—a single file of pack animals journeying together
stirrups—loops or rings hung from either side of a horse's saddle to support the rider's foot in riding and mounting
lateen sail—a triangular sail
sternpost rudder—a paddle-like device under a ship for steering sailing ships
magnetic compass—a device used to determine geographical direction using a magnetic needle that is free to pivot until aligned with the magnetic field of the earth

➤ *Place names, political boundaries.*

10

L E S S O N 2

The Expanding Horizon

THINKING FOCUS

How and why did people travel in the years between A.D. 150 and 1500?

Key Terms

- caravan
- stirrups
- lateen sail
- sternpost rudder
- magnetic compass

➤ *Compare this map to the maps on pages 522–524 of the Atlas. What has changed? Can you find any of these towns on the modern maps?*

10

Isidore of Charax wrote the passage on the right around 10 B.C. for the Roman emperor Augustus. In this first known travel guide, *Parthian Stations*, Isidore describes the trade route from Antioch, on the eastern shore of the Mediterranean Sea, to the borders of India. He names the supply stations and states the distances between them in schoeni *(SKEE nee)*, or the distance people could travel in one hour by camel. Schoeni could vary in length from two and one-half to three and one-half miles, depending on the difficulty of the landscape.

As you read the passage, notice how Isidore points out physical features, such as temples, canals, and villages, to help the traveler follow the route. On the map below, try to find some of the places he mentions.

Then a royal place, a temple of Artemis, founded by Darius, a small town; close by is the canal of Semiramis, and the Euphrates is dammed with rocks, in order that by being thus checked it may overflow the fields; but also in summer it wrecks the boats; to this place, 7 schoeni. Then Allan, a walled village, 4 schoeni. Then Phaliga, a village on the Euphrates (that means in Greek 'half-way'), 6 schoeni.

Who else might have used this particular route, and how would they have traveled? You will learn that, from A.D. 150 to 1500, improvements in transportation encouraged more people to travel. And as travel increased over time, the horizon of people's known world was extended and their world view expanded.

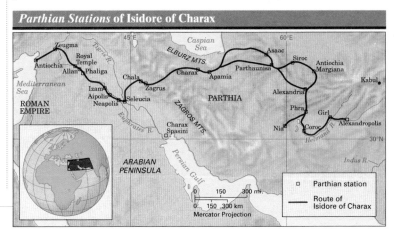

Parthian Stations of Isidore of Charax

Chapter 1

Objectives

1. List the major reasons for long-distance travel in the years between A.D. 150 and 1500.
2. Describe the early inventions that made traveling by land and sea easier.
3. Assess the influence of early travelers.
4. Summarize the limitations of early mapmaking.

Graphic Overview

Travel was slow, difficult, and undependable → **Advances in Travel Technology** →
- Travel became safer and more reliable
- More people began to travel
- People's world view expanded

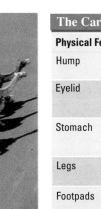

The Caravan Camel		
Physical Feature	Advantage	Effect
Hump	stores fat	provides energy for long journeys
Eyelid	protects eye but lets light shine through when closed	able to see during sandstorms
Stomach	in 3 parts, can hold 50 gallons of water	able to make long journeys without water
Legs	strong, can carry up to 1,000 pounds	able to carry freight
Footpads	spread out when camel steps on them	helps with walking in sand

Merchants, Soldiers, Explorers, Pilgrims

Many who used Isidore's guide were merchants. But throughout history, people also have traveled on religious quests, to conquer other lands, and to explore unknown realms. And all travelers depended on the means of traveling available in their time.

Merchants

From about 1100 B.C., merchants trading in arid regions of Asia and the Middle East used camels to transport their goods. The sure-footed animals could carry up to 1,100 pounds and withstand both intense heat and extreme cold.

Traders often used long halters to tie many camels together to form **caravans.** Great caravans of as many as 5,000 camels trudged along various portions of a rugged 4,000-mile route between the Mediterranean Sea and the Chinese capital at Luoyang.

Soldiers

Soldiers and others who also needed swift transportation rode horses. Three inventions improved horseback riding: the stirrup, the bit, and the horseshoe. **Stirrups** are loops that hang down on both sides of a saddle. They hold the rider's feet and make it easier for riders to use their legs to control a horse. By A.D. 400, the Chinese had developed rigid metal stirrups which gave the rider more security in the saddle.

Another invention, the bit, originated in the Middle East, in about 1400 B.C. A bit is a metal piece that fits in the horse's mouth. It is attached to straps, or reins. Pulling on the reins moves the bit and signals the horse to stop or to turn.

The hard, paved roads of the Roman Empire damaged horses' hooves. So to protect their horses, the Romans developed the third invention, horseshoes. At first, Roman soldiers tied an iron plate over each hoof. But by A.D. 100, they nailed on iron shoes.

Though many people traveled on horseback, the most dramatic use of horses was for warfare. For example, the Mongols of central

▲ *For thousands of years, camels have enabled people in dry and desert regions to travel and ship goods over long, difficult terrain. Review the features of the camel that made it suitable for such journeys.*

Across Time & Space

Dates can sometimes reveal the thinking of those who use them. The most common historical dating system in the United States is B.C. and A.D. This system begins the year 1 at the supposed year of Jesus' birth. Thus B.C. means "Before Christ" and A.D. is Latin for "In the year of our Lord." Modern scholars often use C.E. for "Common era" and B.C.E. for "Before the common era."

11

A Changing World View

Critical Thinking

Ask students what kinds of people were most likely to sail between A.D. 150 and 1500. (*Soldiers, merchants.*) Then consider why Horace regarded ocean travel as dangerous. Generate a list of potential dangers on the board. (*Unknown regions, bad weather, uncooperative wind, difficulty of navigation by stars, cumbersome steering.*) Then discuss the innovations in sea travel that addressed some of these difficulties.

► *It enabled ships to sail more easily in any direction, regardless of the direction of the wind.*

Asia used stirrups to control their horses with their legs so that their hands were free. Experts with bow and arrow, they struck quickly and rode away before their victims could return the attack.

Explorers

Despite fragile ships and the dangers of the open seas, daring explorers set sail to discover what lay beyond the horizon. But, as the Roman Horace wrote in about 65 B.C., "Surely oak and threefold brass surrounded his heart who first trusted a frail vessel to the merciless ocean." Early sailing ships required good weather to reach their destinations. Rigged with rectangular sails, these ships had difficulty sailing against the wind. Also, sailors needed clear skies to see the stars and the shoreline by which they navigated.

Three innovations freed sailors from dependence on the weather: the lateen sail, the sternpost rudder, and the magnetic compass.

Around A.D. 150, a triangular sail known as the **lateen sail** was first used on the Mediterranean Sea. As shown below, the lateen sail enabled ships to sail more easily in any direction, regardless of the direction of the wind.

As early as 200 B.C., the Chinese used the **sternpost rudder** to steer their ships. It was a paddle-like device under the ship that could be moved from side to side. The rudder replaced the steering oar, which was cumbersome and ineffective on large ships. For centuries, sailors were unable to navigate through bad weather. But by the 1100s, the Chinese began to use the **magnetic compass.** A compass needle always points north, so sailors could navigate in any kind of weather.

Such innovations as these revolutionized sea transport.

▼ *Sailing ships travel against the wind by tacking, or often changing directions in a zigzag path. Compare the turning movement of the ship with a lateen sail to that with a rectangular sail. Why was the lateen sail such an important improvement?*

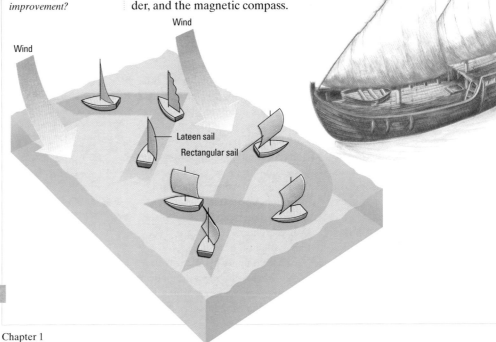

Wind
Wind
Lateen sail
Rectangular sail

12

Chapter 1

Visual Learning

Point out the diagram on p. 12. Have two students demonstrate the paths of the two kinds of ships by walking in the diagrammed patterns across the classroom. Be sure they understand that each pattern continues back and forth. Finally, discuss which ship would have the easier trip—fewer turns, shorter path—to its destination. (*The lateen-sailed ship.*)

Collaborative Learning

Have students work in small groups to chart routes across the gymnasium, school yard, or a field. Mark a starting point and the direction of true north. Each group should choose a destination, mark it, and then plot a route to it by recording the direction and distance to travel for each leg of the route. Each route must involve at least three changes in direction. Have the groups trade charts and try to follow the directions they have received to reach the correct destination.

Science Connection

In Columbus's time, navigators could determine their direction by observing the stars or using a compass. But technology could not tell them what lay ahead in unfamiliar waters. Columbus relied on his experience and observation skills to adjust his ships' course. He noted bird migrations, watched for branches or leaves in the water, and observed changes in the color of the clouds or water—all indications of the direction in which land might be found.

Longer voyages became safer and more dependable. Now adventurous sea captains could sail into unknown regions of the seas. More important, they could find their way back.

Pilgrims

As transportation became safer and more reliable, more people began to travel. Pilgrims and adventurers traveled throughout the world and many wrote about their experiences.

From A.D. 629 to 645, Xuanzang *(shoo ahn DZAHNG)*, a Chinese pilgrim, journeyed over 5,000 miles from China to India and back to collect Buddhist teachings. He recorded fantastic tales of his adventures. This excerpt describes the Hindu Kush mountains.

T his mountain pass is very high; the precipices are wild and dangerous; the path is tortuous, and the caverns and hollows wind and intertwine together. At one time the traveler enters a deep valley, at another he mounts a high peak, which in full summer is blocked with frozen ice. By cutting steps up the ice, the traveler passes on, and after three days he comes to the highest point of the pass. There the icy wind, intensely cold, blows with fury; the piled snow fills the valleys. Travelers pushing their way though dare not pause on their route.

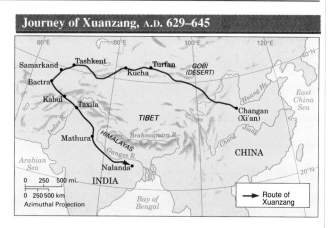

Journey of Xuanzang, A.D. 629–645

Another traveler motivated by religious beliefs was Ibn Battuta, a Muslim. In 1325, Ibn Battuta left his home in Tangier to journey to the Muslim holy city, Mecca, in Arabia. But the sights he saw and the people he met so fascinated him that he devoted the rest of his life to travel.

For 30 years, Ibn Battuta traveled in Arabia, Asia, Africa, and Spain. Like Xuanzang, he recorded many exciting adventures. These accounts shed new light on the world away from home. Describing the Nile River, Ibn Battuta wrote, "This river is most pleasant for navigating, most beautiful in aspect, most productive in fishes, abounding in birds, and its water is most wholesome and pleasant to drink. . . ."

Mapmakers used travelers' information like this to update their own maps of the world. Read A Moment in Time on page 14 to learn more about mapmakers. ■

◄ *Xuanzang's tales of his travels became a popular part of Chinese folklore. What do you think was the most difficult part of his journey? Why?*

◄ *Xuanzang is reported to have been a handsome man who liked to wear colorful clothing. This portrait of him, from about A.D. 800, is painted on silk. His backpack is filled with some of the Buddhist writings he brought back to China from India.*

■ *In what ways did travel become easier between A.D. 150 and 1500?*

13

A Changing World View

GEOGRAPHY
Map and Globe Skills

Have students use the map on p. 13 to list some of the geographic regions Xuanzang crossed. Ask them what challenges he might have faced in each region, and for what reason(s) people were willing to face such difficulties. Point out that Xuanzang's journals provided the Chinese with new information about India's geography, climate, and people as well as religion.

◄ *Sample answer: Crossing the Gobi because it was hot and dry.*

■ *The stirrup and bit gave riders better control; horseshoes protected horses' feet from wear. The lateen sail enabled ships to sail against the wind; the sternpost rudder made steering easier; and the compass let sailors navigate by night or day in any weather.*

13

Religious Context

After 16 years of study in India, Buddhist philosopher Xuanzang (602–64) returned to China with copies of Buddhist manuscripts. There he directed teams of scholars to translate the texts into Chinese. Within 18 years they had completed 1,338 chapters, one quarter of the 5,084 chapters translated over the next 600 years by 185 teams of translators. Thanks to these works, scholars have been able to reconstruct the history of Buddhism in Asia.

Writing

Have each student choose to be a merchant, soldier, explorer, or pilgrim. Students should write an autobiographical sketch that includes the following details: year and place of birth; reasons for becoming a merchant, soldier, explorer, or pilgrim; places visited; means of transportation used and why; and plans for the future. Point out that students may be creative except when discussing means of transportation.

Critical Thinking

Discuss this statement: Advances in communication have greatly reduced the need for travel, yet at the same time they have increased people's desire to travel. *(They have reduced need by sending information without someone making a journey; increased desire by stimulating interest in unfamiliar regions and making contact between distant areas easy.)*

Note: You may want to use this Moment in Time in conjunction with a discussion of the Early Maps section on p. 15.

Early Maps section on p. 15.

GEOGRAPHY
Visual Learning

Ask students how the mapmaker knew how to draw the new world. *(He copied from the globe and used information from Columbus's letter and Columbus's journal with its map of Hispaniola.)* Mapmakers like the one in the picture often accompanied explorers on their jouneys to the new world. This mapmaker may well have had notes and sketches of his own.

More About Mapmaking The map in this picture was called a "portolan chart," because the major ports were laid out first. Then the mapmaker filled in the remaining coastlines freehand, according to nautical charts or navigators' descriptions. Mapmakers usually followed strict rules of color, making coastlines black and harbors red. But in this case, the mapmaker colored the map of the new world green, probably to show how lush it was. Mapmakers often added banners and pictures of ships and battles to identify special landmarks.

14

A MOMENT IN TIME

A Mapmaker

*8:47 A.M., August 27, 1500
In the mapmaker's house,
Santoña, Spain*

Globe
It gave the mapmaker a pattern for the northern part of the New World. Now he is adding the southern part to his new map. The map will change the way Europeans view the world.

Dividers
The mapmaker uses this instrument to plot distances on his map. He just read in Columbus's journal that the island of Hispaniola, where Columbus first landed in the New World, is bigger than Spain.

Smudge
Tracing Columbus's map of Hispaniola left a few carbon marks, but the mapmaker will rub them out with bread crumbs.

Letter
A letter from Columbus is the source of his information for the southern part of his map.

Rhumb Lines
Carefully drawn from the center circle, they'll be used by pilots to direct a ship's course.

Portrait
The mapmaker used this picture of a saint to connect the Northern and Southern hemispheres. He has no idea how they should be joined, and he hopes people will find his solution clever.

Visual Learning

Have the students find the island Columbus named Hispaniola on a modern map. What is Hispaniola called today? *(Haiti and the Dominican Republic.)* Ask students this: If the mapmaker were making the map today, how would he join the two large land masses? *(With Central America.)*

Research

Have students read selected excerpts from Columbus's journal, describing his first voyage and discovery of the new world. Point out that Columbus determined from the beginning to "fudge" the mileage he reported to his sailors each night, telling them they hadn't gone as far as they really had. He did this to calm down the sailors, who were terrified because people had never before sailed out of sight of land for so long.

Mapmaking

Have the students make a freehand map of their school or neighborhood. As ancient mapmakers did, they can embellish their maps with landmarks, drawings of people, or sketches to commemorate special events. They may also wish to use dots or crosses to signify "navigational hazards." If they use such symbols, they should explain them in a key.

Early Maps

Xuanzang, Ibn Battuta, and other travelers collected a wealth of information. Each new journey provided mapmakers with another small piece of the world. Chinese, Indian, Persian, Arab, African, and Polynesian peoples also used their geographic knowledge to make maps.

The greatest geographer and mapmaker of the Roman Empire was Ptolemy (*TAHL uh mee;* 90–168). He collected information from travelers to draw a remarkably accurate map of the world the Romans knew or knew about in 150.

In Europe, Ptolemy's work was neglected as the Roman Empire declined. For the next 1,000 years, European maps gave a distorted view of the world. The most common of these are called T-O maps. They show the continents of Europe, Asia, and Africa separated by bodies of water that together formed a "T." An ocean, which is the "O," encircles the three continents.

From the 1200s on, European mapmakers benefited from the study of others. Ptolemy's work, for example, was well known, translated, and thoroughly analyzed in the Muslim world. In the 800s, the astronomer Ahmad al-Faraghani

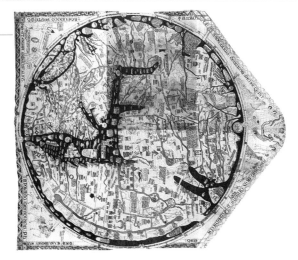

(*ahl fahr uh GAHN ee*), working for the ruler of the Muslim Empire, led a team of scientists in measuring a degree of longitude in order to accurately calculate the size of the earth. Technical knowledge also came from the East, and included the astrolabe, compass, and quadrant.

In Spain in the 1100s, Muslim, Jewish, and Christian scholars prepared translations of scientific material on medicine, astronomy, geography, cartography, and mathematics. From there the books were brought to the new universities of Europe. This knowledge helped Europeans explore and map the world beyond their shores. ■

▲ *Many Christian mapmakers put Jerusalem at the center of their maps. Find three or four landmarks that appear on this map and on the map on pages 518 and 519. How do their locations here differ from the map in the Atlas?*

■ *How did travelers and explorers change people's view of the world?*

Ask students what conclusions they can draw about early mapmaking based on the map shown here. (*European mapmakers knew little about regions beyond home; Christianity influenced how European mapmakers depicted the world.*) Have students compare this map to the map on p. 3 and discuss the differences between the two.

◄ *Answers will vary depending upon landmarks noted. But students should note that the Black and Caspian seas are not long branches of the Mediterranean, that Africa is not rounded at the bottom, and that the Americas are not even shown.*

■ *They brought back information about the places they had visited, thus helping mapmakers create more accurate maps and expanding people's knowledge of the world.*

CLOSE

Draw the Graphic Overview from p. 10 on the board. Have students expand the chart by discussing specific disadvantages of early travel (*for example, impossible to navigate in fog*) and by listing the inventions that overcame those disadvantages (*the magnetic compass*). Write their ideas on the chart on the board.

15

REVIEW

1. **FOCUS** How did geographic knowledge increase in the years between A.D. 150 and 1500?
2. **CONNECT** How would the stirrup, the bit, and horseshoes have affected communications by A.D. 500?
3. **GEOGRAPHY** What areas of early maps were most likely to be accurate? Why?
4. **ECONOMICS** Why did traders choose camels instead of horses as pack animals on trade routes through Asia and the Middle East?

5. **CRITICAL THINKING** Explain this statement: Since A.D. 150, the knowledge gathered from many different peoples helped produce changes in travel and communication.
6. **WRITING ACTIVITY** Write a "travel guide" telling someone how to get to a certain place. Use physical features, directions, and estimates of time to describe the route. Do not use mileage, number of blocks, road signs, or other modern conveniences.

Answers to Review Questions

1. People who traveled to trade, conquer other lands, explore unknown regions, or make religious pilgrimages brought back knowledge of the world. In the 1100s knowledge came from books translated by scholars in Spain.
2. The stirrup and bit gave riders more control over their horses. Horseshoes protected horses' hooves. As a result, by A.D. 500, messengers on horseback could travel more swiftly and securely.

3. The most accurate areas were those closest to the mapmaker's home. This was the area the mapmaker knew best.
4. Camels could travel in extreme weather and over rough terrain. Also, a camel could carry much heavier loads than a horse.
5. As the central government and economy declined, schools may have lost funding and scholars may have lost the respect of others. Fewer traders or travelers would bring news of new ideas or inventions.

Homework Options

Have students write a paragraph on travel methods in the ancient world that incorporates all of the key terms for the lesson.

Study Guide: p. 3

INTRODUCE

Have students read the Thinking Focus and suggest some methods historians might use to reconstruct the past. Mention specific details from Lessons 1 and 2 and ask how historians know them. For example, written accounts tell about Xuanzang's travels. Have students read to learn more about how historians reconstruct the past.

Key Terms

Vocabulary Strategies: T36–T37

history—a record of past human events; the study of the past, including explanations of the events

prehistory—history that took place before the development of writing

archaeology—the recovery and study of physical remains from past human life and culture

primary source—a source for historical study written by someone who participated in or observed the event recorded

secondary source—a source for historical study written after the event it describes, usually with the aid of a primary source

16

B.C. A.D.

3000 TODAY

LESSON 3

Traveling Through the Past

THINKING FOCUS

How do historians reconstruct the past?

Key Terms

- history
- prehistory
- archaeology
- primary source
- secondary source

➤ *An Aztec artisan crafted this mask by covering the front of a human skull with pieces of turquoise and lignite.*

*T*hen Moctezuma . . . pointed out his great city and all the others standing in the water and on the land around the lake.

That huge . . . temple stood so high that from [the top] one could see over everything: three causeways leading into Mexico . . . the aqueduct of Chapultepec which supplied the city with the finest water, the wooden bridges built certain distances apart on the three causeways through which the lake water flowed. We beheld on that great lake a multitude of canoes loaded with provisions. We saw how it was impossible to pass from house to house . . . except by drawbridges . . . or in canoes. We saw in those cities . . . oratories all gleaming white and wonderful to behold.

From Cortés and the Conquest of Mexico by the Spaniards in 1521

Twenty-seven years after Columbus first landed in the West Indies, a band of Spanish adventurers arrived in Mexico. They had come to find fortunes of gold.

In 1519, the Aztec and their leader, Moctezuma, welcomed Hernando Cortés and 650 explorers to their capital at Tenochtitlán *(tay nawch tee TLAN)*. In the above description of the arrival of the Spanish, Spanish explorer Bernal Díaz gives us a look at the astonishing Aztec city, built over the shallow waters of Lake Texcoco.

Just two years later, Tenochtitlán lay in ruins, its once magnificent buildings burnt to the ground, its causeways and canals filled with rubble. Cortés's army had destroyed the city in his quest to conquer the Aztec.

How do we know about the ruined city, the Aztec, Cortés, and the Spanish conquest? The relic on this page tells us, wordlessly, of the Aztec's skill and artistry. The words of the Spanish explorer Bernal Díaz also speak to us, across almost 500 years, of the glorious city.

Chapter 1

Objectives

1. Describe the sources of information historians use to learn about the past.
2. Explain how point of view affects our interpretation of historical sources.

Graphic Overview

Find written and nonwritten sources. → Carefully study primary and secondary sources for authenticity. → Evaluate accuracy and meaning of sources. → Reconstruct history.

Studying the Past

Just as early explorers and mapmakers expanded the world view of their time, historians expand our view of the past. **History** is the record of past human events. To reconstruct history, historians must study nonwritten and written sources. To reconstruct the history of the Aztec, they studied both.

Nonwritten Sources

To study **prehistory,** or history before the development of writing, historians must rely on silent remains, such as fossils, ruins, and artifacts. **Archaeology** is the science of finding and studying these physical remains. Some people wrongly use "prehistoric" to mean "uncivilized," but to archaeologists, "prehistory" is a useful term.

Written Sources

Written sources date back only to about 3200 B.C., when writing was developed in the Middle East.

A wide variety of written materials exists, including scrolls, tablets, inscriptions, calendars, maps, letters, documents, and books.

Primary sources are those written by people who participated in or observed the events they describe. For example, in the last lesson, Ibn Battuta's account of the Nile is a primary source. **Secondary sources** are written after an event, usually with the aid of primary sources. A story that retold Ibn Battuta's experience would be a secondary source.

Historians prefer primary sources, because the people who observed or took part in events usually tell a more accurate story. Historians carefully check the accuracy of every source to make sure they get a true view of the past.

In some cases, careful study of historical evidence leads to changes in our view of the past. For example, a document known as the *Donation of Constantine* gave the Roman Catholic popes power over Italy and western Europe. The docu-ment was sup-posedly written during Constantine's reign (c. A.D. 274–337). In 1440, Italian historian Lorenzo Valla ana-lyzed the text to prove that it was a forgery, written hundreds of years after Constan-tine's death! ■

▲ *Archaeological teams remove and study tiny pieces of earth bit by bit to reveal clues about the past. The workers below are excavating an ancient tomb in Peru.*

■ *Explain the difference between primary and secondary sources.*

17

A Changing World View

DEVELOP

Point out that this lesson discusses how we learn about past human events. Have students look at the visuals in the lesson to list some potential sources of information about the past. *(Written accounts, artifacts, archaeological sites, and artistic depictions.)* Tell students that they will also learn about some of the difficulties historians may face when using such sources.

HISTORY
Study Skills

Draw two columns on the board and label them History and Prehistory. Have students name sources of historical information and tell whether they help us learn about history, prehistory, or both. Write each in the appropriate column(s) on the chart. *(Sources may include legal documents, diaries, news accounts, relics, art, architectural remains and photographs.)*

■ *A primary source is written by someone who witnessed or experienced the event. A secondary source is written after the event, usually with the help of a primary source.*

17

Access Strategy

Tell students to imagine that they are going to write a history of their own lives. Discuss the meaning of the term *history* and what kinds of information should be included in a history of an individual.

Then ask students to help generate a list of potential sources of historical information about themselves. Be sure students recognize that both written and nonwritten sources may be used. *(Lists may include items such as the following: birth certificate, health records, report cards, photos, art work, favorite posses-sions, old letters written by or about them, and stories told about them by relatives.)* Discuss some of these sources to determine just how accurate or misleading they may be.

Access Activity

Show students pictures of artifacts found in a tomb (for example, the Mayan death mask on p. 407). Discuss what such artifacts reveal about the people who buried them. Remind students that people of some civilizations buried their dead with the necessities and trappings they possessed while alive.

Critical Thinking

Write the passages from the Aztec poet and Bernal Díaz del Castillo side-by-side on the board. For each excerpt, help students generate a list of words that show bias. *(crushed, ruins, grief, suffering; rob, fighting, profit, wounds.)* Have them summarize what each excerpt implies about its writer. *(poet overcome with grief; Díaz del Castillo sorry he didn't get more loot.)* Ask students whether either excerpt alone would be an accurate source of historical information, and how they might view the fall of Tenochtitlan differently if they had access to only one of these sources.

Interpreting the Past

How Do We Know?

HISTORY *In 1978, a Mexico City utility worker struck a stone slab that lay 15 feet below street level. He had discovered the Aztec capital of Tenochtitlán, buried for more than four centuries. Project Great Temple exposed over 5,500 objects created by Aztec laborers and artisans.*

➤ *This page was copied from an Aztec tribute roll, a kind of book with pages made of bark. It shows some of the varied goods that came into Tenochtitlan from the empire: jade beads, birds and feathers, animal skins, and pots of honey.*

Like Lorenzo Valla, a good historian has to be a good detective, evaluating the accuracy and the meaning of all sources. A historian must also be a judge, choosing among conflicting interpretations of the past.

Differing Views of the Past

People's backgrounds clearly affect the way they see an event as well as how they choose to tell the story. For example, in Chapter 16 you will read about the mighty empires of the Aztec and Inca peoples and how they were destroyed by a combination of factors. In the 1500s, the Europeans came with advanced weaponry, horses, and disease. They brought about the downfall of Tenochtitlan *(tehn ouch tiht LAHN)*, the Aztec capital. As you might imagine, Aztec and Spanish primary sources describe these events very differently.

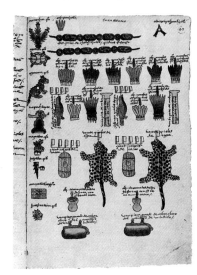

UNDERSTANDING HISTORY

*A*fter Cortés's conquest of Tenochtitlán, an Aztec poet lamented the destruction of his city. "The ways are strewn with broken lances," he wrote. "The houses are without roofs." The Aztec poet's name is not known to us, but his words give us a valuable glimpse of Mexican history.

Changing History

History is the study of past events, such as the Spanish conquest of the Aztec. Traditionally, we learn history from the point of view of the winners—in this case, the Spanish. However, hearing an Aztec voice helps us to understand another important part of the story.

The study of history is not just the discovery and listing of facts and events. Historians also attempt to find meaning in those facts and events. But most facts can be interpreted many different ways, so history can never be purely factual. Both the source's and the historian's point of view influence the way history is eventually written.

Future History

Just as history can never be completely objective, a "final" history can never be written. New historians will discover new sources to study and find new questions to ask of the old sources. People will always debate what history means. And as long as people exist, they will be creating history for future historians.

18

Chapter 1

Critical Thinking

Guide a class discussion of why a one-sided view of history is inadequate. Begin with a familiar example, such as news coverage of your school's loss in an important competition. Should the news story be written by the winners? Why or why not? What are the dangers of choosing to read only the winners' accounts of historic events?

Historical Context

The world's oldest written history comes from China, where archaeologists have found historical records written before 1000 B.C. The grand historian of the Han court, Sima Qian (c. 145–c. 85 B.C.), compiled all the records of the Chinese into a single standard history called *Shih-chi,* or *Historical Records.* The first great Western historian, Herodotus (c. 480–c. 425 B.C.), relied on oral history to write about the wars between Greece and Persia that took place from 500 to 449 B.C.

Collaborative Learning

Arrange for someone to interrupt class without warning by rushing in, taking something, and rushing out. Then, without discussion, have each student write an account of what transpired. Share and discuss these accounts. How do they differ? Why might they differ? Have any students who missed the transaction altogether write a secondary source account of what happened based upon these primary sources. Compare these with the primary sources.

During the 1400s, the Aztecs had seen tremendous advances in the arts, crafts, and learning. Poetry was an Aztec strength. It is not surprising that after the fall of Tenochtitlan, a now-unknown Aztec poet wrote these lines:

We are crushed to the ground;
we lie in ruins.
There is nothing but grief and suffering
in Mexico and Tlatelolco
where once we saw beauty and valor.

Compare the Aztec poet's feelings with those of the Spanish soldier and adventurer Bernal Díaz del Castillo. He was with Cortés on his journey and later wrote his memoirs, which also described the fall of Tenochtitlan:

Some [soldiers] would rob [the Aztecs] of everything they had. We soldiers, on the other hand, who were fighting on the causeways and on land, gained no profit, but plenty of arrows and lance-thrusts and wounds from darts and stones.

Historians must ask when, where, why, and by whom a source was written. The answers to these questions help them evaluate how accurate or biased a source is.

Expanding Views of the Past

History has been called a jigsaw puzzle, with some of the pieces missing. As time passes, new pieces are found. Historians continually revisit the past and reinterpret history in light of new information. In doing so, they change our world view as much as the early geographers who changed the world's map. ■

■ *How do historians evaluate the accuracy of their sources?*

◄ *This Spanish map dates from 1556 and shows Lake Texcoco and the Aztec capital of Tenochtitlan. What reasons do you think the Spanish had for mapping Mexico?*

■ *Historians ask who wrote a source and when, where, and why it was written.*

◄ *Since Mexico was now a colony, the Spanish needed maps for transportation and communication. Equally important, they needed good maps in order to allocate land and establish proof of ownership among themselves.*

CLOSE

Restate the Thinking Focus. On the chalkboard, incorporate students' answers into a flow chart similar to the Graphic Overview on p. 16. Stress that the study of history is an ongoing process in which new techniques, additional evidence, and fresh insights often force us to reevaluate our view of the past.

R E V I E W

1. **FOCUS** How do historians reconstruct the past?
2. **CONNECT** What kinds of primary sources are being created today with the use of electronic communications devices?
3. **HISTORY** Name three sources from which historians have learned about the Aztec civilization.
4. **CRITICAL THINKING** How do you think changing our view of the past affects our world view today?
5. **WRITING ACTIVITY** Choose an event at your school that could have two or more interpretations. Write either an accurate or a biased account of the event. Then exchange papers with a classmate. As a historian, would you use your classmate's account as a reliable primary source? Why or why not? Give examples to support your decision.

Answers to Review Questions

1. Historians gather and study written and nonwritten sources for information about the past. They evaluate the sources for purpose, accuracy, and bias. As new information is discovered, they evaluate it and add it to the body of knowledge about the past.
2. Some of today's primary sources that are created using electronic communications devices include recorded messages, faxes, videotapes, photographs from space, and computer files.
3. Historians have learned about the Aztecs from Aztec poetry, art, relics, personal accounts of explorers, and from the remains of Aztec cities.
4. Answers will vary but should mention that learning new things about the past gives us a new understanding of events in the world today.

Homework Options

Pair students and have each tell the other about something they did or experienced. Direct each listener to repeat to their partner the story they heard. Then have the students write a brief description of what they learned about storytelling from this exercise.

Study Guide: p. 4

DISCOVERY PROCESS

Students will use the following steps in the discovery process to complete the activity:

Get Ready Gather trash items from home that provide clues about their family.

Find Out List items in another student's trash and guess what they reveal about that family.

Move Ahead Make a chart of the clues in the trash and the facts or guesses based on each clue.

Explore Some More List everything in the classroom that could be a clue to 20th-century life for future archaeologists.

Materials needed: Trash items, trash bags, paper, and pen or pencil.

CULTURE
Visual Learning

Have students read the caption for the photograph on p. 20. Explain that an anthropologist studies people to learn more about their origins as well as various aspects of their culture such as religion, diet, social organization, and language. Ask students to give examples of the items they found in their trash bags and link each with one area of a people's culture. *(Sample answer: Church newsletter would show religious affiliation.)*

20

EXPLORING

Archaeology: Clues and Connections

Pieces of a bowl, broken tools, rusted coins—when archaeologists dig up things like these, they study them eagerly. Everyday items are clues to the lives of the people who used them: What did they eat and drink? How did they travel? Did they play games?

▼ *What people throw out tells as much about a society as what people keep. Mountains of garbage give contemporary anthropologists ample material for study.*

Get Ready

Gather items for a "trash" bag from your trash at home. Be sure they are "clean" items, because a classmate will study them to find clues about your family. Rinse out any jars, bottles, or cans. Include anything that gives hints about your family's life—pets, number or age of children, hobbies, or work. Cut the labels off magazines and the address portion off letters.

Find Out

Your teacher will hand out one bag of trash to each student. Make a list of the items in the bag you receive. What does each item tell you? Is there any indication of a family pet: An empty dog-food box? A kitty litter bag? What about ages of

20

Objective

Analyze everyday items for clues to the lives of the people who used them. (History 2; Culture 1; National Identity 3)

Activity

Arrange a field trip for the class to a local historical society or museum. Explain to students before the visit that they are going to see everyday items from centuries ago that give clues to how the people lived then. Suggest that as they view the various exhibits they imagine they are a boy or girl their own age living during the time represented by the exhibit.

After the field trip, have a class discussion about the exhibits that interested students most. Ask if anyone would have liked to live in one of the time periods they saw and why. Have students make general statements about the education, employment, religion, or language of the people who lived in the time periods that interested them.

Every level of this archaeological site dates from a different time period. Archaeologists dig through the layers, sifting the dirt through a fine screen. In this way they catch even the tiniest clues about the past.

the family members: A baby-food jar? A letter from a Cub Scout leader? Did you find anything that suggests work or a hobby: Computer printouts? Pieces of yarn? *Popular Mechanics* magazine? Does anything reveal the family's size: A giant catsup jar? A jumbo container for laundry detergent?

Move Ahead

Make a chart listing the clues you found. Next to each clue, list what you learned or guessed from it. For example:

Clues	*Facts and Guesses*
cat-food can	pet cat
pieces of yarn	someone knits
baby-food jar	baby in house
sawdust	woodworking

Be sure that every fact or guess is supported by a clue.

Explore Some More

Take a look around the classroom. Suppose it were frozen exactly as it is at this moment. If archaeologists were to dig it up in 1,000 years, what might they conclude? List everything in the room that could be a clue to 20th-century life in your school, in your town, or in the United States.

For what purpose might this Peruvian pottery vessel have been created? Note the stone and shell designs pressed into the clay.

21

A Changing World View

NATIONAL IDENTITY
Visual Learning

Explain that it is possible to guess people's national identity and language from clues in their trash. Ask students what clues to national identity and language they might look for in their trash samples. *(Sample answer: Stamps on letters, language on trash items, ethnic food items.)*

HISTORY
Study Skills

To review, have students list several investigation methods or types of observations they have learned to use to obtain clues about the way people live. *(Sample answer: Look for club names, national symbols, types of food, sizes of containers, and types of reading material.)* Ask them how they might use the investigation methods on their lists to study their classroom from a future archaeologist's point of view. *(Students' answers should reflect the same techniques they used to examine their trash samples.)*

It might have been used for wine at social gatherings, because it is decorated and shaped for pouring.

21

Answers to Reviewing Key Terms

A. Sample answers
1. The **lateen sail** helped ships to travel more easily in any direction at any time.
2. The **sternpost rudder** could steer large ships.
3. Using a **magnetic compass,** sailors always knew their direction.
4. The invention of **stirrups** enabled soldiers to shoot while riding horses.
5. **Satellites** transmit radio and television signals anywhere on earth by relaying the signal from its source to its destination.
6. Today, **electronic communications** provide instant communication around the world.

B. Sample answers:
1. Early merchants tied camels together to form **caravans.**
2. Written records give a more complete picture of **history** than other artifacts.
3. When written records are available, historians begin with **primary sources.**
4. "Silent remains" enable us to study **prehistory.**
5. **Archaeology** is the science of finding and studying fossils, ruins, and artifacts.
6. **Secondary sources** pull together information taken from primary sources and other observations.

Answers to Exploring Concepts

A. Students' examples may include any four of the following: trade, exploration, war, inventions, electronic communications, mapmaking, writings, study of the past or study of history.

Chapter Review

Reviewing Key Terms

archaeology (p. 17)
caravan (p. 11)
electronic communication (p. 7)
history (p. 17)
lateen sail (p. 14)
magnetic compass (p. 14)

prehistory (p. 17)
primary source (p. 17)
satellite (p. 7)
secondary source (p. 17)
sternpost rudder (p. 14)
stirrups (p. 11)

A. On your own paper, explain why each invention below is important.
1. lateen sail
2. stern-post rudder
3. magnetic compass
4. stirrups
5. satellite
6. electronic communications

B. Answer each question below. Use the key term that is in parentheses in your answer.
1. How did merchants of Asia and the Middle East transport goods overland? (caravan)
2. Why was the invention of writing important to our study of the past? (history)
3. How do historians piece together written evidence of the past? (primary sources)
4. What do "silent remains" contribute to our study of the past? (prehistory)
5. How might we discover and describe a lost city of which there is no written record? (archaeology)
6. Why do we need more than just eyewitness accounts of history? (secondary sources)

Exploring Concepts

A. In this chapter, you read how people in the past expanded their view of the world. Copy and complete the cluster diagram below. Add examples from the chapter of inventions, historical events, and other things that helped expand our world view.

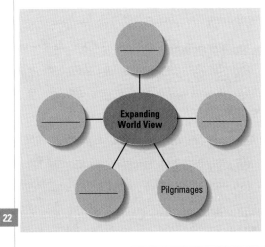

B. Answer each question using information from the chapter.
1. Why did the distance between Rome and Paris, or Lutetia, seem greater in the time of the Roman Empire than it does today?
2. Why was sea travel during the time of the Roman Empire unreliable and dangerous?
3. Compare the speed of communication in the Roman Empire with today.
4. What common role did early soldiers, explorers, merchants, and pilgrims play in expanding the world view of their time?
5. What did travelers such as Ibn Battuta and Xuanzang contribute to mapmaking?
6. How did European geographers benefit from the learning of others?
7. How do historians determine how reliable a primary source is?
8. How do historians affect our world view?
9. Describe how we can "travel" into the past.

Chapter 1

B. Sample answers:
1. Today people fly from Paris to Rome in about two hours. In the time of the Roman Empire, the same trip took days.
2. There were no aids to navigation in bad weather. Sailing ships depended on favorable winds.
3. In the Roman Empire, it took a month to send a message from Rome to Britain. Today, communication is instant.
4. By traveling to unknown lands, these people increased knowledge of the world and opened the way for further exploration.
5. Their detailed descriptions of their travels to new places opened these places to further mapping.
6. Travelers' and traders' stories and diaries provided descriptions of faraway places. In the 1100s, European mapmakers got new information from translations of books from the East.
7. Historians determine whether the primary source conflicts with other primary sources and whether it is biased.
8. They provide information about and interpretations of the past.
9. We "travel" to the past by studying history and picturing life long ago.

Reviewing Skills

1. Use the map at the right to answer the following questions.
   a. When it is 10 A.M. in Seattle, what time is it in Mexico City?
   b. What is the time difference between Detroit and Honolulu?
2. Look at the map on pages 8–9. How many time zones does Africa have? Count from Dakar to Nairobi.
3. Twins are born on a ship. The child who is born first has a birth date one day later than the child who is born last. Where is the ship, and in which direction is it traveling?
4. Suppose you are going to fly from Dallas, Texas, to Paris, France. Your flight is scheduled to arrive in Paris at 7:58 A.M. What could you use to determine the time your

Time Zone Map of North America

watch will show on your arrival in Paris, if you don't reset it during the flight?

Using Critical Thinking

1. A writer has described our world today as a "global village" that has resulted from electronic communications. Based on what you know from the chapter about the limited world view of people of the past and about electronic communications, make an inference about what a global village is. Write a paragraph to explain what led you to this inference.
2. The Romans didn't know that such a place as Australia existed. In fact, they knew nothing of the entire Pacific Ocean. Suppose that somehow a Roman had learned of the existence of the rest of the earth and reported it to the emperor. Imagine the impact such a discovery would have made on Roman society. Now try to imagine what kind of a discovery would have the same impact today. Write a paragraph describing the discovery. Then write another paragraph explaining why you think this discovery would have such an impact.

Preparing for Citizenship

1. **COLLECTING INFORMATION** The telegraph was one of the first forms of electronic communication. Research the different ways messages were sent before the invention of the telegraph in 1837. Make a notebook that shows as many different methods of communication as you can find. Arrange your notebook from the earliest method to the most recent. Be sure to tell where and when each method was used and how it worked.

2. **COLLABORATIVE LEARNING** Read about the history of your community or school and discuss it as a class. Locate a primary source that describes an event in your community or school's history. Form committees. Each committee should write its own description of the historical event based on the information in the primary source. As a class, compare the secondary sources written by the committees. Does each secondary source portray the event accurately? In what ways do they differ?

23

A Changing World View

Planning at a Glance
Empires of the Ancient World

	Objectives	Reading Support *and* Other Resources	Diverse Learning Strategies
Lesson 1 The Fall of the Roman Empire *pp. 26–31* 4–5 days	• Discuss the role that the provinces played in strengthening and weakening the Roman Empire. • Explain the causes for the collapse of the Western Roman Empire. • Explain why the Eastern Roman Empire survived and prospered.	• **Workbook** or **Reading Support:** pp. 15–18 Review p. 4 Lesson Support/Transition p. 4 Multi-lang. Sum. pp. 7–8 • **Other Resources:** Poster 1, Study Guide p. 5	Access Act. **(SDAIE)** TE p. 27 Research **(GATE)** TE p. 28 Visual Learning **(Visual)** TE p. 31 Audiotapes of Multi-language Lesson Summaries **(Auditory)**
Lesson 2 Acquainted Cultures *pp. 32–37* 4–5 days **Literature** "A King's Advisor" *pp. 38–41*	• Discuss the major Asian civilizations in existence at the fall of Rome and their accomplishments. • List how the cultures of Persia, India, and China came into contact with each other. • Describe how the Persians, Indians, and Chinese used what they learned from other cultures in their own societies.	• **Workbook** or **Reading Support:** pp. 19–22 Review p. 5 Lesson Support/Transition p. 5 Multi-lang. Sum. pp. 9–10 • **Other Resources:** Geography Kit, Study Guide p. 6	Access Strat. **(Extra Support)** TE p. 33 Access Act. **(SDAIE)** TE p. 33 Map and Globe Skills **(Visual)** TE p. 34 Homework Options **(Visual)** TE p. 37 Audiotapes of Multi-language Lesson Summaries **(Auditory)**
Lesson 3 The Rise of the Byzantine Empire *pp. 42–45* 2–3 days	• Discuss major Byzantine accomplishments. • Describe the relationship between the Byzantine Empire and Persia.	• **Workbook** or **Reading Support:** pp. 23–26 Review p. 6 Lesson Support/Transition p. 6 Multi-lang. Sum. pp. 11–12 • **Other Resources:** Study Guide p. 7	Access Act. **(SDAIE)** TE p. 43 Visual Learning **(Visual)** TE p. 44 Research **(GATE)** TE p. 44 Audiotapes of Multi-language Lesson Summaries **(Auditory)**
Chapter Review *pp. 46–47*		Chapter 2 Test pp. 5–8 *(See facsimiles on TE p. 560.)*	Assessment Multiple-Use Masters pp. 73–80

Reading Support Resources *for Every Lesson*

Reading and Review	Multi-language Summaries	Lesson Support /Transition
		S D A I E

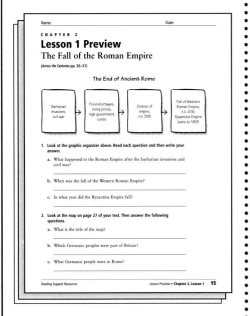

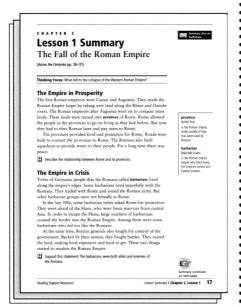

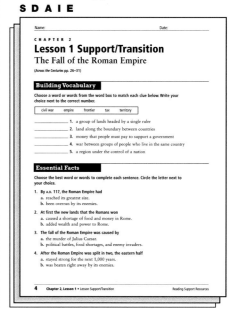

Activities for SDAIE
Specially **D**esigned **A**cademic **I**nstruction in **E**nglish

Reading and Review

- **Chapter Overview*** p. 14
- **Lesson Previews*** using graphic organizers from the Teacher's Edition pp. 15, 19, 23
- **Reading Strategies*** pp.16, 20, 24
- **Lesson Summaries*** pp. 17–18, 21–22, 25–26
- **Lesson Reviews** pp. 4, 5, 6

  * **Workbook** includes starred items.

Multi-language Summaries

Lesson Summaries in:
- English (See Reading and Review.)
- Spanish pp. 17–18, 21–22, 25–26
- Chinese pp. 7–12
- Hmong pp. 7–12
- Khmer pp. 7–12
- Vietnamese pp. 7–12

 Summaries available on audiotapes

Lesson Support /Transition

- **Lesson Support/Transition** pp. 4, 5, 6

 ## Technology Options

Internet Support
http://www.eduplace.com

Social Studies Center at Education Place

Internet support for Chapter 2:
- *Lesson at a Glance*
- *Conserving Mosaics*

Software
Student Writing Center ® (CD-ROM) (Macintosh® or Windows®)

School to Career

Over time, art pieces from the ancient world often have become damaged. See if a local museum, gallery, or university has an art restoration program. Arrange for someone from the program to come in and speak with the class. Have students prepare questions for the speaker.

Character Education

The Justinian Code became a model for the legal systems of many nations because it was seen as firm but just. Ask students to think about the rules of their school and community. Create a list. Why is having an established set of rules important? Why is it important that people respect them?

CHAPTER
PREVIEW

Have the students read the chapter title and the paragraph that follows it. Review with students the events in the ancient world leading up to the time of the Roman Empire. *(Ancient civilizations in Mesopotamia, Egypt, and Greece had risen and fallen, while civilizations evolved in India and China.)* Then point out that the Roman Empire had dominated the world around the Mediterranean Sea, but when it fell in the west, other empires battled for power.

Looking Back

Remind students that the Romans had developed military and trade contacts throughout the ancient world.

Looking Forward

Tell students that when they study Lessons 1–3—The Fall of the Roman Empire, Acquainted Cultures, and The Rise of the Byzantine Empire—they will read about a shift in power in the ancient world.

Lesson 1 details the fall of the Western Roman Empire.

Chapter 2
Empires of the Ancient World

What was happening to the mighty Roman Empire? The Persians challenged its eastern borders. Wave after wave of barbarian tribes swept down from Europe and central Asia. Political quarrels and economic problems forced leaders to split the empire in two. Even so, conditions in the western half of the empire worsened. But the eastern empire—the Byzantine Empire—prospered. Power in the ancient world was shifting to the east.

Barbarian invaders, shown on the bronze clasps above, overran the Western Roman Empire in the 400s. Yet the empire remained strong in eastern areas like Jordan (left).

527–548 Empress Theodora (above), considered the most powerful woman in Byzantine history, rules with her husband Justinian.

250	B.C.	A.D.		250	500

24

27 B.C.

C. A.D. 200 Bantu-speaking peoples continue expansion through eastern and southeastern Africa.

300–525 During the Gupta Dynasty, India trades with the Eastern Roman Empire, Persia, and China.

BACKGROUND

The ancient civilizations of Eurasia shared a common military problem—how to defend themselves against barbarian raiders who were pushing down from the steppes of central Europe and eastern Asia.

Barbarians as Nomads

Barbarians were small bands of nomads who first migrated to the central European and Asian steppes between 800 B.C. and A.D. 100. Most were herders who moved from place to place in search of good pasture land for their animals. Because of their skill with animals, the barbarians often served as employees on the trade caravans that linked the Eurasian civilizations. Some even supplied horses to transport trade goods along the Silk Road and other trade routes. But the barbarian nomads eventually became a threat to Eurasian civilizations as they fine-tuned their skills as warriors and began raiding villages, towns, and farming settlements.

Defense Strategies

The Roman Empire and China, at opposite ends of Eurasia, suffered the most attacks. This was partially because the Persians, located in central Eurasia, had developed a successful strategy to guard their frontiers. The Persians developed a special breed of horse that was larger and stronger and so

During this period, the Byzantine Empire recaptured Roman lands in the West. This ivory carving shows an emperor, thought to be Justinian, triumphantly returning from battle.

867–1057 The Byzantine Empire expands. This gold and silver container, used in Christian ceremonies, shows the domes typical of Byzantine architecture.

750　　　1000　　　1250　　　1500

732 Christian forces in France defeat Muslim invaders.

A.D. 1453

The clasps (p. 24) were used by barbarian horsemen in the 500s to fasten their cloaks.

The ivory carving from the 500s (top, p. 25) celebrates Byzantine prowess in battle and trade. The figures along the bottom carry such goods as ivory and casks of aromatic myrrh.

The Byzantine reliquary, a container for sacred relics, (bottom, p. 25) is from the 800s. The onion-shaped domes and the lion designs show the influence of Persia and Islam on the Byzantines.

Understanding Chronology

Ask the students to look at the timeline. Point out that the beginning date marks the start of the Roman Empire; the end date marks the fall of the Eastern Roman Empire, or Byzantine Empire.

could carry soldiers clad in heavy armor and their weapons. The heavy armor worn by the cavalry repelled the arrows of the steppe nomads.

To finance their cavalry, the Persians set up a system whereby soldiers could support themselves by collecting rent from peasants who lived in the areas they defended. Because Sassanian Persia abutted India on the east, the Sassanian cavalry also helped to defend India, providing the Gupta Empire with a relatively long period of peace.

The Romans and Chinese did not adopt the Persian method of defending their borders with their own countrymen. Instead, the Romans drafted barbarians, a move which eventually weakened Rome's military defenses. China, under the Han, did the same. Chinese rulers sometimes even resorted to bribery, in the form of expensive gifts, to keep the barbarians at bay.

26

INTRODUCE

Point out the lesson title. Tell students that the Romans built a powerful empire that lasted 500 years. Explain that at its peak the Roman Empire provided peace, order, and a high standard of living to the people living within its borders. However, as internal and external problems mounted, the empire began to weaken and crumble. Ask students to read the Thinking Focus and section headings, and determine what problems may have contributed to the empire's breakdown. As students voice their speculations, draw the chart in the Graphic Overview on the chalkboard.

Key Terms

Vocabulary Strategies: T36–T37
province—in the ancient Roman Empire, any of the lands outside Italy conquered and ruled by Romans
barbarian—in the ancient Roman Empire, people living along the empire's borders; a person considered by another group to have a primitive culture

B.C.	A.D.						
250		500	750	1000	1250	1500
	27	476				

L E S S O N   1

The Fall of the Roman Empire

THINKING
F O C U S

What led to the collapse of the Western Roman Empire?

Key Terms

- province
- barbarian

➤ *Roman emperors were often depicted in military dress. The carved figures on the breastplate of Augustus's armor represent a Roman victory over a Persian army.*

26

*T*he world has grown old and lost its former vigor. . . . Winter no longer gives rain enough to swell the seed, nor summer enough to toast the harvest . . . the mountains are gutted and give less marble, the mines are exhausted and give less silver and gold . . . the fields lack farmers, the seas sailors, the encampments soldiers . . . there is no justice in judgments, competence in trades, discipline in daily life.

This description, written in about A.D. 250 by one of the Roman Empire's church leaders, foretells the fate of that mighty empire. Within 200 years of the writing of this description, the Roman Empire would suffer great military and economic crises, weaken, and eventually collapse.

The Empire in Prosperity

From 27 B.C. to A.D. 14, Julius Caesar's adopted son Octavian ruled as Rome's first emperor. Octavian was given the name Augustus, which means the revered or exalted one. As emperor, Augustus put an end to the chaos and power struggles that had occurred within the Roman Empire after Julius Caesar's assassination. Caesar and Augustus also expanded the empire by conquering the territory that ran along the Rhine and Danube rivers.

Chapter 2

Objectives

1. Discuss the role that the provinces played in strengthening and weakening the Roman Empire.
2. Explain the causes for the collapse of the Western Roman Empire.
3. Explain why the Eastern Roman Empire survived and prospered.

Graphic Overview

| Barbarian invasions, civil war | → | Food shortages, rising prices, high government costs | → | Division of empire, A.D. 395 | → | Fall of Western Roman Empire, A.D. 476; Byzantine Empire lasts to 1453 |

Germanic Kingdoms
- Angles, Saxons, and Jutes
- Burgundians
- Franks
- Ostrogoths
- Vandals
- Visigoths
- Suevi and Alemanni
— Boundary of Western Roman Empire, c. 400

0   150   300 mi.
0   150   300 km
Azimuthal Equidistant Projection

Expanding the Empire

Roman conquests of new territory continued under the emperors after Augustus. By A.D. 117, the Roman Empire had reached its greatest size. It extended from Britain in the north to Africa in the south and from Spain in the west to Syria in the east.

The lands and peoples captured by the empire were organized into **provinces,** or territories, of Rome. Rome maintained peace in its provinces by allowing individuals to continue living and working as usual. However, Roman officials did institute Roman laws in these territories. In addition, they appointed governors to rule the provinces and make sure that Roman law was enforced there.

Profiting from the Provinces

Rome benefited from its empire in many ways. Since enemies could reach Rome only by crossing the provinces, these territories pro-

tected Rome by acting as a buffer zone. They also produced food and other goods for the city of Rome. For example, Egypt and North Africa supplied Rome with most of

▲ *As powerful as it was, the Roman Empire did not last. How did its boundaries change as it weakened?*

▲ *Here Egyptian grain is loaded on a barge for shipment to Rome.*

27

Empires of the Ancient World

DEVELOP

In this lesson students will learn that managing such a large empire had advantages as well as disadvantages. Ask students to study the map on this page. What do they notice about the Roman Empire? *(Divided in two—Eastern and Western parts.)* On how many continents did the Romans have territory? *(Three.)* What body of water was surrounded by Roman territory? *(Mediterranean Sea.)* Ask students to locate the capital of the Western Roman Empire *(Rome)* and the Eastern Roman Empire *(Constantinople).* Ask students to determine the approximate distance from the eastern edge of the empire to the western edge using the map scale. *(2,800 miles.)*

ECONOMICS
Visual Learning

What does the illustration on this page illustrate? *(Rome received grain from Egypt.)*

27

Access Strategy

Write the words *high taxes, inflation, water and air pollution, crime, drugs,* and *corruption in government* on the chalkboard. Ask students what these words mean to them. *(They should indicate that they are problems or issues facing society today.)* Then ask how these problems might be solved by individuals, their parents, the community, or the government. *(Discussion will probably determine that in a large society some government involvement is necessary to cope with these* problems.) Tell students that in Lesson 1 they will learn about the problems the Roman Empire faced nearly 1,800 years ago and the solutions they came up with. Ask them to determine which problems are similar to those we face today and to evaluate the Romans' solutions to them. Were they effective? Should we—or have we—tried any of these same kinds of solutions?

Access Activity

Rome imported gold and fruit from Spain, wheat from Egypt, tin from northern Europe, wild animals from Africa, and perfume and spices from the eastern provinces. Have students cut pictures from magazines of these goods and paste them in the proper place on a map of the Roman Empire.

■ *The provinces supplied Rome with food, tax money, and natural resources. In turn, Rome defended the provinces and provided roads, buildings, and aqueducts.*

■ *Describe the relationship between Rome and its provinces.*

Across Time & Space

The word barbarian *was originally used in the Roman Empire to describe people from outside the empire who spoke a different language and had a different culture. Over time, the term* barbarian *has come to mean a person who is uncivilized and warlike.*

▼ *Roman impact on the provinces can be seen in the ruins of a city built by the Romans in Palmyra, Syria.*

its wheat. Trade with the provinces brought wealth to Roman citizens. The people in the provinces also paid taxes, which supported the government and the army of about 300,000 men distributed along the empire's frontiers. For a long time, the empire was well fed, strong, and wealthy.

Because Rome was strong, the empire was peaceful and stable, which benefited everyone in it. The government built roads that connected the provinces to Rome. It also funded the construction of aqueducts. Aqueducts were used to pipe drinking water from wells and springs to the people. ■

The Empire in Crisis

The Roman army along the frontiers managed to protect the Romans for many years. But, beginning in A.D. 161, some enemies broke across the frontiers to

invade the Roman Empire itself. This became a serious problem for the Romans.

HISTORY
Critical Thinking

After discussing the major reasons for the collapse of the empire, have students rank them in order of their importance with "1" being the most important. Write the results on the chalkboard. Ask students if they think the empire would have survived if the most important problem could have been solved. What would their solution to the problem have been?

Study Skills

Remind students that while this lesson focuses on the Roman Empire, Rome and the land it controlled was called the Roman Republic between 509 B.C. and A.D. 27. Have students do research to find out why and how the Roman Republic became an empire.

Political Context

Life in the Roman provinces centered around the towns and cities. The Romans encouraged and often helped to finance the building of these cities as centers for their provincial governments. The Roman provinces were not all governed in the same way. Provinces that had a long record of loyalty to Rome were governed loosely by civilian officials. The Romans even allowed some North African kings to completely control their own internal affairs as long as they adhered to

Roman foreign policy. On the other hand, in those provinces that were recently conquered or at risk from invasion or internal uprisings, the Romans installed governments that exercised strict control. This flexibility helped create a long period of peace and prosperity for the empire.

Border Problems Increase

Along the empire's central and eastern borders lived tribes of Germanic peoples who were not all content to live peacefully with Rome. The Romans called these peoples **barbarians,** meaning people who speak a different language. Tacitus, a Roman historian from the first century, described the barbarians as having "blue eyes, and reddish hair; great bodies, especially powerful for attack, but not equally patient of hard work."

By the 200s, some of these Germanic peoples had established villages along the Rhine and Danube rivers and were peacefully exchanging goods and ideas with Romans. Some became allies of the Romans. Many barbarian men entered the Roman army and helped to defend the frontiers against invasion by hostile barbarian tribes. In return, they and their families were granted land within the empire and a yearly salary. Some even adopted Latin as their language.

Then, in the late 300s, thousands of barbarians began seeking refuge within the empire to escape the Huns. The Huns, a fierce group of nomadic warriors, were sweeping west from the central plains of Asia, conquering everyone in their path. Roman border patrols were unable to limit the number of barbarians entering the empire during this massive migration. So, many hostile barbarians were actually able to enter the empire's borders and still keep their weapons.

Barbarian invaders reached deep into the empire.

Internal Problems Mount

To complicate the situation further, a struggle for political control was occurring in the empire. From A.D. 193 on, many men tried to claim control of the empire. Many of them were generals who, backed by their armies, took the throne by force. Rivals for the throne began to promise higher salaries to the armies in return for their support, but this strained the empire's treasury.

The combination of barbarian invasions and fighting between Roman armies for control of the empire ruined the countryside. Such unrest made it very difficult for farmers to produce enough food. Food shortages resulted, making available food very costly.

In an attempt to cope with the economic problems of the empire, the government minted more coins. But, because government stores of gold and silver had been reduced, the new coins were filled

▲ *In this early third-century relief, country people wearing typical hooded cloaks bring money to a tax collector who is surrounded by his staff.*

◄ *Ostrogoths wore helmets similar to the one at left in the 500s.*

How Do We Know?

HISTORY *The coin pictured below gives us visual evidence that the barbarians had an impact on the Roman Empire. The coin, from A.D. 8, illustrates Roman Emperor Augustus receiving a child from a barbarian.*

29

Critical Thinking

Explain to students how the barbarians became a threat to the empire's security. Ask them to discuss why the barbarians would be attracted to the Roman Empire. *(Wealth, land, security.)*

Science Connection

Archaeologists have learned much about the barbarians from well-preserved corpses discovered in northern European peat bogs. More than 400 finds dating from between 100 B.C. and A.D. 500 have been made. The people were probably sacrificial victims in religious rituals or criminals punished by drowning. In some cases the fine detail of facial features is still visible. Skin has remained intact and hair is present on the face and head. Clothing made from animal skins and wool is still partially intact.

By examining stomachs and intestines, scientists have found that the barbarians' diet consisted mostly of grain. They also ate small amounts of meat, wild fruits, milk, and cheese. Ask students why this physical evidence might be more accurate than the Romans' written descriptions of the barbarians. *(The Romans might have written biased descriptions of the barbarians.)*

Critical Thinking

Every year thousands of people cross the border into the United States illegally. Why? *(To seek work and wages they cannot get at home.)* Ask students how illegal immigration to the U.S. is similar to or different from that of barbarians coming to the Roman Empire. *(Barbarians sought work in the Roman army.)*

■ *Friendly barbarian tribes were allowed to settle within the empire and often served as soldiers fighting for Rome against hostile barbarian tribes. Thus, barbarians were both allies and enemies of the Romans.*

■ *Support this statement: The barbarians were both allies and enemies of the Romans.*

with other, less precious metals as well. The new coins weighed the same as the old ones, but they were actually worth less. If merchants had been willing to accept these new coins at their face value, minting such coins might have solved the financial troubles of the empire. But they would not do so. Instead, merchants charged more coins to exact the same value for their goods. ■

The Empire in Transition

When Diocletian became emperor in 284, he made some changes in an attempt to correct the empire's problems. He divided rule over the empire among four men. With two rulers to oversee the east and two to oversee the west, he hoped to make governing the empire an easier task. Each ruler had his own capital and administrative staff. He established four capitals because from Rome alone he could not adequately govern the vast territory belonging to the empire. Diocletian moved his capital from Rome to Nicomedia, a city a few miles south of Byzantium in Asia Minor.

Diocletian hoped that this division of the empire would help prevent civil wars caused by rivals for the throne. He also hoped that it would make the empire easier to manage and defend.

In response to barbarian pressures on the empire, Diocletian increased the size of the Roman army from 300,000 men to 500,000. The increases of both the civil administration and the military meant large increases in government spending. This further emptied the empire's treasury.

The Rise of the East

Diocletian's successor, Constantine, also worked to stabilize the empire. To this end, he decided to establish a stronger eastern capital city. Constantine chose the old Greek trading town of Byzantium as the site for his new capital in 324. Find this city on the map on page 27.

Byzantium possessed great military and economic advantages. With water on three sides and the Balkan mountains on the fourth, enemies would find the city difficult to attack. Its location also made it a perfect stopping place both for merchants traveling overland and for those traveling by sea between Europe and the East Indies.

From 324 to 330, Constantine had Byzantium completely rebuilt

▼ *Look at the map on page 27 to see which tribes took over the Western Roman Empire.*

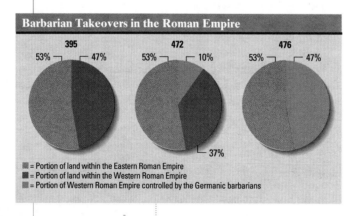

Barbarian Takeovers in the Roman Empire

395 — 53% / 47%
472 — 53% / 10% / 37%
476 — 53% / 47%

■ = Portion of land within the Eastern Roman Empire
■ = Portion of land within the Western Roman Empire
■ = Portion of Western Roman Empire controlled by the Germanic barbarians

Chapter 2

Map and Globe Skills

Have students locate Rome and Constantinople on the map on p. 27. Ask them to discuss the geographic advantages and disadvantages of choosing these cities as capitals of the Roman Empire. Also discuss the advantages and disadvantages of having two capital cities. Find countries with two capitals on pp. 522 and 527. *(Netherlands, Bolivia.)*

Writing

Ask students to imagine that they are Emperor Diocletian. Have each student write a letter to the citizens of the empire explaining why the empire must be divided if it is to survive. Tell the students to use a convincing tone and imaginative incentives to win the citizens' approval. Read several letters out loud (anonymously) and ask students to vote on the one that they think is most convincing.

Historical Context

By 476, all that remained of the Western Roman Empire, Italy, fell to the barbarians. Western Europe was divided into Germanic kingdoms that blended Roman and barbarian lifestyles. Barbarians learned the games of wealthy Romans such as hawking and dice. They learned Latin and rewrote their Germanic law codes in this new language. Many also converted to Christianity.

to resemble Rome. On May 11, 330, he renamed it "New Rome which is Constantine's City." The people called it Constantine's City. In Greek this is *Konstantinoupolis.* Thus, the city eventually became known as Constantinople.

Constantinople suffered from political quarrels and barbarian invasions, but it was the western half of the empire that suffered most. So, in an attempt to solve these problems, Emperor Theodosius I wrote into his will that upon his death the eastern and western sections of the empire should be declared separate empires. Use the map on page 27 to find the border between the two empires. When Theodosius died in 395, his will officially split the Roman Empire in two. Today, scholars use the term *Roman Empire* for the Western Roman Empire and the term *Byzantine Empire* for the Eastern Roman Empire.

The Fall of the West

The Byzantine Empire prospered for the next 1,000 years. However, the Roman Empire never recovered from its troubles. Spain, Gaul, and North Africa were overrun by barbarian invaders. As shown on the map on page 27, the barbarians set up their own kingdoms. In 410, the city of Rome was raided. By the late 400s, emperors of the Roman Empire were little more than puppets. In 476, a barbarian general overthrew the last of these Roman emperors, bringing the Roman Empire to an end. ◼

◀ *The oldest surviving view of Constantinople was created in 1420. How many years earlier had Constantine established the city as Constantinople?*

◼ *What did Diocletian do to strengthen the empire?*

Refer students to the picture on this page and ask them to describe Constantinople. Then have them turn back to the map on p. 27 to explain why Constantinople's location was ideal for trade and defense. *(Defense: surrounded on three sides by water; trade: crossroads between Europe and Asia.)*

◼ *Diocletian divided the empire in two parts so that each half would be easier to defend and manage.*

CLOSE

Refer to the chart from the Graphic Overview on the chalkboard. Ask students to expand on the list of causes for the fall of Rome. Review how each of these factors chipped away at the strength of the empire.

REVIEW

1. **FOCUS** What led to the collapse of the Western Roman Empire?
2. **CONNECT** In what ways might the roads, aqueducts, and buildings that the government funded have improved the living conditions in the provinces?
3. **HISTORY** Why did the government limit the number of barbarians entering the empire at any one time?
4. **ECONOMICS** Why didn't minting more coins solve the empire's economic problems?
5. **CRITICAL THINKING** Why was the Eastern Roman Empire able to survive and prosper while the Western Roman Empire crumbled?
6. **ACTIVITY** Make a list of the problems that led to the collapse of the Roman Empire. Rank the items in your list from most important to least important. Compare your list to those made by other members of your class and defend your ranking.

Answers to Review Questions

1. Barbarian invasions, internal fighting over succession, disruption of trading and farming, food shortages, and financial crises.
2. Roads facilitated travel and trade, aqueducts piped water into the provinces, and at public buildings people were provided with much needed services.
3. Not all barbarians were willing to live peacefully with the Romans.
4. These coins were worth less. Prices rose and economic conditions declined further.

5. The Eastern Roman Empire survived because it had more economically productive provinces, was a crossroads of trade, and was easily defended. The Western Roman Empire failed because of economic problems, political quarrels, and an inability to defend itself.

Homework Options

Have students find and bring in a page of excerpts from the writings of Tacitus, Pliny the Younger, and/or Juvenal. Then have them read these aloud.

Study Guide: p. 5

INTRODUCE

H ave students read the lesson title. Ask them how they would define the term *acquainted cultures.* Explain that it refers to cultures that come into contact with each other. These encounters often result in the exchange of ideas. Ask them to speculate on how one culture might become acquainted with another. *(Trade, war, migration.)* Tell them that this lesson will discuss acquainted cultures that existed at the time of the fall of the Roman Empire.

Key Term

Vocabulary Strategies: T36–T37
dynasty—a succession of rulers from the same family

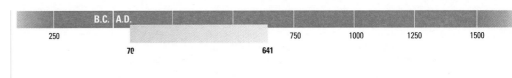

	B.C.	A.D.					
250				750	1000	1250	1500
	70			641			

L E S S O N   2

Acquainted Cultures

THINKING
F O C U S

In what ways did the peoples of various cultures benefit from their contact with each other?

Key Term

* dynasty

▲ *This image of a Sassanid king is made from gold and silver.*

32

I t's hard to imagine any benefits arising from war. Yet, all around the Mediterranean, as Romans, Germans, Persians, Arabs, Berbers, and other peoples fought, they also learned from each other. In fact, any encounter between people of different cultures, whether in war or in trade, leads to an exchange of ideas. Thus, the peoples of Rome, Persia, India, and China, being acquainted, or in touch with one another, influenced each other's beliefs, customs, arts, and sciences. Look at the timelines on page 33 to see how these cultures came into contact.

Sassanid Persia

Perhaps no two Mediterranean peoples encountered each other as frequently in battle as did the peoples of the Roman and Persian empires. Two of the major causes of conflict between Rome and Persia were fights about the border between these two empires and disagreement about political control of Armenia. Armenia acted as an important buffer zone between the two powers. It was in the best interest of both Rome and Persia to have some control over the leadership in Armenia. As long as both countries had some control over this leadership, neither one could use Armenia as a base for a full-scale invasion of the other's territory or as a starting point for a surprise attack.

At War

Eventually, Armenia was split between the Romans and the Persians. In the 300s, Armenia was the first country in the world to make Christianity its state religion, and a "golden age" followed. Armenia fell under the rule of the Ottomans, which later proved disastrous. In spite of foreign rule, however, Armenians—who achieved modern-day independence in 1991—have held onto their unique culture and their Armenian Church. There are now some six million Armenians in the world.

From the beginning of the Persian Sassanid **dynasty,** or family rule, in A.D. 224, until its end in 641, the Persians and Romans often fought for control of Armenia. At the same time, the Persians were also busy defending their borders against invasions by barbarians from the plains of Europe and against the Huns from Asia.

Chapter 2

Objectives

1. Discuss the major Asian civilizations in existence at the fall of Rome and their accomplishments.
2. List how the cultures of Persia, India, and China came into contact with each other.
3. Describe how the Persians, Indians, and Chinese used what they learned from other cultures in their own societies.

Graphic Overview

	Sassanid Persia	Gupta India	Han China
Trade Partners	China, India, Roman Empire	China, Persia, Roman Empire, S.E. Asia	India, Persia, central Asia, Roman Empire
Enemies	Huns, Roman Empire	Huns	Huns and other tribes

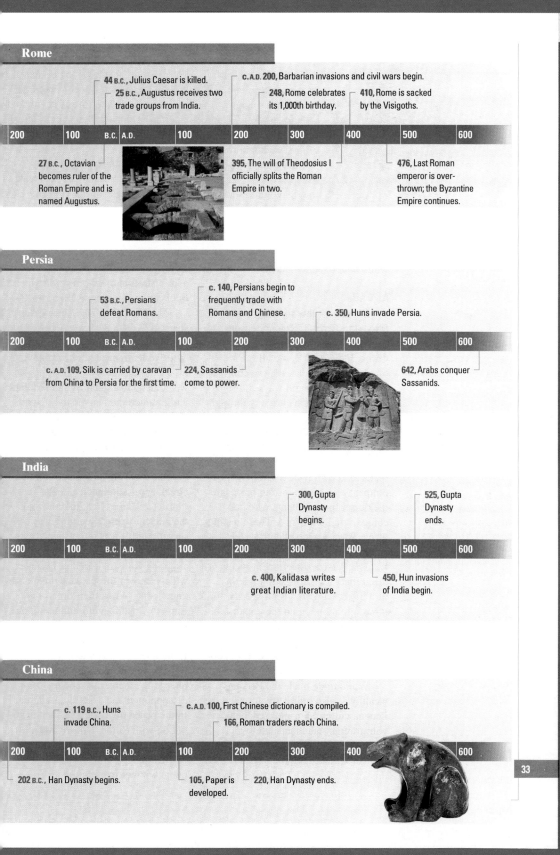

Rome

44 B.C., Julius Caesar is killed.

25 B.C., Augustus receives two trade groups from India.

C.A.D. 200, Barbarian invasions and civil wars begin.

248, Rome celebrates its 1,000th birthday.

410, Rome is sacked by the Visigoths.

| 200 | 100 | B.C. | A.D. | 100 | 200 | 300 | 400 | 500 | 600 |

27 B.C., Octavian becomes ruler of the Roman Empire and is named Augustus.

395, The will of Theodosius I officially splits the Roman Empire in two.

476, Last Roman emperor is overthrown; the Byzantine Empire continues.

Persia

53 B.C., Persians defeat Romans.

c. 140, Persians begin to frequently trade with Romans and Chinese.

c. 350, Huns invade Persia.

| 200 | 100 | B.C. | A.D. | 100 | 200 | 300 | 400 | 500 | 600 |

c. A.D. 109, Silk is carried by caravan from China to Persia for the first time.

224, Sassanids come to power.

642, Arabs conquer Sassanids.

India

300, Gupta Dynasty begins.

525, Gupta Dynasty ends.

| 200 | 100 | B.C. | A.D. | 100 | 200 | 300 | 400 | 500 | 600 |

c. 400, Kalidasa writes great Indian literature.

450, Hun invasions of India begin.

China

c. 119 B.C., Huns invade China.

c. A.D. 100, First Chinese dictionary is compiled.

166, Roman traders reach China.

| 200 | 100 | B.C. | A.D. | 100 | 200 | 300 | 400 | 500 | 600 |

202 B.C., Han Dynasty begins.

105, Paper is developed.

220, Han Dynasty ends.

33

CULTURE
Map and Globe Skills

Have students locate the Roman Empire, Persia, India, and China on the map on pp. 36 and 37. Have them determine, based on location, which cultures would be likely to have the most contact with one another. Which empire is most likely to depend upon waterways as its major means of trade and communication? *(Roman Empire—Mediterranean Sea.)* Which empires were best protected by physical features? *(India—Himalayas; China—deserts.)*

■ *Persia became a wealthy trading nation by establishing a common currency in the country, by maintaining its roads, assigning soldiers to keep roads and travelers safe, and by taxing goods entering and leaving the country.*

34

A Sassanid warrior mounted for battle rides across this silver bowl from c. 364.

Across Time & Space

"Nothing stops these couriers from covering their allotted stages in the quickest possible time— neither snow, rain, heat, nor darkness." This saying closely resembles the motto of the United States Postal Service, but it was actually written in the 400s B.C. by the Greek historian Herodotus to describe a mail delivery system developed by the Persians in about 500 B.C.

■ *How did Persia become a wealthy trading nation?*

34

Chapter 2

The Persians were well prepared to defend themselves against these attackers. Their soldiers fought on horseback and wore armor to protect themselves. In addition, they built large walls around their towns and fields. These walls enabled them to maintain possession of their food supply and shelter while under enemy attack.

At Trade

Despite all this fighting, trade thrived in Persia for many reasons. The overland trade routes connecting China, India, and Rome all ran through Persia. Also, the government aided trade in several ways. It established one common currency throughout the country so that anywhere in Persia a traveler could use the same money. It maintained the roads and even assigned soldiers to patrol those roads to keep travelers safe. The government also set up resting places in the desert for merchants who had come to trade in Persia. These resting places were equipped with water, supplies, and meeting halls.

The Persian government recognized that any increase in trade in turn increased Persia's prosperity, for it brought money into the country. In addition, the government found a way to make even more money by charging a tax on any goods that were carried in or out of the country.

While trade made the Persians wealthy, it also indirectly enriched the Persian culture. For most encounters with foreign merchants led to an exchange of ideas that increased Persian knowledge. The Persians used this knowledge in a variety of ways.

For example, they adopted Roman building techniques to construct bridges, towns, and forts. They modeled their ships after the single-sail vessels of Greece.

Persian Learning

Since the 500s B.C., the Persians had, in the words of one scholar, "behaved like a great cultural sponge." Over a thousand years of Persian art, learning, and culture nourished new conquerors and cultures. This was especially true for the administration of empires, for which the Persians became well known.

The Sassanid King Khusru Anusharvan *(KOOS roo an a SHAR van)* studied Plato and Aristotle. He had their works translated into Pahlavi, the Persian language of the time. He welcomed Greek and Syrian scholars and founded the University of Jundishapur *(juhn DISH a poor)*. Christians fleeing persecution from other Christians came there and opened up a medical school. For 200 years it was the most advanced in the world. Greek and Latin medical texts were translated. It was here that much of the ancient world's learning was preserved until it was retranslated by the Muslim rulers of the 800s.

King Khusru, it seems, became widely known for his wisdom and knowledge. When the Roman Emperor Justinian closed the famous school of philosophy at Athens and persecuted the non-Christian scholars, Khusru invited them to Persia. Expecting to find a kind of "philosopher-king" there, the scholars were disappointed and asked to go home. In the peace treaty he was then negotiating with Rome, Khusru added a special section so the scholars would be free to express their beliefs at home without persecution. ■

Basic Study Skills

Have students research the history of Armenia, paying particular attention to current problems faced by the Armenian people. Why have various empires struggled for control of this area? *(Strategic location at crossroads of more powerful empires.)*

Historical Context

Remind the students of their studies of ancient Athens and the philosophers who lived and taught there. By the 300s B.C., the various Greek scholars' schools functioned something like the colleges in a university. The School of Athens was the leading center of advanced education until disbanded by Justinian in A.D. 529. By that time the "university" of Alexandria had supplanted it. Other schools of the ancient world included the one at Jundishapur as well as the Chinese Imperial University founded in 124 B.C.

Political Context

To handle the day-to-day work of government, the Persian rulers introduced a chief minister, a government official who depended entirely upon the Sassanid emperor for his job. If this official's policies proved disastrous, he could be dismissed or even executed, while the prestige of the emperor would be untarnished. The Ottoman Turks copied this idea with their grand viziers (see Chapter 7, p. 172).

Gupta India

Not long after the founding of the Sassanid dynasty in Persia, a thriving economy and culture began developing in India. The well-run government of the Gupta dynasty existed from A.D. 300 to 467. It maintained the roads to ensure that traders had easy passage to and from India. In addition, the government did not subject its people to heavy taxes, so they had a decent standard of living.

Many of India's merchants also engaged in a prosperous trade with the Eastern Roman Empire, Persia, China, and the countries in Southeast Asia. India sold brassware, ivory, jewels, and even monkeys. The Gupta government profited from this trade by taxing both imports and exports.

The arts and sciences received great attention in this prospering society. Both painting and writing flourished. One of the greatest Indian writers and poets, Kalidasa, describes the results of a battle between the war god Kumara (*koo MAH rah*) and the demon Taraka (*tah RAH kah*) in the following excerpt.

*T*he sun put on a ghastly robe
of great and terrible snakes,
curling together,
as if to mark his joy
at the death of the enemy
demon.

Kalidasa, "Kumara's Fight Against the Demon Taraka," c. 400

UNDERSTANDING CIVILIZATION

*T*he civilizations of Rome, Persia, India, and China were all very different. But they shared common traits. According to historians, a civilization is a society that has cities, a written language, specialized jobs, an organized government, technology, and skilled craftspeople.

Not all societies are complex enough to be civilizations. Early hunter-gatherers never settled long enough in one place to build cities or organize a government. They had a distinctive culture, but not a civilization.

Not all societies are civilizations. It depends on how complex they are. Once, Europeans judged that more complex civilizations were more valuable than simpler ones. They used "uncivilized" to mean "inferior." But we know that is not true.

Development

Civilizations first developed as people learned how to increase their food supply. Farming freed people from looking for food. With more spare time, people developed specialized skills. Soon they produced surplus goods as well as surplus food. People traded surpluses for things that they did not have.

People needed places to meet and trade goods, so they built towns and markets. To keep business records, they developed systems of writing and numbers.

Today, trade still plays a major role in the way civilizations grow and change. Through trade, civilizations exchange ideas, inventions, and goods and they learn about each other.

35

Social Context

According to rule books which Brahmans (priests) wrote to tell Hindus in the various castes how to behave, women of one caste did not have the same privileges as men of the same caste in Gupta India. While some women ruled India as queens, the law books stated that women generally should spend their time serving the men of their families. A girl should be directed by her father, a wife by her husband, and a widow by her son. Hindu widows were not supposed to remarry. Sons as well as daughters were supposed to be directed by their fathers, but adult men had more social freedom than adult women, and widowed men were allowed to remarry. Although some upper-class women were allowed to go to school for pleasure and could own personal property, even sometimes control their family's wealth, they were not supposed to engage in business. There were rules for the work of men as well. Upper-class men were not supposed to do manual labor. Women and men at the bottom of society all had to work hard to feed themselves and their children.

Study Skills

The period of Gupta rule is considered the "Golden Age" of India. Have students do research and prepare a short written or oral report focusing on Gupta achievements in art, science, medicine, mathematics, or literature. Encourage students choosing art or literature as their topic to bring in pictures or excerpts from literary works.

► *The Huns.*

■ *Prosperity brought great creativity in poetry, art, mathematics, and science. The Guptas also built public institutions such as hospitals, maintained good roads, and taxed the people fairly.*

HISTORY

Map and Globe Skills

Have students look at the map on pp. 36–37 as you point out the distances between China, India, Persia, and the Roman Empire. Then have students look at the map of Eurasia on pp. 522–523. Ask students what would be the fewest number of countries one would have to cross today to get from the territory occupied by the former Sassanid Empire to China. *(Three: Iran, Afghanistan, China.)* How many countries by following the coastline? Which ones? *(10: Iran, Pakistan, India, Bangladesh, Myanmar, Thailand, Malaysia, Cambodia, Vietnam, and China.)*

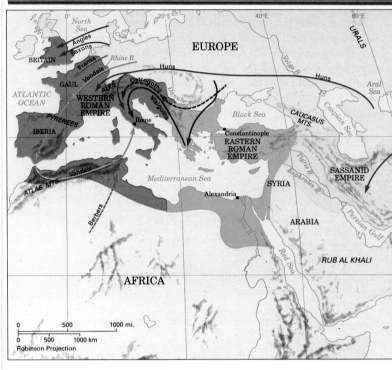

Invasions at the Fall of Rome

► *Which invading group attacked both China and the Western Roman Empire?*

■ *In what ways did India's culture benefit from the prosperity that existed between 300 and 500?*

▼ *The Hun invasions of China are documented by these Chinese statues of Huns from the 500s.*

In the sciences, Indians created a number system, developed the concept of zero, and discovered that the earth rotates on its axis.

However, in 480, Hun invasions began to weaken the prosperous Gupta dynasty. By 525, the Hun invaders had conquered India. They ruled over the people there for the next 200 years. ■

China

To the north of Gupta India lay the vast lands of China. Look at the map on page 37 to find China's boundaries. The Silk Road, a major overland trade route for Chinese silk and other goods, ran through northwest China, Persia, and the Roman Empire. Chinese junks, or ships, also sailed to India to trade their valuable silk and gold for glass and pearls.

The Chinese learned the teachings of Buddhism from Indian traders and missionaries they encountered. Indian ideas also influenced Chinese religious art. Large Chinese statues of Buddha are similar in pose and style to those created by Indian sculptors.

Visual Learning

Ask students to examine the Chinese sculptures on this page and p. 37. Using them as an example, ask students to bring in pictures of art and sculpture from Persia, China, and India that reveal one of these cultures' influence on another.

Art Connection

Bring in examples of Chinese paintings to illustrate differences between Chinese and Western art. Point out that some Chinese painters used ink instead of paint and mixed it with water to get a variety of shades. For drawing lines and creating texture they used different brush shapes. Painters usually chose landscapes or animals as their subjects, and painted on long scrolls of silk. The landscape painter's perspective was often from a high point looking down.

Social Context

One import that the Chinese particularly valued was the horse from central Asia. Chinese and barbarian warriors both fought on horseback. And, in fact, the Chinese were probably the first to use a padded saddle and rigid metal stirrups, which made fighting on horseback quite effective. The horse was a popular subject for Chinese artists as the statues on this page show. Chinese poets praised the horse in their works, calling them Flying Dragons and Horses of Heaven.

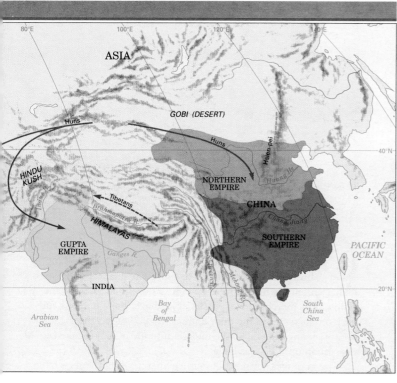

India was not the only area from which China imported goods. From the Middle East, the Chinese imported grapes, beans, and nut trees for their gardens. From Central Asia, they imported horses, which were extremely useful in warfare.

Like India, China was plagued by Hun invaders. In fact, emperors of the Han dynasty, who ruled China from 202 B.C. to A.D. 220, had to fight long and costly wars against the Huns. By 220, the Han dynasty had lost control of China completely. Chinese generals and upper class families, as well as Huns and other invading tribes, then fought each other for control of the country. For the next 360 years, China remained in a state of disunity. ■

■ *What were some of the goods China traded? What are some of the goods they obtained in exchange for these items?*

■ *China traded silk and gold for such goods as glass, pearls, grapes, beans, and horses.*

C L O S E

On separate slips of paper, list characteristics of the three cultures discussed in this lesson. Put the slips of paper into a container and have each student draw one. Have each student tell the class whether that characteristic describes the culture of Sassanid Persia, Gupta India, or Han China.

R E V I E W

1. **FOCUS** In what ways did the peoples of various cultures benefit from their contact with each other?
2. **CONNECT** How might Rome's battles with Persia have contributed to the Western Roman Empire's decline?
3. **CULTURE** In what ways did the peoples of Persia, India, and China influence each other's cultures, and how did they come into contact with one another?
4. **CULTURE** What are some aspects of Chinese culture

that were influenced by Gupta Indians?
5. **CRITICAL THINKING** How might the barbarians and Huns have furthered the cultural exchange between Rome, Persia, India, and China?
6. **WRITING ACTIVITY** The cultures of Rome, Persia, India, and China have all influenced the United States. Write about how one of these cultures has influenced our beliefs, customs, arts, or sciences.

Empires of the Ancient World

Answers to Review Questions

1. Students might say that contact with other cultures led to the exchange of goods and ideas.
2. Constant battles with the Persians weakened the Roman Empire.
3. They influenced each other's religion, arts, and sciences. They had contact with one another through war and trade.
4. The Indians influenced Chinese religion and art. Many Chinese converted to

Buddhism and much of their art is modeled after Indian art.
5. They adopted some of the skills and ideas of the people they conquered. They then passed them on to other cultures that they invaded.

Homework Options

Have students extend the chart shown in the Graphic Overview to include left-hand columns for Art and Religion. They should fill in the boxes under each country with a related culture that influenced it, e.g., for the Religion box under China they should write India.

Study Guide: p. 6

INTRODUCE

Explain that this fable originated in India and evolved to its final form only after being translated and adapted into Arabic and Persian. This particular version was translated into English by Hassan Tehranchian. It serves as an example of how cultures adopted traits from other cultures and of how they shared ideas, inventions, goods, and even stories. This sharing and exchanging motif is central to the focus on acquainted cultures in Lesson 2 of Chapter 2.

READ AND RESPOND

"A King's Adviser" contains several morals, including one presented in a story-within-a-story. For this reason, students need to read this selection very carefully, possibly with some guidance. As they read it, remind students to think about the purpose-setting question. Also ask them if the story teaches more than one lesson, and if so, to try to identify them.

Some words that students may need to know are: *jackals*, small Old World dogs related to wolves; *lineage*, a family background or progression; and *substance*, the physical or mental presence of a person.

In Lesson 2 you learned that countries become "acquainted" through trade, war, and cultural exchange. The following fable is an example of that mixing of cultures.

Shanzibah
(SHAN zih bah)
Nanibah (NAN ih bah)

Kalilah (KAH lih lah)
Dimnah (DIHM nah)

LITERATURE

A King's Adviser

Translated and adapted by Hassan Tehranchian

This fable, from Kalilah and Dimnah, originated in India, and from there passed in translation to Arabia and on to Persia. What lesson does the fable teach, and is there any meaning in it for you today?

Once upon a time there was a merchant who owned two bulls, Shanzibah and Nanibah. The merchant and his bulls were on a journey to a faraway land when Shanzibah accidentally fell into a deep hole. After much tugging and pulling, the merchant was finally able to get Shanzibah out and back on his feet. But the poor animal was so injured that he could not travel any farther. So the merchant found a man to take care of Shanzibah until he was better.

The man was supposed to return Shanzibah to the merchant when the bull had recovered. But, after only one day, the untrustworthy man became tired and bored. He left the poor, unhappy animal all alone and returned to the merchant, telling him that Shanzibah had died.

But fortune smiled on Shanzibah and he recovered all by himself, and set out to find food. To his amazement, he came upon a beautiful field that was full of brightly colored flowers and vegetables of all kinds. Shanzibah rested, and ate so well that he soon became healthy again. He felt so lucky and happy that one day, out of pure joy, Shanzibah let out a very loud bellow.

At the same time there was a lion who lived near the field. This lion was the king of many other animals. Although he was strong and brave, he had never seen a bull or heard one bellow before, so when he heard Shanzibah's loud voice he became very frightened. But since the lion did not want the other animals to know that he was afraid, he decided to stay close to home, instead of roaming far and wide all over his kingdom, as he used to.

Among the lion's subjects were two clever jackals named Kalilah and Dimnah. One day Dimnah, who was more ambitious and greedy, asked Kalilah, "Why do you think the lion has been staying at home so much lately?"

Puzzled by the question, Kalilah answered, "Why are you so interested in the king? It's really none of our business. We are

---

Thematic Connections

Social Studies: Literature as a reflection of human behavior and values

Houghton Mifflin Literary Readers: Accepting a Challenge

Background

The use of animals with human characteristics is very common in the literature of ancient cultures. Jackals often show up as participants in Indian fables, although they are not always given names, as Dimnah and Kalilah were.

This particular fable was passed from India to Arabia to Persia. As it passed through these three acquainted cultures, each culture added to or changed parts of the story. This mixing and adding probably

account for the somewhat uneven narrative flow of the story and the sense that a number of stories are being pieced together here. In fact, these techniques of stories within stories and multiple narrators are fairly common in the oral tradition of storytelling.

comfortable and rich under the lion's rule, and besides, we're not friendly enough with the king to give him advice. It would be better to mind your own business and leave the king's alone. . . ."

Dimnah answered cleverly, "Only ambitious and hardworking people reach high positions. If someone works very hard he can raise his position in life. On the other hand, a weak person will cause his own downfall. We should seek higher positions and not be satisfied with what we have now."

"Then," demanded Kalilah, "tell me what you have in mind."

Dimnah explained: "I would like to introduce myself to the lion. He is upset, and I'm sure I can make him happy with my advice. By doing that I will win his confidence."

"But," asked Kalilah, "how do you know that the lion is upset?"

"I know it because I am so intelligent," said Dimnah. "An intelligent man can sense when something is wrong."

"But," answered Kalilah, "how are you going to become an adviser to the lion? You have never served a king before."

Dimnah had a ready answer. "The king's attendants were not given their ranks and positions all at once; they slowly were moved up from lower positions. If I can get close to the lion I will try to understand him and I will be honest and obedient. I will encourage him to act in a way that will help his people. And when I disagree with his plans, I will try, without offending him, to show what will happen if he follows his own plan. I will be so honest and helpful that I will become his most important adviser. When the lion recognizes my knowledge and skill, he will appreciate me much more."

But Kalilah was still uneasy. "If you have really decided to do this," he advised Dimnah, "you must be aware that what you want to do is very dangerous. According to wise men, only foolish men do these three things: become involved in the king's business; taste poison in order to see what it is; and tell secrets to women!"

Dimnah answered, "That is all true. But the one who never takes chances never becomes great. Let me remind you that only a strong and courageous man could do these three things: enter into the king's business; do business by sea; and face one's enemy."

So Dimnah went to court and introduced himself to the lion. The lion asked his attendants if they knew who Dimnah was, and they told him all they knew about Dimnah and his family. The lion remembered Dimnah's father and so was friendly. He asked Dimnah where he lived. Dimnah replied, "I am staying at my lord's court, waiting for a position so that I can prove myself to you. For any servant, no matter how poor he is, can be of some use one day."

The lion was pleased with Dimnah's response and told his

◄ Are Dimnah's and Kalilah's views of becoming involved in a king's affairs conflicting? Why or why not? *(Yes; Kalilah believes it's better to mind your own business and leave the king's alone; Dimnah believes he can raise his position in life if he is hard working, honest, and obedient.)*

Access Strategy

Ask students if they have certain principles that they try to live by *("do unto others as you would have them do unto you," "it's better to give than to receive")* or important lessons that they have learned in their lives *("mind your own business," "practice makes perfect," "don't leave everything until the last minute").*

Most people develop ideas like these about life. In the story "A King's Adviser," all the important characters seem to have a lesson or two about how people should conduct their lives. Tell students that they need not agree with any of the lessons, but it would be interesting for them to think about why they do or don't agree.

attendants that "a wise man, even if he is of low rank, stands out in a crowd because of his honesty and wisdom."

When he heard this remark, Dimnah became very happy. He realized that he had already impressed the lion, so he dared to suggest, "Let all the subjects present their advice to my lord and show their knowledge openly. If my lord does not know how much knowledge his subjects have, he cannot really benefit from their service. Knowledge is like a seed that is ignored as long as it is hidden beneath the earth. After it grows, people can enjoy taking care of it and gain profit from it. It is important that my lord give his subjects positions based on knowledge and ability, not only on family lineage. He should not prefer careless, unskilled people over learned and wise men. Surrounding himself with friends who have no skills is dangerous. Great things are accomplished by knowledgeable and experienced men; not only by friends or those who stay close to you. Remember, a man who carries a small ruby does not become tired, and the ruby can be very valuable in a time of need. On the other hand, a man who carries a bag of heavy rocks soon becomes tired, and when he is needy his rocks aren't worth anything. And mice, though they live close to people, are hated because they do harm, but a falcon, though it is wild, because of its grace and ability is welcomed by the people, and he even finds himself on the hand of a king."

By the time Dimnah finished talking, the lion had become very fond of him and welcomed his friendship. As time passed, the lion's trust in Dimnah increased.

One day Dimnah asked the lion why he had been staying at home and had given up the joy of hunting. The lion was still trying to hide his fear, but suddenly Shanzibah gave another loud bellow. The noise scared the lion so much his trembling was easy to see. He had no choice but to tell his secret to Dimnah.

"The reason I stay at home is because of this roar. I don't know where it comes from, but an animal with such a loud voice must be very strong and wild, and if he is, then it is not safe for us to live here anymore!"

Dimnah asked if there was anything else besides the roar that frightened the lion, and the lion said, "No."

Then Dimnah said, "It doesn't seem right for my lord not to leave his own land because of a loud roar. Besides, not every powerful voice or large body means something is strong. "What do you mean?" asked the lion. Dimnah explained.

The Fox and The Drum

Once a fox crossing a field saw a drum fall near a tree. The wind caused a branch of the tree to pound on the drum, making a loud noise. The fox, who was impressed by the size of the drum and the loud sound it made, thought it would surely have lots of

➤ Rephrase the two lessons taught in this paragraph. *(Sample answers: It is better to possess a small but valuable skill or thing than a large useless skill or thing; great rulers take risks and surround themselves with skillful and knowledgeable advisers, not with unskilled friends and relatives.)*

Collaborative Learning

Was Dimnah right or wrong to go to the lion with advice? Some students may agree with Dimnah, and some may agree with Kalilah. Divide the class into small groups of students with like opinions. Have each group discuss the reasons for those opinions, including examples or anecdotes to support their views. Within each group, have a student make an official record of the group's opinions. When the groups are satisfied with the written account of the discussion, have them report to the entire class. Students may then discuss and/or debate their stands.

juicy meat. So the fox tried to tear the drum apart, but he only found a little thin skin. Then the fox told himself, "I should have known that the larger the body and the louder the voice, the less substance it would have."

"I told this story," said Dimnah, "so that my lord would see that he has no reason to be afraid. And, if my lord wishes, I will go to investigate the habits of this wild thing." The lion thought this was a good idea indeed.

When Dimnah came back, the lion rushed to ask him what he had found out. Dimnah reported, "I saw an ordinary bull, without the proud looks that go with great strength."

But this did not comfort the lion. He replied, "What you saw does not prove the bull is weak, either. As you know, a strong wind that can knock down huge trees may not be able to uproot a small bush."

So Dimnah went to Shanzibah and said, "I have been sent by the lion, who has ordered me to take you to him. If you come with me, I will ask him to forgive you for not introducing yourself to him sooner. But if you refuse, I will return at once and report your disobedience."

"Who is this lion?" asked Shanzibah.

"The king of all the wilds," answered Dimnah.

The title "king of all the wilds" terrified Shanzibah. He asked Dimnah whether he would protect him if he went with him. Dimnah promised him he would be safe, so Shanzibah went along.

The lion welcomed Shanzibah warmly. He asked him when and why he had come to the kingdom. Shanzibah told his story to the lion, who liked Shanzibah so much he invited him to stay in the field as his guest. Shanzibah was so thankful he offered his services in return. After testing Shanzibah's knowledge in various ways, the lion decided he could trust him and made him a close friend. Day by day, Shanzibah's rank and position became higher and higher, until he became the lion's most trusted adviser.

Further Reading

The Fables of India. Retold by Joseph Gaer. This book contains beast tales from the *Panchatantra*. It also has tales from two other collections of Indian fables, *Hipotadesa* and *Jatakas*.

Persian Folk and Fairy Tales. Retold by Anne Sinclair Mehdevi. The book includes eleven fables and tales of magic, romance, and adventure.

Tales of India: Magical Adventures of Three Indian Princes. Marie Ponsot, translator. These twelve stories were selected from the *Mabharata*. They tell the story of the epic's hero, Prince Ardjuna, and his brothers.

◄ Rephrase the lesson in these paragraphs. *(Sample answer: Appearances can be deceiving. Things may not be as simple as they appear to be.)*

EXTEND

Remind students that this story resulted from the mixing of three cultures. Ask them what aspects of a culture besides literature are affected when cultures mix? *(Architecture, music, food, art, religion, language.)* Have them choose one of these areas of culture and find an effect of cultural mixing in our society today. *(Classical architecture for government buildings; rock n' roll; Native American names for cities, rivers; foreign cuisines.)*

Bulletin Board

Students will be able to identify many different lessons, or morals, from this story. As a class, compile a list of these lessons on the board. When the class considers the list complete, have each student choose one lesson and make a small poster illustrating it. The moral itself should be printed prominently on the poster. After the posters are finished, display them on a bulletin board entitled "A King's Adviser."

Further Reading

You may want to have your students look in the school or local library for more collections of fables and tales to read.

INTRODUCE

Ask students to read the lesson title. Tell them that this lesson will examine life in the Eastern Roman Empire after the fall of the Western Roman Empire. Have students turn to the map on p. 27 as you point out the boundaries of the Eastern Roman Empire and its capital at Constantinople. Using the map, have students discuss the geographical advantages of Constantinople.

Key Terms

Vocabulary Strategies: T36–T37
mosaic—a picture or design made from small pieces of colored material, usually quartz or glass, embedded in plaster
commerce—the buying and selling of goods

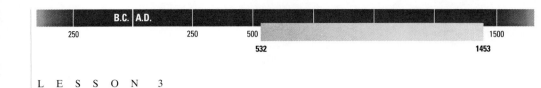

B.C. | A.D.

250   250   500   1500

532   1453

L E S S O N 3

The Rise of the Byzantine Empire

THINKING FOCUS

What were some of the accomplishments of the Byzantine Empire?

Key Terms

- mosaic
- commerce

➤ *This carved horn was probably blown to announce the beginning of entertainments at the Hippodrome.*

In January 532, Constantinople erupted into riot and flames. As the largest city of the Byzantine Empire, it had 350,000–500,000 people. Taxes were high and city officials took bribes on an everyday basis. There were plans to overthrow Emperor Justinian and Empress Theodora. The Hagia Sophia *(ah YEE uh soh FEE uh)*, the Church of the Holy Wisdom, where the emperors, supreme heads of the Church, were crowned, had been torched.

Justinian tried but failed to put down what are now called the Nike Riots. As the crowd chose a new emperor, and Justinian was about to flee, Theodora stopped him with the speech below. After hearing it, the Emperor recovered his nerve and gave orders to put down the riots. Within weeks there were over 30,000 dead. The Empire had survived.

As to the belief that a woman should not be daring among men or assert herself boldly, I consider the present crisis does not allow us to debate that. My opinion is that now is a poor time for flight, even though it bring safety. . . . If now you wish to go, Emperor, nothing prevents you. There is the sea, there are the steps to the boats. But take care that after you are safe, you do not find that you would gladly exchange that safety for death. For my part, I like the old saying that "The Empire is fine burial cloth."

Recorded by Procopius, c. 550

Byzantine History and Culture

Byzantium had been the name of this former Greek colony, founded in 667 B.C. In A.D. 330, the Roman Emperor Constantine built his "new Rome," and named it Constantinople (now called Istanbul). It remained under the control of his heirs until 1453, when the Turks captured it.

While rule in western Europe was decentralized and the population scattered, Constantinople and the great cities of Asia and Africa were thriving.

The borders of the Byzantine Empire changed often over its thousand-year history. The empire fought

42

Objectives

1. Discuss major Byzantine accomplishments.
2. Describe the relationship between the Byzantine Empire and Persia.

Graphic Overview

JUSTINIAN'S EMPIRE

Art	Law	Military	Religion
mosaics / church architecture	Justinian Code	regains land in West / fights Persians	strengthens Christianity / persecutes non-Christians

off Slavs and Bulgars in the west, and Persians in the east. It was held together by Christianity, the state religion, which saw the emperor as God's representative on earth. Slave-holding still existed, but it was forbidden for a Christian to own a Christian slave. Slavery declined in Europe after the fall of the Roman Empire, but slaves continued to be domestic servants. Germanic peoples and Slavs made up the majority of slaves in the Middle East.

In an effort to shore up unity, and for what they thought were the best interests of their faith, the Byzantines forced Christianity on others. Since around 500 B.C., large Jewish communities had existed in Turkey, Mesopotamia, Persia, and Palestine. When the Romans destroyed Judaea in A.D. 70, hundreds of thousands of Jews were shipped off as slaves. Others escaped to set up new lives. By Justinian's time, there were great Jewish centers in what are now Egypt, Spain, France, Germany, Italy, Turkey, and the Balkans.

Justinian's treatment of Jews and other non-Christians (there were then no Muslims) was brutal. Following the anti-Jewish rulings of Church councils beginning in 312, the Byzantines did not allow Jews to build synagogues or join in city life. Justinian forbade Jews to study the works of the rabbis. There were forced conversions and anti-Jewish massacres. Many Jews later moved to more tolerant lands.

Justinian's Contributions

Justinian's passion and effort all went to the church. To glorify the church was to glorify God. To do this, Justinian commissioned religious art and architecture on a grand

scale. He rebuilt Hagia Sophia with columns and walls of polished marble of many colors, and many glittering mosaics. **Mosaics** are colored fragments of glass or quartz embedded in plaster. Read A Closer Look on the next page to see how people restore, or repair, mosaics today. Most awe-inspiring was the Hagia Sophia dome—18 stories high and 108 feet wide. Through its stained-glass windows, light flooded into the church.

In 528, Justinian gave 10 men the task of condensing the 1,600 books of classic Roman law. A year later they came up with a well-organized system of 4,652 laws. The new legal system was called the Justinian Code. It extended the rights of women, children, and slaves, but also called for harsher penalties for crimes. Criminals could have their property taken away, lose an eye or a hand, or even be put to death, depending on their crime. Nevertheless, the laws proved to be very effective at maintaining order.

In fact, Roman law, in the form of the Justinian Code, was so effective that many nations in Europe and Latin America used it as the model for their legal systems.

Mosaics like these from 547 give us some idea of how the Byzantine emperor Justinian and his empress Theodora actually looked. These mosaics were found in Ravenna, Italy.

▼ *A gold bracelet from Constantinople.*

43

Empires of the Ancient World

More About Mosaics Greek mosaics are among the oldest, some of which date from the 5th century B.C. These are called pebble mosaics, and as their name implies they are made of rounded stones set closely together. The Greeks were also responsible for inventing the technique of making mosaics out of pieces of stone or glass cut into squares or cubes. These pieces, called *tesserae* (Latin for dice), could be set much more closely together than pebbles. With this method, mosaic pictures could be much more detailed and have sharper images. Most Byzantine mosaics are made in this way.

A CLOSER LOOK

Conserving Mosaics

Mosaic art once covered floors and walls in the ancient Roman and Byzantine empires. Today conservators in museums work to make sure the mosaics that survive can still be enjoyed.

Solvent—special chemicals sometimes used to dissolve dirt

Animals of the Nile, a mosaic from Pompeii, c. first century B.C.

Fine-art jigsaw puzzle is one way to describe a mosaic. Mosaics are made of little bits of colored glass, tile, or stone set into plaster. Over time, the pieces may come loose. To repair mosaics, conservators first cover the pieces with cloth and glue to keep them in place. Then they fix the plaster.

Palette knife—used to work with tiny pieces of mosaic

Spatula—used to separate the mosaic from the wall or floor

Sponge—used to apply water or solvent to the mosaic

Some mosaics get flipped over on their faces so that conservators can clean and repair the backs. After repairs, mosaics can be returned to where they were, or moved to museums for display.

44

Chapter 2

Visual Learning

Ask students to look closely at the photographs of conservators at work. Do students feel they would enjoy a career of conserving and protecting artwork? Ask them which subjects a professional conservator would need to study. *(History, art, science, and mathematics are among the answers students might give.)*

Critical Thinking

Mosaics are not the only things conservators work with. There are old and delicate paintings, sculptures, buildings, books—almost anything you can think of that previous ages left behind. Why would a government spend lots of money to fund conservation efforts when it could use the money in so many other ways?

Research

Have students look for photographs of mosaics at the library. They will find mosaics were made throughout history, from early Greece to the modern era. Ask each to choose a mosaic and write a paragraph about it showing how it was characteristic of the time it came from and what it shows us about the people who made it.

A New Empire

Justinian also considered it his duty to recover Roman lands in the West that had been lost, as he said, "through indolence [laziness]." From 533 to his death in 565, Justinian's armies did regain parts of Spain, all of Italy, and North Africa. But, after his death, some lands were lost again to outsiders. What's more, battling over these lands distracted the Byzantine military and distracted it from another more serious enemy, the Persians. ■

▲ *This is a view of the interior of Hagia Sophia.*

The Persian Threat

Although barbarian tribes ultimately regained some lands in the West, the Persians were a greater threat to the Byzantine Empire. The Persians most closely matched the Byzantines in strength. They were also committed to battling the Byzantines for control of Armenia as well as to regaining control of Turkey, Syria, and Egypt. For 500 years, the Persians and Byzantines fought, but neither ever won an advantage for long.

In the early 600s, the Persians made their move. In a campaign lasting 17 years, they conquered part of Mesopotamia, occupied Asia Minor, and finally took Syria, Jerusalem, and Egypt.

This victory was short-lived. In 627, Byzantine Emperor Heraclius (*hehr uh KLY uhs*) defeated the Persian army. The Persians had to give up all the land they had recently won.

Until 1453, the Byzantine Empire was an important center of **commerce,** or trade, and culture. But constant warfare had weakened both empires. The Persians, in particular, soon had trouble mustering the strength to fight off new invaders. ■

■ *What distinctive elements of Byzantine culture developed under Justinian's rule?*

◄ *This cameo shows a Persian ruler taking a Roman emperor prisoner.*

■ *How did the constant battling between Byzantium and Persia affect the two empires?*

R E V I E W

1. **FOCUS** What were some of the accomplishments of the Byzantine Empire?
2. **CONNECT** In what ways was Constantinople like Rome? How was it different?
3. **HISTORY** How has the Justinian Code affected the modern world?
4. **GEOGRAPHY** Why and how did Justinian rebuild Constantinople?
5. **CRITICAL THINKING** Why do you think two countries might battle for centuries over control of a certain territory? What are some of the things people fight about today?
6. **ACTIVITY** Imagine that you have been asked to help revise the laws in your town. In small groups, make a list of laws in existence that you think ought to be changed. Revise each law on your list. Then as a class, vote on the laws to determine which should be added to your legal system.

45

Empires of the Ancient World

HISTORY
Critical Thinking

Have students describe the rivalry that existed between the Byzantine Empire and the Persians. Ask them to discuss how the outcome of the battles suggests that the two forces were evenly matched. *(They fought for 500 years, with neither gaining a lasting advantage.)*

■ *Under Justinian's rule, the mosaic art form was fully developed and Byzantine architecture reached its height.*

■ *The constant battles between Byzantium and Persia left both empires very weak and open to attack by other enemies.*

CLOSE

Design a question-and-answer game to test students' knowledge of the lesson on Byzantine achievements under Justinian. Draw category squares on the board, and assign each square a different point value. Make up a list of questions that match these categories. Divide the class into teams and have them select questions by point value and category. Keep track of each team's score on the chalkboard.

45

Answers to Review Questions

1. The Byzantines created new forms of religious art and architecture, developed the Justinian Code, and expanded the boundaries of their empire.
2. Constantinople was a planned city with many beautiful buildings and public conveniences like Rome. It was easier to defend than Rome.
3. The Justinian Code formed the model for later legal codes in Europe and Latin America.
4. Rioting destroyed much of Constantinople. Justinian rebuilt the city with stronger defenses.
5. Students may mention that countries fight to gain control of natural resources, because of religious differences, or to expand their boundaries.

Homework Options

Ask students to imagine that they are tour directors for the city of Istanbul (Constantinople). Tell them to write a short history to present to their tour group and make a list of interesting places to visit. Students might also point out buildings that have survived from the Byzantine period.

Study Guide: p. 7

Answers to Reviewing Key Terms
Answers:
1. b. The chapter uses **province** to refer to a place.
2. a. The chapter uses **commerce** to mean trade.
3. b. The chapter uses **dynasty** to mean a ruling family.
4. b. The chapter discusses **mosaics** as an art form.
5. b. The chapter uses **barbarian** to mean a person who speaks a different language.

Answers to Exploring Concepts
A. Sample answers:
1. Peace they maintained in their provinces.
2. Roads, aqueducts, and bridges.
3. Prosperous trade.
4. Common currency.
5. Concept of zero.
6. Poems and folktales by early Indian writers.
7. Sculptures of Buddha.
8. Silk and gold.
9. Justinian Code.
10. Mosaics.
B. Sample answers:
1. Egyptians and North Africans supplied Rome with wheat and paid taxes.
2. Thousands of barbarians migrated into the Roman Empire, many armed and eager to fight for control. Fighting resulted in ruined fields, causing food shortages.
3. When roads became unsafe in the Roman Empire, merchants and craftspeople living along trade routes went out of business. The Indian and Persian governments aided trade by keeping roads well maintained, and Persia further aided trade by assigning soldiers to patrol roads to protect travelers.
4. Persians modeled ships after single-sailed vessels of Greece.

46

5. Persians borrowed ideas from Indian mathematics. Chinese learned Buddhism from Indian missionaries.
6. Rome maintained peace in the provinces by allowing people to continue living as usual, but under Roman law. Justinian condensed the 1,600 books of Roman law into an effective legal system.
7. Both Constantine and Justinian rebuilt the Byzantine capital.
8. The Persians most closely

Chapter Review

Reviewing Key Terms

barbarian (p. 29)   mosaic (p. 43)
commerce (p. 45)   province (p. 27)
dynasty (p. 32)

In each pair of sentences below there are two meanings for one key term. The key term in the first sentence has a different meaning than it does in the second sentence. Explain which sentence describes the key term's meaning as used in this chapter.
1. a. Making laws was the *province* of the Roman emperor.
   b. The captain was assigned to a far-off *province*.
2. a. Caravans kept *commerce* strong.
   b. The Persians and the Indians carried on a vast *commerce* of ideas.
3. a. A family that discovered oil could start a financial *dynasty* in the modern-day Middle East.
   b. Henry Pu-yi was the last ruler of the Manchu *Dynasty*.
4. a. Justinian did not include the *Mosaic* law of the Hebrews in his code.
   b. A popular subject of early *mosaics* was Mary with Jesus.
5. a. The rioters showed they were *barbarians* by burning and looting.
   b. Marcus knew by the strangers' language that they were *barbarians*.

Exploring Concepts

A. Complete the paragraph by writing in each blank an accomplishment of an early civilization. Two have been completed for you.

Historians and other scholars still study the accomplishments of ancient civilizations. Romans are remembered for the *peace they maintained in their provinces* by allowing people there to live as usual but under Roman law. They are also known for the ___2___ that they built. The Persians are known for the ___3___ they carried on, which enriched their culture. They encouraged trade by establishing a ___4___. Mathematicians today can be grateful to Indians for developing the ___5___. And readers still admire the *poems and folk tales by early Indian writers*. Even today, the Chinese are known in religious art circles for their ___7___, and in commercial circles for their ___8___ trade. The Byzantine Empire influenced modern law with its ___9___ and modern artists with its ___10___.

B. Support each statement with facts and details from the chapter.
1. Rome benefited from having Egypt as a province.
2. Barbarian invasions helped to cause the fall of the Roman Empire.
3. The economies of both India and Persia benefited from safe roads.
4. The Persian navy had the Greeks to thank.
5. Indians made religious and mathematical contributions to other cultures.
6. Law played a key part in the governments of the Roman Empire and the Byzantine Empire.
7. Constantine and Justinian accomplished something similar during their reigns.
8. The Persians were a greater threat to the Byzantine Empire and weakened it more than the barbarians.
9. Julius Caesar's adopted son, Octavian, was a successful ruler when he took over Rome after his father's assassination.

Chapter 2

matched the Byzantines in strength. The Persians were committed to battling the Byzantines for control of Armenia and to regain control of Turkey, Syria, and Egypt.
9. Octavian ended chaos and power struggles and expanded the empire by conquering territory that ran along the Rhine and Danube rivers.

Using Critical Thinking

1. Many ancient cultures have contributed nuggets of wisdom that sound strangely familiar even today. For example, in the first century A.D., a Roman named Pubilius Syrus wrote the following sayings:
   a. The loss that is unknown is no loss at all.
   b. While we stop to think, we often miss our opportunity.
   c. For a good cause, wrongdoing is virtuous.
   d. When fortune is on our side, popular favor bears her company.
   e. It is a consolation to the wretched to have companions in misery.
   f. Practice is the best of all instructors.

   All of these sayings have counterparts in our language today. List the present-day sayings with similar meanings.
2. Perhaps the Romans should have considered the following Chinese proverb from the fifth century B.C. before they expanded their empire: "To go beyond is as wrong as to fall short." Support this statement with an example from your own life or one from current events. Explain your answer.
3. Read a story from or about India from this century. You might choose one by Rudyard Kipling or Rumer Godden, for example. Do you see any similarities between the story and the literature in Lesson 2? What does the story you chose tell you about Indian beliefs, customs, or way of life?
4. Imagine that the towns in your county cannot agree on where the county seat of government should be located. In order to be selected as the "capital" of the county, your town must prove that it has enough important qualities to merit this honor. Write a one-page report boasting about the strengths of your town that will win it the county seat.

Answers to Using Critical Thinking
1. a. What you don't know won't hurt you.
   b. He who hesitates is lost.
   c. The end justifies the means.
   d. Everybody loves a winner.
   e. Misery loves company.
   f. Practice makes perfect.
2. Answers will vary. Students should select relevant examples and explain the application of the proverb.
3. Students should justify any similarities they find between the pieces of literature. They might discuss and compare the different beliefs and customs they read about.
4. Students might discuss whether each writer has really emphasized a strength of the town or whether it is just a strength in the eyes of the writer.

Preparing for Citizenship

1. **COLLECTING INFORMATION** The land that was once known as Persia is called Iran today. Look through newspapers and magazines for stories that answer the following questions about the country of Iran: Is the area still a center of trade? Do the people who live there still welcome ideas from other cultures? What is life like in Iran today? Collect everyone's stories and display them on a bulletin board under headings such as "Persia Yesterday, Iran Today," "Trade in Iran Today," or "Iran and Its Neighbors."
2. **ARTS ACTIVITY** Create a three-dimensional mosaic design that is at least six inches wide and eight inches long. You may use colored cellophane, paper, clay, stones, or other materials to develop a mosaic picture. Your creation could show a person from an ancient civilization, a battle, or just an interesting pattern. As you design and create your mosaic, think about the talent, materials, effort, and imagination that ancient people put into their colorful and often large-scale mosaic pieces. Imagine how much time it took to cover an entire wall or floor in a mosaic pattern or picture.
3. **WRITING ACTIVITY** Write a short, humorous dialogue that takes place between a hostile barbarian armed with a knife and a Roman official. The barbarian fears the conquering Huns and wants to take refuge in the empire. The Roman official is not so sure about the idea and insists on filling out certain paperwork before permitting the barbarian to cross the border. Use what you know about immigration and other government procedures today to write the scene.
4. **COLLABORATIVE LEARNING** As a class project, create a multi-cultural display entitled "Cultural Contributions of the Ancient World." Divide into groups of four and have each member choose one of the following ancient civilizations to research: Rome, Greece, India, or China. Write down as many contributions as you can think of for the civilization you have chosen.

47

Answers to Preparing for Citizenship
1. **COLLECTING INFORMATION** Students should search past and present newspapers and other sources to gain an understanding of the lifestyle, trade policies, and other pertinent information.
2. **ARTS ACTIVITY** You may choose to display the students' mosaics for the school. This might coincide with a trip to an art museum.
3. **WRITING ACTIVITY** You might have students perform their humorous dialogues for the class.
4. **COLLABORATIVE LEARNING** Instruct students to draw or include photocopies of art that is representative of the cultures they are researching to accompany their writings. You might decide to feature the display in a central location at school.

UNIT
OVERVIEW

After students have read the unit title and noted the dates of the unit's time span, have them read the passage below the title.

As students look at the opening photograph, point out that Islam is one of the five major world religions. Ask them if they can name the other four. *(Buddhism, Christianity, Hinduism, and Judaism.)*

Looking Back

Remind students that the Roman Empire once controlled the land around the Mediterranean, including the Middle East, North Africa, and Spain. Point out that the Muslim Empire expanded in these areas.

Looking Forward

Tell students that in the next two chapters they will learn how Islam spread as a religious and political empire:

Chapter 3 *The Roots of Islam*

Chapter 4 *The Empire of Islam*

Unit 2
The Growth of Islam

Covered in silver and gold, the walls of the house of worship shimmer in the light. The people turn toward the niche in the wall that tells them they are facing Mecca, their holy city. They pray. These Muslims are carrying on a religious tradition that dates to the A.D. 600s. That was when Arabian peoples united behind Muhammad, whom Muslims believe was sent as a prophet with the message of Islam. Within 150 years of his death, Muslims ruled lands from the Atlantic Ocean to central Asia. During the following centuries, Islam continued to spread into Africa, Asia, and Europe.

500

48

Muslims at prayer, Mashad, Iran. Photograph by Roger Wood

GEOGRAPHY PROJECT

Journey to Mecca

Geography Skill Make a Map
Students use the skill of Organizing geographic information.

Geography Themes Movement/Regions

Geography Standards 6, 13 culture and experience affect perception of place; cooperation and conflict among people shape earth's surface

Activity *Create a Travel Journal*
Materials writing paper, pens
Management: Individual/Small Group

Have students imagine that they are sightseers in the year 900 traveling through Spain, Egypt, Persia, and ending in Mecca. Have the travelers keep a travel diary of at least four entries about these places.

Have students:
- write clear, concise journal entries and/or draw detailed illustrations of the places.
- describe or show both geographic characteristics and human activity.
- make a route map, showing the places described in the travel journal.

1492

Understanding the Photograph

The photograph shows Muslims at prayer at the Shrine of Imam Riza in Mashad, Iran. Worshipers must face Mecca, the Muslim holy city, which is located in Saudi Arabia. The niche in the wall, called the *mihrab*, indicates the direction of Mecca. Prayer consists of reciting passages from Muslim holy scripture and making movements such as bowing from the hips and kneeling with face to the ground. Mosques are often decorated with art and verses from Muslim holy scripture.

Have students compare the interior and worshipers of the mosque in the photograph with other worshipers and places of worship that they have observed.

Understanding Chronology

This unit covers the rise of Islam and the rise and fall of the Muslim Empire. Point out that this time period is roughly the same as the time period for the Byzantine Empire.

For research support activities, see the *Research Handbook.*

For simulations correlated to this unit, see *Citizenship Simulations*, p. vii.

HOUGHTON MIFFLIN SOCIAL STUDIES

Bookshelf II

Magid Fasts for Ramadan

by Mary Matthews

A story of contemporary life in Egypt that introduces the beliefs and practices of Islam through the activities of a young boy.

Motivate Read aloud pp. 5–10 about Magid's family preparing for the first day of Ramadan. Ask students what Giddu told Magid about why Muslims fast. Then have students look at the opening pages of the unit and explain what they think they will learn about Islam in this unit.

To connect this book with the unit content, use the planning guide and student activity blackline masters beginning on p. iv of the *Bookshelf II Teacher's Resources.*

For additional books that are Easy, Average, and Challenging, see the Unit Bibliography on p. T43. See bibliography updates at www.eduplace.com/ss/hmss.

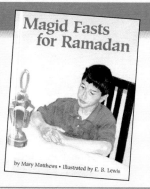

Magid Fasts for Ramadan

by Mary Matthews • Illustrated by E. B. Lewis

Planning at a Glance
The Roots of Islam

	Objectives	Reading Support *and* Other Resources	Diverse Learning Strategies
Lesson 1 Desert Bloom–Caravan Cities *pp. 52–57* 2–3 days	• Analyze the effect of geography on the lifestyle of the early Arabs. • Describe the conditions that led to the growth of trade in the Arabian Peninsula. • Explain the religious significance of Mecca to the early Arabs.	• **Workbook** or **Reading Support:** pp. 28–31 Review p. 7 Lesson Support/Transition p. 7 Multi-lang. Sum. pp. 13–14 • **Other Resources:** Geography Kit, Poster 1, Study Guide p. 8	Access Strat. **(Extra Support)** TE p. 53 Access Act. **(SDAIE)** TE p. 53 Visual Learning **(Visual)** TE p. 54 Map and Globe Skills **(Visual)** TE p. 55 Audiotapes of Multi-language Lesson Summaries **(Auditory)**
Lesson 2 Muhammad and Islam *pp. 58–64* 2–3 days	• Identify Muhammad and explain how he came to found the religion Islam. • Describe the Qur'an and explain its significance to Muslims. • List and explain the Five Pillars of Islam. • Explain how Islam, like other religions, affects all aspects of life.	• **Workbook** or **Reading Support:** pp. 32–35 Review p. 8 Lesson Support/Transition p. 8 Multi-lang. Sum. pp. 15–16 • **Other Resources:** Geography Kit, Study Guide p. 9, Study Print 2	Access Act. **(Extra Support)** TE p. 59 Visual Learning **(Visual)** TE p. 62 Study Skills **(GATE)** TE p. 63 Audiotapes of Multi-language Lesson Summaries **(Auditory)**
Lesson 3 Early Islam *pp. 65–68* 2–3 days	• Explain the origin of the caliphate. • Describe how the Muslim Empire expanded under the first four caliphs. • Describe the issue that divided the Islamic religion.	• **Workbook** or **Reading Support:** pp. 36–39 Review p. 9 Lesson Support/Transition p. 9 Multi-lang. Sum. pp. 17–18 • **Other Resources:** Geography Kit, Study Guide p. 10	Access Act. **(SDAIE)** TE p. 66 Writing **(GATE)** TE p. 67 Social Participation **(Auditory)** TE p. 68 Audiotapes of Multi-language Lesson Summaries **(Auditory)**
Skill: Making Parallel Timelines *p. 69* 1 day	• Make and use parallel timelines.	• **Other Resources:** Study Guide p. 11	Making Timelines **(Visual)** TE p. 69
Chapter Review *pp. 70–71* 1 day		Chapter 3 Test pp. 9–12 *(See facsimiles on TE p. 561.)*	Assessment Multiple-Use Masters pp. 73–80

49A

Reading Support Resources *for Every Lesson*

Reading and Review	Multi-language Summaries	Lesson Support /Transition
		S D A I E

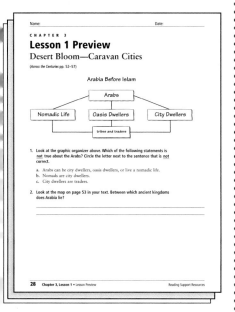

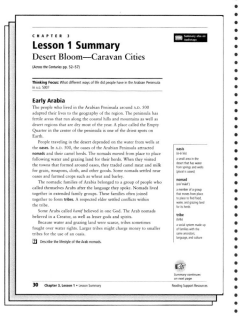

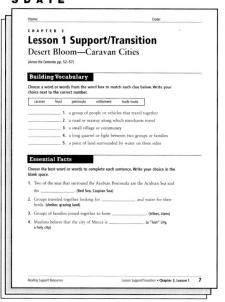

Activities for SDAIE
Specially **D**esigned **A**cademic **I**nstruction in **E**nglish

Reading and Review

- **Chapter Overview*** p. 27
- **Lesson Previews*** using graphic organizers from the Teacher's Edition pp. 28, 32, 36
- **Reading Strategies*** pp. 29, 33, 37
- **Lesson Summaries*** pp. 30–31, 34–35, 38–39
- **Lesson Reviews** pp. 7, 8, 9

* **Workbook** includes starred items.

Multi-language Summaries

Lesson Summaries in:
- English (See Reading and Review.)
- Spanish pp. 30–31, 34–35, 38–39
- Chinese pp. 13–18
- Hmong pp. 13–18
- Khmer pp. 13–18
- Vietnamese pp. 13–18

 Summaries available on audiotapes

Lesson Support /Transition

- **Lesson Support/Transition** pp. 7, 8, 9

Technology Options

Internet Support
http://www.eduplace.com

Social Studies Center at Education Place

Internet support for Chapter 3:
- *Lesson at a Glance*
- *Irrigation Technology*

Software
Student Writing Center ® (CD-ROM) (Macintosh® or Windows®)

School to Career

Most businesses that supply goods are part of the retail industry. Divide the class into small groups, and have each select and research a specific type of retail industry such as clothing or food. What are the responsibilities of the individuals who work there?

Character Education

Muslims fast at Ramadan to promote self-discipline, humility, and sympathy for the hungry. Divide students into three groups. Have each group create a public service campaign promoting one of these qualities. Have them present their campaign to the class. Later, discuss how each campaign was or was not effective.

CHAPTER
PREVIEW

Ask students to read the chapter title. Then have them briefly discuss what they know about Islam. Bring out the idea that Islam is a major force in world events today and that this chapter provides a foundation for understanding Islam.

Have the students read the narrative. Point out on a map the location of the Arabian Peninsula.

Looking Forward

Tell students that they will learn about the rise of Islam when they read the next three lessons: Desert Bloom—Caravan Cities; Muhammad and Islam; and Early Islam.

Lesson 1 describes what life was like for the early Arabs, before the time of Muhammad.

Chapter 3
The Roots of Islam

Dried fruits, vital for long desert treks, became important trade goods.

The Arabian Peninsula is a region of contrasts. By about 1000 B.C., camel caravans crossed the desert, mountains, and grasslands of Southwest Asia carrying trade goods from East to West. Before Roman times, Arab ships had sailed the Red Sea the Indian Ocean. Arabs of town, oasis, desert, and seaport, al played an important part in the exchange of goods and ideas among Asian, European, and African cultures. The Arabian Peninsula also shared in the religious history of Southwest Asia going back to biblical times. In the 600s, a religious leader nan Muhammad brought the message of Islam. United by their beli the desert Arabs came to rule parts of Asia, Africa, and Europe

500s Mecca, with its holy sites and its fresh-water well, grows as the most important stop along Arab trade routes. This scenic river valley (above) is near the city of Abha, Saudi Arabia.

500	540	580

c. 550 Japanese rulers allow their subjects to practice the Buddhist faith.

50

500

BACKGROUND

Islam today is a major world religion, stretching far beyond Arabia and embracing a large number of countries and cultures. Islam, like Judaism and Christianity, was born in the Middle East. All three religions recognize the same God, and although they developed centuries apart, they have a common history and share some traditions.

Islam, Judaism, and Christianity

Islam, Judaism, and Christianity all are monotheistic religions. They each worship one God. In addition, all three groups possess a sacred book. The Jewish Bible consists of the five books of Moses. Christians call this the Old Testament and add to their Bible the New Testament, which includes the Gospels. Of the 28 prophets mentioned in the Qur'an, 21 appear in the Christian Bible. Because they share a common history, many events described in the Bible also appear, with variations, in the Qur'an. Early in their history,

Muslims called Jews and Christians "People the Book" because both groups have sacred texts concerning the God of Abraham.

Jerusalem—Sacred to Three Religions

Muslims, Jews, and Christians all regard Jerusalem as a holy place. For Muslims, the Dome of the Rock—a building with a gold dome, considered by some to be the most beautiful structure in all of Jerusalem—is sacred. This structure was built over the ro from which, Muslims believe, Muhammad rose to heaven with Gabriel.

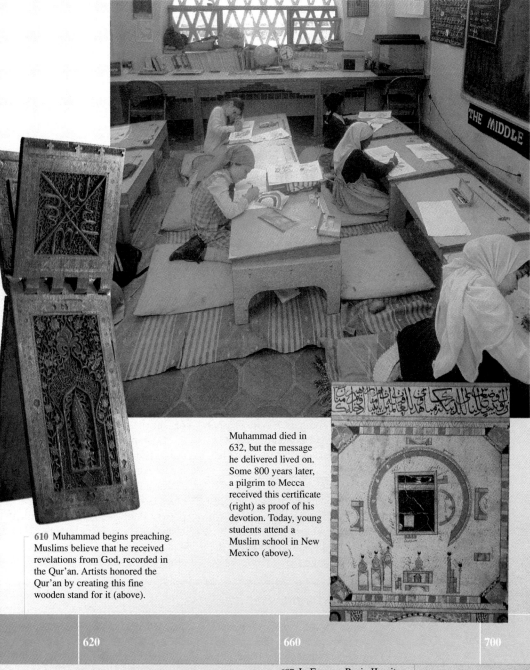

Understanding the Visuals

Direct students to examine the pilgrimage certificate, which dates from 1432. Ask them to speculate on the black rectangle at the center. When students have read p. 57 and its description of the Ka'bah, return to this certificate and revisit their speculations.

Muhammad died in 632, but the message he delivered lived on. Some 800 years later, a pilgrim to Mecca received this certificate (right) as proof of his devotion. Today, young students attend a Muslim school in New Mexico (above).

610 Muhammad begins preaching. Muslims believe that he received revelations from God, recorded in the Qur'an. Artists honored the Qur'an by creating this fine wooden stand for it (above).

620

660

700

687 In Europe, Pepin II unites the Franks and rules until 714.

51

661

Understanding Chronology

Refer the students to the timeline. Point out that throughout the book, entries listed above the timeline will illustrate events discussed in the chapter; events listed below will tell students what is happening elsewhere in the world during the same time period.

Ask students to find c. 550 on the timeline, when the Japanese were permitted to practice Buddhism. This item serves as proof of the spread of ideas—in this case, from India, to China, to Japan. Next, ask students to find 610 on the timeline and tell them to consider, as they read the chapter, how Islam spread.

Jews believe that it was on this same rock that Abraham prepared to sacrifice his son Isaac at God's command. The Wailing Wall in Jerusalem is also a sacred place to Jews. This wall on Mt. Moriah, some 160 feet long, is all that remains of the Jewish holy temple of biblical times. For centuries it has been a symbol of faith and unity for the Jewish people. To Christians, the Church of the Holy Sepulchre in Jerusalem is sacred because it stands on the hill of Calvary, where they believe Jesus was crucified and buried.

INTRODUCE

Point out the lesson title. Have students discuss what they think the word *bloom* suggests about cities in the desert. *(They are a source of life and activity.)* Ask students how they think cities thrived in Arabia in the A.D. 500s. Have them read the Thinking Focus and then the lesson to find out more about Arabia and how early Arabian cities developed.

Key Terms

Vocabulary Strategies: T36–T37
oasis—a small area in the desert watered by springs and wells
nomad—a member of a group that moves from place to place in search of food, water, and grazing land for their herds
tribe—any system of social organization made up of villages, bands or other groups with a common ancestry, language, culture, and name
idol—an image used as an object of worship
pilgrimage—a journey to a sacred place or shrine

---

500   599   620   660   700

LESSON 1

Desert Bloom— Caravan Cities

Site of Uba
Old Caravan Routes
Modern Ro

THINKING FOCUS

What different ways of life did people have in the Arabian Peninsula in A.D. 500?

Key Terms
- oasis
- nomad
- tribe
- idol
- pilgrimage

➤ *The ancient caravan routes (above, right) can be seen with a satellite radar photograph, but are invisible to those standing on top of them.*

In 1984, the space shuttle Challenger roared into Earth's orbit. In one of the first uses of "space archaeology," Challenger's radar equipment beamed down microwaves to the southern Arabian Peninsula and digitally recorded any signals that bounced back. Historians were looking for the "lost" city of Ubar. What they saw—invisible to people on the ground—was a thin black line that showed what lay under the surface of the sand. What they found was a line of compacted earth underneath the desert. The compacted earth showed the centuries of beaten-down tracks of trade caravans. The tracks all led to one place.

Historians knew that many ancient peoples burned an incense called frankincense that came from trees in the mountains near the Arabian Sea. Caravans brought the incense through the desert to Ubar, where it was traded and continued its journey to other lands. Could this line in the desert actually be the long-lost Frankincense Road leading to the ancient marketplace of Ubar?

Looking for answers, archaeologists and historians gathered on the site of this ancient village in 1990 and began piecing together clues from the buried fortress and pottery samples that they unearthed. Ubar, once a stop for merchants and travelers, began to reappear slowly from beneath the sand.

Early Arabia

Ubar was only one of the many settlements located in the Arabian Peninsula. Although the Peninsula's Empty Quarter is one of the driest deserts on Earth, the region consists of fertile ranges of mountains and coastal hills that run along the Red and Arabian seas. To the north, the sparse Syrian Desert separates the Peninsula from Palestine and

Chapter 3

Objectives

1. Analyze the effect of geography on the lifestyle of the early Arabs.
2. Describe the conditions that led to the growth of trade in the Arabian Peninsula.
3. Explain the religious significance of Mecca to the early Arabs.

Graphic Overview

ARABS
- Nomadic Life
- Oasis Dwellers
- City Dwellers

tribes and traders

the Mediterranean coast. At its western edges the region borders the Tigris-Euphrates river system. The dry region in the center of the peninsula, however, is dotted with oases. An **oasis** (plural: oases) is a small area in a desert that is watered by springs or wells. Almost all regions except the Empty Quarter receive some rainfall.

At an Oasis

Ubar thrived from around 900 B.C. to A.D. 300. By the 500s, however, the demand for incense had fallen, and Ubar had been destroyed by the collapse of its underground water reservoir. Water determined where people gathered and on what routes they traveled. Journeys were planned from well to well, or oasis to oasis. Towns and cities grew around these sources of water.

Throughout the peninsula's interior, oases attracted families of **nomads** who were herders. They migrated in regular patterns, following water and grazing land for their camel herds. Their lives revolved around the seasons, as they waited for the rainfall to make the grazing land green. As they traveled, they kept watch for the many wells that had been dug and were maintained to provide water for the people and animals who traveled the land.

▲ *Dates are still raised in groves like this one near the city of Al Ula in Saudi Arabia.*

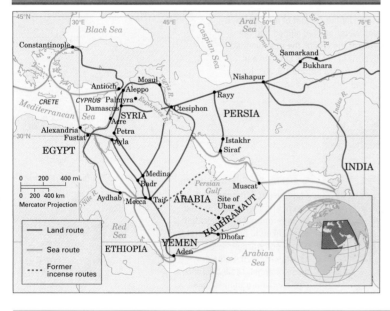

Trade Routes, A.D. 570

◀ *Arabia was at the center of many early trade routes. Goods from Africa, Asia, and Europe crossed Arabia. If you had been a trader, what routes would you have wanted to travel and why?*

The Roots of Islam

D E V E L O P

Have students study the map on this page. Point out that while Arabia is surrounded by bodies of water, there are no river valleys cutting across the peninsula. Discuss what effect this would have on the environment. (*There would be no rivers so the land would be very dry.*) Draw the Graphic Overview on the chalkboard. Have students speculate about the environment of each of the groups. Explain that this lesson describes the geography of Arabia and how it affected the people.

◀ *The advantage of sea travel was that a ship could hold more than a camel caravan could. Land travel was the only way to reach interior towns.*

53

Access Strategy

Read aloud the opening of the lesson and the description of how Ubar was rediscovered. Point out to students that without such advanced technology as microwave radar systems, the location of Ubar might have remained unknown.

Point out also that new technologies are being applied to archaeology in ways that could not have been imagined not long ago. The way the *Titanic* was located and explored is a good example that students may be familiar with. This means that the future of archaeology is wide-open and vibrant. Students may want to look at back issues of *National Geographic* magazine to get a sense of the unfolding advances in archaeology and think about the archaeological riddles they would like to solve. Invite students to brainstorm careers in archaeology.

Access Activity

Have students study a globe to get a sense of Arabia's location and geography. Ask: What type of land mass is Arabia? (*Peninsula.*) What bodies of water surround it? (*Mediterranean Sea, Red Sea, Arabian Sea, Persian Gulf.*) Based on its location, what type of climate and type of land does Arabia have? (*Arid, desert.*)

Note: Use this Closer Look when discussing the ways people in Southwest Asia and North Africa responded to the challenge of building a thriving agricultural system in environments where farming might be difficult.

Visual Learning

The photograph of the water wheel at Hama, Syria, on the Orontes River shows how a noria lifts water up into the air in buckets, but students may have trouble seeing the details of the process. Use the diagram to make clear how the pots around the rim of the wheel pick up water from the river and empty it out into a trough after reaching the highest part of the wheel.

Ask students how the wheel is powered. *(By the force of the water flowing beneath it.)*

More About the Qanat Tell students that the qanat system of transporting water underground is quite ancient. The original forms were developed in what is now Iran, the oldest of which can be dated back as much as 2,500 to 3,000 years. Qanat technology spread both eastward and westward, into Afghanistan and across the Mediterranean to Spain. Despite its ancient origins, qanats are still used today. Ask students if they know of any water transportation systems in use in their state.

Irrigation Technology

Ever since humans settled down and began raising crops for food, they have been building canals and irrigating fields. The Muslims used science and technology to raise water and move it from one place to another. By organizing resources and spreading knowledge among the many groups that made up Muslim culture, they brought great areas of dry land into agricultural production.

aqueduct

stream

The *noria,* or water wheel, was a Roman invention that spread throughout the Muslim world. Driven by the current of the stream, it was fitted with pots that filled with water as they dipped into the stream. When they reached the top of the wheel, the pots emptied into an aqueduct or channel that carried the water to fields and towns. The windmill first appeared in Persia around A.D. 300. It was later copied in Spain and then spread throughout Europe.

54

In Algeria, Iran, parts of Oman, Afghanistan, Morocco, and Spain, irrigation was often fed by underground channels that were linked to natural aquifers, where underground water had become trapped. Some of these channels, called *qanats,* stretched more than 40 miles. Shafts spaced along the channel allowed air pressure to keep the water flowing.

Visual Learning

Have students inspect closely the photograph of the qanat system. Ask them if they can see the channel. *(No, it's underground.)* What are the series of stone circles? *(Tops of air shafts spaced out along the qanat.)*

Bulletin Board

Post recent information and articles on irrigation news from around this country. Use this to explore issues surrounding local water resources and the importance of balancing the irrigation of farmland with other uses. Have students compare modern-day conduits and aqueducts with qanats.

At oases, the nomads would often visit towns and villages. Sometimes they came to groves of date trees, or fields of wheat, barley, or other crops. The fields were irrigated from the area's springs or wells. The nomads often brought products such as camel meat and milk to trade. In exchange, villagers supplied the nomads with grain, and city merchants sold manufactured wares, including weapons, carpets, and cloth, as well as goods for trade such as sugar and tea.

Nomadic Life

The nomadic families of Arabia belonged to a group of people who called themselves Arabs after the language they spoke. Some Arabs settled on oases where they lived as farmers. Others lived in villages and were traders or artisans. Farmers and herders supplied these village-dwellers with food and transport animals.

In order to survive in their desert environment, nomads lived in close family groups with grandparents, parents, and children. Families often joined together to form **tribes.** Each tribe was headed by a respected elder called a *shaikh (shayk).* With the help of family leaders, the *shaikh* settled family and tribal disputes.

While the nomads seem to have believed in a Creator, they also believed in lesser gods that they thought influenced their lives. They made **idols** to represent these "sons and daughters of God." They also believed in spirits that could inhabit natural objects and forces.

Among the groups living in Arabia in A.D. 500 were Arabs called *hanif* who believed in one God. Jewish tribes had existed in Arabia for centuries, while Christian tribes had lived in the northern part of the peninsula. Both Jews and Christians earned their livelihoods as farmers, herders, and artisans.

Because water and grazing land were so scarce, feuds broke out occasionally between tribes. Larger tribes sometimes forced payment from smaller tribes to use the oases. For a price, these larger tribes would also protect traders' caravans from danger. ■

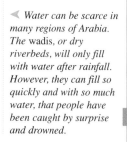

■ *Describe the lifestyle of the Arab nomads.*

◄ *Water can be scarce in many regions of Arabia. The* wadis, *or dry riverbeds, will only fill with water after rainfall. However, they can fill so quickly and with so much water, that people have been caught by surprise and drowned.*

The Roots of Islam

55

GEOGRAPHY

Critical Thinking

Ask students how geography affected lifestyles in pre-Islamic Arabia. *(Oases could be cultivated; seaports were built on natural harbors; grazing lands supported herds of livestock.)* Then ask why cooperation between groups was necessary. *(Each person provides complementary goods or skills.)*

■ *Nomads had to travel year-round to find water and grazing land for their herds. They traded camel products and other goods for food and other products at oases.*

Geographic Context

Most of Arabia consists of hot desert dotted by small oases. However, the southwestern fringe of Arabia—today made up of the Yemen Arab Republic—is mountainous and receives abundant rainfall from the monsoons blowing off the Indian Ocean. The land in this region is quite unlike any other part of Arabia; it is green and fertile. While most nomads were constantly on the move in search of food and water, the southern Arabs lived in densely populated towns and villages surrounded by mountain vegetation, including myrrh, carob, fig trees, mango trees, date palms, and evergreens. These populations developed into highly prosperous and culturally advanced civilizations.

Language Arts Connection

In Arabia, poetry was a favorite form of expression. Poets wrote of romance and love, of tribal loyalty and feuds, and the desert environment. Have students write a poem that deals with Arab life.

Map and Globe Skills

Refer students to the map on p. 53. Why was Arabia crisscrossed by so many trade routes? *(Central location relative to rest of known world.)* At what Arabian cities do the trade routes meet and why do they meet there? *(Probably located at oases.)* Have students trace the route from Yemen to Damascus and calculate the length of the route.

Critical Thinking

Using the example of spices that are grown in India, shipped across Arabia, and will eventually be used in a kitchen in Rome, ask students how transporting this commodity made Arabia prosperous. *(At every trans-shipment point, traders make a profit for their portion of the transport; taxes may have been paid, also.)* Ask students how the long process of bringing spices to Rome, with so many people involved, could be profitable. *(The spices were so highly valued at the final destination that they could demand high prices.)*

■ *Life for the town-dwellers would have been shaped by the trade that brought prosperity to many towns. For instance, goods from many different countries were bought and sold there. Also, the towns were centers of trade for local agricultural products, and visited by nomads who needed such products.*

56

Towns and Trade

➤ *The treasury building of Petra, like most of the city, is carved into a mountainside. This treasury is built in the Hellenistic style, a sign of the conquest of Alexander the Great.*

■ *Describe the lifestyle of the Arab town-dwellers.*

Carrying all kinds of local and exotic goods, merchants crisscrossed Arabia on travel routes stretching between the Mediterranean Sea, the Red Sea, the Arabian Sea, and the Persian Gulf. Some of these merchants chose to stay in the trading centers they passed through, settling and specializing in the trade and transportation of goods. Others became artisans, scholars, and judges. Between A.D. 500 and 600, the Arabian peninsula was inhabited by three types of communities. They were made up of either city-dwellers, people living in agricultural villages, or nomadic tribes. Although each group had a different way of life, they cooperated to make the society run smoothly.

The towns were built along the many trade routes that crossed the Arabian peninsula. Local goods as well as luxuries from Indian Ocean trade routes to the east passed through these villages on their way to Mediterranean lands. As traders crossed the desert, they stopped at the oases for supplies. The Arabs who lived in these oasis villages became leaders among the Arabs throughout the region because of the wealth that such trading brought.

Seaports linked Arabia with Africa and Asia, and travelers and traders came from these continents. Arabs could buy goods and meet people from their own region as well as from distant lands. Various people traveled the desert routes, bringing exotic cloth and fragrant spices from India; ivory, gold, and ebony from Africa; as well as Arabian horses and camels. Many

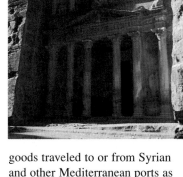

goods traveled to or from Syrian and other Mediterranean ports as well as across the Red Sea toward Egypt and the port of Alexandria.

Petra

In the northwest corner of the Arabian peninsula are the remains of Petra. A former trading city nestled at the foot of a high cliff, it is now known for its beauty. Attracted by Petra's ample supply of spring water, travelers began stopping at this center as early as 300 B.C. The city took its name from the Greek word for "rock" from which some of its earliest buildings were carved.

In the open-air marketplace, or *suq (SOOK)*, of Petra, wheat, olive oil, wine, hides, slaves, precious stones, and spices were abundantly available. Here, merchants would stock local products and wares, and compete with each other to attract customers to their stalls. ■

Study Skills

Have students research prominent oasis cities that developed in northern Arabia like Petra and Palmyra. They should try to find out when the city came into existence, what trade routes it lay on, and other important facts. Then have students do similar research on a port city like Aden or Muscat. Students can present comparisons in short oral reports.

Cultural Context

Frankincense and myrrh, along with other perfumes and food spices, made up the very profitable Arabian spice trade. These two rare and expensive aromatic gums, derived from trees, were in great demand in early Arabia. They were also used by a number of civilizations such as the Sumerians, Egyptians, Minoans, Greeks, and Romans. These groups probably obtained most of their frankincense and myrrh from Arabia, where the most highly valued varieties of

these trees grow (on the southern coastal fringe). Frankincense and myrrh had diverse and important uses, ranging from religious rites to the cremation, embalming, and buri of the dead to the anointing of rulers. Perhaps their most important use was in pharmacology. They were mixed with other spic to make tonics and lotions thought to cure, among other things, headaches, the pains o childbirth, ulcers, and earaches.

The Holy City of Mecca

The city of Mecca grew in a well-protected valley at the crossroads of two long-distance trade routes. The routes stretched north and south between Yemen and the Mediterranean, as well as east and west between the Persian Gulf and the Red Sea. Travelers quenched their thirst and watered their animals at Mecca's fresh water well.

A Sacred Meeting Place

Muslims believe that the founding and settling of Mecca is related to the story of Abraham and his son Ishmael. According to Islamic teachings, Abraham and Ishmael built a cube-shaped shrine called the Ka'bah *(KAH buh)* about 4,000 years ago. Islam teaches that Abraham was commanded to build the Ka'bah as a house of worship and a reminder of Abraham's firm belief in one God.

Worshipers honored the Ka'bah and over time placed idols in it for safekeeping. They honored the gods in it by performing religious rituals. Although the Arab tribes still considered themselves to be descendants of Abraham, they introduced the worship of idols to the Ka'bah. By A.D. 500, there were more than 360 different idols in and around it. There were even some Christian pictures placed

▲ *The city of Mecca was the location of the Ka'bah, which for centuries has held religious symbols. The city was also a prosperous trade center and an excellent source of fresh water.*

there. A tradition continued of visiting the Ka'bah and walking around it.

The Quraysh, a local tribe, settled in Mecca sometime before A.D. 500. Their role as keepers of the Ka'bah gave them great prestige and helped them to make treaties with neighboring tribes. This ensured the safe passage of caravans during the months of pilgrimage and travel. A **pilgrimage** is a journey to a sacred site. The treaties prevented fighting and raiding during this time. By A.D. 500, Mecca had become the most successful trade center in Arabia, prospering from the flow of merchants and pilgrims. ■

■ *How was Mecca different from other Arab trading cities?*

R E V I E W

1. **FOCUS** What different ways of life did people have in the Arabian Peninsula in A.D. 500?
2. **CONNECT** What contact did the Arabs make with peoples beyond Arabia?
3. **GEOGRAPHY** Why did many families in Arabia keep moving?
4. **BELIEF SYSTEMS** Describe why the Ka'bah was an important site for pilgrims.
5. **CRITICAL THINKING** Do you think religious pilgrimages were necessary for trade to continue? Explain your answer.
6. **ACTIVITY** Use an atlas to describe or show the geography of the countries now within the Arabian Peninsula.

57

The Roots of Islam

Divide students into pairs. Have one student assume the role of a member of the Quraysh tribe and the other assume the role of a poor trader. They are in the city of Mecca. Tell the member of the Quraysh tribe to try to convince the trader to leave his or her tribal idol in the Ka'bah. Have the trader explain his or her opinion.

■ *Mecca was not only a trading center but also an important religious center. Arabs came from all over the Arabian Peninsula to worship their gods in the Ka'bah.*

C L O S E

Have students make a cluster diagram for each of the key terms listed on p. 52. For each term have them list and cluster as many related details as they can think of from their reading of the lesson.

57

Answers to Review Questions

1. There were three major ways of life: that of the Arab nomads, that of the agricultural villagers, and that of city-dwellers.
2. There was a great deal of contact, especially through trade. Arabia served as a major trading crossroads between the Mediterranean Sea region and the Indian Ocean. Arabia was also linked through trade to the east coast of Africa.
3. Arab nomads moved their herds in search of the best seasonal grazing lands. Also,

with much of the Arabian economy based on transporting and trading goods, some traders moved a great deal as well.
4. According to Islamic teaching, Abraham and Ishmael built the Ka'bah about 4,000 years ago as a sign of their monotheism. Idol worshipers also used it as a holy site.
5. Trade existed in Arabia before the tradition of religious pilgrimages gained strength.

Homework Options

Have students write a diary entry from the point of view of a merchant in Mecca awaiting the arrival of travelers making their pilgrimage to the Ka'bah.

Study Guide: p. 8

Point out the lesson title. Ask students if they know what a prophet is. *(A person who speaks for God or a god; one who is divinely inspired.)* Explain that in Mecca in the 600s, a man named Muhammad, convinced that God spoke to him through an angel, sparked the religion of Islam. It would take its place next to Judaism and Christianity. Have students read to find out more about Muhammad and his religion.

Key Terms

Vocabulary Strategies: T36–T37
Qur'an—the sacred book of Islam that is believed to contain the revelations made to Muhammad by Allah through the angel Gabriel
monotheism—the belief that there is only one God
Islam—a religion based on the teachings of the prophet Muhammad; "submission to God"
Muslim—a believer in Islam
mosque—a Muslim house of worship
Sunna—traditional Islamic conduct observed by orthodox Muslims, based on the example of Muhammad

500	540	580		660	700
			610 **650**		

L E S S O N 2

Muhammad and Islam

Find details to support the statement, "Islam, like other religions, is not only a system of beliefs but also a way of life."

Key Terms

- Qur'an
- monotheism
- Islam
- Muslim
- mosque
- Sunna

➤ *Today pilgrims visit the Prophet's Cave on Mount Hira.*

Chapter 3

Each year, a Meccan trader named Muhammad would spend a month in quiet thought while inside a desert cave on Mount Hira. In the year A.D. 610, something extraordinary occurred. The first verses of the **Qur'an,** believed by Muslims to be the written record of God's words, were revealed to him at that time.

The story of how Muhammad received these messages was later told by his wife, Aisha *(AY ee shah).* Aisha was the daughter of Abu Bakr, a wealthy trader who was the first person outside Muhammad's family to become a Muslim.

Aisha tells that even before Muhammad's experience in the cave at Hira, he had had "good dreams which came true like bright daylight." Then, in the cave, something more far-reaching happened.

A being he later identified as the angel Gabriel, or Jibril *(juh BREEL)* in Arabic, came to him, telling him to read, or recite. Trembling, Muhammad responded that he didn't know how to read or what to read. "Thereupon [the angel] caught me and pressed me so hard that I could not bear it any more." Three times the angel pressed Muhammad, finally commanding him to

Read! In the name of your Lord who created.
Created man from a clot of congealed blood.
Read! And your Lord is the Most Bountiful.
He who has taught by the pen.
Taught man that which he knew not.

Qur'an 96:1–5

1. Identify Muhammad and explain how he came to build the religion Islam.
2. Describe the Qur'an and explain its significance to Muslims.
3. List and explain the Five Pillars of Islam.
4. Explain how Islam, like other religions, affects all aspects of life.

Graphic Overview

Gabriel	**Muhammad**	**Qur'an**	**Sunna**
The angel reveals Allah's words to Muhammad.	→ The prophet recites Allah's words to the people.	→ Allah's words are recorded in the Qur'an.	→ A record of the example, traditions, and customs of the prophet.

The Life of the Prophet

Muhammad was born into the Quraysh tribe around A.D. 570. Orphaned at an early age, he found work in the caravan trade. At 25, he married a wealthy widow in the trading business. This wealth gave him the freedom to visit Mount Hira each year to think.

On one of these visits in 610, Muhammad is believed by his followers to have had a vision of Gabriel. The angel told him to recite in the name of God. Followers of Muhammad believe the angel then told Muhammad the first of many messages from God.

Muhammad's followers believe that in another vision, the angel Gabriel took Muhammad to meet Abraham, Moses, and Jesus in Jerusalem. From Jerusalem, both Muhammad and Gabriel ascended into heaven, where Muhammad spoke to God.

These revelations confirmed both Muhammad's belief in one God, or **monotheism,** and

his role as the last messenger in a long line of prophets sent by God. The God he believed in—Allah— is the same God of other monotheistic religions, Judaism and Christianity. *Allah,* the Arabic word for God, is the word used in the Qur'an.

Spreading the Word

Muhammad began to preach, first to members of his family, then to the leaders of his tribe and others. When members of some prominent families accepted Islam, the Meccan leaders became hostile. Failing to convince Muhammad and his followers to give up their beliefs, the Quraysh leaders refused to trade with them, causing the Muslims great suffering. Finally, when Arabs from outside Mecca became attracted to the message during the pilgrimage, the Quraysh leaders plotted to kill Muhammad.

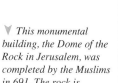

This monumental building, the Dome of the Rock in Jerusalem, was completed by the Muslims in 691. The rock is believed to be the place from which Muhammad ascended into heaven.

DEVELOP

Review with students what kind of religion most Arabs practiced around the A.D. 600s. *(Polytheism.)* Explain that a man named Muhammad at that time began to teach a religion that is centered around belief in one God. Have students review the major headings in the lesson. Point out that this lesson traces the life of Muhammad and the development of his religion, Islam, and describes the beliefs and practices of Islam.

Draw the four stages of the Graphic Overview on the chalkboard. Explain that Muslims believe Allah spoke to Muhammad through the angel Gabriel and that Muhammad's followers recorded that message in the Qur'an. The customs of the Muslim community are based on the Sunna.

Access Strategy

Muhammad was able to convince his neighbors that he had been in a cave and that an angel of God had appeared before him and had given him messages from God about how people were to live their lives. Have students discuss what personal qualities Muhammad must have possessed in order to have his neighbors accept what he was saying as the truth. *(Muhammad must have already enjoyed a reputation for honesty in his community. He must also have been known as a good person. Students might describe Muhammad with such words as honest, sincere, convincing, and a leader.)*

Access Activity

Divide the class into groups of four and ask each group to discuss what they already know and what they would like to know about Islam. Ask each group to share three points with the class. Help students frame questions they hope to have answered through their study of this section.

Critical Thinking

Ask students how polytheist business leaders of Mecca were affected by Muhammad's preaching. *(By denouncing polytheism, the Meccans' source of income—polytheistic pilgrims—was endangered.)* Then ask students how Muhammad appealed to Jews and Christians of Mecca and Medina. *(He claimed to be God's prophet and that the message revealed to him was the same basic message as that brought by Abraham, Moses, and Jesus.)*

➤ *As you can see from the script on the right, Arabic is written with an alphabet different from English. The passage tells of people who reject the message of Muhammad.*

In 622, Muhammad and his followers migrated to Medina, an oasis city about 200 miles north of Mecca. They had been invited and offered safety by the people of the city. This migration to Medina, known as the Hijrah *(HIJ ruh),* marks the beginning of the Islamic lunar calendar. Thus, the year A.D. 622 is also the year 1 A.H. (after Hijrah). Muhammad called the new faith **Islam,** which means "submission" to Allah. Believers in Islam are called **Muslims**—"those who submit to Allah's will."

Returning to Mecca

The Jews and Arabs of Medina welcomed Muhammad and his followers. Their city was on the verge of civil war, and they hoped that Muhammad could unite them. Muhammad hoped that Islam would be accepted by all the people of Medina. Muhammad told the Jews that Islam was not a new religion. The message revealed through him was the same basic message that had been brought by Abraham, Moses, and Jesus, among other prophets. He told them that the true religion is to follow one God and submit to his will. However, some Jewish leaders would not accept Muhammad as God's latest prophet.

Over the next eight years, support for Islam grew. Resistance to the changes introduced by Muhammad also grew. The enemies of the Muslims, led by the Quraysh, continued to try to eliminate Islam and its followers. The Quraysh, fearing that their power and wealth would be lost, tried to make alliances against the Medinans and their supporters. Eventually, many Arab nomadic tribes and leading Meccans joined the Muslim cause. With their support, Muhammad was able to put together an army of more than 10,000. In 630, this army marched on Mecca and the city surrendered without a battle.

One of the first things Muhammad did was to forgive all those who had opposed Muslims for so long. He also removed the idols from the Ka'bah. Thus the Ka'bah was again dedicated to the one God, as it had been in the time of Abraham. The area around the Ka'bah became the first **mosque,** or Muslim house of worship.

After appointing a Muslim governor, Muhammad returned to Medina. Following the defeat of the Quraysh, many tribes in Arabia decided to join the Muslims. They

Study Skills

Have students research the Muslim calendar, which is based on the phases of the moon. Research might include the following: the names of the months, how months that occur in one season one year might occur in another season in another year, and the religious significance of the months.

Historical Context

According to tradition, Muhammad's early life was filled with signs that pointed to his future greatness. At his birth it is said he brought forth a dazzling light, by which his mother could see the castles of Bostra in Syria. On one occasion, he accompanied his uncle Abu Talib on a caravan journey to Syria. Legend says that when a Christian monk laid eyes on Muhammad, he became very excited, for he recognized that Muhammad was destined to be a prophet.

had waited to see how the contest would turn out. Now they sent delegations to offer allegiance and accept Islam. Muhammad also sent letters to leaders outside Arabia, inviting them to Islam. By the time of Muhammad's death in 632, Islam had encompassed the central and western coastal regions of Arabia. ■

■ *How was the religion of Islam founded, and how did it spread?*

The Teachings of Islam

Muslims believe that the Qur'an is the word of Allah. After Muhammad took over the city of Medina, he began to establish an Islamic community with unique customs.

The Qur'an

Muhammad's revelations occurred from 610 until his death in 632. Although he was not literate himself, Muhammad had his revelations written down by his companions. Many of them memorized the whole Qur'an and recited it in his presence. By the time of his death, all the revelations had been compiled into one collection, the Qur'an. In addition, the hadith *(hah DEET)*, or words and deeds of Muhammad, were passed down in oral form through several generations, and compiled into authoritative collections. Together, the Qur'an and collections of hadith, called the **Sunna,** make up the authentic sources of Islamic beliefs and practices.

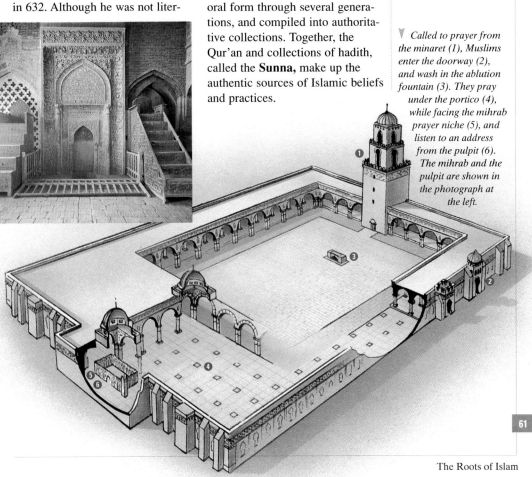

▼ *Called to prayer from the minaret (1), Muslims enter the doorway (2), and wash in the ablution fountain (3). They pray under the portico (4), while facing the mihrab prayer niche (5), and listen to an address from the pulpit (6). The mihrab and the pulpit are shown in the photograph at the left.*

The Roots of Islam

61

■ *Islam is the religion taught beginning in A.D. 610 by Muhammad, who is believed to have had revelations from God and as a result began to preach. His followers waged war against Muhammad's enemies, and, by the time of Muhammad's death in 632, his armies controlled most of the Arabian Peninsula.*

BELIEF SYSTEMS

Critical Thinking

Be sure that students understand why the Qur'an is the single most important guide to practicing Muslims. Explain that many non-Muslim scholars have tried to trace the sources of the Qur'an to other religious texts such as the Bible. Ask students why Muslims might think that trying to trace the sources of the Qur'an is blasphemous. *(To Muslims, the Qur'an is the Word of Allah, given directly to Muhammad.)*

61

Religious Context

According to Muslim tradition, Muhammad's followers wrote his utterances on anything that was available, such as palm leaves, pieces of wood or parchment, or even the shoulder blades of camels. However, even after the Qur'an had been written down, the majority of Muslims, until the 1600s, learned the scripture by word of mouth. The scripture was originally written in Arabic script, which at the time could easily be misread. (It lacked marks for some vowels, and the vowel marks it did have were very similar.) Several schools of law, or opinions on interpreting the sacred texts, emerged from the interpretations of major legal scholars. The Qur'an consists of about 300 pages, divided into 114 chapters called suras. Each sura has a name, such as "The Cow" or "The Bee." The chapters are not ordered chronologically but rather by length, with the longest chapter first.

Critical Thinking

Point out that after Muhammad died, his companions collected all of his revelations into one complete book. Ask students why Muhammad's followers thought it important to write his revelations. *(Parts might have gotten lost; those who memorized his words might have died before they could pass them on; people might lose faith with no scripture to rely on.)*

Critical Thinking

Mecca lies in western Saudi Arabia in a barren valley surrounded by majestic mountains. In the heart of Mecca lies the Great Mosque. The mosque has a courtyard that measures about 600 feet by 800 feet. In the middle of the courtyard is the Ka'bah, a stone building that to Muslims is the house of God. Ask students why Muslims believe that this is the house of God. *(Students could answer that according to tradition the Ka'bah was built by Abraham, believed to be the father of all Arabs. Abraham was commanded to build it as a house of worship and a reminder of his belief in one God.)*

For the followers of Islam, the Qur'an completes the earlier revelations of Old Testament prophets and Jesus. The Qu'ran is the final revelation, just as Muhammad is the final prophet.

Islam has close ties to Judaism and Christianity. Many prophets and holy people who are important figures in the Bible are also described in the Qur'an. For example, Abraham is thought to be the father of Jews through his son

Isaac. Abraham is also considered to be the father of Arabs through his other son Ishmael.

The Jews' and Christians' holy book, the Bible, is considered by Muslims to be based on God's revelations. But Muslims considered these other religions to be less correct. That is because the Qur'an teaches that the Bible has suffered loss and change with time. Christians and Jews are respected as "people of the book" by Mus-

▼ *All Muslims in good health and with enough money must make a pilgrimage to Mecca once in their lifetime.*

Visual Learning

Refer students to the picture of Mecca on p. 62 and the picture of the Ka'bah on p. 63. what building is at the center of the picture of Mecca? *(The Ka'bah.)* Why is there such a huge crowd of people surrounding the Ka'bah? *(They are on a pilgrimage.)* What are the people wearing, and why? *(White garments, a symbol of purity.)*

Religious Context

The pilgrimage to Mecca, called the *Hajj,* is the peak religious experience of a Muslim's life, for it satisfies a deep desire to behold at least once the Ka'bah—the house of God and the actual focal point of a lifetime of prayer. During the week of the pilgrimage, the following rituals are observed: circling the Ka'bah seven times to indicate that God is at the center of all

activity; going to the Mount of Mercy where Muhammad delivered his last sermon; and, most importantly, standing on the plain of Arafat. At Arafat many pilgrims stand from just after noon until just before sunset in serious self-examination and penance. Many Muslims say that during the standing a Muslim comes as close to God as one can on earth.

lims, and all their prophets are revered.

The Arabic word Qur'an can be loosely translated as "recitation." In fact, the very first word the angel Gabriel spoke to Muhammad was "Recite." By reciting aloud, many Muslims memorize as much of the Qur'an as they can.

The Sunna

The Sunna were the guiding rules for Islam and were based on the way the prophet Muhammad lived his own life. The most basic of these rules were the Five Pillars of Islam. The principles and commandments behind these five duties came from the Qur'an, but it was in the Sunna that the prophet explained them by his example.

The first of these pillars is the profession of faith. To express their acceptance of Islam, Muslims repeat the phrase, "There is no god but Allah, and Muhammad is his prophet."

The second pillar is prayer. Muslims must pray five times a day. Prayers follow special rituals, including washing before praying, bowing, and then kneeling while praying. Muslims face the Ka'bah in Mecca when praying. Every Friday at noon, Muslims congregate in mosques for prayer and a sermon by the prayer leader.

The third pillar is giving alms, or showing charity to the poor. Muslims must also contribute to public charities, such as the building of mosques and hospitals.

The fourth pillar is the ritual

fast during Ramadan, the ninth month of the Muslim year. Ramadan is a holy time, because in this month Muhammad received his first message from Allah. During Ramadan, Muslims must not eat or drink from the break of dawn until the setting of the sun. Muslims hope that their fast, which teaches self-discipline, humility, and sympathy for the hungry, brings them closer to Allah.

The fifth pillar of Islam is Hajj—the pilgrimage to Mecca. All Muslims who can afford it must make the pilgrimage at least once. The pilgrimage involves elaborate rites that take place over many days. Before arriving at Mecca, the pilgrims bathe, cut their hair and nails, and take off jewelry. They then put on a white seamless garment, symbolizing a state of purity. Because Muslims from all over the world make pilgrimage, Hajj is a symbol of Muslim unity and equality. ∎

▲ *Pilgrims circle the Ka'bah in the Great Mosque in Mecca. The heavy black covering that protects the shrine is replaced each year. The cloth covers a single doorway that leads into a room inside the Ka'bah.*

∎ *Why are the Qur'an and Sunna important to Muslims?*

An Islamic Way of Life

The five pillars lay at the foundation of what it is for Muslims to

be good human beings in obedience to God's will. But the Qur'an

Critical Thinking

Draw a two-column chart on the board that lists the Five Pillars of Islam. Have students help you fill in details describing each pillar. Next ask students, based on what they have learned about Islam so far, why each pillar is important to Muslims. *(Example: the second pillar, daily prayer, is important because it demonstrates a Muslim's willingness to submit to Allah and recognition of Allah's greatness.)*

∎ *The Qur'an is the written record of Allah's messages revealed through Muhammad. The Sunna is a description of the guiding rules of Islam as based on the way Muhammad lived his own life. Together they constitute a religious and social framework for Muslims.*

Historical Context

Explain to students that Muslims are also guided by the *Hadith,* a book that describes what Muhammad said and did during his life. One narrator relates that "his face shone like the full moon." Another states that in speech, Muhammad was "more truthful than all other men; by nature he was gentler than all, in social life nobler than everyone. Whoever happened to see him suddenly was struck with awe; and whoever came to know him by association could not help loving him."

Study Skills

Have students use reference books to research the modern city of Mecca. Research should include its population, how many pilgrims visit it annually, and what other landmarks in it and surrounding it are important to the rituals of the fifth pillar of Islam—the pilgrimage to Mecca.

Critical Thinking

To help students understand how religions can influence daily life, have them write an hourly log of a Muslim during the month of Ramadan. Students should record at what times they pray (see p. 95) and at what time they eat.

■ *In addition to the five pillars of faith, Islam contains many specific laws that describe how a person should live his or her daily life, based on the Sunna.*

CLOSE

With the help of students, construct a flow chart in which you show how Allah's messages got to Muhammad, to the community of Mecca, and to Muslims today. Use the ideas in the Graphic Overview (Allah, Gabriel, Muhammad, the Qur'an, and the Sunna) to help you.

64

▲ *This street scene from Essaouira, Morocco, shows a variety of Muslim women's dress. The majority of Muslim women do not cover their faces. Some have abandoned traditional Islamic dress for Western styles. Still others have returned to wearing modern forms of modest dress as an expression of Islamic values.*

■ *How does Islam affect many aspects of daily life for Muslims?*

and the Sunna cover many additional moral standards that a Muslim must live by in his or her everyday life. The Qur'an and the Sunna cover diet, marriage, divorce, business contracts, and even the proper way to clean one's teeth. Muslims are forbidden to eat certain foods such as pork, to drink alcohol, or to gamble. Islam, like most other religions, also prohibits murder and theft.

An Islamic term that is often misunderstood is *jihad (jee HUHD)*. The term means "to struggle," to do one's best to resist temptation and overcome evil. Under certain conditions, the struggle to overcome evil may require action. The Qur'an and Sunna allow self-defense and participation in military conflict, but restrict it to the right to defend against aggression and persecution. *Jihad*, for example, was first carried out against the Meccans who had forbidden Muslims to practice or preach their religion. While Islam forbade forced religious observance in the 600s, most rulers in the world at the time decided what religion their subjects would follow and persecuted those who refused.

In contrast to some other societies of the time, Muslim women were also given clear rights in marriage and the right to an education. They had the right to control the earnings from their work, to make contracts, and to serve as witnesses in court.

Many of these rights have become established law in Muslim countries to the present day. In other places, many of these rights have faded over time and have been replaced by oppressive local traditions. Customs of individual countries, some of them originating before Islam, often have determined women's roles more than Islamic principles.

Islam, like other religions, does influence the everyday lives of believers, from birth to death. Muslim parents chant the profession of faith over each newborn baby. Children use the Qur'an as they learn to read and write.

Many Muslims carry prayer beads that they use during free moments of the day as they think of Allah. Most Islamic prayer beads have 33 beads. Some people use the beads to count off the names of God or to praise God. These customs of both formal and informal worship often develop along regional lines, though in Islam the Qur'an and Sunna help unify practices. When someone is about to die, the Qur'an is recited at the person's bedside. ■

REVIEW

1. **FOCUS** Find details to support the statement, "Islam, like other religions, is not only a system of beliefs but also a way of life."

2. **CONNECT** In what ways is Islam similar to Judaism and Christianity?

3. **SOCIAL SYSTEMS** How did Islam affect the rights and status of women?

4. **CRITICAL THINKING** Why do you think the Arabs and others in Southwest Asia would have been attracted to Islam? Explain your reason.

5. **ACTIVITY** Interview your classmates or use the encyclopedia to find out what these rituals have in common: Yom Kippur (among Jews), Lent (among Christians), and Ramadan (among Muslims).

64

Chapter 3

Homework Options

Have students use the terms *Qur'an, Islam, Muslim,* and *Sunna* in a paragraph that describes daily life of a Muslim.

Study Guide: p. 9

Answers to Review Questions

1. Islam is also a way of life because it sets forth ethical standards that Muslims must follow in all aspects of life including diet, marriage, divorce, personal hygiene, and business transactions.

2. All three religions are monotheistic, revere the ancient Hebrew prophets, have a set of sacred writings, and offer a guide as to how followers should lead their lives.

3. The Qur'an gave women clear rights in ma[r]riage, as well as the right to an education, t[he] earnings from work, to make contracts, an[d] to serve as witnesses.

4. Some Arabs already believed in one God. Some had already been exposed to Judais[m] and Christianity. Islam began in Arabia, a[n] a "home-grown" religion may have appealed to some. Some may have desired the sense of unity Islam could bring.

500	540	580	620		700
			632	**661**	

L E S S O N 3

Early Islam

According to the Qur'an, one day in 632, Muhammad received one of his last messages from Allah: "This day, have I perfected for you your religion and completed my favor to you." Islam teaches that Muhammad was overcome with joy, for he realized that this meant he had accomplished his mission on earth. He had preached and spread Islam throughout the land. Most of Arabia had embraced Islam. He also realized that, with his mission complete, he would soon join Allah in heaven.

Muhammad's success in spreading Islam was due in large part to his strong character. His followers were attracted to his morality, courage, and compassion, perhaps as much as they were attracted to his teaching.

When Muhammad died suddenly in 632 without naming a successor, his followers were stunned. Panic swept the community. Some groups, reasoning that the Muslim community would die without Muhammad, renounced Islam. What would Muslims do without their inspired leader and prophet of Allah? Could someone who was not Allah's prophet guide them?

Abu Bakr *(AH boo BAH kur),* one of Muhammad's advisers,

offered wise counsel. He stressed the fact that Muslims worshiped Allah, not Muhammad:

> *And Muhammad is no more than a Messenger; all messengers before him have passed away.*
>
> Qur'an, 3:142

Abu Bakr's words restored calm and faith in the hearts of Muslims. The Muslim leaders now had to choose a successor to the prophet Muhammad.

THINKING FOCUS

What challenges did Muslims face after Muhammad's death?

Key Terms

- caliph
- council
- Shiite
- Sunni

◄ *The teachings of Muhammad lived on after his death. Here a muezzin, or Muslim crier, calls the hour of prayer from the minaret of a mosque in Sille, Turkey.*

65

The Roots of Islam

INTRODUCE

Review Muhammad's role in establishing and spreading the religion of Islam (Lesson 2). Have students read the lesson title and the Thinking Focus. Encourage students to speculate as to what Muhammad's followers might do after his death and whether Islam would continue to spread. Have them read to discover how Islam developed after Muhammad died.

Key Terms

Vocabulary Strategies: T36–T37
caliph—the successor to Muhammad as political leader of the Muslim community; the civil and religious ruler of a Muslim state
council—an assembly called to help pick the next Muslim caliph
Shiite—a member of the branch of Islam that supports the descendants of Muhammad as his rightful successors
Sunni—the branch of Islam that follows the caliphs elected to succeed Muhammad

65

Graphic Overview

```
The Death          The
of        →    Establishment   →    The Expansion
Muhammad        of the              of Islam
                Caliphate
                                →   The Division
                                    of Islam
```

Objectives

1. Explain the origin of the caliphate.
2. Describe how the Muslim Empire expanded under the first four caliphs.
3. Describe the issue that divided the Islamic religion.

DEVELOP

Refer students to the map on p. 67 and ask them what it tells them about the Muslim Empire after Muhammad's death. *(It spread beyond Arabia's borders.)* Point out that along with this expansion came a division in the community of Muslims. Draw the chart in the Graphic Overview on the chalkboard. Briefly explain the key term *caliph* and the word *caliphate*. Ask students what led up to both the expansion and division of the Muslim population.

■ *Muhammad's advisers called for a council to choose his successor. Abu Bakr received the most support.*

ETHICS
Critical Thinking

Ask students why Muhammad's advisers thought it so important to name a successor immediately after his death? *(So followers would not lose faith; to prevent enemies from gaining the upper hand because of lack of Muslim leadership.)* Why did three of the four contenders for the caliphate relinquish their claims? *(Disunity among Muslim leaders might weaken the community; they acknowledged that Abu Bakr had the strongest claim.)*

The First Caliph

▶ *Copies of the Qur'an were often richly decorated. This manuscript page was produced in Egypt during the Mamluk dynasty in the early fourteenth century and is now in the Chester Beatty Library in Dublin.*

■ *How was the problem of Muhammad's successor resolved?*

Soon after Muhammad's death, his most trusted advisers met to choose a **caliph,** an Arabic word meaning "successor." This caliph, Muslims realized, could not give the same kind of spiritual leadership as Muhammad had. The new caliph would not be the prophet of Allah, as Muhammad had been. Rather, he would act as the political and military leader of the Muslims.

Four contenders for the position stood out. Abu Bakr was Muhammad's father-in-law and one of his most respected companions. Two other contenders were Umar and Uthman, Muhammad's long-time friends and advisers. The fourth was Ali, a blood relative. Ali was Muhammad's cousin, his son-in-law, and the father of his grandsons.

An assembly of tribal leaders in Medina chose Abu Bakr as Muhammad's successor. Abu Bakr's first task was to put down revolts by tribes in the area who had renounced Islam after the

death of Muhammad. Thus, he convinced these tribes that the state was still strong. Under Abu Bakr's leadership, the Arabs were united again. The Muslim state began to extend its rule to areas outside Arabia, north into Syria and east into Mesopotamia. ■

The Next Two Caliphs

Abu Bakr, who became caliph at age 59, was caliph for only two years. Before his death in 634, Abu Bakr appointed Umar as his successor. An energetic and spirited leader, Umar encouraged his armies to conquer more lands.

The Muslims were extremely tolerant of those they conquered, as long as they were "people of the book." The Muslims allowed Christians and Jews to keep their churches and synagogues and

promised them security. In fact, some peoples who were persecuted by Persian and Byzantine conquerors, such as the Christians in Egypt and the Jews in Syria, welcomed Muslim rule. They even aided the Muslim takeovers.

Non-Muslims who were not Christians or Jews were also tolerated. Even some other non-Judeo-Christian groups were granted the status of people of the book.

Chapter 3

Access Activity

Ask students what qualities they would look for in a person who was to take over Muhammad's role as leader of Islam. Discuss how they would handle the selection of a new leader. Would it be important that the new leader be related to Muhammad?

Access Strategy

Ask students if they know what a family tree is. Draw one on the chalkboard using your own family. Then have students draw their own family trees at their seats. Ask them how many generations they were able to include, and why they could only list as many as they did. Then explain that Muslims trace the genealogy of Muhammad and his Quraysh tribe to Abraham (Lesson 1), who

lived around the year 2000 B.C. Ask them why they think the Muslims of Muhammad's time put so much emphasis on family ties. *(Their society was based on family, clan, and tribe.)* Explain that a dispute that erupted when it came time to name Muhammad's successor, after his death, centered around whether or not Muhammad's blood relatives were the only ones who could rightfully take his place.

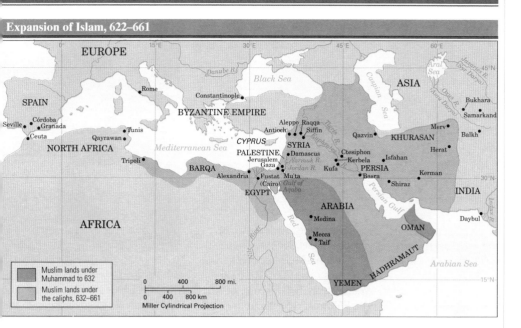

Expansion of Islam, 622–661

EUROPE
SPAIN
Seville • Córdoba • Granada
Ceuta •
NORTH AFRICA
Rome •
Constantinople •
BYZANTINE EMPIRE
Tunis •
Qayrawan •
Mediterranean Sea
Tripoli •
Danube R.
Black Sea
CYPRUS
Aleppo • Raqqa
Antioch • • Siffin
SYRIA
PALESTINE • Damascus
Jerusalem • Yarmuk R.
Gaza • Jordan R.
BARQA
Alexandria • • Fustat Mu'ta
(Cairo) Gulf of
EGYPT Aqaba
Kufa
AFRICA
Red Sea
ARABIA
• Medina
• Mecca
• Taif
YEMEN
Caspian Sea
ASIA
Aral Sea
Jaxartes R. (Syr Darya) 45°N
Oxus R. (Amu Darya)
Bukhara •
Samarkand •
Qazvin •
KHURASAN
Merv •
Balkh •
Ctesiphon • • Kerbela
PERSIA
Isfahan •
Herat •
• Basra
• Shiraz
Kerman •
Persian Gulf
OMAN
HADHRAMAUT
Arabian Sea
30°N
15°N
INDIA
Daybul •
Indus R.

Muslim lands under Muhammad to 632
Muslim lands under the caliphs, 632–661

0   400   800 mi.
0 400 800 km
Miller Cylindrical Projection

15°E   30°E   45°E   60°E

In 644, on his deathbed, Umar named a **council,** or an assembly, to choose the next caliph. This council appointed Uthman. He, in turn, continued to conquer other lands and expand the empire. As you can see on the map above, Muslim forces had pushed into North Africa and had completed the conquest of Persia by 661. ■

Early Political Division

During the time of the empire's rapid expansion, internal troubles plagued the Muslim government. Uthman made enemies at home by appointing members of his own family as regional governors of the empire. This caused bitter jealousy among other families. In 656, an angry mob of about 500 murdered Uthman.

This situation threatened the unity of the Muslim state. Ali was the natural choice for leadership, having participated in the election of previous leaders. He had been among Muhammad's most trusted and loyal companions. Muawiya ('mu AH wih ya), a relative of Uthman, developed a following in

Syria, where he was governor.

Muawiya challenged Ali by demanding that the murderers be punished immediately. He then challenged Ali's right to rule. This forced Ali to oppose him for the sake of unity. Before the two opposing camps came to battle, Ali agreed to negotiate, but talks failed to solve the conflict. Ali ruled for only two years before he was murdered by an angry former supporter. In 661, Muawiya became caliph.

The Shiites

The problem that had caused the civil war remained. Who was Muhammad's rightful successor—

The four caliphs after Muhammad greatly expanded the Muslim Empire. About how many times larger was it in 661 than in 632?

■ *Why was the expansion of the Muslim Empire so successful?*

Across Time & Space

The largest Muslim communities today are in South and Southeast Asia, Africa, and the Middle East. In 1995 there were approximately 1.2 billion Muslims in the world. There are about 5 million Muslims in North America.

67

The Roots of Islam

Critical Thinking

Emphasize the fact that Muslim forces enjoyed huge success and expanded the Muslim Empire with lightning speed. Ask students to speculate as to what factors helped Muslims in expanding their empire. *(Warriors were inspired by their religion and their hope to spread it to other peoples; continuity of leadership; Byzantine and Sassanid empires wore each other out with fighting; discontented Byzantine and Sassanid citizens were tired of being overtaxed and poorly treated.)*

◄ *It was about three or four times larger by 661.*

■ *The Muslim army was a strong force that had been united by Muhammad. The Muslim forces conquered lands in the name of Allah. The Muslims could share in the riches of the lands they conquered.*

67

Writing

Have students assume the role of a newly converted Muslim who has learned that Muhammad has just died. Ask them to write a journal entry that describes their thoughts and feelings. Also have them react to Abu Bakr's words on p. 65, and the naming of Abu Bakr as the first caliph.

Map Skills

Have students use the scale on the map on this page to determine the length and width of the empire at its greatest extent in 632 and in 661.

ETHICS
Social Participation

To help students understand the key issues that divided Islam, divide students into those for and against the succession of Ali, and have them debate the issue of succession.

▶ *Muslims are 19.4%.*

■ *The division developed over the question of Muhammad's successor: Sunnis believed that Muslim leadership passed to caliphs elected from Muslim families; Shiites believed that leadership was limited to descendants of Muhammad.*

CLOSE

Have students help you draw a timeline that details the events that followed Muhammad's death. This activity could directly follow the debate suggested above.

68

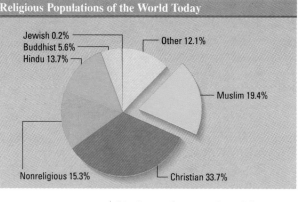

Religious Populations of the World Today

Jewish 0.2%
Buddhist 5.6%
Hindu 13.7%
Other 12.1%
Muslim 19.4%
Nonreligious 15.3%
Christian 33.7%

▲ *What percentage of the world religious population is Muslim?*

■ *How did the division of Muslims into Sunnis and Shiites come about?*

his descendants, such as Ali, or elected caliphs, such as Uthman?

Ali's followers became known as **Shiites** *(shee EYETZ),* from the Arabic meaning "the party of Ali." The Shiites accepted only members of Muhammad's family as his successors. It was their opinion that Ali should have been chosen over Abu Bakr from the beginning. Later, Shiite scholars denied the legitimacy of the first three caliphs, who had not been blood relatives of the prophet.

The Shiites gave Ali the title of the first Imam, meaning divinely guided successor of Muhammad. This concept of the Imam took on a strong sense of spiritual authority.

The Sunnis

Those who claim to follow the Sunna, or example of the prophet Muhammad, are known as **Sunni** Muslims. They accept the election

of the first four caliphs, called the Rightly-Guided Caliphs. They do not attach the same meaning to the Shiite idea of the Imam. Sunnis emphasize Muhammad's teaching that every individual has a direct relationship with God.

The two groups still exist in the Muslim world today. Sunnis make up more than 80 percent of all Muslims. Iran has the largest number of Shiites. Out of a total population of 60 million, over 90 percent are Shiites.

The differences between Sunnis and Shiites have become public knowledge today, but all Muslims remain united by their common faith in Allah. They also share a reverence for the Qur'an as Allah's word and recognize Muhammad as Allah's prophet. ■

R E V I E W

1. **FOCUS** What challenges did Muslims face after Muhammad's death?
2. **CONNECT** Why were many Muslims fearful after the death of Muhammad?
3. **GEOGRAPHY** How far did the Muslim Empire extend under the four caliphs?
4. **CRITICAL THINKING** Do you think the conflict between

Ali and Muawiya was related to the Muslim state's rapid expansion? Give reasons for your answer.

5. **WRITING ACTIVITY** Assume you are a Muslim soldier on your way to conquer Syria in the year A.D. 635. Write three journal entries that reveal your thoughts about Islam, fighting in battle, or life in the desert.

Chapter 3

Homework Options

For each of the key terms in this lesson, have students write a one-sentence definition.

Study Guide: p. 10

Answers to Review Questions

1. The Muslims had to decide who should succeed Muhammad as the leader of Islam. They also felt the call to expand the community of Muslims.
2. Muslims believed that Muhammad, as a prophet, was guided by Allah. Without his strong leadership, they feared that the Muslim community would not hold together.
3. Beyond Arabia, it extended to Syria, Egypt, present-day Iraq, northern Africa, and Persia.

4. The empire's growth must have added urgency to the succession issue. People might have still resented Uthman's appointments. A larger empire might mean more groups struggling for power. A new leader was urgently needed to restore control after Uthman's assassination. The borders had to be defended.

UNDERSTANDING SEQUENCE

Making Parallel Timelines

Here's Why

Most timelines show you dates from a single culture or nation. Some timelines show links between cultural or geographical groups. Parallel timelines show parallels between events and are lined up in parallel.

Some of the events you studied in the Muslim Empire happened at the same time as events in Chapter 2. Parallel timelines help compare different events that happened at the same time.

Here's How

You can make a parallel timeline that helps you see events side by side:

1. Decide what you want to see. You may want to compare the histories of several groups. Or you may have noticed a pattern of events. The timelines below show events in the Muslim Empire and events in other parts of the world.

2. Decide what span of time your timelines will cover. Make sure your timelines are divided into equal and parallel parts. The timelines below cover A.D. 450–700. They are divided into five 50-year segments.

3. Gather dates and information about events for each part of the timeline.

4. Plot the events near the appropriate dates on the timeline. What was going on in the world during the Hijrah?

Try It

Copy the timeline below and plot these events:
- 661, Muslim Empire in North Africa and Persia
- 528, Justinian Code
- 630, Muhammad arrives in Mecca
- 537, New Hagia Sophia in Constantinople

Apply It

Create a parallel timeline. On one part, show events in your own life; on another part, show some significant events that happened in the United States. Find the U.S. dates in a yearbook or an almanac.

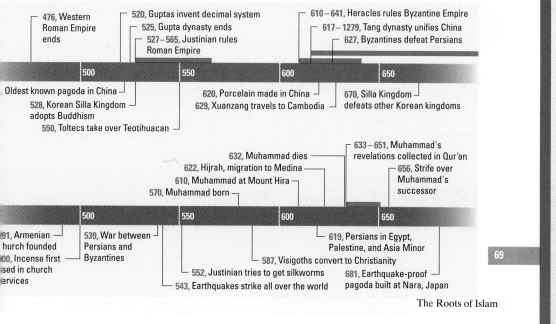

The Roots of Islam

UNDERSTANDING SEQUENCE

This skills feature uses two parallel timelines to show different events at the same time. The top timeline shows events from Chapter 2 above the line, and events elsewhere in the world below it. The bottom timeline shows the same for Chapter 3.

HISTORY

Visual Learning

Have students first cover the top timeline and concentrate on the bottom timeline. Ask which part shows events in Arabia *(the upper part)* and which part shows events elsewhere *(the lower part)*.

Then do the same with the top one. The upper part shows events from Chapter 2 (Byzantines, Guptas, and Chinese) and the lower, events elsewhere.

Explain that the timelines are arranged in order to show parallels between events that happened at the same time.

Have students lay a ruler vertically over both timelines. Point out how the divisions of the timelines line up. Ask what events took place around the years 610–620. *(Heracles rules Byzantine Empire, porcelain made in China, Muhammad at Mount Hira, Persians in Middle East.)* Then review the steps in Here's How.

Making Timelines

Divide the class into small groups. Have each group make a parallel timeline. On the top timeline, they should show events in their classroom or community that occurred during the last year. On the bottom timeline, they should show events that happened anywhere in the world except the United States.

Answers to Try It

These events should be above the top timeline: 528, Justinian Code; 537, New Hagia Sophia in Constantinople. These events should be above the bottom timeline: 630, Muhammad arrives in Mecca; 661, Muslim Empire includes North Africa and Persia.

Answers to Apply It

Answers will vary.

Objective

Make and use parallel timelines. (Visual Learning 2)

Answers to Reviewing Key Terms

A. Answers:
1. nomad
2. pilgrimage
3. oasis
4. Islam

B. Sample answers:
1. Muhammad destroyed the **idols** in the Ka'bah because they represented many gods, and he believed only in Allah.
2. The **Qur'an** is a collection of Muhammad's revelations from Allah.
3. **Monotheism,** the belief in one God, is a key part of Islam.
4. A **Muslim** is a follower of Islam.
5. The **Sunna** includes the example, customs, and traditions that Muhammad practiced and taught.
6. A **mosque** is a Muslim temple.
7. A **council,** or assembly, chose Muhammad's successor.
8. The **caliph** acts as the political and military leader of Muslims.
9. A **Shiite** believes that only a descendant of Muhammad can lead Muslims.
10. A **Sunni** accepts the succession of the first four caliphs.
11. Families formed **tribes** to protect themselves from raiders.

Answers to Exploring Concepts

A. Answers:
500: Mecca is most important stop along the caravan routes.
622: Hijrah marks beginning of Muslim calendar.
630: Muhammad returns to Mecca.
632: Muhammad dies.
633: Collecting of revelations for Qur'an begins.
661: Muawiya becomes caliph.

70

B. Sample answers:
1. Trade, water, and pilgrimage first attracted people to Mecca; today Muslims go there on pilgrimage.
2. Quraysh demanded payment from travelers for the right to worship and trade there; made treaties with nearby peoples to ensure caravans' safe passage; sponsored caravans themselves.
3. Nomadic herders and townspeople exchanged goods and information.

Chapter Review

Reviewing Key Terms

caliph (p. 66)
council (p. 67)
idol (p. 55)
Islam (p. 60)
monotheism (p. 59)
mosque (p. 60)
Muslim (p. 60)
nomad (p. 53)

oasis (p. 53)
pilgrimage (p. 57)
Qur'an (p. 58)
Shiite (p. 67)
Sunna (p. 61)
Sunni (p. 68)
tribe (p. 55)

A. The following quotations express the feelings of various people. For each statement, identify the key term most closely associated with it.
1. "With my family always moving to the next pastureland, I look forward to seeing old friends."
2. "I enjoy traveling to religious sites."
3. "They say it's green and fertile enough there to grow crops."
4. "Muhammad taught that the faith was named 'submission to Allah.'"

B. Write one or two sentences telling how each key term below is related to Islam.
1. idol
2. Qur'an
3. monotheism
4. Muslim
5. Sunna
6. mosque
7. council
8. caliph
9. Shiite
10. Sunni
11. tribe

Exploring Concepts

A. Many important events occurred between 500 and 700 in the history of Mecca and Islam. Copy the timeline on your own paper. Then fill in the event that goes with each date.

B. On your own paper, write one or two sentences to answer each of the following questions. Use facts and details from the chapter for your answers.
1. Why were people first attracted to Mecca, and why do they still go there today?
2. How did Quraysh make Mecca the most prosperous trade center in Arabia by the late 500s?
3. What did early nomadic families and townspeople offer each other?
4. What important belief do Muslims share with Jews and Christians?
5. Why did the Sunnis and Shiites disagree about who should be caliph?
6. How did trade introduce Arab city dwellers to other cultures?
7. How did the Quraysh ensure peaceful pilgrimages?
8. How did the Arabs bring Islam to Africa and Asia?
9. Why did Muhammad think he was a messenger of God?

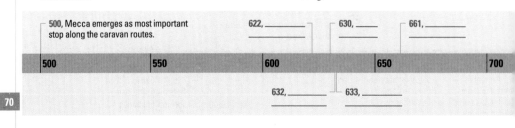

500, Mecca emerges as most important stop along the caravan routes.
622, _____
630, _____
661, _____
632, _____
633, _____

500 550 600 650 700

70

Chapter 3

---

4. Muslims believe in only one God.
5. Shiites believed only members of Muhammad's family should be successors. Sunnis believed in the succession of the first four caliphs.
6. Merchants sold many wares from faraway lands and brought foreign traders to Arabia.
7. Quraysh forbade fighting along trade routes four months of each year.
8. They united as Muslims, formed armies, and fought to take over foreign lands and spread their religion.

9. He received revelations from God through the angel Gabriel.

Reviewing Skills

1. Create a parallel timeline comparing events that took place in the Muslim Empire during the time period from A.D. 630 through 670. You read about the following events in the expansion of the Muslim Empire in Lesson 3:
   - 633, Muslim forces move north into Syria and east into Mesopotamia.
   - 648, Muslim forces push into North Africa.
   - 661, Muslims complete conquest of Persia.

   Find and list dates from Lesson 3 for the following problems of the Muslim government after 630:
   - Muhammad dies suddenly.
   - First caliph Abu Bakr dies.

   - Caliph Umar dies.
   - Caliph Uthman murdered by angry mob of 500 people.
   - Ali is murdered, and Muawiya becomes undisputed caliph.

   Plot the dates of all these events from Lesson 3 in the appropriate places on your timeline.
2. When it is 7 A.M. on Tuesday in Teheran, Iran, what time and day is it in New York City? You may need to look at the time-zone map on pages 8 and 9 to find the answer.
3. What would you draw to show the events that took place during several specific times in history?

Using Critical Thinking

1. Think about the geography of Arabia and the people who lived there. Some people were nomadic herders, some were settled farmers, and some were city-living merchants or artisans. Why do you think these three ways of life grew up? How did they work together to create a successful society?
2. Anwar el-Sadat, a Muslim and the late president of Egypt, once said: "There can be hope only for a society that acts as one big family, not as many separate ones." How would the Muslims in A.D. 630 to 660 have responded to this statement?
3. Ali, Muhammad's son-in-law, wrote: "He who has a thousand friends has not a friend to spare; and he who has one enemy will meet him everywhere." How could you apply this to nations today? Give some examples from today's news that support your opinion.
4. Imagine you are a nomad with a family to support living around A.D. 500. You must decide whether to continue wandering or to settle down at an oasis. What is your future plan for you and your family? What are the dangers you face living at that time in history?

Preparing for Citizenship

1. **WRITING ACTIVITY** You leave your home in Alexandria for the pilgrimage to Mecca. Using the map on page 53 and other atlases, write a letter describing your route, the landscapes and peoples you see as you travel, and any incidents that happen along the way. Describe what you see in Mecca.
2. **COLLABORATIVE LEARNING** Form small groups of students to build a miniature mosque. You may decide to use cardboard, papier-mâché, or other materials. Have one member do research at the library to find out what the insides of mosques look like. Have another member design a building plan. And have two members collect the building materials. Together, construct the mosque according to your plan.

The Roots of Islam

1. Problems of Muslim government:
   632: Muhammad dies.
   634: First caliph Abu Bakr dies.
   644: Caliph Umar dies.
   656: Caliph Uthman murdered by angry mob of 500 people.
   661: Ali is murdered, and Muawiya becomes undisputed caliph.
2. 10 P.M. on Monday.
3. A timeline.

Answers to Using Critical Thinking
1. Students should mention geographical influences such as presence of water and irrigation, location of trade routes and sea ports, adaptability of herding animals, etc. They should also mention dependence of each group on the other for various goods and services.
2. Muslims in 630 to 660 might have said that being right was more important than acting as a family.
3. Students' responses will vary. While the United States has many allies around the world, there are some countries that present problems for us. For example, illegal drugs come into the United States in alarming numbers from other countries. As hard as the United States tries to stop the flow of drugs, they continue. So one "enemy," or negative situation, seems to be everywhere.
4. Students might answer that they will settle down at an oasis and begin farming to support their families. They will address the problems of having enough food, dealing with raiders, and other matters of daily survival.

Answers to Preparing for Citizenship
1. **WRITING ACTIVITY** You might direct students to the library to consult geography books about Egypt, the Sinai Peninsula, and Arabia.
2. **COLLABORATIVE LEARNING** Have the researchers go to the library and consult the *Readers' Guide to Periodical Literature* to find issues of *National Geographic* and other magazines with pictures of mosques. Allow groups to decide how to divide up the tasks prior to the actual construction, in which all share. Also, supply them with sample floor plans of houses to help them draw their plans. Suggest that the "builders" leave the back of the miniature mosque open so that details they add to the inside can be displayed.

Planning at a Glance
The Empire of Islam

	Objectives	Reading Support *and* Other Resources	Diverse Learning Strategies

Lesson 1
A Century of Expansion
pp. 78–84 2–3 days
 	
Literature Selections of **Medieval Muslim Literature** *pp. 74–77*
	• Describe the growth of the Muslim Empire and the Umayyad rise to power.
	• Identify the Umayyad system of government.
	• Analyze the impact of the Umayyad rule on Muslim culture and commerce.
	• Explain the decline of Umayyad control in the eastern Muslim Empire.
		• **Workbook** or **Reading Support:** pp. 41–44
		  Review p. 10
		  Lesson Support/Transition p. 10
		  Multi-lang. Sum. pp. 19–20
		• **Other Resources:** Geography Kit; Posters 1, 3; Study Guide p. 12
			Access Strat. **(SDAIE)** TE p. 79
			Access Act. **(Extra Support)** TE p. 79
			Writing **(GATE)** TE p. 80
			Music Connection **(Auditory)** TE p. 81
			
			Audiotapes of Multi-language Lesson Summaries **(Auditory)**

Lesson 2
The Golden Age
pp. 85–92 2–3 days
	• Analyze the strengths of the Abbasid government.
	• Describe the commercial wealth of Baghdad.
	• Summarize Abbasid achievements in art, literature, and science.
	• Explain the decline and eventual demise of the Abbasid Empire.
		• **Workbook** or **Reading Support:** pp. 45–48
		  Review p. 11
		  Lesson Support/Transition p. 11
		  Multi-lang. Sum. pp. 21–22
		• **Other Resources:** Geography Kit, Study Guide p. 13
			Access Act. **(SDAIE)** TE p. 86
			Map and Globe Skills **(Visual)** TE p. 87
			Collaborative Act. **(Kinesthetic)** TE p. 88
			Role Playing **(Auditory)** TE p. 91
			
			Audiotapes of Multi-language Lesson Summaries **(Auditory)**

Exploring **Origins of Sports and Games** *p. 93*	• Describe the equipment and rules of sports and games. • Explain the origins of sports and games and their development over time.		Activity **(Kinesthetic)** TE p. 93
Skill: **Identifying Main Ideas** *p. 94* 1 day	• Identify main ideas and supporting details in paragraphs.	• **Other Resources:** Study Guide p. 14	

Lesson 3
Islamic Spain
pp. 95–100 2–3 days
	• Explain the success of the Umayyads in unifying Spain under Muslim rule.
	• Assess Cordoba's position as the cultural and intellectual center of the Muslim West.
	• Describe the decline of the Muslim state in Spain.
		• **Workbook** or **Reading Support:** pp. 49–52
		  Review p. 12
		  Lesson Support/Transition p. 12
		  Multi-lang. Sum. pp. 23–24
		• **Other Resources:** Geography Kit, Study Guide p. 15
			Access Act. **(Extra Support)** TE p. 96
			Access Strat. **(SDAIE)** TE p. 96
			Social Participation **(Kinesthetic)** TE p. 98
			Interviewing **(Auditory)** TE p. 98
			
			Audiotapes of Multi-language Lesson Summaries **(Auditory)**

Skill: Using the *Readers' Guide* *p. 101* 1 day	• Identify elements of an entry to the *Readers' Guide to Periodical Literature* and use the *Readers' Guide* to make a list of entries for a given topic.	• **Other Resources:** Study Guide p. 16	
Chapter Review *pp. 102–103* 1 day		Chapter 4 Test pp. 13–16 *(See facsimiles on TE p. 562.)*	Assessment Multiple-Use Masters pp. 73–80

Reading Support Resources *for Every Lesson*

Reading and Review

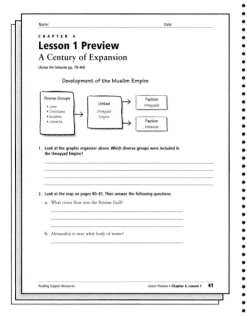

- **Chapter Overview*** p. 40
- **Lesson Previews*** using graphic organizers from the Teacher's Edition pp. 41, 45, 49
- **Reading Strategies*** pp. 42, 46, 50
- **Lesson Summaries*** pp. 43–44, 47–48, 51–52
- **Lesson Reviews** pp. 10, 11, 12

* **Workbook** includes starred items.

Multi-language Summaries

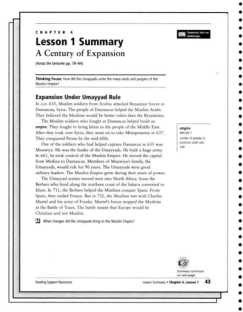

Lesson Summaries in:

- English (See Reading and Review.)
- Spanish pp. 43–44, 47–48, 51–52
- Chinese pp. 19–24
- Hmong pp. 19–24
- Khmer pp. 19–24
- Vietnamese pp. 19–24

 Summaries available on audiotapes

Lesson Support /Transition
S D A I E

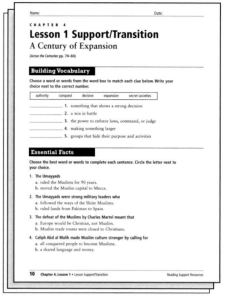

Activities for SDAIE
Specially **D**esigned **A**cademic **I**nstruction in **E**nglish

- **Lesson Support/Transition** pp. 10, 11, 12

 ## Technology Options

Internet Support

http://www.eduplace.com

Social Studies Center at Education Place

Internet support for Chapter 4:

- *Lesson at a Glance*
- *The Great Mosque at Cordoba*
- *An Abbasid Scholar*

Software

Student Writing Center ® (CD-ROM) (Macintosh® or Windows®)

School to Career

The Abbasids helped spread bookmaking throughout the Muslim world. Ask students to create a chart comparing how books were made in the past and how they are made today. How have the skills and responsibilities of the people in the profession changed over the years?

Character Education

A country's military not only has the responsibility of protecting its borders, but also of defending and preserving its ideals. Ask students to think about the ideals the U.S. military defends. What would students be willing to fight for and defend?

CHAPTER
PREVIEW

Tell the students to read the chapter title and the paragraph that follows. Locate Baghdad and Cordoba on a large map of Eurasia. Point out that these two cities were two of the focal points of the vast empire controlled by the Muslims.

Looking Back

What was the extent of the Muslim Empire under the first four caliphs? *(It extended throughout the Arabian peninsula, Egypt, and northern Africa just west of Egypt, and northeast to just beyond the Caspian Sea.)*

Looking Forward

Tell students that they will read about the Muslim Empire and the flourishing of Muslim culture in the cities of Baghdad and Cordoba in Lessons 1–3: A Century of Expansion, The Golden Age, and Islamic Spain.

Lesson 1 describes how the Umayyads rose to power and what life was like under Umayyad rule.

Chapter 4
The Empire of Islam

To the east in Mesopotamia, the grand city of Baghdad arose. "It will surely be the most flourishing city in the world," boasted the caliph. To the west in Spain, an equally grand city blossomed. "Do not speak to me of the court of Baghdad nor of its magnificence. . . ," wrote a poet, "because there is no place like Cordoba anywhere on this earth." As Muslim influence spread from the Near East to the Atlantic Ocean, these two cities became centers of Muslim trade, art, and learning.

During the 600s, Muslims conquered much of the Middle East. People converted to Islam and built mosques, like this one in Qum, Iran.

c. 650 Muslims conquer Persia and take treasures such as the gold and silver Sassanid dish (above) showing a lion hunt.

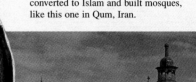

| 600 | 800 | 1000 |

768 Germanic leader Charlemagne becomes emperor of the former Western Roman Empire.

72

635

BACKGROUND

As the Muslim Empire evolved between A.D. 600 and 1250, rulers faced the ongoing problem of combating religious, cultural, and political fragmentation. Disunifying forces led to periodic political breakdowns, which, in turn, gave rise to new states under new leaders or in a new form.

Forces of Fragmentation

The eastern Umayyad, Abbasid, and Spanish Umayyad dynasties shared a common problem: unifying a diverse empire. All of them had to deal with subjects who were neither Muslim nor Arab. Although conversion of nonbelievers to Islam would have reduced religious disparity in the empire, Muslim rulers were reluctant to open the door to non-Arab influences on the Islamic faith. In addition, rulers relied on the taxes paid by non-Muslims to support large standing armies and an

extravagant imperial lifestyle.

Even among the Muslims themselves, a dispute over succession resulted in a major schism between the Abbasids and the Umayyads. The fall of the eastern Umayyad leaders in 750 led to the establishment of an independent Umayyad state in Spain in 756.

Steps Toward Unity

Muawiya, the first caliph of the Umayyad Dynasty, moved the Muslim capital from Medina to the more central city of Damascus He began the practice of appointing a son as

By the late 1300s, when this woman and child were painted, there were huge Muslim states throughout Asia and Africa.

Understanding the Visuals

The mosque (p. 72), the Shrine of Hazrat Ma'sumeh, shows the onion-shaped dome and minarets typical of Muslim architecture. Qum is an especially holy city for Shiites. Some ten kings and 400 saints are buried in and around the city. Built in the early 1600s, the Hazrat Ma'sumeh, or Shrine of Fatima, honors the sister of the Imam Riza.

The casbah ruins are near the city of Ouarzazate in southwestern Morocco.

Understanding Chronology

Tell students to note on the timeline the date 1492, which marks the end of Muslim rule in Spain. Discuss how this date relates to United States history.

1492 Sultan Muhammad XI surrenders, ending Muslim rule in Spain. His gold ceremonial sword is shown to the right.

1200	1400	1600

c. 1277 Invaders from central Asia conquer China.

1453 The Byzantine Empire falls to the Ottoman Turks.

73

1492

73

the next caliph, thus providing for the stable transmission of power. A later caliph then declared Arabic the official language for government and religious affairs. He also instituted a common system of coinage, thereby promoting trade among all regions of the empire.

The Abbasids, who seized control of the Muslim Empire in 750, moved the capital to Baghdad, closer to their own center of power. The new capital became a thriving international trade center that brought great wealth to the empire and its rulers. Baghdad also became a center of learning and the arts.

The Abbasids welcomed non-Muslim contributions to learning and art as well as participation in local and imperial government by Persians and other non-Arab Muslims.

In Muslim Spain, the Umayyads continued the traditions of building mosques and establishing an elaborate and strategically located capital. Like Baghdad, Cordoba became a cultural and intellectual center in which

non-Muslims and non-Arabs played important roles.

The Spanish Umayyads established a large army to protect the empire from attacks by northern Christians or Muslim rulers of North Africa.

INTRODUCE

As the Muslim Empire grew, peoples from varied cultures became part of the empire. In making Arabic the language of the empire, however, the Umayyads saw to it that these cultures could converse with each other. In this short collection of medieval Muslim writings, there are samples of three different genres. The first piece is a story, an example of Muslim Adab literature, which aims at moral education. The second is a letter, perhaps more of an essay, in which the author argues for the new invention of paper by way of disparaging the old writing matter, parchment. Finally we have three poems from Muslim Spain that show not only depth of thought but beautiful imagery.

READ AND RESPOND

Most students will enjoy reading these selections independently. After the students have read them, discuss the purpose-setting questions with them, referring to the background information.

Before students read this story, introduce the word "cadi," or judge. Ask them how important they think judges are, and what might be proper behavior for a judge.

In Chapter 3 you learned about the rise and expansion of Islam. These writings are examples of the great cultural flowering that Islam brought to Asia, Africa, and Europe.

cadi (KAH dee), **magistrate** a judge

sedate calm
composed not excitable
impassive showing no emotion

compelled forced

tenure a period of time in a particular position

assessors officials to evaluate property for taxation

LITERATURE

Medieval Muslim Writings

With the great explosion of learning in Baghdad and Cordoba and the love of Muslims for the beauty of the Arabic language, stories, essays, and poems were a natural way for people to organize what they had learned and to express their feelings. These short pieces on various topics could be used to teach a moral, to send information to friends, to provoke a response from other scholars, or just to express what was in the heart. What values are expressed by these medieval Muslim writings?

The Cadi and the Fly

Al-Jahiz

Al-Jahiz (ahl JAH heeth) was born in the port of Basra about 776, when the city was at its height of cultural and commercial importance. He traced his family roots to East Africa and became a famous figure in Muslim culture. He lived for many years at Baghdad and became a writer, scholar, and adviser at the court of the caliphs. His story titled The Cadi and the Fly *(a cadi is a judge) is a story with a moral, a piece of wise teaching that comes at the end.*

There can never have been a magistrate as sedate, composed, dignified, impassive, self-controlled or precise in his movements as a cadi we had at Basra called 'Abd Allah Ibn Sawwar.

He used to say the morning prayer at home, though he lived quite near the mosque, and then go to his court, where he would wrap his robes around him and sit down without supporting himself on anything as he did so. He sat bolt upright and stock still, neither turning round in his seat, opening his coat, crossing his legs, or leaning on either arm of the chair; he was like a statue.

He would remain thus until the noon prayer compelled him to rise, then sit down again and take up the same posture until the time of the afternoon prayer; having accomplished that, he would remain motionless until sunset, when he would get up, say his prayers, and sometimes (what am I saying? often, rather) return to his seat and deal with a multitude of deeds, contracts, and miscellaneous documents. Then he would say his evening prayer and go home. If the truth be told, he never once got up to go to the lavatory during the whole of his tenure of office: he did not need to, since he never felt like a drink of water or other beverage. Such was his routine all the year round, winter and summer, whether the days were long or short. He never so much as lifted his hand or inclined his head, but limited himself to moving his lips.

One day, when his assessors and the public had taken their place beside him, in front of him and in the gallery, a fly settled on his nose. It lingered there awhile, and then moved to the corner of his eye. He left it

---

Background

Al-Jahiz's real name was Abu Othman Amr ibn Bahr. Al-Jahiz is how he was known; it means "the goggle-eyed one." He was born to an African family living at Basra of *mawla* status, that is, of a slave or client tribe. His education was ordinary, but his sharp, probing mind helped him rise to a high position at court. He lived in Baghdad during the years immediately after it was built and certainly observed and took part in the tremendous growth in Abbasid culture. He must have seen the water-powered Baghdad paper factory being built. As a literary man, his interest in paper versus parchment went beyond the theoretical, since for him they were the tools of his trade.

alone and endured its biting, just as he had armed himself with patience when it settled on his nose, neither twitching his nostrils, shaking his head, or waving it away with a finger. However, since the fly was becoming really persistent, causing him acute pain and moving towards a spot where it was beyond bearing, he blinked his eyelid. The fly did not go away. This persistence drove him to blink repeatedly, whereupon the fly moved away until the eyelid stopped moving, then returned to the corner of the eye even more fiercely than before and stuck its sting into an already sore spot. The cadi's endurance was weakening and his irritation growing: he blinked harder and more rapidly. The fly went away for a moment, then settled again and became so persistent that our cadi, his patience completely at an end, was reduced to driving it away with his hand: Everyone in court was watching this and pretending not to see it. The fly went away until he dropped his hand, then returned to the charge and compelled him to protect his face with the hem of his sleeve, not once but several times.

The magistrate realized that no detail of this scene was escaping his assessors and the public. When he caught their eye, he exclaimed: "I swear the fly is more persistent than the cockroach and more presumptuous than the crow! God forgive me! How many men are infatuated with their own persons! But God acquaints them with their hidden weakness! Now I know I am but a weakling, seeing that God's most feeble creature has vanquished and confounded me!" Then he recited this verse: "And if the fly should rob them of aught, the gods of the idolaters would be unable to restore it to them. Worshipper and idol are both powerless." [Qur'an, 22:72–73].

endurance the ability to withstand hardship

presumptuous going beyond what is right or proper
infatuated to be so in love as to lose one's reason
aught (AHT) anything

◄ Why do you think the cadi didn't want to move? *(He wanted to show people that his devotion to justice was so great he could not be distracted.)* How would you explain the quotation from the Qur'an? *(The gods of the idol-worshippers are so powerless that they couldn't even restore something stolen by a fly.)*

Further Reading

Muhammad: His Life Based on the Earliest Sources. Martin Lings. An engaging narrative of the life of the prophet Muhammad, based on the biography by Ibn Hisham.

Anthology of Islamic Literature: From the Rise of Islam to Modern Times. James Kritzeck. A useful compendium of literature, poetry, tales, historical treatises, and other genres of writing.

The Travels of Ibn Jubayr. R.J.C. Broadhurst. Follow the adventures of a 12th-century Muslim from Spain as he journeys throughout the Mediterranean world on his way to Mecca.

Access Strategy

Tell students that *The Cadi and the Fly* is an example of literature that is meant to teach a lesson about values. The cadi learns that his great pride is simply vanity, and can be dislodged by something as small as a fly.

Good teaching stories usually end with a moral or proverb, but the stories themselves must also illustrate that teaching. Collect such sayings and pass them out to students. Then have the students write short stories that illustrate the sayings and end with someone giving voice to the saying itself.

► What are Al-Jahiz's main arguments against parchment? *(heavy and awkward, useless in wet weather, distorts writing, smells, expensive, turns yellow, etc.)* Ask students to imagine two friendly writers, one of whom writes on paper, the other on a computer. Have them write two letters, each of which argues for a different writing medium.

cumbersome difficult to handle because of size or weight

suffice to be enough

provisions supplies

palimpsest (puh LIHMP sehst) a manuscript, usually papyrus or parchment, that has been erased and written over many times; often the old writing still shows through

The Disadvantages of Parchment

Al-Jahiz

Al-Jahiz lived at a time when paper had just been brought from China to the Muslim world. Most people still wrote on parchment, animal skins that had been scraped clean and treated for taking ink. In this letter, Al-Jahiz argues to a friend against using it anymore. Paper came to be made at Baghdad by factories along the Tigris River. There, water-powered trip hammers processed the pulp. It was many years before Europe could stop importing paper from the Muslim world and make its own.

What is it to you that all my books are written on China paper or Khurasan paper? Explain why you have pressed on me the advantages of using parchment and urged me to write on hide, when you know very well that parchment is heavy and cumbersome, is useless if it gets damp, and swells in wet weather— so much so that were its sole disadvantage to make its users hate rainy days, and its owners regard a shower as a nightmare, this alone would be reason enough for giving up the stuff. You know very well that on rainy days copyists do not write a single line or cut a single skin.

Parchment has only to get moist, let alone left out in the rain or dipped in water, for it to bulge and stretch; and then it does not return to its original state, but dries noticeably shrunk and badly wrinkled. What is more, it smells worse, is more expensive, and lends itself more readily to fraud: Wasit skins are passed off as Kufa ones, and Basra ones as Wasit ones. You are obliged to leave it to age in order to get rid of the smell and for the hair to fall out; it is fuller of lumps and flaws, more is wasted in scraps and clipping, it turns yellow sooner, and the writing very quickly disappears altogether. If a scholar wished to take with him enough parchment for his journey, a camel-load would not suffice, whereas the equivalent in *qutni* [cotton-fiber paper] could be carried with his provisions.

You said: "You should use parchment because it stands up better to scratching out and correction, and also to repeated borrowing and handling; then unwanted sheets are still worth something, palimpsests can be re-used, and second-hand parchment does the same job as new. Writing-books of *qutni* are of little value on the market, even if they contain the most original texts, the choicest rarities, and the most priceless learning. If you went to sell books of an equivalent number of parchment pages containing nothing but the feeble poetry and the idlest gossip, they would be in much greater demand." And you added: "Hide is entrusted with the accounts of the administrative system, with title-deeds, diplomas, contracts and surveys; sculptors' sketches are made on it, postal pouches are made out of it, and it is used for making bags, lids for jars and stoppers for bottles." You did me a grave disservice when you made me take to using parchment instead of paper, and were the cause of my misfortune when you made me exchange light writing-books for volumes too heavy to hold, that crush people's chests, bow their backs, and make them blind.

76

Holding a Debate

Arabic was declared the official language of the Muslim Empire in the early 700s. While most people spoke their own languages, Arabic was required for government business and religious affairs. In addition, scholars and thinkers all over the Muslim Empire were able to converse with each other because Arabic was the language of intellectual pursuits.

Ask students to look at the map of world languages on p. 529. Compare it with the map on pp. 80–81, and check that they understand

that people from Spain to Afghanistan could all share a common language.

Ask if there is any language nowadays that compares to Arabic in the Muslim Empire. Tell them that with the great growth of the Internet, English is fast becoming a universal language. Divide the class in two and hold a debate on the following issue: "Resolved, that making English the official language of the Internet will harm the development of other languages around the world."

Poems from Muslim Spain

Ibn Sa'id al-Maghribi was born in Granada, Spain, in 1213, but during his life traveled to such places as North Africa, Cairo, Baghdad, and Mecca. He completed a 15-volume anthology of poems that his great-grandfather had begun and which had taken over 100 years to complete. Here are three works by poets from the 11th, 12th, and 13th centuries. The poems give evidence of the water-related technology that eventually spread from Muslim lands to Europe. As you read these poems, ask yourself what water represents in each of them.

Good Deeds At Random

Scatter your good deeds all around, not caring
    whether they fall on those near or far away,
Just as the rain never cares where the clouds pour it out,
    whether on fertile ground or on rocks.

Ibn Siraj, Cordoba
died 1114

The Spinning Water Wheel

How wonderful is the water wheel! It spins around like a celestial
    sphere, yet there are no stars on it.
It was placed over the river by hands that decreed that it refresh others'
    spirits as it, itself, grows tired.
It is like a free man, in chains, or like a prisoner marching freely.
Water rises and falls from the wheel as if it were a cloud that draws
    water from the sea and later pours it out.
The eyes fell in love with it, for it is a boon companion to the garden, a
    cupbearer who doesn't drink.

Ibn al-Abbar, Valencia
died 1260

celestial heavenly, planetary
decreed commanded

boon companion best friend

The Fountain

Oh, the beauty of the fountain, pelting the horizon with
    shooting stars, leaping and jumping around playfully;
Bubbles of water burst out of it, gushing into its basin
    like a frightened snake,
as if it used to move back and forth beneath the earth, but
    when it has the chance, it quickly escaped,
And settled into the basin, happy with its new home, and
    in amazement kept smiling, showing its bubbles.
And the branches hover overhead, about to kiss it as it smiles,
    revealing the whiteness of its teeth.

Ibn al-Ra'i'ah, Seville
flourished in 13th century

hover to float in the air

77

◄ Have students write about what water represents in each of these poems. *(In the first poem, rainfall represents the freedom and randomness with which one should do good deeds. In the second poem, water is a treasured commodity, dispensed by a water wheel that works tirelessly for us. In the last poem, water creates images of shooting stars and a darting, bubbling snake.)*

EXTEND

Have students pick one genre from this collection—stories with morals, letters, or poems—and find examples of similar pieces from other cultures. They should pick the piece they feel is most similar to the Muslim work and read it aloud in class. Students can look through literature anthologies, or ask a librarian's help in tracking down literature from other cultures. Students should find other stories that clearly illustrate and then spell out a moral; other letters that argue clearly for or against something; or other poems that use water imagery.

77

Writing Poetry

Bring in some music that is evocative of water. You might try Debussy's *La Mer*, Dvořák's *The Moldau*, or Respighi's *Fountains of Rome*. Explain that each of these is a painting in music of a body of water. Have students close their eyes and put their heads down and picture the water. When the music is over, while the students' eyes are still closed, ask them to pick one image of water that came to them while listening and focus on that. After they have had some time to fix that image in their minds, ask students to write poems that convey those images to others.

Further Reading

You may want to find more examples of Muslim literature. A good collection is *Beyond A Thousand and One Nights Literature Sampler*, published by the Council on Islamic Education, P.O. Box 20186, Fountain Valley, CA 92728-0186.

78

INTRODUCE

Encourage students to think about the title of the lesson. Discuss who or what is expanding. *(Muslim Empire.)* Then ask students to restate the title. *(Perhaps "100 Years of Growth.")* Have students read the Thinking Focus and make predictions about which other lands and peoples became part of the Muslim Empire. Have students look for information related to their predictions as they read the lesson.

Key Terms

Vocabulary Strategies: T36–T37
empire—a political unit often made up of peoples or provinces ruled by a single supreme authority
bureaucracy—a type of organization structured like a pyramid, with one person at the top and many at the bottom; workers at each level supervise those below them
emir—a prince, chieftain, or governor, especially in the Middle East
dissent—to disagree, especially with the accepted doctrine of an established religion

78

| 600 | 635 | 750 | 800 | 1000 | 1200 | 1400 | 1600 |

LESSON 1

A Century of Expansion

How did the Umayyads unite the many lands and peoples of the Muslim Empire?

Key Terms

- empire
- bureaucracy
- emir
- dissent

Muslim soldiers from Arabia attacked Damascus, Syria, in A.D. 635. The Persians and Byzantines had fought back and forth over the territory of Syria for generations. Many inhabitants of Damascus helped the Muslims, expecting their rule to be better than the previous rulers'.

Some soldiers, with their lances, flung small pots of burning oil over the wall, creating smoke and flames that could not be put out. Others loaded catapults with rocks to rain down on the citizens. By nightfall the battle was won. A treaty was drawn up:

In the name of Allah, the compassionate, the Merciful. This is what Khalid ibn al-Walid would grant the inhabitants of Damascus if he enters: he promises security for their lives, property, and churches. Their city wall shall not be demolished, nor shall any Muslim be quartered in their houses. We give them the pact of Allah and the protection of His prophet, the Caliph, and the believers. So long as they pay jizya tax, nothing but good shall befall them.

Expansion Under Umayyad Rule

The Muslim soldiers who fought the Byzantines at Damascus helped to create an **empire,** a number of peoples or provinces ruled by one central authority. After capturing Syria, the victorious Muslim armies went on to conquer Mesopotamia in 637.

By the middle of the 600s, Persia fell to the Muslims. The Muslim Empire then expanded farther to the east by securing the lands that are today known as Turkmenistan, Afghanistan, and Pakistan.

The Umayyads

The Umayyads *(oo MAY yahds)* fought for Islam in these eastern conquests. The Umayyad leader, Muawiya *(mu AH wih ya),* was one of the soldiers who had helped capture Damascus in 635. He had served for 25 years as the Muslim governor of Syria. During that time, Muawiya had built up a devoted army of followers. After the assassination of the fourth caliph, Muawiya had enough support to take control of the empire in 661.

Chapter 4

Objectives

1. Describe the growth of the Muslim Empire and the Umayyad rise to power.
2. Identify the Umayyad system of government.
3. Analyze the impact of the Umayyad rule on Muslim culture and commerce.
4. Explain the decline of Umayyad control in the eastern Muslim Empire.

Graphic Overview

This Graphic Overview shows major changes in the Muslim Empire during its century of expansion.

Diverse Groups
- Jews
- Christians
- Muslims
- converts

→ **United**
Umayyad Empire

→ **Faction**
Umayyads

→ **Faction**
Abbasids

Umayyad Changes

Muawiya moved the capital from Muhammad's home, Medina in Arabia, to his own, more central city of Damascus in Syria. From this political and military center, he could control the empire.

Muawiya began the practice of appointing a son as the next caliph. He founded a tradition of continuous rule by one family. The Umayyads ruled for 90 years.

Westward Expansion

The Umayyads were talented military leaders, and during their years in power, 661 to 750, the Muslim Empire expanded. Their armies advanced west into Africa. Soon the Berbers who lived along the northern coast and the Sahara, converted to Islam.

In 711, with the help of the Berbers, the Muslims moved northward across the Strait of Gibraltar *(juh BRAWL tur)*.

The Muslims were so determined to conquer the Iberian Peninsula that upon landing at Gibraltar, they burned all of their own boats. Retreat was not possible. Now they could only march forward. The conquest of Spain took seven years or less. The Catholic Visigoths, whose rule was no longer popular with the common people, were not able to raise a large enough army. The persecution of Jews and of Christians who disagreed with the church of the rulers, also helped cause their defeat. In the end, the Muslims drove out the Visigothic leaders. Almost the entire peninsula had become Umayyad territory.

From their bases in Spain, Muslim armies repeatedly crossed the Pyrenees *(PIHR uh neez)* and raided France. In 732, the Muslims confronted Charles Martel and his army of Franks. Martel, whose name means "the Hammer," repeatedly attacked the Muslims.

Martel's troops stopped the Muslims at the Battle of Tours in 732. This battle was one of the most decisive in European history. It determined that Europe would be Christian and not Muslim. Trace the Umayyad conquests and their expansion of the Muslim Empire on the map on page 80. ■

■ *What changes did the Umayyads bring to the Muslim Empire?*

▼ *Buildings in Morocco were often made of dried mud bricks. The same material was used to build walls around Moroccan cities to protect them from enemy attack.*

DEVELOP

Tell students that this lesson follows the rise to power of the Umayyads, a group of Muslims committed to the expansion of the Muslim Empire. It examines their achievements and shortcomings and then describes their downfall. Ask students to look at the map on pp. 80–81. Point out the areas ruled by the Muslims during the Umayyad period, 661 to 750.

■ *The Umayyads moved the empire's capital to Damascus, established a family dynasty, created a bureaucratic government, and expanded Muslim control into Africa and Spain.*

79

Access Strategy

Ask students to imagine that they have been put in charge of their school. How might they organize the school so that they achieve a balance between student happiness and safety? How would they permit people the freedom to do whatever they want and et at the same time see that students eceive an education? This is the kind of roblem that the leaders of the Umayyad Empire faced. They wanted to give people freedom of choice, but at the same time they had to protect the public order. They had to make decisions about whether non-Muslims should have to convert to Islam or be allowed to practice their own religion. They had to decide how to charge people for the protection that the Muslim armies provided them.

Access Activity

Divide the class in groups. One set of groups represents the citizens of a conquered city; the other represents the conquerors. Tell the students to negotiate a treaty, but first, each group must decide what are its needs, wants, and fears. Then have representatives debate and prepare a treaty. Comment on the Treaty of Damascus, p. 78.

► *The greatest expansion occurred under Muhammad and the first four caliphs.*

GEOGRAPHY
Map and Globe Skills

Have students study the map on this page and the next. Direct them to read the map key and then identify the areas conquered by A.D. 661 and by 750. Have students consult a political map in the Time/Space Databank to learn which modern countries were included in the Muslim Empire of 750. Ask students what challenges the size and diversity of the empire were apt to present to the Umayyads.

POLITICAL SYSTEMS
Critical Thinking

Ask students to state at least one advantage of a system of hereditary rule. *(Stability.)* Then ask students to state at least one disadvantage of such a system. *(Possibility of heirs being unfit leaders.)* Discuss with students whether the advantages of hereditary rule outweigh the disadvantages.

80

► *Use the map to compare the amount of land under Muslim rule during Muhammad's life and during the time of the first four caliphs with the land ruled during Umayyad times. During which time period did the greatest expansion occur?*

Further Expansion of Islam

Key:
- Islamic Empire, 661
- Conquests, 661–750

0   150   300 mi.
0 150 300 km
Mercator Projection

An Empire of Many Peoples

As the Muslims conquered new lands, the borders of the Muslim Empire expanded far beyond Arabia. Among the peoples conquered by the Arabs were Christians and Jews. The Arabs also conquered people whose religion involved the worship of many different gods.

Treatment of Non-Muslims

Over the centuries that followed, many people in the lands under Muslim rule converted to

Map and Globe Skills

Direct students to look at the map. Remind them that Muslims face Mecca during prayer. What directions do Muslims in the following cities face as they pray: Baghdad, Jerusalem, Alexandria, Cordoba? *(Southwest, southeast, southeast, southeast.)* Ask students why Mecca is a holy city for Muslims. *(Location of Ka'bah.)*

Writing

Ask students to write letters describing the Umayyad treatment of non-Muslims within the Muslim Empire. In their letters students should assume the viewpoint of a Christian, a Jew, or a non-Muslim of another religion. The letters should be addressed to friends or relatives living outside the empire and should explain the advantages and disadvantages of living under the Umayyads. Encourage students also to imagine the everyday routines of non-Muslims and include descriptive details in their letters.

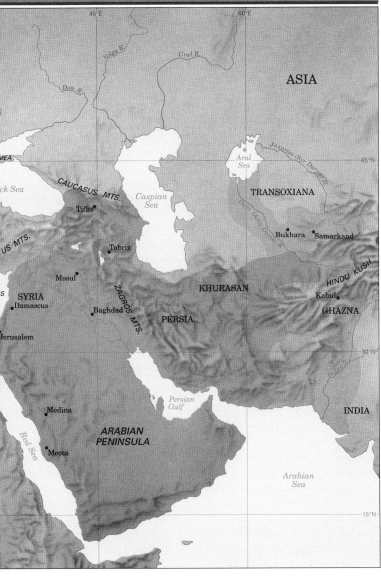

Islam. Some rulers forced people to take on Muslim ways. Many Christians and Jews kept their traditional faiths. Spain became known for its mixing of cultural traditions. When non-Arabs began to convert to Islam, they were sometimes not accepted socially by the Arab community. Some Arabs wanted to keep their culture free of outside influences. In time this changed, and a Muslim culture developed that included the customs and traditions of non-Arabs.

The Umayyad Muslims were generally tolerant of people, such as Christians and Jews, who believed in a single God. Muslims considered Jews and Christians to be "people of the book."

81

The Empire of Islam

Ask students to assess the strengths of Muawiya's government. Point out that his capital was more centrally located and his government's orderly departments exercised strong control in such a diverse empire. In addition, Muawiya began the tradition of hereditary rule, which stabilized the Umayyad power base. Ask students to speculate how such power might be abused. *(Corruption, nepotism.)*

81

Music Connection

Many of our current-day musical instruments have their roots in the Muslim Empire. Ask students where the guitar came from and surprise them with the answer: the Abbasid-period lute, called an 'ud *(uhd)*. Kettledrums and violins, too, have Muslim ancestors. Assign students small research projects finding out the history of these instruments. You might want to bring in a book of musical instruments from around the world.

In addition, you may want to tell students that under the Abbasids, some musical performers became famous throughout the Muslim world. Ishaq al Mausili (d. 850) was a renowned performer and teacher, though opposed to secular music. His pupil, Ziryab, is supposed to have left Baghdad because of his teacher's jealousy. Ziryab went to Spain, where he introduced new teaching methods. Muslim theorists also studied notes and intervals, calculated concordant and discordant intervals, and organized sounds into musical systems.

Study Skills

Ask students to choose one of the cities shown on the map on pp. 80–81. Direct them to this book's gazetteer, an atlas, and a current almanac and instruct them to find the following information: the contemporary name of the city, the country in which it is located, and its population. Then challenge students to find the city's approximate latitude and longitude.

Critical Thinking

Help students to compare the reign of Muawiya to that of Abd al Malik. Note that Muawiya set up a bureaucratic pattern of government and discouraged dissent among conquered subjects. Abd al Malik created a feeling of unity in the empire by adopting a common language and common coinage.

Critical Thinking

Have students study the two quotations on this page. Ask them if there is a difference in style of governing between ibn Abihi and Omar. Make a word web for each that describes his style of governing. *(ibn Abihi: demands obedience, governs by threats; Omar: concerned with fairness, justice, impartiality.)* Ask students to speculate on how these different styles of governing might affect the empire and its peoples. *(Threats inspire resentment; fairness inspires trust.)* Compare them with the first quotation by Abd al Malik in "Political Context," below.

■ *Christians and Jews who didn't accept Muhammad as a prophet of God were taxed but did not have to serve in the Muslim army.*

82

Christians and Jews had full religious freedom. They built churches and synagogues, and several were financed by the state. The state did not ask Christians and Jews to perform military service, but it required them to pay a head-tax, called *jizya.* Many Christians, Jews, and other non-Muslims held key positions in government. Everyone paid taxes on the produce from the land and trade. In addition, all Muslims were required to pay *zakat,* the 2.5 percent charity tax.

Many different peoples benefited from Muslim tolerance. Jews lived in Mesopotamia since the 500s B.C. When the Romans destroyed Judaea in A.D. 70, these Jewish communities grew very important. Their academies helped build Judaism as a religion defined by the Torah (the Jewish Bible), the rabbis (teachers), and the synagogue (temple). By 500, scholars had collected a vast amount of learning about the Torah in a work called the Talmud. This text became one of the great cornerstones of Judaism. Sassanid and Christian rulers had persecuted Jews, but Muslim rulers often protected them.

Government

The Umayyad caliph Muawiya patterned his highly organized government on the Byzantine model that he had first seen when he captured Damascus. He even kept some of the Christians in their old government posts. This system of rule and order was a **bureaucracy,** many different departments managed by workers appointed by the caliph or his representatives.

Under Muawiya, the provinces were ruled by **emirs,** or governors, appointed directly by the caliph.

82 ■ *How did Muslims treat people of different beliefs?*

Chapter 4

One new emir of Mesopotamia gave his subjects this stern warning:

> I demand obedience from you, and you can demand uprightness from me. . . . Do not be carried away by your hatred and anger against me, it would go ill with you. I see many heads rolling; let each man see that his own head stays upon his shoulders!
>
> Ziyad Ibn Abihi, c. 670
> *(zih YAHD IHBN ah BEE hih)*

Muawiya encouraged his emirs to rule strictly in order to stamp out **dissent,** or disagreement. Mesopotamia had been a center of resistance to Umayyad rule.

Compare Ibn Abihi's warning with that of the Caliph Omar, who ruled before Muawiya, from 634 to 644. In an open letter to a provincial judge, he wrote,

> Be just between the two opponents in the way you look at them, your fairness and the way you seat them, so that neither the wealthy take advantage because of their class nor the poor lose faith in your justice. . . . Don't hesitate to correct your verdict if you found out that a previous judgment was wrong, because it is never too late to reinstate that which is right, and it is always better than perpetuating [continuing] the wrong. . . . Don't ever be restless or impatient during a dispute. Verily, God multiplies the reward for putting justice where it belongs. And whoever obeys his good intention and disregards the call of his desires, God will take care of his relations with people.
>
> Caliph Omar Ibn al-Khattab
> ruled 634–664

Study Skills

Ask students to search in an encyclopedia or reference book for more information on the Jews of Mesopotamia and the Talmud. Have students construct a parallel timeline from 600 B.C. to A.D. 900, noting on one timeline events in Jewish history and on the other events in Christian and Muslim history.

Political Context

Abd al Malik's definition of statesmanship reveals the strength of his leadership: "To win the respect and sincere affection of the upper classes; to bind the hearts of the common people by just dealing; to be patient with the lapses of your underlings." Another quotation shows the high standards Abd al Malik set for his assistants. When he heard that one of his department directors had accepted a gift in office, Abd al Malik removed him from his position, saying, "By God, if you have accepted a gift and do not intend to reward the giver, you are blameworthy and vile; if you have accepted it and will do something for a man which you would not have done without the gift, then you are a traitor." Both of these quotations have application today. You might ask students to assess whether Abd al Malik's definition of leadership would fit most national leaders today or have them compare current standards of political conduct with those of Abd al Malik.

Umayyad Unity

Under the Umayyad dynasty, there was a succession of one caliph after another. There also developed a new Muslim culture for the empire. Abd al Malik *(ahb dul mah LIHK)*, caliph from 685 to 705, was influential in shaping this culture.

A Common Language

Abd al Malik declared Arabic to be the official language of the empire. This enabled the Umayyads to bring the diverse cultures of their empire under control. Until Abd al Malik adopted Arabic as the official language, local government workers had been mostly non-Arabic. They had spoken the languages of their local communities. Now all government business and religious affairs were conducted in Arabic. Anyone who wished to participate fully in the culture had to speak Arabic.

A Common Coinage

Not only was the language the same throughout the empire, but the coins the people used were the same too. Muslims borrowed the idea of coinage from the Persians and the Byzantines. The govern-ment began minting coins around 640. Abd al Malik was responsible, around 700, for the first purely Muslim coins. They had no images but were inscribed in Arabic with important quotations from the Qur'an. The coins gave Muslims a symbol of the power of their empire. Having a common coinage also made commerce between parts of the empire easier.

Religious Architecture

One of the first things the Arabs did when they took over a new land was to build a mosque, so they could give thanks to Allah. Muslims throughout the empire could always find a mosque. The mosque would be built from materials that were common to the area.

In 688, during the caliphate of Abd al Malik, North Africa was conquered. In North Africa mosques were made of adobe and wood, because that is what was available for construction. A mosque of this type can be seen on page 116. But the same features that were important to the Islamic religion would be present in every mosque: a minaret, a mihrab, and an ablution fountain. ■

■ *How did Abd al Malik unify the Umayyad Empire?*

◄ *Muslim coins were inscribed with sayings from the Qur'an.*

The Empire of Islam

83

CULTURE

Social Participation

Direct students to look again at the map on pp. 80–81 and identify the probable languages spoken within the Muslim Empire. Then instruct them to write a letter from one of the emirs to Abd al Malik, encouraging the caliph to make Arabic the language of the empire. Tell students to make their case politely but as strongly as possible.

▶ *By about 45 percent.*

■ *A lack of income from conquests and taxes and a schism between Umayyads and Abbasids led to the downfall of the Umayyads.*

CLOSE

Draw the Graphic Overview on the chalkboard. Ask students to provide details about each stage shown in the flow chart. Ask students what territories were part of the Umayyad expansion. What diversity came with that expansion? How did the Umayyads try to unify their empire? What caused the schism within the empire?

84

The Umayyad Downfall

The Umayyads conquered many new lands and peoples for Islam. However, by 750, after 90 years of continuous rule, they faced serious economic and political problems.

Many non-Muslim subjects had by this time converted to Islam. After they converted, they paid fewer taxes than they did before they converted. Consequently, as the number of conversions to Islam increased, the amount of tax money available for the empire to spend decreased.

By 732, the Muslim armies were making fewer new conquests. This stopped the flow of captured wealth that had enriched the empire's economy. The decline in tax revenues and the decrease in captured wealth helped contribute to the money shortage the Umayyads experienced. Examine the chart at the left to find how the percentage of the population paying full taxes varied in 727 and 738.

In addition, the Umayyad Empire had gained the reputation of being too much of a worldly kingdom and not interested enough in the religious ideals of the prophet Muhammad. In the last years of the dynasty, the Umayyads' opponents formed secret societies that were devoted to bringing about the downfall of the Umayyads.

One such group, the Abbasids (*AB uh sihdz*), was named after a family headed by al Abbas. Some historians say that al Abbas was an uncle of Muhammad. The Abbasids started a successful rebellion against the Umayyad rulers from their stronghold northwest of Persia, in a land called Khurasan.

According to some accounts, one of the Abbasid generals, Abdullah (*ahb du LAH*), invited 80 Umayyad leaders to a banquet. While his Umayyad guests were eating, Abdullah ordered his men to kill them. By 750, the Abbasid family was able to gain control of the Muslim Empire in the East.

Only one of the Umayyads, whose name was Abd al Rahman (*ahbd al rah MAHN*), escaped from the Abbasids. He leaped out of a window at Abdullah's deadly dinner, swam across the Euphrates River, and fled in disguise. Then he wandered all the way across Arabia and Africa and crossed into Spain. Once in Spain, Abd al Rahman began to unite the warring Muslim groups there and to build a new Umayyad government.

Now the Muslim state was split between two ruling groups, the Umayyads in Europe and the Abbasids in Asia and Africa. Unified rule was over, but Muslim culture continued to grow. ■

Umayyad Tax Revenues, A.D. 727 and 738

Percentage of Population Paying Full Taxes

100 90 80 70 60 50 40 30 20 10 0

727 738

Year

▲ *By approximately what percent did the population that paid full taxes decline between the years 727 and 738?*

■ *What political problems led to the downfall of the Umayyad Empire?*

REVIEW

1. **FOCUS** How did the Umayyads unite the many lands and peoples of the Muslim Empire?
2. **CONNECT** In what ways did the Umayyads carry out the ideals of Muhammad?
3. **ECONOMICS** What economic problems contributed to the collapse of the Umayyads?
4. **CRITICAL THINKING** Since the Muslims did not necessarily encourage people to convert to Islam, why did they bother expanding their empire?
5. **ACTIVITY** Examine some of the coins of your country. What do the images and inscriptions on the coins tell you about your country?

Homework Options

Have students use each of the key terms in a sentence that gives a fact about the Umayyad dynasty.

Study Guide: p. 12

Answers to Review Questions

1. The Umayyads united the people with a common language, coinage, and religion. Their long-lasting family dynasty gave stability to the empire.
2. The Umayyads were committed to spreading Islam and took their empire into Africa and Spain, giving the people there the chance to convert.
3. As their conquests came to an end, the Umayyads were no longer getting income from the lands they had invaded. Also as people converted to Islam, they no longer had to pay the non-Muslim tax.
4. Students might suggest that the Umayyads did it for the glory of Allah, to give people a chance to hear about Islam, and to get tax money from the lands they conquered.

600   750   1258   1400   1600

L E S S O N   2

The Golden Age

*How did the same wealth
that brought the Abbasids
power lead to their
downfall?*

Key Terms

- calligraphy
- faction

*T*his island between the Tigris in the east and the Euphrates
in the west is a marketplace for the world. All the ships that
come up the Tigris will go up and anchor here; wares brought
on ships . . . will be . . . unloaded here. It will be the highway for the
people. . . .

Praise be to God who preserved it for me and caused all those who
came before me to neglect it. . . .

It will surely be the most flourishing city in the world.

Abu Jafar al Mansur, 752

With these words, the second
Abbasid caliph described his
reasons for building Baghdad as
the new capital of the Muslim
Empire.

Baghdad, in Mesopotamia,
was ideally located to become a
world marketplace. It was situated
along ancient trade routes serving
both the East and the West. Soon
Baghdad, somewhat like an island
between the Tigris and Euphrates
rivers, grew into a huge city that
was the center of trade, learning,
and government.

River traffic passed up and
down the Tigris and Euphrates
rivers. On it traveled the produce
of the heavily irrigated lands of
Mesopotamia. From the plains
at the northern ends of the rivers
came grain. The old Persian Royal
Road still stood, and on it messengers rode from city to city.
Camels and carts were loaded at
river ports and headed to provincial

towns and on to Damascus and
Antioch. South of Baghdad, ships
sailed to and from China, India,
and Africa. Their precious cargoes
were traded in Baghdad, throughout the Abbasid Empire, and
beyond.

▼ *Between which two
rivers did Baghdad
develop?*

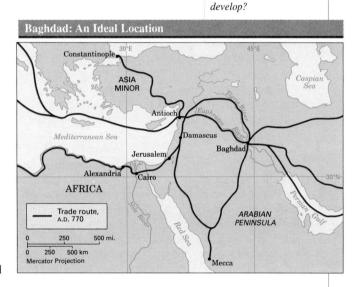

Baghdad: An Ideal Location

Constantinople · 30°E · 45°E

ASIA
MINOR

Caspian
Sea

Antioch

Mediterranean Sea

Damascus

Jerusalem

Baghdad

Alexandria · Cairo

AFRICA

Trade route,
A.D. 770

0   250   500 mi.
0   250   500 km
Mercator Projection

ARABIAN
PENINSULA

Persian Gulf

30°N

Mecca

Red Sea

Nile River

The Empire of Islam

INTRODUCE

*P*oint out the lesson title.
Discuss with students
what the term *golden age*
suggests about a civilization.
*(Peace, a growing economy,
great achievements in the arts.)*
Then have students read the
Thinking Focus. As they read
the lesson, have them look for
ways in which the Abbasids
used their wealth.

Key Terms

Vocabulary Strategies: T36–T37
calligraphy—the art of fine
handwriting
faction—a group of persons
forming a minority in disagreement with the larger group.

◄ *Tigris River and Euphrates
River.*

Graphic Overview

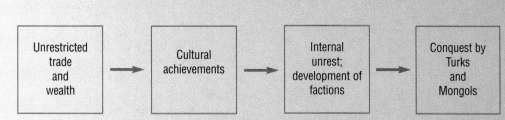

Unrestricted
trade
and
wealth
→
Cultural
achievements
→
Internal
unrest;
development of
factions
→
Conquest by
Turks
and
Mongols

Objectives

1. Analyze the strengths of the
   Abbasid government.
2. Describe the commercial wealth
   of Baghdad.
3. Summarize Abbasid achievements in art, literature, and
   science.
4. Explain the decline and eventual demise of the Abbasid
   empire.

DEVELOP

Ask students to read the headings for the lesson and look at the illustrations. Help them use their observations to list the numerous and varied areas of activity in a flourishing civilization. Based on the lesson's illustrations, students should expect to read about thriving commerce revolving around many different products, recreational pursuits, and advances in both art and medicine.

Draw the four stages of the Graphic Organizer on the chalkboard. Talk about the stages the Abbasid Empire passed through. Have students read Understanding Empire and have them discuss the stages that empires can pass through. Compare the Abbasid Empire's stages with those of other empires they have studied.

Under Abbasid Rule

The Abbasids forcibly took over the territories that had been conquered originally during the time of the old Umayyad Empire. This new Abbasid Empire lasted from 750 to 1258.

One of caliph Abu Jafar al Mansur's first actions was to move the capital of the Muslim Empire from Damascus in Syria to Baghdad in Mesopotamia, where the Abbasid family had much support. Mesopotamia was also the richest province in the empire in tax revenues and in agricultural production. It was an ideal location for a capital city.

Once the Abbasids had achieved power, they were able to hold onto it because of their strong standing army. Abu Jafar al Mansur also used the postal communication system that the Umayyads had developed. However, he also used it as a spy network that would relay information about any dissent in the empire back to the caliph's palace.

The Muslim Empire began to absorb the traditions of the many different cultures that were a part of the empire. As the power center of the empire moved farther east, it was no longer possible for

UNDERSTANDING EMPIRE

An empire is a group of peoples or provinces ruled by the strongest one of them. Not all the subjects, or the people, of an empire have the same language, religion, or physical appearance. They do not earn their livings in the same ways, nor might they even live under the same laws. But they do have the same ruler.

The Life of an Empire

Historians have traditionally seen different stages in the life of an empire. An empire usually begins when a number of regions unite under one ruler, either willingly or by force. The beginning period is one of expansion. Soldiers of the empire might conquer other peoples. Appointed governors represent the ruler. The governors often replace the local and provincial administrators and judges.

During the height of an empire, culture and the economy usually flourish. As in many ancient empires, the civilization of the region of the rulers often absorbs some other cultures.

Empires Decline

Political and economic problems often lead to the weakening and downfall of empires. Regions that have long been part of the empire may rebel against the powers that control them. War may disrupt the empire when region after region breaks free of the control of the nation that once ruled them. While empires can decline, the cultures within them often continue to develop long after the empires have ended.

86

Chapter 4

86

Access Activity

Show students a sample of Arabic script and then have them look at the photograph at the bottom of p. 88. Point out that many Muslim designs are based on Arabic lettering and are highly stylized. Discuss with students why people put designs on buildings. Ask students what designs on buildings tell us about people. (*They love beauty and they have money and time to decorate their world.*)

Access Strategy

Point out that the title of this lesson refers to the golden age of the Abbasid Empire. Discuss with students why a period of time could be called a golden age. Have students think about what books, movies, television shows, scientific achievements, and news events during their own lifetime could be considered part of a present-day golden age.

Discuss whether a society that is made up of people from many different ethnic groups is more likely to have a golden age than one in which everyone has the same cultural background. Compare living in a society which forces everyone to be the same with living in a society which allows for differences among people.

the Arabs to dominate completely the government, the cultural life, or the economy.

The new culture that developed was Muslim, but it was open to ideas from many different countries and cultures, especially those of Persia. However, the Arabic language continued to be the vehicle of government, education, poetry, and, of course, religion. ■

■ *How did the Abbasids get and keep control of their empire?*

The New Capital of Baghdad

At the heart of this Arab-Persian culture was a city with a strong economy. Baghdad's economy relied on taxes and wealth generated by trade and manufacturing. It was also a city of great science and technology.

The empire was rich in the gold, silver, copper, and iron used in trade. Pearls from the Persian Gulf and precious gems from other Muslim lands were in great demand in the Baghdad market.

The Abbasids preserved and improved the ancient network of wells, underground canals, and water wheels. Food production improved under the Abbasids. Dates, rice, and other grains flourished in the rich soil between the Tigris and the Euphrates. In addition, the Abbasids introduced new breeds of livestock and hastened the spread of cotton.

Traders from Scandinavia to Africa came to Baghdad for the products of its industries as well. Leather goods, textiles, paper, metalwork, and perfumes were produced and sold in the city.

▼ *The Round City was a government complex, with administrative offices and residences for the caliph's relatives. The caliph's palace was topped with a dome, and on top of that was the figure of a mounted horseman, which could be seen from the outskirts of the city. The dome collapsed in a storm in 941, and the entire city was destroyed by the Mongols in 1258.*

Baghdad and the Round City, c. A.D. 820

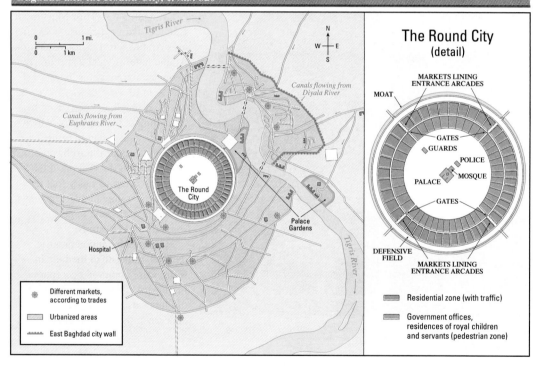

The Round City (detail)

MARKETS LINING ENTRANCE ARCADES
MOAT
GATES
GUARDS
POLICE
PALACE
MOSQUE
GATES
DEFENSIVE FIELD
MARKETS LINING ENTRANCE ARCADES

Residential zone (with traffic)

Government offices, residences of royal children and servants (pedestrian zone)

Different markets, according to trades

Urbanized areas

East Baghdad city wall

■ *The Abbasids took over the Umayyad territories; they kept power with the help of a strong army, a spy network, and the inclusion of local people in the empire's government.*

GEOGRAPHY

Map and Globe Skills

Using the map on p. 85, have students locate Baghdad. Tell them that Baghdad is located on the Tigris River at a point only 20 miles away from the Euphrates River. The city's location was ideal for trade. Ask students to use the map scale to determine the approximate distance along the trading routes from Baghdad to each of the following trading centers: Constantinople *(1000 miles),* Alexandria *(900 miles).*

87

Writing Poetry

Remind students of the poems they read from Muslim Spain (p. 77). If time permits, read one or more of these poems aloud to the students. Then challenge them to write their own poems about the wonders of Baghdad. Students should use information from the text or illustrations to develop their imagery.

Historical Context

Records of the city plan for Baghdad, the city in the round, can be found in such sources as *Baghdad During the Abbasid Caliphate* by Guy LeStrange and *The Topography of Baghdad in the Early Middle Ages* by J. Lassner.

Critical Thinking

A late-9th-century Muslim geographer said this about Baghdad: "I begin with Iraq only because it is the center of this world, the navel of the earth, and I mention Baghdad first because it is the center of Iraq, the greatest city, which has no peer in the east or the west of the world." Discuss with students whether this is fact or opinion.

> *This ivory chess piece was presented to Charlemagne, king of the Franks from 768 to 814, by Harun al Rashid, fifth caliph of the Abbasid Empire.*

■ *Why did Baghdad become such an important center of world trade?*

To handle this great volume of business, the Muslims developed something very similar to a banking system throughout their empire. They had no bank buildings yet, but business people invested in long-distance trade, and goods were bought on credit.

Muslim rule unified most of the eastern world. Boundaries were no longer an obstacle. The Muslims introduced a uniform coinage system, which made commerce even easier. Soon brisk international trade brought great wealth to the whole Abbasid Empire and to its rulers.

The caliphs and the upper classes grew rich, and they enjoyed spending their money on lavish

homes, fine clothing, and elaborate amusements. Horse racing and polo playing were popular activities. People with leisure time could engage in the sport of falconry—training falcons to hunt other birds which the trainer might eat. Wealthy families invited each other to elegant banquets with entertainment by dancers and poets. Such games as chess and backgammon were played during leisure time. ■

Abbasid Culture

Their great wealth enabled the Abbasids to support the arts and learning. The years from about 800 to around 1000 were a period of high achievement in the areas of art and literature.

> *Plaster moldings laced with an intricate leaf design cover the walls and ceilings of this Muslim palace.*

Art and Design

The unique style of Muslim art is unmistakable, because it so often uses Arabic script as its inspiration. Arabic lettering had a special significance for Muslims, because it was used to write down God's words as they had been given to Muhammad. **Calligraphy,** which means beautiful handwriting, flourished under the Abbasids. When used as decoration, the letters were often so fancy that they were almost unreadable. Examples on this and the next page show some of these designs.

Calligraphy and geometric designs, rather than the human form, were common decorations in mosques. The reason Muslims did this was because they were concerned that human images

Chapter 4

■ *Baghdad was between two major rivers, and international trade routes from the East and the West passed through the city.*

Basic Study Skills

Remind students that the Abbasid government was able to survive for 500 years. Have students make a four-column chart and record Abbasid achievements as they read. Suggest they include political, intellectual, economic, and cultural achievements.

Critical Thinking

Ask students to consider the elements necessary for a golden age in the arts. *(Strong economy, inspiration, talented individuals, encouragement from leaders.)* Ask students why a strong economy is required. Help them understand that patronage of the arts requires money to support and reward the artists' efforts.

Research

Divide the class into small groups of three or four students each. Ask each group to prepare an illustrated report about one form of Muslim art. Topics might include ceramics, metalwork, miniature painting, calligraphy, rugs, or carvings.

Collaborative Learning

Remind students that the wealthy Abbasids spent much of their leisure time playing chess and backgammon. Instruct all students to learn the rules for one of these games, and then select two students per game to demonstrate an actual game, giving instructive comments as they play. Finally, schedule a game day, when students can try out their skills. If students wish, periodic game days might be scheduled throughout the remainder of the year.

making. These Chinese prisoners won their freedom in exchange for revealing the secrets of papermaking. In time the skill of papermaking spread throughout the Muslim world, making books more available.

The availability of books contributed to the general interest in all types of learning. Caliph al Ma'mun, who ruled from 813 to 833, founded a school in Baghdad called the House of Wisdom (see p. 91). In the school, scholars translated Greek classics in philosophy into Arabic.

These books and thousands of others were brought to Muslim Spain and Sicily from the east. New works were produced in Spain as well. The Abbasid scholars of Baghdad helped preserve Greek classics that might otherwise have been lost or destroyed.

The Abbasids also became famous for their sensitive poetry:

*Y*ou departed
from my sight
and entered my thoughts,
travelled from my eyes
to my heart.

Al Abbas Ibn al Ahnaf, c. 800

Many poets and writers from far away flocked to Baghdad, where the caliph welcomed them. ■

would distract worshipers from praying to Allah. Most Muslim scholars agreed that creating images of living things like humans and animals, which have souls, is forbidden. They cautioned against worshiping created images.

Muslim artists often used decorative designs made up of plant patterns. The most common of these floral designs was the arabesque, a winding stem, leaves, and flowers, that formed a spiraling design.

Bookmaking and Literature

In 751, during a raid into central Asia, Abbasids captured some Chinese artisans skilled in paper

◄ *In this painting of a coeducational classroom of the time, overseen by a bearded master, some students are reading and writing. The border of the painting is decorated with calligraphy and geometric designs.*

Across Time & Space

The craft of papermaking was developed in China around 150 B.C. Paper was made by soaking flattened plant fibers and then allowing them to dry on a screen. The first papermaking factory in the Muslim Empire was built in Baghdad in A.D. 792.

■ *What achievements in culture led to this period being known as the Golden Age?*

Abbasid Achievements in Learning

The interest in reading also extended to learning about science, mathematics, and medicine. The excellent reputation of Muslim scholars spread across the empire into Europe.

The Empire of Islam

Critical Thinking

Have students share the items they included in their four-column charts on the Abbasid caliphate. List their suggestions in columns on the chalkboard. Then have students arrange the items in each column in a descending order of importance, according to their long-term impact on the rest of the world. Challenge students to reach consensus on the most important achievement of all.

CULTURE
Critical Thinking

Over 1,000 years ago, the people of the Abbasid Empire had a high rate of literacy among both men and women. Have students discuss how the ability to read and write contributes to progress in culture.

■ *It was called the Golden Age because of the accomplishments in decorative art, architecture, poetry, and literature.*

Language Arts Connection

Explain to students that Muslim accomplishments have influenced our modern language. Mix up the words listed here, all of which came originally from Arabic or Persian, and write them on the chalkboard. List the category headings separately. Have students look up any words they don't understand and then arrange the words under their appropriate headings. Discuss any difficult terms.

Math and Science: logarithm, algebra, cipher, alkali, caliber, zenith, amalgam, elixir, nadir
Food: lemon, soda, rice, syrup, coffee, sherbet
Cloth: taffeta, damask, cotton
Economics: bazaar, check
The Arts: lute, guitar, tambourine

Study Skills

Help students see that the title and four major headings of this lesson provide its organizational structure. Review with students the basic principles and format of outlining. Then direct students to the subsection Abbasid Culture, on pp. 88 and 89 and ask them to outline it. Suggest that they use three levels of detail (*I, A, 1*).

90

CULTURE

Critical Thinking

Scholars generally acknowledge that the genius of Islam was its ability to take elements from many different sources and make something entirely new—and clearly Muslim—from them. Discuss this concept with students, and ask whether they think the Abbasid period exemplifies this idea. Encourage students to cite specific details to support their opinions.

Science and Mathematics

Muslim scholars of the Abbasid period were interested in further developing the findings of the ancient Greeks, Africans, and Asians in science, mathematics, and medicine. For example, Muslim astronomers mapped the solar system and believed, long before Columbus's time, that the earth was round.

Modern algebra is based on explorations in mathematics in the early 800s by one of the most famous Abbasid mathematicians, al Khwarizmi *(al KWAH rihz mee)*. Today, we call this type of mathematics *algebra* after the title of one of al Khwarizmi's books, *al jabr*, meaning "the addition of one thing to another."

Medicine

Muslim doctors who lived during the Abbasid reign became skilled at diagnosis and treatment of disease. One doctor, ar-Razi, a Persian-born physician of the 900s, wrote the first accurate description of the diseases that we know today as measles and smallpox. Other doctors performed surgery on patients in clean hospitals that were free to the public. At this time, Muslims were also experimenting with the treatment of disease

▼ *A window (below) at Princeton University honors Abbasid doctor ar-Razi. Muslims also honored the Greek Aristotle, painted as a Muslim (bottom), for his study of plants, such as coriander, shown at top.*

through herbal medicines. Plants, such as coriander, were used for their medicinal powers. One of the leading Abbasid figures of medicine was Ibn Sina, known in Europe as Avicenna *(av ih SEHN uh)*. In his autobiography Avicenna wrote:

> Medicine is not one of the difficult sciences, and therefore I excelled in it in a very short time, to the point that distinguished physicians began to read medicine with me. I cared for the sick, and there opened up to me indescribable possibilities of therapy which can only be acquired through experience. At the same time, I was also occupied with jurisprudence and would engage in legal disputations, being now sixteen years of age.
>
> Ibn Sina, c. 1000

In addition to law and medicine, Avicenna had a number of other interests—philosophy, mathematics, and astronomy. He also wrote a vast medical encyclopedia called *Canon of Medicine*. It summed up the medical knowledge of the time and accurately described diseases and treatments.

Study Skills

Muslim advances in science make interesting report topics. Ask students to choose one of the following topics and prepare a brief research report: the work of Al Razi, Alhazen, or Al Biruni or the invention of the astrolabe. Encourage several students to present their reports orally to the class.

Cultural Context

Caliph al Ma'mun, who ruled from 813 to 833, was intellectually curious. He was interested in religious debates, he built observatories, and he encouraged the study of both astronomy and geometry. Legend says that al Ma'mun at first was afraid to support scholars and scientists in their efforts to uncover the secrets of God's creation. However, in a dream Aristotle came to al Ma'mun and convinced him that reason and religion need not be in conflict.

Mathematics Connection

Ask students what they think algebra is. After listening to their ideas, send one or two students to the dictionary to read its definition aloud. Be sure students understand the word *variable*. Then invite a math teacher at your school to present a beginning lesson in formulating and solving algebraic equations. Thereafter, direct students to think of three different story problems that require algebraic solutions. Challenge them to set up the equations and try to solve them.

An Abbasid Scholar

*3:20 p.m., February 15, 832
In a study at the Bayt al-Hikmah
Baghdad's new "House of Wisdom"*

Turban
The scholar's turban is wrapped from many yards of fine, cotton muslin. His robe is damask, a specialty of the Damascus weavers.

Ink, Pen and Paper
The scholar writes with a pen that has been cut and trimmed from a reed, ink that has been made from lamp-black and gum arabic, and paper made from cotton fiber in a Baghdad paper factory.

Bookshelf
Many of the books in the Bayt al-Hikmah have been translated, copied, and bound right here in the building. Calligraphers and artists have beautified these books, too.

Stomach
This scholar is hungry. He has been fasting since dawn, because Ramadan is the month for fasting for all Muslims. He is looking forward to sundown, when he will pray and then enjoy dinner.

Works
He is taking notes from books on religious and secular subjects, including philosophy, astronomy, mathematics, and medicine. The books are translations from Greek, Hebrew, Syriac, and Persian.

Qur'an
As a sign of respect, the Qur'an has its own stand made of fragrant, carved sandalwood imported from Southeast Asia. The scholar's copy of the Qur'an is illuminated with geometric designs.

91

Note: Use the Abbasid Scholar picture when discussing the cultural achievements of the Abbasids and the transfer of learning (pp. 85–100).

Visual Learning

Ask students how they can tell this is a place of learning *(books everywhere)* and which is the most important book *(the Qur'an has a special stand)*.

Have students examine the furnishings. Do they give the impression of wealth or poverty? *(Wealth; richly decorated and probably took many hours to create.)* Tell students that there were many libraries in Baghdad. Some were even "climate controlled" by water flowing through pipes.

More About the Bayt al-Hikmah The House of Wisdom was begun in 830 by Caliph Ma'mun. At its height it served as museum, library, translation office, school, and meeting center. Jewish, Christian, Persian, and Hindu scholars worked with Arabic-speaking Muslim scholars to translate books into Arabic from Hebrew, Greek, Persian, Syriac, and other languages. The art of translation reached great heights in the 300–400 years after A.D. 800. Translators debated with scholars, scientists, and religious leaders to make sure their translations reflected accurately what the original authors meant.

91

Writing

Ask the students to pretend they are Muslim scholars working at the Bayt al-Hikmah. Have each write a letter to a non-Muslim colleague inviting him or her to come work in the translation office. Students should give reasons why a Jew, Christian, Persian, or Hindu would want to come to Baghdad.

Role Playing

Some of the caliph's critics are complaining that he is spending too much money on the Bayt al-Hikmah. They feel that unnecessary spending must be cut back. Have students prepare points for and against supporting the Bayt al-Hikmah. Then have volunteers role-play a scene in which the caliph's advisers debate this issue.

■ *Abbasid scholars of Baghdad were encouraged to further develop the findings of the ancient Greeks in science, mathematics, and medicine.*

Critical Thinking

Ask students to identify the Fatimids and Seljuk Turks and state their connection to the Abbasids. Have students compare the downfall of the Abbasids with that of the Umayyads, citing both similarities and differences. Then ask students to assess the state of the Muslim Empire at the conclusion of this lesson.

■ *The Fatimids and other factions broke away from the Abbasids. The Seljuk Turks then invaded a weakened Baghdad.*

CLOSE

Ask students to identify the primary sources of Abbasid wealth. List their suggestions in a column on the chalkboard. Then ask students to identify the positive and the negative results of that wealth, and list those suggestions in separate columns on the board. Have students discuss whether the Abbasid wealth was well used.

92

■ *How was Abbasid Baghdad famous as a center of scientific, mathematical, and medical achievements?*

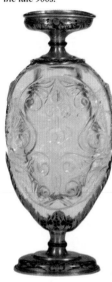

▼ *This delicate crystal vase, decorated with an arabesque floral design, is from the early Fatimid period in Egypt during the late 900s.*

■ *What led to the division of the Abbasid Empire?*

Interest in treating illness went back to the earliest days of Muslim history. It was the prophet Muhammad himself who stated that Allah had provided a cure for every illness. ■

A Divided Empire

The years 800 to 1000 were a golden cultural period for the Abbasid Empire. The end of this period was also a financially difficult time for the government. Tax money was increasingly important to the caliphs because the Abbasids had lost control of several important trade routes. This hurt Baghdad's economy and led the caliphs to increase taxes to support their costly style of living.

Factions and Revolt

During the same period, several **factions,** or opposing groups, began either to leave the empire for other lands or to take control of distant parts of the empire away from the Abbasids. For example, the Fatimids, who were descendants of the Prophet's daughter Fatima, were unhappy about the costly lifestyle of the Abbasids. The Fatimids felt this lifestyle was corrupt compared to the simple lifestyle of Muhammad.

The Fatimids broke away from the Abbasids by the 900s and then migrated into North Africa. By 969, they had conquered most of North Africa and claimed the city of Cairo as their capital.

Seljuk Turks

Groups continued to break away from the weakened Abbasid Empire and opened it to invasion from outside forces. In 1055, Baghdad was conquered by nomadic Turks from Central Asia, who were descended from a warrior named Seljuk.

These Seljuk Turks captured the weak Abbasid caliph, plundered his palace, and took over the government. The Turks allowed the caliph and those who followed him to remain in Baghdad, but only as religious leaders of Islam. Once in control of the government, the Seljuk Turks took their responsibilities as rulers seriously. They began to govern the empire in the tradition of Islamic law.

The Abbasid-Seljuk Empire continued for 200 years but received its death blow when Baghdad fell to Mongol invaders from central Asia in 1258. Thus ended the Abbasid Empire, which, it is said, began with the violent assassination of nearly 80 Umayyad leaders in 750. Only one Umayyad leader had survived, and that was Prince Abd al Rahman, who had escaped to Spain. ■

REVIEW

1. **FOCUS** How did the same wealth that brought the Abbasids power lead to their downfall?
2. **CONNECT** In what ways did the Abbasids further develop Muslim culture?
3. **POLITICAL SYSTEMS** How were non-Arabs treated by the Abbasids?

4. **CRITICAL THINKING** How were the Muslim trade routes important in spreading new ideas and knowledge?
5. **ACTIVITY** Write your first name in the center of a sheet of paper. Then work the letters into a design in the way that Muslims make Arabic letters become part of an intricate design.

92

Chapter 4

Homework Options

For each primary source included in the lesson, have students record who the writer is and what the primary source reveals about Abbasid culture or society.

Study Guide: p. 13

Answers to Review Questions

1. The extravagant spending of the Abbasids caused other factions in the empire to withdraw their support.
2. The Abbasids made an effort to include local people in the government and absorbed the traditions of many different cultures. The resulting Muslim culture gained widespread respect for its contributions to art and learning.

3. The Abbasids welcomed non-Arabs and other cultures into their empire creating a new Muslim culture that was less Arabic than that of the previous Umayyad Empire.
4. As traders moved along trade routes, they spread the ideas and cultures of the various countries they visited.

Origins of Sports and Games

People around the world have always found ways to relax and play. Abbasid rulers enjoyed falconry and backgammon. Find out about these and other games and sports.

Get Ready

Collect a pen, pencil, and notebook. Look for reference books, magazines, or local experts to help you explore the origins of a particular sport or game. You need information about the game's equipment and rules. Also, find out where and how the game originated.

Football is one outgrowth of games that go back centuries. All the related games involved kicking a ball, but the ball's shape and the rules of the game varied.

Find Out

Use your reference materials to find the origins of the game you chose. You may want to show how a game has changed over time. You might want to follow a game to its origins. Some games began as work. The Abbasids, for example, made a sport of hunting with a trained falcon.

Move Ahead

Tape a large sheet of paper to the classroom wall. As you and your classmates share your information, each of you should draw a timeline on this sheet. Each timeline should show the origins of a game and how its rules and equipment changed over time.

Make two lists, one of games that began as recreations, the other of games that grew out of some necessary activity such as work or self-defense.

Explore Some More

Climate, animals, and terrain often affect the development of games. The horse-loving Abbasid rulers enjoyed polo and horse racing. Where did ice hockey develop? Why? Can you think of another sport or game affected by geography?

▼ *Chess has challenged people around the globe for centuries. This Spanish engraving, dating from the late 1500s, shows Arabs playing chess.*

DISCOVERY PROCESS

Students will use the following steps in the discovery process to complete the activity:
Get Ready Gather information from books, magazines, and local experts on a sport or game.
Find Out Find the game's origins, equipment, and rules.
Move Ahead Make timelines to show when each game began and how its rules and equipment changed over time.
Explore Some More Think of games or sports whose development was affected by geography.

Materials needed: Books and magazines about sports, paper, tape, and markers.

HISTORY
Visual Learning

Although no one is certain about the way chess began, historians believe it originated in India in the A.D. 600s. Arab invaders took the game to Spain in the 700s. Have students use the picture to learn more about the history of chess. *(Sample answers: Arab players took chess seriously; their facial expressions show this. Playing was a social event—the people around the players are chatting, eating, and listening to music.)*

93

Activity

Once students have begun their research for the feature, have them work in groups of five or six to invent games of their own. Encourage them to be imaginative in creating rules and equipment but not to get too sophisticated. Once they have their games planned, have them explain the origins of their games (although these may be imaginary), the reasons for their rules, and the shapes of their equipment.

Objectives

1. Describe the equipment and rules of sports and games. (Culture 4)
2. Explain the origins of sports and games and their development over time. (History 1, 2, 6)

UNDERSTANDING WHAT YOU READ

This skills feature uses a summary of Lesson 1 to teach students to identify main ideas in written material.

CULTURE
Critical Thinking

Have students read the summary of Lesson 1 to themselves. Ask them to state its main idea briefly in their own words. *(Possible answer: From 661 to 750, the Umayyads took over nearby countries and gave them a common culture.)* Next, ask volunteers to supply facts from the reading that support the main idea. *(Started a tradition of continuous rule; expanded into Africa, Spain, and Portugal; made Arabic the language of the empire; instituted a common coinage; shared religious architecture.)* Explain that students can understand a book or a story better if they pause after every paragraph to briefly restate the main idea of that paragraph to themselves. Ask them to name ways they can use identifying main ideas in their personal reading.

Identifying Main Ideas

Here's Why

When you read, you need to determine what the writer wants you to understand. Identifying the main idea is the key to getting the most from anything you read. For example, if you were asked to tell someone what you read in Lesson 1 about how the Umayyads united the Islamic Empire, you would need to use this skill.

Here's How

The main idea of a paragraph is often stated in a topic sentence. This sentence, which is usually the first or last sentence, tells what the paragraph is about. The other sentences of the paragraph provide facts and details that support the main idea.

In a large section of text, you may find a topic paragraph. Like a topic sentence, a topic paragraph tells you the main idea of the section. The other paragraphs in the section build on and support the topic paragraph.

Look at the summary of Lesson 1 (to the right). In this case, a topic paragraph begins the passage. As you can see from the green highlighting, the passage is about how the Umayyads expanded and unified the Islamic Empire. Supporting details, highlighted in blue,

explain how the Umayyads accomplished this.

The main idea of a passage is not always stated in a topic paragraph. For example, if the passage below did not include the first paragraph, you would need to look in the rest of the passage for a common idea or ideas. You would study the supporting details to determine the unstated main idea.

Look back at the passage. The blue highlights the part of each sentence that tells something about how the Umayyads expanded or unified their empire. When you determine what these sentences have in common, you

can come up with the main idea of the section.

Try It

Turn to page 83 and reread "A Common Coinage." Write the main idea of that section on your paper. Now list several supporting facts or details that reinforce the main idea.

Apply It

Find a magazine article about a topic that interests you. Identify the topic sentence or topic paragraph of the article. Describe how the other sentences or paragraphs in the article support the main idea.

The Umayyad Empire

In 661, the Umayyads began a 90-year period of rule. During their years in power, from 661 to 750, the Umayyads expanded and unified the Islamic Empire.

Muawiya, the first Umayyad caliph, moved the capital from Medina, in Arabia, to Damascus, in Syria. Muawiya also started the practice of appointing a son as the next caliph. Thus began a tradition of continuous rule by one family.

During their years in power, the Islamic Empire expanded into Africa and present-day Spain and Portugal. In conquered territories, Umayyad Muslims tolerated other religions but gave special privileges to Muslims.

Abd al Malik, caliph from 685 to 705, took other steps to unify the empire. He made Arabic the language of the empire and instituted a common coinage. Mosques built in conquered lands shared a common religious architecture that also provided unity to the empire.

Objective

Identify main ideas and supporting details in paragraphs. (Critical Thinking 1)

Writing an Outline

Have half of the class outline Lesson 1 by listing in order the main ideas of its paragraphs, leaving two empty lines under each. Tell the other half to do the same with Lesson 2. Then, ask the students who did Lesson 1 to exchange papers with the students who did Lesson 2. Have them fill in the missing details, using their textbooks.

Answers to Try It

Main idea: A common coinage helped to unify the Muslim Empire. Supporting details: government minted coins; coins with quotes from the Qur'an were a tangible symbol of power; a common coinage made commerce easier.

Answers to Apply It

Answers will vary.

600   750   1492   1600

L E S S O N 3

Islamic Spain

R*egularly perform thy prayer at the declension [descent] of the sun, at the first darkness of the night, and the prayer of daybreak; for the prayer of daybreak is borne witness unto by the angels.*

Qur'an, 17:80

According to the Qur'an, faithful Muslims are directed to pray at not only these three times of day but also in the afternoon and evening. Mosques were built by the Muslim rulers so that the faithful could answer the Qur'an's call to face Mecca and pray five times every day.

The Great Mosque of Cordoba, Spain, described in A Closer Look on page 97, was begun in 786 by Abd al Rahman. The mosque, completed nearly 200 years later in 976, was a religious, social, and educational center.

THINKING
F O C U S

How did Muslim culture influence Spain?

Key Term

• legacy

The Return of the Umayyads

When Abd al Rahman fled to Spain in 750, he discovered that since the time the Arabs and Berbers had invaded Spain from North Africa in 711, rival factions had been competing for control. No group had succeeded for long. Although there were many Muslims in Spain, there was no unified Muslim government.

Uniting Muslim Spain

By 756, the Umayyad forces in Spain, who did not support the new Abbasid caliphate back in Baghdad, accepted Abd al Rahman as their leader. With this Umayyad help, Abd al Rahman was able to establish an independent Muslim kingdom. He made the ancient Roman city of Cordoba his new capital.

◄ *The arches of the Great Mosque of Cordoba are supported by more than 1,000 pillars of marble, jasper, and alabaster.*

95

The Empire of Islam

INTRODUCE

A sk students to read the Thinking Focus. Then ask them to list as many questions as they can that relate to it. (*How did Muslim culture reach Spain? When did it arrive? What had Spain been like before? How long did the Muslim influence last?*) Tell students to look for answers to their questions as they read the lesson.

Draw the Graphic Overview on the chalkboard. Discuss with students how the right side of the graphic (culture) relates to the left side (administration). (*Basically, a strong and unified and stable political situation provides an opportunity for cultural development.*)

Key Term

Vocabulary Strategies: T36–T37
legacy—something handed down from an ancestor; something from the past

Graphic Overview

```
                    MUSLIM SPAIN
           ┌────────────────┴────────────────┐
     Administration                        Culture
      ┌──────┴──────┐                 ┌───────┴───────┐
    unity        commerce         universities       arts
   ┌───┴───┐        │              │                  │
government army  trade and     translations    poetry and music
                agriculture
```

Objectives

1. Explain the success of the Umayyads in unifying Spain under Muslim rule.
2. Assess Cordoba's position as the cultural and intellectual center of the Muslim West.
3. Describe the decline of the Muslim state in Spain.

DEVELOP

List the following dates and events on the chalkboard: 756—Abd al Rahman becomes leader of Umayyads in Spain; 929–961—reign of al Rahman III brings the high point of Umayyad Spain; 1236—Cordoba falls to Christian forces. Tell students that these dates provide a broad outline of the political information in the lesson. Tell them that much of the lesson concerns the legacy, or cultural heritage, of Muslim Spain.

■ *The Umayyads had a strong central government and a large army.*

HISTORY

Critical Thinking

Ask students to review the career of Abd al Rahman. Remind them of the story of his escape from the Persian massacre. Ask students what they think would have been Abd al Rahman's highest priority for his new kingdom. *(Probably unity, to avoid another disastrous schism.)*

► *Madrid, Toledo, Cordoba, Seville, Granada, and Cádiz, Northern Spain.*

96

Abd al Rahman's goals were to unify Spain under a central government, and to protect his realm from Islamic invaders to the south and Christian forces to the north. He succeeded so well that until 1000, there were few invasions.

■ *How did the Umayyads unify and protect Spain?*

Strengthening Cordoba

The high point for Umayyad power in Spain came about 200 years after the first Abd al Rahman, during the 49-year reign of Abd al Rahman III, which was from 912 to 961. He was the first Umayyad ruler of Spain to adopt the title of caliph, rather than simply governor. He patterned his government after the Abbasids' strong, centralized caliphate in the east, in Baghdad.

During his reign, Abd al Rahman III increased the strength of the army. The caliph bought Scandinavian, African, and German slaves to serve in his forces. This vast army protected his kingdom from the same two forces that had threatened the first Abd al Rahman: Christians in the north and Muslim rivals to the south, especially the Fatimids who had started an empire in Africa. ■

Islamic Spain

► *Orchards of figs, almonds, and sweet cherries covered the countryside of the Islamic Empire of Spain. What Spanish cities were part of the Islamic Empire of Spain? What area of Spain was still controlled by the Christians?*

Glory of Cordoba

With his borders well protected, Abd al Rahman III turned his energies toward making Cordoba a thriving cultural center. Prosperous and well run, the city attracted scholars and artists. Many had come from the Abbasid cultural center of Baghdad. The city's most famous attraction was the Great Mosque, the largest of the city's 3,000 mosques. For A Closer Look at the mosque, see page 97.

In the 900s, Cordoba was western Europe's largest city with a population of 200,000 people.

Access Activity

Ask students to look at each illustration in the lesson, including the map, and by reading only the captions, to identify the subject of the lesson *(Spain under Muslim rule)* and the kinds of things they will be learning about. Then ask them to read the main headings in the text and tell how they think the chapter is organized. *(Rise and decline of a kingdom.)*

Access Strategy

Ask students what large cities they have lived in or visited. Discuss with students what was good about these cities and what was bad. Could any of the cities have been called great? What qualities would a great city have? *(Students may answer that a great city would have beautiful buildings and parks, interesting things for people to do, and good restaurants. They may also say that a great city is one that helps people who live in it.)*

Tell students that in this lesson they will be reading about the glorious city of Cordoba, Spain, which was the capital of the Umayyad state in Spain.

The Great Mosque at Cordoba

The great city of Cordoba demanded a great mosque. The building begun by Abd al Rahman I in A.D. 785 eventually became the third largest mosque in the world. Twice the wall facing Mecca was pushed outward. With the third addition, the wall and its jewellike mihrab had almost reached the river, so the fourth extension had to be added onto one side.

Did you notice that the pillars don't match? The marble and alabaster pillars under the candy-striped arches came from many different Roman buildings. Above this "forest" sparkled a turquoise- and gold-enameled "sky."

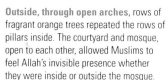

Outside, through open arches, rows of fragrant orange trees repeated the rows of pillars inside. The courtyard and mosque, open to each other, allowed Muslims to feel Allah's invisible presence whether they were inside or outside the mosque.

Orange branches

More About the Great Mosque

Because Islam forbids the making of images, the interior and exterior of the mosque must remind worshipers of God in other ways than with pictures of Mohammad or Muslim saints. The rows and rows of orange trees and massive stone arches stand for the disciplined perfection of Allah. The lines of pillars and trees lead the eye gradually toward the arched doorways in and out of the mosque. This teaches a visual lesson about the shifting relationship between the inner and outer world, between body and spirit, between this world and the garden of the next world. For this reason the Great Mosque has been called "a meditation in stone."

Study Skills

Have students research other famous houses of worship around the world. These might include a Buddhist temple, a Roman Catholic cathedral, a Jewish synagogue, a Quaker meeting house, or a Shinto shrine. Students should make sure they have information about both the specific site they are researching and about the typical characteristics of synagogues or cathedrals. Have them present their findings in oral report form, with visuals.

Visual Learning

Ask students to look carefully at the photograph of the arched gate into the mosque beside the orange trees. Do they see anything that seems out of place in the mosque? *(Figures of saints over the doorway.)* Ask students to read more at the library about the Great Mosque, and write a page explaining how the images came to be there.

CULTURE
Critical Thinking

Ask students to compare Cordoba under the Umayyads with Baghdad under the Abbasids. They might focus on their trade, attractions, and achievements. Then ask students whether Cordoba would have flourished if Baghdad had not also flourished. Help students to see the strong influence of the many merchants, scholars, and artists who traveled to Cordoba from Baghdad.

➤ *In the 900s, there were two Muslim states, the Umayyads' in the west and the Abbasids' in the east. There were also two Christian empires, those of the Roman Catholic Church in the west and the Eastern Orthodox Church in the east.*

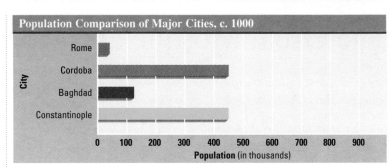

Population Comparison of Major Cities, c. 1000

Population (in thousands)

The size and splendor of Cordoba, with its paved and lighted streets and public plumbing in 300 bathhouses, was truly remarkable for a European city of the Middle Ages. Over 100,000 shops and houses filled the city. But it was the 60,000 richly decorated palaces with gardens and fountains, public courtyards, and broad avenues that made Cordoba an urban jewel in Muslim Spain's crown.

A Center of Learning

Poetry and music thrived in Cordoba. Poets and musicians were regarded as important figures in the court of the caliphs, for they produced poems and songs to glorify the empire and its rulers. Cordoba was the cultural and intellectual center of western Islam.

The Muslims brought thousands of books to Spain. New works were written, too. From the 1100s on, Jewish and Christian scholars worked with Muslims to translate these works into Latin. Scholars brought these books back to Christian Europe, where they stimulated the growth of knowledge and learning at the new universities. In the late 900s, the largest of the 70 libraries in Cordoba contained 500,000 volumes. This was at a time when a Christian monastery would have been

➤ *This carved ivory box shows two young men listening to a lute player. The inscription tells us that it was presented in 968 to al-Mughira, a son of Abd al-Rahman III.*

Chapter 4

proud to house several hundred books. A host of clerks, many of them women, carefully handcopied 70,000 books a year to satisfy the citizens' literary appetites.

Thousands of men and women attended the university and the law school at Cordoba. Scholars from Baghdad traveled to Spain, bringing knowledge and seeking new ideas. Much of this learning was then shared with western Europe by visiting scholars, merchants, and pilgrims who came to Cordoba. This love of learning was Cordoba's greatest **legacy,** or gift, to cultures and civilizations of the future.

Social Participation

Divide the class into several small groups of students. Ask each group to present a short skit about life in Cordoba. The setting should be a public place. Some possible roles include a poet, a government official, a student, a translator, a farmer, and a craftsperson.

Religious Context

Jews were very active in the intellectual life of Muslim Spain. They excelled as physicians, scholars, and artists. Many Jews kept their own beliefs but adopted Arab customs, including Arab names. However, they kept Hebrew names for religious use. The Jewish philosopher Maimonides studied the writings of Aristotle and tried to reconcile Aristotle's teachings with the teachings of the Jewish religion. His work influenced many other philosophers, including Thomas Aquinas.

Interviewing

Group students in pairs and instruct them to enact an imaginary interview of Abbas Ibn Firnas. The setting for the interview should be the hospital where Ibn Firnas was recovering from the back injury he sustained in his flight experiment. Remind students, however, that Ibn Firnas left Baghdad to teach music in Cordoba. They may want to ask about his interest in music, his reaction to Cordoba, or his construction of a Cordoba planetarium, in addition to his flight experiences.

The Intellectual Community

Cordoba was an open center of learning in which non-Muslims and Muslims from other lands were welcome to share in the intellectual community. One of the first of the visiting scholars was Abbas Ibn Firnas. He came to Cordoba from Baghdad in the early 900s to teach music at the court of Abd al Rahman III. His interests were diverse, however, and Ibn Firnas soon began to explore the mechanics of flight. He constructed a pair of wings out of feathers on a wooden frame and made an attempt at flight. Ibn Firnas survived his flight experiment with only a back injury. Later, he went on to build a famous planetarium in Cordoba that was complete with revolving planets.

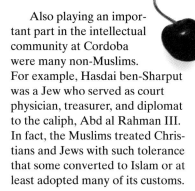

Also playing an important part in the intellectual community at Cordoba were many non-Muslims. For example, Hasdai ben-Sharput was a Jew who served as court physician, treasurer, and diplomat to the caliph, Abd al Rahman III. In fact, the Muslims treated Christians and Jews with such tolerance that some converted to Islam or at least adopted many of its customs.

A City of Merchants

If Cordoba was a center of culture and learning, it was also a city of merchants. Cordoba supported a great many workshops for the production of its famous leatherwork, prayer carpets, ivory boxes, and other handicrafts. Spanish leather goods and textiles were in great demand throughout Europe because of the craftsmanship with which they were made. The art of papermaking, brought from Baghdad, was practiced here also.

Agriculture also flourished under Abd al Rahman III. He encouraged the use of irrigation, which enabled farmers to grow new and exotic crops such as figs, almonds, cherries, bananas, and cotton. Over 4,000 thriving markets sold these agricultural and manufactured products. ■

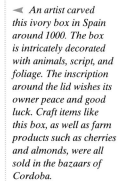

◀ *An artist carved this ivory box in Spain around 1000. The box is intricately decorated with animals, script, and foliage. The inscription around the lid wishes its owner peace and good luck. Craft items like this box, as well as farm products such as cherries and almonds, were all sold in the bazaars of Cordoba.*

■ *What were the greatest achievements of Cordoba?*

The Loss of Spain

By the 1000s, however, a small pocket of Christian resistance had begun to grow larger. Christian forces from the north of Spain began to move southward. The map on page 96 shows the strip of northern territory that remained

Christian throughout the first 250 years of Umayyad reign.

The Reconquest
The late 1000s mark the beginning of a period that Christians call the Reconquest. Knights and

Direct students to the map on p. 96. Ask why Toledo was such a significant victory for the Christians. *(Located in the center of Spain.)* Have students look at a map showing the entire Mediterranean coastline and estimate the distance the Moors had to travel from Spain to North Africa. *(Less than 50 miles.)*

■ *Cordoba's greatest glories were its large population, the Great Mosque, its university and law school, and its artists and scholars.*

Writing

Ask students to compare the conditions existing in Spain when Abd al Rahman arrived and those after Cordoba fell to the Christians. Help students understand that at both times rival groups were struggling for control. In the earlier time Abd al Rahman united the Muslims; in the later time Ferdinand and Isabella united the Christians. Ask students to write two descriptions of the Christian conquest: the first from the Christian point of view and the second from the Muslim's.

Visual Learning

Have students draw or trace an outline map of Spain. Ask them to locate the following: Gibraltar, Toledo, Cordoba, Granada, Mediterranean Sea, Atlantic Ocean, Pyrenees. Then have students create a key for their map and show the Islamic Empire in Spain. Encourage students to decorate the borders of their maps with Islamic-style decorations.

➤ *In 1492, King Ferdinand of Aragon and Queen Isabella of Castile are on their way to the city of Granada to welcome it as part of their united kingdom.*

■ *What were the threats to the Islamic Empire in Spain?*

adventurers from all over Europe journeyed to Spain to fight the Muslims. In 1085, the Spanish Christian ruler Alfonso VI seized the Muslim city of Toledo, whose king was friendly to the Christians. The loss of Toledo marked the point of no return in the battle for Spain.

An Empire Lost

After the attack on Toledo, the rest of Islamic Spain gradually fell to Christian soldiers. The Muslim government dissolved into quarreling factions. Just as the Abbasid Empire had begun to collapse when it could no longer unite its parts, the Umayyad Empire in Spain began to die. The Muslims retreated farther and farther to the south as Christian forces invaded from the north.

Cordoba fell to the Christian forces in 1236, almost 500 years after Abd al Rahman had established it as the capital of his empire. In 1236, the last Islamic kingdom in Spain was that of the Berbers in Granada.

The Catholic kingdoms of Aragon and Castile ruled northern and central Spain. When King Ferdinand of Aragon married Queen Isabella of Castile, their combined kingdoms had enough power to expel the Muslims from Spain entirely. In 1492, the forces of Ferdinand and Isabella of Spain drove out the last Berbers.

Most refugees settled in North Africa, particularly in Morocco where the Berbers had originally come from in 711. Today, 98 percent of the Moroccans are Muslim. The official language is Arabic, but many people speak Spanish. ■

R E V I E W

1. **FOCUS** How did Islamic culture influence Spain?
2. **CONNECT** How did the Abbasid Empire influence the start and the development of the Umayyad government in Cordoba?
3. **POLITICAL SYSTEMS** What problems led to the fall of central Islamic governments?
4. **CRITICAL THINKING** How was Cordoba able to become

the center of culture for western Europe in the 800s and 900s?

5. **ACTIVITY** Muslims translated many important books of Greek knowledge into Arabic. What English books would you suggest be translated into Arabic? Make a list of books that should be available in Arabic. Tell why each book is significant.

Left sidebar

■ *Muslim factions within the empire and Christian forces to the north threatened Umayyad control.*

C L O S E

Refer students to the Thinking Focus. Tell them to identify as many influences as they can to answer the question. List their suggestions on the board. When all ideas have been recorded, ask students to refine the list, eliminating duplicates and any invalid responses and combining similar suggestions. Then have students organize the list, fitting all of the remaining ideas into several categories.

Homework Options

Have students write a response to the following statement in a paragraph that cites specific examples: "The real Islamic conquest of Spain was cultural."

Study Guide: p. 15

Answers to Review Questions

1. The Muslims influenced the religion in Spain, the architecture, and the fine arts. They also made great advances in science and learning.
2. The Umayyad leader Abd al Rahman fled from the Abbasids to Spain. In later years, Abd al Rahman III followed the Abbasid pattern of government, and the Umayyads of Spain attracted many Abbasid merchants, scholars, and artists.
3. Islamic governments were troubled by factions. When factions broke away, they weakened the central government and left it open to invasion by non-Muslims.
4. Cordoba's cultural life was far more diverse and developed than that of other medieval European cities. Cordoba featured many palaces and public courtyards; its numerous poets and musicians were prominent and prolific; and its literate populace had the advantage of a great library, a university, and a law school.

UNDERSTANDING REFERENCE SOURCES

Using the *Readers' Guide*

Here's Why

To find current information about a topic, you need to use reference resources other than encyclopedias and books. Magazines, or periodicals, can provide recently written information about events. Suppose you want to find information about Islam today. How would you find the periodicals you need?

Here's How

The *Readers' Guide to Periodical Literature* is a set of reference books that lists magazine articles by topic. The box below contains two pages from the *Readers' Guide* for the year 1989.

To find an article about Islam, look under the topic **Islam.** There you find a cross reference: *See also* **Muslims.** This reference tells you that

more articles about Islam are listed under the heading **Muslims.**

As you can see, there are three other subject headings with *Islam* in the title. These headings also refer you to different subject listings. Where should you look for an article on Islam and Christianity?

If the listings under **Islam** do not have what you want, then look up the heading **Muslims.** There are several subheadings under the subject **Muslims.** One or more articles are listed under each subheading. Each article is a separate entry. An entry includes the name of the article, the magazine that published it, and the date. Then look for that issue of the magazine in the periodicals section of the library.

Try It

Look again at the *Readers' Guide* entries on this page. In what magazines can you find articles about Muslims in the Soviet Union? Who wrote each article? What is the title of the most recent article about Muslims in the Soviet Union?

Apply It

Think about a special holiday or tradition associated with your ethnic background. Use the *Readers' Guide* to make a list of articles about this topic.

1. Title
2. Joint author
3. Subject heading
4. Author
5. Illustrations, portraits, maps
6. Periodical, volume, page numbers, date

ISENBERG, DAVID
① Reforming the Joint Chiefs of Staff: a timid first step. il *USA Today (Periodical)* 117:12-15 Ja '89
ISIKOFF, MICHAEL
② (jt. auth) See Hosenball, Mark, and Isikoff, Michael
ISLAM
See also
Muslims
ISLAM AND CHRISTIANITY
See Christianity and other religions
ISLAMIC PAINTING *See* Painting, Islamic
ISLANDS
See also
Barrier islands

MUSLIMS **③**
Afghanistan
Afghanistan: Soviet occupation and withdrawal. il maps *Department of State Bulletin* 89:72-90 Mr '89
Afghanistan's uncertain fate. B.R. Rubin. **④** il *The Nation* 248:264-7+ F 27 '89
Target: Kabul. D. Lorch. il pors map *The* **⑤** *New York Times Magazine* p32-5+ F 12 '89
Egypt
See Also Muslim Brotherhood [Egypt]
Soviet Union
Central Asia: the rise of the Moslems. D. Doder. il map *U.S. News &* **⑥** *World Report* 106:48+ Ap 3 '89
Islam regains its voice. R.N. Ostling. il *Time* 133:98-9 Ap 10 '89

101

The Empire of Islam

UNDERSTANDING
REFERENCE SOURCES

This skills feature teaches students how to obtain specific, current information using the *Readers' Guide to Periodical Literature.*

HISTORY
Critical Thinking

After reading the feature, discuss with students why the *Readers' Guide* is important. (*It can lead to much more current and specific information than can be found in encyclopedias and books.*) Discuss why it might be important to have the most current information on a subject.

101

Research

Ask students to think of a subject in which they are interested. Have them use the *Readers' Guide* to locate four recent articles that will enhance their understanding of the subject.

Answers to Try It

U.S. News & World Report, Time; D. Doder, R. N. Ostling; "Islam Regains Its Voice."

Answers to Apply It

Answers will vary, but the articles should relate to the students' chosen topic.

Objectives

Identify elements of an entry to the *Readers' Guide to Periodical Literature* and use the *Readers' Guide* to make a list of entries for a given topic. (Study Skills 1, Critical Thinking 1)

Answers to Reviewing Key Terms
Sample answers:
1. **factions:** Two **factions** fought against each other during the civil war.
2. **calligraphy:** The book jacket was decorated with **calligraphy.**
3. **dissent: Dissent** in the country led to civil war.
4. **legacy:** The beautiful mosaics are a **legacy** of the Muslim Empire.
5. **emir:** The caliph gave a lot of power to each **emir.**
6. **bureaucracy:** The Byzantine government was a **bureaucracy.**
7. **empire:** The Muslim **Empire** was ruled by a caliph.

Answers to Exploring Concepts
A. Sample answers:
   I.–A century of expansion
   A.–Expansion under Umayyad rule
   B.–*An empire of many peoples*
   C.–Umayyad unity
   D.–The Umayyad downfall
   1.–*Shortage of money*
   2.–*The Abbasids*
   II.–The golden age
   A.–Islam under Abbasid rule
   1.–*Gaining power*
   2.–*Holding power*
   3.–*A new culture*
   B.–The new capital of Baghdad
   1.–*Gaining wealth*
   2.–*Using wealth*
   C.–Abbasid culture
   D.–*Abbasid achievements in learning*
   E.–A divided empire
   III.–Islamic Spain
   A.–The return of the Umayyads
   B.–*The glory of Cordoba*
   C.–*The loss of Spain*

Chapter Review

Reviewing Key Terms

bureaucracy (p. 82) empire (p. 78)
calligraphy (p. 88) faction (p. 91)
dissent (p. 82)   legacy (p. 98)
emir (p. 82)

On your own paper, write the key term hinted at by each sentence below. Write a different sentence that contains the key term.
1. Opposing groups broke away from the empire and left it weak.
2. Many pieces of Muslim artwork are adorned with beautiful writing.
3. Some emirs did not allow citizens to disagree with them.
4. Scientific discoveries were one of the gifts that the Muslim Empire passed on to other cultures.
5. A ruling governor reported to the caliph.
6. The Muslim Empire government had different divisions that were managed by workers appointed by the caliph.
7. Syria, North Africa, Spain, Persia, and parts of India were among the group of countries ruled by the Muslims.

Exploring Concepts

A. Copy and complete the following outline using information from the chapter.

  I. A century of expansion
    A. Expansion under Umayyad rule
    B. _____
    C. Umayyad unity
    D. The Umayyad downfall
      1. _____
      2. _____
  II. The golden age
    A. Islam under Abbasid rule
      1. _____
      2. _____
      3. _____
    B. The new capital of Baghdad
      1. _____
      2. _____
    C. Abbasid culture
    D. _____
    E. A divided empire
 III. Islamic Spain
    A. The return of the Umayyads
    B. _____
    C. The loss of Spain

B. Decide whether each statement below is true or false. Support your decision in writing, using facts and details from the chapter.
1. The Umayyad rulers made changes that both expanded and unified the Muslim Empire.
2. The rulers of the Umayyad Empire were tolerant and did not discriminate against non-Muslims.
3. A political split helped bring about the downfall of the Umayyads.
4. Under the Abbasids, culture and learning flourished.
5. The way the Abbasids used their great wealth contributed to the downfall of their empire.
6. Because of their different locations, Baghdad and Cordoba had almost nothing in common.
7. The Muslim peoples did not share their culture of knowledge with any other peoples.
8. Both the Abbasid Empire and Islamic Spain declined and were conquered when their rulers could no longer maintain unity among the people.

B. Sample answers:
1. True. They moved the capital from Medina to Damascus, established inherited rule, expanded the empire, set up a bureaucracy, appointed emirs, declared Arabic the official language of the empire, started a system of coinage, and built mosques.
2. False. They were tolerant of other religions, but they taxed non-Muslims and never fully accepted non-Arabs who converted to Islam.
3. False. The split occurred within Islam. The Shiites were opposed to the rule of the Umayyads.
4. True. Their great wealth allowed them to support artists and scholars.
5. True. The lavish lifestyle of the Abbasids made many of their subjects resent the taxes. Other factions, disillusioned by the extravagance, broke away from the empire.
6. False. Both were centers of Muslim power as well as world trade. Prosperous and well-run, both cities attracted merchants, scholars, and artists from all over the world. Commerce, literature, art, music, and scholarship flourished in both places.
7. False. Merchants, scholars, and pilgrims visited Cordoba and took what they had learned back to western Europe.
8. True. Weakened when some factions broke away, both were less able to defend themselves against outside invaders.

Reviewing Skills

1. Read the section headed Art and Design on page 88 of Lesson 2. Where in the section does the main idea appear? Write down this main idea. Then list three details or facts that support the main idea.
2. Reread the section headed Strengthening Cordoba on page 96 of Lesson 3. What is the main idea of the section? How can you identify the main idea in this section?
3. Use the *Readers' Guide* excerpt on page 101 to answer the following questions:
   a. In what magazine would you look to find an article describing Muslims in Indonesia? What are the title and the date of publication for the article?
   b. Under what entry would you find information about elections in the Middle East?
4. Use the information in Lesson 2 to make a timeline showing events of the Abbasid Empire. Can you make your timeline into a parallel timeline using events of the Umayyad Empire for the same time period?
5. Taking notes and outlining are two ways of studying. If you were outlining or taking notes on the contents of Chapter 4, what two kinds of information would you be writing down?

Using Critical Thinking

1. An empire is formed when one central authority takes control of several other regions. Being ruled by another country affects the government and way of life of the people. The people also affect the ruling country and the empire. What effects did the Byzantines, Persians, and others have on Muslims and their empire? What positive effects can empires have on progress and on society in general?
2. Baghdad and Cordoba were prosperous, well-run centers of commerce that also became centers of great art and learning. Judging from the example of these two cities, what are two or three comments you can make about places in which art and learning flourish?
3. Arabic was declared the official language of the Muslim Empire. What were the positive effects of this policy? What negative effects can you think of? Keeping both types of effects in mind, do you think English should be declared the official language of this country? Defend your position.

Preparing for Citizenship

1. **COLLECTING INFORMATION** Persian and Byzantine coins bore pictures of emperors. Muslim money bore quotations from the Qur'an. Do research to find out what images and words are used on the currency of the United States. Make a scrapbook of the decorations on the money, including drawings and explanations.
2. **COLLABORATIVE ACTIVITY** Although mosques do not all look alike, certain features are the same. This is also true for churches and synagogues and other temples. Working in groups of four, prepare an illustrated report on the architecture of these religious buildings. Decide among yourselves who will research each kind of building. One person can find out more about Muslim mosques. Another person can find out about Christian church architecture, the third person should find out about Jewish synagogues, and the other person should find out about Buddhist temples. The group can choose two members to compile the information and write a description of each kind of building. The other two people can illustrate the descriptions. The whole class should decide whether to use the reports in a scrapbook or bulletin board display.

The Empire of Islam

103

Write the title of the unit on the chalkboard and have students look at a large map of Africa on which the Sahara is clearly marked. Ask students to distinguish, according to the title, which parts of Africa they will study in this unit. *(Western and south central Africa, south of the Sahara.)*

Looking Back

Remind students that the Romans and Byzantines had set up wide-ranging trading networks, and that Muslim culture was an important force in North Africa.

Looking Forward

Have students read the passage below the unit title and note the time span of the unit. Tell students that in the next two chapters they will learn about the great ancient trading empires of Africa and how they established traditions that still exist today:
Chapter 5 *West Africa*
Chapter 6 *Central and Southern Africa*

Unit 3
Sub-Saharan Africa

Traders from faraway Europe, Asia, and the Middle East journeyed to the ancient trading empires of Africa seeking gold, ivory, and other exotic goods. They found well-organized states with noble cavalries. The empires fell, but the traditions of the past live on in Africa today. This cavalry brigade, dressed in ceremonial battle gear, parades through Niger just as ancient cavalrymen rode down the trade routes of the early African empires.

500 B.C.

Niger cavalry procession. Agence Hoa-Qui, Paris

104

GEOGRAPHY PROJECT

African Profile

Geography Skill **Reading a Vertical Profile**
Students use the skill of Acquiring geographic information.

Geography Themes Regions/Human-Environment Interaction

Geography Standards 5, 12 regions help interpret earth's complexity; human settlement

Activity *Create Annotated Maps*
Materials construction paper, colored pens and pencils

Management Whole Class/Individual

Choose two sub-Saharan states or empires covered in the unit, and make annotated maps and vertical profiles. Use the map on p. 140 along with any of the maps on pp. 121, 146, and 150 to create the vertical profile.

Have students:
- draw and annotate two maps and accompanying vertical profiles and/or create two illustrated maps of two states in sub-Saharan Africa.
- write clear annotations about the geography and economics of places shown on the vertical profile map.
- use leader lines to connect annotations to map locations.

A.D. 1700

Understanding the Photograph

The cavalry tradition in West Africa can be traced to the time of the Ghana empire, when horsemen patrolled the trade routes. Elite cavalry corps, trained by Arabs, developed rituals and elaborate uniforms; these traditions are still carried on today.

Understanding Chronology

This unit begins with the early cultures in West Africa and follows the migration of Africans through central, eastern, and southern Africa. It also covers the contacts with Arab and European peoples and shows how those contacts affected the African empires.

For research support activities, see the *Research Handbook.*

For simulations correlated to this unit, see *Citizenship Simulations,* p. vii.

HOUGHTON MIFFLIN SOCIAL STUDIES

Bookshelf II

The African Mask

by Janet E. Rupert

This story is about a young Yoruba girl's struggle to convince her parents that making traditional pottery is an important part of her life.

Motivate Read aloud the Foreword and Chapter 8, pp. 78–87. Then ask students to name some traditional American crafts or activities such as quilting, woodworking, or folksinging. Ask what Layo and her friend see people doing in the Yoruba village. Have students look at the photograph on this page. Tell them that they will read about the African empires from which many of today's traditions originate.

To connect this book with the unit content, use the planning guide and student activity blackline masters beginning on p. iv of the *Bookshelf II Teacher's Resources.*

For additional books that are Easy, Average, and Challenging, see the Unit Bibliography on p. T43. See bibliography updates at www.eduplace.com/ss/hmss.

THE AFRICAN MASK

by Janet E. Rupert

Planning at a Glance
West Africa

	Objectives	Reading Support and Other Resources	Diverse Learning Strategies
Lesson 1 The Roots of Mighty Empires *pp. 108–111* 2–3 days	• Identify the major land regions in West Africa. • Explain the significance of the Nok Iron Age. • Evaluate the importance of trade to Jenne–jeno.	• **Workbook** or **Reading Support:** pp. 54–57 Review p. 13 Lesson Support/Transition p. 13 Multi-lang. Sum. pp. 25–26 • **Other Resources:** Posters 1, 3, 5; Study Guide p. 17	Access Act. **(SDAIE)** TE p. 109 Map and Globe Skills **(Visual)** TE p. 109 Visual Learning **(Visual)** TE p. 110 Homework Options **(Visual)** TE p. 111 Audiotapes of Multi-language Lesson Summaries **(Auditory)**
Lesson 2 The Empire of Ghana *pp. 112–117* 2–3 days	• Identify what made Ghana a successful trading empire. • Explain why Koumbi was divided into two sections. • Evaluate the effects of the Muslim Arab traders on Ghana. • Summarize the events that led to Ghana's downfall.	• **Workbook** or **Reading Support:** pp. 58–61 Review p. 14 Lesson Support/Transition p. 14 Multi-lang. Sum. pp. 27–28 • **Other Resources:** Geography Kit, Study Guide p. 18	Access Act. **(SDAIE)** TE p. 113 Visual Learning **(Visual)** TE pp. 115, 116 Writing a Travel Log **(GATE)** TE p. 114 Audiotapes of Multi-language Lesson Summaries **(Auditory)**
Lesson 3 The Empires of Mali and Songhai *pp. 118–122* 2–3 days	• Evaluate the geographic and political factors that made Mali a great empire. • Assess the impact and economic significance of the adoption of Islam. • Analyze the factors that made Songhai a trading empire. • Identify the major cause of Songhai's decline.	• **Workbook** or **Reading Support:** pp. 62–65 Review p. 15 Lesson Support/Transition p. 15 Multi-lang. Sum. pp. 29–30 • **Other Resources:** Geography Kit, Study Guide p. 19, Study Print 3	Access Act. **(SDAIE)** TE p. 119 Visual Learning **(Visual)** TE p. 121 Study Skills **(GATE)** TE p. 121 Audiotapes of Multi-language Lesson Summaries **(Auditory)**
Skill: Interpreting Proverbs *p. 123* 1 day	• Evaluate and interpret proverbs.	• **Other Resources:** Study Guide p. 20	
Lesson 4 Village Society In West Africa *pp. 124–127* 2–3 days **Literature** "The Cow–Tail Switch" *pp. 128–131*	• Demonstrate how West Aftrican farmers adapted to their land and climate. • List components of West African religions. • Describe the government of rural African villages.	• **Workbook** or **Reading Support:** pp. 66–69 Review p. 16 Lesson Support/Transition p. 16 Multi-lang. Sum. pp. 31–32 • **Other Resources:** Geography Kit, Study Guide p. 21	Access Act. **(SDAIE)** TE p. 125 Map and Globe Skills **(Visual)** TE p. 125 Homework Options **(Visual)** TE p. 127 Audiotapes of Multi-language Lesson Summaries **(Auditory)**
Chapter Review *pp. 132–133* 1 day		Chapter 5 Test pp. 17–20 *(See facsimiles on TE p. 563.)*	Assessment Multiple-Use Masters pp. 73–80

Reading Support Resources *for Every Lesson*

Reading and Review

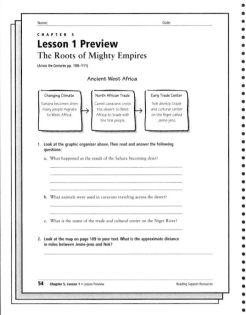

- **Chapter Overview*** p. 53
- **Lesson Previews*** using graphic organizers from the Teacher's Edition pp. 54, 58, 62, 66
- **Reading Strategies*** pp. 55, 59, 63, 67
- **Lesson Summaries*** pp. 56–57, 60–61, 64–65, 68–69
- **Lesson Reviews** pp. 13, 14, 15, 16

* **Workbook** includes starred items.

Multi-language Summaries

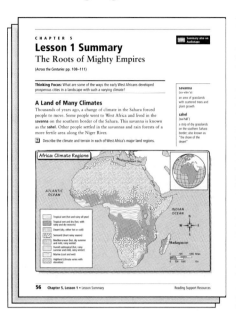

Lesson Summaries in:
- English (See Reading and Review.)
- Spanish pp. 56–57, 60–61, 64–65, 68–69
- Chinese pp. 25–32
- Hmong pp. 25–32
- Khmer pp. 25–32
- Vietnamese pp. 25–32

 Summaries available on audiotapes

Lesson Support /Transition
S D A I E

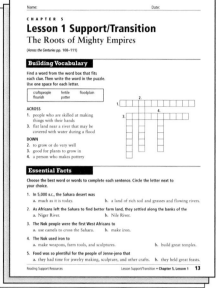

Activities for SDAIE
Specially **D**esigned **A**cademic **I**nstruction in **E**nglish

- **Lesson Support/Transition** pp. 13, 14, 15, 16

 ## Technology Options

Internet Support
http://www.eduplace.com

Social Studies Center at Education Place
Internet support for Chapter 5:
- *Lesson at a Glance*
- *Trading Gold and Salt*

Software
Student Writing Center ® (CD-ROM) (Macintosh® or Windows®)

School to Career

Salt and gold are both minerals mined from the earth. Have students each select and research a mineral obtained through mining. Then have them create a flow chart of the mining process from extraction through final processing. Students should list the job skills required at each stage.

Character Education

Setting a good example is important. Divide students into small groups. Have each group create a skit about setting a good example, such as saying no when offered a cigarrette. Discuss with students how effective each example was. How can this behavior be taken out into their school and communities?

CHAPTER PREVIEW

Ask students to read the chapter title. Then ask a student to read aloud the first sentence of the narrative. Let the students discuss whether they would be willing to trade a pound of gold for a pound of salt, and if so, under what conditions. Then have them read the rest of the text and study the pictures to give them an idea of what life must have been like in West Africa.

Looking Forward

Tell students that they will read about the small villages and the trading empires of West Africa in Lessons 1–4: The Roots of Mighty Empires, The Empire of Ghana, The Empires of Mali and Songhai, and Village Society in West Africa.

Lesson 1 explores the climate and geographic features of West Africa and explains how they influenced West African development.

106

BACKGROUND

Modern historians have run into many difficulties trying to reconstruct Africa's past. Until the 16th century, there were few written records revealing the history of sub-Saharan Africa.

Chapter 5
West Africa

Would you trade a pound of gold for a pound of salt? West Africans did. Salt was scarce, and they needed it to survive. Africans also exchanged other goods as they built trade networks from about 250 B.C. through the A.D. 1500s. Across the Sahara and along the Niger River, traders carried ivory, cloth, baskets, iron tools, jewelry, and much more. While most of West Africa stayed a land of small villages, trade empires grew around splendid cities.

Throughout this period, West Africans carved brightly colored figures like this one to represent gods, spirits, and ancestors. Such figures were often used in religious ceremonies.

A.D. 500–600 The rulers of Ghana store grain in mud huts like these. Built on high, steep land, the huts keep the grain dry and safe from animals.

| 500 | B.C. | A.D. | 500 |

c. 570 Muhammad, founder of the Islamic faith, is born in the Arabian city of Mecca.

106

500 B.C.

Written vs. Oral History

Unlike North Africa, which was influenced by its regular contact with traders and conquerors, western, southern, and central African societies did not develop a writing system until after the arrival of the Muslims and Europeans. Most Africans relied on oral tradition to pass on information about social behavior, codes of law, history, and literature.

The absence of a written record does not mean, as some 19th-century European scholars once suggested, that Africa had no history of its own. These scholars ignored the fact that there were many organized pre-colonial African societies, states, and empires long before the arrival of Muslims and Europeans.

Clues to Africa's Past

Much of the information that historians have gathered on the empires of Ghana, Mali, and Songhai is based on the accounts of visiting or resident Muslims. These early historians, however, were often prone to exaggeration and, at best, presented the

Throughout this period, religion, dance, and music played an important part in West African village life. Even today villagers like these Dogon people perform religious dances in traditional clothing.

c. 800–1050 Ghana controls West Africa's rich trade.

c. 1580 The Songhai control West Africa's wealthiest empire, trading for valuable goods like the Ashanti gold badge above.

1000

1500

Today

c. 1500 With 80,000 people, Tenochtitlan is the largest city in the Americas and is more populous than London.

A.D. 1590

107

Understanding the Visuals

Ask the class to look at the photo of the granaries. A grain called millet was a staple food of many of the peoples of West Africa. Storing the grain until it could be used was important to maintaining a stable food supply. The Dogon people of West Africa devised an ingenious method for storing millet by adapting the environment to suit their needs. Making use of the natural terrain, they built the granaries on the sides of an embankment using sun-baked clay and supporting the structures with timber and gravel (mixed in with the mud). The pointy roofs are made of papyrus or other grass thatch.

Understanding Chronology

Refer students to the timeline entry c. 800–1050. Ask them what was going on elsewhere in the ancient world during this time period. *(The ascent of Muslim culture; the Byzantine Empire was an important center of commerce.)*

African world through Muslim eyes. Historians still question some Muslim accounts of Mansa Musa's pilgrimage that refer to the tons of gold the king distributed on his trip through Cairo.

Most of the non-Muslim historical information on West Africa comes from archaeological finds. Discoveries at Nok and Jenne-jeno, for example, revealed that West Africans possessed iron-working skills and had established societies in which trade was of key importance.

The analysis of African language has also helped to unlock the mysteries of Africa's past. By pinpointing areas where similar languages are spoken, it is possible to trace paths of migration and lines of ancestry.

The Oral Tradition Continues

The oral tradition is still a part of many African societies and continues to provide historians with information about early African life. Oral literature, in the form of rhythmic prose and song, is passed down

from generation to generation. Religious ceremonies, legends, and political and cultural institutions are preserved in the spoken word. In parts of West Africa, details about the Battle of Kirina, where Sundiata is said to have outwitted Sumangaru with his magic, continue to be a part of African oral tradition.

INTRODUCE

Briefly review how the Arabs adapted to their desert environment (Chapter 3). Then ask students to read the Thinking Focus. Explain that in West Africa people learned to adapt not only to climate but to new ideas introduced by outsiders. Have them speculate on what the Sahara's climate and vegetation are like today. Ask them if they think the Sahara has always been a desert. Finally, have students read the lesson to confirm or reject their assumptions.

Key Terms

Vocabulary Strategies: T36–T37
savanna—a region of grasslands containing scattered trees and vegetation
sahel—a strip of dry grasslands on the southern border of the Sahara; also known as "the shore of the desert"
delta—a triangular-shaped landform made by mud and silt deposited at a river's mouth

108

L E S S O N   1

The Roots of Mighty Empires

THINKING FOCUS

What are some of the ways the early West Africans developed prosperous cities in a landscape with such a varying climate?

Key Terms

- savanna
- sahel
- delta

▼ *Although it is as large as the United States, the Sahara has fewer than two million inhabitants.*

Imagine being on a trip by van across the Sahara in North Africa. After hours of travel, your guide sets up camp in an oasis. Its palm trees offer a refuge of shade from the sun-baked sand of the desert.

While you're relaxing by a stream, your guide proposes a hike. To those hardy enough for the walk, she promises scenes of lush plant life and full rivers.

You decide to go. The sun-baked sand burns through your sneakers, and rocks cut your hands as you scramble over a hill. Finally your guide leads you into a cave. Here, she says, are the scenes promised.

Paintings cover the cave walls. Images of wide rivers teeming with fish, vast plains of tall grasses, thick forests, and people herding cattle. The guide explains that these scenes were painted thousands of years ago—and that they represent the ancient Sahara. Could that barren desert really have been such a paradise? Were the paintings of real life?

A Land of Many Climates

Dried-up riverbeds as well as cave paintings indicate that in 5000 B.C., the Sahara was indeed a land of flowing rivers, lush green pastures, and forests. However, over time, its climate began to change. By about 4000 B.C., rain fell less often, and average temperatures had risen. As a result, the

Objectives

1. Identify the major land regions in Africa south of the Sahara.
2. Explain the significance of the Nok Iron Age.
3. Evaluate the importance of trade to the development of Jenne-jeno.

Graphic Overview

Changing Climate
Sahara becomes drier; many people migrate to West Africa.

→

North African Trade
Camel caravans cross the desert to West Africa to trade with the Nok people.

→

Early Trade Center
Nok develop trade and cultural center on the Niger called Jenne-jeno.

rivers dried up, and fertile pasture land became bare and bleak. By 2500 B.C., the desert looked much as it does today.

As the desert became drier, many people moved to search for more fertile land. Many Africans journeyed south to West Africa.

Some of those who migrated to West Africa settled on oases located along a strip of grasslands, or **savanna,** on the Sahara's southern border. This region is known as the **sahel** *(suh HAYL),* or "shore of the desert." Its landscape ranges from desert in the north to scattered vegetation in the south. On the sahel, scant rainfall and occasional oases make some farming possible. There are eight climate zones in Africa. Use the map below to determine the sahel's climate region.

Other Africans went farther south of the sahel to settle in the

▼ *Africa's climate ranges from heavy rainfall in central and parts of southern Africa to scant rainfall in the north.*

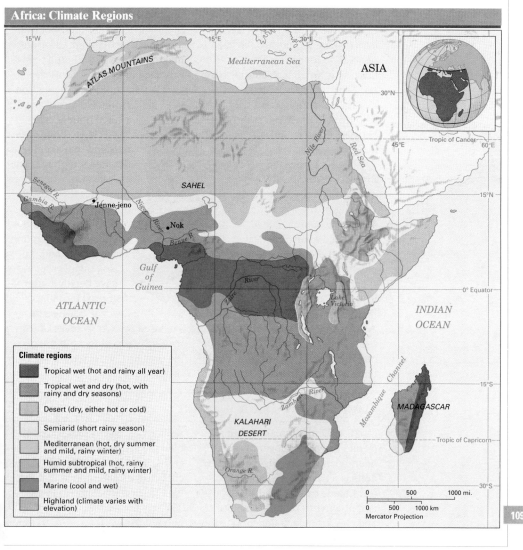

Africa: Climate Regions

Climate regions
- Tropical wet (hot and rainy all year)
- Tropical wet and dry (hot, with rainy and dry seasons)
- Desert (dry, either hot or cold)
- Semiarid (short rainy season)
- Mediterranean (hot, dry summer and mild, rainy winter)
- Humid subtropical (hot, rainy summer and mild, rainy winter)
- Marine (cool and wet)
- Highland (climate varies with elevation)

0   500   1000 mi.
0   500   1000 km
Mercator Projection

West Africa

DEVELOP

Have students trace an outline map of Africa using the map on this page. Tell them that as the class discusses the geography of West Africa, as well as its cities and kingdoms, they should mark these sites on their maps. Suggest that they begin by drawing in the Niger River. Point out to students that geography played a major role in shaping the early history of West Africa.

GEOGRAPHY
Map and Globe Skills

Use the map on this page to indicate the boundaries of West Africa. Explain that the modern boundaries and country names are different from those of ancient West Africa. Define the key terms and show where these geographic features occur on the map. Have students point out other areas of Africa that have climate zones similar to West Africa.

Access Strategy

Begin a discussion of how landscapes change by asking students about their own neighborhoods. Perhaps over the last few years new buildings or businesses have been constructed in their area. Have students discuss the ways in which their town or city has changed. Bring in photographs from books or magazines that illustrate what the town's main streets looked like 50 or 100 years ago. See if they can name an old building or landmark that is still standing from those days.

Finally, find out what the town or area looked like one thousand years ago or more and share this information with the class. Discuss how people might have lived in this different environment. Ask the students to suggest why some people might have moved away from, or migrated to, the area as it changed.

Access Activity

Divide the class into small groups. Provide each with a "country" in which a different list of environmental conditions is described. Ask each group to draw how people could adapt to this particular environment. The drawing should show a dwelling made with available materials, livelihoods based on available natural resources, and tools or crafts.

■ *West Africa's three major land regions are the sahel, the savannas, and the rain forests. The sahel is a strip of dry grasslands relieved by the occasional oasis and scant rainfall. The savannas and rain forests south of the sahel are more fertile areas and have heavy annual rainfall.*

GEOGRAPHY
Critical Thinking

The Hittites who lived in the country known today as Turkey were probably the first people to shape iron into tools and weapons. They began working with the metal around 1500 B.C. Traders and soldiers eventually brought the iron-making technology to other parts of Asia, Europe, and Africa. Why were soldiers and traders so effective in spreading the new technology to different lands? *(Soldiers brought the new iron weapons to fight wars in foreign lands; traders sold iron tools to customers in different areas along different trade routes.)*

■ *The people of the Nok culture knew how to make iron. Because iron was produced earlier by the North Africans, historians assume that the technology spread through contact with traders from that area.*

110

■ *Describe the climate and terrain in each of West Africa's major land regions.*

► *The Nok sculpted humans, animals, and religious figures. Many such sculptures were discovered by tin miners in the 1930s.*

■ *What aspect of Nok culture demonstrates that trade had a major impact on Nok life?*

savannas and rain forests of a more fertile area along the Niger River. There they found relief from the barren Sahara. And along the banks of the Niger, they built some of Africa's greatest empires. ■

A New Technology

Although the vast, scorching Sahara made travel difficult, it did not cut West Africa off from traders to the north. Camel caravans regularly traveled across the desert from North Africa to exchange goods and ideas.

From these North African traders, the West Africans learned iron-making technology. Archaeologists have found iron tools near the city of Nok in present-day Nigeria. The artifacts were made by the Nok people, who lived in the area between 500 B.C. and A.D. 200.

The Nok were the first West Africans to make iron. They began working with it as early as 450 B.C. and, in time, had discovered many practical uses for it. For example, by fitting their spears with iron points instead of stone ones, the spears lasted longer. Also, iron tools were better than stone ones for farming. Using iron-making technology, the Nok vastly improved their lives.

To make iron, the Nok placed rocks rich in iron ore in a clay furnace with charcoal. They then heated the mixture to a high enough temperature to liquefy it.

After the wastes were poured off, a chunk of molten iron remained. A Nok iron maker would then shape that soft, red-hot iron into a tool or weapon. This iron-making process is still used today in some parts of West Africa.

In addition to being iron makers, the Nok were also skilled potters. They used clay to build their huts and to make finely detailed sculptures. The clay head shown here illustrates the artistry of the Nok.

Little is known about why the Nok civilization came to an end. The Nok people seem to have begun to move at least by 300 B.C. However, because they shared their knowledge of iron making and pottery with the people they met, we can trace the path they took. ■

An Ancient Trade Center

In 1977, the remains of an ancient city were discovered on the inland delta of the Niger River. A **delta** is a triangular-shaped landform made by mud and silt deposited at a river's mouth. The iron and clay artifacts found among the remains of the city closely resembled the articles made by Nok craftspeople to the east. Thus, archaeologists determined that some Nok people had come to this site. The city, called Jenne-jeno, was inhabited from 250 B.C. to A.D. 1400.

Chapter 5

Visual Learning

Have students draw a graphic organizer to illustrate the characteristics of the Nok and Jenne-jeno cultures. It should include common characteristics such as trade and iron-making. It should also pinpoint differences in such areas as geography. Have several students copy their diagrams on the chalkboard for discussion and comparison.

Historical Context

The discoveries made at Jenne-jeno show that African history is still being written. Jenne-jeno was discovered only a short time ago in 1977 by anthropologists Susan and Roderick McIntosh. They found the site after aerial photographs revealed a series of mysterious large mounds in the area. When they uncovered the mounds they found thousands of artifacts. Animal bones and charred grains revealed information about people's diets. Fragments of pottery, statues, and containers

for smelting gold and copper revealed the skills of Jenne-jeno craftspeople. Foundations, walls, and hearths provided details about the early dwellings. Iron knives, spearheads, harpoons, and fishhooks revealed that the people fished and hunted. Gold earrings and copper hair ornaments showed that trade was an important part of Jenne-jeno's economy. Copper came from the Sahara, and gold was mined 480 miles (800 km) to the south of Jenne-jeno.

110

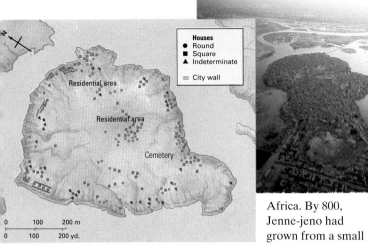

Houses
● Round
■ Square
▲ Indeterminate

= City wall

Residential area

Residential area

Cemetery

0   100   200 m
0   100   200 yd.

It lies about two miles from the modern city of Jenne in the Republic of Mali.

As you can see in the photo above, the city was built on a flood plain on the river's inland delta. The Niger flooded this plain yearly, and when the waters fell back, they left behind rich, moist soil ideal for farming rice. Indeed, the first people to settle there were rice farmers, who also raised cattle and fished in the Niger.

In addition, the Niger acted as a natural highway for trade. People carried rice, fish, baskets, and pottery to river cities in the north and brought back salt, copper, and stone. Traders went south on the river to bring back gold.

Traders also traveled over land. In fact, camel caravans eventually linked Jenne-jeno with North

Africa. By 800, Jenne-jeno had grown from a small settlement into a bustling trade center of about 10,000 people.

Because the people of Jenne-jeno had such an abundant supply of food and other products, many were free to do other things besides farm. Iron tools, copper and gold jewelry, and clay animals have been unearthed in the city. From these finds, archaeologists have determined that well-trained craftspeople lived there.

Despite its flourishing culture and fine location, by 1400, Jenne-jeno was completely abandoned. Archaeologists do not know why this happened. However, at about this time, the nearby city of Jenne was founded. Perhaps many of the people of Jenne-jeno settled in Jenne, which would make them the ancestors of the people who live there today. ■

▲ *This photograph shows the modern city of Jenne on the left and the ancient city of Jenne-jeno in the upper right-hand box. The illustration on the far left is of ancient Jenne-jeno and is based on the research of archaeologists who uncovered artifacts there.*

■ *How did the people of Jenne-jeno obtain the resources they could not produce?*

R E V I E W

1. **FOCUS** What are some of the ways the early West Africans developed prosperous cities in a landscape with such a varying climate?

2. **CONNECT** What things other than goods were exchanged between North African traders and West African traders?

3. **ECONOMICS** In what ways did the inhabitants of Nok benefit from learning the technique of iron making?

4. **GEOGRAPHY** How did the people of Jenne-jeno adapt to the geography south of the Sahara?

5. **CRITICAL THINKING** What would have been the impact on West Africa if the Sahara's climate had not changed so dramatically?

6. **ACTIVITY** Use the clay head pictured on page 110 to make your own Nok-style sculpture of a human or animal head.

West Africa

111

Answers to Review Questions

1. The early West Africans left the dry Sahara to settle in areas where the environment was less harsh. To obtain resources they could not produce, the West Africans traded with North Africans. Goods as well as ideas were exchanged.

2. North African traders brought their technology, their traditions, and a new religion across the Sahara—Islam.

3. Iron-tipped farm tools and weapons were more efficient than stone ones.

4. Fertile soil enabled them to raise abundant food which they traded for products not available to them, such as salt and copper. They used the Niger River to transport goods.

5. If the Sahara had remained lush and fertile, people might not have migrated and settled in West Africa. The trade centers along the Niger probably wouldn't have been developed, and new ideas might not have reached that region.

Homework Options

Have students draw a map that shows the modern boundaries of countries in West Africa. Ask them to compare this with their outline maps and determine what countries Nok and Jenne-jeno would be in today. *(Nigeria and Mali.)*

Study Guide: p. 17

112

INTRODUCE

Explain that although the Sahara made travel difficult, it did not cut off West Africa from North Africa. Large trade empires, such as Ghana, developed along the southern edge of the desert as a result of the trade routes that crisscrossed the desert. See if students can predict what effects trade had on the people of Ghana. Then have them read the lesson to find out how Ghana grew to be a wealthy trade empire.

Key Terms

Vocabulary Strategies: T36–T37
matrilineal—a system of tracing descent through the females of the family
patrilineal—a system of tracing descent through the males of the family

---

	B.C.	A.D.			
500				1500	TODAY
		300	1235		

L E S S O N   2

The Empire of Ghana

THINKING FOCUS

What effect did trade have on the people of Ghana?

Key Terms

- matrilineal
- patrilineal

➤ *This present-day village in the Sahel is called Chadawanka, in Niger. People still exchange salt for milk or grain at its market.*

Chapter 5

Ghana was an ancient agricultural kingdom of the Soninke *(suhn IHN kay)* people with a rich trans-Saharan trade. It began in the southeast corner of what is now Mauritania, along the Senegal River, and later grew along the Niger River. People farmed, built cities, formed social classes, produced art and music, and created trade networks. While agriculture flourished along the rivers, in drier areas people raised livestock. Some moved with the seasons to better grazing land. In the Sahel, on the southern edge of the Sahara, Berber tribes from North Africa raised horses and camels. They led traders and carried goods across the desert by camel to trading towns on the northern edge of the desert. It was a two-month, 1,200-mile trip filled with hardship, yet worth the effort. There was money to be made.

The rulers of Ghana controlled the trade of their kingdom and collected taxes on the salt that came from the north. Large numbers of cavalry and archers made Ghana's army the most powerful in the region. The monarch's power arose from a number of sources: First, he had the loyalty and support of local nobilities. Second, the Soninke religion made him a god to be worshiped. The king's great wealth, however, came from south of the kingdom, from the gold-bearing upper reaches of the Niger and Senegal rivers. This gold (which was in great demand across the Sahara) and its production, trading, and pricing, were all controlled by the king.

Objectives

1. Identify the factors that helped make Ghana a successful trading empire.
2. Explain why Koumbi was divided into two sections.
3. Evaluate the effects Muslim Arab traders had on Ghana's people.
4. Summarize the events that led to Ghana's downfall.

Graphic Overview

Ghana's location helps it become a major trade center. → Ghana's strength lies in its monarchy, army, gold, and agriculture. → North Africans and desert tribes overthrow the king of Ghana.

A Center of Trade

Ghana was in an ideal position for trade. It lay between the Sahel and Sahara in the north, and the highlands and tropical rain forests in the south. The Senegal and Gambia rivers also helped communication and transport. From the south came kola nuts, palm oil, copper, and gold. From the north, came imported items like ceramics, glass and oil lamps—and, of course, salt.

Under the Soninke kings, Ghana became a wealthy trading empire. The Soninke easily conquered neighboring peoples because their iron weapons were far superior to the stone ones of their opponents. By the late 900s, Ghana controlled more than 100,000 square miles of land and hundreds of thousands of people. Ghana's location—between the northern Saharan salt mines and the gold fields of Wangara to the south—helped it become a major trade center. Traders from both areas had to pass through Ghana to exchange goods. And the empire acquired much wealth from the taxes collected on the goods.

West Africans used salt to preserve and flavor food. They also needed to include a lot of salt in their diet to replace that lost from the body through perspiration.

Salt was scarce in southern Ghana, but gold was not. West African gold became important to Europe, the Middle East, and

In parts of central Africa, salt is still considered to be as valuable as gold.

North Africa, for use as money and in jewelry. Since the supply from the few gold mines in Europe and Asia had been exhausted, gold had to be found elsewhere. The trading city-states on the northern edge of the Sahara later accumulated so much gold from this trade that they minted gold coins. These coins were used as far away as Egypt and Syria. During the Middle Ages, two-thirds of all the gold circulating in the Mediterranean area had come across the Sahara.

Fortunately, people in Wangara were glad to trade some of their gold for salt from the north. Gold had limited value for them. Tools, for example, could not be made out of the soft metal. But salt was vital to good health. To the people of southern Ghana, salt and gold were of equal value. And so they made the trade in equal amounts—a pound of gold for a pound of salt. You can learn more about the gold and salt trade in A Closer Look on page 114. ■

Across Time & Space

Salt was also valued in ancient Rome. In A.D. 500, soldiers transported salt on a highway called Via Salaria, or Salt Road. The term salary comes from the Latin salarium, *which means money paid to soldiers to buy salt. Soldiers "worth their salt" were paid a salary.*

■ *What combination of geographic and economic factors made Ghana an ideal trade center?*

113

Point out that this lesson traces Ghana's development as a powerful trading and agricultural empire of West Africa. Write the Graphic Overview on the chalkboard and preview the causal events in the lesson. Suggest that students use the maps of trade empires on p. 121 to help them draw the kingdom of Ghana on their outline maps of Africa. Ask students to refer to the map in Lesson 1, p. 109, to describe Ghana's climate.

GEOGRAPHY
Critical Thinking

Use a map to illustrate how Ghana's location contributed to its success as a trade empire. Show students where Ghana's capital was located. How did Koumbi become a wealthy trade center without any important natural resources of its own? *(Located between salt and gold resources or trade routes; king collected taxes on goods exchanged by traders.)*

■ *Ghana was at the center of a trade route that ran from the salt mines of the northern Sahara to the gold fields south of Ghana. Salt and gold were then considered to be of equal value.*

113

Access Strategy

To demonstrate how value is determined, have students come up with a list of things that have value to people their age. *(Examples: a video of a favorite movie, a tape recording by a particular group, a favorite book, or a favorite food.)* Ask students to consider why some things become valuable and others do not. Suggest that an item that is valuable in one society may not be so regarded in another. Explain that the value of any kind of goods is based on how much of it is available and how many people want it. Point out that in our society gold and diamonds are highly valued because they are scarce and because of their decorative uses. Invite students to imagine a society in which gold and diamonds are plentiful, but salt is not. Which item would be the most valuable? *(Salt.)*

Access Activity

Point out that trade is an important part of the world's economy. Ask students to prepare a list of items they have at home that are imported from other countries: cars, foods, clothing, and household items. With the students' help, list all the countries and their exports on the chalkboard. Use a globe or world map to point out each country's location.

Note: You may wish to use this Closer Look after students have completed A New Trade Center on p. 113.

More About Ghana's Gold It has been said that Ghana's underground gold deposits were so close to the surface that gold was often exposed by heavy rains. Possibly to limit the plentiful supply and thus keep the price up, the king ruled that every gold nugget found in Ghana belonged to him. He allowed people to keep only the gold dust they found. Even so, there was still plenty of gold to go around.

Gold merchants used spoons to keep other people from touching the gold dust with their hands and perhaps walking away with some of the precious dust under their fingernails.

Trading Gold and Salt

Trading gold and salt was not an easy way to make a living. Merchants risked dying of thirst almost every time they made the 1,200-mile journey across the Sahara. But those who overcame the hardships got rich and brought great wealth to the south Sahara kingdoms.

Gold masks could hide more than faces. Sometimes the gold in molded objects—like masks, jewelry, or coins—was mixed with cheaper metals. To avoid being cheated, merchants liked to trade their salt for pure gold dust.

Gold pendant, Baule tribe, Ivory Coast

The king of Ghana and the small-scale societies of the Berbers kept the Saharan trade routes safe. They considered stealing a serious crime and punished thieves severely. "Neither the man who travels nor he who stays at home has anything to fear from robbers men of violence" wrote traveler Ibn Battuta.

Pass the salt! For centuries, North Africans have been getting their salt from the Atlantic Ocean, just like the person in this picture. First, they filled shallow pools with salt water. Then they let it evaporate. The piles of moist sea salt dried quickly under the blazing African sun.

114

Salt

Chapter 5

114

Visual Learning

Have students get current prices of salt (at a supermarket) and gold (from a newspaper or radio). Ask them to make a bar graph comparing the two prices. How many times more expensive is gold than salt?

Research

Throughout history, salt has been important. Ask students to go to the library to find out more about why people use salt. Have them write a short report about uses of salt. Tell them to include an explanation of why refrigeration sharply reduced the need for salt. Ask students to identify foods that are still preserved in salt.

Writing a Travel Log

Ask students to write travel log entries for an imaginary five-day trip across the Sahara, with details about supplies used, people met, trades made, and other things done or seen. Entries should be dated and need not be for consecutive days. Point out that trades may be made only near the beginning or end of the trip, and that the use of supplies will be of greater concern in the middle of the journey. Tell them to comment on why each event is of interest or importance.

A Diverse Capital

From about 800 to 1050, the gold and salt trade made Koumbi, Ghana's capital, the busiest and wealthiest marketplace in West Africa. Gold and salt were the most sought-after items, but in Koumbi's market people also bought and sold cattle, honey, dates, cloth, ivory, and ebony. In other shops at the market, local farmers sold their produce and craftspeople sold their wares.

Most of the traders in Ghana were Muslims who practiced the religion of Islam. Although Ghana's Soninke kings weren't Muslims, they were tolerant of Islam. Still, they tried to keep Islam separate from the traditional Soninke religion. So they divided many of Ghana's trading towns, including Koumbi, into two sections. One section housed the Muslims, and the other section housed the local people.

A six-mile-long boulevard linked the two sections of Koumbi. The Muslim side had 12 mosques and the homes of Muslim traders. Many of the buildings there were constructed of stone, and some had two stories. This section was also home to the huge Koumbi market.

The Soninke section of the capital looked very different. It was a walled city, and most of its one-story houses were made of wood or clay, with straw roofs. The king lived in this section in a large wood and stone palace.

The king was Ghana's religious and military leader and highest judge. The Ghanaian people came to him to settle their disputes.

> When the king gives [an] audience, . . . he sits in a domed pavilion around which stand 10 horses covered with gold-embroidered cloths. Behind the king stand 10 pages holding shields and swords decorated with gold. . . . At the door of the pavilion are dogs of an excellent breed. . . . Round their necks they wear collars of gold and silver.
>
> al-Bakri, historian, from
> *Book of the Roads and Kingdoms*, 1068

Thus, while administering justice, the king could also demonstrate his great wealth and power. ■

A New Religion

In the 900s, as trade in West Africa grew more profitable, many Arab merchants came to live in Ghana. With the trading of goods came the trading of ideas. Arab traders brought the first system of

▲ Most modern markets in West Africa are operated entirely by women. The woman in the main picture is selling yams. The baskets below the yam seller were woven by West African women. Why do you suppose they designed them to fit snugly into one another?

■ *How did the two sections of Koumbi differ from each other?*

West Africa

115

SOCIAL SYSTEMS
Visual Learning

Have students draw a diagram of the capital city of Koumbi on the chalkboard. Invite different students to draw buildings and structures in the Muslim and Soninke sections. Students should illustrate the market, the king's palace, mosques, and houses described in this lesson.

◄ *So they would be easy to store in a small house and easy to carry when empty.*

■ *One section of Koumbi housed the Muslims and the other was reserved for the Soninke people and the king. The Muslim section contained the capital's large market, mosques, and many homes made from stone. The homes in the Soninke section were smaller and made mostly of wood and clay.*

115

Religious Context

The grounds around the king's palace in the Soninke section of Koumbi was considered to be a sacred place by Ghana's people. According to the Muslim historian al-Bakri, the thick groves of trees surrounding the king's palace sheltered "the idols and the tombs of their kings. These groves are guarded, so that no one can enter them or discover their contents." Of the burial customs for Ghana's kings al-Bakri says, "When their king dies, they build over the place where his tomb will be an enormous dome of wood. At his side they place his ornaments, his weapons, and the vessels from which he used to eat and drink, filled with various kinds of food and beverages. Then they dig a ditch around the mound so that it can be reached only at one place." Point out that the burial customs of Ghana's kings were similar to those of the Egyptian pharaohs and of the pre-Columbian societies in Mexico and Central and South America.

Critical Thinking

Explain that traders in Ghana used salt and gold dust as currency. Kings controlled the gold to keep it from losing its value. Only Ghana's kings were allowed to own gold nuggets. Lead a discussion to help students understand that if gold had been allowed to circulate freely, it would have become too common. As a result, its value would have decreased.

BELIEF SYSTEMS

Visual Learning

Have students look at the picture of the African mosque on this page. Tell them that it reflects a blend of two cultures, African and Muslim. Ask them to describe the elements that are African *(use of clay and African style of building, and clothing)* and those that are Muslim *(minarets on mosques, kneeling for prayer).*

This mud mosque in Mali is called the Great Mosque. Muslims must pray at a mosque once a week on Fridays. At other times Muslims even pray in the street but always remove their shoes first. Men and women pray separately.

writing and numbers to West Africa. The Ghanaian kings adopted the Arab writing system and even hired Arabs as government officials to help them take care of trade matters.

By 750, Muslim Arabs had created a huge Islamic Empire in the Middle East. And, as the Arabs gained more influence in West Africa, they taught the people of Ghana about their religion. However, reactions to these teachings were mixed. Although Ghana's Soninke rulers held tightly to their traditional religion, many other government officials and merchants eventually converted to Islam, some spending large sums to build expensive mosques for Muslim worship.

Conversion to Islam

Among the first of the converts to Islam were the Mandinke *(man DIHN kuh)* people from the southern Sahara, who served as middlemen in trade between Arab caravans and Wangara gold miners. The Mandinke formed small trade companies that made contact with many different people. They spread Islamic ideas throughout West Africa.

Many West Africans converted to Islam because it stressed belief in the "brotherhood of all believers." This sense of brotherhood encouraged trust and peaceful trade between people of different nationalities. Muslim traders often extended credit to each other simply because they practiced the same faith.

Visual Learning

Define the key terms *matrilineal* and *patrilineal.* Have students draw two family trees. One should illustrate inheritance through the maternal side of the family and the other, inheritance through the paternal side of the family. Ask students to discuss whether our society is patrilineal or matrilineal.

Social Context

The people of Ghana believed that their king was a sacred person who had divine powers. The king did not appear in public, and it was taboo to watch him eat, drink, or perform other bodily functions. When the king sneezed, members of his court would slap their thighs as a sign of respect. This worship of the king was one reason that Ghana's people found Islam hard to accept. Islam requires Muslims to worship only God.

Art Connection

The Muslims not only influenced the religious beliefs of the people of Ghana but also their art. An Arabic text from the 11th century describes decorative pages with inscriptions from the Qur'an hung on walls in the center of Koumbi. To protect the precious parchment pages of the Qur'an, wood carvers made parchment boards that served as protective coverings. The book covers were made from planks of wood and intricately carved and chiseled with geometric designs.

Traditional Practices

Other Islamic practices were harder for the Ghanaians to accept. Muslims, for example, had their own idea about the succession of kings. In Ghana when a king died, he was not succeeded by his own son but by the son of his sister. This system of tracing succession through the females of the family is known as **matrilineal** succession. Muslims, on the other hand, practiced **patrilineal** succession, in which the throne passes from father to son.

The people of Ghana continued to practice matrilineal succession to determine who inherited family property. This practice was too well established to abandon. Still, many Ghanaians considered themselves Muslims. They were just selective about the ideas they would adopt. ■

■ *In what ways did Ghanaians benefit from their contact with Arab traders?*

A Fallen Empire

Along the northernmost coast of Africa, Berber peoples ruled the region called the Maghreb *(muh GRUHB)*. By the late 1100s they had long been Muslims, and now rival reform movements battled for power. The Almoravids, and later the Almohads, were political and spiritual movements. The wars that followed their rise took large amounts of gold to finance.

Saharan Berbers including the Sanhaja and the Taureg operated the caravans across the desert. By the 900s, the Ghanaians had forced tribute from the Sanhaja's southernmost trading center, Awdaghust *(ah dah GOOST)*. As the Almoravid movement spread, the Sanhaja joined it, and they retook Awdaghust. Then they continued, taking over the lands to the south, conquering Koumbi in 1076.

In 1087, the Soninke regained control from the Almoravids. However, in reestablishing their empire they faced many problems. Some of the states they once ruled had adopted Islam and supported the Almoravids. Others broke away to form separate kingdoms.

King Sumanguru, who wanted to rebuild Ghana's empire, ruled one of these kingdoms. In 1203, he overthrew the Soninke king and took over Koumbi. Meanwhile, a new kingdom to the east called Mali, ruled by the Mandinke, was steadily gaining power. In 1235, the king of Mali defeated Sumanguru and Mali replaced Ghana as the major power in West Africa. ■

■ *How did the brief takeover by the Almoravids lead to Ghana's downfall?*

REVIEW

1. **FOCUS** What effect did trade have on the people of Ghana?
2. **CONNECT** How did the Nok culture help the Soninke defeat neighboring peoples?
3. **GEOGRAPHY** How did the location of the West African gold and salt mines benefit Ghana?
4. **BELIEF SYSTEMS** What Islamic practice was particularly difficult for the Ghanaians to accept? Why?
5. **CRITICAL THINKING** The Ghanaians who practiced the Soninke religion were tolerant of the Muslims who settled in Ghana. How might Ghana's empire have differed if they had not been tolerant?
6. **WRITING ACTIVITY** Imagine that you are visiting Koumbi in the 1100s. This is your first trip to this part of the world, and you don't speak the language. In your journal, record what you see in each section of the city. What does the marketplace look like? Why do you think the city is divided as it is?

HISTORY

Study Skills

List the events that led to Ghana's downfall on separate cards large enough for the class to read. Place the cards in random order on the blackboard's chalk tray. Have volunteers come to the board. Then explain to the volunteers that they have two minutes to arrange the cards in order of occurrence. After the two minutes are up, have the class vote on whether or not they think the order is correct. Rearrange the cards according to the students' suggestions.

■ *Arab traders shared their system of writing and numbers, and Arabs served as government officials in matters of trade.*

■ *When the Soninke tried to reestablish their empire, some of the states that had adopted the Islamic faith supported the Almoravids.*

CLOSE

Trade created a strong link between two very different cultures. Discuss the advantages and disadvantages of Ghana's relationship with the Muslims.

Answers to Review Questions

1. Trade provided the people of Ghana with necessities, such as salt, and was a source of wealth for the empire. Trade attracted Arabs whose religion had a great effect on many of Ghana's people.
2. The Soninke's iron weapons were superior to their opponents' stone ones. Iron-making was first introduced in West Africa by the Nok.
3. Ghana lay between the salt mines of the northern Sahara and the gold mines south of Ghana. Traders from both areas had to pass through Ghana's capital and pay taxes on all goods exchanged there.
4. Muslims practiced patrilineal succession, and the people of Ghana practiced matrilineal succession. The tradition was too fundamental to abandon.
5. Answers may vary, but might stress the idea that a less tolerant climate could have harmed the trans-Saharan trade, which enriched Ghana.

Homework Options

Have students research the people who live in the area that was once ancient Ghana. Point out that the borders of modern Ghana do not overlap those of the early kingdom of Ghana.

Study Guide: p. 18

INTRODUCE

Have students review the factors that helped make Ghana a great trade empire. Explain that when the kingdom of Ghana broke up, it was replaced by the empire of Mali and later the empire of Songhai. Use the Graphic Overview to trace the events in the lesson. Ask students to read the Thinking Focus and predict what Mali and Songhai had in common with Ghana. Have them read the lesson to find similarities and differences among the three empires.

Key Term

Vocabulary Strategies: T36–T37
griot—person who passes down customs, history, legend, art, and poetry through storytelling

B.C. | A.D.

500   500   1000   **1235**   **1590**   TODAY

L E S S O N   3

The Empires of Mali and Songhai

THINKING FOCUS

What events led to the development of the great trade empires of Mali and Songhai?

Key Term

• griot

▼ *Trade still thrives in Mali on the shores of the Niger River.*

In 1235, the Battle of Kirina marked the fall of Ghana and the end of King Sumanguru's reign. But it also meant the rise of the kingdom of Mali and the beginning of King Sundiata's reign. The battle is rich in legends that are retold today.

According to legend, Sumanguru and Sundiata were magicians. Their magic would decide the battle's victor. In the heat of the match, King Sundiata furiously roared at the warriors of King Sumanguru, and they scurried for cover. When Sumanguru bellowed in return, the heads of eight spirits magically appeared above his head.

However, Sundiata's magic was more powerful, and he defeated the spirits. Then Sundiata fixed Sumanguru with his gaze and aimed an arrow at him. The arrow only grazed Sumanguru's shoulder, but it drained him of all his magical powers.

A present-day Mandinke **griot,** or storyteller, finishes the tale:

The vanquished Sumanguru looked up towards the sun. A great black bird flew over above the fray. . . . "The bird of Kirina," [the king] muttered. Sumanguru let out a great cry and, turning his horse's head, he took to flight.

Recorded by D.T. Niane of Mali, from a griot in Guinea, Africa

To the griot who described this battle, Sundiata was a hero.

Mali Develops a Prosperous Trade

Sundiata became king of the new empire of Mali, which had once been a part of Ghana. And he established its capital at Niani, on the upper Niger.

Sundiata never fought again after Kirina. He relied on his army to extend Mali's boundaries. The king focused on restoring prosperity to his kingdom.

Objectives

1. Evaluate the geographic and political factors that made Mali a great trading empire.
2. Assess the impact and economic significance of West African rulers' adoption of Islam.
3. Analyze the factors that paved the way for the emergence of the great Songhai trade empire.
4. Identify the major cause of Songhai's decline.

Graphic Overview

Battle of Kirina	**Empire of Mali**	**Mansa Musa's Rule**	**Songhai Empire**	**Songhai's Defeat**
Muslim king of Mali wins the battle.	Mali takes over Ghana's trade, expanding overland routes.	Muslim culture flourishes, trade increases, and borders expand.	Songhai conquers Mali, becoming West Africa's greatest empire.	Moroccans conquer Songhai.

Sundiata first concentrated on improving agriculture. His soldiers cleared land for farming, and they planted rice, yams, onions, beans, grains, and cotton. In a few years, Mali became a productive farming region.

However, as in Ghana, Mali's economy was based on trade. The many years of fighting in Ghana had interrupted trans-Saharan trade—trade that crossed the Sahara. So, once Mali controlled Ghana's gold mines, Sundiata set about restoring the salt and gold exchange with Niani as the kingdom's new trade center.

Sundiata and his successors expanded Mali's trade routes north and east across the Sahara to Cairo, Egypt, and to Tunis in Tunisia. You can locate these cities in the Atlas on the map on page 525. Mali controlled salt mines in the north at Taghaza and copper mines in the east at Takedda.

In addition to the gold mines at Wangara, the people of Mali had discovered a new source of gold at Bure, not far from the new capital on the Niger River. From Bure they easily shipped gold along the Niger to interested traders. The Niger became a busy highway for trading gold and other goods.

Less than 100 years after the victory at Kirina, Mali had become the most powerful kingdom in Africa. By the late 1300s, Mali was three times as large as Ghana had ever been. ■

▲ *Onions may have been such an important crop because their strong flavor can be used to season other foods.*

■ *How did Sundiata and his armies extend Mali's trade empire?*

Mansa Musa Enriches the Empire

Mali's greatest ruler, Mansa Musa, succeeded to the throne in 1307. Mansa Musa was a devout Muslim, but he respected all his subjects' beliefs. He allowed those who desired it to worship their traditional gods. However, many of the people who lived in trade centers had been influenced by the Arab traders and had already converted to Islam. Under Musa's rule, conversions greatly increased, mainly due to Mali's expanding trade.

The North African writer, Ibn Battuta, praised the newly converted Muslims for faithfully "observing the hours of prayers, studying the books of law, and memorizing the Qur'an." However, as a traditional Muslim, Ibn Battuta was shocked by some West African customs that survived despite Islamic influence. For example, West African women were quite independent. He also found that people still scarred their faces to show their clan affiliations.

Nevertheless, in accordance with Islamic teachings, some of Mali's rulers made pilgrimages to the holy city of Mecca in the Middle East. Mansa Musa made the 3,500-mile journey in 1324.

According to some accounts, which may have become exaggerated over time, Mansa Musa was accompanied on this journey by as many as 50,000 people—friends, family members, doctors, advisers, and 500 slaves carrying golden staffs. In addition, 80 to 100 camels, each

▲ *Mansa Musa in a close-up from the map on the next page.*

119

West Africa

Refer students to the timelines at the beginning of Lessons 2 and 3 to illustrate the chronology of West Africa's three great trade empires. Explain that the text covers these empires in chronological order, beginning with Ghana in Lesson 2, followed by Mali and Songhai in Lesson 3. Have students turn to the three maps on p. 121 to compare the area controlled by each empire. Ask them to mark the boundaries of the empires on their outline maps.

■ *Sundiata's armies extended the borders of Mali's empire, and the king expanded the empire's trade in all directions. Eventually Mali controlled new salt, copper, and gold mines.*

Critical Thinking

Stress that the battle between Sundiata and Sumanguru is steeped in legend. Explain that Sundiata was a hero but that his accomplishments were not all based on legend. He helped to restore and strengthen Ghana's economy. With students' help, make a list of Sundiata's accomplishments on the chalkboard.

119

Access Strategy

Ask students if they have family stories that have been passed down to them by an adult relative. Explain that such stories tend to be told and retold at family gatherings. Find out if one person in particular usually retells the stories. Then tell the students that the role of the griot in African states is similar to that of the family storyteller. Point out that ancient Africa had no written language to record its history. Griots passed down histories, stories, and poems from generation to generation, often at the service of the government. Explain that griots often used musical instruments and songs to accompany their retelling of ancient legend. In addition to providing information and entertainment, their stories often reinforced a society's values. Have students discuss the advantages and disadvantages of relying on the oral transmission of information.

Access Activity

Read the story of the Battle of Kirina on p. 118 while the students follow along in their texts. Then have students enact the battle. Divide the class into two groups, one representing Sundiata, the other, Sumanguru. Have each group work together to assign their roles and prepare their parts. Encourage creativity.

BELIEF SYSTEMS

Visual Learning

Discuss the impact that Mansa Musa's conversion to Islam had on Mali's people. Have students study the map of West Africa showing the figure of Mansa Musa. What details on the map were used to show the presence of Islam? *(Mosques, Arab trader.)* What does the portrait of Mansa Musa on the map suggest about the king? *(The gold crown, orb, and scepter show his wealth; his portrait on the map suggests his power and prominence as an African leader.)*

■ *As Muslims, their empire became a part of the larger Muslim world because of the belief in the "brotherhood of all believers." The empire could fully take part in trade with Muslim countries and take advantage of Muslim scholarship.*

▲ *Detail from a map of Mali made in Spain around 1375. Mansa Musa is drawn with scepter and throne, showing he is the equal of European kings.*

■ *What effect did West African rulers' conversion to Islam have on the empire?*

loaded with 100 pounds of gold dust, are said to have traveled with him to Mecca. Hundreds of other camels carried the other supplies.

Mansa Musa's pilgrimage drew the attention of Mediterranean merchants to Mali's economic importance. European mapmakers began to include Mali on maps because of its role in international trade.

Under Mansa Musa, culture and learning flourished in Niani and other trade centers such as Timbuktu. When Musa returned from Mecca, he brought Arab scholars back with him. Mansa Musa invited these scholars to teach in Mali's learning centers. As Muslims, they welcomed the opportunity to instruct their brothers in scholarship and religion.

Likewise, Muslim traders welcomed the opportunity to trade with fellow Muslims in different states. Thus, they helped to increase Mali's trade empire as well as their own profits.

Even Mali's borders expanded under Mansa Musa's rule. New land was acquired both peacefully and as the result of war. Most of Mali was divided into states, which were under Musa's control. Some regions were allowed to remain independent as long as their rulers pledged their loyalty and a portion of their wealth to Mali. ■

Power Shifts to Songhai

After Mansa Musa died in 1332, Mali was ruled by a series of kings who were unable to protect its vast territory. Berber nomads attacked caravan routes in the desert and threatened to take Timbuktu. People from the southern rain forests raided Mali's southern border. And in the west, the Songhai on the middle Niger River began to revolt.

The Songhai were a mixture of farmers, traders, fishermen, and warriors who lived along the Niger near the city of Gao. For hundreds of years, the Songhai had fought off Mali's control. Sometimes they succeeded; sometimes they failed.

Under Mansa Musa, Mali ruled Gao and most of the Songhai kingdom for about 50 years. However, when he died, the Songhai stopped

120

Study Skills

Have students research what was happening in Europe during the height of Mali's empire in the 1300s. Have students choose one aspect of European life, such as economy, government, or religion, and compare it with its counterpart in Mali in a written or oral report.

Historical Context

In the mid-1300s, the Muslim chronicler Ibu Fadl Allah al-Omari wrote this description of Mansa Musa's court:

The Sultan presides in his palace on a great balcony where he has a huge seat of ebony: on either side it is flanked by elephant tusks turned towards each other. His arms stand near him, being all of gold: sabre, lance, quiver, bow and arrows. He wears wide trousers made of about twenty pieces of cloth of a kind which he alone may wear. Behind him there stand about a score of Turkish or other pages which are bought for him in Cairo: one of them, at his left, holds a silk umbrella surmounted by a dome and a bird of gold: the bird has the figure of a falcon. His officers are seated in a circle about him, in two rows, one to the right and one to the left; beyond them sit the chief commanders of his cavalry. In front of him there is a person who never leaves him and who is his executioner.

Ancient African Empires: 700-1600

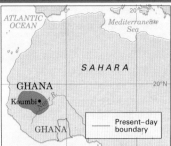

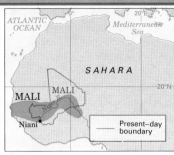

paying taxes to Mali. In 1435, a Songhai prince named Sunni Ali declared Gao's independence. Aided by the Songhai warriors, he successfully fought off Mali's attempts to regain the city.

Under attack on all sides after 1400, Mali gradually weakened. Mali's rulers were unable to drive off the invaders. Berbers took over the trade and learning centers of Timbuktu and Walata in the mid-1400s. In 1464, under the guidance of Sunni Ali, the Songhai began conquering their neighbors and expanding their kingdom.

A new Songhai empire thus grew out of a region that had once been part of Mali, just as Mali had grown out of a state in the empire of Ghana. Gao became Songhai's capital and Sunni Ali its king.

Sunni Ali was a Muslim, but he was not a devoted believer. After he died, his son, a non-Muslim, took over the throne. The new ruler was intolerant of Muslims, so many Muslims joined forces to overthrow him. The Muslims wanted a ruler who shared their beliefs. The ruler they supported was Askia Muhammad. In the 1490s, Askia overthrew Ali's son and declared Islam the state religion.

Askia's armies expanded the borders of Songhai and encouraged many non-Muslims to convert. The new king invited Muslim scholars to his empire, and its cities became great centers of culture and learning once again. At the height of its power in the late 1500s, the Songhai empire was larger and wealthier than Mali had ever been. In time, as the number of Muslims and Muslim traders increased, Songhai would become the greatest trade empire of West Africa. ■

▲ *Compare the growth of ancient Ghana, Mali, and Songhai. Note that although a present-day Ghana and Mali exist, there is no longer a Songhai.*

■ *How did Askia Muhammad's strong rule help Songhai become such a great trade empire?*

▼ *Under the leadership of Askia Muhammad, Timbuktu flourished, attracting scholars, traders, and craftspeople from all over the Muslim world.*

121

Science Connection

Askia Muhammad encouraged the people of Songhai to develop the empire's natural resources. He had them dig many new wells for water, and his engineers designed waterways to bring water to desert regions. The waterways made farming possible far to the north of the Niger and prevented the desert from slowly spreading south to this area. Ask students to locate the area on the climate zone map on p. 109. Use the map to discuss the climate north of the Niger.

Political Context

To please the king of Songhai, each group of people under his rule was obliged to give him gifts. This was usually done once or twice a year when a group's chief visited the capital city or when a government representative or tax collector made his rounds in the provinces. Groups skilled at iron-making might offer iron-tipped spears or arrows for the king's army. Farmers would give food for the king's horses, and Songhai fishermen would ship fish by canoes.

Study Skills

Divide students into pairs and assign each pair a major trade city that existed during the empires of either Ghana, Mali, or Songhai. Instruct the students to work together to prepare a report entitled "[City Name]: Yesterday and Today." If a city no longer exists, the students should choose a town or city near that area for the "Today" section of their report.

HISTORY

Critical Thinking

Refer to the weapons described on this page as you discuss the Moroccan raid on Songhai. Ask students to consider what the outcome of the battle might have been if both sides had used similar weapons. *(Songhai's army would most likely have defeated the Moroccan soldiers because they significantly outnumbered the Moroccans.)*

■ *The ruler of Morocco had already captured salt mines that had been under Songhai's control. He also wanted to control Songhai's source of gold and thereby monopolize the lucrative salt-gold exchange.*

C L O S E

In random order on the board, list the events that contributed to the rise and fall of the empires of Mali and Songhai. As you read each event, ask students to match it to the appropriate empire. Record their responses in a two-column chart. Then have students number the events in chronological order or arrange them on a timeline.

122

Songhai Collapses

▼ *Timbuktu's location at the edge of the Sahara Desert and only eight miles from the Niger River led to the popular saying of the day "Timbuktu, meeting point of the camel and canoe."*

■ *Why did the ruler of Morocco fight for control of Songhai?*

Askia's heirs succeeded him to the throne. Over time, however, these rulers created a small but powerful Islamic group at the top of the ruling society. This group distanced itself from people who were not Muslims. As a result, certain states broke away from the empire, resentful of the Muslim kings.

But the major threat to Songhai came from Morocco in North Africa. In 1585, Morocco's ruler captured Songhai's salt mines in Taghaza. The Moroccan ruler also wanted to control Songhai's source of gold in West Africa. Ownership of both these two important resources would ensure a control of trade. The ruler of Morocco decided that this was worth fighting for.

In 1590, he sent 4,000 soldiers under Muslim Spaniard Judar Pasha to conquer Songhai. After a five-month-long journey across the Sahara, Pasha arrived in Songhai with only 1,000 men. But his soldiers carried something new to the region, something they had acquired in the Middle East—guns.

Songhai's soldiers outnumbered Pasha's by at least 25,000 men. But swords and arrows were no match for guns. Gao fell, and then Timbuktu, and finally most of Songhai.

Pasha destroyed the gold-producing system. Gradually the North Africans lost interest in making Songhai a colony, although they stayed there another 150 years. What had once been a peaceful, well-organized empire became a series of military camps.

Songhai was the last great trading empire of West Africa. No other West African kingdom ever rivaled its power or strong hold on trade. In the towns and villages, however, people went on paying taxes, providing labor, and showing up for military service. The Songhai monarchs still ruled, but now only in a few of their former lands. ■

R E V I E W

1. **FOCUS** What events led to the development of the great trade empires of Mali and Songhai?
2. **CONNECT** What are some of the things the empires of Ghana, Mali, and Songhai had in common?
3. **ECONOMIC GEOGRAPHY** Why do you suppose all the capitals of the great West African trade empires were located on the Niger River?
4. **CRITICAL THINKING** In what ways were Mansa Musa and Askia Muhammad alike? In what ways were they different?
5. **CRITICAL THINKING** How might the war with Morocco have destroyed Songhai's gold-producing system?
6. **WRITING ACTIVITY** Sundiata's victory over Sumanguru is the story that *The Lion King* is based upon. Write your own version of this tale. You can set it in any time or place.

Chapter 5

Homework Options

Ask students to write a paragraph describing a piece of West African art created at the time of the Ghana, Mali, or Songhai empires.

Study Guide: p. 20

Answers to Review Questions

1. Under strong Muslim leaders, both empires expanded their borders and control of trade. Scholarship and trade flourished because of their belief in the brotherhood of all Muslims.
2. These three empires all had strong leaders and a well-organized government. They controlled the salt-gold exchange and were influenced by Muslim traders.
3. The Niger was used as a trade highway. Kings could exercise better control of trade from cities central to this activity.

4. Both were strong rulers who supported the arts and learning. Askia made Islam the state religion and encouraged conversions. Mansa Musa allowed people to believe as they chose.
5. One possible answer is that warfare destroyed the safety of the trans-Saharan trade routes. Without the government's salt-for-gold trade, there was no reason to continue producing gold.

UNDERSTANDING CRITICAL THINKING

Interpreting Proverbs

Here's Why

People sometimes repeat stories or fables in order to teach wisdom or moral lessons. A proverb is similar to the moral of a story; it is a short saying that expresses a well-known truth. Many proverbs can apply to any place in the world and at any time. Others are more specific and reveal something about the particular culture or historical period from which they originated.

If you read a West African proverb, for example, you may learn something about West African culture. You may also learn that West Africans share some values with your own culture.

Here's How

The proverbs in the box below originated among the Ewe tribe of Ghana in West Africa. The proverb about the blacksmith means that when you go to another place, you must learn to behave according to the customs of that place. What clues does the proverb provide about West African

Stool of an Ashanti king

culture? The reference to blacksmiths suggests their importance. Think of a similar saying from your own culture, such as: You can be a big fish in a small pond or a small fish in a big pond.

Now look at the mask on the right, of a European from the west coast of Africa. Think about the second proverb about the hat. One interpretation of this proverb might be that if people want to give you something, you should beware of why they are giving it to you. The proverb gives you a clue that West African culture is a nonwhite culture and that West Africans do not always find white people trustworthy. "Beware of Greeks bearing gifts" is a saying you may know from your own culture that has a similar meaning.

Try It

Examine the last two proverbs. Analyze each of them, asking the same

kinds of questions and using the same kind of thinking applied to the proverbs in Here's How.

Apply It

Your culture has proverbs of its own. Analyze the following proverbs from various cultures, asking questions like those posed in Here's How.

- Haste makes waste.
- A watched pot never boils.
- Anything that can go wrong will go wrong.
- Wisdom is not like money, to be tied up and hidden.

T he blacksmith in one village becomes a blacksmith's apprentice in another.

If a whiteman wants to give you a hat, look at the one he is wearing before you accept it.

You do not become a chief simply by sitting on a big stool.

A stump that stays in a river for a hundred years does not become a crocodile.

Ewe Proverbs, Ghana

123

West Africa

UNDERSTANDING CRITICAL THINKING

This skills feature examines two West African proverbs to teach students how proverbs reflect the wisdom and morality of the culture from which they came.

CULTURE
Study Skills

To get students started, write "A stitch in time saves nine" on the board. Ask volunteers to share other proverbs they know. List them on the board. Discuss each proverb in turn. Pay attention to the details each proverb reveals about its culture. Can it apply to another culture?

Writing Proverbs

After studying the formula of proverbs, ask each student to write three proverbs. Encourage them to share their proverbs with the rest of the class. Discuss their cultural significance.

Answers to Try It

1. Possible interpretation: You cannot designate yourself as great. Cultural clue:

Having a stool to sit on must be a sign of the rank of chief in West African culture.
2. Possible interpretation: You can move to a foreign place, but you will not become a native by simply moving there.

Answers to Apply It

Interpretations may vary according to cultural orientation.

Objective

Evaluate and interpret proverbs. (Critical Thinking 2)

INTRODUCE

Read the lesson title aloud to the class. Stress that the majority of West Africans did not live in cities such as Timbuktu, Gao, or Koumbi. They lived in small villages, and their lives were quite different from the lives of those who lived in the great cities. As they read, though, students should remember that empires like that of the Songhai were highly organized states whose policies affected village life directly. For instance, villagers often paid taxes to the empire, and were called to perform military service.

Key Terms

Vocabulary Strategies: T36–T37
diviner—a person who communicated with the spirit world and helped people to interact with their gods
ancestor worship—honor and reverence paid to one's deceased relatives based on the belief that their spirits live on after death and can influence the gods in one's favor
kinship—the relationship among family members

B.C. | A.D.

500   300   1590   TODAY

LESSON 4

Village Society in West Africa

THINKING FOCUS

How did the people in the rural villages of West Africa survive in their often unpredictable environment?

Key Terms

- diviner
- ancestor worship
- kinship

➤ *Masked Dogon dancers move to the rhythm of drums.*

The young man waits on a hillside. When the drums begin beating, he and the other Dogon dancers will descend to the village. He will wear the mask of Gomintogo, the antelope.

This is the story the dance will tell: An antelope ate a farmer's seeds. The angry farmer killed the antelope. But then the animal's spirit made the farmer's son very ill. To heal his son, the father made a mask of the antelope. The mask captured the antelope's spirit so that it could no longer harm his son. Soon his son was well again.

Now the young man dances, wearing the wooden mask he has carved himself—an antelope head with jagged horns three feet long. As he dances, he feels the spirits of Gomintogo and his ancestors.

Farming: A Way of Life

Symbols of agriculture often appeared in the religious stories of the early West Africans. Most of these people did not live in the large trading cities of Ghana, Mali, and Songhai. They lived in small villages on riverbanks, on the savanna, or in the rain forests.

The most important activity in every village was raising food. People who fished the Niger River also cultivated gardens. Skilled iron makers and blacksmiths also raised crops, chickens, and goats. Even cattle-raising nomads grew a wheat-like grain called millet.

Chapter 5

Objectives

1. Demonstrate how West African farmers adapted to their land and climate.
2. List the common components of West African religions.
3. Describe the government of rural African villages.

Graphic Overview

| agriculture | religion | dance and music | family system | cooperation |

WEST AFRICAN VILLAGE LIFE

In the dry regions of the sahel, farmers grew millet and sorghum *(SAWR guhm)*. These grains are well suited to dry climates because during dry periods they remain alive. In the wetter regions south of the sahel, people grew rice, especially in the delta of the Niger.

In the dense West African rain forests, farmers made small clearings and grew edible roots. The people of the rain forests could not raise livestock, however, as the forest was filled with insects that were deadly to herd animals.

West African farmers devel-oped different farming methods to suit the different types of land. The Dogon, for example, who lived on cliffs south of the Niger, found that pools of rain-water formed in crevices among the rocks. Farmers brought fertile soil from the valley below and turned the pools into gardens.

In each area, most farm-ers grew a small surplus of the crops that flourished in their regions and traded this for the food they could not produce. ■

▲ *Nigerian village women pound palm kernels to extract palm oil, used in making soap.*

■ *How did farming methods differ in different geographic regions?*

Religion, Dance, and Music

*B*ut the year had gone mad. Rain fell as it had never fallen before. For days and nights together it poured down in violent torrents, and washed away the yam heaps. Trees were uprooted and deep gorges appeared everywhere....

That year the harvest was sad, like a funeral, and many farmers wept as they dug up the miserable and rotting yams. One man tied his cloth to a tree branch and hanged himself.

Chinua Achebe, *Things Fall Apart*

Life in the villages of West Africa was often unpredictable. A drought, a flood, or an outbreak of disease could mean disaster. People thought that there were greater powers, or gods, who could protect them from such disaster.

Since earliest times, humans have had religious experiences. These often take vastly different forms. Indigenous religions, or religions that have not been brought by an outside group, flourished in African society. Africans believed that the physical world in which they lived was influenced by a spirit world. Their religion was meant to bring the two together.

Priests and diviners, they believed, helped people interact with the gods. **Diviners** communicated with the spirit world and had healing powers. Diviners also knew how to please the gods through rituals and dancing.

The people of the villages also believed in honoring their relatives through **ancestor worship.** They believed that the spirits of their ancestors lived on after death and could influence the gods in their favor—or punish the living with bad luck, sickness, or even death.

Villagers also tried to contact and please spirits through music and dancing. The Dogon people believed that when a person died,

▲ *Figures such as this one are thought to protect the bones of especially distinguished ancestors.*

West Africa

Explain that even in areas controlled by the great trade empires, most West Africans lived in small communities devoted to farming. Emphasize that there were hundreds of different villages in early West Africa, each with its own unique characteristics. The lesson gives an overview of practices that many villages had in common. Ask students to look at the photos in the chapter to get a feel for this diversity. Use the Graphic Overview to acquaint students with the topics that will be discussed in this lesson.

■ *In the sahel farmers grew grains that were well-suited to a dry climate. Rice was grown in wetter regions south of the sahel. The rain forests had to be cleared of dense vegetation and supported only root crops.*

GEOGRAPHY
Map and Globe Skills

Describe the different crops and methods of farming in West Africa's four main climate zones, desert, semiarid, tropical wet and dry, and tropical wet (see map on p. 109). Have students make a key that describes each zone's climate, farming methods, and crops.

Access Strategy

Divide the class into two groups. One group should imagine that they have been stranded on a desert island. Have the other group imagine they have been stranded on an isolated mountain peak. Tell each group that they will have to work together to gather food and devise a rescue plan. Require each group to come up with a system or method to deal with these tasks. Suggest that they elect a leader or agree on a list of rules before they get started. After a set amount of time, have each group describe how they organized their activities. Discuss how their plans differed because of geography. Tell students that in this lesson, they will learn that West African village societies also had to rely on cooperation for their survival.

Access Activity

Read aloud to the class the story about the Dogon dancers at the beginning of the lesson. Then ask for volunteers to act out the story using mime and dance. Cast one student to narrate the antelope dance. When finished, have the students reflect on what the dance tells us about the relationship between the Dogon and nature.

BELIEF SYSTEMS
Visual Learning

Discuss the role of religion in West African village society. Explain that religion influenced every aspect of village life. To illustrate, have students examine the photos that appear in the Religion, Dance, and Music section of this lesson. Ask them to explain how each is linked to a traditional African religious belief.

POLITICAL SYSTEMS
Critical Thinking

Describe the role of kinship in village government. Ask students to discuss how family ties would increase cooperation within the village society. Have students compare the structure of their family with the structure of family life in West African villages. Who is considered their family leader? What are the family rules and how are they enforced? How do they work together to accomplish household tasks? Ask students whether they can think of any problems that might come from such strong family ties. Use an example that students might recognize, such as a children wanting to be or do something that their parents don't agree with.

126

▲ *These women of the Fante tribe from Ghana call spirits with ritual.*

■ *In what ways were the various religions of West Africa similar?*

their spirit needed a place to stay. So they created masks that looked like the person that had died. When a dancer put on the mask, he was able to touch the spirit that lived within it. The masked dancers felt the spirits as they moved to the beat of the drums. ■

Village Life

People who lived in rural villages were members of large related families, or clans. The members of a clan could trace their origins to a common founding ancestor.

Kinship, or family relationship, was the basis of government. The male head of each clan became one of the village chiefs and often one of the religious leaders. Sometimes a council of family elders made up the village government. Within the family, everyone had jobs and responsibilities according to age, skills, gender as well as tradition. Older people were highly respected.

UNDERSTANDING KINSHIP

The settled farming communities of early West Africa were organized around kinship, or blood relationship, and marriage. People were also adopted, and lived among tight-knit, large, multi-generational families, with siblings (brothers and sisters), parents, grandparents, aunts, uncles, and cousins.

A clan was made up of a number of related families. Larger alliances might occur, too, with clans who spoke the same or related languages. Land was owned by the families or clans; it was rare that individuals owned land. The majority of sub-Saharan Africans lived in rural areas, usually in villages of at most a few hundred people. Others, such as the Yoruba people, lived in big cities. But whether in a city or a village, families and clans became one of the most important organizing forces in African society.

Rights and Responsibilities

The village was made up of many clans and families. Clans protected their members and provided for them when they were sick or old. The clans educated members and found work for them. In return for these benefits, members also had responsibilities. For example, if the clan had certain work to be done, or owed a debt to another clan, it was the members' responsibility to pitch in and help. Jobs were handed out according to age and ability. In places out of reach of a state government, clans might ask members to share in defense duties, too.

The Family in Society

In the United States, children are linked to both of their parents' families equally. This is called a bilateral system; in it both sides of a person's family are important.

In other cultures, relatives of one parent may be given more importance. The Ashanti people of modern West Africa are matrilineal. Children inherit property through their mother.

Kinship determines one's position in the family and even in society. This is because the family reflects the customs and traditions of a society.

126

Chapter 5

Study Skills

Have students research and present an oral report on any cultural group that exists today in West Africa. Explain that in modern-day Nigeria alone, there are more than 300 different cultural groups with almost as many different languages. Require that the reports include descriptions of lifestyle, religion, government, and art. Encourage students to include visuals.

Music Connection

Music was a vital part of religious rituals and social events in village society. Often an entire village would participate by dancing, singing, or playing instruments. This community participation differed from the European style of musical performances in which a sole performer played to a quiet audience. West African music provided the basis for African American spirituals, gospel, blues, and modern jazz, disco, and rock.

Social Context

Craftspeople were given special status in village society. For instance, because objects made of iron played such an important part in daily life, the blacksmith held a high position in West African society. The farmer depended on him for his tools, soldiers and hunters relied on him for weapons, and diviners called on him to make religious objects. Blacksmiths never ate or drank with other villagers, and many were also diviners and medicine men.

Slavery

Under extreme hardship, if a clan was in debt or had promised to provide workers, members could be loaned out to fulfill the family's obligations. A clan might temporarily transfer its rights to a member to another clan in return for goods. When the debt was paid, the worker was returned. If the debt was not paid off, however, the status of temporary "slave" became permanent. Even then, individuals were still people, never property. They had only lost their political rights, not their personal rights. Usually the new family would accept them as members. Former slaves' children were not born slaves, nor did one group enslave other groups.

The majority of slaves, however, were captives of war. While today we find slavery unthinkable, historians remind us that for ancient peoples around the world, slavery was an improvement over death after capture. With rising prosperity in the Middle East and Asia after the 700s, slaves came to be in demand. Some African states exported slaves. Between 1200 and 1500, about 2.5 million Africans were taken across the Sahara or the Red Sea bound for slavery. It was

not just the labor of the slaves that made them valuable but their skills and talents.

Slaves were used for various jobs. Many military leaders and soldiers were slaves. Some slaves became rich and powerful. Most served as domestic servants or did physical labor, like those who mined copper in Mali. Some slaves became the servants of kings and had power and money but they had no freedom. ■

▲ *In current-day Mopti, Mali, goods are traded from boats on the Niger River.*

■ *Why was kinship important in West African village life?*

■ *The religions had several things in common: the belief in a supreme being as a creator of the world; the belief in lesser gods of nature that controlled everyday life; and the belief in life after death with ancestral spirits returning to watch over the living.*

■ *Kinship defined one's village and clan. Since clans were responsible for members' lives, kinship directly affected everything one did and had in life, including education, work, and possibly even freedom.*

R E V I E W

1. **FOCUS** How did the people in the rural villages of West Africa survive in their often unpredictable environment?
2. **CONNECT** Many city dwellers in Mali and Songhai converted to the Islamic faith, but most villagers did not. Why do you think the villagers tended to keep to their traditional religion?
3. **BELIEF SYSTEMS** Clans were responsible for their members. What did a clan provide for its members? What were members expected to do in return?
4. **SOCIAL SYSTEMS** What role did the family play in the religious and political life of the village?
5. **CRITICAL THINKING** People in rural West African villages depended on each other for survival. Do you think this is true of people in the United States today?
6. **ACTIVITY** Imagine you are a village leader. One of the village members has damaged another's home. You need to punish the offender and compensate the victim. What exactly do you do to restore harmony?

West Africa

127

INTRODUCE

Like other cultures in their early stages, the West African culture explained many ethical and moral principles through stories. "The Cow-Tail Switch" not only taught a lesson but also entertained. This retelling by Harold Courlander and George Herzog puts into writing a tale that was part of the oral tradition of West Africa. This selection adds narrative detail to the portrait of West African village life in Lesson 4 of Chapter 5.

READ AND RESPOND

Many students will enjoy reading this story independently, but the dialogue lends itself to oral reading also. In fact, you may wish to replicate the storytelling situation discussed in the headnote. If so, read the story aloud, but stop at the point Ogaloussa is making a decision. Engage the students in a discussion of who should receive the cow-tail switch. Then complete the story and compare decisions.

Before students read the story, tell them that *sinews* are supporting tissues in the body, and *cowry shells* are the brightly colored shells of mollusks that live in warm water oceans.

128

West African chiefs and other important village leaders often carried symbols of their authority. A decorated cow-tail switch, as in this story, was one of those symbols.

cassava (kuh SAH vuh) an edible root

Ogaloussa (oh gah LOO suh)

manioc cassava

128

LITERATURE

The Cow-Tail Switch

Retold by Harold Courlander and George Herzog

West African villagers told stories to teach lessons and for community entertainment. Often, in telling this story about the cow-tail switch, the storyteller would stop before the end. He would then ask the audience to participate by working out the ending. As you read it, think about how you would end this story and what arguments you would make to support your decision.

Near the edge of the Liberian rain forest, on a hill overlooking the Cavally River, was the village of Kundi. Its rice and cassava fields spread in all directions. Cattle grazed in the grassland near the river. Smoke from the fires in the round clay houses seeped through the palmleaf roofs, and from a distance these faint columns of smoke seemed to hover over the village. Men and boys fished in the river with nets, and women pounded grain in wooden mortars before the houses.

In this village, with his wife and many children, lived a hunter by the name of Ogaloussa.

One morning Ogaloussa took his weapons down from the wall of his house and went into the forest to hunt. His wife and his children went to tend their fields, and drove their cattle out to graze. The day passed, and they ate their evening meal of manioc and fish. Darkness came, but Ogaloussa didn't return.

Another day went by, and still Ogaloussa didn't come back. They talked about it and wondered what could have detained him. A week passed, then a month. Sometimes Ogaloussa's sons mentioned that he hadn't come home. The family cared for the crops, and the sons hunted for game, but after a while they no longer talked about Ogaloussa's disappearance.

Then, one day, another son was born to Ogaloussa's wife. His name was Puli. Puli grew older. He began to sit up and crawl. The time came when Puli began to talk, and the first thing he said was, "Where is my father?"

The other sons looked across the ricefields.

"Yes," one of them said. "Where is Father?"

"He should have returned long ago," another one said.

"Something must have happened. We ought to look for him," a third son said.

Thematic Connections

Social Studies: Legends of a Society

Houghton Mifflin Literary Reader: Strange and Mysterious Happenings

Background

In the culture of West Africa, as in many ancient cultures, stories were used to entertain, explain, and teach. In African village society, a person's status was determined by his or her lineage, or family line. Who your ancestors were—father, grandfather, great-grandfather—meant a great deal, so remembering and honoring them were extremely important. "The Cow-Tail Switch" teaches a lesson about the importance of remembering.

"He went into the forest, but where will we find him?" another one asked.

"I saw him go," one of them said. "He went that way, across the river. Let us follow the trail and search for him."

So the sons took their weapons and started out to look for Ogaloussa. When they were deep among the great trees and vines of the forest they lost the trail. They searched in the forest until one of them found the trail again. They followed it until they lost the way once more, and then another son found the trail. It was dark in the forest, and many times they became lost. Each time another son found the way. At last they came to a clearing among the trees, and there on the ground scattered about lay Ogaloussa's bones and his rusted weapons. They knew then that Ogaloussa had been killed in the hunt.

One of the sons stepped forward and said, "I know how to put a dead person's bones together." He gathered all of Ogaloussa's bones and put them together, each in its right place.

Another son said, "I have knowledge too. I know how to cover the skeleton with sinews and flesh." He went to work, and he covered Ogaloussa's bones with sinews and flesh.

A third son said, "I have the power to put blood into a body." He went forward and put blood into Ogaloussa's veins, and then he stepped aside.

Another of the sons said, "I can put breath into a body." He

◄ Why didn't Ogaloussa's family look for him before Puli asked his question? *(They were too busy with the routine of their lives to do anything about it; they were used to him going on long hunting trips; sometimes it takes a new person to recognize a problem.)*

129

Access Strategy

All cultures have traditions and rituals for remembering their ancestors, though the traditions vary a great deal from culture to culture. Ask students to describe a tradition from their culture or religion relating to remembering their ancestors. *(Visiting cemeteries, lighting candles, special remembrance events or celebrations.)*

These traditions are important because they keep us in touch with our family histories. Tell students that in "The Cow-Tail Switch" they will see just how much importance the African villagers placed on remembering their ancestors.

did his work, and when he was through they saw Ogaloussa's chest rise and fall.

"I can give the power of movement to a body," another of them said. He put the power of movement into his father's body, and Ogaloussa sat up and opened his eyes.

"I can give him the power of speech," another son said. He gave the body the power of speech, and then he stepped back.

Ogaloussa looked around him. He stood up.

"Where are my weapons?" he asked.

They picked up his rusted weapons from the grass where they lay and gave them to him. They then returned the way they had come, through the forest and the ricefields, until they had arrived once more in the village.

Ogaloussa went into his house. His wife prepared a bath for him and he bathed. She prepared food for him and he ate. Four days he remained in the house, and on the fifth day he came out and shaved his head, because this was what people did when they came back from the land of the dead.

Afterwards he killed a cow for a great feast. He took the cow's tail and braided it. He decorated it with beads and cowry shells and bits of shiny metal. It was a beautiful thing. Ogaloussa carried it with him to important affairs. When there was a dance or an important ceremony he always had it with him. The people of the village thought it was the most beautiful cow-tail switch they had ever seen.

Soon there was a celebration in the village because Ogaloussa had returned from the dead. The people dressed in their best clothes, the musicians brought out their instruments, and a big dance began. The drummers beat their drums and the women sang. The people drank much palm wine. Everyone was happy.

Ogaloussa carried his cow-tail switch, and everyone admired it. Some of the men grew bold and came forward to Ogaloussa and asked for the cow-tail switch, but Ogaloussa kept it in his hand. Now and then there was a clamor and much confusion as many people asked for it at once. The women and children begged for it too, but Ogaloussa refused them all.

Finally he stood up to talk. The dancing stopped and people came close to hear what Ogaloussa had to say.

"A long time ago I went into the forest," Ogaloussa said. "While I was hunting I was killed by a leopard. Then my sons came for me. They brought me back from the land of the dead to my village. I will give this cow-tail switch to one of my sons. All of them have done something to bring me back from the dead, but I have only one cow-tail to give. I shall give it to the one who did the most to bring me home."

So an argument started.

"He will give it to me!" one of the sons said. "It was I who did

Collaborative Learning

List on the board what each of the sons of Ogaloussa did to bring him back to life. Divide the class into as many groups as there are sons. Have each group prepare an argument stating why that son should receive the cow-tail switch. After students have finished reading the story, have them consider what the moral of the story would have been if their "son" had been given the cow-tail switch. Their arguments should be logical. Have one student in each group take notes from the group's discussion and present the argument to the class. After all groups have presented their arguments, discuss them as a class, noting the use of logic but avoiding judging the arguments as "right" or "wrong."

the most, for I found the trail in the forest when it was lost!"

"No, he will give it to me!" another son said. "It was I who put his bones together!"

"It was I who covered his bones with sinews and flesh!" another said. "He will give it to me!"

"It was I who gave him the power of movement!" another son said. "I deserve it most!"

Another son said it was he who should have the switch, because he had put blood in Ogaloussa's veins. Another claimed it because he had put breath in the body. Each of the sons argued his right to possess the wonderful cow-tail switch.

Before long not only the sons but the other people of the village were talking. Some of them argued that the son who had put blood in Ogaloussa's veins should get the switch, others that the one who had given Ogaloussa breath should get it. Some of them believed that all of the sons had done equal things, and that they should share it. They argued back and forth this way until Ogaloussa asked them to be quiet.

"To this son I will give the cow-tail switch, for I owe most to him," Ogaloussa said.

He came forward and bent low and handed it to Puli, the little boy who had been born while Ogaloussa was in the forest.

The people of the village remembered then that the child's first words had been, "Where is my father?" They knew that Ogaloussa was right.

For it was a saying among them that a man is not really dead until he is forgotten.

Further Reading

African Myths and Legends. Kathleen Arnot. These tales are about animals, humans, and superhumans.

Behind the Back of the Mountain. Verna Aardema. These are black folktales from Southern Africa.

The Cow-Tail Switch and other West African Tales. Retold by Harold Courlander and George Herzog. Additional West African tales and legends that have been passed down through oral tradition.

The King's Drum and Other Stories. Harold Courlander. Here are tales from many different peoples of Africa. Each story identifies the tribe it came from.

The Magic Drum: Tales From Central Africa. W.F.P. Burton. The very short stories in this book are similar to fables. They are favorites in the Congo.

◄ What is this really saying to us? *(That someone can stay alive in our memories even after they have died. But when someone is no longer remembered, then he or she is truly dead.)*

EXTEND

The story of the cow-tail switch touches the importance of remembering and caring for ancestors in West African village society. Have students find more information about African customs regarding lineage and prepare short oral reports to be shared with the class.

131

Writing a News Account

Have students imagine that they are writers for the *West African Gazette* sent to cover the miraculous reappearance of Ogaloussa. Have them write their accounts as news stories, including quotes from any of the characters in the story. Students should write catchy headlines for their stories. After they have written rough drafts of their articles, have students proofread and revise, making sure they have corrected all errors and that the story is done in newspaper style with short, succinct, factual statements. Students should make final copies of their news articles to be displayed or shared.

Further Reading

You may want to have your students look in the school or local library for more collections of African myths, fables, and folktales.

Answers to Reviewing Key Terms

A. Sample answers:
1. The **griot** said, "Once upon a time. . . ."
2. **Diviners** communicated with the spirit world.
3. They moored the boat on the fertile bank of the **delta.**
4. Some grasslands of the **savanna** are farmed.
5. In the **patrilineal** system, ancestry is traced through the male members of the family.
6. **Kinship** was the basis of government in the villages.
7. Abdul settled in the **sahel.**
8. In a **matrilineal** society, ancestry is traced through the women of the family.

B. Sample answers:
1. *Matri-* means "mother" (from the Latin *mater*). Related words: *matriarch, matrimony, maternity.*
2. *Ancestor* comes from the Latin *ante,* "before," and *cedere,* "to go." Words with the same root: *secede* and *precede.* The same prefix: *anteroom* and *anterior.*
3. A shore is usually land on the edge of a body of water. The *sahel* is land along the edge of a desert, a vast, dry "ocean" of sand.
4. The adjective *divine* means "godlike"; the verb *to divine* means "to foretell." Both are from the Latin *divus,* "god," and *divinus,* "inspired by the gods."

Answers to Exploring Concepts

A. Sample answers:
Jenne-jeno: abundant food, trade center, crafts center.
Ghana: ideal location, capital—Koumbi, Soninke rulers.
Mali: gold mines, part of Ghana, Muslim rulers.
Songhai: Farmers, largest trade center, capital—Gao.
Villages: agricultural, nature gods, kinship-based government.

B. Sample answers:
1. Many villages had ties to a broader state that entailed rights and responsibilities. For example, the state provided defense and villagers sometimes served in the defense forces. When villages were not aligned with a broader state, defense was their own concern.
2. Trade caravans came from North Africa to exchange

Chapter Review

Reviewing Key Terms

ancestor worship (p. 126)   matrilineal (p. 117)
delta (p. 110)   patrilineal (p. 117)
diviner (p. 126)   sahel (p. 109)
griot (p. 118)   savanna (p. 109)
kinship (p. 127)

A. Use each word below in a sentence that shows what the word means.
1. griot
2. diviner
3. delta
4. savanna
5. patrilineal
6. kinship
7. sahel
8. matrilineal

B. Write answers to the following questions. You may need to refer to a dictionary.
1. What does the root word *matri-* in *matrilineal* mean? What are some other words that contain *matri-* or a related form?
2. What root word and prefix combine to form the word *ancestor*? What are some other words with the same root? The same prefix?
3. *Sahel* means "shore of the desert." How is this kind of shore similar to that bordering a body of water?
4. What are the different meanings of the adjective *divine* and the verb *to divine*? What root words do they share with *diviner*?

Exploring Concepts

A. Copy the following cluster diagram on your paper. Then fill in the blanks with three important details about each society. Three details are done for you.

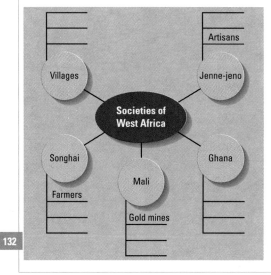

B. Support each of the following statements with facts and details from the chapter.
1. West Africans created city, regional, and state governments. Some villages fell outside these structures.
2. Despite the hardships of desert travel, West Africa was not cut off from the outside world.
3. The Niger helped Jenne-jeno grow into a bustling trade center.
4. Ghana became a powerful trading empire because of its location and government.
5. Traders brought more than goods to Ghana.
6. The success of Mali's trade empire affected the spread of Islam.
7. Askia Muhammad expanded the Songhai kingdom and advanced the spread of Islam.
8. The nature of West African village life helped shape the people's religious practices.
9. Kinship was the most important element in West African village life.

goods and ideas. The Nok people may have learned iron working from traders.
3. The annual flooding left behind rich soil for growing rice. The river was a highway for shipping rice and other products in exchange for salt and gold.
4. Ghana's strong government protected the trade routes that developed between the salt-producing and gold-producing regions.
5. Trade exposed Ghana to new systems of writing and numbering, and brought exposure to Islam, as well.
6. Under Mansa Musa, its Muslim leader, Mali's expanding trade led to more converts to Islam.
7. Askia declared Islam the state religion, expanded Songhai's borders, and turned the cities into centers of culture and trade.
8. Villagers believed that nature gods and ancestors' spirits could protect them from droughts, floods, and diseases.
9. Each villager belonged to a clan, which could trace its origin to a founding ancestor. Kinship was the basis of government.

Reviewing Skills

1. Give one interpretation of the following West African proverb: "When you are carrying beef on your head, you do not use your feet to catch grasshoppers." What does it tell you about West African culture?
2. Give one interpretation of this West African proverb: "You change your steps according to the change in the rhythm of the drum." Can you think of a proverb with a similar meaning? An opposite meaning?
3. Review Understanding Kinship at the bottom of page 126. What is the main idea of this section? What supporting details do you find in the Rights and Responsibilities section? What supporting details do you find in The Family in Society?
4. Suppose you wanted to read an article about the West African trade empires. Where would you look to find the names of magazines that cover that subject?

Using Critical Thinking

1. Ideas are carried along trade routes together with goods and products. Therefore, the direction of trade routes can affect the course of history in very important ways. Suppose trade caravans had been unable, or traders unwilling, to cross the Sahara. How might West African society be different today? What effect might such isolation have had on the spread of religions?
2. Suppose a young person harms another young person. How would the punishment in American society now differ from that in a West African village in the year 1000? Which punishment do you think would be more effective? Why?
3. How did the Nok people make iron, and how did this skill benefit their culture? Do you think the culture you live in would be very different if we did not have metal-working skills? If the world ran out of metal ores completely and our supply of new metal was cut off, how do you think society would be affected? What kinds of adjustments would you have to make in your own life?

Preparing for Citizenship

1. **WRITING ACTIVITY** In Lesson 3 you read part of the story of the battle between Sumanguru and Sundiata, as told by a modern-day Mandinke griot, or storyteller. The language was colorful and the facts were somewhat exaggerated. Choose a recent event of importance in your life or in the world at large and retell it in the style of a modern-day American storyteller. After you write your story, practice reading it and then telling it aloud.
2. **GROUP ACTIVITY** Suppose you lived in West Africa in the time of one of the great trade empires, shown on page 121 of this chapter. Would you prefer to live in the exciting capital city of one of the empires, with its great culture, its exchange of people and ideas, and its many goods and services? Or would you prefer life in a small, rural village? Organize a debate on the question and prepare arguments for your side.
3. **COLLABORATIVE LEARNING** In all the West African cultures this chapter talked about, the importance of cultivating enough food to survive and to trade was stressed. Read through the chapter and list all the foods that were mentioned. Then divide into groups of three or four students. Have each group choose a food (two examples are rice and yams) and find a recipe for it in a cookbook. Then meet with the members of your group to prepare the dish and bring it to school for a potluck lunch.

West Africa

Answers to Reviewing Skills
1. Sample answer: Learn the value of what you have; don't waste time chasing lesser things. Culture clue: Beef is valuable in West Africa.
2. Sample answer: Change your actions to meet changing circumstances. Similar: "Go with the flow." Opposite: "Keep your hand on that plow and hold on!"
3. Main idea: Kinship practices reflect the society. Supporting details in Rights and Responsibilities: West African families include grandparents, aunts, uncles, and cousins; U.S. families have far fewer people. Supporting details in The Family in Society: In America, both parents' sides of a family matter; in West Africa, relatives of one parent or the other are more important.
4. The *Readers' Guide*.

Answers to Using Critical Thinking
1. Students might answer that Islam would probably not have spread as far and as fast in West Africa and might be less important there today.
2. Students might answer that punishment is emphasized in America, but social pressure would curb villagers' behavior. Some may say social pressure is more effective and fair than prison. But the village system would be hard to carry out in our large, complex society.
3. The Nok liquefied iron ore in a clay furnace, then shaped it into tools, weapons, and sculptures. Students might answer that without metal we wouldn't have many common products such as cars, lamps, and locks on doors. Toys and tools would be replaced by plastic or wood objects.

Answers to Preparing for Citizenship
1. **WRITING ACTIVITY** Students' stories should be historically accurate but told in an embellished storytelling style.
2. **GROUP ACTIVITY** Students' arguments should effectively support one side or the other.
3. **COLLABORATIVE LEARNING** Among the foods listed are fish, rice, beef (cattle), salt, yams, honey, dates, onions, beans, chicken, goat meat, millet, sorghum, edible roots, palm oil, and herbs. Guide students in choosing fairly simple recipes and working out the logistics of where to cook the meal—perhaps one group member's home, the school's home economics department, or the school's kitchen.

133

Planning at a Glance
Central and Southern Africa

	Objectives	Reading Support and Other Resources	Diverse Learning Strategies
Lesson 1 The Spread of Bantu *pp. 136–139* 2–3 days	• Assess the impact of geography on the movement of early peoples in central and southern Africa. • Explore how the study of languages can be used to improve our understanding of the past. • Describe how the Bantu speakers diversified as they came into contact with other African cultures.	• **Workbook** or **Reading Support:** pp. 71–74 Review p. 17 Lesson Support/Transition p. 17 Multi-lang. Sum. pp. 33–34 • **Other Resources:** Geography Kit; Posters 4, 5; Study Guide p. 22	Access Strat. **(SDAIE)** TE p. 137 Access Act. **(SDAIE)** TE p. 137 Map and Globe Skills **(Visual)** TE p. 138 Audiotapes of Multi-language Lesson Summaries **(Auditory)**
Skill: Relief Maps: Making a Vertical Profile *p. 140* 1 day	• Construct a vertical profile using information provided on a relief map.	• **Other Resources:** Study Guide p. 23	
Lesson 2 The Rise of Coastal Trading States *pp. 141–144* 2–3 days	• Analyze the effect of the monsoon winds on the development of trade in East Africa. • Describe the contacts among international cultures in the coastal trading centers of East Africa. • Summarize the reasons behind the prosperity and decline of the East African trading centers.	• **Workbook** or **Reading Support:** pp. 75–78 Review p. 18 Lesson Support/Transition p. 18 Multi-lang. Sum. pp. 35–36 • **Other Resources:** Geography Kit, Study Guide p. 24	Access Act. **(Extra Support)** TE p. 142 Social Participation **(Auditory)** TE p. 143 Homework Options **(Visual)** TE p. 144 Audiotapes of Multi-language Lesson Summaries **(Auditory)**
Lesson 3 The Rise of the Zimbabwe State *pp. 145–148* 2–3 days	• Use historical evidence to characterize the early people of Zimbabwe. • Assess the effect of gold mining on the economy and politics of Zimbabwe. • Describe the events that occurred during the breakup of Zimbabwe.	• **Workbook** or **Reading Support:** pp. 79–82 Review p. 19 Lesson Support/Transition p. 19 Multi-lang. Sum. pp. 37–38 • **Other Resources:** Study Guide p. 25	Access Act. **(SDAIE)** TE p. 146 Access Strat. **(Extra Support)** TE p. 146 Social Participation **(Visual)** TE p. 148 Audiotapes of Multi-language Lesson Summaries **(Auditory)**
Lesson 4 The Kongo Kingdom *pp. 149–153* 2–3 days	• Describe the origins of the Kongo Kingdom. • Assess the impact of the Portuguese on the Kongo economy. • Explain how the Portuguese slave trade caused civil war in Kongo.	• **Workbook** or **Reading Support:** pp. 83–86 Review p. 20 Lesson Support/Transition p. 20 Multi-lang. Sum. pp. 39–40 • **Other Resources:** Study Guide p. 26	Access Act. **(Extra Support)** TE p. 150 Access Strat. **(SDAIE)** TE p. 150 Role Playing **(Auditory)** TE p. 151 Visual Learning **(Visual)** TE p. 152 Audiotapes of Multi-language Lesson Summaries **(Auditory)**
Making Decisions: Trade Between the Kongo and Portugal *pp. 154–155*	• Identify the alternatives available to the Mani–Kongo regarding trade with the Portuguese. • Analyze the Mani–Kongo's alternatives and choose the best one.	• **Other Resources:** Poster 8, Study Print 4	Activity **(Auditory)** TE p. 154
Chapter Review *pp. 156–157* 1 day		Chapter 6 Test pp. 21–24 *(See facsimiles on TE p. 564.)*	Assessment Multiple-Use Masters pp. 73–80

133A

Reading Support Resources *for Every Lesson*

Reading and Review

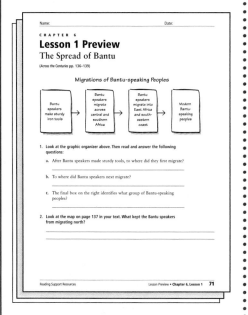

- **Chapter Overview*** p. 70
- **Lesson Previews*** using graphic organizers from the Teacher's Edition pp. 71, 75, 79, 83
- **Reading Strategies*** pp. 72, 76, 80, 84
- **Lesson Summaries*** pp. 73–74, 77–78, 81–82, 85–86
- **Lesson Reviews** pp. 17, 18, 19, 20

* **Workbook** includes starred items.

Multi-language Summaries

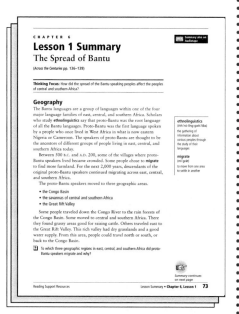

Lesson Summaries in:
- English (See Reading and Review.)
- Spanish pp. 73–74, 77–78, 81–82, 85–86
- Chinese pp. 33–40
- Hmong pp. 33–40
- Khmer pp. 33–40
- Vietnamese pp. 33–40

 Summaries available on audiotapes

Lesson Support /Transition
S D A I E

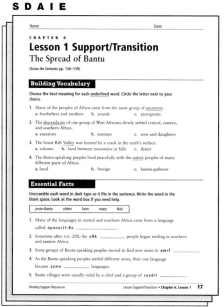

Activities for SDAIE
Specially **D**esigned **A**cademic **I**nstruction in **E**nglish

- **Lesson Support/Transition** pp. 17, 18, 19, 20

 # Technology Options

Internet Support
http://www.eduplace.com

Social Studies Center at Education Place

Internet support for Chapter 6:
- *Lesson at a Glance*
- *A Kongo King*

Software
Student Writing Center ® (CD-ROM) (Macintosh® or Windows®)

School to Career

Cowrie shells served as money for the Kongo traders. Today we have coins and paper bills. Divide students into two groups. Have one group research how coins are minted and the other how paper bills are printed. What job responsibilities are involved? What materials are needed? What techniques are used to discourage counterfeiting?

Character Education

For most cultures, the family is the basic social and political unit. Have students create a family album, including pictures and text showing what makes a family special and unique. What positive qualities and abilities does each family member bring to the whole?

CHAPTER
PREVIEW

Have the students read the chapter title and narrative. Then have the students examine the images and captions. Ask them what the Kikuyu, Zulu, and Shona have in common. *(They are all Bantu-speaking groups.)*

Looking Back

Why did the early West Africans leave the Sahara to settle in other areas? *(They wanted to live where life would be less harsh.)*

Looking Forward

Tell students they will read about the kingdoms of central and southern Africa in the next four lessons: The Spread of Bantu, The Rise of Coastal Trading States, The Rise of the Zimbabwe State, and The Kongo Kingdom.

In Lesson 1 students will read about how the Bantu-speaking peoples settled in central, eastern, and southern Africa.

Chapter 6
Central and Southern Africa

They called themselves Bantu, which means "the people." They spread out from West Africa over 2000 years ago, settling in the grassy savannas and the steamy rain forests of central and southern Africa. Some traveled to the coasts, where they built trading empires. But European traders plundered these empires and took many people away as slaves. Nevertheless, the heritage of "the people" continues. Most central and southern Africans today still think of themselves as Bantu.

During this period, a Bantu group called the Kikuyu became cattle raisers. They used shields like this one to defend their grazing land.

c. A.D. 200 Bantu migrate southward and begin farming and herding. Zulu people living in South Africa today, like this boy, trace their heritage to the early settlers.

| 500 | B.C. | A.D. | | 500 |

134

A.D. 476 A barbarian general overthrows the last emperor of the Western Roman Empire.

500 B.C.

134

East African Traders

The Bantu speakers who settled in East Africa developed a livelihood based on trade. From about A.D. 900, East Africans played a growing role as middlemen who prepared African goods for sale to Arab traders in the Indian Ocean network. The descendants of Bantu-speaking farmers became brokers, warehouse owners, laborers, dock workers, and shopkeepers.

Africans, Arabs, Indians, Persians, and southeast Asians intermingled in East African ports. East African culture assimi-lated many aspects of other cultures. In particular, the religion of Islam and the Arabic language influenced the evolution of a rich, unique culture known as Swahili.

Zimbabwe Miners

In southern Africa, Bantu-speaking migrants settled in an area well suited to farming and herding. Their descendants grew sorghum, owned cattle and sheep, and used iron tools. They were excellent craftsworkers in metal, wood, and ivory.

Centuries-old traditions continue today. This young Kenyan woman, adorned with gold, bronze, and beads, participates in a ritual celebrating her coming of age.

A.D. 1000–1300 Bantu people called the Shona build the Great Zimbabwe, which means "Houses of Stone" (above). This grand city becomes Zimbabwe's capital and trade center.

1000	1500	Today

A.D. 786 Islamic ruler Abd al Rahman III begins building the Great Mosque in Cordoba, Spain.

A.D. 1300 Mali becomes the largest West African trading empire.

A.D. 1700

135

Understanding the Visuals

The ruins of the Great Zimbabwe (p. 135) are located near Masvingo (formerly Fort Victoria), Zimbabwe. Remaining are a 30-foot-tall tower and an 800-foot-long wall that in places is 32 feet high.

Understanding Chronology

Have students note on the timeline that at about the same time that Mali became the largest West African trading empire, Zimbabwe was an important center of trade in eastern Africa.

The discovery of gold and the recognition of its trade value led the Bantu speakers to develop efficient mining techniques. Wealth obtained from the gold trade helped establish a great kingdom, Zimbabwe, between A.D. 1000 and 1300.

Kongo Craft Specialization

On a fertile plateau south of the Congo River, descendants of Bantu-speaking migrants planted crops, gathered forest products, and hunted game. Their central location and access to river transport allowed the Kongo people to develop a prosperous kingdom based on inter-African trade. Craftsworkers excelled in boatbuilding, weaving, woodcarving, and other crafts.

Scholars have only begun to examine Kongo traditions and myths, archaeological remains, and linguistic evidence to learn more about Kongo history before 1500. Evidence suggests the Kongo developed a system of government earlier than most sub-Saharan groups. Some scholars theorize that the rich environment of the tropical forest satisfied the material needs of the Kongo people and thus allowed them to focus their attention on state formation.

Exploitation

In each of these cultures, the arrival of the Portuguese in the 1400s brought exploitation and disaster. While East Africa and Zimbabwe gave up trade profits, Kongo became involved in trading slaves, the beginning of the Atlantic slave trade.

INTRODUCE

Point out central and southern Africa on the map on p. 137. Explain that the terms refer to geographic regions rather than political units. Have students read the Thinking Focus. Point out that, despite cultural, geographical, and political diversity in central and southern Africa today, most of the people share a common ancient history. Have them read to find out why the proto-Bantu-speakers' migrations are the key to this history. Make sure that students understand that Bantu is a language group.

Key Terms

Vocabulary Strategies: T36–T37
ethnolinguistics—the study of the relationship between cultural and linguistic behavior
migrate—to move from one area or country to another and settle there

B.C.	A.D.				
500	280	500	1000	1500	TODAY

LESSON 1

The Spread of Bantu

THINKING
FOCUS

How did the spread of the Bantu-speaking peoples affect the peoples of east, central and southern Africa?

Key Terms

- ethnolinguistics
- migrate

➤ *Bantu-speaking peoples, such as these Kikuyu women, now live in much of eastern, central, and southern Africa.*

Historians have many ways of studying the past. They can study stories that are passed down orally through the generations, or others that are written down. Music and dance, too, sometimes reflect a culture's history. Finally, artifacts and fossils give us physical proof of past events. In the study of central and southern Africa, however, another tool has proved most useful—language.

Consider the English word "continent." English developed from an old Germanic language, but through learning from the French, English-speaking people adopted the French word "continent" *(kahn tee NAHN).*

French developed from Latin, the language of the Roman Empire.

In Latin, the phrase *"terra continuens" (tayr uh kahn TIHN yoo enz)* means "continuous land." By tracing word histories, we learn how cultures interacted. In east, central, and southern Africa, historians are doing just this with the approximately 800 non-European languages spoken there.

Linguistics is the study of languages, and **ethnolinguistics** is the study of various peoples through their languages. In east, central, and southern Africa, scholars have found four major language families: the Khoisan *(KOY sahn),* Afro-Asiatic, Nilo-Saharan *(NEYE loh suh hayr uhn),* and Congo-Kordofanian *(kohr doh FAN yan).*

Perhaps the best studied languages are from one subgroup of the Congo-Kordofanian language family. These are called Bantu languages. Among different Bantu languages, scholars recognized words and grammatical structures that came from the same source.

Scholars now believe that proto-Bantu, the root language of all the Bantu languages, was the first language spoken by a people who lived in what is now eastern Nigeria or Cameroon between 500 B.C. and A.D. 200. These West Africans are believed to be the ancestors of diverse groups of people in many parts of Africa.

136

Chapter 6

Objectives

1. Assess the impact of geography on the movement of early peoples in central and southern Africa.
2. Explore how the study of languages can be used to improve our understanding of the past.
3. Describe how the Bantu speakers diversified as they came into contact with other African cultures.

Graphic Overview

| Proto-Bantu speakers make sturdy iron tools | ▸ | Proto-Bantu speakers migrate across central and southern Africa | ▸ | Languages develop; migration into East Africa and southeastern coast | ▸ | Modern Bantu-speaking peoples |

Geography

During this time, most of east, central, and southern Africa was inhabited by various groups of hunting and gathering peoples. Two non-Bantu peoples are the Khoikhoi *(KOY koy)* and the San (Khoisan). Their language has a distinctive "click" sound unlike any other language in the world. For the proto-Bantu speakers, villages eventually became crowded, and some people moved to find additional agricultural lands. They traveled down the Congo River. From the basin of the Congo, they began to branch out. Some **migrated,** or moved to resettle, to the south, some to the east. For the next 2,000 years, descendants of the original proto-Bantu speakers migrated across east, central, and southern Africa where they settled in diverse lands.

Travel Across Africa

The expanse of savanna and dry grasslands that cover much of central and southern Africa provided a travel route, as well as good grazing ranges for domesticated herds. The migrants learned to avoid areas infested with tsetse *(TSET see)* flies that could infect both humans and cattle with a fatal illness.

To the east, the Great Rift Valley extended across the string of Great Lakes and valleys. This fertile valley, some 4,000 miles long and 20–30 miles wide, was formed in prehistoric times by a crack, or rift, in the earth's crust. Stretching north from Mozambique to Jordan in Asia, the valley welcomed migrating groups with its

dry grasslands and plentiful water. Because it had few disease-carrying insects, this valley provided an excellent place for cattle to graze and an ideal passageway for travel to the north or south.

Along the equator, in the rain forest area of the Congo Basin, a large variety of animals and people inhabited the dense forest. With the thick undergrowth, travel by foot was difficult. For this reason, people who lived there used the network of rivers for their system of transportation. ■

■ *To which three geographic regions in east, central, and southern Africa did proto-Bantu speakers migrate and why?*

▼ *Compare this map with the one on page 525 of the Atlas. Which present-day countries are now in the regions where Bantu-speaking people migrated?*

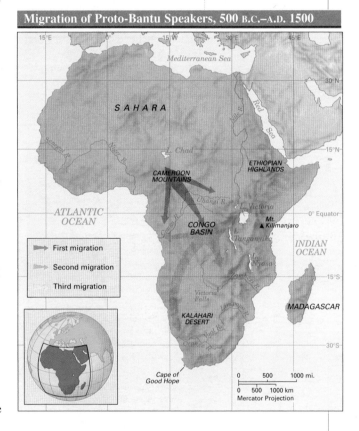

Migration of Proto-Bantu Speakers, 500 B.C.–A.D. 1500

First migration
Second migration
Third migration

Central and Southern Africa

DEVELOP

Draw the Graphic Overview on the chalkboard. Explain that it shows the chain of events that resulted in the diversity of sub-Saharan African peoples. Point out that the lesson explores the historical link among the peoples of sub-Saharan Africa. Lessons 2–4 present the history of a few representative groups.

Although only a few African societies are covered here, the theme of similarity and diversity applies to most of modern sub-Saharan Africa.

■ *The proto-Bantu speakers moved from western Africa and into the savannas of central Africa, the Great Rift Valley, and the Congo River Basin. With a growing population, they were looking for additional agricultural land.*

GEOGRAPHY

Map and Globe Skills

Ask students to use the maps on pages 109 and 137 to describe the terrain and climate the proto-Bantu speakers encountered as they moved south *(rain forest)*, east, *(savanna)*, and west *(savanna)*. Why did they not migrate north? *(Sahara.)*

◄ *All countries in central and southern Africa have Bantu-speaking people.*

137

Access Strategy

Let students share their experiences of moving away from their old home to a new home or of their friends moving away. Especially encourage students who have moved to the United States from another country to talk about the move. With the class, make a list of reasons that people might move. Guide students to generalize that people often move because they want to take advantage of new opportunities, such as better jobs, better schools, or the

chance to build a better life. Tell students that they will be learning about a group of people who lived in ancient Africa and how their descendants moved away from their homes to settle throughout the central, eastern, and southern parts of the continent.

Access Activity

Ask students to imagine they are members of an ancient African farming village moving from their home. Let them discuss the things they will take on the journey. Then divide the class into four groups. Assign each group one environment: grassland, rain forest, seacoast, or mountains. Let them discuss how they will make a new life in that environment.

138

HISTORY
Critical Thinking

Point out to students that the migration of the proto-Bantu speakers proved to be a powerful means of spreading technologies and practices, like iron tools and weapons and cattle herding, that improved productivity and made life more secure for many peoples. Ask students whether their families have moved, or know families that have, and talk about differences they noted in their new locations.

CULTURE
Study Skills

Assign students to research the culture of various Bantu groups important in Africa today. Such groups might include the Ambo, the Chaga, the Ganda, the Hutu, the Kikuyu, the Ngoni, the Shona, the Xhosa, and the Zulu. Have them collect information about their population and distinguishing aspects of their culture and find out where the people live and what languages they speak. Let the students combine their information in a class chart.

The Spread of Bantu Culture

Across Time & Space

Insects continue to pose a problem in Africa today. The anopheles (uh NAHF uh leez) mosquito, which causes malaria, breeds in areas with standing water. The tsetse fly spreads sleeping sickness, and locusts can destroy a field of crops in minutes.

▼ *Use this chart with maps on pages 137 and 525 to trace the order and routes of migrations of the Bantu-speaking peoples.*

About 2,000 years ago, proto-Bantu-speaking people lived in what is today the eastern part of Nigeria. They relied primarily on fishing, farming, hunting, and trading. Using iron, they made hoes, spears, axes, and fishhooks that proved to be much stronger and longer-lasting than tools made from stone, wood, or bone. With better tools, they were able to clear more land and grow plentiful crops. They were also able to catch more fish and game than ever before.

As their ability to produce food increased, the proto-Bantu speakers' communities grew. Some scholars believe that overcrowding may have caused people to migrate. Others think that, with their iron weapons and farming tools, the proto-Bantu-speaking people would have met with little resistance from the hunter-gatherers they encountered. Many of the people they met may have adopted the farming methods and language of the Bantu speakers. The Khoikhoi, for example, began to herd cattle. The San, however, were forced out of their normal hunting grounds into the Kalahari desert.

Making New Contacts

As the migrants moved to new areas, they continued to influence the people they met. Some hunter-gatherers may have adopted the migrants' lifestyle when they married into their families. Noting the appearance of similar words in the languages of these groups, scholars believe that the hunters learned not only the language of the farmers but also many customs.

By now, proto-Bantu was giving way to the beginnings of the Bantu languages we know today. We can trace the migrations of these ancient people by observing where Bantu languages are spoken today. They are mostly south of a line drawn from Cameroon on the west coast of Africa to Kenya on the east coast. Today, this language family includes Swahili, Luba, Kongo, Kikuyu, Ruanda, Sotho, Zulu, and Xhosa, and more.

The Bantu-speaking people also adapted to their new environment by taking on the lifestyles of the local people. For example, like the local herders, the Bantu speakers who settled in the Great Rift Valley started to raise cattle. In the Congo Basin rain forest, heavy rains and dense vegetation

Routes of Bantu-speaking Migrants	
Dates	**Migration Routes**
3000–2500 B.C.	along the Sagha River, among others, into the areas around the Congo and Ubangi rivers; some groups move east along the middle of the Congo River into the northeastern parts of the equatorial rain forest
2500–2000 B.C.	some groups move downstream into the areas where the Kwa-Kasai and Congo rivers meet
2000–1000 B.C.	"Savanna Bantu" move east along the southern edge of the rain forest as far as the Western Rift and Great Lakes region (Lakes Victoria, Tanganyika, and Nyasa)
200 B.C.– A.D. 200	from the Western Rift, "Eastern Bantu" move across eastern and southeastern Africa; others spread south into Angola and Zambia or the heart of the Congo Basin

138

Chapter 6

Map and Globe Skills

Have students use the map on p. 137 to estimate how far some of the Bantu-speaking groups migrated. Let them trace the route some groups might have followed. Ask them which geographic features might have been barriers. (*Ethiopian Highlands, Victoria Falls, Kalahari Desert.*) Which would have been avenues of transportation? (*The rivers.*)

Cultural Context

The Bantu speakers lived near the edge of the forest, fished, hunted, and cultivated yams, palm trees, and grains. They lived in villages, made pottery, and kept dogs, cattle, and goats. Scholars have learned about the ancient Bantu speakers by studying words that are similar in all modern Bantu languages.

prevented Bantu-speaking farmers from raising crops. So many began fishing instead. They also developed crafts such as weaving, woodcarving, boat-building, and basketry.

From the people they met in east Africa, the Bantu speakers learned how to grow crops that had been brought from Asia, including bananas, new kinds of yams, rice, coconuts, and sugar cane. By A.D. 280, descendants of the Bantu-speaking people were farming near the southeastern coast of Africa, on the fertile slopes of Kilimanjaro and in the highlands around Lake Victoria. By 1400, Bantu-speaking groups populated much of sub-Saharan Africa. ■

Related Bantu Words		
Ethnic Group	**Words**	
	person	*people*
Botatwe	muntu	bantu
Swahili	mtu	watu
Tonga	muntu	bantu
Xhosa	umntu	abantu
Zulu	umuntu	abantu

◄ *Ethnolinguists study African history through language. In proto-Bantu, the word for "person" was* mantu *and the word for "people" was* bantu. *Compare the words for "person" and "people" in the present-day languages shown here.*

■ *How did Bantu-speaking groups continue to migrate across Africa?*

Society of the Bantu Speakers

Among Bantu-speaking people, as with all Africans, the family was the basic social and political unit. Families and clans formed villages, and some villages belonged to states and kingdoms. These villages were commonly led by one man or a council of elders. In densely populated areas, some Bantu-speaking people formed empires, such as Zimbabwe.

Some Bantu speakers lived near the edge of the forest, fished, hunted, and cultivated yams, bananas, and grains. Others lived in villages and farmed, traded, made pottery, and kept cattle and goats. The wealth of the villages came from their agriculture. Men, women, and children all worked. Men also herded, hunted, or were artisans, and sometimes performed military duties. Besides their work, women maintained the household and raised the children. ■

■ *Describe the most common political structure among the Bantu-speaking groups.*

R E V I E W

1. **FOCUS** How did the spread of the Bantu-speaking peoples affect the peoples of east, central, and southern Africa?
2. **CONNECT** What did the people of ancient Ghana have that the proto-Bantu-speaking people did not? What effects do you think this had on their descendants?
3. **CULTURE** What changes in lifestyle did the proto-Bantu speakers adopt as they migrated? What changes in lifestyle did the people they meet adopt?
4. **CRITICAL THINKING** In the Indian language Sanskrit, the word for mother is *matar.* In Latin it's *mater,* and in German it's *mutter.* What conclusions might you draw from these similarities?
5. **ACTIVITY** Pick one region of central or southern Africa and collect pictures or draw original ones showing its geography. Then create an illustrated map that shows the geographic conditions the Bantu speakers encountered.

Central and Southern Africa

Critical Thinking

The tsetse fly thrives in areas with heavy vegetation and a large population of wild animals. In such places the flies and animals are constantly reinfecting each other, and in turn, the flies infect humans and domestic animals. In fact, one of the most effective ways of controlling the tsetse fly and the sleeping sickness it spreads is by deforestation and the loss of wild animal populations. Ask if this a good way of stopping sleeping sickness?

■ *The Bantu-speaking groups migrated throughout central, eastern, and southern Africa. In each region they adopted suitable techniques for living from local populations, and local people also adopted their ways of life.*

■ *The most common political structure was the village, which was governed by a chief and a council of elders.*

List the following headings on the chalkboard: geographic region, livelihood, social structure. Have students provide several specific examples under each heading to illustrate the diversity of central and southern Africa.

Answers to Review Questions

1. Bantu-speaking peoples spread their cultural traditions throughout much of the region. This is especially important in the case of their languages.
2. The people of ancient Ghana and the proto-Bantu speakers each had a common language, but the Ghanaians had a settled, agricultural state, while the proto-Bantu speakers migrated. This may have led to more different languages and cultures among the descendants of the proto-Bantu speakers.
3. The Bantu-speaking peoples brought new agricultural practices, and dispersed them in their migration, along with other customs. In return, the Bantu-speaking peoples adopted many new customs from local societies, such as cattle herding, and new ways of fishing.
4. The similarities between these forms of *mother* suggest a common root language.

Homework Options

Have students use a world almanac to gather three significant facts about a modern country in central or southern Africa.

Study Guide: p. 22

UNDERSTANDING
RELIEF MAPS

This skills feature uses a relief map of Africa to teach students the principles of vertical profile maps.

GEOGRAPHY
Critical Thinking

Discuss how a vertical profile map could be of use to travelers. *(Finding the best route to travel, in looking for topography desirable for sports such as skiing or sailing.)* What benefits might a farmer derive from a vertical profile? *(Deciding where to plant and what methods of farming to use.)*

UNDERSTANDING RELIEF MAPS
Making a Vertical Profile

Here's Why

Relief maps use color to show the elevations of landforms. A vertical profile gives a graphic view of the same information. Suppose you wanted to study the early people of Africa. Having a vivid picture of the lands on which these people lived could help you understand them. Could you construct a vertical profile to get this picture?

Here's How

Look at the map on this page. A line has been drawn at 3°S. Use the key to see how the elevation changes along this line. Then look at the vertical profile below the map. It shows the elevations along the 3°S line.

To construct a vertical profile first choose a line along which to draw it—in this case, 3°S. Draw a horizontal line on your paper to represent the profile line. Use the same scale as the map scale. Next look at the map key to see what elevations are represented on the map. Draw a vertical line at one end of your horizontal line. Use the elevation key as the vertical scale along this line. Then use the map to note elevation changes along the profile line. Do this by placing points on the profile to show where and to what degree the elevation changes. Finally, connect the points to complete the profile.

Try It

Construct a vertical profile of the African continent at 15°S. Use graph paper to help you mark elevation segments and place the points of elevation. What is the highest elevation? The lowest?

Apply It

Construct a vertical profile of a location in your state. Use your town as the place to locate your profile line. What is the highest elevation along your line? The lowest?

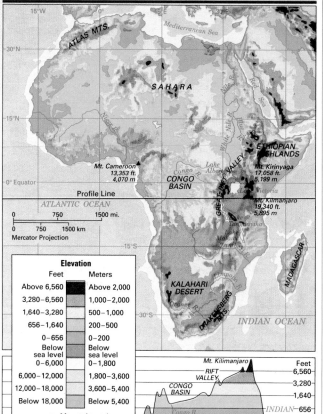

Africa: Physical Regions

Elevation

Feet	Meters
Above 6,560	Above 2,000
3,280–6,560	1,000–2,000
1,640–3,280	500–1,000
656–1,640	200–500
0–656	0–200
Below sea level 0–6,000	Below sea level 0–1,800
6,000–12,000	1,800–3,600
12,000–18,000	3,600–5,400
Below 18,000	Below 5,400

▲ Mountain peak

Objective

Construct a vertical profile using information provided on a relief map. (Map and Globe Skills 5, Critical Thinking 3)

Answers to Try It

Students should construct a vertical profile map whose highest elevation is around 5,000 feet and lowest elevation is approximately sea level.

Answers to Apply It

Answers will vary, but maps should demonstrate an understanding of how to make a vertical profile.

B.C. A.D.

500

200

TODAY

1600

L E S S O N 2

The Rise of Coastal Trading States

The last mainland market-town . . . is called Rhapta, a name derived from the small sewn boats. Here there is much ivory and tortoise shell. . . . The people of Mouza . . . send their small ships, mostly with Arab captains and crews who trade and intermarry with the mainlanders of all the places and know their language.

Into these market-towns are imported lances made especially for them at Mouza, hatchets, swords, awls, and many kinds of small glass vessels; and at some places wine and not a little wheat, not for trade but to gain the goodwill of the barbarians. Much ivory is taken away from these places . . . and also rhinoceros horn and tortoise-shell, different from that of India, and a little coconut oil.

This passage, taken from *The Periplus of the Erythraean Sea,* describes trade between the Arab city of Mouza and Rhapta, an East African port. It was written in about A.D. 100 by a Greek merchant. He had been sent by the Romans occupying Egypt to investigate rumors of a booming trade between Indian Ocean ports.

THINKING FOCUS

How did East Africa become part of an international trade network?

Key Terms

- monsoon
- city-state

Sailing with the Winds

This Greek merchant was writing about the Indian Ocean trade network between East Africa, Arabia, India, Ceylon, and the East Indies. Although trading between Arabs and East Africans probably began in about 900 B.C., the Indian Ocean trade network wasn't really established until about 200 B.C. For it wasn't until then that the Arabs learned to use the seasonal winds known as **monsoons** to sail across the Indian Ocean.

Every year without fail the monsoon blows from the northeast between November and March

▼ *Sailors on the Indian Ocean still sail dhows much like those that Arab traders once used.*

INTRODUCE

Have students read the lesson title and locate East Africa on the map on p. 137. Point out that some Bantu speakers migrated east across the savanna and settled along the coast. Like other groups, these people quickly adapted to a new environment. In East Africa this meant adapting to foreign influences of Arab traders as well as to geography and climate. Tell students they will find out how the Bantu speakers and other peoples who settled on the eastern coast of Africa developed a unique new culture that still exists today.

Key Terms

Vocabulary Strategies: T36–T37
monsoon—a wind system that switches direction seasonally and brings wet and dry seasons
city-state—an independent state made up of a city and the territory that surrounds it.

141

Graphic Overview

SWAHILI CULTURE

| coastal Bantu speakers | Arab traders | Asian immigrants | inland Shona | Portuguese sailors |

Objectives

1. Analyze the effect of the monsoon winds on the development of trade in East Africa.
2. Describe the contacts among international cultures in the coastal trading centers of East Africa.
3. Summarize the reasons behind the prosperity and decline of the East African trading centers.

DEVELOP

Ask students to study the map on p. 142. Using a classroom map, let volunteers locate the coast of East Africa, Arabia, Persia, India, southeast Asia, and China. Have students name some of the products traded by the people bordering on the Indian Ocean. Let students trace the direction of the monsoon winds on the larger map and discuss the reliability of these winds.

GEOGRAPHY
Study Skills

Ask students to explain why the monsoon winds were essential to the development of the Indian Ocean trade network. *(The alternating winds made it possible for Arab ships to sail to and from any port on the Indian Ocean in certain seasons.)* What geographic regions were linked in the Indian Ocean trade network? *(East Africa, Arabia, Persia, India, southeast Asia.)*

■ *Monsoons are winds that regularly change direction with the seasons. Arab dhows sailed with the winds back and forth across the Indian Ocean.*

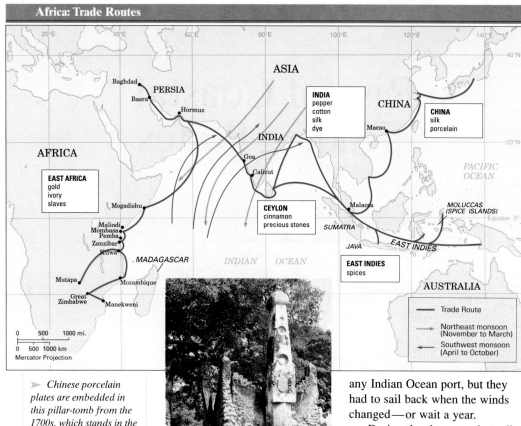

Africa: Trade Routes

ASIA

Baghdad
PERSIA
Basra
Hormuz

INDIA
pepper
cotton
silk
dye

CHINA

CHINA
silk
porcelain

Macao

AFRICA

INDIA

Goa
Calicut

EAST AFRICA
gold
ivory
slaves

Mogadishu

CEYLON
cinnamon
precious stones

Malacca

MOLUCCAS
(SPICE ISLANDS)

SUMATRA

PACIFIC
OCEAN

Malindi
Mombasa
Pemba
Zanzibar
Kilwa

JAVA

EAST INDIES

MADAGASCAR

INDIAN   OCEAN

EAST INDIES
spices

Mutapa
Mozambique
Great
Zimbabwe
Manekweni

AUSTRALIA

0 500 1000 mi.
0 500 1000 km
Mercator Projection

— Trade Route
→ Northeast monsoon
(November to March)
← Southwest monsoon
(April to October)

➤ *Chinese porcelain plates are embedded in this pillar-tomb from the 1700s, which stands in the ancient trading settlement of Kunduchi in present-day Tanzania. The plates are reminders of the vast trade network that once crisscrossed the Indian Ocean.*

■ *Describe the monsoons and explain why they were so important to the Indian Ocean trade network.*

and from the southwest between April and October. So Arab merchants used these winds to propel their ships, called dhows *(dowz)*, from Arabia down the African coast. They could reach Kilwa before the winds died down in March. Then the winds carried them from Kilwa back home again in April. With proper planning, Arabian ships could sail to nearly

any Indian Ocean port, but they had to sail back when the winds changed—or wait a year.

During the short, yearly trading season, the traders would stay with the African merchants. In time they intermarried and settled there. The people on the mainland spoke Bantu languages. After several centuries, their culture merged with the Arabian, Persian, and Indonesian traders', producing the Swahili language and culture. "Swahili" is the Arabic word for "people of the shore." Swahili-speaking people live throughout east and central Africa. ■

The Rise of City-States

Beginning in about A.D. 900, this new immigration of people began to affect the character of the coastal cities. Arab, Persian, and Indian traders came to share in the profits from preparing goods to

Chapter 6

Access Activity

Encourage students to make up a skit about Arab traders trading in a Bantu-speaking port city for the first time. Have students represent the different cultures, values, languages, and religions of the people involved and indicate possible misunderstandings that could arise. Have them show how cooperation can be achieved when people have common goals.

Access Strategy

Direct students to locate the coast of East Africa and the Indian Ocean on the map on p. 142. Ask volunteers to name African cities along this ocean. You may wish to go over the pronunciation of each of these cities. Then ask students to name some of the Asian islands and Indian cities that ring the Indian Ocean. Tell students that a profitable trade developed among the cities along the Indian Ocean. Point out that this exchange of goods and ideas

greatly influenced the development of East African culture and customs.

Prompt students to recall the trading empires they read about in Chapter 5. *(Ghana, Mali, and Songhai.)* Guide students to realize that the location of these kingdoms in the sahel—the shore of the Sahara—allowed them to control trade across the Sahara. Help them make the analogy that the people along the coasts of the Indian Ocean also could control trade by virtue of their location.

sell to incoming ships.

In the hundreds of Swahili fishing and farming villages scattered along the coast, people established a complex economic system. Women, children, and a few men worked in the fields, while men and boys fished. Both men and women were traders and artisans.

The Swahili served as the link between foreign traders and inland Africans. One such group of inland Africans was the Shona, who lived in what is now Zimbabwe, between the Zambezi and Limpopo rivers. Find Zimbabwe on the map on page 525. The Shona had found large deposits of gold and other minerals there. By 1100, they were shipping these precious metals from Sofala, a southern port city, to Kilwa and other Swahili ports to

be exchanged for foreign goods. Other inland Africans brought ivory, grain, and sometimes slaves to the coastal cities to trade for foreign knives, farming tools, fabrics, and porcelain (*PAWR suh lihn*).

Soon the merchants of one port city were in competition with those of another. There were great riches to be made in import-export trade, and each group of coastal merchants tried to attract a larger share of the business.

At this time, too, many ports became **city-states,** or independent states made up of a city and its surrounding territory. The rulers of the city-states grew rich from trade and from taxes they required merchants to pay on the goods that passed through their port. ■

■ *Describe a typical East African trading town of the 1300s.*

From Riches to Ruin

The most prosperous city-state was Kilwa, the southernmost port on the Indian Ocean trade route. By 1100, traders in Kilwa controlled the export of gold and ivory from southern kingdoms. The local rulers and merchants became very wealthy from this trade.

The North African traveler Ibn Battuta

visited Kilwa in 1331. He described it as "one of the most beautiful and well-constructed towns in the world." He claimed, "The whole of it is elegantly built." In addition to the mosque shown below, Kilwa had a huge

▼ *The Great Mosque at Kilwa was built in the mid-1400s. Although most of it is now in ruins, the domes and cloister recall how glorious the East African city-states once were.*

143

Central and Southern Africa

143

Critical Thinking

Ask students what they think might have been the appeal of Islam to the coastal Bantu traders. (*Students might mention that Arab traders, who were Muslims, were wealthy; that through the Muslims, Africans learned to read and write; that Arab Muslims had access to goods and ideas from all over the world. Each of these features might have made Islam a prestigious religion. Accept all answers that show students have grasped the nature of trading societies and some of the features of Islam.*)

■ *The typical trading town was a self-governing city-state ruled by a king. It had an international population, impressive buildings, and a wealthy merchant class.*

Cultural Context

Today the Swahili language is spoken along the east coast of Africa, from Somalia to Mozambique. Several East African countries, including Kenya and Tanzania, have adopted Swahili as the official language for business, trade, and communication.

Modern Swahili has numerous Arabic words. Arabic has always been an important influence on the Swahili language and culture. In fact, the oldest surviving examples of written Swahili were written in Arabic script.

Language Arts Connection

The Swahili literary tradition is young compared to those of China, Europe, and India. The oldest known Swahili poems, composed in the 1600s, were not written down until the 1880s. Read aloud the selection on p. 144. It is the first verse of an anonymous poem called *Stringing Pearls* that was composed in the 1700s. Explain that the Swahili verb for "stringing pearls" also means "composing poetry." Help students discover the metaphor of the diver as an author.

Social Participation

Divide students into three groups: Bantu-speaking gold miners, Swahili traders, and foreign merchants visiting East African ports. Let each group meet to determine the goods and the conditions under which they will trade. Then pick a student from each group to trade. Remind students that traders may not speak the same language.

ECONOMICS
Critical Thinking

Have students explain how the location of the East African coastal cities was responsible for both their rise and their fall as trading centers. *(Location allowed the cities to become prosperous trading centers but also made them vulnerable to Portuguese takeover.)* Ask which were more significant in the long run, the benefits or the disadvantages of location. *(Allow for varied opinions.)*

■ *The Portuguese caused the destruction of many East African trading cities in trying to take control of the cities to monopolize trade.*

C L O S E

Draw the Graphic Overview from p. 141 on the chalkboard. Ask students to describe how each of the groups listed influenced Swahili culture.

144

palace, vast irrigated gardens, and houses many stories high that were built of stone.

Gedi, a trading town built in the 1300s, also had a mosque, a palace, and large houses built of stone. These houses had bathrooms with drains and overhead basins to flush toilets. In addition, the city was obviously well planned. The streets were not only laid out at right angles, but they had drainage gutters as well.

Then, in 1498, the first Portuguese explorer arrived. His name was Vasco da Gama. The Portuguese government had commissioned da Gama to find a way to sail from Portugal around southern Africa, into the Indian Ocean. They hoped that by developing such a trade route they would seize control of the Far East spice trade. But as Vasco da Gama piloted his ship northward along the East African coast, he realized that controlling East African trade would be quite profitable, too.

In 1505, a well-armed Portuguese fleet attacked Kilwa and then Mombasa. Neither city was able to defend itself against the Portuguese cannon. An observer aboard one of the ships that attacked Mombasa recorded the event. He described how the admiral ordered his men to destroy the city and carry off whatever they wanted. As a result, the observer says, " . . . everyone started to plunder the town and search the houses, forcing doors with axes and bars."

After conquering Kilwa, Mombasa, and other city-states, the Portuguese tried to monopolize trade in East African ports. But they did not have enough ships and men to maintain control over the entire Indian Ocean trade network. And by the late 1500s, Swahili groups had regained control of several ports from the Portuguese.

▲ *The carvings on this doorway from Lamu, near Kilwa, speak of the rich Swahili culture that dominated the coastal city-states of East Africa.*

■ *Who caused the destruction of many East African trading centers, and why?*

> *H*e who wants to string pearls
> must be an excellent diver;
> he who manages to succeed
> is a [pearl] diver, a fisherman;
> the soul is a vast ocean;
> in it there is the treasure-trove
> of mother-of-pearl;
> he that is afraid of drowning,
> [for him] the oyster shells
> produce no pearls.
>
> Swahili poem, 1700s

The cities never again saw the prosperity of earlier times. But the unique Swahili culture and language are still a vital part of the African tradition. ■

R E V I E W

1. **FOCUS** How did East Africa become part of an international trade network?
2. **CONNECT** How was the growth of trade in East Africa similar to the growth of trade in West Africa?
3. **CULTURE** Who were the Swahili, and how did their culture develop?
4. **CRITICAL THINKING** How might Swahili life in inland villages differ from that in coastal trading towns?
5. **ACTIVITY** Imagine you are a sailor on a merchant ship sailing from India to East African ports in the 1100s. Describe, or map out, the voyage you might make. Include dates, names and descriptions of ports, and cargoes your ship would carry back to India.

144

Chapter 6

Homework Options

Have students use a modern map to select two East African countries they would like to visit. Have them write or call a travel agent for information.

Study Guide: p. 24

Answers to Review Questions

1. Arabs visited East African ports to trade eastern spices, fabrics, and porcelain for African gold, ivory, and slaves. Residents of port cities served as the link between foreign traders and inland African producers.
2. In both East and West Africa, Arabs traded with African cities on the edge of an environmental zone. *(Indian Ocean, Sahara.)* Arabs influenced the cultures of both areas, especially by introducing Islam.
3. The influence of Muslim Arabs might have been stronger along the coast than inland. On the coast people were merchants, traders, and fishers, while inland people were herders, farmers, and hunters.
4. The Swahili are descendants of Bantu people who migrated to East Africa before A.D. 700. The Bantu adopted elements of Arab culture from the Arabs who traded there. The resulting blend of cultures is called Swahili.

B.C. A.D.

500

300

1700

TODAY

LESSON 3

The Rise of the Zimbabwe State

At its peak around 1400, the stone enclave known as Great Zimbabwe spread over almost 200 acres and held up to 18,000 people. It was the capital city of a major state. Unfortunately only a few records remain of the Shona people who lived in this enclave. There are miles of ruins at Great Zimbabwe, however, that hold much information for archaeologists. In the Shona language, "zimbabwe" means "houses of stone."

There are two large building sites at Great Zimbabwe. One is a hill covered with enormous boulders. Over time, people linked the boulders together with stone walls, making courtyards and narrow passages. The other, is called "the Great Enclosure." Here, a narrow, cone-shaped stone tower rises three stories high. Long corridors gently curve between walls over 15 feet high. Inside the walls are the remains of buildings where the rulers, priests, and artisans of Great Zimbabwe probably lived.

Archaeologists have also found evidence of metal working and trade in copper, iron, and gold. Many gold and copper ornaments were found in the sites—the miner-

THINKING FOCUS

Describe some of the ways the Shona benefited from their decision to settle on the site now known as the Zimbabwe Plateau.

Key Terms

- plateau
- oral tradition
- malaria

◄ *This view of Great Zimbabwe shows the outside wall that surrounded the king's court and measured more than 820 feet long. The cone-shaped tower rises above the wall.*

145

Central and Southern Africa

INTRODUCE

Tell students that in this lesson they will examine a prosperous African kingdom in southern Africa called Zimbabwe. Explain that the people who settled in Zimbabwe were part of the Bantu speakers' migration. Ask students to imagine that they are migrants looking for a place to settle. What type of land and climate would they find desirable? What would they want to avoid? Have them read the lesson to find out the reason why the Bantu speakers chose to settle in this area.

Key Terms

Vocabulary Strategies: T36–T37
plateau—a raised and relatively flat surface of land
oral tradition—the legends, myths, and beliefs that a culture passes from generation to generation by word of mouth
malaria—a tropical disease carried by the anopheles mosquito and characterized by chills, fever, and sweating

Graphic Overview

First Stage 300–1000		Second Stage 1000–1450		Third Stage 1450–1600
Bantu speakers settle in area; take the name Shona.	→	Shona establish trade with East Africans based on gold mined in Zimbabwe; build Great Zimbabwe.	→	Civil war over control of gold trade; Zimbabwe kingdom breaks up.

Objectives

1. Use historical evidence to characterize the early people of Zimbabwe.
2. Assess the effect of gold mining on the economy and politics of Zimbabwe.
3. Describe the events that occurred during the breakup of Zimbabwe.

Remind students that Swahili traders exported gold from Sofala. Point out that Zimbabwe was the major source of this precious metal. Ask students how this might have influenced Zimbabwe's history. (*Zimbabwe probably became wealthy because of this economic power.*)

HISTORY
Critical Thinking

Ask students to use their knowledge of the geography of Zimbabwe to determine if the following statements in head-line form could have been true.

1. Zimbabwe Craftspeople Discover New Way to Work Silver
2. Cattle Raisers Announce That Animals Are Disease-Free
3. Forest Fire Hampers New Construction
4. Ocean Erodes Shoreline Near King's Palace

➤ *They are similar in size.*

■ *They examined artifacts found at Great Zimbabwe, studied documents written by Portuguese explorers, and listened to accounts from modern Shona about the history of Great Zimbabwe.*

146

▼ *How do the sizes of the empires of Zimbabwe and Monomutapa compare with those of modern African nations?*

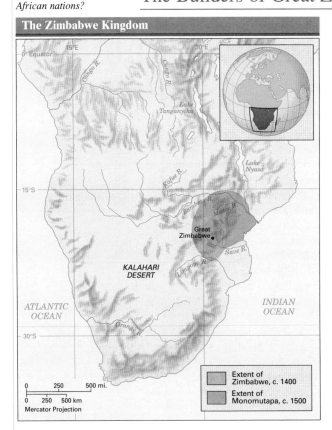

The Zimbabwe Kingdom

How Do We Know?

We know that non-African archaeologists who visited Great Zimbabwe in the 1800s had racist attitudes, because they refused to believe that Africans could have built the impressive site.

■ *Trace the growth and decline of Great Zimbabwe.*

146

al wealth of the lands ruled from Great Zimbabwe. Trading this gold made Kilwa an important Swahili city. Archaeologists also found at Great Zimbabwe items from beyond Africa, including Chinese, Persian, and Syrian artifacts that date back to the 1300s.

The Builders of Great Zimbabwe

Historians now know that Great Zimbabwe was built by the Shona between A.D. 1000 and 1300. The Shona are Bantu-speaking farmers and cattle raisers who had come to this area in about A.D. 300. They might also have brought mining techniques to the region.

The Shona chose to settle in this area for a number of reasons. The **plateau,** or raised, flat surface of land, had abundant rainfall for crops and plenty of trees for build-ing material and firewood. Also, the plateau was free of deadly tsetse flies. And the earth there was rich in granite, iron, copper, and gold.

People lived at Great Zimbabwe long before the great walls were built. The foundations of the hilltop fortress date back to the A.D. 300s. The population grew, and by the late 1100s the Shona had developed a complex society that included agriculture, cattle herding, mining, metalworking, and trade, as well as political and religious structures.

Some historians suggest that the Shona used diplomacy to rule the small surrounding states. They may have demanded tribute from them in food, gold dust, or ivory. But where did their power come from? The great riches produced by the gold and ivory trade allowed the Shona to maintain their rule and expand their influence. Some historians also believe their power was derived from their priests, who commanded great respect.

The power of Great Zimbabwe was not to last. Historians think that decades of drought or poor crops brought about the state's decline. As people planted fields and grazed cattle year after year, the nutrients in the soil ran out. The people cleared more forests and repeated the process of wearing out the land. People. eventually had to move away to better land. ■

Chapter 6

The Gold Mines of Zimbabwe

When the Shona, a Bantu-speaking people, came to the Zimbabwe Plateau, they used gold to make jewelry and other ornaments. But to them, gold was just another metal, like copper or iron. It wasn't as useful as iron, because it was so soft. But coastal traders valued gold highly. The Shona found they could exchange their gold for Chinese silk, Indian glass beads, and fine Persian pottery.

The Search for Gold

The Shona found some of their gold in rivers and streams, but in the 1100s, they began digging to mine gold underground. Archaeologists have found more than 60,000 mine shafts on the Zimbabwe Plateau. They have also discovered that mostly women and children mined these shafts.

The miners built fires next to the large gold-bearing rocks. When the rocks were hot, they threw cold water on them. This caused a sudden temperature change that split the rocks, making it easier for the miners to remove the gold.

The Gold Capital

Through mining and trading gold, Zimbabwe became a wealthy kingdom. By the 1400s, the rulers of Zimbabwe controlled most of the country between the Limpopo River on the south to the Zambezi on the north and from the Indian Ocean west to the Kalahari Desert. Great Zimbabwe was Zimbabwe's capital and trade center.

In the heart of Great Zimbabwe is a large hill where the Shona built a huge granite fortress with 20-foot-thick walls. People lived nearby in clay huts with thatched roofs.

Near the foot of the main hill a thick wall enclosed the king's compound. The significance of the cone-shaped tower is not known to outsiders. At the height of the kingdom in the 1400s, Portuguese historian João de Barros described

How Do We Know?

HISTORY *The oral tradition of one African culture speaks of a strange darkness during chief Bo Kama Bomenchala's reign. Scientists know that an eclipse of the sun occurred in 1680. No other recorded event would account for such a strange darkness. Thus, historians could determine that Bo Kama Bomenchala's reign included the year 1680.*

◄ *Zimbabwe remains an important producer of gold. Mines such as this one use railroad cars to carry ore from underground.*

147

Central and Southern Africa

■ *The people of Zimbabwe become wealthy and powerful by trading gold and by expanding the kingdom's boundaries.*

HISTORY
Social Participation

Ask students to discuss the role that the Portuguese played in the breakdown of the Monomutapa empire. Have them make a chart that examines and compares the Portuguese influence in Zimbabwe to the Portuguese influence on Africa's east coast.

■ *The Portuguese wanted to control the trade markets and gold mines.*

CLOSE

Ask students to discuss the three major stages of the Zimbabwe kingdom as shown in the Graphic Overview. Then have them determine if information gathered by historians about each of these stages would most likely be gleaned from archaeological evidence, oral tradition, written accounts by explorers, or knowledge of the area's geography. *(Example: Information on Zimbabwe's trade with other countries came from archaeological artifacts found in the area.)*

148

■ *How did Zimbabwe become a wealthy and powerful kingdom?*

the king's complex: "The floors, ceiling, beams and rafters are all either gilt or plated with gold . . ." and there were candlesticks "made of ivory inlaid with gold."

Scholars have learned a great deal about Zimbabwe's past from the ruins and also from the Shona's rich oral tradition. In the **oral tradition,** stories are passed down through time by one generation telling them to the next. An oral tradition preserves the history of a people without written records. ■

The Breakup of Zimbabwe

In about 1450, the chiefs of Zimbabwe's gold-producing provinces declared independence from Great Zimbabwe. One of these groups, a northern group led by King Mwene Mutapa, conquered neighboring kingdoms and formed a new empire called Monomutapa.

But civil wars that began to break out in 1490 weakened Monomutapa. In the early 1500s, the empire split in two. The northern half remained Monomutapa, but a rival dynasty, the Changamire, took over the south.

At the same time, Portuguese traders engaged in friendly trading with Monomutapa. But before long, the Portuguese sought increased wealth and power by taking control of Monomutapa's markets and gold mines. In 1570, they attacked the empire.

However, Portuguese forces had been greatly diminished by **malaria.** Carried by mosquitoes, this disease causes fever and chills, and often death. The Portuguese lost so many soldiers to malaria that their conquest attempt failed.

During the next 100 years, the Portuguese continued to undermine the central government. With civil wars and the disruption of gold production, Monomutapa was seriously weakened. By the late 1600s, southern kingdoms had conquered it. ■

➤ *Mwene Mutapa founded and ruled the empire called Monomutapa.*

■ *Why did the Portuguese undermine Monomutapa?*

REVIEW

1. **FOCUS** Describe some of the ways the Shona benefited from their decision to settle on the site now known as the Zimbabwe Plateau.
2. **CONNECT** Describe the trade relationship between the Shona of Zimbabwe and the trading centers on the East African coast.
3. **CULTURE** Why didn't European scholars believe that Africans had built the structures at Great Zimbabwe?
4. **CRITICAL THINKING** Do you think the culture of the United States has an oral tradition? Explain.
5. **ACTIVITY** Imagine archaeologists 1,000 years in the future have discovered the ruins of your school. List three artifacts that the archaeologists might find and explain what the artifacts tell about your culture.

Homework Options

Have students look up any unfamiliar words in this lesson in a dictionary and write their own definitions.

Study Guide: p. 25

Answers to Review Questions

1. The Shona chose to settle in Zimbabwe because of plentiful rain, rich mineral deposits, and the absence of tsetse flies. Zimbabwe's abundance of gold led to gold trade with the East Africans and the Portuguese and helped Zimbabwe become a wealthy kingdom.
2. The Shona people mined gold and traded it with people in the coastal trading centers for goods from India, China, Persia, and other Indian Ocean countries.

3. Many Europeans thought that Africans lacked the ability to build a city like Great Zimbabwe.
4. Because we have a written language, we do not rely on oral tradition to record our history. But oral tradition does exist in the United States. For example, many stories and legends are passed down through families.

B.C. | A.D.

500   500   1000   TODAY

1300   **1600**

L E S S O N   4

The Kongo Kingdom

The lone Portuguese ship inched along off the west coast of Africa. It was 1482 and Captain Diego Cão had gone farther south than any other European. But right now his crew needed rest. Cão spotted the mouth of a mighty river and anchored a few miles upstream. Then he and his men stepped ashore.

The Africans there had never seen white men. So, curious, they gathered around the sailors. One rubbed Cão's arm with water, trying to wipe off what he thought was white paint. They offered to take Cão to their king, but he wanted to sail farther south, so he had four servants go for him.

When Cão returned to the river, he found no trace of his servants. Fearing the worst, he captured four local people and sailed for home. But Portugal's King John hoped to impress their king, so he treated the hostages like princes.

About three years later, King John sent Cão and the hostages back to Africa with gifts and letters for their king. Cão's servants were waiting for him with tales of the vast kingdom of the Kongo. Cão returned to Portugal with his servants and a friendly letter to King John from the Kongo king.

THINKING FOCUS

How did Kongo change after the arrival of the Portuguese?

Key Terms

- currency
- missionary
- plantation

◄ *This column, left by the Portuguese on the African coast, says the king has "ordered this land to be discovered."*

149

The Growth of Kongo

Cão was the first European to encounter the Kongo kingdom. Like the Shona people of Zimbabwe, the people of Kongo descended from Bantu-speaking farmers. Specifically, during the

Central and Southern Africa

INTRODUCE

Have students read the lesson title and use the map on p. 150 to locate the Kongo kingdom. Tell them to read the Thinking Focus and predict an answer to it using what they know about the history of East Africa and Zimbabwe. Have them read the lesson to confirm or modify their predictions.

Key Terms

Vocabulary Strategies: T36–T37
currency—any form of money being used as a medium of exchange
missionary—a person sent to a foreign country to do religious or charitable work
plantation—a large farm where crops are grown

149

Graphic Overview

Causes		**Effects**
• Mani-Kongo wants to trade with the Portuguese • Portuguese most interested in trading for slaves	→ **Kongo Slave Trade** →	• Slave market expands • Africans go to war and take prisoners to sell as slaves • Kongo kingdom declines in power

Objectives

1. Describe the origins of the Kongo kingdom.
2. Assess the impact of the Portuguese on the Kongo economy.
3. Explain how the Portuguese slave trade caused civil war in Kongo.

DEVELOP

Point out that this lesson traces the history of the Bantu-speaking people who settled in the Congo River Basin. Draw the cause and effect diagram in the Graphic Overview on the chalkboard and point out that it describes the kingdom of Kongo from 1500 to the early 1600s. Guide students to realize that contact with the Portuguese brought about the steady decline and eventual breakup of Kongo in the early 1600s.

➤ *People's Republic of the Congo, the Democratic Republic of Congo, and Angola.*

CULTURE
Study Skills

Ask students to explain where the people of Kongo came from. *(Descendants of Bantu-speaking farmers who migrated to the Congo Basin.)* Have students make a chart to compare and contrast the people of Kongo with the peoples of East Africa and Zimbabwe, including origin, livelihood, trade products, and government.

■ *Kongo began in the 1300s when two Bantu clans united. Over the next 100 years, the kingdom of farmers and traders grew large and prosperous.*

150

➤ *Compare this map of the Kongo kingdom with the map on page 525 of the Atlas. What modern nations were once part of the Kongo kingdom?*

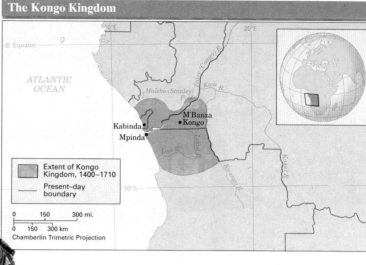

The Kongo Kingdom

Extent of Kongo Kingdom, 1400–1710
Present-day boundary

0   150   300 mi.
0   150   300 km
Chamberlin Trimetric Projection

▲ *This Kongo mask is decorated with cowry shells that were valuable as well as beautiful. Cowry shells were used as money by some African tribes.*

➤ *This carved wooden figure from the Kongo region was used in rituals.*

150 ■ *Describe the early development of Kongo.*

1300s, two Bantu clans had joined together to form what became the kingdom called Kongo.

By the 1400s, Kongo's king, the Mani-Kongo, ruled six provinces and about two million people. Chiefs appointed by the king controlled each province. Find Kongo lands on the map above.

The People of Kongo

Kongo's royal capital, Mbanza, was built on a fertile plateau surrounded by rain forests, 100 miles east of the coast and 50 miles south of the Congo River. The people of Mbanza lived in straw huts scattered around the walled palace of the king.

Farmers planted millet and sorghum on the land around Mbanza. They gathered bananas, coconuts, dates, and citrus fruits from the surrounding forests, and they made

oil, wine, vinegar, and bread from the fruit and sap of palm trees. In addition, the people hunted game for meat.

Trade in Kongo

Mbanza was not only a rich farming area but a prosperous crossroads for trade. The people of Kongo traded with people to the north, east, and west both by land and river. They traded salt from the sea, iron, copper, ivory, and raffia—a fiber made of palm leaves.

As **currency,** or money, the Kongo traders used small seashells, called cowries, from the coast. But when Kongo people began trading with the Portuguese, seashells were the last thing the Portuguese wanted as payment for their goods. They wanted gold. The Kongo region had no gold, so Portugal asked the Mani-Kongo for another form of payment—slaves. To learn more about a Mani-Kongo, see A Moment in Time on page 151. ■

Chapter 6

Access Activity

Have students use the map on this page to point out important geographic characteristics of the Kongo, such as it's central location and nearness to the equator. Ask how they think people lived in a tropical rain forest in the 1300s. If possible, show pictures of a rain forest and its inhabitants today.

Access Strategy

Have students bring in samples or pictures of food products and natural resources that are produced in your area. Items might include wheat, cotton, oranges, soybeans, milk, meat, coal, oil, copper, etc. Ask which products are cultivated and which are simply gathered from the environment.

Bring in pictures or samples of the products that were available in Kongo (see p. 150). Ask students to guess which food products were cultivated and which

grew wild in the forests. Encourage students to discuss what the assortment of Kongo products reveals about the environment and lifestyle of the early Kongo people. Ask students to recall which products the Portuguese were most interested in obtaining from Monomutapa and East Africa. Note that the Kongo traded ivory, salt, iron, copper, and fiber for weaving. Ask students which, if any, of these products the Portuguese might have been eager to trade for.

A Kongo King

11:47 A.M., May 15, 1544
Mbanza, capital of the Kongo kingdom

Salt
The heavy block, worth its weight in gold, was just presented to him by the governor of one part of the kingdom. The gift proves the governor is still loyal to the king.

Zebra Skin
The king is pleased that this gift is wrapped in a valuable skin. At the feast after this ceremony, the king will strengthen his ties to the governor by giving him an elegant drinking glass from Venice. The king trades for jewelry with the Portuguese.

Boots
Of all the European goods the king gets from the Portuguese, these are his favorites. He paid for them with beautiful African cloth he received at last year's tribute ceremony.

Collar
He's wearing his finest African gold for today's tribute ceremony. He wants to show everyone—his subjects and the Portuguese traders—his power and authority. He has to be clever to balance the demands made on him from all sides.

Throne
Gleaming with ivory and inlaid gold, his chair is the only seat in the room. The king's men-at-arms stand at attention with their spears. The governors cluster in small groups, waiting for their chance to kneel before the king.

151

Note: Use the Kongo King picture as a springboard for discussing the influence of European culture on Africa.

CULTURE
Visual Learning

Ask the students what elements referred to or pictured are of European origin *(Portuguese boots and jewelry, Venetian drinking glass)*, and which are of African origin *(inlaid throne, grass mat, shirt, gold collar, salt, zebra skin, African cloth)*. Tell students that a Portuguese chandelier hangs above the king's throne; at the feast, he will cut his food with an iron knife made in Europe.

More About the Tribute Ceremony
The provincial governors offer their king the products of their various regions. Among these items is a finely woven cloth, made from the leaf stalks of a palm tree. The Portuguese use this African cloth, raffia, as sails for their ships.

151

Writing

Ask the students to pretend they are Portuguese traders in the court of the Kongo King. Have each write a letter home, telling about the tribute ceremony and the feast that follows it. They may also wish to describe the fine craftsmanship of the African weavers, wood carvers, and metal workers.

Role Playing

Some of the king's governors feel the king has become too dependent upon the European trade. They feel that the growing Portuguese interest in slaves will soon tear their kingdom apart. Have interested students role-play this scene at the tribute ceremony: one of the governors, after giving the king his gift, respectfully expresses concern about the slave trade to the king, who replies.

Visual Learning

Like the Kongo King, we also wear clothing that comes from many different places. Have each student draw a picture of himself or herself wearing a favorite outfit, including shoes. They should draw a line from each article to the name of the country where the clothing or accessory originated.

GEOGRAPHY
Visual Learning

Have students make posters or charts contrasting Kongo trade in the 1400s with trade in the late 1500s. *(Shift from salt, minerals, fruits, and ivory to slaves and guns.)* Ask them to explain how the Portuguese were responsible for this change.

➤ *Student answers might include that the carver may have felt suspicious, afraid, or mistrustful of the Portuguese.*

■ *The Portuguese traded European goods in exchange for slaves—African war prisoners—to work on plantations.*

The Portuguese in Kongo

Portuguese traders developed a prosperous and friendly relationship with the Kongo people. In 1490, the Portuguese king sent teachers and missionaries to educate the Mani-Kongo and members of his court. A **missionary** is someone who goes to a foreign place to teach religion.

Under the missionaries' guidance, the Mani-Kongo converted to Christianity and even sent his son to a missionary school. Later, his son became king and was baptized with the Christian name of Affonso I.

Affonso continued his father's contact with the Portuguese. He adopted many Portuguese customs and encouraged members of his court to attend school. Some even began to wear European clothes and to import European furniture.

However, some people resented the Portuguese influence. They wanted their king to adhere to local traditions.

Nevertheless, the alliance between the Kongo and King John remained strong until the early 1500s. By then Portugal had begun

➤ *An African artisan from the kingdom of Benin, near the mouth of the Niger River, was employed by the Portuguese to carve this salt container from ivory. It represents explorers and their ships. Look at the faces on the carving. How do you think the carver felt about the Portuguese?*

■ *What European nation led in the African slave trade?*

settling the island of São Tomé, 250 miles off the Kongo coast. Most of the settlers were criminals being deported from Portugal. They had little regard for the African people and a great desire to improve their own lives.

When the Portuguese governor of São Tomé discovered that sugar grew well there, he immediately began looking for workers for the large farms, or **plantations.** He knew slave labor would cost the least and thereby leave more money as profit. So the governor turned to nearby Africa to find slaves.

At first, Affonso supplied him with slaves, not realizing that the Portuguese had a different notion of slavery than he did. Enslaving war prisoners was an accepted practice in Africa. But Africans did not mistreat their slaves or separate them from their families, and slaves could eventually earn their freedom. The Portuguese, however, treated slaves like beasts of burden, working them so hard that many died. When this occurred, they simply bought more. ■

Slaves, Guns, and Civil War

The merchants of São Tomé were not satisfied with the limited number of slaves they could obtain from the Kongo. The buying and selling of slaves had become

quite a profitable business. And with a new Portuguese colony in South America, called Brazil, the demand for slaves was greater than ever.

Chapter 6

Art Connection

Wood sculpture was the most significant art form in the Kongo. Since wood deteriorates with age, many early pieces of Kongo sculpture have been destroyed. But artists today continue to create carvings that are similar to those of their ancestors. Masks, figures of ancestors, musical instruments, and everyday items such as bowls, boxes, combs, and tools are among the objects carved from wood by modern craftspeople. Have students bring in pictures of some of these items.

Religious Context

Portuguese missionaries established a school in the royal capital of Kongo in 1490. As in West Africa, it was the elite who accepted the new faith. Many Kongo leaders became Christians. Rulers who became Christians usually did not give up their old beliefs. They simply added the Christian God to their vision of the spiritual world. This vision acknowledged the existence of many earth spirits and ancestral gods as well as a god of creation.

The Portuguese merchants stopped at nothing to get slaves. Since Africans customarily enslaved prisoners they took in war, the merchants tried to get village chiefs to declare war on each other. And since native criminals were punished with slavery, they encouraged crime among the people. The Portuguese also supplied rival villages with guns and even bribed officials to encourage revolts against the Mani-Kongo. They offered European goods and guns to any chief who would supply them with slaves. Some missionaries even became slave traders.

The Kongo rulers were trapped in a tangled web. A chief needed guns for protection from slave raiders. But the only way to get guns was to trade slaves for them.

Desperate to put an end to this problem, Affonso wrote a series of letters to King John. In one, written in 1526, he pleaded:

> Merchants are taking every day our natives, sons of the land and sons of our noblemen. . . . So great is the corruption and licentiousness [immorality] that our country is becoming completely depopulated.

In letter after letter, Affonso asked the Portuguese king to ban slave trade in Kongo. But King John did nothing. And, by 1540, King Affonso had even decided to support the slave trade in order to increase his own wealth and power.

By the 1600s, the Kongo kingdom was breaking apart. The Portuguese pressured Kongo chiefs in the provinces to rebel against the Mani-Kongo. As a result, the chiefs of some provinces declared their independence from the kingdom. Civil wars erupted as villages staged raids against each other to capture slaves and sell them to the Portuguese.

Thus, contact with the Portuguese had a severe and long-lasting effect on the people of Kongo and all of Africa. The Portuguese destroyed Kongo's trade in goods and replaced it with trade in human beings. Kongo lost many strong and able people to slavery. Finally, civil wars sparked by the Portuguese brought an end to the Kongo kingdom. ■

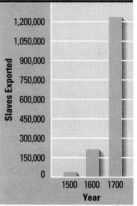

Kongo Slave Trade

Slaves Exported

1,200,000
1,050,000
900,000
750,000
600,000
450,000
300,000
150,000
0

1500 1600 1700
Year

▲ *Queen Nzinga Mbande (c. 1580–1663), is today a national heroine in Angola. She once worked against the Portuguese. One story says that she called a slave to sit upon when the Portuguese governor refused her a chair.*

■ *Why did civil war erupt in Kongo?*

R E V I E W

1. **FOCUS** How did Kongo change after the arrival of the Portuguese?
2. **CONNECT** Compare the relationship of Portugal and Kongo with that of Portugal and Monomutapa.
3. **HISTORY** Describe the actions of the Portuguese to develop the slave trade.
4. **CRITICAL THINKING** Why do you think King John ignored Affonso's plea for help?
5. **WRITING ACTIVITY** Write a letter from King Affonso of Kongo to King John of Portugal in which King Affonso describes the effects of the slave trade in Kongo and asks King John to put a stop to it.

153

Central and Southern Africa

HISTORY
Critical Thinking

Ask students to explain how activities in Portuguese colonies affected the people of Kongo. *(The colonists needed slave labor so they encouraged slave raids and civil wars in Kongo to generate a steady supply of slaves.)* Ask why the Kongo couldn't simply stop selling slaves. *(Africans needed slaves to trade for guns to protect themselves from slave raids.)*

■ *The Kongo village chiefs declared war on each other in order to capture prisoners to sell as slaves.*

CLOSE

Reintroduce the Thinking Focus and discuss the predictions the students made. If the predictions were inaccurate, allow students to revise them. If they were accurate, discuss how students came up with their predictions. You may wish to use the illustrations on pp. 152 and 153 when discussing Kongo and Portuguese perceptions of each other.

153

Answers to Review Questions

1. At first the Kongo had friendly relations with the Portuguese. But soon the Portuguese demand for slaves changed the Kongo economy, ruined its political system, and destroyed the social order.
2. The Portuguese arrived in both places as friends and became enemies who sought only profit.
3. The Portuguese encouraged villages to declare war on each other, encouraged crime among the people, supplied guns, and bribed officials to encourage revolts.
4. Answers will vary. Students may say John would not end the slave trade because Portuguese plantations required slave labor. They may say John wanted to profit from the slave trade.

Homework Options

Have students write a paragraph comparing Portuguese intervention in Kongo with that in East Africa or Monomutapa.

Study Guide: p. 27

DECISION-MAKING PROCESS

1. Recognize the need for a decision.
2. Define the goals and values involved.
3. Acquire and evaluate necessary information.
4. Identify and analyze possible alternatives.
5. Choose the best alternative.

This Making Decisions lesson, Trade Between the Kongo and Portugal, uses steps 4 and 5 of the decision-making process.

ETHICS
Critical Thinking

Explain that the Kongo didn't have to trade its people into slavery; alternatives for dealing with the Portuguese were available to them. Have students think of as many alternatives as they can. *(Not trading with the Portuguese at all; trading only copper with them.)*

MAKING DECISIONS

Trade Between the Kongo and Portugal

Put all the Guinea countries *[African countries along the west coast north of the Kongo kingdom]* on one side and only Kongo on the other and you will find that Kongo renders *[offers]* more than all others put together. . . . No other king in all these parts esteems Portuguese goods so much or treats the Portuguese as well as we do."

Mani-Kongo Affonso I in letter to King John III of Portugal, 1540

Background

The kingdom of the Kongo was established in the early 1400s. From its beginning, trade was the key to power in that kingdom. The Kongo kingdom was located at the crossroads of two trade routes. Copper was traded on a north-south trade route; shells and salt were traded on an east-west trade route. The first Mani-Kongo centered his kingdom

➤ *Seated on a throne above his subjects, Affonso, the Mani-Kongo, meets with a representative sent by the king of Portugal.*

154

Chapter 6

154

Objectives

1. Identify the alternatives available to the Mani-Kongo regarding trade with the Portuguese. (Study Skills 1; Economics 1, 3)
2. Analyze the Mani-Kongo's alternatives and choose the best one. (Critical Thinking 2; Ethics and Belief Systems 2)

Activity

Divide the class in half. Tell students they are going to be participants in a high-level meeting with the Mani-Kongo to decide whether they will trade with Portugal. Half the class will represent the chief council members, who oppose trade with Portugal. The other half will be the Mani-Kongo's personal staff, who favor the trade agreement. Explain that both sides should consider and list the probable consequences of the alternatives they propose. Allow both sides time to meet in their groups to formulate their presentation strategies. If time permits, they might gather supplemental information in the school's library. Conduct the meeting in debate form, giving each member in both of the groups a certain amount of time to express his or her point, and the opposing side a specified amount of time to respond.

where these two trade routes intersected. This enabled him to gain control of the distribution of all of these products.

The Mani-Kongo used his control over trade, his army, and his system of administration and justice to hold power over local chiefs. To those who were loyal to him, he gave gifts—trade goods from the far corners of the kingdom. From those who opposed him, he withheld such goods.

Expanding Trade

Soon after the Portuguese arrived in the Kongo in the late 1400s, the Mani-Kongo offered them high-quality copper. In return, he expected that the Portuguese would offer technology, including guns, knives, and cloth. The Portuguese refused to sell the Kongo people goods that would benefit their society. Instead, the Portuguese only traded worthless items such as china, mirrors, and hats. The trade the Portuguese built up with Kongo only benefited the Portuguese.

The decision to trade with the Portuguese had short-term benefits for the Mani-Kongo. In the long run, however, it had serious negative consequences. In the early 1500s, the Portuguese began trading with the Mani-Kongo for slaves. This led to the destruction of the kingdom.

▲ *The map of western Africa, created in 1502, reveals how little Portuguese explorers had learned about Africa by this time.*

Decision Point

1. For the Mani-Kongo, what were some immediate benefits of trading with the Portuguese? Eventually, what were the negative consequences?
2. Do you think the Mani-Kongo could have foreseen these negative consequences? Why?
3. If the mani-Kongo had refused to trade with the Portuguese, what might have been some of the consequences? Consider both short-term and long-term benefits and drawbacks.
4. Currently the United States trades with many foreign countries, including Japan, China, and South Africa. Look in newspapers and magazines for information about our trade relationships with one of these countries. Discuss some of the short-term and long-term consequences of trading with these nations.

◄ *This African mask, made in the Kongo, is covered with cowry shells. These shells were valuable to the Kongo people.*

155

Central and Southern Africa

155

Answers to Decision Point

1. The luxury items from Europe gave the people of the Kongo status, but the people of the kingdom were eventually sold into slavery and the kingdom was destroyed.
2. Sample answers: Yes: he should have known that no good could come from trading the lives of his people for mere status symbols. No: he could not have foreseen the negative consequences.
3. The Portuguese might have invaded his kingdom. The Mani-Kongo would have had to seek European luxury items from other traders or gone without them, but his people might not have become slaves, and the Kongo might not have been destroyed.
4. Consequences include increasing the mounting foreign debt and trade imbalance, gradually losing our self-reliance, and obtaining some financial leverage to affect decisions made about human rights issues in other countries.

Collaborative Strategy

A recommended strategy for this lesson is heterogeneous grouping. For further information, turn to pp. T34–T35.

Answers to Reviewing Key Terms

A. Sample answers:
1. This is an example of an **oral tradition** because the mother is passing on something that is handed down through generations.
2. The gold coin is an example of a **currency** because it is being used to pay for something else.
3. This is an example of a **city-state** because Kilwa was a city-state.

B. Sample answers:
1. False. The Bantu-speaking people **migrated** in search of land to settle.
2. False. Arabs used the **monsoons** to sail for East Africa between November and March.
3. True.
4. False. Christian **missionaries** taught African natives about Christianity.
5. True.
6. False.
7. False. Zimbabwe is located on a high **plateau.**

Answers to Exploring Concepts

A. Sample answers:
Answers will vary for the third column of the chart.
Kikuyu: Farming. They lived in villages but not kingdoms.
Swahili: Trading. They served as the link between foreign traders and inland Africans.
Shona: Farming, raising cattle, mining. They built Great Zimbabwe.
People of Kongo: Farming, hunting, trading. King Affonso tried to ban slave trade between Portugal and Kongo.

B. Sample answers:
1. Savannas, valleys, and rain forests.

2. Proto-Bantu-speaking people from West Africa migrated across central, east, and southern Africa. Over time different languages developed from this root language.
3. Rhapta imported lances, hatchets, swords, awls, small glass vessels, wine, and wheat. Mouza imported ivory, rhinoceros horn, tortoise-shell, and coconut oil.
4. Local rulers and merchants controlled the trade and became wealthy.

5. The Shona were Bantu-speaking farmers and cattle raisers who reached Zimbabwe about 300.
6. The Shona made gold jewelry and ornaments. Miners heated gold-bearing rocks, threw cold water on them to split them, and removed the gold.
7. They traded salt from the sea, iron, copper, ivory, and raffia.
8. The Portuguese promoted civil wars which weakened Monomutapa. It was then conquered by southern kingdoms.

Kongo lost many people to slave trade with Portugal. Civil wars sparked by the Portuguese brought an end to the Kongo Kingdom.

Chapter Review

Reviewing Key Terms

city-state (p. 143)
currency (p. 150)
ethnolinguistics (p. 136)
malaria (p. 148)
migrate (p. 137)

missionary (p. 152)
monsoon (p. 141)
oral tradition (p. 148)
plantation (p. 152)
plateau (p. 146)

A. For each sentence below write whether it is an example of a city-state, an oral tradition, or a currency. Explain your answer.
1. A mother sings songs to her children that she learned as a child.
2. At the restaurant the man pays for his dinner with a gold coin.
3. In addition to a mosque, Kilwa had a huge palace and houses of many stories.

B. Write whether each statement below is true or false. Then rewrite the false statements to make them true.
1. Bantu-speaking people migrated because the climate grew cold.
2. To sail by the monsoons, Arabs left for West Africa between April and October.
3. The Europeans treated African slaves harshly.
4. Christian missionaries taught Africans about Islam.
5. Many of the people in Africa suffered from malaria.
6. No Africans had large cities or well-organized states.
7. Zimbabwe is located on a low plateau.

Exploring Concepts

A. In this chapter, you read about several groups of African people. The chart below compares four of the groups. Copy the chart on your own paper. Then complete the chart using information from the chapter. The first section has been done for you.

Peoples of Central and Southern Africa

	Occupations	Additional Information
Kikuyu	Farming	They lived in villages but not kingdoms.
Swahili		
Shona		
People of Kongo		

B. Answer each question with information from the chapter.
1. What are three kinds of terrain in central and southern Africa?
2. Why do most people of central and southern Africa speak a Bantu language?
3. What products did the city of Rhapta import around A.D. 100? What did Mouza import from Rhapta?
4. How did the Indian Ocean trade between 1100–1500 affect the town of Kilwa?
5. What do we know about the people who lived at Great Zimbabwe?
6. How did the Shona use the gold of Zimbabwe? How did they mine the gold in the 1100s?
7. What products did the people of the Kongo trade with the people around them before the Portuguese arrived?
8. What were the long-term effects of the Portuguese on Monomutapa and Kongo?

Chapter 6

Reviewing Skills

1. Look at the map on this page. Construct a vertical profile of the land at 20° S. What is the highest elevation shown on your vertical profile? The lowest?
2. Use the following entry from the *Readers' Guide* to answer the questions.
   Monsoons
   Seasonal winds: a blessing or a curse?
   R. A. Borthwick. il maps *Journal of Economic Development* 129:21–7+ Ap '89
   a. What is the title of the article?
   b. Who is the author?
   c. What is the title of the periodical?
   d. On what pages does the article appear?
3. Imagine that African villagers are explaining a truth about life to their children. How might the villagers communicate this truth?

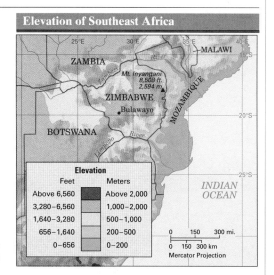

Elevation of Southeast Africa

ZAMBIA
MALAWI
Mt. Inyangani
8,508 ft.
2,594 m
ZIMBABWE
Bulawayo
MOZAMBIQUE
BOTSWANA
Limpopo River
INDIAN OCEAN

Elevation

Feet	Meters
Above 6,560	Above 2,000
3,280–6,560	1,000–2,000
1,640–3,280	500–1,000
656–1,640	200–500
0–656	0–200

0   150   300 mi.
0 150 300 km
Mercator Projection

Using Critical Thinking

1. If you wanted to know whether early African people suffered from sleeping sickness, what information in the chapter might help you to determine this?
2. What were the trading practices of the Arabs of Mouza around A.D. 100? What values of the Arab people do these trading practices reveal? Do you think these values are still important today? Explain your answer.
3. Imagine that you came upon the ruins of Great Zimbabwe. You arrive at a city on a high plateau. You see a tower and a 30-foot wall around the city. Inside the buildings, you eventually discover hidden passages. What would you determine about the Shona's relationships with other groups from these observations?

Preparing for Citizenship

COLLECTING INFORMATION Alex Haley was an African American who traced his family's history back to a village in West Africa. Look in Haley's book, *Roots, the Saga of an American Family,* to find out how he used oral tradition to trace his family's roots.

INTERVIEWING Villages of Bantu speakers were commonly ruled by a chief and a council of elders. Interview an official in your city or town. Find out how your town's government is organized. Is there anyone who functions like a chief? Is there any group that acts like a council of elders? If there are, what are their titles and responsibilities?

3. **COLLABORATIVE LEARNING** Work in committees to research one or two cities in your state or region that were founded as centers of trade. Locate the cities on a map. Find out what products were exported and imported by these cities, and whether this trade is the basis of their economy today. If not, find out how the economy of the city has changed. Each committee should decide what information is important and report it to the class.

1. The highest elevation is between 3,280 and 6,560 feet (1,000 and 2,000 meters). The lowest is between 0 and 656 feet (0 and 200 meters).
2. a. "Seasonal Winds: A Blessing or a Curse?"
   b. R. A. Borthwick.
   c. *Journal of Economic Development.*
   d. 21–27+.
3. Cite a proverb.

Answers to Using Critical Thinking

1. The discussion of the Bantu-speaking migrants in Lesson 1 says that wherever the migrants went, they avoided areas infested with tsetse flies. The bite of these insects spreads a disease called sleeping sickness that is fatal to humans and cattle. This information is evidence that early African people suffered from sleeping sickness.
2. Arab traders intermarried with the mainlanders in areas where they traded. They knew the languages the people spoke. The Arabs also gave the Africans wheat to gain their good will. The Arabs must have valued long-term relationships of good will. Students may say that such values are important today because people need long-term relationships.
3. Students should infer that the Shona needed protection from some other group(s) in the area.

Answers to Preparing for Citizenship

1. **COLLECTING INFORMATION** Haley researched his grandmother's stories in historical records to find his African ancestor. In his ancestor's village in West Africa, the man who recited the oral history of one of the villages recited parts of the same story that Haley's grandmother had told about Haley's African relative.
2. **INTERVIEWING** Students should be able to describe their local government so that their classmates understand who runs the local government and how it is run.
3. **COLLABORATIVE LEARNING** Encourage students to work within their groups to decide what contribution each member will make. Students should use a map to locate each city they study. They should describe how the cities became centers of trade and tell whether the same trade still exists. If it does not, students should report how the economies of the cities have changed.

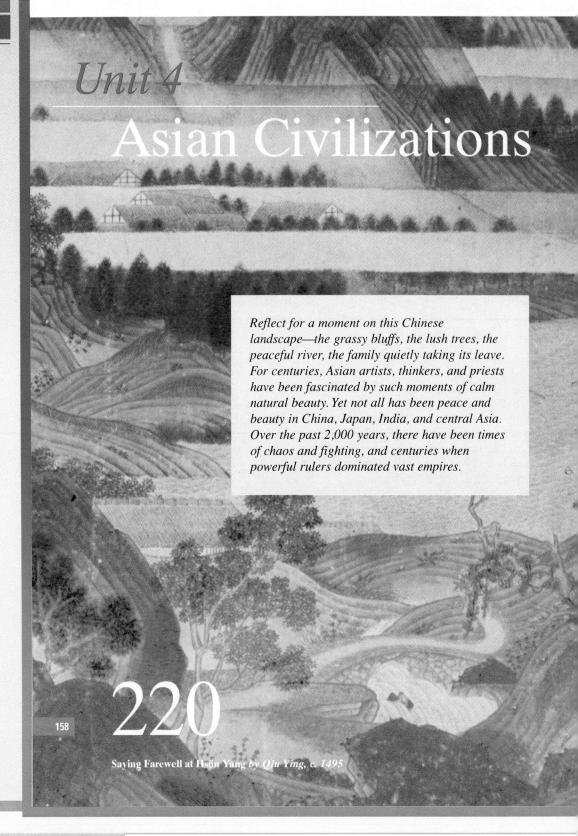

UNIT OVERVIEW

Have the students read the unit title and the passage below it. Explain that Asia is the world's largest continent, covering almost one-third of the world's land area and containing about three-fifths of its people. Then point out on a large map the locations of central Asia, Southeast Asia, India, China, and Japan.

Looking Back

Remind students that the civilizations around the Mediterranean were in contact with Asian civilizations through trade.

Looking Forward

Tell students that in the next three chapters they will study different civilizations that developed in Asia:
Chapter 7 *Three Empires*
Chapter 8 *China*
Chapter 9 *Japan*

Unit 4

Asian Civilizations

Reflect for a moment on this Chinese landscape—the grassy bluffs, the lush trees, the peaceful river, the family quietly taking its leave. For centuries, Asian artists, thinkers, and priests have been fascinated by such moments of calm natural beauty. Yet not all has been peace and beauty in China, Japan, India, and central Asia. Over the past 2,000 years, there have been times of chaos and fighting, and centuries when powerful rulers dominated vast empires.

158

220

Saying Farewell at Hsün Yang *by Qiu Ying, c. 1495*

GEOGRAPHY PROJECT

Early Asia Tour

Geography Skill Comparing Maps
Students use the skill of Analyzing geographic information.

Geography Theme Place/Location

Geography Standards 4, 11 physical and human characteristics of places; economic interdependence

Activity *Create a Brochure*

Materials construction paper, markers and pens

Management Individual/ Small Group

Choose a city, town, or region from each of the Asian empires described in this unit and create a travel brochure written from a modern point of view including maps and illustrations of each place.

Have students:

- write descriptive text for a brochure and/or create a diorama of each place.

- create a locator map for each brochure or diorama and then compare the maps.

- draw illustrations of geographic features and cultural sites.

1923

Understanding the Painting

Qiu Ying was one of the foremost painters of the "blue-green" school of Chinese landscape painting, so called because of the dominant color shadings. Although this painting was created in the late 1400s, landscapes were already the chief subject of Chinese painting by the 900s.

Understanding Chronology

Have students look at the two dates to determine the number of years covered in the unit. *(1703.)* Stress that the unit focuses on five different civilizations or empires during the time span—Mongol, Ottoman, Mughal, Chinese, and Japanese. At different points during the 1700-year period, several of these empires interacted through war, trade, religious conversion, and cultural exchange.

For research support activities, see the *Research Handbook.*

For simulations correlated to this unit, see *Citizenship Simulations,* p. viii.

HOUGHTON MIFFLIN SOCIAL STUDIES

Bookshelf II

Sweet and Sour: Tales from China

retold by Carol Kendall and Yao-wen Li

This anthology of Chinese tales from many time periods includes stories that vary from witty and clever to philosophical.

Motivate Read aloud the story on pp. 60–63 about a Chinese god who comes to earth to try to find the perfect human being. The ending can lead to a discussion about the great cultural achievements that come from China. Ask students how a culture's literature and art are reflective of the culture. Have them look at the Chinese painting on the unit opener pages and predict what they will read about in Unit 4.

To connect this book with the unit content, use the planning guide and student activity blackline masters beginning on p. iv of the *Bookshelf II Teacher's Resources.*

For additional books that are Easy, Average, and Challenging, see the Unit Bibliography on p. T43. See bibliography updates at www.eduplace.com/ss/hmss.

CHAPTER 7 Planning at a Glance
Three Empires

	Objectives	Reading Support and Other Resources	Diverse Learning Strategies

Lesson 1
The Mongols
pp. 162–169 2–3 days
	• Describe the geography of the steppe and its effect on the life of the Mongols.
	• Discuss the social organization of the Mongols.
	• Describe the expansion of the Mongol Empire under Genghis Khan and his successors.
	• Assess the accomplishments and impact of the Mongols.
		• **Workbook** or **Reading Support:**
		  pp. 88–91
		  Review p. 21
		  Lesson Support/Transition p. 21
		  Multi-lang. Sum. pp. 41–42
		• **Other Resources:** Geography Kit, Poster 5, Study Guide 27, Study Print 5
			Access Act. **(SDAIE)** TE p. 163
			Study Skills **(GATE)** TE p. 164
			Social Participation **(Auditory)** TE p. 165
			Map and Globe Skills **(Visual)** TE p. 166
			
			Audiotapes of Multi-language Lesson Summaries **(Auditory)**

Lesson 2
The Ottoman Empire
pp. 170–177 2–3 days
	• Trace the growth of the Ottoman Empire under the early sultans.
	• Detail the highly developed social and military institutions of the empire.
	• Describe the accomplishments of the Ottomans under Suleiman.
	• Discuss the reasons for the gradual decline of the empire after the death of Suleiman.
		• **Workbook** or **Reading Support:**
		  pp. 92–95
		  Review p. 22
		  Lesson Support/Transition p. 22
		  Multi-lang. Sum. pp. 43–44
		• **Other Resources:** Geography Kit, Study Guide p. 28
			Access Strat. **(Extra Support)** TE p. 171
			Access Act. **(SDAIE)** TE p. 171
			Visual Learning **(Visual)** TE pp. 172, 173
			Homework Options **(GATE)** TE p. 177
			
			Audiotapes of Multi-language Lesson Summaries **(Auditory)**

Lesson 3
The Mughal Empire
pp. 178–185 2–3 days
	• Describe the role of geography in the development of India.
	• Evaluate the impact of Akbar's policies on the empire.
	• Discuss the reasons for the gradual dissolution of the Mughal empire.
		• **Workbook** or **Reading Support:**
		  pp. 96–99
		  Review p. 23
		  Lesson Support/Transition p. 23
		  Multi-lang. Sum. pp. 45–46
		• **Other Resources:** Study Guide p. 29, Study Print 6
			Access Act. **(SDAIE)** TE p. 179
			Map and Globe Skills **(Visual)** TE p. 179
			Language Arts Connection **(Kinesthetic)** TE p. 182
			Collaborative Learning **(Visual)** TE p. 183
			
			Audiotapes of Multi-language Lesson Summaries **(Auditory)**

Skill: Reading Mughal Paintings *pp. 186–187* 1 day	• Interpret information presented visually in paintings.	• **Other Resources:** Study Guide p. 30	Creating a Play **(Kinesthetic)** TE p. 186
Chapter Review *pp. 188–189* 1 day		Chapter 7 Test pp. 25–28 *(See facsimiles on TE p. 565.)*	Assessment Multiple-Use Masters pp. 73–80

Reading Support Resources *for Every Lesson*

Reading and Review

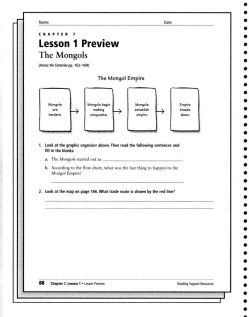

- **Chapter Overview*** p. 87
- **Lesson Previews*** using graphic organizers from the Teacher's Edition pp. 88, 92, 96
- **Reading Strategies*** pp. 89, 93, 97
- **Lesson Summaries*** pp. 90–91, 94–95, 98–99
- **Lesson Reviews** pp. 21, 22, 23

* **Workbook** includes starred items.

Multi-language Summaries

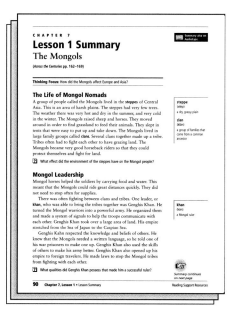

Lesson Summaries in:
- English (See Reading and Review.)
- Spanish pp. 90–91, 94–95, 98–99
- Chinese pp. 41–46
- Hmong pp. 41–46
- Khmer pp. 41–46
- Vietnamese pp. 41–46

 Summaries available on audiotapes

Lesson Support /Transition
SDAIE

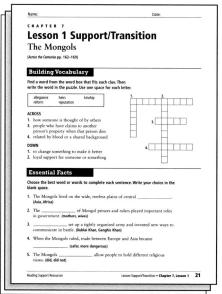

Activities for SDAIE
Specially **D**esigned **A**cademic **I**nstruction in **E**nglish

- **Lesson Support/Transition** pp. 21, 22, 23

 # Technology Options

Internet Support
http://www.eduplace.com
Social Studies Center at Education Place
Internet support for Chapter 7:
- *Lesson at a Glance*
- *The Taj Mahal*

Software
Student Writing Center® (CD-ROM) (Macintosh® or Windows®)

School to Career

The Mongols, Ottomans, and Mughals each built incredible buildings that still fascinate people today. Have students study buildings in their communities. Then have students design a model community, assigning pairs of students a specific building or buildings. What materials would students use?

Character Education

Throughout human history domesticated animals have played important roles, from the practical to the pleasurable. Discuss with students why the humane treatment of animals is important. Contact a local animal shelter to arrange for a speaker to come visit the class to talk about his or her job.

160

CHAPTER PREVIEW

Ask the students to read the chapter title and the paragraph that follows. Using a map of Asia, ask students to identify the areas conquered by the Mongols, Ottoman Turks, and Mughals. Discuss why ruling with tolerance rather than harshness might contribute to building an empire. *(Subjects who are treated harshly would probably try to undermine the people governing them; resources that would otherwise be used to keep people oppressed can be used in building up the empire.)*

Looking Forward

Let students know that in Lessons 1–3 they will be reading about the rise of three powerful empires: The Mongols, The Ottoman Empire, and The Mughal Empire.

Lesson 1 describes the rise of the Mongol Empire and the exploits of Genghis and Kubla Khan.

Chapter 7
Three Empires

This ceremonial sword belonged to an Ottoman sultan.

The conquerors came from homelands in central Asia. The Mongols swept down and captured lands from China to the Middle East. The Ottoman Turks migrated to Asia Minor and then set their sights on new frontiers. The Mughals trekked over the steep passes of the Himalayas and invaded India. Through strong leadership and tolerance toward the people they conquered, the Mongols, Ottomans, and Mughals built great empires.

1260–1294 Led by Kublai Khan, the Mongol Empire reaches its height. Mongol warriors (left) take control of the Middle East from Egypt.

| 950 | 1100 | 1250 | 1400 |

160

997

1235 Mali defeats Ghana to become the major power in West Africa.

1096–1291 European Christians fight Arab Muslims for control of Jerusalem and the Holy Land.

BACKGROUND

The unity and geographical span of the Muslim Empire that was achieved under the Umayyad and Abbasid dynasties was never again matched. The empire continued to split up when, in 1037, the Seljuk Turks invaded. Less than 20 years later, they controlled Baghdad. After an initial expansionary period, the Seljuk Empire itself fell apart. The Abbasid caliph continued to rule in name only, until the Mongols, fresh from having elected a new Great Khan for themselves (Hulagu), destroyed Baghdad and the last caliph in 1258.

The Mongols were not Muslims when they conquered the Muslim states. They were Buddhists. By the 1260s, however, the Mongol leader in Russia declared himself a Muslim. The Europeans, seeing an opportunity to drive Muslims out of the Holy Land, tried their hand at international politics. There was a brief correspondence between Pope Nicholas IV and the Mongol court and an exchange of ambassadors. The Christians hoped to ally with the Buddhist Mongols against the Muslim Mongols. However, in 1295, before this plan could be put into effect, Ghazan Khan, who ruled Persia, announced that he, too, was a Muslim. Most Mongols followed his example. Ghazan Khan had been convinced to convert by his prime minister and friend Rashid al-Din.

During the 1400s and 1500s, the Ottomans built a powerful and wealthy empire. Sultan Sulieman wore the jewels at the right on his turban. Sultan Bayezid wore the silk caftan at left as he sat on his throne.

1556–1605 The Mughal Empire prospers under Akbar. In the painting at the right, Akbar directs the building of a fort in his capital.

1550   1700   1850

c. 1600 The Kongo kingdom breaks apart due to civil wars sparked by the Portuguese.

1923

Understanding the Visuals

The battle scene (p. 160) shows Mongol forces led by Mahmud Ghazan defeating the Egyptian army. Mahmud Ghazan was an Il-Khan (subordinate khan) in the Mongol dynasty that ruled Iran from 1246–1353.

The miniature painting (p. 161) shows Akbar supervising the building of the Red Fort in Agra about 1566. Akbar was a patron of the arts; miniature paintings, which often illustrated manuscripts, frequently depicted Akbar's achievements.

Understanding Chronology

Refer students to the timeline and the images. Ask them to name time periods in which each of the three empires prospered. *(Mongols, 1260–1294; Ottomans, 1400s and 1500s; Mughals, 1556–1605.)*

Rashid al-Din

Rashid al-Din Fadl Allah (1247–1318) was born to a Jewish family, studied medicine, and was eventually physician to the court of the Mongol ruler of Persia. At age 30 he converted to Islam. He became vizier to Ghazan Khan in 1298 and was responsible for building an astronomical observatory, a hospital, numerous schools, and a group of religious buildings, all of which attracted scholars from all over the world.

Rashid was an outstanding statesman. For years the Mongol economy had been faltering. Based on his advice, Ghazan Khan introduced paper money into his empire. However, paper money was entirely new to the Middle East, and people rapidly lost confidence in it. Rashid also developed a philosophy of governing in accordance with the moral principles of a majority of the population.

As if all this were not enough, Rashid al-Din is one of the great world historians. In fact, his is the first attempt to write a history of the world. His book, published in 1307, contains the earliest known general history of Europe, which he based on information from European monks. His history of India came from a Buddhist monk of Kashmir. The history of the Mongols was told to him by Ghazan Khan. This huge work also included a geographical compendium, now lost. He drew on sources in Arabic, Chinese, Greek, Latin, Mongolian, and Persian. Editions of his book were profusely illustrated, with artwork mimicking the artistic style of the region under discussion.

| 950 | 1100 | | 1550 | 1700 | 1850 | TODAY |

1200   **1447**

L E S S O N   1

The Mongols

THINKING FOCUS

How did the Mongols affect Europe and Asia?

Key Terms

- steppe
- clan
- khan

➤ *The Mongols took excellent care of their horses. Here, a Mongol grooms the tail of his horse.*

In the early 1200s, a group of people known as the Mongols began a series of rapid conquests throughout Asia. They would soon control the largest empire in the world. Ibn al Athir wrote about the events of 1220 to 1221, "These Tartars [Mongols] conquered most of the habitable globe and the best, the most flourishing and most populous thereof . . . in about a year."

How were the Mongols able to conquer so much so quickly?

There are several reasons for the Mongol successes. They had outstanding leadership, military skill and, most important, horses. On horseback, the Mongols could advance up to 200 miles a day. Good horsemanship was so important to the Mongols that children, both male and female, learned to ride before they could walk.

The Life of Mongol Nomads

The world that horses enabled the Mongols to inhabit was the wide, treeless plains—or **steppes**—of central Asia. To the north lies the Siberian forest and to the south is desert.

Chapter 7

162

Direct students to look ahead to the map on p. 166 in their texts. Point out that the Mongol Empire, at its largest, encompassed almost all of the landmass of Asia, as well as some of eastern Europe and most of the Middle East. Ask students what difficulties the Mongols might have faced in ruling such a large area. *(Need for a physical presence in many areas; difficulty of communication; widely varying customs and beliefs of conquered peoples.)*

Winter in the steppes is long and bitterly cold, and summer is dry and burning hot. The temperature ranges from –100°F in the winter to 100°F in the summer. The Mongols were nomadic herders who migrated according to the seasons, in search of good grazing land for their flocks of sheep and horses.

Since the Mongols moved so frequently, they didn't have one permanent settlement. Instead, they lived in tents called yurts. Yurts were made of felt, a material made from wool, and so were easily transportable and yet strong enough to offer protection from the extreme weather.

The Mongols traveled in patrilineal family groups called **clans.** Clan members were related by kinship. Clans had a formal leader who was usually the eldest male. They were normally made up of several three- or four-generation family groups. Each clan could trace its descent from an actual or mythical founding

ancestor. The tribe united the clans either through kinship or treaty. The Mongol practice of *anda,* or sworn brotherhood, allowed people to swear allegiance to a clan other than the one they were born into. The chart below shows the social organization of the Mongols.

If the reputation of a tribal leader was very impressive, men from other tribes would swear

▲ *Yurts are still used by many nomads on the steppes of central Asia.*

▼ *Mongol social organization was based on family ties, sworn brotherhood, and sworn oaths to leaders. When a man swore allegiance to a new leader, he forswore his blood loyalty to his own clan and to the tribe.*

Social Bonds Among the Mongol

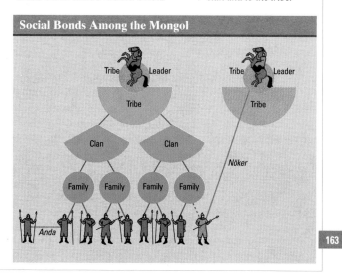

163

Three Empires

Critical Thinking

Explain that the Mongols were loyal to their clans, their tribes, and sometimes to a stronger tribe and its leader. What would be some advantages and disadvantages of this system? *(Ties of loyalty would help to unify the physically separate groups of nomads. They might also contribute to rivalries between clans and tribes.)* Ask students to list their own loyalties—to family, friends, team, school, city, state, and country, and discuss which are strongest.

163

Access Strategy

Direct students to look at the illustrations on pp. 160, 162, and 163 and create with them a word web about the climate of the steppes of central Asia. Then reread the text on p. 163 and confirm or correct students' speculations. You might want to have some of the students report on conditions of life in modern-day Mongolia.

Explore with students the ruggedness of outdoor living for the Mongols and the intense interrelationship between humans and geography. Call students' attention to the importance of the horse.

Access Activity

The Mongols' primary dwelling was a collapsible tent called a yurt. It was 15 feet in diameter and was made from willow poles lashed together with rawhide to form latticework. The yurt frame was covered with layers of greased felt. Have students work in small groups to build yurt models from toothpicks, dental floss, and fabric.

■ *The harsh environment of the steppe made the Mongols very hardy, and since the land was suited to herding rather than agriculture, the Mongols became nomadic herders.*

164

allegiance to him. They would then become the new leader's *nöker,* or followers. Their allegiance to him outweighed any allegiance to clan or tribe.

For all Mongol groups, the need to protect themselves and compete for grazing lands was crucial. To do so, the Mongols developed incredible skill on horseback.

■ *What effect did the environment of the steppes have on the Mongol people?*

Across Time & Space

The present-day country of Mongolia lies between China and Russia. Nearly all the people of Mongolia are descendants of the Mongols, who built an empire in the 1200s.

Mongols had such control over their mounts that they could ride long distances using only their feet. Their hands, then, were free to wield weapons in battle. Their exceptional riding skill and their great ability in using weapons while on horseback gave the Mongols a distinct advantage over their less-skilled enemies. ■

Mongol Leadership

Horses also helped the Mongols in another way. Each soldier had at least three or four extra horses carrying food and water. Because he didn't have to stop for fresh food, water, or horses, the Mongol soldier could travel vast distances quickly.

A Mongol soldier carried an array of weapons into battle: two or three bows; three quivers of arrows; and an ax, rope, and sword. His bow was short enough to be used while riding, yet it was strong enough to launch an arrow into a target 350 yards away.

Although clans and tribes often fought with each other, once in a

while a strong leader could unite them all against a common enemy.

The Great Khan

Temujin *(TEHM yoo jihn),* known today as Genghis Khan, was born in 1167. When Temujin was 12 years old, his father, a tribal chief, was murdered by a rival chief. Fearing he would be next, Temujin fled with his mother and brothers. Mothers of princes and rulers played important roles in government. Although it was nearly impossible for very small groups to survive the environment of the steppe, Temujin, with the help of his mother,

➤ *The energy of Mongols in battle is shown in this painting from a manuscript page. Notice how the artist has used swirling figures to give a feeling of movement to the scene.*

164

Chapter 7

kept the family alive. Thus began his reputation as an intelligent and resourceful leader.

Temujin's reputation continued to grow, and in 1206, an assembly of tribal chiefs elected him the great **khan,** or leader, of the Mongols. They gave Temujin the name Genghis Khan, which means "ruler of all within the seas." He was 39 years old.

Genghis Khan the Warrior

Genghis Khan shaped the powerful Mongol warriors into a tightly structured army. He grouped soldiers into units of 10,000 troops. These units were subdivided into smaller groups of 1,000, 100, and 10. The smaller groups had individual leaders who reported to the group leader above them. This type of military leadership created a clear chain of command within the larger army and helped create order on the battlefield. Genghis further strengthened the Mongol army by incorporating defeated enemy troops who would swear allegiance to the Mongol ruler.

Genghis Khan also devised elaborate signals to be used as communication amid the noise and confusion of battle. Soldiers used drums, horns, shouts, and even bird calls to communicate with each other. Mongol leaders could then direct and organize their troops as situations developed on the battlefield.

Using this highly skilled and structured army, Genghis Khan added vast areas to his empire. The Mongols conquered all the lands between Beijing and the Caspian Sea.

Genghis Khan the Ruler

Although Genghis Khan knew the strength of his warriors, he realized that there were areas where the Mongols were weak. The Mongols lacked a written language. So Genghis used a captured scribe to create a written language for them. He also used the skills of foreign craftspersons and specialists

▲ *The great Mongol ruler Genghis Khan is pictured in this portrait from a Turkish manuscript. Most representations of Mongol rulers come from other cultures.*

Three Empires

Mathematics Connection

In one attack in western Asia, Genghis Khan led 200,000 troops. Each unit contained 10,000 men. Ask students to compute the number of fighting units. *(20)* In addition, each 10,000-man fighting unit was subdivided into smaller groups of 1,000; 100; and 10. Each smaller group had a leader who reported to the leader of the next larger group. What was the maximum number of men reporting to any leader? *(20)* Suggest that students create an organizational chart to help them visualize Genghis Khan's chain of command.

Social Participation

Mongol men were herders and warriors. Mongol women were responsible for most domestic chores, for making clothing, and producing felt. Some women traveled with the Mongol cavalry, preparing food and equipment. Divide students into small groups, and have each group prepare a simple skit depicting the daily life of a Mongol clan, using imaginative props.

■ *Genghis Khan's qualities include intelligence, resourcefulness, political and military leadership skills, organizational skills, tolerance, respect, and inclusiveness.*

► *The Empire was divided into the Khanate of the Golden Horde, the Chagatai Khanate, the Ilkhan Khanate, and the Khanate of the Great Khan.*

GEOGRAPHY

Map and Globe Skills

Have students look at the map on this page to find the original Mongol area and the four later khanates. Have students use the map scale to estimate the east-west extent of the entire Mongol Empire. Also, have students use recent maps to identify the modern countries included in the empire.

166

■ *What qualities did Genghis Khan possess that made him a successful ruler?*

▼ *The Mongol Empire grew rapidly and eventually covered much of Asia. Name the four sections that the Mongol Empire was divided into after the death of Genghis Khan.*

to improve his army. From them he learned how to use catapults and gunpowder bombs. These weapons helped the Mongols besiege enemy fortresses.

Genghis respected the knowledge and beliefs of others. During his rule, Genghis Khan opened his empire to foreign travelers.

Missionaries and merchants were allowed to journey through Mongol lands. He also made a series of laws forbidding fighting among tribes. Despite the fact that Genghis Khan introduced several reforms, he is said to have admitted that "man's highest joy is in victory: to conquer one's enemies." ■

The Later Khans

Genghis Khan died in 1227. In 1229, the empire was divided into four sections, called khanates. His four sons were each assigned a khanate. His third son, Ogodei *(ahg ah DY)*, was elected the Great Khan, the overall ruler of the Mongol Empire. One khanate included the eastern part of Europe. Another occupied the middle part of Russia and Central Asia. The third was in Persia, and the khanate

of the Great Khan held China, Mongolia, and eastern Russia.

The growth of the Mongol Empire continued after Genghis's death. China was conquered in 1234. In 1237, Ogodei sent Mongol horsemen to conquer the rest of southern Russia, as well as Poland and Hungary. Upon Ogodei's death in 1241, the Mongol leaders ended their attacks in Hungary and returned to Mongolia to elect

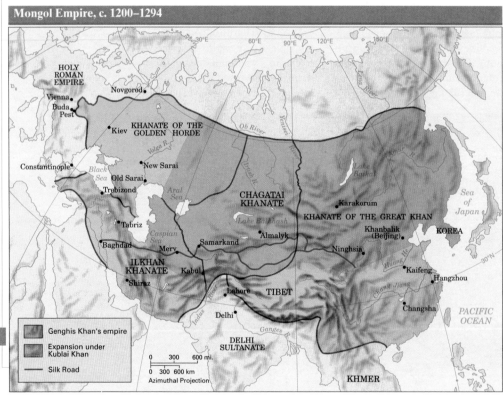

Mongol Empire, c. 1200–1294

166

Genghis Khan's empire

Expansion under Kublai Khan

— Silk Road

0   300   600 mi.
0 300 600 km
Azimuthal Projection

HOLY ROMAN EMPIRE · Novgorod · Vienna · Buda · Pest · Kiev · KHANATE OF THE GOLDEN HORDE · Constantinople · New Sarai · Old Sarai · Trebizond · CHAGATAI KHANATE · Karakorum · KHANATE OF THE GREAT KHAN · Tabriz · Almalyk · Khanbalik (Beijing) · KOREA · Baghdad · Merv · Samarkand · Ninghsia · ILKHAN KHANATE · Kabul · Kaifeng · Shiraz · Lahore · TIBET · Hangzhou · Delhi · Changsha · PACIFIC OCEAN · DELHI SULTANATE · KHMER · Black Sea · Volga R. · Aral Sea · Caspian Sea · Lake Balkhash · Lake Baikal · Sea of Japan · Ob River · Yenisei River · Ural River · Ganges · Indus · Huang He · Chang Jiang

Critical Thinking

Genghis Khan said, "When the Mongols are unoccupied by war, they shall devote themselves to hunting. The objective is not so much the chase itself as the training of warriors, who should acquire strength and become familiar with drawing the bow." Ask students what this reveals about Genghis Khan's commitment to the warrior lifestyle.

Historical Context

Mongol troops were well trained, strictly disciplined, and superbly organized. In addition, they used Chinese catapulting machines to increase the likelihood of their success in a raid on a city or fortressed area. From the Chinese the Mongols also acquired gunpowder, which could be fired in a bamboo tube shot from a bow. But just as important was the Mongols' mastery of more subtle military practices. In battle the Mongols were tactically brilliant. Their armies launched

three-pronged attacks and often faked retreats before launching counterattacks. They also used spies and propaganda. Before an attack, agents were sent into a city to spread tales of Mongol atrocities, thereby instilling panic and fear in the citizens. Before attacking, the Mongols usually asked for voluntary surrender. If Mongol terms were accepted, the population was spared. If the enemy resisted, however, only those with special skills or abilities escaped.

a new Great Khan. This halted the Mongol expansion into Europe.

Kublai Khan

Twenty years later, Genghis Khan's grandson, Kublai Khan, was elected Great Khan. Under Kublai's reign from 1260 to 1294, the Mongol Empire reached its height. The Mongols extended their borders to include eastern Europe, most of the Middle East, China, and the intervening territory. The map on page 166 shows the lands controlled by the Mongol Empire at its height.

Although the Mongol Empire grew, not all Mongol attempts to conquer other lands were successful. Under Kublai Khan, the Mongols tried to invade Japan in 1274 and 1281. Both invasion attempts were stopped by a typhoon, or hurricane, which destroyed most of the Mongol ships.

Like his grandfather Genghis, Kublai developed many programs to help stabilize the empire. Unlike the Chinese, Kublai respected merchants, and under his rule both internal and foreign trade flourished. He also established a postal system with riders covering up to 250 miles a day. Postal stations also served as inns for traveling merchants. Thus, the postal service helped communication and trade.

Breakdown of the Empire

Ultimately, however, the Mongols were better conquerors than rulers. They simply were not able to control the vast area they had won in battle. Communication among the four khanates became increasingly difficult.

◄ *Many people who wrote about the Mongols had been conquered by them. They often portrayed the Mongols as being more violent and brutal than maybe they really were.*

UNDERSTANDING CONQUEST

The Romans in the 2nd century. The Mongols in the 12th century. The British in the 19th century. Each group was famous for conquering vast territories and diverse people.

Reasons for Conquest

What motivates one group to conquer another? There are probably as many reasons as there are human needs—security, food, land, wealth, beliefs, and power. The Mongols, for example, originally conquered to gain grazing land. But over time, they conquered to expand their empire's wealth and power base.

The power that accompanies control of territories and people also motivated many Roman conquests. But the desire for security pushed conquest. The Romans fought three wars over Sicily, an island in the Mediterranean Sea. Rome eventually won control of Sicily in 149 B.C.

In the 1700s and 1800s, the British launched a series of conquests to satisfy a need for resources and markets. The British built an empire that ranged around the world to Africa, Asia, North America, and Australia.

Conquest and Empire

Few great empires exist today. The Mongol Empire broke up because of rebellions by conquered peoples and problems in administering such a large area. Throughout history, successful conquests have not guaranteed successful empires.

Three Empires

CULTURE

Critical Thinking

Have students identify some of the advances attributed to the Mongol khans. *(Military organization, use of gunpowder and catapulting machines, written language, openness to foreign trade and travel, postal service.)* Then direct students to individually rank the Mongol contributions. Encourage discussion of their rankings and try to reach a consensus.

Cultural Context

Even though the size of the Mongol Empire reached its peak under Kublai Khan, its decline began under his rule also. Kublai never enjoyed the universal acceptance enjoyed by his grandfather, Genghis Khan, and he lived a life far different from that of his nomadic ancestors. Kublai grew up in a more civilized environment and was educated by a Chinese Confucian scholar. His palace was plated with gold and silver and was decorated with paintings of dragons, birds, and beasts. He dressed in luxurious silks and jewels. *The Travels of Marco Polo* contains numerous descriptions of Kublai Khan's Mongol splendor, referring to the palace, dress, people, and festivals.

Study Skills

Have students review Breakdown of the Empire to identify the major causes of the decline of the Mongol Empire. Then have students prepare a summary of the key points in verbal or visual form. They may choose to write a paragraph, draw a chart or web diagram, or prepare a conventional outline.

CULTURE
Critical Thinking

In the 1200s and 1300s, Europe lagged far behind China in the arts and sciences. Have students suggest ways in which the Mongol Empire may have made a positive contribution to Western society. *(Students may mention religious tolerance, increased trade and travel, and the spread of ideas between Asia and Europe.)*

■ *Answers will vary but should include information on the rapid growth of the empire and the problems that the Mongols had with administration, such as difficulty of communication and the inability to control vast areas.*

▶ *Timur built Muslim schools and mosques that still stand in the city of Samarkand in present-day Uzbekistan. Note the tigers above the main arch.*

▼ *This representation of Timur's head was created from his skull by an archaeologist who was also a sculptor.*

■ *Support the following statement with details: The Mongols were better conquerors than rulers.*

Moreover, the Mongols were no longer the fierce warriors who had swept down from the steppes. They began to adopt the social customs, languages, and religions of the people they had conquered. Ghazan Khan, who ruled in Persia, made Islam the state religion and adopted much of the Persian culture. In China, the Mongols accepted Tibetan Buddhism, but they were also influenced by the culture of the Chinese.

By 1300, the unity of the Mongol Empire had disappeared. It was then easy for the conquered peoples of the empire to overthrow their invaders. The Persians drove out the Mongols in 1335, and the Chinese followed suit in 1368.

In 1370, Timur the Lame, or Tamerlane as he is known to Europeans, made a final attempt to build a lasting empire. Timur was a Muslim Turk of Mongol descent. He ruled from Samarkand in what is now Uzbekistan. Timur led successful raids throughout central Asia to Persia and Mesopotamia, Asia Minor, southern Russia, and India.

Timur's empire lasted for 45 years. When he died in 1405, his empire was divided among his sons, as Genghis Khan's had been. His heirs fought among themselves for control, and Timur's fourth son, Shahrukh *(shah ROOK)*, won control. After his death in 1447, the empire gradually lost its power. ■

The Impact of the Mongols

Although the Mongols were fearsome warriors who conquered vast territories, that was not their only memorable accomplishment. The Mongols also showed tolerance, or respect, for different religions. They believed that there was truth in each religion. Thus, many religions existed in their empire, including Buddhism, Christianity, Daoism, Islam, and Judaism.

The Mongols also promoted trade and travel throughout their empire. The Silk Road, which had run from China through central Asia to Mesopotamia and Syria

168

Chapter 7

Visual Learning

Have students list on a piece of paper what is shown in each illustration in the lesson. A short phrase is sufficient. Then direct students to jot down the significance of each illustration in a second column. Encourage students to trade and evaluate each other's lists.

Religious Context

Like the majority of Mongols, Genghis Khan was deeply religious. According to most historians, he believed he had been given a divine mission to conquer and rule his empire.

The Mongols believed that spirits lived in fire, in running water, and in the wind. Many Mongols worshiped the god Mongke Koko Tengri, "Eternal Blue Sky," and believed this spirit controlled the forces of good and evil. In addition, each clan worshiped its own animal spirit, or totem. The totem of Genghis Khan's clan was the Blue Wolf.

Despite his own strong beliefs, Genghis Khan decreed that no person would be persecuted for religious reasons as long as that person acknowledged the ultimate authority of the great khan. By the time of Kublai Khan, in the late 1200s, many native Mongols had converted to other religions, primarily Islam and Buddhism.

since the time of the Roman Empire, became active again under Mongol protection.

Travelers from both Europe and the Arab world visited the Mongol Empire. The Italian Marco Polo visited the court of Kublai Khan in the late 13th century. He later described his visit, which was the first accurate record of China by a European.

The 14th-century Moroccan writer Ibn Battuta also described the world of the Mongols in a

book about his travels through Africa, Asia, and Europe. The account that Ibn Battuta made of his many experiences throughout Asia is an important historical resource.

In addition to impressing travelers, the Mongol Empire fostered the spread of ideas from Asia to Europe. Military tactics changed, as single knights in heavy armor saw what squadrons of light horsemen could do. Soldiers in formations (provided the supply lines could be kept up) were more powerful than individual knights in battle. ■

▲ *This painting shows travelers on the well-protected Silk Road during the Mongol reign.*

◄ *This statue of a Chinese goddess was made during the Yuan, or Mongol, Dynasty.*

■ *What were the positive effects of Mongol rule?*

■ *Answers will vary but should include the reopening of the Silk Road, religious tolerance, and the spread of ideas to Europe.*

C L O S E

Read the Thinking Focus aloud. Ask students to create one-sentence headlines that answer the question. A sample might be, "Mongols Build Largest Empire to Date, Spread Technologies Worldwide." Record all student suggestions on the chalkboard. Then have students evaluate, combine, and revise those headings until they can agree on the best one for this lesson.

R E V I E W

1. **FOCUS** How did the Mongols affect Europe and Asia?
2. **CONNECT** Compare social bonds among the Mongols to social bonds among West African villagers.
3. **CULTURE** What qualities contributed to the Mongols' success as conquerors?
4. **CRITICAL THINKING** Ibn Battuta and Marco Polo traveled freely throughout the Mongol Empire. What does this indicate about Mongol rule?
5. **CRITICAL THINKING** Both Genghis Khan and Kublai Khan made significant contributions to the Mongol Empire. Which of the two was the greatest Mongol leader? Why?
6. **ACTIVITY** Read the poem "Kubla Khan," written in 1798, by the English poet, Samuel Taylor Coleridge. What does the poem tell you about the late 18th-century view of the Mongol Empire?

Three Empires

Answers to Review Questions

1. The Mongols imposed their rule on vast areas of Asia and Europe, causing much disruption. They reopened the Silk Road and made trade safer. They also helped spread Chinese discoveries to Europe.
2. In Mongol society bonds were based on blood ties and on personal choices such as *anda* or *nöker*. In West African village society bonds were based on kinship and villages formed the political organization of the society.
3. The Mongols' fierceness in battle, their military skill, and their hardiness all contributed to their success as conquerors.
4. It indicates that the Mongols were tolerant of foreign travelers.
5. Answers will vary but could include Genghis Khan's military and administrative skill or Kublai Khan's military victories and his impact on trade.

Homework Options

Have students draw a scene that illustrates some aspect of daily Mongol life.

Study Guide: p. 27

170

INTRODUCE

Explain to students that the Ottoman Empire began around 1300 and did not end until the 1900s. Read the Thinking Focus aloud and ask why leadership might be the key element in the development and decline of an empire. Have students look through the illustrations and skim the headings of the lesson. Ask which leader might be the most important. *(Suleiman; only his name appears in a heading.)*

Key Terms

Vocabulary Strategies: T36–T37

ghazi—A Muslim warrior who has fought against nonbelievers to expand the frontiers of Islam.

sultan—the ruler of a Muslim country, especially the former Ottoman Empire

grand vizier—the senior adviser or prime minister who advises the sultan on state matters

divan—the governing council in a Muslim country, especially the Ottoman Imperial Council

janissary—a slave/soldier in the elite Ottoman infantry called the janissaries

millet—a partially self-governing group of non-Muslims in the Ottoman Empire; the most common were Armenian, Greek Orthodox, and Jewish

170

| 950 | 1100 | **1257** | **1566** | 1700 | 1850 | TODAY |

L E S S O N   2

The Ottoman Empire

THINKING FOCUS

How important a factor was leadership in the rise and fall of the Ottoman Empire?

Key Terms

- ghazi
- sultan
- grand vizier
- divan
- janissary
- millet

➤ *Flower and spice merchants in the Great Market of Constantinople are shown in this illustration from the 1500s.*

170

By the mid-1500s, the heirs of the Roman emperors no longer ran the great city of Constantinople. The Byzantine Empire had fallen. Now the Muslim Empire of the Ottoman Turks controlled the city as part of a larger empire. Muslim culture provided the lifeblood of the city, and the great Hagia Sophia church had become a mosque. But in one sense, nothing had changed: Constantinople was still one of the great trading cities of the world and the center of an empire of many cultures and religions.

In the Great Market of Constantinople, one could find goods from all over the known world. By the mid-1500s, the market covered an enormous area that was enclosed by a high wall with 18 gates. The Great Market had 67 main streets, each named after the guild working there, as well as dozens of side alleys. There were some 3,000–4,000 shops, as well as mosques, warehouses, workrooms, trade schools, and other services. Outside its walls stood a book market, a flea market, and an open food market. At the time, the Great

Market of Constantinople had the largest concentration and variety of goods for sale anywhere. The city was located on one of the most important international trades routes in the world. It linked such faraway cities as Antwerp and Zanzibar, Kiev and Samarkand, and even Beijing.

Chapter 7

Objectives

1. Trace the early growth of the Ottoman Empire
2. Detail the highly developed social and military institutions of the empire.
3. Describe the accomplishments of the Ottomans under Suleiman.
4. Discuss the reasons for the gradual decline of the empire after the death of Suleiman.

Graphic Overview

This spider chart shows the structure of the lesson.

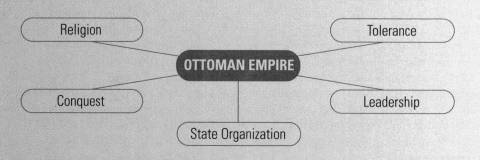

Religion   Tolerance

OTTOMAN EMPIRE

Conquest   Leadership

State Organization

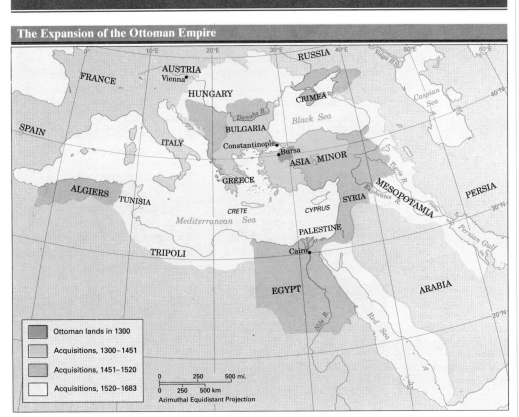

The Expansion of the Ottoman Empire

Ottoman lands in 1300

Acquisitions, 1300–1451

Acquisitions, 1451–1520

Acquisitions, 1520–1683

0   250   500 mi.
0   250   500 km
Azimuthal Equidistant Projection

The Early Ottoman Empire

As a result of the westward movement of the Mongols, many Turkish tribes were driven from their homelands in central Asia. Some of these tribes, who had converted to Islam, settled in Asia Minor and established small states.

Around 1300, one Muslim state was governed by a chief named Osman. Osman and his followers, who became known in the West as Ottomans, were ghazis. **Ghazis** were warriors who fought to expand the frontiers of Islam. As Osman won victories over Christian Byzantine armies, he attracted new followers to his armies.

Osman's armies conquered and united various lands in Asia Minor previously controlled by Byzantium. These conquests formed the core of the Ottoman Empire. Under Osman and his successors, the Ottoman state grew. One of their greatest successes was the capture in 1326 of the Byzantine city of Bursa, which they made the Ottoman capital.

Muslim Ottoman expansion alarmed Christian Europeans, who assembled an army to stop them. But the Ottomans destroyed the European forces in 1389 at Kossovo, in present-day Yugoslavia, and emerged as the most powerful state in the region. In the map above, find this early range of the Ottoman Empire. ■

The Ottoman Empire expanded steadily for four centuries. Use the scale to determine the greatest extent of the empire from east to west.

■ *How did the Ottoman Empire begin and expand?*

Three Empires

Direct students to the map of the Ottoman Empire on p. 171. Have them find the boundaries of the empire at its largest. How does that area compare with the size of the Mongol Empire? *(Mongol Empire was larger.)* Have students recall some of the problems that the Mongols had in governing their empire. Ask students to speculate on whether any of these same conditions might be present in the Ottoman Empire.

GEOGRAPHY

Map and Globe Skills

Ask students to look at the map. Tell them to find Baghdad, the site of the Mongol attack on the Muslim Empire. Then have students locate these early Ottoman acquisitions: Asia Minor, the cities of Bursa and Cairo, and the Danube River. Refer students to a modern map of that same area, and ask them to identify the countries that now exist where the Ottoman Empire once existed.

■ *A small Muslim state led by Osman began to develop. The followers of Osman won territory to add to the empire.*

171

Access Strategy

Have the class do the Access Activity. Discuss the results. Did the team with the appointed leader finish first? What role did the leader play? For example, did that person provide an overall strategy, organize the workers, delegate authority? Did a leader emerge in the second group even though one was not appointed?

Next, ask students to name organizations, teams, or activities in which they participate. List those names on the chalkboard, and beside them list the titles of the leaders within the organizations. *(Examples might include family—mom, dad; football team—coach, quarterback; school—principal, teachers, student council; school newspaper—advisor, editor.)* Have students try to name groups that function without either an official or an unofficial leader. Discuss, also, the layers of leadership that develop within an organization. Have students think of the consequences of inadequate leadership at the top.

Access Activity

Divide the class into two teams. Appoint a leader for one of the groups, but tell the other group that they do not have a leader. Then draw a picture of a spider web on the chalkboard. Give both teams their own ball of yarn, and tell them that they will have three minutes in which to create a replica of the spider web. See which team finishes first.

Critical Thinking

Have students list the advantages and disadvantages of the Ottoman system of winning the sultanship. *(It helped prevent civil war and made the empire more stable; it could be very dangerous if a bad ruler won because there were no replacements.)* Tell students to keep their lists in mind as they read the rest of the lesson.

Rulers and Subjects

In the Ottoman Empire, all campaigns of conquest were either led by the sultan or directed by him. The **sultan** was the ruler of the Ottoman Empire. Although the succession to the sultanship was hereditary, no rules determined which prince should be the heir. Princes fought among themselves to become the sultan. In fact, the winner often killed his brothers to eliminate their possible threat to his power. One of the most powerful sultans, Mehmed, legalized the practice.

To whichever of my sons the Sultanate may be vouchsafed [granted], it is proper for him to put his brothers to death, to preserve the order of the world.

Ottoman legal code, about 1460

State Organization

The sultan was advised on state affairs by the **grand vizier,** or prime minister. The grand vizier oversaw a political system that extended throughout the empire. He also headed the governing council

➤ *The Selim Mosque symbolized the majesty of the Ottoman Empire. It is also known as the Blue Mosque because of the color of its tiles and stained glass. As you can see in the photograph on the left, the mosque is still used for religious services today.*

172

Chapter 7

172

Visual Learning

Have students look at the picture of the mosque on this page. What do they notice about the building? Is it elaborate or simple? What are some of the architectural features? *(Domes, minarets.)* Ask students whether they have ever seen a mosque. Ask them to compare the mosque shown in the text to churches and synagogues typically found in the United States.

Cultural Context

The Turkish bath became an Ottoman institution during the 1300s and 1400s. The public bath, called a *hammam*, was a large central room surrounded by smaller chambers, each with marble-lined walls and mosaics. A dome with glazed window openings covered the central chamber. An Ottoman citizen first sat in the steam bath in the central chamber before bathing in cold water. The outer rooms of the *hammam* were used for refreshments and relaxation.

Because of Islamic laws governing personal hygiene and the popularity of the public bath, the East enjoyed a much higher level of cleanliness than that of medieval Europe. European doctors, as well as church authorities, discouraged bathing, and perfumes were used as substitutes for a daily bath. In later centuries Crusaders returning from the East introduced the custom of the Turkish bath to Europe.

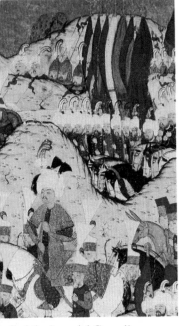

called the Imperial Council, or **divan,** which decided legal and personal complaints. As in the Byzantine Empire, the Ottoman Empire based its civil law on religious law.

From the early 1500s and for the following 150 years, high-ranking women held great political power. The Arabic word **harem** means "sanctuary" or "sacred place." To Muslims a harem referred to the women and the private quarters of a family that were their domain. The women of the royal harem controlled political parties, negotiated with foreign powers, and often acted as rulers in place of their sons. They played a very public role, too, as royal patrons to artists and builders. Wealthy women in Ottoman society who were not members of the imperial family could make their own economic and social decisions. They paid for religious buildings, freed their slaves, and did other charitable acts. Some scholars have called this period "the sultanate of women."

The Janissary Corps

Slaves played a unique role in the Ottoman Empire. Many different ethnic groups were slaves—Africans, eastern Europeans, and especially Russians. One kind of slave, however, was highly unusual. Some parents *wanted* their children to become part of the Janissary Corps, for there they might achieve wealth and power. To be a slave of the sultan could be a mark of honor.

The janissaries were recruited from the provinces as boys between the ages of 8 and 15. The Ottomans sent them to Constantinople for education and training. Most janissaries were Christians who were converted to Islam as soon as they arrived in the capital. They were sent either to the army or to the palace school, and many rose to positions of great power. They learned law, languages, mathematics, literature, and religion as well as a trade. They were considered the emperor's personal slaves. They could be trusted to be loyal, with no other claims to allegiance. The grand vizier and many other important officials were janissaries.

Non-Muslims in the Empire

Jews and Christians were tolerated in the Ottoman Empire. They were not forced to convert to Islam, but they did have to pay a special tax.

Non-Muslims were organized into partially self-ruling groups called **millets.** Each group's religious leader was responsible for the actions of his millet. The main millets were Greek Orthodox, Jewish, and Armenian.

Especially for the people of eastern Europe, the Ottoman conquest

◄ *This image shows the Ottoman armies on a campaign. The men in white turbans are members of the elite Janissary Corps.*

173

POLITICAL SYSTEMS
Critical Thinking

Ask students to describe the Ottoman system of military and civil administration. Be sure they understand that the boys who became janissaries and went to the Palace School were not members of the ruling Muslim group. They were slaves who were trained and educated for important positions. Ask students to evaluate this Ottoman practice.

Social Context

Have students speculate on the effect on the Ottoman Empire of "the sultanate of women." Most Muslim women, however, took care of their children and houses, and managed food preparation. Milking, caring for chickens, weeding a vegetable plot, and reaping crops were jobs delegated to women. Young girls received no formal education; they took care of younger siblings and helped out with other tasks in the home. Marriage commonly occurred between the ages of 12 and 16.

Visual Learning

Point out the picture on this page and ask what life might have been like in the Janissary Corps. *(Rigid, disciplined, prestigious.)* Remind students that boys between the ages of 8 and 15 trained for 7 years before entering the janissaries. Ask students how they think the boys may have felt at varying stages in this process.

Study Skills

Ask students to describe the Ottoman treatment of non-Muslims. Students should understand that millets were self-governing groups of non-Muslims, free to follow their own religious beliefs in exchange for payment of a special tax. Ask students how a policy of tolerance affects minority groups. *(They grow and prosper materially and culturally.)* How does this affect the country? *(Strengthens bonds of loyalty, brings more productive citizens into the system.)* Using Doña Gracia Mendes Nasi as an example, ask students to find other examples of heroes who tried to save victims of persecution. *(Harriet Tubman, Raoul Wallenberg, etc.)*

■ *The janissary system formed an elite military group and trained boys to become administrators. The millet system allowed non-Muslim subjects to retain their religion and some self-rule.*

▲ *This medal in honor of Doña Gracia Mendes Nasi was made in 1553, the year she settled in Constantinople. She became a heroine to many Jews escaping persecution.*

■ *What highly successful political and educational structures did the Ottoman Empire develop?*

➤ *This map of Istanbul dates from the early 1500s. Hagia Sophia is visible in the upper center of the image.*

brought peace and stability, and Ottoman rule was less oppressive than some of the systems it replaced. Paying the sultan's taxes was preferable to life under the harsh laws of some eastern European lords.

While western European countries were persecuting and expelling their Jews, the Ottomans welcomed them. Some Jews held positions of great power, and by 1553 the Ottoman city of Salonika had some 20,000 Jews. Jews were court physicians, ran printing presses, and carried on international trade. Sultan Bayezid II said, "The Catholic monarch Ferdinand was wrongly considered as wise, since he impoverished Spain by the expulsion of the Jews, and enriched Turkey."

Still, there were many who were persecuted and needed to be saved. One heroine for such a campaign was Doña Gracia Mendes Nasi (1510–1569), called "La Señora." Doña Gracia's parents had been forced to convert to Christianity in Portugal, where they lived when she was a child. She and her family practiced Judaism in secret. She later married and helped her husband build up an important banking business. Soon widowed and forced out of Portugal by religious persecution, she went to England, then Belgium, Italy, and finally to Constantinople. During her travels, she helped Jews flee from persecution. Doña Gracia patronized scholars and established schools and synagogues in Constantinople, where she could practice her religion openly. In 1556, she tried to organize a boycott of the Italian port of Ancona because they had executed 26 Jews. Today, a synagogue in Istanbul still carries its original nickname, "La Señora." ■

The Empire at Its Height

While the Ottoman Empire absorbed, trained, and employed its newly conquered people, its military conquests continued. The most famous of these conquests was the capture of Constantinople by the Ottoman Sultan Mehmed the Conqueror in 1453.

The New Capital

The Ottoman Turks had tried to take the Byzantine walled city of Constantinople seven times but had failed each time. The city, defended by only 8,000 men, finally fell to Mehmed and his army of 150,000 on May 29.

Sultan Mehmed's victory fulfilled the call from Muhammad some 800 years earlier for the Muslims to conquer Constantinople. The city

Chapter 7

Social Participation

Have students identify the primary religions found in the Ottoman Empire and list them on the chalkboard. *(Islam, Greek Orthodox, Jewish, Armenian Christian.)* Direct students in groups of four to encyclopedias, other library books, or earlier chapters in this text. Instruct each group to create a chart detailing the major beliefs of each religion.

was called Istanbul by the Muslims and became the new capital of their empire.

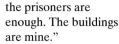

T he hour was already ad-
vanced, the day was declining and near evening, and the sun
was at the Ottomans' backs but
shining in the faces of their enemies. This was just as the Sultan
had wished; accordingly he gave
the order first for the trumpets to
sound the battle-signal and the
other instruments, the pipes and
flutes and cymbals too, as loud as
they could. All the trumpets of the
other divisions, with the other
instruments in turn, sounded all
together, a great and fearsome
sound. Everything shook and
quivered at the noise.

Kritovoulos describing the fall of
Constantinople, circa 1453

Over the next 100 years, Istanbul became a great international
trading city of rare beauty. The
Ottomans took care to preserve
the existing Byzantine architecture,
and they added many new and
beautiful buildings. Legend says
that Mehmed once caught one of his
men trying to remove marble from
the floor of a Byzantine church.
Mehmed said as he stopped the
man, "For you, the treasures and

the prisoners are
enough. The buildings
are mine."

Ottoman expansion
continued during the
reign of Mehmed's son,
Bayezid. The Ottoman
navy defeated the strong navy
of Venice to extend Ottoman control over the Black Sea area. At
the end of Bayezid's reign, he and
his successor, Selim, turned their
attention to the east. Syria, Palestine, Egypt, and Arabia were
added to the empire. With
these areas came control
of three of the holy
places of Islam:
Mecca, Medina,
and Jerusalem.

Suleiman the Magnificent
The Ottoman Empire
reached its height under
Selim's son, Suleiman
(SOO lay mahn), who
reigned from 1520 to 1566.
His empire stretched from
Hungary in the north to Egypt in
the south, and from Algeria in the
west to Mesopotamia in the east.
The capital city of Istanbul, with a
population of about 200,000 and
growing quickly, was one of the
largest cities in Europe at the time.
Foreigners called Suleiman The
Magnificent because of his power,
wealth, and spectacular court life.
The Ottoman Empire was one of the
richest and most powerful empires
in the world. The inscription on the
next page was found carved on a
fortress in Romania. It dates from
1538. The inscription describes
Suleiman's awesome power.

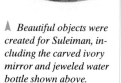

⚊ *Beautiful objects were
created for Suleiman, in-
cluding the carved ivory
mirror and jeweled water
bottle shown above.*

◄ *The official signature
of an Ottoman sultan
was known as a tugra.
Suleiman's tugra, shown
at left, was used on
official documents
during his reign.*

175

Three Empires

GEOGRAPHY
Map and Globe Skills

After Mehmed's victory,
Constantinople was called
Istanbul and became the capital
of the Ottoman Empire. Have
students find Constantinople
on the map on p. 171 and discuss its importance. *(Centrally
located between Europe and
Asia, close to Mediterranean
and Black seas, provides
strategic access to Europe.)*

175

Music Connection

Trumpets, pipes, flutes, and cymbals were
instruments played to announce the siege of
Constantinople. In addition, students at the
Palace School were required to study music,
and the school chorus gave regular concerts
for the sultan. Have students gather information about typical music of this period. Then
have them give oral reports telling about the
types of instruments and the choral and folk
music traditions of the period.

Visual Learning

Have students make a list of the
illustrations and photographs in
the lesson, describing each one in a
short phrase. Then, using the
information in the captions and
what they have learned, have them
state briefly why they think the
illustration was included in the
text. *(Sample answer: the mirror
on p. 175 suggests the "magnificence" associated with Suleiman.)*

Critical Thinking

Ask students why Suleiman was called "The Magnificent." Help them understand that his attention to diverse areas of Ottoman life (*physical conquests, revision of legal code, massive building program, and encouragement of poetry*) and his fairness with non-Muslims should have left few groups anxious to rebel. Suleiman seemed militarily strong, politically wise, and culturally sensitive.

I am caliph in Mecca and Medina. In Baghdad I am the shah, in Byzantine realms the Caesar, and in Egypt the sultan; who sends his fleets to the seas of Europe, North Africa and India. I am the sultan who took the crown and throne of Hungary and granted them to a humble slave.

In addition to being The Magnificent, Suleiman was The Lawgiver to his own subjects. The laws of the empire had been made primarily for a Muslim population. With the rapid growth and conquest of new territories and new peoples, the old legal codes were no longer as useful. Suleiman adjusted the laws to deal with a much larger empire, paying special attention to the fair treatment of non-Muslims. Suleiman's laws remained in use for two centuries.

Suleiman also undertook a massive building program, not only in Istanbul but throughout the empire. Many of these buildings still stand today. They are distinctly Muslim with their domes and minarets. Sinan, Suleiman's architect for 50 years, had been an engineer in the janissaries. As royal architect, Sinan designed over 300 buildings. The most famous one is the Selim Mosque shown on page 172.

In addition, poetry flourished under Suleiman. In fact, next to the Koran, poetry was the most important type of literature in the empire. The court poet Baki wrote this poem praising the deceased Suleiman.

➤ *This gold battle standard was carried by Suleiman's armies. Suleiman is shown above in a detail from a 16th-century painting by Nigari. And at the top right, his army invades Vienna*

176

The infidels of Hungary bowed their heads to the temper of his blade,
The Frank admired the grain of his sword.

He laid his face to the ground, graciously, like a fresh rose petal,
The treasurer of time put him in the coffer, like a jewel.

. . .

This is my prayer: all those who do not weep for you,
Young and old, may their tears be buried in the ground.

May the sun burn and blaze with the fire of your parting;
In grief for you, let him dress in black weeds of cloud.

Chapter 7

Social Participation

Suleiman was nicknamed "The Magnificent" and "The Lawgiver." Mehmed was known as "The Conqueror." Divide students into small groups of five or six students each, and ask them to list five or six contemporary leaders or performers with whom they are familiar. Then tell students to think of descriptive titles that capture the essence of those individuals.

Art Connection

Many beautiful things were produced for Suleiman. Show the video *Suleiman the Magnificent*, produced by the National Art Gallery and the Metropolitan Museum of Art, and discuss with students how "magnificent" Suleiman's reign was.

Research

Mirmar Sinan, Suleiman's royal chief architect for more than 40 years, is considered by many to be one of history's great architects. He designed more than 70 mosques, as well as palaces, public baths, tombs, and schools. Have students read more about Sinan or Ottoman architecture in general and write a brief report, preferably illustrated.

The world around 1550 seemed to belong to the Ottomans. Until 1683, the Ottoman Empire contin- ued to grow. At its peak, it ran almost three-quarters of the way around the Mediterranean Sea. ■

■ *What were Suleiman's accomplishments?*

Decline of the Ottoman Empire

In the centuries that followed, the Ottoman Empire slowly began to lose both its territories and its military superiority. Although the empire lasted until the 20th cen- tury, it never again reached the prominence it had enjoyed under Suleiman.

Several factors contributed to the empire's decline. First, much of the empire's economic strength depended on constant expansion. When the conquests slowed down after 1571, revenues from con- quered lands declined. In addition, a new trade route to India (by sail- ing around Africa) was found. The old trade route through Ottoman territory became less important. Thus, trade revenues declined drastically. The empire underwent considerable financial hardships.

Second, the janissaries began to play a more active and often disruptive role in the government of the empire. Eventually, the sultans lost control over the powerful janissaries. This lack of a strong central leadership had a disastrous effect on the empire. The sultans who followed Suleiman struggled to direct the elaborate political system.

Ottoman rule slowly weakened over the next 350 years. An impor- tant defeat happened in 1683. The Ottoman siege of Vienna was turn- ed back with the help of Polish and German troops under Polish King John Sobieski *(sohb YAY skee)*.

With the dramatic growth of Europe's commercial, military, and industrial strength, the Otto- man Empire began to disintegrate. Egypt achieved virtual indepen- dence in 1805, as did Greece in 1829. France took over Algeria and made it a colony. Russia, with plans to put its navy in the Mediterranean, became an enemy to the Ottomans. From 1853 to 1856, Russia fought the Ottomans for control of the Crimean *(cry MEE uhn)* Peninsula. Russia was defeated when Britain and France, eager to block the Russians, sup- ported the Ottomans. In the 1870s, an uprising against the Ottomans, aided by the Russians, allowed Serbia, Montenegro, and Rumania to become independent in 1878. Piece by piece, the Ottoman Empire was crumbling. ■

■ *Why did the Ottoman Empire decline?*

R E V I E W

1. **FOCUS** How important a factor was leadership in the rise and fall of the Ottoman Empire?
2. **CONNECT** How did the Mongol Empire and Ottoman Empire compare in their treatment of religious groups?
3. **HISTORY** Why did westerners call Suleiman The Magnificent, while his own people called him The Lawgiver?
4. **CRITICAL THINKING** How did Istanbul represent the best qualities of the empire?
5. **WRITING ACTIVITY** Write a poem or passage praising a former United States leader, as Baki did for Suleiman.

177

Three Empires

■ *Suleiman made the laws of the empire more fair to non-Muslim subjects. He also under- took a large building program in Istanbul and the rest of the empire.*

■ *The Ottoman Empire declined because of the loss of trade revenues, the growing political power of the janis- saries, the weak leadership of the sultans who followed Suleiman, and the growing economies of western Europe.*

C L O S E

Read the Thinking Focus aloud. Have students highlight the rise of the Ottoman Empire by citing the accomplishments of the various sultans men- tioned in the text. Place the sul- tans' names and important dates on a timeline drawn on the chalkboard. Students should see that the chain of strong leadership covered most of the years between 1300 and 1570. The absence of such lead- ership helps explain the decline of the empire from 1570 to 1923.

Answers to Review Questions

1. Leadership was an extremely important factor in the rise and fall of the Ottoman Empire. Strong leadership helped the empire to expand. The weak sultans who followed Suleiman were incapable of directing the empire's complex political system and thus contributed to its decline.
2. While the Mongols practiced religious tolerance, the Ottomans both tolerated religious groups and allowed them to be partially self-governing.
3. Suleiman was called The Magnificent in the West because of the splendor of his court and his power as sultan. He was called the Lawgiver by his own people because he updated the laws in the empire.
4. Answers will vary but could include the great trade, the beauty of the city, its wealth, its size, and the religious toler- ance found there.

Homework Options

Have students write an imagina- tive but historically accurate story about some aspect of Ottoman life. Topics could include a day in the life of a janissary, life in the Palace School, a look at women's work, and so on.

Study Guide: p. 28

INTRODUCE

Have students read the Thinking Focus. Ask students to think about the patterns of empires that they read about in the previous two lessons. *(Growth, height, decline.)* Have students predict the factors that they think contributed to the rise and fall of the Mughal Empire and then read the lesson to evaluate their predictions.

Key Term

Vocabulary Strategies: T36–T37
salary—a fixed payment for services paid on a regular basis

---

950   TODAY
997   1858

L E S S O N   3

The Mughal Empire

THINKING FOCUS

What factors contributed to the rise and fall of the Mughal Empire?

Key Term

* salary

➤ *When invaders such as Mahmud crossed into northern India, they were startled by its lush beauty, as in this countryside near Rawalpinda on the Pakistan-India border.*

The whole country of India is full of gold and jewels, and of the plants which grow there are those fit for making apparel, and aromatic plants and the sugarcane, and the whole aspect of the country is pleasant and delightful. Now, since the inhabitants are chiefly infidels and idolaters, by the order of God [Allah] and his Prophet it is right for us to conquer them.

These are the reasons that the Turkish Sultan Mahmud of Ghazna gave for his invasions of India. Between 997 and 1030, Mahmud invaded northern India 17 times.

Mahmud had long heard tales about the riches of India from Muslim scholars and merchants who had traveled there. The scholars went to India to study astronomy, medicine, and mathematics. The merchants brought back Indian gold, jewels, and silks. Eventually, soldiers and conquerors traveled to India for less peaceful purposes.

As Muslims spreading the word of Muhammad to unbelievers, the sultan and his followers felt that their invasion of India was both just and holy. A famous Persian epic poet named Firdausi (the pen name of Abul Kasim Mansur)

lived in Ghazna during the time of the Turkish invasions of India. He had a rather different explanation of the sultan's motive, and it wasn't positive:

To plunder their neighbors and gain all themselves
Is what men desire,
    using God as excuse.

Chapter 7

Objectives

1. Describe the role of geography in the development of India.
2. Evaluate the impact of Akbar's policies on the empire.
3. Discuss the reasons for the gradual dissolution of the Mughal Empire.

Graphic Overview

This organization chart gives the structure of the lesson.

MUGHAL EMPIRE

Beginning	Height	Decline
conquest growth	tolerance civil service	economic problems wars

On the Eve of the Empire

India's geography—with its forbidding mountain ranges and inviting valleys—both discouraged and attracted invaders. The land falls into three distinct geographic regions. Curving across the far north of India from east to west are the Himalayas, the highest mountains in the world. The Himalayas, 200 miles wide in some places, seem to be perfect natural barriers to foreign invasion. Nevertheless, invaders penetrated the mountains through steep passes, such as the 33-mile-long Khyber Pass, located in the northwest.

South of the Himalayas lie the fertile plains of northern India. Many invaders were attracted to the valleys of the Brahmaputra, Ganges, and Indus rivers, which include some of the richest farmland in the world.

Farther south is the Deccan, or southern plateau. The Deccan forms most of the southern peninsula. It is separated from the north by the Vindhya mountains and a series of other low mountain ranges. This rugged southern region with its mountainous terrain and numerous rivers presented an awesome challenge that few invaders chose to take.

The geographic regions of India helped lead to political divisions, especially between the south and north. Hindu states in the south suffered few foreign invasions. However, in the north, Hindu kingdoms had to compete for power with a succession of invaders. The map below shows the side-by-side existence of regional Muslim and Hindu states by the early 1500s. Muslims, such as

▼ *Look at the physical map of India. Using the elevation legend, describe northern and southern India. Had you been a Muslim invader, where in India would you have settled? Why?*

India's Physical Regions and the Kingdom of Northern India

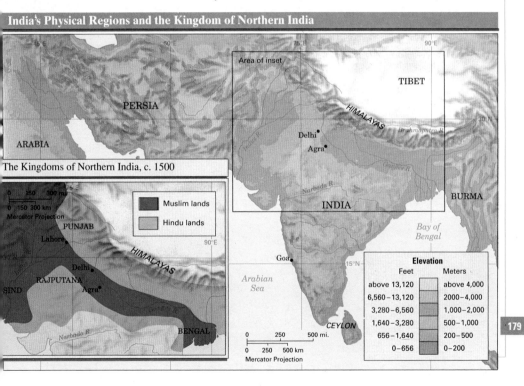

The Kingdoms of Northern India, c. 1500

Muslim lands

Hindu lands

Elevation

Feet		Meters
above 13,120		above 4,000
6,560–13,120		2000–4,000
3,280–6,560		1,000–2,000
1,640–3,280		500–1,000
656–1,640		200–500
0–656		0–200

D E V E L O P

Tell students that this lesson discusses the rise and fall of the Mughal Empire in India. Ask whether the name *Mughal* reminds them of another empire discussed earlier in this chapter. *(Mongol.)* Ask where that earlier empire was located, relative to India. *(East and northeast.)* Tell students that the two empires are related, and encourage them to find the link as they read.

◄ *Answers will vary but should make reference to the physical features of India.*

GEOGRAPHY
Map and Globe Skills

Have students find the three geographical areas of India: the Himalayas in the north, the fertile plains south of the Himalayas, and the southern plateau region, called the Deccan, south of the Narbada River. Point out the inset map showing the various Hindu and Muslim kingdoms in northern India. What does their side-by-side existence suggest about northern India during this time period? *(That very different cultures existed side by side.)*

Access Strategy

On a map locate the Himalayas along India's northern border. Point out that although these mountains seem to protect India from foreign invasion, invaders did manage to penetrate the mountains through high passes. One such invader was Sultan Mahmud of Ghazna, a region that borders India to the northwest. Read aloud the sultan's quotation on p. 178. Why did Mahmud invade India? *(Access to valuable minerals, food source, attractive and hospitable land, a* *sense of divine mission.)* Then read Firdausi's poem on that same page. How did he view Mahmud's invasions? *(As selfish expeditions masked by religious motives.)* Ask students to consider a hypothetical invasion of the United States. Ask students how they would feel about the invaders.

Access Activity

Divide the class into small groups. Have each group make a different type of map of India. Examples include a salt-and-flour topographical map; a religious map, current or past; a map showing all the rivers within India; a population density map; a map of the Himalayas; or a map of natural resources. Have groups share their maps with the rest of the class.

■ *Hindu and Muslim kingdoms existed side by side.*

GEOGRAPHY
Map and Globe Skills

Have students find Delhi in north central India on the map on p. 179. State that Babur gained control of Delhi in 1526. On the inset map, have students find the province of Rajputana, which Babur conquered in 1527. Ask students to find the general area from which Babur came. *(Central Asia.)* What was Babur's background? *(Muslim Turk.)* Why was Babur's empire called Mughal? *(From the Indian word for Mongol.)*

■ *In what ways was northern India a divided country during the 1500s?*

➤ *This painting, on the right, honors the founders of the Mughal dynasty— Timur, Babur, and his son Humayun. Timur wears a turban jewel, like the one above, a symbol of high rank.*

Sultan Mahmud, captured several Indian cities and set up their own governments. In other cities, power remained in the hands of native Hindu princes.

In North India in the early 1500s, many small states competed for more territory. Both Hindu kingdoms and established Muslim states wanted to control the rich agricultural land along the Ganges and Indus rivers. Before the

Mughals arrived, an Indo-Muslim political tradition had accepted Muslim overlords in exchange for Hindus' being left alone to rule their own local lands. Hindu society was able to make a place for a Muslim ruling class by adding another caste-like layer at the top of society for them. The Mughals took advantage of these circumstances to build their own empire. ■

Founders of the Empire

The greatest of the Muslim states was the Sultanate of Delhi in north central India. In 1517, a Muslim Turk from central Asia named Babur invaded India. He conquered the Delhi Sultanate in 1526 and went on to found the Mughal Empire.

Babur's Arrival
Related to Timur on his father's side and Genghis Khan on his mother's side, Babur seemed a fitting conqueror and founder of a world empire. Babur had dreamed of reestablishing a great empire in the Mongol tradition. In 1527, he defeated the Rajputs, the strongest Hindu state in India. During Babur's reign, which lasted until his death in 1530, the

empire covered most of northern India. His empire was called the Mughal, from the Persian-Indian word for Mongol.

Babur was a wise and kind leader. Like many Mughal emperors who followed him, Babur was

Social Participation

Babur missed foods from his native land. Divide students into small groups and have them research the types of food that Babur would have found native to northern India.

Science Context

Before Mahmud's conquest of India, Arabs had traveled to India to study Indian medicine. Classical Indian medicine was called the science of longevity. The Indians believed the body consisted of five natural elements: earth *(bones and muscles)*, water, fire *(gall)*, wind *(breath)*, and space *(hollowness within organs)*. The Indians believed that when the elements worked in harmony, there was health. Illness was caused by a deficiency or excess among the elements.

Writing a News Account

Have students imagine that they are news reporters at the time of Babur's conquest of the Delhi sultanate. Instruct students to write a news account of the conquest, including excerpts from an interview with Babur. Tell students to keep their accounts historically accurate, incorporating some details from the text.

well educated. Throughout his life Babur wrote about the Indian world that he had conquered—its people, animals, landscapes, and customs. But he also seemed genuinely homesick for items from his homeland in central Asia such as good horses, grapes, muskmelons, ice, cold water, good bread and hot baths. Babur wrote in his memoirs, the *Babar-nama*, that "the chief excellency of Hindustan [India] is, that it is a large country, and has abundance of gold and silver."

Akbar the Ruler

Despite his longings for his homeland, Babur remained in India. His grandson, Akbar, who reigned for 49 years (1556–1605) would be remembered as the greatest Mughal emperor.

Akbar's rule began when he was only 13 years old. During his reign the empire expanded to cover most of north and central India and Afghanistan. Look at the map on page 183. Estimate how many miles the empire covered under Akbar.

We know many details about Akbar's life and personality from his biographer, Abul Fazl. For example, we know that "Akbar ate one meal a day—of 40 dishes—and enjoyed ice brought from the mountains." Abul Fazl also tells us that Akbar took great interest in handicrafts. He wrote that Akbar often visited the more than 100 workshops around the palace where crafts and weapons were made.

Perhaps Akbar's greatest political accomplishments were bringing Hindus into the government of the empire and reforming the empire's unfair tax system. Akbar divided the empire into provinces and set up a civil service system to manage its lands. Each job had a salary, or fixed payment, and jobs were given only to qualified men, without regard to their religion. Thus, non-Muslims could enter government service.

Akbar also had the value of land reclassified according to its ability to produce crops. Taxes were lower for those with less productive land. This was fairer than the old system, which made every farmer pay the same rate.

Akbar held a great deal of power, but like other monarchs, he was limited by the power of the nobles, of the cities, and of the army. There were always rebellions or attacks to deal with, and Akbar

▼ *Babur's Mughal army crossed these Himalayas to invade and conquer northern India.*

181

Critical Thinking

Have students point out the growth in the Mughal Empire that occurred during Akbar's reign. Ask students to explain how Akbur showed tolerance to the people of the empire. *(Did not force Hindus to convert to Islam, did not enslave non-Muslims.)* Ask students whether they think Akbar's tolerance was a factor in the growth of the empire. Help them to see that tolerance added stability and minimized rebellion.

181

Research

The Himalayas of Asia include the highest mountains in the world. Have students consult encyclopedias or other reference books to prepare brief reports on the Himalayas. Possible topics include people of the Himalayas, mineral resources, glaciers, types of vegetation, animal life, scientific explorations, and mountain climbing.

Historical Context

Akbar announced a new theory of kingship in 1579. He claimed that a king was God's representative on earth and the impartial ruler of all his subjects. Akbar said that a king must be absolutely tolerant of every creed, establish universal peace in his empire, and work for the welfare of all of his people. Akbar worked hard to implement this ideal. He began work at sunrise and worked past midnight, with only short breaks for meals, rest, recreation, and prayers.

Visual Learning

Ask students to look at the painting of the Mughal rulers on p. 180. Then have students work together to make an illustrated mural that shows each Mughal ruler in the text and his primary accomplishments or characteristics. The finished mural should give a graphic representation of the Mughal Empire from start to finish.

Critical Thinking

Draw a three-column chart on the chalkboard. Label the columns Legislative Reform, Administrative Reform, and Artistic Accomplishments. Have students place Akbar's accomplishments in the appropriate columns on the board. Ask students which accomplishments were the most important and why.

■ *Answers will vary but should mention that Akbar's was an empire of many different religions. He unified it through military strength, religious tolerance, reformation of the tax system, and a civil service with jobs based on merit.*

▲ *Akbar had his new capital city, Fatehpur Sikri, built in 1570. In the painting on the right, Akbar is being welcomed back to Fatehpur Sikri by his sons in 1584. Fatehpur Sikri was abandoned when its water ran out, but the city still stands.*

■ *Evaluate this statement: Religion does not always unify an empire.*

was as skilled a diplomat as he was a military leader.

In Akbar's lands, besides Hindus and Muslims, there were Christians and Jews and many other peoples. Akbar saw that it would not be easy to keep his restless empire together. He abolished the tax on non-Muslims. Whether he truly believed in it, or whether it was only a unifying policy, Akbar developed his own religion for the state. The conflicts between religions prompted him to find a synthesis, or new combination, of all the religions known to him. Born and brought up a Muslim, Akbar turned in 1575 to what he then saw as the essence of all religions. He faced opposition from the Muslim clergy but he proceeded to reduce religious persecution for many of his subjects. Akbar invited scholars of different faiths to his court and sponsored debates on religion.

Akbar the Art Patron

During Akbar's reign, the Mughal court became a center of culture. Akbar invited artists, poets, and musicians to his court and encouraged them to produce works for it.

As trade with the rest of the world continued to grow, there were new influences in art. Some Muslim artists now used naturalism in portraying people and animals, something they had previously kept away from for religious reasons. ■

Inheritors of the Empire

The Mughal Empire continued to grow in size and splendor as Akbar's successors followed his policies. In 1605, Akbar's eldest son Jahangir *(juh hahn GEER)* inherited the throne.

182

Visual Learning

The images on this page give a contemporary historical view and a modern view of Fatehpur Sikri. Ask students to try to find historical and current images of buildings or locations in their community.

Language Arts Connection

Puppet theater is popular in India today and often dramatizes the activities of the kings and princesses of the Mughal period. Have students create a brief puppet show that portrays some aspect of Akbar's rule. Dialogue might feature Akbar and scholars discussing religion, farmers discussing the changes in land tax, or civil servants of many cultures working together on a project. Students could create simple stick or paper bag puppets or construct more elaborate puppets.

Social Context

The city of Fatehpur Sikri was built under the reign of Akbar and became his official residence in 1571. Because two of Akbar's sons were born in the village of Sikri, Akbar decided to develop it into a great city. He built palaces for himself, as well as mansions for his nobles and military officers. The city was protected on three sides by a wall with nine gates and on the fourth side by a large lake.

Jahangir continued to expand the empire, and he also sponsored the repair and rebuilding of schools and monasteries. In 1611, Jahangir married a Persian woman named Mehunissa (MAIR uh NISS uh). She was called "Nur Jahan," or "Light of the World," and she, her father, and her brother dominated Jahangir's court. Nur Jahan's niece, Mumtaz Mahal, married the future emperor. During these years some upper class women studied the arts and sciences. Most women, Hindu and Muslim, generally concentrated on the domestic world, including trades practiced at home such as spinning or weaving. A wide variety of fine Indian textiles became important items of global trade, and their designs were later adapted for factory production.

Jahangir's son, Shah Jahan (SHAH juh HAHN), ruled from 1628 to 1658. Jahan is renowned as the largest Mughal spender and builder. He poured huge amounts of money into construction projects in Delhi, which he made the capital in 1648. The projects included palaces with walls of marble inlaid with precious stones and ceilings of gold and silver.

Shah Jahan also broke with Akbar's religious policies, bringing Mughal laws into closer agreement with some aspects of Muslim law. Shah Jahan also refined Akbar's administrative policies. As the empire grew, productivity rose. The empire's income doubled, and construction projects continued.

Without doubt, Shah Jahan's most famous architectural undertaking was the Taj Mahal. With its inlaid white marble, pointed arches, and domes, the Taj reflects the Mughal style of architecture. To learn more about the splendor of the Taj Mahal, see A Closer Look on page 184.

Only a very wealthy nation could afford such massive building efforts. At one point in the reign of Shah Jahan, "750 pounds of pearls, 275 pounds of emeralds, 5,000 gems from Cathay, corals, topazes, and . . . tubs of uncut diamonds" formed only a part of the Mughal treasury.

But, as time went on, Shah Jahan's spending took its toll on the empire. Shah Jahan added some of the Deccan Hindu states to the Mughal lands. But the cost of military campaigns, combined with huge building projects, seriously drained the treasury. ■

■ *How did the rule of Jahangir and Shah Jahan affect the empire?*

▼ *The Mughal Empire expanded greatly in a relatively short period of time. How much larger was the empire after the death of Akbar?*

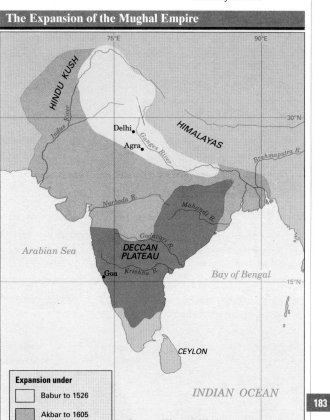

The Expansion of the Mughal Empire

Expansion under
- Babur to 1526
- Akbar to 1605
- Aurangzeb to 1707

0   250   500 mi.
0   250   500 km
Mercator Projection

75°E   90°E
HINDU KUSH
Indus River
Delhi
Agra
Ganges River
HIMALAYAS
Brahmaputra R.
30°N
Narbada R.
Mahandi R.
Godavari R.
Arabian Sea
DECCAN PLATEAU
Goa
Krishna R.
Bay of Bengal
15°N
CEYLON
INDIAN OCEAN

■ *Jahangir took less interest in the administration of the empire, but it was so stable that it did not need his attention. Shah Jahan added some territory to the empire, but his costly building projects weakened the Mughal economy.*

◄ *The empire was about one-third larger.*

Economics Context

The Mughal Empire was a wealthy one. State income was derived from forests, irrigation canals, fisheries, tributes paid by feudal princes, a salt tax, and customs duties. In addition, crops were collected from farmers. The government's share of the farmer's produce was one-third of the farm's average yield.

Collaborative Learning

The Taj Mahal was commissioned by Shah Jahan as a tomb for his wife Mumtaz Mahal. Have students work in small groups of two to four to prepare brief oral reports about the Taj Mahal. All reports should be illustrated and may focus on the materials used in construction of the Taj Mahal, theories about who designed the structure, the gardens surrounding the building, architectural features, details of the construction process, or any other related aspect.

Social Participation

Akbar enjoyed studying religion and held meetings at which scholars from many religions presented their viewpoints. He also sponsored religious debates. Divide students into three groups. Instruct one group to learn all that it can about Islam and another, Hinduism. Tell the third group to prepare questions they will pose to the other two groups.

Note: You may wish to use this Closer Look as an extension to the discussion of the Taj Mahal on p. 183.

More About the Taj Mahal Shah Jahan, well-known for his pomp and opulence, wanted the Taj Mahal to be architecturally perfect since Mughal law allowed no additions, subtractions, or corrections to the original tomb. The entire Taj Mahal is an oblong complex comparable to about five football fields in length and six football fields in width. The complex includes a reflecting pool, a gateway, two mosques, various auxiliary buildings, a garden, and the mausoleum that houses the tomb. Forty-three types of gems decorate the Taj Mahal.

184

A CLOSER LOOK

The Taj Mahal

Mumtaz Mahal was the beloved wife of Shah Jahan. When she died in childbirth in 1631, her heartbroken husband built for her the most glorious tomb in the world—the Taj Mahal.

The rose was her favorite flower. Some say it was a model for the floor plan of the building. Can you see a rose in the design?

From the white marble dome to the precise gardens, every part of the Taj Mahal fits together. Caravans brought rare, colorful jewels from around the world so that the flower designs inside would be the right colors. Craftspeople and architects came from Turkey, Persia, and even Venice, Italy, to work on the tomb.

Courtesy Archeological Survey of India Government of India.

Mumtaz Mahal

Shah Jahan

Mumtaz Mahal and the Shah were constant companions, even on his military campaigns. He trusted her opinion on every thing from art to politics, and showered her with gifts of roses and diamonds. He was so crushed by her death that his beard turned white overnight.

184

Chapter 7

Visual Learning

Have students look at the Taj Mahal picture and find the minarets. They're tall, slender towers, a hallmark of Islamic architecture. From the minaret's balcony, a crier calls the faithful to prayer.

Journal Writing

Scenes of toil hide behind the Taj Mahal's magnificence. Have students brainstorm and write entries for a group journal that recreates those work days. To help them imagine this construction feat, explain that a 10-mile route of pounded earth wound through Agra to the work site. Along it paraded caravans of elephants dragging blocks of white marble from far-off hills. Teams of 20 to 30 bullocks pulled wagons heaped with both marble and red sandstone which came from local quarries. Scaffolding of brick (instead of the usual bamboo) made patterns against a white-hot sky as workers scrambled along it to build the mausoleum. A master calligrapher decorated the facade and burial chamber with Arabic lettering while another craftsman spent all his days carving marble flowers. Persian and Mughal weavers sat at their looms, turning out the finest of carpets for the chamber floors.

End of the Empire

The empire weakened further under Aurangzeb (*AWR ung zehb*), Shah Jahan's son. Aurangzeb, who ruled from 1658 to 1707, was the last to expand the Mughal Empire. Eventually, shrinking resources, loss of control, and growing disorder reduced its size.

Policy Changes

Although Aurangzeb continued his family's military activities, he made important policy changes.

He reinstated the *jizya*, the tax on non-Muslims. He also prohibited the building of new Hindu temples. Many Hindus rebelled, especially in the Deccan, where a Hindu people called the Marathas vied for power with the Mughals. Aurangzeb spent the last 25 years of his reign fighting rebellion.

Foreign Invaders

Aurangzeb was the last Mughal ruler to reign over a great empire. After his death in 1707, successive rulers continued to lose land to various rebelling factions. Still, the Mughal court at Delhi remained famous for its art and sophistication long after its political power faded.

The final blow to the Mughals would come not from neighboring invaders but from Europeans. They were drawn to India for its pepper and spices and fine cotton textiles. The decline of both Mughal and Hindu states was one factor that allowed Europeans to force their own rules for trade. In the 1700s, a trading company from Great Britain took over the government of an Indian province. Great Britain forced the last Mughal emperor from the throne in 1858. ■

◄ *Aurangzeb, the last great ruler of the Mughal Empire, is shown in this painting from a Mughal miniature album.*

■ *Why did the Mughal Empire decline?*

Remind students that Aurangzeb was the son of Shah Jahan and the grandson of Jahangir. Help students trace the deterioration in leadership through these rulers and then ask them to assess the advantages and disadvantages of inherited rule.

■ *The empire declined because of economic problems, Hindu rebellions, and takeovers by European nations.*

CLOSE

Challenge students to create their own graphic organizer of the lesson that reflects the influence of the major Mughal leaders on the empire. Suggest an arrangement that permits Babur to be at the beginning, Akbar at the peak, and the others along a declining path toward the end of the empire. Ask students to review the factors that played a part in the rise and decline of the empire.

REVIEW

1. **FOCUS** What factors contributed to the rise and fall of the Mughal Empire?
2. **CONNECT** How were the early invaders of India similar to the early Ottomans?
3. **GEOGRAPHY** How did India's geography affect invasion attempts?
4. **CULTURE** How does the Taj Mahal represent the height of Mughal architecture?
5. **CRITICAL THINKING** Compare and contrast the rule of Akbar to that of other Mughal rulers. Defend the statement that Akbar was the greatest Mughal ruler.
6. **CRITICAL THINKING** Babur, Akbar, Jahangir, Shah Jahan, Aurangzeb—during whose reign would you have liked to live? Why?
7. **WRITING ACTIVITY** You have now read about the rise and fall of three great empires: the Mongol, the Ottoman, and the Mughal. Write an imaginary conversation between the three great emperors: Genghis Khan, Suleiman, and Akbar. Have them discuss what an empire should be like.

185

Three Empires

Answers to Review Questions

1. An efficient administration, strong treasury, and strong military contributed to the rise of the Mughals. Economic problems and rebellions contributed to the fall.
2. The early invaders of India felt that they were spreading Islam to unbelievers. This is very similar to the ghazi tradition of the early Ottomans.
3. The geography of India made it relatively easy to invade the north, but much more difficult to invade the south.
4. The Taj Mahal represents the height of Mughal architecture with its use of symmetry, pointed arches, and domes.
5. Answers will vary. Students should mention Akbar's religious tolerance, improved administration, and support of the arts.
6. Answers will vary. Students should include the characteristics of the reign they choose.

Homework Options

Have students write a descriptive paragraph telling whether they would rather have lived during the Mongol, Ottoman, or Mughal periods and explaining why.

Study Guide: p. 29

UNDERSTANDING
ART

This skills feature uses a painting of the royal court of Akbar to teach students how to interpret paintings.

CULTURE
Critical Thinking

Discuss with students why this scene could have taken place only in a king's palace. What does it signify about the rest of the kingdom? (*Only a king has the power and influence to encourage such religious tolerance; it indicates the kingdom contains a measure of religious freedom.*)

SOCIAL SYSTEMS
Visual Learning

The facial features of the figures in the painting are very expressive. Ask students to study the face of each man seated in the circle in front of Akbar. Then have them list two or three words (adjectives) that they think describe each man's expression.

186

UNDERSTANDING ART
Reading Mughal Paintings

Here's Why

By studying art from the past, you can learn about the beliefs, actions, values and customs of people who lived long ago. Art flourished under the patronage of the Mughal emperors. Mughal paintings are rich in information. But first, you must learn how to "read" paintings.

Here's How

Like books, paintings often tell a story. When you study a painting, look for the main idea and identify the major characters. Examine how the painter sets the scene and determine what action is taking place. Then look for cultural details and clues to the emotions of the characters.

Study the painting on the opposite page. This scene by Nar Singh was painted to illustrate Abul Fazl's *Akbar-nama,* or history of Akbar.

Akbar's religious and cultural tolerance is the main theme of the painting. The central figure is Akbar, who sits enthroned under a bright red canopy. You may recognize him: on page 182, you saw a painting of his return to Fatehpur Sikri. The key on this page identifies Akbar with the numeral one (1).

The figures who form a circle in front of Akbar are all religious scholars. Find the figures labeled in the key by the numeral two (2). These men are two of the three Jesuit priests whom Akbar had invited to teach about Christianity in 1580. One is Rudolpho Aquaviva, the head of the mission. The other is either the translator Francisco Henriques or the Jesuit priest Antonio Monserrate. The rest of the figures in the circle are thought to be Muslims and Hindus. Outside the courtyard, in the painting's second level, two guards stand watch (3). The bottom level shows horses and passersby (4).

The painting's setting is the Ibadat-Khanah, or House of Worship, located within Akbar's palace at Fatehpur Sikri. Akbar encouraged scholars of diverse faiths to engage in religious discussions at the Ibadat-Khanah. Muslims, Hindus, Christians, Parsees, Zoroastrians, and Jews were all made welcome by Akbar.

This scene shows an evening session at the House of Worship. A heated debate is underway, with participants vigorously discussing the merits and flaws of Christianity and Islam.

In the *Akbar-nama,* Abul Fazl gives a version of what took place that evening. Fazl claims that Father Aquaviva challenged a Muslim

religious scholar to a trial by fire. Fazl says Aquaviva offered to enter a fire holding the Bible if a Muslim scholar would do the same, holding the Koran. Other accounts say that it was actually Akbar or the Muslims who challenged the Jesuits. Although the versions differ, it seems clear that a trial by fire was discussed but rejected.

Now look for important details in the painting. Notice that many of the men hold books, and that books lie scattered on the floor. In this respect, the scene is typical: Akbar enjoyed religious and philosophical debate, and he surrounded himself with learned men.

186

Chapter 7

Objective

Interpret information presented visually in paintings. (Visual Learning 1, 3)

Making a Picture

After students have studied the painting and the diagram of the painting on p. 186, have them draw a picture of a favorite group or activity. Remind students that they should include important details about the group or activity so other students can "read" the drawing using the approach taught in Here's How.

Creating a Play

Have students work in small groups to write and perform a short play based on the scene in the painting on p. 187. Ask each student to write the part for one character. Characters should include Akbar as well as Christians, Hindus, Jews, Muslims, Parsees, and Zoroastrians. Then have each group practice the play and present it to the other groups.

Discuss with students why it was significant that women were excluded from the religious discussions in Akbar's court. *(Education and debate were considered a man's privilege, not a woman's. Women were considered incapable of engaging in such learned discussions.)*

Note how the painter conveys the emotions of the religious scholars and the vigor of the debate. You can see that many of the men are gesturing. This suggests that the scholars were speaking emphatically, and that several conversations were taking place at once.

You have seen how to "read" paintings. Now try to use what you have learned and interpret a painting on your own.

Try It

Look again at the painting of Akbar being welcomed to Fatehpur Sikri, on page 182. What is the painting's main idea, or theme? Who are the major characters? Where does the scene take place, and what is happening in this scene? What cultural information can you gain from examining the painting's details? How does the painter suggest the characters' emotions?

Apply It

Find books that include paintings by American artists of the 1900s, such as Grant Wood, Andrew Wyeth, or John Sloan. Choose a painting that shows an aspect of life in the United States. "Read" the painting, using the approach taught in Here's How.

The fact that Akbar sits above the others symbolizes the power of the emperor. The architecture, decorations, and beautiful floor coverings show the splendor of the royal court. The absence of women in the painting is significant. Women were excluded from the business of the Mughal court, except as entertainers.

187

Three Empires

Answers to Try It

Answers will vary, but should reflect the idea that Akbar, the central figure in the painting, is being welcomed to Fatehpur Sikri. Emotions are shown by portraying both the kissing of Akbar's foot and people with their arms open. The painting reflects a feeling of excitement.

Answers to Apply It

Answers will vary, but should reflect an understanding of the approach to picture "reading" as taught in Here's How.

Visual Learning

Ask students to study the clothing of the various people in the painting above. Then ask them to list the people and the significance of what they are wearing. *(The clothes generally indicate the station in life of the wearer.)*

Answers to Reviewing Key Terms
A. Sample answers:
1. Mongols lived in small groups called **clans.**
2. The **divan** was an Ottoman Imperial Council.
3. **Ghazis** were Muslim warriors.
4. A **janissary** was a member of an elite Ottoman corps.
5. A **khan** was a Mongol ruler.
6. A **millet** was a non-Muslim group in the Ottoman Empire.
7. A **sultan** was an Ottoman ruler.
B. Answers:
1. steppe
2. grand vizier
3. salary

Answers to Exploring Concepts
A. Sample answers:
Mongol Strengths: strong riders, horses, weapons, army, leaders, communication; respect for others' beliefs; willingness to learn skills from others.
Mongol Weaknesses: lived in hard climate, lost unity as empire grew large, then lost discipline as a fighting force.
Ottoman Strengths: unified by religious laws; educated top soldiers and administrators; tolerated non-Muslims; often brought stability to conquered people; made rich conquests; traded and expanded; updated laws; made beautiful buildings; fostered literature.
Ottoman Weaknesses: declining growth hurt economy; lost trade routes, revenues, control over janissaries, and strength of central leadership.
Mughal Strengths: wise, kind leadership of Babur; tolerance, respect for learning, cultural growth, good government, tax reforms under Akbar; good government with his successors, development of architecture.

188

Mughal Weaknesses: military expenses drained treasury; treatment of Hindus caused 25 years of war, rulers lost land, administration and economy grew weak.
B. Sample answers:
1. Genghis Khan subdivided units of 10,000 men to form a chain of command.
2. No law said which son should be sultan. Often, sons who did not claim the throne had to flee or risk being killed.

Chapter Review

Reviewing Key Terms

clan (p. 163)
divan (p. 173)
ghazi (p. 171)
grand vizier (p. 172)
janissary (p. 173)
khan (p. 165)
millet (p.174)
salary (p. 181)
steppe (p. 162)
sultan (p. 172)

4. janissary, Ottoman
5. khan, Mongol
6. millet, Ottoman
7. sultan, Ottoman

A. In the following list, each key term is paired with the name of the empire to which it is related. Write a sentence using each of the pairs, showing how they are related. Use the Glossary on pages 543–549 to check your understanding of the meanings.
1. clan, Mongol
2. divan, Ottoman
3. ghazi, Ottoman

B. Write the key term that is described by each sentence below.
1. Both the winter and summer weather of the vast semiarid plain of central Asia was very uncomfortable.
2. The prime minister had other responsibilities in addition to advising the sultan on state affairs.
3. Workers under Akbar were given a fixed payment for their services.

Exploring Concepts

A. The Mongol, Ottoman, and Mughal empires all had strengths that helped them grow and prosper. They also had weaknesses that caused problems or contributed to their declines. Make a chart like the one below. Use all three lessons in the chapter to complete the chart with important strengths and weaknesses of each empire. If a quality was a strength at one time and a weakness at another, write it in both places on the chart.

Empire	Strengths	Weaknesses
Mongol		
Ottoman		
Mughal		

B. Support each statement with facts and details from the chapter.
1. The structure of Genghis Khan's army showed that one of his strengths was his strong ability to organize.
2. Being the son of a sultan of the Ottoman Empire could be dangerous.
3. Janissaries received an excellent education to prepare them for positions in the Ottoman Empire.
4. Mongol and Ottoman rulers usually practiced a kind of religious tolerance in their empires.
5. Suleiman was known both as The Magnificent in other lands and as The Lawgiver to his own people.
6. Modern leaders could learn many lessons about fair and efficient ways to govern their countries from Akbar.
7. Money played an important role in the decline of both the Ottoman and the Mughal empires.

Chapter 7

3. The Palace School gave instruction in law, languages, mathematics, literature, and religion.
4. The Mongols valued many beliefs. The Ottomans taxed but tolerated non-Muslim groups and allowed partial self-government.
5. Suleiman ruled vast wealthy lands and updated laws as needed.
6. Akbar fostered religious tolerance, freeing prisoners, fair taxes and employment, arts, and healthy economy.

7. Ottoman revenues fell due to declining conquests and loss of trade. Mughals overspent on wars and construction.

Reviewing Skills

1. This painting shows Akbar crossing the Ganges in 1567 on his prized elephant Uduja. He is pursuing Ali Tuli Khan and Bahadur Khan, two brothers with whom treaties had failed. What does the painting tell about ways of war?
2. What do the painting's details tell about the Ganges? Discuss the river, ways of river travel, the natural setting, and its plants and animals.
3. Akbar agreed with this Sufi proverb: "Religious rituals and prayer are good but the dwelling of the Beloved is not in the mosque, temple, or church; it is in a pure heart." Explain this proverb in your own words.
4. If Mongol rulers had had one modern type of map, they would have known the time in all parts of their empire. What kind of map is that?

Using Critical Thinking

1. Many Mongol, Ottoman, and Mughal leaders encouraged religious freedom. Some did not. How did religious freedom benefit the empires? What happened when it was denied? How is it guaranteed in the United States? How does it benefit us?
2. Shah Jahan had a budget deficit because he spent more than his country produced. Compare his budget problem with that of the U.S. in the 1980s and '90s. Who decided what was spent in the Mughal Empire? Who had responsibility to cut back? Who decides and has responsibility in the U.S.?
3. Reread the description of the Great Market of Constantinople on page 170. What goods do you think one could find there? Where would they have come from? Explain your answers. Do the same for the Mongol and Mughal empires. Which cities might have been their great trading cities?

Preparing for Citizenship

1. **COLLECTING INFORMATION** In small groups, study modern maps of areas once held by Mongols, Ottomans, and Mughals. List the names of the modern countries. Collect news articles about them and discuss together the nature of life in these areas today.
2. **COLLABORATIVE LEARNING** Help your class elect members for a Hall of Fame of Mongol, Ottoman, and Mughal leaders. As a class, make a list of leaders. Working in small groups, choose a candidate for each group to promote. Decide how to present your candidate's qualities. For example, let one member make a poster, one a brochure, one a press release, and so on. Carry out a written and illustrated campaign for a class presentation and election. Post the winning candidates' portraits in a Hall of Fame exhibit.

Three Empires

189

Answers to Preparing for Citizenship
1. **COLLECTING INFORMATION** Provide modern maps of Africa, Asia, Europe, India, and the Middle East. Guide students in locating the three empires' boundaries and the modern countries. Announce in advance a date for bringing in the newspaper articles and provide bulletin board or other space for the display.
2. **COLLABORATIVE LEARNING** Guide the class in making up a list of leaders and posting it in the classroom. Provide help as needed to set up dates for preparation, campaigns, and election. Suggest keeping groups down to three or four members so each member can be responsible for a specific task. Provide supplies for posters and announcements; specify an area to post ads and an area for the Hall of Fame display following the class election.

Answers to Reviewing Skills
1. The painting shows that both elephants and horses were used in war. It shows that Akbar himself led his troops.
2. The painting shows that at this location the Ganges was shallow enough and the current not too swift to be crossed. The boat upper left shows that canoe-like crafts were used on the river. The river had large fish. Large birds like cranes nested along its tree-lined banks.
3. Akbar meant that religious forms have value, but God is found in the good within people themselves.
4. A time zone map.

Answers to Using Critical Thinking
1. Students may answer that religious freedom benefited the empires with new ideas, workers, and revenue. When it was denied, rebellions and wars cost money and lives. Our U.S. Constitution provides for religious freedom and thus supports a pluralistic society.
2. Guide students to research as needed. The Mughal ruler decided how much was spent and for what purposes. Solving economic problems was his responsibility. In the United States, we elect leaders to make decisions about spending issues.
3. Answers will vary, but students should show some knowledge of where goods came from, e.g., silk from China, cotton from India, spices from Southeast Asia, agricultural products from nearby regions, etc. For each of the empires' trading cities, students can use the maps on p. 166 (Samarkand, Baghdad), p. 171 (Constantinople, Cairo), and p. 183 (Goa, Delhi).

189

Planning at a Glance
China

	Objectives	Reading Support and Other Resources	Diverse Learning Strategies
Lesson 1 **An Emerging Empire** *pp. 192–197 3–4 days* **Literature:** **"Heaven My Blanket, Earth My Pillow"** *pp. 200–201*	• Identify and explain the factors that made China difficult to govern. • Explain the reasons for the spread of the Buddhist religion in China. • Describe the techniques used by Emperor Wen to unify the Chinese empire.	• **Workbook** or **Reading Support:** pp. 101–104 Review p. 24 Lesson Support/Transition p. 24 Multi-lang. Sum. pp. 47–48 • **Other Resources:** Geography Kit; Posters 5, 7; Study Guide p. 31	Access Strat. **(SDAIE)** TE p. 193 Access Act. **(SDAIE)** TE p. 193 Visual Learning **(Visual)** TE pp. 193, 194 Making a Chart **(Visual)** TE p. 196 Audiotapes of Multi-language Lesson Summaries **(Auditory)**
Making Decisions: **The Great Wall** *pp. 198–199*	• Recognize the dangers to the emperor and the empire. • Define the goals for building the Great Wall. • Evaluate the positive and negative effects of building the Great Wall.		Activity **(Visual)** TE p. 198
Lesson 2 **The Flowering of Chinese Culture** *pp. 202–208 2–3 days*	• Define the *meritocracy* and explain its effect on the political system in China. • Demonstrate how developments in transportation, agriculture, and trade led to the rise of a money economy in China. • Summarize the major accomplishments of the Tang and Song dynasties in the field of art, science, and technology.	• **Workbook** or **Reading Support:** pp. 105–108 Review p. 25 Lesson Support/Transition p. 25 Multi-lang. Sum. pp. 49–50 • **Other Resources:** Geography Kit, Study Guide p. 32	Access Act. **(SDAIE)** TE p. 203 Visual Learning **(Visual)** TE pp. 204, 205 Interviewing **(GATE)** TE p. 204 Science Connection **(Kinesthetic)** TE p. 207 Audiotapes of Multi-language Lesson Summaries **(Auditory)**
Lesson 3 **China and the Larger World** *pp. 209–215 2–3 days*	• Assess the positive and negative effects of Mongol rule in China. • Describe Chinese interactions with other civilizations under the Ming Dynasty. • Evaluate the effect of contacts with the West on the economy of China during the Qing Dynasty.	**Workbook** or **Reading Support:** pp. 109–112 Review p. 26 Lesson Support/Transition p. 26 Multi-lang. Sum. pp. 51–52 • **Other Resources:** Study Guide p. 33	Access Act. **(Extra Support)** TE p. 210 Research **(GATE)** TE p. 211 Art Connection **(Visual)** TE p. 212 Visual Learning **(Visual)** TE pp. 213, 214 Audiotapes of Multi-language Lesson Summaries **(Auditory)**
Skill: Comparing Two Maps of China *pp. 216–217 1 day*	• Compare information on topographic and land–use maps to draw conclusions about how physical features affect land use.	• **Other Resources:** Study Guide p. 34	Collaborative Act. **(Visual)** TE p. 216
Chapter Review *pp. 218–219 1 day*		Chapter 8 Test pp. 29–32 *(See facsimiles on TE p. 566.)*	Assessment Multiple-Use Masters pp. 73–80

Reading Support Resources *for Every Lesson*

Reading and Review

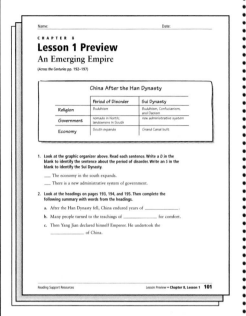

* **Chapter Overview*** p. 100
* **Lesson Previews*** using graphic organizers from the Teacher's Edition pp. 101, 105, 109
* **Reading Strategies*** pp. 102, 106, 110
* **Lesson Summaries*** pp. 103–104, 107–108, 111–112
* **Lesson Reviews** pp. 24, 25, 26

   * **Workbook** includes starred items.

Multi-language Summaries

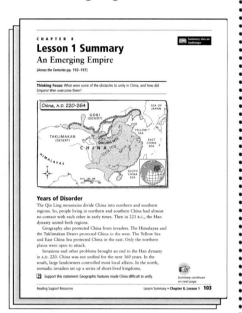

Lesson Summaries in:
* English (See Reading and Review.)
* Spanish pp. 103–104, 107–108, 111–112
* Chinese pp. 47–52
* Hmong pp. 47–52
* Khmer pp. 47–52
* Vietnamese pp. 47–52

 Summaries available on audiotapes

Lesson Support /Transition
S D A I E

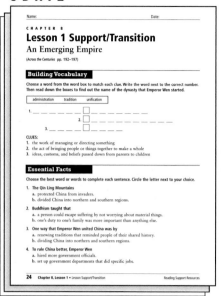

Activities for SDAIE
Specially **D**esigned **A**cademic **I**nstruction in **E**nglish

* **Lesson Support/Transition** pp. 24, 25, 26

Technology Options

Internet Support
http://www.eduplace.com

Social Studies Center at Education Place

Internet support for Chapter 8:
* *Lesson at a Glance*
* *The Voyages of Zheng He*

Software
***Student Writing Center* ®** (CD-ROM) (Macintosh® or Windows®)

School to Career

The Chinese developed a civil service system not all that different from the one used in the United States today. Divide students into small groups. Have each group select and research a form of civil service and create a presentation for the class, perhaps including interviews from civil servants in their field of choice.

Character Education

Ultimately, the teachings of each of China's different systems of thought and practice taught that true happiness was not found through wealth or possessions. Have students write a brief essay on what qualities one needs to be a happy, contributing member of society.

CHAPTER PREVIEW

Have the class read the chapter title and narrative that follows it. Explain that the first dynasty arose in China about 2000 B.C. and that many basic beliefs were well established by the time the Han Dynasty arose about 200 B.C. The Han Chinese invented paper and the seismograph and were known for their creativity. Tell students that the Sui Dynasty had a rich history to build upon when they reunited China.

Looking Back

Remind students that the Mongols conquered China during the 1200s.

Looking Forward

Tell students they will study China and the people who built and strengthened the Chinese Empire in the next three lessons: An Emerging Empire, The Flowering of Chinese Culture, and China and the Larger World.

The first lesson deals with China's reunification after a long period of disorder. Ask students to imagine the difficulties a leader would face trying to reestablish order in a large country.

Chapter 8
China

Throughout this period, scholars wrote using artistic characters. Many characters in Chinese represent whole words. This character, known as yong, means "eternity."

There were troubled times in China after the Han Dynasty fell in A.D. 220. For 360 years, groups battled for power. Still, scholarship survived, and so did beliefs like Daoism and Confucianism. When the Sui Dynasty reunited China in 589, leaders built on such traditions and beliefs to bring the country together. Later dynasties continued to inspire great advances—beautiful works of art, a strong economy, and marvelous new inventions.

617 Taizong (above) begins the Tang Dynasty, a time when art and poetry flower in China. Beautiful ceramic figures like the one at the left are often buried with emperors and nobles.

190			
220	200	550	900

476 The Western Roman Empire collapses.

1066 Normans from northern France conquer England.

BACKGROUND

Trade goods and trade routes were powerful forces in shaping the history of interaction among world civilizations. For China the most important trade product was silk, and the most important trade route to the West was the Silk Road, so named by a 19th-century historian.

Silk Production

Silk fabric is woven from silk filament that the silkworm spins to make its cocoon. Chinese farmers invented sericulture, the rearing of silkworms for the production of filament, more than 4,000 years ago. Chinese rulers collected taxes in the form of silk and controlled silk production in order to preserve silk clothing and furnishings as the exclusive privilege of the aristocracy. They also used gifts of silk to purchase the loyalty of nomadic tribes to the north.

The Silk Road

The Silk Road stretched over 4,000 miles from central China to the eastern shores of the Mediterranean. From 100 B.C., middlemen shuttled silk, porcelain, and spices westbound and wool, silver, and gold eastbound along a series of intermediate stages of the route. People along the route profited by exporting local goods to foreign markets and by taxing goods that passed through their regions. During times of political instability in Asia or the Middle East, trade traffic

During this period, guard towers along the Great Wall of China (below) and geographical barriers helped keep invaders out of China.

1368 Emperor Taizu founds the Ming Dynasty. This Ming dragon, crafted of gold thread on silk later in this period, was a symbol of imperial power. Many even believed that such dragons protected the emperor.

1250

1600

1950

1450s Johann Gutenberg and other Europeans begin using movable type to print books.

1912

Understanding the Visuals

The ceramic figure (p. 190) is made of porcelain, which the Chinese developed during the Tang Dynasty.

The dragon symbol (p. 191) shows a contrast between China and other Eastern cultures because the others saw the dragon as a negative symbol. In China, the dragon remains a symbol of power and good fortune today.

The guard tower along the Great Wall (p. 191) demonstrates a common feature of Chinese architecture—the stacked roof lines that curve gracefully upward at the corners.

Understanding Chronology

Have the students read the timeline. Point out that throughout this long period, China remained relatively isolated from the rest of the world.

---

shifted to alternative routes or ceased until security was restored.

Transmission of Ideas

In addition to trade goods, the Silk Road transmitted ideas and knowledge among the civilizations it served. Chinese knowledge of sericulture, papermaking, printing, and gunpowder was probably carried to the West via the Silk Road. Buddhism, a belief system that attracted many Chinese after the fall of the Han Empire and during the Tang Dynasty, was introduced to China from India by monks who travelled on the Silk Road.

Contact and Isolation

Geographic features such as mountains, deserts, and the Pacific Ocean isolated China from other cultures along most of its borders. In the north the Chinese built the Great Wall to keep out barbarian tribes. Thus the Silk Road in the west and port cities on the southeastern coast were, for the most part, the only avenues of contact between the Chinese and foreign peoples. Rulers were able to limit foreign influence on China by controlling trade traffic at these points. Such decisions made for long periods of political and cultural isolation, which allowed Chinese beliefs, traditions, and political practices to remain essentially unchanged for over 2,000 years.

INTRODUCE

Point out the lesson title and have students discuss the conditions necessary for an empire to become established. Then have students read the Thinking Focus and suggest some elements that would foster disunity. Write their ideas on the chalkboard in two columns—one headed *Order* and one *Disorder*. As students read the lesson, they should see whether any of these conditions existed in China during the years following the Han Dynasty.

Key Terms

Vocabulary Strategies: T36–T37
Confucianism—a set of beliefs, based on the teachings of Confucius, that focused on proper conduct, respect for elders, scholarship, and government service
Buddhism—a religion based on the teachings of Siddhartha Gautama, the Buddha; Buddhism stresses that suffering is a basic part of life, that life is a cycle of death and rebirth, and that suffering can be overcome
Daoism—a belief system based on the teachings of Laozi; Daoists emphasize living in harmony with nature and being content with one's life

192

				900	1250	1600	1950
	220		618				

L E S S O N   1

An Emerging Empire

THINKING FOCUS

What were some of the obstacles to unity in China, and how did Emperor Wen overcome them?

Women gad about in the market place. . . . They go out visiting, to see their relatives, and proceed there by starlight or carrying torches, night after night; they take a large suite with them, setting the street ablaze. . . maids, messengers, clerks, and footmen. . . . These women also make pleasure trips to Buddhist temples, they go out to watch hunting and fishing, they organize picnics on hills and river banks. They even travel . . . in open carriages with the curtains raised, stopping in every hamlet and town they pass through, drinking toasts, singing, and making music on the way.

Ge Hong, third century

Key Terms

- Confucianism
- Buddhism
- Daoism

➤ *This bronze lamp was found in the tomb of a Han dynasty princess.*

While some women in late Han dynasty China might have been enjoying themselves, the huge majority were doing backbreaking work. They were either working alongside men in the fields, weaving at a loom at home while taking care of children, or even working off the yearly stint of required hard labor for the government. Ge Hong was upset by the city-dwelling, fun-

loving ladies, for as the state was falling apart, order and "proper behavior" seemed more and more important.

Lady Ban Zhao *(ban jow)*, the first and greatest of Chinese women scholars, had died in A.D. 116. Ban Zhao was educated in literature, philosophy, business, and politics, and she was given a high position at court. In Han dynasty China, women could still participate in intellectual life. Exceptional women like Ban Zhao could make their mark.

Troubling times followed the overthrow of the last Han emperor, Xian Di *(shehn DEE),* in A.D. 220. Nomadic horsemen attacked from the north, and landowners refused to pay taxes. Army generals with their troops fought each other for power.

Having survived floods, famine, and plagues, peasants now had no money to buy food or seeds.

192

Chapter 8

Objectives

1. Identify and explain the factors that made China difficult to govern.
2. Explain the reasons for the spread of the Buddhist religion in China.
3. Describe the techniques used by Emperor Wen to unify the Chinese empire.

Graphic Overview

This chart compares aspects of life during the period of disorder that followed the Han Dynasty and under the Sui Dynasty.

	Period of Disorder	Sui Dynasty
Religion	Buddhism	Buddhism, Confucianism, and Daoism
Government	nomads in North; landowners in South	new administrative system
Economy	South expands	Grand Canal built

Years of Disorder

Emperor Xian Di, the last of the Han emperors, could not solve the many problems of the empire. In A.D. 220, China's first great empire broke apart. China was fragmented into small, competing kingdoms.

Geography Creates Regions

The Han Empire included the area of China shown in orange on the map below. Though the area makes up only one-third of modern China, it was here that most important events in Chinese history took place.

The eastern third of China, the area around the modern cities of Nanjing, Luoyang, and Changsha, has been the center of China's population throughout history. What natural features shown on the map explain why people settled here? The Qing Ling (chihng lihng) Mountains divide this fertile area into two regions, northern and southern China.

Before the unification of China under the Han Dynasty in 221 B.C., people living in northern and southern China had almost no contact with each other. Even during the Han Dynasty, only traders, soldiers, or government officials were likely to travel from one region to another.

Barriers Protect the Empire

Geography not only divided China but also protected it from the outside world. In ancient times, the Himalayas to the southwest and the Taklimakan Desert to the west limited Chinese contact with

Across Time & Space

Don't be confused if you see the Chang Jiang written as the Yangtze River on older maps. Chang Jiang is spelled according to the Pinyin system for writing Chinese in our Roman alphabet. In 1958, the Chinese officially adopted Pinyin, replacing older systems.

▼ The earliest civilizations in China developed along a river, the Huang He. Find the Huang He and the Chang Jiang on the map.

Division of the Han Empire, A.D. 220–264

- 80°E
- 100°E
- 120°E
- Huang He
- TAKLIMAKAN
- WEI
- Yellow Sea
- Huang He
- QIN LING MTS.
- Luoyang
- 30°N
- Nanjing
- Chengdu
- East China Sea
- Chang Jiang
- Changsha
- HIMALAYAS
- SHU–HAN
- WU
- 30°N

Legend:
- ~~~~ Great Wall
- —— Silk Road

0   200   400 mi.
0   200   400 km
Mercator Projection

China

DEVELOP

Have students look at the map on p. 193 and then discuss the geography of China. Ask them to identify geographic elements that would tend to unite China as well as elements that would make unity difficult. Then have students study the illustrations that accompany Lesson 1, to see whether they can identify any other factors that might affect unification.

GEOGRAPHY

Map and Globe Skills

Ask students to use the map on p. 193 to answer the following: Why was China always invaded from the north? (Open steppes.) What separated north and south China? (Qin Ling Mountains.) What made southern China good farmland? (Yangtze and Yellow River basins.)

Access Strategy

Ask students to think of their own social structure at school. Help them to understand that people naturally group themselves around common interests, common needs, and so on. Then physically divide the students into several groups and ask them to assume they live in China in A.D. 220, when the Han Dynasty ended. Each group is suddenly on its own, and none of the groups trust each other. Suggest that each group elect a leader to help develop a plan for uniting all the groups. Plans may range from friendly persuasion to takeover by force. If some groups select takeover by force, ask them to consider how they would keep subdued groups from rebelling. Will these groups be able to participate in activities, receive recognition, share in the decision making? Have each group share its plan with the rest of the class.

Access Activity

Have students remain in the groups formed for the Access Strategy and work together to design promotional materials for their plans: posters, bumper stickers, buttons, and radio and TV ads detailing the advantages for everyone if that group's plan is adopted. Finally, let the class elect an emperor for the day.

Critical Thinking

Ask students what values Confucianism emphasizes. Point out that Confucianism is less a religion than philosophy, or code of conduct, which—like a religion—guided many aspects of people's lives. Have students compare and contrast the role of Confucius to those of the Buddha, Jesus, and Muhammad.

■ *The Qin Ling Mountains divide China into two distinct regions, north and south, which had little contact with each other and little in common.*

194

Across Time & Space

The Romans saw Chinese silk for the first time in 53 B.C., when they were fighting the Parthians. The Parthians had traded with the Chinese for over 200 years and used the colorful silk in their battle pennants. Within 25 years, silk made up over 90 percent of Rome's imports from China.

➤ *Ban Zhao, charged with teaching manners to the ladies of the emperor's court, writes out some of her rules of conduct. This is an illustration for the scroll* The Admonitions of the Instructress of Court Ladies, *a work from the 200s.*

■ *Find evidence to support this statement: Geographic features made China difficult to unify.*

---

the civilizations of India, Persia, and other areas. Another natural barrier protected China to the east. What was it? China was vulnerable in the north, however. There, a huge open steppe, or grassy plain, left China open to attack by invaders.

A Period of Unrest

Barbarian invasions and other problems finally brought an end to the Han dynasty. Then tribal invaders, Chinese army generals, and aristocratic families were left to struggle for control of various regions. For about 360 years after the Han Dynasty ended, China was in a state of political disunity.

In the south, large landowners controlled local affairs in most areas. They kept private armies to defend their lands, and they fortified their homes. Many small farmers were forced to give up their land and work the landowners' fields in exchange for food and protection.

Control of the central government changed hands often from 220 to 589. Southern China's economy improved during this time of unrest, however. Good harvests and a growing foreign market for silk

helped the capital city, Nanjing, become a center of commerce. By the 500s, merchants from Southeast Asia, India, and Persia traded in the city.

In the north, various groups of nomads from the steppes invaded China and set up a series of short-lived kingdoms. As these nomadic peoples became accustomed to settled life, they willingly adopted the language, traditions, and government structure of the native Chinese. By 589, descendants of the invaders were fully integrated into northern Chinese culture and society. ■

The Spread of Buddhism

For Chinese in all classes, these were years of uncertainty. During the Han Dynasty, most Chinese had been followers of Confucius.

In **Confucianism,** the roles of men and women were further separated. It focused on having respect for elders, completing duties to the family, and attaining virtue by studying the classics or serving the government.

But after the fall of the empire, people began to turn to **Buddhism,** a system of thought and practice based on the teachings of Siddhartha Gautama, the Buddha or "Enlightened One." It offered the promise of escape from suffering. What do the selections on page 195 from the Buddha's teachings say about how one can escape from suffering?

Chapter 8

Visual Learning

Ask students to study the statue of Buddha on p. 195 and relate it to what they have learned about Buddhist teachings. Ask why they think Buddha is often shown in a seated position and with his eyes closed, in a posture of meditation. Ask students what features they might expect on statues or pictures of Confucius.

Historical Context

During the political upheaval that followed the end of the Han Dynasty, southern China was the seat of numerous native Chinese dynasties, all of which were militarily weak. The dynasties seizing power in the north, on the other hand, were non-Chinese and were militarily strong but also inexperienced in administration. They tended to be nomadic, rather than agrarian like the Chinese, and ended up adopting Chinese ways of governing. Ultimately they lost their separate

identities and became totally assimilated into Chinese society, producing a surprisingly homogeneous population. Even Yang Jian, who eventually established the Sui Dynasty, was of mixed Chinese and "barbarian" descent.

*L*ike a spider caught in its own web is a person driven by fierce cravings. Break out of the web, and turn away from the world of sensory pleasure and sorrow.

If you want to reach the other shore of existence, give up what is before, behind, and in between. Set your mind free, and go beyond birth and death

Our life is shaped by our mind; we become what we think. Suffering follows an evil thought as the wheels of a cart follow the oxen that draw it.

Our life is shaped by our mind; we become what we think. Joy follows a pure thought like a shadow that never leaves.

From the *Dhammapada*, translated by Eknath Easwaran

Buddhism originated in India around 530 B.C. Traders and missionaries traveling along the Silk Road introduced the religion to China during the Han Dynasty. However, it attracted few followers then, mostly because it was foreign. Now, in the troubled times at the end of the Han Dynasty, the new religion became attractive.

The Buddha taught that life is a cycle of pleasure and sorrow, of death and rebirth. Suffering, he taught, was a basic part of life. It was caused by paying too much attention to material things in life— to what the Buddha referred to "the world of sensory pleasure."

But a person could escape from suffering, according to the Buddha. Through meditation, he taught, one could achieve enlightenment—a state of complete freedom and peace.

The idea of freedom from the chaos of the earthly world appealed to Chinese people of all classes. It appealed to regional rulers living in constant fear of attack, to landowners worried about crop failure, and to peasants longing for their own plots of land. By the 400s, most regional kings supported Buddhism. Buddhist temples and monasteries thrived throughout China. The Buddhists accumulated much valuable land. They also owned grain mills, and operated hospitals, schools, and inns. ■

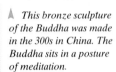

▲ *This bronze sculpture of the Buddha was made in the 300s in China. The Buddha sits in a posture of meditation.*

■ *Why did the Chinese find Buddhism more appealing than Confucianism after the fall of the Han Dynasty?*

The Reunification of China

More than 300 years after the Han Dynasty ended, a northern official named Yang Jian reunited the Chinese Empire. He seized power and declared himself emperor of northern China in 581 and then conquered the south by 589. Yang Jian's title was Emperor Wen, and the dynasty he founded is known as the Sui *(sway)* Dynasty.

A National Identity

Emperor Wen's greatest challenge was to reverse the forces that divided China. He used several techniques to do this.

Critical Thinking

Ask students to read aloud the four excerpts from Buddhist scriptures and reduce each one to a simple do or don't statement. When students are sure they understand the excerpts, ask why Buddhist teachings have appealed to so many people throughout the ages. If time allows, ask students to draw parallels between these teachings and those of other major religions.

■ *Buddhism offered the hope of peace in an unstable time.*

Religious Context

Despite the spread of Buddhism, Confucianism did not disappear. It remained a foundation of culture and gave form to political life. Nonetheless, the Confucian teachings below and in the next column may help to explain both the decline of Confucianism in the chaos following the Han Dynasty and its renewed appeal in the Sui Dynasty.

"It is indeed harmful to come under the sway of utterly new and strange doctrines."

"The Master taught four things: literature, conduct, loyalty, and reliability."

"At home, be humble; at work, be respectful; with others, be loyal. Even among the barbarians you may not abandon these precepts."

"China without a recognized leader is preferable to foreigners with all their leaders."

Study Skills

Research the life of Siddhartha Gautama, the founder of Buddhism. Instruct them to find out about his early years, the visions that changed his life, his understanding of nirvana, and his preaching of the dharma. Let students work in pairs, and encourage them to produce an illustrated report of what they learn.

Critical Thinking

Ask students to identify three ways in which Emperor Wen hoped to unify China. Have them tell in their own words how each of these approaches contributed to a national identity. Then ask students whether any similar elements are a part of the national identity of United States citizens. Encourage students to see the universality of this concept.

➤ *All the way.*

▼ *The Great Wall of China extends 4,000 miles from Inner Mongolia to the sea. If a similar wall was built along the border between the United States and Canada, about how far would it extend from the Atlantic to the Pacific Ocean?*

For one thing, he followed ancient Chinese political practices. For example, when his supporters proclaimed him emperor, he accepted the traditional imperial gifts, including red doors for his house and a robe with a red sash—but only after he had refused them three times, as tradition demanded. By following such ancient traditions, the emperor reminded his people of their common history.

Like emperors of the Han dynasty, Emperor Wen organized public works projects. These projects focused people's attention on the common goals of the empire. Using forced labor crews, the emperor built a grand capital city at Changan. Find this city on the map on page 205. He also oversaw the rebuilding of the Great Wall, which had been built after 214 B.C.,

to protect China from the central Asian nomads who continued to attack the north.

During Emperor Wen's reign, workers began work on the Grand Canal between the Huang He, formerly called the Yellow River, and the Chang Jiang. After the Grand Canal opened in 605, it transported government officials, grain, and silk. Find the Grand Canal on the map on page 205.

Scholarship had been important in earlier Chinese society. Emperor Wen renewed this tradition by founding colleges for the study of the classics. He also set up schools for learning calligraphy, or the writing of Chinese characters, and for accounting and law. Since many ancient manuscripts had been lost after the fall of the Han Dynasty, Emperor Wen collected books from throughout the empire. Scholars organized and classified the texts; then clerks copied them by hand. In this way,

Critical Thinking

Ask students to identify potential areas of disagreement among Buddhism, Confucianism, and Daoism. Help students to see that the Confucian belief in scholarship and government service, for example, might conflict with the Buddhist emphasis on meditation and the Daoist acceptance of things as they are.

Making a Chart

Have students reread the description of Emperor Wen's administrative system and create an organizational chart showing the system's structure. Instruct students to use the specific department and offices cited in the text and then add other departments and offices they think China would have needed in the early 600s.

Mathematics Connection

Have students develop a salary schedule for eight ranks of officials in Emperor Wen's government. (Those in the ninth rank received no salary.) Instruct them to maintain equal increments between all levels, using 900 bushels of grain for the highest rank and 50 bushels for the eighth rank, as described in the text on p. 197.

Emperor Wen ensured the preservation of the Chinese classics.

The Administrative System

Emperor Wen set up a new system of administration to govern his huge empire efficiently. He created several departments for different government functions. Each department was divided into several smaller offices that performed specific duties. For example, within the Department of State Affairs were six offices. They were responsible for the army, finance, punishments, public works, rites, and civil office.

Officials were classified into nine ranks, or levels. Rank determined salary. Officials of the first rank earned 900 bushels of grain per year, while eighth-ranked officials earned 50.

Emperor Wen ordered local governments to send three worthy men to the capital each year. There they were tested in three areas: general literary ability, mastery of a single classic literary work, and the ability to take action in response to certain situations. Those who performed well on the exams were appointed to one of the lower ranks of government.

To prevent officials from showing favoritism or gaining influence in local affairs, Emperor Wen declared that officials could not serve in their home areas. Traveling inspectors, and often even the emperor himself, visited the provinces to check on local officials.

Three Systems of Thought and Practice

Emperor Wen was a Buddhist. He founded many temples and monasteries, and he encouraged support for them. But he recognized that other Chinese systems of thought and practice could help to strengthen his dynasty.

The emperor knew that Confucianism was an important tradition in Chinese government. So he emphasized the Confucian ideas of good conduct, scholarship, and public service.

Emperor Wen also encouraged **Daoism** (*DOW ihz uhm*), based on the teachings of Laozi, a Chinese philosopher who lived from 606 to 530 B.C. Daoists emphasized living in harmony with nature and being content with life.

By encouraging followers of all three systems, Emperor Wen promoted Chinese unity rather than divisiveness. The unified empire that he created continued under the Tang Dynasty, which followed the Sui Dynasty. ■

▲ *This painting of Emperor Wen is a detail from the scroll* Portraits of the Emperors, *completed during the 600s.*

■ *What steps did Emperor Wen take to reunify China?*

■ *To foster unity, he followed ancient Chinese political rituals, organized public works projects, reestablished traditional scholarly pursuits, and allowed older religions to flourish.*

REVIEW

1. **FOCUS** What were some of the obstacles to unity in China, and how did Emperor Wen overcome them?
2. **CONNECT** How does the fall of the Han Empire compare with the fall of the Roman Empire?
3. **GEOGRAPHY** What were the natural barriers that protected China on the east, west, and southwest?
4. **BELIEF SYSTEMS** Why was Emperor Wen wise to allow the practice of Buddhism, Confucianism, and Daoism in his empire?

5. **CRITICAL THINKING** Why might a country benefit from being strongly unified?
6. **ACTIVITY** You are a public relations expert working for Emperor Wen. You have been asked to promote his campaign to unite north and south China. Design a poster that shows some of the factors that have kept northern and southern China separated. The poster should also explain or illustrate the advantages of unity.

197

China

Answers to Review Questions

1. In addition to divisions caused by geographic features, China suffered from social divisions. Also, invasions from the north were a recurring problem.
2. Both the Han Dynasty and the Western Roman Empire fell after repeated barbarian invasions.
3. The sea on the east, the Taklimakan Desert on the west, and the Himalayas on the southwest protected China.

4. Emperor Wen recognized that all three systems of thought and practice were important Chinese traditions. By allowing them to coexist, he could strengthen his dynasty and promote unity.
5. Answers will vary. Students may point out that small, separate groups within a country are seldom able to work together successfully to solve internal or external problems.

Homework Options

If you haven't already assigned the Visual Learning activity on p. 194, do so now.

Study Guide: p. 31

CLOSE

On the chalkboard, fill in the chart shown in the Graphic Overview on p. 192 with students.

DECISION-MAKING PROCESS

1. Recognize the need for a decision.
2. Define the goals and values involved.
3. Acquire and evaluate necessary information.
4. Identify and analyze possible alternatives.
5. Choose the best alternative.

This Making Decisions lesson, The Great Wall, uses steps 1, 2, and 3 of the decision-making process.

HISTORY
Study Skills

Have students identify several reasons given in the text for building the Great Wall. *(Protection along the northern border; a way for the emperor to get rid of enemies, including enemy soldiers, by putting them to work in a distant place.)* What else might the emperor have done to solve his problems? *(Simply have men guard the northern border; have enemies build roads or public buildings; imprison enemies or put them to death.)*

198

The Great Wall

➤ *The Great Wall still snakes for thousands of miles across modern China. However, the wall that is still standing is not Shihuangdi's wall, but a later version, built during the Ming Dynasty.*

H ad the Great Wall not already existed, Yangdi [the second Sui emperor] would certainly have conceived it. As it was, he had to be content with rebuilding it.

Robert Silverberg,
20th-century historian

Background

Records show that Yangdi's rebuilding of the Great Wall in 607 required more than a million workers. Over half of them died of overwork or fled the harsh conditions.

The original building of the Great Wall, begun in 221 B.C., also involved a huge work force. Shihuangdi, the Chinese emperor who conceived of this project, connected shorter walls that had been built along China's northern border centuries before. He also extended the wall for hundreds of miles. The resulting fortified wall was and still is the longest structure on earth.

Before embarking on any massive work, such as the building of the Great Wall of China, a wise decision maker will try to weigh the benefits and the costs of the project. We can look at historical events to try to compare the benefits and the costs of building the Great Wall of China.

▼ *These coins, which were issued by Shihuangdi, were the standard currency throughout the empire at the time when the Great Wall was being built.*

Benefits and Costs of the Great Wall

The most obvious benefit of building the Great Wall was protection. The wall helped prevent nomadic horsemen from invading China's farms along the northern border. Also, it kept farmers living along the border from joining the nomads.

Building the Great Wall enabled Shihuangdi to get rid of his

198

Chapter 8

Objectives

1. Recognize the dangers to the emperor and the empire. (History 3, 5)
2. Define the goals for building the Great Wall. (Critical Thinking 2; History 3, 5)
3. Evaluate the negative and positive effects of building the Great Wall. (Critical Thinking 2; History 5)

Activity

Tell the students to imagine what it might have been like to live in China in 221 B.C., when Shihuangdi decided to begin building the Great Wall. Encourage them to speculate about the following: what the northern farmers' opinions of the Great Wall might have been, the disloyal soldiers' thoughts about it, worker/management problems, the emperor's point of view, the nomads' point of view, and the Chinese people's attitude towards the building project. Then, have students write

news stories about this building project. Tell students that they can use graphs, charts, and political cartoons to make their reports more interesting or that they can work in teams and present their news reports in interview form. Finally, have students present their reports as if they were appearing on the evening news.

enemies. He ordered them to work on distant parts of the wall. He also sent soldiers to work on the wall. As a result, the soldiers could not band together and rise up against the emperor.

However, building Shihuangdi's wall is estimated to have required more than 300,000 workers, most of whom were drafted against their will. Thousands of farmers and merchants were required to supply the workers with food, clothing, tools, and shelter. Most of these supplies never made it

to the work sites; bandits roaming the countryside robbed the supply caravans.

The work of constructing the wall was so difficult and living conditions were so harsh that thousands of workers died. Often they were buried in the wall itself. Thus, the Great Wall of China gained the gruesome title of "the world's longest cemetery."

▼ *Sturdy horses, like the one at the left, carried nomads who raided China's northern border. In response, the Great Wall was built, using labor-intensive construction methods as shown. Study the chart for a comparison of the Great Wall's long-range benefits and short-term costs.*

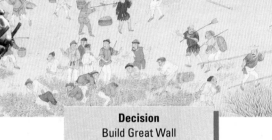

Decision
Build Great Wall

⬇

Outcomes

• People are safer	• Many laborers die
• More farmers stay on farms	• People become poorer
• Fewer threats to emperor arise	• Supply caravans often attacked

Decision Point

1. What were the benefits of constructing the Great Wall of China? What were the costs?
2. Do you think these were the only benefits and costs of the Great Wall? Where would you look to find more information about the role of the Great Wall in Chinese history?
3. Based on the information on these pages and any other information you have found,

do you think the benefits and costs of building the Great Wall balanced out? Explain.
4. Collect information from newspapers and magazines about upcoming plans for large government projects in the United States. Discuss the projected benefits and costs of each project. Decide which projects you would support and which you would oppose.

China

Critical Thinking

Draw students' attention to the chart on p. 199. Have a volunteer read the left side of the chart—the positive outcomes of the building of the Great Wall. Ask if the positive outcomes were long lasting. *(Yes, Emperor Yangdi still relied on the Great Wall for defense 800 years after it was built.)* Then have a volunteer read the right side of the chart. Ask students why they think Emperor Shihuangdi decided to continue building the Great Wall even when its drawbacks became apparent. *(The emperor saw the negative outcomes as short-term costs, while he saw the wall's benefits as longer lasting.)* Discuss with students the values, both positive and negative, reflected in the building of the Great Wall. *(For example, the emperor cared more for his own survival and the survival of his empire than for the lives of the Chinese people.)*

199

199

Answers to Decision Point

1. The benefits were that the people were safer, more farmers stayed on their farms, and there were fewer threats to the emperor. The costs were that many laborers died, the people became poorer, and caravans of supplies traveling to the wall were often attacked.
2. Sample answer: No, additional benefits and costs could be found in encyclopedias and history textbooks.

3. Sample answers: Yes, the benefits of building the Great Wall were much longer lasting than the costs. No, the abuse of human life can never be balanced by any positive outcomes.

Collaborative Learning

For a recommended collaborative learning strategy you can use with this lesson, refer to pp. T34–T35.

INTRODUCE

The poetry of a civilization tells us many things about the life and times of its peoples. These poems describe a uniquely Chinese attitude about nature. Rather than trying to conquer nature or fearing that they would be conquered by it, the Chinese saw themselves as a part of nature. Knowing this may help students understand the development of the Chinese culture as discussed in Lesson 2 of Chapter 8.

➤ How does a poem "search" for a poet? *(Poems don't, but the feelings, stirrings, and spirits of life search for a voice or poet.)*

READ AND RESPOND

Students will be able to appreciate this poetry best if they read it aloud. You may wish to have student volunteers read, or you may want to read yourself. Review the introductory paragraph above the poems with students before reading the poems, emphasizing the focus for the reading given in the last two sentences.

Some words to discuss before reading are: *becalmed,* kept motionless by lack of wind; *gorge,* a narrow passage; and *mainmast,* a sailing ship's principal mast.

200

In the next lesson, you will read about a period of great achievement in Chinese government, trade, science, and art. The poet Yang Wan-Li in many ways symbolized that achievement.

200

LITERATURE

Heaven My Blanket, Earth My Pillow

Poems by Yang Wan-Li

Today our political leaders are usually not poets or artists. In the Song period of Chinese history, which you will study in the next lesson, government officials were also judged on their accomplishments in literature or art. Yang Wan-Li, a respected finance administrator, was also a well-known poet. His poems, like others of the period, express feelings of calm and harmony with nature. As you read, look for examples of these feelings.

Written on a Cold Evening

The poet must work with brush and paper,
but this is not what makes the poem.
A man doesn't go in search of a poem—
the poem comes in search of him.

Evening Lake Scenes

1
The lake seems glued to the sky—
    no banks are visible.
In the middle of the lake, water plants float.
It is evening—geese are forming V's,
    crows are forming flocks;
they land, then fly up again,
    taking a long time to settle for the night.

2
I sit watching the sun set over the lake.
The sun is not swallowed by mountains or clouds:
it descends inch by inch, then disappears completely
leaving no trace where it sinks into the water.

Thematic Connections

Social Studies: Literature as a reflection of how people see their relationship with nature

Houghton Mifflin Literary Readers: Perceptions of Nature

Background

The poems in this selection were written by Yang Wan-Li during the Song Dynasty (A.D. 960–1279). While the Tang Dynasty (A.D. 712–756) is considered a high point of Chinese culture, great urban and commercial expansion took place during the Song period. Under the Song Dynasty, the Chinese made great strides in the arts as well, especially in landscape painting, book printing, and literature. The art of making and decorating porcelains with delicate carvings and glazes was perfected. Innovations in philosophy developed, including neo-Confucianism, entrenching Confucianism into Chinese life.

In the Gorge: We Encounter Wind

Our boat is becalmed in the middle of the river—
the mountains are silent and gloomy at sunset.
Suddenly a clap of thunder sounds in the darkening sky
and the trees along the shore begin to sway.
A powerful wind blows in from the southern sea
and sweeps angrily through the gorge.
The sailors cheer;
  the great drum is beaten.
One man flies to the top of the mainmast.
As a sail unfurls I pull my hands into my sleeves
and watch ripples like goose feathers
  swirl by in the water.

Rain and Cold

I comb my hair and sleep overcomes me:
I dream that all my white hairs are being cut.
I wake up: the wind is leaking through a crack in the window
swinging a spider's web back and forth.

Night Rain at Kuang-k

The river is clear and calm;
  a fast rain falls in the gorge.
At midnight the cold, splashing sound begins,
like thousands of pearls spilling onto a glass plate,
each drop penetrating the bone.

In my dream I scratch my head and get up to listen.
I listen and listen, until the dawn.
All my life I have heard rain,
  and I am an old man;
but now for the first time I understand
  the sound of spring rain
    on the river at night.

Further Reading

Heaven's Reward: Fairy Tales from China. Catherine Edwards Sadler. These stories have been retold for thousands of years in China.

Treasure Mountain: Folktales from Southern China. Catherine Edwards Sadler. These stories tell of greedy officials and noble peasants.

◄ Try to imagine what the poet is feeling and seeing as he stands on the boat in the wind.

◄ Why do you think the poet finally understands the sound of rain on the river? *(Because he is old and has spent many years listening to it. Also, he listens very carefully, even when he is dreaming.)*

EXTEND

Students may better appreciate the poetry of Yang Wan-Li if they know more about the social and cultural context in which it was written. Have them find out more about the Song Dynasty and about other Chinese poets and poems of the period (and the preceding and following dynasties if you wish). Have them share their findings.

Access Strategy

Tell students that a poet does not necessarily describe in realistic details what he or she sees. Instead, the poet often captures the *spirit* of the subject. When you read poetry, you have a chance to understand or see something in a new way. A hair can turn into a spider web, or raindrops can be pearls. Just let your imagination work and see or feel the pictures the poet is painting.

Illustrating

Have students illustrate one of the poems, using Yang Wan-Li's words as guides. Some of the poems lend themselves nicely to water colors and some to ink or charcoal. You may want to give students a choice of media. Have them choose their poems, copy them in their best handwriting on the paper, and then use their illustrations to fill the paper.

Students might be interested in seeing some Chinese art and trying to adopt that style in their illustrations.

Further Reading

You may want to have your students look in the school or local library for more books to read about this period of Chinese cultural achievement.

INTRODUCE

Remind students that the Sui Dynasty had brought order to China and a sense of national identity. Ask whether the lesson title suggests that things are getting better or worse in the years following the Sui Dynasty. Then direct students to the Thinking Focus, and ask what they think the "flowers" of this developing civilization might be.

Key Terms

Vocabulary Strategies: T36–T37
aristocrat—a member of a privileged class having inherited wealth and high social position
meritocracy—a system in which people are chosen for jobs and promoted on the basis of their performance
mandate—a command or instruction from an authority; an order to govern
currency—any form of money being used as a medium of exchange
money economy—an economy in which cash is the most common item exchanged for goods

202

200	550		1600	1950
	618	**1279**		

LESSON 2

The Flowering of Chinese Culture

THINKING FOCUS

What were the most significant achievements of the Tang and Song dynasties?

Key Terms

* aristocrat
* meritocracy
* mandate
* currency
* money economy

➤ *Here is a part of the Chinese text of the poem by Li Bo. This landscape, painted in ink on silk, has been attributed to the Tang artist Li Ssu-hsun. In an essay on painting, Guo Xi, one of the greatest artists of the Song Dynasty, said that enjoying a landscape painting could be a substitute for wandering through the mountains.*

202

Beside my bed the bright moonbeams bound
Almost as if there were frost on the ground.
Raising up, I gaze at the mountain moon;
Lying back, I think of my old home town.

Li Bo, "Quiet Night Thoughts," 701–702

If you were to write a poem about a nature scene near your home, how might your poem be like this one? How would it be different? Before you read on, study the painting and reread the poem.

李　白
望月怀远
窗前明月光
疑是地上霜
举头望明月
低头思故乡

Chapter 8

Objectives

1. Define *meritocracy* and explain its effect on the political system in China.
2. Demonstrate how developments in transportation, agriculture, and trade led to the rise of a money economy in China.
3. Summarize the major accomplishments of the Tang and Song dynasties in the fields of art, science, and technology.

Graphic Overview

This chart shows some achievements of the Tang and Song dynasties.

TANG AND SONG DYNASTIES

Arts	Government	Economy
poetry / painting and sculpture	meritocracy / power for emperor	new crops in South / money

The poem was written by Li Bo, the most beloved poet in China's history. He lived during the Tang Dynasty. The dynasty began when Li Yuan, a rebellious lord who had taken power from the Sui emperor, proclaimed himself emperor in 618. The Tang Dynasty was followed by the Song Dynasty, which lasted until 1279. Together, these two dynasties ruled over the most artistically brilliant era in Chinese civilization.

Poetry and painting are two areas in which Tang and Song artists excelled. A favorite theme of both poets and painters was the harmony they saw in the natural world. In the poem you read, Li Bo remembers the place where he grew up. He notes that the moon that he sees in the poem is the same mountain moon that shines on his home town. Nature unites two different times and places in the poem.

Do you think that the painting shown on page 202 expresses the same mood as the poem? The painting shows a mountainous landscape. But notice the person in the foreground. The size of the figure in relation to the landscape seems to suggest that people, or human activities, are not very important when compared with the beauty of the natural world. Nevertheless, the painter chose to place a human figure in the scene. Perhaps the painter is implying that people can live in harmony with nature, provided they recognize their small place in it.

Chinese painters did not simply draw what they saw. They tried to represent the spirit, or essence, of the subject. This feeling of harmony with their subject helped them to create a sense of life in their work. The Chinese landscape painter and poet Wang Wei explained Chinese painting this way:

◄ During the Tang Dynasty, pottery figures such as this fashionable lady were made in molds and painted. A pale, round face was thought to be most beautiful.

> *Such paintings cannot be achieved by the physical movements of the fingers and the hand, but only by the spirit entering into them. This is the nature of painting.*
>
> Wang Wei, from *Introduction to Painting*, 699–759

▼ Chinese civil service examinations were stamped with seals such as this.

The Civil Service System

Painting and poetry were not the only things the Chinese achieved during the Tang and Song dynasties. They also developed a fair and efficient system of administration.

More Schools for More People

The Sui and early Tang rulers used examinations to find good candidates for public office. But only an **aristocrat,** a member of

Refer students to the many illustrations that accompany this lesson. Then read with students the succession of headings and subheadings found in the text. Encourage students to combine these two elements—graphics and printed words—to predict what took place during this period of Chinese development.

203

Access Strategy

Ask students what they think of when they hear the word *civilization.* Help them to understand that many components make up civilization, or the way of life of a society. Emphasize that *civilization* refers to a more complex lifestyle and social structure than the term *culture.* Tell students to close their eyes and imagine a mural of our current civilization. Have them tell you the different things they "see" in their murals. List those items on the chalkboard, and then have students help you group them into major categories—for example, food, business, government, education, religion, art, and so on. Suggest that students have these broad categories in mind as they read about how Chinese civilization developed in the 600 years that followed the Sui Dynasty.

Access Activity

Divide students into groups of three or four, and have each group create a collage from old magazines and newspapers representing the greatest achievements or best aspects of modern civilization in the United States. Instruct students to include as many different aspects of civilization as possible.

Critical Thinking

Tell students that during the Sui Dynasty more than 90 percent of government workers were members of the aristocracy. Remind them that during the Tang and Song dynasties only about 50 percent of government workers were aristocrats. Ask students to explain why this change took place and to consider why this change would be good for a government. *(Broader support for government policies; increase in quality of work force.)*

■ *The civil service system opened up government positions to social classes other than the aristocracy. The new people who had earned their positions were usually more loyal to the emperor and more efficient in their jobs. Hence they stayed in power.*

a wealthy and influential family, could afford to study for the civil service exams. Preparing for the tests took years and meant traveling to special schools in the capital. As a result, aristocrats held most government jobs.

Later Tang and then Song governments recruited civil servants from other classes. It was still difficult for peasants to spend years studying, but during the Song Dynasty nearly half the civil servants came from classes other than the aristocracy.

This character used by an emperor of the Song Dynasty means "by order of the emperor." Calligraphy was a subject on the civil service examination.

■ *Why did the aristocracy find it more difficult to gain influence under the civil service system?*

A System Based on Merit

Officials appointed under earlier dynasties often held their positions for life, even if they were not very good at their jobs. Under the Tang and Song dynasties, civil servants who did their jobs well were promoted. Those who did poorly were demoted or even fired. Such a system, in which people are chosen and promoted on the basis of their

performance, or merit, is called a **meritocracy.** The Chinese were the first people to establish a meritocracy. Other countries, such as the United States and France, set up similar administrative systems about a thousand years later.

Power to the Emperor

The Chinese had long believed that each emperor received from heaven a **mandate,** or order to govern. This is why one of the emperor's titles was "Son of Heaven." In theory, the emperor had absolute power. In practice, he had always shared his power with wealthy, landowning families.

Under the meritocracy, aristocrats had less power. They held fewer government positions and risked losing their positions if they did not perform well. Officials who were not from the aristocratic class were grateful for their positions and thus more loyal to the emperor. The emperor trusted them to enforce his laws, even in regions far from the capital. ■

The Birth of a New Economy

To manage government business efficiently, official inspectors, tax collectors, and messengers needed to travel throughout the empire. To make this possible, the Tang and Song governments built an extensive system of roads and waterways. These, in turn, spurred trade and encouraged the spread of ideas within China.

Better Roads and Waterways

By the late 700s, relay hostels, or inns, with horses and food for traveling bureaucrats were in use along all main roads. Mounted

messengers and foot runners carried government mail. One observer of the day wrote, "It took only a few days for all the news from distant places to reach the authorities." The roads also made it possible to move grain, tea, and other goods. Some 9,600 runners regularly supplied fresh seafood to the Tang capital of Changan from coastal cities about 800 miles away.

The government also improved canals and waterways for the growing numbers of sailboats, hand-driven paddle-wheel boats, and rowing ships that used them. The

Visual Learning

Ask students to look at the calligraphy on this page. Remind them that this was the symbol of the Emperor, and ask whether they think it appropriately represents the Son of Heaven. Help students to appreciate the strength and forcefulness of the symbol. Encourage students to design their own personal symbol.

Historical Context

The Chinese buried members of the imperial family with a wealth of objects that symbolized their status. Tomb artifacts such as silk and gold clothing, bronze sculptures, ceramics, jade jewelry, and even life-size clay figures of court attendants and warriors have been found. Archaeologists have excavated only a few tombs so far. Hundreds of sites have been identified and designated as protected cultural sites by the Chinese government.

Interviewing

Have students think about the lives of the 9,600 runners who kept Changan supplied with fresh seafood. Tell students to identify four or five questions they would like to ask one of the runners and write their questions and imagined answers in the form of a person-to-person interview.

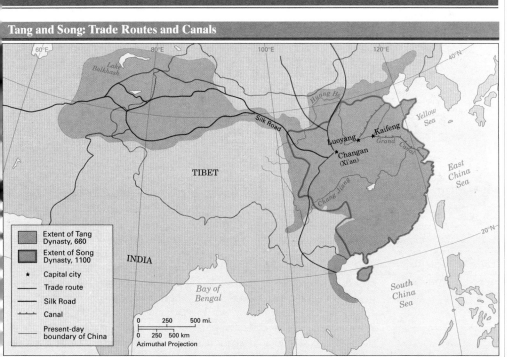

Tang and Song: Trade Routes and Canals

Extent of Tang Dynasty, 660
Extent of Song Dynasty, 1100
★ Capital city
— Trade route
— Silk Road
⊢⊣ Canal
— Present-day boundary of China

0   250   500 mi.
0 250 500 km
Azimuthal Projection

Critical Thinking

Ask students how well any civilization can progress without an efficient system of transportation. Help students to see what new roads and waterways did for China. *(For example, enabled government to stay informed about distant regions, facilitated commerce.)* Ask students to identify the benefits of modern transportation systems.

---

government sponsored hostels along the rivers and extended the canal system. By 850, the rivers and canals formed a vast network of about 1,200 miles extending to much of eastern China.

New Crops and Farming Methods

Though built for government use, roads and waterways promoted trade throughout China. At about the same time, Chinese farming became more productive. Around the year 1000, travelers introduced a new, fast-ripening rice from the area that is now Cambodia. Farmers could plant two or sometimes even three crops of this rice each year instead of just one.

Under both the Tang and Song dynasties, the government assigned plots of land to free peasants. Government officials taught farmers to build irrigation ditches and dams with pumps driven by

human, water, or wind power. Farmers could then turn dry land into paddies, or wet fields, to grow more rice.

A population shift resulted from this boom in agriculture. Southern China was better suited for growing rice than northern China. As more and more land was turned into rice paddies, more and more people could live on what the land produced. The population of southern China grew steadily. Also, Mongol invasions in the north forced many to flee to the south. Many became tenants on large southern farms. The graph above shows this growth in population.

Farmers soon produced more food than they needed. So they sold the extra food, or surplus, to

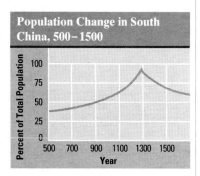

Population Change in South China, 500–1500

Percent of Total Population: 0, 25, 50, 75, 100
Year: 500, 700, 900, 1100, 1300, 1500

▲ *How did the Grand Canal help to unite northern and southern China? What percentage of the total population of China lived in the south around 620? What percentage lived in the south around 1280?*

◄ *The Grand Canal allowed the agricultural products of southern China to be shipped to northern China; about 35 per cent; about 90 per cent.*

205

China

Economic Context

New crops and better agricultural practices enabled farmers to plant the best crops for their local soil and weather conditions. By planting several varieties of early and late-ripening rice as well as cool weather crops like wheat, farmers spread their work out more evenly throughout the year. Staggered planting seasons also reduced the risk of total crop loss due to bad weather.

Visual Learning

Have students analyze the graph of population change on this page. Have them answer questions such as the following: About what year did the population in southern China reach the highest point compared to the total population in the country? *(About 1300.)*

This copper plate was used for printing money during the Song Dynasty.

■ *What factors led to a money economy in China?*

people in other regions, using the new roads and waterways to send crops to market. Market towns grew larger in rural areas.

A Thriving Merchant Class
Using this network of waterways, merchants transported products inexpensively in Chinese sailing ships called junks. Junks also carried goods along the coast, as seen from this description of a Song coastal city:

> Merchants from [southern and central provinces] come to this town in seagoing junks to sell such dutiable goods as spices. . . . [Northern] merchants come bringing copper cash, silk thread, silk floss, silk gauze and thin silk, and do an extremely thriving trade with them.
>
> From *The Continuation of the Comprehensive Mirror for Aiding Government*, 1088

Merchants made copper coins with holes in the center

and strung on a string called a *cash.* Usually there were a thousand coins in a cash. In earlier times, bartered goods, such as lengths of silk, had also been used in trading. As trade increased, merchants found it easier to trade in cash.

But cash was heavy. Imagine carrying 50 dollars in coins in your pocket! In 1024, the Song government used an engraved metal plate like the one shown to the left to print the world's first paper **currency.** As cash and paper currency became the most common items exchanged for goods, a **money economy** developed. Money was now the standard by which people judged the value of a bushel of rice or a length of silk.

The business of trade required more shopkeepers, bankers, inspectors, tax collectors, storehouse workers, and others. As a result, the merchant class grew.

Merchants tended to live in cities and towns, where trading activity was greatest. Cities grew in size as rural workers flocked to the cities to fill jobs related to trade. ■

A Continuing Heritage

Although the Chinese prospered through their thriving new trade network, they continued to value their ancient traditions.

The civil service exams, for example, required candidates to study the Confucian classics. The classics became available after the invention of printing in the late 700s,

Inventions in China and Europe

100, Use of writing paper
(*European writing paper—900, from Cairo*)

577, Matches invented
(*European matches—1500s*)

| 100 | 200 | 300 | 400 | 500 |

200, Fishing reel developed
(*European fishing reel—1650*)

400, Rudder developed
(*European rudder—c.1300*)

■ *Increased trade in China and the development of paper currency led to a money economy.*

ECONOMICS
Critical Thinking

Have students use the information from The Birth of a New Economy to construct a flow chart that shows the interaction among factors such as better roads and waterways, new crops and improved farming methods, increased population in southern China, food surpluses, a thriving merchant class, the use of money and paper currency, and the growth of cities. Many designs are possible. Encourage students to see the cause-and-effect relationships among these developments.

Critical Thinking

Ask students to paraphrase the Neo-Confucian creed cited in the Religious Context note. Encourage them to keep the three verses separate and to put the ideas completely into their own words. Have students share their paraphrases. Then ask whether they can identify the Buddhist, Daoist, and Confucian influences in the creed.

Religious Context

The renewed interest in Confucian ideas naturally built on Buddhist and Daoist concepts, even as it rejected the idea of withdrawal from society. Both Confucians and Neo-Confucians gave social goals a high priority. Many of these elements can be seen in the Neo-Confucian creed:

"Heaven is my father and Earth is my mother, and even such a small creature as I finds an intimate place in their midst."

"Therefore that which fills the universe I regard as my body and that which directs the universe I consider as my nature."

"All people are my brothers and sisters, and all things are my companions."

about 700 years before the development of printing in Europe.

Historians call this renewed emphasis on Confucian ideas Neo-Confucianism. Writers began to find new meanings in Confucian texts and to relate them to problems of the time.

Respect for the past, however, did not keep the Chinese from moving forward. Between 200 and 1200, new inventions improved life in China. Look at the timeline below. Notice that many Chinese discoveries took centuries to reach the West. Chain drives of the type that were later used in bicycles, for example, were in use in China in 976 in silk-making machinery. When was this invention first used in the West?

Printing

Of all the inventions made during the Tang and Song periods, printing was probably the most significant. By making books, calendars, and government pamphlets available to many more people, printing hastened the spread of knowledge throughout China.

Woodblock printing was the earliest form of printing. The Chinese began to use this method in the late 700s, about 600 years before Europeans learned about it. To make a woodblock print, skilled craftspeople carved raised Chinese characters on a wooden "page." They brushed ink onto this page and laid a piece of paper over it to make a print. The entire process was done by hand.

How long do you think it would take you to carve the words in this sentence onto a block of wood? Chinese scholars spent 21 years carving and printing all 130 volumes of the Confucian classics.

Around 1045, a Chinese commoner named Pi Sheng invented a less time-consuming method of printing using movable type. He cut ideograms, the Chinese characters, out of sticky clay and baked them until they were hard. Then he made each page by placing the necessary characters into an iron frame. This method of printing was very quick and efficient for printing many pages of a work.

By 1100, Chinese scholars used books on law, medicine, mathematics, and science to learn from both the past and the present. New techniques for treating disease or planting crops, for example, spread much more quickly in print than by word of mouth. An observer named Fang Tazong wrote the

▼ *About how long after the Chinese first used matches did Europeans make matches?*

c.8th century, Paper money developed
(*European bank note issued–1658*)

1041–1048, Movable type developed
(*European movable type–1450*)

| 700 | 800 | 900 | 1000 | 1100 | 1200 |

976, Bicycle chain drive developed
(*European bicycle chain drive–1770*)

China

207

■ *Printing, warfare, and travel by sea had existed for centuries. Chinese inventors did not seek to change society through their work, but to improve existing processes and functions.*

CLOSE

Review with students the accomplishments of the Tang and Song dynasties by filling in the Graphic Overview. Then have students work together to design and create a mural depicting the accomplishments of the Tang and Song dynasties. Encourage students to use a Chinese art style if they wish, but stress the importance of including the many areas of civilization covered in the text: government, transportation, agriculture, commerce, and technology.

208

▲ *The Chinese first used gunpowder for fireworks during the Tang Dynasty. A Chinese book published in 1044 gives a precise formula for making gunpowder.*

➤ *This compass was made by using a magnetic rock called a lodestone. The compass maker cut a thin sheet of metal into the shape of a fish and rubbed it with the lodestone to make it magnetic.*

■ *Find evidence to support this statement: Chinese inventions showed a respect for the past as well as a desire to improve on it.*

following about education in the province of Fujian during Song times:

Every peasant, artisan and merchant teaches his sons how to read books. Even herdsmen, and wives who bring their husbands food at their work in the fields, can recite the poems of the men of ancient times.

Other Inventions

Another important invention was gunpowder, which may have been discovered as early as the 600s. By the 1200s, the Chinese made and used gunpowder in large quantities. A document written in 1221 states: "On the same day were produced 7,000 gunpowder crossbow arrows, 10,000 gunpowder ordinary arrows, 3,000 barbed gunpowder packages and 20,000 ordinary gunpowder packages." In addition, archaeological evidence shows that by 1288 the Chinese had invented guns, which were later copied in Europe.

Another invention made traveling easier. For travel by sea, the Chinese used charts of the stars and a compass they called a "fish."

Chinese astronomers began mapping the stars as early as 300 B.C. Star charts dating from about 940 show many familiar constellations. The "fish" was a piece of metal shaped like a fish that pointed south when floated in water. This description of how sailors used the magnetic fish was written in 1119:

The sailors are sure of their bearings. At night they judge by the stars. In daytime they tell by the sun. When it is cloudy, they rely on the south-pointing needle.

Europeans learned about these inventions during the years that followed the Song Dynasty. These years were a period of Mongol domination in China. ■

R E V I E W

1. **FOCUS** What were the most significant achievements of the Tang and Song dynasties?
2. **CONNECT** How did the civil service system in the later Tang and Song dynasties differ from that of the Sui Dynasty?
3. **CULTURE** What common theme runs through many poems and paintings of the Tang and Song dynasties? How is this theme related to the religious beliefs of the period?
4. **ECONOMICS** How did Chinese agricultural growth

make necessary the development of a money economy?
5. **CRITICAL THINKING** Would you describe your school as a meritocracy? Explain.
6. **ACTIVITY** Assume that you are the inventor of one of the items pictured in the timeline on pages 206 and 207. Describe your invention and explain its purpose to your classmates, who have never heard of such a device. Be sure to point out how your device could improve their lives.

Chapter 8

Homework Options

If you haven't already assigned the Visual Learning activity on p. 207, do so now.

Study Guide: p. 32

Answers to Review Questions

1. The arts, especially poetry and painting, flourished in China during the Tang and Song dynasties. Other important achievements of this time include the civil service system, an extensive network of roads and waterways, and printing.
2. Under the Tang and Song dynasties, more people from social classes other than the aristocracy worked in the civil service system.
3. Harmony within the natural world was a

popular theme of Tang and Song poets and artists. Buddhism and Daoism also stressed the harmony within nature.
4. Increased crop yields resulted in a surplus of food. Increased wealth resulted in more trade. Trade made necessary a money economy.
5. Answers will vary, but students will probably say that students get ahead in school based on merit or performance rather than by having special privileges.

200   550   900   1950
1234   1912

L E S S O N   3

China and the Larger World

O n this [New Year's] day all the rulers, and all the provinces and regions and realms where men hold land or lordship under [the Great Khan's] sway, bring him costly gifts of gold and silver and pearls and precious stones and abundance of fine white cloth, so that throughout the year their lord may have no lack of treasure and may live in joy and gladness. . . . I can also assure you for a fact that on this day the Great Khan receives gifts of more than 100,000 white horses, of great beauty and price. And on this day also there is a procession of his elephants, fully 5,000 in number, all draped in fine cloths embroidered with beasts and birds. . . . Let me conclude with one more fact, a very remarkable one well worthy of mention in our book. You must know that a great lion is led into the Great Khan's presence; and as soon as it sees him it flings itself down prostrate before him with every appearance of deep humility and seems to acknowledge him as lord. There it stays without a chain, and is indeed a thing to marvel at.

Marco Polo, from *Travels*

This detailed account of a day at the Great Khan's court at Beijing was recounted by Marco Polo, a traveler from Venice, Italy. Polo lived in China from 1275 until 1292. The Great Khan in this report was Kublai Khan, a grandson of Genghis Khan.

Although only 17 years old when he arrived in China, Polo served Kublai as an ambassador and in other ways. At the time of his visit, all of China, as well as much of the rest of the world, was under Mongol rule.

THINKING
F O C U S

What factors caused China to open trade at some times and remain isolated at others?

Key Term

• despot

◄ *In this portrait of Kublai Khan, he is dressed in the traditional clothing of a Chinese emperor.*

209

China

INTRODUCE

R emind students of the accomplishments of the Tang and Song dynasties, but point out the absence of any attention to building military strength. Have students explain why China would have been an appealing target for outside forces. Also ask students why foreign conquest of China would have tended to increase Chinese contacts with the rest of the world.

Key Term

Vocabulary Strategies: T36–T37
despot—a ruler who holds absolute power and uses it abusively

209

Graphic Overview

This chart compares aspects of life under the Yuan, Ming, and Qing dynasties.

	Yuan	Ming	Qing
Relations with West	International trade prospers	Overseas trade restricted	Overseas trade allowed at Guangzhou
Population	Many die in North	New foods introduced	Population grows, territory added

Objectives

1. Assess the positive and negative effects of Mongol rule of China.
2. Describe Chinese interactions with other civilizations under the Ming Dynasty.
3. Evaluate the effect of contacts with the west on the economy of China during the Qing Dynasty.

DEVELOP

Explain to students that this lesson will span three dynasties and 700 years, up to the early 1900s. Tell students that two of the three dynasties were non-Chinese and suggest that they look for similarities and differences between the two foreign dynasties as well as between the foreign and Chinese dynasties.

HISTORY
Critical Thinking

After students have read the lesson opener on p. 209, ask them whether they think Mongol rule would have an overall positive or negative effect on China. Then have them read The Mongols in China and list in two columns all of the positive or negative elements they find. Have students assign a value to each item—for example, from 1 to 5—and determine a total for each column. Call for a show of hands to arrive at a class position on Mongol rule.

The Mongols in China

While southern China prospered under the Song Dynasty, Genghis Khan made life very difficult for people in northern China. His well-organized and skillful

▲ *Mongol warriors, like the one in the upper picture, shot arrows from large bows with force enough to pierce armor. They rode small, sturdy horses like the one shown in the ceramic model above. This ceramic horse was found in a tomb from the Tang Dynasty.*

Mongol horsemen traveled for weeks at a time, making surprise attacks along the Chinese frontier. They learned to use catapults and gunpowder bombs to break through city walls. With few horses and inferior riding skills, Chinese armies were rarely able to defeat the Mongols. In 1234, a few years after Genghis Khan's death, the Mongols completed the conquest of northern China.

A Mongol Dynasty

Kublai Khan was chosen *khan,* or ruler, in 1260. In 1267, Kublai moved his capital from Mongolia to Beijing *(bay JIHNG)* in northern China in order to be closer to his subjects.

Kublai adopted certain Chinese traditions of government to make it easier for him to rule and be accepted by the Chinese. For example, he rebuilt the capital in the traditional Chinese style and declared himself emperor and Son of Heaven. He even founded his own dynasty, called the Yuan *(yu AHN),* which lasted until 1368.

However, unlike many northern barbarians before them, Kublai Kahn and the Mongols did not try to change Mongol culture so that it became more like Chinese culture. They used some Chinese systems of government, but only to strengthen Mongol rule. The most important government positions were held by Mongols or by other non-Chinese, including Marco Polo. The Chinese themselves were given the least important jobs. Government documents were usually written in Mongolian and then translated into Chinese.

Kublai Khan staged many attacks on the Song Dynasty in southern China. His forces finally overpowered the last group of Song defenders in 1279. Kublai thus became the first ruler to control all of China in over 300 years.

An Interruption in Progress

Although the Mongols maintained the basic Chinese government structure, their occupation of China disrupted economic and social development. It also slowed the remarkable progress of Chinese civilization under the Tang and Song dynasties. Millions of Chinese died during the decades of the Mongol invasions, including about half the population of the North. Some were killed by the Mongol attacks while many more

210

Access Activity

Divide students into three groups for a debate. One group will defend China's greater interaction with the rest of the world; another group will defend China's remaining isolated; and the third group will judge the debate. Have students review their arguments after reading the lesson.

Access Strategy

Ask students what they think the word *free* means in terms of one country's relations with another. *(For example, unrestricted trade, unrestricted travel.)* Then ask whether they think the United States is completely free in its relations with other countries. Encourage students to share what they know or have heard of current trade restrictions or immigration quotas. Discuss the value of open versus closed borders.

died from outbreaks of disease that often followed the attacks. Once highly populated areas, such as the eastern province of Anhui, were almost empty of people by the time the attacks ended.

Much of the wealth of the Tang and Song dynasties was lost as the Mongols burned cities and used vast areas of fertile farmland as pastures for their horses. They neglected canals and irrigation systems, and fertile fields soon became parched and barren. Many farmers lost their land to the Mongols, and many civil servants lost their jobs.

In the south, the Mongols hoped to win support from the wealthy landowners by letting them keep their lands. However, the Mongols seized land from the peasants, forcing them to seek work as hired hands on large estates. Thus the rich remained rich, while the poor became even poorer.

A Direct Link to the West

The Mongols disrupted Chinese life and culture. However, they strengthened China's links to the rest of the world. Camel caravans traveled throughout the vast Mongol Empire, from Beijing to central Asia to the Black Sea, carrying silks and ceramics for the Western market. The Mongols expanded the Chinese system of postal relays, establishing stations with supplies and horses for travelers who crossed the Asian steppe.

Travelers who crossed the Indian Ocean to China found thriving port cities, such as Guangzhou *(GWAHNG joh)*, sometimes known as Canton, and Fujien *(FOO jihn)*. Merchants, missionaries, and diplomats from the Arab world gathered in southern China's seaports. Through Arab merchants, many goods from the West and from southeastern Asia were traded in Chinese ports.

Increased contacts with the world not only expanded trade in China but also aided the spread of ideas in the West. For example, knowledge of printing and gunpowder probably spread from China to western Asia and then to Europe during the Mongol period. ■

■ *In what ways did the Mongol conquest of China affect the livelihood of most Chinese people?*

■ *The Mongols used farmland as pastures for their horses, thus eliminating the livelihood of many people involved in farming. However, their active support of trade increased the number of people involved in trading.*

The Ming Dynasty

Merchants prospered under Mongol rule. But most Chinese were eager to expel the foreigners who did not appreciate China's traditions. The Chinese rebelled against the Mongol rulers and founded a new dynasty in 1368. The rebel leader and founder of the Ming Dynasty was Emperor Taizu *(ty TSOO)*. The Ming Dynasty continued to rule China until as late as 1644.

Familiar Traditions

Emperor Taizu turned to familiar traditions for help in restoring the empire. He reestablished the civil service examination system and encouraged promising scholars. He undertook public works projects: repairing irrigation systems, building reservoirs, and extensively rebuilding the Great Wall. He helped homeless people by

◄ *Blue and white ceramics such as this Ming vase became the most popular kind of ceramics for trade. Cobalt, used to make the blue color on this vase, was first imported during the Mongol period.*

China

Research

Have students do research to find out about modern Mongolia. Have them locate information on its boundaries, resources, and population. The results of their research could take the form of a written report or a map.

Critical Thinking

Ask students to write a paragraph in which they discuss the Mongols' values and priorities. For example, why did the Mongols rebuild the capital in traditional Chinese style yet burn other cities and ruin farmland? Why did they remove Chinese from important government positions yet permit wealthy landowners to keep their land?

Study Skills

Ask students to explain China's changing relationship with the rest of the world during the Ming Dynasty. Students should mention that an early interest in showing off China's power was replaced by a distrust of foreign influence and a consequent restraint of trade. However, Ming rulers could not keep China isolated; therefore, both ideas and goods were eventually exchanged with the West.

► *The innermost square of the Imperial City was "forbidden" because most people were not allowed to enter the part of the city where the emperor lived.*

giving them land in regions left devastated by the Mongols. Unlike earlier emperors, Taizu also seized large estates, abolished slavery, and raised the taxes of the rich. Such measures narrowed the gap between rich and poor.

More Power to the Emperor

Ming rulers made themselves extremely powerful. For example, Emperor Taizu abolished the position of prime minister and controlled all departments of government directly.

While earlier emperors had welcomed open discussion of issues, Ming emperors made decisions in secret councils. Emperor Taizu even created a secret police force to spy on officials. Historians estimate that he accused at least 100,000 people of corruption or treason and then executed them. Such a ruler, who holds absolute power and uses it abusively, is called a **despot.**

The Ming emperors ordered a splendid new capital built on the site of the old Mongol capital of Beijing. During the early 1400s, about one million workers labored to complete the new city. Great walls, 40 feet high, surrounded a central area known as the Imperial City. Here grand halls, courtyards, and gardens provided a costly and lavish setting for the business of government.

A Superior Naval Power

At first, the emperors wanted to show the world the power of the Ming Dynasty. Between 1403 and 1433, court official Zheng He gathered a fleet of ships and made seven voyages to the Middle East and to the east coast of Africa. You can read more about Zheng He in A Closer Look on page 213.

But the Ming emperors soon decided that the rest of the world had little of value to offer China. They forbade further explorations and ended the costly voyages after 1433. They even made it a crime for any Chinese subjects to leave the country by sea.

▼ *The Forbidden City was the innermost square of the Imperial City. It was surrounded by a moat and a high wall. The Forbidden City contained palaces for members of the imperial family, and the Hall of Supreme Harmony, shown below, where the emperor held court. Why do you think that this part of Beijing was called the Forbidden City?*

Critical Thinking

Ask students to assess the impact of the Ming Dynasty on everyday Chinese life. Ask students to balance internal improvements *(for example, a return to a civil service examination system, various public works projects, abolition of slavery)* with such things as the secret police force and the construction and maintenance of the lavish imperial city.

Cultural Context

The Ming Dynasty was known for its appreciation of art. The court spent huge sums of money to fill the palace with bronze and porcelain objects. The well-known blue-on-white Ming porcelain first used abstract designs but later portrayed specific scenes. You might bring in a picture of Blue Willow china to illustrate. Ming porcelain became popular throughout China and as far away as Persia and Europe. Later, multicolored pieces predominated.

Art Connection

Have students find pictures of Ming porcelain in library books and then design their own bowls or vases in a style that was popular during the Ming Dynasty. Each bowl or vase should feature a single design that wraps around the entire piece and tells a story pictorially: students will need to show their designs from several perspectives to convey the complete story. Students could draw their designs on paper or, if possible, on real bowls and vases.

The Voyages of Zheng He

Fifty years before Europeans began searching for a sea route to the East, Chinese ambassador Zheng He explored the West. His emperor sent Zheng He to collect presents and to display the splendor and power of China. Under these orders, Zheng He sailed to southeastern Asia, India, Arabia, and Africa in the early 1400s.

Zheng He, detail from a woodcut by Lo Moudeng, 1597

Chinese Pearls

Everywhere he went Zheng He brought pearls and Ming vases to show off China's wealth. Most foreigners had never seen pottery so delicate and beautiful.

Ten times larger than European ships of the period, the junks Zheng He sailed had room for 500 people.

Ming Vase

Zheng He brought back giraffes, zebras, tigers, and ostriches. When they saw the giraffe, people told the emperor Zheng He had brought back a *qilin,* a mythical creature that appeared when the wisest emperor ruled. The emperor is said to have replied, "That is no *qilin,* and I am no wise man."

The Tribute Giraffe with Attendant, by artist Shen Du, A.D. 1414

China

213

Note: You may wish to use this Closer Look when discussing Ming emperors and their various displays of the power of rulers (p. 212).

More About Chinese Junks
These Chinese vessels, of which there were more than 60 in Zheng He's fleet, were much larger than European ships and easily able to weather the harshest ocean storms. They had as many as five masts, with sails that were stiffened with bamboo slats so they could be raised and lowered easily like venetian blinds. Their holds were partitioned with bulkheads, which made it possible to seal off leaking sections until port could be reached and repairs made. Europeans did not develop similar technology for centuries.

Research

Have students read more at the library about the voyages of Zheng He. Ask them to trace the course Zheng He followed on these voyages using a globe, and compare their extent with that of European explorers. Ask students how they think the world would be different today if China had established colonies, as Europeans did, in countries they discovered.

Visual Learning

Ask students to look at the Ming vase on p. 213. Tell them the Chinese called its pattern the "one thousand deer" motif, and that today this vase is considered to be far more valuable than all of Zheng He's pearls would be, because of the vase's beauty, age, and rarity.

Study Skills

Ask students to summarize the social changes that occurred in China during the Qing Dynasty. They should mention the expansion of Chinese territory, the growth of cities, the increasing success of the merchant class, the increase in population, and the improving literacy rate.

■ *At first they increased contact with the West. Later, they restricted trade severely. Trade continued overland and some ships sailed to Southeast Asia.*

Contact with the World

Until the mid-1400s, Chinese were among the best sailors in the world, visiting Africa and India almost 100 years before the Portuguese rounded the tip of Africa. The emperors, however, stopped financing expeditions and for a time outlawed overseas trade. Invasions from the north demanded their attention and money. Confucian attitudes looked down on merchants, and the bureaucrats resented the growing importance of traders and travelers. Still, goods such as tea and silk were shipped by caravan to central Asia and as far north as Russia, while some ships continued to sail to Southeast Asia and India to trade.

The first European ship to reach China was Portuguese, arriving in 1514. In 1557, the Chinese allowed the Portuguese to set up a trading station on the coast of China at Macao, near Guangzhou. As other Europeans arrived, the Chinese restricted them to certain areas along the coast. Some traders brought Jesuit missionaries with them. The missionaries worked at converting some Chinese to Christianity.

European traders seeking Chinese tea, silk, and porcelain brought with them sweet potatoes and corn from the Americas. They introduced beef and dairy cattle, which the Chinese then raised in the fertile pastures of the south. Increased trade also brought more gold and silver to China.

Throughout the Ming Dynasty, despotic rulers tried to restrict trade. Eventually, the people grew tired of heavy taxation and careless government. In the early 1600s, peasants in the southern regions rebelled against the despots. ■

■ *In what ways did the Ming dynasty affect trade and other contacts with the West?*

▼ *Notice the similarity between the imperial headpiece of this Qing Dynasty empress and that of Kublai Khan on page 209.*

The Qing Dynasty

The Ming ruler sent armies to the south to fight the peasants who were rebelling. A tribal people from the north, known as the Manchus, seized this opportunity to invade northern China. In 1644, they defeated the Ming and began the Qing *(chihng)* Dynasty, which was to last until 1912.

Like the Mongols, the Manchus wanted to keep their tribal traditions. Control of the army was kept in Manchu hands. For governing their subjects, however, the Qing adopted Chinese traditions. The Manchus continued the Ming government structure and civil service system. They even allowed many Ming officials to remain in office. Positions in the local government were filled mostly by Chinese rather than by Manchu officials.

Culture and Population

The Qing rulers also assigned scholars to edit Chinese literary and historical works, including the Confucian classics. The shift from woodblock printing to movable type in the 1500s triggered a boom in publishing and a rising literacy rate. In 1726, they sponsored a famous encyclopedia of 5,020 volumes.

Visual Learning

Ask students what the attire of the Qing empress on this page tells about the dynasty's approach to the Chinese people. Help students understand that the Qing rulers adopted many Chinese traditions and supported Chinese literature and arts.

Political Context

It wasn't until the mid-1700s that China was completely free from trouble with foreign nomads from the north. Though the Mongols had close cultural ties with the Manchus, they still loomed as a potentially hostile power on the frontier. To secure their cooperation, the Qing rulers established an institution known as the banner system. This was a system of group leadership in which the strongest leaders of the nomad tribes shared in top decision making. Each leader has his own military company, or banner. Originally made up of the eight most powerful Manchu tribesmen, the system was extended to include Mongols. Gradually the system was modified to suit Chinese institutions. The Grand Council, a body of advisers appointed by the emperor, took over the decision-making role of the banner chiefs. The emperor also allowed the banner chiefs less control over their forces, so that he could control them directly.

The population of China was about 60 million in 1400. By 1580, it had more than tripled, and it continued to increase rapidly during the Qing Dynasty. By 1850, the population was about 430 million. This population growth was partly due to the nutritious foods introduced during the Ming Dynasty. As population grew, China's territory also increased. During the Qing Dynasty, China doubled in size, expanding north into Manchuria and Mongolia, west into Tibet, and south into what is now Burma and Vietnam. Compare the map on page 533 with the map on pages 522 and 523 of the Atlas to see how China grew.

Cities and Trade

As China's population grew, the cities also expanded. Farmers sold their crops locally to merchants, who transported them to the cities. Peasants found work in small handicraft industries, such as weaving.

The Qing emperors allowed a limited amount of trade between China and other nations through the port at Guangzhou. For the most part, however, the Chinese believed that there was little to be gained by contact with other peoples. They preferred to follow the traditional patterns of Chinese life that had been outlined centuries before by Confucius. ■

What flags can you see over Guangzhou's harbor in this 1847 painting?

What aspects of traditional Chinese government did the Qing retain?

■ *The Qing retained the civil service system that the Ming Dynasty had restored. It also allowed many Ming officials to stay in office.*

R E V I E W

1. **FOCUS** What factors caused China to open trade at some times and remain isolated at others?
2. **CONNECT** What impact did Mongol rule have on the economic progress of the Tang and Song dynasties?
3. **ECONOMICS** How did the Ming attitude toward foreigners affect trade?
4. **POLITICAL SYSTEMS** Compare and contrast Mongol rule and the Qing Dynasty.
5. **CRITICAL THINKING** Why did invaders from the North not try to replace the Chinese culture with their own culture?
6. **WRITING ACTIVITY** You are a Portuguese trader who has just returned from Macao, China, in 1500, with a shipload of goods. Write a paragraph in which you describe your purchases and explain why you think Europeans will buy them.

China

C L O S E

Ask students to compare the Yuan, Ming, and Qing dynasties, using a chart like that shown in the Graphic Overview.

Answers to Review Questions

1. China was isolated more under some rulers than others. Mongol rulers fostered trade throughout their empire. Ming emperors first encouraged and then prohibited trade. Under Qing rulers, contacts with the West increased, and traders came to China in large numbers.
2. Mongols burned cities and neglected farmland. Also, many Chinese died from disease. As a result, economic growth was slowed, especially in northern China.
3. Ming rulers did not completely approve of trade, and they felt that foreigners had very little to offer China.
4. Mongols ignored most of Chinese culture. Qing rulers admired the Chinese. Under both dynasties there was increased contact with the West.
5. Answers will vary. Students may say that the Mongols were more interested in the riches to be found in China than in living as the Chinese did.

Homework Options

If you haven't already assigned the Art Connection activity on p. 212, do so now.

Study Guide: p. 33

UNDERSTANDING LOCATION DECISIONS

This skills feature uses topographic and land-use maps of China to teach students how physical features affect land use.

GEOGRAPHY
Map and Globe Skills

Ask the students to look at the maps shown on pp. 216 and 217. Have them use the titles and legends to determine the purpose of each map and the kind of information it provides. Ask specific questions about the maps: What does the topographic map show? (*Physical features.*) How is elevation indicated on the map? (*Colors.*) What does the land-use map show? (*Economic activities.*)

Then ask students to make some generalizations about China's topography. (*Includes mountains, deserts, lakes; elevations to over 10,000 feet.*) Have them do the same concerning China's land use. (*Wide range of economic activity, including farming, fishing, mining, and industry.*)

Comparing Two Maps of China

Here's Why

No single map can show you everything about a region. Maps have many purposes. Often you learn more by comparing maps than by examining them individually.

For example, you can compare topographic and land-use maps of China. Using the two maps together will help you see how China's physical features affect how people use land in China.

Here's How

Look at the topographic map on this page. It shows physical features such as mountains, deserts, lakes, and rivers. A key explains how colors on the map show elevations.

Study the land-use map of China on the facing page. This map helps you see what types of economic activities are most dominant in different areas of China.

Compare the two maps to see how geographical factors have influenced land use in Beijing. Find Beijing on the topographic map. You can see that a river and a connecting canal link Beijing with both the Yellow Sea and the Grand Canal.

Beijing's elevation is fairly low. Notice that deserts lie to the west and northwest of Beijing and that the land rises to the west and north. Beijing itself lies on the northern edge of the North China Plain. The map shows

that Beijing is approximately 40°N. Its latitude and elevation are much like that of central Illinois.

From the topographic map, you have learned that Beijing has water resources, which could be useful for farming, industry, and trade. Because of its latitude and elevation, you can infer that Beijing is in an area that would be a good place to live, work, and farm.

Now look at the land-use map to see what economic activities are important to Beijing. The map's color coding tells you that Beijing is in an urban and industrial area. Most of the surrounding land is used for farming. Find the city of Tianjin, southeast of

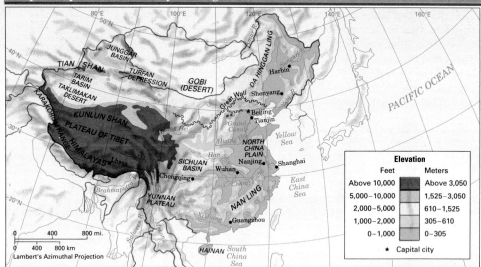

People's Republic of China: Physical Regions

Elevation

Feet	Meters
Above 10,000	Above 3,050
5,000–10,000	1,525–3,050
2,000–5,000	610–1,525
1,000–2,000	305–610
0–1,000	0–305

★ Capital city

Lambert's Azimuthal Projection

Chapter 8

Objective

Compare information on topographic and land-use maps to draw conclusions about how physical features affect land use. (Map and Globe Skills 1, Geography 3, Critical Thinking 3)

Research

Have students use library resources to investigate how topography has affected land use in their community or state. Ask them to report their findings to the class.

Collaborative Learning

Divide the class into small groups. Help each group choose a country or geographic region outside the United States to study. Have them use topographic and land-use maps to determine how physical features have affected land use in that area. Have each group make a brief report of their findings to the class.

Beijing. Goods manufactured in Beijing are shipped from port facilities near Tianjin. The photograph to the right helps illustrate the importance of the Grand Canal to these two cities. Beijing's industries clearly benefit from the water transportation routes that link the city to markets in China and abroad.

Try It

Look at the western area of China on the topographic map. Find the Himalayas, the Karakorum Shan (Range), and the Kunlun Shan. These mountains are located in the most rugged area of China.

Now locate China's cities. What areas have few cities?

What geographical features might account for this?

Study the land-use map. What is the main land use in the western half of China? What is the main land use in China's eastern half? What aspects of China's geography explain these differences?

Finally, locate China's urban and industrial areas on the land-use map. What information from the topographic map might help

explain why these urban and industrial areas are located here?

Apply It

Find topographic and land-use maps of your state in an encyclopedia or atlas. Compare the maps. Then write a short report about how information from the topographic map helps explain the locations of cities and land use.

People's Republic of China: Land Use and Resources

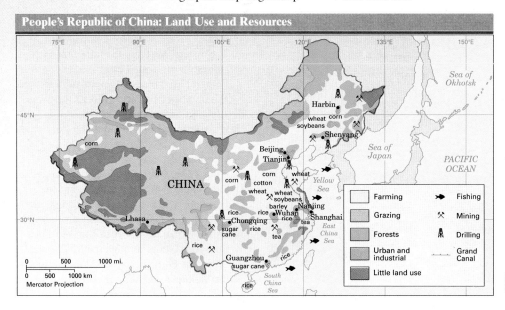

China

Answers to Try It

There are few cities in western China, where most of the land is desert or mountainous.

Grazing is the main land use in the western half of China. Farming is the main land use in the eastern half of China. Because of its deserts, high elevations, and mountains, most of western China is not suitable for farming. The land that can be used is good only for grazing. The land in the eastern half

of China is far less mountainous and more suitable for farming.

Most of China's cities are located in the eastern half of the country, and many of these cities are situated along the rivers.

All of the industrial areas are in the eastern half of China. Many are located along rivers or near the coast.

Answers to Apply It

Answers will vary.

Study Skills

Tell students to choose five locations shown on the maps on these two pages. Have them compare the topography and economic activities of each by summarizing the information in a table. Use *location, topography,* and *economic activities* as table headings.

Answers to Reviewing Key Terms

A. Answers:
1. Daoism
2. Buddhism
3. Confucianism

B. Sample answers:
1. **money economy:** We have a **money economy** and so we pay for things with currency.
2. **aristocrat: Aristocrats** could afford to pursue a higher education.
3. **despot:** One Ming emperor was a **despot** who accused people of treason or corruption and then executed them.
4. **meritocracy:** We are lucky to have a system of **meritocracy,** where people get promotions because of their performance.
5. **mandate:** In China, the people believed that their emperor was directed to rule by a **mandate** from heaven.
6. **currency:** Merchants appreciated paper **currency,** since coins were heavy to carry.

Answers to Exploring Concepts

A. Sample answers:
Imperial China
I.–An emerging empire
A.–Years of disorder
1.–*Geography creates regions*
2.–*Barriers protect the empire*
3.–A Period of Unrest
B.–*The spread of Buddhism*
C.–The reunification of China
II.–*The flowering of Chinese culture*
A.–The civil service system
B.–The birth of a new economy
1.–Better roads and waterways
2.–*New crops and farming methods*
3.–*A thriving merchant class*
C.–A continuing heritage
III.–China and the larger world
A.–*The Mongols in China*
B.–The Ming Dynasty
C.–*The Qing Dynasty*

218

B. Sample answers:
1. Landowners refused to pay taxes. Floods, famine, and plagues occurred. Peasants had no money for food.
2. The Himalayas, the Taklimakan Desert, and the Pacific Ocean provided protection. Steppes exposed the north.
3. China's economy improved. Farmers had good harvests.

Chapter Review

Reviewing Key Terms

aristocrat (p. 203)
Buddhism (p. 194)
Confucianism (p. 194)
currency (p. 206)
Daoism (p. 197)

despot (p. 212)
mandate (p. 204)
meritocracy (p. 204)
money economy (p. 206)

A. The following quotations describe three systems of thought and practice. Identify the key term by which each of these systems is known.
1. "I am content with my life because I live in harmony with nature."
2. "Through meditation, I can find peace and freedom."
3. "I believe in proper conduct, respect for elders, scholarship, and government service."

B. Identify the term that fits each clue below. Then write a sentence for each term.
1. It means the opposite of "a system in which people trade one kind of goods for other goods."
2. It means the opposite of "a member of a poor family with no influence."
3. It means almost the same as "dictator."
4. It means the opposite of a "system in which people are chosen and promoted without having to do their jobs well."
5. It means the same as "a command from someone who has authority."
6. It means the same as "money."

Exploring Concepts

A. Complete the following outline on your own paper. Fill in all the blank spaces.

Imperial China
  I. An emerging empire
    A. Years of disorder
      1. _____
      2. _____
      3. A period of unrest
    B. _____
    C. The reunification of China
  II. _____
    A. The civil service system
    B. The birth of a new economy
      1. Better roads and waterways
      2. _____
      3. _____
    C. A continuing heritage
  III. China and the larger world
    A. _____
    B. The Ming dynasty
    C. _____

B. Support each of the following statements with facts and details from the chapter.
1. The last Han emperor was faced with serious problems in the year 220.
2. Geography divided China but also protected it from invasion, except in the north.
3. The events following the fall of the Han Dynasty were not all bad.
4. Emperor Wen renewed important traditions and organized projects to focus the people's attention on common goals.
5. Chinese merchants found that paper money was an improvement over the old way of carrying their cash.
6. After 1279, many advances made under the Tang and Song dynasties were undone.
7. For many years, Chinese knowledge, inventions, and art passed to Europeans through Indian Ocean traders, and from overland caravans coming through the Middle East. When the Portuguese found the sea route to the Indian Ocean, this all changed.

The foreign market for silk grew. Nanjing became prosperous.
4. Wen accepted traditional gifts after refusing them three times. He organized building a capital city, the Grand Canal, and rebuilding the Great Wall.
5. The old coins, shaped liked doughnuts, were carried on strings. Merchants found them heavy. Paper money made doing business easier.
6. Millions of Chinese died during Mongol invasions. Mongols burned cities, used

farmland as pastures, and let irrigation systems fall into disuse.
7. Goods such as ceramics and silk; inventions such as gunpowder, the compass, and printing; and ideas such as Buddhism were transmitted along the Silk Road or across the Indian Ocean. With a direct sea route to Europe, the Silk Road became less important. The Portuguese also brought missionaries, who introduced Christianity to China.

Reviewing Skills

1. Look at the map on this page. It shows the location of China's Great Wall and Grand Canal. Parts of the canal were built under different rulers. A connecting canal was built to link Ta-tu, now Beijing, with the Grand Canal. Look at the topographic map on page 216. Think about China's topography. What geographical facts made it practical for the Chinese to build the canal where they did? What major rivers are linked by the canal?

2. Note the location of the Great Wall on the map on this page. Now find the Great Wall on the topographic map on page 216. The wall was built to prevent invasions. What geographic features shown on the topographic map are also natural barriers? How does the information on this map help explain the location of the Great Wall?

3. Study color coding on the topographic map of China on page 216. Which would show a greater change in elevation, a vertical profile of China at 110° E or a vertical profile of China at 30° N?

4. Beliefs and values of people in ancient China can be understood by studying some of their sayings. What are those sayings called?

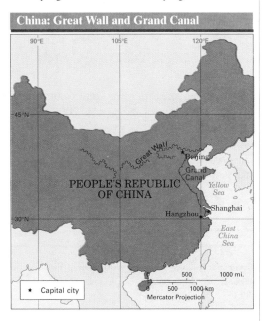

China: Great Wall and Grand Canal

Using Critical Thinking

1. Today, we are affected in important ways by things that were invented in China thousands of years ago. Think of at least three of these inventions you read about in the chapter. Explain how they affect modern people in everyday ways. In your explanation, be sure to mention both positive and negative aspects.

2. The Ming emperor Taizu showed by many of his actions that he was a despot. Citizens of modern nations like ours must constantly be alert to protect themselves from despotic leaders. Recall the despotic actions Taizu took while he was emperor. Then explain how modern citizens can identify leaders who have despotic tendencies.

Preparing for Citizenship

1. **WRITING A REPORT** In the United States, the civil service system is a meritocracy. Most workers in the national government and in many state and city governments belong to this meritocracy. Research the civil service system. Find out how it selects government workers. Then write a report for others who may want to make a career in government.

2. **COLLABORATIVE LEARNING** With your class, plan a large clay or plaster relief map of China. Join in one of these group activities: gather materials; decide which places to show on the map; make the relief map; create labels; prepare a talk to explain the map to visitors. Work out a schedule to show when each task should be finished.

China

Planning at a Glance
Japan

	Objectives	Reading Support *and* Other Resources	Diverse Learning Strategies
Lesson 1 Land of the Rising Sun *pp. 222–226* 3–4 days	• Explain how Japan was influenced by its geography. • Describe the effect of the Shinto religion on Japan. • Evaluate the influence of Chinese culture on Japan.	• **Workbook** or **Reading Support:** pp. 114–117 Review p. 27 Lesson Support/Transition p. 27 Multi-lang. Sum. pp. 53–54 • **Other Resources:** Geography Kit; Posters 5, 7; Study Guide p. 35; Study Print 7	Access Act. **(Extra Support)** TE p. 223 Study Skills **(Visual)** TE p. 224 Homework Options **(Visual)** TE p. 226 Audiotapes of Multi-language Lesson Summaries **(Auditory)**
Lesson 2 A Developing National Culture *pp. 227–230* 2–3 days	• Analyze the social and political events that led to a unique Japanese culture. • Characterize the literature of the Kyoto court. • Evaluate the impact of an isolated court on Japan.	• **Workbook** or **Reading Support:** pp. 118–121 Review p. 28 Lesson Support/Transition p. 28 Multi-lang. Sum. pp. 55–56 • **Other Resources:** Study Guide p. 36	Access Act. **(SDAIE)** TE p. 228 Access Strat. **(Extra Support)** TE p. 228 Writing **(GATE)** TE p. 229 Audiotapes of Multi-language Lesson Summaries **(Auditory)**
Lesson 3 The Power of the Shoguns *pp. 231–236* 2–3 days	• Identify the role of the samurai in Japanese government. • Evaluate the influence of Buddhism on Japanese culture. • Identify the cultural achievements of medieval Japan.	• **Workbook** or **Reading Support:** pp. 122–125 Review p. 29 Lesson Support/Transition p. 29 Multi-lang. Sum. pp. 57–58 • **Other Resources:** Poster 9, Study Guide p. 37	Access Act. **(SDAIE)** TE p. 232 Access Strat. **(Extra Support)** TE p. 232 Bulletin Board **(Visual)** TE p. 233 Art Connection **(Kinesthetic)** TE p. 235 Audiotapes of Multi-language Lesson Summaries **(Auditory)**
Lesson 4 Japan: Unified Yet Isolated *pp. 237–242* 2–3 days	• Evaluate the rule of the Japanese shoguns. • Describe the rise of the merchant class in Japan. • Describe the popular art forms of early modern Japan.	• **Workbook** or **Reading Support:** pp. 126–129 Review p. 30 Lesson Support/Transition p. 30 Multi-language Summaries pp. 59–60 • **Other Resources:** Geography Kit, Study Guide p. 38	Access Act. **(Extra Support)** TE p. 238 Access Strat. **(SDAIE)** TE p. 238 Research **(Visual)** TE p. 240 Role Playing **(GATE)** TE p. 240 Audiotapes of Multi-language Lesson Summaries **(Auditory)**
Skill: Recognizing Assumptions *p. 243* 1 day	• Recognize and evaluate assumptions in decision making.		
Chapter Review *pp. 244–245* 1 day		Chapter 9 Test pp. 33–36 *(See facsimiles on TE p. 567.)*	Assessment Multiple-Use Masters pp. 73–80

Reading Support Resources *for Every Lesson*

Reading and Review

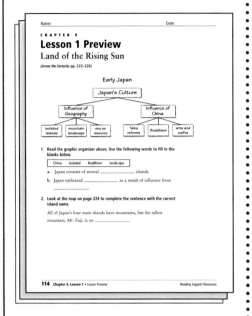

- **Chapter Overview*** p. 113
- **Lesson Previews*** using graphic organizers from the Teacher's Edition pp. 114, 118, 122, 126
- **Reading Strategies*** pp. 115, 119, 123, 127
- **Lesson Summaries*** pp. 116–117, 120–121, 124–125, 128–129
- **Lesson Reviews** pp. 27, 28, 29, 30

* **Workbook** includes starred items.

Multi-language Summaries

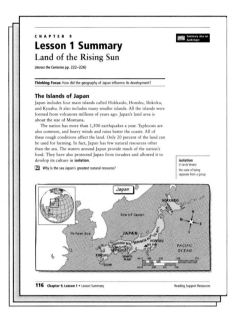

Lesson Summaries in:

- English (See Reading and Review.)
- Spanish pp. 116–117, 120–121, 124–125, 128–129
- Chinese pp. 53–60
- Hmong pp. 53–60
- Khmer pp. 53–60
- Vietnamese pp. 53–60

 Summaries available on audiotapes

Lesson Support / Transition
S D A I E

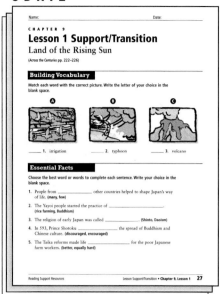

Activities for SDAIE
Specially **D**esigned **A**cademic **I**nstruction in **E**nglish

- **Lesson Support/Transition** pp. 27, 28, 29, 30

Technology Options

Internet Support
http://www.eduplace.com

Social Studies Center at Education Place

Internet support for Chapter 9:

- *Lesson at a Glance*
- *A Samurai*

Software
Student Writing Center ® (CD-ROM) (Macintosh® or Windows®)

School to Career

One way to study a culture is to study its literature, for the written word often represents the values and norms of the culture or those speaking out against it. Have students choose an author or poet on which to report. Is the writer considered "popular"? How did he or she become a published author or poet?

Character Education

Exposure to new and different cultures and ways of life often alters and expands the existing culture. Have students create a chart. On one side, list the benefits of diversity, such as increased tolerance for difference. On the other side, list negative results such as discrimination. How can each student help make the negatives positive?

Chapter 9
Japan

A Buddhist monk tends a simple garden of rocks and sand. A beautiful woman warrior knocks her foe from his horse. A poet writes three lines about a frog in a pond. What can these brief moments tell us about Japan since the 500s? The monk shows religious simplicity. The woman warrior symbolizes both a love of beauty and a respect for combat. And the poet reflects a quiet reverence for nature. Each quality has played an important role in the unfolding of Japan's unique history and way of life.

Throughout this period, Buddhism influenced life in Japan. The bowl and whisk are part of the Zen Buddhist tea ceremony. With the whisk, the drinker stirs and froths the tea.

794 Japan's emperor makes Kyoto the capital. One of the city's loveliest sights is the Golden Pavilion, built 600 years later as a mountain villa for Japan's rulers.

500	700	900	1100

220

552

632 Muslim armies begin building a great empire. By 750, they control lands from Spain in the West to India in the East.

A Land of Beauty and Violence

Japan's majestic mountains and lush green forests instilled in the early Japanese a profound appreciation for nature and beauty that would manifest itself in Japanese arts for centuries. This reverence for nature and an awe of its more violent aspects, such as tidal waves and earthquakes, also gave rise to the first known Japanese religion—Shinto. In Shinto, spirits are everywhere in nature, and Shintoists pray for nature's blessings in the form of good weather and abundant harvests.

The Early Japanese

The first people to settle Japan arrived probably from mainland Asia at least as early as 4500 B.C. In the 200s B.C., other groups came from the mainland, bringing with them the knowledge of how to grow rice.

Rice—Backbone of Japan's Economy

Japan's wet climate is ideally suited to the cultivation of rice. Soon after rice was introduced, it became Japan's primary staple crop. It was also the chief medium of exchange in Japan until the 1200s.

Since the 1300s, the Japanese have enjoyed *Noh* drama, featuring a masked dancer on a darkened stage. This wooden *Noh* mask is more than 500 years old.

Toyotomi Hideyoshi, left, becomes Japan's military ruler in 1585. Probably the most admired Japanese hero, he rises from a peasant background to become a powerful leader.

1800s Ando Hiroshige creates prints like the one above showing a warrior approaching a village in a beautiful setting.

1300	1500	1700	1900

1638–1715 King Louis XIV rules France and drains the treasury with his luxurious lifestyle and many wars.

1854

Understanding the Visuals

Little did the people who built the Golden Pavilion (p. 220) know that they were helping to save Kyoto from destruction more than 500 years later. During World War II, the Allies purposely did not bomb Kyoto in order to spare its historic treasures—among them, the Golden Pavilion.

The Hiroshige print (p. 221) is an example of the type of landscape painting, emphasizing Japan's scenic beauty, for which Ando Hiroshige was famous. In his last will and testament, Hiroshige wrote: "I set forth on a new journey; let me sightsee all the famous views in Paradise!"

Understanding Chronology

Refer the students to the timeline. Point out the long period of cultural continuity it indicates.

Rice-growing drastically changed the way of life in early Japan, for, unlike hunting and gathering, it required the concerted effort of the entire community. Because rice was so precious, feuding clans often destroyed each other's rice fields or irrigation ditches. In the 600s, those caught destroying valuable rice fields received severe punishment.

Chinese Culture in Japan

By the end of the 400s, Japan was using the Chinese writing system, and Chinese Buddhism was introduced into Japan from Korea and China about A.D. 552. Unlike Shinto, Buddhism offered learned scriptures, a caste of priests, an elaborate moral code, and the hope of reaching relief from suffering and the attainment of Nirvana. Shintoists, fearing Buddhism might eclipse Shinto, reconciled their beliefs with Buddhist doctrine. Buddhism and Shintoism coexisted peacefully. Today, the majority of Japanese practice both Buddhist and Shintoist rituals.

Buddhism sparked an interest in all things Chinese. Encouraged by Prince Shotoku, who hoped to strengthen the power of the Japanese emperor by copying the Chinese system of centralized rule, the Japanese began systematically to adopt various aspects of Chinese culture, including government, arts, literature, and architecture, into their own. Chinese influence on Japan waned after a few centuries, but Buddhism continues to play a key role in shaping Japan's culture.

INTRODUCE

Point out the lesson title. Tell students that the country of Japan is made up of many islands. Ask students to describe, using the map, the geographical features of the islands of Japan, and to name the nearby countries or continents. Have them read the Thinking Focus and ask them to predict how the fact that Japan is an island might affect its development. Have students read to confirm or reject their predictions.

Key Terms

Vocabulary Strategies: T36–T37
isolation—the condition of being separated from a group
Shinto—a Japanese religion whose followers believe that all things in the natural world are filled with divine spirits

500		900	1100	1300	1500	1700	1900

552   710

LESSON 1

Land of the Rising Sun

THINKING FOCUS

How did the geography of Japan influence its development?

Key Terms

- isolation
- Shinto

➤ *Izanagi and Izanami stood together on the Floating Bridge of Heaven and held council. "Is there not a country beneath?" they asked. Then they decided to create the islands of Japan.*

In the beginning, there was chaos. Then Heaven and Earth began to separate, and gods came to life. In the seventh generation, two gods— Izanagi and Izanami—decided to create a drifting land on the oceans. Izanagi reached down from heaven and thrust a jeweled spear into the ocean. When he withdrew the spear, drops fell from its point, forming the islands of Japan.

This is how the world began, according to Japanese mythology. The myths go on to tell how the next generation of gods struggled for power. The Sun Goddess gave life to everything around her. But her brother, the Storm God, was wild and fierce. He ruined his sister's rice crop and so upset her that she hid in a cave. Without her, heaven and earth went dark.

Other gods brought the Sun Goddess a beautiful bronze mirror and a sparkling jewel to coax her out of the cave. When she came out and told of the Storm God's mischief, the other gods banished him to the earth. His descendants lived on the Japanese islands.

After many years, the Sun Goddess sent her grandson, Ninigi *(nee NEE gee)* to take control of the island of Honshu. As symbols of his divine power, she sent with him her bronze mirror, her jewel, and a

great iron sword. Two generations later, according to legend, Ninigi's grandson Jimmu conquered the Storm God's descendants and in

222

Chapter 9

Objectives

1. Explain how Japan's geography influenced its early development as a nation.
2. Describe the effect of the Shinto religion on the politics of Japan.
3. Evaluate the influence of Chinese culture on early Japanese culture.

Graphic Overview

The greatest influences on Japan's culture were its geography and China.

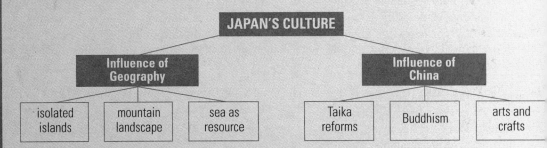

JAPAN'S CULTURE					
Influence of Geography			**Influence of China**		
isolated islands	mountain landscape	sea as resource	Taika reforms	Buddhism	arts and crafts

660 B.C. became the first emperor of Japan. Today, the divine objects described in the legend—the mirror, the jewel, and the sword—are the symbols of the emperor's heaven-sent power.

The Islands of Japan

Millions of years ago, volcanic mountains pushed up out of the Pacific Ocean. The tops of these mountains are the islands of Japan. As you can see from the map on page 224, Japan consists mainly of four large islands—Hokkaido *(hah KYD oh)*, Honshu, Shikoku, and Kyushu *(kee OO shoo)*. Japan also includes many smaller islands.

Together, the major Japanese islands total about 146,000 square miles, about the size of Montana. However, the four main islands are so spread out that their north-south curve covers about 1,200 miles. If the main islands were placed next to the eastern coast of the United States, they would reach from Maine to Georgia.

The Japanese islands lie on a very unstable part of the earth's surface. Each year Japan has more than 1,500 earthquakes, though most are mild. And 60 of its 150 major volcanoes are still active. Typhoons are also frequent in Japan. The heavy winds and rains batter its coasts, flood its valleys, and uproot its trees.

Mountains and hills cover most of Japan, leaving less than 20 percent of it for farming. Japan has few natural resources such as coal, iron, or other minerals. The sea has always been Japan's greatest resource. It provides food for the Japanese as well as transportation routes. Japan's seas have also acted as a natural barrier, keeping Japan in **isolation,** or setting it apart, from much of the world. The seas often shielded Japan from invasion by northern Asian tribes.

Because they live on islands, the Japanese were able to control the flow of people and ideas into their country. As a result, Japanese culture developed with few influences from other countries, except China. ■

Across Time & Space

Although Japan has few natural resources, its economy today is the second largest in the world. To keep its factories humming, Japan must import 99.7 percent of its oil, 96.3 percent of its natural gas, and 94.7 percent of its coal. It is no longer an isolated nation.

■ *Why is the sea Japan's greatest natural resource?*

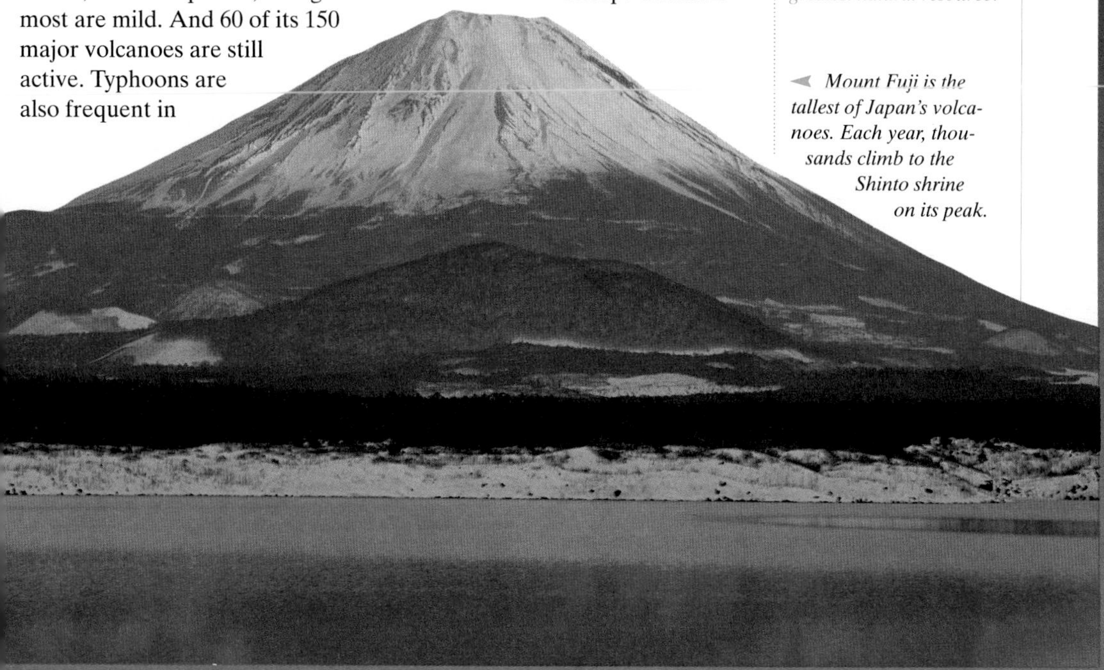

◄ *Mount Fuji is the tallest of Japan's volcanoes. Each year, thousands climb to the Shinto shrine on its peak.*

DEVELOP

Have students read the Japanese legend at the beginning of the lesson. Explain that there are many legends about the first Japanese people and emperor. Point out that Japan's title, "Land of the Rising Sun," comes from a legend about Japan's emperor descending from the sun goddess. Many Japanese legends also explain the geography of Japan. Tell students that in this lesson they will learn how Japan's geography affected the cultural development of its early peoples.

■ *The sea provided Japan with fish, trade and transportation routes, and a natural barrier to hostile invasion.*

GEOGRAPHY

Critical Thinking

Have students describe significant aspects of Japan's geography. *(Volcanoes, earthquakes, typhoons, mountains.)* Then have them list the advantages and disadvantages of living on the islands of Japan, based on its geography. *(Advantages: protected, abundant seafood; disadvantages: little farmland, few resources.)*

Access Strategy

Ask students if they have ever lived on or visited an island. Have them imagine what it would be like if the state they live in were in the middle of the Atlantic or Pacific Ocean. Ask them how the geography of their island state would affect the way they live. For example, if their state has little arable farmland—like Nevada, perhaps—they would be forced to look to the ocean and to the nearest continent for resources needed to survive. Ask students what their major industries would probably be, regardless of the geography of their island state. *(Fishing, tourism.)* Other points of discussion might include transportation, development of culture in isolation, interaction with people from other states, and military significance. Point out that the geography of Japan, a mountainous island nation with little fertile land and few natural resources, greatly affected the development of its people and culture.

Access Activity

Have students use the map on p. 224, as well as a world map, to complete the following activities:

1. Measure the distance from Japan to various places on the Asian mainland.
2. Determine what type of climate each island might have by comparing their latitudes to places in the United States.

➤ *Mount Fuji is on Honshu.*

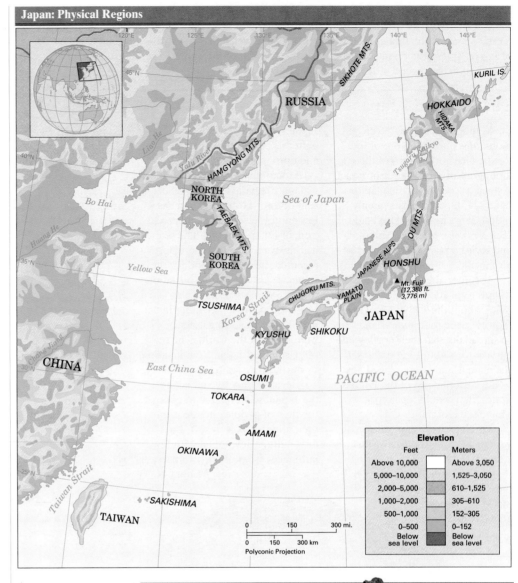

Japan: Physical Regions

Elevation		
Feet		Meters
Above 10,000		Above 3,050
5,000–10,000		1,525–3,050
2,000–5,000		610–1,525
1,000–2,000		305–610
500–1,000		152–305
0–500		0–152
Below sea level		Below sea level

▲ *On which island is Mount Fuji?*

➤ *Stone spearheads such as this show how people of the Jomon culture lived.*

The Early People of Japan

Despite its isolation, many peoples migrated to Japan. Stone tools and weapons found in Japan show that it has been inhabited for thousands of years.

Among the first people were hunter-gatherers who lived over 10,000 years ago. Other immigrants pushed them north about

200 to 100 B.C. The Ainu *(EYE noo)*, who live on Hokkaido, may be descendants of these hunter-gatherers.

Early Cultures

In about 8000 B.C., people of the Jomon *(JOH mahn)* culture, who probably came from Korea

224

Chapter 9

Historical Context

Little is known about Japan's early history. We learn about its history from archaeological remains, and from accounts of early Chinese travelers. In one account from the A.D. 200s, a Chinese traveler described Japan as consisting of 100 countries or regions. These regions were consolidated under one ruler—a queen named Pimiko. The people agreed to choose a woman ruler because under previous male rulers, Japan was torn by violence and war. Pimiko "occupied herself with magic and sorcery, bewitching the people.... She had one thousand women as attendants, but only one man.... When Pimiko passed away, a great mound was raised, more than a hundred paces in diameter. Over a hundred male and female attendants followed her to the grave. Then a king was placed on the throne, but the people would not obey him.... A relative of Pimiko named Iyo, a girl of thirteen, was [then] made queen and order was restored."

and northern Asia, first appeared in Japan. Ancient accumulations of shells, fishhooks, and harpoon points show that the Jomon were fishers and hunter-gatherers.

About 200 B.C., the Jomon culture was gradually replaced by a new, settled society known as Yayoi (yah YOY). The Yayoi settled in the fertile Yamato plain on the largest island, Honshu.

The Yayoi introduced the cultivation of rice in water, after which rice became Japan's most important crop. The islands' summer rains made the climate ideal.

The Yayoi used metal tools to irrigate and level the land. This development changed the Japanese from hunter-gatherers to farmers.

Between A.D. 200 and 300, an even more complex culture began to replace the Yayoi. Archaeologists call this the "tomb culture." The people of this culture left huge graves filled with such things as bronze mirrors, crowns, and clay figurines of armor-clad warriors and horses. These objects suggest that rulers of this culture were from a respected warrior class.

Early Religion

The religion of early Japan, **Shinto**, revolved around nature.

Shinto teaches that the natural world is filled with divine spirits, or *kami*. The highest-ranking *kami*, the Sun Goddess, came to be identified with Japan's emperor.

Sometime after 400, one ruling warrior clan from the plains of southeastern Honshu became more powerful than other ruling clans. From this family came Japan's first emperor. He was the first of a line of emperors from one family that continues even today. You have read how this family was said to be descended from the Sun Goddess. The idea of the emperor being divine may have been influenced by ideas from China. ■

▲ These "wedded rocks" are linked by a straw rope. In the Shinto religion, they are associated with the gods who created the islands of Japan.

■ How did the lifestyles of the peoples of the Jomon, Yayoi, and "tomb" cultures compare and contrast? How do we know?

▲ The Jomon culture takes its name from its pottery, created by pressing cords into the wet clay.

Korea and the Spread of Chinese Influence

By the 800s B.C., native peoples had established small tribal states in Korea, on the Asian mainland across from the Japanese islands. Rice growing had come to southern Korea from China some 2,000 years before. In 108 B.C., northwestern Korea was colonized by Han dynasty China, which set up military posts there. The trade that

followed began a concentrated cultural and commercial exchange between the two areas. In the rest of Korea, three conflicting kingdoms arose, Koryo in the northeast, Paekche (behk CHAY) in the southeast, and Silla in the southwest.

Beginning in Koryo in the 400s, Buddhism spread south from China into Korea. The courts took

225

Critical Thinking

Ask students why a ruling warrior clan in the Yamato region claimed to be descendants of the Sun Goddess. *(They wanted to increase their power.)* Ask them how this claim might have affected their power. *(People would eagerly follow the descendants of the Sun Goddess.)*

■ *We can tell the Jomon were hunter-gatherers by the empty seashells, fishhooks, and harpoon points they left behind. We know the Yayoi were a settled agricultural society from their iron farm tools. From the figurines found in their tombs, we know that the people of the "tomb culture" included armored warriors on horses.*

Collaborative Learning

Tell students that Shinto means "the way of the gods." Have them get into groups to research the Shinto religion. Suggest that they work together to find answers to some or all of the following questions: Why did Shinto merge so easily with Buddhism in the A.D. 500s ? Does Shinto have holy scriptures? How did Shinto evolve from nature worship? What traditions and rituals do Shintoists practice? Where do they worship? How was Shinto linked to Japanese government?

Language Arts Connection

Some scholars believe that the compilation about A.D. 750 of the *Man'yoshu*, a collection of nearly 4,500 poems, marked the true beginning of the Japanese poetic tradition. People from many classes of society—beggars, peasants, frontier guards, and aristocrats—contributed poetry to the anthology; and the anthology contains a huge variety of poetic forms and lengths. You may wish to select some poems for the class to read and discuss.

Critical Thinking

Have students reread the legend at the beginning of the lesson. Ask them what this myth tells us about how the early Japanese felt about themselves and the islands they lived on. *(They thought their land was created by the gods and that their rulers were descended from the gods. Therefore they probably believed that the gods favored them.)*

■ *Chinese culture first spread in Japan because of the introduction of Buddhism, which was popular in China, as well as the efforts of Prince Shotoku. He believed Chinese culture would modernize Japan.*

■ *Why did Chinese culture spread throughout Japan?*

▼ *At Kyongbok Palace in Seoul, South Korea, the Hyangwon Pavilion shows the influence of Chinese architecture. The Chinese influence can also be seen in the Great Buddha Hall (at bottom), one of the largest buildings at Nara, Japan, built in 745.*

on the new religion at first, then the nobles, then the common people. By the 660s, Silla had unified the country and was sending Buddhist scholars and priests to Japan.

The powerful Japanese Soga clan thought Buddhism would strengthen the government, as it had in China. They fought to have it accepted in Japan. In 593, Prince Shotoku, one of their relatives, came to the throne. He encouraged Buddhism and the spread of Chinese culture.

Shinto linked the Japanese to their homeland and their past. But Buddhism was accepted along with Shinto because it met spiritual needs not met by Shinto. Buddhism promised rewards to the faithful and the good.

After Prince Shotoku's death, members of the government imposed a series of Chinese-style changes called the Taika Reforms. Under this plan, the government

declared that all farmland in the provinces—areas outside the capital—was the property of the emperor. The land was divided into small plots, and clan leaders were assigned to oversee the land in their territories. In this way the central government gained more control over the clans as well as wealth from taxes on the land.

In 710, the government established a new capital called Nara in the Yamato plain. Religion and art flourished in Nara.

Although the Taika Reforms reduced the power of the clans, they had little effect on the lives of the peasants, or poor farm workers. In a collection of Japanese poems made about 700 and called the *Man'yoshu*, an anonymous poet described the hardships he faced in the countryside:

*H*ere I lie on straw
Spread on bare earth,
With my parents at my pillow,
My wife and children at my feet,
All huddled in grief and tears.
Must it be so hopeless—
The way of this world?

As before, small farmers still gave up part of their harvest. The difference was that after the reforms, they gave it to government officials instead of to clan leaders. ■

CLOSE

Draw the Graphic Overview on the board. Point out how the two branches reflect the two main influences on Japan's culture. Then have students add details to each branch.

REVIEW

1. **FOCUS** How did the geography of Japan influence its development?
2. **CONNECT** How is the history of Japan's first emperors different from that of China's early emperors?
3. **BELIEF SYSTEMS** Describe the Shinto religion. How is it related to the Japanese emperor?
4. **CULTURE** By what means did Prince Shotoku help

spread Chinese culture in Japan?
5. **CRITICAL THINKING** Contrast the effect of the Taika Reforms on the landowners and on the peasants.
6. **ACTIVITY** Find Japan on the maps on pages 530 and 531 of the Atlas. How much of Japan is used for crops? What else do the maps tell you? Organize this information on the chalkboard.

Chapter 9

Homework Options

Have students trace the development of early Japanese culture by making a timeline using the information in the lesson.

Study Guide: p. 35

Answers to Review Questions

1. Japan was physically isolated from other lands, which caused it to develop a unique culture undisturbed by political events on the Asian mainland.
2. Japanese emperors were believed to be descendants of gods. They ruled over an isolated culture. Chinese emperors were believed to have authority from Heaven. They tried to unite different cultures.
3. Shinto reflects a respect for the natural world. The emperor is said to be descended from the Sun Goddess, the highest-ranking Shinto deity.
4. Prince Shotoku encouraged the spread of Buddhism from China through Korea.
5. A noble with an estate probably had to give part of his land back to the state. The peasant's role would have been unchanged, except that peasants would be working for the state.

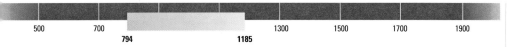

500
700
794
1185
1300
1500
1700
1900

LESSON 2

A Developing National Culture

Lady Dainagon is very small and refined, white, beautiful, and round, though in [behavior] very lofty. Her hair is three inches longer than her height. She uses exquisitely carved hairpins. Her face is lovely, her manners delicate and charming.

Lady Murasaki, *The Diary of Murasaki Shikibu*, c. 980–1015

This portrait tells us a lot about the qualities that were admired at the Japanese court around the year 1000. One important physical characteristic was a woman's hair. People thought the longer her hair, the lovelier the woman.

◄ *Lady Dainagon might have used hairpins such as these.*

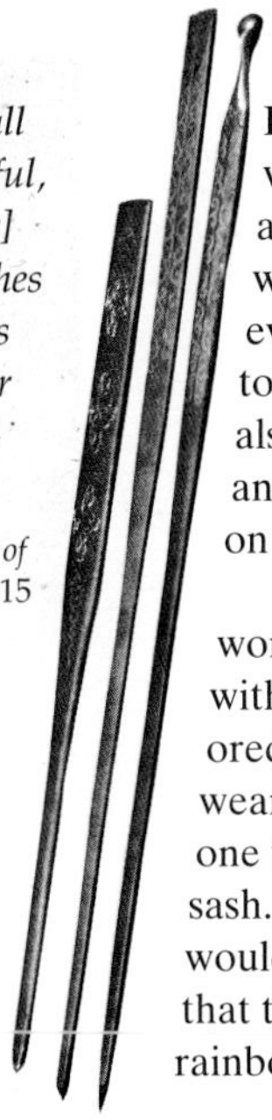

Because lightness of skin was admired, both women and men covered their faces with white powder. Women even blackened their teeth to heighten the effect. They also shaved their eyebrows and painted false ones high on their foreheads.

Members of the court wore clothing embroidered with gold, silver, and multicolored thread. A woman might wear 12 or more silk robes at one time, all tied with a single sash. The sleeve of each robe would be a different length so that the woman's arm was a rainbow of colors.

THINKING FOCUS

How did moving the capital to Kyoto affect the development of Japanese culture?

Key Terms

- regent
- courtier

A Court of Refinement

The finely dressed women and men of the court lived in the new capital of Kyoto, then known as Heian. Here they developed a culture of refinement and luxury. The capital that had been established at Nara in 710 was abandoned because the power of the government was overwhelmed by that of the Buddhist clergy. Buddhist temples and monasteries were a center for cultural activity. However, the clergy tried to interfere in politics. After the move to Kyoto in 794, the emperor strictly limited the number of Buddhist temples and monasteries that could be built. In this way he limited Buddhist influences on his government. Moving the capital also had the effect of isolating Kyoto from events in the provinces.

Even before the court moved to Kyoto, nobles of the Fujiwara

INTRODUCE

Read the lesson title and ask students to define *national.* Explain that in the 700s most of Japan's culture was Chinese in origin. Point out that the Japanese didn't develop a truly national culture until they moved the capital from Nara to Kyoto. Have them read the Thinking Focus and ask them to speculate as to why moving the capital to a new location might have helped Japan to develop its own unique national culture. Draw on the chalkboard the basic structure of the chart in the Graphic Overview. Fill in the headings Unique Culture, Isolation of Kyoto Court, and Provincial Unrest as shown. Then add the students' speculations where appropriate. Have students read to confirm or modify their speculations.

Key Terms

Vocabulary Strategies: T36–T37

regent—person who rules for a monarch

courtier—a person who takes part in the highly refined social life of a court

Graphic Overview

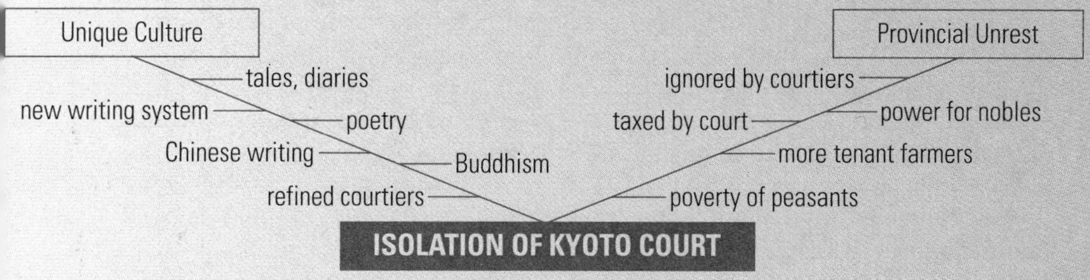

Unique Culture
tales, diaries
new writing system
poetry
Chinese writing
Buddhism
refined courtiers
Provincial Unrest
ignored by courtiers
taxed by court
power for nobles
more tenant farmers
poverty of peasants
ISOLATION OF KYOTO COURT

Objectives

1. Analyze the social and political events that led to the development of a unique Japanese culture in Japan.
2. Characterize the literature and writers of the Kyoto court.
3. Evaluate the impact of an isolated court on life in the provinces.

Point out to students that this lesson shows how the Japanese adapted Chinese culture to form their own uniquely Japanese culture. It focuses on the refined characteristics of this culture and the arts that flourished within it. Have students use a dictionary or thesaurus to find synonyms for *refined (civilized, elegant, tasteful, graceful)* to give them a better idea of what this culture was like.

CULTURE
Critical Thinking

Ask students if they think that Japan's culture would have developed differently if the capital had not been moved to Kyoto. *(Answers should focus on those parts of culture mentioned in the lesson—government, religion, literature, the arts, court life.)*

■ *A class of wealthy nobles, unconcerned with affairs outside of isolated Kyoto, pursued lives of leisure dominated by the arts. The culture of Kyoto was one of highly refined manners and taste.*

▲ *This fragment of a scroll shows a court lady named Kodai no Kimi in her many layers of robes. Their costumes were so heavy that many women found it difficult to move.*

■ *What were some of the activities of the courtiers at Kyoto?*

clan had come to be the most powerful of the emperor's advisers. The Fujiwara were related to the emperor by marriage. To make sure that their power would grow, members of the clan continued to marry into the imperial family. In fact, it became the custom for imperial princes to marry Fujiwara women. Members of the Fujiwara clan served as **regents** for the emperor, exercising power in the emperor's name for most of the time between 858 and 1185. As the Fujiwara clan's power over the imperial family increased, high government offices became increasingly closed to other families. Also, the emperor became much more a religious symbol than a government leader.

During this relatively peaceful period, Japanese culture flourished. Of the 100,000 people in Kyoto, only about 5 percent were **courtiers,** people who took part in the highly refined social life of the court. Nonetheless, it was these courtiers who created the culture of the period. Japanese literature and customs developed, using language and traditions that the courtiers had adopted from China.

The Kyoto court became one of highly refined manners and tastes, a place where delicacy was valued above all. Every action was thought to carry meaning and every event had great potential. Stories from the literature of the age tell of men falling in love with women after just a glimpse of hair from behind a screen.

The Shingon *(SHIHN gahn)* form of Buddhism was popular among courtiers. Shingon Buddhism involved elaborate ceremonies and rituals and stressed the importance of art and learning. Art, especially poetry and literature, became very important at the court of Kyoto. ■

The Literature of the Court

Poetry was the favorite form of writing among Japanese courtiers. They composed short poems for every occasion, and poetry contests were very popular.

The courtiers greatly admired beauty, especially in nature. Their writing expresses a sentimental sadness at the fragile beauty of natural things. This feeling of sadness at the death of beauty is expressed by the Japanese word *aware (ah WAH ray)*. What does this poem describe that might arouse feelings of *aware?*

*T*his perfectly still
  Spring day bathed in
  the soft light
From the spread-out sky,
Why do the cherry blossoms
So restlessly scatter down?

Ki no Tomonori, *Kokinshu,* c. 905

Access Activity

Ask students to list hairstyles and clothing styles that are popular today. Ask them if they know of hairstyles and types of clothing that were popular when their parents were young, in times past, and in other cultures. Have students read the opening of the lesson and then react to the Japanese standards of beauty and clothing described there.

Access Strategy

Ask students to name ideas or things the United States has borrowed from other cultures. Possible categories include food, language, government, sports, and architecture. Then ask them if they think that, despite these borrowings, the United States has developed its own unique culture. Explain that the United States adapted many things from different countries, which, over time, have acquired uniquely American characteristics. For example, we borrowed the English language from Great Britain, but American English differs in pronunciation, spelling, and slang. Ask students for other examples such as football *(from British soccer and rugby)* and Tex-Mex food *(distinctly different from Mexican food)*. Also point out that the United States is unique in having a mixture of so many different cultures. Explain that the Japanese gradually adapted what they borrowed from the Chinese to form their own unique culture.

New Writing Systems

One thing Japan borrowed from China was its writing system. Formal writing was in Chinese, and so was early poetry. But because they wanted to express feelings in their own language, the Japanese developed a set of characters called *hiragana* to represent Japanese. *Hiragana* symbols represent syllables rather than words. Compare Chinese symbols and *hiragana* in the chart on this page. Why do you suppose that writing in *hiragana* allowed the Japanese to be more expressive than writing in Chinese? Women, who were not expected to learn Chinese, used *hiragana* to write some of the greatest literature of the age.

Diaries and Tales

After poetry, diaries were the favorite form of writing. These personal accounts help us understand the values of the times. For example, the diary of Murasaki Shikibu, a lady of the Fujiwaras, tells a great deal about the roles of women. Because she was a girl, she was not taught to read or write Chinese. She tells how she found a way to learn:

Writing Styles of Japan				
Style	**Words** *(shinto)*	*(haiku)*	**Description**	**Origin**
Kanji	神道	俳句	Pictograms of concepts	Writing system adopted from Chinese characters
Hiragana	しんとう	はいく	Phonetic symbols of one syllable each	Writing system originated and simplified in Japan

> When my elder brother Shikubu no Jo was a boy, he was taught to read the Chinese classics. I listened, sitting beside him, and learned wonderfully fast, though he was sometimes slow and forgot. Father, who was devoted to study, regretted that I had not been a son.
>
> Lady Murasaki, *The Diary of Murasaki Shikibu*, c. 980–1015

The crowning literary achievement of this time was Murasaki's *Tale of Genji*, a long account of the life and loves of a fictional prince. Genji has the virtues valued by the Kyoto court: he is handsome and romantic. But the mood of the tale is often one of sadness. ■

▲ Hiragana *was developed during the 800s. Another style of Japanese writing,* katakana, *was developed later to spell words from foreign languages.*

■ *What kinds of literature developed at the court of Kyoto?*

▼ *Two ladies of the court watch as Prince Genji walks in the garden by moonlight.*

229

Study Skills

Emphasize the fact that literature and arts usually reflect the values of the society in which they were produced. Tell students to make a list of specific things that were important to the Kyoto courtiers. Then have them use these lists to determine the courtiers' values. Tell them to support their findings with information from the excerpts and text.

■ *Poems, diaries, tales, and long works of fiction were some of the kinds of literature that developed at the court.*

Writing

Tell students that writing letters was an extremely popular form of communication among the Kyoto courtiers. The courtier chose the color and texture of the paper very carefully, so that it would evoke the right mood in the recipient. Letters almost always contained poems. Penmanship was also extremely important. Have students assume the role of a Kyoto courtier. Tell them to write a letter that describes a day in the life of the court. Encourage them to choose paper whose shade and texture represent the feeling they want to evoke and to include a poem.

Cultural Context

Because the Japanese language is wholly different in structure from the Chinese language, it was extremely difficult to adopt the Chinese writing system to spoken Japanese. Spoken Japanese was much easier to write phonetically, for it had only 47 syllables.

Study Skills

Have students use their text and outside sources to find information about the city of Kyoto. Have them pinpoint its location, including its distance from the old capital of Nara, and describe its geography and how it was designed. *(It was patterned after the Chinese capital.)*

► *The Taira and Minamoto families.*

■ *The people in the provinces were not as interested in the arts as were the courtiers. Provincial nobles acquired more land. Most Japanese commoners were tenant farmers or menial laborers on the nobles' estates.*

CLOSE

Divide the class into groups of three. Have one student assume the role of a courtier, one the role of a landowner, and one the role of commoner. Explain that these three people have been thrown together because of a natural disaster, such as a volcanic eruption or earthquake. Tell students to have a conversation based on their knowledge of each class. For example, the commoner might complain that he could feed his family for a year if he had the money the courtier spent on clothing. The courtier might ignore him and read or write poetry.

230

Life in the Provinces

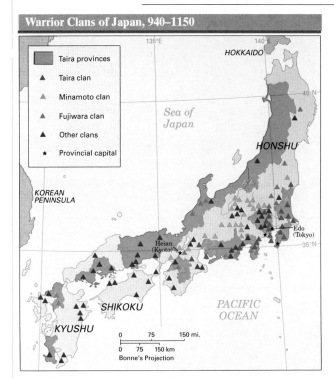

Warrior Clans of Japan, 940–1150

▲ *What families were in power in the provinces?*

■ *How did life in the Japanese provinces differ from life at the Kyoto court?*

The courtiers were able to live as they did because they were supported by what was produced in the provinces. Farmers paid part of what they grew to imperial tax collectors. Courtiers also collected part of what was produced on their private estates. But caught up in the life of the court, courtiers preferred to ignore the provinces. The responsibility for what went on there was in the hands of provincial nobles.

Japan had a long tradition of private ownership of land. In the 600s, clans in the provinces had been unhappy with the Taika Reforms, which had broken up their lands and reduced their power. Taking advantage of the imperial government's involvement with court life, provincial nobles took over more and more land. By 1100, some provincial nobles had acquired large estates that were free of government control.

In order to avoid paying taxes and serving as soldiers in the imperial army, many small landowners gave over their land to the nobles. They ended up as tenant farmers, paying rent in crops for the privilege of farming land owned by the nobles. Others became carpenters or menial laborers on the huge private estates. Most peasants remained as poor and as miserable as ever, spending their days at backbreaking work and their nights in crowded huts.

The Kyoto courtiers were out of touch with all of this. They were isolated in a world of luxury and fine culture at Kyoto. The "dwellers among the clouds," as they were called, probably looked upon lowly workers as barely human. ■

REVIEW

1. **FOCUS** How did moving the capital to Kyoto affect the development of Japanese culture?
2. **CONNECT** Why was Buddhism able to coexist with Shinto in Japan?
3. **HISTORY** How did the central government's involvement with court life affect conditions for Japanese farmers?
4. **CRITICAL THINKING** What do you think might have been the eventual result of the isolation of the ruling class at Kyoto?
5. **WRITING ACTIVITY** Imagine that you are a member of the emperor's court at Kyoto. Write a diary entry that describes either clothing worn by courtiers or your daily life at court.

Chapter 9

Homework Options

Have students write a paragraph describing how the different classes adapted the Buddhist religion to their specific needs.

Study Guide: p. 36

Answers to Review Questions

1. Kyoto was isolated from the common people. A class of wealthy nobles was able to pursue a life of leisure dominated by arts and literature and courtly refinements.
2. Shingon Buddhism was popular at Kyoto. It called for elaborate ceremonies and rituals. It also set a high value on poetry and literature. Yet it did not rule out the Shinto attitude of respect for nature.
3. As the central government weakened, provincial nobles took control and many small farmers became tenant farmers on large estates.
4. Answers will vary. Students should note that isolation would encourage cultural differences between the classes and weaken ties between people in different classes.

L E S S O N   3

The Power of the Shoguns

Jomyo Meishu of Tsutsui . . . was attired in a dark blue hitatare, a suit of black-laced armor, and a five-plate helmet. At his waist, he wore a sword with a black lacquered hilt and scabbard. . . . He let fly a fast and furious barrage from his twenty-four arrow quiver, . . . He abandoned the weapon and fought with his sword.

Anonymous, from
The Tale of the Heike, 1100s

The passage you just read is from a collection of Japanese tales of war. It tells of a warrior monk. Warrior monks, and many more warriors who were not monks, were common in Japan during the 1100s. It was a time when many swords slashed and many arrows struck their marks.

Life for these warriors was clearly quite different from that of the Kyoto courtiers described in *The Tale of Genji*. How had they come to exist in Japan?

What impact did samurai values have on Japanese culture and religion?

Key Terms

* shogun
* daimyo
* samurai
* denomination

◄ *This print of two warriors fighting with swords is from a famous series titled* One Hundred and Eight Popular Heroes *from Shuihu zhuan.*

231

Japan

INTRODUCE

Read the lesson title and ask students if they know or can guess what the word *shogun* means. *(Great general.)* Point out that as the central government at Kyoto lost power, military leaders in the provinces gradually gained power and fought for control of the government. Ask them to predict how the rise of the military class might affect the culture of Kyoto. Have students read the lesson to confirm or deny their predictions.

Key Terms

Vocabulary Strategies: T36–T37
shogun—a line of military leaders who ruled Japan
daimyo—the lord of an agricultural estate in feudal Japan, who supported the shogun
samurai—the feudal military aristocracy of Japan, from the term meaning "those who serve"
sect—a subdivision of a religious group

Graphic Overview

 Decline of power of Kyoto court → Rebellions in provinces → Rule by shogun and samurai class → Religious and cultural change

Objectives

1. Identify the factors that caused the rise of the samurai and explain the effect of the samurai on Japanese government.
2. Evaluate the influence of Buddhism on Japanese culture and explain how Buddhism changed as Japanese society changed.
3. Identify the cultural achievements of medieval Japan.

DEVELOP

Explain to students that this lesson focuses on the rise of a military class as the central government weakens, and the effect of this class on Japanese religion and culture. Draw the Graphic Overview on the chalkboard. Ask students to explain how this sequence of events took place.

POLITICAL SYSTEMS

Study Skills

Have students contribute to a spider map that depicts the structure of the political system under the shoguns. The main branches could include: Samurai, Daimyo, Shogun, Emperor, and Commoners. As students add details to each main branch, be sure they include the function of each group in the political system.

A Warrior Government

As the Kyoto court maintained its isolation, lawlessness spread in the provinces. Rebellions of nobles and even of Buddhist monks were put down by the government.

The central government had long been dominated by the Fujiwara family. But as its income from taxes and its power over provincial nobles decreased, the government came to depend on warlike provincial nobles for help in putting down rebellions. Also, less powerful nobles came to depend on the most powerful clans for protection. It was a dangerous age, one in which men—and even a few women, as this description shows—won fame as warriors:

> *T*omoe was especially beautiful, with white skin, long hair, and charming features. She was also a remarkably strong archer. . . . Tomoe galloped into their midst, rode up alongside Moroshige, seized him in a powerful grip, pulled him down against the pommel of her saddle. . . . She discarded armor and helmet and fled toward the eastern provinces.
>
> Anonymous, from *The Tale of the Heike,* 1100s

In the 1100s, nobles of the Taira and Minamoto warrior clans battled for control. By 1185, the Minamoto were victorious. Led by Yoritomo, they set up a warrior government. In 1192, Yoritomo was given the title **shogun,** meaning "great general," by the emperor.

Because Yoritomo didn't want his warriors to be distracted by court life in Kyoto, he made his headquarters at Kamakura, near present-day Tokyo. The emperor continued to live at Kyoto. But the real power resided in the shogun's headquarters at Kamakura.

The Rise of the Samurai

The shogun was supported by the nobles who owned large estates in the provinces. These nobles became known as **daimyo** *(DY mee oh).* Each daimyo relied on warriors to protect his estate. As reward for their service, the warriors themselves won small pieces of land.

The warriors were called **samurai** *(SAM uh ry),* which means "those who serve." The samurai became a new class in society— mounted, armored warriors who often held positions as officials in the provinces. You can read more about a samurai warrior in A Moment in Time on page 233.

The Impact of Foreign Invasion

Under the Kamakura shoguns, Japan enjoyed stable rule and trade with China flourished. In the late 1200s, however, Japan was threatened by the Mongols under Kublai Khan. In 1274, when Mongol forces launched an attack from Korea across the Sea of Japan, they had to turn back because of a storm. But in 1281, Mongol forces numbering as many as 150,000 landed on Kyushu.

How Do We Know?

HISTORY *For warriors in medieval Japan, the ritual and ceremony of the battle were as important as the battle itself. Stories describing heroism in battle were popular. The Tale of the Heike, for example, tells about battles between the Taira and the Minamoto in the 1100s.*

▼ *Cherry blossoms were sometimes used as a symbol for samurai in the literature and art of Japan. A samurai knew that his time on earth was likely to be as brief as the flowering of a cherry tree.*

232

232

Access Activity

Have students study the picture of the samurai on p. 231. Then have them look at the picture of the Kyoto courtiers on p. 229. Tell students to compare people in the two pictures by listing their characteristics, such as clothing and facial expressions.

Access Activity

Ask students what the United States would be like, politically, economically, and culturally, if the police force was gradually done away with. Students might suggest that anarchy would reign and that the crime rate would be astronomical because people wouldn't worry about getting caught while committing a crime. People would band together for protection. Those who were the strongest—in numbers, weapons, and physique—would control the land and weaker people. Trade would be almost impossible because of raiders, so communities would have to be self-sufficient. Cultural achievements would dwindle as people became more concerned with staying alive rather than expressing creative impulses. Prestige would be measured by military accomplishments. Introduce these possible consequences if students do not suggest them. Ask them what their own lives might be like in such a chaotic society.

A Samurai

*10:06 P.M., November 18, 1274
In a manor house on the Japanese
island of Kyushu*

Note
He has tucked away the small piece of paper the messenger rushed to him. Our samurai's lord writes that the fierce Mongols will land at Hakata Bay tomorrow morning!

Armor
Made of small, strong iron plates, the suit still lets him swing his sword. Putting it on takes hours, but our samurai expected this battle. He assembled the armor days ago and left it waiting on a stand.

Long Sword
Fired red-hot, folded, and hammered sharp a hundred times, the long blade is called the soul of a samurai. He never goes anywhere without it.

Helmet
The lacquered metal smells of incense, which the samurai burns inside the helmet. He does this so that if an enemy cuts off his head, it will smell sweet.

Mask
It was designed to terrify his enemies and it will. The polished iron face is strong enough to stop a spear.

233

Note: In addition to using this Moment in Time when discussing the rise of the samurai, you may wish to use this illustration when introducing Lesson 3 of Chapter 10, Two Feudal Societies.

BELIEF SYSTEMS
Visual Learning

Bushido, the way of the warrior, represented a religious commitment to the military life. A heroic death in battle was the samurai's most honorable goal.

The samurai's training began at the age of five or six when he was taught to shoot at a target using a small bow and bamboo arrows and to ride a horse. As an older boy, he also endured long fasts and barefoot hikes in the snow.

More About the Samurai's Armor
With only 25 pounds of protection (compared to the European knight's 55 or 60), the samurai could trudge through rice paddies or scale castle walls. The suit's scales of lacquered iron, laced together with silk cords, were easily mended if a cord got cut.

Bulletin Board

Each article the samurai wears or carries has a distinct purpose. Ask students to bring in pictures of people who must dress in uniform for a specific sport or occupation. Students should annotate their pictures, describing the purpose of each article of clothing or equipment. Display these on a bulletin board.

Writing

Before tangling with his adversary, a samurai combatant would announce his name, ancestry, and previous deeds of heroism. When the fight was over, the winner complimented his defeated opponent on his bravery before killing him with the smaller of his two swords. Write the speech this samurai will make before and after meeting his Mongol opponent in the morning.

Visual Learning

Ask students to use the picture to explain how this samurai lives up to his military code: "A samurai should live and die sword in hand. . . . To be brave and warlike must be his invariable condition." *(Armor assembled, incense in helmet, mask to terrify enemy, sword ready.)*

■ *The shogun was supported by the daimyo, who in turn was supported by the samurai.*

▲ *This beautifully decorated saddle belonged to a shogun of the 1500s. It symbolizes two arts of samurai tradition—the arts of war and peace.*

■ *How were the warrior governments organized?*

The Mongols used crossbows that shot farther than Japanese arrows, and catapults that hurled flaming bombs. But the samurai, relying on their swords, fought fiercely. After 50 days of battle, a great typhoon helped the Japanese achieve victory. The winds and rains rolled over Kyushu, destroying the Mongol fleet. The Japanese called the typhoon the *kamikaze,* or "divine wind," believing that their gods had aided them.

After the Mongols had been repelled a second time, the Kamakura shogunate was plagued by economic troubles caused by the war. The government was unable

to reward the samurai for their military services. Angry and resentful, a huge army of samurai marched into Kamakura and burned it to the ground. After a series of battles, a new shogunate founded by the Ashikaga family took over Japan. In 1392, it moved the shogun's headquarters back to Kyoto. There the warriors married into noble families and adopted the ways of the Kyoto courtiers, receiving instruction in etiquette, literature, and music.

The Ashikaga shogunate lasted until the late 1500s through times of peace as well as war. Together, the Kamakura and Ashikaga shogunates make up the period of history, from 1185 to about 1600, known as medieval Japan. ■

Development of Religious Denominations

During medieval times, Buddhism changed to reflect the needs of the Japanese people. Different religious groups, or **denominations,** of Buddhism developed.

Pure Land Buddhism, for example, stressed chanting the name of Amida Buddha. Amida is considered to be a spiritual Buddha who lived many eons ago. Amida was supposed to have established a paradise in the west, beyond the setting sun. His believers would chant his name while watching the sun set. This denomination dif-

➤ *This painting on silk represents the Amida Buddha.*

fered from earlier types of Buddhism in stressing happiness in afterlife rather than finding peace, or enlightenment, in life on earth. It taught that believers would be reborn in a blissful, pure land, or paradise. Amida Buddhism became more popular in Japan as disorder increased in the countryside. It was popular among peasants as well as the upper classes.

One of the most controversial denominations in Japan was founded by the monk Nichiren in the 1200s. Nichiren taught that the only truth was to be found in the Lotus

Chapter 9

Critical Thinking

Stress the fact that the samurai were a completely new class that gained in importance because the daimyo needed to protect their estates. Have students assume the role of a daimyo searching for samurai to protect his estates. Tell them to write a want ad describing the qualifications necessary for the job. *(Loyalty, skill in battle, courage.)*

Writing News Reports

Refer students to the description of the Mongol invasion of Japan on pp. 232 and 234. Have them write a news account, complete with headlines and interviews, about the invasion and the effect of the Kamikaze. You might have students include an illustration of the Kamikaze wiping out the Mongol fleet. Have students share their accounts in class.

Cultural Context

During the Kamakura shogunate, Zen temples were austere and plain. However, as Zen became more popular with the ruling class, the temples grew more elaborate, and Zen monks eventually became important patrons of the arts themselves. They sponsored wrestling and archery contests for illiterate samurai, as well as pottery, painting, calligraphy, and flower arranging for their more sophisticated patrons.

Sutra, believed to be the Buddha's last teaching. All other denominations were false, he taught, and unless Japan turned from these false religions, it would perish.

Disciples of Zen Buddhism were concerned with individual enlightenment more than national well-being. Zen taught that physical and mental exercise would produce a sudden recognition of the nature of existence.

As the samurai class became important, Zen became more popular. Zen appealed to many samurai, partly because it stressed exacting spiritual and physical discipline as the path to enlightenment. The samurai themselves had been through harsh physical training, and approved the discipline required of Zen converts.

Also, some Zen masters scoffed at book learning and at logic and other mental skills. They taught that enlightenment would come only by breaking away from logic. Zen students were required to sit still while they meditated for hours on seemingly absurd puzzles such as "What is the sound of one hand clapping?" This form of meditation pleased the many samurai warriors who could not read. ■

■ *How was Japanese society affected by Zen Buddhism?*

CULTURE

Critical Thinking

Emphasize the link between Buddhism and Japanese medieval arts. Have students make a chart that illustrates these links. The major art forms, such as Noh drama and the tea ceremony, should be included.

■ *Buddhism affected the way people studied, the way they fought wars, their government, as well as art and culture.*

A Unified Culture

Buddhism greatly influenced the arts of medieval Japan. Zen, for example, stressed the importance of the moment. It taught that a person who is in a hurry to complete something fails to experience the natural world fully. Zen art stressed the process, the way that activities were performed.

This emphasis on process can be seen in arts and ceremonies that developed in medieval Japan and are still practiced today. For example, the tea ceremony was first developed by Zen priests and then adopted by members of the court. As you can see in the pictures below, the tea ceremony has continued into modern times.

Process, in the form of gestures and dance steps, is emphasized as well in Japanese Noh drama, which

▼ *After many years, every movement in a tea ceremony became formalized and took on special meaning.*

A Japanese Tea Ceremony

After rinsing their hands and mouths with water from a wooden dipper, guests crawl through a small passageway to enter the tea room.

The scroll one sees on entering the alcove is a single line of calligraphy, often drawn by a Zen priest. Guests spend some time examining the scroll, clearing the mind in preparation for the ceremony.

The host enters and serves a light meal, which is followed by tea.

Tea bowls are made by hand. Their shape varies according to the time of the year. The "winter" bowl shown here is deeper than a "summer" bowl would be.

235

Research

Have students find out more about the arts of medieval Japan. You might assign different groups of students to research different kinds of art, such as painting, literature, flower arranging, and dance. Have students bring in pictures or other examples of the type of art they are researching. Encourage them to find out more about Chinese and other influences on Japanese art.

Art Connection

After students have researched the different types of Japanese art (see Research activity on this page), have each group assemble materials to create a work of art. Materials might include rocks and sand for a rock garden, or brush and ink for a painting. Have members of each group work separately or together to make Japanese-style works of art. Have them share their creations with the class.

Critical Thinking

In a paragraph have students compare and contrast the role of the military in Japanese medieval society and in the United States today. Before they write, encourage them to list the traits of both systems in a two-column chart. Categories for comparison could include Influence on Government, Attitude of Soldiers, and so forth.

△ *In this garden established at a Zen temple about 1450, each detail provides a subject for meditation.*

➤ *Most Noh plays concern an encounter between a troubled spirit and a priest or bystander. People dance the action of the plays and chant to the music of a flute and drum. The demon mask was used in Noh dramas of the 1200s.*

■ *What new art forms developed in medieval Japan?*

developed from both Shinto and Buddhist forms of worship. A masked dancer, supported by minor players and a chorus, presents a slow dance-drama. The actors wear lavish costumes of gold brocade and vivid colors, but the stage is bare. The script is very poetic, and the plot is simple.

Another form of art that shows Buddhist influence is the Japanese garden. Buddhism teaches that people are a part of nature, and Buddhist gardeners thus find their art in nature. Rock gardens are often found at Zen temples. The gardens are meant to provide a calm, quiet

place for meditation. Zen emphasizes severity and restraint, as well as appreciation for simple and natural forms. The rock gardens consist only of rocks and of sand raked in patterns. The rocks are placed so as to suggest natural things, such as a mountain canyon, a beach, or a seascape. Gardeners sometimes search for years for just the right rock to place in a garden.

Flower arranging, incense blending, and painting are other medieval art forms influenced by Buddhism. Most of these art forms are still popular in Japan today. ■

R E V I E W

1. **FOCUS** What impact did samurai values have on Japanese culture and religion?
2. **CONNECT** Compare and contrast the values and achievements of the Japanese courtiers with those of the samurai.
3. **CITIZENSHIP** Ceremony is important in all cultures. What are some occasions in the United States

where ceremony is important? What formal gestures are used in these ceremonies?
4. **CRITICAL THINKING** Why might Zen Buddhism have appealed to many samurai?
5. **ACTIVITY** Based on what you have learned about the tea ceremony, develop a ceremony or ritual for serving a beverage or food in your classroom.

Chapter 9

■ *Noh drama, gardening, flower arranging, and incense blending developed in medieval Japan.*

C L O S E

Have students read aloud the two quotes about samurai in battle on pp. 231 and 232 of the lesson. Ask them to list the values represented by these samurai. Then have students list the ways in which these values affected other aspects of Japanese life—religion and culture, for example.

Homework Options

Have students select major events from the lesson and put them on a timeline.

Study Guide: p. 37

Answers to Review Questions

1. The samurai created some trends in Japanese culture, such as an enthusiasm for Zen Buddhism. Zen and other forms of Buddhism, in turn, had a great influence on art and culture.
2. Courtiers valued refined behavior, art, literature. They also developed new writing systems. Samurai valued discipline, strength, and fearlessness in battle.
3. Answers will vary. Students may think of an inauguration or a swearing-in, when a

person is asked to raise his or her right hand and repeat an oath of office.
4. Zen stressed rigid spiritual and physical discipline. The enlightenment attained through that discipline allowed a warrior to rid himself of worldly concerns and concentrate on fighting. Many samurai warriors were illiterate, and thus were attracted to Zen's de-emphasis of book learning.

500   700   900   1100   1300   1500   1900
                                        1570   **1854**

L E S S O N   4

Japan: Unified Yet Isolated

eneral Oda Nobunaga had, by 1591, begun to unify his war-ravaged country. One of his major battles was against a Buddhist monastery whose monks had dared to help an enemy army. He ordered his warriors to destroy all 3,000 buildings of the monastery and kill all 20,000 within. His officers pleaded with him not to do this, but he remained firm.

Nobunaga's forces encircled the monastery. With ferocious cries, they stormed the center, burning the buildings and destroying all within—priceless books and art, monks, soldiers, even children. Nobunaga explained his orders this way:

I have devoted myself to the hardships of warrior life in order that I might restrain the turbulence within the land. [But these monks] are themselves traitors to the country. If . . . they are not destroyed now, they will again become a peril to the nation.

Oda Nobunaga, from
Hoan Nobunaga-ki, c. 1570

This and similar acts of such great violence were not unusual in Japan during the late medieval period. By the late 1400s, both the shogun and the emperor had become dependent on whatever daimyo happened to control the capital.

THINKING FOCUS

Why did the Tokugawa shoguns want to keep Japan isolated?

Key Terms

- succession
- haiku

◄ *Isolated warrior clans throughout Japan made constant raids on enemy camps, as seen in this detail from a scroll*

237

Japan

INTRODUCE

Point out the lesson title and explain that after the mid-1300s, Japan was wracked by civil war that left the country in a state of chaos. Tell students that this lesson focuses on Japan's unification, through war, and on its subsequent isolation from the rest of the world. Ask students to predict why a period of isolation might follow unification of a country.

Key Terms

Vocabulary Strategies: T36–T37
succession—the sequence in which one person after another succeeds to a title, throne, or estate
haiku—an unrhymed Japanese poem consisting of three lines with five, seven, and five syllables, respectively

237

Objectives

1. Evaluate the methods Japanese shoguns used to unite Japan.
2. Describe the conditions that led to the rise of the merchant class in Japan.
3. Describe the popular art forms that emerged in early modern Japan.

Graphic Overview

| Wars of unification | → | Political and cultural isolation | → | Rise of merchant class | → | A new culture |

CHAPTER 9 *Lesson 4*

DEVELOP

Draw the Graphic Overview on the chalkboard. Point out to students that this series of events chain shows the cause-and-effect relationship between developments and reflects the structure of the lesson. Have students think about and discuss the idea of cultural isolation and contrast it to geographic isolation (Lesson 1). Ask how a country might go about enforcing a policy of cultural isolation.

POLITICAL SYSTEMS
Basic Study Skills

Point out that strong and patriotic leaders like Nobunaga guided Japan away from civil war and away from the rest of the world. Have students make a two-column chart that lists the measures taken by Japanese leaders to unify Japan. *(Modernize army, move capital, and so forth.)* Tell students to list each measure taken in column one, and to note its effectiveness in column two.

238

➤ *A samurai warrior would have been proud to own this steel sword, which was made in the 1100s. When did Japan take the final step to isolate itself from the West?*

➤ *This statue of Tokugawa Ieyasu marks his tomb. Ieyasu was from a peasant family, but established a line of rulers.*

▼ *White Heron castle near Kyoto was begun in 1581 by Hideyoshi and completed in 1609 by a member of the Tokugawa clan. To reach it, an enemy would have had to pass through 11 barricades. However, the castle was never attacked.*

Political Struggles in Feudal Japan

1185, The Minamoto clan crushes the Taira family and rules from Kamakura.

1274, Mongols make their first attempt to invade Japan.

| 1200 | 1300 | 1400 | 1500 |

An All-Powerful Shogunate

Weakened by court life in Kyoto, the Ashikaga shogunate had been unable to keep control. Warring nobles had nearly destroyed the capital in a struggle for power. In the provinces, various daimyo fought for control.

Wars of Unification

From the midst of this chaos emerged Oda Nobunaga—a powerful leader, fierce and stubborn. Recognizing the limitations of swords and arrows, he armed his troops with muskets, which had been introduced to Japan by Portuguese traders. With his more modern army, Nobunaga soon controlled more than a third of the country.

After Nobunaga's death, one of his generals, Toyotomi Hideyoshi, took control and within five years conquered all the remaining provinces. When Hideyoshi died in 1598, another power struggle followed. In 1600, Tokugawa Ieyasu *(ih yeh YAH soo)* was victorious. He became shogun in 1603.

The Tokugawa Shogunate

Tokugawa Ieyasu established his shogunate in Edo, now called Tokyo. There he built a nearly indestructible fortress. In 1605, he turned over the shogunate to his son. Ieyasu thus established a line of **succession,** or inheritance, of the shogunate, much like that of a kingship. The Tokugawa shogunate was to last for more than 250 years.

238

Chapter 9

Access Activity

Ask students to imagine that the United States government has just announced a policy of isolation from the rest of the world. No one can leave the United States, and trade and communication with other nations will stop completely. Ask students to discuss how our society would change with such a strict policy of isolation.

Access Strategy

Ask students what their favorite forms of entertainment are. *(Going to the movies, listening to rock music, watching TV, playing or watching sports.)* Then ask them if they think their favorite pastimes are popular with the American general public. Explain that these popular forms of entertainment are part of what is called "popular culture"—the culture created by and for the majority of the public. Ask students what forms of entertainment might not be as popular with the general public. *(Going to the opera or to art museums, listening to classical music.)* Point out that entertainment and art forms that were once part of the popular culture sometimes lose a wide audience but remain important to a small percentage of the population. *(Example: Opera was very popular with European immigrants at the turn of the century.)* Ask students if they can think of a popular art form today that might become less popular within the next 50 years.

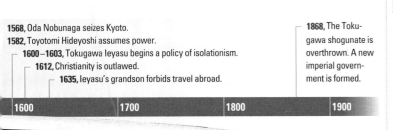

1568, Oda Nobunaga seizes Kyoto.
1582, Toyotomi Hideyoshi assumes power.
1600–1603, Tokugawa Ieyasu begins a policy of isolationism.
1612, Christianity is outlawed.
1635, Ieyasu's grandson forbids travel abroad.

1868, The Tokugawa shogunate is overthrown. A new imperial government is formed.

| 1600 | 1700 | 1800 | 1900 |

Under the Tokugawa each daimyo was required to swear an oath of loyalty to the shogun and to give military aid when called upon. In addition, each daimyo had to spend part of every other year in Edo, serving the shogun. The daimyo were forced to leave their wives and eldest sons in Edo when they returned to the provinces.

Foreigners in Japan

When Portuguese traders reached Japan in 1542, they also brought Catholic missionaries.

By the early 1600s, the shogunate saw these foreigners as a threat. The Tokugawa knew of Europe's religious and political wars. They feared the turmoil might spread to Japan. Also, they feared that if the daimyo became rich from foreign trade, they might rebel.

Between 1612 and 1635, therefore, the shogunate issued decrees that outlawed Christianity, restricted travel, and banned virtually all European trade. In effect, Japan was set on a policy of strict isolation from western influences. ■

■ *What steps did the Tokugawa shoguns take to unify Japan?*

UNDERSTANDING ISOLATION

The islands of Japan were cut off, or isolated, from other countries. Even so, in the 1630s, Japan's government felt the need to adopt a policy of political and economic isolation. How were these kinds of isolation different?

Kinds of Isolation

Mountains, jungles, or seas can isolate a culture. This is geographic isolation. For example, the Hawaiian islands were unknown to

the rest of the world until Captain James Cook landed there in 1778.

Japan's isolation in the 1630s was deliberate. In America today, the Amish deliberately isolate themselves from the culture that surrounds them. Living in farming communities in Pennsylvania and the Midwest, they practice simplicity as a religiously dictated way of life and do not use modern inventions such as electricity or telephones.

Results of Isolation

Geographic, or deliberate, isolation limits the influences of other cultures and often strengthens the unique qualities of a culture.

Also, isolation limits technological and commercial growth. An isolated culture cannot borrow or adapt the ideas of other cultures. For Japan of the 1800s, the lure of increased trade and new knowledge was to make isolation less attractive than it had been.

239

Japan

Critical Thinking

Emphasize the fact that the Tokugawa shogunate took measures to control the four classes and to isolate Japan in order to preserve its traditional economy and social structure. Ask students how these measures affected the merchant class, and how they actually helped Japan's economy and social structure to change dramatically. (*Measures caused commerce to increase and the merchant class to prosper.*)

■ *The shoguns moved the capital from Kyoto to Edo, and established a line of succession. They also began to control landowning daimyo, and isolated Japan from European influences.*

239

Social Context

The Tokugawa shogunate issued laws governing, among other things, military households. The object of these laws was to ensure peace and order within each estate. The laws stressed traditional values that were popular in medieval Japan, and included quotes from earlier rulers:

Visits of the daimyo to the capital are to be in accordance with regulations.

Restrictions on the type and quality of dress to be worn should not be transgressed.

Lord and vassal, superior and inferior, should observe what is proper to their station in life.

Persons without rank shall not ride in covered litters.

The samurai of the various domains shall lead a frugal and simple life.

When the rich make a display of their wealth, the poor are humiliated and envious. Nothing engenders corruption so much as this, and therefore it must be strictly curbed.

Study Skills

Have students research the influence of Christianity in Japan just before Japan's isolation. They should include information about the roles various shoguns played in prohibiting Christianity and their motivations. Ask students how Japanese religion might have developed differently if missionaries had been allowed to stay.

Critical Thinking

Ask students to speculate as to why the merchants were attracted to the new, popular arts, rather than the older, more refined arts. Then ask them how the merchants actually helped to create these new arts. *(The merchants had money to spend on these entertainments.)* Tell students to use examples from the text to support their conclusions.

■ *The merchant class rose as the dominant economic group as Japan developed a money economy.*

Control of the Classes

The shogunate enforced a strict social system designed to preserve a traditional Japan. There were four official classes below the shogun and daimyo. From highest to lowest they were samurai warriors, artisans, peasants, and merchants.

Restrictions on Each Class

To keep the daimyo in line, the shogun made them swear an oath of allegiance. The shogun took away the warriors' lands and instead paid them salaries for their services. The once-illiterate samurai learned to read and write and became educated administrators.

Since artisans didn't threaten the shogun's control, few restrictions were placed on them. They thrived in towns, selling their wares to samurai and merchants.

Peasants made up the bulk of the population. Because they were so numerous, the government placed many restrictions on them. Peasants were forbidden to travel beyond the land on which they worked. Also, tax collectors took about half of their crops, leaving them with just enough to survive.

At the bottom of the social scale were the merchants. Merchants had to live within towns and were excluded from political affairs. Finally, merchants were not allowed to dress lavishly or to live in luxury.

The Rise of the Merchant Class

Despite government regulations, the merchant class prospered. More and more merchants were needed to bring food, cloth, and other goods to Edo. They also traded in other cities where the daimyo and their followers might stop to rest.

Before the Tokugawa era, money was not much used in Japan. But merchants found money much less bulky to carry than the bushels of rice traditionally used for trade. By 1600, gold and silver coins were in use, and by 1700, Japan's economy was based largely on money. Merchants controlled the flow of money by setting prices and charging interest on loans. They grew rich from their trade and their power grew with their wealth. ■

Across Time & Space

In 1996 the tiny, mineral-poor islands of Japan accounted for 17.4 percent of the world's gross domestic product (GDP). GDP is the total value of all the goods and services produced in a country during a single year.

■ *How did Japan's economy change during the Tokugawa era?*

➤ *A daimyo and his samurai warriors make their way to Edo. Daimyo were required to spend part of each year at the shogun's court.*

A New and Different Culture

The merchants had leisure time and money. They spent it on new forms of entertainment that be-

came available in cities. In the late 1600s, areas of cities were set aside as pleasure quarters. There city

240

Critical Thinking

The shogunate ranked the four social classes of Japan from highest to lowest. Ask students to speculate as to why each class was ranked where it was.

Research

Assign groups of students to research one new Japanese art form that became popular in the late 1600s. Have students bring in pictures or prepare other visual aids and present their findings to the class. Give students the option of acting out or performing the art form they've researched.

Role Playing

After students have shared their research about new art forms (see Research on this page), tell them to assume the role of a daimyo or samurai on his first visit to the new pleasure quarter in a city. Have students describe in a letter to the shogun their reactions to the events and activities in this quarter, along with their suggestions to the shogun as to what to do about these new forms of "lower-class entertainment."

dwellers could find theaters, teahouses, gambling houses, wrestling, and public baths.

The upper classes officially scorned these amusements as lower-class entertainment. They clung to the traditional arts such as Noh theater and the tea ceremony. Still, they allowed the pleasure centers to prosper and gradually were attracted there themselves.

Some of the new cultural forms, such as Kabuki theater, were long lasting. Kabuki theater had its origins in performances of wandering ballad singers and dancers, who acted out stories by dancing and gesturing. Kabuki, which is still popular today, was a rich blend of music, dance, and mime, and involved spectacular staging and costumes. The plays' subjects ranged from adventures of brave samurai to tales of romance and broken hearts.

Besides plays for the Kabuki theater, new forms of literature also included epic novels about samurai exploits and short poems called **haiku.** A haiku is a poem of three lines that is intended to create a mood or bring about a sudden insight into human existence. A haiku has 17 syllables. The first line has five syllables, the second seven, and the third five. Matsuo Basho, one of Japan's greatest poets, wrote hundreds of haiku, including the following:

> Old pond:
> Frog jump-in
> Water-sound.
> Matsuo Basho, Untitled, 1686

During the 1500s and 1600s, education spread to all classes, to varying degrees, and the economy boomed. When Japan emerged from its self-imposed isolation and reopened its doors in 1854, the West saw a unique and successful civilization. ■

▲ *Small bunraku puppets were often used in plays performed in the cities. Entertainment and everyday scenes were common subjects of prints such as the one below.*

■ *What role did the new merchant class play in the development of a new popular culture?*

◄ Remind students that the haiku shown here is translated into English from Japanese, so it has lost its syllabic pattern. Here is one by the poet Chora that fits the pattern in English:
   After spring sunset
   Mist rises from the river . . .
   Spreading like a flood.

■ *Wealthy new merchants spent much of their extra time and money on amusements in the pleasure quarters of Japanese cities.*

Southeast Asia

In the first thousand years A.D., Southeast Asia was greatly influenced by China and India. Goods and ideas were exchanged in what are now Burma, Thailand, Laos, Cambodia, Vietnam, Malaysia, Singapore, Indonesia, Brunei, and the Philippines. The earliest towns in the region seem to have been started in Vietnam, as shown by the great stone fortifications at Co Lao *(koh LWAH)*. In addition, there were many trade and religious centers around which farmers or fishers lived.

From early times, Hindu ideas and styles spread into the area, affecting Southeast Asian ideas about monarchy, law, religion, art,

241

Japan

241

Cultural Context

Students may be familiar with the early Khmer *(KMAIR)* Empire, which arose in Cambodia in the 800s. In this Hindu-influenced region, the god-king's position was supreme, and in the 1100s the Khmer began building the great temple complex of Angkor Wat. Later, they built nearby Angkor Tom, a massive temple with a golden tower. The tower rested on four huge carved heads. The temple complexes were spectacular, but they placed a heavy economic strain on the empire.

For building the temples and maintaining the priests, dancers, musicians, and officials, the Khmer needed tens of thousands of villages to work for them. At the height of their prosperity, the Khmer had 12.5 million acres of land under cultivation. At last the Khmer people rebelled against their god-kings. They turned to a type of Buddhism that emphasized poverty and simplicity. By the early 1400s, Angkor had been abandoned.

■ *Hindu ideas about monarchy, law, religion, art, and architecture spread from India to Southeast Asia. Buddhism also spread from India. Chinese influences were political and military. Islam came via Sumatra. Indian Ocean trade brought money, ideas, and eventually, colonization.*

architecture, and language. The states that grew there were often Hindu or Buddhist or both. Chinese influences were more political and military. The mighty rulers of China forced these states to pay tribute or be taken over.

Outside Influences

China ruled Vietnam as a province from about 100 B.C. to A.D. 900. In addition to using Vietnamese trade networks, China was eager to use the expert sailing skills of the local people to export its silk and spices. The Vietnamese would sail to the islands of Indonesia. Ships from Indonesia carried goods to Malaya. From there, Indian ships would take the goods west. Indian traders often settled in the Southeast Asian ports. At the trading city of Oc Eo *(ahk YOH)* in Cambodia, archaeologists found ancient Roman coins and Indian jewelry.

Islam first came to Southeast Asia at Perlak, on the northern coast of Sumatra, in the 1290s. It spread gradually through the islands and into the mainland. Many of the port cities and coastal states welcomed Islam not only as a religion, but also as a way of cementing ties with the Muslim traders who came from Arabia and

■ *How did outside influences from China, India, and the rest of the world affect Southeast Asian civilizations?*

Persia. With the profits of trading, some powerful leaders challenged and overthrew the older inland states, whose wealth was based on agriculture. The richest and strongest of the new Muslim states was Malacca, on the west coast of Malaya.

Trade and Resources

Malacca became the center of trade for Southeast Asia in the 1500s. It lay at the junction of the Indian, China, and Java seas. Here traders from as far away as Europe came for cottons and silks, pepper and cloves, perfumes and dyes. When European powers found a direct sea route to Southeast Asia, they began a period of colonization for many Southeast Asian states.

Besides international trade, there was much trade between regions, the coastal areas, the inland regions, and the islands. Southeast Asia is rich in resources. The people's system of agriculture raised enough rice to feed a large population. They domesticated many plants and exported many, including yams. Some plants were used for dyes, others for medicines, and others to eat. Some regions exported timber, oils, resins (a tree product used for inks and varnishes), or minerals. ■

CLOSE

Write the lesson title on the chalkboard. Divide the class into groups. Have students work together to create an idea web for the entire lesson. Then have the whole class participate in creating a web on the board. The web should show the main ideas, key points, and details of the lesson. *(For example, main ideas: isolation, control of classes, changes in culture.)*

R E V I E W

1. **FOCUS** Why did the Tokugawa shoguns want to keep Japan isolated?
2. **CONNECT** How did the Tokugawa shogunate go about creating stability that had been lacking in medieval Japan?
3. **ECONOMICS** What was the role of the merchants within Japan's early economy?
4. **GEOGRAPHY** How did the geography of Southeast Asia

contribute to its religious diversity?
5. **CRITICAL THINKING** How does the phrase "it takes money to make money" apply to the merchant class under the Tokugawa shogunate?
6. **WRITING ACTIVITY** Write a haiku of your own, following the form explained on page 241. Use a single image from nature as the subject of your haiku.

Chapter 9

Homework Options

Have students research why Japan finally opened its doors in 1854, and how the Japanese adapted to the Western ways.

Study Guide: p. 38

Answers to Review Questions

1. The Tokugawa shogunate feared that Europe's religious and political turmoil would spread to Japan. It also feared rebellion from the daimyo if they became rich from foreign trade.
2. Tokugawa Ieyasu moved the capital, began a line of succession, and took steps to control the daimyo.
3. Merchants were tightly controlled. They lived within towns and were excluded from political affairs. Yet their trade

spurred Japan's transition to a money economy.
4. Hinduism and Buddhism spread overland through Southeast Asia from India and China. Through Korea, Buddhism spread to Japan. Traders brought Islam and Christianity over the Indian Ocean.
5. Merchants controlled money, and thus could buy and sell goods and charge interest on money loaned to samurai.

Recognizing Assumptions

Here's Why

Suppose you are planning a party. You choose pizza for food because you assume that most people like to eat pizza. An assumption is an idea that is accepted as fact without proof or demonstration. Often the assumption is so deeply rooted in a culture or in an individual's beliefs that it is not even stated.

For example, look at the picture of court women from *The Tale of Genji*. You might assume that women played a subordinate role in Japan in the 900s. However, you learned in Lesson 2 that Lady Murasaki contributed greatly to Japanese culture, writing perhaps the world's first novel.

Most assumptions can be proven to be either true or false, depending on the actual facts. In either case, you need to be aware of your unstated assumptions in order to correctly evaluate your conclusions.

Here's How

Assumptions that are correct can help you make sound decisions quickly even when you don't have all the facts. Incorrect assumptions, on the other hand, can cause you to make poor and even harmful decisions. Use the following steps to help you identify and evaluate your assumptions.

First, put your assumptions into words. Try to express in words exactly what ideas you accept as facts that influenced your decision or your feelings.

Second, identify the basis of your assumptions. Think about why you hold certain assumptions. Many useful assumptions are based on experience. Others are an unquestioned part of a culture or of certain religious beliefs. Remember that people in different cultures have different values. Be careful not to apply your assumptions to cultures where they are not appropriate.

Third, check your assumptions for accuracy. Be sure you have enough accurate information to test your assumptions. When you test your assumptions against more accurate or more complete information, you may find that they are incorrect.

Try It

Reread The Impact of Foreign Invasion on pages 232 and 233 in Lesson 3. Think about what assumptions you might make about the intensity and outcome of the battle. Then follow the three steps listed in Here's How. How well did the facts bear out your assumptions? On what factors were your assumptions based? What factors did your assumptions leave out?

Apply It

Write a sentence or two identifying the assumptions that might have led to each of these actions. Explain on what the assumptions might have been based.

1. You expect a homework assignment. However, you make plans to go to a volleyball game.
2. You go with friends to a local park and they suggest swimming in a lake you've never been in before. You dive into the water.

243

Answers to Try It

Assumption: The samurai were greatly outnumbered and overwhelmed by the Mongols. Basis: The Mongols had crossbows and catapults that hurled flaming bombs. The samurai only had swords. Check for accuracy: The samurai were twice victorious over the Mongols. The original assumption did not account for the intimidating nature of the samurai mask and armor nor the effect of the *kamikaze* on battle conditions.

Answers to Apply It

1. Assumptions: The assignment would be short and easy. Basis: The teacher usually gives short, easy assignments; the student usually does the assignments quickly.
2. Assumptions: The lake is deep enough; the lake is safe for swimming. Basis: Belief that the friends have swum and dived in the lake at some other time; belief that lakes in parks are safe for swimming.

Objective

Recognize and evaluate assumptions in decision making. (Critical Thinking 1, 2; Culture 4)

Answers to Reviewing Key Terms

A. Sample answers:
1. **Courtiers** used language and traditions from China to develop literature and art.
2. **Shogun** means "great general."
3. Buddhism had many **denominations.**
4. In 1605, Ieyasu turned over the shogunate to his son and thus established a line of **succession.**

B. Sample answers:
1. True.
2. False. **Shinto** revolved around nature.
3. True.
4. False. The **haiku** of Japan were poems that had 17 syllables.
5. False. Japanese warriors were called **samurai,** which means "those who serve."
6. True.

Answers to Exploring Concepts

A. Sample answers:
593: Prince Shotoku rules and encourages Buddhism.
794: Kyoto becomes capital of Japan.
1281: Kamakura shogunate repels Mongols.
1603: Tokugawa shogunate begins.
1635: Japan forbids travel abroad.
1854: Japan ends its policy of isolation.

B. Sample answers:
1. Around 400, a clan on Honshu, said to be descended from the Sun Goddess, became more powerful than other ruling clans. All of Japan's emperors have come from this family.
2. Buddhism spread from China to Korea in the 400s. In the 660s, the Korean Silla Kingdom sent Buddhist scholars and priests to Japan.
3. Under the Taika Reforms, all farmland in the provinces belonged to the emperor. In effect, the government increased its control over the clans and gained wealth from taxing the land.
4. The Kyoto court was one of refined manners and tastes. The courtiers valued delicacy, and they admired art and beauty.
5. The clan leaders were to oversee the lands for the emperor. Instead, they took over more and more land. By 1100, some nobles had acquired large estates.

Chapter Review

Reviewing Key Terms

courtier (p. 228) samurai (p. 232)
daimyo (p. 232) denomination (p. 234)
haiku (p. 241) Shinto (p. 225)
isolation (p. 223) shogun (p. 232)
regent (p. 228) succession (p. 238)

A. Be sure you understand the meanings of the key terms. Then answer each question by writing one or more sentences.
1. How did courtiers influence the culture of Japan between 858 and 1185?
2. What title means "great general"?
3. Which Japanese religion had many denominations?
4. How was a line of succession to the title "shogun" established?

B. Write whether each statement below is *true* or *false.* Then rewrite the false statements to make them true.
1. Japan's seas have kept Japan in isolation from much of the world.
2. The religion of early Japan, Shinto, revolved around ancient feudal rites.
3. The nobles who owned large estates became known as daimyo.
4. In the 1600s, poets in Japan often wrote haiku, poems with exactly 17 lines.
5. Japanese warriors were called samurai, which means "those who rule."
6. From 858–1185, members of the Fujiwara clan were often regents for the emperor.

Exploring Concepts

A. Copy the timeline below on your own paper. After each date, write the importance of the date in the history of Japan. The first entry is done for you.

B. Answer each question with information from the chapter.
1. How did Shinto lead to a political tradition for the emperors of Japan?
2. What role did Korea play in the spread of Chinese culture in Japan in the late 500s?
3. What changes were made by the Taika Reforms? What were the results?

4. What values characterized the court at Kyoto?
5. What task were the clan leaders given under the Taika Reforms? Instead of performing this task, what did they do while the courtiers were preoccupied?
6. How were the Mongols defeated in 1281? What effect did the Mongol invasion have on the Japanese government?
7. What decrees did the Tokugawa shogunate issue between 1612 and 1635? What was the effect of these decrees?
8. When Japan reopened its doors to foreigners in 1854, how had it changed?

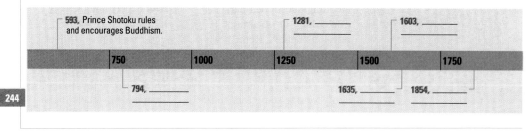

Chapter 9

6. The samurai fought the Mongols. After 50 days of battle, a typhoon destroyed the Mongol fleet and defeated them. The government couldn't repay the samurai, who then burned Kamakura to the ground.
7. Between 1612 and 1635, the shogunate restricted travel, banned European trade, and outlawed Christianity. Japan was isolated from western influences.
8. During the 1500s and 1600s, education spread to all classes, and the economy boomed. When Japan emerged from its isolation in 1854, the West saw a unique and successful civilization.

Reviewing Skills

1. Turn to page 225 and read the paragraphs in the first column that describe the Yayoi culture. The last sentence of this section is, "These objects suggest that rulers of this culture were from a respected warrior class." What assumption does the author make in this sentence?
2. Read the first paragraph on page 239. The Tokugawa shoguns forced the daimyo to leave their wives and eldest sons at the shogun's court in Edo when the daimyo returned to the provinces they governed.

What assumptions did the shogun make about the daimyo?
3. Use an atlas to find out which areas of Japan have few cities. Then look at the topographical map of Japan on page 224. What geographical features might account for the lack of cities in certain areas?
4. You want to summarize the history of Japan on a poster that shows the most important historic events. What graphic device would you use to give visual impact to written facts and dates?

Using Critical Thinking

1. The men and women of the Kyoto court lived very different lives from the rest of the Japanese people. What were the positive effects of their lifestyles at court? What were the negative effects?
2. During the late 1500s, General Oda Nobunaga began to unify Japan. He destroyed a Buddhist monastery and its 20,000 residents because the monks inside had dared to help an enemy army. Do you think his actions were justified? Why or why not?

3. Why did Yoritomo want his warriors to live in Kamakura instead of Kyoto? What do you think he feared might happen if they went to Kyoto?
4. In the early 1600s, the shogunate issued decrees that set Japan on a policy of isolation. When Japan emerged from its isolation in 1854, the West saw a unique and successful civilization. What do you think would happen if the United States began a policy of isolation, including an end to foreign trade, today?

Preparing for Citizenship

1. **COLLECTING INFORMATION** Japan experiences more than 1,500 earthquakes a year, though most are mild. Find out what causes earthquakes and where the world's major earthquakes occur. To what extent can they be predicted? How do people try to control earthquake damage, especially in cities?
2. **WRITING ACTIVITY** Japan, an isolated nation, developed a unique and successful civilization. Locate other island nations on a globe. Choose one to study. Find out for how long, and to what extent, this nation was isolated. How much, in spite of isolation, was it influenced by other nations? Write a brief report describing the nation you chose.

3. **GROUP ACTIVITY** Today most Japanese people live in urban areas. Find out which of the cities mentioned in this chapter are major cities of Japan today. What are Japanese cities like? How are they similar to cities in Western countries? How are they different?
4. **COLLABORATIVE LEARNING** Work in committees to study different kinds of Japanese arts, such as haiku poetry, the tea ceremony, and Kabuki theater. Using information you find, create a sample of the art form you study. One committee might recite a poem and another perform a skit for the class. As a class, discuss how the art forms of a country help its people take pride in their nation.

Answers to Preparing for Citizenship

1. **COLLECTING INFORMATION** The earth contains plates that press each other, causing earthquakes. Most occur in two belts—the circum-Pacific and the Alpide. The history of a region helps predict the next earthquake. Engineers construct buildings that withstand them.
2. **WRITING ACTIVITY** Answers will vary depending on the nations chosen.
3. **GROUP ACTIVITY** Tokyo and Kyoto are major cities. Like Western cities, Japanese cities have tall office buildings, crowded commercial districts, and wide expressways. However, shops include traditional Japanese items as well as modern goods.
4. **COLLABORATIVE LEARNING** Each committee should decide which art form to study. Encourage all students to participate in creating their committee's art form. Help students make their poems and skits reflect Japanese art forms as accurately as possible. With the help of the haiku committee, you may wish to conclude by helping the class write haiku poems.

Answers to Reviewing Skills

1. The author assumes that we can tell what people of a culture are like by analyzing the things they leave in their tombs. Because people of the Yayoi culture left figurines of warriors and horses, along with objects of wealth, such as mirrors and crowns, experts assume that the rulers of this culture were from a warrior class.
2. The Tokugawa shoguns assumed that the daimyo cared enough about the lives of their wives and eldest sons that they would not plan a revolt against the shogun while they were away from court.
3. The interior of Japan has few cities. The mountains in the interior might account for this.
4. Use a timeline.

Answers to Using Critical Thinking

1. On the positive side, the courtiers helped Japanese culture to flourish. On the negative side, they lived lives of extravagance and ignored the poverty under which the rest of Japan lived.
2. Answers will vary. Students may say that Nobunaga's actions were not justified because he could have punished the monks and let the innocent people leave.
3. Yoritomo must have thought his warriors would become weakened by the easy life of the court at Kyoto. He probably feared he would lose control of Japan if his warriors became weak.
4. Students may say that our country would change drastically. We are dependent on foreign trade for fuel and resources that enable us to operate the technology on which our country runs.

UNIT OVERVIEW

Read aloud the unit title. Explain that the Medieval Period, also known as the Middle Ages, covers the period that began after the fall of Rome and lasted until about 1450. Then have a student read the paragraph aloud. Tell the students that in this unit they will learn about what life was like during this period in Europe and in Japan.

Looking Back

Remind students that they learned about the fall of Rome in Chapter 2. Ask them who controlled Europe after the fall of Rome. *(Barbarian tribes controlled individual regions.)*

Looking Forward

Tell students that in the next two chapters they will study changes in society that formed a link from the ancient world to the modern world and that led to developments in art, education, politics, and religion:
Chapter 10 *Feudal Europe and Japan*
Chapter 11 *Europe: Rule, Religion, and Conflict*

Unit 5
Medieval Societies

Today is tournament day, and the squires display the helmets of their knights for all to see. The nobles of the castle gather with the peasants of the countryside to watch the bold warriors. Soon the knights will mount their horses, grab their lances, and demonstrate their battle skills. These are the men who defend the European castles and set out on holy crusades for the glory of their kings and their God.

330

246

The Showing of the Helms Before the Tournament, *from* Livre des Tournois du Roi Rene. *Bibliotheque Nationale, Paris*

GEOGRAPHY PROJECT

Medieval Scrapbook

Geography Skill **Measuring Distances on Maps**
Students use the skills of Acquiring and Analyzing geographic information.

Geography Theme Place

Geography Standards 6, 13 culture and experience influence perception of places; forces of conflict influence the control of earth's surface

Activity *Create a Scrapbook*

Materials construction paper, writing paper, pencils, pens, and markers

Management Individual/Small Group

You are traveling from Paris to Constantinople during medieval times. Create a scrapbook describing the differences and similarities of geography and culture between western and eastern Europe at that time.

Have students:

- write articles, letters and/or prepare to tell a story about a person traveling between regions during the medieval period.

- include a map of the route traveled and a chart that shows the distances between places along the route.

- include illustrations of regional features in Europe and the Middle East.

1450

Understanding the Print

The title of the book from which the print is taken can be translated as *Book of Tournaments of King René.* The king published this treatise on the tournaments that featured contests between knights in about 1460. Such tournaments had been extremely popular in France and England since the 11th century.

Have students reread the passage below the unit title and then study the print to find the elements described in the passage.

Understanding Chronology

This unit concentrates on conditions in Europe during the 1,000 years after the fall of Rome. It also explains the feudal system, which governed life in much of Europe and Japan during this period.

For research support activities, see the *Research Handbook.*

For simulations correlated to this unit, see *Citizenship Simulations,* p. viii.

Bookshelf II

Armor

by Charlotte and David Yue

This nonfiction book gives detailed information and illustrations about medieval armor used in Europe and Asia.

Motivate Read aloud pp. 13–18, describing the first types of armor people made to protect knights in battle. Ask students what sort of protective equipment people use today. Then have them look at the armor pictured on this page and list some questions they have about the Middle Ages. Have students look for the answers to their questions as they read Unit 5.

To connect this book with the unit content, use the planning guide and student activity blackline masters beginning on p. iv of the *Bookshelf II Teacher's Resources.*

For additional books that are Easy, Average, and Challenging, see the Unit Bibliography on p. T43. See bibliography updates at www.eduplace.com/ss/hmss.

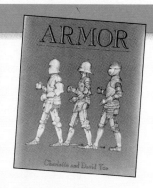

Planning at a Glance
Feudal Europe and Japan

	Objectives	Reading Support *and* Other Resources	Diverse Learning Strategies
Lesson 1 Europe After the Roman Empire *pp. 256–261* 2–3 days **Literature:** "The Story of Roland" *pp. 250–255*	• Characterize the political situation in Europe following the fall of the Roman Empire. • Describe the reign of Charlemagne and assess the political conditions in Europe after the death of Charlemagne. • Explain the importance of Alfred the Great and of William the Conqueror in the history of medieval England.	• **Workbook** or **Reading Support:** pp. 131–134 Review p. 31 Lesson Support/Transition p. 31 Multi-lang. Sum. pp. 61–62 • **Other Resources:** Geography Kit, Poster 3, Study Guide p. 40, Study Print 8	Access Strat. **(Extra Support)** TE p. 257 Access Act. **(SDAIE)** TE p. 257 Study Skills **(GATE)** TE p. 259 Map and Globe Skills **(Visual)** TE p. 260 ▭ Audiotapes of Multi-language Lesson Summaries **(Auditory)**
Lesson 2 Daily Life in Feudal Europe *pp. 262–270* 3–4 days	• Explain the structure of feudalism. • Describe the daily life of people of different classes under feudalism. • Explain the decline of feudalism in England and the importance of the *Magna Carta*.	• **Workbook** or **Reading Support:** pp. 135–138 Review p. 32 Lesson Support/Transition p. 32 Multi-lang. Sum. pp. 63–64 • **Other Resources:** Geography Kit, Study Guide p. 41, Study Print 9	Social Participation **(Kinesthetic)** TE p. 264 Art Connection **(Visual)** TE p. 266 Visual Learning **(Visual)** TE p. 267 Interviewing **(Auditory)** TE p. 269 ▭ Audiotapes of Multi-language Lesson Summaries **(Auditory)**
Lesson 3 Two Feudal Societies *pp. 271–274* 2–3 days	• Identify the major similarities in the development of feudalism in Western Europe and in Japan. • Summarize the reasons that feudalism ended earlier in Europe than it did in Japan.	• **Workbook** or **Reading Support:** pp. 139–142 Review p. 33 Lesson Support/Transition p. 33 Multi-lang. Sum. pp. 65–66 • **Other Resources:** Study Guide p. 42	Access Act. **(SDAIE)** TE p. 272 Access Strat. **(Extra Support)** TE p. 272 Writing a Narrative **(GATE)** TE p. 273 Visual Learning **(Kinesthetic)** TE p. 273 ▭ Audiotapes of Multi-language Lesson Summaries **(Auditory)**
Skill: Group Decisions: How a Guild Works p. 275 1 day	• Evaluate the advantages and disadvantages of accepting and supporting group decisions.	• **Other Resources:** Study Guide p. 43	
Exploring: Japanese and American Schools *pp. 276–277*	• Identify similarities and differences between Japanese and American schools. • Identify the values reflected by each system.		
Chapter Review *pp. 278–279* 1 day		Chapter 10 Test pp. 37–40 *(See facsimiles on TE p. 568.)*	Assessment Multiple-Use Masters pp. 73–80

Reading Support Resources *for Every Lesson*

Reading and Review

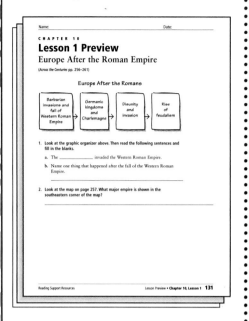

- **Chapter Overview*** p. 130
- **Lesson Previews*** using graphic organizers from the Teacher's Edition pp. 131, 135, 139
- **Reading Strategies*** pp. 132, 136, 140
- **Lesson Summaries*** pp. 133–134, 137–138, 141–142
- **Lesson Reviews** pp. 31, 32, 33

  * **Workbook** includes starred items.

Multi-language Summaries

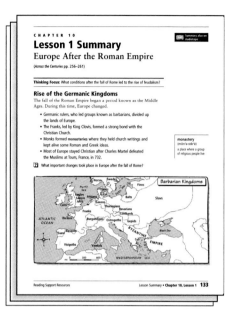

Lesson Summaries in:
- English (See Reading and Review.)
- Spanish pp. 133–134, 137–138, 141–142
- Chinese pp. 61–66
- Hmong pp. 61–66
- Khmer pp. 61–66
- Vietnamese pp. 61–66

  📼 **Summaries** available on audiotapes

Lesson Support /Transition
S D A I E

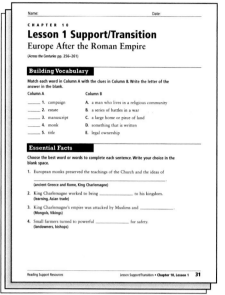

Activities for SDAIE
Specially **D**esigned **A**cademic **I**nstruction in **E**nglish

- **Lesson Support/Transition** pp. 31, 32, 33

💻 Technology Options

Internet Support
http://www.eduplace.com

Social Studies Center at Education Place

Internet support for Chapter 10:
- *Lesson at a Glance*
- *Medieval Farming*

Software
Student Writing Center ® (CD-ROM) (Macintosh® or Windows®)

School to Career

Bakeries in medieval Europe were probably just as tempting as bakeries today. Help students organize their own classroom bakery. They will need to decide what to make, what supplies they'll need, and how much they will need to charge. They can use the money they raise for a class trip or other activity.

Character Education

The feudal codes of chivalry and *bushido* each stressed that a soldier's loyalty must belong completely to his master or lord. Ask students to write a brief essay on what loyalty means to them. Is it similar to the loyalty demanded by the feudal lords?

Chapter 10
Feudal Europe and Japan

A castle rises high on a rocky mount, defended by massive stone walls. Such fortresses protected people in both Europe and Japan from invaders about 1,000 years ago. The sturdy stone walls, three feet thick, shielded peasants from attack. The peasants paid for their safety by serving the lord of the castle or giving him land. This arrangement, called the feudal system, ruled life in Europe and Japan for centuries.

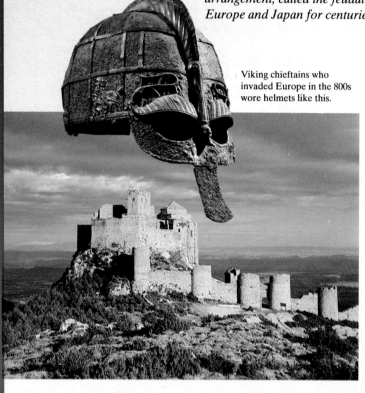

Viking chieftains who invaded Europe in the 800s wore helmets like this.

c. 900–1100 To protect their castles, European landowners build walls with rounded turrets that are difficult to attack. This castle was built along the border of present-day France and Spain.

400	700	1000

c. 700 Ghana becomes the first large West African trading empire.   c. 900

248

476

social structures are called manorialism and feudalism.

Manorialism

During the early medieval period, travel across Europe became difficult and dangerous as many kingdoms fought among themselves for land and wealth. As a result, trading activities diminished and towns—the centers of trade—became depopulated. Many people had to move to the countryside to make their living as peasants on large estates called manors, owned by lords.

The manors consisted of a manor house, surrounding farmland, the peasants' huts, farm buildings, a church, wine press, mill, and other buildings that made the manor a self-contained community. Serfs were bound to the soil and were passed to a new lord if the manor changed hands. For use of land to farm for themselves, peasants paid rent, provided labor, and gave the lord produce. The lord presided over the manor court, which tried minor offenses such as petty theft and made regulations for managing the manor.

Japanese artisans created beautiful war implements for samurai. These sword guards, made in the 1700s, separated the sword handle from the blade.

Understanding the Visuals

The castle (p. 248) was built at Loarre in the Pyrenean foothills in the 900s and 1000s. It was the site of numerous battles between Christian and Muslim forces. Christians finally gained control of the castle in 1070.

The Japanese sword guards (p. 249) are representative of the beautifully designed and crafted war implements carried by samurai. A thriving artisan class developed in Japan to produce these items. Wildlife scenes and scenes from Japanese fables were common motifs on sword guards.

Understanding Chronology

Ask the students to read the timeline. Note that the feudal period in Japan extended far beyond the feudal period in Europe.

c. 1100–1854 Like European knights, samurai defend Japanese estates. This samurai armor, made of steel, silk, and bronze, dates to between 1338 and 1573.

1300

1600

1900

c. 1530 The Inca conquer much of South America.

1854

249

Feudalism

Feudalism, which developed in the 700s, was built upon the manorial system. Feudal society was based on relationships between powerful lords—including kings—and their vassals, who, in exchange for vows of personal loyalty and military service, received an estate of land called a fief, along with its buildings and its peasants. Thus a vassal became the lord of a manor. A vassal held his fief only so long as he remained loyal to his lord. During the 800s possession of fiefs became hereditary, and according to the custom of primogeniture, control of the fief passed to the vassal's eldest son.

Vassals provided their lords with mounted soldiers called knights. There were no standing armies, so when a lord needed to fight a war or defend land, he called upon his knights. Rather than housing the knights himself, a vassal would sometimes grant knights fiefs from his own landholdings.

Since there was no centralized legal system, feudal law courts, made up of all the vassals of a single lord, were formed to settle differences among vassals. The lord presided over his court, and vassals pronounced judgments over their peers, much like a modern judge and jury.

INTRODUCE

This story about Charlemagne's nephew, Roland, gives students a look at some aspects of life in medieval Europe, especially the courtly life of knights and kings. "The Story of Roland" by Katharine Pyle introduces Lesson 1 of Chapter 10. Tell students that they will learn more about Charlemagne and his kingdom when they read Lesson 1.

READ AND RESPOND

You might wish to use "The Story of Roland" in a cooperative reading activity. If so, read aloud with your students, alternating with volunteers and helping students stay aware of the focus question that precedes the story.

Some words that students may need to know as they read are: *excommunicated*, denied membership in the church; *faltered*, stumbled or became unsteady; *retinue*, a group of people that follow a king; *hindered*, got in the way or stopped; and *stealthily*, secretively.

In this chapter you will read about an age of kings, lords, and knights. "The Story of Roland" is one of the most famous tales from that age.

Charlemagne
(SHAHR luh mayn)

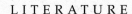

LITERATURE

The Story of Roland

Katharine Pyle

Writers of all times revisit historical stories. The work this story is based upon was written in the 1100s. We know that warriors in the time of Charlemagne, the 800s, were not easy to organize and command. By the 1100s, however, loyalty, obedience, and respect for authority were admired traits. Which attitudes are illustrated in this story of Charlemagne?

King Charlemagne had a sister Bertha whom he loved above all others of his sisters. Gentle she was, and beautiful, and kind, and Charlemagne thought to marry her to some great noble of his land, or to some foreign Prince or King, for she was worthy of the greatest.

But Bertha loved the young Count Milan. He was of noble birth but poor, and Charlemagne, in his pride, forbade the match.

But Bertha and the Count loved each other so dearly that even their awe of Charlemagne could not keep the two apart, and one night they were married secretly by a wandering priest.

When Charlemagne learned of this, as he needs must, his anger was so great he had the young pair driven from the court. He would not speak of them or hear their names. All were forbidden to give them aid or comfort, and they were even excommunicated by the Pope, at Charlemagne's desire.

And now the young couple were in wretched case. They had no home, and none dared shelter them, or even give them food, lest they bring down the wrath of Charlemagne upon their heads. The two wandered away from court, forlorn and desperate, not knowing what to do, or where to turn, until at last they disguised themselves as beggars, and so begged their way through France and into Italy. There they took shelter in a cave near to the town of Sutri, and in that cave their child was born; a son, whom they named Roland.

The people of the town were kind, and brought them food, and clothing for the babe; but Milan said, "I can no longer bear with pity and with alms. I will go forth to some far country, and will there take service under some foreign King who has no fear of Charlemagne. So I will win a home for thee, and for our babe."

Then Bertha wept bitterly, but would not say him nay, for as

Thematic Connections

Social Studies: Resolution of ethical issues in a society

Houghton Mifflin Literary Reader: Overcoming Obstacles

Background

Charlemagne was the first great European king after the fall of the Western Roman Empire. He was a very able and respected ruler. On Christmas Day in A.D. 800, Pope Leo III crowned Charlemagne emperor of the Romans and of what would eventually become the Holy Roman Empire. This coronation illustrates an important point about medieval history—the struggle between church and state. When a pope crowned a king, the pope was also demonstrating his own stature and power.

Charlemagne's empire grew in strength and ultimately included all of Christian Europe. Charlemagne had great respect for education. He is given credit for preserving many classic works of Latin literature for the Western world.

long as they stayed in any land where Charlemagne had power they always must keep in hiding, lest he find them out, and wreak his wrath on them.

So Milan bade his wife farewell and journeyed forth. But he did not journey far, for he was drowned in crossing a river there in Italy.

This news was brought to Bertha, and such was her grief that for a time it seemed that she must die with sorrowing. But time went on, and she had still her son, and all her love was turned to him, so that her grief was eased.

And Roland grew to be a lad of noble bearing, strong and tall, and having eyes strangely like Charlemagne's, they were so brightly blue, and clear, and keen as any hawk's.

Now, as it chanced, the Governor of Sutri had married another sister of King Charlemagne, and had a son Oliver of the same age as Roland. Also the two were much of the same height and strength and noble bearing, and he had the same blue eyes, and ruddy coloring, so that those who saw the two boys together wondered much that they should be so like; for no one guessed that they were cousins. Even Roland had not been told of that, nor told that he was a nephew of the mighty Charlemagne of whom he heard so many wondrous tales. His mother feared that if he learned this some harm might come of it.

And Roland's clothes were scarcely more than rags, but the boys of the town had grown to love him, and two who were the sons of merchants begged for him some cloth, and brought it to the cave. The cloth one brought was red, the other brought him white, and out of these Bertha fashioned a tunic for her son.

Full early he became a leader 'mongst the boys, but Oliver would be a leader too. So he challenged Roland to a wrestling match, that they might prove which was the better, and the fittest for the leadership. The place chosen for the contest was a field outside the town, and many came to watch, but Roland told Bertha naught of what was planned.

The two lads, having reached the place, stripped off their outer clothing and stood forth facing each other eye to eye, and foot to foot. Then suddenly, as with one thought they sprang together and seized each other and they wrestled up and down, each striving to throw the other, but neither could succeed. So for a long time they struggled up and down and back and forth. They put forth all their strength and every trick they knew, but neither could best the other. They strove until the sun, that had been high, sank toward the west, and till their breath came whistling from their throats, and till their hearts seemed like to burst.

Then those who were watching cried, "It is enough. Give over! or ye will kill yourselves. 'Tis plain that neither can best the other." But even as they spoke, Roland gave a sudden twist, and

Access Strategy

Tell students that a story can express a great deal about the attitudes held during a particular time in history. The story might not describe the attitudes directly, but a careful reader can uncover these important pieces of information by reading between the lines.

In the story of Roland, for example, students can learn by carefully observing characters. What kind of behavior is rewarded? What kind of behavior is punished? Answers to these questions can help students uncover medieval attitudes regarding obedience and respect for authority. The story reflects other attitudes and values, too—about loyalty and friendship, about leadership qualities, and about forgiveness. As students discover these attitudes and values, have them consider whether they still apply today or how they have changed.

➤ What does this tell you about the kind of person Roland was? *(Possible answers: It shows he was wise, not greedy for power, fair, humble, and a good friend.)*

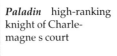

Paladin high-ranking knight of Charlemagne s court

252

shifted his hold, and he caught Oliver by the waist, and threw him down, and held him with his head and back pressed to the earth till Oliver cried, "Enough! I yield me!"

Then Roland drew away and rose, and Oliver too; Oliver said, "Thou art the better one; the fittest for the leadership."

But Roland answered, "Nay, it was by chance I threw thee; thou and I will lead together."

Those who heard shouted with joy of this; and the two lads put on their clothing, and embraced and went away together. And from that very time a friendship sprang up between them, and a love greater almost than that of brothers. It was a love that lasted all their lives, and never changed nor faltered even till that day when both died on the same field of battle.

Now Roland at this time was ten years old, and Charlemagne, his uncle, had become so great and famous that he was to come to Rome and there be crowned as Emperor by the Pope.

The way to Rome led through the town of Sutri, and the King had planned to spend the night there with the Governor.

Roland had gone forth with the other lads to see the Emperor come riding in with all his retinue. The Governor came forth to meet him, and it was a splendid sight.

Roland was standing somewhat apart from all the other boys, and as the King passed it seemed to him that Charlemagne looked at him, kindly, and with more than a passing glance.

And Roland hastened home, and said to his mother, "I have seen King Charlemagne and, mother, he seemed to look at me almost as though he knew me. He is the kingliest man, methinks, of any in the world. I would I were a knight to ride beside him, or a Paladin. How I would love and serve him."

And Bertha said, in a low voice, "He is indeed a man to love and serve, yet he can be cruel, too, unjust and stern."

But Roland heeded not; he said, "My mother, thou hast told me that my father was a knight and of a noble lineage. Why should I not go to Charlemagne and tell him who I am and how I long to serve him? Then, perchance, he would send me as a page to some great house, and I might afterward become a knight, and fight with him in wars."

But Bertha said, "Listen to me, my son. Thou art well grown and wise beyond thy years. Now I will tell thee something thou hast never known. But promise first that thou wilt never tell this thing that I reveal to thee, but keep it secret."

Then Roland promised eagerly, for he was curious to know the secret.

Then Bertha told him that this King he longed to serve was her own brother; told him of how she and her dear husband had been driven from the court, and of his father's death. Last of all she said, "Thou seest now why thou mayst

Reader's Theater

The style and language of "The Story of Roland" is somewhat archaic and classical, and thus less easily accessible than modern prose. To make the story more accessible, have students rewrite it in the format of Reader's Theater.

After you read and discuss the story with the class, divide students into small groups. Have the members in each group collaborate to rewrite the story using contemporary language. After the groups have rewritten the story, they should present their versions for the rest of the class.

never go to the King, nor seek his favor, nor in any way reveal thyself to him."

And Roland's face had grown as red as fire, and his eyes blazed with anger, and his hands were clenched until the knuckles whitened. And Bertha, ending her story, wept, not for herself, but for her husband, who was dead and for their son, who must endure this poverty. But Roland said, between his teeth, "The King is feasting even now off yonder with the Governor, while thou, his sister, scarcely hast a crust. But trust me, thou shalt share this feast, my mother"; and he made as if to leave the cave. But Bertha caught him by the sleeve and cried, "What wouldst thou do, my son?"

Roland made answer, "Naught that I should not do," and freed himself, but gently, and went forth, and made his way to the Governor's castle. There he entered in, and came on to the hall where Charlemagne feasted. And many a noble knight was there, and ladies, richly dressed.

But Roland took no heed of them. He came on through the hall and to the King, and said to him, "My mother is hungry, and it is not meet that she should fast while ye have plenty here, and still to spare." And he took up the dish of food that had been set before the King, also his goblet filled with wine, and turned to leave the hall.

meet proper

But those about cried out and rose and would have caught hold of Roland; but Charlemagne hindered them. "Let the boy go," he said, for suddenly he remembered a dream that he had had not long before.

In his dream he had heard his sister Bertha calling him, and she was in deep distress. Then in his dream the love he once had felt for her returned, and he sought everywhere to find her, but he found her not. Then a lad like to the one who had but now gone from the hall, came to him and took him by the hand and said, "Come now with me, and I will take thee to thy sister Bertha, for she is my mother."

Charlemagne went with him in his dream, and so came to a cave and found his sister there, and she was weeping. Then it seemed to him his heart would break with pity for her grief, and he had cried, "Bertha!" and with that cry had wakened, and it was all a dream.

But it was because of that he had let the lad go free, and now he bade the attendants follow him secretly and see which way he went. If it was to his mother, and the food and wine were indeed for her, then they were to bring both son and mother back with them, not with roughness but as though they honored them.

As they were bidden so the attendants did. They followed Roland but so stealthily that he did not know of it, and so came

◄ What does this paragraph tell you about Roland? *(Possible answers: He is brave, foolish, and/or unselfish.)*

Writing a Report

"The Story of Roland" tells how Charlemagne became acquainted with his nephew. That was just the beginning of their relationship. Have students conduct research to find out more about Roland, Charlemagne, Oliver, and Bertha. Students should take notes and then organize those notes into short written reports. You may want to have volunteers share their reports orally, or you may wish to display the reports in the classroom.

to a cave, and saw him enter there, and afterward they heard him speak and someone answer him. Then they, too, made their way into the cave and saw the Lady Bertha there (but guessed not who she was) and Roland had set the food before her and was urging her to eat; but she would not, and only wept.

When Roland saw the men he thought they had come there for harm, and ran and fetched a staff and made ready to defend his mother. Then the attendants told him that they meant no ill; they had but come to bring him and his mother to the King and that the King intended only good toward them.

Then Roland's heart was lightened, but his mother feared. She feared what Charlemagne might do to them when he discovered she was Bertha. But she rose, and prepared herself as best she could to come before him.

So the attendants brought them back to Charlemagne; and when the King saw that it was indeed his sister Bertha they had brought, he cried aloud, and went and took her in his arms, and there were tears upon his cheeks. And Bertha wept again, but now with joy, and all was forgiven between them.

After that she and Roland were arrayed in garments fitted to their rank, and went with Charlemagne to Rome, and saw him crowned as Emperor. Oliver went with them, riding at Roland's side, and joying in his good fortune.

When Charlemagne returned to France again he brought Bertha and Roland with him, and Roland was trained in all things fitting one of high degree, and he was dear to Charlemagne; so dear, indeed, that none was dearer, not even Charlot the Emperor's own son and heir to France. And Bertha dwelt in the palace, and in time was married to Count Ganelon, the Emperor's counselor and friend.

As for her son, as years went on he came to be the most famous Paladin in all of France, and was beloved alike by high and low; but this was not until years afterward, when Roland had learned the duties of a page, a squire, and then a bachelor, and last of all a knight. And through all this his cousin Oliver was ever his dearest friend, so that a saying rose, "As dear to each other as are Roland and Oliver."

Further Reading

Adam of the Road. Elizabeth Gray Vining. Searching for his minstrel father and his dog, Adam wanders 13th-century England. He meets jugglers, minstrels, pilgrims, and nobles in a journey that shows you the life and customs of the time.

Charlemagne and His Knights. Katharine Pyle. Additional stories about the adventures of Roland and other knights.

Knights in Armor. Shirley Glubok. This art book is based on the collection of armor in New York's Metropolitan Museum of Art. Here you can see exactly what the knights wore.

The Master Puppeteer. Katharine Patterson. A 13-year-old boy in feudal Japan tells his story of everyday existence and life in the theater. The ancient art of Japanese puppetry provides the backdrop for this adventure story.

The Merry Adventures of Robin Hood. Howard Pyle. The book retells the legend of a man who robs from the rich king and gives to the poor peasants.

◄ Do you like the way this story ended? Why or why not?

EXTEND

During his reign, Charlemagne made many conquests and added many lands to his kingdom. Give students an outline map of Europe. Have them go to the library, find what European lands Charlemagne ruled, and draw in those lands on the map.

255

Further Reading

You may want to have your students look in the school or local library for more books to read about Charlemagne and his knights or about life in the Middle Ages in England, France, and Spain.

Ask students to read the Thinking Focus and identify the new term it presents. Write feudalism on the chalkboard. Point out that kings and knights were part of the feudal system. Have students share what they know about these and other aspects of feudalism. Then have students read to confirm or modify their impressions of feudal times.

Key Terms

Vocabulary Strategies: T36–T37
monastery—a place in which a community of religious people lives
feudalism—a political and economic system based on the relationship between a large landowner and people who need his protection
hierarchy—a group of people organized by rank or authority
fief—a large feudal estate
vassal—a person under the protection of a feudal lord
oath of fealty—an expression of loyalty to one's lord
knight—an armed, mounted soldier who served a lord

➤ *Spears, shields, and bows and arrows can be seen in the carving.*

256

---

400   476   1300   1600   1900
1066

L E S S O N 1

Europe After the Roman Empire

Key Terms

- monastery
- feudalism
- hierarchy
- fief
- vassal
- oath of fealty
- knight

➤ *This Anglo-Saxon box lid from the 700s was carved from whalebone. It shows warriors attacking a fortress. What kinds of weapons can you see in the carving?*

256

When the barbarian Odoacer took command of Rome in A.D. 476, he removed the powerless emperor Romulus Augustulus. The Western Roman Empire lay like a skeleton fallen in its own useless armor.

To Romans, it must have seemed the end of the world. All along the 10,000-mile border of the empire, there was war. Orientus, a Roman poet in the 400s, wrote:

See how swiftly death comes upon the world, and how many people the violence of war has stricken. Some lay as food for dogs; others were killed by the flames that licked their homes. In the villages and country houses, in the fields and in the countryside, on every road—death, sorrow, slaughter, fires, and lamentation.

Rise of the Germanic Kingdoms

The fall of Rome marked both the end of the ancient world and the beginning of a new era. Historians call this period, which lasted until about 1450, the Middle Ages, or the Medieval Period. Some have called the early part of this period the "Dark Ages" because little that was written at that time has come down to us. Historians do know, however, that important changes took place in Europe.

Chapter 10

Objectives

1. Characterize the political situation in Europe following the fall of the Roman Empire.
2. Describe the reign of Charlemagne and assess the political conditions in Europe after the death of Charlemagne.
3. Explain the importance of Alfred the Great and of William the Conqueror in the history of medieval England.

Graphic Overview

Help students understand that each box represents a change that took place over many years.

Barbarian invasions and fall of Western Roman Empire → Germanic kingdoms and Charlemagne → Disunity and invasion → Rise of feudalism

New kingdoms were set up in the lands the Germanic invaders had conquered. The map below shows the barbarians' division of rule in Europe. One Germanic group called themselves the Franks, or "the bold." Find the part of Europe where the Franks settled.

A Conquering People

In 481, the 15-year-old warrior Clovis became king of the Franks. He led them for 30 years in wars that widened the boundaries of the Frankish kingdom. Eventually, it included most of what are now France and Germany. Clovis also led the Franks into Christianity. After the collapse of the Western Roman Empire, one of the only ties with the stability of earlier times was provided by the church of

Rome. It continued such traditions of the empire as using Latin and making its center in Rome. It supported many of the Roman traditions that Europeans once knew. Laws set up under Christian rulers included many elements of the Roman systems of property ownership and taxation. In addition, a few of the old Roman trade routes still operated.

Elsewhere in Europe, monks formed religious communities known as **monasteries.** There they devoted themselves to preserving the ideas of ancient Rome and Greece as well as church writings.

The church supported Clovis because it wanted to continue to serve Christians in the area ruled by the Franks. In order to do that, the church had to cooperate with

▼ *Find present-day France and England on the map of Europe on page 524 of the Atlas. Which Germanic tribes settled in the areas that became France and England?*

Barbarian Kingdoms

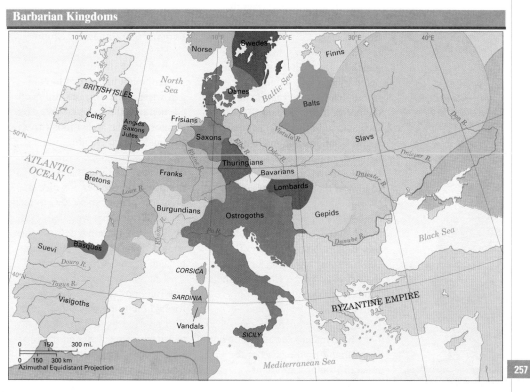

Feudal Europe and Japan

257

Point out that this lesson will focus on developments in the regions of Europe now known as France and England. Have students identify these regions on the map. Then have students compare the kingdoms in France and England on this map with those shown in the map on p. 27 in Chapter 2, Lesson 1. *(They should notice that the kingdom of the Franks is about twice as large on the later map.)* Help students to see that the changes between the maps suggest greater political stability.

◄ *Angles, Saxons, and Jutes settled in the area that became England; Franks, Bretons, and Burgundians settled in what became France.*

HISTORY

Social Participation

Tell students that the Middle Ages, especially the years prior to A.D. 1000, were once known as the Dark Ages. Divide the class into three groups, and tell them to prepare to debate the appropriateness of this description after reading the lesson. One group should defend the phrase, another should refute it, and the third should judge the debate.

257

Access Strategy

Have students look back at the chart on p. 30 of Chapter 2 of this book. Review with them some of the problems of the Roman Empire during its last years. Remind them that the empire officially split into two parts in A.D. 395 and that the Eastern Roman Empire continued as the Byzantine Empire. Ask them what the first circle on the chart shows. *(The Western Roman Empire was about 53 percent of the former Roman Empire.)* Have them estimate from the

second circle on the chart the amount of land that barbarian tribes controlled in 492. *(10 percent of the former Roman Empire; about one-fourth of the Western Roman Empire.)* Ask what the last circle on the chart shows. *(Barbarian tribes controlled all of the former Western Roman Empire by 496.)*

Access Activity

Direct students' attention to the map on this page. Have students count the number of tribes controlling some part of Europe. Ask whether students would expect this medieval Europe to be at peace or at war. Also ask which tribe occupies the most strategic position in Europe. Help students see that the Franks occupied this position.

■ *The Franks enlarged their kingdom and spread Christianity.*

■ *What important changes took place in Europe after the fall of Rome?*

the king. Once Clovis had been baptized and had accepted the support of the church, the leaders of the church encouraged him to spread Christianity. "Every battle you fight is a victory for us," a bishop wrote to Clovis.

A New Royal Family

The sons and grandsons of Clovis were more interested in squabbling among themselves than in ruling the kingdom. A new family rose to power from within the king's household. The Mayors of the Palace, officials of the king, were the kingdom's real rulers.

It was a Mayor of the Palace, Charles Martel, or Charles the Hammer, who defeated Muslim invaders from Spain at Tours, France. Martel's victory against the Muslim armies in 732 meant that northern Europe remained firmly Christian.

In 751, Martel's son, Pepin, asked the head of the church, Pope Zacharias, to recognize him as king. Pepin was the first king to rule with the blessings of the church. King Pepin's son Charles, who was called Charlemagne, would also rule with the church's support. ■

Charlemagne's Empire

Charlemagne was to become more than the king of the Franks. He would become emperor, the ruler of the former Western Roman Empire.

Charlemagne's 48 years of rule, which began in 768, were dominated by war. He fought the Lombards in Italy, the Saxons to the north, the Avars and Slavs to the east, and others, 60 campaigns in all. Charlemagne made his defeated opponents accept the Roman church and swear loyalty to him as their new ruler.

An Emperor Crowned

In 800, Charlemagne marched into Italy to help Pope Leo III put down a rebellion there. Leo knew that he would need Charlemagne's protection and support. On Christmas day, he crowned Charlemagne emperor.

Charlemagne and the pope both knew that only the head of the Eastern Roman Empire at Constantinople could legally claim

▼ *This gold likeness of Charlemagne at the cathedral of Aachen was made to hold his bones.*

the title of emperor. But the title fitted Charlemagne well. As emperor, he dedicated himself to strengthening the church and bringing learning to his empire.

An Age of Learning

Although he learned to read and write, Charlemagne still needed men of letters around him. His greatest scholar was a monk from England named Alcuin.

By Charlemagne's time, most of Europe's libraries had been destroyed during periods of war. Very few people knew how to read the few books that were left. Led by Alcuin, Charlemagne's scholars copied by hand these manuscripts to keep them for future ages.

Charlemagne also made sure that religious services were performed the same way throughout Europe. He forced illiterate clergy to become educated, and tried to rid the church of corruption. As Charlemagne grew old, his empire began to unravel. Enemies were

Critical Thinking

Ask students what Pope Leo III gained by crowning Charlemagne Holy Roman Emperor. What did Charlemagne gain by accepting the title Holy Roman Emperor? Tell students that this relationship between church and state is a theme they will encounter repeatedly as they study the history of Europe.

Political Context

After Clovis, the leadership of the Franks gradually shifted to the mayors of the palace. Originally, a mayor of the palace had been a royal officer whose duty was to sign each royal edict to make it official. Later, mayors took on more of the duties of prime ministers, or chief executives, and also led armies. By the time Charles Martel seized power, the descendants of Clovis, the Merovingians, had become mere puppet rulers and were called "do-nothing kings."

Cultural Context

The great battles of Charlemagne's time are described in more than 80 epic poems, written between the 1100s and 1500s. The most famous of these long poems is the 4,000-line *Song of Roland,* which describes a knight of legendary courage who protected Charlemagne's army from Muslim forces in the Pyrenees. The work is believed to be based on an actual battle that took place in 778.

ammering away at its borders. From the east came a people called the Magyars. From North Africa and Spain, Muslims attacked. And from Scandinavia came a group of fearless warriors known as Vikings. The map on page 260 shows these invasions.

But all of this was to be someone else's problem. In 814, at the age of 72, Charlemagne died.

Jews in Medieval Europe

Jews had lived in Europe since Roman times. They lost many rights, however, when the Empire fell and the Christian church began to rule. Charlemagne granted Jews the right to own land in Gaul (France). Jews also had their own courts and freedom of trade and religion.

Many rulers granted Jews rights in exchange for extra taxes. Jewish culture and economy thrived, and many Jews specialized in handicrafts, finance, and navigation. Thus, some Jews created long-distance trade networks organized around Jewish families and relatives in far-away places. Jewish trade networks also grew because Jews were free to move around Muslim lands, while Christians were not. Christian rulers sometimes relied on these Jewish merchants as advisers on international politics and trade.

Jewish culture blossomed in the centers around the Mediterranean and along the Rhone and Rhine rivers. Great Jewish communities in the Byzantine Empire and Rome continued to develop. New Jewish centers arose in Spires, Worms, Troyes, Paris, and Narbonne, in what is now France and Germany. The Jews there created a culture which they called "Ashkenazic" *(ahsh kuh NUHZ ik)*. This included customs of religious and daily life as well as the beginnings of a new language— a mixture of Hebrew and Old German called Yiddish. Jewish communities were never very secure, however. Rulers often demanded heavy tributes in money or forced them to leave.

From about 900 to 1100, religious writings, law anthologies, histories, and poetry poured out of Jewish academies of higher learning. One important Jewish scholar was **Rabbi Sh**lomo (Solomon) ben **I**saac, known as Rashi. He could not attend religious discussions because he had to support his family, so he wrote out his commentaries about the Torah and Talmud. They remain of great importance to Judaism today. Christian scholars, too, still use his work.

Europe After Charlemagne

Charlemagne's son, Charles the Pious, lacked his father's shrewdness and strength. Long before he died in 840, his sons, Lothair, Charles, and Louis, were fighting for control of the empire. For a while, the empire was divided among them, as you can see on the map on page 260. Their kingdoms came apart as landowners became more independent.

As Europe broke up into smaller kingdoms, people looked to local lords to defend them. With the Magyars, Muslims, and Vikings at their borders, the people needed protection.

After Charlemagne's death, the Vikings found Europe falling apart, and ready for the taking. The

▲ *King Solomon reads the Torah, from a late 12th-century Hebrew Bible and prayer book made in France.*

How Do We Know?

HISTORY *Historians know quite a bit about what Alcuin did and thought while he worked at Charlemagne's court. Many of Alcuin's letters to other churchmen can still be read today.*

259

Feudal Europe and Japan

Ask students to review the accomplishments of Charlemagne. List his achievements in one of three columns on the chalkboard: Military, Cultural, and Religious.

259

Cultural Context

The monks of Charlemagne's court developed a style of writing called Carolingian minuscule which was compact yet legible, allowing them to save valuable paper. Most modern typefaces are based on this writing. Under Alcuin's direction, many manuscripts were copied in minuscule. The manuscripts were decorated with a kind of art called illumination. Illuminators filled the spaces within initial letters and margins with small but exquisite pictures and designs.

Writing a Letter

Charlemagne's greatest scholar was Alcuin, many of whose letters to fellow churchmen still exist. Have students review the information about Alcuin and Charlemagne in the text and then write their own versions of one of Alcuin's letters. Have them address a letter about Charlemagne's cultural programs to a former colleague still living in England. Tell students to include accurate details of the times.

Study Skills

Have students gather additional information about the Vikings. Suggest that they investigate the daily life of the Vikings, their skill as shipbuilders, their battle dress and strategy, their conquests and exploration, and their long-term influence on European development. Ask students to present the highlights of their investigations in oral reports to the class.

GEOGRAPHY
Map and Globe Skills

Refer students to the map on this page. Have them answer questions such as the following: Which of Charlemagne's grandsons inherited the area that is almost entirely in today's France? *(Charles the Bald.)* What country is now largely in the area inherited by Louis the German? *(Germany)* Have students compare this map with a modern-day map of Europe.

➤ *Vikings attacked the British Isles and areas that are now France, Germany, and Spain.*

■ *Charlemagne brought education and culture to his reign and tried to rid the churches of corruption.*

260

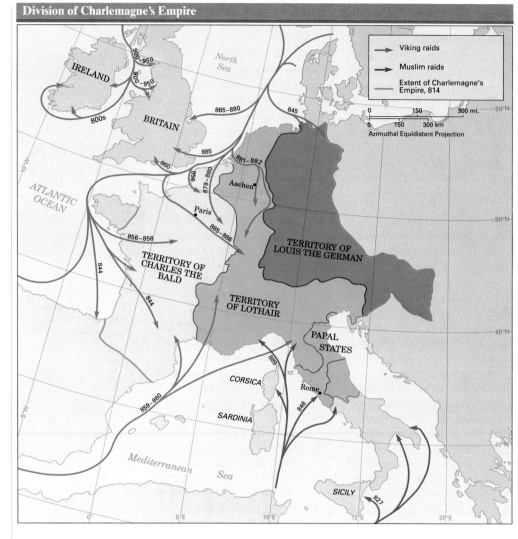

Division of Charlemagne's Empire

Viking raids

Muslim raids

Extent of Charlemagne's Empire, 814

0   150   300 mi.

0   150   300 km

Azimuthal Equidistant Projection

IRELAND

North Sea

BRITAIN

ATLANTIC OCEAN

Aachen

Paris

TERRITORY OF CHARLES THE BALD

TERRITORY OF LOUIS THE GERMAN

TERRITORY OF LOTHAIR

PAPAL STATES

CORSICA

Rome

SARDINIA

Mediterranean Sea

SICILY

▲ *Where in Europe did Vikings attack?*

■ *How did Charlemagne improve learning and the quality of the church in medieval Europe?*

260

Vikings sailed out of Scandinavia into coastal villages throughout Europe, plundering, killing, burning, and taking prisoners. By the time a local army arrived, the Vikings were gone. In time, they grew bolder, establishing camps from which they raided the countryside. ■

Medieval England

During the 800s, England suffered most at the hands of the Vikings, who launched attacks along the coast. England was saved only by the tough resistance of the Anglo-Saxon king, Alfred the Great. From his base in Wessex, Alfred fought the Vikings for three decades until his death in 899.

A New Ruler

When King Edward, a descendent of Alfred, died childless, the right to the English throne came

Chapter 10

Visual Learning

Bring in articles or books that show pictures of the Bayeux Tapestry. This medieval embroidery, 230 feet long, depicts more than 70 scenes from the Norman Conquest of England. Have students analyze the pictures for details about military equipment and tactics, and for other historical details.

Language Arts Connection

A country's history is reflected in its place names. Have students look for Anglo-Saxon names on a map of Great Britain with these endings: *ton, ham, wic* or *wich*—meaning "a settlement or village"; *bury* or *borough*—meaning "a fortified place." Then ask students to find place names of Scandinavian origin with these endings: *by*—meaning "village"; *thorpe*—meaning "a settlement smaller than a village." Have students name towns and cities that have these endings.

into question. An English assembly chose Edward's brother-in-law Harold as king. But Edward's cousin William, Duke of Normandy in France, felt his right to the throne was stronger. He said that Edward had promised him the kingdom. He also argued that Harold had sworn to support his claim.

William and his Norman army invaded England. On October 14, 1066, at the Battle of Hastings, William's Norman forces defeated Harold's Saxon infantry.

King William the Conqueror, as he came to be called, was a descendant of Vikings who had settled in France. He had ruled his territories in France with a firm hand and also took firm control of England. He took the land from Harold's followers and, using an arrangement called feudalism, divided it among his own followers.

A New Order

Feudalism was a social and political arrangement that developed in Europe after the fall of the Roman Empire and lasted until about 1200. It was rooted in the people's need for protection against invaders and in landowners' needs for defense. Without Roman administrators or soldiers, small farmers turned to powerful landowners for protection. People received protection in return for service as soldiers or for turning over title and ownership of their land to the larger landowners. With feudalism came new relationships among people. **Hierarchies** developed; they were orders of rank and authority within different classes of people or organizations.

Under the feudal system he established in England, King William ruled all of England. He gave large estates, called **fiefs**, to the warriors who had served him. The new landowners became his subjects, or **vassals**. In exchange for the land awarded to him, each vassal swore an **oath of fealty** to the king. That is, the vassal promised to remain loyal to his lord. He also promised to provide his lord with armed, mounted soldiers, or **knights**, for military duty.

William's vassals, in turn, granted parts of their fiefs to other people. The king's vassals became lords with vassals of their own. These vassals became lords to individual knights. Each vassal swore an oath of fealty to his lord. All levels of society were bound, by loyalty and by need, to their king. ■

▲ *A flag with this design was carried by William the Conqueror's troops at the Battle of Hastings.*

■ *Describe the condition of Europe after Charlemagne's death.*

REVIEW

1. **FOCUS** What conditions after the fall of Rome led to the rise of feudalism?
2. **CONNECT** Compare and contrast the rule of Charlemagne in western Europe with that of Akbar in India.
3. **CITIZENSHIP** What similarities and differences do you see between the feudal style of governing and our government today?
4. **CRITICAL THINKING** Do you think a law of succession would have prevented the Battle of Hastings? Why?
5. **WRITING ACTIVITY** In the early days of the Middle Ages, Romans and Germanic people lived side by side and influenced each other. In the United States, also, different ethnic groups live side by side. Choose one ethnic group. Describe some of the ways that group has influenced American culture.

Feudal Europe and Japan

INTRODUCE

Ask students to read the Thinking Focus and then look at the illustrations in the lesson. Have students describe the types of people pictured. *(Peasants, clergy, knights, noblewomen, craftspeople.)* Tell them that feudal arrangements affected each class of people in a different way. Have them read to find out how.

Key Terms

Vocabulary Strategies: T36–T37
homage—the ceremonial recognition of allegiance to a lord shown by a vassal
manor—the castle and estate of a feudal lord
serf—a person who was bound to the land and owned by a lord
guild—an association of tradespeople made up of merchants, craftspeople, or artisans

262

---

400   700   1000   1600   1900
1066   **1400**

L E S S O N 2

Daily Life in Feudal Europe

THINKING
F O C U S

How did the feudal system affect the everyday lives of people in Europe?

Key Terms

- homage
- manor
- serf
- guild

➤ *This cutaway view shows the home of a medieval family and their animals. What would you find most uncomfortable about living in this home?*

262

*H*is hood full of holes
  with the hair sticking
  through,
His clumsy knobbed shoes cob-
  bled over so thickly,
Though his toes started out as
  he trod on the ground . . .
Two miserable mittens made
  out of old rags, . . .
He wading in mud almost up
  to his ankles,
And before him four oxen, so
  weary and feeble
One could reckon their ribs, so
  rueful were they.

This description of a medieval peasant is from the poem *Piers the Plowman*, which was written in the late 1300s in England by William Langland. The harsh conditions endured by peasants like the one Langland described in his poem had not improved at all for hundreds of years.

In 1066, the rulers of England changed, but the lives of English peasants remained the same. In the hierarchy of William the Conqueror's feudalism, peasants were at the bottom.

Chapter 10

Objectives

1. Explain the structure of feudalism.
2. Describe the daily life of people of different classes under feudalism.
3. Explain the appeal of life in medieval cities for different groups in medieval society.
4. Explain the decline of feudalism in England and the importance of the *Magna Carta*.

Graphic Overview

MEDIEVAL SOCIETY

Country People — **Townspeople**

lords | clergy | craftspeople | clergy | merchants

knights | serfs

slaves

slaves

The Feudal System

After the victory at the blood-soaked field of Hastings went to William the Conqueror, life in England changed for many. William planned to rule in peace, using the system of feudalism that was already in place in France.

If you think of feudal society as a house with many rooms, then loyalty was the set of beams that held it up. Vassals paid **homage,** or showed honor, to their lords. The word homage comes from the French word for "man." The vassal was to be the lord's man in body, mind, and spirit.

When an oath of fealty was sworn between a king and a lord or between a lord and a knight, the bond of loyalty was formalized in a ceremony. The vassal knelt before his lord. Placing his hands between the lord's hands, he swore to serve his lord in loyalty and love. Then the vassal and his lord kissed, and the lord gave his vassal a clod of earth symbolizing the fief that the vassal would use. When a vassal died, a lord went through the ceremony with the vassal's oldest son.

In 1066, feudalism was not fully developed in England. William and his Norman lords set about to change all that. William ordered a survey to be taken of the ownership of every bit of land in England. The results of the survey were written in *The Great Domesday Book,* which became a valuable source of information for the king's tax agents. Then William distributed the land as fiefs to his Norman followers. ■

■ *Why was loyalty important in the feudal system?*

▼ *These ivory chess pieces from the 1100s show three different classes of medieval society: a knight, a queen, and a member of the clergy—a bishop.*

Life in the Country

William and his Norman lords built fortified castles on their fiefs all over the island kingdom of England. By 1100, several hundred castles had been built throughout the countryside. These Norman fortresses helped to shape the lives of the kings, lords, and knights who made up English nobility.

Nobles

For the lord of a fief, a castle might be home. For others who lived on his land, it was both a

Feudal Europe and Japan

DEVELOP

Tell students that feudalism brought order to the economy and social life of the Middle Ages. Review the relationship between lords and vassals described in Lesson 1. Then draw the Graphic Overview on the chalkboard. Note that the peasants who worked the fiefs of the vassals were dependent on their lords for protection but did not swear an oath of fealty, as did the knights. Have students identify the groups in the Overview.

■ *Bonds of loyalty ensured that each person in the feudal chain fulfilled his obligations.*

SOCIAL SYSTEMS
Critical Thinking

The bond of loyalty between vassal and lord held feudal society together. Discuss the concept of loyalty with students. Ask students to name people or organizations that command their loyalty, such as friends, family, sports teams, school. Have students assess the strengths and weaknesses of a social structure based on loyalty.

Access Strategy

Write the term *daily life* on the chalkboard and ask students what the term means to them. Who are some of the people they come into contact with during their own daily lives? *(Family members, teachers)* Who are some of the people that they might have come in contact with each day if they had lived during the Middle Ages? Remind them that the people they would come in contact with on a country manor would be different from people they would meet in a city. Then have them look at the illustrations for this lesson and tell what aspects of people's daily lives in the Middle Ages the lesson will be about (where they lived, the work they did, what they ate).

Access Activity

Explain how the oath of fealty was conducted (see p. 263) and have two students reenact the ceremony. Have students think of other oaths and pledges that people make today and what they mean, such as the Pledge of Allegiance or the Scout Oath. Note that most modern pledges involve loyalty to values and standards rather than to individuals.

► *Knights and soldiers can be seen in the background.*

► *This painting from Les Tres Riches Heures du Duc du Berry shows a rich feast held inside a castle. A lord and his guests, who are other nobles and clergy, are in the foreground. What can you see in the far background?*

center for feudal life and a place of safety during battle. Castle walls were three feet thick. They were built to withstand blows from battering rams and flaming missiles launched from enemy catapults. Windows were mere slits through which the archers could shoot their arrows. A Norman castle was usually a tower built at the top of a hill and surrounded by a deep trench, or moat.

The Norman castle was built for

UNDERSTANDING HIERARCHY

The knight made an oath of fealty to the lord of the manor. The lord swore to be faithful to the more important lord who had granted him his fief. The hierarchy of the feudal society extended from the humblest peasant all the way up to the king.

Hierarchy as Ranking

A hierarchy is a system by which persons or things are ranked one above another. A group of equals, such as the members of a sports team, cannot be considered a hierarchy.

The meritocracy that

Emperor Wen developed in China was a hierarchy with the emperor at the top. Beneath him stood courtiers, administrators, and clerks. Each group, from the administrators up through the emperor, had greater powers than the group below it.

Other Hierarchies

Hierarchies define where people stand in relationship to each other and define their rights and responsibilities. Most workplaces such as offices and factories are hierarchies, with a boss or president

over several rankings of supervisors and workers. Medieval city dwellers and guild members had their own hierarchies.

Slaves were at the bottom of medieval society. They were usually captives of war or kidnap victims. Slavery continued throughout Europe in spite of the teachings of the Church. Gradually, over the centuries most slaves became **serfs.** While slaves could be sold or given away, serfs were required to stay on and work on a piece of land for anyone who owned the land.

264

Chapter 10

Social Participation

Divide the class into small groups of two or three students each. Ask each group to write and present a skit or monologue describing daily medieval life from one of the following points of view: the lord of the manor, his wife, his daughter, a castle knight, a peasant widow struggling to clothe and feed her children, a local priest.

Political Context

The use of cavalry in warfare contributed to the growth of feudalism. After Charles Martel fought mounted troops in the Battle of Tours in 732, the demand for cavalry grew rapidly. Horses, however, were expensive. Warriors who could not afford to keep horses could not become knights. On the other hand, by carefully managing their land, other warriors gained the means to acquire horses, advance to knighthood, and obtain more land and wealth.

Economic Context

The economy of Europe in the early Middle Ages was based largely on agriculture. Throughout Europe, farmers were becoming more efficient, producing more food with less effort. Most manors used the three-field system. One-third of the land was used for spring planting, one-third for autumn planting, and one-third of the land was allowed to rest, or lie fallow, each year. This approach increased soil fertility and is similar to the crop rotation system of modern agriculture.

Becoming a Medieval Knight

Page	Squire	Knight
• Serving in household • Learning swordplay • Playing chess and other strategy games • Hunting with hawks and falcons • Learning code of courtesy expected of knight	• Acting as personal servant to knight • Learning jousting • Assisting knight in battle • Taking charge of prisoners captured in battle	• Serving lords as warriors • Overseeing land as vassals • Taking part in tournaments
Age 7	Age 13–14	Age 18–22

security, not for comfort. The lord and lady of the castle usually slept behind a curtain in the main dining hall. Also sleeping in the hall might be a small mob of knights, guests, servants, and dogs. The floor was covered with herbs to keep down the smell of bones and other refuse. On a winter morning, inhabitants would wash by plunging their arms through ice-crusted water in a bucket.

Life in a castle was far from glamorous, and few who lived there were the courteous knights and ladies of legend. A knight was often the landless younger son of a lord's vassal. The lord provided the knight with food, lodging, armor, and a horse in exchange for his services. But between wars the castle's knights fought among themselves or bullied the servants unless the lord of the castle kept an eye on them.

The lady of the castle usually had very little power, except over female servants. Medieval women were supposed to be subject to their husbands and fathers, just as vassals were subject to their lords. However, most of the daily life of the castle was within women's domain. Besides cooking and cleaning, women also managed the making of clothing and medical

▲ *The chart shows the stages that a young man went through before he became a knight. Why do you think it was such a long and rigorous process?*

◄ *This woman of the 1300s wears clothing such as that worn by ladies of English or French castles.*

265

Feudal Europe and Japan

Ask students to compare the glamorous view of castle life most Americans acquire from fairy tales and television to the gritty picture presented in the text. Ask students why our view of kings and nobles, knights and ladies has become so glamorized and incorrect. *(Answers may include inadequate knowledge, the beauty of art and costumes seen in illustrations, a desire to escape reality.)*

◄ *Answers will vary. Students may suggest that being a knight was a very serious commitment.*

Have students describe a noble's castle. Have them link the thick walls and the absence of windows to the need for defense and the techniques of warfare of the day. Ask what other features a castle might have. *(Moat, towers, ramparts)* Check that students understand what a catapult is.

265

Language Arts Connection

Divide the class into groups of four to six students each. Ask each group to research and review the legends of Robin Hood or King Arthur. Then have the groups report orally on the various aspects of medieval life they found represented in the legends. Each group should also identify any elements within the legend that seem inconsistent with their knowledge of the feudal structure. Explore with students possible reasons for the inconsistencies.

Reader's Theater

Select a dramatic portion of one of the Robin Hood or King Arthur stories. Distribute copies to students and have them read through the selection silently first. Then assign parts for the dialogue. Involve the rest of the class in reading the narrative sections. Narratives could be read by individuals or by a chorus. Encourage all students to speak expressively and distinctly. When students are comfortable with their parts, invite another class to come for a presentation.

Study Skills

Have students research one of these topics: armor, castle building, medieval agriculture, medieval education, Gothic art, development of Romance languages, or medieval drama. Tell them to organize their notes and then present their findings in an outline in which all items are full sentences.

Visual Learning

What products are the peasants shown in the painting on this page working to produce? *(wool and grain)* Explain to students that most of what was produced on a manor was used by those who lived there. Point out that the woman described in the excerpt from *Piers the Plowman* on this page also worked at the production of wool cloth.

➤ *Answers will vary, but students may say that these peasants look happier than those described in* Piers the Plowman. *In fact, this painting is almost like a vacation poster, hawking the virtues of peasant life. Encourage students to speculate on the reasons for the two different viewpoints. Which seems more accurate?*

266

 In this miniature painting, peasants are shearing sheep and harvesting grain in fields surrounding a castle. Does this picture of peasant life differ from the images conveyed in Piers the Plowman *on this page and on page 262?*

266

care for everyone in the castle. When their husbands were at war, women took over the **manor,** the castle and entire estate.

Some noblewomen controlled fiefs or became abbesses, who ruled over convents and convent lands. Hildegard of Bingen (1098–1179), a Christian woman raised in a convent, had religious visions. She wrote books, founded convents, and preached throughout Germany. She wrote religious music and poetry. She was also a physician and pharmacologist.

Peasants

The lord's castle might be a cold, drafty fortress. But as you can see in the picture on page 262, even a well-off medieval family lived with its animals.

In the early Middle Ages, farming methods improved in Northern Europe and England. See A Closer Look on page 267 for additional information on advances in medieval farming. But farming was still hard, and both men and women were bound to the plots of land that they tilled for their lords. Some were so poor that they would not even have owned the scrawny oxen described by William Langland. Instead they would borrow oxen from their lord or a neighbor.

The peasant woman produced food and clothing for her own household. William Langland wrote of peasant women's work in *Piers the Plowman:*

*W*hat they save from
   their spinning they
   spend on house rent,
on milk and oatmeal to make
   porridge
to fill their children when they
   cry for food.
They themselves suffer the
   sting of hunger
and of winter misery, rising at
   night
to rock the cradle in its
   cramped corner,
to card and comb wool, to
   mend and wash,
to scrub and wind yarn, to
   weave rushlights.
It's painful to read or to write
   verses
on the hard lives of women
   who live in hovels. . . .

Chapter 10

Study Skills

Have a student read aloud the listing of a peasant woman's duties in the primary source on this page. Help students understand any unfamiliar expressions. Then discuss the tasks that are generally not a part of housekeeping today, so that students get a sense of the full extent of such a woman's work.

Art Connection

Have students make a medieval calendar. Tell them that the peasants used the feast days and saints' days of the church year to help them mark the seasons and plan their work. Share the following information: The peasants started spring plowing right after Easter. Their planting had to be completed by Pentecost, which occurred seven weeks after Easter. Harvesting began on Midsummer Day, June 24. By the Feast of the Assumption on August 15, the harvest and haying were finished. From then until St. Michael's Day on September 23, peasants gathered the fruit crop. They gathered the root crops until St. Martin's Day, November 11. Students may design their calendars as one large page with small illustrations, or they may put each section of the calendar on a separate page. Suggest that students study the illustrations in this chapter for ideas. They may also wish to do library research or even visit a nearby museum.

Medieval Farming

The cycle of changing seasons brought an endless round of work to peasant families. But improvements like the wheelbarrow, horseshoes, and new crops slowly began to soften their harsh lives.

Protecting horses' feet from wear and injury, better horseshoes allowed these strong animals to pull metal-tipped plows. Plowing deeper meant farmers could get at the richest soil, grow more crops, and store food for lean times.

Month by month, this page from a 15th-century French "book of hours" shows the activities of the farm year. Read it left to right and top to bottom. In the January snow, peasants cut the winter wheat they had sowed in September. October found the peasant crushing grapes for wine by foot.

Not the same old bean and pea soup! New plants like cabbage, parsley and leeks added flavor and nutrition to the boring peasant diet.

Leeks

Peas

Cabbage

Parsley

Note: You may wish to use this Closer Look after students finish reading the subsection "Peasants" on p. 266.

More About Medieval Farming

Advances in technology helped farmers in the Middle Ages. Two inventions that brought increased farm production were the metal-tipped plow and the improved horseshoe.

Better designs for horseshoes meant that some medieval farmers could replace their oxen with horses. Oxen were strong and cheap to own; for hundreds of years, they had been used to pull plows. Horses cost more to buy, ate more expensive food, and needed protection for their hooves. But horses worked twice as fast as the plodding oxen.

ECONOMICS
Visual Learning

Explain that for hundreds of years, farmers had planted half their land each year and allowed the other half to rest. During the late Middle Ages, this custom changed. In fall, farmers planted winter wheat on a third of their land; they planted barley, oats, peas, and beans on another third in spring; the final third they left to rest. Have students draw a pie graph to illustrate each of these two patterns of land use.

267

Research

Have students research a topic from the month-by-month illustration on this page. Allow time for them to go to the library to find information on their topic. The following list identifies the illustrations shown. January: cutting winter wheat; February: gathering firewood; March: planting trees; April: combing wool; May: a noble hunting with falcons; June: cutting hay; July: binding wheat; August: separating wheat from chaff; September: planting winter wheat; October: squeezing wine grapes; November: beating acorns from trees; December: slaughtering hogs.

Visual Learning

Discuss the illustrations included in the "book of hours." What do they show about the significance of the activities shown for each month? (See list under Research at left.) Then have students create a similar page that might be used to illustrate a "book of hours" showing a year in their own lives.

> ➤ *Here Pope Urban II blesses a church at Cluny in the 1000s. The monastery at Cluny in France was established in 910, and was a leader of the reform movement within the church. By the late 1000s, there were about 200 monasteries administered by the center at Cluny.*

■ *A feudal lord maintained his castle as a fortress. Knights and townspeople were his frequent guests. Peasants labored to support all castle activities.*

■ *How did each class help to keep a feudal manor running?*

▼ *A monk in his study is shown here on an ivory book cover from the Middle Ages.*

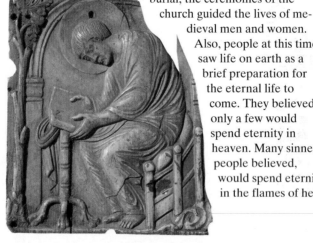

Clergy

Society in the Middle Ages was described by Alfred the Great as consisting of "men of prayer, men of war, and men of work." Perhaps the men and women "of prayer" had the most comfortable lives of any in the Middle Ages.

The influence of the clergy—from pope, archbishops, and bishops to priests, monks, and nuns—extended to every part of medieval life. Most medieval manors included a small church. From baptism to marriage to burial, the ceremonies of the church guided the lives of medieval men and women. Also, people at this time saw life on earth as a brief preparation for the eternal life to come. They believed only a few would spend eternity in heaven. Many sinners, people believed, would spend eternity in the flames of hell.

The power to condemn or to forgive sinners made the church a considerable force in medieval society. Many people entered the clergy because of their deeply held beliefs. Others, however, joined the church to acquire status and influence.

Thousands of monks, nuns, and servants also lived and worked in large stone structures. A monastery was a complex community with many different buildings—granaries, breweries, bakeries with huge ovens, wineries, and the abbey church and library.

Inside the library, monks hunched over tall desks and copied manuscripts in beautiful handwriting, or drew illustrations. With the same devotion and care, monks and nuns of the Middle Ages also taught children, fed the poor, cared for the sick, and provided shelter to travelers. Most of the clergy worked long hours and reaped few earthly rewards. Their devotion to the church mirrored a vassal's dedication to his lord. ■

Study Skills

Some women in the Middle Ages assumed positions of great power and responsibility as heads of convents and religious orders. Ask students to find out more about Hildegard of Bingen and write a summary paragraph about her life and accomplishments. Compile the paragraphs in a class booklet, and encourage students to include illustrations.

Religious Context

In 529 a monk named Benedict started a monastery at Monte Cassino in Italy. His rule, or regulations for conduct, called for a balance of manual labor, intellectual work, and prayer. That rule became the standard for many monasteries throughout Europe and for Benedictine monks even today, though not all monasteries are Benedictine. Locate Monte Cassino on a map of Europe for students. Other important monasteries include Cluny (France), Canterbury, Winchester (both in England), and Assisi (Italy).

Life in the Town

Not all people lived in feudal manors or monasteries. Peasants seeking freedom, younger sons of nobles seeking a fortune, scholars seeking new ideas, and freed serfs left the country manor for towns.

The Growth of Towns

The walls that rose around a medieval town enclosed a jumble. Narrow, crowded streets turned in on each other. Rough wooden houses shoved up against each other, hardly leaving enough space for light to filter through.

After the Western Roman Empire fell, towns had almost disappeared from Europe. The population of Rome, which remained the largest city in Europe, fell from about one million to only a few thousand.

But in the 1000s, trade and town life began to revive. Linen from Italy, woven wool from Flanders, leather from Spain, and other products were traded in towns in Europe and in countries beyond Europe. And the craftspeople who made these products found ways to control their own trades.

Guilds

Shoemakers, blacksmiths, tailors, weavers, and bakers banded together with others of their trade to form guilds. A **guild** was a union of people who practiced a trade. Guilds for each trade limited the number of people they accepted.

A boy who wanted to work at a trade began as an apprentice. He served a guild member for several years until he mastered basic skills. Then he became a journeyman, or skilled worker. A journeyman received pay for his work. Eventually, if he became skilled enough, he would produce a masterpiece and present it for admission into the guild. Only an expert at his trade was allowed to join a guild.

Christian law, unlike Roman law, put women under the control of their fathers and husbands. Women were responsible for the home, children, and most of the trade goods they produced there, such as textiles or foods. Some, however, were merchants or shopkeepers. A craftswoman might be admitted to a guild if her husband was a member. In Paris and Cologne, embroiderers formed all-female guilds.

Many European Jews also lived in towns because they were not allowed to own land. However, they were not allowed to join guilds, either. Many Jews were therefore merchants. Some were moneylenders, the only trade forbidden to Christians.

The town was where feudalism began to die. Powered by trade, the new commercial way of life that developed in the towns looked beyond the simpler and closed world of manor and village. ∎

▲ *The carpenter in this French painting from the late Middle Ages probably belonged to a carpenter's guild.*

■ *Describe the new social order that evolved in medieval towns.*

▼ *This banner was proudly displayed by the boot and shoemaker's guild of a town in Belgium.*

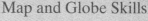
Discuss with students the elements in the medieval town that would give rise to the modern city. *(Commerce, guilds, exchange of ideas, new social order.)* Then ask students to locate the following medieval towns on a political map: Bruges, Cambridge, Genoa, Frankfurt, Ghent, Innsbruck, London, Milan, Oxford, Paris, Venice.

■ *Merchants traded linen, wool, leather, and other products, and craftspeople formed guilds to control their trades.*

269

Persuasive Writing

There were very few ways to leave the hard life of a serf. One way was to escape and hide in a large town. After a year and a day one would be legally free. Life would still be hard, though. Even being apprenticed to a demanding master, for instance, was hardly better than serfdom—except that it carried the promise of freedom. Ask students to imagine themselves in that position. Then have them write a letter advising a relative on whether to risk the escape from serfdom.

Interviewing

Today's version of the medieval guild is a labor union. As a group or individual activity, have students telephone or write a letter to a nearby labor union to ask how the terms *apprentice, journeyman,* and *master* are used today. Students should also inquire about how a worker advances from one stage to the next. If possible, arrange for a union representative to visit the class and answer student questions about union organization, membership, and goals.

Critical Thinking

Present the background information on serfs in the persuasive writing activity on this page. Then discuss the similarities in the conditions facing medieval serfs and those facing escaping slaves in this country several hundred years later. *(Both groups lacked the freedom to control their own destinies, endured physical hardships, and sought comfort in religion.)*

Critical Thinking

Ask students to explain in what way the *Magna Carta* was a product of feudalism. *(It detailed the nobles' rights as vassals of the king.)* Then ask in what way it foreshadowed future developments in political systems. *(It subjected the king to the rule of law in his dealings with the nobles, establishing some degree of personal freedom and due process, both of which would have an impact on future political ideas and systems.)*

■ *The* Magna Carta *established rights that not even a king could take away. It paved the way for rule by law.*

CLOSE

Have students summarize the structure and workings of feudalism and how it affected peasants, clergy, and townspeople. From student comments construct a web graphic organizer on the chalkboard that puts feudalism and all levels of nobility at the center and shows other major groups radiating out from that center. Help students assess the overall impact of feudalism on social progress.

270

The Forces of Change

▲ *This copy of the* Magna Carta *is one of four in England. No one is sure which is the original.*

■ *How did the* Magna Carta *pave the way for a new social system in England?*

Eventually, the feudal monarchy that was established in England by William the Conqueror would also change. After William's death in 1087, the followers he had rewarded with feudal fiefs grew more and more powerful. Their wealth was increased by payments they demanded from towns that grew up on land within their control. Over several generations, the feudal lords' power and wealth grew substantially.

When King John took the throne in 1199, the most powerful landowners had become increasingly outspoken. Then John led England into losing wars and ever-higher levels of taxation. In 1204, John lost all of his lands in the north of France, thus angering those of his vassals who held fiefs in that region.

Also, because of a disagreement between John and the pope, the churches shut their doors to the people of England. Many lords renounced allegiance to John, and a small band of them cornered him in a meadow outside London. In June of 1215, after days of argument, they forced him to affix the royal seal to an amazing medieval document—the *Magna Carta*, or great charter. You can read excerpts form the *Magna Carta* on page 504.

The *Magna Carta* focused on the rights of nobles. It acknowledged the rights of the lords and prevented a king from taking those rights away. It also contained the following condition:

> N *o free man shall be taken or imprisoned or dispossessed, or outlawed, or banished, or in any way destroyed, nor will we go upon him, nor send upon him, except by the legal judgment of his peers or by the law of the land.*

By subjecting the king to the rule of law, the *Magna Carta* became the basis for future reforms. Our own Bill of Rights and the concept of "due process of law" grew out of the *Magna Carta*.

The signing of the *Magna Carta* signaled the beginning of feudalism's decline. The ideas of personal freedom and liberty were now firmly planted. ■

REVIEW

1. **FOCUS** How did the feudal system affect the everyday lives of people in Europe?
2. **CONNECT** How did the Battle of Hastings contribute to the rise of feudalism in England?
3. **BELIEF SYSTEMS** In what ways did the relationship between the clergy and the church resemble the relationship between vassals and their lords?
4. **SOCIAL SYSTEMS** Compare and contrast the life of an apprentice with the life of a serf on a manor.
5. **CRITICAL THINKING** In your opinion, which was the most important class or group of people in feudal times? Why?
6. **WRITING ACTIVITY** The *Magna Carta* guaranteed lords certain rights under laws that even a king had to obey. Think about the elements of respect and consideration that go into running a contented household. Then draw up a household *Magna Carta* to share with the class.

Chapter 10

Homework Options

Have students write a paragraph about medieval Europe that uses each of the key terms.

Study Guide: p. 41

Answers to Review Questions

1. Feudalism provided military support for monarchs and land for vassals. It kept peasants impoverished.
2. After William the Conqueror won the Battle of Hastings, he established the existing French style of feudalism throughout England.
3. The clergy served the church with the same devotion a vassal showed his lord. Members of the clergy were also ranked within a rigid hierarchy.
4. Serfs were at the bottom of the feudal order. Living conditions for serfs were dismal. Apprentices occupied the lowest rank among craftspeople. Their conditions were also bleak, but they could move up in society by developing skills.
5. Answers will vary. Students should support their choice with evidence from the text.

400   700   1900
       732   1854

L E S S O N   3

Two Feudal Societies

The Japanese samurai warrior and the Italian knight on this page face one another across 6,000 miles. Even so, the men are strikingly similar. Like the Italian knight, the samurai rides a horse and wears armor. The samurai's armor consists of lacquered steel plates sewn together with leather strips and fastened across his chest. Although earlier knights had worn heavy chain mail shirts of up to a hundred thousand wire links, this knight is encased in plates of steel.

Both men spent their lives preparing to wage battle for their lords. When the samurai was a boy, he practiced with a long wooden sword and studied martial arts. At 15, he exchanged the wooden sword for a long metal one. The knight, too, began his training young, learning to fight as a page and as a squire.

The samurai practiced Buddhism and Shintoism. The knight prayed to Jesus Christ. But both men followed codes of behavior that stressed loyalty to their lords and serving as examples of virtue to people of lower classes. Despite the miles and years that separate them, the warriors are alike in many ways. Each was a member of a specially trained warrior class that provided protection to people in feudal societies.

THINKING FOCUS

In what ways were feudal Japan and feudal Europe alike and different?

Key Terms

- chivalry
- bushido

▲ *This Italian knight from the 1300s carries a shield with the symbol of Naples, Italy.*

◄ *In this Japanese painting from about 1600, a samurai cleans his sword. Notice that both the knight and the samurai use stirrups. How would stirrups help them in battle?*

271

Feudal Europe and Japan

INTRODUCE

Ask students what they recall about the relationship between the Japanese shogun, daimyo, and samurai from Chapter 9, Lesson 3. Have students name their European counterparts. *(King, lords, and knights.)* List these parallel terms on the chalkboard. Have students read the Thinking Focus and then read to find the reasons behind the similarities and differences between the two feudal systems.

Key Terms

Vocabulary Strategies: T36–T37
chivalry—the idealized code of conduct of medieval knights, emphasizing honor, courtesy, loyalty, and fair treatment of the weak
bushido—a Japanese code of ethics involving courage, loyalty, and commitment to military life; also called "the way of the warrior"

◄ *Stirrups would allow them more freedom of movement, since they would not need to hang onto the horse to remain in the saddle. Thus, they could defend themselves or use weapons.*

271

Objectives

1. Identify the major similarities in the development of feudalism in Western Europe and in Japan.
2. Summarize the reasons that feudalism ended earlier in Europe than it did in Japan.

Graphic Overview

	Knight	Samurai
Society	feudal Europe	feudal Japan
Style of Battle	horseback; lances	swords, arrows
Code of Honor	chivalry	bushido
Period of Importance	800s–1300s	1100s–1800s

DEVELOP

Ask students to study the two pictures on p. 271 to find three similarities in the subjects. *(Both wear armor, have elaborate clothes, carry weapons, ride horses.)* Have students skim Chapter 10 and Lessons 3 and 4 in Chapter 9 for other pictures of knights and samurai. Draw the Graphic Overview on the chalkboard and have students discuss similarities and differences between the two societies. Ask them in which society they think the feudal system would last longer. Then have them read to confirm or modify their predictions.

Similar Societies

Across Time & Space

During the periods of feudalism, massive castles sprang up all over Europe and Japan. In Europe, castles had rounded walls so that ladders would not balance against them and invaders could not get inside. In Japan, the stone walls were curved so they would stay upright through an earthquake. But Japanese castles were palaces—built for beauty as well as protection.

▼ *The Bayeux Tapestry, which was made in the late 1000s by Norman Duchess Matilda and her ladies, is only 20 inches wide but 230 feet long. It tells the story of the Norman Conquest. This section shows William with his Norman lords, some members of the clergy, entertainers, and servants at a banquet.*

In Europe, feudalism developed after the fall of the Roman Empire and especially after Charlemagne's empire collapsed in 814. Lacking a strong central government, landowners came to depend on warrior knights for protection against invaders. These knights became a new class in society.

In Japan of the 1100s, landowners in the provinces depended on samurai warriors to protect their estates and to wage battles against rival clans. In the 1100s, the samurai became an important new class in Japanese society.

Styles of Battle

Frankish warriors of the 700s did not ride horses. The Muslim invaders who threatened France in 732 did ride horses. Therefore, the Franks had great difficulty defeating the Muslims. Later, the Frankish leader Charles Martel granted land to his most trusted warriors and asked them to use income from the land to equip themselves with horses and armor.

When Frankish foot soldiers changed to fighting on horseback, they lengthened the spears they had been accustomed to using into lances. By bracing himself in his stirrups and charging his enemy at a gallop, a warrior could strike a tremendous blow with his lance.

Of course, the armies who fought with Charles Martel and with his grandson Charlemagne continued to be made up mostly of warriors on foot, with only a few mounted knights. But when Vikings and other invaders threatened France, landowners outfitted more and more of their warriors with horses and armor. As a reward for his service as a warrior, a knight was often awarded a fief of land for his own use, thus becoming a vassal to the lord he served.

Japanese samurai did not learn new methods of fighting at the beginning of their feudal period. Japanese armies had included mounted warriors when the ruling clans invaded Japan around A.D 200. But many warriors of the

RVN: PRANDIVM: ET hIC: EPISCOPVS:CIBV:E POTV: BE NE DIC IT ODO:EPS ROT BER WIL LELM:

Chapter 10

Access Activity

Direct students to the illustration on p. 272 which shows different levels of European society. Ask students to work in pairs to identify as many positions in society as they can, based on the picture. Then have them name other positions or levels that are not depicted.

Access Strategy

Point out that Lesson 3 is somewhat different in structure from other lessons they have read in that it has a double focus. State that the lesson compares and contrasts two societies they have read about in Chapters 9 and 10—Europe and Japan—and is mostly a summary of certain information and ideas they have met before. Have students suggest features of these societies they can recall from their reading about the political and social systems of Japan and Europe. Record their comments in the form of two semantic maps on the chalkboard. Then use the timeline on p. 271 to point out that, although these two societies were both feudal in structure, feudalism prevailed in different time periods in the two societies.

Study Skills

Ask students what conditions gave rise to feudalism in Europe *(invasion by outsiders, political disorder)* and in Japan *(wars between clans, general lawlessness).* Then review the similar duties and codes of conduct of knights and samurai. Ask what the price was for failing to fulfill their duties. *(Public disgrace; suicide.)*

1100s fought on foot. Samurai also used bows and arrows.

Codes of Honor

Tales of Middle Ages praised knights such as King Arthur's Sir Lancelot:

> *Y*ou were the [most courteous] knight that ever bore shield! And thou were the truest friend . . . that bestrode horse. And thou were the kindest man that ever struck with sword. And thou were the goodliest person that ever came among [a crowd] of knights, and thou [were] the meekest man and the gentlest who ever ate in hall among ladies.
>
> Thomas Malory, *Le Morte d'Arthur,* 1485

Knights aspired to a code of conduct called **chivalry.** The values of that code were the qualities praised in Sir Lancelot: courtesy, honor, defending the weak, and loyalty to one's lord. Of course, most knights did not live up to these ideals.

The samurai code is today called **bushido** or "the way of the warrior." It required a samurai to give up his life if necessary to protect his lord. If he failed or was captured, a samurai sometimes felt so humiliated by his loss of honor that he would kill himself. Like the code of chivalry, the ideals of bushido included a code of gentlemanly conduct for samurai. Confucian ideas of duty were important in Japan during feudal times. Samurai believed they had a duty to serve as examples of virtue for the lower classes. ■

▲ *In this detail from the* Handscroll of the Heiji War, *painted in the 1200s, warriors defend the gate of a palace.*

■ *How did the system of feudalism meet the needs of both medieval Europe and Japan?*

■ *Feudalism provided security for people at all levels of society and made up for the lack of a strong, centralized government.*

Research

The martial arts of jujitsu and karate are influenced by the philosophy of the samurai. Have students use the library to learn about these martial arts (skills involved, types of contests, recognition, and so forth). Then have students work together to contact an expert in one of these martial arts and arrange a demonstration for the class. Tell students to prepare questions to be answered by the expert.

Writing a Narrative

Ask students to write a brief imaginary biographical sketch of either a samurai or a knight. Help students think about the details that will make their stories come alive. Instruct them to give their subjects families and teachers, overlords, and battles to win or lose. Have students share their biographies with the rest of the class. Encourage them to combine elements from several of the biographies in a class play about the life of a samurai or a knight.

Visual Learning

Tell students that the symbols of the samurai were the sword and the cherry blossom. Ask students to suggest two symbols for European knights. *(Possibilities include a sword, a cross, a lance.)* Suggest that students create cardboard cutouts of a full-size samurai and knight, using their text and outside sources to gather visual details.

CULTURE
Critical Thinking

Ask students to explain the role that technology played in the decay of the feudal system in Europe. Have them discuss other factors involved, such as the growth of cities. Then ask students to identify and explain the role that geography played in the preservation of the feudal system in Japan. Finally, emphasize the evolution of the samurai's role in Japan.

■ *Feudalism lasted longer in Japan because samurai warriors played a greater role in the social and political structure. Also, Japan's isolation provided little need for change.*

CLOSE

Ask students to agree or disagree with this statement: The European knight and the samurai served the same function in their societies. Tell students first to jot down their supporting ideas on paper and then organize them in order of importance. List in two columns on the chalkboard all of the most important reasons for agreement and for disagreement. Guide students to a conclusion.

274

Different Societies

In Japan, the way of the warrior remained a powerful force in society until 1854. In Europe, feudalism ended 400 years earlier.

Why did feudalism die in Europe? For one thing, growing towns offered alternatives to people who did not want to function within the feudal system. Also, military technology changed in the 1300s. Large armies with new weapons—the longbow in the 1300s and guns in the 1400s—made mounted knights less effective in battle.

Knights were often more interested in overseeing their land than in serving as warriors. Sometimes

■ *Why did feudalism last so much longer in Japan than it did in Europe?*

▼ *Part of the wall surrounding this town was originally a castle (top left), built in the 1100s. Compare it with the Japanese castle on page 238.*

they refused to fight when asked to perform military service. When feudalism was strong, this would have resulted in a ceremony of public disgrace. Then, a knight who broke his vows was stripped of his armor, piece by piece. His shield was crushed, his spurs cut off, and his sword broken in half. But after about 1400, kings began to rely on paid armies rather than asking knights to honor their feudal obligations.

In Japan, the ruling shoguns eventually forced samurai to become literate and to learn administrative skills. In Europe, however, most knights did not learn these skills. Administrators in European kingdoms were often members of the clergy.

Feudalism in Japan lasted longer than feudalism in Europe partly because samurai who were not warriors became government administrators. Also, Japan sealed itself off from the West between 1635 and 1854, thus preserving its feudal society. But Japanese shoguns adopted Western military technology after 1854.

Just as in Europe, feudalism arose in Japan to fill a need for government and protection. And just as in Europe, Japanese feudalism declined quickly when things began to change. ■

REVIEW

1. **FOCUS** In what ways were feudal Japan and feudal Europe alike and different?
2. **CONNECT** What role did religion play in the belief system of the knight? Of the samurai warrior?
3. **HISTORY** Why did feudalism decline in Europe? In Japan?

4. **CRITICAL THINKING** In the Middle Ages in Europe, a person born into the peasant class had little opportunity to advance upwards. What are some of the ways people today can improve their status?
5. **WRITING ACTIVITY** Write a story about a meeting between a knight and a samurai warrior.

274

Chapter 10

Homework Options

Have students complete an expanded chart of the main points of the lesson, based on the chart shown in the Graphic Overview.

Study Guide: p. 42

Answers to Review Questions

1. Both cultures supported a rigid hierarchy in which the functions and roles of each class were well defined. However, in Japan, warriors appreciated the value of education and gradually became administrators. In Europe, administrators were often members of the clergy.
2. The knight was a Christian. The samurai practiced Buddhism and Shinto.
3. Advances in warfare made mounted knights less effective. Some knights were

reluctant to accept land from several lords and then became reluctant to leave their estates. Kings began to rely on paid armies rather than on knights. Similar changes took place in Japan after 1876.
4. Answers will vary, but students may mention education, experience, hard work, resourcefulness, and luck.

UNDERSTANDING GROUP DECISIONS

How a Guild Works

Here's Why

Group decisions are effective only when they are accepted and supported by group members. Members of a group need to know how to consider both their short-term and their long-term interests when evaluating group decisions.

You would have needed the skill of evaluating group decisions if you had belonged to a guild in feudal Europe. You need it to be an effective member of a modern group, too, such as a sports team or a scout troop. Do you know how to evaluate and support group decisions?

Here's How

A trade guild benefits its members by making decisions that are good for the group as a whole on a long-term basis. Members of a trade guild are largely dependent upon the guild for their livelihood.

Similarly, the guild depends on the support of its members. The goals of the group may sometimes conflict with the short-term interests of some individual members. When this happens, the individual can either accept the group decision or work to get the decision changed. To disobey the group would probably result in negative consequences over the long term.

Suppose you are a member of a feudal trade guild. Your guild wants you to raise prices on the goods you sell, but you think this will result in a loss of sales for you. What should you do?

You must weigh the negative effects of the price increase on you against the positive effects such a change might have for the entire group. Your reaction to such a decision depends on how the positive and negative effects balance each other. One way to weigh the effects of a decision is to create a chart like the one the students have made in the photograph below.

Try It

Consider the following decisions made by your guild. Make a chart for each decision and then consider what your reaction in each case would be.

1. The guild decides to increase membership dues to support the family of a member who is unable to work.
2. The guild decides to restrict new memberships at a time when it seems there is plenty of business for all.

Apply It

Suppose your study group has decided to meet on the weekend to prepare for a test next week. Make a chart of the advantages and disadvantages of this decision.

Feudal Europe and Japan

275

UNDERSTANDING
GROUP DECISIONS

This skills feature uses feudal trade guilds to teach students how to evaluate and make group decisions.

SOCIAL SYSTEMS
Critical Thinking

Ask students to name a few groups that they consider themselves a member of. *(Family, class, sports team.)* List the names of the groups on the chalkboard. Then ask students how they became a member of the group and how the group affects their life. Now lead a class discussion about possible consequences of leaving one of the groups listed. *(Consequences can range from none to severe.)* Ask students if their degree of attachment to a group influences how they behave in the group.

275

Answers to Try It

Answers will vary but might include:
1. Individual Advantage: security. Group Advantage: loyalty. Individual Disadvantage: deduction from pay. Group Disadvantage: possible low morale.
2. Individual Advantage: less competition. Group Advantage: no time lost in training new members. Individual Disadvantages: friend or relative may be closed out; workload may increase. Group Disadvantage: lack of new people may mean a shortage of new ideas.

Answers to Apply It

Answers will vary, but should demonstrate that students have considered both individual and group advantages and disadvantages.

Objective

Evaluate the advantages and disadvantages of accepting and supporting group decisions. (Critical Thinking 2; Social Participation 2)

DISCOVERY PROCESS

Students will use the following steps in the discovery process to complete the activity:

Get Ready Gather books or magazines that discuss Japanese schools; list interesting questions.

Find Out Look for answers to the questions.

Move Ahead Create categories of questions on a chart and compare the answers found.

Explore Some More Choose another topic and again investigate similarities and differences between Japan and the United States.

Materials needed: Books, magazines, large sheet of paper, tape, and markers.

CULTURE
Study Skills

Draw attention to the top photograph on p. 276 and ask a student to read its caption aloud. Ask students who cleans their school. *(Custodian or maintenance staff.)* How would they feel if they had to clean the school? Then discuss the caption to the lower illustration on p. 276. Encourage students to think about the subjects they spend the most time learning. Is social studies second only to English? How well do they feel they know geography?

276

EXPLORING

Japanese and American Schools

You can learn a great deal about another country by finding out about its schools. Education is one way in which a society passes its values and its knowledge to the next generation. What is school like in Japan?

▲ *Who cleans your school? In Japan, the students themselves sweep the floors of their classrooms daily.*

➤ *This is the cover of a seventh-grade geography textbook popular in Japan. Japanese seventh graders spend more time on social studies than any other subject except Japanese.*

276

Find Out

Look for answers to each of your questions. If an answer gives you an idea for another question, add it to your list.

Divide your information into two groups: ways in which American and Japanese schools are alike and ways in which they are different. Did you find more similarities or more differences?

Get Ready

You'll need a notebook, a pen, and some books or magazines with information about schools in Japan.

Make a list of questions you want to answer: What time does school begin and end for Japanese students your age? Do they have dress codes? What about after-school sports? Do students move from class to class? Does one teacher handle all subjects? What subjects do Japanese schools teach? How much homework do they give?

Chapter 10

Objectives

1. Identify similarities and differences between Japanese and American schools. (Study Skills 1, 2)
2. Identify the values reflected by each system. (Ethics and Belief Systems 1, 2, 4)

Activity

Assign half the students to research the history of Japanese schools and half to research that of American schools. Give each student a question from the categories on the class chart. For example, a student might look for information on the hours in a Japanese school day or week in the 1800s. When the students have finished their research, have them add the facts they found to the class chart in the appropriate areas. Use the information on the chart for a class discussion of the similarities and differences between the two educational systems, and have students speculate on the values represented by some of the facts. Discuss which values are similar and which are different.

Move Ahead

Tape a large sheet of paper to the wall of your classroom. Each student should mention a question that he or she asked. Use the questions to create categories on the chart. For instance, some people may have asked about school hours. If so, a student might write on the chart: "Hours in School per Day (or Week)."

Do everyone's answers agree? If not, find out where the information came from. Is one magazine or book more recent than another? Is one author more knowledgeable and respected than another?

When your chart is complete, discuss the information. What Japanese ideas would you like American schools to adopt? Why?

Explore Some More

Choose another area of American life, one you're very familiar with. It might be sports, games, crafts, music, art, or some current concern—animal welfare, the environment, or political campaigns, for instance.

Find out whether the Japanese share this interest of yours. If so, do they pursue it in the same way? If not, can you find out why not?

▲ May 5, Boys' Day, is a school holiday in Japan. On this day most families fly carp flags outside their homes. The symbol of the carp—a fish that swims against river currents—inspires boys to face life's difficulties with courage.

◄ Like Boys' Day, Girls' Day is also a school holiday in Japan. Celebrated on March 3, Girls' Day centers around dolls. Girls display their dolls and hold tea parties where they serve little cakes iced with cherry-blossom frosting.

277

Feudal Europe and Japan

Critical Thinking

Ask a student to read the italicized introduction to the feature aloud. Then draw students' attention to the illustrations on p. 277, and have them read the captions to themselves. Ask what value the carp flag displayed in Japan on Boys' Day represents. *(Facing life's difficulties with courage.)* Next, ask students to give their opinions about the values expressed by Girls' Day. *(Possible answers: being good mothers, having good manners, being good cooks.)* Ask if students can think of anything in American culture that teaches values similar to those of Boys' and Girls' Days. *(Possible answers: Boy Scouts, Girl Scouts.)* Go on to discuss students' opinions on whether the values taught by Boys' Day and Girls' Day could be shared by both boys and girls. *(Encourage students to see that indeed they could and should.)*

Activity

Divide students into two groups and tell them they are going to debate whether students should clean their own classrooms at the end of each school day. Allow them time to meet in their groups and list the points they want to make. Tell them to support their points with the values they represent and historical facts from their earlier research. During the debate, have the groups take turns introducing their points. Let the opposing team respond to each point. When both groups have stated and rebutted each point, have the entire class vote by secret ballot for or against the issue. Count their votes and declare the winning group.

Collaborative Strategy

One recommended strategy that may be useful in this lesson is heterogeneous grouping. For further information, turn to pp. T34–T35.

Answers to Reviewing Key Terms

A. Sample answers:
1. False. **Monasteries** were religious communities formed by monks.
2. False. **Knights** were mounted soldiers a lord provided to the king for military duty.
3. False. A **hierarchy** was a ranking of people based on their functions in society.
4. True.
5. False. A **fief** was land a lord gave to soldiers who had served him.
6. False. **Feudalism** was a social and political system of rule.
7. False. **Vassals** were soldiers who received land from a lord.
8. True.
9. False. A vassal who received land took an **oath of fealty** promising loyalty to his lord.
10. True.

B. Sample answers:
1. Joshua was an apprentice in a blacksmiths' **guild.**
2. Lady Jane ran the **manor,** the castle and estate, while her husband was away.
3. The vassal paid **homage,** or honor, to his lord.
4. Knights tried to practice a code of conduct called **chivalry.**
5. People near the top of a **hierarchy** have advantages.

Answers to Exploring Concepts

A. Sample answer:
For lesson 1, students might draw a barbarian and write: *Barbarians were the tribes that invaded Europe after Rome fell.*

B. Sample answers:
1. Barbarian tribes fought each other and conquered parts of the empire. Government and learning almost disappeared.
2. Charlemagne's grandsons fought each other, and landowners took over local rule. Vikings conquered the divided empire.
3. Answers should show understanding of the terms *feudalism, hierarchy, lord, fief, vassal, knight,* and *oath of fealty.*
4. A vassal's fief belonged to him only as long as he remained loyal.
5. Residents were protected by thick walls and narrow windows. Everyone slept in the drafty, dirty dining hall.

Chapter Review

Reviewing Key Terms

bushido (p. 273)
chivalry (p. 273)
feudalism (p. 261)
fief (p. 261)
guild (p. 269)
hierarchy (p. 261)
homage (p. 263)

knight (p. 261)
manor (p. 266)
monastery (p. 257)
oath of fealty (p. 261)
serf (p. 264)
vassal (p. 261)

A. Write whether each of the following statements is true or false. Then rewrite the false statements to make them true.
1. Monasteries were simple town churches in the Middle Ages.
2. Knights were monks and nuns on horseback.
3. Most castles had a hierarchy, or tower.
4. Bushido was the samurai code of loyalty and conduct.
5. A fief was a kind of musical instrument.
6. Feudalism was a religious and economic system of rule in medieval Europe.
7. Knights and their lords sailed to battles on warships called vassals.
8. Serfs were the peasants who lived on a lord's estate.
9. A medieval woman had to take an oath of fealty to her husband at her marriage.
10. A guild was a union of tradespeople.

B. Use each word below in a sentence that shows what the word means.
1. guild
2. manor
3. homage
4. chivalry
5. hierarchy

Exploring Concepts

A. Create an illustrated "people summary" of the chapter by drawing pictures of one person from each lesson as listed below. Write a sentence describing each person you draw.

Lesson 1:
barbarian
Charles Martel
Charlemagne
Pope Leo III
Alcuin
Viking
Alfred the Great
William the Conqueror

Lesson 2:
peasant
monk
Hildegard of Bingen
King John

Lesson 3:
samurai
shogun

B. Support each of the following statements with facts and details from the chapter.
1. After the fall of Rome, Europe became a place of warfare.
2. Viking conquests in Europe were made easier by the weakness of Charlemagne's heirs.

3. Under William the Conqueror there developed a highly organized system for ruling England.
4. Loyalty held English feudal society together.
5. Castles in 12th-century England were built for safety but were not very comfortable for those living within.
6. Peasants led difficult lives.
7. The church played a very important role in the lives of most of the people in Europe during the Middle Ages.
8. In spite of their limited legal state, many European women held great responsibilities in the Middle Ages.
9. Japanese feudalism and European feudalism were different but similar.
10. There were several reasons why feudalism endured 400 years longer in Japan than in Europe.

6. Peasants faced hard work in the fields, crude huts for homes, malnutrition, and the threat of disease or warfare.
7. From baptism to marriage to burial, the church guided people's lives. Monks and nuns fed the poor, cared for the sick, and sheltered travelers.
8. This is especially true of privileged women. Sometimes noblewomen controlled whole fiefs. It is also true of women's roles in the church, where women led large convents and abbeys.
9. In both Japan and Europe, the feudal system placed government in the hands of local lords. Warriors followed the code of chivalry in Europe and bushido in Japan.
10. Japan was isolated for centuries, and some samurai became government administrators.

Reviewing Skills

1. Read the group decision below. Then make a chart that gives both the individual and group advantages and disadvantages of the decision.

   Instead of collecting money to donate to a charity, your class decides to spend several Saturdays helping senior citizens in the neighborhood maintain their houses by raking leaves, painting fences, and hauling away rubbish.

2. Review the section called An Age of Learning in Lesson 1 on pages 258–259. What unstated assumption did Charlemagne make about knowledge and learning?

3. Suppose you are outlining a chapter that compares and contrasts the nature of feudalism in Europe with that of feudalism in Japan. What two kinds of information would you need to find and list in your outline?

Using Critical Thinking

1. In this chapter, you learned how the advent of fighting from horseback and using armor changed the nature of warfare. You also learned about the changes in military technology that permitted armies to defeat mounted knights. What were those new inventions of the 1300s and 1400s? Do you think the country with the most sophisticated weapons always wins a war? Explain your answer.

2. "They worked hard, and they were poor. They had almost nothing to their names, and the little they had was not much use in this world." This bleak description, along with the quotes in the chapter from *Piers the Plowman,* might easily describe the peasants of Europe in the Middle Ages. Do the quotations also describe the plight of some people today? If so, who? Where? How are their conditions similar?

3. Craftspeople in medieval Europe began their apprenticeships when they were very young and worked long hours for no pay while they learned the skills they would need for their life's work. Imagine that you are transported back in time to the Middle Ages. What trade would you be interested in learning to master? Which do you think is more important, the kind of vocational training young people received in the Middle Ages or the general education you're getting now? Explain your answer.

Preparing for Citizenship

1. **COLLECTING INFORMATION** Research what happened on that day in June of 1215 when the powerful landowners made King John of England agree to the Magna Carta. Imagine that you are King John and tell the class about your experience in a way colorful enough to make them feel they are witnessing history.

2. **GROUP ACTIVITY** In two groups, draw hierarchies of your school system and of your town government or a local business. Draw organization charts that show who reports to whom. Your finished products will probably resemble pyramids, with many people at the bottom and fewer on each level as you move toward the top.

3. **COLLABORATIVE LEARNING** In groups of five, plan a five-minute TV documentary on one of these topics: Charlemagne's kingdom, William's conquest and rule of England, life on a medieval manor, or feudalism in Japan. Assign one person to research the subject, one to write the script, one to make simple costumes and scenery, one to prepare the ads, and one to direct the documentary. Each student in the group should also play one of the characters. If possible, videotape the documentary.

Feudal Europe and Japan

Answers to Preparing for Citizenship

1. **COLLECTING INFORMATION** Schedule times when students can tell the class about their research. They should present the most important facts about the Magna Carta from King John's point of view.

2. **GROUP ACTIVITY** You might use a corporation as an example in which manual laborers and clerical workers report to supervisors, who report to middle managers, who report to top managers, who report to the company president or CEO, who may report to a board of directors.

3. **COLLABORATIVE LEARNING** Encourage students to supplement the textbook with reference books. Allow time for the planning meeting, work sessions, and rehearsals. If students decide to videotape the documentary, be sure they know how to use the camera and have a VCR available. Help find a place where they can rehearse, film, and present the program.

Answers to Reviewing Skills

1. Answers will vary but might include some of the following elements:

   Advantages: Individual—No one student will be embarrassed about not being able to donate money and each can contribute the tasks he or she can do best; Group—The class can learn how to work together and will see real results of their actions.

   Disadvantages: Individual—Some students may not live nearby and some may be physically challenged and unable to do some of the work required; Group—The class may have trouble agreeing on who to help.

2. Knowledge is power.

3. Main ideas and supporting details.

Answers to Using Critical Thinking

1. The new weapons were longbows in the 1300s and guns in the 1400s. Students might point out that even though the Muslims who invaded France in Clovis's time had the advantage of horses, the French still defeated them. The United States did not win the Vietnam War, despite its superior weaponry.

2. Students might compare the peasants' situation with that of refugees, the homeless, or the very poor.

3. Trade choices will vary. Some students may say that they go to school to be trained for a career, like apprentices in the Middle Ages. Others may say that a general education is more important than vocational training because it teaches them how to think and will be useful even if they change careers.

Planning at a Glance
Europe: Rule, Religion, and Conflict

	Objectives	Reading Support *and* Other Resources	Diverse Learning Strategies
Lesson 1 **The Power of the Church** *pp. 282–288* 2–3 days	• Describe the organization of the Catholic church between 1000 and 1300 and its effectiveness as a unifying force in western Europe. • Account for the conflicts between popes and kings during this period. • Describe the role of the church in everyday life.	• **Workbook** or **Reading Support:** pp. 144–147 Review p. 34 Lesson Support/Transition p. 34 Multi-lang. Sum. pp. 67–68 • **Other Resources:** Poster 3, Study Guide p. 44	Access Act. **(SDAIE)** TE p. 283 Writing **(GATE)** TE p. 284 Music Connection **(Auditory)** TE p. 287 Social Participation **(Visual)** TE p. 287 ▭ Audiotapes of Multi-language Lesson Summaries **(Auditory)**
Lesson 2 **The Byzantine Empire** *pp. 289–294* 2–3 days	• Identify Constantinople's geographical advantage for land and sea trade. • Describe the role of the emperor in the Byzantine Empire. • Compare and contrast Christian churches in the East and the West. • Summarize the events that led to the disruption of the Byzantine Empire.	• **Workbook** or **Reading Support:** pp. 148–151 Review p. 35 Lesson Support/Transition p. 35 Multi-lang. Sum. pp. 69–70 • **Other Resources:** Geography Kit, Study Guide p. 45	Access Act. **(Extra Support)** TE p. 290 Access Strat. **(SDAIE)** TE p. 290 Map and Globe Skills **(Visual)** TE p. 290 Writing a Letter **(GATE)** TE p. 291 ▭ Audiotapes of Multi-language Lesson Summaries **(Auditory)**
Lesson 3 **The Crusades** *pp. 295–302* 2–3 days	• Analyze the reasons for the crusades and the reasons people became crusaders. • Summarize the major crusades to the Holy Land and assess the effectiveness of each. • Evaluate the outcomes and significance of the crusades.	• **Workbook** or **Reading Support:** pp. 152–155 Review p. 36 Lesson Support/Transition p. 36 Multi-lang. Sum. pp. 71–72 • **Other Resources:** Geography Kit, Poster 10, Study Guide p. 46	Access Strat. **(SDAIE)** TE p. 296 Role Playing **(Auditory)** TE p. 297 Making a Mural **(Visual)** TE p. 297 Visual Learning **(Visual)** TE p. 298 ▭ Audiotapes of Multi-language Lesson Summaries **(Auditory)**
Skill: Understanding Historical Maps *p. 303* 1 day	• Draw conclusions in the context of historical geography.	• **Other Resources:** Study Guide p. 47	
Chapter Review *pp. 304–305* 1 day		Chapter 11 Test pp. 41–44 *(See facsimiles on TE p. 569.)*	Assessment Multiple-Use Masters pp. 73–80

Reading Support Resources *for Every Lesson*

Reading and Review

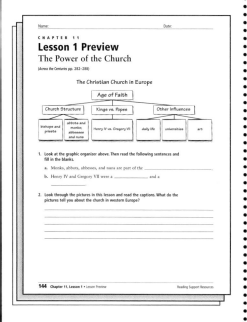

- **Chapter Overview*** p. 143
- **Lesson Previews*** using graphic organizers from the Teacher's Edition pp. 144, 148, 152
- **Reading Strategies*** pp. 145, 149, 153
- **Lesson Summaries*** pp. 146–147, 150–151, 154–155
- **Lesson Reviews** pp. 34, 35, 36

  * **Workbook** includes starred items.

Multi-language Summaries

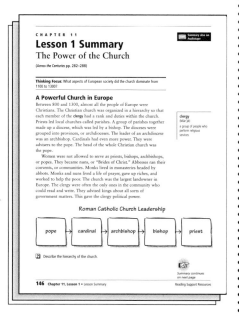

Lesson Summaries in:
- English (See Reading and Review.)
- Spanish pp. 146–147, 150–151, 154–155
- Chinese pp. 67–72
- Hmong pp. 67–72
- Khmer pp. 67–72
- Vietnamese pp. 67–72

 Summaries available on audiotapes

Lesson Support / Transition
S D A I E

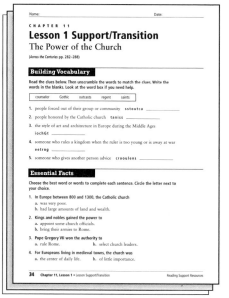

Activities for SDAIE
Specially **D**esigned **A**cademic **I**nstruction in **E**nglish

- **Lesson Support/Transition** pp. 34, 35, 36

 ## Technology Options

Internet Support
http://www.eduplace.com

Social Studies Center at Education Place

Internet support for Chapter 11:
- *Lesson at a Glance*
- *A Crusader*

Software
***Student Writing Center*®** (CD-ROM) (Macintosh® or Windows®)

School to Career

The Byzantines established libraries and schools because they respected learning and education. Organizing information in a library is a large task. Ask your school or public librarian to give students a tour of the library facilities, explaining the education and training needed for a career in library science.

Character Education

During the Crusades, the Muslims and Christians each dedicated their lives and resources for a cause they believed was right. Dedication is still important. Have students create a list of individuals they know who are dedicated to a specific cause. Why do they think these individuals have made this commitment?

Chapter 11

Europe: Rule, Religion, and Conflict

Throughout this period, Christians looked toward Jerusalem as their holy city. This map from late in the period depicts the city at the center of the world.

It was the Age of Faith, as the Catholic church dominated much of Europe from 1000 to 1300. As early as the 800s, the church won power from Europe's kings. Then in 1096, the world truly saw the church's might. That year the pope gathered some 45,000 knights, archers, and swordsmen in Constantinople. This massive army hoped to drive the Muslims out of the holy city of Jerusalem. Yet battles over the Holy City would go on for almost 200 years.

800s The Catholic church becomes the center of life in Europe. Many visit churches to see holy objects, like this jeweled container holding the remains of St. Stephen.

650	750	850	950

900 Cordoba, the largest city in Western Europe, is the center of western Islam.

280

726

The Pope

The pope, also called the vicar of Christ, is the spiritual and temporal leader of the Catholic church. The apostle Peter—whom Jesus called the rock upon whom he would build his church—was the first pope, or bishop of Rome.

Like the prophets of biblical times, medieval popes anointed kings and proclaimed them God's chosen rulers. In this way, a king gained a status higher than that of other leaders or rulers. He also believed he gained protection as well because his authority was divinely sanctioned. The pope, in turn, gained power and prestige as the bestower of the divine sanction. In exchange for the anointing or crowning, the king was duty-bound to protect the church, the defenseless and the poor, to fight unbelievers in the name of Jesus, and to ensure that justice was done.

The Inquisition

Popes used their influence in society to build up the power of the church. They tried to enforce the acceptance of a uniform body

Crusaders in need of money sacked and looted Constantinople in 1204. These bronze horses were among the valuable objects they took.

The map showing the Christian world with Jerusalem as the center (p. 280) is from a 14th-century manuscript.

La Sainte Chapelle (p. 281) was built between 1246 and 1248 to hold holy relics brought from the crusades. The stained glass is the oldest in Paris. Fifty-foot high panels of stained glass cover three sides of the chapel. The panels include 1,134 scenes.

Understanding Chronology

Have the students read the timeline. Note that Cordoba, Spain, thrived as the center of western Islam during the same period the Christian church grew to dominate much of Europe.

1240s Parisians build Sainte Chapelle in their city. Such magnificent chapels with costly stained-glass windows show the wealth and power of the French monarchy.

| 1050 | 1150 | 1250 | 1350 |

1185 The Minamoto family unites Japan under its shogunate rule.

1204

281

of religious beliefs, believing this to be essential in maintaining an orderly society. Thus heretics—those whose religious beliefs or practices varied from those authorized by the church—were seen as socially dangerous, immoral, and punishable. Among the heretics were those who practiced alchemy, witchcraft, and sorcery as well as all non-Christians.

In 1231, Pope Gregory IX established the Inquisition, a special papal court for apprehending heretics and bringing them to trial. Originally, the purpose of the Inquisition was to suppress heretical religious movements that had gained popularity in the 1100s and 1200s. Suspects were brought before the court and encouraged to confess and recant their heretical beliefs. Failing this, they were interrogated and tried. Sometimes torture was used to procure confessions or the names of other heretics. Those who refused to recant were turned over to civil authorities for punishment. Rulers had to carry out the sentences of the Inquisition or face excommunication from the pope.

INTRODUCE

Point out the lesson title and review the growth of the official Christian church in the early Middle Ages (Chapter 10). Have students read the Thinking Focus. Ask them to suggest what the role of Christian churches is in today's society. *(Moral and religious teaching, projects to help the disadvantaged.)* Have them read to find out how the role of the church differed in the Middle Ages.

Key Terms

Vocabulary Strategies: T36–T37
clergy—the group of people who have been ordained for religious service
excommunication—the act that deprives someone of membership in the church
salvation—the deliverance of the soul from the power of sin
tithe—a tenth of one's income paid to support the church
university—an institution of higher learning that replaced monasteries and cathedral schools

| 650 | 750 | 800 | | 1300 | 1350 |

L E S S O N   1

The Power of the Church

THINKING FOCUS

What aspects of European society did the church dominate from 1100 to 1300?

Key Terms

- clergy
- excommunication
- salvation
- tithe
- university

➤ *This painting shows the building of Chartres Cathedral. The cathedral was so important to the people that even noblemen and their ladies helped haul stones.*

Many townspeople stood on the church steps awaiting the decision about the new cathedral. This decision would affect their town's future. At last the smiling bishop appeared at the doorway to announce the long awaited answer. Yes, a cathedral would be built in their town to the glory of God!

An architect was selected to design the cathedral and supervise the beginning of its construction. The expense would be great since many workers would be needed: stonecutters, woodworkers, carpenters, masons, blacksmiths, roofers, glassmakers, sculptors, and more. For hundreds of men in the town this would become their life's work. For a few it would even mean their death, since there was the possibility of falling from the scaffolding on which the workers stood as they built the walls ever higher.

The townspeople knew it could take as many as 100 years to complete the building of the cathedral. However, it was difficult for them to imagine that their great-great-grandchildren would be as old as they were now when the building was finished.

Why would these people, who lived in western Europe in A.D. 1200, spend so much money, time, and labor to begin building something that they would not even live to see completed? Because the cathedral allowed them to celebrate, in stone and glass, the power of the church and of God in their lives.

282

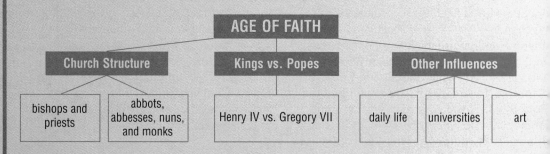

Objectives

1. Describe the organization of the Catholic church between 1000 and 1300 and its effectiveness as a unifying force in western Europe.
2. Account for the conflicts between popes and kings during this period.
3. Describe the role of the church in everyday life.

Graphic Overview

This chart provides an overview of the content of this lesson.

AGE OF FAITH

Church Structure		Kings vs. Popes	Other Influences		
bishops and priests	abbots, abbesses, nuns, and monks	Henry IV vs. Gregory VII	daily life	universities	art

A Powerful Church in Europe

Between 800 and 1300 almost all the people of Europe were Christians. Only one branch of the faith existed in Europe, and it was headed by the pope in Rome. The Christian religion was organized in such a way that it was the center of spiritual life and an important political force.

The Church Hierarchy

The church was organized in a hierarchy so that each member of the **clergy,** or ordained members of the church, had a specific rank. The priest of the local church, or parish, had a certain group of duties. These included leading religious services, visiting the sick, and conducting ceremonies such as baptisms and weddings. Many parishes together formed one diocese (DY uh sihs). Heading each diocese was a bishop, who, in turn, had a different group of responsibilities.

The dioceses were united into provinces, or archdioceses, under the authority of archbishops. Cardinals were second in power to the pope. The cardinals also acted as counselors to the pope and eventually were responsible for electing new popes. Leading the entire church was the pope. *Pope* comes from the Latin word for "father."

Monks lived in monasteries headed by abbots and had lives of thought, prayer, and charitable work. The word monk comes from the Greek word *monos* meaning "alone." Although abbots usually answered to bishops, the abbots ran these religious communities and were responsible for their spiritual life. The monks did physical labor to support their communities. Some monks occasionally preached.

Women were not allowed to be priests, bishops, archbishops, or popes. Still, many women were led by their strong belief to participate in other aspects of the church. Many became nuns, who were "Brides of Christ." They swore never to marry and to devote themselves to lives of poverty and charitable work. Abbesses ran their communities, called convents, which sometimes owned the land around them. Thus many abbesses became skilled managers and farmers, as well as spiritual leaders to the nuns. Most abbesses reported to local bishops.

The Church's Influence

The church brought Christianity to many Europeans. It taught that they could help save their souls

▲ *Popes wear miters with peaks in front and back.*

▼ *Chartres Cathedral, built on a hill 50 miles southwest of Paris, is visible for miles around. The tower on the left was not finished for hundreds of years.*

283

■ *Local churches were headed by priests. Priests were supervised by bishops and cardinals. The pope was the highest authority, and his influence extended over all church members.*

Visual Learning

Point out the cross and the crown in the illustrations on pp. 284 and 285 as symbols of power and influence. Have students discuss why the pope, a religious figure, fought against the king. *(King had political power, pope had religious power.)*

▼ *Hildegard of Bingen wrote music and poetry, tended the sick, preached and ran convents.*

■ *Describe the hierarchy of the church.*

▼ *The jewel-encrusted gold cross reveals the wealth possessed by the church.*

284

284

by giving donations to it. In addition, popes, cardinals, and bishops were often nobles with land of their own who left this land to the church when they died. By 1050, the church was the largest landholder in western Europe.

The clergy were often the only members of society who could read and write. Even most kings were illiterate, so they needed bishops, abbots, and clerks to write documents and keep records. Thus the clergy also had the opportunity to advise kings on all sorts of matters.

The career of Abbot Suger *(SOO zhair)* is an example of how religion and politics were often intermingled during this time. Suger was born in 1081 into a peasant family living near Paris. As a boy he showed high intelligence and was selected by his village priest to be educated in a monastery, where his closest friend happened to be the son of the king

of France. In 1108, that friend was crowned King Louis VI of France.

Suger became a monk and, in 1122, an abbot, or leader of his monastery. As Louis's friend and adviser, he worked to increase cooperation between Louis and his nobles by stressing the fact that they shared a common faith. When King Henry of Germany invaded King Louis's lands in 1124, Abbot Suger loaned the king the sacred banner from the monastery to carry into battle. The banner rallied so many French nobles to the king that Henry retreated before the battle began.

From 1147 to 1149, the new king, the son of Louis VI, left his crown with Abbot Suger and appointed him regent to rule his lands while he, the king, was away at war. During these years, Suger developed fairer methods of taxation and prevented a rebellion from taking away Louis's rule. ■

A Power Struggle Between Kings and Popes

Kings and nobles had gained the power to appoint bishops and other officials of the church during the 800s. They sometimes even sold these positions to the highest bidder. In particular, kings rewarded their allies by appointing them to be bishops of the church. The fact that the kings possessed such great power over the church strengthened their authority. Yet, because these church officials appointed by the kings often behaved immorally and quite selfishly, many people lost respect for the church.

Pope Gregory VII

One monk, named Hildebrand, was part of a movement to free the church from the control of kings and nobles. He wanted the church to be free of this control so that the clergy might concentrate on performing its mission of saving Christians. Hildebrand became pope in 1073 and took the name Gregory VII. In 1075, Gregory issued a document stating that the pope was above kings and only the pope could appoint cardinals and bishops. The document warned that government officials who did not obey the pope could be removed from office.

Writing

Have students assume the role of newspaper reporters in 1075 when Pope Gregory VII claimed that the authority of the church (the pope) was superior to the power of the government (the king). Have students write an editorial in which they describe Gregory's claim, evaluate it, and predict how people will respond to it. Then have students read their articles to the class.

Role Playing

Have students role-play the conflict between Pope Gregory and King Henry. Begin with Gregory's rise to power in 1073 and include Henry's excommunication, Henry's appeal for support from his nobles and bishops, Henry's journey to Italy to ask forgiveness of the pope, and finally Gregory's cancellation of the excommunication. Ask students if they think it was appropriate for the pope to allow Henry to rejoin the church.

King Henry IV

Henry IV, king of Germany and Italy, considered Gregory's document an attack on his power as king. So, while continuing to appoint bishops in his kingdom, Henry fired back a letter to the pope. In it the king demanded that the pope step down from his office.

But Gregory would do no such thing. Instead, in 1076, he announced the **excommunication** of Henry, thus expelling Henry from the church. Henry was condemned to live as an outcast from the church-oriented society of the 1000s. The excommunication also meant that Henry's subjects were no longer obliged to obey him as their king.

Henry looked for support from his nobles and bishops but found little, because Gregory had also threatened them with excommunication it they supported the king. To save his throne, Henry realized he had to give in to the pope. He then traveled to Italy barefoot during the winter to present himself to the pope as a humble beggar. Gregory kept Henry waiting for three days in the snow outside his

castle before finally canceling the excommunication.

The Treaty

Pope Gregory had won this battle, but the struggle between the kings of Germany and the popes continued until 1122. In that year, church leaders, nobles, and representatives of the king and the pope met in Worms, Germany, where they agreed to a treaty called the Concordat *(kuhn KAWR dat)* of Worms. The king agreed to having the pope select church leaders. ■

Henry IV wears a crown and holds the scepter and the orb and cross, symbols of monarchy. The orb and cross theme is repeated on the top of the crown.

■ *Why is the conflict between Henry IV and Pope Gregory significant?*

The Age of Faith

While popes and kings fought for power, the common people of western Europe tried to live their lives according to the principles of the church. The mission of the church was to save the soul of all members so that they would go to heaven after they died rather than hell. This **salvation,** or saving, came through accepting the beliefs of the church, living a moral life, and performing good works.

People also paid one-tenth of the produce from their lands to the church each year. This **tithe** *(tyth)* could be paid in money, produce, or labor. People also had to pay rent to the lord on whose land they farmed.

Daily Life

The church was the center of daily life in every village and town. Church bells announced the time

285

Critical Thinking

Have students consider Gregory's claim to the right to depose Henry in 1075. Was Gregory attempting to purify the church of wealth-seeking bishops or trying to increase his own power—and that of the church—at the expense of kings? *(Answers will vary.)*

■ *It represented a victory for papal authority and for papal control over church offices.*

285

Religious Context

In 1075 Pope Gregory issued the *Dictatus Papae,* a list of 27 statements defending the power of the church and of the pope. Share the following excerpts with students to help them see the basis of the pope's argument. Ask students to evaluate the pope's claims:

1. That the Roman church was founded by God alone.
3. That he [the pope] alone can depose [remove from office] or reinstate bishops.

12. That he [the pope] may depose Emperors.
19. That he [the pope] himself may be judged by no one.

Study Skills

Have students study the picture of King Henry IV of Germany. Have them identify details in the picture that indicate Henry's power. *(Crown, scepter.)* Have students look up *crown* and *scepter* in the dictionary and then write a sentence that incorporates the definitions of both words.

286

CULTURE
Visual Learning

Have students study the illustrations on this page. Ask them to identify the role of the church in each event that is pictured. How important are the events pictured in the lives of people of the Middle Ages? What can students conclude about the importance of the church in everyday life? *(It provided a meaning for life and a way of sharing important events; it also controlled most important events in a person's life.)*

▲ *People are admitted into the church through baptism.*

➤ *During daily mass, the Last Supper of Jesus and his disciples is remembered.*

▲ *The Catholic church teaches that marriage is the formal union of man and woman as husband and wife in the sight of God. In the 1000s, people married as early as the age of 13.*

➤ *At burial ceremonies a priest offered a blessing for the dead and welcomed the soul into heaven.*

286

Chapter 11

for work, meals, rest, and for mass, the worship service. Churches were also centers of community activity. Often large and sturdily constructed, they served as gathering places for town meetings and as places of refuge during wars or heavy storms. The doorsteps or courtyard of a church might even be where the local farmers' market took place.

Church holidays provided the peasants with relief from their sunup-to-sundown farm labors. On these special days, Christians celebrated events in the life of Jesus and remembered famous saints of the church. After attending mass, the people spent the remainder of the holiday visiting, feasting, and dancing in the church courtyard.

A shared faith gave the church members a sense of community, but it also kept those with different beliefs outside this community. For example, Christians did not accept Jews socially and often even persecuted them. Jews were also generally not allowed to participate in trade. Furthermore, Jews were often required to pay a tax whenever the king demanded.

Religious Orders

Many people in the church wanted a religious life that was less secluded than that of monks living in a monastery. As a result, during the 1200s, several new orders, or religious communities, were formed. These new orders did not shut themselves off from the world as other monks and nuns did. Instead, they lived in the towns and worked to bring Christianity directly to the people.

Critical Thinking

Have students share their experiences of baptisms, weddings, funerals, or other Christian services. Have them discuss the purpose of these special events and offer ideas on how they might have developed.

Religious Context

Another religious order begun in the early 1200s was the Dominicans, also called the Order of Preachers. Founded in 1215 by St. Dominic, a Spanish priest, the Dominican order was devoted to preaching against heresies and to theological study. Many teachers in the universities, including St. Thomas Aquinas, were Dominicans.

One new order was founded in 1209 by Francis of Assisi. Francis was born in Italy in 1182, the son of a wealthy merchant. After a carefree youth, he spent a year battling a serious illness. During that time, he had a vision of Jesus that changed him forever.

Francis disowned his father and rejected a large inheritance, making a vow instead to live his life in poverty as Jesus had done. Francis rebuilt churches and served the poor. Many people followed him. He created a new religious order, now called the Franciscans.

Francis was also a talented poet and musician. This is part of one of his poems.

> *B*e praised, my Lord, for all
>   your creatures.
> In the first place for the blessed
> Brother Sun, who gives us the
>   day and enlightens us
>   through you.
> He is beautiful and radiant
>   with his great splendor.
>
> St. Francis of Assisi, from "The
> Canticle of Brother Sun," 1224

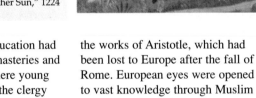

The peaceful landscape and gentle animals are symbols of Francis of Assisi's love for nature and all living things. The halo around Francis's head identifies him as a saint. Francis was declared a saint in 1228, two years after his death.

Universities

Until the 1100s, education had taken place within monasteries and bishops' cathedrals. There young men planning to enter the clergy were educated. As European towns grew during the 1100s, people began wanting to get better educated —often still at bishops' cathedrals. This enthusiasm for learning was partly sparked by the flow of knowledge from the Muslim world. The Muslims had important schools in cities such as Cordoba and Baghdad. Muslims and Jews had studied and translated books by Greek, African, and Asian writers, such as the works of Aristotle, which had been lost to Europe after the fall of Rome. European eyes were opened to vast knowledge through Muslim writings and translations.

In Europe, groups of students gathered in towns to study philosophy, theology, medicine, and law under famous teachers. They began to form **universities,** or guilds of students and teachers. Women were not allowed to teach or study at the universities. By the 1200s, universities had replaced monasteries and cathedrals as the popular centers of learning.

287

Critical Thinking

Have students discuss how the illustration on this page shows the importance of Christianity in the artistic achievements of Europe in the Middle Ages. *(Artist chose religious subject for painting.)* Have students give other examples of how artistic and cultural achievements reflected the importance of religion. *(Cathedrals, sculptures, Christian philosophy.)*

Reader's Theater

Have students form four groups. Have each group research one of the following events from the life of St. Francis: Francis disowning his father, Francis restoring the church of San Damiano, Francis visiting Pope Innocent III in Rome, and Francis visiting the sultan Melek-el-Kamel in Damietta. Have students from each group develop a script from their research and present the event to the class in the form of a reader's theater.

Music Connection

A musical style of the Middle Ages was the Gregorian chant. Named after Saint Gregory I, the Gregorian chant is a combination of speaking and singing. It includes settings of Biblical texts and the liturgy of the Mass— all in Latin. Find a recording of Gregorian chants to play for students, and ask them to describe what they sound like. *(Plain, slow, expressive.)* In a discussion, establish a connection between this musical style and religious feelings and practices of the time.

Social Participation

Have students develop a bulletin board display that illustrates people's intellectual and artistic achievements during the Middle Ages in Europe. Divide the class into three groups. Assign each group a specific area to cover, such as art, literature, and architecture. Have each group create a bulletin board display on its topic and explain it to the class.

➤ *The floor plan of a Gothic cathedral is laid out in the shape of a cross. At the front of the cathedral is a crucifix. A crucifix is a cross with the figure of Jesus on it. This one is made of bronze.*

Religious Art

In the painting and sculpture of this time, artists often vividly portrayed events in the life of Jesus, such as the crucifixion. The artists also generally painted Jesus in a highly stylized, as opposed to realistic, manner. Artists stylized their paintings to express their own spiritual beliefs.

However, the greatest artistic achievement of the age was the designing and building of Gothic cathedrals. The word *cathedral* comes from the Greek word meaning "chair." It was in the cathedral that the bishop had his throne, which was the symbol of the power of his office.

Gothic architecture dominated Europe for the 400 years from 1140 until the 1500s. One of the innovations introduced by architects of these cathedrals was ribbed arches, which emphasized the shape of the pointed ceilings. Another was flying buttresses, which were used outside the cathedral to support the heavy structure. Cathedrals were so large and required so much labor to build, that they often took a hundred years or more to finish completely.

Gothic cathedrals were enormous buildings, generally the largest buildings in any community. Their vast interiors were designed

to fill onlookers with awe at the power of God. In these masterpieces of design and construction, a variety of artistic elements were combined. Among these were elements such as sculptures of Jesus and the saints; paintings that showed scenes from the life of Jesus; and stained-glass windows, which looked like walls of colored light and usually illustrated stories from the Bible.

For believers, the cathedral, which had an interior or immense open spaces, religious images, and colored light, was the closest thing to experiencing heaven on earth. As Abbot Suger, a pioneer in the design of Gothic cathedrals, wrote of the cathedral of St. Denis, "The entire cathedral is pervaded [filled] by a wonderful and continuous light." ■

■ *How did the church influence European culture between the 1100s and 1300s?*

■ *Christian themes were common in many kinds of artworks. Christian Gothic cathedrals represent the era's greatest architectural achievements.*

C L O S E

To show how the church was the most powerful force in western Europe from 1000 to 1300, draw on the chalkboard the diagram shown in the Graphic Overview on p. 282. Have students copy the diagram and add details based on the lesson text. Then have them trade diagrams with a partner for evaluation.

R E V I E W

1. **FOCUS** What aspects of European society did the church dominate from 1100 to 1300?
2. **CONNECT** How does the hierarchy of the Catholic church compare to the hierarchy of feudal society in western Europe?
3. **BELIEF SYSTEMS** What is excommunication? What role did it play in the struggle between popes and kings?
4. **CRITICAL THINKING** Was Pope Gregory justified in excommunicating Henry? Explain.
5. **WRITING ACTIVITY** Prepare a news story describing the building of a new Gothic cathedral in the late 1100s. Be sure to include quotations from at least three people who would be involved in building or using the church.

Chapter 11

Homework Options

Have students use information from the four illustrations on p. 286 to write a summary paragraph explaining the influence of the church on people's daily lives.

Study Guide: p. 44

Answers to Review Questions

1. The church was able to control daily life in nearly every village and town. Because church officials were often the only literate members of the community, they helped to run governments, write documents, and keep records.
2. The church hierarchy was priest, bishop, cardinal, pope; the feudal hierarchy was serf, vassal, lord, king. People paid taxes to those above them in the feudal hierarchy and tithes to their parish church.
3. A person who is excommunicated is banished from the Catholic church. Pope Gregory VII used excommunication to force Henry IV to submit to his authority.
4. Answers will vary. Some students may say the pope was exercising his authority on a purely religious matter. Others might suggest that the pope was using a religious punishment for a political problem.

650   726   1150   1250   1350
                                    1095

L E S S O N   2

The Byzantine Empire

You are a young merchant in the year 1000 seeking your fortune in Constantinople *(kahn stan tuh NOH puhl)*, the capital of the Byzantine Empire. You have endured a 1,500-mile sea voyage from your home in Venice, Italy, to reach this city so rich in works of art and architecture and so busy with commerce. Now, at last, you get your first glimpse of it.

Sailing into port, you see on your left the walls that help protect the city from invaders. Ahead is the Sacred Palace, home of the emperor. Behind it is the towering dome of the great Hagia Sophia

(HAY jee uh soh FEE uh), a glorious Christian church.

Upon docking, you immediately head up Middle Street, the main street of the capital, which leads right to the palace. This street is crowded with peddlers' canopied stalls. You search the stalls, hurrying past fruit, vegetables, and fish.

Then, quite suddenly, you see what you came for—long rolls of Chinese silk cloth, embroidered in rich threads of gold. You will exchange your gold coins for the cloth. You will then take the cloth back to Venice, where you can sell it for a handsome profit.

THINKING
FOCUS

Compare the Eastern Orthodox Church and the Church of Rome.

Key Terms

- literacy
- classic
- patriarch
- icon
- schism

◄ *Constantinople, now called Istanbul, still remains a busy port of trade. The craftsmanship that went into making this silver communion cup was typical of the kind of care artisans took in crafting the goods they sold in Constantinople.*

289

Read the lesson title and ask students to look at the photograph of modern Istanbul. Explain that Constantinople, which was the earlier name for Istanbul, was the capital of the Byzantine Empire. Ask students to read the Thinking Focus and explain that Byzantine society was different in many ways from that of western Europe. Tell students to see how many differences they can find as they read the lesson.

Key Terms

Vocabulary Strategies: T36–T37
literacy—the ability to read and write
classic—a work of art or literature from ancient Greece or Rome
patriarch—the male leader of a family or clan; in the Byzantine Empire, the bishop of Constantinople
icon—a picture or representation of a sacred person
schism—a separation or division into factions, especially within a church

289

Graphic Overview

This Graphic Overview presents the major topics in the lesson.

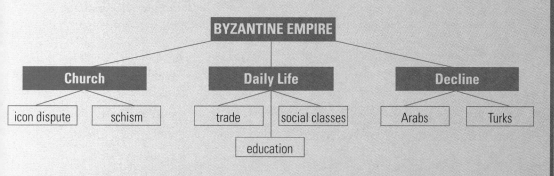

BYZANTINE EMPIRE

Church	Daily Life	Decline
icon dispute · schism	trade · social classes · education	Arabs · Turks

Objectives

1. Identify Constantinople's geographical advantage for land and sea trade.
2. Describe the role of the emperor in the Byzantine Empire.
3. Compare and contrast Christian churches in the East and the West.
4. Summarize the events that led to the disruption of the Byzantine Empire.

Explain to students that this lesson compares Byzantine society with that of western Europe. With the students, look at the text headings in sequence, and encourage them to read for similarities and differences in several areas: government, commerce, religion, and the rise and fall of the empire.

GEOGRAPHY
Map and Globe Skills

Have students refer to the map on p. 290 and make a list of all the cities with which Constantinople traded, noting whether the trade was by land or by sea. Ask students to predict how Constantinople's location might have played both a positive and a negative role in the city's history. Help students to see the great opportunity for trade as well as vulnerability to attack. *(Constantinople could be attacked by ships from Europe and Asia.)*

► *Because it was located between Europe and Asia.*

The Roman Empire in the East

Anyone from the West would have experienced wonder upon arriving at Constantinople. Since Constantine had had Constantinople built to be the eastern capital of the Roman Empire, he also had it modeled after Rome. And, like Rome, it became a magnificent center of the Christian faith.

Two Centers of Christianity

Since the time of Jesus' disciple Peter in A.D. 64, the city of Rome had been the center of the Christian faith. According to Christian tradition, Peter was the first bishop of Rome. Christians regarded the pope as the successor to Peter. The pope was the leader of the Christian faith as well as being the bishop of Rome.

In the late 300s, Emperor Theodosius I went one step further. He made Christianity the official religion of the Roman Empire. In addition, when Theodosius I died in 395, his will formally split the empire, leaving half to each son.

Over the next one hundred years, tribes of barbarian invaders

▼ *Why was Constantinople such an ideal port for trade?*

captured most of the lands that were controlled by the Western Roman Empire. In 476, one of these tribes, the Goths, overthrew the last emperor of the Western Empire, bringing it to an end. However, the pope and the Roman church still existed in the West. Furthermore, the Eastern Roman Empire, or Byzantine Empire, continued to thrive.

The Byzantine emperor became the head of both the government and the Christian religion in the East. The people of the Byzantine Empire believed the emperor's authority came from God and extended to all matters of church and state. Constantinople became a second center of Christianity.

A Center of Trade

The emperor of the Byzantine Empire ruled with the help of a complex system of advisers and officials. Specialized departments handled different tasks, such as collecting taxes.

Constantinople became a center of world trade. From the lands around the Black Sea came furs and hides, grain, and wine. From Arabia came spices, gems, and silk. And from Africa came ivory and slaves. On the map at left, locate the trade routes used by merchants from these countries.

The empire generated vast amounts of money from trade. The government taxed everything that came through the city.

The Byzantines—those who lived in the Byzantine Empire—sold many of their own products, too. In the rural areas of the empire, farmers produced grapes,

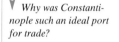

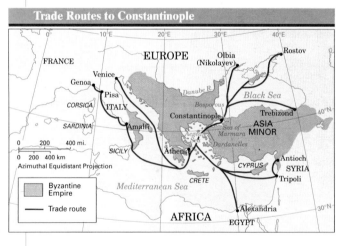

Trade Routes to Constantinople

Chapter 11

Critical Thinking

Have students consider the pros and cons of one ruler serving as the head of both the church and the government. What advantages would a Byzantine emperor have over a king or a pope in western Europe? *(More power to do as he or she wished; no disagreement between church and state.)* How might this benefit, or hurt, the people? *(Emperor could work for people's good or use the threat of excommunication as a tool to pursue selfish goals.)*

olives, and wheat for export. In the capital, manufacturers produced glassware, enamel, ivory, and silk.

Attracted by the wealth to be made in trade and industry, people from all over the world came to live in Constantinople. By the year 1000, one million people lived in this thriving city.

Life in the Empire

What was daily life like for the Byzantines? Many of them worked as farmers in rural areas. Craftspersons and traders, who were heavily taxed by the government, lived in the cities. Except for government officials and wealthy merchants, most Byzantines were poor.

Byzantine women had little freedom. They were kept at home, and seldom received any formal education. However, a few women of the wealthy upper classes were educated at home.

The government set up its own schools and libraries, in addition to those run by the church. As a result, there was a higher rate of **literacy**—knowing how to read and write—than in western Europe. At school, the sons of prosperous Byzantine merchants studied the works of famous Greek and Roman writers such as Homer, Virgil, Plato, and Aristotle. These ancient writings were called the **classics.** Even the name of the magnificent church built in 537 during the reign of Emperor Justinian symbolized Byzantine respect for learning. The church was called the Hagia Sophia, which is Greek for "holy wisdom." ■

▲ *In this mosaic in the church of Hagia Sophia, Mary and Jesus are receiving a model of the church from Emperor Justinian on the left, and a model of the city from Emperor Constantine.*

■ *Why was the Byzantine Empire so powerful?*

■ *Located at the intersection of two seas and two continents, the empire became a center of trade and accumulated vast amounts of wealth. Its powerful armies conquered lands both far and near.*

Writing a Letter

Have students imagine that they are citizens of the Byzantine Empire during the reign of Justinian. Each student should assume a Byzantine identity (man, woman, or child; farmer, craftsperson, merchant, government official), and write a letter to a relative in western Europe, reflecting the outlook of the particular Byzantine citizen. Direct students to use information from the lesson in describing the details of their lives.

Research

Have students become familiar with the following terms: *democracy, plutocracy, theocracy,* and *autocracy.* Then instruct them to write a short paper in which they use these terms to describe the governments of the Byzantine Empire *(autocracy or theocracy),* western Europe in the 1100s *(plutocracy),* and the United States today *(democracy).* Each of the three settings should be the subject of a brief paragraph that explains why the particular term is appropriate.

Visual Learning

Have students study the mosaic on this page. Explain that it is found in the cathedral of Hagia Sophia and pictures an emperor. Have students explain the Byzantine religious attitude that this mosaic reflects. *(Emperor was seen as God's agent here on earth.)*

Visual Learning

Ask students to study the pictures on this page. Have them describe details of both the exterior and the interior of an Eastern church.

▲ *This Byzantine church in present-day Bulgaria shows the continued use of the rounded arch in Eastern Orthodox architecture. The interior is rich in icons.*

The Eastern Church

As the official state religion, Christianity powerfully influenced the lives of the Byzantines. The bishop of Constantinople—called the **patriarch**—dominated the Byzantine church. However, the emperor, the head of both church and state, held more power and authority than the patriarch.

Contrasts with the West

Although the eastern and western churches were both Christian, they differed in many ways. One of these differences was that the Byzantines tolerated much more discussion and debate about religious matters. In the Byzantine church, services were conducted in Greek, the language of the people. The use of their native language allowed the worshipers to become more involved in the service. In the western church, services were conducted in Latin, a language known only to the priests and the well educated.

The architecture of Byzantine churches was also different from that of western churches. Byzantine churches were plainer on the outside, usually featuring a rounded dome, as you can see in the photograph. Their interiors, however, were richly decorated with carvings, painted tiles, and murals. There were **icons** of Jesus and the saints that were nonrealistic, flat images meant to put the viewer in a spiritual frame of mind. Church leaders hoped the faithful would use the icons to worship or honor those religious figures they represented.

Clashes over Authority

Between the years 700 and 1050, the pope still claimed to have

292

Critical Thinking

Have students write a paragraph comparing the dispute between Pope Gregory VII and Henry IV of Germany (Lesson 1) with the dispute between Emperor Leo III and Pope Gregory III. Have students summarize the nature of the disputes, the actions taken by all participants, and the final result in each case.

Historical Context

The struggle over icons—also called the Iconoclastic Controversy—took place from 726 to 843. The Biblical text used against icons comes from the book of Exodus *(Revised Standard Version)*:

"You shall not make for yourself a graven image, or any likeness of anything that is in heaven above, or that is in the earth beneath . . . you shall not bow down to them or serve them."

In 726, Leo III ordered that all images be destroyed or covered. Under Leo's successor, Constantine V, icon worshipers were severely persecuted. In 787, Empress Irene re-established the use of icons, but in 814, Leo V forbade the use of icons once again. This second period of iconoclasm ended in 843, when Empress Theodora permitted the use of icons. In the Eastern Orthodox church, this event is celebrated as the Feast of Orthodoxy.

authority over the entire Christian church—not just the Church of Rome. However, serious differences of opinion existed between the members of the eastern and western churches. The controversy over icons is one case in point.

Byzantines used icons in many ways. They prayed or lit candles before them or carried them in religious processions. However, some Byzantines thought this devotion to the icons went too far. They feared that people worshiped the icons themselves as gods. Others disagreed, saying that the icons only helped them to worship God better.

In 726, Byzantine Emperor Leo III, fearing that the icons were being worshiped as gods, ordered them destroyed. Many Byzantines refused to comply with the order. From Rome, Pope Gregory III, who was in favor of icons, condemned the emperor's actions. Gregory thought that icons were important for honoring holy people of the past and providing a way for those who could not read to learn about their faith.

As the argument between Emperor Leo III and Pope Gregory III intensified, Gregory made allies of the Franks. Gregory needed the friendship of these Germanic tribes so that they would support and protect him in any war with the Byzantine Empire. In 800, to solidify this alliance, the pope crowned the leader of the Franks, Charlemagne, the only true and holy Roman emperor. Thus, Charlemagne became the first Holy Roman Emperor. However, this action outraged the Byzantines, because they believed that the Byzantine emperor was the only true and rightful Roman emperor.

A Schism in the Church

In 1054, the basic question of who was supreme, the western pope or the eastern patriarch, was still a big issue. The matter finally reached a climax over the question of who was responsible for the churches of southern Italy. When the eastern patriarch, Patriarch Cerularius *(seer u LAIR ih uhs),* lost that argument, he retaliated by closing any churches in Constantinople that celebrated the mass in the western style. At this point, Pope Leo IX of the West excommunicated Patriarch Cerularius of the East, who in turn excommunicated the pope. This led to a split, or **schism,** into two separate churches, the Roman Catholic church in the West and the Eastern Orthodox church in the East. ■

Across Time & Space

The mutual excommunication of the leaders of the Eastern and Roman churches lasted until our century. In 1964, the then-current pope and the patriarch met in Jerusalem. The next year, the two leaders made a formal statement that undid the excommunications.

■ *What factors led to the schism between the churches in the East and West?*

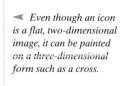

◄ *Even though an icon is a flat, two-dimensional image, it can be painted on a three-dimensional form such as a cross.*

■ *Conflicts over ultimate control of the church and different ways of worship led to the separation of the two Christian churches.*

Illustrating

Have students make posters showing the differences between the Eastern and Western churches. Encourage them to use pictures or articles cut out of newspapers or magazines, original art work, or photographs. If possible arrange a class tour of a representative Eastern and Western church in your area. Permit students to work in pairs if they wish, each member focusing in depth on one of the churches. Have students present their finished posters to the class.

Role Playing

Divide the class into two groups. Have one group defend the position of Emperor Leo III and the other group defend the position of Pope Gregory III. Have each group prepare a list of ideas supporting its position on the use of icons in the church as well as its perception of who is the final authority on this question. Have each group appoint a representative, and have the two representatives assume the roles of Leo and Gregory in debating the issue in front of the class.

Visual Learning

Have students study the photograph on this page and describe what they see. Use the photograph to generate discussion on the role of icons in modern religion. Ask students to describe any religious icons they have encountered. Then have students compare the role of icons in religion today with that of icons during the 700s and 800s.

Critical Thinking

Review with students the geographic location of Constantinople and the Byzantine Empire. Ask them to explain why it was necessary to fortify Constantinople with three sets of walls. *(It was a very wealthy and desirable city.)* On a map have students locate the regions from which major invaders emanated: the Persians, Arabs, and Seljuk Turks. Ask students to predict the outcome of the emperor's plea to the pope for help.

■ *Attacks from the East and the South caused the empire to lose territory and resources.*

CLOSE

Have students create a list of differences between Byzantine and western European society. Write their suggestions on the chalkboard, and then have students organize the differences into categories. *(For example, government, religions, daily life.)* Finally, have students rate the categories of differences in terms of impact on the Byzantine Empire.

294

The Empire Under Attack

Throughout its long history, the Byzantine Empire endured frequent attacks on its borders. Invaders sought to acquire the empire's great wealth, as well as to acquire the territory itself, because it was so well located for conducting trade with many countries. As a result, emperors had to maintain a powerful military. They also had to build defensive walls around the city of Constantinople.

The Decline of the Empire

The walls protected the city of Constantinople, but they did not protect the empire. After Emperor Justinian extended the empire to its greatest size in the 500s, a period of decline began. In the early 600s, Persians attacked from the east and the south. They took Egypt and marched north, but were unsuccessful in taking Constantinople. Furthermore, in the 630s, Muslim Arabs attacked from the south, capturing the empire's lands in Palestine and Syria.

During the 800s and 900s, the empire again prospered. Trade increased and many of the lost territories were regained by the Byzantines.

An Invasion of Turks

But then in 1071, the invasion of a powerful army of Seljuk Turks threw the Byzantine Empire into decline again. The Seljuk Turks came from Turkestan in central Asia. They were named in honor of Seljuk, their first leader. The Seljuks defeated the Byzantines in 1071 at the battle at Manzikert in present-day Turkey.

The Seljuks continued to capture Byzantine lands, and by 1081 established a new capital in Nicaea *(ny SEE uh),* only 200 miles southeast of Constantinople. In 1095, the Byzantine emperor sent a desperate message to Pope Urban II. Just 40 years before, the patriarch of the East had excommunicated the pope of the West. Now the Byzantine emperor had no choice but to risk humiliation and plead with the pope for military assistance from the West in order to defend Constantinople against the Turkish invaders. ■

➤ *Seljuk Turks ride camelback on the bottom of this colorful ceramic bowl from Persia.*

■ *Why did the Byzantine Empire decline in power between the early 600s and late 700s?*

REVIEW

1. **FOCUS** Compare the Eastern Orthodox Church and the Church of Rome.
2. **CONNECT** Explain why the Eastern Orthodox Church became a separate church from the Church of Rome.
3. **HISTORY** Explain why it was difficult but necessary for the Byzantine emperor to ask for the pope's help in 1095.
4. **CRITICAL THINKING** Do you think Pope Gregory III was justified in condemning Emperor Leo III for his decision to have all icons destroyed? Why?
5. **WRITING ACTIVITY** Use a dictionary to discover the meaning of the word *iconoclast.* Put yourself in the role of Pope Gregory III and write a letter to Emperor Leo III in which you use the word *iconoclast.*

Chapter 11

Homework Options

Have students outline the last section, The Empire Under Attack, to use as a study guide. Encourage students to use their outlines for reference during class discussion of that section.

Study Guide: p. 45

Answers to Review Questions

1. East: headed by patriarch, services in Greek, tolerated more discussion, less ornate on outside of church, icons on inside. West: headed by pope, services in Latin, no religious discussion, no icons.
2. The final break came in 1054 over the issue of who was responsible for the churches of southern Italy. The pope and patriarch excommunicated each other over this issue.
3. In 1071, Seljuk Turks took land away from

the empire. In 1081, the Turks moved their capital only 200 miles from Constantinople, further threatening the Byzantines.
4. Answers may vary. Some students may say that Leo III was right since he felt the icons were being worshiped as false gods. Other students may hold the opinion that Leo III had no right to infringe on the authority of the pope regarding a religious issue.

650   750   850   950   1050   1350

1095   **1270**

L E S S O N   3

The Crusades

*J*erusalem is now held captive by the enemies of Christ and is subjected, by those who do not know God, to the worship of the heathen
[unconverted]. She seeks . . . to be liberated, and [implores] you to
come to her aid.
    On whom, therefore, rests the labor of avenging these wrongs and of
recovering this territory, if not upon you?

Jerusalem is a holy city for
Jews, Christians, and Muslims.
Conflict has sometimes erupted
over possession of Jerusalem and
the right to visit its holy sites. The
crusades were such a period.
    From the 900s, many European
Christians made the pilgrimage to
Jerusalem. The region was stable so
the journey was relatively safe.
After 1070 the region became unstable, and some leaders in Europe
saw a chance to win the Holy Land.
In 1095, Pope Urban II spoke to an
audience and inflamed his listeners
with the words above. Many replied, "God wills it! God wills it!"
They began preparing for holy war.

THINKING FOCUS

*What were the crusades,
and why were they
important?*

Key Terms

- crusade
- infidel

◄ *While leading a
religious council in
Clermont, France,
Pope Urban II called
on his fellow Christians
to free the Holy Land
from the Turks.*

295

Europe: Rule, Religion, and Conflict

INTRODUCE

*A*sk students to explain
why the Byzantine
emperor would call the
pope for assistance in defending
the empire against Turkish
invaders (Lesson 2). *(The pope
was the most influential leader
throughout Europe.)* Review
the definition of crusade. *(Holy
War.)* Have students read the
Thinking Focus and then read
the lesson to learn about the
outcome and effects of the
crusades on western Europe.

Key Terms

Vocabulary Strategies: T36–T37
crusade—a military expedition
taken by European Christians
to win the Holy Land from the
Muslims
infidel—one who is an unbeliever in respect to Christianity

Graphic Overview

travel to
foreign lands

Jerusalem
controlled by Muslims

CRUSADES

cities grow
through trade

Jews
persecuted

military technology
improved

Objectives

1. Analyze the reasons for the
   crusades and the reasons
   people became crusaders.
2. Summarize the major crusades
   to the Holy Land and assess
   the effectiveness of each.
3. Evaluate the outcome and
   significance of the crusades.

DEVELOP

Point out that this lesson covers a long series of wars involving three different cultures. Have students study the map on this page. Ask them to locate the homelands of the European Christians, the Byzantines, and the Muslims. Then have them trace the routes of the four crusades described in the lesson.

Write the Graphic Overview on the chalkboard, and refer to it as each appropriate effect of the Crusades is developed in the lesson.

ETHICS
Critical Thinking

Point out the word *infidel*. Ask students to show how this term, in itself neutral, became emotionally charged. What would be the effect of labeling the enemy during wartime? *(It would depersonalize the enemy and imply justification in killing them.)*

■ *Both the Third Crusade and the Fourth Crusade used water routes.*

296

Four Major Crusades

Christian lands, 1080
Muslim lands, 1080
First Crusade, 1096–1099
Second Crusade, 1147–1149
Third Crusade, 1189–1192
Fourth Crusade, 1202–1204

0   150   300 mi.
0 150 300 km
Azimuthal Equidistant Projection

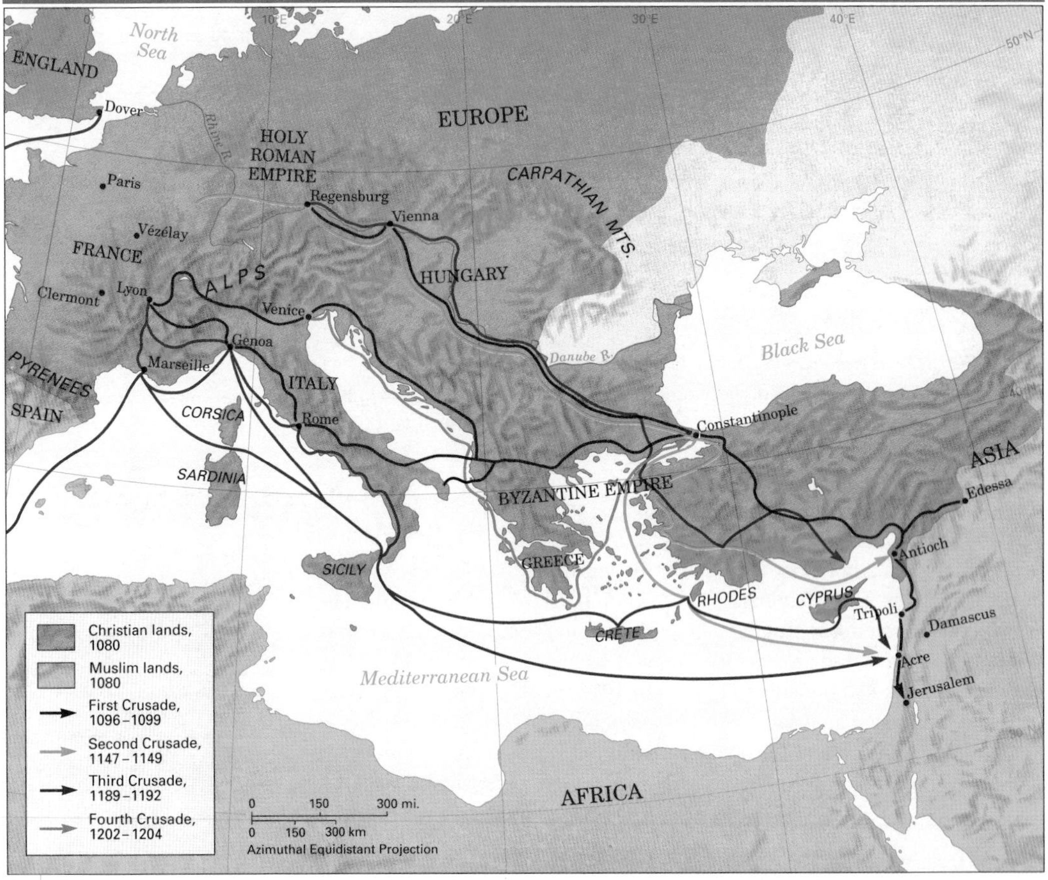

▲ *Look at the map to determine which of the crusades used a water route.*

296

The Crusades Begin

This campaign was actually the first of eight wars Europeans fought to win the Holy Land from the Muslims. These wars, called the **crusades,** occurred between 1096 and 1270. Four of the eight crusades involved Europeans in major warfare. Those who fought were called crusaders, because they vowed to "take up the cross."

The Christians' Motives

Winning the Holy Land from the **infidels** *(IHN fih duhlz),* or non-Christians, was Pope Urban's most obvious motive for war. He also wanted to reunite the Western and Eastern Christians under his rule. Becoming allies to the Byzantines might aid this cause. At home, Urban also wished to turn the European knights away from infighting and to put their energy into Christian service. For their sacrifices, the knights would be granted the land they conquered. This appealed to the younger sons of many nobles because only the first-born son could inherit a father's feudal lands.

Historians estimate that some 45,000 crusaders left western

Chapter 11

Access Activity

Divide the class into three groups. Have one group represent western Europeans, one Byzantines, and one Muslims. Based on earlier readings (Chapters 2, 3, 4, and 10), have each group compile two lists—the first of ways in which their group is similar to the other groups and the second of ways they are different from them. Share and discuss these lists.

Access Strategy

Have students identify places that are important to them, to people in their state, or to people in the United States. Why are these places important? *(Hometown; a place where friends or relatives live; valuable resources; strategic military location; special historical significance of cities, monuments, museums.)* Then have students discuss how they would respond if they were unable to visit these places. Would they feel that they had a right or an obligation to take them back by force? Under what circumstances would they have that right or obligation?

Europe to fight in the First Crusade. About 4,000 of those were knights, who were happy to at last be able to employ their fighting skills. The rest of the crusaders were foot soldiers, archers, and cooks. Women and priests also traveled with the men of the army.

Peasants had any of several good reasons for going on the crusade. One reason was that the church promised immediate salvation in heaven to anyone killed while helping to recover the Holy Land for Christians.

A second reason was that a peasant could be free of the bonds to his feudal lord while on a crusade. In other words, if a peasant left on a crusade, the lord of the manor would accept that as a reasonable excuse for the peasant not to pay his rent. The crusades also offered peasants an adventure.

The March to Jerusalem

The crusaders first made their way by foot and on horseback to the important city of Constantinople. The Byzantine emperor's daughter wrote about this as follows:

> F ull of enthusiasm and ardor they thronged every highway . . . Like tributaries joining a river from all directions they streamed towards us in full force.

Anna Comnena, c. 1097

From Constantinople the crusaders marched to Nicaea, the Seljuk capital, conquering it in June 1097. Then they swept eastward across Turkey. There, in 1098, they established the first of their crusader states.

The Crusader States

Crusader states were small outposts that were run like feudal kingdoms in Europe. The crusaders chose kings of these states, though these kings had no more power than a feudal lord.

The crusade now swept southward towards the Holy Land. In July 1099, the crusaders reached Jerusalem. The crusaders slaughtered its Muslim and Jewish inhabitants and made the city the capital of another crusader state.

Now the crusaders controlled a narrow strip of land about 500 miles long but only about 50 miles wide. This left them vulnerable along the outer strip to continued threats from Muslim forces. They built huge castles on the eastern border to better cope with these threats. Knights lived in these castles. To learn more about these knights of the crusades, look at A Moment in Time on page 298.

For now, the Christians had regained the Holy Land. Pilgrims could come to Jerusalem. Fulcher of Chartres wrote, "Now we who were westerners have become easterners. He who was Italian or French has in this land become a Galilean or Palestinian." ■

How Do We Know?

HISTORY *Fulcher of Chartres, a French priest, kept a chronicle, or record of his experiences, on the First Crusade. His* Chronicle of the First Crusade *has provided historians with many details of the journey and of the crusaders.*

▼ *This cross belonged to a crusader from the first crusade. Roundels, or curved panels, with Arabic inscriptions from the Koran were hung in Hagia Sophia after the Turks turned it into a mosque.*

■ *Why did the Christians want to recapture Jerusalem?*

297

Europe: Rule, Religion, and Conflict

Critical Thinking

Have students describe ideas they associate with the cross and the roundel pictured on p. 297. Which symbol is more familiar or which do they understand better? Ask them if one is likely to be able to understand a culture or religion if one does not understand its basic symbols. Then ask them to judge how well the Christians understood the Muslims, and vice versa.

■ *Jerusalem and other parts of the Holy Land were sacred to Christians because Jesus had lived and died there.*

297

Role Playing

Choose half a dozen students to assume the roles of crusaders (king, knight, foot soldier, archer, cook, priest; boys or girls can play any role) being interviewed upon their return from the Holy Land. Then have the rest of the class ask them questions. Why did you go? Was it hard to leave home? What was your journey like? Was it anything like what you expected? How does it feel to be back? After the interviews, have students discuss their perception of the crusaders.

Making a Mural

Have the entire class work together to make a large mural showing various elements that went into launching the First Crusade. Students could include pictures of the different types of crusaders, the pope, horses, weapons, armor, and other supplies the crusaders might have brought along. Encourage them to include a map as well. When the mural is finished, have students use it to tell the story of the First Crusade.

Critical Thinking

After students study the symbols on this page, have them write a paragraph describing the role of symbols in unifying members of a group and gaining support for a cause. Encourage students to refer not only to the symbols shown here but to other religious and political symbols as well. Have students share their conclusions with the class.

Note: You might wish to use this Moment in Time to preview the clash between Muslims and Crusaders in the Horns of Hattin on pp. 299–300. This illustration can also be used to introduce Lesson 3 of Chapter 10, Two Feudal Societies.

HISTORY
Visual Learning

Use this picture to explain why the crusader only fought on foot in emergencies. *(His armor weighs about 60 pounds, making it hard to handle a sword precisely.)*

Knights usually fought on horseback. They used a lance of wood, tipped with metal.

Explain to the students that the crusades allowed knights from countries typically at war with one another—France and England, for example—to fight a common enemy, the Muslims who controlled the holy places of Jerusalem.

More About the Knight's Armor
The springy mesh of interlocking rings that made up the crusader's chain mail could break the force of a sword blow. But a well-shot arrow could go right through the spaces between the rings.

A Crusader

3:32 P.M., October 20, 1192
In a field outside Temitz, Austria

Sword
This weapon is useful for fighting on foot. On his return trip, he has been attacked by German townspeople who think he might rob or kill them, as some knights have.

Chain Mail
The knight's head-to-toe suit of interlocked metal rings is heavy, hot, noisy, and hard to keep clean.

Shield
Designed as a personal sign, his shield identifies him to friend and foe on the battlefield.

Pebble
He picked this stone off the floor of the Church of the Holy Sepulchre in Jerusalem. Filled with good luck, it's very precious to our knight.

Letter
A commander near Jerusalem wrote this letter to a king in northern Germany. Our knight cannot read the letter, which complains of a water shortage.

Spices
These gifts will amaze his friends in England. Black pepper is unknown in his district; sugar is a once-in-a-lifetime treat.

Quilted Body Suit
Protecting him against the chain mail, this suit hasn't been washed or removed in eight and a half months.

Bandage
The knight's arrow wound is dressed with a sophisticated, soothing ointment, applied by an Islamic doctor.

298

Visual Learning

This picture is bursting with information. Ask students what they can tell or guess about the crusader from looking at the picture. *(He's religious, dirty, wounded, wary, and weighed down with armor.)*

Research

Ask the students to construct a shield that will identify them in the same way the knight's shield told people who he was. They may wish to research the history and meaning of their family's name and their given name. They should describe the symbols on their shields to their classmates. Refer students to p. 513 for examples of heraldry.

Writing

The knight couldn't read or write, but he could have dictated a letter to someone who did know how to write. Ask the students to write the letter that the knight might have dictated to be sent to his wife in England. They should be sure to include descriptions of his adventures in Jerusalem and Germany, and how he feels, living for months in a hot, heavy body suit.

Muslims Regain the Holy Land

During the 1140s, about 40 years after the First Crusade, the Muslims began to overpower the crusader states. The Church urged the people to renew the battle.

The Second Crusade, which lasted from 1147 to 1149, proved unsuccessful. Instead of fighting against the Muslims, armies led by King Louis VII of France and King Conrad III of Germany fought among themselves. Then Muslims almost wiped out the crusader army in Turkey. The small number of men who did make it to the Holy Land could not manage to live peacefully with the local Christian lords, who feared that the newcomers would attempt to set up a new government. While the crusaders argued among themselves, the Muslims continued to recapture lands.

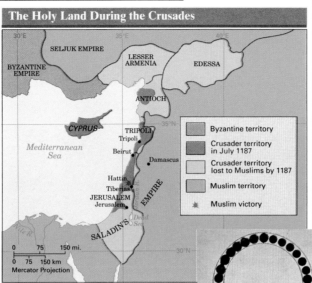

The Holy Land During the Crusades

Legend:
- Byzantine territory
- Crusader territory in July 1187
- Crusader territory lost to Muslims by 1187
- Muslim territory
- ✴ Muslim victory

0   75   150 mi.
0   75   150 km
Mercator Projection

Saladin's Rise to Power

In the late 1100s, Saladin was the leader of the Muslim forces. Saladin had been just a young Muslim schoolboy in Damascus when Christian knights laid siege to his city during the Second Crusade. But Saladin, whose name means "honoring the faith," would become a towering figure in the Muslim world, the greatest leader against the Christian crusaders.

As a young man Saladin served in the army of Syria, a country to the east of the crusader states. When the Syrian army took control of Egypt, south of the Holy Land, the caliph gave Saladin the job of running the government.

Because he was a strong leader, Saladin was able to unite the many small Muslim groups surrounding the crusader states. He became the supreme leader of both Egypt and Syria in 1171.

The Horns of Hattin

Saladin led the Muslims in a siege of Tiberias, the capital city of one of the crusader states near the Sea of Galilee. Knights of the Kingdom of Jerusalem, the southernmost crusader state, headed north to free Tiberias from Saladin. Christians and Muslims met in a decisive battle in July 1187.

The crusader army of about 20,000, including 1,200 knights in full armor and chain mail, was exhausted from marching all day in the desert. So six miles from Tiberias the crusaders camped in a small valley between the Horns of Hattin, twin mountain peaks. During the night the Muslim cavalry, outnumbering the Christian crusaders by several thousand, surrounded the crusaders.

▲ *The portrait of Saladin painted in 1180 is thought to be the only image of him that still exists. Find the lands on the map controlled by Saladin and his forces.*

299

Europe: Rule, Religion, and Conflict

Visual Learning

Have students study the illustration on this page and its caption. From the picture and caption, it is not clear who is attacking Jerusalem. Have students find evidence to suggest whether Muslims or Christians are attacking. *(Since it is a French painting, one could speculate that the Christians are attacking to "free" the city from Muslims. In the 1300s, Jerusalem was controlled by Muslims.)*

▲ *Jerusalem was taken by the Christians in 1099. The Muslims recaptured the city in 1187. This French illustration from the 1300s depicts a battle for control of Jerusalem.*

Just before dawn, the Muslims set fire to the dry grass that surrounded the valley, and the wind blew the flames up to where the crusaders were encamped. The Muslims charged behind the flames, boxing in the crusaders.

After the fire died down, few crusaders escaped death or captivity. Most of the crusader foot soldiers were sold into slavery. But Saladin also had a tremendous sense of honor. He guaranteed the safety of fleeing pilgrims, released husbands from captivity, and gave gifts to widows and orphans.

Saladin had decisively defeated the crusaders. With no opposition left, Saladin retook Jerusalem, and within three months, he had retaken almost all of Palestine. Use the map on page 299 to identify lands held by Muslims.

The Crusade of Kings

When news of the loss of Jerusalem reached western Europe, the pope is said to have died of grief. His successor, Pope Gregory VIII, called for a Third Crusade, which came to be called the Crusade of Kings. Three kings responded to the call: Emperor Frederick I of Germany, King Richard of England, and King Philip II of France. In 1189, these kings and their armies began preparations to regain Jerusalem from Saladin and the Muslims.

From the beginning, this crusade went badly. The 70-year-old Frederick drowned in 1190 while swimming across a river in Turkey. Most of Frederick's army was so discouraged that they returned to Europe.

Richard, who would later be nicknamed "the lion heart," was a military genius famous for his great courage in battle. But he had an unstable character—generous one moment and violent the next. Philip, a skilled politician, was no warrior but was an expert in planning sieges.

In April 1191, Philip began a siege of Acre, a key city on the coast. Richard joined Philip for the siege in June. The following month, the Muslims surrendered and Philip headed back for France. After occupying Acre for a few weeks, Richard became impatient when peace negotiations with Saladin were going slowly. Richard ordered the execution of all 2,700 Muslims within the city's walls.

Richard and Saladin

During the next year, Richard and Saladin fought many battles. Richard regained some territories

Chapter 11

Study Skills

Ask students to point out primary sources used in the lesson. Review the difference between a primary and a secondary source. Then have students go to the library to locate other primary source information on the crusades. Instruct them to copy a short excerpt from one and supply an identification *(author, title, date)*.

Historical Context

A strange and tragic (and perhaps legendary) crusade called the Children's Crusade is said to have taken place in 1212. Thousands of boys and girls from France and Germany became convinced that, because of their innocence, they could do what adults could not. They believed that they could recover the Holy Land. None of the children reached Jerusalem. Many froze to death or starved during the long march to the Mediterranean.

Conducting a Survey

Have students conduct a survey to find out the class's attitudes about the value and effectiveness of the crusades. Hold a discussion to allow students to decide on a series of questions (answerable with yes or no) to use in a poll. *(Examples: Should Pope Urban have called for the crusades? Did the crusaders accomplish their goals?)* After each student has responded, tally the scores and discuss them.

but failed to regain Jerusalem. Each leader made various peace proposals, and in September 1192, the two leaders signed a five-year treaty. Under this treaty, the crusaders could keep their cities along the coast from Jaffa north, and pilgrims could once again freely visit the holy places.

The Fourth Crusade

In 1198, Pope Innocent III called a crusade that proved to be disastrous to the Byzantine Empire. In this Fourth Crusade, the crusaders decided to head east by the Mediterranean Sea rather than by land. The merchants of Venice saw this as an opportunity to strengthen their trade routes. They convinced the crusade leaders to use force if necessary to install the Venetians' choice for the next Byzantine Emperor.

When the crusaders reached Constantinople, where the emperor lived, they kept their promise, but the people rebelled against this imposed ruler. The crusaders then seized Constantinople and pillaged it. Later historians have referred to this incident as "the Sack of Constantinople."

For three terrible days, the crusaders burned libraries; desecrated churches; and stole many valuable works of art, jewels, and gold. They then shipped their bounty back to Venice. In the selection below, you can read a Greek historian's eyewitness record of the pillaging.

> How shall I begin to tell of the deeds done by these wicked men? They trampled the images underfoot instead of adoring them. They threw the relics of the martyrs into filth. . . , They broke into bits the sacred altar of Santa Sophia, and distributed it among the soldiers. When the sacred vessels and the silver and gold ornaments were to be carried off, they brought up mules and saddle horses inside the church itself.
>
> Nicetas Choniates, 1204

The spirit of the crusades had been lost. The "enthusiasm and ardor" that Anna Comnena had seen in the first crusaders had been replaced by a hunger for wealth. ■

▲ *This Egyptian leather shadow puppet showing archers in a river boat celebrates a victory over the crusaders.*

■ *Were the crusades successful? Explain.*

■ *Because the expressed purpose of the crusades was to capture the Holy Land and the Christians failed to do so, they may be judged a failure. However, the First Crusade was temporarily successful.*

The Crusades Affect the West

Since these wars did not achieve their stated purpose, Christians might say they ended in failure. Jerusalem, the "center of the earth," remained in the Muslims' control. Constantinople, the jewel of the Byzantine Empire, was ravaged. People lost respect for the crusaders because of the abuses inflicted upon innocent people.

In Europe, the crusades proved to be a particular disaster for one group—the Jews. Crusaders considered both Jews and Muslims to be infidels. So at the same time that the crusaders set out to fight Muslims in the East, they slaughtered both the eastern and western Jewish population. The crusaders destroyed a number of Jewish towns along the Rhine River.

In some ways, though, western Europe did benefit from the crusades. First, trade, which was

Across Time & Space

Over the centuries, many Arabic words have come into common use in English. Arabic terms for products or ideas that have become part of the English language include tariff, sugar, rice, lemon, pistachio, and cotton. With the crusades, most Europeans got their first taste of sugar, citrus fruits, and many spices.

Europe: Rule, Religion, and Conflict

Historical Context

In the 1200s, Christians launched four other crusades. During the Fifth Crusade (1217–1221), the Egyptian city of Damietta fell to the Christians, but they were unsuccessful in gaining territory elsewhere in the Middle East. Eventually they returned the city to the Muslims in exchange for a truce. The Sixth Crusade (1228–1229) was led by the Holy Roman Emperor Frederick II. Frederick negotiated the return of Jerusalem to the Christians. This gain was short-lived.

In 1244, the Muslims retook Jerusalem. In response, King Louis IX of France launched the Seventh Crusade (1248–1254), which ended with his capture. He was released after the Muslims received a huge ransom. In 1270, Louis led the final crusade. He died when a plague broke out among his troops. A few attempts were made to organize crusades during the 1300s and 1400s, but Europeans were then more interested in westward exploration and expansion.

Critical Thinking

After students read the last section of this lesson, have them divide a piece of paper into two columns. On one side have them list the negative results of the crusades. On the other side have them list the positive results of the crusades. Have them use the lists to write a paragraph in which they evaluate the outcome and effect of the crusades.

Critical Thinking

Point out to students that, although the crusades were motivated by religious differences, one of the results of these crusades was that Christians grew to appreciate Muslims and Muslim culture. Have students give examples of ways in which Christians benefited from this contact. (*They acquired new products and ideas.*)

■ *Europe benefited from the crusades through increased trade, including luxury goods from the East; new military technology; new influences on music and poetry; a focus on exploring new lands, in the Christians' desire to spread their religion; stronger national governments; and a new vision of the wider world.*

CLOSE

Reintroduce the Thinking Focus and have students refer to the Graphic Overview on the chalkboard as they identify the causes and effects of the crusades.

302

▲ *Christians brought this reliquary, or container for relics, from Turkey to Italy in the late 1000s. They believed it held part of the finger of St. Nicholas, which would have made it a holy vessel. The crusaders carried many relics back to western Europe when they returned from the crusades.*

■ *How did the crusades benefit western Europe?*

already growing, expanded as a result of the crusades. As the crusaders passed through Europe, they brought with them a need for goods and services. Business in European towns boomed. In the lands of the Muslim Empire, there was a much higher standard of living. Some crusaders were determined for Europe to have the paved and well-lit streets and other civic improvements of those lands.

Crusaders also brought back many of the luxury goods available in the East—silk, spices, and pearls—and European demand for these fineries grew. The Italian cities of Venice, Pisa, and Genoa negotiated special trade treaties with Muslim rulers. In some cases, they were the sole suppliers of certain goods. In 1277, by special treaty with Muslim Sicily, the Venetians learned glass making.

A second effect of the crusades was a great transfer of military technology. Battles with the more advanced Muslims taught the Europeans about new and better weapons and tactics. It is possible that this is how gunpowder came to Europe.

Third, some scholars say that European poetry and music grew after the crusaders heard Arabic love poetry and music. In literature, chivalry developed a concept called "courtly love." Women received the benefit of this literary style, in which they were seen as holy, pure, and good. This contrasted with the general view of women as weak and inferior.

A fourth effect of the crusades was on the church itself. These wars strengthened the church's desire to spread Christianity and to eventually overwhelm the Muslim Empire. The church also came to see exploration as one of the most useful ways to spread Christianity around the world.

A fifth effect of the crusades was to strengthen Europe's national governments. Thousands of feudal lords were killed, and many landowning families went bankrupt paying for their knights' voyages. Thus their lands returned to the monarchs, whose power grew.

Finally, and perhaps most important, many Europeans now had their eyes opened wide to the world. Before the crusades, most had seen little beyond the next village. Now they knew about life in the Holy Land, other parts of Europe, and the Mediterranean. They now knew there were other ways of doing things—sometimes better ways. And, in some cases, they were willing to try them. ■

R E V I E W

1. **FOCUS** What were the crusades, and why were they important?
2. **CONNECT** Why did the crusades prove disastrous for the Byzantine Empire?
3. **BELIEF SYSTEMS** Why have so many wars been fought over the region called "the Holy Land?"
4. **CRITICAL THINKING** How did the motives of the first crusaders differ from those of the last crusaders?
5. **CRITICAL THINKING** How does using the label "infidel" to describe members of other faiths affect the way people behave toward one another?
6. **ACTIVITY** Prepare a chart of the four major crusades. For each crusade, give the dates when it occurred, the major participants, and the major events that occurred during the crusade.

Chapter 11

Homework Options

If you haven't already assigned the Writing Activity on p. 299, do so now.

Study Guide: p. 46

Answers to Review Questions

1. The crusades were a series of wars started by Pope Urban II to put the Holy Land under Christian control. The crusades were important in spreading the more advanced Byzantine and Muslim cultures back to the West.
2. In 1204, crusaders looted Constantinople of much of its art treasures and books. Byzantine traders lost much of their business to their European counterparts during the crusades.

3. Since the region in general, and Jerusalem in particular, is holy to Judaism, Christianity, and Islam, each faith has sought political control of the area.
4. The first crusaders fought for religious reasons; the fourth crusaders fought to pay off debts.
5. It has the effect of demeaning and dehumanizing the members of other faiths, thereby reducing understanding and kindness towards them.

UNDERSTANDING HISTORICAL MAPS
Drawing Conclusions

Here's Why

Historical maps provide information about the past. Some of this information may be straightforward, such as boundaries or routes. Sometimes, however, you need to use the facts to answer more complicated questions. When you use pieces of information to figure out another idea, you are drawing a conclusion.

Here's How

Look at the map of trade routes in A.D. 1200. It shows products traded and trade routes. You can use one piece of information, products traded, to draw a conclusion about Chinese economy and society.

The products traded from eastern China were perfume, silk, and porcelain. You know that these are products that people need to manufacture, and they are not raw materials, such as iron ore or sheep. Because they are manufactured goods, some complicated technology was probably needed to make them. You can conclude that Chinese society around 1200 had some complex technology.

Try It

Now look at the goods traded from Europe. Based on that information, what conclusions can you draw about European society around 1200? What kinds of goods were they and what was required to produce them? Draw a conclusion about the kinds of technology that might have been available in Europe.

Apply It

Do some research to find out more about making silk and wool. See how the two processes compare, and what kinds of technology were needed. Then look at the conclusion that you drew about European society. How can you find out whether it was correct?

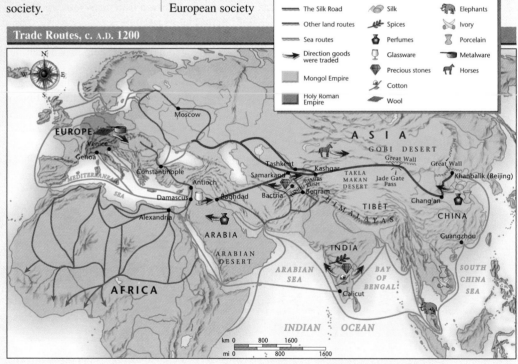

Trade Routes, c. A.D. 1200

Legend
- The Silk Road
- Other land routes
- Sea routes
- Direction goods were traded
- Mongol Empire
- Holy Roman Empire
- Silk
- Spices
- Perfumes
- Glassware
- Precious stones
- Cotton
- Elephants
- Ivory
- Porcelain
- Metalware
- Horses
- Wool

303

Answers to Try It

Answers will vary but should reflect an understanding of the information on the map. For instance, by 1200 metalware and wool were produced in Europe in exportable quantities. This suggests that Europe's technology at the time was advanced enough to produce metal at a high volume, yet at the same time, Europe's economy had a strong agricultural element. Europeans were still unable to produce the highly refined goods available from the East.

Apply It

Answers will vary but should show an awareness that drawing a conclusion is partly speculative and that conclusions need to be checked against an authoritative source. Responses should also show that students are capable of finding authoritative sources to check their answers.

Objective

Draw conclusions in the context of historical geography.

Answers to Reviewing Key Terms

A. Sample answers:
1. The **clergy** worked to achieve the church's purpose, **salvation** of souls.
2. **Patriarch** Cerularius and Pope Leo IX's **excommunication** of each other led to a **schism** in the church.
3. The **crusades** were wars in which Christians considered Muslims to be **infidels.**
4. During the time of the later **crusades,** some Europeans studied Greek and Roman **classics** in the new **universities.**
5. The dispute over **icons** may have been a factor in the **schism** in the church.

B. Sample answers:
1. A **tithe,** or one-tenth of a person's income, could be paid in money, produce, or labor.
2. **Icons** included paintings and figures of Jesus.
3. The **classics** were writings of ancient Greeks and Romans like Aristotle, Plato, Homer, and Virgil.
4. Byzantine schools and churches promoted **literacy.**
5. The first **universities** taught theology, philosophy, law, and medicine.
6. Soldiers marching to the **crusades** were "full of enthusiasm and ardor."
7. The **clergy** led worship services, weddings, and baptisms.
8. Accepting the church's beliefs, living a moral life, and doing good works brought **salvation.**

Answers to Exploring Concepts

A. Answers:
1054: Church schism
1071: Seljuks defeat Byzantines at Manzikert.
1096: First Crusade begins.
1147: Abbot Suger becomes regent in France.
1149: Second Crusade ends.
1182: Francis of Assisi born.
1204: Sack of Constantinople.
1270: Crusades end.
Sample summary:
From 1000 to 1300, the church was more powerful than kings. A schism occurred between the eastern and western branches. When pilgrims could not go to holy sites, the crusades began. This led to the Byzantine Empire's downfall and to

---

Chapter Review

Reviewing Key Terms

classic (p. 291)
clergy (p. 283)
crusade (p. 296)
excommunication (p. 285)
icon (p. 292)
infidel (p. 296)

literacy (p. 291)
patriarch (p. 292)
salvation (p. 285)
schism (p. 293)
tithe (p. 285)
university (p. 287)

A. The key terms in each group are related in some way. Write a sentence or two showing how the words in each pair or group are related to each other.
1. clergy, salvation
2. excommunication, patriarch, schism
3. crusade, infidel
4. classics, crusade, university
5. icon, schism

B. Each phrase below is related to a key term as it is used in the chapter. Write a sentence that includes each phrase and the key term to which it relates. The first one has been done for you.
1. money, produce, or labor: A tithe, or one-tenth of a person's income, could be paid in money, produce, or labor.
2. paintings and figures
3. Aristotle, Plato, Homer, and Virgil
4. Byzantine schools and churches
5. theology, philosophy, law, and medicine
6. "full of enthusiasm and ardor"
7. worship services, weddings, baptisms
8. belief, moral life, good works

Exploring Concepts

A. On your own paper, copy and complete the timeline using information from the chapter. Then write a summary of the chapter based on the dates and events in this timeline.

B. Write a sentence to answer each question using information from the chapter.
1. How did the crusades help bring about the end of the Byzantine Empire?
2. How did the crusades reflect the power of the church in Europe?
3. What positive effects did the crusades have on trade, warfare, and outlook in western Europe?
4. In what way did Christians look upon the crusades as a failure?
5. How did the establishment of religious orders and universities help expand the church and the community?
6. Describe three ways in which the church was the center of community life in Europe around 1000.
7. Why did King Louis the VI appoint Abbot Suger as regent in 1147?
8. How were Byzantine churches different from western European churches?
9. Summarize the dispute over icons between Leo III and Gregory III.

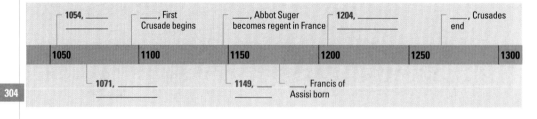

Chapter 11

Europe's enrichment by eastern trade, arts, and knowledge.

B. Sample answers:
1. Crusaders overran Constantinople.
2. Pope Urban could arouse many people, even kings, to go off to war.
3. Crusaders brought back arts, learning, and new technologies and trade.
4. At the end, Christians failed to conquer the Holy Land, and many people were killed.
5. Religious orders brought Christianity to the people. Universities brought learning to those outside the clergy.
6. Churches were gathering places, refuges, and even marketplaces.
7. Louis left to fight in the crusades. Abbot Suger was his trusted adviser.
8. Western churches were elaborate inside and out. Byzantine churches had simple exteriors with detailed interiors.
9. Leo thought icons had become objects of worship. Gregory felt icons helped people learn about their faith.

Reviewing Skills

1. Look at the map on page 142. Your business, located in Alexandria, is planning to send a ship from the Red Sea to Southeast Asia, stopping along the way in India. The voyage one-way to Asia will take four months. The wool you are shipping has arrived late, so your ship won't reach the Indian Ocean until December. Use the map and a calendar to estimate when the ship will arrive in Southeast Asia. Form a conclusion about when the ship will return.

2. The map on page 290 shows trade routes in the eastern Mediterranean during the Byzantine Empire. Venice-to-Trebizond is the longest route under Byzantine control. Now look at the map on page 205. The Silk Road was the longest trade route in the Tang lands. How long is each? Draw a conclusion about trade, government, or transportation technology as you compare Byzantine and Tang trade routes.

3. Look at the map of Baghdad on page 87. What conclusions can you make about Baghdad's dependence on water.

Using Critical Thinking

1. "Many feudal Europeans, most of whom had never traveled beyond the next village, now had their eyes opened to the wide world." Write one or more paragraphs to answer the following questions about the above quotation. Is it a statement of fact, opinion, or reasoned judgment? Why? Given the information in the chapter, what might the statement mean? Is it supported by information in the chapter? How?

2. The beginning of Lesson 2 talks about some of the trade that existed between western Europe and the East before the crusades began. The Seljuks invaded the Byzantine Empire in 1071. That same year, they seized Jerusalem and prevented Christians from entering the city. What effect did the actions of the Seljuk Muslims have on the beginning of the crusades? How did they influence trade between East and West? Write a paragraph or two describing the Seljuk influence and the effect of the crusades themselves on international commerce.

Preparing for Citizenship

1. WRITING ACTIVITY Imagine that you work for King Henry IV as a clerk. As such, you are a member of a very special group of people: you are one of the few individuals in western Europe at this time who can read and write. The king has asked you to record the story of his excommunication by Pope Gregory. Write two or three paragraphs describing this event.

2. ARTS ACTIVITY In the library, find books on European, Byzantine, or Muslim arts and crafts from the period between 1000 and 1300. Choose one style and find a picture that represents that style. For example, it could be a picture of enameled jewelry or embroidered cloth, a carving, a mural, a painting, or a sculpture. Draw a picture of your own that is similar in style to the picture you are looking at.

3. COLLABORATIVE LEARNING Divide into groups of three to four people each. As a group, gather and present visually as much information as you can about the people of Europe and the lands around the Mediterranean from 1000 to 1200. Your presentation should consist of a variety of visuals, such as maps, timelines, charts, or graphs, or any combination of those formats. It also can include written notes, but it should not simply be a report. One person from each group should explain the group's project to the class.

305

Europe: Rule, Religion, and Conflict

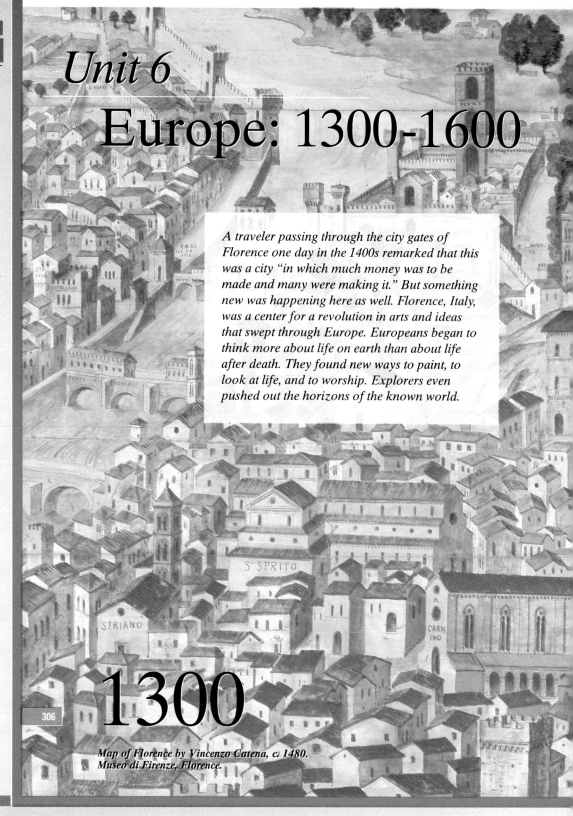

UNIT
OVERVIEW

Have students read the unit title and the paragraph below it. Then ask them if they are familiar with the names Leonardo da Vinci, Michelangelo, and Galileo. Explain that the great artists da Vinci and Michelangelo and the astronomer Galileo did some of their work in Florence. Their accomplishments were part of a rebirth in art and learning called the Renaissance.

Looking Back

Review with students the effects of the Crusades from Lesson 3 of Chapter 11. Emphasize especially the contact with Muslim and Byzantine cultures that opened European eyes to the achievements of other societies.

Looking Forward

Tell students that in the next three chapters they will study several great movements in history that led to changes in education, art, science, religion, and geography:

Chapter 12 *The Renaissance*
Chapter 13 *Reformation and the Scientific Revolution*
Chapter 14 *The Age of Exploration*

306

Unit 6

Europe: 1300–1600

A traveler passing through the city gates of Florence one day in the 1400s remarked that this was a city "in which much money was to be made and many were making it." But something new was happening here as well. Florence, Italy, was a center for a revolution in arts and ideas that swept through Europe. Europeans began to think more about life on earth than about life after death. They found new ways to paint, to look at life, and to worship. Explorers even pushed out the horizons of the known world.

1300

306

Map of Florence by Vincenzo Catena, c. 1480. Museo di Firenze, Florence.

GEOGRAPHY PROJECT

Regional Changes

Geography Skill **Make a Route Map**
Students use the skills of Acquiring and Organizing geographic information.
Geography Theme Regions
Geography Standards 5, 17 interpreting earth's complexity; applying geography to interpret the past

Activity *Create a Documentary*
Materials writing paper, pencils, pens
Management Individual/ Small Group

Choose one of the regions discussed in the unit. Write a documentary script describing the important cultural, political, and economic changes that took place in different locations within the selected region between 1300 and 1600.

Have students:

• create a concise documentary script or storyboard describing major changes in the region.

• include a route map of important trade routes and exploration expeditions that apply to the time period and region.

• provide illustrated storyboards to present the script to another class.

1600

Understanding the Map

The map illustrates what a prosperous Italian city looked like during the Renaissance. A wall with 11 gates encircled Florence, built along both banks of the Arno River. The twisting streets were crammed with tall, narrow buildings featuring shops on the street and living quarters above.

Understanding Chronology

This unit covers events in Europe during the Renaissance. Point out that major changes in art, learning, religion, and exploration occurred during this relatively short time period.

For research support activities, see the *Research Handbook.*

For simulations correlated to this unit, see *Citizenship Simulations,* p. viii.

HOUGHTON MIFFLIN SOCIAL STUDIES

Bookshelf II

Bard of Avon: The Story of William Shakespeare

by Diane Stanley and Peter Vennema

This biography of the world-famous playwright focuses on his use of classical literature and historical events as a source for ideas in his plays.

Motivate Read pp. 26–33 about the types of plays William Shakespeare wrote during his career as a playwright. Ask students why they think Shakespeare turned to classic Greek stories and English histories for the ideas for his plays. Remind students that the time period they are about to study in this unit was called the Renaissance and it was characterized by a revival of interest in ancient Greek and Roman arts, literature, and science.

To connect this book with the unit content, use the planning guide and student activity blackline masters beginning on p. iv of the *Bookshelf II Teacher's Resources.*

For additional books that are Easy, Average, and Challenging, see the Unit Bibliography on p. T43. See bibliography updates at www.eduplace.com/ss/hmss.

Planning at a Glance
The Renaissance

	Objectives	Reading Support and Other Resources	Diverse Learning Strategies
Lesson 1 Europe at the End of the Middle Ages *pp. 310–315* 2–3 days	• Assess the effects of the plague, war, and famine on Western Europe. • Describe the breakdown of feudalism and the rise of central governments.	• **Workbook** or **Reading Support:** pp. 157–160 Review p. 37 Lesson Support/Transition p. 37 Multi-lang. Sum. pp. 73–74 • **Other Resources:** Geography Kit; Posters 5, 7; Study Guide p. 48; Study Prints 10	Access Strat. **(SDAIE)** TE p. 311 Access Act. **(SDAIE)** TE p. 311 Social Participation **(Auditory)** TE p. 312 Making a Poster **(Visual)** TE p. 314 Audiotapes of Multi-language Lesson Summaries **(Auditory)**
Lesson 2 The Italian Renaissance *pp. 316–323* 2–3 days	• Describe how northern Italy gave birth to the Renaissance. • Define humanism and show how it affected Western Europe.	• **Workbook** or **Reading Support:** pp. 161–164 Review p. 38 Lesson Support/Transition p. 38 Multi-lang. Sum. pp. 75–76 • **Other Resources:** Geography Kit, Study Guide p. 49, Study Print 11	Access Strat. **(SDAIE)** TE p. 317 Visual Learning **(Visual)** TE pp. 320, 321 Writing a Dialogue **(GATE)** TE p. 321 Role Playing **(Auditory)** TE p. 322 Audiotapes of Multi-language Lesson Summaries **(Auditory)**
Skill: Reading a DaVinci Sketch *p. 324* 1 day	• Interpret information presented in a technical drawing.	• **Other Resources:** Study Guide p. 50	Making a Drawing **(Visual)** TE p. 324
Lesson 3 Renaissance Life *pp. 325–328* 2–3 days	• Describe life in an Italian city of the Renaissance. • Identify and describe the different social classes of Renaissance Italy.	• **Workbook** or **Reading Support:** pp. 165–168 Review p. 39 Lesson Support/Transition p. 39 Multi-lang. Sum. pp. 77–78 • **Other Resources:** Study Guide p. 51	Access Strat. **(Extra Support)** TE p. 326 Writing **(GATE)** TE p. 327 Social Participation **(Auditory)** TE p. 328 Audiotapes of Multi-language Lesson Summaries **(Auditory)**
Lesson 4 Renaissance in Northern Europe *pp. 329–333* 2–3 days	• Explain how the ideas of the Italian Renaissance spread to northern Europe. • Compare and contrast Northern European humanism and Italian humanism.	• **Workbook** or **Reading Support:** pp. 169–172 Review p. 40 Lesson Support/Transition p. 40 Multi-lang. Sum. pp. 79–80 • **Other Resources:** Geography Kit, Study Guide p. 52	Access Act. **(SDAIE)** TE p. 330 Map and Globe Skills **(Visual)** TE p. 330 Study Skills **(Auditory)** TE p. 332 Reader's Theatre **(GATE)** TE p. 332 Audiotapes of Multi-language Lesson Summaries **(Auditory)**
Chapter Review *pp. 334–335*		Chapter 12 Test pp. 45–48 *(See facsimiles on TE p. 570.)*	Assessment Multiple-Use Masters pp. 73–80

Reading Support Resources *for Every Lesson*

Reading and Review	Multi-language Summaries	Lesson Support / Transition
		S D A I E

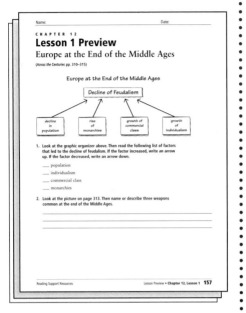

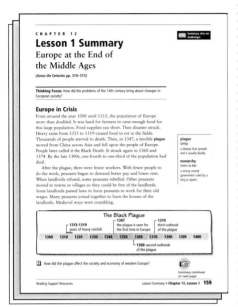

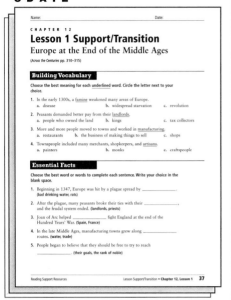

Activities for SDAIE
Specially **D**esigned **A**cademic **I**nstruction in **E**nglish

- **Chapter Overview*** p. 156
- **Lesson Previews*** using graphic organizers from the Teacher's Edition pp. 157, 161, 165, 169
- **Reading Strategies*** pp. 158, 162, 166, 170
- **Lesson Summaries*** pp. 159–160, 163–164, 167–168, 171–172
- **Lesson Reviews** pp. 37, 38, 39, 40

* **Workbook** includes starred items.

Lesson Summaries in:
- English (See Reading and Review.)
- Spanish pp. 159–160, 163–164, 167–168, 171–172
- Chinese pp. 73–80
- Hmong pp. 73–80
- Khmer pp. 73–80
- Vietnamese pp. 73–80

 Summaries available on audiotapes

- **Lesson Support/Transition** pp. 37, 38, 39, 40

 Technology Options

Internet Support
http://www.eduplace.com

Social Studies Center at Education Place

Internet support for Chapter 12:
- *Lesson at a Glance*
- *da Vinci's Notebooks*

Videotape/Videodisc
We the People:
Supports and enhances major topics: **Theme:** *Art of the Italian Renaissance*

Software
Student Writing Center ® (CD-ROM) (Macintosh® or Windows®)

School to Career

Medical techniques have changed since the time of the European Renaissance. With a partner, have students select and research a medical field of study, including the education needed. Then hold a medical career fair, with each pair creating a booth to present their area of specialty to the class.

307B

Character Education

Service Learning: Gutenberg's press allowed many Europeans to read and own books for the first time. Literacy is important for success. Arrange for students to begin a peer reading program with younger, elementary students once a week. Students can read aloud or have the other students read aloud to them.

CHAPTER
PREVIEW

Have the students read the chapter title and the paragraph below it. Discuss with students the idea of rebirth. Point out that a rebirth can indicate a renewed interest in forgotten or neglected ideas (such as those of the Greeks and Romans) as well as an interest in new ideas.

Looking Forward

Tell the students that Lessons 1–4—Europe at the End of the Middle Ages, The Italian Renaissance, Renaissance Life, and Renaissance in Northern Europe—recount how the Renaissance originated in Italy and spread through Europe.

In Lesson 1 the students will read about how life in the Middle Ages began to change, causing feudalism to break down.

308

Chapter 12
The Renaissance

From the 1300s to the mid-1600s, Europe went through a renaissance, or "rebirth." People broke from bonds of the church and feudal structures. Scholars and artists studied the ideas of classical Greece and Rome. Writers told stories of everyday people. Paintings burst with life. To many Europeans, this was the beginning of the modern world.

1434 Cosimo de Medici (above left) begins his rule of Florence, Italy. The wealthy Medicis support architects who design the city's impressive buildings (above).

1300	1350	1400	1450

308

1300

1370 Mongol leader Timur begins a series of raids through central Asia.

1420 The Chinese build the Great Temple of the Dragon in Beijing.

BACKGROUND

The Renaissance was a period of creative experiment nurtured by individualism. Individuals once dominated by the church and the unyielding feudalism of the Middle Ages were now taking control of their own lives.

The Renaissance Man and Woman

The concept of the "Renaissance person" has survived into modern times. A Renaissance person is a versatile and energetic person who uses a variety of talents and skills to pursue personal goals. He or she exceeds the expectations of society in his or her achievements.

During the Renaissance the luxury of pursuing one's individual interests was reserved for the privileged of the middle and upper classes who embraced the principles of humanism. The true Renaissance person strived to be knowledgeable in philosophy, the arts, literature, and music. A well-rounded person was also eloquent and well-mannered. The freedom to express oneself sparked achievements in literature, the arts, and science. Shakespeare used his talents to entertain, while writers such as Machiavelli devoted their talent to political theory. The new individualism encouraged self-promotion. Pride replaced the humility taught by the church as people clamored to attain fame and fortune.

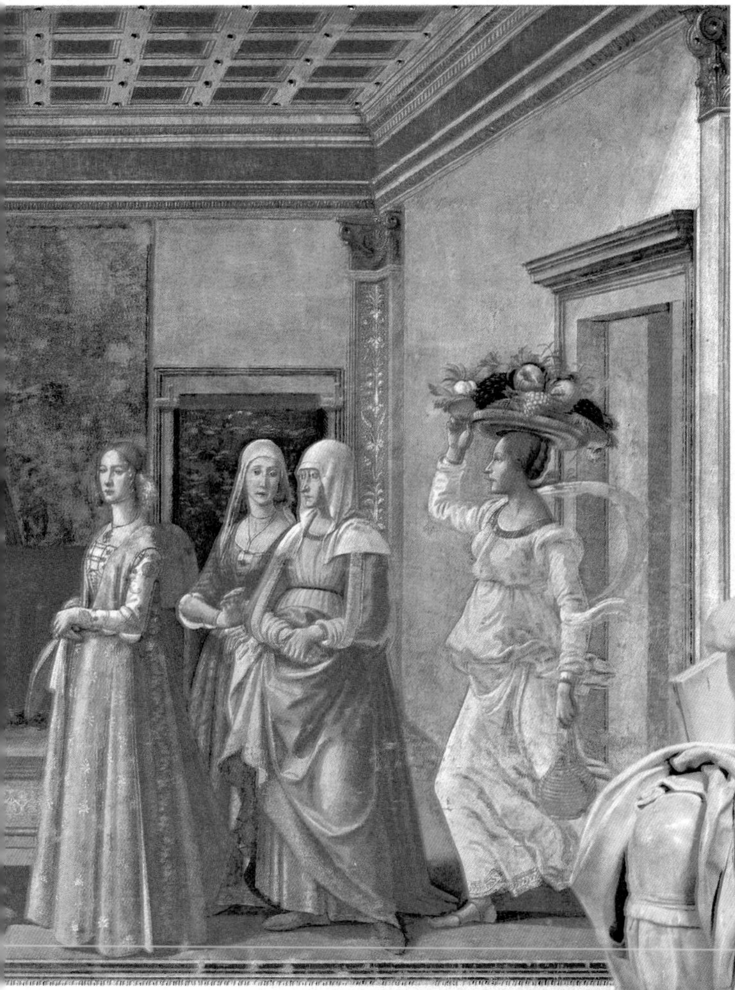

Throughout this period, painters portrayed figures who almost seemed to come alive. This work by Ghirlandaio shows a wealthy young lady of Florence and her attendants.

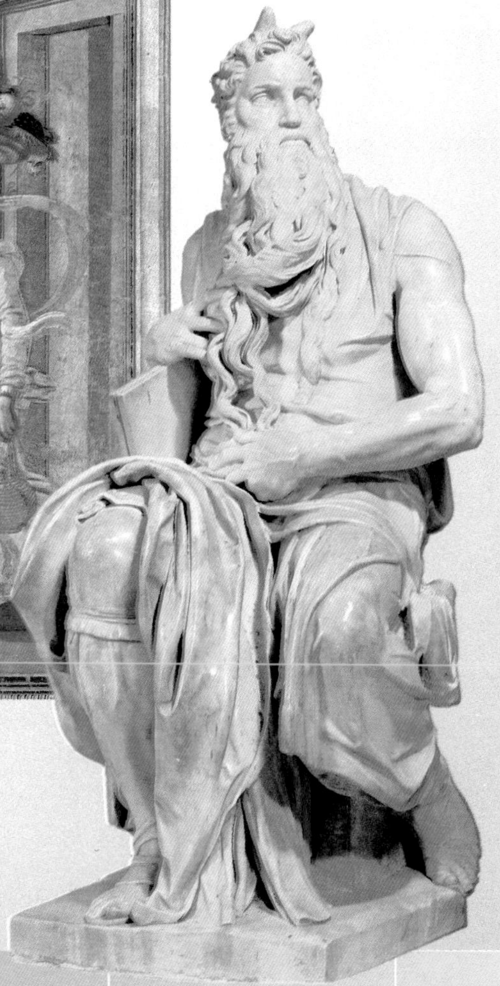

c. 1515 Michelangelo completes the statue *Moses.* This sculpture shows the power and emotion of the aging wise man.

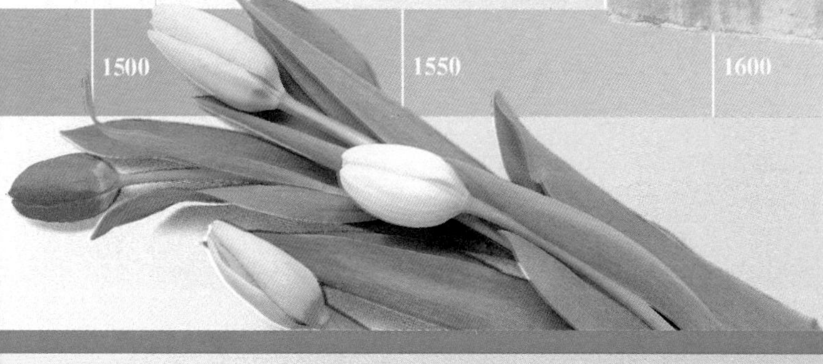

Traders bring tulips to Europe from Constantinople in the 1500s.

1500 | 1550 | 1600 | 1650

1650

Understanding the Visuals

Ask what makes both the picture of the buildings in Florence and the picture of the young woman and her attendants look real. Explain that depth and distance in pictures are achieved through the use of perspective, a technique that had originally been used sporadically by the Greeks and Romans and was rediscovered and further developed during the Renaissance.

Understanding Chronology

Ask students to read the timeline and be aware that while wonderful buildings were being erected in Florence, a beautiful temple, reflecting a very different architectural style and culture from that of the Renaissance, was being built in Beijing, China.

The Renaissance Artist

One group of people who attained that fame was the Renaissance artists. The Renaissance created a new respect for art and artists. Members of a growing middle class with new-found wealth, along with heads of city-states, scrambled to support the arts.

With the elite acting as patrons for the arts, artists became highly paid professionals and part of the elite. Medieval artists, in contrast, earned meager wages and were included among the ranks of the lower-middle class. Artists now took pride in their work as individuals and began signing their paintings and carving their names into their sculptures. Merchants and bankers even used art as a form of financial investment, knowing that the work of some artists was likely to increase in value.

The Renaissance artist was intellectually independent, unlike artists of the Middle Ages who were bound to a guild. Those who were well-respected such as Michelangelo, Leonardo da Vinci, and Titian were quite wealthy, and most artists were at least economically secure. Many patrons of the arts, including Cosimo Medici, thought that artists had "divine" powers, which since the Middle Ages had been attributed only to God.

Read the lesson title and point out that this lesson will focus on Europe in the late Middle Ages (1300s). Point out that as the Middle Ages came to an end there was a new focus on individualism. Ask students what other words and ideas this term suggests. Record their comments in the form of a semantic map on the chalkboard. Tell students to read the Thinking Focus. Have them predict how individualism might have contributed to the breakdown of feudalism in the Middle Ages.

Key Terms

Vocabulary Strategies: T36–T37
plague—a highly infectious, usually fatal, epidemic disease
monarchy—a strong central government ruled by a king or a queen
heretic—a person who has controversial opinions, especially one who publicly disagrees with the accepted beliefs of the Roman Catholic Church
individualism—personal independence; the idea that every person should be free to develop and pursue his or her own goals

1300   1500   1550   1600   1650

LESSON 1

Europe at the End of the Middle Ages

THINKING FOCUS

How did the problems of the 14th century bring about changes in European society?

Key Terms

- plague
- monarchy
- heretic
- individualism

► *The plague overwhelmed Europe during the 1300s. In this painting, The Triumph of Death, by Francesco Traini, a hunting party comes across the coffins of three plague victims. The monk at the far left reminds the hunters of how fleeting life is.*

Ring-a-ring o' roses,
A pocket full of posies,
A-tishoo! A-tishoo!
We all fall down."
The words may be a little different, but you probably still recognize this children's rhyme: "Ring-Around-the-Rosie."

As common as this verse is, few people know that it describes one of the most destructive events of the Middle Ages—the Great Plague. The **plague** was a disease that swept like wildfire through Europe beginning in 1347. It was first seen in China in 1331 and in 15 years had spread across Asia to the Black Sea. People later called it the Black Death, because black spots formed under the skin from internal bleeding.

A rosy rash and sneezing were also symptoms of the disease. People carried bunches of herbs called "posies" in their pockets to try to ward off the illness. Millions of people "fell down" and died as wave after wave of the Black Death struck.

The plague spread quickly, infecting rich and poor alike. On the next page is an Italian man's description of the helplessness he felt as the disease spread.

Chapter 12

---

1. Assess the effects of the plague, war, and famine on the economy of Western Europe.
2. Describe the reasons for the breakdown of feudalism and the rise of central governments.
3. Explain how medieval values changed as a result of increased trade and commerce.

Graphic Overview

This root chart shows the structure of this lesson.

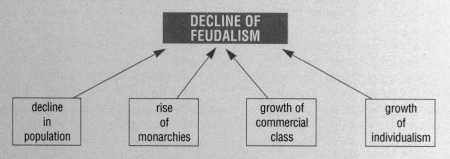

DECLINE OF FEUDALISM

decline in population | rise of monarchies | growth of commercial class | growth of individualism

The Great Plague, 1346–1353

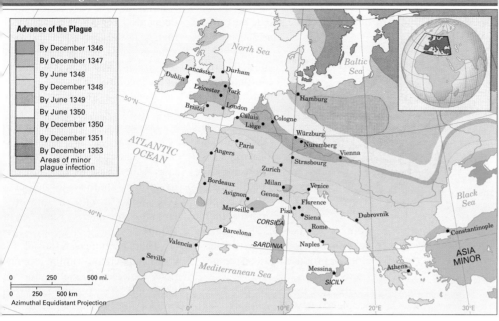

Advance of the Plague

- By December 1346
- By December 1347
- By June 1348
- By December 1348
- By June 1349
- By June 1350
- By December 1350
- By December 1351
- By December 1353
- Areas of minor plague infection

0 250 500 mi.
0 250 500 km
Azimuthal Equidistant Projection

I do not know where to begin describing its relentless cruelty; almost everyone who witnessed it seemed stupefied [stunned] by grief. . . . I, Agnolo di Tura, known as the Fat, buried five of my children with my own hands. . . . Nobody wept for the dead, since each was awaiting death; and so many died that everyone thought that the end of the world had come.

▲ *The Great Plague began in Asia and was carried to Europe by the fleas on black rats. These rats lived on trade ships that traveled between Asia and Europe. In Europe the plague moved from south to north, along trade routes.*

Europe in Crisis

During the 350 years before the plague, the population of Europe had more than doubled in size. Because the agricultural techniques of the Middle Ages were fairly crude, farmers had trouble growing enough food for the large population. Then disaster struck. Unusually heavy rains fell during the years from 1315 to 1319, causing the farmers' grain to rot in the fields. Thousands of people starved to death.

When the plague struck in 1347, it devastated many areas already weakened by the famine. Look at the map above, and follow the progress of the plague as it swept across the continent. The

▼ *Many Europeans used "remedies" for the plague. Two popular remedies were pomanders, which were oranges stuck with cloves, and peeled onions. Neither worked, however.*

DEVELOP

Discuss the effects of destructive events such as war, famine, and disease on a society's value systems, economy, and government. Have the students read aloud the first-person account describing the plague on p. 311. Ask them to speculate on how people would react to a crisis such as the plague. Explain that throughout history these types of events have stimulated changes in society. People begin to reexamine their values as they look for new ways to cope with their changing world.

HISTORY
Visual Learning

Emphasize the impact of the plague on Western Europe by asking one-third of the class to leave their seats and go to the back of the room. Ask them what effect this loss of students could have on how the class is conducted. Discuss how the decline in population caused by the plague and famines affected the economy.

311

Access Strategy

Have students assemble in pairs. Ask them to talk about events that could have a major impact on their lives. These events might include the loss of a family member or friend, a natural disaster such as an earthquake or tornado, or a war. Ask them to discuss how their lives or the lives of others would change as a result of these events. Tell students that in this lesson they will learn about major events that brought an end to the Middle Ages and paved the way for the Renaissance.

These events also caused changes in people's lifestyle and values.

Access Activity

Ask students to imagine that they work at a busy job that employs 25 workers. In one week, half the employees leave, and the boss does not replace them. Ask the students how they would react. *(They would probably ask for higher wages.)* Have them compare their situation to the one medieval peasants were in after the plague.

■ *The plague killed one-fourth to one-third of Europe's population in the mid-1300s. After the plague, there was a shortage of workers. Because of this shortage, peasants began to demand higher wages from their landlords. When they were turned down, many peasants moved to towns to find a better life and to break their ties with the landlords.*

SOCIAL SYSTEMS

Social Participation

Stress that the late Middle Ages was a period of social rebellion. In the aftermath of the plague, landlords clamped down on their peasant tenants. They passed laws to lower wages and tried to restrict their freedom. Divide the class into two groups. One group will represent the lower class peasants, the other will represent the upper class medieval landlords. Have each group air its grievances.

312

▲ *Neither rich nor poor was spared from the plague. These woodcuts from* The Dance of Death *by Hans Holbein show death visiting a poor farmer and a scholar.*

■ *How did the plague affect the society and economy of western Europe?*

▼ *Joan of Arc is still celebrated as a heroine who helped save France from the English, as shown in this French statue.*

population recovered in most areas from the 1347 outbreak. New outbreaks of the plague hit Europe in 1360 and 1374. By the late 1300s, one-fourth to one-third of the population of Europe had died. In some towns, over 50 percent of the people died.

After the plague, there were too few people. There were not enough people to harvest the crops or produce all the necessary goods.

Because there were fewer people to do work, peasants demanded better wages and lower rents. Landlords resisted peasant demands. Like others before them, many peasants moved to towns or villages. There they hoped to find a better life, free from the control of the landlords.

Some landlords passed laws to force peasants to work for their traditional wages. Throughout Europe, bitter resentment brewed as landlords tried to enforce those laws. Many peasants joined forces to storm and burn manor houses. As peasants broke their ties with landlords, the feudal system began to falter.

These economic and social crises chipped away at the foundations of medieval society in the 1300s and 1400s. Conditions were ripe for great social change. ■

Rise of Central Governments

During the Middle Ages, power rested in the hands of nobles who owned feudal estates. But from the 1100s to the 1300s, the power in Western Europe had begun to shift from the nobles to kings. These kings were attempting to form **monarchies,** or strong central governments ruled by a king or queen. Monarchies in countries like England and France began to gain power and authority. Kings and queens collected taxes, raised armies, and ruled their subjects through central governments.

However, the increasing power of some kings was not well received by everyone. Revolts by many nobles against kings and contests between kings for territory produced war. These wars raged almost constantly in the 1300s and 1400s. The longest war of the later Middle Ages was the Hundred Years' War. This war began in 1337, when the king of England claimed to be the rightful king of France. The French king resisted, and war lasted on and off for another 116 years. Finally in 1453, the French troops defeated the English.

Joan of Arc

At the point during the war when French fortunes had sunk to their lowest, a young woman helped bring about a remarkable reversal. Joan of Arc grew up in the small French village of

Critical Thinking

People caught the plague when they were bitten by the fleas that lived on black rats. Ask students what the large number of plague deaths tells us about medieval sanitation. *(Sanitation was poor, rats and fleas were common.)* Hygiene was an important part of Jewish and Islamic religious law. Some scholars say that is why Jews and Muslims may have been less prone to catch the plague than Christians.

Social Context

Joan of Arc shed the customary role assigned to women during the Middle Ages. She dressed in a knight's armor and rode into battle as a commander of French troops. During this time in history, peasant women worked in the house and in the fields. Except for spinning and weaving, most jobs were filled by men. Men were the heads of families and prevailed in wars and politics. Equality of the sexes as we know it today was entirely foreign to the people of this period.

Historical Context

Monarchs were able to increase their power partly as a result of the Black Death. Landed nobles, who had held the growth of central governments in check, lost a great deal of wealth during and after the plague because agricultural prices declined and the cost of finished goods and labor increased.

Donremy. Like most peasants, she never learned to read or write.

Joan left home in 1429 at the age of 17. She insisted that she had received messages from God telling her to help drive the English out of France. Joan asked one of the French nobles to let her speak to Charles, heir to the throne.

Charles decided to test Joan. He had one of his nobles sit on the throne while he stood with the rest of the court. When Joan entered, she went to Charles, although she had never seen him before. This helped convince Charles that Joan spoke the truth.

Charles gave Joan soldiers and supplies and sent her off to Orleans. At this town in northern France, the English and French had been engaged in a fierce battle for several months. Before she left, Joan dictated a message for the English leaders. She hoped to persuade them to leave France without further bloodshed:

> *S*urrender to the Maid [Joan] sent hither by God the King of Heaven, the keys of all the good towns you have taken and laid waste in France.

The letter did not convince the English to surrender. Instead, the 17-year-old Joan rode off to Orleans to fight bravely alongside her soldiers. Joan defeated the English at Orleans and went on to win four other battles against them.

Joan was captured in May 1430. The English army and the Church tried her as a witch and a **heretic,** or one who speaks beliefs different from the accepted church opinion. Her sentence: to be burned at the stake. Joan was only 19 years old when she died.

New Ways of Fighting

The Hundred Years' War was a turning point in medieval war technology. Horse-mounted knights in heavy armor could not survive the armor-piercing arrows shot from the newly developed longbows.

With the crusades and revived trade routes, Europeans learned about Greek, Roman, Indian, Chinese, and Muslim war technology. During the crusades, the Muslim armies had used hand grenades and flame throwers filled with naphtha, a naturally occuring petroleum byproduct. The Chinese had long used gunpowder for fireworks and signals.

The introduction of guns and gunpowder to Europe in the 1320s made the biggest impact on how wars were fought there. By the 1320s, cannons were being made for besieging and bombarding forts and castles. Smaller cannons led to hand-held cannons, and beginning in the 1400s, soldiers carried long handguns known as harquebuses (*HAHR kuh buhs uhs*) into battle.

During the 1300s, rulers also began to raise large armies by hiring professional soldiers. ■

◄ *Warfare changed greatly during the Hundred Years' War. New weapons, such as the longbow and the cannon, made both the knight and the castle obsolete.*

Across Time & Space

Twenty-five years after Joan of Arc was executed, the Catholic Church decided that Joan had not been a witch. Five centuries later, on May 16, 1920, Joan of Arc was declared a saint by the Roman Catholic Church.

■ *Why did the feudal system begin to crumble?*

313

The Renaissance

Describe the new weapons that evolved in the late Middle Ages. Ask students to look at the cannon pictured at left. How would this new type of weapon be effective in attacks on castles and walled cities? (*More powerful ammunition, longer firing distance meant that castles could no longer withstand attacks.*)

■ *There were several reasons why the feudal system began to crumble. Peasants refused to work for their traditional wages after the plague. Many left the manors and moved to towns. As a result, nobles lost some of their power and wealth. Monarchs gained power as the nobles lost it. New weapons made knights obsolete, causing kings to hire armies of professional soldiers.*

313

Language Arts Connection

Despite the fact that knights were gradually replaced by paid soldiers, the nobility of northern Europe clung to the ideals of the knight's code of chivalry, long after their usefulness had faded. The Spanish author Miguel de Cervantes satirized the use of this outdated code in his work *Don Quixote.* Prepare a script for a readers' theater based on a passage from *Don Quixote* and cast students as the characters. Then have students prepare a dramatic reading for the class.

Critical Thinking

Remind students that knights had been powerful socially as well as militarily during the Middle Ages. Ask students what effect the new military technologies had on knights' social status. (*Knights lost their social status as their military power decrease, relative to these technologies.*)

BELIEF SYSTEMS

Critical Thinking

Ask students to write their own definition of *values.* Then read them the dictionary definition. Have them make a list of values that are important in our society, and write them on the board. Compare and contrast these values to the values that were emerging at the close of the Middle Ages. Possible areas of focus might include individualism, personal freedom, success and material wealth, and reward based on hard work instead of noble birth.

SOCIAL SYSTEMS

Visual Learning

Have students look at the painting of *The Moneychanger and His Wife* and discuss how the painting represents a change in the values of the Middle Ages. *(The man and his wife are members of a growing commercial class. The wife is distracted from the religious book she is reading by her husband who is sorting gold and silver coins.)*

314

Trade and Commerce

In spite of the famine, plague, and wars of late medieval society, manufacturing and trade flourished. Goods and services were more in demand than ever.

In Europe, large-scale manufacturing and commercial activity was centered in the towns rather than in the countryside. Towns, especially those on the rapidly developing intercontinental trade routes, were prosperous, bustling with people buying and selling food and goods.

Town society was made up of merchants, shopkeepers, and artisans who were socially above the laboring class and below the nobility. This commercial class tended not to rely heavily on the church for guidance. Instead, they focused on achieving earthly success and wealth. While women were kept out of government and some guilds, their work as merchants, shopkeepers, and artisans was crucial to both family and town economy.

Some of the most prosperous and powerful towns in Europe were Florence and Milan, in Italy. The country's location made trade easier with Asia, Africa, and the rest of Europe.

Italian traders bought and sold fine woolens, colored cottons, and silk woven with gold and silver threads. They also traded wines, furs and leather, jewels, ivory, and metals. They traded spices, too—salt from the coast of France, and cinnamon and peppercorns from the islands of Southeast Asia.

Some of the wealthiest Italian merchants were bankers and moneychangers. Over 500 different currencies were in use in Europe at the time. For a fee, moneychangers would exchange Portuguese coins for French, or Italian coins for English.

▼ *The commercial class became increasingly powerful during the 1300s and 1400s. Members of this class tended to be concerned with making money. They made their money by trading such goods as silk, linen, saffron, and salt.*

Map and Globe Skills

Italians dominated trade and banking in Western Europe. Ask students to look at a map of Italy to see if they can determine why its location made it an important center of trade. *(Mediterranean Sea linked Italy to the East.)*

Social Context

The last names of many of the people who lived in medieval Europe were based on their trade or occupation. The person who baked and sold bread might be known as Thomas Baker. Other common names included Weaver, Potter, and Butcher. Ask students to leaf through a phone book to find other last names that may have had their origin in medieval Europe.

Making a Poster

Tell students that they will be helping an Italian merchant sell his goods. They will have to make a poster advertising these products. The poster should include a description of the products, the country from which they were imported, and drawings that will help attract customers.

Bankers could afford to lend some of their own money. Some banking families were so rich that they even lent money to kings and popes.

International trade brought many upper-class and commercial class Europeans into contact with new ideas and exotic goods from faraway places. Many worked for themselves and earned money to support their families. This freedom to work for one's self, along with the lure of money and success, changed the values of medieval society. **Individualism,** the idea that each person should be free to develop and pursue his or her own goals, became an important value for many of the people of the time. ■

■ *How did medieval values change as trade and commerce grew?*

UNDERSTANDING RELIGIOUS PERSECUTION

Religious persecution is practiced when people of one faith deny those of another the right to their own beliefs. Sometimes, persecution takes the form of denying other people their right to justice, property, or life.

As Christianity in Europe grew stronger, it taught that members of other religions were to be converted, by force if necessary. In the Crusades, many Jewish communities in Europe were slaughtered by Crusaders. Some Crusaders claimed they were trying to strengthen Christianity, but many simply looted and killed in a superstitious frenzy. When Black Death broke out, many Christians blamed Jews for it, leading to more deadly attacks on Jewish communities. Rulers often expelled the Jews from their countries, as did the English in 1290, the French in 1306, 1322, and 1394, and the Spanish in 1492.

Causes of Persecution

Throughout the ages, and especially in Europe in the Middle Ages, people believed in superstitions. These are beliefs or practices that come from ignorance, fear of the unknown, or trust in magic or chance. Many people in troubled times look for scapegoats, too. Scapegoats are people or things that are falsely blamed. Some medieval women who did not fit traditional roles were accused of being witches and burned.

Effects

Christians drove out Jews and other non-Christians from medieval European society. They forbade them to own land, to practice a trade or a profession, or to bear arms. Jewish long-distance trade networks were broken. In 1215, a Church council forced Jews to wear special badges to set them apart from Christians. Can you think of any examples of religious persecution today?

REVIEW

1. **FOCUS** How did the problems of the 14th century bring about changes in European society?
2. **CONNECT** How did the Black Death help weaken feudal arrangements?
3. **HISTORY** How did changes in warfare in the 1300s help to change European society?
4. **CRITICAL THINKING** How did trade help to change the attitudes some Europeans had of the world?
5. **WRITING ACTIVITY** Pretend that you are living in Europe during the 1350s. Write two or three entries in your diary describing the events taking place in your area.

The Renaissance

INTRODUCE

Have students read the major and secondary headings in the lesson and scan the illustrations. Ask them to define Renaissance using these context clues. Have students speculate on how individualism (Lesson 1) might have led to a rebirth of learning and the arts in the Renaissance. Have students read the Thinking Focus and predict how life during the Renaissance might have been different from that of the Middle Ages. Have them read the chapter to confirm or reject their predictions.

Key Terms

Vocabulary Strategies: T36–T37
Renaissance—the revival of attention to classical Greek and Roman art, literature, and learning that originated in Italy in the 14th century
republic—a political order whose head of state is not a monarch and in which supreme power lies in a body of elected citizens
mercenary—a professional soldier hired by a foreign country
humanism—a doctrine or attitude that is concerned with human beings and their values, capacities, and achievements
realism—an artistic style that aims to visually represent people and objects as they exist

316

1300   1650

LESSON 2

The Italian Renaissance

THINKING FOCUS

In what ways did viewpoints about human beings change during the Renaissance?

Key Terms

- Renaissance
- republic
- mercenary
- humanism
- realism

➤ *During the Renaissance, wealthy people began to eat from plates and to use knives and forks. During the Middle Ages, people did not use utensils, and ate from a common plate.*

316

*I*t is wrong to rinse your mouth and spit out wine in public . . . to carry your toothpick either in your mouth, like a bird making its nest, or behind your ear.

Refrain as far as possible from making noises which grate upon the ear, such as grinding or sucking your teeth.

It is bad manners to clean your teeth with your napkin, and still worse to do it with your finger.

A man . . . will take care not to get his fingers so greasy as to dirty his napkin with them, because the sight of it would be unsavory to others.

Anyone whose legs are too thin, or exceptionally fat, or perhaps crooked, should not wear vivid or parti-colored [multi-colored] hose, in order not to attract attention to his defects.

It is not polite to scratch yourself when you are seated at table. You should also take care, as far as you can, not to spit at mealtimes, but if you must spit, then do so in a decent manner.

Your conduct should not be governed by your own fancy, but in consideration of the feelings of those whose company you keep.

A man must . . . not be content to do things well, but must also aim to do them gracefully.

Giovanni della Casa, from
The Book of Manners, 1558

These are some of the social do's and don'ts of a new age as listed in an Italian manners book. A new way of living and thinking was taking hold in Europe as the Middle Ages died out. During this new age, called the Renaissance *(rehn ih SAHNS),* people began to focus on refinement, personal achievement, and learning.

Chapter 12

Objectives

1. Describe the political and economic conditions that made northern Italy the birthplace of the Renaissance.
2. Define humanism and describe how the values of humanism differed from the values of the Middle Ages.
3. Assess the influence of humanism on the arts and sciences.

Graphic Overview

This cause-and-effect chart shows the structure of the lesson.

| Independent republics ruled by wealthy families; supporters of the arts | → | Revival of interest in classical cultures | → | Flowering of arts and learning |

The Birthplace of the Renaissance

The word **Renaissance** comes from a Latin word that means rebirth or revival. The term is used to describe a renewed attention to ideas from classical Greek and Roman culture. This renewal occurred first in northern Italy and then spread through Europe between the 1300s and mid-1600s.

Italian City-States

During the late Middle Ages, the government of Italy was different from those of other countries in Europe. In France and England, for example, strong central governments were forming. However, at the beginning of the Italian Renaissance, Italy was made up of about 250 small states. Most of these states were ruled by cities and were called city-states. Some of the cities were small, but others, like Venice and Milan, had as many as 100,000 people. Look at the map on this page to see how Italy was divided at this time.

Each Italian city-state was independent. All had formed when townspeople began to free themselves from the control of feudal landlords in the 1100s. Some Italian city-states had a republican form of government. A **republic** is a government whose head of state is not a monarch. These cities were not republics like the U.S., as only a few people got to vote, and the cities were mostly run by a few rich families. Other city-states were ruled by a tyrant, or absolute ruler. These tyrants often passed on their jobs to their children, just like kings. Some even ruled so-called "republics," but controlled the elections.

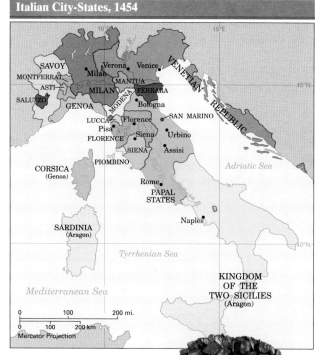

Italian City-States, 1454

The Ruling Class

Florence's ruling class was made up of about 800 of the city's wealthiest families. They were aristocrats or merchants and bankers who often led the major guilds. To maintain their control, members of the ruling families often excluded others from government and guilds.

These families lived in luxurious palaces that often took up an entire city block. They used their wealth to beautify their cities by hiring architects to design and build palaces. Inside these palaces, each family usually had an elaborate court of attendants. The court included family members and political advisers, as well as leading artists and scholars.

▲ *The Italian city-states were often ruled by powerful families. This was especially true of Florence. This guild shield illustrates the trade that made Florence wealthy: wool.*

317

The Renaissance

DEVELOP

Before the students begin reading, show them a painting from the Middle Ages and a painting from the Italian Renaissance. If you cannot locate large, clear, color pictures in library books, refer students to the two paintings at the top of p. 323. Ask them to compare and contrast the style of the paintings. *(The medieval painting seems flat, two-dimensional; people and objects appear to be stacked on top of each other; the Renaissance painting uses linear perspective that draws the eye to the center of the painting.)* Tell them as they read to draw comparisons between life during the Renaissance and life during the Middle Ages.

HISTORY
Map Skills

Use the map on the left to introduce the terms *city-state* and *republic.* Ask students to compare the individual city-states of Italy to the map of Europe in Lesson 4. Contrast the large nations of France and Spain, each under one central government, with the small, independent city-states of Italy. Ask students to locate Florence, Milan, and Venice on the map. Explain how geography helped Italy to become a flourishing trade center.

317

Access Strategy

Ask students to give examples of people they admire or people who are greatly respected by other people. What qualities do they have? *(Likely responses: kind, honest, generous, skillful, talented, beautiful, curious.)* Introduce the word *ideal* (a standard of perfection or excellence). Ask students which combination of qualities would describe the ideal person. Try to get the class to agree on a specific set of qualities. With the students' help, construct a mobile. The mobile should show qualities that our society considers ideal. Explain that in our society, just as in Renaissance society, people strive to achieve goals or ideals. As they read the lesson, ask them to think about the similarities between our society's ideals and Renaissance ideals. Hang the mobile in the classroom and refer to it throughout the lesson.

Access Activity

Bring in an assortment of picture books showing examples of Renaissance art. Include examples of architecture, painting, and sculpture. Have students pick out one work of art that appeals to them and describe what they like about it to the rest of the class.

■ *In northern Italy, the republican style of government and the vast amount of wealth brought in from international trade encouraged new ways of thinking.*

▲ *This French engraving shows Niccolò Machiavelli as a young man.*

■ *Why did the Renaissance begin in northern Italy?*

➤ *The figure in this painting is probably Cardinal Bessarion, who was seen by people of the Renaissance as a model humanist. The cardinal was honored for being devoted to both scholarship and public service.*

The ruling families often struggled among themselves for control of their city. In the 1430s, the Medici family dominated the ruling class of Florence. The Medicis were a talented and ambitious family who controlled an international network of banks in Europe.

City-states also competed with each other for land and power. Frequently they fought to control international trade markets. To defend the city-states, the rulers gathered large troops of **mercenaries,** or paid soldiers. The thirst for power and wealth led to many murders, riots, feuds, and battles within and among city-states.

One of the great political thinkers of the Renaissance was Niccolò Machiavelli (*MAK ee uh VEHL ee;* 1469–1527), who lived in and worked for Florence. His book, The Prince, is a discussion of how a leader should govern his people. In medieval times, the job of government was to administer justice. Machiavelli—having studied ancient Rome—thought the job of government should be the state's growth and expansion. Machiavelli advised his prince to ignore whether actions were good or evil, and to judge them on their benefit to the state. A ruler might be cruel or merciful, generous or deceitful, all to better the state. What do you think of his ideas? ■

The Renaissance and Life

Life in the Italian city-states changed the way some residents viewed the world. Though very religious, these residents concentrated more on this life than on heaven or hell. In doing so, they hoped to understand people and their world better.

In particular, these Italian scholars turned to the works of the ancient Greeks and Romans as their guides. Many of these classics had been reintroduced into Western Europe by Europeans who came into contact with Byzantine and Arab scholars. European

318

Critical Thinking

Review with students the paragraph on Machiavelli. Then write on the board the saying, "The end justifies the means." Have the class debate the meaning of this saying, relating it to Machiavelli's ideas. Divide the class in two and hold a debate on whether Machiavelli was right or wrong.

Social Context

Humanism and its passion for the past was a pursuit of the rich, powerful, and well-educated in Renaissance Italy. It took time, money, and education to research ancient manuscripts, excavate ancient relics, and create artwork that reflected the ideals of the Greeks and Romans. Only the elite class of the Italian city-states could afford to dabble in humanistic pursuits. Although many humanistic ideas spilled over to the lower classes, many Italians were desperately poor and did not have the influence, money, or education to participate in humanistic ventures. In the mid-1400s, it is estimated that approximately seventy-five percent of the population was lower class, of which many were paupers, with no means of support except begging. In Venice, beggars became such a problem that the practice was banned in 1529.

scholars of the Middle Ages had studied some of the classics to deepen their religious faith. Renaissance scholars added to this and now studied to expand their knowledge. Scholars spent many hours learning Greek and Latin in order to read the Greek and Roman sources. They wanted to recreate the spirit of classical arts, literature, and philosophy. Because they studied the classics, or the humanities, they were called humanists. Their concern with the classics was called **humanism.**

During the Middle Ages, many Christians saw themselves as sinful creatures struggling to get into heaven. But humanists did not see people as sinful. They thought people had dignity, worth, and the ability to achieve almost anything. Religion was important to humanists, but they stressed that life on earth was also meaningful.

Renaissance humanists focused on three ideas of the Greeks and Romans. The first was individual worth. The humanists were impressed by the ideas of Romans such as Virgil, and Greeks such as Socrates. These men felt that humans could improve themselves through study and reflection.

The second idea that impressed the humanists was a strong commitment to public service. They read how the Greek aristocrat Pericles had revitalized Athens with public buildings like the Acropolis. They learned how Cicero, a member of a wealthy Roman family, had fought bravely for the Republic of Rome. In a similar spirit, wealthy Italian families spent much of their money constructing public buildings like the Ospedale degli Innocenti, an orphanage in Florence. They also adopted the idea of public service to encourage the arts. As an example, these wealthy families helped to support artists and writers so that all the citizens of the community could enjoy artistic and literary works.

The third idea the humanists encouraged was the development of a variety of skills and talents. They thought people should be well-rounded in their knowledge. They admired individuals like Archimedes (*ahr kuh MEE deez*), who had been a scientist, a mathematician, and an inventor. Humanists saw no limits to what people could achieve. ■

▼ *Renaissance humanists studied the works of ancient Greek philosophers such as Plato, whose bust is shown here.*

■ *What were the basic beliefs held by Renaissance humanists?*

Critical Thinking

As Renaissance men and women became more interested in themselves and their personal achievements, they tried to call attention to themselves. This promotion of self was frowned upon in the Middle Ages but was a common practice in ancient Rome and Greece. Renaissance composers began to sign their music, artists painted self-portraits, and wealthy businessmen had statues erected in their honor. Ask students to list ways in which people call attention to themselves in our society.

■ *Definitions will vary but should emphasize that humanism stresses the value and potential of the individual. Renaissance humanists believed in being well-rounded, providing public service, and exercising individual will.*

The Flowering of Arts and Learning

The new excitement about human potential spilled over into many areas of Renaissance life. It helped to stimulate great artistic and intellectual achievements across the European continent.

The Italian Leonardo da Vinci (*duh VEEN chih*) was one of the greatest figures of the Renaissance. As an artist, he is known for the *Mona Lisa* and many other paintings. He was also one of the greatest scientific thinkers of his day. As you can see in A Closer Look at Leonardo's Notebook on pages 320 and 321, Leonardo was curious about how things worked. With his strong desire to learn and his many talents, Leonardo was the ideal Renaissance man.

319

The Renaissance

Science Connection

In addition to promoting philosophy and art, the revival of classical learning also stimulated interest in science. Translation of the works of the Greek writer and astronomer Ptolemy gave scholars information on geography and mapmaking. The work of the Greek doctor Galen provided insight into anatomy and blood circulation. What the scholars of the Renaissance did not immediately recognize was that many of Ptolemy's and Galen's theories were wrong. Ptolemy estimated that the world was much smaller than it really is, and Galen's description of blood circulation was incorrect. Some historians think that Renaissance people may have relied too much on the ancient Greeks and Romans for their knowledge. Ask students how this practice might impede progress.

Study Skills

Have students research the life of a person whom they consider to have the qualities of a Renaissance man or woman. The person may be a historical or modern figure. Ask them to write a one-page report explaining their choice.

Note: You may wish to use this Closer Look to preview The Flowering of Arts and Literature, which begins on p. 319.

More About Leonardo's Writing
Leonardo da Vinci began his practice of writing backward (mirror-fashion) when he was 21 years old. Some people have speculated that he was unable to write left-to-right. Evidence suggests, however, that he did write left-to-right when communicating with friends or relatives.

A more common theory is that Leonardo da Vinci developed the habit of writing backward to keep his ideas from being stolen. While it is possible to read his notes with the help of a mirror, it certainly makes it more difficult.

A CLOSER LOOK

Da Vinci's Notebooks

Leonardo da Vinci had done everything. At least that's what the people of his time thought. Everybody knew of his successes in painting, medicine, military engineering, and even costume design. What they didn't know was that all his life Leonardo had been writing and drawing even more astonishing ideas in his private notebooks. Looking through these notes, we can see his exciting imagination at work.

Using a quick hand, Leonardo sketched birds in flight. Look at how the top sketches show artistic illustrations of birds soaring in the sky. Then see how he has made the lower drawings more technical. Leonardo seems interested in how wings move up and down. What is he working toward?

Humans had wanted to fly for thousands of years. Leonardo came amazingly close to making that possible. The sketches above and to the left show that he had figured out how wings work and had designed a flying machine. The only problem is that humans don't have strong enough arms to power his invention.

320

Chapter 12

Visual Learning

Suggest that students try their hand at learning from their observations as da Vinci did. Tell them to select and draw an object that they can look at every day. Ask them to carefully observe the object every day and make a new sketch of it or add to the first one. After several days, have students describe differences between their original and final drawings.

Research

Explain that da Vinci represented the ideals of the Renaisssance in terms of his broad range of interests. Da Vinci became an accomplished painter, scientist, inventor, sculptor, musician, writer, and military engineer. Have students each research da Vinci's interest in one of these areas and prepare a brief report for the class.

Collaborative Learning

Make classroom quantities of student reports from the activity described in Research. Have each student put the reports together into a book. Ask students to give a brief oral account of something they learned from a classmate's report.

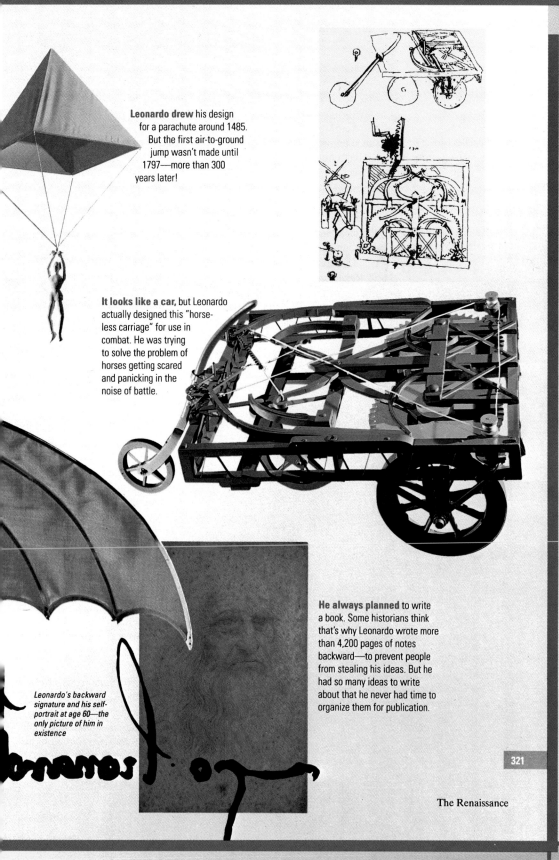

Leonardo drew his design for a parachute around 1485. But the first air-to-ground jump wasn't made until 1797—more than 300 years later!

It looks like a car, but Leonardo actually designed this "horse-less carriage" for use in combat. He was trying to solve the problem of horses getting scared and panicking in the noise of battle.

He always planned to write a book. Some historians think that's why Leonardo wrote more than 4,200 pages of notes backward—to prevent people from stealing his ideas. But he had so many ideas to write about that he never had time to organize them for publication.

Leonardo's backward signature and his self-portrait at age 60—the only picture of him in existence

321

The Renaissance

Writing a Dialogue

Ask students to imagine what it would be like to witness da Vinci's reactions to the following inventions: automobile, airplane, parachute. Have them write a dialogue between Leonardo da Vinci and themselves in which da Vinci expresses his thoughts on one of the inventions.

Visual Learning

The model on p. 324 was created from one of da Vinci's drawings. After students have completed the skill lesson on p. 324, they might enjoy creating their own model of a da Vinci sketch. Suggest that they use one of the drawings on this spread. Display the models for other classes.

Critical Thinking

Point out to students the significance of Cervantes using an elderly, "befuddled" man as the knight at the center of his story. In the Renaissance, a time of intellectual rebirth and renewal, Cervantes wrote his story as a gentle parody of the romanticized chivalry that seemed increasingly out of place in a rapidly changing world. To help familiarize students with the outline of Cervantes' novel, you may want to play a recording of the Broadway musical *Man of La Mancha* and walk students through the story.

▼ *Many Florentines thought this building would collapse. Because Brunelleschi studied Roman architecture and used his knowledge of mathematics to design a dome similar to those built by the Romans, the building has stood for over 500 years. Note how the style of this church differs from that of the Gothic cathedrals of the Middle Ages, shown on page 283.*

Renaissance Literature

Italian writers Francesco Petrarch *(PEH trahrk)* and Giovanni Boccaccio *(boh KAH chee oh)* were two of the first Renaissance humanists. Examining ancient Greek and Roman manuscripts during the 1300s, they discovered letters written by Roman politicians and books written by Greek philosophers. They adapted the clear and graceful style of these Roman and Greek writers.

Literature was one area where Renaissance thinkers excelled. New ideas, new technology for making books, and a growing readership inspired new writers. Some of our greatest works of literature are from the Renaissance. One literary genius was Miguel de Cervantes *(suhr VAHN tehz*; 1547–1616), a Spanish poet, playwright, and novelist. He was also a diplomat, a soldier, and for five years, a captive of pirates. His greatest work is the story of Don Quixote *(kee HOH tay)*, a slightly befuddled old gentleman who thinks he is a medieval knight, and who sets out to rid the world of evildoers. Cervantes' work is both funny and thoughtful, and has been a favorite of readers since it was written.

Renaissance Architecture

Classical styles also influenced Renaissance architects. Florence architect Filippo Brunelleschi *(broo nuh LEHS kee)* built a Roman-style dome on top of the Florence Cathedral, shown at left. Brunelleschi had a good grasp of mathematics and was the first artist known to use linear perspective. Linear perspective is a system that gives a flat surface the feeling of space and depth. Examine the medieval and the Renaissance paintings on the next page, and compare the use of perspective.

Renaissance Art

Greek and Roman styles also influenced many Renaissance artists. Like the ancient artists, Renaissance painters and sculptors wanted to show people and nature as they really were. Such **realism** is evident in sculptures such as the *Moses* by Michelangelo on page 308. Like many artists of the Renaissance, Michelangelo studied anatomy so that he could sculpt and draw the human figure realistically.

Critical Thinking

Renaissance artists invented new techniques to help portray life realistically. Ask students to discuss the aspects of humanism that motivated this quest for realism. *(Worth of individual; focus on personal achievement.)*

Role Playing

Have each student choose a Renaissance artist, architect, or writer. Students will portray that person in an oral presentation to the class. Ask them to describe their work, where they lived, and other interesting facts about their lives. Encourage students to use pictures of their art or read passages from their work.

Renaissance artists depicted subjects other than religious ones. They created realistic portraits,

battle scenes, and country and street scenes using a new technique of mixing paints with oil. Oil paints could be blended easily because they dried slowly. These paints allowed artists to add more subtle colors to their paintings. ∎

▲ *Perspective gives a painting a sense of depth. Notice how the people in the painting from the Middle Ages, shown on the left, all appear to be in one place. In the Renaissance painting, shown on the right, some people appear close while others appear far away.*

∎ *How did Renaissance humanism lead to achievements in the arts and sciences?*

Wealth and the Renaissance

Why did the Renaissance begin amongst the wealthy? Upper-class Italians had enough money to allow them to enjoy their leisure time. This leisure provided them with time to study the ideas of the ancient Greeks and Romans. These upper-class Italians were also highly literate and thus could easily learn about Renaissance ideas.

In addition, increased trade had brought wealthy Italians into contact with other peoples and ideas. Trade had also provided them with money to spend on art.

Not everyone in the city-states felt the influence of the Renaissance. Scholars, painters, and art supporters realized that they were participating in something new and exciting. But life for the average worker remained much the same. Because they could neither read nor afford art, workers were more concerned with making a living than with learning about Renaissance ideas. ∎

∎ *How important was wealth in fostering the Renaissance?*

R E V I E W

1. **FOCUS** In what ways did viewpoints about human beings change during the Renaissance?
2. **CONNECT** How was the commercial class an example of the Renaissance belief in the importance of life on earth?
3. **CULTURE** What values of the Renaissance were similar to the values of Greek and Roman societies?
4. **CRITICAL THINKING** Why was realism important to Renaissance artists and writers?
5. **WRITING ACTIVITY** Look at a piece of art shown in this chapter or in the chapter opener. Study the picture to see how it is typical of Renaissance art. Write your thoughts about the art.

The Renaissance

BELIEF SYSTEMS
Visual Learning

Discuss how humanism influenced the style of Renaissance architects, painters, and sculptors. Have students examine the illustrations in Lesson 2. Ask them to find evidence of realism and the use of nonreligious subject matter.

■ *Members of the patrician class embraced humanism and valued personal achievement. They also believed in using their money to better their city. Thus they gave direct financial support to talented artists and scholars.*

■ *Wealth was extremely important in fostering the Renaissance because it provided wealthy Italians with the leisure time to learn about classical ideas and the money to support the arts.*

C L O S E

Draw the Graphic Overview on the chalkboard. Then ask students to explain how a revival of interest in the classics led to a change in viewpoints about human beings.

Answers to Review Questions

1. During the Middle Ages, many European Christians viewed life on earth primarily as preparation for a better afterlife. They thought people were basically sinful. During the Renaissance, many people thought humans could achieve almost anything in this life. They valued the dignity of individuals.
2. The values of the commercial class centered around wealth and personal achievement. Preparing for an afterlife was no longer the main goal.
3. All three societies shared beliefs in the will of the individual, a devotion to public service, and the development of many skills and talents.
4. Renaissance painters and writers wanted to show people and nature as they really were.

Homework Options

Have students choose an aspect of medieval life such as art, religion, government, or city life. Ask them to write a report comparing it to life in the Renaissance.

Study Guide: p. 49

UNDERSTANDING TECHNICAL DRAWINGS

This skills feature uses the design of a roasting spit drawn by Leonardo da Vinci to teach students how to interpret technical drawings.

Critical Thinking

Ask students to recall occasions when they have used technical drawings to assemble or understand something. Have them describe the experience to the rest of the class. Did the technical drawing help or hinder them? Specifically, what was it about the drawing that helped or hindered? *(Students may make general observations that the drawing was "good" or "bad." Encourage them to be specific.)*

324

UNDERSTANDING TECHNICAL DRAWINGS

Reading a da Vinci Sketch

Here's Why

A technical drawing shows how an object works or how it can be built. Knowing how to read a technical drawing will help you to understand how objects are designed and produced.

The roasting spit below (left) was drawn by Leonardo da Vinci some 500 years ago. You read this drawing just as you would a modern technical drawing.

Here's How

The model in the photograph below (right) is based on the drawing. The chimney has been left uncompleted so

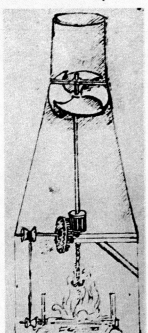

324

you can see some interior parts. Technical drawings will not always be accompanied by models. This time, however, the model will help you to understand the drawing.

Look at the drawing, especially at the gears and the fanlike part in the chimney. Notice that the focus of the drawing is to show how all the elements work together to turn the spit.

Now concentrate on how the drawing describes the working of the spit. Use the labels on the photograph to help you.

Find the part that is labeled "Airscrew." The airscrew operates from the draft caused by the fire. As the airscrew moves, it turns the lantern gear. The lantern gear turns the crown gear, which in turn moves the pulley. The pulley, connected to the spit, then turns the spit.

The turning motion of the airscrew is rotational, or around and around. The gears change the motion to a direction that can turn the spit. Otherwise, the design would not be functional.

Da Vinci introduced many practical features into this design. First this design saves the time of turning the spit by hand. Also, since the spit turns slow or fast depending on the size of the

fire, the design provides a way to control the evenness of the cooking.

Try It

Turn to A Closer Look on pages 320 and 321. Study the drawings and model of the automotive wagon. Explain how the drawings provide information about the design.

Apply It

Use your school or community library to find a technical drawing related to a career or hobby. Describe the focus of the drawing and the information the drawing provides about the design.

Airscrew

Lantern gear

Pulley

Crown gear

Spit

Chapter 12

Objective

Interpret information presented in a technical drawing. (Visual Learning 1, 3)

Making a Drawing

After students have studied the technical drawing and the model, have them choose a simple machine in the classroom (paper cutter, stapler) and make a technical drawing of it. Remind students to label the parts of their drawings and to indicate motion with arrows pointing in the proper direction.

Answers to Try It

The cut-away drawing shows what is needed in order to make the wagon. By showing the internal works, it illustrates the reasons behind the overall design. The top drawing shows what Leonardo expected the battle wagon to look like.

Answers to Apply It

Answers will vary, but should emphasize clear drawings and precise labels.

| 1300 | 1350 | 1400 | | 1650 |

LESSON 3

Renaissance Life

Early in the morning of July 2, 1442, the people of Florence have turned out to salute their city and its patron saint, John. Shops are closed, but peddlers line streets selling fat cherries, golden peaches, and lion-shaped sweets.

As you pop a cherry into your mouth, your eyes move toward the crowd gathering around the jugglers and acrobats on the corner. How gaily everyone is dressed! The ladies' pale silks shimmer. The gentlemen's long cloaks of red, black, or peacock-blue velvet glow in the bright sunlight.

The parade is a wonderful sight. Bishops in long, flowing robes lead the street procession. Trumpeters and drummers in formation play rousing tunes while flagbearers march in step.

The most exciting part of the festivities is the *palio,* a horse race held in Florence's largest square. The crowd gathers to cheer for their favorite riders as they gallop bareback over the rough stone streets. The street curves dangerously close to buildings and spectators. Riders risk their lives to make the hairpin turns that lead to the finish line and glory. The winner of the race basks in the applause of the crowd. The losers limp home with broken spirits and sometimes broken bones.

THINKING FOCUS

How did each of the social classes contribute to the Renaissance in Italy?

Key Terms

- patrician
- patron
- dowry

▲ *In* The Race of the Palio in the Streets of Florence, *Di Francesco showed the excitement of Florence's race.*

325

The Renaissance City

The cities of Renaissance Italy were colorful, lively places. Florence was a typical Renaissance city. The twisting streets were crammed with tall, narrow buildings with shops on the street and living quarters above. The entire city seemed to tumble over itself.

The Renaissance

Have students read the Thinking Focus. Ask them to discuss what they think determines a person's social rank, or class. *(Job, income, influence, education, ethnic background, political standing.)* Review the reasons for the emergence of a commercial class during the Middle Ages. Stress that the Renaissance brought little change for the lower class, which made up three-fourths of the population. Have students read the lesson to learn more about the class structure of Italian Renaissance society.

Key Terms

Vocabulary Strategies: T36–T37
patrician—a member of the highest class of society in Italian city-states during the Renaissance; an aristocrat
patron—a person who financially supports scholars or artists
dowry—money, land, servants, or any other valuable property given by a bride's family to her husband at marriage

325

Graphic Overview

	Employment	% of Population
Upper Class	merchants, bankers	2
Commercial Class	shopkeepers, artisans	23
Lower Class	laborers, farmers, and unemployed	75

Objectives

1. Describe the advantages and disadvantages of living in an Italian city of the Renaissance.
2. Identify and describe the different social classes of Renaissance Italy.
3. Discuss the importance of the family during the Italian Renaissance.

Discuss the role of the three major classes in Renaissance society. Point out that members of the upper class—called patricians—had more wealth and power than members of the lower class. An estimated 75 percent of the people were members of the lower class, and only 2 percent were patricians. Draw the Graphic Overview on the chalkboard but do not fill in the boxes under employment. Have the students fill these in as they read.

■ *Italian Renaissance cities were interesting and lively places to live. Many cities were prosperous. They had paved streets and beautiful public buildings. However, living conditions were usually crowded, and the ruling families often feuded. This often led to outbreaks of violence.*

Ask students to list some of the advantages and disadvantages of living in a Renaissance city as a member of the lower class. Do these advantages and disadvantages still exist today in our modern cities?

▲ *The streets of a Renaissance city were often very muddy. To prevent their skirt hems from dragging in mud, women wore platform shoes.*

■ *What were some of the advantages and disadvantages of living in a Renaissance city?*

▼ *Renaissance Florence was a bustling, prosperous city. Lorenzo di Medici was an important person in the city.*

The palaces of wealthy citizens stood next to the run-down houses of the lower class. Large, open plazas, or squares, stood in the shadows of giant cathedrals and public buildings.

In the 1400s, Florence was one of the largest cities in Europe, with over 38,000 people. Another 200,000 people lived in the countryside around Florence.

Cities were the showcases of Italian city-states, and residents worked hard to make their cities beautiful. New streets were paved and straight and were built much wider than the old alleyways of the Middle Ages. The city government strictly limited the height of new houses so that light and air could reach street level.

The city of Florence was quite prosperous. One 15th-century traveler, when entering one of the 11 gates of Florence, remarked that it was a city "in which much money was to be made and many were making it."

But Florence was also very crowded. Overcrowding often led to friction between city dwellers. Violent feuds between families were common. Assassinations, ambushes, and bloody riots disturbed the peace of the streets and the business of the marketplace.

At night, the gates of the walled city were closed, and a curfew was enforced. Only the police, government officials, and those with special passes were allowed to be out on the streets of Florence after dark. ■

From Peasant to Patrician

The residents of Italy's thriving cities belonged to many different social classes. Each class played a different role in the life of the city.

The Lower Classes

The lower classes were made up of laborers, such as porters, boatmen, and peddlers, who had no association with the powerful guilds. In Florence the lower class made up three-fourths of the population, but the wealthy classes prevented them from having a voice in government.

Peasants were considered the lowest of the lower class in Italy. Leon Battista Alberti, a member

Have students survey the illustrations in Lessons 1 through 4 of the chapter. Ask them to identify one illustration that depicts a member (or members) of the upper, middle, and lower classes. Ask them what clues they used in making their selections.

Prepare 10 to 15 strips of cardboard (about 3 inches x 12 inches) and on each one write the name of a Renaissance occupation such as banker, lawyer, carpenter, blacksmith, or porter. For other occupations refer to the section From Peasant to Patrician. Tie a string to each strip so that it can be worn as a sign around the neck. Distribute the signs at random and ask students wearing signs to line up in front of the class. Discuss the concept of social class and tell students that each occupation falls into either lower, commercial, or upper class in Renaissance society. Instruct the class to arrange the students according to their social rank and explain their choices. Conclude by telling students that in this lesson they will learn more about how each of these classes lived in Renaissance Italy. Be sure to explain any occupations they don't understand.

of one of Florence's oldest families of merchant bankers, referred to farmers as "ploughboys who had grown up among the clods." In spite of prosperity in the cities, Italian peasants remained poor.

Commercial and Upper Classes

The commercial class of the cities consisted of shopkeepers and artisans. Many of them worked for the minor guilds, which included blacksmiths, leather tanners, carpenters, and butchers.

A person could move up in society, especially from the middle to the upper class, but it was not easy. Many members of the commercial class worked long and hard to gain wealth and success but never changed classes.

The **patricians** were at the top of the social ladder. Some were the descendants of medieval noble families. Most were merchants and business people who ran the highly prosperous major guilds. These guilds included cloth manufacturers, bankers, doctors, and lawyers.

Patricians and their families controlled the wealth and government of Italian cities. Some patricians also felt it was their duty to give financial support to local scholars and artists. As **patrons,** they gave money to creative individuals. The artists, in turn, often paid tribute to their patrons in their art.

The First Ghettos

In Renaissance times, Christians still barred Jews from most occupations and from owning land. Many Jews turned to finance, as it was one of the few pursuits open to them. Some Jews were touched by the new learning and formed small groups of poets and philosophers. In Venice, however, in 1517, the city ordered all Jews to live in a particular neighborhood, where they could be gated in behind walls and controlled. Approved by the Church in 1555, this system of forced segregation spread throughout Europe. Inside the ghettos, as they were known, Jews still managed to carry on their own community life, with markets, hospitals, and courts, and their remarkable, high level of education for all. ■

▲ *Isabella d'Este was a member of a family that ruled Mantua, an Italian city-state. She was a patron to some of the finest artists and writers of the Renaissance.*

■ *Describe the people who made up the lower, middle, and upper classes in Renaissance Italy.*

The Importance of Family

Patricians also felt a strong obligation to their families. The family was the center of patrician life, and family members had strong loyalties to each other.

The family was so important in Renaissance Italy that Leon Batista Alberti wrote a *Book of the Family* in 1432–1434. In his book he offered rules for family members to live by. Alberti advised families to own houses rather than to rent them. All branches of the family should live together and take their meals together. He also advised keeping the family business within the family.

True to Alberti's advice, the wealthy families lived in large, high-walled palaces, some of which covered a whole city block. Grandparents, aunts, uncles, and cousins shared a central courtyard, a chapel, and a dining hall.

Critical Thinking

Members of the upper class believed they had special obligations and responsibilities to society. Ask students to discuss how humanism motivated them to serve in public office, contribute to the construction of public buildings, give to charity, and serve as patrons of the arts.

■ *The lower class consisted of farmers and town laborers such as porters, boatmen, and peddlers, who had no connection with the guilds. The middle class was made up of shopkeepers and artisans. The upper class included merchants and business people such as bankers, doctors, and lawyers, who belonged to the major guilds.*

327

Writing

Ask students to decide whether they want to be a member of the lower, commercial, or upper class. From that point of view, have students write a short article for a Renaissance newspaper. They may pick from the topics suggested by the headlines in the corner activity, or select a topic of their own. Suggest that each article answer the basic questions: Who? What? Where? When? Why? How?

Social Participation

Divide the class into groups. Tell each group they are publishers of a Renaissance newspaper. Provide them with the following headlines: Drought Hurts Farmers; Guild Donates Money to Poor; Medici's Son Wins Award; Artist Discovers Linear Perspective. Have each group rank the stories according to their interest to their readers'.

Social Participation

Divide students into two debate teams. One team will represent Renaissance women and one will represent Renaissance men. Have students debate issues such as marriage, family life, and education from their team's point of view.

■ *A closely knit family could keep their wealth and power for generations. At a time when competition for power and wealth was fierce, it was important to have the loyalty and support of family members.*

CLOSE

Compared to the Middle Ages, the Renaissance is often described as the beginning of the modern world. Ask students to define *modern* in their own words. Then have them read the paragraphs on p. 238 that cover women's lives during the Renaissance. Ask if the students recognize a modern attitude in the words of Louise Labé or in the life of Artemisia Gentileschi. If so, have students be specific about the parallels they see.

328

➤ *Artemisia Gentileschi specialized in painting scenes showing strong women. In this self-portrait, how does she give the impression of strength?*

How Do We Know?

HISTORY *Some women were able to move ahead in Renaissance society. Artemisia Gentileschi (GEN tuh LESS kee) was a talented artist. She wrote in a letter to Galileo, "I have seen myself honored by all the kings and rulers of Europe."*

The Role of Men

Boys of patrician families began learning about the family business at an early age. After completing school, they were sent to other countries to learn about international business. After years of training, they would return to the family business.

Men also married with the good of their businesses or families in mind. Often, marriage joined the social and political fortunes of two families. Parents chose suitable mates for their children and arranged the terms of the marriage.

The Role of Women

Members of the bride's family had to provide a **dowry** when she married. The dowry could be money, land, servants, or any other

■ *Why was the family so important in Renaissance life?*

valuable property. Girls whose families could not afford dowries often remained unmarried and were sent by their families to convents.

Following the Roman model, upper-class Renaissance men expected women to confine their activities to the care of the house and the children. Middle- and lower-class women continued to work in trades and prospered with the rise of the economy.

For all women who could read—and many now learned how—the world of books opened up their minds to new ways of thinking, including thinking about their own situation. Cassandra Fedele *(fuh DEL ay)* was famous as a public speaker in Venice and a lecturer at the University of Padua. The French poet Louise Labé *(lah BAY)* requested in her 1555 book that women make their mark by writing:

If any woman becomes so proficient as to be able to write down her thoughts, let her do so and not despise the honor but rather flaunt it instead of fine clothes, necklaces, and rings. For these may be considered ours only by use, whereas the honor of being educated is ours entirely.

REVIEW

1. **FOCUS** How did each of the social classes contribute to the Renaissance in Italy?
2. **CONNECT** How were Italian Renaissance cities different from medieval towns?
3. **HISTORY** Why did peasants and women benefit so little from the Renaissance?
4. **CRITICAL THINKING** What were some advantages and disadvantages of being a tradeswoman?
5. **WRITING ACTIVITY** Write two descriptions of life in an Italian Renaissance city. In the first, imagine that you are a wealthy trader. In the second, imagine that you are a poor dockworker. How do your descriptions differ?

328

Chapter 12

Homework Options

Have students write a report on a Renaissance city that exists today such as Venice, Milan, or Florence.

Study Guide: p. 51

Answers to Review Questions

1. Patricians donated money and time to improve their cities and also ran the guilds. The commercial class worked in the skilled trades. The lower class did much of the work of the city, providing food and unskilled labor.
2. Italian Renaissance cities were larger and had wider streets than medieval cities.
3. Peasants and women had no say in government or in the guilds that regulated trade. Only upper-class men had the freedom to pursue their creative interests and realize their full potential.
4. Answers will vary. With an expanding economy, women were entering the work force in greater numbers than they had previously. Many women prospered in their trades. Students may note that patrician women rarely worked outside the home.

1300	1350	1400		
		1430		**1650**

L E S S O N   4

Renaissance in Northern Europe

Pieter Brueghel the Elder *(BROO guhl)* was a successful artist born in Flanders about 1530. Flanders is now part of the countries of France and Belgium.

Brueghel is best known for his paintings of peasants. His painting *The Peasant Dance,* shown below, is a fine example of the Renaissance art of northern Europe.

The subject of the painting is a village celebration. Brueghel portrays peasants as real people. Some are fat, some have missing teeth, and some have big noses. Like many painters of the Renaissance, Brueghel relied on colorful, vivid detail and realism.

Brueghel's peasants are dancing, drinking, kissing, and talking. Look at the strain on the face of the bagpipe player and the expression in the eyes of his friend, who is trying so hard to get his attention.

Like Italian Renaissance artists, Brueghel painted people as they really were. He showed their flaws as well as their strengths. Such honesty makes his paintings sparkle with life and emotion.

**THINKING
FOCUS**

How was the northern European Renaissance different from the Italian Renaissance?

Key Term

- secular

◄ The Peasant Dance
by Pieter Brueghel illus-
trates the style of northern
European painting.

329

The Renaissance

INTRODUCE

Explain that this lesson will compare and contrast the Italian and northern Renaissance. Ask students to read the Thinking Focus. Have them predict how the ideas of the Renaissance spread to northern Europe. Point out that northern humanism was different, due mainly to the strength of the Church in northern Europe. Have students read the lesson to find out how the Church influenced the northern Renaissance and how Renaissance ideas spread.

Key Term

Vocabulary Strategies: T36–T37
secular—worldly, rather than religious, in nature

329

Graphic Overview

This compare-and-contrast chart illustrates the main idea of the lesson.

	Beginning	Primary Supporters	Character
Italian Renaissance	1300s	patrician families	secular
Northern Renaissance	late 1400s	royal courts	religious

Objectives

1. Explain how the ideas of the Italian Renaissance spread to northern Europe.
2. Compare and contrast northern European humanism and Italian humanism.
3. Describe some of the artists, writers, and scientists of the northern Renaissance and list their achievements.

330

DEVELOP

Have the students compare the timelines in Lessons 1 through 4 to help them understand the chronology of the Renaissance in Italy and northern Europe. Ask them to draw a simple timeline showing the time spans for the Italian and northern Renaissance. Ask them to discuss three ways in which the ideas of the Renaissance were spread from south to north. *(Traveling traders, books, and scholars and artists often sponsored by monarchs.)*

► *Renaissance ideas were spread by Italian businessmen along these trade routes. Thus, the trade routes helped to facilitate the spread of Renaissance ideas.*

GEOGRAPHY

Map Skills

Ask students to examine the trade route map shown on this page. Have them describe Italy's location in relation to northern Europe. Instruct them to make a chart that lists the countries of northern Europe. Next to each country have students list the countries that each traded with.

330

The Spread of Ideas

The Renaissance ideas that inspired Brueghel began to spread to northern Europe in the late 1400s. How did these ideas move from Italy to countries such as France, Germany, England, and Spain?

Trade and Travelers

One way was through travel. Italian businessmen had offices in cities throughout Europe. Whether in Geneva or London, they lived in Italian Renaissance style. They carried this style as they moved through Europe while trading. Other Europeans began to appreciate the Italians' emphasis on wealth, beauty, and personal achievement. The map below shows the major trade routes of Europe. Which of the cities do you

▼ *How did the European trade routes affect the spread of Renaissance ideas?*

think felt the greatest impact of the Italian Renaissance?

While Italians were traveling through Europe, other Europeans made journeys to Italy. Artists such as Brueghel came to Italy to study art. Scholars came to the great library at the Vatican in Rome. And many foreign visitors came to see Rome's ancient ruins.

Words and Books

Renaissance ideas also spread by way of the printed word. Many people had experimented with ways to print type. Then, between 1438 and 1454, Johannes Gutenberg *(GOOT en burg),* a German, invented and perfected a movable type printing press. Because books could now be printed quickly with

Trade Routes

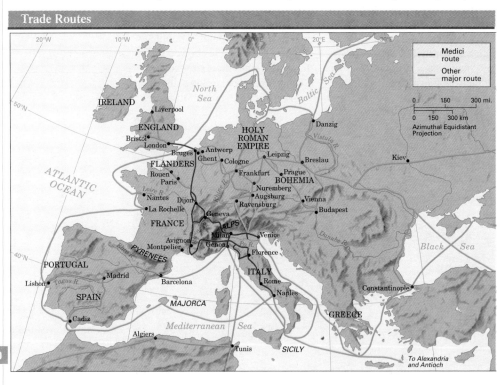

330

Chapter 12

Access Activity

Have students carve their initials in reverse on a cut potato or sponge. Coat the initials with paint or ink and have them print their initials on a piece of paper. Explain the advantages of movable type over this type of block printing (which was done in wood). Use pictures or diagrams to compare the early presses of the Renaissance to modern printing systems.

Access Strategy

Make up a short story that has a lesson or moral, or select one of Aesop's fables that is unfamiliar to most students. In private, tell one student the story and then ask that student to tell another and so on, until all the students have heard the story. Have the last student repeat the story to the class. Then read your original story to show students how it changed as it passed from one student to another. Point out that as information passed from Italy to

northern Europe during the Renaissance, it also changed. The people of northern Europe molded the ideas to fit their own needs, adapting them to fit their lifestyle, values, and religion. Ask students how people learn about new ideas in our society. *(Television, books, word of mouth.)* Tell them to read the lesson to find out how ideas were spread in the Renaissance.

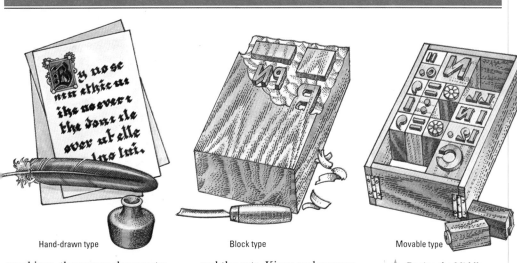

Hand-drawn type   Block type   Movable type

machines, they were cheaper to buy. Books became available to thousands of people. The presses printed everything from the Bible to Greek and Roman classics. By 1500, between 9 and 12 million books had been produced by about 1,000 printers in Europe. The literacy rate began to rise steadily as interest in learning grew.

The book trade then became a major part of trade fairs. Churches, universities, and also individuals bought books printed in many languages. Works by classical and humanist writers were translated and circulated all over the European continent.

Monarchs, Scholars, and Artists

As humanism spread, royal courts of the north, such as those of France and England, began to develop an interest in learning and the arts. Kings and queens eagerly supported the humanist scholars and artists. For example, King Francis I of France brought Leonardo da Vinci and many other Italian artists and scholars to his court. French writer and physician François Rabelais *(rah BLEH)* summarized the outlook of the new age:

L ight and dignity have been restored to the art of letters. Now all branches of science, so long extinct, have been reestablished. . . . The world now is full of scholarly men, learned teachers and ample libraries.

Francois Rabelais,
Gargantua, 1535

Renaissance values and ideas had become firmly rooted in northern Europe by the mid-1500s. ■

Ideas and Ideals

The Renaissance humanism of northern Europe was not simply Italian humanism transplanted. Northern humanism had a character of its own. During the Middle Ages, feudalism had been stronger in northern Europe than it had been in Italy. As a result, the northern Europeans with the most money and power were nobles and

During the Middle Ages, books were hand printed. At first, Europeans printed books by using block printing. In this technique, letters are carved on a block of wood, the block is inked, and the ink is transferred onto paper. For the later movable-type press, a printer joins individual letters together in a case and then inks them. Cases of movable type were easy to put together. Letters could also be reused.

■ *How did the ideas of the Italian Renaissance spread to northern Europe?*

The Renaissance

Political Context

Germany was the first country of northern Europe to adopt the ideals of the Italian Renaissance. The German Renaissance flourished from the end of the 1400s to the early 1500s. Historians think that Germany was the first northern country to embrace humanism because, although its central government was unstable at the time, its cities were strong and relatively independent, like the city-states of Italy.

Critical Thinking

Next to religious texts, the second most popular books in northern Europe during the 1500s were about social behavior and manners. Ask students how this reveals that humanism had spread to northern Europe. *(People wanted to improve their personal lives; there was renewed interest in individual worth.)*

CULTURE

Critical Thinking

Ask students to select a piece of northern Renaissance art or a quotation from this lesson. Have them describe how it reflects humanistic ideals. Do these ideals differ from Italian humanist ideals?

■ *Northern humanists focused on a spiritual interpretation of humanism. They applied humanist ideas to Christianity. Students studied Greek and Hebrew so they could read early Bibles and understand how early Christians practiced their religion.*

➤ *Royal courts, rather than the homes of the wealthy, were the center of Renaissance learning in northern Europe. Here, Francis I of France listens to a lecture in his court.*

■ *Did northern humanism stress the spiritual or the secular? Explain.*

▼ *In this detail from the Ghent altarpiece, Jan van Eyck painted Jesus in a realistic, lifelike way.*

332

royalty, not members of the patrician families. Thus, nobles and royalty became patrons of the arts as were the patrician families in Italy. Renaissance learning in northern Europe centered on the royal courts rather than in the homes of great families.

Northern humanism also differed from Italian humanism in the role of the church. Because northern Europe had fewer large towns to act as cultural centers, the church played a larger, more active role in northern culture. Northern Europeans, like the Italians, valued **secular,** or nonreligious ideas, such as individual achievement and progress. But northern Europeans also emphasized the importance of spiritual life.

Thus, northern humanists studied more than the philosophy and literature of ancient Greece and Rome. Students also learned Greek and Hebrew so they could read ancient Bibles and understand how early Christians practiced their religion.

As northern Europeans began to absorb the ideas of humanism, some began to question the way that church leaders interpreted the Bible. Specifically, humanists

thought church leaders put too much emphasis on ceremony and ritual.

One of these scholars, Desiderius Erasmus *(ih RAZ muhs)*, a Dutch priest and 16th century humanist, wanted to reform the church. He believed that church teachings should be easy for everyone to understand, and that everyone should be able to read the Bible, not just the clergy. Erasmus traveled across Europe and wrote dozens of books, mostly on religion. His works were widely published and read, thanks to the new technology of printing. ■

Achievements

More than just the quest for knowledge and learning spread from Italy. The changing style of the arts and sciences also found its way to northern Europe.

Arts and Literature

Many northern artists expressed religious themes in their work, but they began to represent both people and nature more

realistically. Look at the painting at left by the Dutch artist Jan van Eyck. Note how realistic the figure in the painting looks.

Realism was also important to the humanist writers of northern Europe. They wrote about religion, politics, and the behavior of their fellow human beings.

Sir Thomas More was an English statesman, scholar, author,

Chapter 12

Study Skills

Music flourished during the Renaissance. New instruments were developed, and composers saw it as a time of experimentation. Have students do research to see what instruments were popular at this time. Have them bring in recordings from home or the library that contain Renaissance music played on Renaissance-style instruments.

Science Connection

Despite the renewed interest in scientific thought, many people of the Renaissance held strongly to their beliefs in astrology. Astrologers prepared horoscopes for members of all classes. They advised people on when to travel and when to plant and harvest crops. Governments asked them when to wage war, and doctors administered their medicine at astrologically determined times. Some of the most learned scholars believed in the power of the stars to influence earthly events.

Reader's Theater

Select a scene from Shakespeare's *Romeo and Juliet* (an annotated edition) and assign students to read the different parts. Have students read through the scene on their own. Be sure to go over any unusual words or any lines they have difficulty understanding. It might be helpful to check out a Shakespearean performance on record or tape at the library and let students listen to it as they practice for the reading. Encourage them to speak their lines dramatically and naturally.

and a friend of Erasmus who lived from 1478 to 1535. Based on the Renaissance concept of the individual worth, More proposed that all men should be treated equally.

In his most famous book, *Utopia*, More described the rules of a society in which all men are equal and everyone works together to achieve happiness:

> *T*he second rule of nature is to lead a life as free of anxiety and as full of joy as possible, and to help all one's fellow men toward that end.
>
> Sir Thomas More,
> *Utopia*, 1516

This theme of tolerance was continued by Michel de Montaigne *(mawn TAYN)*, a French writer who felt that no man should be put to death for his beliefs.

Some Renaissance writers tried to entertain as well as educate their audiences. William Shakespeare, born in England in 1564, was a poet, an actor, and a master playwright. Shakespeare's characters are full of life, wit, and passion. They reveal the strengths and weaknesses of people from all walks of life. Many plays are built around historic figures, such as Julius Caesar and the kings of England.

The following passage reflects Shakespeare's attitude toward life and art:

> *A*ll the world's a stage, And all the men and women merely players. They have their exits and their entrances, And one man in his time plays many parts . . .
>
> William Shakespeare,
> *As You Like It*, 1599

Medicine

The achievements of the northern Renaissance were not limited to the arts. Medicine also made advances. In Switzerland, Paracelsus, a physician and chemist, discovered a new way to treat illness. He treated his patients with tiny doses of poisons to destroy diseased tissue.

The surgeons of the 1500s often had to treat injuries caused by firearms and cannons. Ambroise Paré, a French surgeon, developed bandages to replace the common practice of the time of cauterizing, or burning, the edges of a wound. He also was the first to use thread to close a wound. Paré's attitude toward his medical skills might be described as evidence that he was a humanist in the northern tradition: "I treated him, God cured him." ■

▲ *Marguerite of Navarre (1492–1549), a French queen, was a patron of learning and literature.*

▲ *William Shakespeare, shown above, wrote many of the most famous works of the Renaissance.*

■ *Describe some of the achievements of the northern Renaissance.*

■ *Artists learned new ways of painting and sculpting realistically. Writers such as More and Erasmus spoke out for social and religious reform. Playwrights like Shakespeare produced great dramatic works. Scientists made discoveries in medical treatment and surgery.*

CLOSE

On the chalkboard, draw a three-column chart listing names, terms, and achievements associated with the Italian Renaissance and the northern Renaissance in the first column. Label the other columns, Northern and Italian. Then, in the first column ask students whether each item applies to the northern or the Italian Renaissance and place a check mark in the appropriate column(s). As a reteaching tool, draw the Graphic Overview on the chalkboard but do not fill in the center boxes. Ask students to fill these in. Have them use the Overview to answer the focus question.

REVIEW

1. **FOCUS** How was the northern European Renaissance different from the Italian Renaissance?
2. **CONNECT** How did feudalism in northern Europe make the character of the Renaissance different in the north than in Italy?
3. **CULTURE** How did the scholar Erasmus represent northern humanism?
4. **CRITICAL THINKING** Why was the printing press an important part of the Renaissance?
5. **WRITING ACTIVITY** Imagine that you live in Paris in the early 1500s. You have a sister or brother who lives in Florence whom you write to regularly. Write a letter to her or him discussing the changes that the Renaissance has brought to life in your city.

Answers to Review Questions

1. In northern Europe, spiritual values remained more important than in Italy where values such as wealth and personal success were more important.
2. Because feudalism was stronger in northern Europe, nobles and royalty became patrons rather than wealthy merchant families.
3. Erasmus's humanism was religious in nature. He believed that church teachings should be easy for everyone to understand and suggested that changes should be made in the way church leaders conducted themselves.
4. Because of the printing press, more books were available and they were cheaper to buy. Books helped spread Renaissance ideas and increase literacy.

Homework Options

Ask students if they would have preferred to live in Italy or northern Europe during the Renaissance. Have them write a short paragraph explaining their choice.

Study Guide: p. 52

Answers to Reviewing Key Terms
A. Sample answers:
1. Rulers hired **mercenaries** to defend their **republics.**
2. **Patricians** were **patrons** of the arts.
3. **Realism** in art was an important part of the **Renaissance.**

B. Sample answers:
1. The **plague** helped end the feudal system.
2. A **monarchy** is ruled by a king, not a noble.
3. **Individualism** involved the pursuit of one's own goals.
4. The **Renaissance** began in Italy in the 1300s.
5. Northern humanists valued **secular** ideas.
6. **Humanism** involved a concern with the classics.
7. Michelangelo's *Moses* is an example of **realism** in art.
8. A **dowry** had to be provided when a girl married.
9. Joan of Arc was tried as a **heretic** and a witch.

Answers to Exploring Concepts
A. Sample answers:
Joan of Arc helped France win the Hundred Years' War.
Petrarch and Boccaccio believed a writer's style should be easily understood.
Erasmus believed church teachings should be understandable by everyone.
Sir Thomas More proposed equal treatment for all.
Shakespeare wrote to educate and to entertain.
Louise Labé was a poet and writer who urged women to educate themselves and write.
Michelangelo sculpted and drew realistic human figures.
Brunelleschi was the first to use linear perspective.
334
Da Vinci painted the Mona Lisa and other paintings.
Brueghel painted people as they really were.
Gutenberg invented a printing press with movable type.
Paré first used bandages and closed wounds by sewing.
Da Vinci explored how many things worked.

B. Sample answers:
1. People made their own decisions and had the freedom to pursue personal goals.
2. Many people died in the plague, so fewer peasants

Chapter Review

Reviewing Key Terms

dowry (p. 328)
heretic (p. 313)
humanism (p. 319)
individualism (p. 315)
mercenary (p. 318)
monarchy (p. 312)
patrician (p. 327)

patron (p. 327)
plague (p. 310)
realism (p. 322)
Renaissance (p. 317)
republic (p. 317)
secular (p. 332)

A. Write a sentence or two using each pair of words. The sentences should show how the words are related.
1. mercenary, republic
2. patrician, patron
3. Renaissance, realism

B. Each key term can be used to describe a fact about the time in history covered in the chapter. Use each key term in a sentence that gives a fact about this time.
1. plague
2. monarchy
3. individualism
4. Renaissance
5. secular
6. humanism
7. realism
8. dowry
9. heretic

Exploring Concepts

A. During the Renaissance, many individuals developed their skills and talents. Copy the chart on your own paper. Note the information given. Using information from the chapter, add one contribution for each person.

	Name	Contribution
Leaders	Joan of Arc	
Writers	Petrarch and Boccaccio	
	Erasmus	
	Sir Thomas More	
	Shakespeare	
	Louise Labé	
Artists	Michelangelo	
	Brunelleschi	
	da Vinci	
	Brueghel	
Inventors and Scientists	Gutenberg	
	Paré	
	da Vinci	

334

B. Support each statement with facts and details from the chapter.
1. One of the major changes brought about by the Renaissance was the development of a new sense of individualism.
2. The plague ravaged Europe and directly affected the state of feudal society.
3. Greek and Roman art, literature, and philosophy played important roles in the development of Renaissance ideas and ideals.
4. Ruling families were a very important feature of the Italian city-states.
5. During the time of the Renaissance, there were great artistic and intellectual achievements across the European continent.
6. The population of Italian Renaissance cities included three social classes.
7. Life in an Italian Renaissance city had many advantages and disadvantages for all classes of the population.
8. Renaissance ideals did not apply to all people.
9. The ideas of the Renaissance were spread in a variety of ways.

Chapter 12

worked for the feudal landlords. Those who were left demanded higher wages or moved to towns for a better life. Feudalism faltered.
3. Greek and Roman styles influenced many Renaissance artists and writers.
4. Ruling families used their wealth to improve and beautify their cities.
5. Writers and artists, encouraged and supported as individuals, flourished.
6. They were the lower class, the middle class, and the upper class.

7. Advantages: wide, straight, paved streets; regulated construction of new buildings; beautiful cities. Disadvantages: overcrowded cities; feuds; violence.
8. Renaissance men and women needed time and money to cultivate their talents. Lacking both, the poor could not achieve the Renaissance ideal. Women and Jews were not allowed full participation in the culture.
9. Ideas were spread by business travelers to and from Italy, through the printed word, and by visitors carrying ideas home with them.

Reviewing Skills

1. Study the da Vinci drawing of a printing press at the right. The type bed is at the top of the incline. When the press is moved down by turning the operating lever, the type bed is pulled up the incline by a rope tied to the geared axle on the left. Releasing the lever lets the type bed roll down the incline so new type can be put in. Is the press up or down here? What advantages does a wheeled type bed have?

2. Reread Religious Persecution on page 315. How does superstition play a part in religious persecution?

3. If you wanted to find a recent magazine article about Joan of Arc, Leonardo da Vinci, or the city of Florence, where would you look?

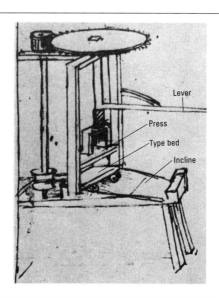

Lever
Press
Type bed
Incline

Using Critical Thinking

1. The invention of a printing press with movable type was a great advancement. What might your classes in school be like if a printing press with movable type had not been invented?

2. Ideas of the Renaissance were spread through travelers on business and by way of the printed word. Review highlights in the history of communication by looking up "Communication" in an encyclopedia. Compare and contrast the ways that ideas were communicated in the Renaissance period with the ways that new ideas are communicated today.

Preparing for Citizenship

1. **WRITING ACTIVITY** Reread the description of Brueghel's painting *The Peasant Dance* on page 329. Pretend that you are a young peasant living in the 1500s. Write a brief essay about Brueghel's painting expressing your feelings about the way the artist has portrayed the characters.

2. **GROUP ACTIVITY** With three classmates, plan a panel discussion on the topic "Should Artists Be Supported by Patrons?" Two classmates take the position that patrons have always been needed for art to flourish. The other two argue that no other profession is given financial support, so why should artists be supported?

3. **COLLABORATIVE LEARNING** Review the information about the Renaissance cities and the different social classes in Lesson 3. Divide into groups of four to eight students each. Each group will be responsible for dramatizing a scene from everyday life at that time. Assign the following tasks to members of the group:
   (1) write the scene,
   (2) get costumes and act out the scene,
   (3) design and create the scenery,
   (4) gather props and prepare advertisements of the production.
   When all preparations have been completed, present the minidrama.

Planning at a Glance
Reformation and the Scientific Revolution

	Objectives	Reading Support and Other Resources	Diverse Learning Strategies
Lesson 1 The Decline of Church Authority *pp. 338–341* 2–3 days	• Analyze the decline in power of the Catholic church. • Compare and contrast the beliefs and practices of early Protestant groups with those of the Catholic church.	• **Workbook** or **Reading Support:** pp. 174–177 Review p. 41 Lesson Support/Transition p. 41 Multi-Lang. Sum. pp. 81–82 • **Other Resources:** Poster 7, Study Guide p. 53	Access Strat. **(Extra Support)** TE p. 339 Access Act. **(SDAIE)** TE p. 339 Visual Learning **(Visual)** TE p. 340 Audiotapes of Multi-language Lesson Summaries **(Auditory)**
Lesson 2 Martin Luther and the Reformation *pp. 342–347* 2–3 days	• Explain the significance of Luther's reforms and the church's reactions. • Explain the reasons behind the spread of Protestantism.	• **Workbook** or **Reading Support:** pp. 178–181 Review p. 42 Lesson Support/Transition p. 42 Multi-Lang. Sum. pp. 83–84 • **Other Resources:** Geography Kit, Study Guide p. 54	Access Strat. **(Extra Support)** TE p. 343 Access Act. **(SDAIE)** TE p. 343 Study Skills **(GATE)** TE p. 344 Visual Learning **(Visual)** TE pp. 345, 346 Audiotapes of Multi-language Lesson Summaries **(Auditory)**
Skill: Identifying Patterns *p. 348* 1 day	• Recognize and identify organizational patterns in text.	• **Other Resources:** Study Guide p. 55	
Lesson 3 Era of Reformation *pp. 349–352* 2–3 days	• Identify and describe the Protestant movements launched during the Reformation. • Assess the impact of the Reformation on the Catholic church.	• **Workbook** or **Reading Support:** pp. 182–185 Review p. 43 Lesson Support/Transition p. 43 Multi-Lang. Sum. pp. 85–86 • **Other Resources:** Study Guide p. 56	Access Act. **(SDAIE)** TE p. 350 Access Strat. **(Extra Support)** TE p. 350 Study Skills **(Visual)** TE p. 351 Audiotapes of Multi-language Lesson Summaries **(Auditory)**
Lesson 4 Scientific Revolution *pp. 353–356* 2–3 days	• Identify and describe the Scientific Revolution. • List and explain the key features of the scientific method.	• **Workbook** or **Reading Support:** pp. 186–189 Review p. 44 Lesson Support/Transition p. 44 Multi-Lang. Sum. pp. 87–88 • **Other Resources:** Study Guide p. 57	Access Act. **(SDAIE)** TE p. 354 Access Strat. **(Extra Support)** TE p. 350 Role Playing **(GATE)** TE p. 355 Audiotapes of Multi-language Lesson Summaries **(Auditory)**
Skill: Making Hypotheses *p. 357* 1 day	• Make and test hypotheses.	• **Other Resources:** Study Guide p. 57	
Making Decisions: Scientific Discoveries *pp. 358–359*	• Identify Jenner's scientific methods.	• **Other Resources:** Poster 8	
Chapter Review *pp. 360–361* 1 day		Chapter 13 Test pp. 49–52 *(See facsimiles on TE p. 571.)*	Assessment Multiple-Use Masters pp. 73–80

Reading Support Resources *for Every Lesson*

Reading and Review

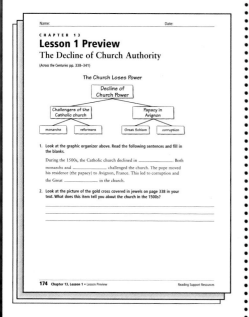

- **Chapter Overview*** p. 173
- **Lesson Previews*** using graphic organizers from the Teacher's Edition pp. 174, 178, 182, 186
- **Reading Strategies*** pp. 175, 179, 183, 187
- **Lesson Summaries*** pp. 176–177, 180–181, 184–185, 188–189
- **Lesson Reviews** pp. 41, 42, 43, 44

* **Workbook** includes starred items.

Multi-language Summaries

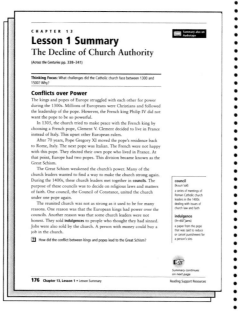

Lesson Summaries in:
- English (See Reading and Review.)
- Spanish pp. 176–177, 180–181, 184–185, 188–189
- Chinese pp. 81–88
- Hmong pp. 81–88
- Khmer pp. 81–88
- Vietnamese pp. 81–88

 Summaries available on audiotapes

Lesson Support /Transition
S D A I E

(Lesson 1 Support/Transition worksheet image)

Activities for SDAIE
Specially **D**esigned **A**cademic **I**nstruction in **E**nglish

- **Lesson Support/Transition** pp. 41, 42, 43, 44

Technology Options

Internet Support
http://www.eduplace.com

Social Studies Center at Education Place
Internet support for Chapter 13:
- *Lesson at a Glance*
- *A Printer*

Software
Student Writing Center ® (CD-ROM) (Macintosh® or Windows®)

School to Career

Have students brainstorm different technologies and equipment used in scientific study today. Then, have pairs of students choose a specific instrument to research, including origin and purpose. What scientific professions would make use of this equipment?

Character Education

The Reformation and the Scientific Revolution opened up new avenues of thought for many. Practicing these ideas often took great courage. Divide students into small groups. Ask each group to research an individual who they believe shows great courage today. They can then present what they learn to the class.

CHAPTER
PREVIEW

A sk students to read the chapter title and the passage that follows it. Point out that today people accept the fact that the Earth orbits the Sun, but at the beginning of this period, some people believed the Earth was the center of the universe. In fact, Catholic church leaders persecuted people who challenged that idea.

Looking Back

Remind students that during the Middle Ages the church was extremely powerful and regulated people's lives.

Looking Forward

Tell the students that in Lessons 1–4 they will read about how people began to question religious and scientific ideas and about the changes that resulted: The Decline of Church Authority, Martin Luther and the Reformation, Era of Reformation, and Scientific Revolution.

In the first lesson, students will read about the kings and commoners who challenged the power of the Roman Catholic Church.

Chapter 13
Reformation and the Scientific Revolution

Handwritten papers nailed to a church door . . . a telescope aimed at the stars . . . an apple falling from a tree: each played a part in a great era of change that swept across Europe. Christian leaders such as Martin Luther and John Calvin tried to reform the Catholic church. Scientists such as Nicolaus Copernicus and Galileo helped launch a scientific revolution.

1319 *The Madonna and Child with Saints* by the Italian artist Simone Martini shows a scene approved by Catholic leaders. Reformers questioned the power of the Catholic church.

1300	1400	1500

336

1302

1492 Christian forces drive out the Moors, the last Islamic kingdom in Spain.

BACKGROUND

Although the Reformation was sparked by corruption among some Roman Catholic Church officials, Protestants ultimately withdrew from the church because of fundamental disagreements about beliefs and practices.

In the wake of the Renaissance, Europe was changing rapidly. In this climate of change, the Roman Catholic Church was essentially a conservative force. It sought to protect its long-established role as the keystone of society.

Apostolic Succession

In defending the church's authority and hierarchic structure, Roman Catholic thinkers depended on the original Christian hierarchy: those disciples of Jesus who came to be known as the Apostles. After the crucifixion of Jesus, they were accorded a special respect in church life as the people who were chosen by Jesus to spread the faith.

As the Apostles traveled throughout the Mediterranean world preaching and founding congregations, their special status was transmitted to those who led the new congregations. The local leaders came to be known as bishops, and as leaders of the fledgling Christian movement one of their most important jobs was to hand over their responsibilities to a worthy successor.

This tradition of bishops handing over authority to new bishops was eventually formalized in the doctrine of Apostolic Succession. According to this doctrine, the

The Italian astronomer Galileo (1564–1642) used the telescopes above to study the stars and planets. Catholic leaders persecuted Galileo for supporting the idea that the earth travels around the sun.

SCUOLA DI SUSTERMANS
RITRATTO DI GALILEO

1619 The German astronomer Johannes Kepler publishes a book explaining how the planets orbit the sun. This pen-and-ink drawing from the book tells how to predict the position of the planets.

1556–1605 In India, Mughal emperor Akbar practices religious tolerance, integrating Hindus into his empire.

1600	1700	1800

1687

337

Understanding the Visuals

The tempera on wood painting (p. 336) shows St. Paul, St. Lucia, the Madonna and Child, St. Catherine, and St. John the Baptist. Simone Martini was one of many artists who made handsome livings painting imagery for the Catholic church illustrating Catholic concepts. Protestant reformers rejected the saint-hood system celebrated in this painting.

Galileo used telescopes like the ones on p. 337 to discover the rings of Saturn, four of the satellites of Jupiter, and the mountains and craters on the moon.

Understanding Chronology

Ask the students to read the timeline and note the contrast between the entries for 1319 and 1619. One reflects the power of the church as the dominating force in most of Europe. The other reflects ideas based on observation and analyses that are independent of church influence.

---

authority of the first Apostles, which they had received directly from Jesus, was passed on through generations of bishops, up to the present day.

Primacy of Rome

Roman Catholic thinkers defended the authority of their church on the grounds of another tradition, as well. Although it was assumed among the early Christians that the bishops were all equals, it was also the case that the bishops of certain cities were thought to carry special authority.

Foremost among these were the bishops of Rome. Just as the city had been the center of the Roman Empire, so too it became the center of the western Christian world. For many centuries now the Bishop of Rome has been known as the Pope.

Conclusion

These claims to authority, resting on ancient traditions, were at the heart of controversies that erupted in Europe during the 1500s and 1600s. Potent religious reform movements and an explosion in

scientific thinking swept Europe in this era, changing the way many people viewed the church.

INTRODUCE

Ask students how the Renaissance (Chapter 12) affected people's attitude toward the Catholic church. Remind students that Renaissance ideals stressed the role of the individual in society. By the 1300s, rulers and common people alike were beginning to rely less on the church for guidance. Have students read the lesson title and Thinking Focus. Encourage them to predict developments that might have caused the church's authority to decline. Then have students read the lesson to see if their predictions were correct.

Key Terms

Vocabulary Strategies: T36–T37
council—a series of meetings of Roman Catholic Church leaders in the 1400s dealing with issues of church law and faith
indulgence—a certificate issued by the pope that was said to reduce or cancel punishment for a person's sins

338

1300   1500   1600   1700   1800

L E S S O N 1

The Decline of Church Authority

THINKING FOCUS

What challenges did the Catholic church face between 1300 and 1500? Why?

Key Terms

- council
- indulgence

➤ *Ornate, gold-encrusted crosses such as this one created in the 1300s reveal how wealthy the church had become.*

We are obliged by the faith to believe and hold . . . that there is one Holy Catholic and Apostolic church, and that outside this church there is neither salvation nor [pardon] of sins. . . . Of this one and only church there is one body and one head—not two heads, like a monster. . . . Furthermore we declare, state, define and pronounce that it is altogether necessary to salvation for every human creature to be subject to the Roman [pope].

Pope Boniface VIII,
Unam Sanctam, 1302

King Philip IV of France knew that this latest decree from the pope was a response to the king's most recent challenge to the Catholic church. He had ordered the clergy to pay taxes. Pope Boniface VIII

replied by issuing a strong statement of his authority—the *Unam Sanctam*.

Furious, King Philip ordered his men to arrest Boniface at his family home in Anagni, Italy, and bring him back to France for trial. Though the aged pope died before he reached France, the king had succeeded in humiliating him. He had also damaged the authority of the once powerful church.

The church drew its authority from people's faith. Millions of Europeans were now Christian, and the great majority of them followed the leadership of the pope.

Conflicts over Power

Between 1100 and 1300, the office of the pope was extremely powerful. Indeed, during this time, the Catholic church had become increasingly involved in political matters, helping to hold Europe together. By the end of the 1300s,

however, monarchs who resented the pope's interference had risen to power. King Philip IV was one of many who refused to bow to the pope's authority.

Chapter 13

Objectives

1. Analyze the internal and external causes of the decline in the authority of the Catholic church between 1300 and 1500.
2. Compare and contrast the beliefs and practices of early Protestant groups with those of the Catholic church.

Graphic Overview

DECLINE OF CHURCH POWER

Challengers of the Catholic church
- monarchs
- reformers

Papacy in Avignon
- Great Schism
- corruption

Challenges from Monarchs

The cardinals, the highest ranking clergy under the pope, were responsible for electing a new pope when the old one died. In 1305, the cardinals attempted to restore harmony between the French monarchy and the church by electing a Frenchman as the new pope. This did improve the relationship between the French monarchy and the office of the pope. But then the new pope, Clement V, did something that angered the monarchs of other European countries. He moved the pope's residence to Avignon *(ah vee NYAWN)*, France, to keep it safe from fighting going on in Italy.

The pope's residence remained in Avignon for 70 years, during which time seven popes were elected. The rulers of such countries as England, Germany, and the Italian city-states thought that these popes were dominated by France. Although this was not entirely true, the monarchs nevertheless resented what they saw as France's overwhelming influence over the church. As a result, the church was less respected and lost some of its power to influence rulers.

In 1376, Pope Gregory XI moved the pope's residence back to Rome. When he died in 1378, Urban VI, an Italian extremely unpopular with the French, was elected pope. In protest the French cardinals elected a Frenchman, Clement VII, who returned the pope's residence to Avignon. Pope Urban VI, however, refused to step down from office. Now the church had two popes!

This split, known as the Great Schism, weakened the church's authority. Many people, not knowing which pope to follow, lost faith in the church's ability to provide spiritual leadership.

Corruption Within the Church

Bishops and other top-ranking clergymen decided it was up to them to restore unity and dignity

▼ *To protect the papal palace at Avignon from attack by bandits, Pope Innocent IV had a four-mile-long wall constructed. Innocent and his successor, Pope Urban V, stayed within its confines. However, by 1365, people wondered whether the pope wasn't actually a prisoner behind the wall.*

339

to the church. During the 1400s, they created a series of **councils,** or groups of church leaders, which met to rule on matters of church law and faith. These councils became much more powerful than the pope. One council, the Council of Constance, finally reunited the church under one pope in Rome in 1417. Thus ended the Great Schism.

Although the councils reunified the church, they did not help it regain its former power. In time, the councils came to be controlled by the European monarchs.

The church collected taxes, property, and court fines to support itself. Some ambitious people were attracted to its wealth and used its

■ *How did the conflict between kings and popes lead to the Great Schism?*

money and power to further their own ends. Some clergy also sold **indulgences** to believers who felt they had sinned. These certificates, issued by the pope, were said to reduce or cancel punishment for a person's sins. With the wealth they obtained, some popes and higher clergy lived like princes.

Furthermore, clerical positions were often sold to the highest bidder, regardless of a person's background. This practice resulted in some clergy who were immoral, uneducated, or even illiterate. As such practices continued, corruption increased in the priesthood. Many people questioned the spiritual leadership of the clergy. ■

The Call for Church Reform

The church had a long tradition of reform. Reformers called for changes among the clergy, including a return to the spiritual ideals set forth in the Bible. By the 1300s, however, many of the clergy had become corrupt. Many people were outraged by the behavior of the church. Others believed the church expressed the true meaning of the Bible. Those who spoke out

▼ *Nicholas Ridley and Hugh Latimer were two Protestant martyrs burned at the stake for heresy in 1555.*

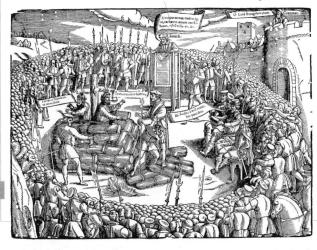

against church practices were sometimes branded as heretics. The church punished heretics with excommunication or execution.

Challengers of the Church

John Wycliffe, a scholar at Oxford University in England, was one such challenger of the church. In his writings in the late 1300s, he declared that monarchs should rule over the church in their own kingdoms. He also translated the Bible from Latin into English, which threatened the clergy's power. Since the clergy was among the small percentage of the population able to read Latin, people depended on it to interpret the Latin Bible. If the Bible could be taught and read in English, people could interpret its meaning themselves.

Wycliffe was not the only reformer who defied the church. His ideas also influenced John Hus, an eastern European priest. In fiery sermons, Hus spoke out against the practice of selling indulgences and called for reform. He went to the Council of Constance for a debate, but was instead burned at the stake as a heretic. This example kept many people from voicing their disagreements with the church.

Spiritual Movements

Spiritual movements also formed in response to the problems of the church. These groups wanted to express religious feelings in their own way. Mystics believed that people could experience God directly in their hearts. They also believed that both men and women could experience God. Margery Kempe and Catherine of Siena were two well-known mystics.

From Philip IV of France to John Wycliffe of London to the mystics of the 1300s and 1400s, people questioned the church's authority. They paved the way for Martin Luther, whose ideas would change the church forever. ■

▲ *Catherine of Siena claimed that she "was chosen and sent on to this earth in order to right a great scandal." That scandal was the Great Schism.*

Then the Archbishop said to [Margery Kempe]: "I have received bad reports about you. They tell me you are a very wicked woman." And she replied: "Sir, they tell me that you are a wicked man. . . ."

Then an important cleric in a furred hood said: "Hold your tongue: talk about yourself, and leave him alone. . . ."

Then the Archbishop said to her: "You will swear that you will neither teach the people in my diocese, nor argue with them."

"No sir, I will not swear that," she said, "because I shall talk about God . . ."

Straight away an important cleric produced a book, and quoted St. Paul against her, saying that no woman ought to preach.

She in reply said: "I am not preaching, sir, I do not get up in a pulpit. I only use conversation and holy talk and I intend to do that as long as I live."

— From *The Book of Margery Kempe*, c. 1432

■ *What church doctrine did the early reformers oppose?*

R E V I E W

1. **FOCUS** What challenges did the Catholic church face between 1300 and 1500? Why?
2. **CONNECT** Why might it be said that the church reformers of the 1300s and 1400s were carrying out the spirit of the Renaissance?
3. **HISTORY** How did corruption within the church contribute to its loss of authority among the people?
4. **BELIEF SYSTEMS** What basic principle did early religious reformers emphasize?

5. **CRITICAL THINKING** Find evidence from the lesson to support this statement: Power corrupts. Do you think this generalization always holds true? Explain.
6. **ACTIVITY** Enact a scene where a monarch and a pope discuss which is more important, the church or the state. Each side should come with its own advisers, split equally between supporters and critics.

341

Reformation and the Scientific Revolution

■ *The early reformers wanted to do away with the many rituals and rites of the Catholic church. They wanted to read the Bible in translation and pray without the interpretation or aid of a priest. They also objected to many church practices that they considered corrupt.*

C L O S E

Ask students to comment on this statement: "One reason Catholic thinkers have for believing in the authority of the Roman Catholic Church is that without that unified authority the Christian movement is prone to splintering into many denominations." Is it good or bad for a religion to have many denominations? Have students research the present status of Christianity to find out if the religion has formed many sub-groups, and have them reflect in writing on what they find out.

Answers to Review Questions

1. Some European monarchs challenged the power and authority of the Catholic church. Because of church abuses, many people began to call for church reforms.
2. During the Renaissance, the individual's role in society and civic life became important. The early reformers carried this value into their religious life as well.
3. When people became outraged at the church's abuses—the sale of indulgences and the sale of clerical positions to immoral, illiterate, or uneducated persons—they began to question the church's authority.
4. Early religious reformers believed the individual could experience God through personal prayer, without church help.
5. Many of the clergy abused their power by selling indulgences and living like royalty on the profits. Students might suggest that corruption depends on the person and cite examples supporting their opinions.

Homework Options

Ask students to select terms from the lesson that represent factors in the decline of church authority. Have them explain their selections.

Study Guide: p. 53

1300   1400   1505   1560   1600   1700   1800

INTRODUCE

Point out that most early reformers initially wanted only to reform, or make changes to improve, the Catholic church. Explain that one reformer, Martin Luther, was a Catholic priest when he began to question the church. Have students read the Thinking Focus and then read the lesson to discover Luther's role in the Reformation and in changing the course of religion in western Europe.

Key Terms

Vocabulary Strategies: T36–T37
Protestant—a reformer who protested against the abuses of the Catholic church in the 1500s; a member of a church descended from those that seceded from the Roman Catholic Church during the 1500s
Reformation—the reform movement of the 1500s that re-sulted in the separation of the Protestant churches from the Roman Catholic Church
pamphlet—an unbound pub-lished work such as an essay, usually on a current topic

L E S S O N   2

Martin Luther and the Reformation

THINKING FOCUS

What was Luther's role in the Reformation?

Key Terms

- Protestant
- Reformation
- pamphlet

➤ *The entrance doors to All Saints Church are now inscribed with Luther's* Ninety-Five Theses.

342

Chapter 13

Martin Luther, a priest and professor at the University of Wit-tenberg, approached All Saints Church in Wittenberg on October 31, 1517. Quickly he nailed some papers, handwritten in Latin, to the church door.

No crowd gathered to see what Luther was doing. However, on the outskirts of Wittenberg, people were gathering around Johann Tetzel, a Dominican monk. Tetzel had been authorized to preach indulgences, for which people donated money.

It was against such practices that Luther was protesting in the papers he nailed to the church door. In these papers, his *Ninety-Five Theses,* Luther explained his objections. He saw the practices as proof of how corrupt the Catholic church had become. Luther chal-lenged the church to defend itself. He read over one thesis:

Why does not the Pope, *whose riches are at this day more ample than those of the wealthiest of the wealthy, build the one Basilica of St. Peter's with his own money, rather than with that of poor believers?*

Luther's *Ninety-Five Theses* were really an invitation to scholars to debate certain church issues. He had no idea that his challenge to the church would capture a growing movement of protest and change that would sweep Europe.

Objectives

1. Explain the significance of Luther's *Ninety-Five Theses.*
2. Summarize Luther's Protestant reforms and the church's reactions.
3. Explain the reasons behind the spread of Protestantism.

Graphic Overview

This chart provides an overview of the material presented in this lesson.

Corruption Some priests sell indulgences and live off the profits.	➜	***Ninety-Five Theses*** Martin Luther posts his theses objecting to the sale of indulgences and other church practices.	➜	**The Reformation** Luther's ideas coincide with others', sparking the Protestant Reformation.

Luther Questions the Church

Martin Luther was born on November 10, 1483, in Eisleben, Germany. Luther's father, a hardworking miner, wanted his son to be a lawyer. So in 1501, Luther began studying law at the University of Erfurt.

A Man of Faith

One day in 1505, Luther was caught in a thunderstorm and thrown to the ground when a bolt of lightning struck nearby. Like most men and women of his time, Luther believed that God could come to the aid of humans. In the storm he cried out, "Help, St. Anne, and I'll become a monk." True to his word, that same year Luther ceased studying law and joined the monastery in Erfurt.

Luther was a model monk, and in 1507, he was ordained a priest. A year later, Luther was selected from among his peers to teach at the University of Wittenberg.

A New Religion

As a monk Luther had struggled to understand the true nature of godliness. The church taught that the performance of religious ritual and good deeds was necessary to ensure the soul's salvation. Luther worked hard to satisfy the church and save his soul. But he worried that his actions might not satisfy God.

◄ *At the University of Erfurt, Luther became known for his long and serious talks. His friends nicknamed him "the philosopher." This engraving depicts Luther as he looked at this time.*

Across Time & Space

Reform is not restricted to either the Middle Ages or the church. In the 1950s and 1960s, Martin Luther King, Jr., led a social reform movement in the United States seeking racial equality. Under the leadership of this Baptist minister named for Martin Luther, the movement for civil rights gained wide support from blacks and whites. His policy of nonviolent protest helped curb racial injustice in the South.

◄ *Johann Tetzel sold so many indulgences that some people made fun of him in a popular rhyme: "As soon as money in the box rings, The soul from Hell's fire springs."*

Have students read the selection from Luther's *Ninety-Five Theses* on p. 342. Explain that much of the riches Luther alludes to were obtained by the sale of indulgences. Like the church reformers before and after him, Luther objected to this and many other church practices. Point out that Luther's publication of his theses inspired many other reformers, sparking the Reformation.

Access Strategy

Help students understand the Reformation by asking them if there's some aspect of school life they would like to change. Ask them what they think they could do to bring about this change. Then offer an example. Have them imagine that one student, who is dissatisfied with the quality of food served in the cafeteria, posts her complaints on the cafeteria door. Encourage the class to guess how the other students, the teachers, and the principal would react. Would some students support her? What would happen if the principal took action against her? Would her supporters continue to defend her? Explain that, in a similar way, Martin Luther called for reform and gained much support. The church's reaction against him only strengthened his followers' determination to bring about change.

Access Activity

Ask students to study the picture on this page. What is Johann Tetzel, the man on horseback, doing? *(He's selling something.)* What might he be selling? *(He might be selling indulgences.)* Encourage students to use details from the picture to determine whether the artist supports or objects to this church practice.

BELIEF SYSTEMS

Critical Thinking

Stress the fact that Luther was prompted to write his *Ninety-Five Theses* because he was outraged by the church's selling of indulgences. How is Luther's opposition to indulgences linked to his belief in justification by faith? *(He stressed that personal faith, not the church, is the key to salvation.)* Why were Luther's theses so powerful? *(Many shared his views about church corruption and wanted something to be done about it.)*

■ *His belief in justification by faith contradicted the church's teaching of good works as the way to salvation.*

■ *How did Martin Luther's beliefs conflict with church doctrine and practices?*

▼ *Luther claimed that his burning the bull was purely symbolic; in reality he thought it was the pope himself who should have been burned.*

Luther's fears vanished, however, when he read St. Paul's letter to the Romans: "He who through faith is righteous shall live" (Romans 1:17). To Luther, Paul's message seemed clear: the path to God is through faith alone. Forgiveness was not something the church could grant, nor was it something individuals could achieve on their own. Instead, it was given by God to each person who accepted Him. This theory became known as justification by faith, meaning that a person could be made just, or good, by his or her faith in God.

Luther's belief in justification by faith led him to question the Catholic church's practice of selling indulgences. He objected not only to the church's greed but to the very idea of indulgences. He did not believe the Catholic church had the power to pardon people's sins. Rather, Luther taught that

salvation could be achieved only through God's mercy. No one needed to seek or buy salvation through the church.

By nailing his theses to the church door, Luther was not acting as a heretic. He was simply inviting other scholars to respond to his ideas in a debate, an ordinary method of learning at universities of his day.

At first, no one accepted Luther's invitation. Over the next few years, however, his *Ninety-Five Theses* sparked a religious movement to reform the Catholic church. Because the reformers were protesting against what they felt to be the abuses of the Catholic church, they came to be known as **Protestants.** And because they wanted to reform the Catholic church, that is, improve it by making changes, their movement is known as the **Reformation.** ■

The Reformation Begins

Luther's *Ninety-Five Theses* were soon translated from Latin into German. Within a year, his

344

Chapter 13

ideas were known throughout Europe. As one historian put it, they spread "as if angels from heaven themselves had been their messengers." Encouraged by this success, Luther wrote hundreds of essays between 1517 and 1546, in which he stressed justification by faith and criticized church abuses.

Finally, in 1520, Pope Leo X issued a bull—a statement of the pope's authority—condemning Luther and banning his works. Defying the pope, Luther publicly burned the bull. The break with the church was then complete. In January 1521, Pope Leo X excommunicated Luther.

However, Charles V, the Holy Roman Emperor, decided to give

Study Skills

Have students research Luther's early life and his career as a law student. Ask them to find out what his family and parents were like and how they reacted to his decision to become a monk. Tell students that Luther was nicknamed the philosopher at law school; have them determine why. Encourage students to give oral reports on their research.

Collaborative Learning

Obtain a copy of Luther's *Ninety-Five Theses.* Select several theses that can be understood by the students. (It may be necessary to paraphrase some passages.) Then divide the class into groups of three or four and give each group a different thesis. Have students work together to interpret the meaning of their thesis and rewrite it in their own words. Then ask each group to share its analysis with the class.

Religious Context

Luther sent copies of his theses to high-ranking members of the clergy. To his theses he attached the following invitation:

"Out of love for the faith and the desire to bring it to light, the following propositions will be discussed at Wittenberg under the chairmanship of the Reverend Father Martin Luther, Master of Arts and Sacred Theology. . . . He requests that those who are unable to be present and debate orally with us may do so by letter."

Luther one final chance. In 1521, at a meeting in Worms, Germany, the emperor demanded that Luther recant, or take back, his teachings. Facing church officials and an excited assembly of people, Luther refused. He said in part:

I do not accept the authority of popes and councils. . . . My conscience is captive to the word of God. I cannot and I will not recant anything. . . . Here I stand, I cannot do otherwise. God help me. Amen.

A near riot broke loose. Luther strode out, his hands raised high in triumph. Yet the emperor later declared him an outlaw whom anyone could kill without punishment.

Fortunately for Luther he had a powerful friend in Frederick the Wise, Prince of Saxony. The prince arranged a pretend kidnapping of Luther and hid him away for about a year in the castle at Wartburg. Here, Luther translated the Bible from Greek into German. His translation allowed the German people to read the Christian Bible without having to rely on the interpretation by the priests.

Luther continued to write works in which he attacked the church or discussed books of the Bible. His teachings eventually led to a separate "Lutheran" church. This and other Protestant churches would continue to oppose the Catholic church. ■

Protestantism Spreads

Why did Luther's ideas, which challenged the centuries-old Catholic church, succeed? First, many people longed for a simpler, more direct relationship with God. Second, the times were changing. Trade was increasing, and many people felt a new individualism and nationalism. The new ideas around showed that change was possible.

The printing press, developed in Europe about 1450, also contributed to Luther's success. Printed **pamphlets** containing unbound essays could spread new ideas quickly to many people. By 1523, about a million copies of Luther's pamphlets were in circulation. The printer in A Moment in Time on page 346 is typical of the craftsmen who ran the early presses.

As the Reformation spread, it gained the support of European peasants. In 1524 and 1525, arguing that everyone was equal under God, a group of poor German peasants took up arms against their wealthy landowners. Known as the Peasants' War, this revolt was badly organized and lacked strong leadership. Government armies quickly crushed the uprising.

The peasants were surprised and disappointed to discover that Martin Luther did not support them in the Peasants' War.

◄ *Turn this woodcut portrait of Luther upside down to see what his opponents thought of him.*

■ *How effective were the church's responses to Luther's teachings?*

▼ *Many people feared that the art of printing, new to Europeans, came from the devil. But by 1500, there were more than 1,000 print shops in Europe.*

Note: Use this Moment in Time to extend discussion of the impact of printing from Protestantism Spreads on p. 345. You may also wish to review the information about printing on pp. 330–331.

More About Printing In London in 1620, the Stationers' Company had complete control of the printing industry; members of this company were the only people who might own a press, print, or train apprentices. The Stationers decided which members had the right to sell all kinds of printed materials, including psalm books, schoolbooks, and almanacs.

By law, the printer could print only 1,500 copies of any book. After each page was printed in the maximum number of copies, the type was broken out and put back in its case, to prevent illegal reprints.

ECONOMICS

Visual Learning

Tell students that during his apprenticeship, this printer must master every single step that goes into making a book. When his apprenticeship ends in about four years, he will become a journeyman printer.

346

A Printer

4:29 P.M., August 24, 1620
Great Hall, Northumberland House, London

Eyes
He can read both English and Latin backward and forward. When he started working for the king's printer at age 14, it was hard for him to read the backwards-facing metal type.

Arms
The printer's arms ache from lifting the heavy iron plate of the press hundreds of times since 7:00 this morning.

Beard
He keeps his London-style beard neatly trimmed. After a country childhood, he enjoys city entertainments like seeing plays by Shakespeare.

Woodcut
Pages with pictures, like the one he just took off the press, are still carved in one piece. Most pages are made with movable type that will be taken apart as soon as all the books are printed.

Title Page
The book's title, *Novum Organum,* and its author's name, Francis Bacon, are surrounded by fancy pictures.

Paper
This sheet was thrown away because a young apprentice mixed up a *p* and a *q*. On this page Bacon says printing, gunpowder, and the magnet have changed the world.

Apron
He tries to keep his clothes free of ink, but our printer is called the "dirty-hands" apprentice. His friend, the "clean-hands" apprentice, gets to handle the paper.

346

Visual Learning

Looking at the picture, discuss all the things the printer needed to learn before he could do his job. (*Read English and Latin backwards and forwards, spot mistakes on a page, mix and spread ink on the type, lift and replace the heavy press.*)

Debate

In the English translation of the book the printer is working on, the author says, "printing, gunpowder, and the magnet . . . have changed the whole face and state of things throughout the world; the first in literature, the second in warfare, the third in navigation." Have students debate which mechanical discovery changed the world the most, giving reasons for their choice.

Research

Ask students to research the stages in the process of bookmaking in the 1500s: the manufacture and preparation of the type, paper, and ink; setting the type; printing a proof sheet; proofreading for typographical errors; folding the printed sheets; gathering the printed sheets; and bundling the pages (books were sold unbound; purchasers would then bind them for their personal libraries). Then have students compare bookmaking past and present.

In the pamphlet *Against the Robbing and Murdering Hordes of Peasants,* Luther criticized the rebels for seeking economic gain in the name of God. As a result, Luther lost the support of many social reformers.

However, Luther's ideas became popular with the German princes. Luther did not believe that the church should own property. He also thought that rulers should appoint clergy members. Thus, Luther favored a more powerful role for rulers and a weaker church authority.

Many German princes who wanted freedom from the pope's authority favored Protestantism. Others remained Catholic because they depended on the support of the pope. Eventually, the differences between these German princes erupted in war. From 1546 to 1555, war raged between the Catholic and Protestant princes.

Finally, in 1555, a compromise, called the Peace of Augsburg, was reached. This compromise permitted each German prince to decide which religion would be allowed in his state. Most rulers of northern Germany chose Protestantism, and most in southern Germany remained Catholic. Many people had to move to states that allowed them to practice their own religion.

Lutheranism in Central Europe

Roman Catholic

Lutheran

By 1560, the Reformation was established in Germany and, as you can see on the map above, in much of the rest of Europe. Compare this map with that on page 529 of the Atlas showing the distribution of religions in the world today. What other countries can trace their religious roots to the ideas of the Reformation? ■

▲ *In what countries did Lutheranism become established by 1555?*

■ *Why did Protestantism spread throughout Germany between 1517 and 1560?*

R E V I E W

1. **FOCUS** What was Luther's role in the Reformation?
2. **CONNECT** What similar task did John Wycliffe and Martin Luther undertake? What was the purpose of their work?
3. **HISTORY** How did Gutenberg's invention help spread Protestantism?
4. **POLITICAL SYSTEMS** How did Luther's reforms affect political events in Germany?
5. **CRITICAL THINKING** How do you think Martin Luther would have advised the European peasants to handle their problems with their landowners?
6. **ACTIVITY** Think of a topic you would like to debate. Then write out your position on the topic and post it on your class bulletin board. As in Martin Luther's time, invite other students to debate your viewpoint and exchange ideas.

347

Reformation and the Scientific Revolution

UNDERSTANDING TEXT ORGANIZATION

This skills feature uses examples of organizational patterns found in Chapter 13 to illustrate how to identify text organization and improve understanding of the content.

CULTURE

Critical Thinking

Discuss with students how understanding the pattern of a text may aid them in understanding the text itself. *(Readers can better organize the text's information when they understand how it is set up; the text's key points are more easily recognized when the pattern is understood.)*

UNDERSTANDING TEXT ORGANIZATION

Identifying Patterns

Here's Why

Writers use different patterns to organize what they write. The chart on this page identifies four text patterns and gives clues for each. You will find examples of all four patterns in this chapter. Recognizing the patterns while reading helps improve your understanding.

Here's How

The section Challenges from Monarchs on page 339 is an example of a chronological or time-related pattern. This pattern describes events in the order in which they happened. Notice that several dates are used: "in 1305," "in 1376," and "in 1378." Dates and phrases that describe time periods, such as "for 70 years," are clues that the pattern is chronological. Words that describe time relationships—before, after, during—are clues too.

A cause-and-effect pattern shows what events made other events happen. Sometimes this pattern begins with the effect and then explains its causes. The section Corruption Within the Church on page 339 is an example of a cause-and-effect pattern. The first sentence alludes to the schism in the church. The rest of the paragraph describes actions taken by the bishops to restore the unity of the church.

Look for the cause-and-effect pattern in the paragraph that focuses on how corrupt practices severely weakened the church (page 340). The cause is the sale of indulgences to raise money. The effect is that some officials kept the money for themselves.

Spatial patterns describe people, places, things, and events. Such a pattern shows the relationship of the characteristics being described. The description of Luther and Tetzel on page 342 is an example of spatial organization.

Compare-and-contrast patterns show similarities and differences between two subjects. On pages 346–347 is a description of two groups' reactions to Luther's ideas. It contrasts the reactions of some social reformers with that of the German princes.

Writers use all of these patterns to organize their work. Often, especially in long passages, you will find a combination of several of these patterns.

Try It

Turn to A New Religion in Lesson 2. Tell what organizational pattern is used in this section. Explain how you identified the pattern.

Apply It

Find an article in a magazine or newspaper that uses one of the organizational patterns explained on this page. Name the pattern and explain how you identified it.

Pattern	Definition	Clue Words
Chronological	Tells the order in which events happened	as soon as, at last, first, second, third, next, then, before, after, finally, while, by 1565, until 7 P.M.
Spatial	Describes people, places, things, or events	above, across, beside, behind, below, beyond, east, farther, in front of, inside, lower, near, next to, north, outside, south, under, within, west; names of places
Cause-and-effect	Tells what events caused others	as a result, because, consequently, if, nevertheless, since, so, therefore, then
Compare-contrast	Compares or contrasts events, ideas, people, and so on	although, by contrast, by comparison, compared to, relatively, similarly, unlike

Chapter 13

Objective

Recognize and identify organizational patterns in text. (Critical Thinking 2)

Writing

After students have read about the patterns described in Here's How, have them write paragraphs about an aspect of the Reformation that interests them, using one of the organizational patterns described. Make sure there is only one pattern per example paragraph. Tell students to exchange their papers and have others identify the patterns used.

Answers to Try it

The cause-effect pattern is used. Luther's studies of the Scripture are the cause; the effect is his questioning of practices of the church. Posting the *Ninety-Five Theses* was a cause; the effect was a movement to reform the Catholic church.

Answers to Apply It

Answers will vary but should include appropriate clues to the pattern.

L E S S O N   3

Era of Reformation

Here's an imaginary scene that might have occurred in 1560. A young Frenchman arrives in Geneva, Switzerland, and enters a Calvinist church—a plain wooden structure one story high. Inside, the people sing a hymn in French.

Looking around, the young man compares this church with the Catholic church he attended as a boy. Absent are brightly colored stained-glass windows, candles, ornate statues, paintings on the walls. The young man sees just one cross, a plain wooden one that hangs above the small altar table.

When the singing stops, the minister delivers a sermon on the importance of living a virtuous life.

The entire service is simple but serious, and the young man feels comfortable in this church.

◄ *Like Luther, Calvin was a persuasive writer and speaker who united many religious reformers.*

THINKING FOCUS

What effect did the Reformation have on religion in Europe?

Key Terms

- predestination
- Counter Reformation
- inquisition

Calvin and the Reformation

In the early 1500s, reform spread throughout Europe. Three of Martin Luther's ideas became the center of debate. One idea was justification by faith. The second was the idea that the Bible was the only authority for Christians, rather than the laws of the Catholic church or papal bulls. The third was a belief in a priesthood of all Christians, denying the special powers that priests had in the Catholic church.

Around 1517, when Luther posted his *Ninety-Five Theses,* Ulrich Zwingli, a Swiss priest working in Zurich, brought the Reformation to that city. He urged Christians to study the Bible on their own and deepen their faith.

After Zwingli's death, John Calvin, a Frenchman educated in law, continued to teach the ideas of the Reformation. Forced to flee France in 1534, where the Catholic church had been harrassing

349

Reformation and the Scientific Revolution

Graphic Overview

Protestant Movements		Many people leave the Catholic church to join Protestant movements.		Counter Reformation
• Lutheranism • Calvinism • Anabaptist movement • Church of England	→		→	• Council of Trent • Founding of new orders • The Inquisition

DEVELOP

Explain that this lesson focuses on the main Christian denominations, besides Lutheranism, that developed during the Reformation. It also discusses the Catholic church's response to these new denominations, including the church's attempt to reform itself from within. Ask the students to speculate as to why, in spite of this response, the Catholic church couldn't halt Protestantism.

■ *Calvinists believed in justification by faith and predestination. Calvinist leaders encouraged believers to lead a simple, virtuous, and disciplined life.*

► *Catholicism: adherence to the traditional sacraments. Lutheranism: justification by faith. Church of England: supremacy of king over pope. Calvinism: justification by faith and predestination.*

BELIEF SYSTEMS

Critical Thinking

Many religious reformers held different beliefs. When they broke away from the Catholic church, many new Protestant churches were formed. How did Calvinists and Lutherans differ in their beliefs? *(Their interpretations of predestination differed.)*

350

▲ *Calvinist churches did not allow ornamentation to distract worshipers. This Dutch Calvinist church was built in the early 1600s.*

■ *What religious ideas and practices were important to Calvinists?*

▼ *Can you list some of the beliefs or practices central to each of these church traditions?*

Protestants, Calvin moved to Switzerland. The city of Geneva soon became the center for a movement called Calvinism.

Calvinism differed from other movements of the Reformation in one important way. Calvin taught that God had already chosen, or predestined, a special group of believers for salvation. This theory is known as **predestination.** Luther also accepted predestination but thought that people could never know whom God had chosen.

Calvinism emphasized being devoted to God and leading a disciplined life. According to Calvinists, a person who could maintain such conduct was probably a member of God's chosen group.

Calvinist church services were plain. No images of saints hung on the walls; no organ accompanied the singing. Nothing appealing to the senses interfered with what the worshiper experienced as his or her spiritual link to God.

Calvinists also followed a strict code of moral behavior. Fortune-telling, gambling, and even dancing at social gatherings were all pro-

hibited. Councils elected by church members enforced this code of behavior, as well as other laws of the Calvinist church. By the time Calvin died in 1564, Calvinism had taken root in many places including Scotland, France, and Bohemia.

While Protestant reformers did not aim to change women's roles in society, their actions had that effect. The reformers did not think that women were equal to men, but the Reformation and other social changes did introduce new ideas about family life that gave women a more important role. With changing ideas about marriage and women's roles, the family became a more loving, spiritual relationship.

When convents were closed, many women lost the safety of all-female communities. Since the Protestant clergy could now marry, however, the wife of a minister became an important person. Protestants also favored public education, with both boys and girls learning reading, arithmetic, writing, and religion. ■

Other Protestant Movements

One Protestant group, called the Anabaptists, lived by an even stricter moral code than that of the Calvinists. The Anabaptist movement began in Zurich around 1525 among a group of dissatisfied followers of Zwingli. They believed that the state was made up of sinners. Therefore, true Christians should withdraw from the state and form a separate community.

Both Catholics and Protestants openly opposed the Anabaptists. They resented the Anabaptists' claim that members of all other religious groups were sinners. Anabaptists were widely harassed,

Major Churches During the Reformation			
Religion	**Time Founded**	**Founders**	**Administrators**
Roman Catholic	500s	Popes	Pope, Councils, Bishops
Lutheran	1529	Martin Luther	Congregation, Local Rulers
Church of England	1534	Henry VIII	King of England
Calvinist	1546	John Calvin	Presbytery (Council of Elders)

Chapter 13

Access Activity

Bring in pictures illustrating the interior of a Catholic church and the interior of a Calvinist, Puritan, or Presbyterian church. Have students compare the two pictures and see if they can tell which is which. Then ask them to support their answers by citing details in the pictures.

Access Strategy

Ask students to imagine that they've had the same group of six or seven friends for many years and that they do everything together. Then ask them what they would do if three of their friends suddenly tried to force their opinions on the rest of the group. Would they argue with their friends? What would the students do if the three refused to be friends any longer unless the rest of the group agreed with them? Explain that the religious reformers

were faced with a similar predicament. Because religious reformers didn't agree with many of the beliefs and practices of the Catholic church, they argued against them. When the church insisted they agree without question, many groups broke off from the church and formed their own churches.

and many were executed. Survivors fled to Poland and Holland.

Not all religious reform movements had religious causes. In 1533, Henry VIII of England argued with the pope that he should be allowed to have a divorce, even though it was against church rules. To get his way, Henry persuaded the English parliament to declare England independent of all foreign authorities, including the pope. The following year, parliament's "Act of Supremacy" recognized the Church of England as a separate body with the monarch of England as its head on earth. Religious practices changed slowly, however. Not until Henry's son, Edward VI, became king in 1547 did Protestant practices gain a strong following in England.

Although these reform movements had different beliefs, they shared the same basic motivation: the desire to bring about changes in the church. And because those changes were not coming from within the church, the reformers created their own churches. ■

■ Find evidence to support this statement: Some Protestant groups wanted to make political as well as religious reforms.

The Catholic Church's Response

During the 1400s, many priests recognized that reforms needed to be made. They realized that selling indulgences was corrupt, and they protested against such abuses.

Reforms came slowly. However, as more and more people left the Catholic church to join the Protestant movement, Catholic leaders urged Pope Paul III to assemble a general council to discuss church reform. The Council of Trent, held from 1545 to 1563, set two main goals: to rid the church of abuses and uphold traditional Catholic beliefs. This movement

UNDERSTANDING REFORM

The leaders of the Reformation first tried to change the Catholic church from within. Reform means to change an existing institution.

Participants in a revolution, on the other hand, seek to destroy or replace an existing institution. Therefore, the actions of the colonists in America against the English in 1776 were a revolution, not a reform movement.

Issues and Leaders

Reform movements start because people want to improve some aspect of society. In the mid-1800s, many people wanted to reform the United States voting system to allow women to vote. Leaders of this reform movement, such as Susan B. Anthony, campaigned for women's rights for more than 70 years. In 1920, the Nineteenth Amendment to the U.S. Constitution guar-

anteed women's right to vote.

The Results of Reform

Sometimes the changes brought about by reform movements go beyond what the reformers had in mind. For example, Luther's religious reformation helped to further the existing climate of questioning that led to many social, political, and scientific changes during the following 300 years.

Study Skills

On the chalkboard create a table of churches that is similar to the table on p. 350. Include Calvinism, the Church of England, the Anabaptist movement, and Lutheranism. Then add another category to the chart—Reason for Development—and call on students to fill it in. In a discussion of these reasons, help students to see that these reform movements were all motivated by the same basic desire to make changes in the church. Since these changes weren't forthcoming, reformers created their own churches.

■ Members of the Anabaptist movement in Zurich, Switzerland, held that the state was made up of sinners and proceeded to form their own community with their own laws. King Henry VIII of England set up the Church of England after the Pope would not allow him to divorce one woman and marry another.

Historical Context

Sir Thomas More (1478–1553) was among those whom King Henry VIII executed for refusing to embrace the Church of England. More, a high-ranking member of the English government, opposed Henry's plan to divorce his queen. He also could not accept the king's authority over that of the Catholic church. As a result, Sir Thomas was arrested and imprisoned for 14 months. Throughout this period, his jailers pressed him to submit to the king, but More steadfastly refused. On July 6, 1535, convicted of high treason, More was beheaded. Unrepentant before he died, More said, "The Church is one and indivisible, and you have no authority to make a law which infringes Christian unity." Exactly 400 years after his execution, the Catholic church declared More a saint.

Critical Thinking

Ask students to speculate as to why members of various Protestant movements did not rejoin the Catholic church after it reformed from within. Help students to understand that by this time, the break with the Catholic church was complete. Protestant beliefs and practices were so different from those of the Catholics that reunification was impossible.

BELIEF SYSTEMS

Critical Thinking

Explain to the class that Jesuit missionaries worked to spread Catholicism, using gently persuasive methods. They first learned about their hosts' culture and then taught the people about Catholicism. The Inquisition, on the other hand, used extremely harsh methods to enforce Catholic beliefs. Which method do you think was more effective in strengthening Catholicism? *(The method used by the Jesuits. Punishing people for their beliefs often only strengthens them in their resolve.)*

■ *The church assembled a general council, the Council of Trent, which set two goals: the abolition of abuses and the reaffirmation of traditional Catholic beliefs. The church also encouraged the founding of new orders whose members worked to spread Catholicism around the world.*

CLOSE

Draw the Graphic Overview on the chalkboard. Then discuss the relationship between the Reformation and the Counter Reformation.

352

Christian Churches in Europe, 1600

▲ *Most Anglicans lived in England in 1600. Anglicans are members of the Church of England.*

■ *In what ways did the Catholic church try to reform from within?*

within the church became known as the **Counter Reformation.**

Reacting to Protestants

To help purify itself, the church also encouraged the founding of new orders, or special religious groups. One new order was the Society of Jesus, founded by a Spanish priest named Ignatius Loyola in 1540. Jesuits (*JEHZ oo*

ihts), as the members of the society were called, took vows of poverty and of obedience to the pope. The Jesuits were noted for their educational and missionary works.

In addition to encouraging the spread of Catholicism, church officials tried to halt the spread of Protestantism. Officials in Rome revived the **Inquisition**—a church court to judge, convict, and punish heretics. Both Catholics and Protestants used death and torture in their battle for supremecy.

In Spain, Ferdinand and Isabella used the Inquisition to consolidate their new Spanish state, which had been slowly conquered from the Muslims. In 1492, after using torture, burning, and forced conversions, Ferdinand expelled all Jews from Spain. It had been a center of Jewish and Muslim culture for over 700 years (see pages 95–100). Portugal's Inquisition followed this example four years later.

The church officials also established the *Index of Prohibited Books*. Prohibited books included works by Calvin and Luther.

The Counter Reformation helped to correct many church abuses. However, it could not stop the spread of Protestantism. Never again would a single church dominate all of Europe. ■

R E V I E W

1. **FOCUS** What effect did the Reformation have on religion in Europe?
2. **CONNECT** In what ways were the religious beliefs of Zwingli and Calvin similar to Martin Luther's beliefs?
3. **GEOGRAPHY** Suppose you were a follower of Martin Luther living in Spain in 1600. Use the map on this page to determine where you could go to live among people who shared your beliefs.
4. **CRITICAL THINKING** Why do you think the Anabaptists were persecuted by other Protestant groups?
5. **CRITICAL THINKING** In your opinion, was the Counter Reformation successful? Explain your answer.
6. **WRITING ACTIVITY** Write a brief essay defending the Catholic Church against the changes of the Reformation.

Chapter 13

Homework Options

Have students select one reform movement discussed in the lesson and write a paragraph summarizing its history.

Study Guide: p. 56

Answers to Review Questions

1. The Reformation fostered the growth of many new churches and forced the Catholic church to reform from within.
2. All three men believed in justification by faith and predestination and in leading a simple, pious life, freed from many of the rituals of the Catholic church.
3. You could go to northern Germany, Denmark, Norway, Sweden, or Prussia to live with other Lutherans.
4. The Anabaptists claimed that all other

religious groups were sinners and that true Christians should not associate with them. Other Protestant groups believed they were God's elect and were deeply offended by the Anabaptists' beliefs.
5. The Counter Reformation can be considered both a success and a failure. It dealt with much of the corruption within the church but failed to halt the spread of Protestantism.

| 1300 | 1400 | 1500 | | 1700 | 1800 |

1543   **1687**

L E S S O N   4

Scientific Revolution

Clearly, by 1543, Nicolaus Copernicus, the Polish physician and astronomer, did not have much longer to live. For years, Georg Joachim, his young assistant, had begged Copernicus to publish his revolutionary theories on planetary motion. Copernicus theorized that the sun, not the earth, was the center of the universe. Copernicus claimed he needed more time to provide mathematical and factual support for these theories. But, on his deathbed, he agreed to publish.

Copernicus died later that year. But on the day he died, Joachim brought him the first copy of his work, *On the Revolution of the Celestial Spheres*.

The publication of Copernicus's theory began a movement that would change people's view of the world. Theories that had been accepted for hundreds of years would be challenged by scientific experiment and observation.

What was the Scientific Revolution?

Key Terms

- Scientific Revolution
- scientific method
- hypothesis

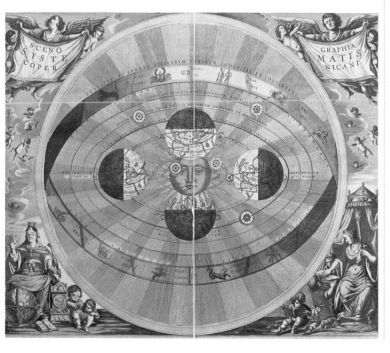

◄ *In Ptolemy's system, the earth is circled by water, air, fire, and seven planets—including the moon and sun. The plan shown here illustrates Copernicus's sun-centered theory.*

353

Reformation and the Scientific Revolution

Graphic Overview

| Copernicus | Vesalius | Galileo | Bacon | Newton |

SCIENTIFIC REVOLUTION

DEVELOP

Point out that this lesson describes the new scientific theories and discoveries that occurred during and after the Reformation. Ask students how the spirit of the Reformation, as well as that of the Renaissance, might have led to new scientific thinking. *(Spirit of challenging old ideas couldn't be confined only to religious and artistic arenas.)*

HISTORY
Critical Thinking

Have students compare the early developments of the Reformation with those of the Scientific Revolution. What do Luther and Wycliffe have in common with Copernicus and Vesalius? *(The religious reformers challenged accepted ideas about the spiritual world. The scientists questioned classical theories about the physical world.)* Encourage students to consider whether the term *revolution* is a good description of the change in scientific thinking at this time.

■ *Copernicus questioned accepted beliefs and sought to test them against data gathered through careful observation. This way of thinking ushered in the Scientific Revolution.*

354

New Visions of the Natural World

▲ *In order to carry out his experiments and make drawings such as this, Vesalius sometimes stole the bodies of people who had been hanged.*

■ *How did the scientific discoveries of Copernicus offer a new view on the world?*

The new Protestants encouraged Bible reading. They taught reading to many people, and thus spread learning and ideas through books. By promoting literacy skills and questioning authority, the forces of the Reformation directly affected the Scientific Revolution.

Copernicus was one of the first European scientists to question theories about the universe. For instance, educated Europeans accepted the theory of Egyptian astronomer Ptolemy that stated that the earth was at the center of the universe.

The Universe

After years of observation and mathematical research, Copernicus concluded that the universe was sun-centered. Drawings demonstrating Copernicus's theory appear on the preceding page and on page 516 of the Minipedia. According to this theory, the planets, including earth, revolve around the sun in circular orbits. The German astronomer Johannes Kepler later proved that the planets' orbits were oval.

Protestant and Catholic leaders alike opposed Copernicus's theory.

The Protestants claimed that the Bible said the earth stood still. The Catholics claimed that the earth and its human beings—not the sun—held the central place in the universe. In 1610, the Catholic church declared that all followers of Copernicus were heretics.

The Human Body

While Copernicus and Kepler explored the universe, Flemish physician Andreas Vesalius explored the human body. His observations challenged the works of Galen, a second-century physician whose theories were widely accepted. Vesalius's thorough dissection of the human body enabled him to describe human anatomy much more accurately. Vesalius's book stimulated new research in the field of anatomy. Some results stemming from continued research are discussed in Making Decisions on pages 358 and 359.

Vesalius and Copernicus questioned and reevaluated accepted theories. Their emphasis on careful observation of the natural world marked a new era in scientific thinking, a period that became known as the **Scientific Revolution.** ■

Galileo and the Church

The Italian astronomer and physicist Galileo continued the work of Copernicus. He greatly admired the Polish astronomer's genius. Like Copernicus and Vesalius, Galileo recognized the importance of relying on observation rather than blindly trusting classical authorities.

Through observation and experimentation, Galileo tested the theory of falling bodies. This theory, which held that heavy objects fall faster than lighter objects, had been accepted since about 300 B.C. Galileo made his own observations by dropping objects of various weights and shapes from different

354

Chapter 13

Access Activity

Have students observe the moon from the same place every night for a week and note its position. Discuss their observations every day. Explain that as the moon circles the earth and the earth circles the sun, the moon appears to change shape. Similar changes in Venus's appearance helped Galileo formulate his sun-centered theory.

Access Strategy

Have students help you conduct an experiment using the scientific method. Take a pencil in one hand and a thick notebook in the other. Hold the objects in front of you at shoulder height. Ask students which one is heavier. Then ask which one they think will hit the ground first when you let them go at the same time. Release the pencil and notebook and have students judge which object reaches the floor first. *(Both should hit at the same time.)* Then use two other objects of differing weights and repeat the experiment. Ask students what they can conclude from these experiments. *(Objects fall at the same speed regardless of weight.)* Explain to students that this method of experimentation was a new idea in the 1500s. Previously scientists had accepted classical theories and did not question them. This new method of gathering data from direct observation revolutionized scientific thought.

heights. He then developed a mathematical formula showing that all bodies—no matter what their shape or weight—would fall at the same speed.

Galileo also applied his method of observation to astronomy. In 1609, he developed a telescope that was larger and more powerful than any made before. Galileo was the first person to observe sunspots, Jupiter's moons, and Saturn's rings. He also provided new information about the rough, crater-marked surface of our moon, which had previously been considered smooth.

Galileo's observations of one planet, Venus, provided strong support for Copernicus's theory. But when Galileo argued the point in his *Dialogue Concerning the Two Chief World Systems*, the

Catholic church reacted. Because the idea of a sun-centered universe went against Catholic beliefs, the publication was placed on the *Index of Prohibited Books*. The inquisition in Rome condemned Galileo in 1616. Threatened with torture, Galileo, now an old man, denied his belief in Copernicus's ideas.

But his spirit was not broken. Upon leaving his trial, he is believed to have said of the earth, "but still it moves." Galileo spent the remaining eight years of his life under house arrest on his estate near Florence, where he continued his scientific activities.

The church's victory was short-lived. By the late 1630s, the theory of the sun-centered universe was well established, and the age of science was under way. ■

▼ *Using this compound microscope, Robert Hooke examined cork, snowflakes, and tiny organisms, such as the tick. His drawings were published in the book* Micrographia *in 1645.*

The Scientific Method

The Scientific Revolution was pioneered by Copernicus, Vesalius, and Galileo. Many other thinkers and writers also contributed to its success.

Francis Bacon

One such thinker was Francis Bacon, an English philosopher. In his book *Novum Organum,* published in 1620, Bacon stressed the importance of observation and experimentation leading to the statement of general principles about the natural world. This way of doing scientific research is now known as the **scientific method.**

A key part of this process, according to Bacon, was forming a

hypothesis. A **hypothesis** is an assumption that can be tested by investigation. For example, Robert Hooke, an Englishman who developed the compound microscope in 1665, hypothesized that a microscope with two lenses could produce a clearer image of a magnified object.

This hypothesis was then tested by an experiment, and the results were recorded. Hooke experimented by adjusting and readjusting the placement of the lenses. Then he made accurate drawings based on his observation of the

355

Research

Divide the class into small groups. Have each group write a report on the contributions of early scientists not mentioned in this lesson. Suggest they study one of the following: English physician William Harvey, Irish chemist Robert Boyle, or French chemist Antoine Lavoisier. Students' research should include facts about how their subject questioned traditional theories.

Role Playing

After students have completed the Research activity on this page, have each group role-play an important event or moment in their scientist's life. For example, those researching Harvey might role-play his discovery of how blood circulates in the body. Encourage students to use primary source quotations they come across in their research for the role-play activity.

Critical Thinking

Have students test the following hypothesis: black absorbs heat; white reflects it. Ask them how they would prove or disprove this hypothesis. *(One suggestion is to place a black sheet of paper and a white sheet of paper in the sun and then test their temperatures.)* Have students carry out their experiments, and record their results. Discuss their conclusions.

CULTURE

Critical Thinking

Emphasize the fact that ideas about the scientific method revolutionized the way scientists approached their research. Then ask students if they can think of ways in which they have used the scientific method in their science classes.

■ *The idea of the scientific method holds that people cannot learn by relying on established truths, but by observing, collecting, and analyzing data.*

CLOSE

Redraw the Graphic Overview on the chalkboard. Have students add details describing the accomplishments and significance of each scientist. Details should also include birth and death dates, field of expertise, and nationality.

356

▲ *Isaac Newton was praised by the English poet Alexander Pope in the following rhyme: "Nature, and nature's laws lay hid in night/ God said, 'Let Newton be!' and all was light."*

➤ *Newton's studies of how light passes through a prism helped explain how rainbows are formed.*

■ *What was revolutionary about the scientific method?*

magnified objects. Finally, the collected data were analyzed and a conclusion was drawn. Hooke's data indeed revealed that objects could be more closely observed using a microscope with two lenses.

Bacon's method helped others in the Scientific Revolution organize and formulate their research. The scientific method is still at the core of scientific research.

Isaac Newton

Sir Isaac Newton, English scientist, astronomer, and mathematician, also used the scientific method. Many scientists before Newton made observations and recorded data. However, Newton's biggest contribution was in providing an explanation for the universe that was very large in scope. His great ability lay in interpreting data and drawing accurate conclusions about the nature of the universe.

Born in 1642, the year Galileo died, Newton expanded and perfected many of Galileo's theories. Like Galileo, Newton was fascinated by falling objects. According to the story, while in the country one day, Newton saw an apple fall from a

tree branch. He hypothesized that there must be some force pulling the apple to the ground. He further hypothesized that the same force that pulls an object to earth keeps the moon and planets in orbit around the sun. After much observation and many experiments, Newton announced that a force called gravity holds the universe together. He described this theory and many others in the *Mathematical Principles of Natural Philosophy* published in 1687.

During the Reformation and the Scientific Revolution, people began to reexamine their spiritual and physical worlds. Freed from having to rely on accepted theories and beliefs, they sought new answers to old questions. This searching set the stage for further reformation in the 18th and 19th centuries. ■

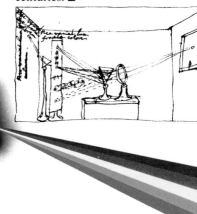

1. **FOCUS** What was the Scientific Revolution?
2. **CONNECT** What did the new scientific thinkers and the leaders of the Reformation have in common?
3. **BELIEF SYSTEMS** Why was the publication of Vesalius's findings considered revolutionary?
4. **SCIENCE** How did Newton use the scientific method?

5. **CRITICAL THINKING** Which scientific achievements do you think were more important, those of Copernicus or those of Galileo? Explain.
6. **ACTIVITY** Use Bacon's scientific method to answer the following question: Which weighs more, a pound of apples or a pound of lettuce?

Chapter 13

Homework Options

Have students write a series of headlines that trace the progress of the Scientific Revolution.

Study Guide: p. 57

Answers to Review Questions

1. The Scientific Revolution was a period of extensive scientific activity in the 1400s and 1500s during which new scientific methods were developed and established beliefs were challenged.
2. Both scientists and Protestant reformers questioned traditional ideas.
3. Vesalius's publication of his findings revealed that he had dared to question and reevaluate the accepted theories of Galen. His publication of these findings was also,

in effect, an admission that he had dissected human beings.
4. Newton applied the scientific method to his ideas about gravity. He formed an hypothesis, collected data, and came to a conclusion about the law of gravity.
5. Answers will vary. Some students will hold that because Copernicus was first, his work was more revolutionary. Other students will note that Galileo expanded and improved upon Copernicus's ideas.

UNDERSTANDING CRITICAL THINKING

Making Hypotheses

Here's Why

You know that a hypothesis is an explanation, based on known facts, that can be tested as more facts become available. To develop a hypothesis, you gather all the information you can about a question or a problem. The hypothesis then becomes the basis of any further testing. You can test a scientific hypothesis through observation or experimentation, as discussed in Lesson 4.

Other subjects, such as history, also invite hypotheses. Some hypotheses about history can never be proved or disproved because of lack of evidence. However, you can continue to test a hypothesis when you find new information.

Suppose you want to explain why the church lost so much of the power it once had. You have read many facts about this in the chapter. You could use these facts to form a hypothesis.

Here's How

Look at the diagram below. It shows the steps involved in making a hypothesis.

The arrows indicate that each step leads to the next. To formulate a hypothesis of your own, follow these steps in order:

1. **Define the question.** You could ask, for example: What was the primary cause of the decline in church authority between 1300 and 1500?
2. **Gather evidence.** Read through the chapter and list events that caused the church's authority to decline. Your list may look something like this:
   - Secular rulers gained power.
   - The Great Schism caused confusion.
   - Corruption existed within the church.
   - Many groups were asking for reform in the church.
3. **Examine the clues.** Analyze the list. Can the clues be placed under a particular heading? How might the ideas be summarized?
4. **Make a hypothesis.** One example of a hypothesis that shows the primary cause of the decline in church authority between 1300 and 1500 is this: The church did not use its power wisely.
5. **Test the hypothesis.** You can test your hypothesis by reading more about the topic, either in your textbook or in outside sources.

Try It

Now form a hypothesis of your own that answers this question: Why did the Calvinists have such a strict code of behavior? Use what you have learned about the Calvinists in Lesson 3 to complete steps 2–4.

Apply It

Formulate a hypothesis which answers this question: Why do some seventh grade students. make excuses about late homework assignments? Use the five-step process to work out your hypothesis. Write down the facts you used to develop your hypothesis. When you learn new facts about the question, examine them and be prepared to alter your hypothesis to account for the new information.

Making a Hypothesis

1. Define the question. → 2. Gather evidence. → 3. Examine the clues. → 4. Make a hypothesis. → 5. Test the hypothesis.

Reformation and the Scientific Revolution

This skill feature draws on information in the chapter to teach students how to formulate and test hypotheses.

HISTORY

Critical Thinking

Give students some statistical information about their school or class. You might, for example, show the number of students absent on different days of the week or how attendance changes from month to month. Then ask students how they might explain these statistics.

Tell them that their explanations are educated guesses or hypotheses. Then explain that they can improve their hypothesizing skills by following certain steps.

Review the five steps involved in making a hypothesis on p. 357. Have students work in small groups to gather evidence from the chapter to answer the question in Try It.

Answers to Try It

Answers will vary but should show evidence of using steps 2–4 outlined:
1. Gather evidence. *(Students should cite facts from the chapter, such as: Calvinists believed those who led a disciplined life would be members of God's chosen group; their services and decor were plain.)*
2. Examine the clues. *(The Calvinists sought things that were strict, plain, and simple.)*
3. Make a hypothesis. *(Calvinists thought it would be easiest to attain their goals if they had strict, uncomplicated rules to follow.)*

Answers to Apply It

Answers will vary. Students should explain the steps used to arrive at their hypotheses.

Objective

Make and test hypotheses. (Critical Thinking 3)

DECISION-MAKING PROCESS

1. Recognize the need for a decision.
2. Define the goals and values involved.
3. Acquire and evaluate necessary information.
4. Identify and analyze possible alternatives.
5. Choose the best alternative.

This Making Decisions lesson, Scientific Discoveries, uses step 3 of the decision-making process.

ETHICS
Critical Thinking

Ask students to find two statements in the text that explain why even the doctors of Jenner's time felt uncomfortable about his idea for a smallpox vaccine. *(Injecting people with the material from infected sores was unsettling, and no one was sure that the injections weren't harmful.)* Have students give their ideas about why Jenner went ahead with the experiment. *(Even though one life was being risked, many could be saved; Jenner's observations and investigations showed that his idea for a vaccine was logical.)*

358

MAKING DECISIONS

Scientific Discoveries

I n all corners of the world, I sought for the true and experienced arts of medicine. Not alone with doctors; but with barbers, surgeons, learned physicians, women, magicians, alchemists . . . , with the wise and the simple, I [gathered information] for a foundation of medicine which should be unspotted by fables or babble.

Paracelsus, a Swiss physician, 1493–1541

Background

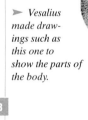

➤ *Vesalius made drawings such as this one to show the parts of the body.*

In 1543, Flemish scientist Andreas Vesalius did a shocking thing. He published a book about human anatomy, showing detailed pictures of the bones, muscles, and organ systems. In doing so, he admitted that he had performed dissections. In those days, dissecting the human body was forbidden by the major religions—Judaism, Christianity, and Islam.

The Scientific Revolution, fueled by the courage of Galileo, Vesalius, and others, created an intellectual climate in which people began to question even the oldest and most accepted ideas. Doctors and scientists rejected what they could not prove to be true and formulated new theories based on their observations of the world.

For example, in 1796, English physician Edward Jenner made an observation about smallpox, a disease that terrorized Europe.

Milkmaids— young girls who milked cows—rarely contracted the disease. Jenner found that these girls had previously suffered from cowpox, a disease similar to smallpox, but much milder. Victims of both diseases developed infected sores on their skin.

Jenner did an experiment to find out if injecting a person with fluid from a cowpox sore prevented the person from contracting smallpox. A young boy volunteered to be the guinea pig. Several weeks after injecting the boy with fluid from a cowpox sore, Jenner injected the boy with material from smallpox sores. Jenner, the boy, and the boy's mother waited anxiously to see if the boy would come down with smallpox, but the boy remained healthy. By recognizing that cowpox and smallpox were related and conducting a daring experiment, Jenner had found a way to protect people from smallpox.

358

Chapter 13

Objective

Identify Jenner's methods of gathering information to develop a smallpox vaccine and evaluate them. (Critical Thinking 2; Ethics 2)

Activity

Have the class count off by twos. Tell them to imagine that they are doctors living in Jenner's time. They have to write about his vaccination experiment for a medical journal. Instruct the "ones" to be in favor of Jenner's methods and the "twos" to oppose it. Explain that they should first report on Jenner's observation, investigation, and experiment, and then give their reasons for supporting or opposing his methods. Remind students that they should not take advantage of hindsight;

none of Jenner's contemporaries knew if his experiment was truly a success or just a single stroke of luck. The articles should end with the doctors' suggestions of what Jenner should do next with his vaccine.

◄ *Magnetic resonance imaging produces pictures of the human body that enable doctors to pinpoint problems before surgery. Today, doctors are also able to use artificial hearts and cell-separation techniques to save lives.*

Knowledge and Responsibility

Jenner's discovery was not easy for people to accept at first. Even physicians found it unsettling to think of injecting people with material from infected sores. Was Jenner taking too many risks? Was he sure that injections could do no harm? Should people wait for more proof before submitting themselves to Jenner's procedure?

Decision Point

1. What were the risks and benefits of Jenner's treatment for smallpox? Do you think Jenner was right to test his procedure the way he did? Why?
2. If you had been alive in Jenner's day, would you have wanted to undergo Jenner's treatment? What would you want to ask him before you agreed to the procedure? List the questions you would ask before making this decision.
3. Suppose a researcher discovers a drug that helps cure heart disease. Its side effects are not yet fully known or understood. What information could help you decide whether this new drug should be given to patients? How could you find this information?

> **What should a doctor do with a new medicine that could save people's lives?**

Withhold it for further tests	Make it available to a select group	Make it available to anyone
• Advantages • Disadvantages	• Advantages • Disadvantages	• Advantages • Disadvantages

Reformation and the Scientific Revolution

Answers to Reviewing Key Terms
A. Answers:
1. False. Martin Luther spread the ideas of the **Reformation** with his many **pamphlets.**
2. False. The Reformation was the **Protestant** movement to improve the Catholic church.
3. True.
4. True.
5. True.

B. Sample answers:
1. The selling of **indulgences** was one of the corrupt practices that Luther was protesting in the **Protestant** movement. **Predestination** was a doctrine of the Protestant movement.
2. A **Protestant** was a reformer who was protesting against the abuses of the Catholic church through the **Reformation.** Protestants were brought before the **Inquisition** and tortured or sentenced to death for refusing to change their beliefs.
3. Forming a **hypothesis** is the first step in the **scientific method,** a development of the **Scientific Revolution.**

Answers to Exploring Concepts
A. Answers:
Individuals in Religion: Pope Boniface VIII, Pope Clement V, Pope Gregory XI, Pope Urban VI, Pope Clement VII, John Wycliffe, John Hus, Margery Kempe, Catherine of Siena, Martin Luther, Pope Leo X, Ulrich Zwingli, John Calvin, Pope Paul III, Ignatius Loyola.
Individuals in Government: King Philip IV, Charles V, Frederick the Wise, Henry VIII, Edward VI.
Individuals in Science: Copernicus, Georg Joachim, Johannes Kepler, Andreas Vesalius, Galileo, Francis Bacon, Isaac Newton.

Answers for names of two individuals and the summary of their contributions will vary.
B. Sample answers:
1. Philip's response to the *Unam Sanctam* showed that government leaders could challenge church leaders. This lessened the authority of the church.
2. Urban VI was already pope, so people could not be sure who was really pope.

Chapter Review

Reviewing Key Terms

council (p. 340)
Counter Reformation (p. 352)
hypothesis (p. 355)
indulgence (p. 340)
inquisition (p. 352)
pamphlet (p. 345)

predestination (p. 350)
Protestant (p. 344)
Reformation (p. 344)
scientific method (p. 355)
Scientific Revolution (p. 354)

A. Write whether each of the following statements is true or false. Then rewrite the false statements to make them true.
1. Martin Luther was a leader in the Counter Reformation.
2. The Reformation was the Catholic movement to improve the Protestant church.
3. The scientific method involves a series of logical steps used in scientific research.
4. Councils of church leaders were created to meet and rule on matters of church law and faith and to restore unity and dignity to the Catholic church.
5. During the Scientific Revolution, accepted theories about the nature of the universe were challenged.

B. Write a sentence or two using the three terms in each group. The sentences should show how the terms are related.
1. indulgences, Protestant, predestination
2. Protestant, Reformation, inquisition
3. scientific method, hypothesis, Scientific Revolution

Exploring Concepts

A. In every age there are individuals who have a strong effect on historical events. Copy the chart below. Then fill in the boxes with the names of individuals who were important participants in this historical period. Add more boxes if necessary. Then choose two names from each category and summarize the contributions of each.

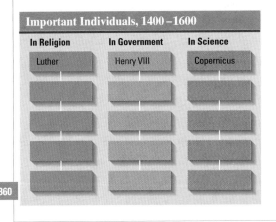

Important Individuals, 1400–1600

In Religion	In Government	In Science
Luther	Henry VIII	Copernicus

Chapter 13

B. Support each statement with facts and details from the chapter.
1. The *Unam Sanctam* eventually led to a lessening of the authority of the Catholic church.
2. Many Catholics were confused by the French cardinals' election of Clement VII to the office of pope.
3. Some clergy engaged in corrupt practices, which further weakened the authority of the church.
4. Copernicus and Newton reached conclusions that changed previous ideas of how the universe worked.
5. The Council of Trent was an important part of the Catholic church's attempt to reform itself.
6. Scientists of the 1500s and 1600s and religious reformers questioned accepted theories and beliefs.
7. In addition to Martin Luther, there were other individuals and groups who broke away from the Catholic church.

3. Some clergy sold indulgences and some sold clerical positions to the highest bidder. As a result, some clergy were immoral or uneducated.
4. Copernicus concluded that the Earth revolved around the Sun, rejecting the common belief in an Earth-centered universe. Newton developed and applied theories about gravity and the movement of planets and other large bodies.

5. The Council set two main goals: to rid the church of abuses and to uphold traditional Catholic beliefs.
6. Religious reformers questioned the teachings and authority of the church. Scientists challenged accepted ideas about the world and the human body.
7. Ulrich Zwingli, John Calvin, the Anabaptists, and Henry VIII also broke away.

Reviewing Skills

1. What system is used to organize the text sections The Reformation Begins and Protestantism Spreads on pages 344–347? Explain what clues you had.
2. Copernicus believed that the sun was the center of the universe and the earth only one of the planets that revolved around the sun. However, he refused to publish the mathematical work and records of observation that supported his hypothesis until he knew that he was near death. Use the five-step process to formulate a hypothesis

that explains why Copernicus did not publish his findings earlier. Read Lesson 4 to review the facts. Explain how your hypothesis accounts for all the facts you list.

3. Reread the quotation from Pope Boniface's *Unam Sanctam* on page 338. What was Pope Boniface's bias?
4. You are reading Protestant and Catholic primary sources on the Reformation. What factors can you think of that might affect factual reporting from both Protestant and Catholic sources?

Using Critical Thinking

1. The events of history are like a chain of causes and effects. What action of King Philip IV caused Pope Boniface VIII to issue the *Unam Sanctam?* What action did Philip take as a result of the pope's decree? What effect did Philip's action have on the Catholic church? If Philip IV hadn't responded to the *Unam Sanctam* as he did, what role might the church play in our lives and government today? Why?
2. "The pen is mightier than the sword" is an old saying. What does it mean? How would you apply the saying to the actions of Martin Luther?

3. Copernicus's theory on planetary motion was strongly opposed by certain leaders of his day. Suppose that a theory that is in direct opposition to a widely accepted scientific theory was proposed today. Do you think it would meet with the same kind of opposition? Why?
4. Modern Americans enjoy many important rights, including the freedom of religion and the freedom of speech. If the people you learned about in this chapter had these two rights, do you think the events in the chapter would have been any different? Explain what you mean.

Preparing for Citizenship

1. **GROUP ACTIVITY** Look at the map of world religions on page 529 of the Atlas. Choose one of the religions shown. Research its development and prepare a timeline showing dates of important events in its history. Display the timelines in the classroom. Also look for and display newspaper and magazine articles about that religion.
2. **INTERVIEWING** Interview a minister, a priest, a rabbi, or someone else in a religious role. Ask questions such as these: Why did you choose this profession? What type of schooling is required? What do you especially like about your work? What are some

disadvantages? Present your information in brief talks called "Meet ____."
3. **COLLABORATIVE LEARNING** Meet with your class to plan a Living History in which important people introduced in this chapter discuss their contributions and achievements. Which people made the most important contributions? Use the chart you completed in Exploring Concepts as a guide. Select students for the following tasks: role-play the historical figures; write their scripts; make costumes and props; design and construct scenery; and make posters advertising the presentation. Then present the Living History.

Reformation and the Scientific Revolution

Answers to Reviewing Skills

1. The Reformation Begins is chronological. Clues: *Within a year, finally, later.* Protestantism Spreads uses a cause-and-effect pattern. Clues: *contributed to, as a result, thus.*
2. Hypotheses may vary. Possibility: Copernicus feared being condemned by the church and prevented from continuing his work. Supporting evidence: In 1610, all who believed his theories were declared heretics. In 1616, Galileo was condemned for writing about Copernicus's theories.
3. The idea of the church's authority being divided is compared to a monster with two heads; thus the pope expresses horror at anyone questioning his authority.
4. The reporter's personal bias.

Answers to Using Critical Thinking

1. Philip IV tried to collect taxes from the church; then had Boniface arrested. The action lessened the church's authority. One might speculate that the church might have more control over government and our lives today because it might have the authority it had then. However, other events in the intervening years would also have had an effect.
2. Interpretations may vary. Luther's writings helped spread the Reformation.
3. Some may say that most people today are more accepting of new ideas. Others may say that proof supporting the theory would be expected.
4. Students may suggest that freedom of religion might have prevented the accumulation of power in the church. Freedom of speech might have permitted open discussion and resolution of the abuses within the church.

Preparing for Citizenship

1. **GROUP ACTIVITY** Suggest that students begin their research in the library. Students' timelines should illustrate the important events in the history of the religion they choose.
2. **INTERVIEWING** Have students prepare their lists of questions and arrange for interviews with local religious leaders.
3. **COLLABORATIVE LEARNING** Have students choose a producer/director to be in charge of the Living History. Have students outline specific goals and establish

deadlines for each of the goals. Schedule time for the planning meeting, the group work sessions, and the presentation. After the presentation, have students evaluate how well they met their goals.

Planning at a Glance
The Age of Exploration

	Objectives	Reading Support *and* Other Resources	Diverse Learning Strategies

Lesson 1
Travel, Trade, and Exploration
pp. 364–370 2–3 days
	• Discuss some of the factors that spurred Europeans' interest in exploring.
	• Tell how European demand for products from the Far East encouraged exploration.
	• Assess the role of religion in spurring exploration.
	• Discuss why Spain and Portugal needed new sources of gold.
		• **Workbook** or **Reading Support:**
		  pp. 191–194
		  Review p. 45
		  Lesson Support/Transition p. 45
		  Multi-Lang. Sum. pp. 89–90
		• **Other Resources:** Geography Kit, Poster 7, Study Guide p. 59
			Access Strat. **(Extra Support)** TE p. 365
			Access Act. **(SDAIE)** TE p. 365
			Map and Globe Skills **(Visual)** TE pp. 365, 366
			Language Arts Connection **(GATE)** TE p. 369
			
			Audiotapes of Multi-language Summaries **(Auditory)**

Lesson 2
Adventure and Profit
pp. 371–376 2–3 days
	• Discuss Prince Henry's role in early European exploration.
	• List important technological advances in navigation in the 1400s.
	• Describe Portugal's exploration of the African coast and its effect on trade.
	• Explain the economic significance of establishing colonial settlements.
		• **Workbook** or **Reading Support:**
		  pp. 195–198
		  Review p. 46
		  Lesson Support/Transition p. 46
		  Multi-Lang. Sum. pp. 91–92
		• **Other Resources:** Geography Kit, Study Guide p. 60, Study print 12
			Access Strat. **(Extra Support)** TE p. 372
			Visual Learning **(Visual)** TE p. 373
			Social Participation **(Auditory)** TE p. 374
			Homework Options **(Visual)** TE p. 376
			
			Audiotapes of Multi-language Summaries **(Auditory)**

Lesson 3
Exploring the Americas
pp. 377–381 2–3 days
 	
Literature:
"The Audience"
pp. 384–389
	• Discuss Columbus's goals in sailing westward.
	• Evaluate the impact of the early Spanish contacts with Indians in the Americas.
	• Describe early European explorations in North America.
		• **Workbook** or **Reading Support:**
		  pp. 199–202
		  Review p. 47
		  Lesson Support/Transition p. 47
		  Multi-Lang. Sum. pp. 93–94
		• **Other Resources:** Geography Kit, Study Guide p. 61
			Access Act. **(Kinesthetic)** TE p. 378
			Access Strat. **(SDAIE)** TE p. 378
			Study Skills **(GATE)** TE p. 380
			Map and Globe Skills **(Kinesthetic)** TE p. 381
			
			Audiotapes of Multi-language Summaries **(Auditory)**

Skill: Reading a Wind and Current Map *pp. 382–383* 1 day	• Form hypotheses from information on a special–purpose map.	• **Other Resources:** Study Guide p. 62	Using a Map **(Visual)** TE p. 382
Chapter Review *pp. 390–391* 1 day		Chapter 14 Test pp. 53–56 *(See facsimiles on TE p. 572.)*	Assessment Multiple-Use Masters pp. 73–80

Reading Support Resources *for Every Lesson*

Reading and Review

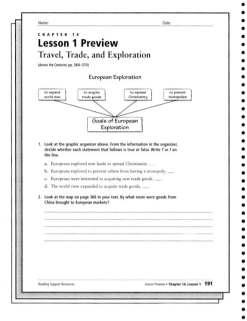

- **Chapter Overview*** p. 190
- **Lesson Previews*** using graphic organizers from the Teacher's Edition pp. 191, 195, 199
- **Reading Strategies*** pp. 192, 196, 200
- **Lesson Summaries*** pp. 193–194, 197–198, 201–202
- **Lesson Reviews** pp. 45, 46, 47

  * **Workbook** includes starred items.

Multi-language Summaries

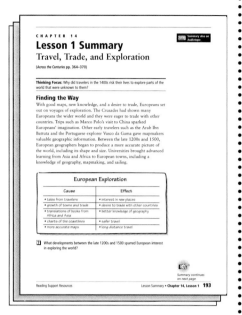

- **Lesson Summaries** in:
- English (See Reading and Review.)
- Spanish pp. 193–194, 197–198, 201–202
- Chinese pp. 89–94
- Hmong pp. 89–94
- Khmer pp. 89–94
- Vietnamese pp. 89–94

   Summaries available on audiotapes

Lesson Support /Transition
S D A I E

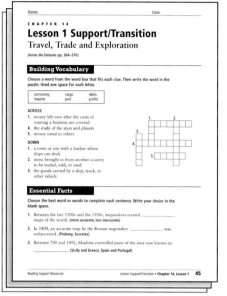

Activities for SDAIE
Specially **D**esigned **A**cademic **I**nstruction in **E**nglish

- **Lesson Support/Transition** pp. 45, 46, 47

 Technology Options

Internet Support
http://www.eduplace.com

Social Studies Center at Education Place

Internet support for Chapter 14:

- *Lesson at a Glance*
- *The Spice Trade*

Software
***Student Writing Center* ®** (CD-ROM) (Macintosh® or Windows®)

School to Career

Create a scenario such as building a space station. Have students think of the jobs they think will need to be filled to design, construct, and operate the space station. Fill each position with a student. Then have each student research skills and training needed for the job.

Character Education

It can be difficult to hold to ideals and beliefs when others disagree. Peer pressure can make people do things they normally might not. But peer pressure need not be negative. Have students select a cause, such as recycling, and then create a "positive peer pressure" campaign to promote their cause to others.

CHAPTER PREVIEW

Have the students read the chapter title and the paragraph below it. Point out that the paragraph describes trade as an important reason for exploration. Ask the students to suggest other reasons European explorers might have set off on their voyages. (*To discover new lands; to spread Christianity; to establish new colonies.*)

Looking Back

Remind students that in the past the oceans had acted as natural barriers to exploration.

Looking Forward

Tell the class that the next three lessons—Travel, Trade and Exploration; Adventure and Profit; and Exploring the Americas—recount dramatic adventures and discoveries.

Lesson 1 explains how mapmaking contributed to the age of exploration and why people were willing to sail unknown seas.

Chapter 14
The Age of Exploration

Gold, silver, and silks glimmered in the North African sun. The fragrance of spices filled the air. The year was 1415. Portugal's Prince Henry, then a crusader, marveled at the riches in the city of Ceuta. These sights gave Henry a dream—to control the rich trade with Africa and Asia. The same dream sparked many adventurers of the 1400s and 1500s. Time after time, they risked voyages on uncharted waters to reach the valuable goods of Africa and Asia.

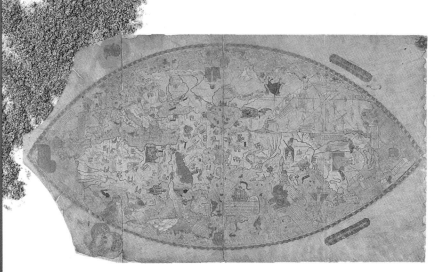

Throughout this period, explorers brave high waves, storms, rocky shallows, and their crews' fears that sea monsters lurk in the ocean.

1292 After 17 years in China, traveler Marco Polo returns to Venice and tells Europeans of China's wonders. A later geographer uses Polo's accounts to draw this map.

| 1250 | 1300 | 1350 | 1400 |

362

1250

c. 1400 Chinese trading ships sail to the Middle East and eastern Africa.

BACKGROUND

The European Age of Exploration is characterized most of all by the quest for knowledge and the application of knowledge to practical situations. In addition, commercial and religious motives played an important role in stimulating exploration by land and water.

The Quest for Knowledge

The Renaissance interest in the individual and in developing human potential set the stage for European exploration and expansion. The learning that came from Spain and Portugal encouraged speculation about the shape and size of the world.

Travelers such as Nicolo de' Conti supplied valuable information to mapmakers. In fact, when this Venetian merchant-adventurer speculated about the possibility of a sea route to the East, many mid-1400s mapmakers altered their maps accordingly. Earlier maps showed southern Africa extending around the globe to join with northern Asia.

Commercial Motives

As European demand for eastern imports grew, some countries had to supplement their exports with gold bullion. Much of this gold came from North African traders, who carried it across the Sahara from the south. The earliest voyages of exploration were part of a Portuguese plan to locate and deal directly with southern African gold producers. The demand for eastern imports also inspire

During this time, scholars and sailors worked to improve the tools of navigation. Their work paved the way for many advances, like this sextant of the 1700s.

1400s and 1500s Monarchs like England's Queen Elizabeth (above) finance exploration in hope of gaining great riches.

| 1450 | 1500 | 1550 | 1600 |

1526 Babur founds the Mughal Empire in India.

1600

Understanding the Visuals

The "sea monster" (p. 362) is an example of what illustrators of the 1400s and 1500s drew based on the tales told by sailors back from long expeditions. These sailors saw species of fish they had never encountered before and described them as monsters. Note the three eyes and the boar's head on this "monster."

The sextant (p. 363) allows navigators to determine the position of their ships by measuring the angular distance between the horizon and the sun or a star.

Understanding Chronology

Have students read the timeline. Point out that the countries of Western Europe were not the only ones at this time who were eager to expand trade by sea. Note that the entry for c. 1400 tells of Chinese trading ships that sailed to the Middle East and eastern Africa.

explorers to seek alternative routes to the East, which resulted in the European discovery of the Americas.

Since the voyages of exploration were designed to find new markets and new sources of wealth, countries jealously guarded the information they obtained. Thus the records of the earliest Portuguese exploration of Africa, for example, are vague and incomplete. Commercial interests served to suppress the dissemination of geographic knowledge.

Religious Motives

Most of the early explorers were also motivated by religious concerns. They sought to convert people to Christianity or to gain allies, such as the legendary Christian king Prester John, in the ongoing fight against Islam. Thus, while Vasco da Gama was rounding Africa on his way to India, two overland travelers were searching for Prester John in the Middle East and Africa. Both expeditions were sent by King John II of Portugal.

INTRODUCE

Ask a volunteer to read the primary source excerpt aloud to the class. Encourage the class to discuss the dangers that 15th-century sailors faced and the fears they might have had when exploring unknown seas. Tell students to read the Thinking Focus and to make predictions to answer the question. Direct them to check their predictions as they read the lesson.

Key Terms

Vocabulary Strategies: T36–T37

monopoly—The total control by one group of the means of producing a service

balance of trade—the difference in value between the total imports and total exports of a nation

bullion—gold or silver in the form of bars or ingots of a specific weight

1250 — 1600

LESSON 1

Travel, Trade, and Exploration

THINKING FOCUS

Why did explorers in the 1400s risk their lives to explore parts of the world that were unknown to them?

Key Terms

- monopoly
- balance of trade
- bullion

The seas rose towards the sky and fell back in heavy showers which flooded the ships. The storm raging thus violently, the danger was doubled, for suddenly the wind died out, so that the ships lay dead between the waves, lurching so heavily that they took in water on both sides; and the men made themselves fast not to fall from one side to the other; and everything in the ships was breaking up, so that all cried to God for mercy.

Gaspar Correa,
from *Lendas da India*, 1561

This print of Vasco da Gama is based on an unknown artist's painting.

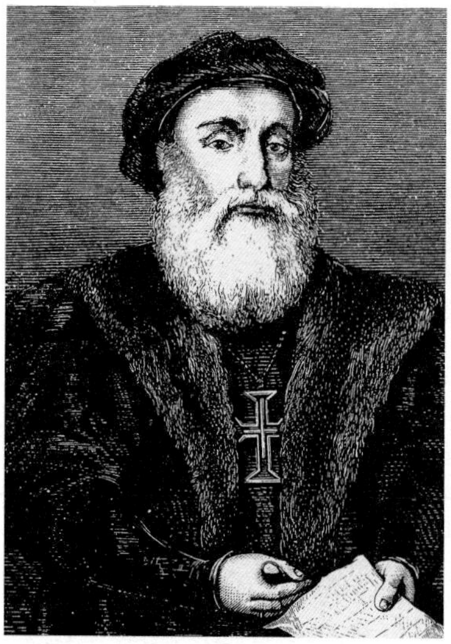

That is how the Portuguese chronicler Gaspar Correa recorded the dramatic events of Vasco da Gama's voyage. The Portuguese explorer sailed around the Cape of Good Hope at the southern tip of Africa to India in the late 1490s.

The voyage took tremendous courage. At one point, da Gama's four ships lost sight of land for 96 days. The sailors thought they were lost. The crew was panic-stricken with fear, and murmurings of mutiny worried the captain.

But da Gama did not turn back, despite storms, sickness, and food shortages. He reached India in May 1498, after 14 months at sea. In 1499, when he finally returned to Portugal, only 44 of the original 170 sailors still survived.

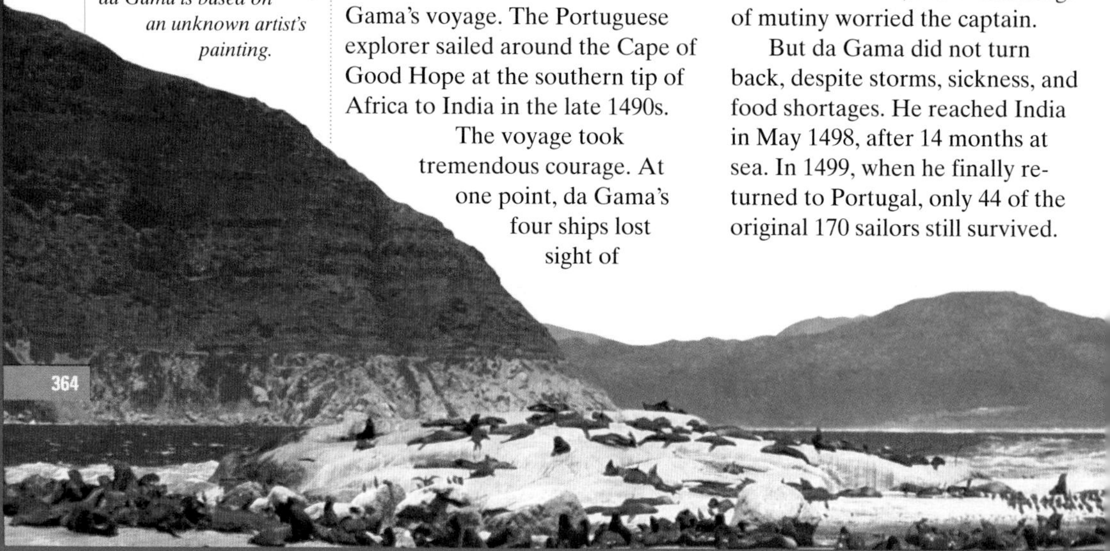

Objectives

1. Discuss some of the factors that spurred Europeans' interest in exploring.
2. Tell how European demand for products from the Far East encouraged exploration.
3. Assess the role of religion in spurring exploration.
4. Discuss why Spain and Portugal needed new sources of gold.

Graphic Overview

to expand world view
to acquire trade goods
to spread Christianity
to prevent monopolies
GOALS OF EUROPEAN EXPLORATION

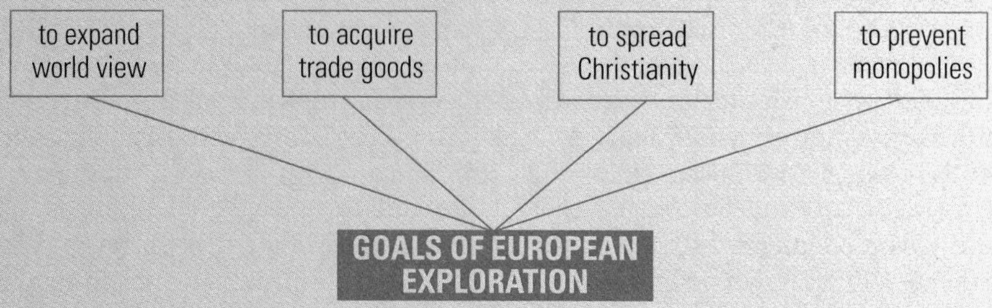

Finding the Way

Great advances in mapmaking helped explorers like Vasco da Gama. Between the late 1200s and 1500, geographers began to produce a more accurate picture of the world. They also developed new theories about its shape and size. And new information gathered by earlier world travelers and traders about the riches of far-away places kindled the desire for travel and exploration.

Early Exploration

Many people knew more about the world than the Europeans did. These included groups from China, India, Southeast Asia, Africa, and the Middle East. The Europeans' interest in exploration now grew. The crusades had shown many people the wider world. Towns were growing, as was trade. Also, the new universities brought advanced learning from Asia and Africa to the attention of Europeans. Marco Polo's written account of his travels was a popular book.

Firsthand observations, like those you have read about from Marco Polo and Ibn Battuta, also provided some mapmakers with valuable information. By the 1300s, pilots were using coastal charts, or portolans, that had been prepared according to information supplied by trading ship captains. These charts showed the sailing courses, ports, and anchorages that were mainly used by traders in the Mediterranean Sea. Portolan charts eventually surpassed earlier maps in accuracy and reliability.

Although the quality of Portolan charts was improving all the time,

travelers needed still better maps. The slow development of understanding of ancient and medieval learning was starting to make a difference in travel to western Europeans.

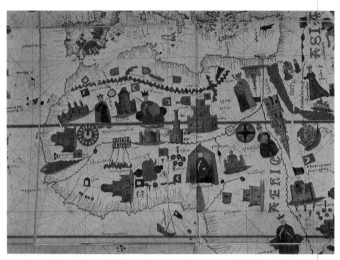

This map from 1493 locates sailing routes and anchorages along the West African coast as well as cities and kings in West Africa.

New Old Learning

The ancient observatory at Alexandria, the imperial geographers of Abbasid Baghdad, even the Byzantine sea traders gathered knowledge of geography, cartography, astronomy, and navigation. From the 1100s on, some translations of their work began filtering through to western Europe. Eventually it spread through the growing university towns of Paris, Padua, Oxford, and others. The T-O maps of medieval European cartographers showed the three known continents separated by T-shaped bodies of water and encircled by an O-shaped ocean. T-O maps were small and did not accurately represent locations. For an example of a

Across Time & Space

Mapmaking has come a long way since the rediscovery of Ptolemy's Geography. Airplanes make it possible to photograph large areas from the air and then map them. Artificial satellites can send pictures of still larger areas, even the whole earth.

The Cape of Good Hope can still be difficult to sail around today.

DEVELOP

Point out that this lesson describes four reasons why the Europeans began to explore new lands. Draw the diagram shown in the Graphic Overview on the chalkboard. Tell students to copy the diagram, fill in the central ideas, and add details for each branch as they read the lesson.

GEOGRAPHY
Map and Globe Skills

Encourage students to study the map on this page. Ask them what the purpose of the map is. *(To show anchorages on the west coast of Africa.)* Let them hypothesize about the purpose of the lines. *(Probably compass settings for navigational purposes.)* Discuss the ways in which the map seems accurate and the ways in which it seems distorted. You may wish to ask them to compare this map to the map on p. 525 to help them make their judgments.

Access Strategy

Ask students to suggest places that are being explored today. *(Space, Antarctica, ocean floor.)* Have them describe some of the risks involved in exploring these areas. Ask them which, if any, of these frontiers they think is important enough to risk one's life to explore. Why? Compile a list of goals or potential rewards that students feel would make taking such a risk worthwhile. Let students discuss whether they think the benefits of exploring each of these frontiers outweigh

the risks. Point out that different people are motivated in many different ways to undertake challenges that others might find far too risky. Tell students to make a list as they read the lesson of the kinds of motivations that sparked the age of exploration.

Access Activity

Allow students to make a bulletin board display of risks that have paid off. The bulletin board should feature people who have taken risks, indicate what they did, and show or tell how the activity paid off. Have students work together to collect pictures, to arrange them, and to write captions to explain them.

■ *Accounts travelers gave of their journeys to distant places, the rediscovery of Ptolemy's maps and writings, and Muslim learning from Spain spurred Europeans' interest in exploring the world.*

► *Genoa, Venice, and Naples.*

T-O map, see page 15 in Chapter 1.

In 1400, a patron brought to Florence the ancient text *Geography*, by the geographer Ptolemy *(TAHL uh mee)*. It was then translated and circulated. Written 1,250 years earlier, in A.D. 150, it contained a remarkably accurate map of the world known to the Romans at that time.

Most people still believed in Ptolemy's idea of how the heavens operated, too. The earth, which was round, was at the center of the uni-

■ *What developments between the late 1200s and 1500 spurred European interest in exploring the world?*

verse. The planets revolved around it. Arab, Persian, and other Muslim mathematicians created advanced calculations in order to be able to predict the locations of the planets. These calculations were necessary if one had to plot a course at sea without landmarks. Surprisingly, Ptolemy's system worked well for a thousand years. Our current understanding of how the planets revolve is now some 400 years old, and there are new discoveries all the time. ■

Meeting the Demand for Goods

In the 1300s and 1400s, many traders were willing to risk their lives for the wealth they would receive by satisfying the demand in Europe for luxury goods. Items such as eastern silks, cotton, dyes, and gems could

▼ *Which Italian ports were located at the western end of the east-west trade routes?*

be sold at high prices. The demand for spices was especially strong. Find out more about the spice trade in A Closer Look on page 367.

Goods from the East were brought by camel caravan or ship.

Eurasian Trade Routes Before Europe's Age of Exploration

Trade route

Map and Globe Skills

Have students use the map of trade routes to locate the sources of eastern trade goods. Ask them how geography helped the people of the Middle East to become the leading long-distance traders. *(Well-situated to control both land and sea traffic between east and west markets.)* Ask how geography favored the Italians. *(Central location, many good seaports.)*

Economic Context

In addition to Antioch and Alexandria, many other cities throughout the Middle East profited from east-west trade. Merchants from as far away as China gathered in places like Jiddeh, a port city on the Red Sea. A merchant named Varthema described Jiddeh in 1503:

"[I saw] a marveylous number of strangers and pylgryms of whiche some came from Syria, some from Persia and others from both [India and] the East Indies. . . . From India . . .

they have pearles, precious stones and plentie of spyces and especially from Bangalla they have a very large quantity of cotton and silks. . . . In the lower part of the Temple were fyve or six thousande men that sell none other thyng than sweete oyntments and from hence all manner of sweet savours are carried into the countryes of all the Mohumetans [Muslims]."

The Spice Trade

Europeans wanted more spice in their lives. Tired of bland food, nobles used spices to lend their dishes an exotic flavor. Spices were expensive because they were rare and passed through many hands on their way to market. The demand for tasty products pushed out the boundaries of the known world, as explorers rushed to find new routes to the spice lands.

Marco Polo in Pepperland shows the explorer helping to harvest the precious berries. Marco Polo tasted pepper for the first time in the East and brought some back to Europe in the 13th century. At one time in England, peppercorns were so valuable they were counted out one by one, and used as money.

Pepper plant, pepper berries, and dried peppercorns—native to India

One of the earliest known spices, pepper became popular because its fiery bite overpowered the taste of spoiled food.

Cinnamon—native to the island of Sri Lanka

Cloves —dried flowerbuds of a tree from Southeast Asia

Merchants, sailing ships like this one, traded Arabian frankincense for Indian pepper.

Peppercorns in meat

More About the Spice Trade

Sometimes eastern merchants made up stories about spices to prevent others from finding out where they grew and how to grow them for themselves. The Chinese claimed that cassia, a spice like cinnamon, was guarded by huge bats in the swamps where it grew. Arabs warned that the aroma in the frankincense fields was so powerful it regularly killed the slaves sent to tend it.

More About the Ship
The 300-year-old ship is carrying frankincense and pepper along the southeast coast of the Arabian Peninsula. The owner's family has traded spice for generations, using this same ship. Arabs have traded in spices for thousands of years. The Romans obtained much of their spice and incense from Arabian traders.

367

Research

Ask your students to name all the spices they can think of besides pepper, cinnamon, and cloves. List these on the chalkboard. Assign one spice to each student and have him or her research the spice's history and its geographical origin. Each student should give a brief oral report on the results.

Visual Learning

In the upper right corner, students can see how pepper looks when it is fresh and when it is dried. Have students research what other spices and condiments look like in their natural state. What does sugar or mustard look like before it comes to the table, and how is it prepared?

Costs of Spices, c.1350 and Today

A.D. 1350 at Master Craftsperson's Wages

One Pound

Cinnamon
Ginger
Pepper

0 1 2 3 4 5 6 7 8 9 10 11 12 13 14
Days

Today at Minimum Wage

One Pound

Cinnamon
Ginger
Pepper

0 1 2 3 4 5 6
Hours

⬆ *This chart compares the amount of time it would have taken to earn enough money to buy these luxury items in 1350 with the amount to time it takes today. Which item is now the most expensive?*

◼ *How did Europeans obtain goods from the East?*

➤ *Ginger.*

◼ *Eastern goods were brought by ship to ports on the Mediterranean such as Antioch, Alexandria, Venice, and Genoa after having been traded many times along the way. The Italians transported most Eastern goods from the Mediterranean throughout Europe.*

Critical Thinking

After students answer the comprehension question in the margin, ask them why Europeans in the late 1300s were no longer satisfied with purchasing eastern goods from Italian merchants. *(These goods were expensive because of the Italian monopoly.)*

Along the way to ports such as Antioch and Alexandria the goods changed hands many times. Each trader covered only a portion of the route and then sold his cargo to the next trader.

Each trader in the long relay through Eurasia raised the price in order to make a profit. Thus, by the time a piece of silk reached the Mediterranean, it might cost more than 100 times its original price.

In the bustling Mediterranean ports, cargoes from the East were loaded onto Italian merchant ships for the passage to Europe. Italian port cities such as Venice and Genoa played a key role in east-west trade.

Because their location was central to Mediterranean markets, the Italian city-states had long been home to the best seafarers, navigators, and shipbuilders in the West. Moreover, Italian merchants had long been involved in overseas trade with commercial centers in Muslim countries. As a result, Italian cities had flourished since the 1100s.

Venice was all-powerful in the eastern Mediterranean, while Genoa dominated western Mediterranean trade in the early 1300s. However, in the late 1300s, the two cities waged war to determine which of them would command trade on the Black Sea and the Aegean Sea. Despite some crushing defeats in battle, Venice maintained a **monopoly,** or complete control, over trade with the East. ◼

Carrying Christianity Across the Sea

Europeans sought goods and profit, but they also wanted to spread Christianity among non-believers in other parts of the world. Some Christian explorers also hoped to find a mythical king named Prester John, who was rumored to rule a Christian kingdom in Africa or Asia. According to legend, Prester John had successfully defended his kingdom from Muslim attack. From the 1100s on, the Portuguese spent great amounts of time, energy, and resources looking for this potential ally in the fight against the Muslims.

The Spanish and Portuguese had long been waging religious warfare against Islam. Since the early 700s, Muslims had invaded and occupied much of Spain and what would later become Portugal. Many battles were fought against the Muslims, but they were not finally driven out of southern Spain until 1492.

Chapter 14

Critical Thinking

Have students define and give examples of a monopoly. *(Only dentist in town.)* Ask who profits from a monopoly and who might suffer from it and why. *(Owner benefits; consumers may suffer high prices, poor quality or service, lack of variety, limited supply.)* Which monopolies are beneficial, common, or necessary? *(Printing money, utilities.)*

Economic Context

The wealth that accumulated in Italian trading centers, including Venice, Genoa, and Florence, led to the rise of modern capitalism. This was because private individuals, not the church or the government, accumulated money from trade. These individuals used their money to make more money. Some invested their profits in industry. Others lent out their accumulated money and charged fees. This practice, begun in 14th-century Italy, led to the rise of the banking industry.

These religious wars influenced Spanish and Portuguese exploration. If people in newly discovered regions converted to Christianity, Spain and Portugal would have new allies in the fight against Islam. This was one reason missionaries usually accompanied the expeditions that explored or settled new regions.

Missionaries used education to convert the nonbelievers to Christianity. In the 1600s, Jesuit missionaries in China studied Chinese language and culture to better understand the people they wanted to convert. They also helped teach the Chinese and Europeans about each other's civilizations.

However, other missionaries were not so gentle. Some used

torture to subdue nonbelievers in foreign lands. For instance, 16th-century missionaries in Central and South America forced native inhabitants to work on church-owned farms. This outraged many Christians. Bartolomé de Las Casas, a defender of the rights of the natives, wrote a book on acceptable methods of conversion. An excerpt from his work follows.

*H*earers, especially pagans, should understand that the preachers of the faith have no intention of acquiring power over them through their preaching. . . . [They] should understand that no desire for riches moves [preachers] to preach. . . . In speaking and conversing with their hearers, especially pagans, the preachers should show themselves so mild and humble, courteous and . . . good-willed that the hearers eagerly wish to listen and hold their teaching in greater reverence.

Las Casas, *The "Only Method" of Converting the Indians,* 1530s

While missionaries on exploratory expeditions sought to make new converts, many of the explorers leading these expeditions were searching for new gold markets. If Spanish and Portuguese explorers could find new sources of gold, their governments might be able to break up the Venetian monopoly on trade. ∎

◄ *This 1422 painting is of a Jesuit missionary-astronomer who predicted an eclipse of the sun in China. The Chinese ruler ordered the missionary to teach his people Western science.*

∎ *What role did religion play during the new era of European exploration?*

Searching for New Markets

The Venetians delivered their cargoes of spices and other eastern goods by land or by sea to cities throughout Europe. In exchange for the eastern imports, Europeans exported wool, linen, timber, tin,

Social Participation

Divide students into small groups to have them discuss the ideas of Bartolomé de Las Casas on conversion. To start the discussion, you may wish to have a volunteer read the primary source on this page aloud to the class.

∎ *The explorers hoped to win new believers for Christianity who would help them in the fight against Islam.*

Language Arts Connection

Have students work in small groups to research legends that spurred explorers or scientists to venture into unknown regions. Suggested legends include Prester John, the Fountain of Youth, El Dorado, the Holy Grail, the Loch Ness Monster, the Abominable Snowman.

Cultural Context

In about 1498, Christopher Columbus asked Spanish rulers for these foods for a voyage to America: biscuits, salted flour, wheat, salted meat and fish, oil, vinegar, cheese, chickpeas, lentils, beans, honey, rice, almonds, and raisins. Water and wine were the only drinks mentioned in his journal. The absence of fresh fruits and vegetables caused many sailors on long voyages to suffer from scurvy. It caused the death of 100 of Vasco da Gama's crew of 170 men.

Critical Thinking

Ask students to imagine themselves as missionaries in a foreign land in the 1400s. What obstacles would confront them? *(No common language, few books or pictures to use as teaching aids, little knowledge about the culture or beliefs of the people you want to convert.)* How would they address those issues?

Visual Learning

Ask students to make diagrams or drawings to illustrate the concept of the balance of trade. Set aside time so that students can show their drawings and explain them to the class. Let students vote to select the drawing or diagram that best illustrates the concept.

■ *The Portuguese sought African sources of gold, grain, and produce to break the Italian monopoly on trade and to help maintain their balance of trade with other nations.*

CLOSE

Have students add specific details to the diagram in the Graphic Overview to answer the Thinking Focus. Students should include details such as better maps, desire to learn about the world, and the search for Prester John as they clarify each of the four central ideas.

370

copper, lead, and guns. Above all, some European countries needed gold to buy imported goods.

Portugal and Spain were active participants in east-west trade. However, the total cost of the goods Portugal imported was often higher than the total value of the goods it exported. Thus, the Portuguese government frequently owed a trade debt to other governments. Portugal had to pay these governments to maintain the **balance of trade,** or the difference between the total value of exports and the total value of imports. European trading countries demanded payment of debts in gold, which often took the form of **bullion.** Bullion was gold that had been melted and then molded into ingots, or bars, of specific weights.

As eastern imports increased, the Portuguese government needed more gold to pay for the goods. Portugal and Spain obtained most of their gold from North African traders at high prices. These traders had bought the gold from central and southern African gold producers and then carried it by caravan across the Sahara. Portugal wanted to bypass the North African traders and deal directly with the source, the gold producers. By trading directly, they could obtain gold more cheaply. So, in 1419, Portuguese explorers began sailing south along the west coast of Africa in search of gold markets.

Portugal needed gold, but it also needed good farmland and workers to cultivate the land. Nobles wanted to claim farmland in overseas regions to increase their wealth. And traders were eager to find new supplies of agricultural produce to sell in Portugal.

Eventually, some Portuguese began to hope for an even greater reward than gold and land: a sea route to the East. If they sailed directly to India and China, Portuguese traders could buy goods at their source and sell them in Europe at huge profits. Portugal could then break the Italian monopoly on east-west trade. Finding a sea route to the East and establishing a direct trading connection became the goal of many European explorers. ■

▲ *Gold bullion is still used by countries today to pay debts and to settle accounts.*

■ *Why did Portugal want to find new markets?*

REVIEW

1. **FOCUS** Why did explorers risk their lives to explore parts of the world that were unknown to them?
2. **CONNECT** Travelers in the age of exploration began to view the world in new ways. How was their view of the world similar to that of thinkers during the Reformation and the Scientific Revolution?
3. **ECONOMICS** Why did the Portuguese want to find new sources of gold?
4. **BELIEF SYSTEMS** What did European Christians hope to achieve by exploring unknown lands?
5. **CRITICAL THINKING** Many "explorers" "discovered" places that were already thoroughly known to the people who lived there. What are the real meanings of the words "explore" and "discover"?
6. **ACTIVITY** Hide a book or other object. Then draw a map that could be used to direct someone to the object's discovery. Be sure to indicate the proper positions and directions of things and places indicated on your map. Finally, see if a friend can use the map to find the object.

370

Chapter 14

Homework Options

Have students select one section of lesson, such as "Searching for New Markets," and outline or graphically map the information presented.

Study Guide: p. 59

Answers to Review Questions

1. Many Europeans sought goods or profit. Others wished to spread Christianity.
2. During the Reformation and the Scientific Revolution, people sought knowledge based on experience. Likewise, the early explorers wanted to expand their knowledge of the world through firsthand experience.
3. Gold carried across the Sahara by North African traders was expensive. The Portuguese hoped to trade directly with gold producers to obtain gold more cheaply.
4. Christian explorers hoped to convert non-believers to Christianity and find new allies in the fight against Islam.
5. Exploring and discovering have to do with seeking beyond the new horizons one's current knowledge. Europeans who sailed to distant seas in the 1500s and 1600s did this, even though other peoples already knew the regions.

| 1250 | 1300 | 1350 | 1400 | | 1600 |

1415   **1550**

L E S S O N   2

Adventure and Profit

P rince Henry of Portugal, or "Henry the Navigator" as he was known, was a leader in the early years of European exploration. In 1453, a historian described him as a curious and adventurous man.

T he noble spirit of this Prince was ever urging him both to begin and to carry out very great deeds. . . .. He had also a wish to know the land that lay beyond the isles of Canary and that Cape called Bojador [BAHJ uh dawr], for that up to his time, neither by writings, nor by the memory of man, was known with any certainty the nature of the land beyond that Cape. . . . It seemed to him that if he or some other lord did not endeavor to gain that knowledge, no mariners or merchants would ever dare to attempt it, for it is clear that none of them ever trouble themselves to sail to a place where there is not a sure and certain hope of profit.

Gomes Eannes de Azurara, from
Discovery and Conquest of Guinea, 1453

Prince Henry was determined to overcome the fear surrounding Cape Bojador. And the unknown beyond the Cape fascinated him.

THINKING
F O C U S

How did Prince Henry's center for navigation help establish Portugal's trading empire in the 1500s?

Key Terms

- caravel
- capital
- colony

◄ *Prince Henry leads troops against the Muslim city of Ceuta in this painting from the 1400s. While in Ceuta, Henry became intrigued by descriptions of Africa's wealth.*

Prince Henry, Navigator

Henry could not guarantee that Portugal would profit from his exploration along the west coast of Africa. But he could vouch that gold and other luxury goods could be found in Africa. In 1415, he had been a crusader in the Muslim port city Ceuta *(SAY oo tah)* in North Africa. He had seen vast quantities of gold, silver, and grain, magnificent silks and tapestries, and fragrant spices. Camel caravans from sub-Saharan Africa brought these sumptuous goods to Ceuta.

371

The Age of Exploration

INTRODUCE

H ave students use the lesson title, the Thinking Focus, and the picture on this page to guess what sort of man Prince Henry was. *(Leader, soldier, well-educated.)* Ask for what reasons a man like Prince Henry might want to explore. *(Students should recall four reasons from Lesson 1: knowledge, religion, new markets, access to cheaper goods.)* Tell them to read the first section to learn which of these reasons was most important to Henry.

Key Terms

Vocabulary Strategies: T36–T37
caravel—a swift, maneuverable sailing ship used for exploration by the Spanish and the Portuguese in the 1500s and 1600s
capital—wealth in the form of money or property used for the production of more wealth
colony—a settlement in a distant land whose citizens keep close ties to their parent country

Graphic Overview

| Prince Henry establishes navigational school at Sagres, Portugal. | → | European shipbuilding, mapmaking, and geographic knowledge improve. | → | The Portuguese sail around the coast of Africa. | → | The Portuguese increase their trade network and establish colonies. |

Objectives

1. Discuss Prince Henry's role in early European exploration.
2. List important technological advances in navigation in the 1400s.
3. Describe Portugal's exploration of the African coast and its effect on trade.
4. Explain the economic significance of establishing colonial settlements.

DEVELOP

State that this lesson will describe how Henry's interest in exploration eventually led to the building of the Portuguese trade empire. Draw the Graphic Overview on the chalkboard to illustrate the structure of the lesson. Refer students to the map on p. 374. Point out that it took 15 years for Henry's expeditions to round Cape Bojador. Emphasize that Henry's dedication and preparation for exploration were historically far more significant than the short range of his expeditions indicates.

GEOGRAPHY
Map and Globe Skills

Have students use a map of modern Europe to locate Sagres on Cape St. Vincent. Ask them to explain why this town was so important during the early years of exploration. How did its geographic location contribute to its significance? (*At the southwestern tip of Portugal, it was ideally located for study of seafaring on the Atlantic.*)

■ *Henry founded a center for the improvement of shipbuilding, navigation, and mapmaking; and organized and financed voyages down the African coast.*

372

▲ *This astrolabe dates to 1532. G. Hartmann, the name of the maker, is inscribed on it.*

➤ *This woodcut of a mapmaker in his study shows the tools he used. The lodestone shown on the small, round table had magnetic properties and so served as a compass.*

■ *Why was Prince Henry of Portugal nicknamed "the Navigator"?*

372

Henry hoped to find the source of African gold by sailing south along the coast. He hoped to find new markets and new goods for Portugal as well. Perhaps he would even find the legendary Prester John or new believers for the Christian faith.

Henry was an unusual man—intensely religious and fascinated by the mystery beyond known boundaries. When he left Ceuta, he did not return to Lisbon and the luxurious life of a prince. Rather, Henry sailed to the small town of Sagres (*SAH greesh*)

on Cape St. Vincent, the southernmost point of Portugal. There, on the rocky, windswept peninsula, Henry established a center for navigation and exploration. He summoned shipbuilders, mapmakers, sea captains, and instrument makers from all over Europe to live and study in Sagres.

Henry also invited sailors, travelers, and scholars from Europe, Africa, and the Middle East to share their geographical knowledge. He financed expeditions to West Africa. Bit by bit, Henry's scholars added information to the maps developed at Sagres. ■

Preparations for Sailing

Explorers needed more than improved maps to find their way to unknown destinations in Africa and beyond. Out on the open sea, they had only the sun, moon, and stars to guide them. Ocean-going seafarers also had to deal with unpredictable winds and unseen

currents that could send them far off course. They didn't know what hardships lay ahead of them or how long it might take to get to their destination.

Prince Henry's experts improved and adapted for navigation such instruments as the compass

Chapter 14

Access Activity

Read aloud from a brochure describing a cruise on an ocean liner. Have students list the facilities such a ship must have. (*Electricity, water and sewer systems, communication systems, area for recreation and accommodations.*) Then ask them to speculate as to how the voyages of the early explorers differed from such a cruise.

Access Strategy

Ask students to imagine that they are planning an exploratory expedition to an unknown region in the late 1400s. What kinds of resources will they require to carry out their plan? (*Reliable means of transportation, directions to their destination, supplies for the trip, people to accompany the expedition.*) Ask students how they might finance the trip. (*Use personal funds, ask investors for money, ask government for money.*) What questions would investors have about the expedition?

(*What is the purpose? What can I expect in return for my money? Are you likely to be successful?*) What sorts of problems might be encountered along the way? (*Bad weather, technical breakdowns, getting lost, running low on supplies.*) Help students to recognize what great courage, conviction, resources, and resourcefulness were necessary to undertake voyages of exploration.

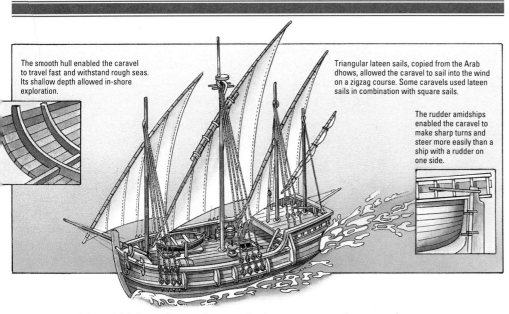

The smooth hull enabled the caravel to travel fast and withstand rough seas. Its shallow depth allowed in-shore exploration.

Triangular lateen sails, copied from the Arab dhows, allowed the caravel to sail into the wind on a zigzag course. Some caravels used lateen sails in combination with square sails.

The rudder amidships enabled the caravel to make sharp turns and steer more easily than a ship with a rudder on one side.

and the astrolabe, which is used to determine latitude. They also devised methods that would help guide a ship when it sailed out of sight of land. For example, they designed mathematical tables that could be used to determine latitude from the angle of the North Star or the sun's elevation. A cross-staff measured this angle. A sailor held the long shaft of the cross-staff to his eye and pointed the instrument heavenward. He then moved the crosspiece until the horizon was at one end and the star was at the other. The sailor measured the angle that the cross-piece formed and used the mathematical table to determine his location's latitude.

Henry also required his sailors to keep accurate accounts of all the things they saw while sailing along a coastline. This information was added to information brought by travelers and scholars invited to Sagres to make maps more accurate.

In addition, Henry's ship designers built a new kind of ship better suited to voyages on the open sea. The ships used for coastal trade had square sails and steering oars. These ships were hard to maneuver on the open sea and had difficulty tacking, or changing course, with the wind.

Prince Henry's ship designers borrowed the best features from other sailing vessels to create the swift and maneuverable **caravel,** which is pictured above. This vessel was large enough to hold the supplies for a crew of about 20. One Venetian seaman called it "the best ship that sailed the seas." The caravel became the standard ship of explorers of the 1400s and 1500s.

▲ *The caravel's ability to sail into the wind meant the vessel also had the ability to return its passengers home. Explorers going out in a caravel were more willing to risk longer voyages.*

▼ *Prince Henry could not improve the food his explorers ate on their voyages. Foods like the cheese, salt pork, and oats shown here often spoiled as a result of the ship's dampness.*

Critical Thinking

Refer students to the picture of the caravel. Have students explain how the caravel serves as proof of interaction among different cultures in the 1400s. *(It exhibits features from Arab and northern European ships.)*

Science Connection

A knot is a modern unit of speed used for ships and airplanes. It equals one nautical mile per hour, or 1.15 land miles per hour. A plane traveling at 100 knots will cover 100 nautical miles or 115 land miles in one hour. The term *knot* comes from a device called a log line that was developed in the late 1500s to measure a ship's speed. A log or board was attached to a cord that was knotted at fixed intervals of 47 feet 3 inches, or 7/1,000 of a nautical mile. Sailors dropped the log behind the ship and allowed the cord to play out for 28 seconds, or 7/1,000 of an hour, as the ship moved away from the board. The number of knots that passed over the edge of the ship equalled the ship's speed per hour: 5 knots = 5 nautical miles per hour. The readings from the log line were recorded in a special log-book. Today, the word *log* refers to a general record of a trip or voyage.

Visual Learning

Have students work in groups to make models or draw pictures of navigational instruments from the 1400s and 1500s. *(Examples: quadrant, cross-staff, compass, astrolabe, hourglass.)* Students should explain when their instrument was invented and for what purpose. If possible, students should demonstrate or explain its use.

■ *New navigation instruments (cross-staff, compass, and astrolabe), better maps, and the caravel made sea exploration possible.*

■ *What technological improvements made exploration by sea possible in the 1400s?*

On the open ocean, strong winds and currents made ships travel much faster than they did in the calmer areas along the shore. Speedier passage meant ships could travel farther on fewer supplies. ■

The Portuguese Explorations

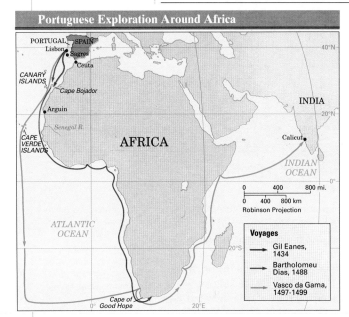

Portuguese Exploration Around Africa

Voyages
→ Gil Eanes, 1434
→ Bartholomeu Dias, 1488
→ Vasco da Gama, 1497–1499

▲ *Find Cape Bojador on the map. Do you think it was primarily a physical or mental barrier to the Portuguese explorers? Why was rounding the cape so important?*

Even with these technological advances, it took many years and many voyages before the seafarers of Portugal became experts on the open sea. The first expeditions down the African coast, organized and financed by Prince Henry, probably began around 1419. The goal of these voyages was to round the dreaded point of land called Cape Bojador, just south of the Canary Islands.

Arab geographers called the waters there the "Green Sea of Darkness" because of violent waves and currents, frequent fogs, strong winds, and dangerous shallows. Beyond Bojador was the unknown, feared by even the most daring and skillful seafarers. In 1453, the chronicler Azurara

explained why no ship had ventured beyond Cape Bojador.

[T]he mariners said] that beyond this Cape there is no race of men nor place of inhabitants . . . and the sea [is] so shallow that a whole league from land it is only a fathom [six feet] deep, while the currents are so terrible that no ship having once passed the Cape, will ever be able to return. . . .

Gomes Eannes de Azurara, from *Discovery and Conquest of Guinea, 1453*

By 1433, Henry had sent 15 expeditions to pass the cape, but each one returned to Sagres without success. Finally, in 1434, a Portuguese captain named Gil Eanes (*zhil YA nihsh*), rounded Bojador and landed on the African coast south of the cape. The barrier of fear had been broken.

Year by year, Henry sent ships farther down the African coast. In 1448, the explorers established the first Portuguese trading post at Arguin. Merchants there exchanged wheat, cloth, and glass beads for African gold, slaves, pepper, and ivory. By the time Prince Henry died in 1460, 25 caravels a year carried goods between Portugal and West Africa.

Later Portuguese rulers continued to support exploration of the West African coast. As the expeditions pushed down the coast, some rulers began to think it might be possible to sail all the way around

Chapter 14

Africa to the East. In 1485, the king of Portugal, Dom João *(zhwown)* II, announced that his ships would soon open up the sea route to India.

The king's hunch proved correct. In 1488, Bartholomeu Dias rounded the Cape of Good Hope at the southern tip of Africa. In 1498, Vasco da Gama became the first European to sail around Africa and reach the city of Calicut in India, proving the existence of a sea route to the East. ■

◄ *With this bronze figure, a West African artist "recorded" Portuguese exploration of his land. How do you think it reflects the West Africans' impression of the Portuguese explorers of the 1500s?*

■ *Why did the Portuguese want to explore the west coast of Africa?*

◄ *Students might respond that to the West Africans the Portuguese might have seemed evil, threatening, or hostile.*

■ *The Portuguese wanted to explore the west coast of Africa to increase trade and to find a new sea route to the East.*

Commerce and Colonies

Long-distance voyages like those of da Gama and Dias were expensive and risky. Explorers needed huge sums of money to build ships and equip their expeditions, which often lasted several years. Thus, the first problem most explorers faced was finding someone to finance their voyages.

Investing in Overseas Trade

Prince Henry, a wealthy member of the royal family, paid for his early projects with his own money. However, eventually it became clear that trade with Africa could be highly profitable. Then Portuguese kings and wealthy merchants were willing to contribute **capital,** or money and materials, to finance later voyages. But the large fleets that sailed to the East after da Gama's first voyage in 1498 required more money than the Portuguese could supply.

To finance these longer voyages, Portuguese investors turned to foreign bankers in southern Germany and the Italian city-states of Genoa and Florence. In exchange for their investment, the bankers became part owners of the valuable cargoes. When their agents sold the goods in Europe, the bankers often received more than twice as much money as they had invested.

Establishing Colonies

The Portuguese lost a large percentage of their profits to foreign investors. But Portugal profited from exploration by establishing **colonies,** or settlements of their own citizens, in the lands they explored.

Prince Henry's voyagers had discovered several uninhabited islands off the coast of West Africa between 1419 and 1470. Among these were Madeira, the Cape Verde Islands, and São Tomé *(sown tuh MAY)*. The Portuguese sent settlers to these islands to grow sugar and wheat for export back to Portugal.

Crusaders had created a demand for sugar in Europe after tasting it in the Middle East during the 1000s. As a result, Italian merchants established huge farms, called plantations, on several

ECONOMICS

Study Skills

Direct students to prepare a diagram showing the flow of capital due to the establishment of Portuguese colonies. Diagrams could include the source of capital for the voyages, the return investors received on their money, the effect on the Venetian spice trade, the source of capital for setting up colonies, the return on the crops exported, and the reinvestment of the profits. Students might use arrows of various thicknesses to indicate the relative size of investments and returns.

375

Geographical Context

Portuguese traders found only scattered fishing villages along the West African coast. Since civilizations in this area traded via the trans-Saharan caravan routes rather than via the Atlantic, major cities were located in the interior. However, in time, the increased flow of gold to Europe via Portuguese ships led to the gradual decline of the trans-Saharan caravan routes.

Reader's Theater

Have students work in small groups to research the accomplishments of one of the men who sailed for Portugal in the 1400s: Gil Eanes, Bartholomeu Dias, Vasco da Gama, or Diego Cao. Have students choose one significant event in the explorer's life, such as reaching his goal, surviving hardships at sea, or announcing success or failure to a king or other sponsor. Students should write a script depicting that event, assign roles, and perform their piece for the class.

Map and Globe Skills

Tell students to trace both the land and sea routes from India to Europe using the maps on pp. 366 and 374. Have them estimate the total length of each complete route. Discuss why goods transported by Portuguese ships were cheaper than goods sent overland. *(Middlemen along land routes raised prices.)*

Mediterranean islands and grew sugar. These merchants brought slaves from Russia and Africa to the islands to cultivate and harvest the sugar.

During the 1400s, Portuguese explorers bought, traded, and

▲ *The sugar obtained from sugar cane stalks such as these remained a luxury throughout the 1700s. Sugar was often listed with diamonds among the gifts given to European monarchs.*

captured African slaves. Many of these slaves were shipped to Europe. Many others were sent to Portuguese colonies to work on the sugar plantations. Frequently, colonists enslaved the islands' native inhabitants and forced them to work on the plantations.

The European demand for sugar, however, soon exceeded the supply the plantations could produce. Sugar could, therefore, be sold in Europe at a very high price. Since the price paid for the sugar far surpassed the cost of growing it, plantation owners made great profits. They used these profits to buy more slaves and expand their sugar plantations. As a result, by 1550, the

■ *How did Portugal profit from the colonies it established off the coast of West Africa?*

island of São Tomé was producing 30 times as much sugar as it had produced in 1530.

Trading in the East

The early Portuguese traders were also active in the East. In the early 1500s, they established naval bases and trading stations at strategic locations along the eastern spice routes. They hoped to ruin the Venetian spice trade by preventing Arab and Indian merchants from carrying spices overland to Egyptian and Syrian ports.

Meanwhile, Portuguese fleets brought gold and Indian cotton to trade in busy spice ports such as Malacca, on the south coast of Malaysia. These important trade ports are shown on the map of trade routes on page 366.

Although Portuguese explorers conquered important port cities such as Malacca, Goa in India, and Hormuz in the Middle East, they never completely cut off the Venetian spice trade. Many Arab and Indian merchants continued to use traditional routes to trade with Venetian merchants in the Mediterranean. However, Portugal's conquests in the East and in the Atlantic enabled it to control a large part of eastern trade for nearly 100 years. ■

REVIEW

1. **FOCUS** How did Prince Henry's center for navigation help establish Portugal's trading empire in the 1500s?
2. **CONNECT** Why did Prince Henry want to find a new source of African gold for Portugal?
3. **HISTORY** Why weren't technological advances enough to launch the new era of European exploration?
4. **ECONOMICS** Why was the tiny island of São Tomé important to the Portuguese?

5. **CRITICAL THINKING** If you were a Portuguese ruler in the 1400s, would you support exploration? Why or why not?
6. **ACTIVITY** Make a timeline of the explorers of the great age of European discovery. Add other explorers by looking at "Exploration" on page 514 in the Minipedia.

Chapter 14

Left sidebar

■ *It increased its direct trade with the Africans and set up plantations to grow sugar for export to Europe.*

CLOSE

Have students write or talk about each illustration in this lesson. Students should identify the person or object, give an approximate date, and tell how the illustration relates to the history of exploration. Then have students illustrate each stage in the process of exploration given in the Graphic Overview.

Homework Options

Have students draw and illustrate a timeline showing important events in the early years of European exploration.

Answers to Review Questions

1. Advances in the science of navigation made at Prince Henry's center enabled the Portuguese to send the first expeditions down the African coast. These voyages led to the opening of the route to the East, which, in turn, helped Portugal to establish its trading empire.
2. The Portuguese needed gold to help pay for their imports. Henry wanted to find the source of African gold so that Portugal could obtain it more cheaply.
3. Seafaring explorers had to overcome the fear of the unknown and obtain financial backing for their expeditions.
4. The Portuguese set up plantations on São Tóme. They produced sugar economically and sold it at great profit in Europe.
5. Answers will vary. Students should mention that rulers had to weigh risks and expenses against the potential benefits.

1250   1300   1350   1400   1451   1600

L E S S O N   3

Exploring the Americas

Columbus's plan was so exciting, and hiring on as a ship's boy seemed like such a good idea at the time. You were ready for an adventure. But how could you have known that it would be like this?

You work hard, the days are monotonous, and you're not sure if you will ever see home again. It's been 52 days since you left Spain, but there's no land in sight. . . .

The last grains of sand slip through the sandglass. Another half hour gone. You turn the glass. Ring the bell. Make your mark. One more mark to go, then your four-hour watch is over.

Waves rock the ship. Sleep is impossible now. Whoever sees land first will receive 10,000 maravedis.

Enough to change your life, at least for a little while.

A dark twig bobs in the foamy water. A small flock of birds passes overhead, moving southwest. The captain must be right. Land must be near. The sun on the water hurts your eyes as you strain to make out a tree, a hill, a sandy beach. Nothing. Just green sea.

The glass is empty. You turn the glass. Ring the bell. Make your mark. Rodrigo takes over the glass. The new watch charts the speed of the bobbing twig in the green sea.

There's space on deck in the shade of the mast. A short nap might stop the burning in your eyes. Maybe later you'll lower a line and catch a fish for dinner. You close your eyes and dream of home.

THINKING FOCUS

What role did Christopher Columbus's voyages play in the colonization of North America?

Key Term

• circumnavigation

◄ *When the sand measuring the last half-hour of a seaman's watch ran out of the glass, he'd call the next men on duty: "On deck, on deck, gentlemen mariners of the starboard watch . . . shake a leg!"*

Christopher Columbus

Like the boy described above, but about 30 years earlier, Christopher Columbus probably began his seafaring career as a ship's boy.

Although very little is known about his early life, most scholars think that Columbus was born in Genoa, Italy, in 1451.

377

The Age of Exploration

INTRODUCE

Direct students to read the lesson title and Thinking Focus. Point out that while the Portuguese were sailing eastward to India, Columbus was trying to sail westward to the same goal. Ask students who they think was more successful in reaching the goal and which aim was more significant in history. Have students read to confirm or reject their predictions.

Key Term

Vocabulary Strategies: T36–T37
circumnavigation—the act of sailing around the world

377

Graphic Overview

WHY EUROPEANS WENT TO AMERICA

Search for Western Sea Route to Asia

Atlantic route

Northwest Passage

Set Up Plantations and Settle New Lands

South America

North America

Caribbean

Objectives

1. Discuss Columbus's goals in sailing westward.
2. Evaluate the impact of the early Spanish contacts with Indians in the Americas.
3. Describe early European explorations in North America.

DEVELOP

Point out that this lesson will describe some of the highlights of the European exploration and colonization of the Americas. Draw the branching diagram in the Graphic Overview on the chalkboard. Point out that the reasons for trans-Atlantic expeditions changed between 1492 and the 1600s.

► *Magellan.*

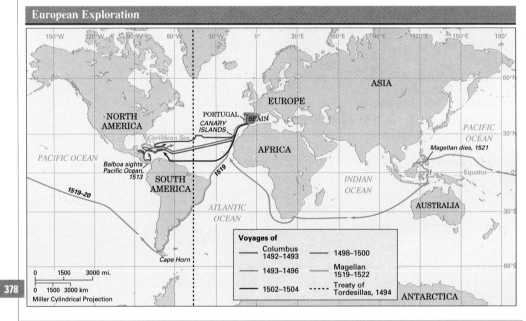

▲ *Columbus's notes in a geography book (now in a Seville library) show that he forgot that his and al-Faraghani's "miles" were different lengths.*

▼ *Both Columbus and Magellan sailed west. Which one found a westward route to India?*

While still a young man, Columbus became a seaman on Genoese merchant vessels. When he was 25 years old, Columbus was shipwrecked off the coast of Portugal. By good fortune, he landed close to Sagres and Prince Henry's center for navigators. Columbus decided to stay. For eight years Columbus read books about geography, history, and travel. He studied the charts of Portuguese pilots who had sailed to Africa's west coast. He calculated that the distance from Spain to Asia would be no more than 4000 miles. It is, in fact, about 15,000 miles, with the Americas in between. Columbus misunderstood the unit of measure used in 861 by the Muslim astronomer al-Faraghani, when he calculated the earth's circumference (and fell short by less than one mile!).

In 1484, Columbus asked the Portuguese rulers to finance his voyage. When they refused, Columbus turned to King Ferdinand and Queen Isabella of Spain. They rejected his idea at first, but finally, in 1492, agreed to pay for the expedition.

On August 3, 1492, Columbus set sail from Palos, Spain, with three ships and 88 men. After eight weeks at sea, the crew feared that they would never see land again. They were afraid that the strong east winds would prevent them from sailing back home. On September 24, Columbus made the following entry in his journal.

European Exploration

(map)

ASIA
EUROPE
PORTUGAL SPAIN
NORTH AMERICA
CANARY ISLANDS
Caribbean Sea
PACIFIC OCEAN
AFRICA
PACIFIC OCEAN
Magellan dies, 1521
Balboa sights Pacific Ocean, 1513
SOUTH AMERICA
1519
INDIAN OCEAN
1519–20
Equator
AUSTRALIA
ATLANTIC OCEAN
Cape Horn
ANTARCTICA

Voyages of
Columbus
1492–1493 ———
1493–1496 ———
1502–1504 ———
1498–1500 ———
Magellan 1519–1522 ———
Treaty of Tordesillas, 1494 - - - -

0 1500 3000 mi.
0 1500 3000 km
Miller Cylindrical Projection

378

Chapter 14

Access Activity

Read the first section of Lesson 3 aloud to the class. Ask volunteers to mime the actions described. Then talk about what might have happened on the next few watches. Have volunteers mime these scenes. Discuss the combination of boredom and excitement Columbus's crew might have felt on the voyage.

Access Strategy

Tell students to imagine that they have the opportunity to work as ship's boys on one of Columbus's ships. They know that their captain is a good mariner whose plan to reach the East by sailing west has gained the support of the king and queen of Spain. But they don't know just where they are going, how to get there, how long the trip will take, what dangers they will encounter enroute, whether they will have enough food during the trip, what they will find at the end of their voyage, or whether they will ever see home again. If Columbus is right, they will have the chance to make money by using their wages to purchase some goods to sell at home. If Columbus is wrong, they might die at sea. Ask students if they would join the expedition. Have them give reasons why they might have been willing to participate in such an adventure.

I am having trouble with the crew, . . . complaining that they will never be able to return home. They have said that it is insanity and suicidal on their part to risk their lives following the madness of a foreigner. . . . I am told by a few trusted men (and these are few in number!) that if I persist in going onward, the best course of action will be to throw me into the sea some night.

Christopher Columbus,
from his journal, 1492

Despite this threat of mutiny, Columbus stayed on course. Two hours after midnight on October 12—two very long months after they'd set sail—land was sighted. At dawn, the sailors went ashore. They named the new land San Salvador and claimed it for Spain.

San Salvador is a small island in the Bahamas, located about 50 miles off the east coast of Florida. Columbus thought he had landed on an island off the coast of Japan or China. Columbus also visited two other islands: Cuba, which he believed to be part of China, and Hispaniola. People knew within 30 years of his expedition that Columbus had not discovered a westward route to India. But people continued to call the native inhabitants of America "Indians" and the islands he reached the "West Indies."

The name "America" was chosen by Alsatian geographer Martin Waldseemüller (*VAHLT say myoo lur*), when he laid out a new map of the world in 1507. Amerigo Vespucci (*vehs POO chee*) made voyages after Columbus, and while Columbus died forgotten, Vespucci wrote a best-selling book about "the New World." ■

How Do We Know?

HISTORY *On his maps in the early 1500s, Waldseemüller named America after Amerigo Vespucci. The mapmaker thought that Vespucci had discovered the North American mainland in 1497. When he found out that Columbus had arrived first, "America" had already been printed in thousands of books.*

■ *Why did Columbus continue to explore the islands in the Caribbean and the coasts of South and Central America?*

▼ *Exports of gold and silver from the New World were very important to Spain. By law, one-fifth of the silver and gold mined in the regions claimed by Columbus belonged to the king of Spain.*

The Spanish in the Americas

Columbus made four voyages in all, to the Caribbean and the coasts of South and Central America. After his first, the Spanish rulers acted quickly to prevent their chief rivals, the Portuguese, from profiting from his discovery. The Spanish asked Pope Alexander VI to grant them control of navigation and settlement in the regions Columbus had visited.

The pope had drawn an imaginary line from north to south in the Atlantic. All land and sea west of the line would belong to Spain, and all land east of the line would belong to Portugal. In 1494, the rulers of the two countries signed the treaty of Tordesillas (*tawrd uh SEE yuhs*) to establish this boundary.

Rumors that the lands were rich with gold and silver attracted many Spanish adventurers to the Americas. Wherever they found riches, Spanish conquerors killed

Silver and Gold Exported from the Americas, 1520–1650

Silver and Gold (in millions of pounds) — vertical axis: 0, 3, 6, 9, 12

Year — horizontal axis: 1520, 1540, 1560, 1580, 1600, 1620, 1640

379

The Age of Exploration

Critical Thinking

Ask students to suggest reasons why Columbus made careful observations of floating debris and of flocks of birds. (*Evidence of land.*) Why was it significant that the birds were moving southwest? (*Indicated land would be found in that direction; Columbus assumed it would be Asia.*)

■ *Columbus continued to explore these lands to find proof that he had reached Asia.*

Geographic Context

Economic Context

The actual total cash expense of Columbus's expedition was 1,167,542 maravedies. The Spanish monarchs paid 1,000,000 maravedies and Columbus himself paid the rest. It is difficult to compare purchasing power in 1492 with that of today, but scholars estimate that the cost of Columbus's expedition was equal to about 88,000 of today's dollars. More importantly, they estimate that, during the 16th century, the Spanish received 1,733,000 maravedies for each one they invested.

Visual Learning

Refer students to the line graph on this page. Ask them to identify the year the most gold and silver was exported from the Americas (*1600*); discuss how the exportation rate rose before 1600 (*quickly*); and talk about how it declined after 1600 (*fell off slowly*).

Critical Thinking

The Treaty of Tordesillas of 1494 established that Portugal could claim all land discovered east of 48° W longitude and Spain could claim all the land west of that line. Have students locate this line on the map on p. 378 and make a chart of all the present-day countries granted to Portugal and Spain according to this treaty. You may wish to point out that other European countries neither signed the treaty nor abided by its rules.

■ *Many Spanish colonists exploited the Indians by forcing them to work on plantations or in mines or killed them to steal their gold and silver.*

■ *Why was it necessary to create laws designed to protect the Indians from the Spanish colonists?*

➤ *In this engraving, Magellan holds the world and uses a navigator's instrument to plot a course.*

the local people and stole their treasures. In the 1540s, the Spanish discovered silver deposits in Peru, on the Pacific coast of South America. They opened mines and forced the Indians to work in them.

Spain also sent explorers and colonizers to the new territories. Eager for profit, the colonists set up plantations to grow sugar cane, tobacco, and other crops for export to Europe. These plantations required great numbers of laborers to plant, harvest, and pack the crops. The Spanish colonists forced the Indians to do the work. These workers were poorly fed, overworked, and beaten by the Spanish. Many died from this abuse.

Even more death, however, was brought to many Native Americans through the introduction of European diseases. Europeans, Africans, and Asians had endured centuries of plagues, and those who had survived developed immunities. Their bodies were able to fight off these diseases. Native peoples, however, had no such immunities, and the diseases spread like wildfire. There were nearly 80 million native people in North and South American when Columbus arrived. Probably more than 75 percent had died by 1600.

Some Spanish priests, who attempted to convert the native peoples to Christianity by gentle means, tried to enforce laws designed to protect the Indians. However, these priests were few in number, and rarely succeeded. ■

Europeans in North America

Spain was only one of many European countries that explored the Americas. Around the year 1000, almost 500 years before Columbus's voyage, Vikings led by Leif Ericson landed in Newfoundland and explored part of the coast of North America. In the 1480s, Basque and other European fishermen fished and whaled near the coast of Canada.

The English were the first to send an organized expedition in Columbus's wake. In 1497, the Italian John Cabot, sailing for England, reached Newfoundland, which he thought was part of Asia. On a second voyage, he explored the coast of North America. When the English began to establish colonies in North America in the 1600s, they claimed possession of the areas Cabot had visited.

In 1513, Vasco Núñez de Balboa, sailing for Spain, crossed the Isthmus of Panama and saw the Pacific Ocean. From 1519 to 1521, a Spanish fleet under the command of Ferdinand Magellan made the first **circumnavigation,** or voyage around the earth. You can trace that voyage on the map on page 378.

By 1521, Balboa and Magellan had proved that a huge, newly discovered continent blocked the westward route to Asia. Explorers who followed were determined to find a way around or through that continent.

Study Skills

Assign each pair of students a Central or South American country. Students should find out about its location, geography, people, language, and the impact of European exploration on that country. Have students prepare written or oral reports.

Religious Context

Many Spanish missionaries wanted to teach the Indians and gain their trust, not just make them conform to Christian practices. Thus they established mission towns built around a church. You might want to have students research life in the early mission towns of the American southwest.

Writing

Have each student choose to be an explorer, a missionary, or a colonist. Tell them to write a journal entry or a letter to a friend or relative in Europe about their experiences in the new land. Alternatively, some students may choose to be Indians who live in mission towns or work on plantations. They could explain how they feel about the beliefs, customs, and demands of the new colonists.

The hope of finding such a route, called the Northwest Passage, drew Europeans across the Atlantic. In 1524, King Francis I of France sent an expedition to America. The Italian commander of the voyage, Giovanni da Verrazano, sailed from the coast of present-day North Carolina north to Newfoundland. Another expedition was led by the French explorer Jacques Cartier. In 1535, he sailed up the Saint Lawrence River to the future site of Montreal, Canada. Verrazano and Cartier's voyages gave the French a claim to part of North America.

In the late 1500s, the Europeans realized that the vast continent offered a wealth of resources: land, timber, minerals, fur, and much more. Colonists from England, France, and Holland began to arrive in North America to farm, search for gold, trap animals for fur, or seek religious freedom. The native population in North America was not taken advantage of as rapidly as in the Spanish colonies. Northern colonists had no need for cheap labor. But as more settlers claimed American Indian land, the Indians were pushed westward.

As colonies and trading empires were established in North America, the importance of Mediterranean trade with the Far East declined. Sugar raised on Caribbean island plantations became the main export of the North American colonies. Because of the rising demand for sugar, the focus of trade in Europe shifted from the Mediterranean nations to nations along the North Atlantic that had colonized the New World. Thus, in the 1600s and 1700s, Holland, France, and England became the major powers in European commerce. ■

◄ *John White, the English governor of an American colony, painted watercolors depicting American Indian life. This man is wearing ceremonial body paint.*

■ *What was the result of France's search for the Northwest Passage?*

REVIEW

1. **FOCUS** What role did Christopher Columbus's voyages play in the colonization of North America?
2. **CONNECT** How were the goals of Prince Henry and Columbus similar? How were their goals different?
3. **CRITICAL THINKING** Review the maps on pages 374 and 378. Which of the five explorers, in your opinion, was most important? Why?
4. **ECONOMICS** How did Europe's exploration and colonization of North America affect Mediterranean trade?
5. **CRITICAL THINKING** Do you think the harsh treatment of native peoples was a necessary result of European exploration? Explain why or why not.
6. **ACTIVITY** Trace the map of North America in the Atlas on page 526. With different-colored markers, trace the routes European explorers followed between 1497 and 1550 in their search for the Northwest Passage. Then try to "discover" the actual Passage, which was not conquered until 1906.

NATIONAL IDENTITY

Map and Globe Skills

Have the students list the European nations that took part in the exploration and colonization of the Americas. Put up a world map on the wall or on a bulletin board. Have students use yarn of different colors to show where people from various European nations settled in the Americas. You may wish to have them indicate where various North American Indians lived during the time that Europeans first explored North America.

■ *The French did not find the Northwest Passage but laid claim to the northern part of North America.*

CLOSE

Have students draw the Graphic Overview from p. 377. Under the branches for exploration, have students fill in names of explorers, the dates of their expeditions, and their accomplishments. Under the branches for colonization, have students fill in descriptive details from the lesson.

Answers to Review Questions

1. Columbus's voyages led others to discover the resources of North America.
2. Both da Gama and Columbus sought a direct sea route to India and China. Da Gama sought an eastward route; Columbus searched westward.
3. Accept all answers students support with logical reasons.
4. The importance of Mediterranean trade with the Far East declined as trade with the Americas grew.
5. Answers will vary. Some students may say that both the Europeans and the Indians could have profited from plantations and investments if the colonists had been willing to learn from the Indians and treat them fairly. Others may think the European attitude of superiority and desire for profit made exploitation inevitable.
6. Routes should be traced around islands in the Arctic Ocean.

Homework Options

Write a paragraph describing how and why the reasons for sailing to America changed from 1492 to the 1600s.

Study Guide: p. 62

UNDERSTANDING
MAP SYMBOLS

This skills feature uses a map of Vasco da Gama's voyage to India to teach students how to read and interpret information on a special-purpose map.

GEOGRAPHY
Map and Globe Skills

Ask students to explain why accurate map making and map reading are important. *(Small errors can lead to large mistakes. The ability to read a map keeps people from getting lost.)*

Reading a Wind and Current Map

Here's Why

Wind and ocean currents affect many things from the weather and climate to ocean transportation. Maps like the one shown here describe the flow of these currents around the world. Of course, Vasco da Gama did not have such a map when he sailed to India in 1498. Knowing how to read this map, however, can help you understand some of the conditions da Gama faced on his voyage.

Here's How

The map on this page shows the major ocean currents of the world and the prevailing winds around the world in July. Locate Portugal on the map. Then follow the line that shows da Gama's route to India.

Now look at the arrows on the map that show wind currents. These arrows represent prevailing winds, or winds that usually blow from the same direction. Wind currents in the Northern Hemisphere tend to move in a clockwise direction. In the Southern Hemisphere, winds tend to move counterclockwise.

Focus your attention on the Atlantic Ocean. You will see that winds moving clockwise in the Northern Atlantic would have helped move da Gama's ships south to a point about midway down the

coast of Africa. Here, the wind moves in a counterclockwise direction. These winds would have slowed the progress of the ships.

To see how the winds affected the rest of the voyage, look at the arrows showing wind direction in the Indian Ocean. The winds blow from Africa's west coast toward the east. This means that the wind was blowing with the ships as they crossed the Indian Ocean.

Besides the wind, da Gama depended on ocean currents to move his ships along. Like the wind, water tends to circulate clockwise in the Northern Hemisphere and counterclockwise in the Southern Hemisphere.

Look back to the Atlantic Ocean near Portugal. As you can see, da Gama's ships would have started off their voyage by being carried down the coast of Africa, first by the Canary Current

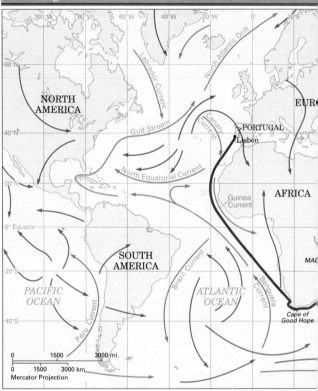

Prevailing Winds and Ocean Currents

Objective

Form hypotheses from information on a special-purpose map. (Map and Globe Skills 1; Critical Thinking 2)

Using a Map

Have students choose two locations they want to travel between by sea. Using information provided on the map above, have them chart the best route to travel and be able to defend their decisions.

Writing a Report

Ask students to research and write a report on Vasco da Gama's voyage to India. Students should avoid discussion of da Gama's route, but should instead concentrate on other elements of the trip (people, places, preparation, planning, equipment.)

and then by the Guinea Current.

About halfway down the coast of Africa, however, da Gama would have encountered the Benguela Current. This current runs in the opposite direction of the route of da Gama's ships. What current affected the ships after they went around the tip of Africa?

For the final leg of the voyage, da Gama's ships crossed the northern Indian Ocean. The currents in this portion of the Indian Ocean change direction in response to strong seasonal winds called monsoons. From April to October, monsoons blow from the southwest, creating a current that flows in a clockwise direction. From November to March, monsoons create a current that runs in a counterclockwise direction. Since da Gama completed this last leg of the voyage in May, we can assume that he was helped by both the wind and ocean currents in the northern Indian Ocean.

Try It

Look back at the map on page 378 that shows the routes taken by Christopher Columbus from Portugal to the Americas. Use that map with the one below to describe how wind and ocean currents affected one of the voyages.

Apply It

Suppose you wanted to sail from a port about halfway down the western coast of North America to the Philippines, and then back. Assume that you are making the voyage during the summer. What route would you take in order to use wind and ocean currents to speed your voyage? Suppose you wanted to sail from the tip of Florida to the coast of West Africa and back. What route would you take?

Map labels: 100°E, 120°E, 140°E, 160°E, 180°, 160°W, 140°W, NORTH AMERICA, ASIA, Japan Current, PACIFIC OCEAN, California Current, Equatorial Current, PHILIPPINES, Equatorial Currents, INDIAN OCEAN, AUSTRALIA, East Australian Current, West Wind Drift

Legend:
→ Ocean current
→ Wind current
→ Da Gama's route

383

The Age of Exploration

Discuss with students the ways in which people use maps other than for travel. *(Locating resources, designing landscapes, finding one's way around a building, attacking another army.)*

383

Answers to Try It

The Canary and North Equatorial Currents as well as prevailing east-to-west winds indicate a positive effect on his voyages to the Americas, but a negative effect on his return trip to Spain.

Answers to Apply It

Students should describe a route that follows the clockwise pattern created by the California, Equatorial, and Japan Currents. Wind currents would be favorable for the voyage from North America to the Philippines. On the return voyage, wind currents would be blowing in the opposite direction of the course of the boat. Catching the Gulf Stream and Canary Current loop is the best route for sailing from Florida to West Africa.

Visual Learning

Ask students to study the map above, paying close attention to da Gama's route from Portugal to India. Based on information provided by the map, can students identify a better route to India than da Gama's?

INTRODUCE

Students have learned that when Christopher Columbus made his voyage to what he hoped was India, he was financed by King Ferdinand and Queen Isabella of Spain. Obtaining this financing was no easy matter, as shown in "The Audience" by C. Walter Hodges. This selection helps students view what they learned in Chapter 14, Lesson 3 from the perspective of an imaginary firsthand observer.

READ AND RESPOND

Most students will enjoy reading this selection independently, though some may need you to read with them. As students read, remind them to consider the focus question as raised in the paragraph preceding the story.

Some words to discuss before reading are: *antechamber,* a small outer room that leads to a more important room; *dais,* a raised platform; *adversity,* suffering or hardship; *assented,* agreed; and *aghast,* shocked.

In Lesson 3 you learned about Columbus's appeal to Ferdinand and Isabella. Here is an imaginative recreation of his second appearance before that King and Queen.

384

LITERATURE

The Audience

C. Walter Hodges

As you have learned in this chapter, the dream of wealth and the lure of riches drove Columbus and other explorers like him. They undertook journeys of unknown dangers and uncertain outcomes to pursue that dream. But they needed financial support. As you read this story, play the role of the audience— the King or Queen. Would you support Columbus? Why or why not?

The town was taken, the Moors were driven out, the wars were at an end. Now, now at last there must be time to hear Columbus. Now at last the victorious Sovereigns would give him ships to sail in quest of his new horizon.

He went to his friend Alonzo de Quintanilla and implored him to obtain audience for him soon. The Accountant-General promised to do so, and on the following day Columbus was summoned into the presence of Their Majesties.

Father Juan Perez, Luiz de Santangel and I went with him to the audience. The antechamber was full of people, little groups talking in low voices, Court officials, men and women with petitions to present. Presently an usher called the name of Columbus, and he went in.

Ferdinand and Isabella were seated on a low dais, surrounded by the councillors and members of the Royal Household. Prominent among them was Fernando de Talavera, recently made Archbishop of Granada, the King's most trusted adviser. Near the dais, a little to one side, was a table at which were seated the Court notaries. There was a subdued light in the room, a feeling of many people gathered in a warm silence. Their dresses seemed to melt into the rich colors of the surrounding tapestries. A blade of sunlight dazzled upon the helmet of a soldier, and its reflection nodded in an opposite corner of the room.

From the table a little man rose halfway to his feet and read from a paper:

"Señor Christopher Columbus of Genoa, making application to Your Majesties for ships to seek out certain lands which he claims to stand yet undiscovered beyond the seas."

Having gabbled his formality he sat down again. The Queen smiled gently at Columbus and inclined her head towards him.

Thematic Connections

Social Studies: Historical empathy; analysis of cause and effect

Houghton Mifflin Literary Reader: A Helping Hand

Background

In 1485, Christopher Columbus first approached King Ferdinand and Queen Isabella about finding a short route to India and the Far East. Because the Spanish treasury was severely strained by the struggle to push the Muslims from Spain, Columbus did not get the financing. For six years, Columbus and his brother, Bartholomew, tried to obtain the money from England and France. Finally, in 1492, Spain reconsidered Columbus's plan and gave him the ships and money for his voyage. Unfortunately, Columbus never found what he was looking for. Instead of finding a faster route to the Far East, he landed in the "New World." Columbus made three voyages to the "New World" but gradually lost credibility and favor with the king and queen, and he died in 1506, a broken man.

Then the King spoke:

"Señor Columbus is well known to us, I think; but if I remember rightly his proposals were examined by a Special Commission some years ago. Was it not so?"

"At Salamanca, sire."

"And the Commissioners rejected them," continued the King, "on the grounds that you could not bring forward sufficient evidence in support of your theory. Again, was it not so? And was not the Archbishop of Granada here in charge of that Commission?"

Columbus looked across at Talavera, and said nothing. The King continued:

"But since you bring your case again before us, señor, we must presume that you have fresh evidence in support of it. Or that you have fault to find with the method by which it was previously examined."

"Sire, it is not with the method but with the verdict that I have fault to find," said Columbus. "I believe that the members of the commission were all men of great renown for learning and scientific knowledge. But the greater their learning the greater was their error. They were wrong in their conclusions, and I dispute their verdict."

"And what says the Archbishop to that?" asked the King. Talavera shrugged.

"What can I say, sire, more than Señor Columbus has said? The men whom I assembled numbered among them some of our greatest scholars. Upon my word the hearing was fair and unprejudiced. Señor Columbus has his project much at heart, and it is natural that he should disagree with our findings upon it. Indeed I am sorry. But if he can bring forth further evidence . . ." He was silent. The King looked questioningly at Columbus. "Can you do that, señor?"

Columbus seemed for a second to be tongue-tied. Then he said, rather slowly:

"I can bring forward a few more traveler's tales, more strange reports; what else had I to do in all these years but to seek and collect them wherever they were to be found? I have no more real proofs than you have heard already. Nor will any man have, until he goes to find them where they exist beyond the horizons of the Ocean itself. Only give me my ships sire, and I will bring you proof enough."

There was whispering among the company, and someone laughed softly. But the King was obviously impatient. Drumming with his fingers on the arm of his chair, he said:

"We do not doubt your personal sincerity, señor. But you have heard the Archbishop. Without fresh evidence we cannot think it would be justifiable to re-open the inquiry."

Suddenly the Queen spoke.

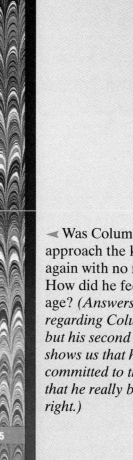

◄ Was Columbus foolish to approach the king and queen again with no new evidence? How did he feel about the voyage? *(Answers may vary regarding Columbus's wisdom, but his second appearance shows us that he was totally committed to the project and that he really believed he was right.)*

Access Strategy

Have a discussion with students about persuasion. Ask students to think of a time when they really wanted something and convinced another person or persons to give it to them. Ask how they did it. With logic? Emotion? Something else? Now have students think of a time when someone wanted them to do something and convinced them to do it. How did that person succeed? Is there one best way to persuade, or do different methods work with different people?

As they read this story, have students watch how Columbus works to get what he wants. Can they learn any methods from him?

Writing a Letter

After reading "The Audience," students have some idea of the difficulty Columbus had in getting financing for his voyage. Have students imagine that they are Columbus. Instead of having an audience with Ferdinand and Isabella, tell them to write a letter to the king and queen asking for the financial backing. Before they write the letters, students should list their arguments. Then they should organize the list in a logically persuasive way. You may want students to proofread and revise the letters and then make final copies to be displayed in the classroom or shared aloud.

"My Lord," she said, "perhaps Señor Columbus has not been quite fair to himself. He says he has no further proofs to bring. But since his proposals were first rejected by us he has faced much adversity without foregoing his convictions. Also he has made many friends who believe in him, men whose opinions should carry some weight. If constancy of itself is proof of nothing, at least it has the merit to be heard, even a second time."

The King looked at her and smiled slightly.

"I stand rebuked, madam," he said. "Certainly, if Señor Columbus wishes to speak, he shall be heard."

Again Columbus bowed; and he began to speak, at first slowly, then with increasing force.

"It is true what I have said. The evidence you have previously examined is still the only evidence I have to offer. But, sire, upon that very evidence I am willing to venture my life. I have shown you maps, drawn up not only by me, but by some of the greatest authorities ever known to have studied the mysteries of the Western Ocean; and I have offered to follow those maps till I have found a way for you across that ocean to the very shores of the Indies. I repeat, to do so is to venture my life; and not only my life, but the reputation I have spent so much of it to build. I can offer no other guarantee. But if Your Majesties will give me three ships, and accept the hazard, then it must be, if God so wills it, that according to all the known laws of science we shall find those shores that I have promised you, and Spain will become as wealthy as she is now victorious."

The King interrupted: "Spain is victorious, but she is also poor. The wars against the Infidel have drained the treasury dry. You say you demand three ships only. But what you really ask is for ships, men, provisions, cannon, ammunition, a thousand things, for a voyage lasting perhaps a year, perhaps even longer. It may be, as you yourself suggest, that I shall never see those ships again. Where is the money to come from?"

"From the Indies, sire!" cried Columbus, "where there is wealth enough in one province to beggar the combined treasuries of all Europe! This is testified by Marco Polo and Sir John Mandeville, and many other travellers from the East. They have seen kingdoms where swineherds fasten their rags with belts of gold and where the little street boys play in the mud with pearls. They have seen with their own eyes the princes of India riding in procession upon elephants whose thick hides are inset with jewels patterned like a carpet, whose tusks are carved to the fineness of lace, and whose ears are hung with bells of silver and gold which chime with every step in confused and wonderful harmonies! They say these beasts would seem like gods of splendor were it not for the splendor of the kings who ride them, under the tinkling and perfumed canopies that shade them from the sun. Is there another nation in Europe that would not gamble three ships for all that treasure? I tell you, for the people who first discover the Western way to the Indies, a thousand ships will not suffice to carry home the riches they will find, not even though their holds are crammed so full they spill upon the decks! All this I offer to Spain. But there is little time for Spain to choose. My plan is no secret. It is talked of everywhere, and is plainly written down for anyone to study. Am I the only man to consider the undertaking? Perhaps even now in Portugal, or France, or England, they are preparing ships for just such a voyage as mine. Perhaps in a few years the Atlantic will be an open road. Perhaps some other man, not I, will sail the ship that opens it. If this should happen it will be God's punishment for my pride, for I have lived all these years dreaming of the pride I should have when I, the first, shall strike the Spanish flag into the soil of the Indies.

"I have only one thing to add. Upon the floor here between us is a carpet. It is an Indian carpet such as has great value for us in Europe. The merchants who trade in such things grow richer every year. And from whom are they obtained? Not from the Indians. They are bought from the Muslims of Aleppo and

387

387

Bulletin Board

Have students prepare a bulletin board illustrating the life of Christopher Columbus. They should first find out more about Columbus at the school or public library. Then help students compile their research into a list of facts that tell Columbus's story chronologically. Finally, have students print the facts on cards and find or make pictures that illustrate the facts.

➤ Why do you think the king shows signs of changing his mind? *(Columbus's argument is starting to "hit home" because he is talking about saving money by controlling channels of trade with the East.)*

Alexandria, who alone control the channels of trade with the Far East. Thus, though you have driven the Infidel out of Spain, you must still buy in his bazaars and pay the price he asks. And as your ships return home from the Muslims of Aleppo they may be plundered and sunk by the Muslim pirates of Barbary, and their crews sold into slavery. Will you pay that price, and still not grant three ships for a venture such as mine?"

It was plain, long before he finished speaking, that Columbus held the imagination of the Court. Even those who could not believe him to be more than a half-crazy fanatic were moved by the forcefulness of his address. After his concluding words the assembly became aware of its own hesitancy, kept awkwardly silent and waited for the King to establish them again in their former opinions. But the King himself was hesitant. He cleared his throat and looked round at the Archbishop of Granada, and somehow it began to be clear, even from this, that Columbus had made his mark. In a moment the silence was relieved by the mutterings of conversation, and when at last the King spoke it was to make certain the good opinion in which the petitioner now found himself. The King inquired if Columbus had with him the papers and other material relating to the expedition, particularly of the estimated cost. Columbus produced two closely written scrolls, saying that the greater bulk of the material was at his lodging.

"Then señor," said the King, "if you will deliver it this evening to my secretary, I will see that the Council meets to discuss the matter within the next day or two, and I promise that it shall have every consideration."

More than this Columbus could not have desired. His joy was evident to everyone, and we, his friends, standing in the doorway of the room felt that at last his success was assured.

Our hopes were high. But in a few minutes they were to be brought down even lower than before! Where success had seemed certain, failure became inevitable out of the mouth, as it were, of Columbus himself. For, as we were about to leave the audience, the Archbishop spoke suddenly:

"Señor Columbus has stated his requirements for the expedition," he said, "but nothing for himself. Before the matter goes to Council we should know what reward he proposes to ask for his services. Supposing," he added, "that they are fruitful."

To this the King immediately assented, and the Court again waited for Columbus to speak. After a moment's hesitation he made the following demands:

"Firstly, my lords, I request that I receive a knighthood and the title of First Admiral. Secondly, if the expedition is successful, that I should be accorded the hereditary vice-regency of all the lands I may discover. And thirdly, that I receive a tenth part of all the revenues obtained from them."

388

Role Playing

The main characters in "The Audience" are Columbus, Ferdinand, Isabella, and Talavera. The story consists primarily of dialogue between these main characters. Divide the class into groups of four, one student for each character. Have these groups reread the story and write dialogue that tells the story in more contemporary language. After the groups have written their dialogues, have them choose characters and play their roles for the rest of the class.

The entire audience was aghast. No one had expected such extravagant demands. When he finished speaking Columbus found himself the center of a silence so deep that it seemed as though a blanket of deafness had enclosed the room. Not even the voice of anger could find itself. At last the King spoke, quietly, his words magnified by the hush.

"Can you not moderate those terms, señor?"

Columbus spread his hands. "They are reasonable, my lord," he said.

"Reasonable indeed!" a thick red-faced man spluttered out suddenly, unable to hold his wrath. "They are outrageous, monstrous, an insult! Has not this crazy adventurer the wits enough to know his place before the nobility of Spain? What is he but a weaver's son from the gutters of Genoa, and he demands to be made an Admiral and a knight! A peddler of inaccurate maps! He, an Admiral! And since when did tradesmen receive knighthoods? He should be whipped for his impertinence!"

"Sire," cried Columbus, addressing the King. "From whom should Spain most proudly accept her Empire: from the hands of a tradesman, or from her own Admiral, duly appointed by the State?"

The King shrugged his shoulders and said:

"Very well, señor. The Council shall consider the matter."

The audience was at an end. Columbus bowed and walked quickly from the room. We, his friends, went with him into the bright evening street through the crowd of idle soldiers at the gate. Here we parted company, no one saying a word.

Further Reading

Argosies of Empire. Ralph Bailey. Here are stories of sailors who explored the world's sea routes before Columbus.

Columbus Sails. C. Walter Hodges. The rest of Columbus's story by the writer of "The Audience." A sailor and a monk describe his story.

He Went with Vasco da Gama. Louise Andrews Kent. This is a story of how da Gama sailed around the Cape of Good Hope to reach the Indies. It also tells the story of Portuguese history.

I Challenge the Dark Sea. Olive W. Burt. Based on the life of Henry the Navigator, this story describes how Henry's support of science above superstition paved the way for many of the discoveries of his time.

Son of Columbus. Hans Baumann. Columbus's youngest son sails with his father and tells the story of his fourth and final voyage to the New World.

◄ Why do you think the friends did not talk after the audience? *(They still did not know what the king and queen were going to decide, and they were probably too nervous, depressed, anxious, or exhausted to speak. They may also have been quite surprised, even shocked, by Columbus's "extravagant demands" and statements at the end of the audience.)*

EXTEND

On his first voyage, Columbus's ship the *Santa Maria* was wrecked on a coral reef near Haiti. He and his men built a fort there. Have students find out more about this fort. Questions they might want to answer include the following: From what was the fort built? *(The wreckage of the ship.)* What was the fort's name? *(Navidad.)* Why was the fort named that? *(They were shipwrecked on Christmas Eve.)* What was the fort for? *(To house a garrison that was to look for gold.)* What happened to the fort? *(It was destroyed and the men killed after they had started robbing the inhabitants of the island.)*

Further Reading

You may want to have your students look in the school or local library for more books about Columbus and other explorers featured in Chapter 14.

Answers to Reviewing Key Terms

A. Answers:
1. colonies
2. bullion
3. monopoly
4. circumnavigation
5. caravel
6. balance of trade
7. capital

B. Sample answers:
1. If explorers could find new sources of gold, they could make more **bullion.** Governments felt they could then break up the Venetian **monopoly** on trade in the Mediterranean.
2. The **caravel** made **circumnavigation** possible.
3. If Portuguese kings and merchants contributed **capital** to finance voyages, Portugal could establish **colonies** in other lands.

Answers to Exploring Concepts

A. Sample reasons:
1. Maps, Muslim and Ptolemy's; travelers' tales (Marco Polo, Ibn Battuta).
2. Improvements in compass, astrolabe; latitude and longitude charts; development of caravel.
3. Spanish enslavement; diseases; lands and riches stolen by Spanish.
4. Christian explorers believed God wanted them to teach nonbelievers; hoped to find mythical king, Prester John; waged religious warfare against Islam in Spain and Portugal.
5. European demand for sugar; low supply drove prices higher; cheap source of labor exploited in West Africa.

B. Sample answers:
1. From 1200 to 1500, geographers made world maps and developed ideas about its size and shape. By 1300, sailors were using coastal charts, or portolans, from information supplied by trading ship captains.
2. In 1498, Vasco da Gama reached India.
3. Ptolemy wrote a book with a very accurate map of the world as Romans knew it. The map was helpful to European mapmakers.
4. During the 1200s and 1300s, European demand for eastern goods was great.
5. The central location of Venice and Genoa gave traders easy access to the Mediterranean. These cities made huge profits by trading with the Middle East.
6. Jesuit missionaries were very interested in understanding the Chinese. They even learned about Chinese language and culture and taught the Chinese about their own society.
7. Prince Henry wanted very much to explore other lands—to find new sources of African gold, trade goods, find markets for Portuguese products, and find African converts to Christianity.
8. Spain founded many colonies in the Americas where Spaniards grew sugar cane, tobacco, and other crops on large plantations.
9. Portugal, England, France, and Holland also sent explorers to America.

Chapter Review

Reviewing Key Terms

balance of trade (p. 370)
bullion (p. 370)
capital (p. 375)
caravel (p. 373)
circumnavigation (p. 380)
colony (p. 375)
monopoly (p. 368)

A. Each of the sentences below has words in italics that describe a key term. Read each sentence, and replace the words in italics with the correct key term from the list above.
1. Spain, Portugal, England, and France founded *settlements of their own citizens in foreign lands they explored.*
2. Portugal paid its foreign debts in *bars or blocks of gold.*
3. Spanish explorers in South America searched for gold so that Venice's *complete control of business activity* might be destroyed.
4. Ferdinand Magellan of Spain made the first *voyage around the earth.*
5. Prince Henry's ship designers created a *swift and easily maneuverable ship that could sail on the open sea.*
6. Portugal had to pay other countries to maintain the *difference between the total value of exports and the total value of imports.*
7. The rulers of Spain contributed the *money and material* to finance Columbus's voyage.

B. Write a sentence or two using each pair of words below. The sentences should show how the words are related.
1. bullion, monopoly
2. caravel, circumnavigation
3. capital, colony

Exploring Concepts

A. Copy the following chart on the age of exploration on your paper. List one or more reasons for each historical fact.

Historical Fact	Reason
1. Knowledge about the world grew (1200–1500).	Maps, travelers' tales
2. Portuguese exploration became easier.	
3. Spanish mistreated natives of Central and South America.	
4. Christianity spread.	
5. Portuguese sugar plantations were profitable.	

B. Tell why each statement below is false using facts and details from the chapter.
1. From 1200 to 1500, geographers had no idea of the size and shape of the world.
2. Vasco da Gama reached Mexico in May 1498.
3. Ptolemy's map was of little use to European mapmakers.
4. Few Europeans wanted to buy goods from the East during the 1200s and 1300s.
5. Venice and Genoa were isolated from profitable trade with the Middle East.
6. Jesuit missionaries in the 1600s were not interested in understanding the Chinese people whom they wanted to convert.
7. Prince Henry of Portugal had little interest in exploring other lands.
8. Spain had no colonies in the Americas.
9. Only Spain explored North and South America.

Reviewing Skills

1. Look at the wind and ocean current map on pages 382 and 383. In what direction do the prevailing winds blow in the Pacific Ocean off the eastern coast of South America? Would you expect this for wind currents in this area of the world? Why?
2. Look again at the map. Would it be difficult to sail from Australia to the southern tip of South America? Describe the winds and currents and their directions on such a voyage.

3. Suppose you are a partner in an English trading company in the early 1500s. Your company has just voted to finance an expedition to find the Northwest Passage. What are the advantages and disadvantages of such a decision? How did you vote?
4. If you wanted to find out how terrain helped people decide how to use land, what two types of maps would you compare?

Using Critical Thinking

1. As in Columbus's time, some people today argue that the exploration of the solar system and the universe is a waste of time and money. If you agree with these people, explain your reasons. If you do not agree, write down some arguments that could be used to convince them that they are mistaken about space exploration.
2. An old saying states that the people of one generation build on the accomplishments of the generations who lived before them. Explain how this saying was true of the European explorers between 1200 and 1500. Then discuss how the saying applies to the generations living today.

3. Prince Henry and Christopher Columbus both reached important goals in their lives. Examine and compare the lives of Prince Henry and Christopher Columbus. Think of what character trait or traits may have helped them succeed. Now think about goals you want to reach sometime in your future. How could you use one of the traits that helped them succeed to achieve your goal? Explain your answer.
4. Suppose you could travel back in time and live in Europe during the age of exploration described in this chapter. Would you like to live during that era? If so, what things would you like to do? If not, why not?

Preparing for Citizenship

1. ARTS ACTIVITY Choose an event from each lesson of this chapter that interests you. Draw or paint a picture to illustrate each event. You may want to select one of these: Vasco da Gama's voyage to India; Bartolomé de Las Casas defending the rights of native people to the King of Spain; Prince Henry's shipbuilders inspecting their first caravel; sailors on a ship in the "Green Sea of Darkness" near Cape Bojador; enslaved Africans working on a sugar plantation on Madeira; Cabot, Verrazano, or Cartier searching for the Northwest Passage.

2. COLLABORATIVE ACTIVITY Meet with your class to plan a book of mini-biographies of people you learned about in this chapter. Have each biography explain how the person was involved with European exploration. First, decide on a title for the book. Then, choose groups to do the following jobs: research and write an introduction and the biographies; illustrate the biographies and design a cover; photocopy the biographies and bind them together in a book; distribute copies of the finished book to other classes in your school. Have all the groups work together to produce your book.

391

The Age of Exploration

Answers to Reviewing Skills
1. Counterclockwise; yes, because winds in the Southern Hemisphere tend to blow in a counterclockwise direction.
2. No, if a southeast course is taken. Air currents and the West Wind Drift both head from Australia east to South America's southern tip.
3. Possible answers include advantages implicit in actually finding Northwest Passage, and disadvantages associated with Atlantic crossing and ocean exploration at that time. Also, familiarity with North America was advantageous to English trading company.
4. Land use and topographic maps.

Answers to Using Critical Thinking
1. Time and money might be used instead to solve problems on Earth. Those disagreeing may indicate needed resources on other planets; colonization to solve overcrowding on Earth; natural desire to explore unknown; importance that United States keep pace with Soviet Union space exploration.
2. Students might say that European explorers between 1200 and 1500 learned about other parts of world from writings of earlier travelers and about the earth's geography from past scholars. Examples applying to today may include the value of learning from experience, possibly mistakes, of elders.
3. Columbus's and Prince Henry's traits: curious, imaginative, adventurous, determined, courageous. Goals will vary.
4. Reasons for going back in time: thrill of adventure, satisfaction of discovery. Reasons against: difficult life.

Answers to Preparing for Citizenship
1. ARTS ACTIVITY Students should create three pictures, depicting one event from each lesson in the chapter. Allow time for students to show and talk about their pictures.
2. COLLABORATIVE LEARNING Allow time for the class planning meeting and group working sessions. Suggest that the "biographers" use the encyclopedia for research. Be sure the biographies are brief and that they explain how the subjects were involved with European exploration.

Suggest that the students printing or typing the book use word processors or typewriters and copiers to reproduce them.

Have students read the unit title and the paragraph below it. Ask them what they think the Americas were like before the European explorers "discovered" them. Explain that they will learn about the earliest settlers and the advanced civilizations that developed before contact with Europe.

Looking Back

Review with students what they learned about the exploration of the Americas by Europeans in Chapter 14. What had happened by the 1500s? *(European nations, in particular Spain and Portugal, had sent explorers to seek adventure and riches in the then unexplored lands.)*

Looking Forward

Tell students that in the next two chapters they will learn about unique civilizations that developed in their own hemisphere (western) and how European explorers influenced these civilizations:
Chapter 15 *Early American Civilizations*
Chapter 16 *Two American Empires*

392

Unit 7
Civilizations of the Americas

Richly colored, this South American weaving is made of tropical bird feathers. What was it for? Archaeologists think it is an Inca cape of the A.D. 1400s, perhaps worn by priests. Such objects, left by small groups or great civilizations, tell of life in the Americas before 1500.

1800 B.C.

392

Detail of a feathered poncho with cotton base, Inca culture, north or central coast of South America, 15th century. The Textile Museum, Washington, D.C., 91.7.

GEOGRAPHY PROJECT

American Cultures

Geography Skill Make an Annotated Map
Students use the skill of Analyzing geographic information.

Geography Themes Human/Environment Interaction

Geography Standards 14, 17 humans modify environment; apply geography to interpret the past

Activity *Create a Museum Catalog*

Materials writing paper, construction paper, colored pens, markers

Management Individual/Small Group

Choose one of the cultures from the Americas discussed in the unit to create a museum catalog that describes the achievements of the Olmec, Mayan, Tiwanakan, Moche, Incan, or Aztec cultures.

Have students:
- select artifacts or art from photos in the text and look in library books for other ideas for the museum exhibit.
- write clear, concise museum catalog text and/or create exhibits.
- make an annotated map of the region where the culture originated and key illustrations of selected artifacts or art to the map.

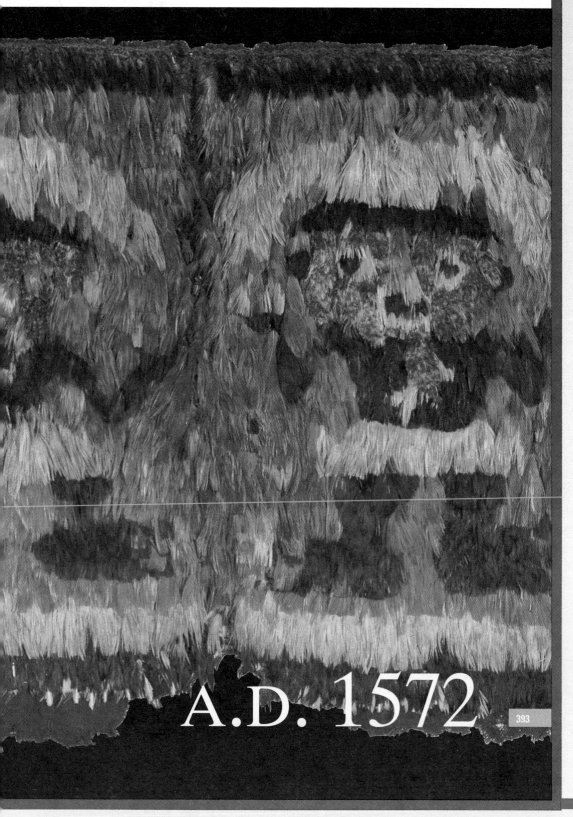

Understanding the Weaving

The images on the cape are Inca diety figures. Each colored feather comes from a different type of bird. The turquoise feathers are from the quetzal, a bird that was considered sacred in early American civilizations.

Understanding Chronology

This unit covers the origins of human settlement in the Americas and the pre-Columbian civilizations. Point out to students that the early history extends back to the time of hunter-gatherers thousands of years before any of the civilizations they have studied in this book.

A.D. 1572

393

For research support activities, see the *Research Handbook.*

For simulations correlated to this unit, see *Citizenship Simulations*, p. viii.

Bookshelf II

City of the Gods: Mexico's Ancient City of Teotihuacán

by Caroline Arnold

Color photographs and clear text explore the ancient ruins of Teotihuacán and illuminate what life was like there two thousand years ago.

Motivate Read aloud pp. 4–11, showing the photographs as you read. Then ask students why they think archaeologists and the Mexican government were interested in finding out more about this city that was built two thousand years ago. Have students look at the photograph of the Incan feathered poncho above and tell them they will be reading about the variety of American cultures in this unit.

To connect this book with the unit content, use the planning guide and student activity blackline masters beginning on p. iv of the *Bookshelf II Teacher's Resources.*

For additional books that are Easy, Average, and Challenging, see the Unit Bibliography on p. T43. See bibliography updates at www.eduplace.com/ss/hmss.

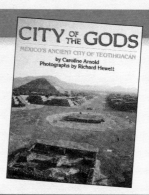

CITY OF THE GODS

MEXICO'S ANCIENT CITY OF TEOTIHUACÁN
by Caroline Arnold
Photographs by Richard Hewett

Planning at a Glance
Early American Civilizations

	Objectives	Reading Support *and* Other Resources	Diverse Learning Strategies

Lesson 1
Origins
pp. 396–399 2–3 days
	• Describe the lifestyle of the early hunter–gatherers.
	• Explain how the adoption of agriculture led to a sedentary lifestyle.
		• **Workbook** or **Reading Support:** pp. 204–207
		  Review p. 48
		  Lesson Support/Transition p. 48
		  Multi-lang. Sum. pp. 95–96
		• **Other Resources:** Poster 5, Study Guide p. 63
			Access Act. **(SDAIE)** TE p. 397
			Study Skills **(Visual)** TE p. 397
			Art Connection **(Visual)** TE p. 398
			
			Audiotapes of Multi-language Lesson Summaries **(Auditory)**

Lesson 2
The Olmec
pp. 400–403 2–3 days
	• Evaluate the role of environment in Olmec civilization.
	• Compare and contrast the contributions of the Olmec social classes.
	• Summarize the main features of Olmec religion.
	• Describe the evidence of Olmec trading with other peoples.
		• **Workbook** or **Reading Support:** pp. 208–211
		  Review p. 49
		  Lesson Support/Transition p. 49
		  Multi-lang. Sum. pp. 97–98
		• **Other Resources:** Study Guide p. 64
			Access Strat. **(Extra Support)** TE p. 401
			Social Participation **(Visual)** TE p. 402
			Homework Options **(GATE)** TE p. 403
			
			Audiotapes of Multi-language Lesson Summaries **(Auditory)**

Lesson 3
The Maya
pp. 404–409 2–3 days
	• Locate and describe the area of Maya settlement.
	• Assess the effectiveness of Maya agricultural techniques.
	• List important Maya achievements and their significance.
		• **Workbook** or **Reading Support:** pp. 212–215
		  Review p. 50
		  Lesson Support/Transition p. 50
		  Multi-lang. Sum. pp. 99–100
		• **Other Resources:** Geography Kit, Study Guide p. 65
			Access Act. **(SDAIE)** TE p. 405
			Map Skills **(Kinesthetic)** TE p. 405
			Study Skills **(Visual)** TE p. 406, 407
			
			Audiotapes of Multi-language Lesson Summaries **(Auditory)**

Exploring **Nonverbal Communication** *pp. 410–411*	• Define and give examples of nonverbal communication.		Activity **(Kinesthetic)** TE pp. 410, 411

Lesson 4
The Tiwanakans and the Moche
pp. 412–415 2–3 days
	• Compare the regions in which the Tiwanakan and Moche civilizations developed.
	• Compare and contrast the lifestyles of the Tiwanakans and Moche.
		• **Workbook** or **Reading Support:** pp. 216–219
		  Review p. 51
		  Lesson Support/Transition p. 51
		  Multi-lang. Sum. pp. 101–102
		• **Other Resources:** Study Guide p. 66
			Access Strat. **(Extra Support)** TE p. 413
			Map and Globe Skills **(Visual)** TE p. 413
			Visual Learning **(Visual)** TE p. 415
			
			Audiotapes of Multi-language Lesson Summaries **(Auditory)**

Skill: Note Taking: **Recording Information** *pp. 416–417* 1 day	• Explain how to extract information from resources and record it efficiently.	• **Other Resources:** Study Guide p. 67	
Chapter Review *pp. 418–419* 1 day		Chapter 15 Test pp. 57–60 *(See facsimiles on TE p. 573.)*	Assessment Multiple-Use Masters pp. 73–80

393A

Reading Support Resources *for Every Lesson*

Reading and Review	Multi-language Summaries	Lesson Support /Transition **S D A I E**
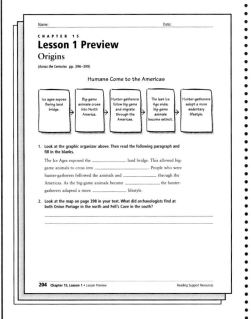	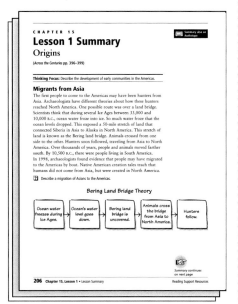	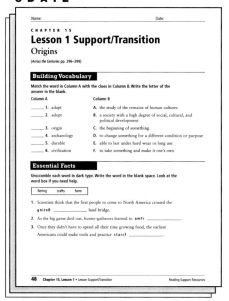

Activities for SDAIE
Specially **D**esigned **A**cademic **I**nstruction in **E**nglish

- **Chapter Overview*** p. 203
- **Lesson Previews*** using graphic organizers from the Teacher's Edition pp. 204, 208, 212, 216
- **Reading Strategies*** pp. 205, 209, 213, 217
- **Lesson Summaries*** pp. 206–207, 210–211, 214–215, 218–219
- **Lesson Reviews** pp. 48, 49, 50, 51

* **Workbook** includes starred items.

Lesson Summaries in:
- English (See Reading and Review.)
- Spanish pp. 206–207, 210–211, 214–215, 218–219
- Chinese pp. 95–102
- Hmong pp. 95–102
- Khmer pp. 95–102
- Vietnamese pp. 95–102

Summaries available on audiotapes

- **Lesson Support/Transition** pp. 48, 49, 50, 51

 # Technology Options

Internet Support

http://www.eduplace.com

Social Studies Center at Education Place

Internet support for Chapter 15:
- *Lesson at a Glance*
- *The Mayan Calendar*

Videotape/Videodisc

We the People:
Supports and enhances major topics: **Theme:** *Ancient Cultures of America*

Software

Student Writing Center ® (CD-ROM) (Macintosh® or Windows®)
MayaQuest® Trail (CD-ROM) (Macintosh® or Windows®)

School to Career

Today we are able to see and study how early Americans lived through the work done by archaeologists. If possible, arrange for a local archaeologist to come speak with the class. Afterward, students may wish to organize their own archaeological dig.

Character Education

The first Americans needed to be self-sufficient and self-reliant. Divide students into small groups. Give each group a scenario in which they would need to be self-sufficient and self-reliant, such as being lost in the woods. What skills and character qualities would students need to survive their scenario?

CHAPTER PREVIEW

Have students read the chapter title and the paragraph that follows it. Ask them to define *prehistoric. (Relating to the time before written history.)* Explain that this chapter deals with the growth of civilizations in the Americas before the development of writing systems. Point out that archaeological evidence is an important source of information about prehistoric times.

Looking Forward

Tell students they will learn about the people who settled North and South America when they read Lessons 1–4: Origins, The Olmec, The Maya, and The Tiwanakans and the Moche.

Lesson 1 describes the very first Americans, those who crossed the land bridge from Asia to Alaska.

Chapter 15

Early American Civilizations

A prehistoric bone, a spear, a carved jade figure—all are clues in an age-old mystery: What were the earliest Americans like, those who settled North and South America between about 40,000 B.C. and A.D. 1300? Ancient tools and bones found by archaeologists help trace the paths of these first settlers. Carvings and sculptures, ornaments and massive temples show how later groups farmed, hunted, fought, and worshiped. All of these objects help unravel the mysteries of prehistoric America.

During this period, hunters migrated as far as southernmost South America. In Texas's Bonfire Cave archaeologists have found weapons and bones from about 13,000 to 10,000 B.C.

1200–400 B.C. The Olmec people build a great civilization in Mexico. Religion is important to the Olmec, who carve jade religious figures like the one shown here.

| 2000 | 1500 | 1000 | 500 |

563 B.C. Religious leader Siddhartha Gautama, later called the Buddha, is born in India.

394

1800 B.C.

BACKGROUND

With the exception of the Mayan codices, few written records remain of ancient American civilizations. Historians have had to rely mostly on archaeological findings to compile their histories of the early hunter-gatherers and the first American civilizations.

Searching for Clues

Archaeological sites provide three different types of evidence—artifacts, features, and ecofacts. Artifacts are usually handmade items such as tools, pottery, or art objects. Features are the large structures of a society such as tombs, aqueducts, and buildings. Ecofacts are the natural objects that are found among the artifacts and features. Ecofacts might include dried grains of corn, seeds, or animal bones. Ecofacts can reveal information about diet, as well as the environment in which ancient people lived.

Dating Objects

Archaeologists use two methods to date historical evidence—relative dating and absolute dating. Relative dating is used to determine the age of an object in relation to another object. This type of dating does not reveal actual age but establishes a comparison between two objects. One method of relative dating analyzes the fluorine content of bones. Bones absorb this chemical element from ground moisture. The older the bone, the higher the level of fluorine. If several bones are found at a site, the archaeologist

During this period, the Maya built great pyramid-temples, like this one at Chichen Itza in Mexico.

Understanding the Visuals

Bonfire Cave (p. 394) is located in southwestern Texas. Although the region is now dry and landlocked, 15,000 years ago it was a marshy region adjacent to the Gulf of Mexico. Over thousands of years, however, gulf waters have receded.

The ceramic sculpture (p. 395) dates to between 700 and 900. The bracelets, necklace, and the pet bird on its perch indicate that this figure is intended to be a noblewoman.

Although the Mayan pyramid (p. 395) has a shape similar to the pyramids of Egypt, it had a different function. The Egyptian pyramids served as burial chambers for kings; the Mayan pyramids were temples.

Understanding Chronology

Ask the students to look at the timeline. Draw their attention to the entry about the Olmec. Note that the Olmec civilization developed before the Roman Empire existed. (According to legend, Rome was founded in 753 B.C.)

Tiwanakans abandon their great city between A.D. 1100 and 1300. They leave behind traces, such as gold ornaments of condors and other religious figures.

A.D. 250–900 Mayan culture reaches its height in Mexico and Central America. Brilliant Mayan wool and cotton are treasured trade goods. The sculpture (above) shows a Mayan noblewoman weaving.

B.C.	A.D.	500	1000	1500

A.D. 312 Roman Emperor Constantine becomes a Christian. Before the century ends, Christianity is the empire's official religion.

A.D. 1300

395

can tell which ones have been there the longest by using this method.

To determine the actual age of an object, archaeologists use absolute-dating methods. Radiocarbon dating, invented in the 1940s, can date an object back 50,000 or 60,000 years. This technique measures the amount of a certain type of carbon present in once-living matter such as bones, wood, or ash. As an object decays, the amount of carbon it contains decreases at a measurable rate. The older the object, the fewer carbon particles remain. By measuring how much carbon is in

an object, it is possible to determine its age. Scientists determined the age of the earliest Mayan settlements by carbon dating the wooden beams used in building.

Another technique, potassium-argon dating, is used to date objects found in rock formations that contain radioactive potassium and argon. Over time, radioactive potassium changes to argon. By knowing the rate of change and measuring the amount of radioactive potassium and argon in a rock sample, scientists can determine the age of the rock formation and thus the age of the objects

found with it. This method was used to date the 1¼ million-year-old bones and tools found in eastern Africa.

Dendrochronology is the most accurate of the absolute-dating methods, but it can only be used to date wooden objects. By counting the growth rings on trees in the area where an object is found, archaeologists can determine age, but only as far back as 8,000 years.

396

INTRODUCE

Use a world map to locate the North and South American continents. Explain that scientists believe that the first inhabitants came to the Americas from northern Asia across the Bering Strait. As these people wandered in search of food, many made their way south into Central and South America. Ask students to read the Thinking Focus. Have them speculate on how the first communities evolved in the Americas. Tell them that Lesson 1 will trace this development.

Key Terms

Vocabulary Strategies: T36–T37
hunter-gatherer—early people who obtained their food by hunting wild animals and gathering wild plants, roots, nuts, and berries
extinct—no longer existing or living
sedentary—characterized by remaining in one place and not migrating

40,000 B.C.   33,000   8000   5000

LESSON 1

Origins

THINKING FOCUS

Describe the development of early communities in the Americas.

Key Terms

- hunter-gatherer
- extinct
- sedentary

➤ *Many mammoths stood as tall as 14 feet at the shoulder. Their tusks grew to more than 13 feet in length.*

His heart was beating fast. Was it excitement or fear? Today, as a young man, he would finally join the hunt.

The men had sighted a herd of mammoths. Now they would try to drive the mammoths toward a steep ravine. Armed with flint-tipped wooden spears, they hoped to force some of the huge beasts off the cliff.

The boy gasped when he saw the mammoths. They were at least three times his height. Giant, curved tusks jutted from their jaws.

He tightened his grip on his spear. With a signal from his father, he rushed with the others toward the animals, startling them into a full run.

The mammoths pounded toward the cliff, but most of them veered to avoid the edge. One turned too late. When the hunters found their reward at the bottom of the cliff, the boy's eyes gleamed with pride. He had left the camp a boy; he would return a hunter.

Migrants from Asia

Archaeologists believe the first people to come to the Americas were hunters such as those described above. These hunters traveled across the Bering land bridge, which connected Siberia and Alaska during several Ice Ages. Native American creation tales teach that humans were created in North America.

Today, the Bering land bridge is under water. But this was not the case between about 33,000 and 10,000 B.C. During those years, glaciers one to two miles thick covered much of the northern hemisphere. So much water froze into ice that the ocean level dropped, exposing the 50 miles of land between Asia and North America.

Chapter 15

Objectives

1. Describe the lifestyle of the early hunter-gatherers using archaeological evidence.
2. Discuss the theories that explain the disappearance of the big-game animals in ancient America.
3. Explain how the adoption of agriculture led to a sedentary lifestyle.

Graphic Overview

This chart outlines the migration of hunter-gatherers through the Americas and their eventual shift to a more sedentary lifestyle.

| Ice ages expose Bering land bridge. | Big-game animals cross into North America. | Hunter-gatherers follow big game and migrate through the Americas. | The last Ice Age ends; big-game animals become extinct. | Hunter-gatherers adopt a more sedentary lifestyle. |

Animals wandered across the land bridge to graze on the plants growing on each continent. From time to time, hunters from east Asia followed the animals across to North America. Over thousands of years, hunters and animals traveled south to the warmer forests and grasslands of North and Central America. Follow their migration routes on the map on page 398. By 10,500 B.C., people were living at Monte Verde in South America.

Archaeologists traced the path these early migrants took by studying ancient bones and artifacts, such as tools, pottery, and orna- ments. They have discovered tools dating from 32,000 to 17,000 B.C. that are very similar to ancient stone tools found in Asia. In 1998, archaeologists found evidence that humans may have also migrated to the Americas by boat. ■

▲ *Islands between Siberia and Alaska are the parts of the Bering land bridge that are still above water.*

■ *Describe a migration of Asians to the Americas.*

Early Hunter-Gatherers

The hunters who migrated to North America made their own weapons and tools. They pounded pieces of stone into sharp points and attached them to long wooden spears or bones. As the hunters learned more about working with stone, they developed improved tools, like those shown below. Some of these tools have sharp edges, which means other stones were used as chisels to chip off one or both edges of the stone. Sharp points such as these were an improvement over the points used earlier in Asia. These improved points have been found at hunting sites, along with the bones of hundreds of animals apparently killed in one hunt.

These people moved from place to place following big-game animals. They hunted huge tusked mammoths like the one

shown on page 396, mastodons, ground sloths as big as modern-day elephants, sabre-tooth cats, and bison. Usually they hunted these animals in groups of 20 to 50 people, since it took several spear points to kill a big-game animal.

The hunters also stalked smaller animals, such as bears, deer, foxes, and turkeys. And they gathered nuts, wild berries, and other foods from plants. Because these people obtained their food by hunting wild animals and gathering fruits of wild plants, scholars call them **hunter-gatherers.**

▼ *Early hunter-gatherers used points like these as tools and weapons. Each one could fit easily in your hand.*

Early American Civilizations

Have students study the map on p. 398. Ask them to discuss why people migrate. *(To find food, better farmlands.)* Point out that the Asian migration took place over thousands of years. People's lifestyles changed as their food sources changed and as they had to adapt to new surroundings. Stress that the process of adaptation is a gradual process that takes many years and extends over many generations. Refer students to the timeline on pp. 394 and 395 to emphasize this point.

■ *Asians migrated across the Bering land bridge from east Asia to what is now Alaska. They followed big-game animals who wandered across the bridge in search of food.*

HISTORY
Study Skills

Assist students in drawing a graphic organizer on the chalkboard that lists the archaeological discoveries—stone tools, animal bones—that have provided information about the lifestyle of early hunter-gatherers. Have students draw extensions to indicate the significance of these finds.

Access Strategy

To help students understand the life of hunter-gatherers, divide the class into three groups. Tell them to imagine that each group has been stranded, with just the clothes they are wearing, in a forest wilderness. Each group should plan how they will get food and water, provide shelter, and fulfill any other needs for survival. They should also list any information they lack that would help them survive in the wilderness, for example, which plants are edible. Have the groups share their ideas with the class.

Finally, point out that the earliest Americans faced many of the same challenges the students faced in their groups. Ask students to compare the hunter-gatherers' life with that of their imaginary groups. *(Hunter-gatherers had a history of living off the land. Students have a background of modern technology that hunter-gatherers lacked.)* Have students suggest who might survive better: they themselves or the hunter-gatherers.

Access Activity

The tools shown on p. 397 were used for hunting and to prepare the carcasses of animals to be eaten and made into clothing. Ask students to look carefully at the different tools and speculate on how each was used. Ask what modern tools we have for these purposes. *(Knives, tanning machines.)*

■ *They mostly ate moose, bear, and other game animals; fish; and nuts, berries, and other foods from wild plants.*

➤ *Migration routes avoided areas covered by sheets of ice. People didn't settle in most of Canada early on.*

Critical Thinking

Discuss how the hunter-gatherers were affected by the gradual extinction of big-game animals. *(Had to find new source of food, gradually developed farming, lifestyle changed.)* Ask students to discuss how modern society is affected when animals become extinct.

■ *What did early hunter-gatherers eat, and how did they get their food?*

▼ *While the first Americans were migrating into South America, sheets of ice covered most of what is now Canada. How did this affect the migration routes of these people?*

By dating bones of big-game animals, archaeologists have established that the big game had died out by 8000 B.C. No one is certain why they disappeared, or became **extinct.** Some experts think that as the last Ice Age ended at about 8000 B.C., the climate grew warmer and drier. The grass fields where animals grazed turned brown and dried into dusty deserts. The lakes where hunter-gatherers fished, shrank or dried up. And as food and water supplies dwindled, so did the great herds. Others think the hunters killed off too many of the big animals when they developed better hunting methods. ■

Early Farmers

As the big game died out in the Americas, the hunter-gatherers adapted to their changing environment. They hunted smaller animals and gathered food within a smaller area than they had before. As they began to spend time in one place, they adopted a more **sedentary,** or settled, lifestyle.

To support this new lifestyle, the hunter-gatherers developed new tools. Those who lived near water wove nets and fashioned harpoons to catch fish. To store the food they gathered, they wove baskets from plant fibers. Using rocks, the hunter-gatherers crushed nuts and seeds into coarse meal to make flat cakes something like tortillas *(tawr TEE yuhs).*

As people searched for food closer to where they lived, they noticed that many of their food plants grew in the same places year after year. They probably saw plants sprout from discarded seeds. Eventually, they found they could grow their own plants using seeds from wild plants.

They probably also noticed that their plants grew best in open, sunny areas, so they began to create clearings with their stone axes. To plant their seeds, these first farmers used long, sturdy digging sticks. They harvested plants by hand. Gradually, as would happen all over the world, the hunter-gatherers became food producers. In the chart on page 399, you can see how their lives changed as

Routes of Migration, 18,000–500 B.C.

Chapter 15

Critical Thinking

Have students identify the types of evidence needed to prepare the chart on this page. Ask what they think is missing from the chart due to a lack of evidence. *(Example: religious practices.)* Discuss how the evidence is gathered *(archaeological digs)*, and by whom. *(Archaeologists, historians.)*

Collaborative Learning

As the hunter-gatherers became more sedentary, populations increased and social systems began to develop. In small groups, have students discuss the social groups they belong to—family, school, team, town. How are these groups alike? How are they different? Why do groups need structure and rules? One person of each group should take notes on the discussion. Another should use these notes to share the results of the discussion with the class.

Art Connection

Explain that archaeologists have learned much about early people from their cave paintings. Have students find pictures or make drawings of cave paintings to share with the class. Have them explain how, when, and where the paintings were made and how each painting documents the lifestyle of early humans and the animals they depended upon. Display these paintings on a bulletin board.

Life in the Americas

	Hunter-Gatherers, c. 12,000–8500 B.C.	Sedentary Villagers, c. 8500–500 B.C.
Food	Some large game, but primarily smaller animals, such as moose and bear; fish; wild plants; and limited cultivated plants	Cultivated crops, including maize (corn), beans, squash, and chili peppers; domesticated animals, such as sheep, goats, and llamas; and some small wild game
Homes	Portable and easy to assemble (probably made of animal hides and wood)	Sturdy, built to endure over time (hardwood frames and foundations)
Tools	Projectile points, axes, scrapers (made of stone), wooden mortars, grinding stones, and small implements (made of shell and bone)	Cultivating tools, such as digging sticks and simple hoes; cooking pottery; weaving looms; and polished stone tools

◄ *What clues can you find on this chart to indicate that the people in the Americas lived a more settled life after about 8500 B.C.?*

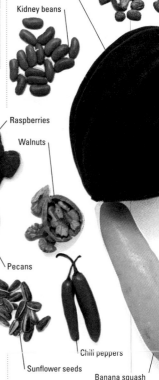

Pinto beans
Acorn squash
Kidney beans
Raspberries
Walnuts
Pecans
Chili peppers
Sunflower seeds
Banana squash

they began to rely more heavily on farming.

Farmers in regions now known as Mexico, Peru, and Bolivia began growing maize (corn), beans, and squash around 8500 B.C. These new foods were especially important because people could eat them fresh, or they could dry them and store them for later use.

People also domesticated wild animals that roamed near their settlements. In early Bolivia and Peru, for instance, people raised llamas and alpacas for food and wool. They also used such animals to transport heavy loads.

Freed from the demands of constant hunting, people had time for other activities. They used their free time to build durable dwellings and to perfect their crafts and toolmaking. They also built special

structures for religious ceremonies. Religion became a community-wide activity, and religious events became social events as well.

As the settlers worked in their fields, good farmland became important, and people created permanent homes in fertile areas where they settled. Neighboring farmers began sharing duties and dividing up tasks. Some settlers developed specialties and traded tasks or goods with their neighbors. Thus, their simple settlements grew into established villages. As the villages prospered, their populations increased. These early communities became the basis for the first civilizations in the Americas. ■

■ *How did hunter-gatherers become food producers?*

REVIEW

1. **FOCUS** Describe the development of early communities in the Americas.

2. **CONNECT** In what ways did the arrival of the early migrants in America differ from the arrival of the European explorers?

3. **GEOGRAPHY** What do you think caused big-game animals and hunters to migrate as far as South America?

4. **ECONOMICS** What did having a surplus of food enable

the early hunter-gatherers to do?

5. **CRITICAL THINKING** How did the lifestyle of hunter-gatherers differ from that of early farmers?

6. **ACTIVITY** Look at the chart, Life in the Americas, on this page. On a separate sheet of paper, create a third column with a heading that describes your lifestyle, for example, Urban Dweller, and the year. Then list your food, home, and tools under this new heading.

399

Early American Civilizations

◄ *Cultivating crops, domesticating animals, building homes, making tools for cultivating.*

CULTURE
Visual Learning

Have students use the information in the chart on this page to write a short essay to explain how an increased reliance on farming led to a sedentary lifestyle. Ask them to discuss the relationships between food, shelter, tools, and lifestyle. (*The food available determines lifestyle, and lifestyle determines shelter.*)

■ *As the big game died out, they hunted smaller animals closer to one place. Eventually, they saw that the same plants always came up in the same place and that they could grow their own plants with seeds from wild plants.*

CLOSE

Draw the Graphic Overview flow chart on the chalkboard and use it to review the main points presented in the lesson. Ask students to follow the progress of the early Asian migrants, starting with their migration across the Bering Strait and ending with the development of the first communities.

Answers to Review Questions

1. Hunter-gatherers followed big game from Asia through the Americas. As big game died out, people learned to farm. They eventually settled into villages and began specializing and sharing labor.

2. The early migrants came following game and made America their homeland. Europeans came to find new trade routes and resources for their homelands.

3. Answers should include a reference to the warmer climate and an abundance of

forests and grasslands to the south.

4. It meant that people had time for activities such as perfecting crafts and building more permanent homes.

5. Hunter-gatherers constantly moved and hunted to supply food. Farmers had a regular food supply; more permanent homes; and more highly developed tools, crafts, and social systems.

6. Charts might include frozen dinners, fast foods, apartments, and computers.

Homework Options

Ask students to decide if they would have rather been an ancient hunter-gatherer or a farmer. Ask them to write a one-page explanation of their answers.

Study Guide: p. 63

INTRODUCE

Tell students that this lesson will focus on the Olmec, the first complex civilization in the Americas. Have students read the Thinking Focus and define *civilization* in their own words. Ask them how they think a complex civilization would differ from the groups of hunter-gatherers and farmers discussed in Lesson 1. Have them read the lesson to confirm or disprove their predictions.

Key Terms

Vocabulary Strategies: T36–T37
elite—a small, privileged group at the top of a society
hieroglyph—a system of writing that uses picture symbols for concepts, objects, or words

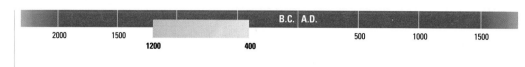

| | | | | B.C. | A.D. | | | |
| 2000 | 1500 | 1200 | 400 | | | 500 | 1000 | 1500 |

L E S S O N   2

The Olmec

THINKING FOCUS

What evidence suggests that the Olmec civilization was complex?

Key Terms

- elite
- hieroglyph

▼ *Huge stone heads such as this were first unearthed in 1862. They weigh 18 to 24 tons and stand 6 to 10 feet tall.*

"*About a league and a half's distance [four and a half miles] from a sugarcane hacienda (hah see EHN duh), on the western slopes of the Sierra de San Martin, a worker on this hacienda who was clearing jungle noticed on the surface of the ground what he took to be the bottom of a huge pot lying upside down. He told the owner of the hacienda of this discovery, and the latter ordered this object to be unearthed.... As a work of art, it is, without exaggeration, a magnificent sculpture...."*

This notice appeared in 1869 in a bulletin of the Mexican Geographical Society. The news it told introduced the modern world to a mysterious ancient world, one of the first American civilizations, the Olmec of Mexico.

The object was a colossal head, carved from stone. It was taller than a person and weighed several tons. Archaeologists wondered about the person with the helmet and stern face. Was he a king, a soldier, a priest, or some combination of the three? More mystifying, how had the Olmec obtained the massive stone that was used in the sculpture?

Archaeologists knew there were no large boulders in the area where the Olmec had settled. The closest stones were about 50 miles away in the Tuxtla (*TOOST luh*) Mountains. The Olmec must have brought the stones from the mountains. But how had they managed to move these huge stones?

After studying the geography of the area, archaeologists found an answer to their question. The Olmec probably rolled the huge slabs of rock on logs or dragged them 25 miles on wooden sleds down the mountainsides to a tributary of the Coatzacoalcos (*koh aht suh koh AHL kuhs*) River. Then they must have floated their cargo on rafts to the Gulf of Mexico and along the coast to the Tonala River. There they battled their way upriver 12 miles to their site at La Venta.

Chapter 15

Objectives

1. Evaluate the role of a fertile environment in a complex civilization.
2. Compare and contrast the contributions of the upper and lower classes in Olmec society.
3. Summarize the main features of Olmec religion.
4. Describe the evidence of Olmec trading with other peoples.
5. Locate the Olmec on a map.

Graphic Overview

This chart shows some of the features that made the Olmec civilization complex.

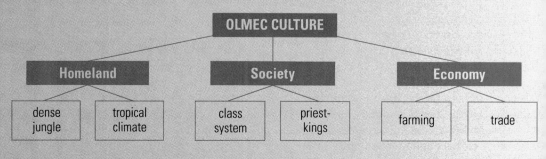

```
                    OLMEC CULTURE
         ┌──────────────┼──────────────┐
     Homeland         Society         Economy
     ┌───┴───┐       ┌───┴───┐       ┌───┴───┐
   dense  tropical  class   priest-  farming  trade
   jungle climate   system  kings
```

A Fertile Environment

Archaeologists now think that the Olmec civilization developed around 1200 B.C. It occupied the region from the Gulf of Mexico on the north to the Tuxtla Mountains in the south. The two major centers of the Olmec, La Venta and San Lorenzo, were built on rivers. La Venta, in fact, was located on an island in the Tonala River.

The Olmec home was a challenging land of rivers and jungle. Heavy rains caused the rivers to flood each year. And because of the tropical climate, much of the land was swampy and covered with dense jungle. Whenever farmers cleared the land, the jungle sprang back almost overnight.

But the Olmec adapted to the land. The floods deposited fertile soil ideal for raising their squash, gourds, beans, avocados, peppers, and maize. And the rivers provided game such as crocodiles, fish, shellfish, and aquatic birds.

The Olmec also learned to farm the jungle. They cut down and burned one section of thick

jungle vegetation and planted there for several years. Then they moved on and cleared the next section of jungle for farming.

The Olmec even developed a calendar of their growing seasons. They used the calendar to track the passing of the seasons, so they knew when to sow and harvest each crop. In addition to the food they raised or caught in the rivers, the Olmec ate deer, wild pigs, pheasants, and wild monkeys from the jungle.

Thus, the Olmec became efficient producers of their own food. Soon they even had surpluses, or extra supplies, of food. In turn, their population grew rapidly. And as their population increased, the Olmec developed the class system, rituals, and networks of trade that are features of a complex society. ■

▲ *The region the Olmec occupied is shown on the locator map above. The lush jungle vegetation seems to swallow up everything. In fact, the tangled vines that grew over Olmec ruins hid them for centuries.*

◄ *This aerial view of southeastern Mexico shows the jungle rainforest that lies in the lowlands near the Gulf of Mexico.*

■ *What environmental factors helped the Olmec develop a complex society?*

Elite and Commoners

Archaeologists believe that at its height, the Olmec population numbered tens of thousands of people and covered from 6,000 to 7,000 square miles. That is slightly less than the area of New Jersey. These people were probably divided into at least two classes of society—the upper, or **elite,** class and a lower class, the commoners.

Early American Civilizations

Tell students that Lessons 2, 3, and 4 will examine early American civilizations and will show how the Olmec, in this lesson, and three other peoples adapted to geography to create complex societies. Explain that little or no written history has survived from these cultures, but scholars have pieced together information from artifacts that remain. Have students examine the photos of Olmec artifacts in this lesson before they begin to read.

GEOGRAPHY
Critical Thinking

Point out the Olmec region on a map and explain that the land there provided fertile soil and abundant plant and animal life. But it was hard work to live in the harsh environment, especially with its extreme heat, humidity, insects, and snakes. Have students imagine they are Olmec farmers or hunters and ask them to describe a typical day.

■ *Rich soil and rivers and forests filled with game gave the Olmec food surpluses. So the population grew and the society became more complex.*

Access Strategy

Ask students what they would bury in a time capsule to let people in the future know how we lived, worked, and entertained ourselves. Have each student make a list of five to 10 items and then share it with the class. Keep track of these items on the chalkboard to see if common items occur. Have students rank the items in their order of importance.

Then tell students that because of the moisture and acidic soil in the area where the Olmec settled, only a small number of artifacts from their culture survived. Stone columns and figures survived, but articles made of wood, cloth, plant fibers, animal skins, and even bones and shell decayed quickly. Point out that the picture historians can draw from these artifacts is incomplete. For example, religion may have played only a small part in a culture. But if all that remains of that civilization are its religious artifacts, scholars might tend to overemphasize the importance of religion in that culture.

Access Activity

Have students look at the Olmec head on p. 400 and the jungle landscape on p. 401. Tell them to imagine they are archaeologists who have just discovered the stone head in this jungle setting. Ask them what questions the artifact raises. Then have students discuss what conclusions they might draw about the Olmec from this artifact.

SOCIAL SYSTEMS

Critical Thinking

Have students describe the evidence that suggests there were at least two classes in Olmec society. Ask the students if they think there may have also been an Olmec middle class. What role might a middle class have played? *(Supervisors of laborers.)*

■ *Because of the discovery of elaborate tombs and simple graves, archaeologists believe the Olmec had both upper and lower classes.*

■ *They were warriors and rulers and were expected to ensure that the gods protected the village and sent good weather for crops.*

BELIEF SYSTEMS

Social Participation

After discussing the role of religion in Olmec society, have students study the jade figurines pictured on this page. Ask them to build a story around what the figures in the photo are doing. (Note: Scholars speculate that the figures represent a sacrificial victim awaiting death or a priest leading a religious ceremony.)

Across Time & Space

The colossal heads were monuments to honor the Olmec rulers. The great stone faces of Mount Rushmore in South Dakota are 10 times larger than the Olmec heads. They pay tribute to four U.S. presidents.

■ *What do the artifacts found at Olmec burial sites reveal about Olmec society?*

■ *What role did priest-kings play in Olmec society?*

▼ *These jade figurines were found buried in this arrangement in 1955 at La Venta.*

This idea is based on inferences about the carving and moving of the giant Olmec heads.

In general, when archaeologists find evidence such as the giant Olmec heads, they conclude that hundreds of workers must have labored to carve and move these monuments. These laborers were probably directed by a smaller group of supervisors. They, in turn, followed the dictates of a single ruler or group of rulers. Such a division of labor suggests that the Olmec divided their society into distinct classes of people.

Archaeologists believe that many of the massive heads found at sites in La Venta are probably heroic portraits of Olmec leaders. Each helmet is marked with unique symbols that probably represent the different ruling families.

Olmec burial sites provide further clues about the different Olmec classes. Some burial sites consist of simple, crudely prepared graves that contain few or no ornaments. These are most likely the graves of commoners. At other sites, elaborate stone tombs contain intricately carved figures and finely crafted ornaments made from jade, amethyst, and other semiprecious stones. Some even contain mirrors that were made from iron ore. These tombs probably belonged to members of the elite class. ■

Power and Religion

Olmec rulers were priest-kings who came from the ranks of the elite. They were not only brave warriors and civil leaders, they were also religious leaders. The Olmec believed that the priest-kings were direct descendants of their gods. They also believed the priest-kings had the power to ensure that the gods would protect them from their enemies. And they looked to the priest-kings to influence the gods to send good weather for their crops.

The Olmec had as many as 15 gods, but the jaguar-man was probably the most important god. It represented the mystery of life and death. The Olmec made small jade sculptures of jaguars and other images of gods to use in their religious rituals.

They performed these rituals in an attempt to please their gods. Many ceremonies took place at stone altars, which were adorned with intricate carvings. The priest-kings sacrificed animals, and even human beings, as offerings to their gods. They often sacrificed soldiers captured in battle to demonstrate their own power as warriors. Archaeologists have discovered knives, axes, and other sharp tools that may have been used in these sacrifices. ■

Study Skills

The Olmec made religious objects, jewelry, and sculpture from raw materials that were obtained in and around where they settled. Have students do research and make a list of natural materials available in their own area. Ask them which of these materials might have been useful to the Olmec.

Historical Context

La Venta was once surrounded by lush, tropical vegetation. La Venta, once an important center of Olmec society, has been transformed by modern industrialization. Now, the land has been cleared for an oil refinery. An airstrip cuts across the site where Olmec artifacts were once discovered. Waste clogs the swamps as the search for oil under the surface of La Venta continues.

Language Arts Connection

No one knows what the Olmec called themselves. The name *Olmec* was given to this ancient people by archaeologists. It comes from the Aztec root *ollin,* which means "rubber." Olmec means the "rubber people" and reflects the fact that these people lived in a land where rubber is produced. The sap from these rubber trees was later used by the Maya to waterproof their clothing.

Trade and Competition

For the Olmec, jade was extremely valuable. They obtained jade and other raw materials for their crafts by trading with people in nearby regions. Olmec-style pottery, statues, and cave paintings have been found in Mexico, Guatemala, and El Salvador. This suggests that the Olmec traveled to these places to find and trade for resources. Archaeologists have found both Olmec artifacts and **hieroglyphs,** written signs that represent concepts and objects, as far as 500 miles from the Olmec area.

Archaeologists have also found scenes of war carved on stone monuments. This suggests that the Olmec sometimes fought neighboring tribes—and each other—for materials and control of trade routes.

This competition for resources may have caused the destruction of Olmec civilization. In fact, evidence of vandalism has led archaeologists to conclude that the Olmec center of San Lorenzo was purposely destroyed around 900 B.C.

After San Lorenzo, La Venta seems to have become the center of Olmec art and religion. But mutilated and buried stone heads found at La Venta suggest that it, too, was destroyed by enemies around 400 B.C. After eight centuries of growth, the Olmec civilization, the first civilization of the Americas, was in decline.

Regional Powers

As traders and keepers of religious centers, the Olmecs transferred many elements of their culture to the growing civilizations around them.

Beginning around 200 B.C., a strong empire and a great city grew in the Valley of Mexico called Teotihuacan *(tay oh tee wah KAHN).* Lasting until around A.D. 650, Teotihuacan attracted people from the countryside to city life, with broad streets, markets, plazas, temples, palaces, and apartments. The city also had waterways, reservoirs, sewers, and slums. Irrigated fields surrounded the city, but in its center stood two gigantic, pyramid-shaped temples, now called the Temples of the Sun and Moon.

After Teotihuacan's fall, people from northern colonies moved back into the central region, bringing with them a group called the Toltec. The Toltec later came to rule lands north and west of the Valley of Mexico. They passed on legend and lore to the Aztec. ■

▲ *Jade figures like this axehead were more valuable than gold to the Olmec. Jade figures have been found as far as 500 miles from the Olmec's territory. The jade had been used in trade.*

■ *How did Olmec competition for goods and trade routes affect their civilization?*

Critical Thinking

Describe the evidence that led archaeologists to speculate that the Olmec had a system of trade. Ask students how they think archaeologists determined that artifacts and cave paintings found in other areas were products of the Olmec. *(The artifacts would have typical Olmec features such as Olmec hieroglyphics, physical features, Olmec gods.)*

■ *Competition led to battles among the Olmec and other peoples. These battles probably led to the destruction of the Olmec civilization.*

C L O S E

Remind students of the factors that contributed to the complexity of Olmec society by showing them the Graphic Overview chart for this lesson. Have them discuss ways each of the bottom entries influenced Olmec culture. *(Fertile soil, warm weather for crops, workers for civic projects, abundant food supply, variety of goods available.)*

R E V I E W

1. **FOCUS** What evidence suggests that the Olmec civilization was complex?
2. **CONNECT** In what ways were Olmec farming techniques better than those of the early farmers?
3. **SOCIAL SYSTEMS** How did archaeologists determine that the Olmec probably had at least two social classes?
4. **SOCIAL SYSTEMS** In what ways were the priest-kings important to Olmec society?
5. **CRITICAL THINKING** How might the course of Olmec civilization have differed if it had never developed a trade network?
6. **WRITING ACTIVITY** Imagine that you and your family are in the Americas in 1200 B.C. searching for a new place to settle. Write a paragraph describing the type of area that you are looking for, including the sources of food and the climate. Also describe what your lifestyle would be like there.

403

Early American Civilizations

403

Answers to Review Questions

1. Evidence includes the existence of different social classes, elaborate religious rituals, and a large network of trade.
2. The Olmec planted crops in rich soil near rivers. They used calendars to plan their growing seasons.
3. Because work on the giant Olmec heads was so difficult and complex, archaeologists believe a system of supervisors from an upper class and workers from a lower class must have existed. In addition, two different types of burial sites, some crude, some elaborate, suggest the existence of two social classes.
4. They were civic, military, and spiritual leaders of the society.
5. The Olmec civilization might not have ended if competition for resources and control of trade routes had not led to war and the destruction of San Lorenzo and La Venta.

Homework Options

List archaeologists who explored Olmec sites, including Hermann Beyer, George Vaillant, and Matthew Stirling. Have each student research one archaeologist and write up an imaginary interview with that person.

Study Guide: p. 64

404

INTRODUCE

Tell students that, like the Olmec, the Maya began as a farming society. Ask them to read the Thinking Focus and predict how the Mayan culture changed as its farming methods improved. You might also help students compare the two cultures by showing them the Graphic Overviews for Lessons 2 and 3. Both charts list features of these complex civilizations. Have students look for more similarities between the Olmec and Maya as they read.

Key Terms

Vocabulary Strategies: T36–T37
stele—an upright stone column with inscribed hieroglyphs used as a monument, particularly by early peoples of Central America
codex—a manuscript volume; record books kept by early Central American peoples such as the Maya and Aztec

---

| 2000 | 1800 | | B.C. | A.D. | | 900 | 1000 | 1500 |

LESSON 3

The Maya

THINKING
FOCUS

In what ways were the Maya an advanced civilization?

Key Terms

- stele
- codex

➤ *The seven-inch-tall ceramic ballplayer at top right is part of the religious art of the Maya. Real players on the losing side sometimes became sacrifices to the gods. The large Mayan temple, on the right, was built between A.D. 600 and 800. Artist Frederick Catherwood, who accompanied explorer Stephens, painted this view of the Mayan temple.*

I t is impossible to describe the interest with which I explored these ruins. The ground was entirely new. . . . We could not see ten yards before us, and never knew what we should stumble upon next. The beauty of the sculpture, the solemn stillness of the woods, disturbed only by the scrambling of monkeys and the chattering of parrots, the desolation of the city, and the mystery that hung over it, all created an interest higher, if possible, than I had ever felt among the ruins of the Old World.

With these words, John Lloyd Stephens described his discovery in 1839 of a ruined city in the jungles of Central America. Among the ruins and tangled vines, he found a temple with a broad stairway that was inscribed with thousands of strange symbols. He also found a ball court watched over by six enormous stone parrots. And he found heavy stone columns carved with images of jaguars, birds, serpents, and men in fabulous feathered headdresses. Stephens had no idea who the builders of this city were, but he was sure he had found evidence of a magnificent civilization.

A Growing Civilization

Stephens had discovered the ruins of Copan, an ancient Mayan city. Like the Olmec, the Maya settled in a fertile region. Notice on the map on page 405 that this region stretched south along an extended finger of land that is surrounded by water.

The 125,000 square miles that the Maya occupied contained both highlands and lowlands. The highlands in the south ran along a mountain range that included active volcanoes. A long rainy season and deep, fertile soil made this area good for farming.

Chapter 15

404

Objectives

1. Locate and describe the area of Mayan settlement.
2. Assess the effectiveness of Mayan agricultural techniques.
3. Describe the role of priest-kings in Mayan society.
4. List important Mayan achievements and their significance.
5. Name the present-day countries that occupy the region where the Maya settled.

Graphic Overview

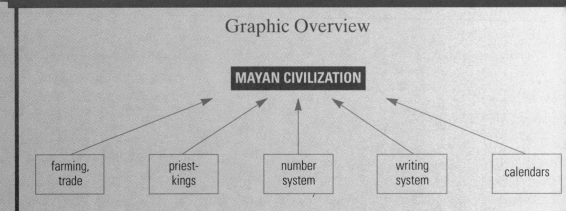

MAYAN CIVILIZATION

| farming, trade | priest-kings | number system | writing system | calendars |

The lowlands were located in the central and northern part of the region. Some lowlands were covered with dense tropical forests with fertile soil. Others had only rough, dry grass or cactus and were not good for farming. But they were rich in the limestone the Maya needed for building and in the flint they used in stonework.

Archaeologists think the Maya may have begun farming the fertile areas of the lowlands as early as 1800 B.C. Between 1800 and 500 B.C., the Maya established small farming villages. They gathered food from the forests and also raised crops. Between 100 B.C. and A.D. 200, some of the villages grew into cities with impressive palaces and pyramids. Mayan artisans carved huge stone figures and pillars to adorn their cities.

During the height of Mayan civilization, between A.D. 250 and 900, about three million people lived in Mayan cities scattered through the region. Look at the map at the above right to find the major cities.

Mayan cities were built around religious centers. At the heart of

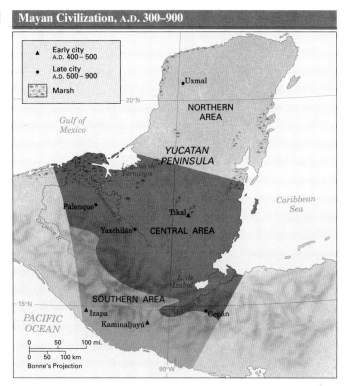

Mayan Civilization, A.D. 300–900

- ▲ Early city A.D. 400–500
- ● Late city A.D. 500–900
- Marsh

Uxmal
NORTHERN AREA
Gulf of Mexico
YUCATAN PENINSULA
Palenque
Tikal ▲
Yaxchilán
CENTRAL AREA
Caribbean Sea
L. de Izaba
SOUTHERN AREA
PACIFIC OCEAN
Izapa ▲
Kaminaljuyú ▲
Copán

0   50   100 mi.
0   50   100 km
Bonne's Projection

the city, the Maya usually built tall limestone pyramids that were surrounded by large, open plazas. At the top of the pyramids they built temples. The Mayan priest-kings climbed the steps of the pyramids to perform religious ceremonies at these temples. ■

▲ *Find Copan on the map. Look at the Copan ball court below. Guess the size of the buildings by comparing them with the car in the background.*

■ *What were Mayan cities like?*

DEVELOP

Have students study the map on this page showing the growth of the Mayan civilization. Ask students to use the information on the map and on page 401 to compare and contrast the geography of the Olmec and Maya regions. Refer students to the timelines in Lessons 2 and 3 to compare the dates of each civilization's development.

GEOGRAPHY
Map Skills

Have students trace the map of the Maya territory shown here. Remind them that the Maya occupied both highlands and lowlands. Then refer them to a physical map of Central America and have students indicate the highland and lowland regions on their traced maps. Finally, discuss which Mayan cities were in the highlands *(those in the south)* and which were in the lowlands. *(Those in the north.)*

■ *They had huge buildings with statues and pillars carved of stone. Many were built around religious centers, with tall limestone pyramids and large open plazas.*

405

Access Strategy

Brainstorm with students about the kinds of activities that take place in the center of their community. *(Shopping; government administration; social, sporting, and religious events.)* Then tell them to look at the aerial view of Copan on this page. Explain that this Mayan city is arranged much like many modern cities. People gathered there to engage in the same kinds of activities we do today. Point out that at least 10,000 people lived in Copan. As you read aloud the following details about

the ancient city, have students try to relate the description to their own community.

There were two types of housing in Copan. Those who were wealthy lived in stone homes clustered in groups near the main plaza. Away from the plaza the land was less densely settled. The lower class farmers and servants of the rich lived in pole and thatch houses scattered near the river. On the other side of the river were the farmers' fields.

Access Activity

Some Mayan towns, such as Copan, were built along rivers for the fertile soil and easy transportation and trade. Ask students to draw a map of their community, showing the main buildings and centers of activity, as well as natural features such as rivers and mountains. Discuss why community centers may be built in these locations.

■ *Highland farmers used terraced farmland and farmers in wet lowlands built raised fields. To clear land in dense forests, farmers burned vegetation. To make thin soil more fertile, they covered it with rich soil from river beds and banks. They also developed a system of irrigation.*

ECONOMY

Critical Thinking

Point out the variety and sophistication of the Mayan farming methods. Help students see that these methods helped to support a large Mayan population. To provide a better understanding of these methods, give students a list of different land types. Have students come up with a Mayan farming technique that would have solved the problem of raising crops on these types of land. Drawings may be helpful.

406

An Economy Based on Agriculture

■ *What techniques enabled highland and lowland farmers to become more efficient?*

▼ *Mayan farmers built flat terraces on the slopes of the highlands to stop topsoil from being washed downhill. They built canals that descended the hills. The canals were an efficient way to provide water for irrigating the crops in the terraces.*

As the population of Mayan cities increased, farmers had to produce more food. To meet this demand, they devised ways to farm hillsides and other land that they had not been able to farm before. You can see in the diagram below that the Maya built flat terraces into the slopes of the highlands. In the wet lowlands, they built raised fields to improve drainage and, thus, water fields without flooding them. In densely forested areas, they burned off vegetation to clear land.

In the hot, dry region of the lowlands, where the soil was thin, the Maya used yet another technique. They scooped rich soil from the banks and the bottom of rivers and spread this over the rocky plains to create farmland. They also dug canals and moats to bring water to dry areas. Using these techniques, the Maya grew their crops of maize, beans, avocados, melons, and squash.

As the Maya became more efficient farmers, they developed a surplus of food. They traded their excess food and other products with other peoples living in Central America and Mexico. Mayan traders carried their goods on foot or in dugout canoes to places as far away as present-day Mexico City. In this way, they obtained things they could not produce themselves. For instance, they traded salt, honey, finely decorated cotton, and jaguar pelts with people in regions we know today as Guatemala and Honduras. In return, they received jade, brightly colored bird feathers, and cacao beans. From jade they carved jewelry and statues. They used the cacao beans to make chocolate and also as a form of money in trade. ■

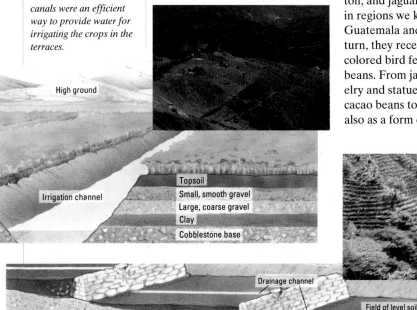

High ground

Irrigation channel

Topsoil
Small, smooth gravel
Large, coarse gravel
Clay
Cobblestone base

Drainage channel

Field of level soil

Embankment

Limestone mountainside

Ask students to research Mayan trade and draw a map showing trade routes and products. Suggest they use a current map since modern countries are referred to in many sources on Mayan trade. The maps should indicate incoming and outgoing routes, and the imports and exports should be listed on the routes or in the map's legend.

Economic Context

Growing food, especially in the lowlands, took a tremendous amount of work. With an average of 10 feet of rain a year, farmers had to work feverishly to plant and harvest during the few dry periods. Climate was not the only problem. Farmers also had to fight off tropical animals and insects. Overfarming drained the soil of nutrients, which meant that fields often had to lie fallow for five to ten years before they could support more crops. Cleared fields were quickly overrun by jungle growth. The Maya had no wheeled vehicles or farm animals to make their work easier. They carried everything on their backs. Maize was the important crop and staple food. The Maya ate it every day with every meal. Women did all the cooking. They ground corn kernels that had been soaked in water into dough to make flat cakes or tortillas. They also prepared a type of corn porridge. Mayan farmers also raised cotton, tobacco, and cacao.

Priests as Kings

The Maya worshiped many gods and believed their gods controlled the sun, rain, and other elements of nature. They sought to please the gods, hoping in return they would be blessed with good weather and bountiful harvests. They also worshiped their rulers, because they believed their rulers could influence the gods.

The Maya told about their rulers in hieroglyphs painted on tomb walls and carved into stone **steles,** or columns. One such ruler, named Pacal, began ruling the city-state Palenque at the age of six, with help from his mother. In A.D. 65, when he turned 12, he became king in his own right. During his 68-year reign, the city of Palenque flourished.

From pictures carved on the walls of Pacal's tomb, scholars have concluded that Pacal, like other Mayan rulers, was a priest as well as a warrior and ruler. As priests, Mayan kings sacrificed food, animals, and even human beings to please the gods. Sometimes the priest-kings pierced their own skin and shed their own sacred blood in the belief that this would keep their society healthy and productive. ■

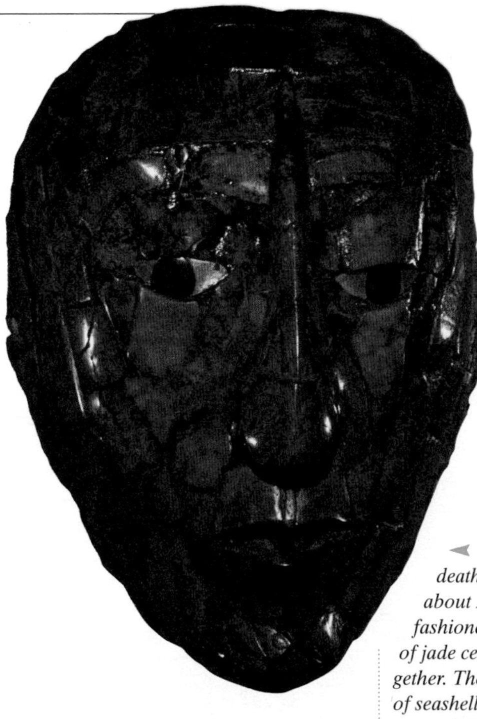

This Mayan death mask from about A.D. 700 was fashioned out of pieces of jade cemented together. The eyes are made of seashells. The Maya covered their king's face when he went to live with the gods.

■ What do we know about Mayan rulers?

Mayan Achievements

The Mayan civilization developed many cultural achievements, such as a number system and a writing system of hieroglyphs like those on the stele at the right. The priest-kings also created two calendars to record and plan their years. To learn more about the Mayan calendars, read A Closer Look on page 408.

The number system enabled the priest-kings

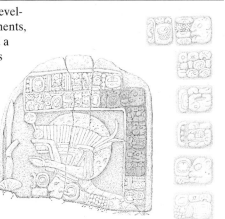

Mayan hieroglyphs are read from left to right, top to bottom. Scholars think this stele describes a person named Jaguar Claw, who is about to be sacrificed. The person shown here is probably the ruler of the Mayan city of Dos Pilas.

BELIEF SYSTEMS

Critical Thinking

Discuss the role of priest-kings in Mayan culture. Ask students to speculate on why priests were also kings. *(Importance of religion, divine leadership.)* Ask students how the architecture and art of the Maya reflects the importance of religion in this culture. *(Large temples, sacrifices shown in art.)*

■ *The Maya greatly honored their rulers, who served as priests and warriors as well as kings. These rulers developed sophisticated systems of writing and numbers, and two calendars. As priests, they led religious rituals, including ceremonies of sacrifice. The Maya believed their rulers could influence the gods.*

Collaborative Learning

Bring in pictures of Mayan artifacts and architecture. Have students analyze the artifacts and guess how they were used and what materials they were made from. You may want to divide the class into two teams. Have one team read a description and then ask the other team to match it to the artifact it describes. Keep score on the chalkboard.

Cultural Context

Ball games were an important ritual in Mayan society. The games were similar to soccer, but the ball was smaller and made of hard, solid rubber. Players propelled the ball with their hips, knees, and waist, all of which were covered with leather padding. Even with padding, players often died from internal injuries. Players scored by bouncing the ball off a target at either end of the stone courts. Winners were considered heroes, and losers were often killed.

Study Skills

The core of the Mayan civilization was religion. Religion influenced government, art and scientific achievement, and agricultural production. Have students construct a graphic overview that shows how religion was linked to almost every aspect of Mayan life.

Note: You may wish to use this Closer Look after students have studied Mayan Achievements on pp. 407 and 409.

More About Mayan Calendars
New Year's Day took place on the same day on both Mayan calendars only once every 52 solar years. This 52-year period was called a calendar round.

Scholars believe that the Maya understood that their solar calendar should have been 365¼ days rather than 365 days. Yet they chose to ignore this slight inaccuracy.

CULTURE
Visual Learning

Point out on the number wheel that a dot stands for one and a bar stands for five. Have students identify each number on the wheel and write additional numbers through 19. (For additional information on the Mayan numerical system, see the chart on p. 409.)

A CLOSER LOOK

The Mayan Calendar

Why do people have good days and bad days? Why do crops grow well one year and poorly the next? The Maya believed it was because different gods ruled each day. By consulting their two calendars and using the right mathematics, Mayan priests knew which gods ruled which days. Then the priests had to figure out what influence the gods would have.

On the 260-day religious calendar, each day was given a name and a number. The name *Imix* meant "water lily," and represented the ocean. *Ik* was named for the wind, and *Akbal* was named for the darkness of night.

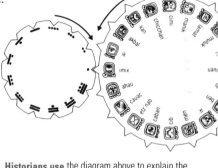

Historians use the diagram above to explain the 260-day religious calendar. Each name and each number was a divine being—two gods for every day. When you turn the wheels, you discover that the same name and the same number only fall together once every 260 days. Then the cycle starts all over again.

1 Imix—the New Year's day of the Mayan 260-day year

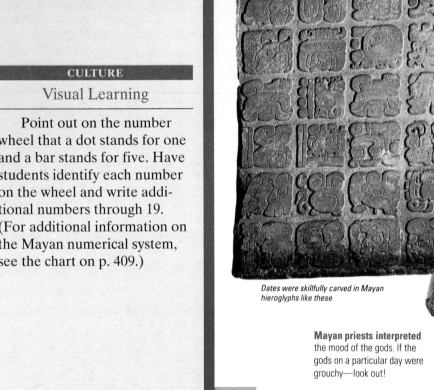

Dates were skillfully carved in Mayan hieroglyphs like these

Mayan priests interpreted the mood of the gods. If the gods on a particular day were grouchy—look out!

The other Mayan calendar was based on the earth's orbit around the sun and had 365 days like ours. Each of these days had a god, too. This calendar had 18 months of 20 days each, plus 5 extra days. It was considered bad luck to do anything on those 5 days, so people did very little. They didn't even eat!

Chapter 15

Critical Thinking

Have students use information from this page to determine how many days off the Mayan calendar would be after one calendar round. *(13 days.)* Ask a volunteer to explain the significance of this inaccuracy. *(13 days, or almost two weeks, can make a difference in planting and harvesting crops.)*

Research

Ask students to look in the library for more information on Mayan hieroglyphics. Have them write a paragraph or two explaining what kinds of information has been gained from these carvings.

Bulletin Board

Explain that many different cultures developed calendars based on astronomical observations. Divide students into groups to research information on different kinds of calendars. Suggest that they prepare a bulletin-board display using the information from their research.

to record information about astronomical events. The detailed astronomical charts and tables that they made using this system are quite accurate. Their system was based on the number 20 instead of 10, which is the basis for our decimal system. As you can see at the top of this page, they used dots and dashes to represent numbers and even had a symbol for zero.

To record important dates and events in the lives of their rulers, the Maya developed hieroglyphs. Each hieroglyph represents a sound. When the pictures are put together, they can make up part of a word or a whole word. Some hieroglyphs represent ideas, such as "life" or "happiness." Others represent objects like "corn" or "water."

The Mayan priest-kings used hieroglyphs to write record books, each of which was known as a **codex.** Archaeologists have studied the three existing codices and deciphered part of them to learn about religious ceremonies, astronomy, and Mayan calendars.

The codices reveal that the Maya had two calendars. They used them to determine the best time to plant crops, hunt, and perform religious ceremonies. The Mayan priest-kings developed the

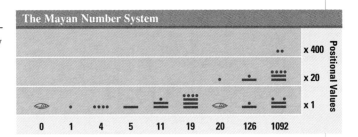

The Mayan Number System

									Positional Values
								••	x 400
						•	⎯•⎯	⠶⠶	x 20
👁	•	••••	⎯	⎯•⎯	⠶•	👁	⎯•⎯	⠶⠶	x 1
0	1	4	5	11	19	20	126	1092	

calendars from their close observations of the movements of the sun, moon, and stars.

Mayan cultural achievements also included the magnificent architecture of their cities and beautiful works of decorative art. For example, Mayan artisans made jewelry out of jade, gold, and shells. King Pacal, in his tomb at Palenque, was found wearing a life-size mosaic mask made from jade. He also wore jewelry of jade and mother-of-pearl. The Maya were also accomplished weavers, and they communicated nonverbally through their weaving designs. (See Exploring Nonverbal Communication on pages 410–411.)

These are only some of the achievements of the ancient Mayan civilization. The Mayan culture has survived, however, unlike many other early American cultures. Today, Mayan people live in Guatemala, Belize, and parts of Mexico. ■

▲ *In the Mayan number system, symbols represented basic numerical values. Find the bar above that equals 5. Vertical positions also indicated that the basic value was multiplied by a certain number (1, 20, 400, and so on). Thus, the representation above for 1,092 translates into this equation: 12 + (14 x 20) + (2 x 400) = 1,092. Translate the representation for 126 into a numerical equation.*

■ *Describe the Mayan writing and number systems.*

R E V I E W

1. **FOCUS** In what ways were the Maya an advanced civilization?
2. **CONNECT** What agricultural techniques made Mayan farming more efficient than Olmec farming?
3. **BELIEF SYSTEMS** What did the Maya worship? What important role did the priest-kings play in the Mayan religion?
4. **CULTURE** How have archaeologists learned so much about King Pacal?

5. **CRITICAL THINKING** Why was the invention of a number system important in Mayan society?
6. **WRITING ACTIVITY** Write a message for a classmate using your own hieroglyphs. First, write out the message you want to send. Then create simple pictures for each sound, word, or idea you want to get across. Remember, when someone looks at your picture, they will need to be able to guess the sound, word, or idea it represents. Trade messages, and decipher them.

Early American Civilizations

Critical Thinking

Explain that the Maya had many outstanding achievements, but some historians are puzzled that the Maya failed to come up with such practical inventions as the wheel, the arch, and measuring the weight of objects. Ask students how these inventions would have helped the Maya. *(For example, they would have made building easier.)*

◄ *6 + (6 x 20) = 126*

■ *The writing system used hieroglyphs, each of which represented a sound. Hieroglyphs were read left to right, top to bottom. The number system was based on 20, with specific symbols for one, five, and zero. The Maya combined these symbols in vertical columns to indicate higher numerical values.*

CLOSE

Ask students to write an epitaph for the Mayan culture. Remind them that an epitaph is an inscription on a tombstone in memory of the person buried there. The epitaph should be a single paragraph that touches on the important features of the Mayan world.

Answers to Review Questions

1. The Maya developed a variety of farming techniques for many kinds of soil, writing and number systems, and two calendars. Mayan engineers and artisans created impressive cities and beautiful artwork.
2. They built terraces into highland slopes and raised fields in the lowlands to improve drainage. They covered rocky plains with rich river soils and dug canals and moats to irrigate dry areas.

3. The Maya worshiped many gods. The priest-kings offered sacrifices to please the gods.
4. They studied the artifacts and carvings in his tomb.
5. Answers will vary but should refer to the importance of the number system in recording information about astronomical events.

Homework Options

Ask students to draw a chart comparing and contrasting the Maya and the Olmec.

Study Guide: p. 65

DISCOVERY PROCESS

Students will use the following steps in the discovery process to complete the activity:

Get Ready List several forms of nonverbal communication and gather references to use in explaining them.

Find Out List and illustrate messages that one form of nonverbal communication can convey.

Move Ahead Display and read the messages.

Explore Some More Be alert to all forms of nonverbal communication in use in everyday life.

Materials needed: Reference books, magazines, sketch paper, construction paper, and markers.

CULTURE
Study Skills

Ask students to find a definition of *nonverbal communication* in their texts. *(Facial expressions, gestures, and codes using symbols or sounds.)* Explain that nonverbal communication conveys messages without using spoken words. Have students find examples of nonverbal communciation in their text and explain how not having to speak might be advantageous. *(Sample answer: Basketball referees communicate with hand gestures; don't have to be heard in noisy crowd to be understood.)*

410

EXPLORING

Nonverbal Communication

Mayan weaving contains messages, but only people who can recognize and understand its colorful symbols can read them. For centuries people have used various kinds of nonverbal communication to convey their thoughts to others.

Get Ready

Get a notebook, a sketch pad, and a pencil. List several forms of nonverbal communication: facial expressions, gestures, and codes using symbols or sounds. Include some visual arts, such as Mayan weaving or another art form that communicates through colors and symbols. Choose one form.

➤ *Using a traditional back-strap loom, this Mayan woman weaves patterns used in her village for generations. For the Mayan weaver, snakes symbolize the earth, toads symbolize saints, and eagles symbolize life and death.*

410

Chapter 15

Objectives

1. Define and give examples of nonverbal communication. (Culture 1, 3)

2. Identify, compare, and contrast examples of nonverbal communication. (Culture 3, 4)

Activity

Divide students into small groups and have them embark on an imaginary journey in which their very lives will depend on the success of their nonverbal communication. Explain the following situation: They have been in an ocean shipwreck, and they are now afloat on a vast sea in tiny lifeboats. Although their little boats are within sight of shore, they are too far for sound to carry to the people there. The lifeboats are equipped with flashlights and enough food and water

for three days. Among each group's survivors are an artist; a tailor with needles, thread, and fabric; and a sales representative whose traveling case contains novelties such as balloons and firecrackers.

Tell the groups that each must devise a system to send a message to either the people on the shore or airplane pilots above them. When the groups have finished, have each explain to the rest of the class their message and their method for conveying it.

You are going to explain and illustrate an example of nonverbal communication. You may need reference books to help you with this exploration. Sports and art magazines can also be good sources of ideas.

Find Out

Make a list of messages that can be delivered using the form of nonverbal communication that you chose. For instance, you might list the various messages that a basketball referee can deliver through gestures: personal foul, traveling, or time out. Draw simple sketches to show how some of these messages would be expressed.

What are the limits of the form of nonverbal communication you chose? What kinds of messages could not be communicated using this form?

Are your examples of nonverbal communication easy to understand, like a smile or a shrug?

Or do people need special knowledge in order to understand them, as they would for the signals of the basketball referee?

Move Ahead

Display your sketches of nonverbal messages on the bulletin board. Try to "read" the messages your classmates drew. Can they "read" yours?

Did you find any nonverbal

signs that had more than one meaning? For instance, waving is a way of saying "Good-bye." But waving very forcefully or with a downward movement of the hand can mean "Go away!"

Explore Some More

Be alert to all forms of nonverbal communication in your everyday life. Notice a traffic officer stopping traffic or signaling it to move on. Sometimes families have special signals too. For example, some parents ring a bell or flash a porch light to call children home.

◄ *Its beacon flashing in the night, this lighthouse transmits information to incoming sailors about conditions close to shore.*

◄ *Wandering in a foreign city, how can you find the local train station or a place to exchange money? These signs, which use international symbols, will help guide you.*

▼ *Many deaf people use American Sign Language to communicate. Combining hand signs, body movements, and facial expressions, this language is as expressive and complex as spoken English. Below is the sign for the letter "h".*

Critical Thinking

Have students choose two forms of nonverbal communication that are similar in some way and explain the similarity. You may wish to have them choose as one of these forms a type of nonverbal communication pictured or discussed in the text. *(Sample answer: A traffic officer and a deaf person both use hand signals.)* Then, tell them to find two examples that are different in some way and describe the difference. *(Sample answer: A lighthouse beacon flashes its message and must be seen, while a bell is rung and must be heard.)* To clarify the advantages of different forms of nonverbal communication, ask students why certain types of nonverbal communication wouldn't work for some people or in certain situations. *(Sample answer: Deaf children wouldn't be able to hear a phone ring.)*

Activity

Have students work in groups to report on international forms of nonverbal communication. Assign research topics such as art symbols, religious symbols, Morse code, ship signals, international traffic and safety signs, national flags and other symbols, or body language. Tell the groups that their reports should consist mostly of illustrations, having only enough text to explain their meanings. Provide the groups with construction paper and colored markers. Display the completed reports in a place where all the students can look at them.

Collaborative Strategy

One recommended strategy that may be useful in this lesson is heterogeneous grouping. For further information, turn to pp. T34–T35.

Have students examine the pictures of the Tiwanakan and Moche landscapes as well as the cross-sectional map at the bottom of pp. 412 and 413 and compare and contrast these two geographic areas. Tell them that each area was home to a civilization that evolved at about the same time as the Maya. Like the Maya, both civilizations had to develop specialized farming methods to feed their large populations. Have students speculate on the farming methods used by the Tiwanakans and Moche.

Key Terms

Vocabulary Strategies: T36–T37
altiplano—the land on a high, flat plateau in South America
adobe—bricks formed of mud mixed with straw

B.C. | A.D.

2000   1500   1000   500
300   1400

L E S S O N   4

The Tiwanakans and the Moche

THINKING FOCUS

In what ways did the Tiwanakans and Moche adapt to the land?

Key Terms

* altiplano
* adobe

Y ou've worked your way to the top of a magnificent peak high in the Andes. The air is thin but clear at 12,000 feet. A large condor circles the high, flat, and barren plateau called the **altiplano.** Its wings catch the dry wind blowing across the sun-baked rock. As you scan the vast stone wilderness, you glimpse a huge lake surrounded by snow-covered mountains.

This is the land of the ancient Tiwanakans *(tih WAHN ah kahns),* a civilization that prospered from 300 B.C. to A.D. 1200. At its height, the Tiwanakan culture occupied 1,500 square miles from the plateaus of Peru and Bolivia down the southern coast of Peru and into northern Chile.

About 400 years after the Tiwanakan culture began, another culture, called the

Moche *(MOH chay),* developed along the northern coast of Peru.

The Moche homeland was very different from the altiplano. North along the Pacific coast of Peru is a thin strip of desert where rain almost never falls. The land is stark, with barren foothills that rise into the Andes. Small rivers flowing down the Andes to the ocean irrigate the sparse vegetation. These river valleys were home to the Moche from about A.D. 100 to 700, when Moche culture flourished.

As the Tiwanakans adapted to the cold, high plateaus, the Moche adapted to the dry desert coast. To survive, both had to develop efficient farming techniques.

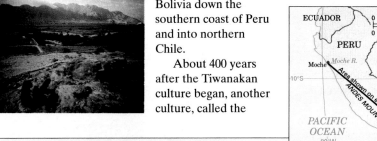

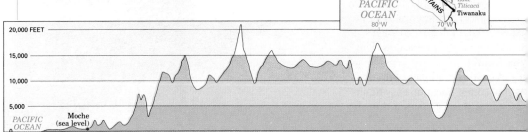

---

1. Compare regions in which the Tiwanakan and Moche civilizations developed.
2. Compare and contrast the lifestyles of the Tiwanakans and Moche.
3. Interpret artifacts for information about how ancient peoples lived.

Graphic Overview

This chart compares and contrasts the Tiwanakan and Moche cultures.

	Tiwanakans	Moche
Homeland	cold, high plateau	dry, desert coast
Farming	irrigation canals, raised soil beds	aqueducts, terraced fields
Lifestyle	social classes, honored the condor	social classes, worshiped many gods
Fate	abandoned city of Tiwanaku by 1300	abandoned city of Moche by about 600

Adapting to the Land

The Tiwanakans and Moche developed different ways to grow their crops that were well suited to their different environments. Look at the cross-sectional map below to get a sense of the terrain and elevation in the Tiwanakan and Moche regions.

Tiwanakan Adaptations

On the high plateau where the Tiwanakans lived, the nights are cold and the daylight sun is scorching. Water is scarce, except near the lakes. The Tiwanakans channeled water to their fields from nearby Lake Titicaca and from other lakes. They dug broad irrigation canals to enable water to flow around large raised beds of soil.

To make the soil beds, the Tiwanakans built a cobblestone base and covered it with a thick layer of clay. They poured on top of this three layers of gravel, each finer than the next. Finally, they covered the entire mound with a rich layer of soil. These raised beds provided a quality of both irrigation and drainage that today's technology cannot surpass.

The canals around the beds not only provided water for the plants but also protected them from the killing nightly frosts. Water and algae in the canals absorbed the sun's heat during the day and then radiated that warmth throughout the chilly nights.

The Tiwanakans could not grow maize, beans, squash, and other warm-climate crops. Instead, they grew hardy crops such as potatoes and grain suited to the cool climate.

Moche Adaptations

Because the land was too dry for farming, the Moche had to invent ways to get water to their crops. Using mud as their building material, the Moche constructed miles of aqueducts to carry river water to their fields. At least one of these channels was 70 miles long. Many are still in use today.

The Moche also found a way to grow crops on the steep slopes of the Andes foothills. They terraced the slopes into flat beds like steps of a giant staircase. In these fields the Moche grew corn, beans, peanuts, hot peppers, and squash. They also gathered shellfish from the sea and rivers and ate llama and guinea pig. ∎

■ *Describe the methods the Tiwanakans and Moche used to bring water to their farmlands.*

▼ *Melting snow from the Andes forms a river that created the Moche Valley (previous page, left) leading into the Pacific coast. The Moche lived alongside the river. The environment below is called an "altiplano," or high plain. It is a windswept plain with a lake. Compare the elevation of the Moche and the Tiwanakans.*

Lake Titicaca
•Tiwanaku
(12,645 ft./ 7,857m)

ALTIPLANO

413

DEVELOP

Point out that the high levels of achievement of the Olmec, Maya, Tiwanakans, and Moche were directly related to their ability to adapt to their environment. Explain that Lessons 2 and 3 examined civilizations in Mexico and Central America. This lesson will focus on two cultures in South America. Help students draw a timeline that includes all four civilizations.

■ *The Moche built mud aqueducts to carry river water to their crops, while the Tiwanakans built canals from nearby lakes to water their fields.*

GEOGRAPHY
Map and Globe Skills

Use a topographical map to point out the areas where the Tiwanakan and Moche settled in South America. Point out the Andes Mountains, Lake Titicaca, deserts, plateaus, and other geographic features mentioned in the text. Ask students to compare the topography of the Moche and Tiwanakan settlements.

Access Strategy

Discuss with students the ways people in the United States have adapted to their environment. Do people who live in the South have the same types of houses as people who live in the North? Are the farms in Iowa different than those in New Mexico and Arizona? Do people from southern California eat different foods than people in Maine do? Ask students how often they think about where their food comes from. Does the fact that many people take the food supply for granted indicate our level of achievement in food production? How has successful food production freed people to do other things?

Restate that a civilization's success depends upon its ability to adapt to its environment and produce enough food to support its population. As food production becomes more efficient, people can focus on other things besides farming, such as religion, government, and crafts.

Access Activity

Emphasize the role geography plays in determining lifestyles. Write the regions of the United States on the board—Northwest, Southwest, Midwest, South, and East. Then give some details about the lifestyle in each area. Include popular local foods, outdoor sports, or farming methods. Call on students to match the lifestyle to the region.

HISTORY

Critical Thinking

Ask students to discuss the role of government in Tiwanakan trade, agriculture, religion, and art. *(The government built and patrolled roads for trade and maintained raised fields. The sacred bird, the condor, was associated with rulers, and artisans crafted beautiful objects for the rulers.)* Next, ask students how a powerful government might contribute to the success or failure of a civilization. *(It could manage efficiently and encourage growth, or it could waste resources and bring about destruction.)*

▲ *This four-cornered, brightly dyed Tiwanakan hat is made of llama wool. Hats like these were used by all for extra warmth at high elevations.*

How Do We Know?

HISTORY *By studying the images in Moche pottery, archaeologists have discovered that the lima bean was sacred to the Moche. They have also found that when Moche artists painted the beans on pottery, they gave the vegetables heads, arms, and legs. Some are even depicted as warriors and messengers. Lima beans may have been considered so sacred that they were used only in rituals and never eaten at all.*

➤ *Viracocha was the Tiwanakans' god of the sky and creation, and was often shown as the condor god with snake hair, as in this sandstone image.*

414

Living and Working

As the Tiwanakans improved their farming methods, their harvests grew in size. Their population also increased, and soon social classes began to form. Moche civilization also shows evidence of social classes.

Tiwanakan Lifestyle

Among the Tiwanakans, as in other early civilizations, the common people performed the hard labor. They also paid two types of taxes to support the government. They gave part of the food they harvested to the state and spent time each year working for the state. The women usually worked as weavers, and the men helped to build and maintain the raised fields and roads.

The Tiwanakan rulers ordered many miles of roads to be built to connect the villages and to make trading easier. To further promote trade, the government supplied llamas as pack animals in trade caravans and patrolled the roads to protect caravans from attack.

The llama caravans brought tropical fruits, wood, monkeys, and colorful bird feathers from the jungles of Bolivia. From Chile and Peru, they carried seafood, corn, hot peppers, copper, and gold dust. Outbound caravans hauled potatoes, grains, locally crafted textiles, pottery, and jewelry.

The holy city of Tiwanaku was the center of both trade and religion. Pilgrims came to worship

Chapter 15

at the Gateway of the Sun in this holy city. Archaeologists who have studied this carved gateway and other Tiwanakan carvings have deduced that the Tiwanakans honored the condor. This is not surprising, since great numbers of stately condors must have soared over Tiwanaku, seeming to watch over its land and subjects.

The condor is also associated with the ruling elite. Perhaps like the Maya, the Tiwanakans thought their rulers could influence the gods and, out of respect, treated them much like gods. Artisans crafted fine jewelry, crowns, pottery, and vivid textiles to honor them. What happened to these strong, creative people? How did their civilization come to an end?

Between 1100 and 1300, the city of Tiwanaku was abandoned.

Critical Thinking

Historians are still looking for reasons to explain why the Tiwanakan and Moche civilizations declined. Ask students to select one of these civilizations and formulate their own theory on why it came to an end. Their theory should incorporate information in the lesson. Encourage a wide variety of student theories.

Geographic Context

Tiwanaku, with an elevation of 12,600 feet, was the highest city in the ancient world. It was surrounded by some of the tallest peaks in the Andes. Lake Titicaca, the Tiwanakans' source of irrigation water, lies 12,507 feet above sea level, the highest navigable lake in the world. It is 110 miles long and nearly 50 miles wide. Some parts of the lake are more than 900 feet deep. The lake water is slightly salty, which posed problems for ancient farmers and still troubles farmers today.

Social Context

Weaving was a highly developed craft in Moche civilization. Paintings on pottery indicate that it was primarily done by women. The Moche spun cotton and also mixed it with wool from the llama, alpaca, and vicuna. Moche men wore loincloths, shirts, and jackets made from brightly embroidered fabric. Women wore plain, knee-length dresses but painted their faces and feet. They also wore colorful jewelry. Homes were decorated with brightly colored blankets.

Those who lived in and around Tiwanaku resettled in small groups on the mountainsides.

Archaeologists disagree about why people deserted the city. Some think a drought destroyed the city's fragile agricultural system. Others speculate that Lake Titicaca may have flooded and made the nearby fields unusable. Still others believe that outsiders invaded the city. Whatever the reason, by 1400, all that was left of Tiwanakan culture were ruins high in the Andes.

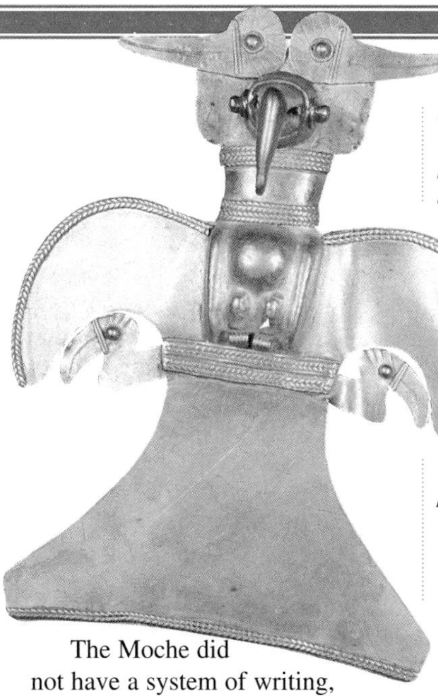

◄ The figure at left is a Tiwanakan condor god made of a beaten sheet of gold. The one-foot tall Moche pot below is decorated with the ruler's head at the top of the vessel. Examine each artifact carefully. What does each imply about that civilization, its people and their beliefs?

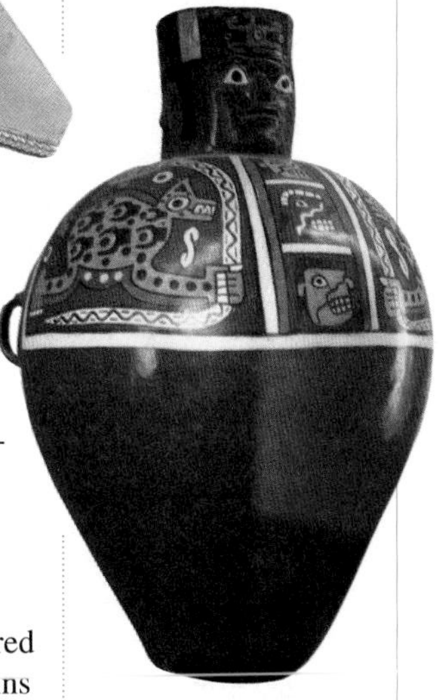

Moche Lifestyle

The ancient city of Moche was the civic and religious hub of the Moche civilization. It was located on Peru's Pacific coast in the midst of irrigated farmlands.

Much like the Tiwanakans, the Moche probably used great numbers of laborers from the lower class to do their work. These workers dug and maintained aqueducts and built great pyramids and temples. To build temples, the Moche mixed river mud and straw to form bricks called **adobe** *(uh DOH bee)*.

Most commoners farmed or fished and hunted for food. Priests, artisans, warriors, and engineers were members of the elite. The 1987 discovery of the tombs of the "Lords of Sipan," the richest tomb found in the Americas, has added to our knowledge of Moche crafts.

The Moche did not have a system of writing, but Moche pottery recovered from tombs reveals much about their culture. Clay figures and painted pottery jars show people farming, cooking, weaving, and giving birth. These ceramics tell of war and sacrifice, of glorious rulers and many gods.

Some experts think that the Moche culture was absorbed by other Andean cultures. Others believe the Moche were conquered by outsiders. But the truth remains unknown. In about 600, the Moche abandoned their city and moved to nearby areas. Six hundred years later, the Tiwanakans would do the same. ■

■ Compare and contrast Tiwanakan and Moche lifestyles.

REVIEW

1. **FOCUS** In what ways did the Tiwanakans and the Moche adapt to the land?
2. **CONNECT** What did the Tiwanakan lifestyle have in common with other early civilizations in the Americas?
3. **CULTURE** What does Moche pottery tell us about Moche culture?
4. **CRITICAL THINKING** In what ways were the Moche and the Tiwanakans similar?
5. **ACTIVITY** The condor was an emblem of a Tiwanakan god. What symbols do we use in our society to represent important things? Make a list of modern symbols such as the American eagle and the American flag. Tell what each symbol represents.

HISTORY

Visual Learning

Much of what historians have learned about the Moche comes from their finely detailed pottery. Ask students to study the Moche artifact on this page and tell what it reveals about the Moche way of life. *(The Moche honored their rulers.)*

■ Both civilizations show evidence of social classes and a religion based on the worship of many gods. While the Tiwanakans depended heavily on trade, it seems the Moche relied more on agriculture, hunting, and fishing.

CLOSE

Draw the chart shown in the Graphic Overview on the chalkboard. Have students extend the chart by adding other features of the Moche and Tiwanakan civilizations.

Answers to Review Questions

1. The Moche used terrace farming and aqueducts to grow crops because their land was hilly and dry. The Tiwanakans used raised beds and irrigation canals warmed by the sun because their land was hard and dry and the temperatures were extreme.
2. The Tiwanakans, like other early peoples, had a complex civilization with upper and lower classes. They developed farming techniques suitable for their environment.
3. It shows Moche people farming, cooking, weaving, and giving birth, and provides evidence of war, sacrifice, and the worship of many gods.
4. They both developed very specialized farming techniques, believed their rulers influenced the gods, and used lower class labor. Both ended mysteriously.
5. For example, stripes on the American flag represent the 13 original states and the stars stand for the current states.

Homework Options

To review the concept of civilization, have students make a chart showing characteristics of the Olmec, Maya, Tiwanakans, and Moche.

Study Guide: p. 66

This skills feature uses information about the Maya in Chapter 15 to teach students how to take and organize notes quickly and efficiently.

CULTURE

Critical Thinking

Ask students to explain how the methods of note taking described in this skills feature might work for writing a speech or editorial.

Recording Information

Here's Why

You may have made use of reference books, magazines, newspapers, or computer databases in the library or on the Internet. To make the most effective use of such sources, you need to develop the skill of taking and organizing notes. Taking good notes will help organize your information and make the task of writing a report easier. It will improve the quality of your reports.

Suppose you had to prepare a report about how the ancient Maya lived. Would you know how to take notes and organize them for your report?

Here's How

As you begin to gather information for your report, skim several general sources. This will give you an idea of some of the key topics and subtopics. You might begin by reading about the Maya on pages 404 through 409 of this book. Another general source would be an encyclopedia. From these general ideas, develop several questions you want your report to answer. For example, you might decide to answer these questions: What did Mayan houses look like? What were they made of? How were they made? Revise and add to these questions as you do

further reading for your report.

Once you have several questions to answer, begin the note-taking process. Writing your notes on 4" x 6" cards will make it easy for you to keep track of your information and organize it.

The text shown on the computer screen in the illustration is an example of a source you might use for notes. It tells about the homes of the Maya. This will be a subtopic in your report. Write the name of the subtopic on the first line, as shown on the

sample note card at the top of the next page.

On the note card under the subtopic name, list important details from the text. If you are listing many details about a subtopic, use a separate card for each category. Look again at the sample note cards. Notice that one card has information about how the Mayan huts were divided for use. What category of details does the other card contain?

As you make notes, be sure that you paraphrase what you have read. This means you must write the

Chapter 15

Objective

Explain how to extract information from resources and record it efficiently. (Study Skills 1, 2)

Writing a Review

Have students write a review of a movie, record, or television show, using the methods of organization described in this skills feature. Students should turn in their notes as well as the finished review.

Writing a Report

Ask students to write a short report about a well-known person. Have them record their initial information in the manner described on pp. 416 and 417. Have students turn in their notes before they start to write the report. Critique students' notes for content and organization and then return them to students for use as they write their papers.

5. Mayan Huts
   Single room
   Partition divides sleeping area
   from living area

5. Mayan Huts
   Walls of poles covered with mud
   Palm leaf roofs
   Packed earth floors

   The Mayans, p. 15

notes in your own words. Reread the information about Mayan huts shown on the computer screen below. Notice how this information has been condensed to three short phrases on the note card. The card simply notes the main ideas from the sentences.

Paraphrasing will help you to take notes more quickly and efficiently. It will also help to ensure that the report you turn in is your own work. You should copy directly from a source only if you want to use an exact quotation.

If you plan to include a quotation in your report, be sure you have copied the spelling, punctuation, and grammar from your source precisely. On your note card, be sure to put quotation marks at the beginning and the end of the quotation, so that you will be able to tell it from your paraphrased notes.

On each note card, include information about just one subtopic. If the source you are using includes information on more than one subtopic, put the information on separate cards. Keeping the information on different subtopics separate will make sorting your note cards much easier.

After you have written all of the details about one subtopic from a single source, write the source information on the card. Source information includes the source title and the page number on which you found the information. By recording this information, you make it easy to refer to the source again.

When you finish writing note cards, you might want to use a number-coding system to help organize your cards. Assign each subtopic a number, and write that number on any cards with notes about that subtopic. For example, the number 5 on the note cards above indicates that both cards contain information about the subtopic "Mayan huts."

You could also code your note cards with color. Use a magic marker of a different color to highlight each subtopic, or use note cards of different colors for each subtopic.

Try It

Turn to Lesson 3, page 406. Find the paragraph that begins with the sentence "As the Maya became more efficient farmers, they developed a surplus of food." Write a note card summarizing the information in the paragraph. Be sure to include a subtopic, notes that are paraphrased, and source information.

Apply It

Suppose you were writing a report about one of the groups you have read about in this chapter. Prepare five or six note cards on the material you find for your report. Remember to include the source of your information on each card. Organize your note cards using one of the methods mentioned in Try It.

417

Early American Civilizations

CULTURE

Critical Thinking

Point out to students that organized note taking is only one of many steps in preparing to write a report. Point out, for example, what can happen if students choose too broad a topic. *(The report will lack focus.)* Ask students to create a list of additional topics for a report about the Maya.

417

Answers to Try It

Subtopic: Mayan Trade.
Notes: traded surplus food; carried goods by
   foot, dugout canoes.
Goods traded—salt, honey, cotton, pelts.
Goods received—jade, feathers, cacao beans.
Source: *Across the Centuries*
Page reference: 406

Answers to Apply It

Answers will vary.

Visual Learning

Have students study the illustrations on pp. 416 and 417. How does each picture represent the organized taking of notes? *(Both show information being paraphrased and put into specific subtopics.)*

Answers to Reviewing Key Terms

A. Answers
1. **Hieroglyph** comes from Greek words meaning "sacred carving." Originally given to symbols carved on ancient Egyptian monuments; later it meant any form of picture writing. Mayan hieroglyphs were carved into stele or painted on temple walls.
2. **Altiplano** comes from Latin words meaning "high plain." It is a flat region 12,000 feet above sea level.
3. **Adobe** is a Spanish word coming from Arabic words meaning "the brick."
4. **Codex** is a Latin word meaning "a writing."
5. **Stele** is a Greek word meaning "pillar."
6. **Extinct** is from the Latin meaning to "extinguish" or "put out."

B. Sample answers:
1. People who relied on wild types of food such as game and naturally-growing plants, nuts, and berries followed many animals that don't exist today.
2. When farming began, people settled in one place for long periods of time.
3. Olmec tombs filled with fine things probably were the tombs of a small, wealthy class of people.
4. People living on high plains in the Andes in South America do not migrate from place to place.
5. Translating a book of Mayan picture writings requires tremendous patience and perseverance.

Chapter Review

Reviewing Key Terms

adobe (p. 415)   hieroglyph (p. 403)
altiplano (p. 412)   hunter-gatherer (p. 397)
codex (p. 409)   sedentary (p. 398)
elite (p. 401)   stele (p. 407)
extinct (p. 398)

A. Use a dictionary to find the origins of the following words. On your own paper, write one or two sentences explaining how each word got its meaning.
1. hieroglyph
2. altiplano
3. adobe
4. codex
5. stele
6. extinct

B. Each sentence below includes one or two key terms. Rewrite each sentence. Do not use any of the key terms in your new sentence.
1. Hunter-gatherers followed mammoths and other animals that have long been extinct.
2. The development of farming enabled people to adopt a sedentary way of life.
3. Fancy, complicated tombs found at Olmec burial sites probably belonged to members of the elite class.
4. The people who live on the altiplano today live a sedentary way of life, farming and keeping small herds.
5. Translating a Mayan codex requires tremendous dedication.

Exploring Concepts

A. The diagram below should show ways that each of the two groups, hunter-gatherers and sedentary villagers, adapt to their environment. Copy the diagram on your paper, and fill in four behaviors and characteristics of both hunter-gatherers and sedentary villagers. Use information from the chapter to complete the diagram.

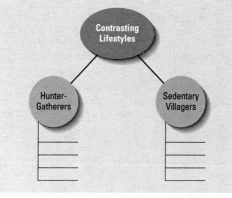

B. Write a sentence giving a piece of archaeological evidence that supports each statement below. The first one has been done for you.
1. People first came to the Americas from Asia. Answer: Tools found in South America are very similar to stone tools from the same time period found in Asia.
2. Olmec society was divided into classes.
3. In their rituals, Olmecs sacrificed people and animals.
4. Many ancient American cultures worshiped animals.
5. The Olmec traded with people as far away as 500 miles.
6. Mayan priest-kings developed two calendars, an understanding of astronomy, and a number system.
7. Food surpluses led to increasingly complex societies and cultures.
8. The Tiwanakans built raised beds of soil for farming that provided an exceptional quality of irrigation and drainage.

Chapter 15

Answers to Exploring Concepts

A. Sample answers:
Hunter-Gatherers: developed improved spearpoints, fishnets, harpoons, baskets.
Sedentary Villagers: developed engineering projects, terracing, raised fields, aqueducts, numbers, calendar.

B. Sample answers:
1. Tools found in South America are very similar to stone tools from the same time period found in Asia.
2. Class structure was necessary to create colossal stone heads created by the Olmecs. Objects found in Olmec graves vary.
3. Archaeologists found knives, axes, and other sharp tools at altar sites.
4. Olmec jaguar and half-human, half-jaguar representations were found in Olmec

ruins. Many Tiwanakan carvings depict the condor.
5. Olmec artifacts and hieroglyphs were found 500 miles from where Olmec lived.
6. Calendars, astronomical observations, and a number system were recorded in the Mayan codices.
7. Evidence of advanced farming methods was found. Evidence of trade and scientific and religious activities indicate that some people lived on surplus food.
8. Layers of cobblestone, clay, and gravel were found in Tiwanakan areas.

Reviewing Skills

1. Find the heading Moche Adaptations on page 413. Read the first two paragraphs that appear under the heading. Write a separate note card explaining each paragraph. Be sure to write your notes in your own words.

2. Read the paragraphs that appear under the heading Moche Lifestyle on page 415. Write a note card for each paragraph explaining the information, again in your own words. What subtopics will you need? How many note cards will you need to use to explain the information?

3. Suppose you wanted to find out if any recent articles have been written about the Mayan civilization of Central America. What subject headings might you look under in the *Readers' Guide to Periodical Literature* to find information about the Maya? What subject headings might you look under to find information about the areas of Peru, Bolivia, and Chile once inhabited by the Tiwanakan and the Moche?

4. Suppose you were reading a difficult primary source account of an exploration of a Mayan ruin in the jungles of Central America. What would help you better understand a passage from this account?

Using Critical Thinking

1. In what ways were the Olmec, the Mayan, the Tiwanakan, and the Moche civilizations similar? If you can identify major differences between the civilizations, do so. If not, explain why. Were there no major differences, or do you not have enough facts to make a comparison?

2. Some of the civilizations described in the chapter had class systems. For each society, list evidence of a class system. Then explain whether you think a class system is the only explanation for this evidence and why. If you think the evidence might point to some different kind of system, describe it.

3. When the Olmec civilization vanished, there were few clues as to why. State one hypothesis given in the chapter to explain the Olmec's disappearance. Describe evidence that supports that hypothesis. How would you further test that hypothesis?

Preparing for Citizenship

1. ARTS ACTIVITY Research the Olmec or Mayan civilization's artifacts, art, and hieroglyphs in the library. Then use a variety of symbols like these to create a poster. Show things you like and are interested in, something interesting you have done or that you hope to do. Or you might show some skill or ability you have.

2. COLLABORATIVE LEARNING Form a group of three or four people. In your group, choose one of the artistic or engineering feats that was accomplished by one of the civilizations from the chapter. Then figure out a plan for accomplishing this feat. The task to be performed can be the creation of an artistic work such as one of the huge stone heads the Olmec created, a land engineering project such as raised beds or terraces, or a water transportation project involving the creation of aqueducts or irrigation canals. As a group, make a list of questions you will need answered in order to plan the project. Then have each group member research the answers to assigned questions and present those answers to the group. This will require estimation and hypothesis-making. Have the group figure out a way to present the plan to the whole class as clearly and in as much detail as possible. Then have each group member complete the presentation of his or her information and conclusions according to the group's plan.

419

Early American Civilizations

Answers to Reviewing Skills
1. Subtopics: Irrigation, Terracing References: *Across the Centuries*, p. 413.
2. Subtopics: City of Moche, Labor, Social Classes, Artifacts, Decline of Moche References: *Across the Centuries*, p. 415 Total note cards: 5
3. Mayan civilization: Maya, Central America, ancient civilizations, Mayan cities. Tiwanakans and Moche: Peru, Bolivia, Chile, ancient civilizations.
4. Identifying the organizational pattern of the written account.

Answers to Using Critical Thinking
1. Similarities: worshiped many gods, some with non-human characteristics; sophisticated solutions to farming problems; religious leaders also political. Differences: only Olmec made giant stone heads, only Maya and Moche seem to have built pyramids. Lives of commoners not well known, nor whether spoken languages were similar.
2. Evidence of class system: burial sites, completed projects, priests' power. Data suggests class systems.
3. Hypotheses: Olmec cities destroyed by enemies; Evidence: Olmec carvings depicted warfare; evidence of vandalism; no evidence of drought or flooding. Test invasion and absorption hypothesis: Look for evidence of possible nearby groups that might have had contact with destroyed or assimilated culture. Test natural disaster hypothesis: Look for evidence of drought or flooding during that time.

419

Answers to Preparing for Citizenship
1. ARTS ACTIVITY When posters are completed, let other students try to decode them by trying to figure out what the student who made each poster was saying about himself or herself.
2. COLLABORATIVE LEARNING Olmec stone heads: students should research the weight and dimensions of rocks used and the types of tools used to carve the rocks. They should make educated guesses about the number of people, length of time, and division of labor involved in the moving and carving process. Each group should devise a plan such as the following: "To make one of these stone heads will require 2,000 people and will take 10 years." Discuss how groups arrived at conclusions. Award a "contract" for well-thought out plans. Students might bid on one contract that will go to the winner.

Planning at a Glance
Two American Empires

	Objectives	Reading Support *and* Other Resources	Diverse Learning Strategies
Lesson 1 The Aztec *pp. 422–428* 2–3 days	• Describe the geography of the Aztec environment and explain how it affected Aztec agricultural techniques. • Identify the Aztec social classes and describe the economic relationship between them. • Analyze the relationship between war and religion in Aztec society.	• **Workbook** or **Reading Support:** pp. 221–224 Review p. 52 Lesson Support/Transition p. 52 Multi-Lang. Sum. pp. 103–104 • **Other Resources:** Geography Kit; Posters 5, 7; Study Guide p. 68	Access Strat. **(SDAIE)** TE p. 423 Map and Globe Skills **(Visual)** TE p. 423 Visual Learning **(Visual)** TE p. 425 Audiotapes of Multi-Language Lesson Summaries **(Auditory)**
Lesson 2 The Inca *pp. 429–435* 2–3 days	• Describe the location and geography of the Inca Empire. • Explain the methods the Inca used to expand and control their empire. • Describe how Inca agricultural techniques were suited to different types of terrain. • Describe the importance of ancestor worship in Inca religion and culture.	• **Workbook** or **Reading Support:** pp. 225–228 Review p. 53 Lesson Support/Transition p. 53 Multi-Lang. Sum. pp. 105–106 • **Other Resources:** Geography Kit, Study Guide p. 69	Access Strat. **(Extra Support)** TE p. 430 Map and Globe Skills **(Visual)** TE p. 430 Social Participation **(Auditory)** TE p. 432 Research **(GATE)** TE p. 434 Audiotapes of Multi-Language Lesson Summaries **(Auditory)**
Skill: Analyzing Elevation *p. 436* 1 day	• Read and use a topographic map and a vertical profile.	• **Other Resources:** Study Guide p. 70	
Lesson 3 The Arrival of the Spanish *pp. 437–442* 2–3 days **Literature:** **"The Legend of the Lake"** *pp. 444–445*	• Compare and contrast the internal problems of the Aztec and Inca empires. • Describe the events that led up to the Spanish conquest of the Aztec and Inca empires. • Summarize the reasons for the rapid Spanish conquest of the Aztec and Inca empires.	• **Workbook** or **Reading Support:** pp. 229–232 Review p. 54 Lesson Support/Transition p. 54 Multi-Lang. Sum. pp. 107–108 • **Other Resources:** Study Guide p. 71	Access Strat. **(Extra Support)** TE p. 438 Math Connection **(Visual)** TE p. 440 Science Connection **(GATE)** TE p. 441 Audiotapes of Multi-Language Lesson Summaries **(Auditory)**
Skill: Identifying Values *p. 443* 1 day	• Identify values that underlie people's actions.	• **Other Resources:** Study Guide p. 72	
Chapter Review *pp. 446–447* 1 day		Chapter 16 Test pp. 61–64 *(See facsimiles on TE p. 574.)*	Assessment Multiple-Use Masters pp. 73–80

Reading Support Resources *for Every Lesson*

Reading and Review

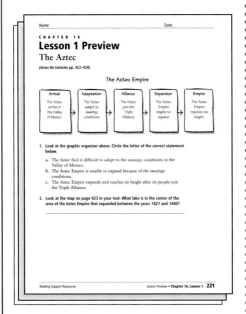

- **Chapter Overview*** p. 220
- **Lesson Previews*** using graphic organizers from the Teacher's Edition pp. 221, 225, 229
- **Reading Strategies*** pp. 222, 226, 230
- **Lesson Summaries*** pp. 223–224, 227–228, 231–232
- **Lesson Reviews** pp. 52, 53, 54

* **Workbook** includes starred items.

Multi-language Summaries

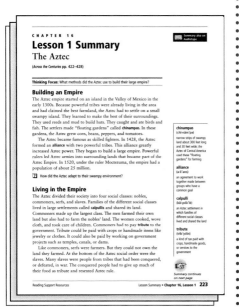

Lesson Summaries in:
- English (See Reading and Review.)
- Spanish pp. 223–224, 227–228, 231–232
- Chinese pp. 103–108
- Hmong pp. 103–108
- Khmer pp. 103–108
- Vietnamese pp. 103–108

 Summaries available on audiotapes

Lesson Support / Transition
S D A I E

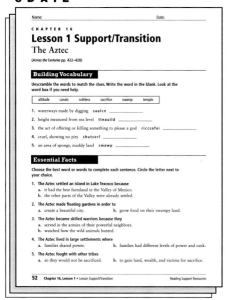

Activities for SDAIE
Specially **D**esigned **A**cademic **I**nstruction in **E**nglish

- **Lesson Support/Transition** pp. 52, 53, 54

 Technology Options

Internet Support

http://www.eduplace.com

Social Studies Center at Education Place

Internet support for Chapter 16:
- *Lesson at a Glance*
- *Machu Picchu*

Videotape/Videodisc

We the People:
Supports and enhances major topics: **Theme:** *Ancient Cultures of America*

Software

Student Writing Center ® (CD-ROM) (Macintosh® or Windows®)
The Amazon Trail® II (CD-ROM) (Macintosh® or Windows®)

School to Career

It is still a mystery how some of the larger Aztec and Incan structures were built. Have students create a word web using terms related to the construction industry. What are the many jobs in construction?

Character Education

Would the Spanish have been as successful in conquering the Aztecs and the Incas if these groups had had the support of the groups they had conquered? Have students create a list of qualities they feel a good leader should possess. What individuals in today's world do they feel exemplify these qualities?

CHAPTER
P R E V I E W

Read the chapter title to the students. Then have them read the narrative and identify the two empires. Use a large map to point out the locations of the Aztec and Inca empires. Then ask the students if they can guess who the "strange invaders" from the East might be.

Looking Back

Remind students that they learned about European exploration of the Americas in Lesson 3 of Chapter 14.

Looking Forward

Inform students they will read about the Aztec and Inca civilizations and the Spanish conquerors in the next three lessons: The Aztec, The Inca, and The Arrival of the Spanish.

Lesson 1 describes how the Aztec built their empire and what life was like under Aztec rule.

Chapter 16
Two American Empires

Floating gardens of sunlit yellows, reds, and greens—in the 1300s and 1400s, the Aztec created such gardens on the swampy land outside their capital in Mexico. By the 1100s, the Inca were engineering terraced fields in the high, cold mountains of South America. Until the 1500s, these two powerful empires ruled vast lands in the Americas. It seemed as though they would rule forever, but then strange invaders appeared from the East.

During this time the Inca rule a vast empire and craft striking works of art, like this gold and turquoise knife handle.

c. 1300 The Aztec settle on an island in Lake Texcoco, Mexico. Their empire grows rich and powerful, and artisans craft works like this two-headed turquoise serpent.

| 1200 | 1300 | 1400 |

420

1230

c. 1330s Bubonic plague, or Black Death, hits Asia and then Europe.

BACKGROUND

The written information we have concerning Aztec and Inca civilizations comes from the Aztec and Inca themselves, as well as those who conquered their empires—the Spanish. Using both Indian and Spanish accounts, we obtain a clearer picture of Aztec and Inca history and culture.

Aztec Sources

Perhaps the most important Aztec sources on Aztec civilization are the codices—native books of deerskin or bark paper. In these books, Aztec scribes used a combination of colorful pictography, ideograms, and phonetic symbols to record a multitude of things, including calendars of religious ceremonies and the amount and nature of tribute paid by subject tribes. Other Aztec sources of information include works written by Aztec chroniclers in the Latin alphabet, which they learned from the Spanish.

Spanish Sources on the Aztec

Many Spanish missionaries were eager to learn about Aztec culture and history, thinking it would assist them in converting the Aztec to Catholicism. One priest, Father Bernardo de Sahagun, devoted his life to documenting Aztec history and culture in an encyclopedia. He questioned Aztec noblemen and priests and, with the help of Aztec scribes, interpreted Aztec codices. Other Spanish sources include accounts of Aztec life and the Spanish conquest written by Spanish conquistadors and soldiers.

Throughout this period, the Inca wove colorful works of art. Many had everyday uses, such as this combination child's doll and good-luck charm.

The Inca ruled an empire of about 13 million people during the 1500s. Their ruins stand today. The "baths of the Inca" above were used by Inca priests for religious ceremonies.

1521 Spanish conquerors, led by Hernando Cortés (right), defeat and plunder the mighty Aztec Empire.

1500

1600

1700

1518 Traders begin sending shiploads of African slaves to the West Indies.

1572

Understanding the Visuals

The Inca ceremonial knife (p. 420) represents an Inca divinity. It is 15 1/2 inches tall.

The two-headed serpent of shell and turquoise (p. 420) was a breast ornament worn by an Aztec high priest during religious rituals.

The ruins of the "baths of the Inca" (p. 421) are located near Cuzco, Peru, the ancient Inca capital.

Understanding Chronology

Have the students read the timeline. Ask them to determine how long it took from the time Columbus landed in the New World to the time Cortés and his men destroyed the Aztec Empire. *(29 years.)*

Using Aztec and Spanish Sources

Many Spanish and Aztec accounts of the Spanish conquest and of various aspects of Aztec life differ tremendously. For example, most Spanish chroniclers explain that Montezuma was stoned to death by his own people, while many Aztec accounts point to the Spanish soldiers as Montezuma's murderers. Even Sahagun's work must be read with skepticism because he received his information from a group that represented a very small percentage of the Aztec population, the noblemen of one Aztec community.

Scholars find the Aztec codices difficult to interpret exactly because the Aztec system of hieroglyphs was not developed enough to express complex ideas, because the hieroglyphs are cluttered with religious mythology, and because Aztec scribes might have tampered with records for political reasons. Therefore, in order to get a true understanding of Aztec history and life and the events of the conquest, it is necessary to consult a variety of both Spanish and Aztec sources.

Inca Sources

The Inca had no writing system. With no written history to turn to, Spanish and Inca chroniclers had to rely on the memories of the official rememberers. These official rememberers served the government, changing the content of Inca history when it suited the government. In addition, many subject tribes kept their own historical records, providing us with different perspectives on Inca history.

INTRODUCE

Have students name different empires that they have studied thus far in the text. Tell them that the Aztec were natives of the Americas who built a large empire. Then have students read the Thinking Focus and recall methods used to build an empire. Ask students to predict how the Aztecs were able to build a large empire in the Valley of Mexico. Then have them read to confirm or disprove their predictions.

Key Terms

Vocabulary Strategies: T36–T37
chinampa—narrow strips of land about 300 feet long and 30 feet wide in swampy land and used for farming in Central America, particularly by the Aztec
alliance—a pact or union made between states in a common cause
calpulli—an Aztec settlement in which families of different social classes lived and shared the land
tribute—a kind of tax paid in goods or services to the ruling government

422

| 1200 | 1300 | 1520 | 1600 | 1700 |

L E S S O N   1

The Aztec

THINKING FOCUS

What methods did the Aztec use to build their large empire?

Key Terms

- chinampa
- alliance
- calpulli
- tribute

➤ *The eagle on a prickly pear cactus is an important symbol in Mexican history. The eagle shown here was used on a plan of Tenochtitlan from the 1500s. Today, the eagle symbol forms the center of the Mexican flag.*

According to legend, the Aztec received this command from the god Huitzilopochtli *(wee tsee loh POHCH tlee)*. "Go where the cactus grows, on which the eagle sits happily . . . there we shall wait, there we shall meet a number of tribes and with our arrow or with our shield we shall conquer them."

The Aztec were a band of hunter-gatherers living on a small island in northwestern Mexico, when their god summoned them to leave their homeland. Guided by Huitzilopochtli, they journeyed through deserts and over steep mountains. They fought hunger and thirst, hoping at every turn to see the promised sign, an eagle perched on a prickly pear cactus, eating a snake. There

was no time to grow food, so they ate fly eggs and snakes to survive. There was no time to weave cloth, so they wore animal skins for clothing.

They journeyed through the fertile lands of tribes that were larger and stronger. These tribes looked down on the Aztec, calling them Dog People because of their barbarian ways. They did not allow the Aztec to settle. Besides, the Aztec still had not seen the sign.

After 200 years of wandering, the Aztec came upon the promised sign. They found the eagle on a small, swampy island in Lake Texcoco in the Valley of Mexico. They named their new home Tenochtitlan *(tay nawch tee TLAHN)*, "Place of the Prickly Pear Cactus." There they started to build a powerful empire.

Building an Empire

No one knows exactly why the Aztec came to the Valley of Mexico. Perhaps they were attracted to the valley's climate and fertile soil. Its high altitude gives the valley a mild climate. By the time the Aztec arrived in the Valley of

Mexico in the early 1300s, powerful tribes had already claimed the most fertile lands in the area. So they settled on a soggy, uninhabited island in Lake Texcoco. The island was about 12 miles square in size.

Chapter 16

Objectives

1. Describe the geography of the Aztec environment and explain how it affected Aztec agricultural techniques.
2. Identify the Aztec social classes and describe the economic relationships between them.
3. Analyze the relationship between war and religion in Aztec society.

Graphic Overview

This flow chart shows the structure of the lesson.

| **Arrival** The Aztec arrive in the Valley of Mexico. | **Adaptation** The Aztec adapt to swampy conditions. | **Alliance** The Aztec join the Triple Alliance. | **Expansion** The Aztec Empire begins to expand. | **Empire** The Aztec Empire reaches its height. |

Expansion of the Aztec Empire

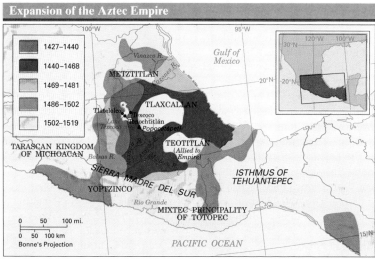

Legend:
- 1427–1440
- 1440–1468
- 1469–1481
- 1486–1502
- 1502–1519

METZTITLAN · Gulf of Mexico · TLAXCALLAN · Tlatelolco · Texcoco · Tenochtitlán · Popocatepetl · Lake Texcoco · TARASCAN KINGDOM OF MICHOACAN · Balsas R. · SIERRA MADRE DEL SUR · YOPTZINCO · TEOTITLÁN (Allied to Empire) · ISTHMUS OF TEHUANTEPEC · Rio Grande · MIXTEC PRINCIPALITY OF TOTOPEC · PACIFIC OCEAN

0 50 100 mi.
0 50 100 km
Bonne's Projection

◄ *The Aztec Empire expanded greatly over a 92-year period. During what periods did it expand the most?*

Adapting to the Land

The future looked grim for the Aztec. Because the land on their island was mostly swamp, they couldn't grow crops such as corn for food or cotton for clothing. Also, the timber and stone they needed to build huts was scarce on the small island.

The Aztec, however, learned to use what was around them to their advantage. They used reeds and mud from the swamp to make huts. They caught and ate birds and fish that lived on the island or in the water around it. From the tribes around them, the Aztec learned a method of farming that was especially suited to the swampy areas in which they lived.

This way of farming made use of **chinampas,** or "floating gardens." Chinampas are narrow strips of land about 300 feet long and 15 to 30 feet wide, almost completely surrounded by canals. The Aztec built these floating gardens around their central city. They used the rows of canals to tend the chinampas by boat. Look at the pictures of the floating gardens below. On these floating gardens, Aztec farmers were able to produce such vegetables as corn, squash, chili peppers, beans, and tomatoes.

▼ *The Aztec were able to turn swampy ground into usable farmland with chinampas. Notice the types of soil that were piled in layers. Which layer do you think would have been most fertile? In the photograph at left, modern farmers are tending chinampas in south central Mexico.*

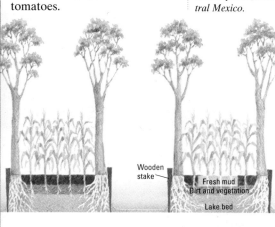

Wooden stake · Fresh mud · Dirt and vegetation · Canal · Lake bed

DEVELOP

Point out to students that this lesson traces the development of the Aztec from a small, migratory band of hunter-gatherers to a superior military power that controlled a huge empire in and around the Valley of Mexico. Using the map on this page, have students describe the geographical features of the Valley of Mexico and surrounding regions.

◄ *The empire expanded most from 1440 to 1468 and from 1486 to 1502.*

◄ *The mud layer is the most fertile.*

GEOGRAPHY
Map and Globe Skills

Refer students to a current map of Central America and to the map on this page that shows the extent of the empire. Ask students questions such as the following: What countries today lie in what was once the Aztec Empire? *(Mexico, Guatemala.)* Why do you think much of Mexico has a temperate climate? *(Much of Mexico is made up of plateaus high in altitude.)*

Access Strategy

Have students look at each photo or illustration in Lesson 1 to get an idea of what kinds of information will be covered. Ask them what they see in each photo or illustration and help them figure out what larger category or idea each picture relates to. For example, on p. 424 they see a picture of a chief's headdress; this photo is a clue that they will be learning something about Aztec leaders, government, or war. Other topics indicated by photos and illustrations include geography, agriculture, people (society), cities, art. Encourage students to also scan the major headings, as well as the pictures for clues to the content of the chapter.

Finally, examine the illustration on p. 422. Point out that this image has become an important symbol of the origins of the Mexican people, many of whom are descended from the Aztec. Bring in a Mexican flag (or a picture of one) so students can see that this image is still important in modern Mexico.

Access Activity

Have students role-play the story of the Aztec's journey to their new home as told on p. 422. Tell students that the island the Aztec finally settled on was marshy and offered little food or clothing or shelter. Point out that, despite these difficult beginnings, the Aztec were able to build a huge empire.

Critical Thinking

Ask students why Aztec leaders encouraged technological as well as military achievements. Have them use examples from the lesson to back up their opinions.

■ *The Aztec built floating gardens in the lake beds. They also built homes from reeds and mud, and ate birds and fish that lived in the area.*

The Aztec used the canals around the chinampas to travel by canoe to the city of Tenochtitlan and to nearby islands. They also built three great causeways, or raised roads, to the mainland so they could also travel back and forth on foot. One causeway was over five miles long.

The Aztec traded with peoples in these nearby areas. Besides food items, they also obtained timber and stone, which they used in building. The Aztec had succeeded in adapting to their environment.

Rising to Power

The Aztec not only adapted to the land, they also found ways to get along with their neighbors. According to Aztec legend, more powerful and more civilized tribes forced the Aztec to serve as soldiers in their armies. From these more powerful tribes, the Aztec learned to be skilled warriors.

As the number of Aztec warriors increased, so did the Aztec reputation for military skill. In 1428, the Aztec formed an **alliance,** or union, with two other powerful tribes. This Triple Alliance increased Aztec military strength, and they began to build a huge empire that would one day cover the southern third of Mexico and extend into what is today Guatemala. The Aztec empire covered an area about 375 miles wide and 315 miles long.

One of the greatest rulers of the empire was Ahuitzotl *(ah WEE soh tl)*. From 1486 until his death in 1502, he led Aztec armies in conquest throughout Mexico and Central America. He launched lightning-quick attacks that took his enemies by surprise. Ahuitzotl also oversaw the completion of the pyramid of the Great Temple, which he dedicated to the god Huitzilopochtli.

When Ahuitzotl died in 1502, his nephew, Moctezuma, became the new ruler. Like Ahuitzotl, he led his warriors into battles of conquest. Under his rule, which lasted until 1520, the empire reached its greatest size, with a population of about 25 million people. ■

■ *How did the Aztec adapt to their swampy environment?*

➤ *Only Aztec nobility could wear clothing made of quetzal feathers like the headdress shown here. Quetzal feathers, from the quetzal bird shown above, were sacred to the Aztec and had to be obtained through trade.*

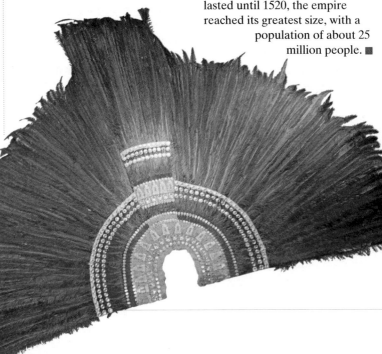

Critical Thinking

Have students look at the picture of Montezuma's headdress and read the caption. Point out that it is over four feet tall. Ask them why Montezuma might have been at a disadvantage when wearing this headdress into battle. *(Makes him an easy target; enemies would know he was the chief; hard to fight and move quickly.)*

Art Connection

The painting on the next page is by Mexican painter Diego Rivera. Have students research him and bring in samples of his paintings that depict Aztec life. You might have them research other artists who use Aztec culture as subjects, such as José Orozco and David Siqueiros.

Social Context

At the top of the social pyramid was the Aztec ruler. He was always chosen from the same family, and was usually the brother or son of his predecessor. A general and military council advised him on matters of state and war. He usually dwelled in luxury in a huge palace and was surrounded by hundreds of servants. By the end of the 1400s, the ruler was no longer regarded as human but as a living god. No ordinary citizen could touch him or look upon his person.

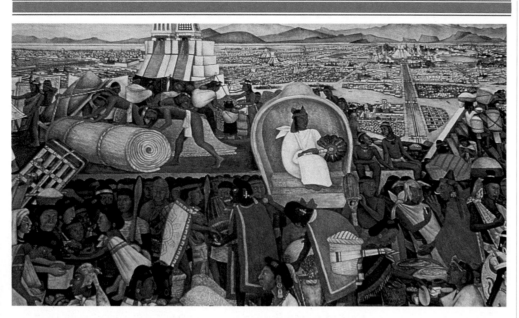

Living in the Empire

As the empire expanded, Aztec society became more complex. An intricate class structure had developed over a period of more than 200 years.

Social Classes

The Aztec lived in large settlements called **calpullis.** Families of different social ranks—nobles, commoners, serfs, and slaves— lived in each calpulli. They all shared the land of the calpulli.

Commoners made up the majority of the Aztec population. They farmed their calpulli land but were also required to farm the nobles' land. While the men of the calpulli worked in the fields, the women cooked and wove cloth and cared for the younger children. At about age 10, commoner boys were sent to a school run by the calpulli, where they learned, among other things, Aztec religion and history.

Aztec commoners had to pay tribute to the government. **Tribute** was a kind of tax paid in goods or services. Tribute could be paid in crops, in handmade items such as jewelry or clothing, and by work on state projects, such as temples, canals, and dams.

Like commoners, serfs had to work the land, but they could not own it. Serfs made up about one-third of the Aztec population.

Slaves occupied the lowest rung of the Aztec social ladder. Many slaves were captives of war. Others were Aztec who had committed crimes or who had not repaid debts.

The nobles were the smallest class, but they controlled the other classes. Nobility was hereditary, and members of the noble class served as government officials, priests, and warriors. Nobles lived off tribute paid by commoners and conquered peoples.

▲ *The Mexican painter Diego Rivera painted* Great Tenochtitlan *from 1929 to 1945. It shows his imaginative view of the color, excitement, and people in an Aztec market. The statue below helps us know what Aztec commoners actually looked like.*

425

Two American Empires

425

Refer students to the Diego Rivera painting on this page. Have students identify at least one member from each class in Aztec society. They should give reasons for their selections. Then ask them to list items that the people are trading.

Cultural Context

The language of the Aztec, Nahuatl (*NAH waht uhl*), reflects a highly civilized people. It is logical and clear. Nahuatl also gives us insights into Aztec society and values. The word for wife, for example, means "one who is owner of a man." Children were always called "beloved children." Nahuatl has given us such words as *avocado, tomato, chocolate, tamale,* and *chili.* Today, thousands of Mexicans with Aztec ancestors speak a modern form of Nahuatl.

Writing

Have students choose one class of Aztec society and write a paragraph that describes their life as a member of that class. The paragraphs may be written as a diary entry or a letter to a friend.

Critical Thinking

Ask students to list the advantages and disadvantages of being a member of each Aztec social class.

Critical Thinking

Ask students to evaluate the Aztec's treatment of conquered peoples. Have them draw conclusions as to why the Aztec allowed the conquered peoples to keep their own religion, language, social structure, and customs.

Conquered peoples made up the majority of those living in the Aztec Empire. The Aztec allowed each conquered tribe to keep its own religion, language, social structure, and customs.

But not all aspects of Aztec rule were so positive. Most of the wealth of the empire was made up of tribute paid by subject, or conquered, tribes. Many tribes were forced to give up so much of their food as tribute that they lived on the brink of starvation. The endless demand for tribute made subject tribes resent Aztec rulers.

Trade and Markets

Aztec merchants lived in separate calpullis. They traveled throughout the empire and beyond to bring back exotic goods such as colored feathers, jade, and cocoa for the nobles. The merchants employed many carriers, usually slaves, who walked in long caravans carrying heavy loads for trips of 250 miles or more.

Merchants sold many of their goods in city markets throughout the empire. The marketplace was an important center in Aztec cities. The Spanish explorer Hernando Cortés later reported that more than 60,000 people visited the city market daily in Tlatelolco (*tlah tehl OHL koh*).

The Aztec Universe

The Aztec believed that the world was alive with spirits. Every aspect of nature had been created by the self-sacrifice of the spirits of wind and rain, or rocks and corn, and more. These spirits still lived in nature. The Aztec believed that humans must live by the rules of the spirits, or the universe would be destroyed.

The Aztec gods represented these spirits who controlled the world. They were more like African gods than Greek or Roman gods. The Aztec gods did not share human characteristics, did not marry or have children, and did not have emotions. The gods required prayer, thanksgiving, rituals, and sacrifices to keep the world from destruction.

The Aztec dealt with the gods in their everyday lives, in the fields and on the lakes. They respected nature. An early Spanish missionary named Bernard de Sahagun (*sah hah GOON*) recorded that when Aztec women cooked corn, "first of all they breathed upon [the corn]. . . . In this way it would not take fright; thus it would not fear the heat."

Cultural Achievements

From archaeologists' findings, we know the Aztec built elaborate palaces, temples, and government storehouses out of stone and brick. We have also recovered many everyday objects, including jewelry, pottery, carvings, and even the remains of sacrifices. We also know Aztec craftworkers produced beautiful feather headdresses, stone sculptures, and jewelry set with precious stones.

Perhaps the most important Aztec artifacts that archaeologists have discovered are the Aztec codices, or codes. Each codex is a kind of book, with pages made from bark. The pages open and close like folding screens and include brightly colored hieroglyphs.

At one time there were hun-

Geographic Context

The city of Tenochtitlan covered more than five square miles in the middle of Lake Texcoco. The population in 1519 was about 400,000 people, the largest in Meso-American history at that time. Today, Mexico City stands where Tenochtitlan was. Lake Texcoco no longer exists—the Spaniards drained it in the 1600s to provide more room for settlement.

Language Arts Connection

On the board write this poem about the Aztec god of nature:
He mocks us.
As he wishes, so he wills.
He places us in the palm of his hand,
He rolls us about;
Like pebbles we roll, we spin. . . .
We make him laugh.
He mocks us.
Have students speculate on how the Aztec felt about their position in the world.

dreds of these books. Unfortunately, Spanish missionaries and settlers in the Aztec region burned many of the codices. Other books rotted in the humid climate. From the few that remain, historians have learned about aspects of Aztec life. What kind of scene is on the codex page shown below? ■

■ *Describe the different classes in Aztec society and the effect that tribute had on each of them.*

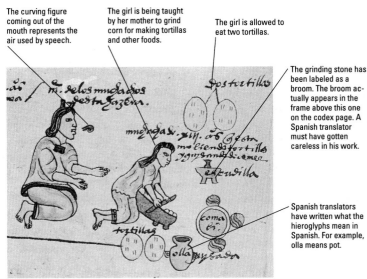

The curving figure coming out of the mouth represents the air used by speech.

The girl is being taught by her mother to grind corn for making tortillas and other foods.

The girl is allowed to eat two tortillas.

The grinding stone has been labeled as a broom. The broom actually appears in the frame above this one on the codex page. A Spanish translator must have gotten careless in his work.

Spanish translators have written what the hieroglyphs mean in Spanish. For example, olla means pot.

◀ *This codex page shows some of the tasks that Aztec girls learned to perform.*

▼ *The rain god Tláloc was one of the major Aztec gods. This is only one of many different Aztec representations of the god.*

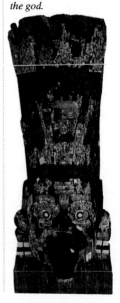

Fighting for the Gods

The everyday lives of all classes of Aztec society revolved around religion. Many Aztec gods are depicted in the codices.

The two most important gods in the Aztec world were Huitzilopochtli, the god of the sun and of war, and Tláloc *(tlah LOHK),* the god of rain. The Aztec especially feared the god Huitzilopochtli, because he could destroy the world whenever he wanted.

Human Sacrifices

The Aztec held many religious ceremonies throughout the year. At these occasions, Aztec priests offered sacrifices to the gods to help ensure good harvests. Human sacrifice was common. When the Temple of the Sun in Tenochtitlan was dedicated to the sun and rain gods, the Aztec sacrificed as many as 10,000 people.

The reasons for the human sacrifices are still not clear. Many historians believe that the Aztec used these human sacrifices to frighten their enemies. Most of the people sacrificed by the Aztec were captives of war. The Aztec believed that whatever one's station in life, if he were sacrificed he would become a divine being. Many victims went willingly. A sacrificed warrior would live happily forever, they said, like a hummingbird. Some scholars think that the Aztec arranged wars to capture sacrifices for the gods.

427

Two American Empires

■ *The classes in Aztec society were the commoners, the serfs, the slaves, and the nobles. Commoners had to pay tribute to the government in crops, handmade items, or by work on state projects. Serfs had to work the land also. Nobles lived off tribute paid by commoners and conquered peoples.*

427

Research

Have students find photos and sketches of Aztec art and architecture. Tell them to describe each picture with a short list. They should include, for example, what material was used, what purpose it served, and, if it is a carving or painting, who or what it depicted. Have them number each photo or sketch and share their findings with the class.

Writing

Have students write a news account of a battle between the Aztec and a neighboring tribe in which the Aztec emerge victorious. The account should include interviews from successful Aztec warriors, prisoners of war, and the survivors of the neighboring tribe. You might have students research Aztec fighting methods.

Study Skills

Have students research the Aztec religion. Tell them to make a chart listing important Aztec gods, their function, physical description, and how they influenced the everyday lives of the Aztec.

▲ *This Aztec codex page shows different types of Aztec warriors. Notice how the warriors carry shields. Warriors' shields were made from quetzal feathers and would have resembled the feather shield shown above.*

■ *How were war and religion linked in Aztec culture?*

War and Religion

The Aztec's reasons for war, however, were not strictly religious. They wanted to control the Valley of Mexico, so they waged war on any tribes who resisted their rule. As the number of people in the empire grew, the Aztec required more land to grow crops and more tribute to support the expanding government. To meet this demand for resources, they conquered more and more tribes.

The Aztec needed a well-trained army to keep expanding. At the calpulli schools, the boys learned ruthless fighting methods and became strong warriors. When the Aztec attacked a city, they killed warriors and townspeople alike. They plundered homes and captured victims for sacrifice.

Aztec warriors fought without fear of death. They believed their deaths would help keep the world going.

> I n the midst of the plain
> my heart craves death
> by the obsidian edge.
> Only this my heart craves:
> death in war.
>
> From an Aztec codex

Warriors also fought hard because the more captives they took, the higher their social rank would be. The ruthless tactics of the Aztec helped them build an empire. But like their ever-increasing demand for tribute, their cruelty led to deep resentment among subject tribes. Later, Spanish adventurers would use this resentment to their advantage. ■

REVIEW

1. **FOCUS** What methods did the Aztec use to build their large empire?
2. **CONNECT** What did the Moche, the Tiwanakan, and the Aztec all have to overcome in order to farm?
3. **HISTORY** Why was the Triple Alliance important?
4. **CULTURE** What do the Aztec codices tell us about Aztec life?
5. **CRITICAL THINKING** Did the Aztec use the tribute system wisely? What changes would have improved the system?
6. **ACTIVITY** Study the codex pages shown on page 427 and on this page. Choose an aspect of everyday life in the United States and then draw your own codex page to describe it.

Chapter 16

■ *Aztec warriors believed the gods would reward them for being successful in battle. Also, captives of war were sacrificed in religious ceremonies.*

CLOSE

Draw the Graphic Overview from p. 422 on the chalkboard. Have students get into groups and copy the Graphic Overview on a sheet of paper. Point out that there are arrows between each main head. Have them explain the connection between each pair of main heads linked by arrows. Then have them make additions to the diagram based on what they have learned in the lesson.

Homework Options

Have students write a paragraph about the expansion of the Aztec empire that includes each key term listed on p. 422.

Study Guide: p. 68

Answers to Review Questions

1. The Aztec produced enough food to allow the population to grow. They developed a trade system that supplied goods throughout the empire. The Aztec also had an army that added people, land, and tribute to the empire.
2. The Moche, the Tiwanakan, and the Aztec all had to overcome geography that was not well suited to agriculture.
3. The Triple Alliance enabled the Aztec to unite with two powerful tribes. This alliance increased the size of the Aztec armies, allowing them to conquer more tribes and land.
4. The Aztec codices tell us such things as how the Aztec fought, how they worshiped, and how they taught their children. The codices also reveal that the Aztec had a writing system of hieroglyphs.
5. Answers will vary, but should judge the effects of tribute and suggest changes that would improve the tribute system.

1200
1230
1525
1600
1700

L E S S O N 2

The Inca

The young Inca and his fellow workers walked up to the next boulder to be moved. It was as tall as three men. Working side by side, the men wrapped a thick rope around the massive rock. At the leader's signal, they gripped the rope and began to pull. The young man grunted. His muscles strained and the palms of his hands burned. Sweat poured down his face. Slowly the boulder inched closer to the fortress. Finally, the leader signaled them to stop.

The man sat down to rest. He watched as other workers pounded and sculpted the boulder with big stone hammers. Then, with a mixture of sand and water, they all rubbed the rock until it was very smooth on four sides. When joined, the squared boulder would fit tightly with the others.

The Inca built the massive stone fortress of Sacsahuaman *(sak sa wah MAN)* during the 1400s. It was built just north of their capital city Cuzco in western South America. The fortress not only protected the Inca from their enemies but survived several powerful earthquakes. This is a remarkable fact, since the Inca used no mortar to join the boulders together. The fortress was one of the many technological achievements of the Inca, who conquered and ruled one of the largest empires in the Americas.

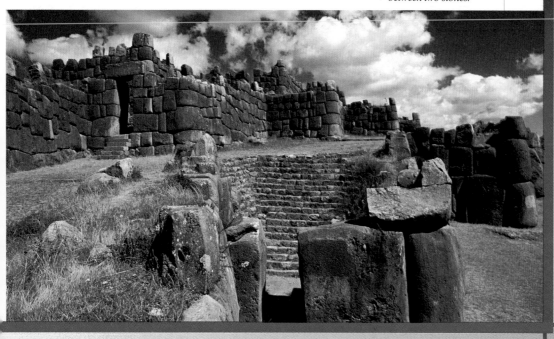

THINKING FOCUS

In what ways were the Inca a technologically advanced civilization?

Key Terms

- vertical economy
- terrace farming

Inca stonework was so finely made that a piece of paper cannot fit between two stones.

INTRODUCE

Tell the students that at about the same time the Aztec were building their empire in Mexico, the Inca were constructing their own empire in South America. Have students read the Thinking Focus. Review the methods the Aztec used to build a technologically advanced empire. Point out that the Inca and Aztec empires developed, in many respects, along parallel lines, but that there were differences. Have students read to discover similarities and differences between the two empires, and the reasons for them.

Key Terms

Vocabulary Strategies: T36–T37

vertical economy—the growing of crops according to the altitude of the land, particularly in South America

terrace farming—the building of raised banks of earth on steep land for farming

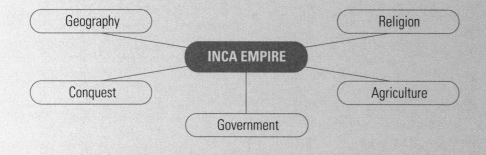

Graphic Overview

This spider chart shows the flow of the lesson.

Geography
Religion
INCA EMPIRE
Conquest
Agriculture
Government

Objectives

1. Describe the location and geography of the Inca Empire.
2. Explain the methods the Inca used to expand and control their empire.
3. Describe how Inca agricultural techniques were suited to different types of terrain.
4. Describe the importance of ancestor worship in Inca religion and culture.

430

DEVELOP

Tell students this lesson follows the development of the Inca from one of many small tribes in the Cuzco Valley to the supreme military power in the region controlling one of the largest empires in the Americas. Have students look at the map on this page. Ask them to describe the geographical features of the Inca Empire and to point out how they differ from those of the Aztec Empire.

➤ *The empire developed between the Pacific Ocean and the Andes.*

GEOGRAPHY

Map and Globe Skills

Have students locate the Inca Empire on a world map. Then ask questions such as the following to help them describe its location and geography: On what continent was the Inca Empire located? (*South America.*) What ocean does it border? (*Pacific.*) What major mountain chain runs through it? (*Andes.*)

■ *The Inca ruled an area covering most of what is now Ecuador, Peru, and Bolivia, plus parts of Argentina and Chile.*

Rising to Power

■ *What was the extent of the Inca Empire?*

▼ *The Inca Empire grew over about a 200-year period. Between what two geographic features did the empire develop?*

The Inca competed with other tribes for control of the fertile Cuzco Valley. By 1230, they controlled the area shown in red-violet on the map below.

The Cuzco Valley lies in the Central Andes, a land of very diverse terrain. Mountains surrounding the valley reach heights of more than 22,000 feet above sea level. Rivers cut deeply into these mountains as they plunge north toward the Amazon River. Bare, windblown plateaus lie above the tree line of the fertile valley.

Very little is known about the early history of the Inca. Unlike the Olmec and the Maya, the Inca had no writing system. Their history was passed down orally from one generation to the next by "official rememberers" called quipu camayocs. Because of this oral tradition, legend, myth, and fact overlapped in Inca history.

We do know that it was not until 1438 that the Inca began to gain dominance over the Cuzco Valley. The seventh ruler of the Incas, Pachacuti (*PAH chah koo tee*), whose name means "he who transforms," launched a sweeping campaign of conquest. First, the Inca armies took over the smaller states in and around the Cuzco Valley. Next, they marched into the Andes highlands and conquered other tribes there.

By 1525, the Inca Empire covered most of what is now Ecuador, large areas of modern-day Peru and Bolivia, and parts of modern-day Argentina and Chile. The map shows the greatest extent of the Inca Empire. How many miles did it extend from north to south?

The Inca called their powerful empire Tihuantinsuyu (*tee wahn teen SOO yoh*), or the "Land of the Four Quarters," because they believed they had conquered the entire world. At its height, the population of the Inca Empire reached about 13 million. ■

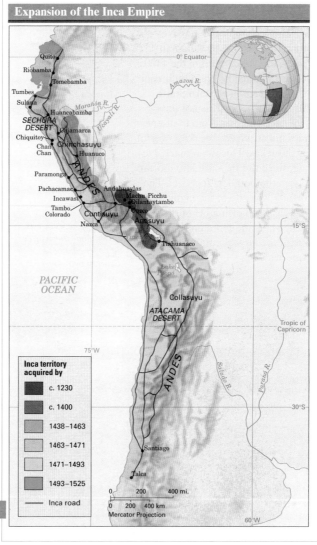

Expansion of the Inca Empire

Quito
Riobamba
Tomebamba
Tumbes
Sulana
SECHURA DESERT
Huancabamba
Chiquitoy
Cajamarca
Chan Chan
Chinchasuyu
Huanuco
Paramonga
Pachacamac
Incawasi
Tambo Colorado
Cuntisuyu
Nazca
Andahuaylas
Machu Picchu
Ollantaytambo
Cuzco
Antisuyu
Tiahuanaco
PACIFIC OCEAN
Collasuyu
ATACAMA DESERT
ANDES
Santiago
Talca

0° Equator
Amazon R.
Marañón R.
Ucayali R.
15°S
Tropic of Capricorn
30°S
75°W
60°W

Inca territory acquired by
c. 1230
c. 1400
1438–1463
1463–1471
1471–1493
1493–1525
— Inca road

0   200   400 mi.
0 200 400 km
Mercator Projection

Access Activity

After students have studied the map on p. 430, ask them:
1. How does the length of the Inca Empire compare with that of the western United States? (*Inca Empire is more than twice as long.*)
2. Why do you suppose the Inca expanded north to south rather than east to west? (*The Andes are in the way.*)

Access Strategy

Find out if any of your students hold jobs. Explain that most children in the Inca Empire—the commoners' children—were required to work all day long by the time they were seven or eight years old. They usually helped their parents with family chores, including farming, herding, weaving, and preparing food. Ask students what their lives would be like if they had to work all day helping their parents rather than attending school.

Then tell them that although they were required to work, Inca commoners rarely went hungry or lacked for anything. Even if their crops failed, the government would see to it that they received proper food and shelter. Discuss the advantages and disadvantages of living in such a carefully controlled empire.

Conquering and Controlling

Conquering a Region

The Inca ruler first sent scouts to the region he wanted to take over. The scout judged the fertility of the region's land and the strength of its armies and defenses, and memorized its geography. Then the ruler and his military advisors devised a plan of attack based on the scout's report. Before attacking, though, the Inca ruler sent ambassadors to the enemy tribe to try to persuade them to join the empire peacefully. Usually, the tribes refused, and then the massive Inca armies attacked.

Once they conquered a region, the Inca made certain that it stayed under their control. They held both local religious idols and local princes hostage in Cuzco to discourage rebellion. The Inca also forced members of conquered tribes to join their army. The Inca offered rewards to new soldiers who proved successful in battle to ensure their loyalty. These rewards were taken from newly conquered areas.

The Inca stationed troops throughout their empire. If an uprising occurred far away from Cuzco, the Inca ruler could easily send a messenger to his army in that region to put it down. The rebellious people were then relocated closer to Cuzco or to another area where Inca rulers could keep a close eye on them. When tribes were peaceful, the Inca allowed the local rulers to stay in power. They also held feasts and festivals for loyal subject tribes.

The Inca also used other methods to maintain control of subject peoples. They made the Inca religion the official religion of the empire and they required all of their subjects to learn Quechua *(KEHCH wuh)*, their native language. This helped promote unity in the empire.

Organizing the People

Inca rulers totally controlled the lives of their peoples. The Inca believed that their ruler was lord of all things—the land, the animals, the water, and the people. Everything belonged to him. A rigid social structure helped the emperor exercise this control.

The Inca had two classes—the nobility and the commoners. Most of the people in the empire were commoners. They lived in cramped adobe huts and worked the land from sunrise to sunset. This work was their tribute to the government. The nobles lived off the tribute but also served as governors of Inca subject tribes, political advisers, and public administrators. Government administrators organized huge public projects. Those commoners not needed for farming had to pay tribute by helping with these projects.

One such project was a highway system that spanned the

> ▲ *One of the first steps in organizing an area is to find out what exists there. The Inca used counting devices called quipus to keep track of everything from soldiers to food.*

> ▼ *Tribes conquered by the Inca generally had well-developed cultures of their own. This ceremonial cup was created by the Chimu people of northwest Peru.*

431

Two American Empires

Critical Thinking

Ask students to compare and contrast the Inca methods of conquering a region and controlling the people with the Aztec methods. Have them list the advantages and disadvantages of both systems. *(Possible advantages include that the Inca system was more organized and it allowed tribes to surrender to the Inca. Possible disadvantages include that the Aztec system caused much more death and resentment among subject tribes.)*

Cultural Context

The Inca did not have an alphabet or a system for writing numbers. Instead, employing a decimal system like ours, they used the quipu, pictured above, for counting. The quipu consisted of about 100 brightly colored strings with knots in them (quipu literally means "knots"). The color, length, and thickness of a string symbolized what was being counted (a thick yellow string might be corn or gold), and the strategically placed knots represented the actual numerical amount.

The quipu camayocs counted and recorded a huge variety of commodities, including corn production, llamas, weapons, enemies killed, and a census of a newly conquered region. Modern interpreters are still not sure what the countless strings and knots mean. The quipu is still used today for counting in the Andean highlands.

Study Skills

Have students research the duties and responsibilities of the Inca ruler. They should obtain information on how he was chosen, how he lived, and how he ruled.

POLITICAL SYSTEMS

Critical Thinking

Emphasize the fact that it was through strict control of the people that the Inca were able to make such extraordinary technological advancements. Also point out that the Inca used their technology (e.g., their road system) to obtain even greater control and to further expand their empire.

■ *Answers will vary but could include: the Inca held local idols and local princes hostage to discourage rebellion. They forced subject tribes to join their army. They spread their army throughout the empire. The Inca also made the Inca language and religion standard in the empire.*

Across Time & Space

The Inca built many rope bridges that spanned steep-cliffed canyons and crossed over fast-flowing rivers. Today, many Inca descendants still rely on rope bridges. They often spin as much as 20,000 to 30,000 feet of rope from grass to build or repair their bridges.

■ *What methods did the Inca use to control their empire?*

▼ *The llama was very important to the Inca. Its wool, shown here, was spun into thread, which was used to make beautiful fabrics like the weaving below. These fabrics were used by all levels of society.*

length of the empire. Roads were built in the highlands and along the coast. When necessary, the roads included tunnels, causeways, and stone or even rope bridges. Built to quickly move the Inca army, the highways also helped transport crops and other goods throughout the empire. Scholars estimate that the Inca built nearly 10,000 miles of roads.

Under Inca rule, the commoners had few individual freedoms. They weren't allowed to travel without government approval. The government also decided when and whom they married. Marriage was encouraged, because only married couples were assigned plots of land

from which goods for tribute could be raised. ■

Working the Land

Though they enjoyed little freedom, Inca subjects rarely went hungry. The Inca's clever farming techniques allowed them to make full use of their varied lands. In addition, their strong organizational skills made them efficient producers and distributors of food.

Once the Inca conquered a region, they took total control of the land. They sent administrators, who were members of the nobility, to evaluate the geographic resources of the region. Then they divided the region's farmland into three parts. The commoners harvested one part of the farmland for government workers, one part to support Inca religious leaders, and one part for themselves.

The farmland varied greatly from region to region because the Inca Empire lay in and around the Andes. Some valleys lie as high as 8,000 feet above sea level. Others are only a few hundred feet above sea level.

Because soil, temperature, and other conditions change as altitude increases, only certain crops could be grown in

Social Participation

Group students into pairs. Tell one student to assume the role of a loyal Aztec commoner and the other to assume the role of a loyal Inca commoner. Have them debate about which empire is better to live in. Tell them to back up their opinions with facts from each lesson.

Geographic Context

The Inca subject tribes of the Andean highlands raised llamas and alpacas. Both the llama and alpaca are members of the camel family. The llama stands about four feet tall at the shoulder and has thick long hair that may be brown, gray, white, or black. The llama is sure-footed on mountain trails and can carry up to 200 pounds and travel up to 20 miles a day with a full load. It will lie down and refuse to move if it feels it has worked hard enough.

At one time in the early 1500s, the Inca used as many as 500,000 llamas to carry silver from mines. The llama lives on low shrubs and other mountain vegetation. It can survive for weeks without water, obtaining moisture from green plants.

The alpaca resembles the llama; it is a few inches shorter and its hair is much longer. Because its hair is much longer, finer, and straighter than the llama's, alpacas were raised mainly for making warm cloth.

Diagram a mountain slope on the chalkboard. Have students individually label the slope with the names of crops produced at each level. Point out the vertical distribution of the crops. Emphasize the fact that the Inca took advantage of their diverse environment by using various farming techniques, including terracing and chinampas.

certain areas. In the low valleys, farmers grew maize (corn), beans, and squash. In the mountains, they raised llamas and alpacas for wool and meat. This growing of crops according to the height of the land is called a **vertical economy.**

The Inca were able to grow surplus amounts of food by using very productive farming techniques. One of these techniques was **terrace farming.** The soil on the mountain slopes in the highlands was thin and didn't receive enough rainfall. The Inca carried topsoil and gravel from the more fertile lowlands to the hillsides. There, they packed it into narrow farming terraces like the ones pictured above. To protect against drought, the Inca constructed elaborate canal systems for irrigation.

The government built huge warehouses to store surplus food in case of emergencies such as crop failure or war. The quipu recorded how much food was stored and where it was stored. Because the government distributed food and goods to the people, free trade and huge markets like those the Aztec enjoyed did not exist in the Inca Empire. ■

Inca terraces were such an effective farming technique that they are still used in modern-day Peru.

■ *Why was Inca agriculture so productive?*

■ *The Inca used advanced farming techniques such as terrace farming. In addition, they grew their crops in the areas for which they were best suited.*

Praying to the Ancestors

Not all of the commoners worked to produce food for the empire. Some commoners helped to build massive cities. To learn more about an Inca city, see A Closer Look on page 434.

Other commoners paid their tribute by making pieces of art and

433

Two American Empires

433

Social Context

Inca society was made up of clans called *ayllus.* Members of each ayllu believed that they descended from a common ancestor. The descendants of Inca rulers formed the royal ayllus in Cuzco. They held the most important posts in the government and religious hierarchy, which were handed down to their sons after they died. Nobles who belonged to lesser nobility included members of Inca peoples surrounding Cuzco and chieftains of conquered peoples.

The nobility enjoyed numerous rights and privileges. Cuzco nobles wore earplugs as symbols of their positions. Only they could wear fine clothing and gold and silver jewelry. Only noble children went to school, where they learned about Inca religion, law, history, poetry, music, and astrology. Nobles were punished less severely than the ordinary citizen for the same crime. They were also exempt from agricultural labor and lived off the revenues of the land that they owned.

Critical Thinking

Ask students to list the ways a common language might have promoted unity within the Inca Empire. *(Government officials could communicate with the leaders of subject tribes; members of the army could understand their superiors and each other.)*

Note: Use this Closer Look as a preview to Praying to Ancestors which begins on p. 433.

More About Life at Machu Picchu
Enough food was grown on the terraces just outside Machu Picchu to feed the whole community of about one thousand people. The farm families who grew the food both lived and worked on the terraces, never entering the city.

Living inside the city were probably four groups of people: nobles, commoners, soldiers, and *mamaconas,* "chosen women" who took part in religious ceremonies.

Nobles and commoners lived in homes—the nobles' homes were of polished stone. Soldiers lived in barracks and the mamaconas in community houses. The city also included a temple for worship of the sun, a cemetery, and a prison.

SOCIAL SYSTEMS
Critical Thinking

Lead a discussion about what it is like to live in a resort town visited mainly by wealthy or famous people. Have students describe what they would like about living in Machu Picchu. Then ask what the disadvantages would be.

434

A CLOSER LOOK

Machu Picchu

Almost touching the clouds, the Inca city of Machu Picchu sits one and a half miles high on a mountaintop in Peru. Forgotten for hundreds of years, Machu Picchu was rediscovered in 1911 by explorer Hiram Bingham, who wrote: "It fairly took my breath away."

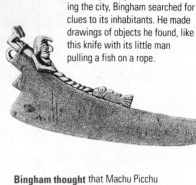

Clearing away the vines covering the city, Bingham searched for clues to its inhabitants. He made drawings of objects he found, like this knife with its little man pulling a fish on a rope.

Bingham thought that Machu Picchu must have been a special religious city because of the fine stonework. Archaeologists now think it may have been a kind of vacation resort for Inca nobles.

Climbing stairs was a way of life for the people who lived here. Over 3,000 steps connect the levels of the city and the farming terraces. Machu Picchu could only be reached by a log bridge on a sheer cliff. If enemies threatened, citizens could simply draw back the bridge.

434

Many mysteries about Machu Picchu remain. When, exactly, did people live here? Why were more women buried here than men? Historians still study Bingham's discoveries, like this jar which may have held a corn drink, to try to find answers.

Chapter 16

Visual Learning

Have students draw pictures or create collages depicting life on the farm terraces of Machu Picchu. Tell students that they should use information from this page, from other parts of the chapter, and from their research. Explain that their illustrations should show how they think it felt to live at the time of the Inca Empire.

Research

Have students find out more about Hiram Bingham's discovery. Suggest that they use the *Readers' Guide* and the card catalog to locate articles and books about Hiram Bingham, Machu Picchu, and Inca Technology.

Journal Writing

Tell students to try to imagine what it was like to be with Hiram Bingham when he came upon Machu Picchu. Ask them to write a journal entry describing what they saw and did and how Bingham might have reacted. Encourage students to write detailed entries, including comparisons with familiar objects and places to try to capture some of the excitement of the discovery.

jewelry from precious metals. Many of these precious works of art were placed in the palaces of dead rulers as well as the temples of the gods. In order to assure that their crops would grow, the Inca prayed to both gods and ancestors. They believed that there was life after death, and that dead rulers and nobility played a role in deciding the fate of the empire.

When an Inca ruler died, the Inca mummified, or preserved, his body. His relatives looked after his palace and estate. They believed the mummy's spirit would harm them if they didn't. The Inca believed mummies spoke to the living and to each other through priests. Mummies were brought out of their palaces for important ceremonies held during the harvest and planting seasons. A Spanish chronicler in the 1500s witnessed one of these ceremonies.

They sat them [the royal mummies] all down in a row, in order of seniority, and the servants who looked after them ate and drank there. . . . In the fire they burned the food they had set before the mummies to eat; it was the same meal that [the family] themselves ate.

Inti, the god of the Sun, was the most important god of the Inca state. In all major cities of the empire, the Inca built temples for Inti, whom they portrayed as a golden disk with a human face. The Inca made animal or special food sacrifices to their gods. Only in times of crisis, such as flood or famine, did the Inca sacrifice humans.

Priests performed these sacrifices. In fact, priests played a large role in Inca everyday life. In Cuzco, the priests began each day with prayers, offerings to the gods, and predictions of the future. They predicted the future by "reading" the remains of animal sacrifices or flames in a fire. No matter how small the issue, Inca rulers often based their decisions on predictions of the priests.

The Inca were optimistic about the world and their place in it. They believed that, under the rule of their divine king, their empire would continue into eternity. The arrival of the Spanish, however, would prove them wrong. ■

▲ *Fine gold jewelry, like this necklace, was placed in the palaces of dead rulers. Inca children were often buried with dolls like the one below.*

■ *Why were mummies important to the Inca?*

R E V I E W

1. **FOCUS** In what ways were the Inca a technologically advanced civilization?
2. **CONNECT** How did the Inca method of conquering other tribes differ from the Aztec method?
3. **GEOGRAPHY** How did altitude and terrain affect Inca agriculture?
4. **SOCIAL SYSTEMS** What was everyday life like for the common people who lived in the Inca Empire?
5. **CRITICAL THINKING** Why do you think the Inca worshiped their ancestors?
6. **ACTIVITY** Choose a city that you feel best illustrates life in the United States. Make A Closer Look for the city you chose using photographs from magazines.

Two American Empires

435

Answers to Review Questions

1. The Inca produced an elaborate system of roads, almost 10,000 miles long. They also developed efficient agricultural techniques, such as terrace farming. In addition, they constructed massive buildings, using expert masonry techniques.
2. The Inca ruler would send a scout to evaluate a territory. Based on the scout's report the Inca would draw up a plan of attack. If the enemy tribe refused to surrender peacefully, the Inca would invade.
3. The Inca adapted farming to altitude and terrain, growing the crops and using farming techniques best suited to each area.
4. Commoners had little control over their lives. They worked the land or labored to build roads and buildings. They lived in small huts. Travel and marriage required government approval.
5. Answers will vary. The Inca believed in the power of the dead to influence the future of the living.

Homework Options

Have students write a paragraph for each major heading in the lesson. Each paragraph should contain three or four key points.

Study Guide: p. 69

UNDERSTANDING TOPOGRAPHY

This skills feature uses an elevation map and a vertical profile to teach students how elevation affects topography.

GEOGRAPHY
Map and Globe Skills

Have students use the map key of the Inca Road on p. 436 to determine the range of elevations shown on the map. *(From below 15,000 feet below sea level to above 15,000 feet above sea level.)*

Then refer students to the elevation line shown on the map. Point out that the vertical profile is a cross section of the landforms along the elevation line. Remind students that they made a vertical profile for the Chapter 7 skills feature (p. 140).

Read Here's How aloud while students trace the route from Lima to Jauja. Discuss how topography might have affected the Inca. *(Methods of transportation, crops grown, type of shelter.)*

Analyzing Elevation

Here's Why

You already know about topography, the natural surface features of the land. If you plan a bicycle route to avoid hills or to go around a lake, you are considering topography.

Studying topography doesn't only provide information about possible routes. Topography can also help you explore cultures and history. For example, you can learn about the Inca culture by analyzing the elevation of the Inca Road.

Here's How

Suppose you want to go from Lima to Jauja on the Inca Road. The map below uses color to show different ranges in elevation, or height above sea level.

Elevation is part of the topography of a region. The key beside the map shows the elevations represented by each color.

From Lima, you travel south for about 35 miles. The elevation during this portion of your trip is low and unchanging.

Now you turn to the east, toward Huarochiri. In the 45 miles to Huarochiri, you climb first to an elevation of over 5,000 feet and then to over 10,000 feet. This is higher than Mount St. Helens in Washington.

In Huarochiri, you continue east and soon reach an elevation of over 15,000 feet. This is higher than Mount Whitney in California.

As you leave Huarochiri, the elevation drops to the 10,000-foot range. In the 50 miles between Huarochiri and Jauja, you are never below 10,000 feet and are often as high as 15,000 feet.

Try It

Suppose you wanted to travel from Nazca to Cuzco,

going through Andahuaylas, on the Inca Road. Use the map to trace your route. Use the vertical profile to describe the topography that you would encounter.

Apply It

Locate a topographic map of your state in an atlas. Use the map to describe a bicycle or hiking route between two areas that show either a very great or very small change in elevation over 50 miles.

The Inca Road in Central Peru

Elevation	
Feet	Meters
Above 15,000	Above 4,572
10,000–15,000	3,048–4,572
5,000–10,000	1,524–3,048
0–5,000	0–1,524
Sea level	Sea level
0–5,000	0–1,524
5,000–10,000	1,524–3,048
10,000–15,000	3,048–4,572
Below 15,000	Below 4,572
—— Inca road	

Objective

Read and use a topographic map and a vertical profile. (Map and Globe Skills 2, 3)

Research

Have the students use library resources to find out more about how the Inca Road was made.

Answers to Try It

Cuzco is about 225 miles northeast of Nazca. It is about 125 miles from Nazca to Andahuaylas, and in the first 50 miles of the trip the elevation rises from below 5,000 feet in Nazca to above 15,000 feet. The elevation

for the remainder of the trip is between 10,000 and 15,000 feet. From Andahuaylas to Cuzco the elevation ranges between 5,000 and 15,000 feet. Students should use the vertical profile to supplement their answers.

Answers to Apply It

Answers should demonstrate an awareness of distance, direction, and topography.

1200   1300   1400   1500   1600   1700
                              1519   1572

L E S S O N 3

The Arrival of the Spanish

A *thing like a ball of stone flies out of their bellies and flashes sparks and rains fire. . . . If the ball hits a tree, it blows away in splinters, as though a magician had blown it away from inside. Their battle dress and their arms are all made of iron. . . . They are carried on the backs of stags wherever they like to go. Their skin is white, as though made of chalk. . . . Their dogs are great monsters with flat ears and long tongues which hang out."*

An eyewitness account of
the Spanish arrival, as told to
Bernardo de Sahagun, 1528

Hernando Cortés, the Spanish **conquistador,** or conqueror, landed on the shores of central Mexico in April 1519, seeking adventure and wealth. With him were over 550 men, 16 horses, 14 cannons, and a few dogs. He was greeted by messengers of the Aztec ruler Moctezuma. Wanting to show the Aztec his power, Cortés had the ships' cannons fired. The Aztec were stunned. They rushed back and reported to Moctezuma.

This was the first time the Aztec had seen cannons or horses or men with white skin. According to Sahagun's account, which was based on reports by Aztec who had been with Moctezuma: "When Moctezuma heard this report, he was seized with fright. His heart grew weak to the point of faintness. . . . And despair overcame him."

THINKING FOCUS

Why were the Spanish able to take over the Aztec and Inca empires so quickly?

Key Terms

• conquistador
• civil war

 *This drawing from a codex shows the Aztec view of the arrival of the Spanish.*

437

Two American Empires

Graphic Overview

	Aztec	**Inca**	**Spanish**
Internal Condition	civil war	civil war	not applicable
External Condition	Spanish invade	Spanish invade	not applicable
Impact of Disease	enormous	enormous	minimal
Weapons	bows, arrows, clubs	bows, arrows, clubs	guns and cannons

---

INTRODUCE

Point out the lesson title and review with students the early Spanish expeditions to the Americas and the reasons behind them. Have students read the Thinking Focus and point out that the Spanish clashed with and conquered both the Aztec and the Inca. Ask students to speculate on how the Aztec and Inca would react to meeting Europeans for the first time.

Key Terms

Vocabulary Strategy: T36–T37
conquistador—the Spanish term for conqueror used in reference to Spaniards who came to the New World in the 1500s in search of wealth
civil war—a war between factions or regions within one country

Objectives

1. Compare and contrast the internal problems of the Aztec and Inca empires.
2. Describe the events that led up to the Spanish conquest of the Aztec and Inca Empires.
3. Summarize the reasons for the rapid Spanish conquest of the Aztec and Inca Empires.

DEVELOP

Tell students that in this lesson they will read about how the Aztec and Inca Empires came to an end when the Spanish arrived and conquered them. Ask students to skim the lesson and read the three major headings. Help students to see the cause-and-effect structure of the lesson and point out that the first section deals with internal causes and the second with external causes. You may wish to use the Graphic Overview shown on p. 437.

■ *Civil war, food shortages, and increasing costs were common in both the Aztec and Inca Empires.*

POLITICAL SYSTEMS
Critical Thinking

Have students compare and contrast the causes of internal weakening in the Aztec Empire with those of the Inca Empire. Ask them why rebellion was a greater problem in the Aztec Empire.

438

The Empires Weaken

The Spanish appeared on American shores in the early 1500s. At that time, **civil war,** or fighting between parts of the empire, plagued both the Aztec and the Inca.

In the Aztec Empire, a number of subject tribes began to rebel against their harsh Aztec rulers. Led by the Tlaxcalans, these rebel tribes put up a bitter struggle. Infuriated, Moctezuma launched huge attacks against them.

Rebellion was so widespread that the Aztec were forced to fight in many areas at once. Because their armies were spread so thinly, they won few battles. Also, waging so many battles caused war costs to soar. There were few resources left for making new conquests.

Increasing war costs, decreasing tribute from new conquests, and a famine in 1505 prompted Moctezuma to demand more tribute from his subject states. This demand led to even more resentment and rebellion among subject tribes.

The Inca were also facing internal unrest when Spanish adventurers, led by Francisco Pizarro, arrived in 1532. When the Inca ruler died in 1525, his two sons, Huascar *(WAHS kahr)* and Atahualpa *(ah tah WAHL pah)*, fought each other for the throne. The northern half of the empire supported Atahualpa, and the southern half supported Huascar. After three years of bloodshed, Atahualpa emerged as the ruler of a greatly weakened empire. ■

■ *How were the internal problems of the Aztec and Inca empires similar, and how did they contribute to their downfall?*

438

Old and New Worlds Clash

Because of internal division, the Aztec and Inca could not keep out the Spanish invaders. When the Spanish saw the wealth of the two American empires, they set out to conquer them.

Cortés Conquers the Aztec

When Moctezuma first learned of the Spanish arrival, he believed that Cortés might be Quetzalcoatl *(keht sahl koh AHTL)*, an ancient god come to reclaim his earthly kingdom. He welcomed the strangers into Tenochtitlan, saying, "It appears that our Lord has returned to his country. Go hence and receive him worthily."

But he soon learned he had made a grave mistake. Within days, Cortés took Moctezuma hostage. Moctezuma ordered vast

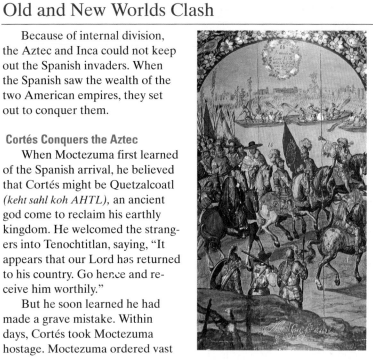

Access Activity

Continue to use the hypothetical situation described in the Access Strategy. Have students debate about what the U.S. government should do, giving reasons for their opinions.

Access Strategy

Ask students what the United States government might do if a small fleet of spaceships from an unknown planet in another solar system touched down in the United States. Have them imagine that the aliens inside the ships resemble human beings but have blue skin. They state that they have come in peace. Ask students what their reactions might be to finding out about such an incident. Would they feel curious? Mistrustful? Threatened? Excited? How do they

think the government might react? Would they welcome the strangers? Fight them? Arrest them?

Tell them this imaginary situation is not unlike the situation the Aztec and Inca faced when the Spanish explorers landed on their shores. Point out that the huge difference between the cultures of the Spanish and the native Americans played a key role in deciding the fate of the native empires.

amounts of gold and silver brought to the palace. But the foreigners stayed. Moctezuma remained a prisoner. Many people blamed him for the Spanish takeover.

Some people blamed an Aztec slave girl named Doña Marina by the Spanish and called "La Malinche" *(lah mah LEEN chay)* by the Aztec. She translated the Aztec language, Nahuatl *(naw WAT uhl),* to Mayan. A shipwrecked Spaniard named Aguilar *(ah GWEE lar),* whom Cortés rescued, then translated from Mayan to Spanish. With La Malinche and Aguilar at his side, Cortés was able to negotiate with the Aztec. In modern Mexican vocabulary, a *malinchista (mah leen CHEES tah)* is someone who betrays one's country or friends.

Six months later, one of Cortés' deputies massacred thousands of Aztec people, triggering a rebellion. Moctezuma died in the rebellion, but sources disagree as to who killed him—the Spanish, or his own people. After the rebellion the Aztec drove the Spanish out.

The remaining Spanish escaped to a Tlaxcalan camp. The Tlaxcalans hated the Aztec, so Cortés persuaded them to help him. Other tribes eagerly joined the army.

In May 1521, with a huge army behind them, the Spanish laid siege to the Aztec capital. They blocked boat traffic and stranded the city without supplies. Then an epidemic broke out among the Aztec.

Finally, on August 13, 1521, with most of their warriors dead from disease, starvation, or war wounds, the Aztec gave up. Thousands of them were enslaved, but most fled to the countryside.

Pizarro Conquers the Inca

The Inca Empire ended similarly 11 years later when the Spanish conquistador Francisco Pizarro arrived. Leading about 150 men, Pizarro landed in Tumbes on the northern coast of the Inca Empire in early 1532. The Spanish assured Inca messengers that they wished only to admire the empire. The Inca ruler Atahualpa then allowed the Spanish to advance as far as his military stronghold in Cajamarca.

Pizarro decided on a quick, brutal attack. He called for a meeting with Atahualpa, but waited safely behind and sent a Spanish monk in his place. The monk offered Atahualpa a Bible and told the chief to give up his beliefs. Outraged, Atahualpa threw the Bible to the ground, saying, "I will be no man's tributary. . . . As for my faith, I will not change it."

When the monk reported that the Inca chief could not be converted, Pizarro and his troops attacked, killing more than 5,000 Inca. Atahualpa was taken prisoner. The Inca gave Pizarro 24 tons of gold and silver as a ransom for Atahualpa, but he was not released. The Spanish later strangled him.

▲ *This image shows the Aztec view of the war against the Spanish invaders. Notice the difference in weapons and armor used by the Aztec and the Spanish.*

▼ *This standard was carried by Hernando Cortés on all his campaigns in the New World. Notice that the Madonna is the central image.*

439

Two American Empires

■ *The Aztec ruler welcomed the Spanish believing they might be gods. The Inca, while more cautious, allowed the Spanish to bring troops into their empire.*

Critical Thinking

Have students rank the reasons for the destruction of the Aztec and Inca Empires from most important to least important, and explain the reasons for their choices.

■ *How did the Aztec and Inca rulers receive the Spanish conquistadors?*

➤ *These portraits at right and above show the Spanish conquistador Francisco Pizarro, who conquered the Inca empire, and the last Inca ruler, Atahualpa. The Inca used rope slings, similar to those above, as weapons against the Spanish invaders.*

In February 1536, Manco Inca, the last heir to Huascar's throne, led an army estimated at 200,000 Inca to Cuzco. But the Inca siege soon failed because most supplies had been used up in the civil war. Manco Inca retreated with his army into the Andes. There they held out until 1572, when the Spanish finally defeated them.■

Two Empires Destroyed

Scholars give many reasons for the rapid Spanish conquest of the Aztec and Inca empires. First and foremost, the Spanish weapons were technologically superior. They fought with cannon and crossbow, as well as spears and swords made of iron. The Aztec, with bronze and copper shields, stone knives, and woven-cloth armor, were no match for them.

Second, the Spanish and the Aztec came from drastically different cultures. They had different ways of living and believing. Moctezuma believed that Cortés might have been a god and allowed him to walk freely into the capital city. Cortés, on the other hand, saw the Aztec culture as something pagan to be destroyed and replaced by the Christian faith.

The two groups even fought by different rules. The Aztec usually fought only to take captives for sacrifice. The Spanish, however, fought to kill.

The Spanish also took advantage of the weakened and rebellious state of the American empires. They used resentful subject tribes to guide them through unfamiliar territory and to help them win their battles. The Spanish turned on the subject tribes once their goals were achieved.

Finally, disease brought by the Europeans had a disastrous effect on the Aztec and Inca. Smallpox and measles, which the Aztec and Inca had never been exposed to, spread rapidly through their

Chapter 16

Critical Thinking

Ask students to speculate as to what might have happened in the Aztec and Inca Empires if the natives had attacked the Spanish forces as soon as they stepped on land, rather than welcoming them.

Research

Have students find out more about Hernando Cortés or Francisco Pizarro. Help them develop a list of questions to focus their research, such as: What drew them to the Americas? What other expeditions did they make? Where did they get the money to make their journeys?

Math Connection

Refer students to the chart of population decline on p. 441. Ask them to write down the size of the Aztec population before and after the arrival of the Spanish. Have them subtract the second number from the first to determine the total population decline. *(Approximately 20 million.)* Then have them divide that number by the first number to come up with the percentage of decline. *(Approximately 83 percent.)* Do the same for the Inca.

empires. Not only did disease drastically reduce their armies, it killed off many leaders, leaving the Aztec and Inca even more vulnerable.

The Spanish conquest devastated the Aztec and Inca populations. Spanish nobles took over the land and forced the Aztec and Inca into slavery. As slaves, they labored on farms and in silver mines. In some areas more than 90 percent of the population died as the result of the Spanish takeover. The chart on this page shows the population decline among the Aztec and the Inca after the arrival of the Spanish.

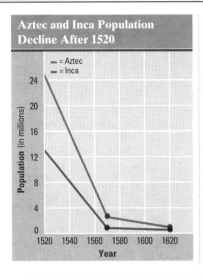

Aztec and Inca Population Decline After 1520

◄ *Note the dramatic drop in both the Aztec and Inca populations after the Spanish arrived.*

UNDERSTANDING EPIDEMICS

I t attacked people, beat them down all over the city and killed enormous numbers. Those afflicted lay about helpless, like corpses on their beds. . . . If they tried to move they cried out in pain." A Spanish chronicler describes the effects of a smallpox epidemic that killed millions of Aztec and Inca in the 1500s. An epidemic is a highly contagious disease that infects many people at the same time. Because of the numbers they affect, epidemics disrupt societies and help shape history.

The Spanish had built up immunity, or resistance, to diseases like the measles and smallpox. Native Americans had no immunity to

the diseases, which devastated their peoples.

Epidemics in History

Major epidemics have had significant impact on other civilizations. An outbreak of the bubonic plague, or Black Death, swept through Europe in the 1300s. Nearly half the population of Europe died. Due to the plague, life in both cities and the countryside was hard hit. Trade and production slowed, and governments found it difficult to raise money.

Epidemics Now

Epidemics still occur today. In late 1997, over 1.6 million people in the world were living with Acquired

Immune Deficiency Syndrome, or AIDS. Researchers are looking for a cure, but experts predict that by the end of the year 2000, over 60 million adults will have been infected with HIV (the virus that causes AIDS). No one knows what the full impact of the epidemic will be in this country, but in some parts of Africa, entire villages have been wiped out.

In general, epidemics are much rarer today. Medicines now exist that prevent the diseases that devastated the Aztec and the Inca. But the discovery of such drugs came too late to prevent epidemics from playing a role in the conquest of the New World.

441

Two American Empires

Critical Thinking

Ask students why the Spanish destroyed as much as they could of Aztec and Inca architecture, idols, and anything else that represented their culture. *(Possibly to destroy cultural unity.)* Then ask them what effect the Spanish destruction of these things has had on our understanding of the Inca and Aztec civilizations. *(It made current knowledge of the Aztec and Inca much more limited because primary source information was destroyed.)*

Language Arts Connection

Have small groups of students analyze the meaning of the Aztec poem on p. 442. To get them started you might ask these questions: What is the cause of the grief and suffering mentioned in the poem? *(The destruction caused by the Spanish conquistadors.)* To whom is the poem addressed? *(An Aztec god, called Giver of Life.)* What tone, or attitude, does the poet express? *(Grief, sadness.)*

Science Connection

Epidemics have changed the course of history. Have students find out more about the causes of epidemics, how they spread, and why they are rarer today than in the past. They might focus on the plague, the flu, typhoid, or the measles.

Critical Thinking

The outbreak of disease among the Aztec and the Inca contributed to their downfall. Ask students if they think the Aztec and Inca would still have been defeated if disease had not been a factor.

442

CULTURE

Study Skills

Have students find out more about the descendants of the Aztec and how they live today. (The Inca are already discussed in the lesson.) Students should discover, among other things, what aspects of Aztec society, such as religion and agricultural techniques, still survive today.

■ *Answers will vary. An example could be: Disease killed many Aztec and Inca leaders and drastically reduced their armies, leaving the empires more vulnerable to Spanish attacks.*

C L O S E

Using information from the section Two Empires Destroyed, have students develop a web that summarizes the reasons for the rapid destruction of the Aztec and Inca Empires. You may wish to use the Graphic Overview on p. 437 as a base; let students add to it. Be sure they categorize each cause as internal or external and explain why.

442

The Aztec and Inca, however, responded differently to the invaders. The capture of Tenochtitlan meant the end of Aztec civilization, because the city had been the center of Aztec life. When it fell, they ceased all resistance and allowed the Spanish to take over their land and people.

An anonymous poet described the feelings of the Aztec just after the Spanish conquest in 1521:

> There is nothing but grief and suffering
> in Mexico and Tlatelolco,
> where once we saw beauty and valour.
> Have you grown weary of your servants?
> Are you angry with your servants, O Giver of Life?

The Inca, on the other hand, did not give up after their capital city was conquered. Resistance to Spanish rule continued for 40 years. Some scholars believe this is because the Inca rulers took much better care of their subject tribes. They provided their subjects with both food and land. By spreading their culture, religion, and language throughout their empire, the Inca bonded their subjects together.

The Spanish destroyed temples, artwork, and anything else that represented Inca culture. But Inca traditions survived. Today, some 20 million Inca descendants still speak Quechua, celebrate ancient religious ceremonies, and farm in small villages. The Inca people below live much as their ancestors did. ■

■ *Which of the following contributed most significantly to the defeat of the Aztec and Inca empires: disease, civil war, cultural differences, or Spanish military strength? Defend your answer.*

➤ *Both the Aztec and the Inca continued to exist after the Spanish conquest. The people in the near photo are descendants of the Aztec. Those to the far right are descendents of the Inca.*

R E V I E W

1. **FOCUS** Why were the Spanish able to take over the Aztec and Inca empires so quickly?
2. **CONNECT** Why did civil wars occur in the Aztec and Inca empires?
3. **HISTORY** Spaniards wrote most accounts of the conquest. Why do you think it would be hard for historians to reconstruct the truth about what happened?
4. **CRITICAL THINKING** Do you think the defeat of the Aztec and Inca by the Spanish could have been prevented? Explain.
5. **WRITING ACTIVITY** Write a news broadcast describing either the arrival of Cortés in the Aztec Empire or the arrival of Pizarro in the Inca Empire.

Chapter 16

Homework Options

Have students make two timelines—one for the Aztec and one for the Inca—that trace the Spanish conquest.

Study Guide: p. 71

Answers to Review Questions

1. The Spanish had technologically superior weapons such as guns and cannons. They also took advantage of the political situation by enlisting the help of tribes who resented their Aztec rulers. European disease also hastened the conquest of the Aztec and Inca. It spread through the empires and wiped out large segments of the populations.
2. Subject tribes were unhappy with their harsh Aztec and Inca rulers. Specifically, they were tired of paying huge tributes to their rulers.
3. Spanish accounts would probably not present fairly the Aztec or Inca side of the story, thus losing not only detail but objectivity.
4. Answers will vary but should indicate an understanding of the Spanish advantages and of the internal problems of the Aztec and Inca.

UNDERSTANDING CRITICAL THINKING

Identifying Values

Here's Why

Do you sometimes wonder why people act as they do? If you can identify the values that underlie their actions, you may better understand those actions.

When the Aztec and the Spanish conquistadors first faced each other in 1519, they knew nothing about each other's values. As the painting below shows, the Aztec welcomed Cortez with gifts, as they would a returning hero or a god. Compare the weapons carried by the Aztec and by the Spanish soldiers. What does this suggest to you?

The reasons why the Spanish were able to conquer the Aztec within two years are complex: technical advantages of cannons and muskets over stone knives,

political instability of the Aztec Empire, and a disastrous outbreak of smallpox among the Aztec.

If the Aztec and the Spaniards had known more about each other's values, that might not have been enough to change the outcome of the battles. However, from your viewpoint, looking back into the past, you can see how their values influenced their actions.

Here's How

Turn to page 440 and read the section Two Empires Destroyed. Identify statements that refer to values of the Spanish and the Aztec. Explain the differences in values and how these might have affected their actions. For example, look now at the statement,

"The two groups even fought by different rules." The Aztec valued the taking of captives in battle; the Spanish did not. Therefore, the Spaniards who were captured frequently escaped and could fight again. Because of the differences in values, the Aztec were more likely to die on the battlefield.

Try It

Use the text on pages 431, 432, and 442 to identify values of the Inca. List those you think affected the Inca's responses to the Spaniards.

Apply It

Write down the values you and your classmates hold in common on these topics: air pollution, environmental waste, diet, clothes, exercise. Compare your list with others'.

443

443

Answers to Try It

Before attacking, Inca rulers sent ambassadors to the enemy tribe to try to persuade them to join the empire peacefully. Though they enjoyed little freedom, Inca subjects rarely went hungry. The Inca rulers took much better care of their subjects, providing them with both food and land. By spreading their culture throughout the empire, the Inca gave many of their subjects a common bond. Thus resistance to Spanish rule continued for 40 years after the Spanish conquest.

Answers to Apply It

Answers will vary, but students should take care to compose their lists of values independently before comparing them with the lists of their classmates.

Objective

Identify values that underlie people's actions. (Critical Thinking 2)

INTRODUCE

Students have read how the empires of the Aztec and Inca flourished and then were destroyed by Spanish Conquistadors. The Spanish, however, did not destroy memories of those civilizations, memories that are rooted in their respective myths and legends. "The Legend of the Lake," from *Warriors, Gods and Spirits* by Douglas Gifford, is an example of an Inca legend that has been passed down. It follows Lesson 3, in Chapter 16, in which students learned about the conflict between the Conquistadors and the Aztec and Inca civilizations.

READ AND RESPOND

Most students can probably read this short legend independently. As students read the selection, ask them to think about what the legend says to us about being too proud and not listening to other people.

Words that students may need to know before reading are: *arrogant*, exaggerating one's own worth; *prophesying*, predicting the future; *persisted*, did not stop; and *flogged*, beaten with a rod or whip.

Although the Conquistadors destroyed much of the Aztec and Inca civilizations, the people live on. Sometimes that living is more in memory than in reality, as in this Inca legend.

444

LITERATURE

The Legend of the Lake

Retold by Douglas Gifford

Lake Titicaca, the largest freshwater lake in South America, lies nearly 4,000 meters up on the Altiplano. There it straddles the border between Bolivia and Peru. To the Inca, the lake was a holy place. According to legend, it was there that the children of the Sun first descended to earth. This story, set in a region where earthquakes are still a common occurrence, tells how the lake first came into being.

L ong ago in the high plains lay a vast, rich city built by a proud and arrogant people. They were so pleased with their city and so satisfied with their progress that they would never admit that any improvement was possible. "We are the lords of all creation," they said loftily, "and all people must obey us. There is no city like ours in all the world."

One day a group of ragged Indians arrived in the city. Although they looked poor, they soon began to attract attention to themselves by prophesying that the city would be destroyed. "Prepare," they told the people, "for ruin will come by earthquake and flood and fire. The smell of death is on this city!"

"What nonsense," scoffed the city people. "Why don't you go away? We are the greatest of all people. Look at our buildings. There are none like them in the world. Look at our water system and irrigation. Where will you find any to equal them? We are a modern, progressive race: we know how to deal with floods and earthquakes. Go away with your old wives' tales."

The ragged band of Indians persisted in their warnings and eventually, tired of their nagging, depressing voices, the city people had them flogged and thrown out of the city. Only the priests were anxious.

"These were holy men," they said, "and who knows, they may be right. Perhaps they can see further than we can."

Some of the priests took the Indians' words so seriously that they, too, left the city and retired to their temple on the hill. There they lived as hermits, cutting themselves off from the city people completely.

"Look at them," mocked the city people. "What good do they think they are doing up there? All they can do is preach; they've

Thematic Connections

Social Studies: Legends of a Society

Houghton Mifflin Literary Readers: Tales of Long Ago

Background

By the end of the 15th century, the Inca Empire stretched about 3,000 miles along the coast and mountains of western South America. Even though the Inca did not have a system of writing, they were very skilled in medicine, agriculture, weaving, and pottery. They were also skilled rememberers, especially those designated as quipucamayocs. Because of these official rememberers, many Inca legends survive today. Above all else, though, the Inca were expert engineers and builders. Inca ruins existing today are so precisely built that a knife will not fit between the huge, perfectly carved stone blocks (some weighing hundreds of tons).

The Inca religion was a mixture of beliefs from conquered tribes. The Inca worshiped many gods in both elaborate and simple ceremonies. The gods of the sun, moon, and earth were especially popular.

never done an honest day's work in their lives. If anyone is doomed it is they. That hill is the very place for lightning to strike. How we'll laugh when that happens."

Then, one peaceful afternoon, one of the city people saw a small red cloud on the horizon. At first he could not tell whether it was a real cloud or just a puff of smoke from a burning house but it grew larger and larger. Soon it was obvious that it was a real cloud and that there were others massing together with it, red clouds and dark clouds the color of lead. When night came there was no darkness, for the sky and the earth below were lit up by a glaring red light from the clouds. An eerie silence hung over the whole land.

Suddenly, there was a flash and a rumble, then an ear-splitting crash as the earth jolted violently. Many of the buildings stood firm, for they had been well constructed of stone but almost immediately a red rain started to pour from the clouds and the earth shook again, more violently even than before. Building after building crashed to the ground and the red rain grew to a continual cloudburst. The carefully constructed water and irrigation systems were completely destroyed; mountain rivers were jolted from their courses and a great flood rose over the buildings of the city.

Today the great Lake of Titicaca covers the proud city. Not one of its mocking inhabitants survived and it is said that some died with their unbelieving smiles still on their faces. Only the priests in their humble straw huts were saved. Their temple on the hill stood firm against the earthquake and the hill itself rose above the flood waters. Today it is the Island of the Sun.

The ragged prophets, too, survived for they watched sadly from a high place as the waters rose and the city was destroyed. Some of their descendants became the Callawayas, the wise men of the valleys by the Altiplano, travelling doctors and healers famous for their skills.

Further Reading

The Captive. Scott O'Dell. A young seminary student joins a Spanish expedition to the New World. He joins the Maya and assumes the identity of a Mayan god.

The Feathered Serpent. Scott O'Dell. This book continues the chronicle begun in *The Captive*.

Temple of the Sun. Evelyn Lampman. This is a story of how the Aztec Indians tried to resist being conquered by Cortés.

Warriors, Gods and Spirits from Central and South American Mythology. Retold by Douglas Gifford. A collection of stories about Central and South American peoples.

◄ The humble prophets who had tried to help were ridiculed and beaten, but they survived the flood. The people of the city had been arrogant and proud and had died. What lesson does this teach us? *(Possible answers: Humility is a strength, and arrogant pride a weakness; helping others will be rewarded; nothing is indestructible.)*

EXTEND

The Inca left a rich heritage of legends and myths as well as impressive ruins. Have students research in the school or public library to find specific examples of Inca ruins. Have them prepare short oral reports on their findings.

445

445

Writing a Narrative

A narrative is a story or a description of an event. Have students assume the identity of one of the ragged Indians who visited the city and write a narrative about the experience. They need not give themselves names, but can if they wish. Students should retell the story as if they were involved. Encourage students to describe how things looked and how they felt about the events in the story. After the stories are finished, students may want to share them aloud or display them.

Further Reading

You may want to have your students look in the school or local library for more books about Inca and Aztec civilizations, as well as other Central and South American peoples, such as the Moche, Tiwanakans, and Maya.

Answers to Reviewing Key Terms
A. Sample answers:
1. **civil war:** The Aztec Empire was weakened by **civil war.**
2. **vertical economy:** In the **vertical economy,** farmers grew grain at low altitudes while herders raised llamas at higher altitudes.
3. **tribute:** Aztec nobility did not pay **tribute** to anyone.
4. **chinampa:** Aztec farmers could use canals to travel from **chinampa** to **chinampa.**
5. **calpulli:** Serfs and slaves worked in a **calpulli.**
6. **conquistadors:** Spanish **conquistadors** quickly destroyed the Aztec Empire.
7. **alliance:** The Aztec formed an **alliance** with other tribes.
8. **terrace farming:** The Inca used **terrace farming** to farm at high altitudes.

Answers to Exploring Concepts
A. Sample answers:
I.–The Aztec
A.–Building an empire
B.–*Living in the empire*
C.–Fighting for the gods
II.–The Inca
A.–Rising to power
1.–*Controlling Cuzco Valley*
2.–*Conquering a vast area*
B.–*Conquering and controlling*
C.–Working the land
D.–*Praying to the ancestors*
III.–The arrival of the Spanish
A.–*The empires weaken*
B.–Old and new worlds clash
C.–Two empires destroyed
1.–*Superior Spanish weapons*
2.–*Different cultures*
3.–*Disease*
B. Sample answers:
1. The Aztec grew crops in floating gardens, or chinampas, which were surrounded by water. The Inca grew crops according to the height of the land.

2. Some Aztec history was recorded in codices and can be decoded. Inca history was passed down orally.
3. The Inca Empire covered parts of Ecuador, Peru, Bolivia, Argentina, and Chile. The Aztec Empire was limited to parts of Mexico and Guatemala.
4. The Inca offered enemies a chance to join the empire

Chapter Review

Reviewing Key Terms

alliance (p. 424)   conquistador (p. 437)
calpulli (p. 425)   terrace farming (p. 433)
chinampa (p. 423)   tribute (p. 425)
civil war (p. 438)   vertical economy (p. 433)

The following sentences contain clues to the key terms. On your own paper, write the key term each sentence suggests. Then use the key term in a different sentence.
1. Fighting between different parts of the empire was a problem for both the Aztec and the Inca empires.
2. Inca living at different altitudes grew products and raised livestock suited to different altitudes and conditions.
3. In the Aztec Empire, nobles lived off a kind of tax that could be paid to them in goods and services.
4. The Aztec converted swampy land to floating gardens.
5. Aztec families of different social ranks lived in each settlement.
6. Cortés and Pizarro were Spanish conquerors who conquered the Aztec and Inca.
7. To enlarge their empire, the Aztec formed a union with other tribes.
8. In order to grow crops at high altitudes, the Inca carried rich topsoil from low areas and packed it into flat-topped mounds of earth in the higher areas.

Exploring Concepts

A. Copy and complete the following outline using information from the chapter.

```
I. The Aztec
   A. Building an empire
   B. _____
   C. Fighting for the gods
II. The Inca
   A. Rising to power
      1. _____
      2. _____
   B. _____
   C. Working the land
   D. _____
III. The arrival of the Spanish
   A. _____
   B. Old and new worlds clash
   C. Two empires destroyed
      1. _____
      2. _____
      3. _____
```

B. Support each of the following statements with facts and details from the chapter.
1. Both the Aztec and the Inca used imaginative farming methods to grow crops.
2. Historians have a different way of learning about early Aztec history than they do about early Inca history.
3. The Inca Empire was larger than the Aztec Empire.
4. The Inca and Aztec behaved differently when they conquered other tribes.
5. The Inca used various methods for maintaining control over conquered tribes.
6. Everyday life differed for Inca nobility and commoners.
7. The Aztec and the Inca had different reasons for human sacrifice.
8. More social classes existed in the Aztec Empire than in the Inca Empire.
9. The Inca engaged in ancestor worship.
10. Conquistadors conquered the Aztec and the Inca for many of the same reasons.

before conquering them. The Aztec just wanted to conquer enemies.
5. The Inca held local religious idols and princes hostage, made them soldiers, rewarded new soldiers, made Inca religion and language required.
6. The nobility did not work, but ruled commoners who labored and farmed.
7. The Aztec sacrificed thousands, mostly captives of war. The Inca sacrificed humans only in times of extreme crisis.

8. Social classes of the Aztec Empire were nobles, commoners, serfs, and slaves. The Inca had two main social classes—the nobility and the commoners.
9. The Inca prayed to their ancestors. They believed dead rulers and nobility helped decide the fate of the empire.
10. These reasons included costs of war, civil war, disease, repressive tribute demands, food shortages, and inferior weapons.

Reviewing Skills

1. Refer to the map of the Inca Road on page 436. Use this map to trace a route from Chincha Alta to Andahuaylas. Then describe what this route is like as if you were telling a group of travelers what they can expect.
2. Study the overall network of roads shown on the map of the Inca Road. In general, do you think it is easier to travel east-west or north-south on the Inca Road? Explain your answer.
3. Find the heading Rising to Power on page 424. Reread this part of the chapter and explain what values the Aztec seem to have learned from neighboring tribes.
4. Tell how each of these sections of Lesson 1 helps to identify the moral values of the Aztec people:
   Social Classes—pages 425 and 426
   Human Sacrifices—pages 427 and 428
   War and Religion—page 428
5. How were different attitudes toward conquered peoples in the Aztec and Inca empires shown?
6. Before the arrival of the Spanish in the Inca Empire in 1532, the Inca were confident that their empire would continue on into eternity. Form a hypothesis to explain this belief. Be sure to give evidence from the chapter to support your hypothesis.
7. If you were planning a trip from one side of the Andes to the other and you wanted to see where mountain peaks and valleys were located, what kind of map would you use?

Using Critical Thinking

1. Both the Aztec and Inca solved the major problem of feeding their people in spite of poor farming conditions. Modern farmers have also had to solve problems to grow crops. For example, the dry climate in the American Southwest presented problems, so farmers developed ways to irrigate crops. How does this solution compare to that of the Aztec and Inca?
2. The Aztec government allowed only certain goods to be sold in each market. There might have been one market for feathers and jewels and another market for slaves. Evaluate how this system might affect store owners and shoppers today in your community if all the shoe stores were in one area, sporting goods stores in another area, bookstores in still another, and so on.

Preparing for Citizenship

1. **WRITING ACTIVITY** Write a report in which you compare the way the Inca emperors ruled with the way our leaders govern today. For example, how would each type of leader accomplish large building projects such as the construction of roads, sewage treatment plants, or large public monuments?
2. **COLLABORATIVE LEARNING** The Aztec created beautiful hieroglyphic books called codices that told about various aspects of Aztec life. Create a codex to tell about life in your school. As a class, decide which aspects to include, such as school sports, the art department, the choir or chorus, the band or orchestra, the school newspaper, and various clubs such as language clubs. Then break into small groups to cover each aspect. Each group should decide what each member will contribute. One might research the various school departments for ideas about what to draw; another might draw the hieroglyphs; another might write translations of the hieroglyphs. All the codices can then be bound into a book for the whole class to use.

447

Two American Empires

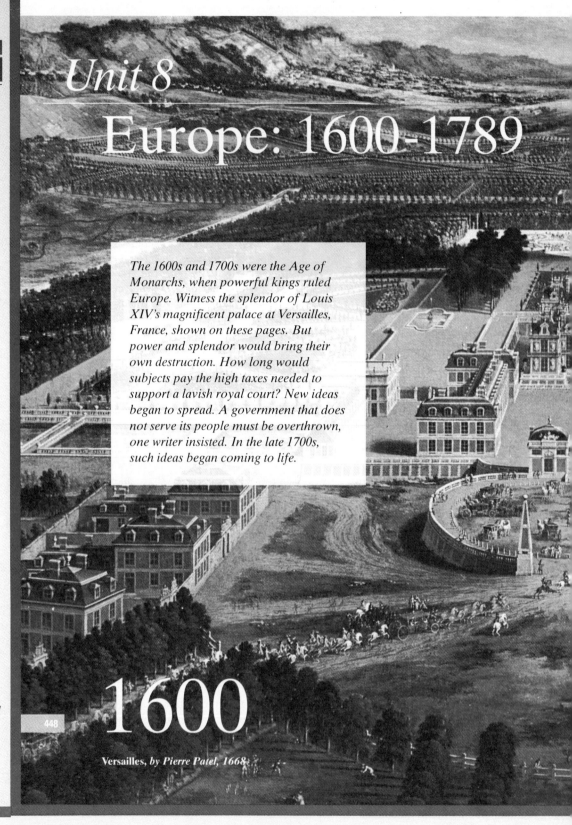

UNIT
OVERVIEW

Have students read the unit title and the passage below it. Explain that Louis XIV, who reigned from 1643 (when he was 4) to 1715, was an absolute ruler. He said "L'état, c'est moi," or "I am the state." Point out that during this period people in France and England began to reject the notion that one person should hold all the power.

Looking Back

Remind students that in the previous two units they learned about the split between Catholics and Protestants and about European exploration. Explain that in this unit they will study the effects these actions had on Europe.

Looking Forward

Tell students that in the next two chapters they will learn different ways in which European nations governed themselves, how these nations expanded their control, and how new ideas led to changes in these governments, as well as in how people lived and worked:
Chapter 17 *European Rule and Expansion*
Chapter 18 *The Enlightenment*

448

Unit 8
Europe: 1600-1789

The 1600s and 1700s were the Age of Monarchs, when powerful kings ruled Europe. Witness the splendor of Louis XIV's magnificent palace at Versailles, France, shown on these pages. But power and splendor would bring their own destruction. How long would subjects pay the high taxes needed to support a lavish royal court? New ideas began to spread. A government that does not serve its people must be overthrown, one writer insisted. In the late 1700s, such ideas began coming to life.

1600

448

Versailles, *by Pierre Patel, 1668*

GEOGRAPHY PROJECT

Monarchy Mapping

Geography Skill Make a World Map
Students use the skill of Acquiring and Organizing geographic information.

Geography Theme Location

Geography Standards 5, 9 interpreting earth's complexity; characteristics and distribution of populations on Earth's surface

Activity *Create a World Map Mobile*
Materials construction paper, colored pencils, coat hangers, tape, yarn or string
Management Whole Class/Small Group

Create a mobile showing six different regions during the age of absolutism and enlightenment. Make smaller pieces that hang below each region to detail the political, economic, and cultural situations in the time period.

Have students:
- make an annotated or illustrated world map mobile divided into 6 continents (excluding Antarctica) or regions.
- write clear, concise annotations or captions about economic, political, cultural climate of monarchies that are based on geography elements.
- include a legend and a compass rose on the maps.

1789

449

Understanding the Painting

Pierre Patel was a French artist who was known for his landscape paintings. This painting is an example of the many works Louis XIV commissioned to glorify his own accomplishments.

Understanding Chronology

This unit covers the events and ideas that shaped Europe during the same period the colonies were developing in America. Point out that by the end of this period the United States had become an independent nation.

For research support activities, see the *Research Handbook.*

For simulations correlated to this unit, see *Citizenship Simulations*, p. viii.

HOUGHTON MIFFLIN SOCIAL STUDIES

Bookshelf II

A Murder for Her Majesty
by Beth Hilgartner

An adventure mystery that takes place in York, a large cathedral city in England, during the Elizabethan Age.

Motivate Read aloud pp. 126 (second paragraph) to 130 to orient students to the time period of the story. Before reading, explain that Alice is walking through an English market town during the time that Queen Elizabeth I ruled England. Then have students look at the illustration of the Spanish Armada on p. 460. Ask them how victory at a great sea battle would affect the mood of a country. Tell them they will be reading about an age of monarchs, or kings and queens, who used their power to change the world.

To connect this book with the unit content, use the planning guide and student activity blackline masters beginning on p. iv of the *Bookshelf II Teacher's Resources.*

For additional books that are Easy, Average, and Challenging, see the Unit Bibliography on page T43. See bibliography updates at www.eduplace.com/ss/hmss.

A Murder for Her Majesty
Beth Hilgartner

17 Planning at a Glance
European Rule and Expansion

	Objectives	Reading Support *and* Other Resources	Diverse Learning Strategies
Lesson 1 **The French Monarchy** *pp. 452–456* 2–3 days	• Summarize Henry IV's attempts to promote religious tolerance in France. • Identify Cardinal Richelieu and explain how his policies increased the power of the French monarchy. • Compare and contrast peasant life and the life of the mobility under Louis XIV. • Defind absolute monarchy.	• **Workbook** or **Reading Support:** pp. 234–237 Review p. 55 Lesson Support/Transition p. 55 Multi-Lang. Sum. pp. 109–110 • **Other Resources:** Poster 7, Study Guide p. 73, Study Print 13	Access Strat. **(SDAIE)** TE p. 453 Access Act. **(Extra Support)** TE p. 453 Research **(GATE)** TE p. 455 Visual Learning **(Visual)** TE p. 455 Audiotapes of Multi-Language Lesson Summaries **(Auditory)**
Skill: Predicting **Consequences** *p. 457* 1 day	• Predict consequences based on evidence and experience.	• **Other Resources:** Study Guide p. 74	
Lesson 2 **The English Monarchy** *pp. 458–463* 2–3 days	• Evaluate Elizabeth I's efforts to achieve religious unity. • Describe the series of events that led to the English Civil War. • Explain the significance of the Restoration and the Glorious Revolution. • Compare and contrast constitutional monarchy and absolute monarchy.	• **Workbook** or **Reading Support:** pp. 238–241 Review p. 56 Lesson Support/Transition p. 56 Multi-Lang. Sum. pp. 111–112 • **Other Resources:** Geography Kit, Study Guide p. 75	Debate **(Auditory)** TE p. 460 Music Connection **(Auditory)** TE p. 461 Map Skills **(Visual)** TE p. 462 Visual Learning **(Visual)** TE p. 462 Audiotapes of Multi-Language Lesson Summaries **(Auditory)**
Lesson 3 **European Expansion** *pp. 464–470* 2–3 days	• Identify the major European powers competing for trade and colonies between 1500 and 1700. • Analyze the reasons behind European colonialism. • Describe the methods used by the European powers to manage their overseas territories. • Evaluate the effects of European colonialism on native peoples.	• **Workbook** or **Reading Support:** pp. 242–245 Review p. 57 Lesson Support/Transition p. 57 Multi-Lang. Sum. pp. 113–114 • **Other Resources:** Geography Kit, Study Guide p. 76	Access Act. **(SDAiE)** TE p. 465 Writing **(GATE)** TE p. 466 Map and Globe Skills **(Visual)** TE p. 467 Interviewing **(Auditory)** TE p. 469 Audiotapes of Multi-Language Lesson Summaries **(Auditory)**
Skill: Identifying **Stereotypes** *p. 471* 1 day	• Identify stereotype in photographs and pictures.	• **Other Resources:** Study Guide p. 77	Visual Learning **(Visual)** TE p. 471
Chapter Review *pp. 472–473* 1 day		Chapter 17 Test pp. 65–68 *(See facsimiles on TE p. 575.)*	Assessment Multiple-Use Masters pp. 73–80

449A

Reading Support Resources *for Every Lesson*

Reading and Review

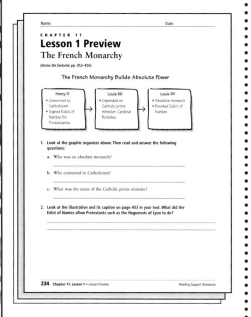

- **Chapter Overview*** p. 233
- **Lesson Previews*** using graphic organizers from the Teacher's Edition pp. 234, 238, 242
- **Reading Strategies*** pp. 235, 239, 243
- **Lesson Summaries*** pp. 236–237, 240–241, 244–245
- **Lesson Reviews** pp. 55, 56, 57

* **Workbook** includes starred items.

Multi-language Summaries

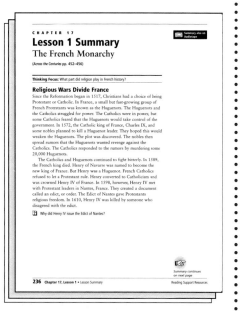

- **Lesson Summaries** in:
  - English (See Reading and Review.)
  - Spanish pp. 236–237, 240–241, 244–245
  - Chinese pp. 109–114
  - Hmong pp. 109–114
  - Khmer pp. 109–114
  - Vietnamese pp. 109–114

  Summaries available on audiotapes

Lesson Support /Transition
S D A I E

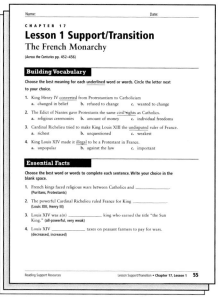

Activities for SDAIE
Specially **D**esigned **A**cademic **I**nstruction in **E**nglish

- **Lesson Support/Transition** pp. 55, 56, 57

 ## Technology Options

Internet Support
http://www.eduplace.com

Social Studies Center at Education Place
Internet support for Chapter 17:
- *Lesson at a Glance*
- *Morning at Versailles*

Software
***Student Writing Center* ®** (CD-ROM) (Macintosh® or Windows®)

School to Career

The governments of Europe underwent many changes throughout the 1600s and 1700s. Politics is a complex and ever-changing profession. Ask students to research politics and different forms of government and then create a classroom government.

Character Education

Charles I appears to have had little concern for those he ruled. Individual actions do affect others. Sharing one's time, knowledge, and resources is important. Divide students into small groups. Have each group research a cause. How could they help this cause? What benefits would they themselves receive?

CHAPTER
PREVIEW

Have the students read the chapter title and the paragraph following it. Ask students to define Reformation. *(The movement to reform the Catholic church.)* Point out that differences between Catholics and Protestants had major effects on France and England during this period. Religious differences also played a role in the settling of new colonies.

Looking Forward

Inform students that in the next three lessons they will read about the struggle between the monarchy and the people in both France and England and the establishment of colonies by a number of European nations: The French Monarchy, The English Monarchy, and European Expansion.

Tell students that Lesson 1 describes what life was like for the kings of France and how the French Protestants were treated.

Chapter 17
European Rule and Expansion

"I have loved war too much," confessed King Louis XIV of France. The period after the Reformation was a stormy time in Europe. Catholics and Protestants fought for their beliefs. Kings plotted against their enemies. Nations battled for land. Meanwhile, European explorers tested uncharted waters and claimed new lands. In time, the Europeans carried their disputes across the ocean to the New World.

During the 1500s, Spanish officials in the Americas forced Indians to work on farms and in mines. This emerald-studded cross was made of gold mined in the Americas.

1498 Portuguese explorers make Goa, a port in India, a center for trade and Catholic missionaries. This painting shows St. Francis Xavier sailing into Goa in 1542.

1400	1475	1550

450

1400

1505 Portuguese ships attack key African ports and try to control East African trade.

BACKGROUND

Following the Protestant Reformation, European governments became more and more centralized and bureaucratic. Due to religious pluralism, the political influence of the church declined. As a result, power struggles between rulers and nobility dominated political events.

France and England

During the 1600s, the power of the French kings grew steadily at the expense of the nobles, as a bureaucracy made up of members of the middle class expanded. In England the nobles retained their power in Parliament, and in the English Civil War of the 1640s, they successfully resisted Charles I's attempts to establish an absolute monarchy. In 1688, Parliament replaced James II with William and Mary, who were prepared to rule on more equal terms with Parliament.

The Holy Roman Empire

In the mid-1500s, the lands of the Holy Roman Empire included Spain, Italy, the Netherlands, the Americas, and Austria-Hungary-Bohemia. To make them more manageable, Emperor Charles V divided them between his son Philip II and his brother Ferdinand. Over the next century, the goal of emperors—to have a religiously united (Catholic) empire with centralized authority—was never realized. In Bohemia, in southeast Germany, powerful Protestant nobles resisted the emperor's attempts to

Understanding the Visuals

The gold cross (p. 450) was recovered in 1955 from the cargo of a Spanish ship that sank on the reefs near Bermuda in the 1590s.

The portrait of King Charles I and Queen Henrietta (p. 451) was painted by Sir Anthony Van Dyck, one of the most prominent Flemish painters of the 1600s. In 1632, King Charles appointed him "principalle Paynter in ordinary of their Majesties" and knighted him. He painted many portraits of European aristocracy, as well as religious and mythological scenes.

King Charles I of England, shown with Queen Henrietta, lost a power struggle with Parliament. He was beheaded for treason in 1649.

In the 1700s, the kings of France held grand parties at the palace in Versailles. Women dressed in the latest fashions, such as this silk and lace gown from about 1770.

1661–1715 King Louis XIV outlaws the Protestant faith and wages war against England and Spain. This portrait of the king was painted on the lid of a snuffbox.

1625

1700

1775

1635 The Japanese shogunate bans European trade.

1763

Understanding Chronology

The timeline notes that King Louis XIV waged a war against England and Spain between 1661 and 1715. Point out that while England and France were fighting each other in Europe, they were fighting each other in North America as well.

451

451

impose Catholicism. This conflict grew into the Thirty Years' War (1618–1648), which resulted in the defeat of the Holy Roman Empire.

Prussia

Before the Thirty Years' War ended, the Great Elector Frederick William began uniting territories across northern Germany into the state of Prussia. To build up the army needed to protect and unify Prussia, he forced the Estates—a representative assembly dominated by nobles called Junkers—to allow him to levy taxes without their consent. In exchange he gave the Junkers more power over their serf tenants, whose numbers had been reduced by the war. Junkers also found employment as officials in the state bureaucracy or as army officers. Thus, in contrast to nobles in France, they preserved their powerful role in government.

Russia

In Russia during the 1600s, developments paralleled those in Prussia. The tsars increased their power over the nobles, but in exchange gave the nobles more power over their serfs. Under Peter the Great, the army, administration, educational system, and industry were modernized along western lines. The nobles retained their influence by serving as military officers or civil servants.

INTRODUCE

Point out the lesson title and review the concept of monarchy. Have students identify the roles of monarch, nobility, and peasants in a society governed by a monarch. Have students discuss how they think an absolute monarch differs from a monarch.

Draw the Graphic Overview on the chalkboard and then direct students to read the Thinking Focus. Ask them to predict what part religion played in French history. Have students read to confirm or reject their predictions.

Key Terms

Vocabulary Strategies: T36–T37
prime minister—the chief government official appointed by a ruler
absolute monarch—a ruler who has no restrictions of any kind on his or her power
divine right—the right of a monarch to rule, based on the belief that this right comes directly from God and that the monarch is responsible only to God

1400 1475 1550 **1572** **1715** 1775

LESSON 1

The French Monarchy

THINKING FOCUS

What part did religion play in French history?

Key Terms

- prime minister
- absolute monarch
- divine right

> All three of Catherine's sons became kings of France. Catherine was the mother and unofficial adviser of Francis II, Charles IX, and Henry III.

452

Within weeks after the wedding, it became known as the "scarlet nuptials," because of the amount of blood that had been spilled. But at first it had seemed like a chance to unite French Catholics and Protestants.

In 1572, Henry, King of Navarre, arrived in Paris to marry Marguerite, the sister of the Catholic king of France, Charles IX. Henry was a leader of the French Huguenots *(HYOO guh nahts),* or French Protestants, a small but fast-growing group that some Catholics feared would eventually control the government.

One person who had much to lose if the Huguenots gained power in France was Catherine de Medici, the mother of the bride. But Catherine was also the niece of the Pope, the widow of the French king, Henry II, and the mother and adviser of King Charles IX. She pressured her son to have one of the Huguenot leaders killed so that the others would flee Paris.

King Charles submitted to the pressure and ordered a few of his nobles to commit murder. When

the plot failed, Charles's nobles spread rumors that Huguenots were seeking revenge against all Catholics.

The following morning, St. Bartholomew's Day, Catholics who

were convinced the Huguenots were about to kill them murdered hundreds of Huguenots in their beds. The Huguenots fought back, but in one month's time 20,000 Huguenots died. Henry, the new husband of the king's sister, was spared on the condition that he renounce his Protestant faith and become a Catholic.

Chapter 17

Objectives

1. Summarize Henry IV's attempts to promote religious tolerance in France.
2. Identify Cardinal Richelieu and explain how his policies increased the power of the French monarchy.
3. Compare and contrast peasant life and the life of the nobility under Louis XIV.
4. Define absolute monarchy.

Graphic Overview

Henry IV	**Louis XIII**	**Louis XIV**
• Converted to Catholicism • Signed Edict of Nantes for Protestants	• Depended on Catholic prime minister, Cardinal Richelieu	• Absolute monarch • Revoked Edict of Nantes

Religious Wars Divide France

Since the Reformation began in 1517, Christians had a choice of being Protestant or Catholic. Making the choice often involved serious consequences, even death.

After convincing his French in-laws that his conversion to Catholicism was sincere, Henry returned to Navarre in 1576. There he resumed his leadership of the Huguenots and his membership in the Protestant church.

In 1589, Charles IX's brother, King Henry III of France, was dying without a direct descendant. The dying king named his sister's husband as his successor. Henry of Navarre became King Henry IV of France.

Henry's Second Conversion

But Catholics refused to allow a Protestant to rule France. So Henry took religious instruction, converted to Catholicism, and was crowned at Chartres Cathedral.

Both Catholics and Huguenots claimed Henry had given up his faith for political gain. But Henry replied, "I wish to give peace to my subjects, and rest to my soul."

The Edict of Nantes

In 1598, Henry met with Protestant leaders in Nantes (nants), France. Together they created a

document known as an edict, or order, that gave Protestants the same civil rights as Catholics:

> **A**nd we permit those of the so-called Reformed religion to live and dwell in all the towns and districts of this our kingdom and the countries under our rule, without being annoyed, disturbed, molested.
>
> Edict of Nantes, 1598

In 1610, a religious fanatic who did not agree with the edict assassinated Henry IV. ■

▲ *The Edict of Nantes allowed Protestants such as the Huguenots of Lyon to build a church and worship openly.*

■ *Why did Henry IV issue the Edict of Nantes?*

Cardinal Richelieu Builds the Monarchy

At the time of Henry IV's death, his son, Louis XIII, was only nine years old. Louis XIII depended upon a council of advisers. By 1624, the king's chief adviser, or **prime minister,** was a cardinal named Richelieu (*RISH uh loo*).

From 1624 to 1642 he ruled France for Louis XIII.

Gaining Power for the King

Richelieu was both a cardinal of the Catholic church and a brilliant politician. His goals were to

453

European Rule and Expansion

D E V E L O P

Point out that religious wars were one of the problems faced by the French monarchs. Identify the two opposing groups: Protestants and Catholics. Have students recall differences between those two religions (refer to Chapter 13). Ask them to consider how a ruler might try to end religious conflicts.

BELIEF SYSTEMS

Critical Thinking

Be sure students understand that Henry IV became Catholic for political reasons. Have students discuss the appropriateness of Henry's decision and consider what might have happened if Henry had not declared himself a Catholic.

■ *Henry IV wrote the Edict of Nantes to secure religious freedom for Protestants.*

453

Access Strategy

Have students assemble in groups of three or four. Ask them to discuss times when they have had to do things they didn't want to do, or felt pressured to hide or change their thoughts or beliefs. Examples might be having to be home at night by a certain time, having to spend time with people you dislike, or being required by law to wear a seatbelt when riding in a car. Ask students how they felt in such situations. Then ask the class how they would feel about having one person in a

country deciding what everyone should think and do. Tell students that such a person was called an absolute monarch.

Access Activity

Discuss with the class whether their national citizenship or their religion is more important. The French Protestants during the reign of Louis XIV were given the choice of becoming Catholic or of leaving France. If the students were given the choice of changing religions or changing countries what would they do?

These three views of Richelieu were painted as a study in preparation for a sculpture of him.

■ *Why did Richelieu want to limit the nobles' power?*

■ *One of Richelieu's goals was to make the king absolute ruler of France. By taking power away from the nobles, he increased the power of the king.*

CULTURE

Social Participation

Divide the class into two groups: nobles and peasants. Have each group compile a list of their grievances about the treatment they are receiving under Louis XIV. Have representatives from each group read the lists to the class. Record the points of each group in the form of a chart on the chalkboard.

---

make the king the undisputed ruler of France and to increase the power of France in Europe.

Richelieu did not want the nobility to share the king's power. In 1626, he ordered the army to destroy the nobles' castles, except those border and coastal castles needed for defense against invasion. He felt that their castles gave the nobility too strong a power base.

Richelieu thought that the Huguenots also threatened the king's power. He personally led the French troops in taking the Huguenots' weapons. But he allowed the Huguenots to keep their freedom of worship.

Waging War on Spain

In the 1630s, Richelieu turned his attention to the Thirty Years War, involving France in this conflict. This war had started in 1618 as a religious dispute between the Catholic and Protestant nations of Europe. By the 1630s, it had become a political battle to obtain land.

Richelieu commanded the French Catholic forces to fight the Spanish Catholic forces. Since Spain and its territories in the Netherlands nearly surrounded France, Richelieu was worried about the possibility of Spain invading France. He was also anxious to increase French landholdings. Although France acquired more land through these battles, Richelieu had to triple taxes between 1635 and 1638 to finance the war. ■

Louis XIV Reigns Supreme

When Louis XIII died at age 42 in 1643, his son, Louis XIV, was only 4 years old. For 18 years, he was advised by Cardinal Mazarin, who had succeeded Richelieu as prime minister. When Cardinal Mazarin died in 1661, Louis—then 22 years old—announced that he would rule without a prime minister, although he would have advisers.

Louis was an **absolute monarch,** an all-powerful king. For the next 54 years, he devoted himself to his task eight hours a day (and often longer), controlling everything from court etiquette to troop movements. He described the position of monarch in a letter to his son:

A Huguenot cartoon shows King Louis XIV, the "Sun King," as the "Sun Avenger" out to bring death to all Protestants.

I n a well-run state, all eyes are fixed upon the monarch alone. . . . Nothing is undertaken, nothing is expected, nothing is done except through him alone.

Louis XIV stated the theory that he ruled by **divine right,** that his power came from God and he was responsible only to God. Louis XIV's great power earned him the title "the Sun King."

Nobles and Huguenots

The nobility of France could have challenged Louis's power. But in 1661, Louis began to build a new palace near Paris. Find out about Louis's life at Versailles (*vuhr SY*) by studying A Closer Look on the next page.

454

Chapter 17

454

Study Skills

Have students research the Frondes—the civil wars that took place during Louis XIV's youth. Have them present their findings to the class, and ask them to suggest a connection between the Frondes and the building of Versailles. (*Louis could watch the nobles more closely at Versailles and anticipate rebellions.*)

Speaking and Listening

Select two teams of students for debate. The proposition for debate is whether a king rules by divine right and is accountable only to God. Have the teams argue for and against this claim. When each team has presented its views, allow students in the audience to ask the teams questions. Then submit the proposition to a vote.

Cultural Context

The 1600s are considered the classical age of French literature. Two of France's most famous playwrights, Racine and Molière, wrote during the reign of Louis XIV. Racine wrote tragedies, modeled after those of Greek writers. Molière wrote comedies in which he satirized the social and religious hypocrisy of his time.

Morning at Versailles

All France revolved around the palace at Versailles, and life at Versailles revolved around King Louis XIV. Every morning a crowd of nobles gathered anxiously outside the king's bedroom. Inside, the ceremonial "Rising of the King" was beginning.

If the king woke up in a bad mood, the news spread throughout the palace in minutes.

The best time to ask the king a favor was early in the morning.

At about 7:45, royal fire starters and the royal watch winder entered the bedroom. They were followed by the royal wig maker, who brought the king's early-morning wig from the royal wig room.

At 8:00, when the clock rang, the valet approached the king, who pretended to still be asleep and officially woke him. Then the two top doctors entered with Louis's childhood nursemaid, who gave him a kiss.

At 8:15, the most privileged nobles and priests entered to watch Louis get dressed. To be in this group was the highest honor at Versailles. Whoever was the king's favorite noble at the time got to hand the king his shirt.

This chest held the king's clothes for the day

455

Note: You may wish to use this Closer Look in connection with a discussion of Louis XIV's attitude regarding the role of the monarch (p. 454).

More About Louis XIV's Court
The king's rising was not the only odd feature of life at court. Court etiquette was very rigid. For example, one couldn't knock at a door in the palace, but had to scratch lightly on it with the left little fingernail. The king was once so angry at a woman who had taken the wrong seat at dinner, it took two people to calm him down afterwards. On the other hand, if he took a liking to someone he might make them a Duke or a Duchess. That was why everyone at the palace was so interested in every little thing the king did. One of his courtiers was so impressed with just seeing Louis XIV that he wrote that he had seen the king putting on his pants in the morning, "which he did very cleverly and gracefully."

Research

The photograph above shows only a small part of the grand display at Louis XIV's center of power. Ask students to read more about Versailles at the library, paying special attention to photographs of the palace and its furnishings. Students should write a one- or two-page paper on life at Versailles.

Visual Learning

Have students look carefully at the photograph of the palace at Versailles. Point out to them how opulent and disciplined the architecture and topiary are. Everything about Versailles, inside and out, was designed to be as magnificent and awe-inspiring as possible, to show off the power and authority of the king.

> ➤ *This print, made in 1789, the year of the French Revolution, calls for everyone, (from left to right) the peasants, the clergy, and the nobility, to share in the great burden of taxes.*

Louis invited many nobles to come live with him in his palace at Versailles. There he could keep the nobles under watch while entertaining them with frequent banquets and festivals.

The other challenge to Louis's power might have come from the Huguenots. For in 1685, he abolished the Edict of Nantes. Since Louis was convinced he ruled by God's authority, he believed that his first duty as ruler was to uphold the Catholic faith. Therefore, he made it illegal to be Protestant in France. Nearly 200,000 Huguenots moved to other countries.

■ *In what ways did Louis XIV govern as an absolute monarch?*

Peasants

Louis wanted to make France the greatest military power in

Europe. Thus, he increased taxes to finance wars against England and Spain.

Peasant farmers had the most difficulty paying taxes, since they also paid rents to their landlords for use of the land they farmed. The peasants lived in fear of bad harvests that would limit their produce and leave little money for taxes. Many of the peasants' noble landlords lived at Versailles with the king and were out of touch with the peasants.

By 1715, at the end of Louis XIV's 72-year reign, wars had killed many Frenchmen and the government was bankrupt. On his deathbed, Louis XIV confessed, "I have loved war too much." ■

■ *Louis XIV ruled without a prime minister. He made Protestantism illegal in France. He built Versailles in order to closely watch the French nobles.*

CLOSE

Draw the Graphic Overview on the chalkboard. Ask students to answer the Thinking Focus by mapping the causes and effects of the signing of the Edict of Nantes by Henry IV and its revocation by Louis XIV.

REVIEW

1. **FOCUS** What part did religion play in French history?
2. **CONNECT** In what ways were Louis XIV's idea of divine right and the beliefs of the Incas about their ruler alike?
3. **POLITICAL SYSTEMS** How did Cardinal Richelieu increase the power of the monarch?
4. **HISTORY** Compare the ways in which Louis XIII

and Louis XIV ruled France.

5. **CRITICAL THINKING** Was building the palace at Versailles an appropriate use for the tax money that Louis XIV collected from the people? Why?
6. **WRITING ACTIVITY** Look at the picture of Louis XIV on this page. Write a paragraph describing your impressions of the personality of this absolute monarch.

Homework Options

Have students write a sentence using each key term. Each sentence should correctly incorporate the meaning of the term.

Study Guide: p. 73

Answers to Review Questions

1. Henry IV had to convert to Catholicism to become king. Once king, he wrote the Edict of Nantes, making Protestantism legal. Richelieu took away the weapons of the Protestants. Louis XIV made Protestantism illegal in France.
2. Both the French and the Inca rulers were absolute monarchs. The French ruled by divine right, and the Inca priest-king was thought of as a god.
3. Richelieu ordered the army to destroy all

the nobles' castles that weren't needed for defense, took away Huguenots' weapons, and fought to increase French landholdings.

4. Louis XIII had a strong prime minister, Cardinal Richelieu. Louis XIV did not want to share his power with anyone.
5. Answers will vary. Students might say that taxes shouldn't have gone to support a lavish lifestyle while peasants struggled to earn enough to eat.

UNDERSTANDING CRITICAL THINKING

Predicting Consequences

Here's Why

When you read a mystery novel, you constantly think about what will happen next. The same thing can happen when you read history. When you read about Henry of Navarre as you did in Lesson 1, you wonder what will happen next. The French Catholics resist Henry, and you wonder who will win.

Knowing the result of one struggle can help you predict what might happen in a similar struggle later. Could you have predicted what Henry would do to become king of France?

Here's How

To predict consequences accurately, follow these steps:

1. **Review the facts stated.** In Lesson 1, you read that Henry of Navarre first converted to Catholicism to save his life after the St. Bartholomew's Day Massacre. Then he became a Huguenot again. You also learned that only a Catholic could rule France and that Henry was next in line to become king.

2. **Add other knowledge and experience.** This information may come from your own experience or from something you have read. As you know, Catholics and Protestants behaved violently toward each other at this time. The engraving below of Henry's assassination several years later helps illustrate the depth of religious feeling. Notice the assassin climbing up on the wheel to attack Henry.

3. **Make a prediction.** Use what you know and your additional knowledge to decide what you think will happen. Henry had previously converted to Catholicism for political reasons, so you can predict that Henry might do the same thing again.

4. **Check for accuracy.** You can check your prediction by further reading.

Predicting Consequences

1. Review the facts stated.
2. Add other knowledge and experience.
3. Make a prediction.
4. Check for accuracy.

Try It

Read the first sentence in the Huguenots and Nobles section of Lesson 1. Follow the first three steps in Here's How to predict a possible consequence after Louis XIV revoked the Edict of Nantes. After you finish reading the section, write a statement analyzing the accuracy of your prediction.

Apply It

Write a sentence predicting how your classmates might respond to each of these situations. Use the four steps to make each prediction.

1. You and a friend enter the same essay contest and you win first place.
2. The administration decides to cancel the end-of-the-year school party because too many students have not turned in their missing assignments.

457

European Rule and Expansion

UNDERSTANDING CRITICAL THINKING

This skills feature uses the events in Lesson 1 to teach students to predict consequences.

HISTORY
Critical Thinking

Begin the lesson by asking the students to make some predictions about an upcoming event at school or in the community. Have them explain the reasons for their predictions. Point out that predictions are most likely to be accurate if they are based on evidence or facts.

Answers to Try It

1. Louis XIV revoked the Edict of Nantes.
2. Catholics and Huguenots had lived in peace under the Edict of Nantes. Without the Edict, the Catholics and Protestants didn't get along.
3. Answers may vary. Sample answers: The Huguenots could convert to Catholicism; they could rebel against the King and lose; they could rebel and establish a Protestant country; or they could leave the country. Statements of accuracy will vary, but should relate to the answers given here or by students.

Answers to Apply It

Students' predictions will vary for both situations. Answers should be based on facts or evidence and should reflect the use of the steps used on the skills page.

Objective

Predict consequences based on evidence and experience. (Critical Thinking 2)

458

| 1400 | 1475 | 1550 | | 1700 | 1775 |
| | | **1558** | | **1689** | |

L E S S O N   2

The English Monarchy

THINKING FOCUS

What events led to Parliament's becoming a major power in the English government?

Key Terms

- Parliament
- commonwealth
- constitutional monarchy

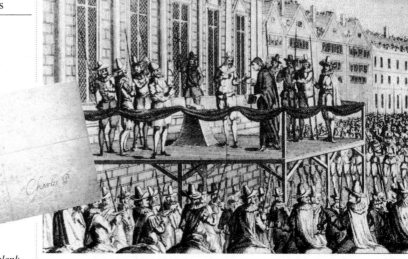

▲ *By signing this blank piece of paper, Charles's son gave Parliament the freedom to set its own terms for sparing the king's life. But they beheaded the king instead.*

458

"At last he laid down his head, stretched out his hands as the sign, and the executioner let drop the hatchet." This event in 1649, described in a book of memoirs by Sir Philip Warwick, had until then been thought impossible. The king of England, Charles I, had been tried and executed for betraying his own country.

The members of **Parliament,** an elected group of representatives, did not have any constitutional authority to sentence the king to death. However, backed by the soldiers nicknamed "Roundheads," they did have the military power to do so. The story of how the English Parliament became so powerful begins at least 100 years before the execution of the king.

The Reign of Elizabeth I

The 45-year reign of Elizabeth, which began in 1558 when she was 25, is known as the Elizabethan Age. One of the subjects in Queen' Elizabeth's kingdom was William Shakespeare. He wrote poetry and plays in an atmosphere that was open to literary creativity.

Chapter 17

Objectives

1. Evaluate Elizabeth I's efforts to achieve religious unity.
2. Describe the series of events that led to the English Civil War.
3. Explain the significance of the Restoration and the Glorious Revolution.
4. Compare and contrast constitutional monarcy and absolute monarchy.

Graphic Overview

| Monarchy with active Parliament | → | Monarchy without active Parliament | → | Commonwealth and protectorate | → | Constitutional monarchy |

Elizabeth, the lords and ladies of her court, and the common people of London all responded enthusiastically to the very lively though sometimes violent works of Shakespeare. But he was only one of many who produced and dedicated works of literature to the queen.

The Church of England

When Elizabeth I became queen of England in 1558, she took over a kingdom divided by religion. Her half-sister Mary, an older daughter of Henry VIII, had ruled England before her. Mary, who was a Roman Catholic, opposed the way her father had broken away from the pope's Catholic church and started a separate English church. Mary tried to reimpose Catholicism on England. She put non-Catholics on trial for heresy and had some of them executed. Other Protestants fled, nicknaming the queen "Bloody Mary."

Elizabeth was the daughter of Henry VIII's second wife and had been raised a Protestant. When Elizabeth became queen, she made the Church of England the official state religion. It followed a middle ground between Catholicism and Calvinism. However, Elizabeth persecuted Catholics and tortured and executed a number of Catholic priests.

The Spanish Armada

In the 1580s Elizabeth decided to support the Dutch Protestants in their war against Spain. To put a stop to that, the Catholic ruler of Spain, Phillip II, decided to invade England with an armada, or armed fleet, of 130 warships.

The big Spanish ships, however, were slow. The English ships were

faster and easier to maneuver. Also, English guns shot more rapidly.

The armada entered the English Channel between England and France on July 30, 1588. In the first few days, the English captured and destroyed only a few Spanish ships. Then on August 8, before dawn, the English set eight of their own unmanned ships on fire. A favorable wind carried the fire ships toward the Spanish fleet. Astonished, the Spanish cut anchor and sailed out to sea.

As the Spanish fled, the English pursued them and badly damaged the Spanish fleet. A violent storm finished off the armada.

▲ *Elizabeth I is painted in her coronation robe with crown, orb, and scepter. The orb is a globe of gold topped by a cross, signifying the rule of Jesus over the world.*

459

European Rule and Expansion

Before students read the lesson, have them look at the pictures on pp. 462 and 463 of the nine English monarchs who ruled while Louis XIV was king in France. Mention that in England, as in France, struggles over religion and over the possession of political power dominated the 1600s, but that in England these conflicts were resolved very differently.

Access Strategy

Have students study the picture on p. 458 to identify various elements. What is the center of the crowd's attention? Where is this event taking place? Who are the onlookers and how are they dressed? Point out that this event, the execution of King Charles I of England, took place in 1649. Describe the structure of the lesson to students: it begins with an important and dramatic event in 1649 and then goes back in time about 100 years (to 1558) to explain the chain of events that led to this dramatic event. The lesson then moves forward in time to the year 1688. Refer students to the timeline at the top of p. 458.

Access Activity

Have students compare the portraits of Louis XIV (p. 456) and Elizabeth I (this page). How are they similar? *(Both hold the scepter in the right hand, are wearing flowing garments, and look powerful.)* Ask students to read to find out ways in which these two rulers were quite different.

HISTORY
Visual Learning

Have students point out the opposing fleets in the picture of the battle scene involving the armada. Ask students whether they think the painter was English or Spanish. Why do they think so? *(Since the picture shows the Spanish under attack by the English, it was probably painted by an English artist.)*

■ *Elizabeth cooperated with Parliament and gave England a long period of stable government. During her reign, the English navy beat the Spanish Armada in a battle that made England the major sea power of the world.*

▲ *The Spanish used a crescent formation to fight the English at sea. But the English were victorious and made medals like this to remember their victory.*

■ *What were some of Elizabeth's accomplishments as the queen of England?*

Only half of the original 130 ships made it home. Spain, which had been a sea power since the voyages of Columbus in the 1490s, ruled the seas no longer.

The Power of Parliament

Before Elizabeth could use any funds from the English treasury to fight the Spanish Armada, she needed approval from Parliament.

Even before the Magna Carta was accepted in 1215, monarchs summoned nobles to advise them in making laws. By the 1500s, this group, Parliament, had become a part of the English government.

Parliament was made up of two houses. Members of the House of Lords were titled members of the nobility who by birthright received an invitation to attend Parliament. The House of Commons was made up of landowners, merchants, and lawyers elected to serve in Parliament whenever the king called it into session. Parliament could disapprove taxes or laws that the monarch wanted. In addition, Parliament could suggest new laws. ■

The English Civil War

Elizabeth I died in 1603 without an heir. The crown passed to her Protestant cousin James, who had ruled Scotland since 1583 as an absolute monarch. James wrote, "The state of monarchy is the supremest thing on earth."

Monarchs Oppose Parliament

James and Parliament quarreled when he wanted to raise taxes. They again argued when he wanted to arrange a marriage between his son, Charles, and a Catholic princess of France.

After Charles became king of England in 1625, he simply dismissed Parliament whenever it opposed him. He also persecuted the Puritans, who were another Protestant religious group that wanted simpler forms of worship than the Church of England had.

In 1628, Charles wanted to increase taxes for a war with Scotland to force them to belong to the Church of England. Before the Parliament would grant its consent to another tax increase, its members insisted that Charles approve the Petition of Right. This petition made it illegal for the king to imprison citizens, such as the Puritans, without cause. Desperate for

460

Study Skills

Have students find out more about the lives and careers of one of the nine leaders shown on pp. 462 and 463. Direct students to present their findings to the class in an oral report.

Debate

Have students debate this proposition: A king cannot be tried by his own subjects. One side will defend Charles I, the other will defend Parliament under Cromwell's leadership. Help students prepare for the debate by asking them who decides who has power within government. After the debate, put the proposition to a vote by the class.

Political Context

The treason of which Charles I was accused and for which he was beheaded was regarded as an agreement he had made with Scotland in order to overthrow Parliamentary forces. In December 1647, he offered to accept Presbyterianism in Scotland and make England Presbyterian for three years if the Scots would support his return to power. In August 1648, the Civil War ended with the final defeat of Charles's Scottish supporters.

money, Charles agreed to the Petition of Right. But the following year, he dismissed Parliament again when it refused to approve more war funds. For the next 11 years, Charles ruled alone and did not call Parliament.

In 1640, Charles needed money to fight the Scots, who were invading England. He was forced to accept Parliament's demands to get the money. By now, Puritan candidates had gained power in Parliament. They introduced laws to make the king call Parliament into session every three years.

In 1642, Charles made a final effort to assert his power. He ordered the arrest of five powerful members of the House of Commons. To defend itself, Parliament took control of the army. Charles fled north with his own army, and Parliament took over the central government. The clergy and most of the nobles, who benefited from Charles's religious policies and taxes, supported the king. Puritans and many merchants supported Parliament. Thus began the English Civil War.

Cromwell Leads Parliament

The war lasted seven years until Oliver Cromwell, a devout Puritan and a brilliant military leader, led Parliament's forces to victory. At the end of the war in 1649, Parliament put Charles on trial. They accused him of treason, charging "that by a tyrannical power he had endeavoured to overthrow the rights and liberties of this people." Charles claimed that, because he was king, no court had authority over him. Nevertheless, Parliament found him guilty and ordered him beheaded.

For the next four years, Cromwell and a Parliament dominated by Puritans ran the government. The leaders called the nation a **commonwealth,** because the government was a group working for the common good of all people.

However, in 1653, Cromwell was angered by the failure of Parliament to adopt proposed reforms. He responded by dismissing Parliament and abolishing the commonwealth. He then formed a new government, called the Protectorate, gave himself the title Lord Protector, and continued to rule England.

Cromwell ruled much like a military dictator. He imposed his Puritan values on England, limiting freedom of the press and enforcing strict moral standards. He

A memorial locket picturing Charles I contains a piece of linen stained with his blood.

prohibited gambling, horse racing, dancing on the village greens, fancy dress, and going to the theater. Because of such harsh policies, the public hated him as much as they ever hated Charles. However, Cromwell still controlled the military.

This is a portrait of Charles I in three poses. Studies of this type were usually done in preparation for a sculpture of the model.

461

European Rule and Expansion

461

Economic Context

Although Charles I could not raise taxes during the 11 years he ruled without Parliament, he did find ways of managing his expenses. He forced people to house soldiers in their homes, and he collected in peacetime taxes that were supposed to be collected only in wartime. One of the most famous of his devices was to collect ship money—money used to outfit warships—not only from coastal, port towns, but also from inland towns.

Music Connection

Henry Purcell (c. 1659–1695) was an English composer who wrote coronation music, dance music, and operas during the time of the English civil wars. Among his works is also a funeral march for Queen Mary. Find recordings of his music at the library and play selections for the class. Point out that only members of the royal court and other wealthy people would have heard his music.

Critical Thinking

Have students consider this question: Why were the nobles in England able to maintain their power while those in France lost theirs? (*English monarchs needed Parliament's cooperation to run government, and nobles in England were an important part of Parliament. In France, the monarch reigned with absolute authority.*)

Critical Thinking

Help students to see that the English people must have become very dissatisfied with the Protectorate to be willing to return to a monarchy. Have them compile a list of events that brought the English people to that point.

■ *Like his father, James I, Charles I thought of the English crown as an absolute monarchy in which it was not necessary for him to consult with Parliament. Parliament expected to be consulted and given the right to reject some of the king's proposals.*

Map Skills

On a map of Europe, have students determine the distance from England to the Netherlands, where William and Mary came from, and from England to France, where James II fled.

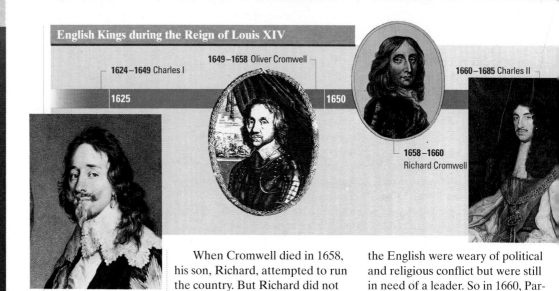

English Kings during the Reign of Louis XIV

1624–1649 Charles I

1649–1658 Oliver Cromwell

1658–1660 Richard Cromwell

1660–1685 Charles II

1625

1650

■ *Why did Charles I and Parliament quarrel?*

Across Time & Space

Today, about 75 percent of the French people are members of the Roman Catholic Church, and just 2 percent are Protestant. In England at present, 85 percent of the people are Protestant, and only 13 percent are Catholic.

When Cromwell died in 1658, his son, Richard, attempted to run the country. But Richard did not have the leadership ability to manage the new government, and in 1659, Parliament took sole control of the government. By that time, the English were weary of political and religious conflict but were still in need of a leader. So in 1660, Parliament invited Charles, the son of the executed king, to return from exile in France to become King Charles II. ■

The Glorious Revolution

Historians call this return to monarchy the Restoration. It was not an absolute monarchy, however. When Charles II became king, the authority to govern was divided more equally between the monarch and Parliament.

A Period of Uncertainty

After what happened to his father, Charles II knew better than to try to force Parliament to do as he willed. He ruled England peaceably for 25 years. During his reign, many people rejected the Puritan ways that had dominated the country under Cromwell's rule. Parliament restored the Church of England as the state church and passed laws restricting the religious practices of Puritans, preventing them from assembling in groups of five or more persons.

After Charles II died in 1685, he was succeeded by his brother, King James II. However, at the age of 25, James had converted to Catholicism. Many in England feared that he would try to make England Catholic again. He did appoint Catholics to public office, against Parliament's wishes. He also stationed soldiers near London to scare Parliament.

To many, it looked as if James was preparing to rule as an absolute monarch. However, the people were willing to put up with James, because they expected that eventually he would be succeeded by his Protestant daughter, Mary. Mary had been raised a Protestant by James's first wife. Then, in June 1688, James's second wife, a Catholic, had a son. Because males succeeded to the throne before females, the new heir to the throne would be Catholic.

Parliament was unwilling to govern in partnership with another

Visual Learning

Refer students to the row of portraits at the top of pp. 462–463. Have them create a timeline showing when each monarch ruled. Above the timeline they should indicate which monarch was reigning. Below it they should list a significant event that occurred during each monarch's reign.

Bulletin Board

Have students locate books containing large portraits of the monarchs shown on pp. 462–463 and make photocopies to bring to class. On a separate sheet of paper, in large letters, they should write out an important fact about the monarch's reign. Have them attach the "fact sheet" to the portrait with tape and post them on a bulletin board. Then order the portraits chronologically.

Reader's Theater

Have students reenact events from the English civil war up to the Glorious Revolution. Instruct students to develop a script from the information in their textbook. Have them assign parts for the monarchs involved as well as members of Parliament, nobles, clergy, merchants, and the common people. Encourage students to create props and costumes for their parts.

1685–1688
James II

1689–1702 William; 1689–1694 Mary

1702–1714 Anne

1700

1714–1727 George I

1725

Have students point out differences between an absolute monarchy and a constitutional monarchy. Ask students how Louis XIV might have responded if the French people had required him to accept the Bill of Rights.

Catholic king.

A group of lords invited Mary, daughter of James II, whom they had originally hoped would become their monarch, to become the new queen. They also asked Mary's husband, the Protestant William of Orange, to be their king. William was the ruler of the Netherlands.

William arrived on English shores with an army of 14,000 soldiers and was welcomed by the English people. King James II, powerless, fled to France without putting up a fight. This became known as the Glorious Revolution because power changed hands without blood being shed.

A Constitutional Monarchy

Although William and Mary became joint rulers of England in 1689, they did so only after agreeing to accept Parliament's Bill of

Rights. This document limited the power of the English monarch in a number of ways.

First, the monarch could appoint to public office only persons who were acceptable to a majority of Parliament. Second, the monarch could not keep an army in peacetime, nor could he suspend any laws without the consent of Parliament. Third, Parliament was required to hold regular meetings so that the king could never govern without Parliament. Finally, a Catholic could no longer become king of England.

With the passage of this Bill of Rights, Parliament finally had direct political power over the government of England, making England a **constitutional monarchy.** A constitutional monarchy is one in which the monarch's power is limited by law. ■

▲ *King Louis XIV ruled France for 72 years. During that time England had nine leaders.*

■ *What was the Glorious Revolution, and why was it so named?*

■ *The Glorious Revolution was the nonviolent exchange of power in England between James II and William of Orange.*

Draw the Graphic Overview on the chalkboard and have students review what events happened in England to cause two dramatic changes in the form of government in about 40 years time.

463

REVIEW

1. **FOCUS** What events led to Parliament's becoming a major power in English government?
2. **CONNECT** How did the power of the English monarchs in the 1600s and early 1700s compare with the power of the French monarchs during the same period?
3. **HISTORY** Why did Parliament want William of Orange, rather than James II, to be king?
4. **CRITICAL THINKING** In what ways is a constitutional monarchy different from an absolute monarchy?
5. **WRITING ACTIVITY** Study the portrait of the young Queen Elizabeth I on page 459. Imagine you have just written a book of poems dedicated to the queen. Write a flattering description of the queen that could serve as an introduction to the book.

463

European Rule and Expansion

Answers to Review Questions

1. Since Parliament could disapprove taxes, Elizabeth I worked with the body. Charles I refused to co-operate and ordered the arrest of Parliament members. This resulted in the English Civil War and Charles's execution. Later, when James II produced a Catholic heir, Parliament replaced him with rulers willing to accept Parliament's power—William and Mary.
2. The French monarchs had absolute power.

The English kings were to share their power with Parliament.
3. James II fathered a Catholic heir. Unwilling to face another Catholic king, Parliament invited William of Orange, a Protestant, to rule England.
4. In an absolute monarchy, the power of the monarch is unlimited. In a constitutional monarchy, the monarch's power is limited by law.

Homework Options

Have students do research to learn more about the ships of the Spanish Armada.

Study Guide: p. 75

464

1400   1775
1763

L E S S O N   3

European Expansion

Shielding their eyes from the blazing African sun, the men from the Portuguese ship approached the chief of the tribe. After an exchange of greetings and some gifts, the ship's captain got down to business: Did the chief have any slaves to sell? Yes, there were slaves.

With a signal from the chief, guards brought the slaves forward, chained to each other at the wrists. The captain inspected them carefully to find the healthy ones, for only healthy ones would survive the trip back to Lisbon. Then he pointed to the ones he wanted, and the barter began. When the dealing was finished, weapons and trinkets were exchanged for human beings, and families were separated forever.

On board ship, the slaves had to lie on planks that were stacked between the decks. Each was in a space only two feet by five feet. They were allowed to walk around the deck once each day for exercise. They ate twice a day if there was enough food. Those who rebelled on the way were killed by being

tossed overboard. One out of six died anyway from disease, spoiled food, or starvation.

Slave trade was only one part of a trading empire that linked the small country of Portugal to colonies in Africa, South America, India, and China. In the 1400s, Portugal's Prince Henry, known as the Navigator because of his interest in sea exploration, led all other European monarchs in setting up an overseas empire.

464

Chapter 17

Graphic Overview

The information in this graphic overview compares colonizing countries in the lesson.

	Colony Location	Colony Resources
England	North America	crops, furs
France	North America	furs
Netherlands	North America	furs
Portugal	South America	crops, metals
Spain	N. and S. America	crops, metals

Portuguese Slave Trade, 1500-1800

Map legend:
- Portugal and its colonies
- Trade route

Locations on map: EUROPE, PORTUGAL, *Mediterranean Sea*, AZORES (Port.), NORTH ATLANTIC OCEAN, MADEIRA IS. (Port.), Mazagan, CAPE VERDE ISLANDS (Port.), AFRICA, FERNANDO PÓO (Port.), Equator, SOUTH AMERICA, slaves, guns, sugar, ANGOLA, BRAZIL, SOUTH ATLANTIC OCEAN

Scale: 0 500 1000 mi. / 0 500 100 km / Orthographic Projection

◀ *The exchange of goods and slaves among Africa, South America, and Europe formed a triangle of trade.*

▼ *The Portuguese brought back cinnamon, peppercorn, and cloves from the Indies.*

Growth of the Portuguese Empire

The Portuguese wanted to establish a sea route to the Indies. Most Europeans at that time used the term *East Indies* to refer to India and the islands southeast of it. The Portuguese were tired of relying on Italian merchants who, since the Crusades, had dominated trade in spices and other products from the East Indies.

The Portuguese also wanted to spread Christianity. By the mid-1200s, Muslims had been expelled from Portugal. The Christian government was eager to spread the Catholic faith to new lands.

Exploring the Seas

On their early voyages in the mid-1400s, Portuguese explorers cautiously hugged the west coast of Africa as a way of directing their course. By 1488, explorers had rounded the southern cape, or tip, of Africa and headed up the east coast. The Portuguese exploration voyages reached India in 1498.

In 1500, a Portuguese ship captain supposedly drifted off course and landed on the east coast of South America in an area known today as Brazil. However, he may have been secretly exploring lands south of where the Spanish had been. The Portuguese laid claim to a large area of South America for their king. On the map above, estimate how close Africa and South America are to each other.

465

European Rule and Expansion

Point out to students that this lesson covers the overseas expansion of five European countries: Portugal, Spain, England, France, and the Netherlands. Have students recall early explorations by any of these countries in Chapter 14. Point out that the developments discussed in this lesson were built on these explorations.

465

Access Strategy

Ask students what it would be like if they had to leave their present home and go to a faraway place that they had never seen and about which they had heard almost nothing. What would they take along? Who would they want to go with them? How would they decide where to settle, and how would they build new homes? How would they deal with people from new cultures that they had never encountered before? Help students to understand the many unknown and dangerous elements in the lives of the overseas explorers. Note that the traders and especially the colonizers who followed knew more about where they were headed but still faced the unknown. They had to develop a new life as they adapted to their new surroundings. Explain that in this lesson they will be following the journeys of European peoples to North and South America, Africa, India, the East Indies, and China.

Access Activity

On a world map or globe, point out western Europe. Trace a line from Portugal to the East Indies and tell (or have students compute) how far the Portugese traveled by sea. Then have students locate themselves on the map or globe, and find a place as distant from them as the East Indies are from Portugal.

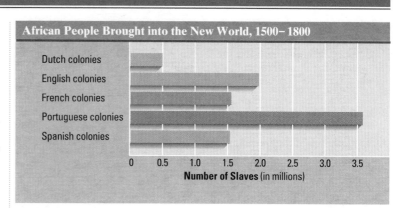

African People Brought into the New World, 1500–1800

Dutch colonies
English colonies
French colonies
Portuguese colonies
Spanish colonies

0   0.5   1.0   1.5   2.0   2.5   3.0   3.5
Number of Slaves (in millions)

➤ *All countries having colonies in the New World imported slaves to the Americas. The largest percentage of the slaves were brought to Brazil by the Portuguese. Which country was second in bringing slaves to the New World?*

➤ *England.*

How Do We Know?

HISTORY *We know about the Portuguese involvement in the spice trade through* The Book of Duarte Barbosa, *written by a government official in India between 1501 and 1517. He noted where each spice grew and the price it sold for in different markets.*

■ *Why did the Portuguese seek new trade routes to the Indies?*

SOCIAL SYSTEMS
Collaborative Learning

Divide up the class into pairs. Have each student write three questions about the graph at the top of the page. Then have students exchange questions with their partners and privately write out answers. When both students are done, have them return their answers to the question writer, who should review them for correctness and go over any incorrect answer with his or her partner.

■ *They sought new trade routes to control trade from the East Indies, increase Portugal's power, and spread the Catholic faith.*

Setting Up Trade

Portuguese merchants following the newly mapped routes began to establish a far-reaching trade network. The Portuguese government supported merchant expeditions with money, ships, and sailors, because the government wanted to set up a monopoly over trade. If the Portuguese held a monopoly, the government could make more money. The government got a share of the profits made by merchants, so when merchants made more money, the government also made more money.

The Portuguese set up their first trading posts along the west coast of Africa. Portuguese merchants stationed agents at the posts to trade with the local people. The merchants traded items such as guns, knives, and cloth. In exchange they received gold and ivory from the Africans.

Portuguese colonists began to settle Brazil in the 1530s. They set up large sugar cane plantations and forced the native people to work on them. Many native people died from diseases brought by the Europeans, such as smallpox and measles. As the native population dwindled, Portuguese traders brought slaves from Africa to Brazil. These slaves were then forced to work on the plantations in place of the natives. ■

Expansion of the Spanish Empire

From 1492 to 1504, Columbus made four voyages to and from the Americas. During each voyage, he explored and claimed islands, including those now known as the Bahamas, Cuba, and Haiti. He called these islands the West Indies and the inhabitants Indians.

The Encomienda System

News of Columbus's discoveries attracted many Spanish explorers to these new lands. By 1550, Spain controlled Mexico, Central America, part of South America, most islands in the Caribbean, and part of what is now the southwestern United States.

The Spanish government ruled with the **encomienda** *(ehn koh mee EHN dah)* **system,** named after a Spanish word meaning "to entrust." Under this system, a Spanish colonist received from his government the grant of a group of Indians who had to work for him. In exchange,

---

Map and Globe Skills

Have students locate the West Indies, especially the Bahamas, Cuba, and Haiti, on a map. Have them find out what the major exports of those countries are today, and present their findings to the class.

Language Arts Connection

Read an excerpt from *The Book of Duarte Barbosa,* or another account of trade in India or the East Indies. After reading, have students write a paragraph in which they describe, on the basis of what they heard, the background of the author and the audience for whom the author was writing.

Writing

Have students imagine they are either Native Americans observing the activities of the Spanish or Africans observing the activities of the Portuguese. Ask them to write a letter to the king of Spain or Portugal protesting the treatment of their people. Challenge students to find a solution to the problems to which the king will agree. In their letters, they should try to convince the king of another way of trading.

he was entrusted to house and feed the Indians and instruct them in the Catholic faith. For their part, the Indians were expected to mine and farm the land and to pay tribute.

However, many Indians died from the hard labor, as well as from the diseases carried by the Spaniards. In fact, so many Indians died that the Spaniards, like the Portuguese, eventually imported slaves from Africa to replace Indian laborers.

Mercantilism

The Spanish and Portuguese governments both followed an economic policy called **mercantilism** *(MUR kuhn tee lihz uhm).* According to this policy, a country set up colonies for the purpose of obtaining raw materials and developing new markets that would trade only with the ruling country. The colonies provided the ruling country with the raw materials they produced. Likewise, the colonies bought manufactured goods from the country that ruled them.

By 1600, vast amounts of silver had been shipped back to Spain. When the supply of precious metals declined, the Spaniards concentrated on agriculture as a source of income.

Slavery and Race

Spanish slave traders bought sugar, tobacco, and cotton and shipped them to Spain. There they traded these agricultural products for manufactured goods, such as cloth and guns. Then the traders took these goods to Africa and exchanged them for slaves to bring to the Americas. This "Triangle Trade" lasted from 1520 to 1800. European traders shipped as many

as 12 million slaves from Africa to the mines and plantations of the New World.

As you have already read, many different forms of slavery have existed throughout the world in many different cultures. The Triangle Trade grew from a desire for cheap labor in the Americas. More and more enslaved Africans were brought to the Americas, and slavery itself again changed.

As Europeans colonized and traded in slaves, they came to divide the peoples of the world into those who were "white" and those who were "colored." Soon they came to think that dark skin color meant "inferior." In time, racism, the dividing of people according to skin color, came to dominate many parts of the Americas. Great Britain led the campaign to abolish slavery in the early 1800s. The U.S. abolished slavery in 1865. Brazil was the last country in the Americas to abolish slavery, in 1888. ■

The Spanish used slaves to mine gold during the 1500s in South America. Slave laborers on plantations produced cash crops such as sugar, tobacco, and cotton (below).

■ *Describe the encomienda system and the policy of mercantilism.*

European Rule and Expansion

Critical Thinking

Have students explain why the encomienda system, which was supposed to ensure that the Indians were taken care of, contributed to their depopulation and to the need to import slaves. *(The Indians were overworked and caught European diseases for which they had no immunity.)*

■ *In the encomienda system, Spanish colonists were granted control of groups of Indians who had to work for them. Under mercantilism, countries set up colonies in order to get raw materials and to control the trade of the colonies.*

Religious Connection

The harsh treatment of the Indians was protested by Spanish missionaries. The missionaries were sent to convert the Indians to Christianity, but when the Indians virtually became slaves of the Spanish, attempts at conversion appeared hypocritical. The missionaries' protests were heard by the Spanish government, but the great distance between the Spanish government and the colonial encomiendas made enforcement of protective measures difficult.

Visual Learning

Have students identify the roles of the people shown in the illustration on this page. Ask them how this picture supports the idea that Europeans exploited the new lands and people to increase their own wealth.

Map and Globe Skills

On a large map that shows North and South America, Africa, and Europe, have students use yarn and thumbtacks to show the origins and destinations of slaves taken from Africa to the New World. Refer them to the graph at the top of p. 466, the text, and outside resources if necessary.

CULTURE

Visual Learning

Have students study the visual on this page. Ask them to speculate on why the painting was made and by whom. (*Students may answer that the painting was done by Indians to flatter Europeans as being influential, or that it was done by Europeans to flatter themselves.*)

➤ *A painted cotton wall hanging from India, done in the 1600s, shows the Portuguese in India. The Portuguese can be identified by their European dress.*

▲ *This coat of arms of the East India Company includes the Latin motto "God shows the way."*

468

Dutch, English, and French Competition

Because they were busy with civil and national wars, the Dutch, English, and French lagged behind Portugal and Spain in developing overseas trade and establishing colonies. However, beginning in about 1600, the Dutch began taking control of Portuguese colonies along the African coast, in the East Indies, and in China. They also began setting up new colonies in North America.

Trade in the East

Not only did the Dutch take over many of Portugal's colonies, they also took over Portugal's trade routes. The Dutch, English, and French founded large trading companies. Private investors joined together to finance these companies, such as the East India Company. They could invest more money than the government or an individual alone could afford.

Furthermore, the government granted **charters,** official documents that gave companies the right to do things that normally only a government would do. They could maintain an army and navy, declare war, and govern new territories. The Portuguese, more limited in power, were no match for these well-equipped rivals.

In 1662, the English won trading rights to Bombay, an important colony on the west coast of India. In 1690, they founded another major colony, Calcutta, on the east coast of India. Meanwhile, in 1674, the French set up a post near Madras on the Indian south coast. England and France then battled each other throughout the next century for control of trade in

Critical Thinking

Have students do research into Colbert, the French minister of finance during the reign of Louis XIV. Have them explain why the policy of mercantilism, which Colbert supported, would have been attractive to Louis XIV. (*It would provide government with greater profits and control.*)

Research

Have students do research to find the emblems for the English and French trading companies. Ask them to tell what the various parts of the emblem represent, and what purpose the emblem served. Have them cite or show examples of the emblems (logos) that are used by modern-day businesses or corporations.

India. In 1763, British troops decisively defeated the French forces.

Colonies in the West

Spain's hold over its colonies in the Americas proved strong. Therefore, the other European powers began to establish colonies away from the Spanish on the Atlantic coast of North America.

England was the first to establish a North American colony. In 1607, the English made a permanent settlement at Jamestown. The London Company, granted a charter by King James I, provided the money for the ship and crew. Some people came to seek wealth, while others, such as the Puritans, came to escape religious persecution. By 1763, the British colonies had nearly two million inhabitants. Under mercantilism, people in the colonies exchanged raw materials, such as tobacco and furs, for manufactured goods from Britain, such as cooking utensils, tools, and cloth. Colonists were not allowed to manufacture any product that Britain could sell to them.

The Dutch also settled in North America. In 1624, they founded New Netherland, which covered parts of today's states of New York, New Jersey, Connecticut, and Delaware.

Many colonists in New Netherland made a living by trapping animals and selling the pelts to merchants. The furs were shipped to the Netherlands to be made into hats and coats for the Dutch. However, the Netherlands and England competed for the fur trade. In 1664, the Dutch lost New Netherland to England,

▼ *The English boasted the sun never set on their Union Jack flag. A jack is a small flag flown at the front of a ship on a jack, or a staff.*

UNDERSTANDING COLONIALISM

Colonialism did not begin with the Portuguese in Africa in the 1400s. The Greeks established colonies along the coast of Italy in 750 B.C.

Why Colonies Existed

Colonialism is a policy in which one country forcibly takes control of the people and land of another country, known as its colony. The ruling country often uses the colony as a source of wealth.

A colony is a separate country; however, a colony is not a separate nation, because it does not govern itself.

During the 1800s, Europeans explored and claimed land in Africa's interior. Parts of Africa were ruled by Italy, Belgium, France, Britain, Germany, Spain, and Portugal. By 1914, the only independent countries left in Africa were Liberia and Ethiopia.

Colonialism Runs Its Course

In the early 1900s, many African colonies began to demand self-government. In 1975, Portugal, the last European country with holdings in Africa, gave up its colonies. The last British colony, Hong Kong, returned to Chinese control in 1997.

In the Western Hemisphere, most colonies won their independence in the 1700s and early 1800s. In many cases the struggle for independent status involved a colony in a war with the ruling country. Freeing its colony meant a loss of economic benefits to the ruling country.

469

European Rule and Expansion

GEOGRAPHY

Map and Globe Skills

Have students study the map on this page. Ask students why the English would be unhappy with the Dutch colony of New Amsterdam. (*The Dutch colony divided the English colonies.*)

■ *They were unable to break Spain's hold on her colonies, so they set up colonies of their own in North America, which had not yet been colonized.*

CLOSE

Draw the outline for the Graphic Overview on page 464 on the board. Have different students help fill in the second and third columns with the correct answers.

➤ *The colonies increased the territory of the monarchs and produced new resources for Europe.*

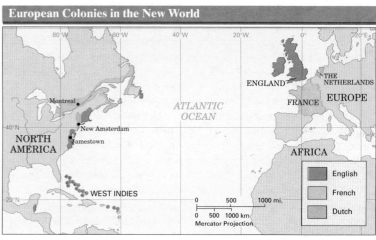

European Colonies in the New World

ENGLAND · THE NETHERLANDS · FRANCE · EUROPE · ATLANTIC OCEAN · Montreal · New Amsterdam · Jamestown · NORTH AMERICA · AFRICA · WEST INDIES

0   500   1000 mi.
0 500 1000 km
Mercator Projection

English
French
Dutch

■ *Why did the Dutch, English, and French settle in North America?*

when English warships entered the harbor of New Amsterdam and demanded the city's surrender.

In 1608, England's other rival, France, founded its first North American settlement of Quebec in present-day Canada. Later, Louis XIV did not allow Huguenots to settle there, because he wanted colonists to be loyal to the king and to the Catholic faith. Although sparsely populated, French territory included all the land along the Mississippi River Valley down to the Gulf of Mexico.

Conflict in the West

Native Americans still controlled the vast lands of North America. However, conflict between the English and French spilled into their territory. In 1756 the two world powers fought in the Americas as well as Europe and Asia. The French and Indian Wars, or the Seven Years' War, were fought in what are now New York and Pennsylvania, and the Canadian provinces of Ontario, Québec, New Brunswick, and Nova Scotia.

The English finally defeated the French in 1763. As a result, the American colonies felt less dependent militarily on the English, who had been protecting them from the French and the Indians. Now, the American colonists began to question the rules of mercantilism which limited their rights to trade and manufacture. ■

REVIEW

1. **FOCUS** Why did European nations establish colonies throughout the world?
2. **CONNECT** Compare the way the French and English monarchs felt about religious minorities in their colonies.
3. **GEOGRAPHY** What valuable resources did the Spanish export from South, Central, and North America?
4. **ECONOMICS** Why did the Dutch, English, and French set up trading companies?

5. **CRITICAL THINKING** Was the encomienda system a good way to manage Spain's colonies in the New World? Why?
6. **WRITING ACTIVITY** Suppose that you have been asked to establish a colony for your country. What type of site would you choose? How would you manage the colony? What would you do if natives already lived on the site? Write a proposal discussing these three issues.

Homework Options

Have students choose one of the spices that Europeans traded for, such as cloves, cinnamon, nutmeg, ginger, mace, or turmeric. Ask them to bring in a sample of the spice and to tell (or find out) how it is used.

Study Guide: p. 76

Answers to Review Questions

1. They established overseas colonies to increase their wealth through trade, to increase their power by controlling overseas territories, and often to spread their faith.
2. The English monarchs allowed religious minorities to inhabit the colonies. The French monarch would not permit religious minorities in the colonies.
3. They exported gold and silver and cash crops such as sugar, tobacco, and cotton.

4. They set up trading companies to finance their colonies in the New World because their governments did not have enough money to finance them on their own.
5. Answers will vary. Students may point out that the system was probably efficient but that it exploited the laborers.

UNDERSTANDING RELATIONSHIPS

Identifying Stereotypes

Here's Why

A stereotype is an over-simplified idea about a group of people. For example, "Scandinavians are blond" is a stereotype. It is oversimplified. Not all Scandinavians are blond.

Because they are often based on partial truths, stereotypes can be hard to recognize. You may have some oversimplified and only partly true ideas about people from a certain country or of a certain race, religion, age, or sex. Some stereotypes, such as that of blond Scandinavians, may be harmless; others are not. During the 1500s, Europeans made slaves of the peoples of Africa and the Americas. Because these Europeans accepted the stereotype of Africans and Indians as less than human, they did not treat them as fellow humans.

Relating to people as individuals rather than as members of groups will help you to overcome stereotypes. Many of the events described in this chapter would not have been possible if people of the 1500s and 1600s had been able to recognize and overcome the stereotypes they held about people of certain religions or people of certain races.

Here's How

The picture below shows an American family from the 1960s packing its car for a vacation. What does the picture tell you about the stereotypes people had about boys and girls at that time? Notice that the girl holds a doll; the boy, a baseball bat. Like her mother, the girl wears a skirt and dressy shoes. The boy wears clothing more suitable for play. Some stereotypes that this picture suggests are that boys play active games and girls wear pretty dresses and play quietly with dolls.

Try It

What stereotypes about sex roles did people have during other periods in history?

Look through this textbook for pictures of men or women. Think about what the men and the women are doing in the pictures. Notice that many pictures include no women at all.

What stereotypes about sex roles do the pictures represent? Write a paragraph about one or two of the most interesting examples. Compare your observations with those of your classmates.

Apply It

Much of the humor in television situation comedies is based on stereotypes. Make a list of stereotypes that you see in a show you watch. Discuss your list with others in your class.

UNDERSTANDING RELATIONSHIPS

This skills feature uses both 17th- and 20th-century examples to teach students to recognize stereotypes.

NATIONAL IDENTITY
Visual Learning

Have students use the photograph on this page to find stereotypes of the "typical" American family. *(Two children, one [collie] dog, father taller than mother, brother older than sister, family is well-dressed, neighborhood that has lawns and flower beds.)* Then explain that the photograph does not accurately portray most American families.

SOCIAL SYSTEMS
Visual Learning

Stereotypes may have changed since this photograph was taken in the 1960s. Ask students which ones have changed. *(Women and girls don't have to wear skirts; boys and girls share more playthings and games; many single-parent families.)* Then ask students to find magazine pictures that show present-day families and bring them to class to discuss the stereotypes represented.

471

Answers to Try It

Answers will vary.

Answers to Apply It

Answers will vary.

Objective

Identify stereotypes in photographs and pictures. (Visual Learning 1)

Answers to Reviewing Key Terms
A. Sample answers:
1. An **absolute monarch** has complete freedom of rule and answers to no one.
2. Louis XIV ruled by believing in **divine right.**
3. The **Parliament** made the laws in England.
4. England was called a **commonwealth.**
5. An **encomienda system** might not be popular with the natives.
6. Under a **constitutional monarchy,** power is restricted by a constitution and laws.
B. Sample answers:
1. a ruler appoints a **prime minister.**
2. Under **mercantilism,** the ruling country benefited more than its colonies.
3. To protect their own interests, governments gave **charters** to rich companies that would represent them.

Answers to Exploring Concepts
A. Sample answers:
French
  Main Religions: Catholic. Protestant (Huguenot).
  Countries Fought: England, Spain.
  Lands Colonized: North America, India, Africa.
English
  Main Religions: Catholic. Protestant (Church of England), Protestant (Calvinism), Protestant (Puritanism).
  Countries Fought: France, Spain, Scotland, Netherlands.
  Lands Colonized: North America, India, Africa.
Spanish
  Main Religions: Catholic,
  Countries Fought: England, Netherlands.
  Lands Colonized: Central America, North America, South America, Caribbean, Africa.
Portuguese
  Main Religions: Catholic.
  Countries Fought: (not in chapter).
  Lands Colonized: South America, India, China, Africa.
Dutch
  Main Religions: Protestant.
  Countries Fought: England, Spain.
  Lands Colonized: North

Chapter Review

Reviewing Key Terms

absolute monarch (p. 454)
charter (p. 468)
commonwealth (p. 461)
constitutional monarchy (p. 463)
divine right (p. 454)
encomienda system (p. 467)
mercantilism (p. 467)
Parliament (p. 458)
prime minister (p. 453)

A. Rewrite the sentences below using key terms in place of the underlined words.
1. A <u>ruler who believes in doing whatever he or she wants</u> has complete freedom of rule and answers to no one.
2. Louis XIV ruled by believing in <u>God-granted power</u>.
3. The <u>members of an elected group of representatives</u> made the laws in England.
4. England was called a <u>government where people governed for their common good</u>.
5. A <u>system that allows foreigners to take over and enslave locals</u> must have been hated by the local people.
6. Under a <u>government where a king or queen rules a country</u>, power is restricted by a constitution and laws.

B. The statements below are false. Rewrite them to make them true.
1. A ruler owes allegiance first to the prime minister who appoints him or her.
2. Colonies receive more benefits than the ruling country under mercantilism.
3. The only reason that governments granted charters to private investors was out of a desire to help businesses grow.

Exploring Concepts

A. Copy and complete the following chart on your own paper.

People	Main Religions	Countries Fought	Lands Colonized
French	Catholic Protestant (Huguenot)	England Spain	N. America India Africa
English			
Spanish			
Portuguese			
Dutch			

B. Answer each question with information from the chapter.
1. Henry IV of France took an important step for religious freedom. What was it?
2. Richelieu wanted to increase the king's power. How did he do this?
3. Louis XIV ruled by divine right, with no prime minister. What was the form of government?
4. Was Elizabeth considered a successful Queen of England? Explain.
5. What did Charles I do when Parliament would not approve his requests for money?
6. What was it called when William arrived to take over England and James II fled? Why?
7. Why did Portugal encourage exploration?
8. Were the Spaniards in the Americas fair or unfair rulers? Explain.
9. Why did the English, French, and Dutch establish colonies away from Spain's in North America?

America, China, Caribbean, Africa.
B. Sample answers:
1. Henry IV passed the edict of Nantes, giving Protestants the same civil rights as Catholics.
2. Richelieu ordered the army to destroy castles, except those needed for defense; took weapons from Huguenots to remove threat to the king's power.
3. This made France an absolute monarchy.
4. Yes; she unified the country, defeated the Spanish Armada, and cooperated with Parliament.
5. Charles I stopped calling meetings of Parliament for 11 years.
6. Glorious Revolution. No blood was shed when power changed hands.
7. Portugal wanted a sea route to the East Indies for spices, to increase its power, and to spread Catholicism.
8. Unfair; they forced Indians to work in mines and on plantations.
9. They couldn't compete with Spain's strong hold over its colonies.

Reviewing Skills

1. Read the first paragraph in the text section on page 458 of Lesson 2 that begins with The Reign of Elizabeth I. Predict what actions Elizabeth will take to solve the religious problems in England. Explain the stated facts and other knowledge that you used to make your prediction.
2. Under the encomienda system, the Spanish government gave Spanish officials grants of land with power over all the Indians who lived on it. What might you predict could happen when a person has this much power over other people?
3. How did the Spanish government view Indians? How might that have made it easier for the Spanish to adopt a policy of giving away Indians with land grants?
4. When there is a struggle for power in a war or over succession to a throne, people often view those on the other side in a stereotyped way. How might this make it easier for one side to fight the other?
5. Read pages 452 and 453. How did the religious values of the leaders of France affect the citizens of France? How did these values make it hard for the people to understand each other?
6. When reading about the actions of a character in a story, what skill would you use to guess what will happen?

Using Critical Thinking

1. When kings were absolute monarchs they caused much bloodshed and turmoil. Do you think it is possible for an absolute monarch to be a wise, fair, honest king or queen? Would an absolute monarchy work in today's world? Explain your opinion.
2. When a Spanish official received land and the Indians living on that land, he was expected to provide something in return: to care for them and teach them Catholicism. Evaluate the strengths and weaknesses of this system. Do you think people would want to live under this system today?
3. Choosing a religion in the 16th century was a dangerous business. If your choice was not the accepted religion, you might face death. Think about why some people chose to practice unpopular religions they knew might endanger their lives. Were they stereotyped because of their religious choices? Are all people the same who practice a certain religion?

Preparing for Citizenship

1. **WRITING ACTIVITY** Imagine you live in England during the Glorious Revolution. Today you witnessed the arrival of William of Orange accompanied by 14,000 soldiers. A group of lords invited him to rule peacefully with his wife, Mary, the Protestant daughter of James II. Describe the scene and express your thoughts about this revolution.
2. **COLLABORATIVE LEARNING** Your class will stage two debates set in England in 1642. Both debates will present the Puritans and merchants who support Parliament against the nobles and clergy who support King Charles. But the two debates will have different outcomes: the first debate will stage the actual outcome—the English Civil War; and the second debate will stage an imaginary outcome—peace. Divide the class into four sections. The first two sections' debate will lead to the actual outcome. The other two sections will "rewrite" history and show a peaceful outcome. In each section, have some students research the information (or create new ideas for the peaceful outcome), some moderate the debate, and some do the actual debating. You might create simple costumes and a painted mural background for your debates.

473

European Rule and Expansion

Answers to Reviewing Skills
1. She might set up a compromise religion. Facts: Her kingdom was divided by religion; her father started new English church; her sister returned nation to Catholicism.
2. Indians might be overworked and mistreated.
3. Indians were not viewed as human beings with the same rights as Europeans. The Spanish considered Indians as property instead of people.
4. If the other side is seen as less than human, it is easier to mistreat or kill them.
5. Because of the religious values of the leaders, many people died. Since the leaders of France were Catholic, the Huguenots were feared and persecuted. Huguenots and Catholics mistrusted each other.
6. Predicting an event.

Answers to Using Critical Thinking
1. No matter how wise, one person couldn't fairly represent and rule a large group. Nobody can eliminate self interest. People need to feel represented.
2. Strength: Indians were supposed to be cared for by Europeans. Weakness: Spaniards did not know what was best for Indians and were more concerned with what was desirable for themselves. Today, people probably would be more vocal about personal freedom.
3. Consider the importance of religion to people in the 16th century. Discuss pros and cons of standing up for religion and the unfairness of stereotyping someone because of religion.

473

Answers to Preparing for Citizenship
1. **WRITING ACTIVITY** Encourage students to use sensory details to describe the scene. You might brainstorm first as a class, perhaps creating a cluster diagram with visual objects, then filling in details for each visual.
2. **COLLABORATIVE LEARNING** In addition to researching, moderating, and participating in the actual debates, students may want to create stage props and paint some sort of background that is appropriate to the time period. Other students may be interested in researching and creating simple costumes for the debating students to wear. If possible, and after sufficient rehearsals, invite parents or other classes to view the debates.

Planning at a Glance
The Enlightenment

	Objectives	Reading Support *and* Other Resources	Diverse Learning Strategies

Lesson 1
A New Order of Ideals
pp. 476–479 2–3 days
	• Trace the origins of Enlightenment.
	• Discuss the philosophers and their reforms.
	• Explain Locke's concepts of government.
		• **Workbook** or **Reading Support:** pp. 247–250
		    Review p. 58
		    Lesson Support/Transition p. 58
		    Multi-Lang. Sum. pp. 115–116
		• **Other Resources:** Poster 7, Study Guide 78, Study Print 14
			Access Strat. **(Extra Support)** TE p. 477
			Speaking and Listening **(Auditory)** TE p. 478
			Homework Options **(SDAIE)** TE p. 479
			
			Audiotapes of Multi-Language Lesson Summaries **(Auditory)**

Lesson 2
Ideas in Action
pp. 480–485 2–3 days
 	
Literature
"To the Assembly for Protection"
pp. 486–489
	• Explain how the philosophers affected European governments.
	• Show how the Declaration of Independence incorporated many Enlightenment ideals.
	• Discuss the causes and effects of the French Revolution.
		• **Workbook** or **Reading Support:** pp. 251–254
		    Review p. 59
		    Lesson Support/Transition p. 59
		    Multi-Lang. Sum. pp. 117–118
		• **Other Resources:** Geography Kit, Study Guide 79
			Access Strat. **(Extra Support)** TE p. 481
			Access Act. **(SDAIE)** TE p. 481
			Visual Learning **(Visual)** TE pp. 483, 484
			
			Audiotapes of Multi-Language Lesson Summaries **(Auditory)**

Lesson 3
Economic Changes
pp. 490–493 2–3 days
	• Explain the agricultural and industrial revolutions.
	• Discuss how the agricultural and industrial revolutions affected peoples' lives.
		• **Workbook** or **Reading Support:** pp. 255–258
		    Review p. 60
		    Lesson Support/Transition p. 60
		    Multi-Lang. Sum. pp. 119–120
		• **Other Resources:** Study Guide 80
			Access Strat. **(Extra Support)** TE p. 491
			Access Act. **(SDAIE)** TE p. 491
			Making a Mural **(Visual)** TE p. 493
			
			Audiotapes of Multi-Language Lesson Summaries **(Auditory)**

Making Decisions: Industrial Growth *pp. 494–495*	• Define the goals and values of industrialization.	• **Other Resources:** Poster 8	Activity **(GATE)** TE p. 494 Visual Learning **(Visual)** TE p. 495
Skill: Presenting Primary Sources *p. 496* 1 day	• Explain how to incorporate primary sources in an oral report.	• **Other Resources:** Study Guide 81	Collaborative Act. **(Auditory)** TE p. 496

Lesson 4
After the American Revolution
pp. 497–500 2–3 days
	• Discuss the ideals embodied in the Constitution of the United States.	• **Workbook** or **Reading Support:** pp. 259–262
		    Review p. 61
		    Lesson Support/Transition p. 61
		    Multi-Lang. Sum. pp. 121–122
		• **Other Resources:** Study Guide 82
			Access Act. **(Extra Support)** TE p. 498
			Access Strat. **(SDAIE)** TE p. 498
			Visual Learning **(Visual)** TE p. 499
			
			Audiotapes of Multi-Language Lesson Summaries **(Auditory)**

Chapter Review *pp. 501–502* 1 day		Chapter 18 Test pp. 69–72 *(See facsimiles on TE p. 576.)*	Assessment Multiple-Use Masters pp. 73–80

Reading Support Resources *for Every Lesson*

Reading and Review

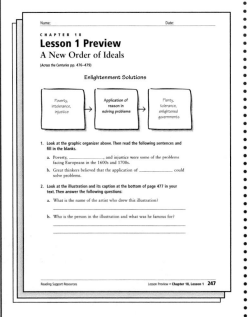

Multi-language Summaries

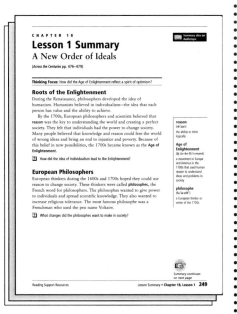

Lesson Support /Transition
S D A I E

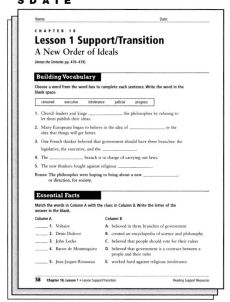

Activities for SDAIE
Specially **D**esigned **A**cademic **I**nstruction in **E**nglish

- **Chapter Overview*** p. 246
- **Lesson Previews*** using graphic organizers from the Teacher's Edition pp. 247, 251, 255, 259
- **Reading Strategies*** pp. 248, 252, 256, 260
- **Lesson Summaries*** pp. 249–250, 253–254, 257–258, 261–262
- **Lesson Reviews** pp. 58, 59, 60, 61

  * **Workbook** includes starred items.

- **Lesson Summaries** in:
  - English (See Reading and Review.)
  - Spanish pp. 249–250, 253–254, 257–258, 261–262
  - Chinese pp. 115–122
  - Hmong pp. 115–122
  - Khmer pp. 115–122
  - Vietnamese pp. 115–122

   **Summaries** available on audiotapes

- **Lesson Support/Transition** pp. 58, 59, 60, 61

 # Technology Options

Internet Support
http://www.eduplace.com

Social Studies Center at Education Place

Internet support for Chapter 18:
- *Lesson at a Glance*
- *A Parisian Market Woman*

Software
***Student Writing Center*®** (CD-ROM) (Macintosh® or Windows®)

School to Career

The agricultural and industrial revolutions each had a dramatic impact upon the economies of many nations. Examining historic economic data is one thing economists do. Have students research the field of economics. Then have them write a job description for a specific economics position, such as teaching.

Character Education

The French and American Revolutions occurred in part because people decided it was time for a change. This doesn't mean they didn't love their country. Have students study the primary source documents in the Time/Space Databank, and have them select an ideal, such as **equality,** and write an essay on how this ideal relates to how they see patriotism in the United States.

CHAPTER
PREVIEW

Have students read the chapter title and the narrative that follows it. Then instruct them to read the captions and look at the images. Point out that Voltaire, Rousseau, and Jefferson represent what was happening in Europe and North America during the Age of Enlightenment—people were demanding power over their own lives rather than allowing themselves to be ruled by monarchs.

Looking Back

Ask students what happened in England in the 1600s that shows people had already begun to limit the power of the monarchy. *(A constitutional monarchy was instituted. William and Mary had to agree to limits on their power before they were permitted to take the throne.)*

Looking Forward

Tell the students they will learn about how the ideas of the Enlightenment led to changes in government, agriculture, and industry in Lessons 1–4: A New Order of Ideals, Ideas in Action, Economic Changes, and After the American Revolution.

Lesson 1 introduces leading thinkers of the Enlightenment.

474

Chapter 18
The Enlightenment

To enlighten *means "to shine a light on." During the 18th century, the time known as the Enlightenment, great thinkers did just that. They shed new light on old ideas by using their powers of reasoning and helped bring about great change. Scientists made great discoveries. Inventors created marvelous new machines. Revolutionaries even overthrew kings and built new governments with the inspiration of Enlightenment ideas.*

Jean Jacques Rousseau (right) comes to Paris and meets Enlightenment thinkers in the 1740s. Rousseau's ideas help spark the French Revolution.

1717 At the age of 23, the writer Voltaire is jailed for making fun of the French government. Voltaire goes on to become a great Enlightenment thinker.

| 1700 | 1720 | 1740 |

474

1700

1733 Georgia becomes Britain's 13th colony along North America's Atlantic coast.

BACKGROUND

The 1700s were a time of growing optimism in Europe. Thinkers of this time put aside pessimistic views about original sin and human depravity. They asserted that human beings were fundamentally good and that, through improving the human environment, they would become better and happier people. These thinkers suggested numerous reforms in religion, law, and economics.

Religion

Because members of various religions persecuted each other as well as nonbelievers, many intellectuals of the 1700s advocated a religious outlook called *deism*. Deists held that all human beings were naturally religious, and that by a rational study of nature—rather than through divinely inspired scriptures—people could learn all they needed to know about God and human morality. Deists saw God as the rational architect of the universe who had created it to run according to certain laws that could be discovered by science.

Deists identified a core of common religious beliefs: that there is a supreme being, that this being deserves to be worshiped, that a life of virtue is the best form of worship, that one must repent for one's sins, and that in the next world one is rewarded or punished according to one's behavior in this life. By focusing on these similarities, deists hoped to promote tolerance among religious

Understanding the Visuals

The painting on p. 474 is an allegory honoring Rousseau that shows icons relating to the Enlightenment and the French Revolution. The eye in the center symbolizes seeing new ideas; the section on the right shows a soldier of the revolution, a heaven-lit monument to the revolution and, behind it, a pale image of a guillotine; the two female figures on the left represent Goodness and Good Faith.

The painting of Marie Antoinette (p. 475) shows some of the symbols of decadence and excess that brought down the monarchy, such as her elaborate hairstyle and expensive silk and lace dress, and the elaborate furnishings.

1776 Thomas Jefferson, influenced by Enlightenment ideas, writes America's Declaration of Independence. Also an inventor, he later creates this polygraph, which copies a letter as the original is written.

1789 A revolution begins in France. In 1793, revolutionaries execute King Louis XVI and later his queen, Marie Antoinette (above).

1760   1780   1800

1750s Slaves are Africa's major export, replacing gold.

1784 The British government takes control of India from the British East India Company.

1800

Understanding Chronology

Ask the students to read the timeline. Point out that in only 13 years' time—1776–1789 —two revolutions occurred that would affect future generations worldwide.

475

groups. Many early Americans, including Jefferson, Franklin, and Washington, held deist beliefs and helped to form a government that allowed for a wide range of religious beliefs and practices.

Law

Reforms of legal practices were encouraged by Cesare Beccaria, an Italian philosophe. In his influential treatise *On Crimes and Punishments,* published in 1764, Beccaria argued against torture, the bribing of judges, and the use of cruel or degrading punishments. He suggested many reforms that are taken for granted today: scaling penalties according to the offense, abolishing torture and capital punishment, and establishing uniform judicial procedures.

Economics

In reaction to the policies of mercantilists, who neglected agriculture to pursue wealth in trade and industry, French philosophe Francois Quesnay developed a new theory of economics. In his *Tableau Economique,* published in 1758, Quesnay argued that land was the true source of wealth and national prosperity. Like Adam Smith after him, Quesnay argued that economic regulations by the government were unnecessary and that individuals, in pursuing profit, would follow the natural, divinely appointed order to everyone's benefit.

INTRODUCE

Point out the lesson title and explain that this "new order" in Europe followed the reign of Louis XIV in France and the Glorious Revolution in England. Clarify the term *ideals. (Patterns, models, or values to follow.)* Have students read the Thinking Focus and discuss the term *optimism.* Have them read the lesson to see what these new ideals were and how they reflected greater optimism.

Key Terms

Vocabulary Strategies: T36–T37
reason—the capacity for logical thought
Age of Enlightenment—a movement in Europe and America in the 1700s that analyzed ideas and institutions using human reason
philosophe —a European thinker or writer of the 1700s from either the aristocracy or the middle class
contract—an agreement between two or more parties
natural rights—rights believed by many to be guaranteed to all people by nature, including life, liberty, and the right to own property

476

1700   1800

L E S S O N   1

A New Order of Ideals

> **THINKING**
> **F O C U S**
>
> *How did the Age of Enlightenment reflect a spirit of optimism?*

Key Terms

- reason
- Age of Enlightenment
- philosophe
- contract
- natural right

➤ *Enlightenment thinkers were fascinated by the universe. Scientists had shown that the movements of the planets and stars were orderly and predictable. This painting from 1765 by Joseph Wright shows people studying a model of this orderly universe.*

The 1700s must have been an exciting time in which to live. Everywhere in Europe, philosophers and scientists tried to solve old problems with a new approach. These thinkers believed that **reason,** or logical thought, was the key to understanding the world and creating a perfect society. The belief in the power of reason to change the world was first seen in science. During this Age of Reason, one scientific discovery seemed to follow on the heels of another. Whole new fields of science were born. In France, Antoine Lavoisier's *(lah vwah ZYAY)* experiments led

to the invention of chemical equations and, eventually, to the study of modern chemistry. Charles Coulomb *(KOO lahm)* invented several instruments for measuring electrical and magnetic forces. Pierre Laplace developed a theory about the origin of the solar system.

Some people found the era threatening, as many long-held beliefs were disproved. But others looked to the future with confidence. They hoped that, just as reason helped people understand the physical world, so it could help them understand their social and political world. Once people understood this human world, they

476

Chapter 18

Objectives

1. Trace the origins of Enlightenment thought back to earlier Renaissance humanism and 17th-century scientific advances.
2. Discuss the philosophes and the reforms they wanted to make.
3. Explain the new concepts of government developed by Locke, Montesquieu, and Rousseau.

Graphic Overview

| Poverty, intolerance, injustice | → | **Application of reason in solving problems** | → | Plenty, tolerance, enlightened governments |

could then improve it. Governments could be changed to better serve the people. Poverty, intolerance, and injustice could be ended.

In this new age, anything seemed possible. This spirit of optimism spoke for the century, which was named the **Age of Enlightenment.**

Roots of the Enlightenment

This new way of thinking about the world had its roots in the Renaissance. Beginning in that period, a number of European traditions came under examination. The philosophy of humanism paved the way. Renaissance humanists believed in the dignity and potential of the individual. They argued that people could improve their world by understanding it and changing it.

Many Renaissance thinkers began to reexamine critically a number of long-held beliefs. The growing European exploration and understanding of the world helped call into question the belief that the ancient civilizations had been superior to modern Europe in all ways. Humanists began to realize that they had surpassed the Greeks and Romans in exploration, trade, and science. They began to believe in progress. Perhaps advances in learning and science would improve life. ■

▲ *During the Scientific Revolution, scientists learned a great deal about the physical world. Using a telescope like the one shown, Isaac Newton studied the universe and helped change people's views of the world during the Enlightenment.*

■ *How did the idea of individualism lead to the Enlightenment?*

▼ *Voltaire was one of the most versatile of the Enlightenment figures. Here the artist Hubert has drawn the many faces of Voltaire, from writer and philosopher to spokesman for democracy.*

European Philosophers

European thinkers during the 1600s and 1700s hoped that they could use reason to achieve progress in other areas besides science. Made up of members of the aristocracy and middle class, these thinkers called themselves **philosophes** *(fee luh ZAWFS)*, from the French word for philosophers.

Both the Catholic and Protestant churches and many monarchies of Europe distrusted the philosophes. In order to solve problems, the philosophes made proposals that challenged traditions and promised to give more power to individuals. Neither the churches nor the monarchies of Europe were willing to give up their power. They censored and even imprisoned the philosophes to discourage these thinkers from trying to spread their new ideas. The most famous philosophe was François Marie

Arouet *(a REH)*, known by his writing name, Voltaire *(vohl TAIR).*

Voltaire

Although he was born into a middle-class family, Voltaire knew firsthand about the injustices of his day. While in his twenties, he had been arrested and jailed for being the supposed author of verses making fun of the government. In his thirties, he was beaten and

DEVELOP

Draw the Graphic Overview on the chalkboard and explain the relationship between the three parts. Have students discuss the term *reason*, identify its various meanings, and clarify its meaning in this lesson. Then discuss the term *Enlightenment.* What is the opposite of enlightenment? *(Darkness, ignorance.)* What image does this term suggest? *(Turning on a light, making something clear.)*

HISTORY
Critical Thinking

Referring to the picture of Newton's telescope, point out that Newton's discovery of natural laws led the philosophes to hope to discover natural laws governing society. Ask students to identify other basic similarities between Newton and the philosophes. *(Belief that the world makes sense and that we can use our reasoning to understand it.)*

■ *Individualism stresses the dignity and potential of the individual. Greater confidence in the individual's ability to think and judge for himself or herself promoted a desire for freedom from ignorance, superstition, and tyrannical authority.*

Access Strategy

Have students study the picture on p. 476. Ask them to describe the expressions on the faces of the people watching the experiment. *(Fascination.)* Ask them how Europeans at the time might have felt about the new discoveries they were making about their world. Point out that at the time many people were threatened by the new knowledge that was becoming available. Ask students to think of inventions or new knowledge that has changed the way we live in our own century.

(Internet, television, cars, jets, computers, electric light.) Are there some people who resist these changes, who prefer to live as they did beforehand? *(Yes.)* Have students discuss how change often involves both positive and negative effects. Have them read the lesson to see the sorts of social and political changes that some people wanted in the 1700s, why they wanted those changes, and how some people resisted those changes.

Access Activity

Tell students that this lesson will cover a period that built upon the achievements of the Renaissance, the Reformation, and the Scientific Revolution. Ask students to recall (from Chapters 12 and 13) the major figures, events, accomplishments, and ideas of those periods. Write their responses on the chalkboard in a cluster diagram.

Critical Thinking

Ask students what institutions were most threatened by the changes suggested by the philosophes. *(Church and state.)* Why were they so threatened by these changes? *(They would lose power and wealth because the beliefs on which these institutions were based were being challenged.)* How did the ideas of Locke, Montesquieu, and Rousseau potentially threaten governments? *(These three philosophes did not automatically accept a government just because tradition was on the monarchy's side. Instead they believed that government was based on a contract that could be dissolved if the ruler failed to protect the rights of his or her subjects.)*

■ *The philosophes wanted to give power to individuals, rather than governments, spread scientific knowledge, and increase religious tolerance.*

478

▲ *During the 18th century, philosophes spread their ideas through salons, books, and pamphlets. Salons, such as the one shown above, were held one day a week in the home of a weathy woman. Here philosophes would read their work to the audience.*

➤ *Not only did women become important in salons, they also became professional artists.* Lady at Her Dressing Table *is a miniature painting by Rosalba Giovanna Carriéra, who lived from 1675 to 1757.*

■ *What changes did the philosophes want to make in society?*

jailed for remarks made to a French nobleman. These events made a deep impression on Voltaire. He fought all his life for freedom from censorship and for the rights of the individual.

Voltaire worked especially hard against religious intolerance. He saw that intolerance led to violence. He urged people to be tolerant of each other's beliefs:

> **B**y what right could a being, created free, force another to think like himself? . . . Tolerance has never brought civil war; intolerance has covered the earth with carnage.

The *Encyclopédie*

Another of the philosophes, Denis Diderot *(DEE dih roh),* spread the ideas of the philosophes

and the new scientific knowledge. He spent more than 20 years writing and editing the *Encyclopédie (ahn sy kluh PAY dih).* Diderot hoped the *Encyclopédie* would help ". . . change the general way of thinking." The first volume, published in 1751, was followed by 21 others, and over 160 authors contributed. No such vast collection of learning had existed before the *Encyclopédie.* By 1789, nearly 16,000 copies had been sold, and people all over Europe and America learned about the ideas of the philosophes.

Both the government and the church recognized that the *Encyclopédie* was a powerful voice for change. The French king banned the *Encyclopédie,* and the pope placed it on the *Index of Prohibited Books.* ■

Chapter 18

Study Skills

Have students define *encyclopedia* and tell the difference between a dictionary and an encyclopedia. How was the purpose of the *Encyclopédie* different from the purpose of modern encyclopedias? *(Encyclopédie: "to change the general way of thinking"; modern encyclopedias are informational.)* Ask: Would a government today ban a modern encyclopedia?

Religious Context

Following the revocation of the Edict of Nantes in 1685, Protestants in France were subjected to increasing persecution. A Protestant named Jean Calas had been accused of murdering his son to prevent him from becoming a Catholic. Calas was found guilty. Voltaire, convinced that the accusations were based on rumors and anti-Protestant feelings, worked to reverse the verdict. Although Voltaire was too late to save Calas's life, he did clear Calas's name.

Speaking and Listening

Arrange students into a circle similar to that shown in the picture of a salon. Have students discuss the new ideas of the Enlightenment, such as religious tolerance, the importance of science, new forms of government, and the rights of individuals. Ask some students to adopt a skeptical attitude toward these ideas and to ask questions. After the discussion, ask students how the activity helped them to understand the importance of the salons.

New Ideas about Government

Among the thinkers whose ideas were included in the volumes of *Encyclopédie* were three philosophes—John Locke of England, Baron de Montesquieu of France, and Jean-Jacques Rousseau of Switzerland. These three men concerned themselves with the question of what the best form of government was.

In *Two Treatises of Government* (1690), Locke wrote that government was a **contract,** or agreement, between the people and their ruler. The people allowed the ruler power as long as he or she governed fairly. Locke believed that if a ruler did not honor this contract, then the people had a right to overthrow the ruler.

Locke was willing to accept a monarch as ruler as long as he or she protected the rights of the people. Locke considered these **natural rights**—the rights every person was entitled to by nature—to be life, liberty, and the protection of property.

Baron de Montesquieu thought that government worked best when the power of the monarch was limited. Montesquieu argued that good government was best divided into three equal branches—legislative, executive, and judicial. If government were not divided, he feared:

> There would be an end of everything, were the same man or the same body . . . to exercise those three powers, that of enacting laws, that of executing the public resolutions, and of trying the causes of individuals.
>
> Montesquieu,
> *The Spirit of the Laws,* 1748

Rousseau criticized the idea of an absolute monarch even more strongly than Montesquieu. Rousseau believed that the people should participate directly in the government they elected:

> The deputies of the people . . . are not and cannot be its representatives. . . . Every law the people have not ratified [approved] in person is null and void—is, in fact, not a law.
>
> *The Social Contract,* 1762

Like Locke, Rousseau believed that government was a contract between the rulers and the people. He argued that the people could cancel the contract if they believed the government was not serving their needs. However, they could not sever the contract for trivial reasons. ■

▼ *Rousseau was an important philosophe during the Enlightenment. This playing card from the 1700s shows Rousseau dressed as a champion of democracy.*

■ *How were Locke, Montesquieu, and Rousseau alike and different in their philosophies of government?*

■ *They all agreed that the main purpose of government was to improve life for its people. Locke felt that a contract existed between the ruler and the people and that the people could break the contract if the ruler failed to protect the people's rights. Montesquieu believed in limiting the government's power by dividing it into three parts. Rousseau also believed that government involved a contract, but he argued that the people should participate directly in their government.*

CLOSE

Reintroduce the Thinking Focus. Have students discuss why the Scientific Revolution led to a greater faith in human reason. *(Evidence that world could be understood through human reasoning.)* Then have students identify elements of the enlightened society that the philosophes hoped for. *(Religious tolerance, individual freedom, scientific progress.)*

R E V I E W

1. **FOCUS** How did the Age of Enlightenment reflect a spirit of optimism?
2. **CONNECT** Why do you think the philosophes were critical of Louis XIV's absolute monarchy?
3. **HISTORY** What role did the *Encyclopédie* play in spreading the views of the philosophes?
4. **CRITICAL THINKING** How was the focus of the Enlightenment different from the focus of Renaissance humanism?
5. **WRITING ACTIVITY** Imagine that you have just been at one of the famous salons in Paris in the 1700s. Write a brief description of what you heard.

Answers to Review Questions

1. During the Age of Enlightenment people began to feel that many of society's problems could be solved using reason and that virtually anything was possible.
2. The philosophes were critical of Louis XIV's absolute monarchy because he persecuted Protestants and did not protect the rights of the people.
3. The *Encyclopédie* was very important in spreading the views of the philosophes.

Between 14,000 and 16,000 copies sold throughout Europe.

4. Renaissance humanism focused on improving the individual. Improving society was a secondary interest to humanists. Enlightenment thinkers focused on improving society, not necessarily the individual.

Homework Options

Based on their reading of the lesson, have students write definitions of each of the key terms and show how each term relates to the optimism of this period.

Study Guide: p. 78

Point out the lesson title and have students review the ideals of the Enlightenment thinkers (Lesson 1). Emphasize that as these new ideals grew in popularity, some reformers attempted to put them in action. Have students read the Thinking Focus and ask them to predict the types of changes that would take place and who would support or resist them. Have them read to check their predictions.

Key Term

Vocabulary Strategies: T36–T37
enlightened despot—a European ruler in the 1700s with absolute power who tried to support Enlightenment ideals such as tolerance and freedom

480

1700   1720
    1740   1799

L E S S O N   2

Ideas in Action

THINKING
FOCUS

How did the ideas of the Enlightenment affect governments in Europe and America?

Key Term

• enlightened despot

➤ *Voltaire, the figure on the left in the engraving, often provided advice to Frederick the Great, shown at right.*

He [the king] should often remind himself that he is a man just as the least of his subjects." With these words, Frederick II of Prussia, shown here with Voltaire, defined the new type of leader envisioned by the philosophes. An avid reader of the philosophes, Frederick especially admired Voltaire. Frederick even invited Voltaire to come live at his court. Voltaire must have thought highly of Frederick as well, for he called him the "Philosopher King." Eventually they quarreled, but not before Frederick had adopted many of the ideas of the philosophes. In an essay, he wrote:

If [a king] is the first judge, the first general, the first financier, the first minister of the nation . . . it is in order to fulfill the duties which these titles impose upon him. He is only the first servant of the state, obliged to act with fairness, wisdom, and unselfishness, as if at every instant he would have to render an account of his administration to his citizens.

Essay on the Forms of Government, 1788

Attempts at Reform

Frederick wanted to use his power and wisdom to improve the lives of his people. Because Frederick supported the ideals of the Enlightenment while remaining an all-powerful ruler, or despot, he is called an **enlightened despot.** But

Frederick was not the only European monarch to adopt Enlightenment ideals. Catherine the Great of Russia and Joseph II of Austria were also enlightened despots of the late 1700s. Locate the areas they ruled on the map on page 481.

Chapter 18

Objectives

1. Explain how the ideas of the philosophes affected European governments of the 1700s.
2. Show how the Declaration of Independence incorporated many Enlightenment ideals.
3. Discuss the causes and effects of the French Revolution.

Graphic Overview

ENLIGHTENMENT IDEALS

Enlightened Despots
- legal reforms
- religious tolerance

American Revolution
- natural rights
- contract between ruler and ruled

French Revolution
- natural rights
- religious tolerance

Reform in Europe

Frederick made important changes in Prussia during his rule from 1740 to 1786. His interest in recent scientific advancements resulted in the use of new crops, such as potatoes and clover in Prussia. He also encouraged the use of new planting methods and new equipment, such as crop rotation and iron plows.

As an enlightened ruler, Frederick also worked to increase religious tolerance. He welcomed Catholics into Lutheran Prussia and gave them nearly full equality. He even built a large Catholic church in Berlin and once said that he would erect a mosque if Muslims came to Prussia.

Under Frederick's rule, Prussia's legal system was vastly improved. The laws were simplified, and Frederick worked to ensure just sentences by trying to end the bribing of judges.

Elsewhere in Europe other enlightened despots supported reforms. In Russia, Catherine the Great ruled from 1762 to 1796. She tried to modernize Russia by importing architects, musicians, and intellectuals from western Europe. When the French government banned Diderot's *Encyclopédie,* Catherine offered to publish it. Catherine also restricted cruel punishment of serfs and allowed some religious tolerance.

Most progressive of all the enlightened despots was Joseph II of Austria, who ruled from 1780 to 1790. Determined to improve life for his subjects, he abolished serfdom and allowed peasants to own land. He taxed all classes equally and offered complete religious freedom to all faiths.

The Failure of Reform

Although these monarchs tried up to a point to help their people, most of the gains they made were small or short-lived. In Prussia, Frederick was intolerant of Jews. He made Jews pay special taxes, and tried to keep them from holding government offices. In Russia,

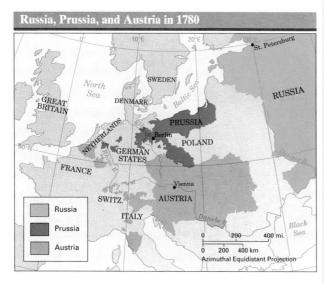

Russia, Prussia, and Austria in 1780

Russia

Prussia

Austria

Azimuthal Equidistant Projection

a peasant revolt caused Catherine to strengthen oppression of the serfs. And in Austria, nearly all of Joseph's reforms were reversed after his death at the age of 49. Nobles regained their privileges, and peasants lost their rights.

It was clear that the European nobility, who held the power and the money, were not going to give up their favored position easily. Since a monarch's power depended on the nobility's support, enlightened despots found it difficult to fulfill Enlightenment ideals. Montesquieu described this interdependence between the monarch and the nobles in a brief phrase: "No monarchy, no nobility; no nobility, no monarchy." ■

▲ *The rulers of Russia, Prussia, and Austria all tried to use the ideas of the philosophes when governing their countries. Where were these countries in relation to France?*

■ *Why were the reforms of enlightened despots largely unsuccessful?*

481

The Enlightenment

481

DEVELOP

Point out to students that the impact of the Enlightenment varied in different countries. In some places change took place peacefully; in others it did not. Draw the Graphic Overview on the chalkboard. Have students add details to the diagram as they read the lesson.

POLITICAL SYSTEMS
Critical Thinking

Ask students to identify the particular reforms made by Frederick II *(agricultural advances, tolerance of Catholics, legal reform)* and show which Enlightenment ideal each exemplifies. *(Scientific advancement, religious tolerance, respect of individuals' rights.)*

◄ *Austria is east of France, and Prussia and Russia are northeast.*

■ *The reforms of the enlightened despots were not supported by the nobility who held the money and power in Europe.*

Access Strategy

Engage students in a discussion of the types of oppressive events that lead people to revolt. As an example, list a series of increasingly oppressive policies that might be adopted in their school. These might include eliminating free periods, assigning seats in the cafeteria for lunch, making students wear signs indicating offenses (being tardy, forgetting homework), taking away their choice of activities, showing favoritism to blonde-haired students, doubling their homework assignments, adding a full school day on Saturday, and extending the school day to 12 hours. Have students tell how they would respond to each of these changes or restrictions, whether by complaining to friends, resisting their enforcement, taking their grievances to a higher authority, going on strike, or staging some type of revolt. Ask students: When would a rebellion be justified? Have them draw up a list of students' rights that they think should be protected.

Access Activity

Briefly define the traits of an enlightened ruler. *(Tolerates religious diversity, promotes rights of individuals.)* Help students to make a list of all the kings and queens and other rulers discussed in Chapter 17. Have students rank them from least enlightened to most enlightened and provide reasons for their ranking.

Critical Thinking

Point out that the revolutionaries made use of Locke's contract theory to justify their Declaration of Independence. Have students identify the revolution in England just prior to the time that Locke published his book (1690). *(Glorious Revolution.)* How was the turn of events in the English colonies ironic? *(English had earlier developed the revolutionary theory that was used against them.)*

■ *The Declaration of Independence incorporates Locke's ideas about natural rights and his idea that the people can dissolve the contract between themselves and their ruler.*

Influences in America

Leaders of the British colonies in North America adopted Enlightenment ideas with more success. Two leaders, Thomas Jefferson and Benjamin Franklin, had studied European ideas and traveled in Europe. The philosophes' ideas impressed them.

Like the philosophes, Jefferson and Franklin had a wide range of intellectual, political, and scientific interests. Jefferson was a writer and a student of the classical languages, literature, and architecture. Franklin—a talented printer, writer, scientist, politician, and inventor—corresponded with many of the philosophes.

Since the mid-1760s, Jefferson, Franklin, and other British colonists in North America had been enraged by attempts to raise taxes. Parliament wanted the colonists to pay a share of the expense from fighting the Seven Years' War with France. The colonists disagreed. Since they were British citizens,

▲ *Some Americans, such as Franklin, were influenced by Enlightenment thought. Here Franklin, at right, is shown on a snuff box with Rousseau and Voltaire to illustrate that all three shared many of the same ideals.*

■ *How does the Declaration of Independence reflect the influence of Enlightenment thinkers?*

they reasoned, they should not be taxed unless they were represented in Parliament.

Convinced that their rights were being violated, the colonists made a bold decision. In 1776, they decided to reject British rule. Then Thomas Jefferson headed a committee to draft a Declaration of Independence. On July 4, 1776, the Declaration was formally adopted.

In this document the colonists declared that "governments are instituted among men" to secure "certain inalienable rights, that among these are life, liberty, and the pursuit of happiness." These guaranteed rights follow directly from Locke's belief in natural rights.

The Declaration also stated that "governments [derive] their just powers from the consent of the governed." Therefore, when a government fails to respect the people's rights, "it is the right of the people to alter or to abolish it and to institute new government." This again echoes Locke's belief that the people have a right to overthrow a king who violates the contract between subjects and ruler. The American Revolution would be fought to defend these declarations of Enlightenment thought. ■

The French Revolution

In 1787, France's government was deeply in debt from supporting the colonists during the Revolutionary War. Poor harvests in 1788 led to food shortages, rising food prices, unemployment, and starvation. But still the government continued to collect taxes

from the poor, while French nobles paid almost no taxes. The anger of the French people grew.

In 1789, King Louis XVI, needing money to pay off his debts, decided to raise taxes. He called a meeting of the Estates General. The Estates General was made up of representatives from three groups of people, or estates. The First Estate was the clergy, the Second Estate was the noblility, and the Third Estate included everyone else. Members of the Third Estate had virtually no power in the government but paid almost all the taxes.

A Struggle for Power

On June 17, 1789, the representatives of the Third Estate broke away from the Estates General and formed a new group called the National Assembly. They swore to meet separately until France became a constitutional monarchy. Some members of the First and Second Estates joined them. In need of a unified group to have new taxes passed, Louis gave in to the Assembly's demands. He then urged the rest of the nobles and clergy to join the Assembly.

In July 1789, Louis gathered troops near Paris. The people of Paris feared that he was going to seize power from the Assembly and go back to his old methods of absolute rule. In retaliation, on July 14, a crowd stormed the Bastille, a fortress-prison that held arms and a few prisoners. They tore down the prison, took the weapons, and liberated its prisoners. This event marked the beginning of the French Revolution. The French woman in A Moment in Time on page 484 is part of a group that is presenting the demands of the people to King Louis XVI.

Waging a Revolution

In August 1789, the Assembly began drafting a new constitution. They adopted the Declaration of the Rights of Man and of the

▲ *The poor in France paid almost all the taxes. This French cartoon from the 1700s shows a poor person carrying a noble and a churchman.*

▼ *Governor De Launay (center) is arrested by the angry crowd during the storming of the Bastille.*

483

Note: Use this Moment in Time when discussing the events leading to the French Revolution (p. 483).

Visual Learning

Explain to students that this woman participated with thousands of other market women in the march on Versailles. She was one of only a few marchers who were allowed an audience with the king.

Set the scene for the students by explaining that the market women were traditionally great supporters of the king, marching in ceremonial processions to honor him. But today the women are upset. The bread shortages in Paris made it impossible for the women to feed their families.

More About Demonstrations

Less than a month before the march to Versailles, a group of market women at Chaillot, west of Paris, had stopped five carts filled with grain. The angry women brought the flour to bakers who were complaining that they had no flour to make bread.

484

A MOMENT IN TIME

Parisian Market Woman

*7:19 P.M., October 5, 1789
In the royal clock room of the palace at Versailles*

Eyes
She's amazed by the bright, white room decorated with real gold. Never in her life did she dream that she would be demanding the king's help.

Apron
She had no time to change before she joined the huge march to see the king. She sells the fish her husband catches, and a fishy smell clings to her clothes.

Stomach
She's hungry, very hungry. It's not just because she hasn't eaten since early morning today. It's been weeks since she's been able to put bread on her family's table.

Hand
Trembling with excitement and fear, she is holding her skirt to bow to her king. She wishes her hands weren't so chapped from her hard daily work.

Pamphlet
Tucked under her apron, a crudely printed page demands, "We want bread!" In the market people say that the king's army is not letting wheat wagons into Paris.

Skirt
Her hem got caked with mud on the rainy 12-mile march from Paris to Versailles. The angry marchers waited for hours at the gates of the palace before a small group of women was allowed inside.

484

Visual Learning

Find a book with pictures of the palace at Versailles to show the class. (Also see "A Closer Look: Morning at Versailles" on p. 455.) Ask them how the market woman might have felt when she saw the splendor of the king's living quarters.

Writing

Have students write the market woman's speech to the king. They should remember that she is respectful, but her family's situation is desperate. She fully expects the king to help her because, to her, he is almost a god.

Critical Thinking

The queen, Marie Antoinette, is supposed to have answered "Let them eat cake," when people like the market woman begged the king for bread. But there is no evidence she ever said anything like this. Ask students why they think this rumor might have begun in the hotly-charged economic and political climate of pre-revolutionary France.

Citizen. At the top of their list of natural rights, they placed "liberty, property, security, and resistance to oppression." They wrote that "the source of all sovereignty [power] resides essentially in the nation" rather than the king. Read more from the Declaration on p. 506.

In the next few years, the Assembly began numerous reforms in France. The nobility and clergy now had to pay taxes. In 1791, the Assembly established a constitutional monarchy. In 1792, Louis plotted with the rulers of Austria and Prussia to overthrow the new government. The plot was discovered. In September, the people ended the monarchy, and France became a republic. Louis was guillotined for treason in January 1793.

After Louis' death, disorder and violence swept through France. This Reign of Terror lasted almost a year. Anyone suspected of treason or hostility to the revolution was imprisoned and, sometimes, executed. More than 18,000 men, women, and children were killed.

The revolutionary period ended when General Napoleon Bonaparte seized control of the government in 1799. He defeated the Austrians and convinced the other European powers to make peace. Although the revolution had been bloody, it marked a turning point for France.

The Declaration of the Rights

◄ *The artist Jacques Louis David drew this pencil sketch of Marie Antoinette on the way to the guillotine during the Reign of Terror.*

of Man prompted Olympe de Gouges *(duh GOOJ)* to write a Declaration of the Rights of Woman in 1791. The following year, in Britain, Mary Wollstonecraft echoed her call. In 1791, the French National Assembly gave Jews and Protestants full and equal rights. In Berlin, German Jewish philosopher Moses Mendelssohn sparked a new reform movement within Judaism. He asked Jews to remain Jewish but to share in the culture of the nations they lived in.

Yet for both Christian women and Jews, the French Revolution brought few real changes. To them, the Revolution meant a new way of looking at the world—as future citizens with full rights still to be obtained. ■

Across Time & Space

The storming of the Bastille is celebrated in France on Bastille Day. Observed on July 14, it is France's most important national holiday. This day of remembering freedom and independence, much like the Fourth of July in the United States, is traditionally celebrated with parades, music, and dancing.

■ *How are the reforms that took place during the French Revolution representative of Enlightenment ideals?*

REVIEW

1. **FOCUS** How did the ideas of the Enlightenment affect governments in Europe and America?
2. **CONNECT** How did the enlightened despots in Europe differ from the constitutional monarchs in Britain?
3. **ECONOMICS** What were some of the economic and agricultural crises that helped to bring about the French Revolution?
4. **CRITICAL THINKING** Montesquieu wrote: "No monarchy, no nobility; no nobility, no monarchy." What do you think he meant by this statement?
5. **WRITING ACTIVITY** Imagine you have participated in the events in France of July 14, 1789. Write a letter in which you describe your day to a friend.

485

The Enlightenment

Have students recall the meaning of the term constitutional monarchy. *(The monarch's power is limited by law.)* Have them point out the type of monarchy that France had been prior to the revolution. *(Absolute monarchy.)* Ask them how a republic differs from a constitutional monarchy. *(Republic has no monarch; citizens hold ultimate power.)*

■ *Removing tax advantages for the clergy and nobles promoted equality. Establishing a republic gave the people more power in government. Extending religious tolerance reduced persecution.*

CLOSE

Reintroduce the Thinking Focus. Draw the Graphic Overview on the chalkboard and have students continue branching the diagram with specific details.

Answers to Review Questions

1. Enlightenment thought inspired the efforts of enlightened despots, helped lay the groundwork for the French Revolution, and greatly influenced the writing of the Declaration of Independence.
2. The reforms instituted by the enlightened despots were largely temporary while those of the constitutional monarchy were more permanent. Also the constitutional monarch ruled together with the Parliament while the enlightened despot had more absolute power.
3. Bad weather led to poor harvests in France. Even though many people were starving, Louis XVI still raised taxes to pay off the government's debt from the American Revolution.
4. Nobles supported the monarch only when the monarch protected the nobles' privileged status.

Homework Options

Have students use the text to draw a timeline of the important events that occurred during the French Revolution.

Study Guide: p. 79

INTRODUCE

The French Revolution was a violent uprising, as students learned in Lesson 2. The king and queen were the focus of the protests of the people. "To the Assembly for Protection" describes the royal family's hiding during the Revolution. This story, by Elizabeth Powers, is from a book based on the real diary of the king and queen's daughter.

READ AND RESPOND

The language and the French names might make this selection difficult for students. Read it with them, offering assistance as needed. Have students keep in mind the reading focus suggested in the paragraph preceding the story.

Some words students may need to know are: *passive,* not resisting; *constraint,* the holding back of one's feelings; *compelled,* driven or urged with force; *rogues,* dishonest or worthless people; *impudence,* a bold disregard for others; *vile,* foul or repulsive; and *oppressors,* people who unjustly or cruelly use authority.

In Lesson 2 you read about both liberation and terror during the French Revolution. The following story recreates a part of that stormy period.

Roederer (reh DRAIR)
Tuileries
(TWEE luh reez)

Mme Madame

M. Monsieur

LITERATURE

To the Assembly for Protection

Elizabeth Powers

Fifteen-year-old Marie Therese Charlotte began writing the story of her life in a journal when she and her family were imprisoned in revolutionary France. The daughter of Louis XVI and Marie Antoinette, Madame Royale, as Marie Therese was known, gives us an eyewitness account of the French Revolution. This story is from The Journal of Madame Royale, *a book based on the real journal kept by Marie Therese. What are Madame Royale's feelings about the French Revolution?*

At midnight on the ninth of August, Attorney General Roederer and others came to my father and warned him that there would be another march on the Tuileries. He urged my father to take his family to the National Assembly hall that adjoined the Tuileries and had been, in fact, the indoor riding school of the palace. There we would be under the protection of the deputies. My father left the room without answering.

My mother sent a message for Mme de Tourzel to awaken my brother and me and bring us to her. We came, along with kind Mme de Lamballe who had been safely out of the country but who had returned from England to be with my mother in her bad moments.

It was so hot that the leaves had fallen off the trees, and my mother had not been able to sleep.

Now she said, "This is a conflict of forces. We have come to the point where we must know which is going to prevail—the King and the Constitution, or the rebels."

At this point there was shouting and booing in the garden and drummers were beating the call to arms. M. Roederer put his head out of the window. He said, "My God, it is the King they are booing! What the devil is he doing down there? Come quickly, let us go to him!" He and his men ran down the stairs.

My father was brought back, out of breath and red in the face. It seems he had gone down to rally his guards, but when he got there he did not know what to say, so he only made matters

---

Thematic Connections

Social Studies: Historical empathy

Houghton Mifflin Literary Readers: Building a Country

Background

This story recounts the storming of the royal palace in August of 1792. The royal family fled from the enraged mob into the National Assembly and listened as testimony was presented against them. The monarchy was suspended, and the king was charged with treason, tried, and found guilty. He was beheaded on January 21, 1793. Marie Antoinette was similarly executed in October of the same year. She had been extravagant and frivolous, earning the hatred of the

French people by indulging herself at their expense.

We hear this story from Marie Therese Charlotte, the young daughter of the French king and queen. Because a family member tells the story, we get a new perspective. For example, Louis XVI is usually described as slow-witted and hesitating. In this story, though, Marie Antoinette, the queen, attributes his hesitation to shyness.

worse. Some artillery men had even dared to turn their cannon against their King!

My poor father. I remembered then what I had heard my mother say once to Mme Campan, her first lady of the bedchamber: "The King is not a coward; he possesses an abundance of passive courage, but he is overwhelmed by an awkward shyness, a mistrust of himself, which proceeds from his education as much as from his disposition. He is afraid to command, and above all things, dreads speaking to assembled members. He lived like a child, and was always ill at ease under the eyes of Louis XV until the age of twenty. This constraint confirmed his timidity."

After M. Roederer returned with my father he pleaded, "Sire, your Majesty has not five minutes to lose."

My mother said that we had a strong force in the palace but he answered, "Madame, all Paris is on the march." Then he turned to my father, who was sitting staring at the floor, and asked permission to escort us to the Assembly.

My father raised his head and looked at M. Roederer. Then he turned to my mother and said, "Let us be going." As he rose to his feet, my aunt came from behind his chair and said, "M. Roederer, will you answer for the life of the King?"

He said yes, that he would walk in front, but that there should be no one from the Court, and there should be no other escort than the members of the department who would surround the Royal Family, and the men of the National Guard who would march in line on both flanks as far as the National Assembly.

"Very well," my father said. "Will you give the orders?"

My mother said, "What about Mme de Tourzel, my son's governess? And Madame de Lamballe?"

Yes, he said. They could come, too.

When we reached the bottom of the great staircase my father stopped and said, "What is going to happen to all the people remaining up there?" No one answered.

Mme Campan had remained in my mother's apartments. We learned later that some men with drawn sabres rushed up the stairs, seized her and thrust her to their feet. But some of the Queen's other waiting women threw themselves at the ruffians' feet and held their blades away from her. Just then someone called from the bottom of the staircase, "What are you doing up there? We don't kill women." Her assailant quitted his hold on her and said, "Get up; the nation pardons you."

When we were under the trees we sank up to our knees in the piled up leaves. "What a lot of leaves," my father remarked, "they have begun to fall very early this year."

My brother, holding my mother's hand, was amusing himself by kicking the leaves against the legs of the persons walking in front of him. My aunt was holding tight to my hand and Mme de

Lamballe (lah BAHL)

◄ The king might be comparing himself to the leaves here. How can he be compared to the leaves? *(They both are falling sooner than expected.)*

Access Strategy

Ask your students to try to imagine their lives completely changing overnight. One day everything is perfectly normal; the next day, nothing is. Your life has been comfortable and secure; now suddenly you have to leave your home, you have nothing to eat or drink, you hear gunfire all around you.

You might not even understand why this was happening. All you could really tell was that it had something to do with your mother and father and that it was scary. No one explained anything to you, but you tried to make some sense out of the little you could see and hear. Tell students that in this literature selection, they will read the impressions of a fifteen-year-old woman who had just such an experience.

Tourzel and her daughter were supporting Mme de Lamballe who was trembling so she could hardly walk.

When we reached the hall, my father made an address. He said: "I have come here to prevent a great crime from being committed, and I am convinced that I could not be in a safer place than in your midst, gentlemen."

The president of the Assembly replied that the King could depend on the firmness of the National Assembly, but that they were sworn to defend with their lives the rights of the people and the constitutional authorities. They also said that it was against the rules for them to proceed with their debates with us there.

They then took us to the minute-writer's office. This room was so low the grown-up people could not even stand up straight. It had two or three stools and a bench, and an iron grating separated it from the hall. Not a breath of air could enter, and we were compelled to spend eighteen hours in this steaming cubbyhole.

All at once the boom of the gunnery was heard and men were saying it was coming from the Tuileries. Then someone shouted, "Here come the Swiss Guards!" Soon we heard the rattle of gunfire. There were shouts and cries coming from outside and inside now, saying that the King's Swiss Guards had fired on the people—had lured the citizens and then shot them down. There were curses and shouts demanding the death of the King.

My father sent an order for the Swiss Guards to cease firing, but before morning more than a thousand lives had been lost.

All at once, to our horror, we saw some of the faithful guards and nobles being chased into the Assembly hall by rogues who struck them down without mercy. They brought in my father's own servants who, with the utmost impudence, gave false testimony against him, while others boasted of vile things they had done. These were followed by looters who triumphantly strewed silverware, cashboxes, letters, even our toys, and anything else they could pick up over the desk of the president of the Assembly.

We listened as men mounted the tribune to lie about and denounce my mother and father. They cried, "Death to the Austrian woman!" "Death to the King!" and "Death to the Aristocrats!" We heard my father, the King, deposed and his veto abolished.

At last some one brought us food and water. My mother took a glass of water; my father ate; my brother and I fell asleep. My mother did not break her fast until we were taken to the Convent of the Feuillants, which had been confiscated and where bedrooms were made up for us. Next day we were taken back and heard the King and Queen branded as oppressors of the people. We heard them discuss what should be done with the King and where he should be kept.

Feuillants
(fuh YAHNTS)

Conducting an Interview

"To the Assembly for Protection" is an imaginary recreation of a first-hand account of a historic event. We witness it through the eyes of a participant, Marie Therese Charlotte. Newspaper reporters often interview participants in events to find information for their stories. Have students imagine that they are reporters interviewing Marie Therese about the events in "To the Assembly for Protection." Have them list the questions they would ask. Then you might want to pair students and have them take turns playing the roles of the reporter and Marie Therese.

For three long days we listened until it was declared that the King was suspended from his functions and a new municipal government, the Commune, was formed.

It was decreed that the Temple was the only place to ensure our safety. We were to be conducted there "with all the respect due to misfortune." The attorney for the new Commune, M. Manuel, was to accompany us. The Temple—so-called because in olden days it had been the fortress of the Knights Templar—was as sinister-looking as the Bastille. It consisted of a small castle with a round tower at each corner, narrow windows, and an inner court which, we would find, the sun hardly ever reached. We were to live in this fortress.

Towards three in the afternoon, Manuel, accompanied by Petion, came to take the Royal Family away. They made us all get in a carriage with eight seats. Then they crowded in with their hats on their heads, shouting "Long Live the Nation!" They had the driver go slowly, as throngs pressed themselves against the carriage, shrieking, spitting, and hurling insults. They had the cruelty, too, to point out to my parents things that would distress them—for instance, the statues of the kings of France thrown down from their pedestals, even that of Henri IV, before which they stopped and compelled us to look.

We learnt that the guillotine, the official instrument to cut off people's heads, had been set up in the Place du Carrousel.

Further Reading

Fear No More. Hester Chapman. This story is about the mysterious life and death of Louis Charles, the son of Louis XVI.

Jacobin's Daughter. Joanne S. Williamson. This story about the French Revolution focuses on its leaders and the conflicts among the political factions of the time.

Marie Antoinette, Daughter of an Empress. This biography focuses on the life of the woman who was queen of France in the 18th century. It also tell the story of her mother, the dominating Maria Theresa, Empress of Austria.

Victory at Valmy. Geoffrey Trease. This is an adventure story that takes place in the early days of the French Revolution.

◄ These final two paragraphs give us a clue as to the final outcome of this story. What do you think happens? *(The king and queen will probably have their heads cut off.)*

EXTEND

Students know what happened to Louis XVI and Marie Antoinette, but not much has been said about Marie Therese Charlotte. Have them find out what happens to her after her imprisonment. You might want to refer students to *The Journal of Madame Royale*, from which "To the Assembly for Protection" was excerpted.

Writing a News Article

The flight of the royal family and their subsequent capture were big news in France in 1792. Using the information students have gathered from reading, have them write articles for a newspaper. You may want them to base their articles on the questions they devised for the interview with Marie Therese. Remind students to write succinct, factual sentences and to include an attention-getting headline. After students proofread and revise the articles, you may want to organize them in a newspaper-like format on the bulletin board, under a fictitious masthead such as *The Paris Times* or *The Revolution Gazette*.

Further Reading

You may want to have your students look in the school or local library for more books on this topic or about other events and people from the Enlightenment period.

INTRODUCE

Point out the lesson title. Tell students that economics involves the production and distribution of goods, including food. Have students skim the illustrations and headings in the lesson. Then have them read the Thinking Focus and discuss possible answers. *(New farming tools and techniques increased the amount of food grown, which supported the increasing population; industrialization brought the growth of cities and new methods of working.)* Have them read to confirm or revise their opinions.

Key Terms

Vocabulary Strategies: T36–T37
agricultural revolution—a series of developments in Europe during the 1700s that improved farming methods and the yield of the land
crop rotation—the planting of crops such as turnips, wheat, and clover in alternate years to keep soil fertile
enclosure—the fencing in of common land to form larger estates in Britain during the 1700s
industrial revolution—the improvements in industry that began occurring in Britain during the 18th century
capitalist—an investor of money, or capital, in business

490

1700   1800

L E S S O N   3

Economic Changes

**THINKING
FOCUS**

How did the agricultural and industrial revolutions change life in Britain during the 1700s?

Key Terms

- agricultural revolution
- crop rotation
- enclosure
- industrial revolution
- capitalist

➤ *Gleaners are seen hard at work in this painting by Jean François Millet. Gleaning was backbreaking labor. But some families could not grow enough on their small plots for their own needs. So they gleaned to survive.*

The British farm women bent over to gather the gleanings, or the grain remaining on the ground after harvest. These women and their families before them had gathered gleanings from these fields, which were owned by an aristocratic family, for hundreds of years. The women's families farmed small plots of land. But they depended on gleanings because their own lands were simply too small to provide their families with enough food.

But these were perhaps the last gleanings that the women would ever collect. Parliament had decreed that large landowners could fence in and redistribute the land. The women and those like them had staged demonstrations, complained, argued and pleaded, but with no result.

Where would they go in the spring? Perhaps their families would go to the city to look for work. Perhaps they could be hired hands for a wealthy neighbor. Neither future appealed to them. They wanted things to stay the same.

The Agricultural Revolution

The French Revolution was not the only revolution that occurred during the 1700s. In Britain two different revolutions would change life in Europe forever.

The first major change took place on farms. By the end of the 1700s, British farmers had learned how to increase the amount of food they could grow by using a number of new methods. These new methods were so significant that together they are called the **agricultural revolution.**

Chapter 18

490

Objectives

1. Explain the agricultural and industrial revolutions.
2. Discuss how the agricultural and industrial revolutions affected the lives of people in the 1800s.

Graphic Overview

	Elements	Positives	Negatives
Agricultural Revolution	new tools and crops, enclosure	produced more food with less labor	displaced small farmers
Industrial Revolution	new machines, division of labor	provided jobs and made goods efficiently	caused poor working and living conditions

The agricultural revolution began in Britain in the 1500s. It started slowly and gathered momentum in the 1600s. By 1750, when the population of Britain began to grow rapidly, the changes were well under way. Experimentation resulted in more food to feed a hungry population.

Crop Rotation

In medieval Britain, farmers had used a three-field system when planting their crops. Each year, they would plant one field with wheat or rye and another with barley or oats. They would not plant any crop on the third field, allowing the soil to rest. The next year they would switch which crops were grown in which field. Under this system, called **crop rotation,** the soil in a field rested every third year.

Beginning in the 1500s, British farmers introduced changes in crop rotation. In the 1600s, they began to grow new crops, such as turnips or clover, on the field that had previously been left unplanted. Such crops actually nourished the soil, making it more fertile. Now fields were productive every year instead of lying unused every third year.

Turnips and clover also increased the amount of fodder, or food for animals, that was grown. The new crop rotation allowed farmers to raise more cows, sheep, and horses than before, making meat more plentiful. More animals also meant more manure, an important soil fertilizer. The more fertile soil produced more food.

Farm Tools

Another change in farming during the 1700s was the use of more efficient farming tools. One such tool was the horse-drawn seed drill pictured above. Developed by Jethro Tull in the 1730s, the drill planted evenly spaced seeds at a consistent depth and immediately covered them with soil. Space was left between rows so that the ground could be broken by a horse-drawn hoe. In this way the soil absorbed more air and water, helping plants grow better.

Enclosure

Perhaps the most significant change accompanying the agricultural revolution was **enclosure** of land—breaking up large unfenced common fields into smaller, fenced-in plots. Traditionally, peasants held their land scattered equally in the three fields in their village. Once the grain in one field was harvested, poor farmers could collect gleanings from the lands. Once the gleaning was finished, villagers could pasture their animals on the stubble. They also had

Across Time & Space

Historians are not sure why the population of Britain increased during the 1700s. One reason for the increase was that fewer people were catching the plague and dying.

491

The Enlightenment

DEVELOP

Ask students to compare the pictures on pp. 490 and 491. How are they similar? *(Subject is farming.)* How are they different? *(Level of technology.)* Draw the Graphic Overview on the chalkboard, but do not fill in the boxes. Explain that because advances in agriculture and industry brought such dramatic changes to society and to the way the average person lived, these advances are described by the term *revolution.* Have students read to identify the elements of each revolution and their positive and negative results.

CULTURE
Critical Thinking

Point out the picture on this page, and ask students what theme of the Enlightenment is depicted. *(Using science to improve lives.)* What is the effect of such machinery on human labor? *(Makes work easier, requires fewer workers.)* Point out that since fewer workers are needed, unemployment can result.

Access Strategy

Have students describe what it would have been like to live as farmers 200 to 300 years ago, when there were no cars, planes, electricity, refrigerators, air conditioners, or indoor shopping malls. What would it be like for them to have to grow their own food, make their own clothing and furniture, and travel by foot or on horseback? How would their relationship with the earth (or nature) be different? How would the pace of their lives be different? What would they like or dislike about their lives? Then have them imagine suddenly having that life taken away and moving to a town. How would city life be different? What type of work would they probably find? *(Business, factory.)* Would the change be difficult to make? What advantages and disadvantages would city life offer? Have them read the lesson to see how people dealt with such changes 200 years ago.

Access Activity

Have students bring to class items or pictures of items that reduce human labor. *(Appliances, tools, vehicles, computers.)* Have each student explain how the particular item saves time or effort, and how the work would be done if that item did not exist. Ask students to think of the effects of these time- or labor-saving devices on their lives.

■ *The enclosure of common land, new farm machinery such as the horse-drawn seed drill, and crop rotation all affected agriculture.*

Critical Thinking

Have students look at the chart on this page. Have students identify the positive and negative effects of the use of a division of labor. *(Positive—increase in productivity; negative—monotonous work.)* Ask students how they would feel about having a job in which they performed a limited task over and over. Discuss the term *assembly line* and the use of robots in today's factories to handle routine tasks. Ask what effects robots would have on workers today. *(Fewer dull, routine jobs.)*

■ *What developments changed agriculture in Britain?*

▼ *Adam Smith's idea of specialization of labor can be applied to making shoes. By specializing in a particular step, each worker becomes faster at it. Also, dividing the process into simple steps opens the door to mechanization. The cotton gin (right), invented by Eli Whitney in 1793, separated cotton fiber from seed 50 times faster than workers could do it by hand.*

common rights to village pastureland and meadowland. Without these sources of food, farmers had trouble providing for their families.

But during the 1600s and 1700s, large landowners began buying up the holdings of small landowners and then fencing in, or enclosing, the land. Once the land was enclosed, the owner could

farm it any way he liked. Landowners introduced new agricultural techniques, which boosted the amount of food produced on the same amount of land. But many peasants were left without land of their own. They bitterly resented enclosure but could not stop it. Deprived of land, many headed to cities to find work. ■

The Industrial Revolution

As the population of Britain grew, the demand for goods, such as clothing, also increased. British manufacturers could not meet this demand using only the traditional method of making cloth by hand. In response, inventors began producing machines that could manufacture goods faster and more cheaply. Some were operated by people

who had been driven off the land by the agricultural revolution. These improvements brought about an **industrial revolution,** a change in the way goods were produced and the way people lived.

New Technology

Like other Enlightenment figures, British inventors hoped to apply scientific principles to the problem of producing more goods. Many inventions in the 1700s affected the textile industry. Prior to the 1700s, spinning and weaving had been done with spinning wheels and hand looms. In 1733, John Kay invented a flying shuttle, a mechanical loom that allowed one person to do the work of two.

With the flying shuttle, workers used up thread so quickly that a better machine was needed for spinning. In 1764, James Hargreaves invented the jenny, a device that spun eight spools of thread at once. Between 1750 and 1800, England went from importing 3 million to 50 million pounds of raw cotton per year to make cloth.

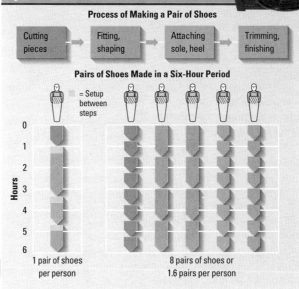

Specialization of Labor

Process of Making a Pair of Shoes

Cutting pieces → Fitting, shaping → Attaching sole, heel → Trimming, finishing

Pairs of Shoes Made in a Six-Hour Period

👤 = Setup between steps

Hours: 0, 1, 2, 3, 4, 5, 6

1 pair of shoes per person

8 pairs of shoes or 1.6 pairs per person

Chapter 18

Have students find out more about the inventions discussed on pp. 492 and 493. Have them identify the year in which each machine was invented, its inventor, its function, the machine it replaced, and the effect the invention had on the industrial revolution.

Iron production in Britain also grew through technological advances. Furnaces for smelting iron were heated by charcoal made from hardwood. When hardwood became scarce around 1700, production declined. During the early to mid-1700s, Abraham Darby and his son developed a way to produce a cheaper substitute from coal, called coke. Coal was plentiful in Britain, and as a result of the new technology iron production tripled between 1788 and 1806.

Have students make a mural of pictures of inventions, beginning in 1700 and going up to the present day. Divide the mural in three parts headed 1700s, 1800s, and 1900s. Have students bring in pictures or make drawings of inventions from each period. Below each picture, have them provide a caption indicating the invention's name, inventor, and year of invention. Have students link similar inventions to show that progress is based on previous accomplishments.

Capital and Labor

Capital and labor, or money and workers, were two of the important elements in the industrial revolution. The British government encouraged individuals called **capitalists** to invest their money in new industries. Competition among individual producers led them to produce the best product at the cheapest price. It was important for producers to do this, so that they would have the most customers and make the greatest profit.

A British economist named Adam Smith wrote about some of the changes in the economy. Smith showed how having workers specialize in a task could increase the number of goods they could produce. The chart on page 492 illustrates Smith's argument.

Conditions of Life

Although the new industries provided jobs, they damaged the living and working conditions of many laborers. Workers—even children under 10 years of age—spent 12 or 14 hours, six days a week, performing monotonous tasks. Some children were crippled by unsafe machines.

The increase in the number of people in British cities caused new problems. So many people burned coal for heat that the skies turned black with smoke. Charles Dickens described the intense overcrowding and dirtiness of these cities:

*I*t was a town of machinery and tall chimneys, out of which interminable [never ending] serpents of smoke trailed themselves for ever and ever. . . . It had a black canal in it, and a river that ran purple with ill-smelling dye, and vast piles of buildings.

Charles Dickens, *Hard Times*

For better or worse, the industrial revolution made Britain the workshop of the world. ■

▲ *The first steam-powered loom was invented by Edmund Cartwright in 1786. Early power looms were most effective for weaving tough cotton fibers.*

■ *What conditions contributed to the growth of industry in the late 1700s?*

■ *The invention of new machines such as the steam engine and the spinning jenny plus the availability of a labor force contributed to industry's growth.*

C L O S E

Reintroduce the Thinking Focus and have students suggest answers. Draw the Graphic Overview on the chalkboard and have students fill in the boxes. Ask: How did the Agricultural Revolution contribute to the Industrial Revolution? *(Supply of labor and increased food supply that could support a larger population.)* Finish by asking whether this time of great technological change was an era of progress.

R E V I E W

1. **FOCUS** How did the agricultural and industrial revolutions change life in Britain during the 1700s?
2. **CONNECT** How did crop rotation in Britain during the 1700s differ from that used during the Middle Ages?
3. **ECONOMICS** How did an increase in the population during the 1700s help bring about changes in agriculture and industry?
4. **CRITICAL THINKING** If you had been a British peasant in the late 1700s, would you have preferred to remain a farmer or work in a textile factory? Explain.
5. **WRITING ACTIVITY** Referring to the text and a dictionary, write a definition of *capitalist* in your own words, and give an example from the present or the past.

493

The Enlightenment

Answers to Review Questions

1. New farming tools and techniques allowed the food supply to increase, thus keeping pace with the growing population but also decreasing the number of workers necessary to farm. This forced small farmers off the land and into the cities. In cities new manufacturing provided jobs for these workers but in other ways diminished the quality of their lives.
2. Using the new crop rotation, farmers no longer left one field unplanted every third year. Instead, they planted the third field with a crop that would replenish the soil, such as turnips or clover.
3. The population increase led farmers to experiment with new techniques to increase the food supply. These new techniques required fewer laborers to produce more food, thus freeing many workers for industry.
4. Answers will vary. Students may suggest that neither option was appealing.

Homework Options

Have students make a timeline listing all of the new inventions discussed in the text and their year of invention.

Study Guide: p. 80

DECISION-MAKING PROCESS

1. Recognize the need for a decision.
2. Define the goals and values involved.
3. Acquire and evaluate necessary information.
4. Identify and analyze possible alternatives.
5. Choose the best alternative.

This Making Decisions lesson, Industrial Growth, uses steps 2 and 3 of the decision-making process.

HISTORY
Critical Thinking

Discuss the advantages and disadvantages of industrialization both during the English industrial revolution and in present-day communities. *(Both provided jobs and made various businesses and forms of entertainment available; both caused overcrowding and made life in the industrialized areas unpleasant.)*

Industrial Growth

▼ *The textile factory below was one of the first examples of industrial growth in England. Notice the huge machines in this cloth factory. Modern industrial growth often results in other community projects, such as schools, museums, and shopping centers like the one at the right.*

> The city's destiny and expanse finally bred a sense of captivity. . . . Its ugliness finally obscured its grandeur; the wretchedness of most of its inhabitants mocked the luxury of the few. In the workers' quarters it was a sink of vice and disease. . . . It was crowded with rootless, anonymous strangers.
>
> Richard D. Altick, 20th-century historian

Background

The English agricultural and industrial revolutions led to higher living standards and new expectations and desires. Thousands of people moved from rural areas to cities in search of work and a brighter future. The cities, however, were not ready to accommodate them. London, Birmingham, and other English cities were filled with people desperate for work. As described in the quote at the top of this page, poverty and overcrowding made these industrial cities places that bred despair.

On the other hand, industrialization affected the people in some very positive ways. Because of improvements in agricultural technology, food production increased. The increase in the number of new industries gave people a wider choice of how to make a living.

In cities, people were exposed to music, art, and other forms of culture that were less available in the countryside. Nevertheless, debates raged over whether the advantages of industrialization actually outweighed the disadvantages.

494

Objectives

1. Define the goals and values of industrialization. (Critical Thinking 1; Economics 1, 5)
2. Acquire and evaluate the information necessary to make a decision on industrialization. (Critical Thinking 2)

Activity

Ask students to imagine that they have just moved to London with their families during the beginning of the Industrial Revolution. Job opportunities have become scarce in the rural villages where they grew up; their parents have come to find jobs in the city.

After setting the scene, have the students make several journal entries about what it's like to adjust to their new life in London. What kind of place does the family find to live in? Do the parents find work? Is this a time of prosperity or of overcrowding and poverty? Encourage students to be creative as they write their entries.

Concerns About Growth

The same debate rages today. When a major industry considers opening a plant or large office in a small or medium-sized community, some people in the community are for such growth; others are against it.

Those who welcome the new facility promote it with a number of arguments. For one thing, new industry creates new jobs. Its owners and the people who move to the town to work at the new facility will pay taxes to the town. These taxes can be used to build new schools, repair streets, and improve city services. The larger population will attract other new businesses: restaurants, hotels, clothing stores, groceries.

Those who do not want the new industry in their community have other arguments. A larger population will require more city services, such as more teachers, wider streets, more sewers, and larger police and fire departments. To get enough money to pay for all this will involve increasing taxes, at least at first. Opponents also argue that heavier traffic may lead to congestion, confusion, and frustration. Life may become more hectic and less enjoyable for the people in the town.

▲ *Greater job opportunities result from industrial growth.*

Decision Point

1. What goals and values would cause residents to support the bringing of a new industrial facility to their community? What goals and values would cause these residents to oppose the idea?

2. Suppose a manufacturing company plans to build a new factory in your town or city. What do you think you would want to know about this new facility? Where could you find the information you want?

3. Imagine that a new industry is going to be based in your community. What one problem could this help to solve? (Consider unemployment, young people leaving the community, inadequate support for local businesses.)

4. What is one problem that a new industry in your area might create? Can you think of a way to prevent this problem from arising and still allow the industry to develop in your area?

UNDERSTANDING
REPORTS

This skills feature teaches students how to use primary sources to make oral reports more accurate and interesting.

CULTURE
Critical Thinking

Ask students to imagine they are giving an oral report about a famous movie star. Discuss the primary sources they could incorporate in their reports. *(Interviews with the star or associates; autobiographies, biographies; etc.)*

UNDERSTANDING REPORTS
Presenting Primary Sources

Here's Why

You will probably speak to groups several times while you are in school. If you know how to prepare an interesting oral report, your presentations will be less stressful and more well received.

One way to make oral reports more accurate and interesting is to use primary sources. As you know, primary sources are documents that are produced at the time of the event, like newspaper articles. Many people you have read about in this chapter left written accounts of events that occurred during their lifetimes. Benjamin Franklin, for example, is well known for his fascinating autobiography. John Locke, Jean Jacques Rousseau, Adam Smith, and Voltaire also wrote extensively about events and ideas of their time. Suppose you wanted to make an oral report about one of these people. How would you use primary sources to make your report interesting?

Here's How

You can use primary mary sources in any of several different ways. You would not use all of these methods in

496

one report, but using any one of them will certainly improve your report.

1. Use a primary source to limit your topic. For example, a specific journal entry could become the basis for an oral report about Benjamin Franklin.

2. Use quotations from a primary source to help bring your report alive. For example, you could frame your report with quotations at the beginning and the end. Or you could use quotations throughout the report to support specific points.

3. Broaden the perspective of your report by using several primary sources. For example, if you were preparing a report about the Constitutional Convention, you might choose

quotations from the writings of Thomas Jefferson, Benjamin Franklin, and John Adams.

Review the steps below for preparing and presenting an oral report. Think about how you might use primary sources as you work your way through the steps.

Try It

Use the steps listed below to prepare an oral report about one of the people mentioned in Here's Why. Be sure to use primary source materials that will spark your listeners' interest.

Apply It

Find examples of primary sources used in oral reports on radio or television. Explain how the reports used those primary sources.

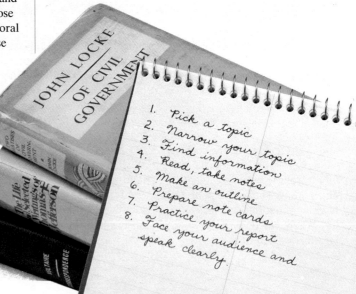

1. Pick a topic
2. Narrow your topic
3. Find information
4. Read, take notes
5. Make an outline
6. Prepare note cards
7. Practice your report
8. Face your audience and speak clearly.

Chapter 18

Objective

Explain how to incorporate primary sources in an oral report. (Study Skills 1)

Collaborative Learning

Group students in pairs. Ask one student in each pair to imagine that he or she is a television reporter covering a late-breaking news item. Have the other student pretend to know inside information about the story. Set up a "live" interview (either scripted or not) that enhances the audience's understanding of the pair's story.

Answer to Try It

Answers will vary.

Answers to Apply It

Answers will vary.

1700   1720   1740   1760

1777   1800

L E S S O N   4

After the American Revolution

A fter the North American colonists overthrew Britain's authority, government in the new nation was founded on the Articles of Confederation. Adopted in 1777, the Articles only loosely united the 13 states. Each state was like a separate country, with its own government, army, trade, and currency.

Many leaders, including George Washington, felt that the nation needed a more powerful central government than it had. They hoped that such a government would unite the states. The leaders also believed that the natural rights of the people had to be outlined to protect the freedoms that had so recently been won. In 1787, the leaders of the nation met to provide the nation with a new and responsive government.

THINKING

F O C U S

What Enlightenment ideals did the founders of the government of the United States share with the philosophes?

Key Terms

- checks and balances

◄ *George Washington was unanimously approved as president of the Constitutional Convention held at Philadelphia in 1787.*

A New Constitution

W e the people of the United States, in order to form a more perfect union, establish justice, insure domestic tranquility, provide for the common defense, promote the general welfare, and secure the blessings of liberty to ourselves and our posterity, do ordain and establish this Constitution for the United States of America.

497

The Enlightenment

Graphic Overview

CONSTITUTION, BILL OF RIGHTS

| Social contract | Checks and balances | Freedom of religion | Freedom of the press | Division of power |

DEVELOP

Draw the chart in the Graphic Overview on the chalkboard to show that the influence of the Enlightenment did not end with the Declaration of Independence. Explain that the lesson discusses the ideals of the United States Constitution. Point out that all of the ideals listed in the Graphic Overview were beliefs that the Founding Fathers shared with the philosophes. You may wish to extend the discussion by reading the Bill of Rights to students. Point out that such Enlightenment ideals as freedom of religion and freedom of the press are protected in these amendments, not in the actual Constitution.

BELIEF SYSTEMS

Critical Thinking

To discuss the Preamble to the Constitution, separate it into phrases. Have students discuss the meaning of each phrase. Clarify any words that are unfamiliar. What are the "blessings of liberty"? Ask: Has the Constitution succeeded in its stated purpose?

■ *The two share the ideals of a social contract existing between ruler and ruled and of a government with branches that check and balance each other.*

498

▲ *The three branches of the U.S. Government are also separated physically in Washington D.C.—the executive White House (top right), the judicial Supreme Court (top left), and the legislative Capitol (bottom).*

How Do We Know?

HISTORY *In 1792, British author Mary Wollstonecraft extended the theory of natural rights to include women. In her book* A Vindication of the Rights of Women, *she stresses the importance of education in bringing about equality between men and women.*

498

■ *What ideas in the Constitution are similar to the ideals of the philosophes?*

The quote you just read begins the Constitution. It expresses the purpose of the document. The influence of the Enlightenment can be clearly seen in the first three words, "We the people." Americans had come to believe in Locke and Rousseau's theory that government is basically a "social contract" between the people and their ruler.

The Constitution goes on to identify the branches of government and to define these branches' roles. The three branches were the legislative, executive, and judicial. The framers of the Constitution wanted to keep any one of the branches of government from becoming too powerful. As the French philosophe Montesquieu had written, "It is necessary from the very nature of things that power should be a check to power."

Those writing the Constitution developed a system of **checks and balances** between government power centers. For example, the president can veto, or refuse to pass, bills passed by the Congress. But if Congress passes the bill again by a two-thirds vote, it becomes law.

Similarly, the president can nominate judges to the Supreme Court, but the Senate can refuse to approve the persons chosen by the president. The Supreme Court can also cancel laws that have been passed by Congress if they are judged to be in conflict with the Constitution. ■

Chapter 18

Access Activity

Ask students what it would be like if each teacher at their school suddenly decided to teach subjects without regard to what was being taught by other teachers. What would be missing from such an environment? *(Order, consistency.)* Compare this lack of centralization to the situation the colonies were in under the Articles of Confederation.

Access Strategy

Ask students to give examples of situations they have been in that required compromise. *(Siblings disagreeing about who uses the stereo or what kind of music they play; teacher and student disagreeing about what grade an assignment deserves.)* Have them role-play the interaction between the two disagreeing parties. Ask: Why do disagreements come about? *(Two or more people have differing needs, desires, or viewpoints.)* What are the possible outcomes when people disagree?

(One party gives in; both parties compromise; the issue is referred to a higher authority; the parties clash physically; the issue is submitted to a vote.) Have students define *compromise.* Help students to see that compromise helps to stabilize situations of potential conflict. State that the writers of the Constitution formed a government that allowed the different branches to reach a solution by compromising.

Ideas flowed from Europe to the United States. So did symbols of those ideas. The Statue of Liberty was built in France and was given to the United States. The workers in the photo were working near the left arm of the statue.

Referring to the illustration on p. 498, ask students to identify which building represents which branch of government. How does the diagram suggest a balance of power? *(Each part is linked to the other two, all are roughly equal in size.)* Have them identify checks and balances between branches of the government and discuss the purpose of having checks and balances.

UNDERSTANDING PROGRESS

When Alexander Hamilton, one of the delegates at the Constitutional Convention, tried to convince Americans to ratify the Constitution, he used a typical philosophe argument. The government of the United States would be better than past governments, he argued, because "the science of politics . . . like most other sciences, has received great improvement." Much like other thinkers of the Age of Enlightenment, Hamilton believed in progress. What is progress? And how do we measure progress?

What Is Progress?

Progress implies improvement, or forward movement toward a desirable goal. Although progress involves change, not all change involves progress. When the Roman Empire broke up, most of western Europe became isolated from the learning and culture of the larger world community. The Middle Ages were certainly a time of change but, in many ways, not a time of progress.

How Is Progress Measured?

Progress is not always easy to measure, because in some societies it occurs for some people but not for others. Ancient Greece is often considered a model of political, economic, and social progress. But this progress applied only to free white men, not to women or slaves. The opening up of the American West brought progress to pioneers but certainly not to American Indians.

Is Progress Always Good?

The philosophes of the 18th century looked forward to a perfect world. They did not realize that progress often has a cost. For instance, although the Industrial Revolution provided many people with jobs and goods, it also brought pollution, oppressive working conditions, and overcrowding to the cities. It is important to evaluate progress in terms of its benefits as well as its costs.

499

The Enlightenment

Political Context

At the Constitutional Convention, difficulties in resolving issues threatened to end the convention before its goal was achieved. Delegates differed on such issues as the strength of the federal government, the power of the president, and the composition of the representative assembly. In the end, Congress was divided into two houses. One was based on population—House of Representatives—and the other was made up of two representatives from each state—Senate.

Speaking and Listening

Organize a debate on the issue of how strong the federal government should be. Students might consider the statement, "A loose association of states is a guard against tyranny," or "A strong federal government is needed to guard against chaos." Choose a team of debaters to research the arguments on each side. Have them present the debate to the class. Then put the issue to a vote. Have students decide if the framers of the Constitution made the right decision.

Study Skills

Provide students with a copy of the Constitution (without amendments). Have students develop an outline of this document in which they identify the major headings and topics discussed under each heading. Then have students describe the structure of this document and tell why they think it was organized this way.

Social Participation

Read aloud, or have student volunteers read aloud, the second to last paragraph, beginning "For the great majority . . ." Make sure students understand that what was going on in British North America and France was unlike anything elsewhere in the world.

You might want to make a chart listing down the side the various rights and freedoms mentioned in this paragraph, and across the top various countries and cultures that students have studied over the year. Compare which human rights people had in, for example, the Byzantine Empire, Mughal India, and Tokugawa Japan with the rights demanded by people in British North America and France.

■ *People were forming their own government and governing themselves.*

CLOSE

Reintroduce the Thinking Focus, and have students discuss how the lesson has clarified their ideas. Have students discuss how their perception of the Constitution has changed from reading this lesson.

500

Around the World in 1790

■ *What was happening in the United States at this time that was so unusual?*

▼ *The Statue of Liberty has been a symbol of liberty, freedom, and democracy for over a hundred years.*

While Americans chose to form their own nation and to govern themselves, we should remember that this was an extremely unusual step for those times. With the adoption of the U.S. Constitution in 1788, Americans chose for themselves a system of government based on Enlightenment ideals and lessons learned from history. In the Constitution as in the French Declaration of the Rights of Man and the Citizen, are ideas from the *Magna Carta*, and the English Bill of Rights.

Yet most people around the world had no idea of these changes. When the power of the Indian Mughal emperors fell in the 1770s, European trading companies established treaties that often led to colonization. As their power grew, the British took over more and more Asian lands. When Britain won the Seven Years' War in 1763, it became the world's largest and most powerful empire.

In China, Emperor Qianlong ruled an empire closed to outside influences and threats. During his reign, China came to be the most populous and largest nation on earth. China also ruled parts of Vietnam and Burma. In Japan, the Tokugawa clan still ruled as shoguns.

Society was also closed to outsiders, except for trade with the Dutch.

Europe's demand for the high-quality silks, cottons, lacquers, porcelains, rugs, and eventually tea that came from Asia, had to be paid for in gold and silver. That came either from Spanish-American mines or Africa's Gold Coast. In Spanish America, many people worked in mines in order to support this trade. Others worked on large cattle-ranching estates, also owned by the Spanish.

For the great majority of people around the world, ideas of full citizenship, equal rights, freedom of speech and belief, and democratic decision making, would have been extremely foreign. It was in British North America and France, however, that large segments of the merchant or middle class, working class, and peasantry began to believe in democratic republicanism.

The American experiment meant democracy on a scale that had never been tried before. The Constitution created by these early Americans gave them and continues to give us today the opportunity to reform and change our government, ensuring that in all ages it is "of the people, by the people, and for the people." ■

500

R E V I E W

1. **FOCUS** What Enlightenment ideals did the founders of the government of the United States share with the philosophes?
2. **CONNECT** What were the similarities between the Constitution and the Declaration of the Rights of Man and of the Citizen?
3. **HISTORY** How did the United States Constitution reflect a belief in progress?

4. **CRITICAL THINKING** How does the separation of powers into three branches of government, and checks and balances among those branches, help to guarantee freedom?
5. **WRITING ACTIVITY** Imagine that you are an immigrant arriving in the United States in the 1800s. Write a description of why you left your home and what you hope to find when you arrive in the United States.

Chapter 18

Homework Options

Have students write a few paragraphs on why studying world history is important to understanding the United States of America.

Study Guide: p. 82

Answers to Review Questions

1. They shared such ideals as beliefs in individual freedom, religious tolerance, existence of a social contract, and importance of a checks-and-balances system to guard against tyranny.
2. Like the Declaration, the Constitution reflected the belief in Enlightenment ideals such as the existence of a social contract and the protection of natural rights.
3. The Constitution reflects a belief in

progress because the Founding Fathers believed that, because people knew more about the science of politics, they would be able to create a better government than all previous governments.
4. The separation of powers into three branches of government helps to guarantee freedom by preventing any one branch from achieving absolute power. This guards against tyranny.

Chapter Review

Reviewing Key Terms

Age of Enlightenment (p. 477)
agricultural revolution (p. 490)
capitalist (p. 493)
checks and balances (p. 498)
contract (p. 479)
crop rotation (p. 491)
enclosure (p. 491)

enlightened despot (p. 480)
immigrant (p. 500)
industrial revolution
(p. 492)
natural right (p. 479)
philosophe (p. 477)
reason (p. 476)

A. Rewrite each sentence. Use a key term in place of the phrase in italics.
1. Sir Isaac Newton used *logical thought* to discover the laws of motion.
2. Joseph II was an *absolute ruler who supported the ideals of the Enlightenment.*
3. Many *people from foreign lands* came to the United States seeking jobs and land.

4. The framers of the Constitution developed a system of *maintaining a balance of power between the three branches of government.*
5. *Breaking up large open, common fields into smaller, fenced-in plots* was an important part of the agricultural revolution.
6. *People willing to invest their money in new industries* were essential to the industrial revolution.

B. Write a sentence or two for each pair of words showing how the words are related.
1. Age of Enlightenment, philosophe
2. contract, natural right
3. agricultural revolution, crop rotation
4. industrial revolution, capitalist

Exploring Concepts

A. Copy the diagram and fill in the names of the people or documents.

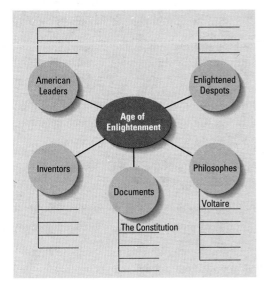

B. Support each statement with facts and details from the chapter.
1. Many of the philosophes hoped to discover a better way to govern.
2. Both Martin Luther and Thomas Jefferson challenged authority in order to make positive changes in their world.
3. Frederick II admired Voltaire and adopted many of his ideas.
4. During the reign of Joseph II, many Austrians were freer than ever before.
5. The Declaration of the Rights of Man and the Citizen included ideas from the writings of John Locke and Jean-Jacques Rousseau.
6. One of the effects of the agricultural revolution was an increased supply of workers for the Industrial Revolution.
7. Ideas expressed by the philosophes can be found in American government.
8. Many immigrants came to the United States seeking religious and political freedom.

The Enlightenment

Answers to Reviewing Skills

1. Answers will vary. Students should include outline topics such as the name of the inventor, date of invention, its effects on the industrial revolution, and how it increased production. They should name their primary source and indicate where they would use it.

2. Note card 1:
The Agricultural Revolution
Crop Rotation
Crops grown that help replenish the soil.
No longer need to leave field barren every third year.
Increased fodder for animals.
Across the Centuries, p. 491.
Note card 2:
The Agricultural Revolution
Farm Tools
More efficient tools developed.
Seed drill.
Horse-drawn hoe.
Across the Centuries, p. 491.
Note card 3:
The Agricultural Revolution
Enclosure
Common fields broken up and enclosed with fences.
Poor farmers forced off the land.
Across the Centuries, pp. 491–492.

3. A primary source.

Answers to Using Critical Thinking

1. Students may say that our government seems to demand high taxes, but all have to pay taxes, and all receive the benefits.

2. Students may say that people should be educated so they can work at better jobs. Education can also help end intolerance. People can vote to remove corrupt public officials.

3. Answers will vary depending on the inventions chosen.

Reviewing Skills

1. Reread the section in Lesson 3 entitled The Industrial Revolution. Choose one invention that would make a good oral report. What would you want to cover in your report? Make an outline. What primary sources might you use? Indicate in your outline where you would use information from primary sources.

2. Turn to Lesson 3, page 490. Find the section of the lesson with the heading The Agricultural Revolution. Use note cards to take notes summarizing the information found in this section. Remember to include subtopics, the source of information, and your page references.

3. You have to give an oral report on a recent event that occurred in your city, state, or country. What might you use as a source of information for your oral report?

Using Critical Thinking

1. In 1764, Voltaire wrote: "In general, the art of government consists in taking as much money as possible from one class of citizens to give to another." He was referring to the way that the king of France taxed the Third Estate. Does this statement describe government in the United States today? Why?

2. People living during the Age of Enlightenment believed that poverty, intolerance, and injustice could be ended. But we still have those problems today. What can citizens of this century do to help end them?

3. Inventions such as the flying shuttle greatly changed the British textile industry. Goods were produced more cheaply and quickly, but under terrible working conditions. Think of other inventions that have had a profound effect on other industries. Name some positive effects of those inventions. Name some negative effects.

Preparing for Citizenship

1. **GROUP ACTIVITY** Stage a panel discussion between philosophes and enlightened despots. You may portray Locke, Voltaire, Catherine the Great, or other figures from the chapter. Your purpose should be to include the points that the two groups agreed on, but also show how they differed. You may want to consult other resources such as biographies or the encyclopedia for additional ideas.

2. **WRITING ACTIVITY** Analyze a part of the Declaration of Independence to find ideas from the philosophes. On the left half of a large poster, write passages from the Declaration. On the right half, write the name of the philosophe on whose ideas the passage is based.

3. **COLLABORATIVE LEARNING** As a class, choose a recent period from history and put together a three-volume encyclopedia of the thinking from that period similar to Diderot's *Encyclopédie*. Each volume will be about one of these categories: government, business, or science. Decide as a class what the page size and the cover design of the encyclopedie will be. Team up with three other people. Divide the team into two pairs. Each pair is responsible for providing an illustrated article in one of the three categories. Each pair should choose a topic and research it in periodicals, encyclopedias, and other resources. The topic may be related to people, ideas, events, inventions or discoveries. Then one person should summarize the findings and the other illustrate the summary. Get together with other teams who have chosen the same category, bind all the pages into one volume and cover them.

502

Answers to Preparing for Citizenship

1. **GROUP ACTIVITY** Have panel members reread the chapter to review the passages by the figures whom they will represent. Suggest they find more quotations by these figures in Bartlett's *Familiar Quotations*.

2. **WRITING ACTIVITY** Direct students to write the passages from the Declaration of Independence in blue and the philosophes' names in red. Students may also be encouraged to paraphrase the passages from works that contain ideas used in the Declaration of Independence.

3. **COLLABORATIVE LEARNING** Each student should first decide which of the three categories—government, business, or science—he or she wants to research. After the teams are formed, refer students to the various resources mentioned for information. Remind students to summarize, not copy, the information. The illustrations should be related to the information. Let students decide how they would like to share their finished products with the whole class.

Time/Space Databank

★ ★ ★ ★ ★ ★ ★ ★ ★

Excerpts from the

Magna Carta (1215)

The *Magna Carta* brought constitutional monarchy to England by limiting the power of the rulers. Since the time of William the Conqueror, the law of the land held that ordinary people had rights; the *Magna Carta* made that law official. It established that no one is above the law, even the king. This is called the rule of law. The *Magna Carta* also balanced the monarch's power by putting the right to tax people into the hands of the people's representatives. It set the rights of private property so that kings or lords could not simply take away others' property. The *Magna Carta* also set a system of justice that called for proper trials and juries. Here are some excerpts from the *Magna Carta* (1215).

---

freeman someone with the rights and privileges of a citizen
gravity seriousness
saving except for
freehold property held for life
villein a kind of serf
wainage agricultural tools
bailiff officer of the law
chattels personal, movable property

The king cannot seize people, put them in jail, or expel them from the kingdom without a fair trial with a jury, according to the law.

A **freeman** shall not be fined for a small offense, except in proportion to the **gravity** of the offense; and for a great offense he shall be fined in proportion to the magnitude of the offense, **saving** his **freehold;** and a merchant in the same way, saving his merchandise; and the **villein** shall be fined in the same way, saving his **wainage,** if he shall be at our (i.e., the king's) mercy; and none of the above fines shall be imposed except by the oaths of honest men of the neighborhood.

No constable or other **bailiff** of ours [i.e., the king] shall take anyone's grain or other **chattels** without immediately paying for them in money, unless he is able to obtain a postponement at the good will of the seller.

No sheriff or bailiff of ours [i.e., the king] or any one else, shall take horses or wagons of any free man, for carrying purposes, except on the permission of that free man.

No free man shall be taken, or imprisoned, or banished, or in any way injured, nor will we go upon him, nor send upon him, except by the legal judgment of his peers, or by the law of the land.

Neither we nor our bailiffs will take the wood of another man for castles, or for anything else which we are doing, except by the permission of him to who the wood belongs.

To no one will we sell, no one will we deny or delay, right to justice.

Excerpts from the

English Bill of Rights (1689)

Almost 500 years after the *Magna Carta* was signed, the English Bill of Rights extended more individual rights to English citizens. In the Glorious Revolution of 1689, England's new king and queen had to accept the English Bill of Rights before they could take the throne. This law guaranteed basic freedoms, like the freedom from cruel and unusual punishment, the freedom for members of parliament to speak openly, and the freedom of parliament to meet often and without the influence of the crown. The Bill of Rights established the principle that the monarchy was limited by the parliament. Now the ruler was simply another official in the service of the state. Here are some excerpts from the English Bill of Rights (1689), in which the parliament declares.

That the **pretended** power of suspending of laws or the execution of laws by regal authority without consent of parliament is illegal.

pretended supposed

That the pretended power of dispensing with laws or the execution of laws by regal authority as it hath been assumed and exercised of late is illegal.

That the **levying** money for or to the use of the crown by **pretence** of **prerogative** without grant of parliament for a longer time or in other manner than the same is or shall be granted is illegal.

levying raising *pretence* a right that is claimed without basis in law *prerogative* an exclusive right or privilege

That it is the right of the subjects to petition the king and all commitments and prosecutions for such petitioning are illegal.

That the raising or keeping a standing army within the kingdom in time of peace unless it be with consent of parliament is against law.

Parliament limits the power of the king to raise or keep an army. Now the monarch needs the parliament's agreement to do this.

That the subjects which are Protestants may have arms for their defence suitable to their conditions and as allowed by law.

That election of members of parliament ought to be free.

That the freedom of speech and debates or proceedings in parliament ought not to be **impeached** or questioned in any court or place out of parliament.

impeached challenged

That excessive bail ought not to be required nor excessive fines imposed nor cruel and unusual punishments inflicted.

And that for **redress** of all **grievances** and for the amending, strengthening and preserving of the laws parliament ought to be held frequently.

redress setting right; correcting
grievances complaints or protests

505

Excerpts from the

Declaration of the Rights of Man and of the Citizen (1789)

The Declaration of the Rights of Man and of the Citizen was stro
influenced by the English Bill of Rights, the writings of Rousseau, an
the American Declaration of Independence. The rule of law is suppo
in the French Declaration, and France's rulers now lead only by the
agreement of the nation. To balance power, the Declaration establishe
national assembly which will also control the country's taxation. Also
down in the Declaration are the right to private property and the rig
a fair trial according to the law. For those who believed in the French
Revolution, the Declaration of the Rights of Man and the Citizen (178
was practically a holy document.

---

calamities disasters
solemn serious
inalienable cannot be
removed or transferred to
others

grievances complaints or
protests
incontestable
unquestionable
redound contribute
auspices protection

imprescriptible cannot be
removed

*The representatives of the French people, organized as a Nation
Assembly, believing that the ignorance, neglect, or contempt o
rights of man are the sole causes of public **calamities** and of t
corruption of governments, have determined to set forth in a **solemn**
laration the natural, **inalienable**, and sacred rights of man, in order
this declaration, being constantly before all members of the social bod
shall remind them continually of their rights and duties; in order tha
acts of the legislative power, as well as those of the executive power, n
be compared at any moment with the objects and purposes of all polit
institutions and may thus be more respected; and lastly, in order that
grievances of the citizens, based hereafter upon simple and **incontestable** principles, shall tend to the maintenance of the constitution
redound to the happiness of all. Therefore the National Assembly rec
nizes and proclaims, in the presence and under the **auspices** of the
Supreme Being, the following rights of man and of the citizen:*

1. *Men are born and remain free and equal in rights. Social dist
tions may be founded only upon the general good.*

2. *The aim of all political association is the preservation of the n
ural and **imprescriptible** rights of man. These rights are libe
property, security, and resistance to oppression.*

3. *The principle of all sovereignty resides essentially in the nation. No body nor individual may exercise any authority which does not proceed directly from the nation.*

4. *Liberty consists in the freedom to do everything which injures no one else; hence the exercise of the natural rights of each man has no limits except those which assure to the other members of the society the enjoyment of the same rights. These limits can only be determined by law.*

Liberty means that people are free to do anything as long as it does not harm others. People have the right to pursue their own goals, as long as they recognize that other people have the same rights, too.

5. *Law can only prohibit such actions as are hurtful to society. Nothing may be prevented which is not forbidden by law, and no one may be forced to do anything not provided for by law.*

6. *Law is the expression of the general will. Every citizen has a right to participate personally, or through his representative, in its formation. It must be the same for all, whether it protects or punishes. All citizens, being equal in the eyes of the law, are equally eligible to all dignities and to all public positions and occupations, according to their abilities, and without distinction except that of their virtues and talents.*

7. *No person shall be accused, arrested, or imprisoned, except in the cases and according to the forms prescribed by law. Anyone **soliciting**, transmitting, **executing**, or causing to be executed, any **arbitrary** order, shall be punished. But any citizen summoned or arrested **in virtue of** the law shall submit without delay, as resistance constitutes an offense.*

soliciting trying to get
executing carrying out
arbitrary not limited by law
in virtue of according to

8. *The law shall provide for such punishments only as are strictly and obviously necessary, and no one shall suffer punishment except it be legally inflicted in virtue of a law passed and **promulgated** before the **commission** of the offense.*

promulgated put into effect by formal announcement
commission carrying out

9. *As all persons are held innocent until they shall have been declared guilty, if arrest shall be deemed **indispensable**, all harshness not essential to the securing of the prisoner's persons shall be severely repressed by law.*

indispensible absolutely necessary

10. *No one shall be **disquieted** on account of his opinions, including his religious views, provided their **manifestation** does not disturb the public order established by law.*

disquieted troubled; made anxious
manifestation presentation

People have the right to speak, write, or publish their thoughts freely. The law may set limits to this freedom of speech, and people must respect the limits of the law.

duration length of time

inviolable unable to be broken or changed

indemnified compensated

11. *The free communication of ideas and opinions is one of the most precious of the rights of man. Every citizen may, accordingly, speak, write, and print with freedom, but shall be responsible for such abuses of this freedom as shall be defined by law.*

12. *The security of the rights of man and of the citizen requires public military forces. These forces are, therefore, established for the good of all and not for the personal advantage of those to whom they shall be intrusted.*

13. *A common contribution is essential for the maintenance of the public forces and for the cost of administration. This should be equitably distributed among all the citizens in proportion to their means.*

14. *All the citizens have a right to decide, either personally or by their representatives, as to the necessity of the public contribution: to grant this freely; to know to what uses it is put; and to fix the proportion, the mode of assessment and of collection and the* **duration** *of the taxes.*

15. *Society has the right to require of every public agent an account of his administration.*

16. *A society in which the observance of the law is not assured, nor the separation of powers defined, has no constitution at all.*

17. *Since property is an* **inviolable** *and sacred right, no one shall be deprived thereof except where public necessity, legally determined, shall clearly demand it, and then only on condition that the owner shall have been previously and equitably* **indemnified***.*

★ ★ ★ ★ ★ ★ ★ ★ ★

The Declaration of Independence

In Congress, July 4, 1776
The unanimous declaration of the thirteen united States of America

INTRODUCTION*

When, in the course of human events, it becomes necessary for one people to dissolve the political bands which have connected them with another, and to assume, among the powers of the earth, the separate and equal station to which the laws of nature and of nature's God entitle them, a decent respect to the opinions of mankind requires that they should declare the causes which impel them to the separation.

In the Declaration of Independence, the colonists explained why they were breaking away from Great Britain. They believed they had the right to form their own country.

powers of the earth *other nations*
station *place* **impel** *drive*

BASIC RIGHTS

We hold these truths to be self-evident: That all men are created equal, that they are **endowed** by their Creator with certain unalienable rights; that among these are life, liberty, and the pursuit of happiness; that, to secure these rights, governments are instituted among men, **deriving** their just powers from the consent of the governed; that whenever any form of government becomes destructive of these ends, it is the right of the people to alter or to abolish it, and to institute new government, laying its foundation on such principles, and organizing its powers in such form, as to them shall seem most likely to effect their safety and happiness. **Prudence,** indeed, will dictate that governments long established should not be changed for light and **transient** causes; and accordingly all experience hath shown that mankind are more disposed to suffer, while evils are sufferable, than to right themselves by abolishing the forms to which they are accustomed. But when a long train of abuses and **usurpations,** pursuing invariably the same object, evinces a design to reduce them under **absolute despotism**, it is their right, it is their duty, to throw off such government, and to provide new guards for their future security. Such has been the patient sufferance of these colonies; and such is now the necessity which **constrains** them to alter their former systems of government. The history of the present King of Great Britain is a history of repeated injuries and usurpations, all having in direct object the establishment of an absolute tyranny over these states. To prove this, let facts be submitted to a candid world.

The opening part of the Declaration is very famous. It says that all people are equal. Everyone has certain basic rights that are unalienable. That means that these rights are so basic that they cannot be taken away. Governments are formed to protect these basic rights. If a government does not do this, then the people have a right to begin a new one.

endowed *given* **deriving** *receiving*
prudence *wisdom* **transient** *temporary*
usurpations *seizing powers unjustly*
absolute despotism *complete and unjust control* **constrains** *forces*

Forming a new government meant ending the colonial ties to the king. The writers listed the wrongs of King George III to prove the need for their actions.

*Titles have been added to the Declaration to make it easier to read. These titles are not in the original document.

Colonists said the king had not let the colonies make their own laws. He had limited the people's representation in their assemblies.

assent agreement **inestimable** *immeasurable* **formidable** *causing fear* **compliance** *giving in to a request or a demand*

The king had made colonial assemblies meet at unusual times and places. This made going to assembly meetings hard for colonial representatives.

In some cases the king stopped the assembly from meeting at all.

annihilation *complete destruction* **convulsions** *disturbances* **endeavored** *tried*

The king stopped people from moving to the colonies and into new western lands. **hither** *here* **appropriations** *grants* **judiciary powers** *system of law courts*

The king prevented the colonies from choosing their own judges. Instead, he sent over judges who depended on him for their jobs and salaries.

tenure *term* **multitude** *large number* **harass** *bother, cause trouble*

The king kept British soldiers in the colonies, even though the colonists had not asked for them.

render *make* **jurisdiction** *authority* **quartering** *providing housing for* **mock** *false* **imposing** *forcing* **depriving** *taking away*

The king and Parliament had taxed the colonists without their consent. This was one of the most important reasons the colonists were angry at Great Britain.

★ ★ ★ ★ ★ ★ ★ ★ ★

CHARGES AGAINST THE KING

He has refused his assent to laws, the most wholesome and necessary for the public good.

He has forbidden his governors to pass laws of immediate and pressing importance, unless suspended in their operation till his **assent** *should be obtained; and, when so suspended, he has utterly neglected to attend to them.*

He has refused to pass other laws for the accommodation of large districts of people, unless those people would relinquish the right of representation in the legislature, a right **inestimable** *to them, and* **formidable** *to tyrants only.*

He has called together legislative bodies at places unusual, uncomfortable, and distant from the depository of their public records, for the sole purpose of fatiguing them into **compliance** *with his measures.*

He has dissolved representative houses repeatedly, for opposing, with manly firmness, his invasions on the rights of the people.

He has refused for a long time, after such dissolutions, to cause others to be elected; whereby the legislative powers, incapable of **annihilation,** *have returned to the people at large for their exercise; the state remaining, in the mean time, exposed to all the dangers of invasions from without and* **convulsions** *within.*

He has **endeavored** *to prevent the population of these states; for that purpose obstructing the laws for the naturalization of foreigners; refusing to pass others to encourage their migration* **hither,** *and raising the conditions of new* **appropriations** *of lands.*

He has obstructed the administration of justice, by refusing his assent to laws for establishing **judiciary powers.**

He has made judges dependent on his will alone, for the **tenure** *of their offices, and the amount of payment of their salaries.*

He has erected a **multitude** *of new offices, and sent hither swarms of officers to* **harass** *our people and eat out their substance.*

He has kept among us, in times of peace, standing armies, without the consent of our legislatures.

He has affected to **render** *the military independent of, and superior to, the civil power.*

He has combined with others to subject us to a **jurisdiction** *foreign to our constitution and unacknowledged by our laws, giving his assent to their acts of pretended legislation:*

For **quartering** *large bodies of armed troops among us;*

For protecting them, by a **mock** *trial, from punishment for any murders which they should commit on the inhabitants of these states;*

For cutting off our trade with all parts of the world;

For **imposing** *taxes on us without our consent;*

For **depriving** *us, in many cases, of the benefits of trial by jury;*

★ ★ ★ ★ ★ ★ ★ ★ ★

For transporting us beyond seas, to be tried for pretended offenses;

For **abolishing** the free system of English laws in a neighboring province, establishing therein an **arbitrary** government, and enlarging its boundaries, so as to render it at once an example and **fit instrument** for introducing the same absolute rule into these colonies;

abolishing getting rid of **arbitrary** *tyrannical* **fit instrument** suitable tool *invested* having

For taking away our charters, abolishing our most valuable laws, and altering fundamentally the forms of our governments.

For suspending our own legislatures, and declaring themselves **invested** with power to legislate for us in all cases whatsoever.

He has **abdicated** government here, by declaring us out of his protection and waging war against us.

The colonists felt that the king had waged war on them.

abdicated given up **plundered** robbed

He has **plundered** our seas, ravaged our coasts, burned our towns, and destroyed the lives of our people.

He is at this time transporting large armies of foreign **mercenaries** to complete the works of death, desolation, and tyranny already begun with circumstances of cruelty and **perfidy** scarcely paralleled in the most **barbarous** ages, and totally unworthy the head of a civilized nation.

The king had hired German soldiers and sent them to the colonies to keep order.

mercenaries hired soldiers **desolation** *misery* **perfidy** treachery **barbarous** *uncivilized* **insurrection** revolt

He has constrained our fellow-citizens, taken captive on the high seas, to bear arms against their country, to become the executioners of their friends and brethren, or to fall themselves by their hands.

He has excited domestic **insurrection** among us, and has endeavored to bring on the inhabitants of our frontiers, the merciless Indian savages, whose known rule of warfare is an undistinguished destruction of all ages, sexes, and conditions.

RESPONSE TO THE KING

In every stage of these oppressions we have **petitioned** for **redress** in the most humbles terms; our repeated petitions have been answered only by repeated injury. A prince, whose character is thus marked by every act which may define a tyrant, is unfit to be the ruler of a free people.

The colonists said that they had asked the king to change his policies, but he had not listened to them.

petitioned requested **redress** relief **unwarrantable** unfair **magnanimity** *generosity* **conjured** requested earnestly *disavow* turn away from **consanguinity** *kinship* **acquiesce** agree **denounces** condemns

Nor have we been wanting in our attentions to our British brethren. We have warned them, from time to time, of attempts by their legislature to extend an **unwarrantable** jurisdiction over us. We have reminded them of the circumstances of our emigration and settlement here. We have appealed to their native justice and **magnanimity;** and we have **conjured** them, by the ties of our common kindred, to **disavow** these usurpations, which would inevitably interrupt our connections and correspondence. They, too, have been deaf to the voice of justice and of **consanguinity.** We must, therefore, **acquiesce** in the necessity which **denounces** our separation, and hold them, as we hold the rest of mankind, enemies in war, in peace friends.

★ ★ ★ ★ ★ ★ ★ ★ ★

The writers declared that the colonies were free and independent states, equal to the world's other states. They had the powers to make war and peace and to trade with other countries.

rectitude moral rightness *absolved* freed *allegiance* loyalty *levy* declare *contract* make *mutually* together

The signers pledged their lives to the support of this Declaration. The Continental Congress ordered the Declaration of Independence to be read in all the states and to the army.

INDEPENDENCE

We, therefore, the representatives of the United States of America, in General Congress assembled, appealing to the Supreme Judge of the world for the **rectitude** of our intentions, do, in the name and by the authority of the good people of these colonies, solemnly publish and declare, that these United Colonies are, and of right ought to be, FREE AND INDEPENDENT STATES; that they are **absolved** from all **allegiance** to the British crown, and that all political connection between them and the state of Great Britain is, and ought to be, totally dissolved; and that, as free and independent states, they have full power to **levy** war, conclude peace, **contract** alliances, establish commerce, and do all other acts and things which independent states may of right do. And for the support of this declaration, with a firm reliance on the protection of Divine Providence, we **mutually** pledge to each other our lives, our fortunes, and our sacred honor.

John Hancock

NEW HAMPSHIRE	PENNSYLVANIA	VIRGINIA
Josiah Bartlett	Robert Morris	George Wythe
William Whipple	Benjamin Rush	Richard Henry Lee
Matthew Thornton	Benjamin Franklin	Thomas Jefferson
	John Morton	Benjamin Harrison
MASSACHUSETTS	George Clymer	Thomas Nelson, Jr.
John Adams	James Smith	Francis Lightfoot Lee
Samuel Adams	George Taylor	Carter Braxton
Robert Treat Paine	James Wilson	
Elbridge Gerry	George Ross	SOUTH CAROLINA
		Edward Rutledge
NEW YORK	DELAWARE	Thomas Heyward, Jr.
William Floyd	Caesar Rodney	Thomas Lynch, Jr.
Philip Livingston	George Read	Arthur Middleton
Francis Lewis	Thomas McKean	
Lewis Morris		CONNECTICUT
	MARYLAND	Roger Sherman
RHODE ISLAND	Samuel Chase	Samuel Huntington
Stephen Hopkins	William Paca	William Williams
William Ellery	Thomas Stone	Oliver Wolcott
	Charles Carroll of	
	Carrollton	GEORGIA
NEW JERSEY		Button Gwinnett
Richard Stockton		Lyman Hall
John Witherspoon	NORTH CAROLINA	George Walton
Francis Hopkinson	William Hooper	
John Hart	Joseph Hewes	
Abraham Clark	John Penn	

Heraldry

Symbols of heraldry

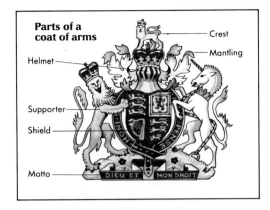

Parts of a coat of arms

Crest

Mantling

Helmet

Supporter

Shield

Motto

DIEU ET MON DROIT

The displaying of arms

Coats of arms were first displayed on the shields of knights. Later, arms appeared on flags, clothes, and other possessions.

WORLD BOOK illustrations by Oxford Illustrators Limited

Symbols used on a coat of arms

Coats of arms were developed during the 1100's as a way to help a knight's followers recognize him on the battlefield. The colors, designs, lines, and *cadency* (status) symbols shown below became standard and were used in different combinations according to specific rules.

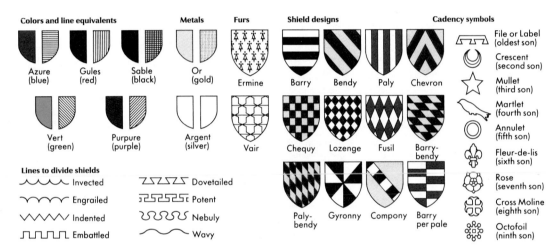

Colors and line equivalents

Azure (blue)   Gules (red)   Sable (black)

Vert (green)   Purpure (purple)

Metals

Or (gold)   Argent (silver)

Furs

Ermine

Vair

Shield designs

Barry   Bendy   Paly   Chevron

Chequy   Lozenge   Fusil   Barry-bendy

Paly-bendy   Gyronny   Compony   Barry per pale

Cadency symbols

File or Label (oldest son)

Crescent (second son)

Mullet (third son)

Martlet (fourth son)

Annulet (fifth son)

Fleur-de-lis (sixth son)

Rose (seventh son)

Cross Moline (eighth son)

Octofoil (ninth son)

Lines to divide shields

 Invected

Engrailed

Indented

Embattled

Dovetailed

Potent

Nebuly

Wavy

Kinds of charges

A charge is a symbol of an object or figure that appears on a shield. Animals are among the most popular charges.

Swords   Ship   Tower

Unicorn   Lion   Dragon

Arms   Wolf's head   Tortoise

Patterns of family relationships

Two or more arms were sometimes combined on one shield in order to show family relationships. The earliest methods of *marshaling,* as this procedure is called, are shown below. The arms of two families are placed side by side or one within the other.

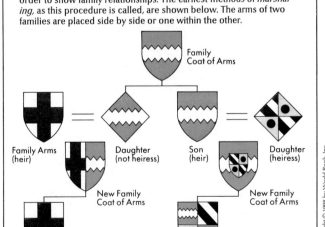

Family Coat of Arms

Family Arms (heir)   =   Daughter (not heiress)   Son (heir)   =   Daughter (heiress)

New Family Coat of Arms   New Family Coat of Arms

Son (heir)   Son (heir)

Famous ancient and medieval explorers

Explorer	Nationality	Main achievements	Date
* Alexander the Great	Macedonian	Reached Afghanistan, western India.	c.331 B.C.-326 B.C.
* Eric the Red	Norwegian	Sailed to Greenland from Iceland.	c.982
* Ericson, Leif	Norwegian	Probably the first European to reach mainland North America.	c.1000
* Ibn Batuta	Arabian	Traveled through the Middle East and India; visited China and the East Indies.	1325-1354
Odoric of Pordenone	Italian	Traveled in Turkey, Iran, across central Asia, and in the Indian and South Pacific oceans.	c.1314-c.1330
* Polo, Marco	Italian	Visited Sri Lanka, China, India, Iran, and Sumatra.	1271-1295
* Pytheas	Greek	Sailed from the Mediterranean Sea to the North Atlantic Ocean.	c.300 B.C.
Rubruck, William of	Flemish	Traveled through central Asia to Mongolia.	1253-1255
Zhang Qian	Chinese	Traveled from China to central Asia.	128-126 B.C.

*Has a separate biography in WORLD BOOK.

Explorers of the great age of European discovery

Explorer	Nationality	Main achievements	Date
* Balboa, Vasco Núñez de	Spanish	Led expedition across Isthmus of Panama; sighted Pacific Ocean.	1513
* Cabeza de Vaca, Álvar Núñez	Spanish	Explored Gulf Plains from Texas to Mexico.	1528-1536
* Cabot, John	Italian	Sailed across the North Atlantic to what is now Canada.	1497-1498
* Cabot, Sebastian	Italian	Explored South American coast to the Río de la Plata.	1526-1530
* Cabral, Pedro Álvares	Portuguese	Reached Brazilian coast; sailed around Africa to India.	1500-1501
* Cartier, Jacques	French	Sailed up the St. Lawrence River.	1535
* Columbus, Christopher	Italian	Made four voyages to the West Indies and Caribbean lands.	1492-1504
* Coronado, Francisco de	Spanish	Explored the American Southwest.	1540-1542
* Cortés, Hernando	Spanish	Conquered Mexico.	1519-1521
* Da Gama, Vasco	Portuguese	First European to reach India by sea.	1498
* De Soto, Hernando	Spanish	Explored American Southeast; reached Mississippi River.	1539-1542
* Dias, Bartolomeu	Portuguese	First European to round the Cape of Good Hope.	1487-1488
* Drake, Sir Francis	English	First English explorer to sail around the world.	1577-1580
* Frobisher, Sir Martin	English	Searched North American coast for a Northwest Passage.	1576-1578
* Magellan, Ferdinand	Portuguese	Commanded first globe-circling voyage, completed in 1522 after his death.	1519-1521
* Oñate, Juan de	Spanish	Explored American Southwest.	1598-1605
* Orellana, Francisco de	Spanish	Explored Amazon River.	1541
* Pizarro, Francisco	Spanish	Conquered Peru; founded Lima.	1531-1535
* Ponce de León, Juan	Spanish	Explored Florida.	1513
* Verrazano, Giovanni da	Italian	Searched for a Northwest Passage.	1524
* Vespucci, Amerigo	Italian	Sailed to the West Indies and South America.	1499-1504

*Has a separate biography in WORLD BOOK.

Famous explorers of Africa

Explorer	Nationality	Main achievements	Date
Bruce, James	Scottish	Rediscovered source of the Blue Nile.	1770
* Burton, Sir Richard	English	Explored Arabia and East Africa; reached Lake Tanganyika.	1853-1858
Caillié, René	French	Explored western Africa; crossed the Sahara.	1826-1828
Clapperton, Hugh	Scottish	Explored northern Nigeria and Lake Chad region.	1822-1827
* Emin Pasha	German	Explored east-central Africa.	1878-1892
Laing, Alexander Gordon	Scottish	Explored Niger River Basin; reached Timbuktu.	1822; 1826
* Livingstone, David	Scottish	Traced upper course of the Zambezi River; reached Victoria Falls and Lake Ngami.	1849-1873
* Park, Mungo	Scottish	Explored course of the Niger River.	1795-1797; 1805-1806
Speke, John Hanning	English	Reached Lake Tanganyika and Lake Victoria.	1858
* Stanley, Sir Henry	Welsh	Explored the Congo River.	1874-1889

*Has a separate article in WORLD BOOK.

Explorers of Australia and the Pacific Ocean

Explorer	Nationality	Main achievements	Date
Bougainville, Louis Antoine de	French	Led first French expedition around the world.	1766-1769
Burke, Robert O'Hara	Irish	One of the first explorers to cross Australia from south to north, with William John Wills.	1860-1861
* Cook, James	English	Explored South Pacific.	1768-1779
* Dampier, William	English	Explored coasts of Australia, New Guinea, and New Britain.	1691-1701
Eyre, Edward John	English	Explored southern coast of Australia.	1840-1841
Jansz, Willem	Dutch	First known European to sight and land in Australia.	1606
Stuart, John McDouall	Scottish	Made six trips into the interior of Australia.	1858-1862
Sturt, Charles	English	Explored southeastern Australia; reached Darling River.	1829-1830
* Tasman, Abel Janszoon	Dutch	Sailed to Tasmania and New Zealand.	1642
Warburton, Peter Egerton	English	Crossed Australia from Alice Springs to Roebourne.	1873
Wills, William John	English	One of the first explorers to cross Australia from south to north, with Robert O'Hara Burke.	1860-1861

*Has a separate article in WORLD BOOK.

Extracted from the Exploration article in *World Book*. Copyright © 1998 by World Book, Inc.

Major developments

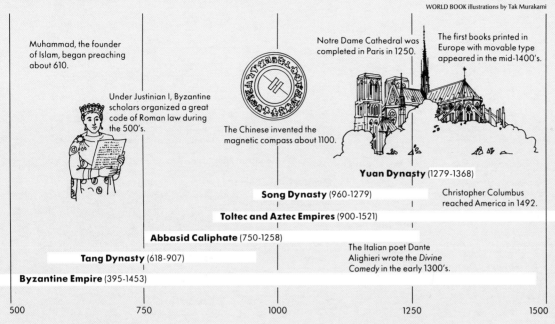

WORLD BOOK illustrations by Tak Murakami

Muhammad, the founder of Islam, began preaching about 610.

Under Justinian I, Byzantine scholars organized a great code of Roman law during the 500's.

The Chinese invented the magnetic compass about 1100.

Notre Dame Cathedral was completed in Paris in 1250.

The first books printed in Europe with movable type appeared in the mid-1400's.

Yuan Dynasty (1279-1368)

Song Dynasty (960-1279)

Christopher Columbus reached America in 1492.

Toltec and Aztec Empires (900-1521)

Abbasid Caliphate (750-1258)

The Italian poet Dante Alighieri wrote the *Divine Comedy* in the early 1300's.

Tang Dynasty (618-907)

Byzantine Empire (395-1453)

| 500 | 750 | 1000 | 1250 | 1500 |

Between 300 and 1500, new civilizations appeared in Africa and the Americas. In the Middle East, the Muslim Arabs rose to power and conquered a huge empire by the mid-700's. In the 1200's, Mongol warriors swept through Asia, creating one of the largest empires in history.

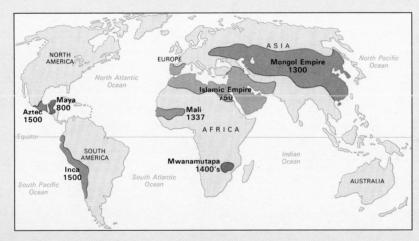

WORLD BOOK map

Important dates

300's-mid-1000's The Ghana Empire, the first great black empire in western Africa, existed as a trading state.

527-565 The Byzantine Empire reached its greatest extent under Emperor Justinian I.

622 Muhammad, prophet of Islam, fled from Mecca to Medina. His flight, called the Hegira, marks the beginning of the Islamic calendar.

732 Charles Martel and the Franks defeated invading Muslims in fighting in west-central France. The victory prevented the Muslims from overrunning Europe.

750 The Abbasids became the caliphs of the Islamic world.

800 Pope Leo III crowned Charlemagne, ruler of the Franks, emperor of the Romans.

c. 988 Vladimir I (also spelled Volodymyr) established

Christianity among the East Slavs, ancestors of the Belarusian, Russian, and Ukrainian people.

1054 Rivalries between the church in Rome and the church in Constantinople resulted in their separation as the Roman Catholic Church and Eastern Orthodox Churches.

1192 Yoritomo became the first shogun to rule Japan. Shogun rule lasted until 1867.

1215 English barons forced King John to grant a charter of liberties called Magna Carta.

1279 The Mongols gained control of all China.

1300's The Renaissance began in Italy.

1368 The Ming dynasty began its nearly 300-year rule of China.

1453 The Ottoman Turks captured Constantinople (Istanbul) and overthrew the Byzantine Empire.

World, History of the

Major developments

WORLD BOOK illustrations by Tak Murakami

Nicolaus Copernicus proposed in 1543 that the sun is the center of the universe.

Michelangelo completed painting the ceiling of the Sistine Chapel in the Vatican in 1512.

William Shakespeare wrote many of the world's greatest dramas between 1590 and 1616.

Charles Darwin published his theory of evolution in 1859 in *The Origin of Species*.

European Colonial Expansion in Africa and Asia (1870-1914)

Latin-American Wars of Independence (1791-1824)

French Revolution (1789-1799)

Revolutionary War in America (1775-1783)

Industrial Revolution (1700-mid-1800's)

Manchu Rule of China (1644-1912)

Tokugawa Shogunate in Japan (1603-1867)

Mogul Empire (1526-1707)

Ludwig van Beethoven composed many of his greatest symphonies between 1800 and 1815.

Alexander Graham Bell invented the telephone in 1876.

Voyages of Discovery (1400's-1500's)

Ottoman Empire (1326-1922)

Renaissance (1300-1600)

| 1500 | 1600 | 1700 | 1800 | 1900 |

European colonial empires had spread over much of the world by the late 1800's. The largest empires of the period belonged to Great Britain, France, and Germany.

- Belgium
- France
- Germany
- Great Britain
- Italy
- Netherlands
- Portugal
- Spain

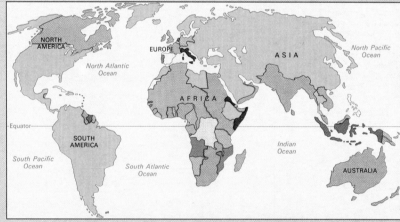

NORTH AMERICA
EUROPE
ASIA
North Pacific Ocean
North Atlantic Ocean
AFRICA
-Equator-
SOUTH AMERICA
South Pacific Ocean
South Atlantic Ocean
Indian Ocean
AUSTRALIA

WORLD BOOK map

Important dates

1500's The Reformation led to the birth of Protestantism.

1519-1521 Ferdinand Magellan commanded the first globe-circling voyage, completed in 1522 after his death.

1521 The Spanish conquistador Hernando Cortés defeated the Aztec Indians of Mexico.

1526 Babar, a Muslim prince, invaded India and founded the Mogul Empire.

1588 The Royal Navy of England defeated the Spanish Armada, establishing England as a great naval power.

1644-1912 The Manchus ruled China as the Qing dynasty.

1776 The 13 American Colonies adopted the Declaration of Independence, establishing the United States of America.

1789 The French Revolution began.

1815 Napoleon Bonaparte was defeated in the Battle of Waterloo, ending his attempt to rule Europe.

1853-1854 Commodore Matthew Perry visited Japan and opened two ports to U.S. trade, ending Japan's isolation.

1858 Great Britain took over the rule of India from the East India Company after the Sepoy Rebellion.

1865 Union forces defeated the Confederates in the American Civil War after four years of fighting.

1869 The Suez Canal opened.

1871 Germany became united under the Prussian king, who ruled the new empire as Kaiser Wilhelm I.

1898 The United States took control of Guam, Puerto Rico, and the Philippines following the Spanish-American War.

Major developments

WORLD BOOK illustrations by Tak Murakami

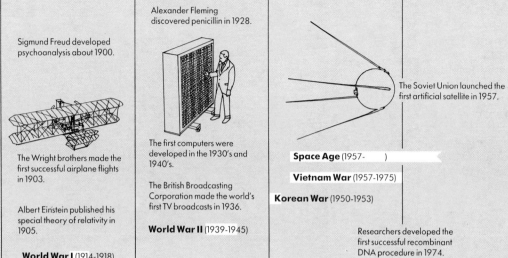

Sigmund Freud developed psychoanalysis about 1900.

The Wright brothers made the first successful airplane flights in 1903.

Albert Einstein published his special theory of relativity in 1905.

World War I (1914-1918)

Alexander Fleming discovered penicillin in 1928.

The first computers were developed in the 1930's and 1940's.

The British Broadcasting Corporation made the world's first TV broadcasts in 1936.

World War II (1939-1945)

The Soviet Union launched the first artificial satellite in 1957.

Space Age (1957-   )

Vietnam War (1957-1975)

Korean War (1950-1953)

Researchers developed the first successful recombinant DNA procedure in 1974.

| 1900 | 1925 | 1950 | 1975 | 2000 |

The wealth of nations can be compared on the basis of each country's *gross domestic product* (GDP). The GDP is the value of all goods and services produced within a country in a year. The developing countries of Africa and Asia have the lowest GDP per person.

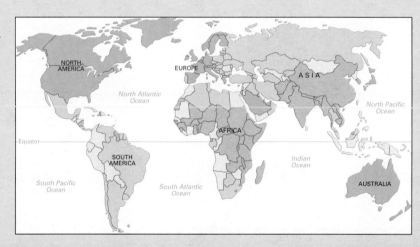

High GDP per person

Medium GDP per person

Low GDP per person

Very low GDP per person

WORLD BOOK map;
1991 GDP estimates.

Important dates

1914 The assassination of Archduke Francis Ferdinand of Austria-Hungary started World War I.

1917 The Bolsheviks (Communists) seized power in Russia.

1933 Adolf Hitler became dictator of Germany.

1939 Germany invaded Poland, starting World War II.

1941 The Japanese attacked Pearl Harbor, and the United States entered World War II.

1945 The United Nations was established.

1945 The first atomic bombs used in warfare were dropped by U.S. planes on Hiroshima and Nagasaki.

1945 World War II ended in Europe on May 7 and in the Pacific on September 2.

1949 The Chinese Communists conquered China.

1950 North Korean Communist troops invaded South Korea, starting the Korean War.

1957 The Vietnam War started when South Vietnamese rebels attacked the U.S.-backed South Vietnamese government.

1969 U.S. astronauts made the first manned moon landing.

1989-1990 Democratic reforms spread across Eastern Europe, and several non-Communist governments replaced Communist dictatorships.

1990 East Germany and West Germany were reunited, ending the division of Germany that had begun soon after the end of World War II.

1991 The Communist Party of the Soviet Union lost control of the Soviet government, and the Soviet Union ceased to exist.

WORLD: *Political*

ABBREVIATIONS

BOS. AND HERZ.
  Bosnia and Herzegovina
CEN. AFR. REP.
  Central African Republic
DEN. Denmark
FR. France
GR. Greece
IT. Italy
N. North, Northern
NETH. Netherlands
N.Z. New Zealand
PORT. Portugal
S. South
SP. Spain
U.A.E. United Arab
  Emirates
U.K. United Kingdom
U.S. United States
W. Western

— National boundary

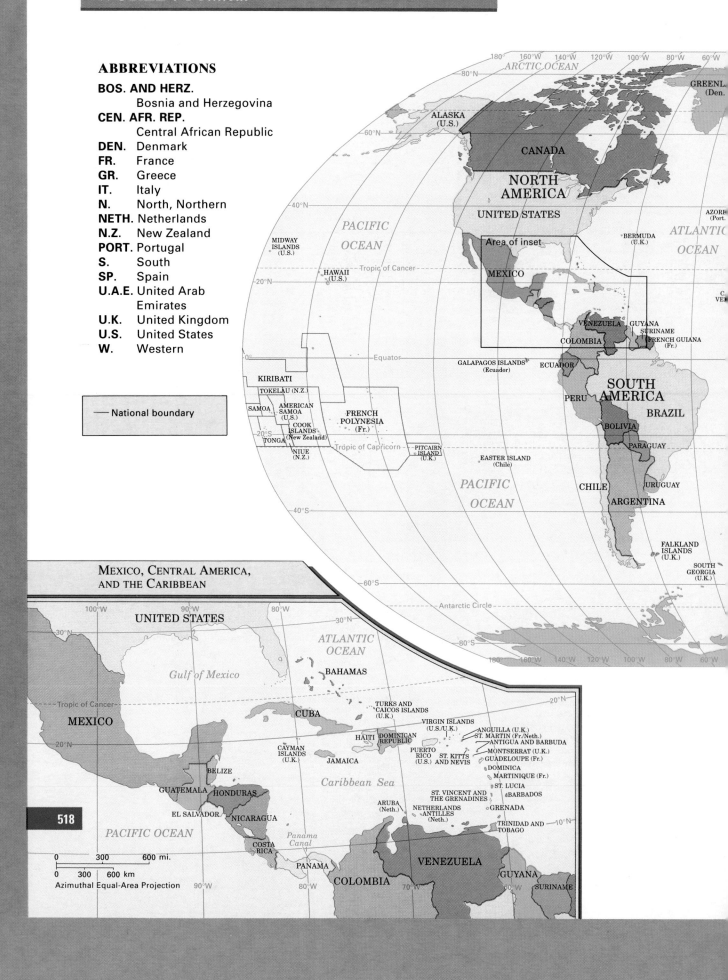

MEXICO, CENTRAL AMERICA, AND THE CARIBBEAN

518

0   300   600 mi.

0   300   600 km
Azimuthal Equal-Area Projection

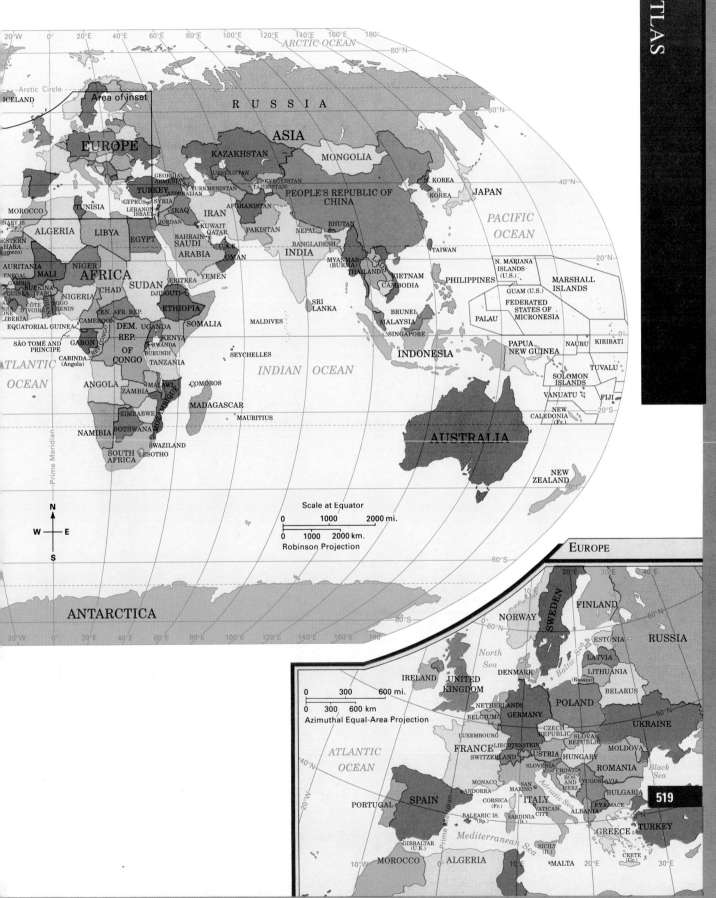

20°W 0° 20°E 40°E 60°E 80°E 100°E 120°E 140°E 160°E 180°

ARCTIC OCEAN

80°N

Arctic Circle

ICELAND

Area of inset

RUSSIA

60°N

EUROPE

ASIA

KAZAKHSTAN

MONGOLIA

40°N

GEORGIA
ARMENIA
TURKEY
AZERBAIJAN

UZBEKISTAN
TURKMENISTAN
KYRGYZSTAN
TAJIKISTAN

N. KOREA
S. KOREA

JAPAN

CYPRUS
LEBANON
ISRAEL
SYRIA
IRAQ
JORDAN

IRAN

AFGHANISTAN

PEOPLE'S REPUBLIC OF
CHINA

PACIFIC
OCEAN

MOROCCO

TUNISIA

NARY IS.
(Sp.)

ALGERIA

LIBYA

EGYPT

SAUDI
ARABIA

KUWAIT
QATAR
BAHRAIN
U.A.E.
OMAN

PAKISTAN

NEPAL

BHUTAN

BANGLADESH

INDIA

TAIWAN

20°N

ESTERN
HARA
(orocco)

AURITANIA
NIGER

MALI

AFRICA

CHAD

SUDAN

ERITREA

DJIBOUTI

YEMEN

MYANMAR
(BURMA)
THAILAND
LAOS
VIETNAM
CAMBODIA

PHILIPPINES

N. MARIANA
ISLANDS
(U.S.)

GUAM (U.S.)

MARSHALL
ISLANDS

ENEGAL
SENEGAL
GAMBIA
GUINEA
BURKINA
FASO
NIGERIA
TOGO
BENIN
CÔTE
D'IVOIRE

RRA
ONE
LIBERIA

CAMEROON

CEN. AFR. REP.

ETHIOPIA

SOMALIA

SRI
LANKA

MALDIVES

BRUNEI
MALAYSIA

FEDERATED
STATES OF
MICRONESIA

PALAU

0°

EQUATORIAL GUINEA

SÃO TOMÉ AND
PRINCIPE

GABON

REP. CONGO

DEM.
REP.
OF
CONGO

UGANDA
RWANDA
BURUNDI

KENYA

TANZANIA

SEYCHELLES

SINGAPORE

INDONESIA

PAPUA
NEW GUINEA

NAURU

KIRIBATI

CABINDA
(Angola)

INDIAN OCEAN

TUVALU

ATLANTIC
OCEAN

ANGOLA

ZAMBIA

MALAWI

MOZAMBIQUE

COMOROS

MADAGASCAR

MAURITIUS

SOLOMON
ISLANDS

VANUATU

FIJI

20°S

ZIMBABWE

NEW
CALEDONIA
(Fr.)

NAMIBIA

BOTSWANA

SWAZILAND

SOUTH
AFRICA

LESOTHO

AUSTRALIA

N
W — E
S

Scale at Equator

0 1000 2000 mi.

0 1000 2000 km.

Robinson Projection

NEW
ZEALAND

40°S

60°S

Prime Meridian

ANTARCTICA

80°S

20°W 0° 20°E 40°E 60°E 80°E 100°E 120°E 140°E 160°E 180°

EUROPE

20°E 30°E 40°E

10°E

SWEDEN

FINLAND

NORWAY

60°N

0°

ESTONIA

RUSSIA

North
Sea

DENMARK

Baltic Sea

LATVIA

LITHUANIA
(Russia)

BELARUS

IRELAND

UNITED
KINGDOM

NETHERLANDS

POLAND

0 300 600 mi.

0 300 600 km

Azimuthal Equal-Area Projection

BELGIUM

GERMANY

CZECH
REPUBLIC

SLOVAK
REPUBLIC

UKRAINE

50°N

LUXEMBOURG

FRANCE

LIECHTENSTEIN

SWITZERLAND

AUSTRIA

HUNGARY

MOLDOVA

ATLANTIC
OCEAN

40°N

SLOVENIA

CROATIA

BOS.
AND
HERZ.

YUGOSLAVIA

ROMANIA

Black
Sea

MONACO

SAN
MARINO

Adriatic Sea

BULGARIA

PORTUGAL

SPAIN

ANDORRA

ITALY

F.Y.R. MACE.

ALBANIA

519

CORSICA
(Fr.)

VATICAN
CITY

GREECE

TURKEY

BALEARIC IS.
(Sp.)

SARDINIA
(It.)

Prime Meridian

20°W

10°W

GIBRALTAR
(U.K.)

Mediterranean Sea

SICILY
(It.)

CRETE
(Gr.)

10°W

MOROCCO

ALGERIA

10°E

MALTA

20°E

30°E

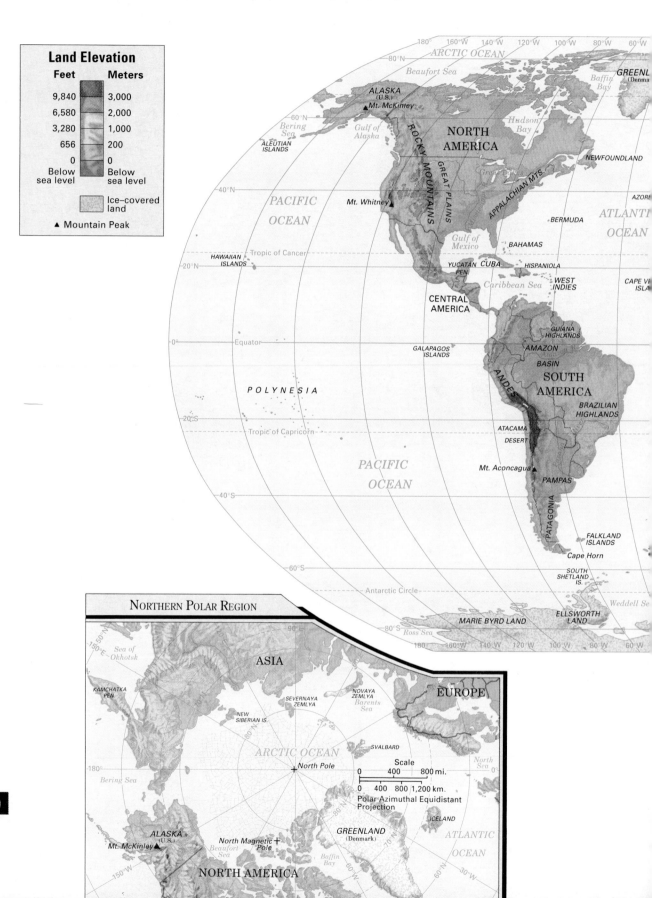

Land Elevation

Feet		Meters
9,840		3,000
6,580		2,000
3,280		1,000
656		200
0		0
Below sea level		Below sea level

Ice–covered land

▲ Mountain Peak

ARCTIC OCEAN
Beaufort Sea
GREENL (Denma
Baffin Bay
ALASKA (U.S.)
▲ Mt. McKinley
Bering Sea
Gulf of Alaska
ROCKY MOUNTAINS
NORTH AMERICA
Hudson Bay
NEWFOUNDLAND
ALEUTIAN ISLANDS
GREAT PLAINS
Gr
AZOR
PACIFIC OCEAN
Mt. Whitney ▲
APPALACHIAN MTS.
BERMUDA
ATLANTI OCEAN
Tropic of Cancer
Gulf of Mexico
BAHAMAS
HAWAIIAN ISLANDS
YUCATAN PEN.
CUBA
HISPANIOLA
WEST INDIES
CAPE VE ISLA
CENTRAL AMERICA
Caribbean Sea
Equator
GALAPAGOS ISLANDS
GUIANA HIGHLANDS
AMAZON
BASIN
SOUTH AMERICA
POLYNESIA
ANDES
BRAZILIAN HIGHLANDS
ATACAMA DESERT
Tropic of Capricorn
PACIFIC OCEAN
Mt. Aconcagua ▲
PAMPAS
PATAGONIA
FALKLAND ISLANDS
Cape Horn
SOUTH SHETLAND IS.
Antarctic Circle
Weddell Se
MARIE BYRD LAND
ELLSWORTH LAND
Ross Sea

NORTHERN POLAR REGION

Sea of Okhotsk
ASIA
KAMCHATKA PEN.
SEVERNAYA ZEMLYA
NOVAYA ZEMLYA
Barents Sea
EUROPE
NEW SIBERIAN IS.
SVALBARD
North Sea
ARCTIC OCEAN
North Pole
Bering Sea
Scale
0   400   800 mi.
0   400   800 1,200 km.
Polar Azimuthal Equidistant Projection
ICELAND
ALASKA (U.S.)
Mt. McKinley ▲
North Magnetic Pole +
Beaufort Sea
GREENLAND (Denmark)
ATLANTIC OCEAN
Baffin Bay
NORTH AMERICA

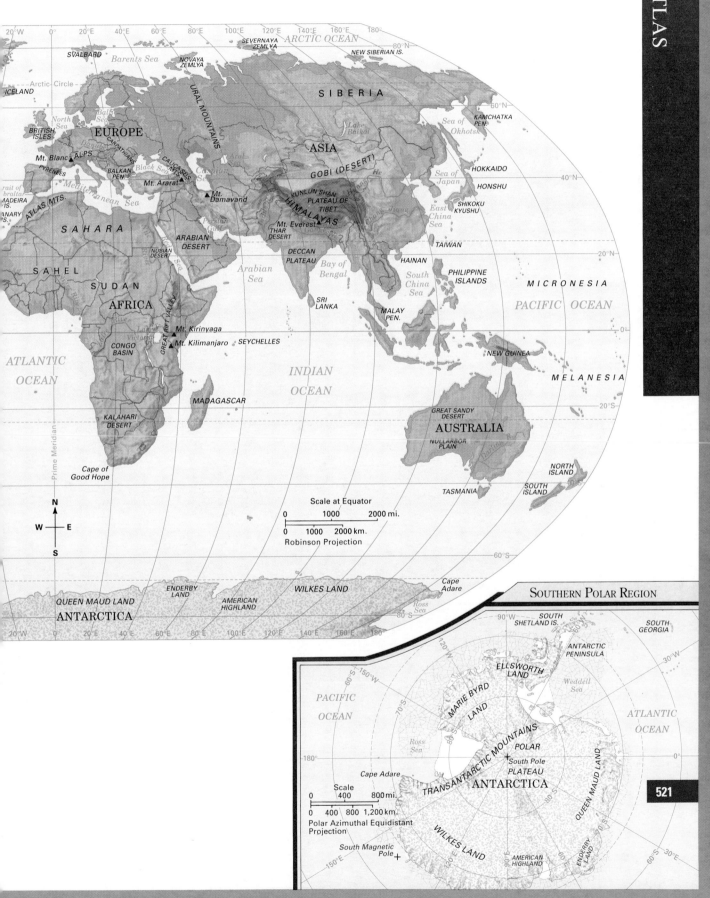

ARCTIC OCEAN

SVALBARD
Barents Sea
NOVAYA
ZEMLYA
SEVERNAYA
ZEMLYA
NEW SIBERIAN IS.
80°N

ICELAND

Arctic Circle

North
Sea

BRITISH
ISLES

EUROPE

URAL MOUNTAINS

SIBERIA

60°N

Lake
Baikal

Sea of
Okhotsk

KAMCHATKA
PEN.

ASIA

ALPS
Mt. Blanc
CARPATHIANS
PYRENEES
BALKAN
PEN.
Black Sea
CAUCASUS
MTS.
Mt. Ararat

Caspian
Sea

GOBI (DESERT)

HOKKAIDO

40°N

Mediterranean Sea

Strait of
Gibraltar
MADEIRA
IS.
CANARY
IS.
ATLAS MTS.

Mt.
Damavand

KUNLUN SHAN
HIMALAYAS

PLATEAU OF
TIBET

Sea of
Japan

HONSHU

SHIKOKU
KYUSHU

East
China
Sea

Mt. Everest
SAHARA
ARABIAN
DESERT

THAR
DESERT

TAIWAN

20°N

SAHEL

SUDAN

NUBIAN
DESERT

Arabian
Sea

DECCAN
PLATEAU

Bay of
Bengal

South
China
Sea

HAINAN

PHILIPPINE
ISLANDS

MICRONESIA

AFRICA

GREAT RIFT VALLEY

SRI
LANKA

MALAY
PEN.

PACIFIC OCEAN

0°

Lake
Victoria

Mt. Kirinyaga
Mt. Kilimanjaro

SEYCHELLES

NEW GUINEA

ATLANTIC
OCEAN

CONGO
BASIN

INDIAN
OCEAN

MELANESIA

MADAGASCAR

20°S

KALAHARI
DESERT

GREAT SANDY
DESERT

AUSTRALIA

Prime Meridian

NULLARBOR
PLAIN

NORTH
ISLAND

Cape of
Good Hope

N
W   E
S

TASMANIA

SOUTH
ISLAND

Scale at Equator

0   1000   2000 mi.

0   1000   2000 km.

Robinson Projection

60°S

ENDERBY
LAND

WILKES LAND

Cape
Adare

QUEEN MAUD LAND
ANTARCTICA
AMERICAN
HIGHLAND
Ross
Sea
80°S

20°W   0°   20°E   40°E   60°E   80°E   100°E   120°E   140°E   160°E   180°

SOUTHERN POLAR REGION

SOUTH
SHETLAND IS.
90°W

SOUTH
GEORGIA

PACIFIC
OCEAN

60°S
150°W

70°S

ELLSWORTH
LAND

ANTARCTIC
PENINSULA

Weddell
Sea

ATLANTIC
OCEAN

30°W

MARIE BYRD
LAND

Ross
Sea

180°

TRANSANTARCTIC MOUNTAINS
POLAR
South Pole
PLATEAU

QUEEN MAUD LAND

0°

Cape Adare
ANTARCTICA

Scale
0   400   800 mi.

0   400   800   1,200 km.

Polar Azimuthal Equidistant
Projection

WILKES LAND
AMERICAN
HIGHLAND

ENDERBY
LAND

60°S
30°E

South Magnetic
Pole

521

90°W   75°W   60°W   45°W   30°W   15°W   0°   15°E   30°E   45°E   60°E

75°N

NORTH AMERICA

Arctic Circle

60°N

ATLANTIC OCEAN

45°N

30°N

Tropic of Cancer

15°N

AFRICA

0° Equator

15°S

SVALBARD (Norway)

FRANZ JOSEF LAND

NOVAYA ZEMLYA

Barents Sea

Murmansk

Norwegian Sea

White Sea

R U S S I A

Reykjavik★ ICELAND

Trondheim

SWEDEN

FINLAND

Gulf of Bothnia

Lake Ladoga

URAL MOUNTAINS

Ob River

Novosib

Helsinki

Oslo★ Stockholm★ Tallinn★

St. Petersburg

Volga River

Moscow★

Samara

NORWAY

ESTONIA

North Sea

Copenhagen★ Riga★ LATVIA

LITHUANIA

Vilnius★

Aqmola★

Edinburgh

UNITED KINGDOM

Baltic Sea

Gdansk

Minsk★ BELARUS

Don River

Volgograd

KIRGHIZ STEPPE

Lake Balkhash

Dublin★ IRELAND

Amsterdam The Hague NETH.

Berlin★

Warsaw★

Kiev★ Kharkhiv

KAZAKHSTAN

London BELG. GERMANY POLAND UKRAINE

Aral Sea

Brussels★ LUX. Bonn Prague★ CZECH REP.

MOLDOVA

Almat★

Paris★ Rhine River SLOVAK REP.

Dniester

Chisinau

Bishkek★

Sea of Biscay FRANCE Bern★ SWITZ. LIECH. Vienna★ AUST. HUNG. Budapest★ ROMANIA

Sea of Azov

Caspian Sea

UZBEKISTAN

Tashkent★ KYRGYZSTAN

Venice ALPS Zagreb★ CRO. BOS.

Bucharest

Black Sea

GEORGIA

CAUCASUS MTS.

Tbilisi★ PAMIRS

MONACO SAN MARINO

Sarajevo★ Belgrade★ BULGARIA

Dushanbe★ TAJIKISTAN

Barcelona

ANDORRA CORSICA (Fr.)

Rome★ ITALY APENNINES YUGO. Sofia★ Skopje★ FYR. MACE.

ARMENIA Yerevan★ Baku★ TURKMENISTAN Ashgabat★

HINDU KUSH

PORTUGAL Lisbon Madrid★ SPAIN

SARDINIA (Italy)

Tirane★ ALB. GREECE

Istanbul

Ankara★ ASIA MINOR TURKEY AZERBAIJAN

Kabul★ AFGHANISTAN Islamabad★

Tyrrhenian Sea Athens★

ELBURZ MTS.

KURDISTAN

KU

BALEARIC ISLANDS (Sp.)

SICILY (Italy) Ionian Sea Aegean Sea

Nicosia★ CYPRUS

SYRIA

ZAGROS MOUNTAINS Tehran★ PLATEAU OF IRAN

HIMAL

MALTA

Mediterranean Sea

Beirut★ LEBANON Damascus★

Baghdad★ IRAN

New Delhi★

Jerusalem★ ISRAEL JORDAN Amman★ IRAQ

Kuwait★ KUWAIT

PAKISTAN THAR DESERT

Karachi

INDIA

Red Sea Riyadh★

BAHRAIN QATAR U.A.E.

Persian Gulf

OMAN Abu Dhabi★ Muscat★

DECCAN PLATEAU

SAUDI ARABIA Mecca

RUB AL KHALI (DESERT)

OMAN

Mumbai (Bombay)

Sanaa★ YEMEN

Arabian Sea

Prime Meridian

Aden SOCOTRA (Yemen)

WESTERN GHATS EASTERN GHATS

Cha (Ma

Gulf of Aden

LACCADIVE ISLANDS (India)

SRI LAN

Colombo★

Male

MALDIVES

INDIAN OCEAN

N
W ✦ E
S

| ★ National capital |
| • Major city |
| − National boundary |

0   400   800 mi.
0   400   800 km.
Robinson Projection

0°   15°E   30°E   45°E   60°E   75°E

ARCTIC OCEAN

75°N

NORTH
AMERICA

SIBERIA

60°N

River

Lena River

STANOVOI RANGE

Bering Sea

Sea of
Okhotsk

Irkutsk

Lake Baikal

ALTAI MTS.

DA HINGGAN LING

SAKHALIN

45°N

KURIL ISLANDS

Ulaanbaatar

MONGOLIA

Harbin

Vladivostok

Sapporo

GOBI (DESERT)

Beijing

N. KOREA
Pyongyang

Sea of
Japan

SHAN

Huang He

Seoul
S. KOREA

JAPAN

Tokyo

PLATEAU
OF
TIBET

PEOPLE'S REPUBLIC
OF CHINA

Yellow
Sea

Osaka

30°N

Jiang

Shanghai

Thimphu
BHUTAN

East
China
Sea

BANGLADESH
Dhaka

Ye Jiang

Taipei
TAIWAN

PACIFIC

Calcutta

MYANMAR
(BURMA)

LAOS

Guangzhou
MACAO
(Port.)

HONG
KONG

OCEAN

Hanoi
Gulf
of
Tonkin

HAINAN

Philippine

Bay
of
Bengal

Vientiane

Yangon
(Rangoon)

THAILAND

Da Nang

VIETNAM

Manila

Sea

15°N

ANDAMAN
ISLANDS
(India)

Bangkok

CAMBODIA

PHILIPPINES

Phnom
Penh

Ho Chi Minh City
(Saigon)

NICOBAR
ISLANDS
(India)

South China
Sea

Bandar Seri
Begawan
BRUNEI

MALAYSIA

Kuala Lumpur

MALAYSIA

Singapore
SINGAPORE

BORNEO

0°

SUMATRA

CELEBES

INDONESIA

Java Sea

NEW GUINEA

Jakarta
JAVA

Arafura Sea

523

Timor
Sea

15°S

AUSTRALIA

90°E   105°E   120°E   135°E   150°E   165°E   180°   165°W   150°W   135°W   120°W

90°E   105°E   120°E   135°E   150°E   165°E

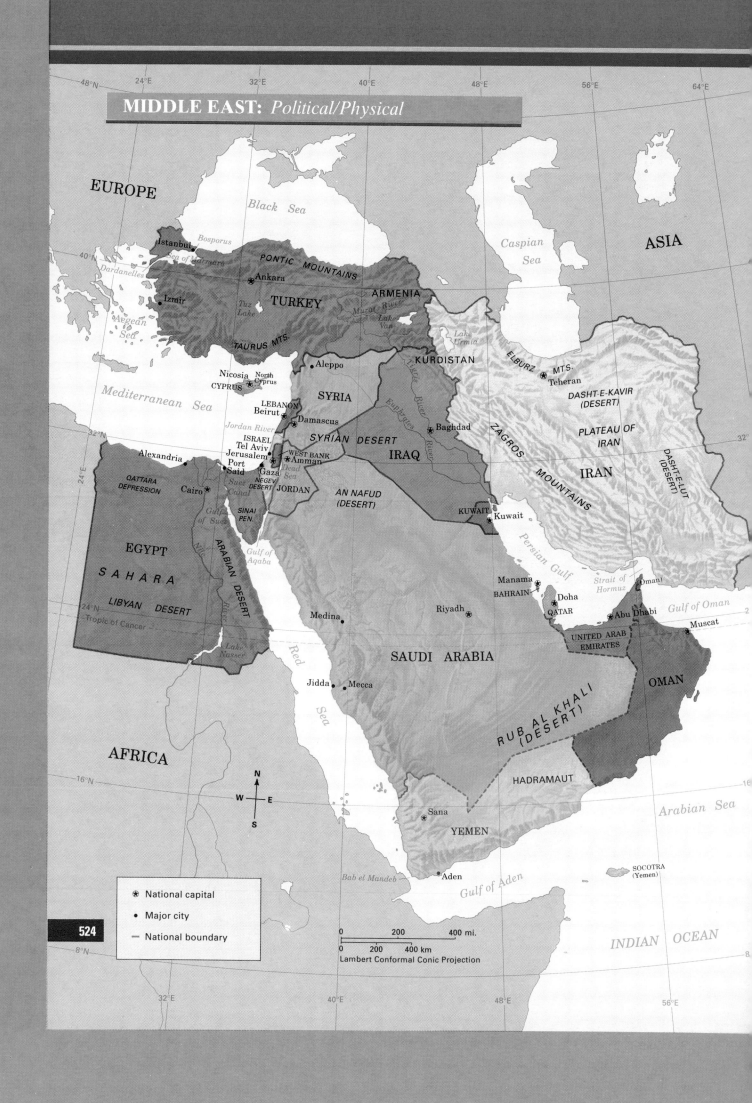

MIDDLE EAST: *Political/Physical*

EUROPE

ASIA

Black Sea

Caspian Sea

Istanbul
Bosporus
Sea of Marmara
Dardanelles
⊛ Ankara
PONTIC MOUNTAINS
ARMENIA
ELBURZ MTS.
⊛ Teheran

Izmir
TURKEY
Tuz Lake
Murat River
Lake Van
KURDISTAN
DASHT-E-KAVIR
(DESERT)

Aegean Sea
TAURUS MTS.
Aleppo
Lake Urmia
PLATEAU OF IRAN
DASHT-E-LUT
(DESERT)

Mediterranean Sea
Nicosia North Cyprus
CYPRUS ⊛
SYRIA
Tigris River
ZAGROS MOUNTAINS
IRAN

LEBANON
Beirut ⊛
Damascus ⊛
Euphrates River
⊛ Baghdad

Jordan River
SYRIAN DESERT
IRAQ

ISRAEL
Tel Aviv
Jerusalem ⊛
Port Said
WEST BANK
Amman ⊛
Dead Sea

Alexandria
NEGEV DESERT
Gaza
JORDAN
AN NAFUD (DESERT)

QATTARA DEPRESSION
Cairo ⊛
Suez Canal
SINAI PEN.
KUWAIT
Kuwait ⊛

Gulf of Suez
Gulf of Aqaba
Persian Gulf
Strait of Hormuz
Oman

EGYPT
ARABIAN DESERT
Manama ⊛
BAHRAIN
Doha ⊛
QATAR
⊛ Abu Dhabi
Gulf of Oman

SAHARA
Nile River
Medina
Riyadh ⊛
UNITED ARAB EMIRATES
Muscat

LIBYAN DESERT
Tropic of Cancer
Lake Nasser
SAUDI ARABIA
OMAN

AFRICA
Red Sea
Jidda • Mecca

RUB AL KHALI (DESERT)

HADRAMAUT

Arabian Sea

N
W — E
S

Sana ⊛
YEMEN

SOCOTRA (Yemen)

Bab el Mandeb
Aden •
Gulf of Aden

⊛ National capital

• Major city

— National boundary

INDIAN OCEAN

524

```
0        200      400 mi.
0    200   400 km
```
Lambert Conformal Conic Projection

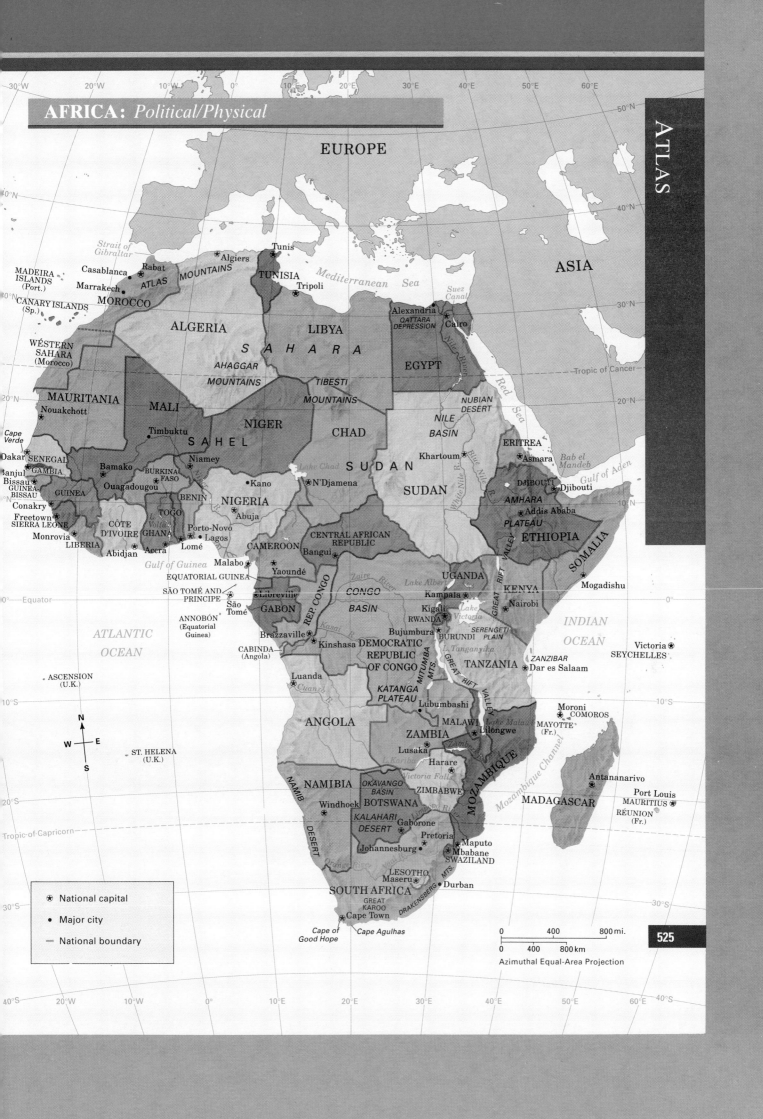

AFRICA: *Political/Physical*

EUROPE

ASIA

Strait of Gibraltar

MADEIRA ISLANDS (Port.)

Casablanca   Rabat

CANARY ISLANDS (Sp.)

Marrakech   *ATLAS*   *MOUNTAINS*

MOROCCO

Algiers   Tunis

TUNISIA   Tripoli

Mediterranean   Sea

Suez Canal

Alexandria

QATTARA DEPRESSION   Cairo

ALGERIA   LIBYA

S A H A R A

EGYPT

Nile River   *Red Sea*

WESTERN SAHARA (Morocco)

AHAGGAR MOUNTAINS

Tropic of Cancer

MAURITANIA

Nouakchott

MALI

SAHEL

Timbuktu

NIGER

TIBESTI MOUNTAINS

CHAD

NUBIAN DESERT

NILE BASIN

Cape Verde

Dakar   SENEGAL

Banjul   GAMBIA

Bissau   GUINEA-BISSAU

Conakry   GUINEA

Freetown   SIERRA LEONE

Monrovia   LIBERIA

Bamako

BURKINA FASO

Niamey

Ouagadougou

Kano

N'Djamena

S U D A N

Khartoum

SUDAN

ERITREA

Asmara   *Bab el Mandeb*

Blue Nile R.

White Nile R.

Gulf of Aden

DJIBOUTI   Djibouti

BENIN

NIGERIA

Abuja

TOGO

GHANA

CÔTE D'IVOIRE

Abidjan

Accra   Lomé   *L. Volta*

Porto-Novo   Lagos

CAMEROON

Bangui

CENTRAL AFRICAN REPUBLIC

AMHARA

Addis Ababa

PLATEAU

ETHIOPIA

SOMALIA

Malabo

Yaoundé

EQUATORIAL GUINEA

SÃO TOMÉ AND PRINCIPE

São Tomé

Libreville

Equator

GABON

REP. CONGO

CONGO BASIN

Zaire River

Kasai R.

Brazzaville

Kinshasa

Mogadishu

Lake Albert

UGANDA

Kampala

CONGO

Lake Victoria

Kigali

RWANDA

Bujumbura   BURUNDI

SERENGETI PLAIN

Nairobi

KENYA

GREAT RIFT VALLEY

INDIAN OCEAN

ANNOBÓN (Equatorial Guinea)

ATLANTIC OCEAN

ASCENSION (U.K.)

CABINDA (Angola)

Luanda

Cuanza R.

DEMOCRATIC REPUBLIC OF CONGO

KATANGA PLATEAU

Lubumbashi

MITUMBA MTS.

L. Tanganyika

TANZANIA

Dar es Salaam

ZANZIBAR

Victoria

SEYCHELLES

ST. HELENA (U.K.)

ANGOLA

ZAMBIA

Lusaka

MALAWI

Lilongwe

Lake Malawi

MAYOTTE (Fr.)

Moroni

COMOROS

Zambezi R.

Harare

Antananarivo

Port Louis

MAURITIUS

RÉUNION (Fr.)

NAMIBIA

NAMIB DESERT

Windhoek

OKAVANGO BASIN

BOTSWANA

ZIMBABWE

Victoria Falls

L. Kariba

MOZAMBIQUE

Mozambique Channel

MADAGASCAR

KALAHARI DESERT

Gaborone

Limpopo River

Pretoria

Maputo

Johannesburg   Mbabane

SWAZILAND

Orange River

Vaal R.

LESOTHO

Maseru

Durban

SOUTH AFRICA

GREAT KAROO

DRAKENSBERG MTS.

Cape Town

Cape of Good Hope   Cape Agulhas

Legend

⊛ National capital

• Major city

— National boundary

N
W   E
S

Tropic of Capricorn

| 0 | 400 | 800 mi. |
| 0 | 400 | 800 km |

Azimuthal Equal-Area Projection

525

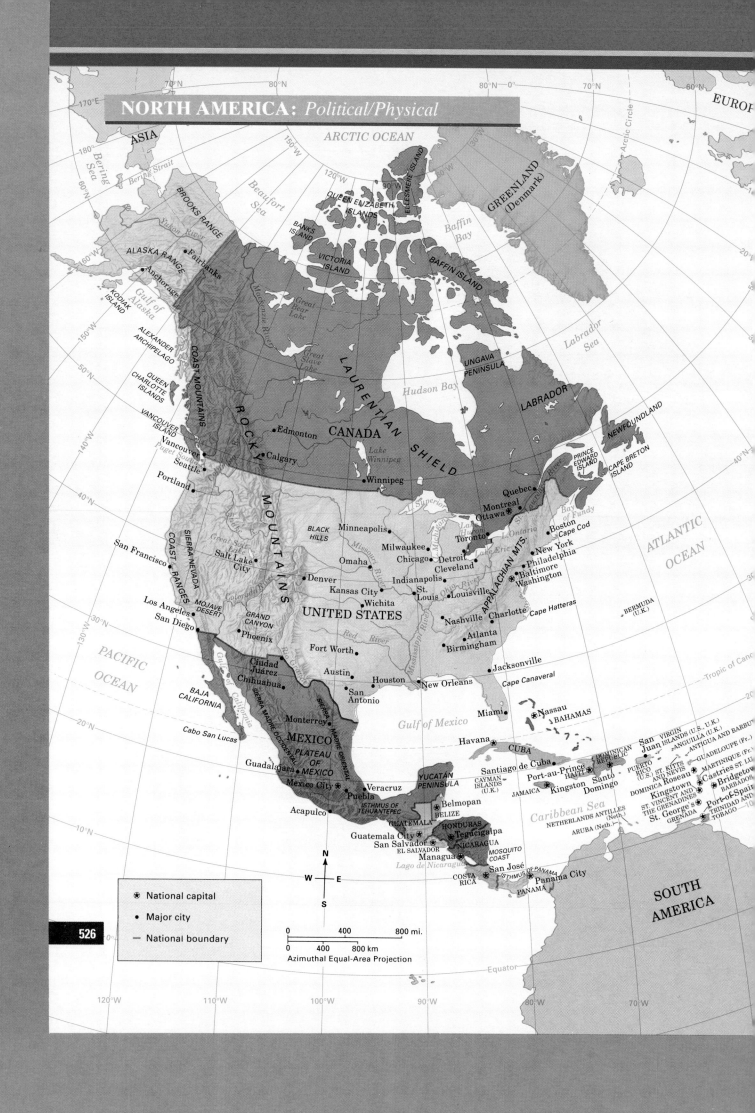

NORTH AMERICA: *Political/Physical*

ASIA

ARCTIC OCEAN

Bering Sea

Bering Strait

Beaufort Sea

BROOKS RANGE

Yukon River

ALASKA RANGE •Fairbanks

•Anchorage

Gulf of Alaska

KODIAK ISLAND

ALEXANDER ARCHIPELAGO

QUEEN CHARLOTTE ISLANDS

VANCOUVER ISLAND

COAST MOUNTAINS

Vancouver•
Puget Sound
Seattle•

Portland•

San Francisco•

COAST RANGES

SIERRA NEVADA

Salt Lake City•
Great Salt Lake

Los Angeles• MOJAVE DESERT

San Diego•

Phoenix•

BAJA CALIFORNIA

Cabo San Lucas

Gulf of California

Ciudad Juárez•
Chihuahua•

SIERRA MADRE OCCIDENTAL

Monterrey•

MEXICO

PLATEAU OF MEXICO

Guadalajara•

SIERRA MADRE ORIENTAL

Mexico City⊛
Puebla•

Acapulco•

ISTHMUS OF TEHUANTEPEC

QUEEN ELIZABETH ISLANDS

BANKS ISLAND

VICTORIA ISLAND

ELLESMERE ISLAND

GREENLAND (Denmark)

Baffin Bay

BAFFIN ISLAND

ROCKY MOUNTAINS

Mackenzie River

Great Bear Lake

Great Slave Lake

LAURENTIAN SHIELD

Hudson Bay

UNGAVA PENINSULA

Labrador Sea

LABRADOR

•Edmonton CANADA

•Calgary

Lake Winnipeg

•Winnipeg

NEWFOUNDLAND

PRINCE EDWARD ISLAND

CAPE BRETON ISLAND

Quebec•
Montreal•
Ottawa⊛

Bay of Fundy

Columbia River

BLACK HILLS

Minneapolis•

Milwaukee• L.Superior

Omaha• Missouri River

Chicago• Lake Michigan

Detroit• Lake Huron

Toronto• L.Ontario

Cleveland• Lake Erie

Boston• Cape Cod

New York•

Philadelphia•

Denver• Kansas City•

Colorado River

GRAND CANYON

Wichita•

St. Louis• Ohio River

Indianapolis•

Louisville•

APPALACHIAN MTS.

Baltimore•
Washington⊛

ATLANTIC OCEAN

UNITED STATES

Nashville• Charlotte•

Cape Hatteras

BERMUDA (U.K.)

PACIFIC OCEAN

Red River

Fort Worth•

Austin•

San Antonio•

Rio Grande

Houston• •New Orleans

Atlanta•
Birmingham•

Jacksonville•

Cape Canaveral

Miami•

Gulf of Mexico

Havana⊛ CUBA

Nassau⊛
BAHAMAS

Santiago de Cuba•

CAYMAN ISLANDS (U.K.)

JAMAICA

Port-au-Prince⊛
HAITI

DOMINICAN REPUBLIC

Kingston⊛ Santo Domingo⊛

PUERTO RICO (U.S.)

VIRGIN ISLANDS (U.S., U.K.)

San Juan⊛

ANGUILLA (U.K.)

ST. KITTS AND NEVIS

ANTIGUA AND BARBUDA

GUADELOUPE (Fr.)

DOMINICA Roseau⊛

MARTINIQUE (Fr.)

Castries⊛ ST. LU

Kingstown⊛ BARBADOS

ST. VINCENT AND THE GRENADINES

St. George's⊛
GRENADA

Bridgeto

Port-of-Spain⊛
TRINIDAD AND
TOBAGO

NETHERLANDS ANTILLES (Neth.)

ARUBA (Neth.)

Caribbean Sea

YUCATÁN PENINSULA

Veracruz•

⊛Belmopan
BELIZE

GUATEMALA

Guatemala City⊛
San Salvador⊛
EL SALVADOR

HONDURAS

⊛Tegucigalpa

NICARAGUA

MOSQUITO COAST

Managua⊛

Lago de Nicaragua

San José⊛

COSTA RICA

ISTHMUS OF PANAMA

PANAMA

Panama City⊛

SOUTH AMERICA

N
W — E
S

Legend

- ⊛ National capital
- • Major city
- — National boundary

526

0   400   800 mi.

0   400   800 km

Azimuthal Equal-Area Projection

EUROP

Arctic Circle

Tropic of Canc

Equator

SOUTH AMERICA: *Political/Physical*

CENTRAL
AMERICA

Caribbean Sea

ATLANTIC
OCEAN

Barranquilla
Cartagena
Maracaibo
Caracas
Orinoco River
LLANOS
VENEZUELA
Angel Falls
Georgetown
Paramaribo
GUYANA
Cayenne
Medellín
GUIANA HIGHLANDS
SURINAME
FRENCH
GUIANA
(Fr.)
Bogotá
COLOMBIA
MALPELO
(Colombia)
Rio Negro
Quito
ECUADOR
AMAZON
Belém
Guayaquil
Solimões
Manaus
Amazon River
*Gulf of
Guayaquil*
Iquitos
BASIN
Fortaleza
GALÁPAGOS
ISLANDS
(Ecuador)
Equator
Madeira River
Tapajós River
Xingu River
Trujillo
BRAZIL
Recife
PERU
A
N
D
E
S
Lima
Cuzco
PLATEAU OF
MATO GROSSO
BRAZILIAN
São Francisco River
Salvador
Arequipa
Lake Titicaca
La Paz
Brasília
HIGHLANDS
ALTIPLANO
BOLIVIA
Sucre
PACIFIC
OCEAN
Belo Horizonte
Antofagasta
ATACAMA DESERT
GRAN CHACO
PARAGUAY
Paraguay River
São Paulo
Rio de Janeiro
Tropic of Capricorn
SAN FÉLIX
ISLAND
(Chile)
SAN AMBROSIO
ISLAND
(Chile)
Asunción
Santos
Paraná River
Salado River
Pôrto Alegre
Córdoba
CHILE
A
N
D
E
S
Rosario
URUGUAY
Valparaíso
Santiago
Buenos Aires
Montevideo
Rio de la Plata
JUAN FERNÁNDEZ
ISLANDS
(Chile)
ARGENTINA
PAMPAS
Concepción
Colorado R.
Bahía Blanca
Valdivia
Gulf of San Matías

N
W   E
S

Comodoro Rivadavia
PATAGONIA
Gulf of San Jorge

⊛ National capital
• Major city
— National boundary

ATLANTIC
OCEAN

0   400   800 mi.
0   400   800 km
Azimuthal Equal-Area Projection

*Strait of
Magellan*
FALKLAND
ISLANDS
(U.K.)
TIERRA
DEL FUEGO

527

Cape Horn
SOUTH GEORGIA
(U.K.)

Drake Passage

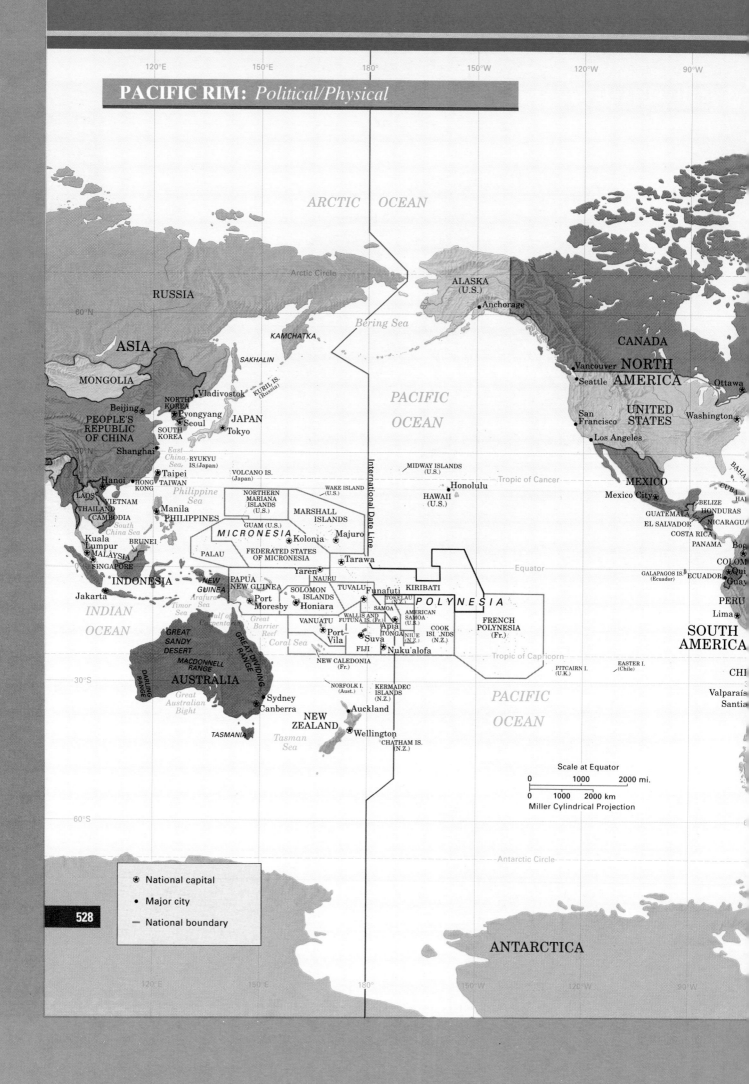

PACIFIC RIM: *Political/Physical*

ARCTIC OCEAN

RUSSIA

ASIA

MONGOLIA

Beijing

PEOPLE'S
REPUBLIC
OF CHINA

Shanghai

Hanoi
HONG
KONG
LAOS
TAIWAN
VIETNAM
THAILAND
CAMBODIA
Kuala
Lumpur
BRUNEI
MALAYSIA
SINGAPORE

INDONESIA

Jakarta

INDIAN
OCEAN

KAMCHATKA

SAKHALIN

Vladivostok
KURIL IS.
(Russia)

NORTH
KOREA
Pyongyang
Seoul
SOUTH
KOREA

JAPAN

Tokyo

East
China
Sea
RYUKYU
IS.(Japan)

Taipei

Philippine
Sea

VOLCANO IS.
(Japan)

South
China Sea

Manila
PHILIPPINES

NORTHERN
MARIANA
ISLANDS
(U.S.)

GUAM (U.S.)

MICRONESIA

PALAU

FEDERATED STATES
OF MICRONESIA

Kolonia

WAKE ISLAND
(U.S.)

MARSHALL
ISLANDS

Majuro

Yaren
NAURU

Tarawa

Bering Sea

ALASKA
(U.S.)

Anchorage

PACIFIC

OCEAN

MIDWAY ISLANDS
(U.S.)

Honolulu

HAWAII
(U.S.)

International Date Line

PAPUA
NEW
GUINEA
NEW
GUINEA

Port
Moresby

Arafura
Sea
Timor
Sea

Gulf of
Carpentaria

GREAT
SANDY
DESERT

MACDONNELL
RANGE

DARLING RANGE

AUSTRALIA

Great
Australian
Bight

TASMANIA

Great
Barrier
Reef

Coral Sea

GREAT DIVIDING RANGE

Sydney
Canberra

SOLOMON
ISLANDS
Honiara

TUVALU
Funafuti

VANUATU

Port-
Vila

WALLIS AND
FUTUNA IS. (Fr.)

Suva

FIJI

NEW CALEDONIA
(Fr.)

NORFOLK I.
(Aust.)

NEW
ZEALAND

Auckland

Wellington

Tasman
Sea

KERMADEC
ISLANDS
(N.Z.)

CHATHAM IS.
(N.Z.)

KIRIBATI

TOKELAU
(N.Z.)

SAMOA

Apia

TONGA

Nuku'alofa

AMERICAN
SAMOA
(U.S.)

NIUE
(N.Z.)

POLYNESIA

COOK
ISLANDS
(N.Z.)

FRENCH
POLYNESIA
(Fr.)

PITCAIRN I.
(U.K.)

EASTER I.
(Chile)

Tropic of Cancer

Equator

Tropic of Capricorn

PACIFIC

OCEAN

Antarctic Circle

ANTARCTICA

CANADA

NORTH
AMERICA

Vancouver
Seattle

San
Francisco

Los Angeles

UNITED
STATES

Ottawa

Washington

MEXICO

Mexico City

BELIZE
GUATEMALA
HONDURAS
EL SALVADOR
NICARAGUA
COSTA RICA
PANAMA

CUBA
HAI

BAHA

COLOM
GALAPAGOS IS.
(Ecuador)
ECUADOR
Qui
Guay

PERU

Lima

SOUTH
AMERICA

CHI

Valparaís
Santia

Bog

Arctic Circle

60°N

30°N

120°E

150°E

180°

150°W

120°W

90°W

30°S

60°S

Scale at Equator

0   1000   2000 mi.

0   1000   2000 km

Miller Cylindrical Projection

⊛ National capital

• Major city

— National boundary

528

WORLD: *Religions*

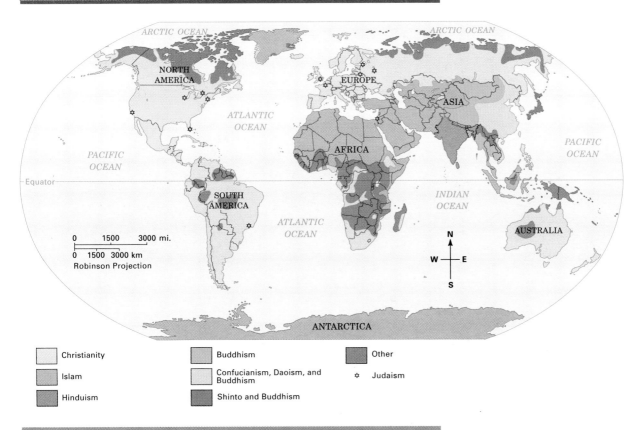

Christianity	Buddhism	Other
Islam	Confucianism, Daoism, and Buddhism	☆ Judaism
Hinduism	Shinto and Buddhism	

0   1500   3000 mi.
0   1500 3000 km
Robinson Projection

WORLD: *Languages*

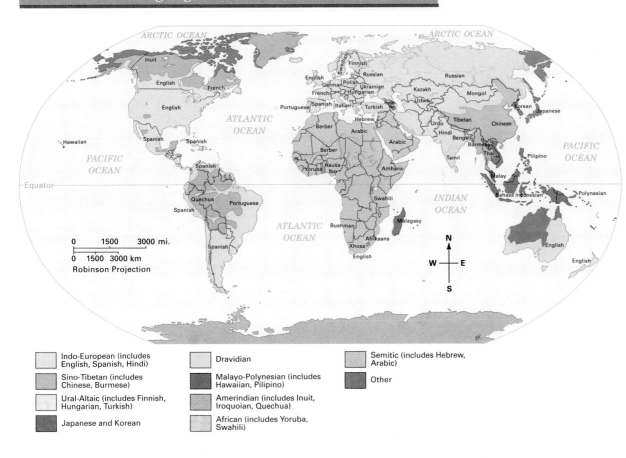

Indo-European (includes English, Spanish, Hindi)	Dravidian	Semitic (includes Hebrew, Arabic)
Sino-Tibetan (includes Chinese, Burmese)	Malayo-Polynesian (includes Hawaiian, Pilipino)	Other
Ural-Altaic (includes Finnish, Hungarian, Turkish)	Amerindian (includes Inuit, Iroquoian, Quechua)	
Japanese and Korean	African (includes Yoruba, Swahili)	

0   1500   3000 mi.
0   1500 3000 km
Robinson Projection

WORLD: *Vegetation*

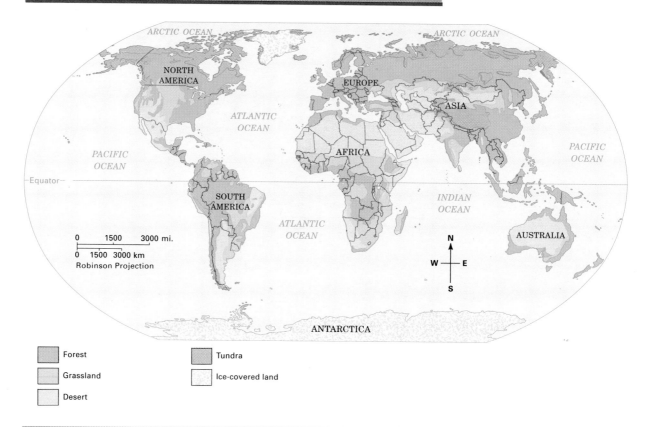

- Forest
- Grassland
- Desert
- Tundra
- Ice-covered land

WORLD: *Climate*

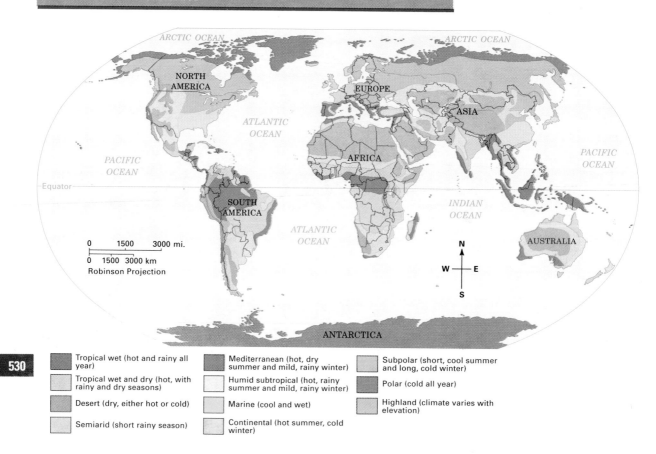

- Tropical wet (hot and rainy all year)
- Tropical wet and dry (hot, with rainy and dry seasons)
- Desert (dry, either hot or cold)
- Semiarid (short rainy season)
- Mediterranean (hot, dry summer and mild, rainy winter)
- Humid subtropical (hot, rainy summer and mild, rainy winter)
- Marine (cool and wet)
- Continental (hot summer, cold winter)
- Subpolar (short, cool summer and long, cold winter)
- Polar (cold all year)
- Highland (climate varies with elevation)

WORLD: *Population*

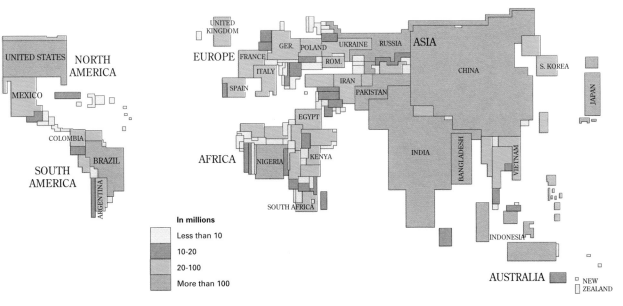

In millions

- Less than 10
- 10-20
- 20-100
- More than 100

Each country's size in the cartogram represents the size of its population compared with those of other countries in the world. Based on information in *Statistical Abstract of the United States 1995*.

WORLD: *Land Use, Land and Ocean Resources*

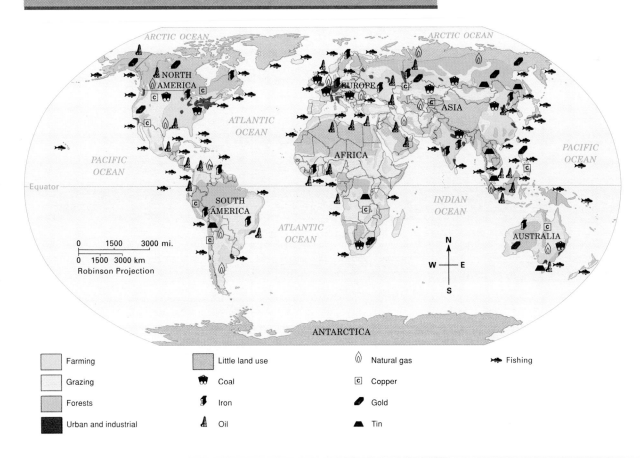

Farming	Little land use	◊ Natural gas	⤞ Fishing
Grazing	Coal	c Copper	
Forests	Iron	Gold	
Urban and industrial	Oil	Tin	

Robinson Projection

0   1500   3000 mi.
0   1500 3000 km

THE WORLD: A.D. 750

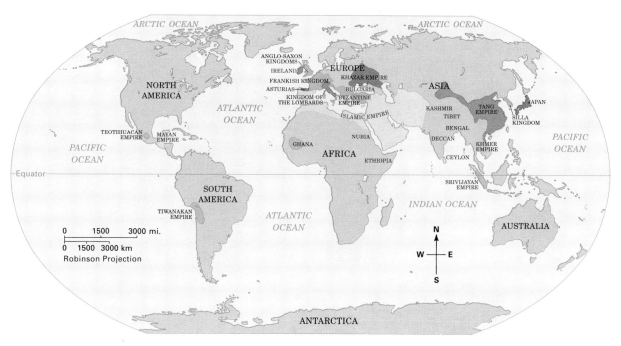

World Civilizations: A.D. 500–1700

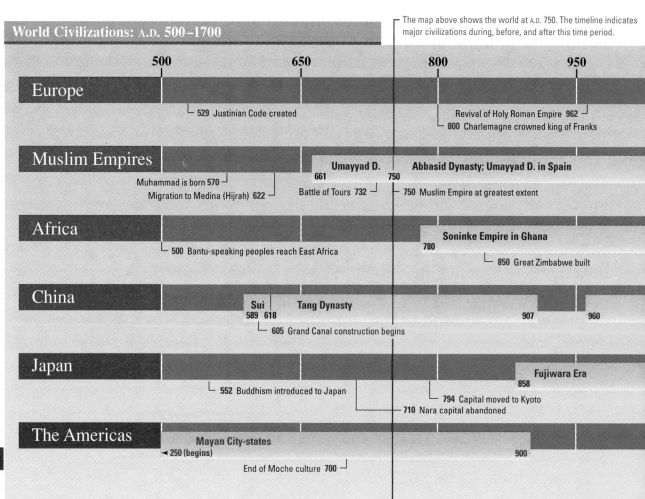

The map above shows the world at A.D. 750. The timeline indicates major civilizations during, before, and after this time period.

	500	650	800	950
Europe	529 Justinian Code created		Revival of Holy Roman Empire 962 / 800 Charlemagne crowned king of Franks	
Muslim Empires	Muhammad is born 570 / Migration to Medina (Hijrah) 622	661 Umayyad D. 750 / Battle of Tours 732	Abbasid Dynasty; Umayyad D. in Spain / 750 Muslim Empire at greatest extent	
Africa	500 Bantu-speaking peoples reach East Africa		780 Soninke Empire in Ghana / 850 Great Zimbabwe built	
China		Sui 589 618 Tang Dynasty / 605 Grand Canal construction begins	907	960
Japan	552 Buddhism introduced to Japan		794 Capital moved to Kyoto / 710 Nara capital abandoned	Fujiwara Era 858
The Americas	Mayan City-states ◄ 250 (begins) / End of Moche culture 700		900	

THE WORLD: *A.D. 1492*

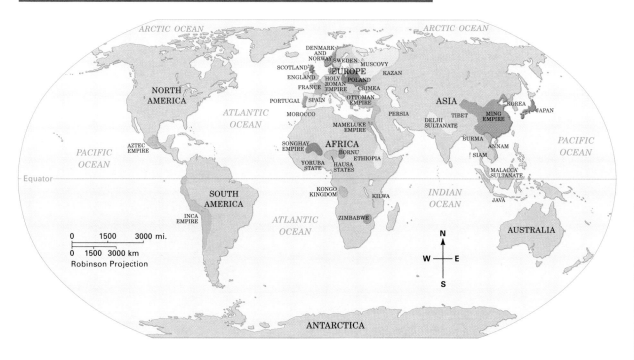

The map above shows the world at A.D. 1492. The timeline indicates major civilizations during, before, and after this time period.

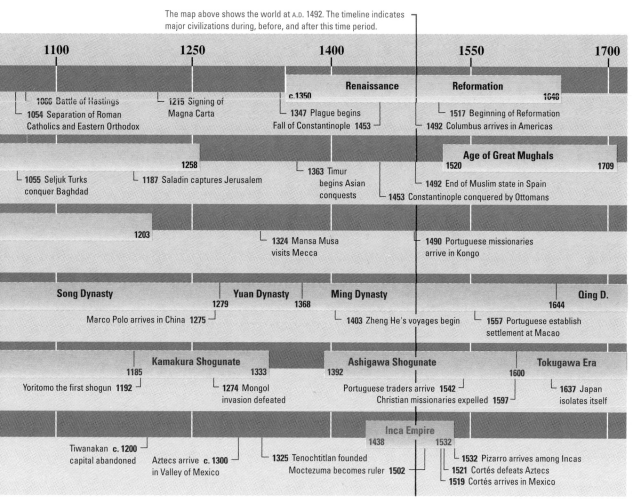

1100	1250	1400	1550	1700

Renaissance c.1350 — 1648 **Reformation**

1066 Battle of Hastings
1054 Separation of Roman Catholics and Eastern Orthodox

1215 Signing of Magna Carta

1347 Plague begins
Fall of Constantinople 1453

1517 Beginning of Reformation
1492 Columbus arrives in Americas

Age of Great Mughals 1520 — 1709

1258

1055 Seljuk Turks conquer Baghdad
1187 Saladin captures Jerusalem

1363 Timur begins Asian conquests

1492 End of Muslim state in Spain
1453 Constantinople conquered by Ottomans

1203

1324 Mansa Musa visits Mecca

1490 Portuguese missionaries arrive in Kongo

Song Dynasty — 1279 — **Yuan Dynasty** 1368 — **Ming Dynasty** — 1644 **Qing D.**

Marco Polo arrives in China 1275
1403 Zheng He's voyages begin
1557 Portuguese establish settlement at Macao

Kamakura Shogunate 1185 — 1333 — **Ashigawa Shogunate** 1392 — 1600 — **Tokugawa Era**

Yoritomo the first shogun 1192
1274 Mongol invasion defeated
Portuguese traders arrive 1542
Christian missionaries expelled 1597
1637 Japan isolates itself

Inca Empire 1438 — 1532

Tiwanakan c.1200 capital abandoned
Aztecs arrive c.1300 in Valley of Mexico
1325 Tenochtitlan founded
Moctezuma becomes ruler 1502
1532 Pizarro arrives among Incas
1521 Cortés defeats Aztecs
1519 Cortés arrives in Mexico

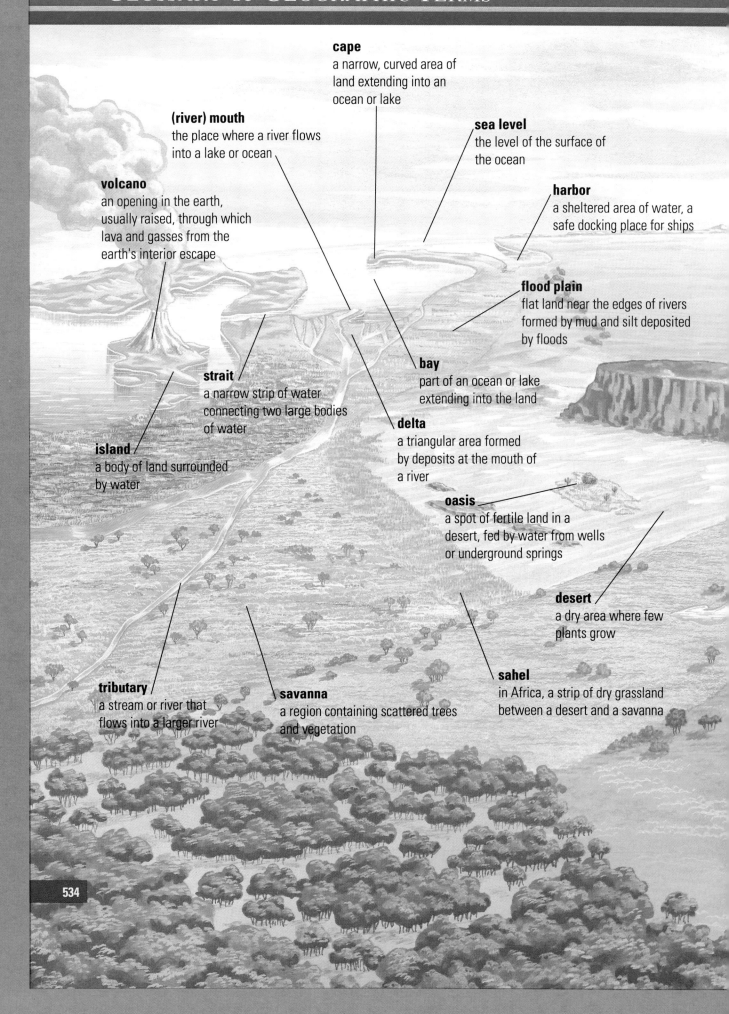

cape
a narrow, curved area of land extending into an ocean or lake

(river) mouth
the place where a river flows into a lake or ocean

sea level
the level of the surface of the ocean

volcano
an opening in the earth, usually raised, through which lava and gasses from the earth's interior escape

harbor
a sheltered area of water, a safe docking place for ships

flood plain
flat land near the edges of rivers formed by mud and silt deposited by floods

strait
a narrow strip of water connecting two large bodies of water

bay
part of an ocean or lake extending into the land

delta
a triangular area formed by deposits at the mouth of a river

island
a body of land surrounded by water

oasis
a spot of fertile land in a desert, fed by water from wells or underground springs

desert
a dry area where few plants grow

tributary
a stream or river that flows into a larger river

savanna
a region containing scattered trees and vegetation

sahel
in Africa, a strip of dry grassland between a desert and a savanna

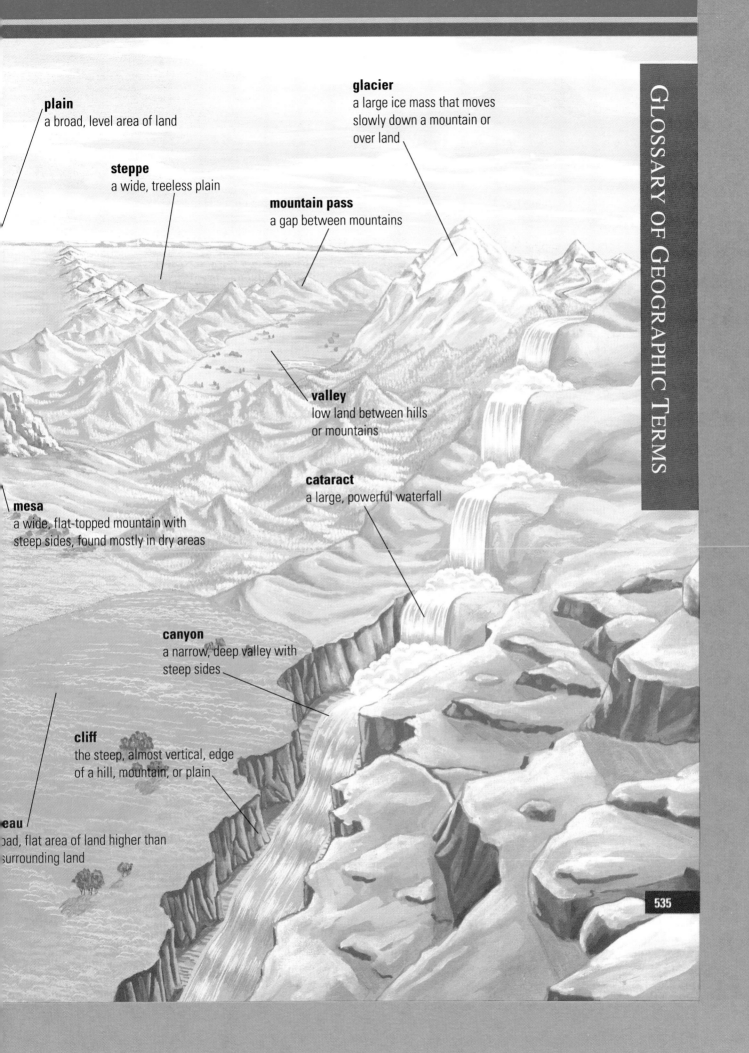

plain
a broad, level area of land

steppe
a wide, treeless plain

glacier
a large ice mass that moves
slowly down a mountain or
over land

mountain pass
a gap between mountains

valley
low land between hills
or mountains

mesa
a wide, flat-topped mountain with
steep sides, found mostly in dry areas

cataract
a large, powerful waterfall

canyon
a narrow, deep valley with
steep sides

cliff
the steep, almost vertical, edge
of a hill, mountain, or plain

eau
ad, flat area of land higher than
surrounding land

This Gazetteer will help you locate many of the places discussed in this book. Latitude and longitude given for large areas of land and water refer to the centermost point of the area; latitude and longitude of rivers refer to the river mouth. The page number tells you where to find a map with each place located.

PLACE	LAT.	LONG.	PAGE
A			
Aachen (Charlemagne's capital; Germany)	51°N	6°E	**260**
Aegean Sea (part of Mediterranean)	39°N	25°E	**290**
Agra (early capital of Mughal Empire; India)	27°N	78°E	**179**
Alps (mountain range in S. and central Europe)	46°N	9°E	**296**
Antioch (ancient Syrian capital; Turkey)	36°N	36°E	**10**
Arguin (island trading post of Portuguese off of W. Africa)	21°N	17°W	**374**
Augsburg (city connected with Reformation; Germany)	48°N	11°E	**347**
Avignon (papal city in France)	44°N	5°E	**311**
B			
Baghdad (capital of Abbasid caliphate; Iraq)	33°N	44°E	**85**
Bering Strait (waterway that separates Asia and N. America)	65°N	170°W	**398**
Berlin (capital of Prussia; Germany)	53°N	13°E	**481**
Black Sea (opens onto Aegean Sea through Bosporus)	43°N	32°E	**36**
Bojador, Cape (W. Africa; W. Sahara)	26°N	15°W	**374**
Bombay (city in W. India where English first traded)	19°N	73°E	**522**
Bosporus (waterway connecting Black Sea and Sea of Marmara; Turkey)	41°N	29°E	**290**
Bruges (important trading city in Flanders; Belgium)	51°N	3°E	**330**
Bursa (early capital of Ottoman Empire; Turkey)	40°N	29°E	**171**
C			
Cairo (capital of Fatimid caliphate; Egypt)	30°N	31°E	**171**
Calcutta (English colony in India)	23°N	88°E	**523**
Calicut (city da Gama visited first in India)	11°N	76°E	**374**
Caribbean Sea (W. Indies, Central and S. America)	15°N	76°W	**378**
Caucasus Mts. (mountain range between Black and Caspian seas)	43°N	45°E	**36**
Ceuta (North African port important in the gold trade; Morocco)	36°N	5°W	**96**

PLACE	LAT.	LONG.	PAGE
Chang Jiang (Yangtze R.; major river of China)	32°N	120°E	**193**
Changan (Xi'an; capital of China under Han and Tang dynasties)	34°N	109°E	**205**
Clermont (city where call for crusades originated; France)	46°N	3°E	**296**
Congo Basin (central Africa)	6°N	20°E	**525**
Constantinople (Istanbul; capital of Byzantine and Ottoman empires; Turkey)	41°N	29°E	**67**
Cordoba (capital of Umayyad caliphate; Spain)	38°N	5°W	**96**
Cuzco (capital of Inca Empire; Peru)	14°S	72°W	**430**
D			
Damascus (capital of Umayyad caliphate; Syria)	34°N	36°E	**81**
Dardanelles (waterway connecting Sea of Marmara and the Aegean Sea; Turkey)	40°N	26°E	**290**
Delhi (capital of Mughal Empire; India)	29°N	77°E	**179**
E			
Edessa (Urfa; city held by crusaders; Turkey)	37°N	39°E	**296**
Edo (Tokyo; center of Tokugawa shogunate; Japan)	36°N	140°E	**230**
F			
Fernando Póo (island off W. Africa)	4°N	9°E	**465**
Flanders (region noted for woolen trade; France, Belgium)	51°N	3°E	**330**
Florence (cultural center of Renaissance Italy)	44°N	11°E	**317**
Fustat (Cairo; capital of Fatimid caliphate; Egypt)	30°N	31°E	**80**
G			
Gao (capital of Songhai Empire; Mali)	16°N	0°	**121**
Geneva (center of Calvinism; Switzerland)	46°N	6°E	**352**
Genoa (port on Mediterranean; Italy)	44°N	9°E	**290**

PLACE	LAT.	LONG.	PAGE
Ghent (cloth weaving city in Flanders; Belgium)	51°N	4°E	**330**
Goa (Portuguese colony in India)	16°N	74°E	**142**
Good Hope, Cape of (S. Africa)	34°S	18°E	**374**
Granada (capital of Muslim kingdom; Spain)	37°N	4°W	**96**
Great Rift Valley (stretches from Jordan to S.E. Africa)	0°N	36°E	**525**
Great Zimbabwe (capital of ancient Zimbabwe; Zimbabwe)	20°S	31°E	**146**
Guinea, Gulf of (part of Atlantic; W. Africa)	2°N	1°E	**109**

H

PLACE	LAT.	LONG.	PAGE
Hangzhou (capital of China during late Song dynasty)	30°N	120°E	**166**
Hattin (battle where crusaders were defeated; Israel)	33°N	36°E	**299**
Heian (early name for Kyoto; Japan)	35°N	136°E	**230**
Himalayas (mountain range in Asia)	30°N	85°E	**179**
Hindu Kush (mountain range in Afghanistan)	36°N	72°E	**522**
Horn, Cape (tip of S. America)	56°S	67°W	**527**
Huang He (Yellow R.; N. central China)	34°N	117°E	**193**

I

PLACE	LAT.	LONG.	PAGE
Izapa (early Mayan city; Mexico)	15°N	92°W	**405**

J

PLACE	LAT.	LONG.	PAGE
Jamestown (English settlement in Virginia)	37°N	77°W	**470**
Jenne-jeno (Djénné; trading city in W. Africa; Mali)	14°N	5°W	**109**
Jerusalem (holy city of Jews, Christians, and Muslims; Israel)	32°N	35°E	**299**

K

PLACE	LAT.	LONG.	PAGE
Kaifeng (capital of China under Song dynasty)	35°N	114°E	**205**
Karakhoto (caravan city; N. China)	42°N	101°E	**366**
Karakorum (capital of Genghis Khan's empire; Mongolia)	47°N	103°E	**166**

PLACE	LAT.	LONG.	PAGE
Khanbalik (Beijing; Kublai Khan's capital; China)	40°N	116°E	**166**
Kilwa (port in E. Africa)	9°S	39°E	**142**
Koumbi (capital of ancient kingdom of Ghana)	15°N	8°W	**121**
Kyoto (Heian; city that was early home of Japan's emperors)	35°N	136°E	**230**

L

PLACE	LAT.	LONG.	PAGE
La Rochelle (port and Huguenot center; W. France)	46°N	1°W	**330**
Lisbon (capital of Portugal)	39°N	9°W	**374**
Luoyang (capital of China under Tang and Song dynasties)	35°N	113°E	**205**

M

PLACE	LAT.	LONG.	PAGE
Machu Picchu (Inca citadel; Peru)	13°S	73°W	**430**
Madras (city in S. India; fought over by British and French)	13°N	80°E	**522**
Malacca (trading city; Malaysia)	2°N	102°E	**142**
Malindi (ancient E. African port; Kenya)	3°S	40°E	**142**
Marmara, Sea of (separates Europe and Asia; Turkey)	41°N	28°E	**290**
Mazagan (Al-Jadida; port founded by Portugal; Morocco)	33°N	9°W	**465**
M'Banza (capital of Kongo Kingdom; central Africa)	5°S	15°E	**150**
Mecca (holiest city of Islam; Saudi Arabia)	21°N	40°E	**67**
Medina (holy city of Islam; Saudi Arabia)	24°N	40°E	**67**
Milan (city-state in N. Italy)	45°N	9°E	**317**
Moche (site of ancient civilization; N. Peru)	8°S	79°W	**412**
Mombasa (E. African port)	4°S	40°E	**142**
Montreal (French settlement; Canada)	46°N	74°W	**470**
Mpinda (port on Zaire [Congo] R.; Angola)	6°S	12°E	**150**

N

PLACE	LAT.	LONG.	PAGE
Nanjing (southern capital of Ming emperors; China)	32°N	119°E	**193**
New Amsterdam (Dutch settlement; New York)	41°N	74°W	**470**

This dictionary lists many of the important people introduced in this book. The page number refers to the main discussion of that person in the book. For more complete references see the Index.

Pronunciation Key
This chart presents the system of phonetic respellings used to indicate pronunciation in the Biographical Dictionary and in the chapters of this book.

Spellings	Symbol	Spellings	Symbol	Spellings	Symbol
pat	a	kick, cat, pique	k	thin, this	th
pay	ay	lid, needle	l	cut	uh
care	air	mum	m	urge, term, firm, word, heard	ur
father	ah	no, sudden	n		
bib	b	thing	ng	valve	v
church	ch	pot, horrid	ah	with	w
deed, milled	d	toe	oh	yes	y
pet	eh	caught, paw, for	aw	zebra, xylem	z
bee	ee	noise	oy	vision, pleasure, garage	zh
life, phase, rough	f	took	u		
gag	g	boot	oo	about, item, edible, gallop, circus	uh
hat	h	out	ow		
which	hw	pop	p	butter	ur
pit	ih	roar	r		
pie, by	eye, y	sauce	s	Capital letters indicate stressed syllables.	
pier	ihr	ship, dish	sh		
judge	j	tight, stopped	t		

A

Abd al Malik *(ahb dul mah LIHK)* c. 646–705, Umayyad caliph, 685–705 (p. 83).

Abd al Rahman I *(ahb al ra MAHN)* 731–788, founder of Umayyad dynasty in Cordoba, 756–788 (p. 95).

Abd al Rahman III 891–961, Umayyad caliph of Cordoba, 929–961 (p. 96).

Abu Bakr 573–634, first caliph after death of Muhammad, 632–634 (p. 65).

Affonso I ?–c. 1550, ruler of the Kongo Kingdom in Africa (p. 152).

Ahuitzotl *(ah WEET soh tl)* ?–1502, Aztec ruler, 1486–1502 (p. 424).

Akbar, Akbar the Great 1542–1605, emperor of Mughal Empire, 1556–1605 (p. 181).

Alcuin 735–804, English monk (p. 259).

Alfonso VI, Alfonso the Valiant ?–1109, king of Castile in Spain, 1072–1109 (p. 100).

Ali c. 600–661, fourth caliph of Muslim Empire, 656–661 (p. 66).

Anna Comnena c. 1083–1148, Byzantine author (p. 297).

Atahualpa *(ah tah WAHL pah)* c. 1500–1533, last ruler of the Inca Empire in Peru, killed by Pizarro's troops (p. 438).

Augustus 63 B.C.–A.D. 14, first Roman emperor, 29 B.C.–A.D. 14 (p. 26).

Aurangzeb *(AWR ung zehb)* 1618–1707, emperor of Mughal Empire, 1658–1707 (p. 185).

B

Babur 1483–1530, founder of Mughal dynasty of India, emperor, 1526–1530 (p. 180).

Bacon, Francis 1561–1626, English philosopher (p. 355).

Balboa, Vasco de 1475–1519, Spanish explorer of Isthmus of Panama and Pacific Ocean (p. 380).

Bayezid II 1447–1513, son of Mehmed II, Ottoman sultan, 1481–1512 (p. 175).

Boniface VIII c. 1235–1303, pope, 1294–1303, had power struggle with Philip IV of France (p. 338).

Brueghel, Pieter, the Elder *(BROY guhl)* c. 1530–1569, Flemish artist (p. 329).

Brunelleschi, Filippo *(broo nuh LEHS kee)* 1377–1446, Italian Renaissance architect (p. 322).

C

Cabot, John 1450–1498, Italian navigator and explorer of North America for English (p. 380).

Calvin, John 1509–1564, French theologian and reformer (p. 349).

Cão, Diego c. 1400s, Portuguese navigator and explorer of Congo River (p. 149).

Cartier, Jacques 1491–1557, French explorer (p. 381).

Catherine II, Catherine the Great 1729–1796, Russian empress, 1762–1796 (p. 480).

Cervantes, Miguel de 1547–1616, great Spanish writer of the Renaissance, wrote *Don Quixote* (p. 322).

Charlemagne, Charles the Great 742–814, king of the

Franks, 768–814, and emperor of the West, 800–814 (p. 258).

Charles I 1600–1649, king of England, 1625–1649, executed by English Parliament (p. 460).

Charles II 1630–1685, king of England, 1660–1685, invited to be king after Cromwell's death (p. 462).

Charles V 1500–1558, Holy Roman Emperor, 1519–1556, king of Spain during conquests (p. 344).

Charles Martel, Charles the Hammer c. 689–741, Frankish ruler, 715–741 (p. 258).

Clement V 1264–1314, pope, 1305–1314, moved papacy from Rome to Avignon, France (p. 339).

Clement VII ?–1394, pope, 1378–1394, pope in Avignon during the Great Schism (p. 339).

Clovis I c. 466–511, king of the Franks, 481–511 (p. 257).

Columbus, Christopher 1451–1506, Italian explorer for Spanish (p. 377).

Conrad III c. 1093–1152, king of Germany, 1138–1152 (p. 299).

Constantine, Constantine the Great c. 280–337, Roman emperor, 306–337 (p. 30).

Copernicus, Nicolaus 1473–1543, Polish physician and astronomer (p. 353).

Cortés, Hernando 1485–1547, Spanish conqueror of Mexico (p. 437).

Cromwell, Oliver 1599–1658, lord protector of England, c. 1649–1658 (p. 461).

D

Dias, Bartholomeu c. 1450–1500, Portuguese navigator, rounded Cape of Good Hope (p. 375).

Díaz, Bernal c. 1492–c. 1581, Spanish soldier and historian (p. 16).

Diderot, Denis *(DEE dih roh)* 1713–1784, French encyclopedist (p. 478).

Diocletian 245–313, Roman emperor, 284–313 (p. 30).

E

Edward VI 1537–1553, king of England, 1547–1553 (p. 351).

Elizabeth I 1533–1603, queen of England, 1558–1603, defeated Spanish Armada (p. 458).

Erasmus, Desiderius *(ih RAZ muhs)* c. 1466–1536, Dutch priest and humanist (p. 332).

Ericson, Leif c. 1000, Norse mariner, explored Newfoundland (p. 380).

F

Faraghani, Ahmad al died c. 861, Muslim astronomer, mathematician, and engineer (pp. 15, 378).

Ferdinand II, Ferdinand the Catholic 1452–1516, king of Spain, 1479–1516 (p. 378).

Francis of Assisi c. 1182–1226, Italian founder of the Franciscans (p. 287).

Francis I 1494–1547, French king, 1515–1547, king during Renaissance in France (p. 381).

Franklin, Benjamin 1706–1790, American statesman, scientist, and philosopher (p. 482).

Frederick I c. 1125–1190, king of Germany, 1152–1190, drowned on Third Crusade (p. 300).

Frederick II, Frederick the Wise 1482–1556, prince of Saxony, 1544–1556 (p. 345).

Frederick II, Frederick the Great 1712–1786, king of Prussia, 1740–1786, student of Voltaire (p. 480).

G

Galileo 1564–1642, Italian astronomer and physicist (p. 354).

Gama, Vasco da c. 1469–1524, Portuguese navigator, sailed to India (p. 364).

Gautama, Siddhartha, "the Buddha" c. 563–483 B.C., Indian philosopher and founder of Buddhism (p. 194).

Genghis Khan, Temujin *(TEHM yoo jihn)* 1162–1227, Mongol conqueror (p. 164).

Gregory III ?–741, pope, 731–741 (p. 293).

Gregory VII, born Hildebrand ?–1085, pope, 1073–1085, quarreled with Henry IV of Germany (p. 284).

Gregory VIII ?–1187, pope, 1187, initiated Third Crusade (p. 300).

Gregory XI 1330–1378, pope, 1370–1378, returned papacy to Rome from Avignon, France (p. 339).

Gutenberg, Johannes *(GOOT en burg)* c. 1397–1468, German inventor of movable type printing (p. 330).

H

Hargreaves, James ?–1778, English inventor of the spinning jenny, 1764 (p. 492).

Henry, Henry the Navigator 1394–1460, prince of Portugal, patron of sea exploration (p. 371).

Henry IV 1050–1106, king of Germany, 1056–1105, quarreled with Pope Gregory VII (p. 285).

Henry IV 1553–1610, king of France, 1589–1610, signed Edict of Nantes (p. 452).

Henry V 1081–1125, king of Germany, 1111–1125, made pact with pope, Concordat of Worms (p. 284).

Henry VIII 1491–1547, king of England, 1509–1547, established Church of England (p. 351).

Heraclius c. 575–641, emperor of the Eastern Roman Empire, 610–641 (p. 45).

Hooke, Robert 1635–1703, English scientist (p. 355).

Huascar *(WAHS kahr)* c. 1495–1533, son of Inca, put to death by his brother Atahualpa (p. 438).

I

Ibn Battuta, Muhammad 1304–1377, greatest Arabian traveler of Middle Ages (p. 13).

Ibn Sina, Avicenna *(av ih SEHN uh)* 980–1037, Abbasid doctor (p. 90).

Ignatius Loyola 1491–1556, Spanish priest, founder of Jesuits (p. 352).

Isabella I, Isabella the Catholic 1451–1504, queen of Aragon and unified Spain, 1479–1504 (p. 378).

J

Jahangir *(juh hahn GEER)*, Conqueror of the World 1569–1627, Mughal emperor, 1605–1627 (p. 182).

James I 1566–1625, king of England, 1603–1625, began colonization of America (p. 460).

James II 1633–1701, king of England, 1685–1688, deposed in Glorious Revolution (p. 462).

Jefferson, Thomas 1743–1826, third president of the United States, 1801–1809 (p. 482).

Joan of Arc 1412–1431, French farm girl who led French against English in 1429 (p. 312).

John 1167–1216, king of England, forced by barons to set his seal to the *Magna Carta* (p. 270).

John II, John the Perfect 1455–1495, king of Portugal, 1481–1495, supported exploration (p. 149).

Joseph II 1741–1790, Austrian king, 1764–1790 (p. 480).

Julius Caesar 100–44 B.C., Roman general and dictator, 49–44 B.C. (p. 26).

Justinian I 483–565, Byzantine emperor, 527–565 (p. 42).

K

Kay, John 1742–1826, English inventor of the flying shuttle, 1733 (p. 492).

Kepler, Johannes 1571–1630, German astronomer (p. 354).

Khwarizmi, al *(al KWAH rihz mee)* c. 780–850, Arab mathematician, developer of algebra (p. 90).

Kublai Khan 1216–1294, Mongol leader, 1260–1294 (p. 167).

L

Labé, Louise c. 1520–1566, French poet and writer, called for women to educate themselves (p. 328).

Laozi 606–530 B.C., Chinese philosopher and founder of Daoism (p. 197).

Las Casas, Bartolomé de 1474–1566, Spanish Dominican missionary and historian (p. 369).

Leo III c. 680–741, Byzantine emperor, 717–741 (p. 293).

Leo III c. 750–816, pope, 795–816, crowned Charlemagne emperor of Holy Roman Empire (p. 258).

Leo IX 1002–1054, pope, 1049–1054, excommunicated patriarch of Constantinople (p. 293).

Leo X 1475–1521, pope, 1513–1521, pope during start of Protestant Reformation (p. 344).

Leonardo da Vinci *(VEEN chih)* 1452–1519, Italian artist and scientific thinker (p. 319).

Li Yuan 565–635, founder and first emperor of Tang Dynasty of China, 618–626 (p. 203).

Locke, John 1632–1704, English philosopher (p. 479).

Louis VI, Louis the Fat, 1081–1137, king of France, 1108–1137, friend of Abbot Suger (p. 284).

Louis VII, Louis the Young c. 1120–1180, king of France, 1137–1180, joined crusade (p. 299).

Louis XIII 1601–1643, French king, 1610–1643, assisted by Cardinal Richelieu (p. 453).

Louis XIV 1638–1715, king of France, 1643–1715, absolute monarch; built Versailles (p. 454).

Louis XVI 1754–1793, French king, 1774–1792, executed during French Revolution (p. 482).

Luther, Martin 1483–1546, German religious reformer (p. 341).

M

Machiavelli, Niccolò 1469–1527, Italian political thinker and writer of *The Prince* (p. 318).

Magellan, Ferdinand c. 1480–1521, Portuguese navigator of the world (p. 380).

Mahmud of Ghazna c. 971–1030, Turkish sultan, 997–1030 (p. 178).

Mansa Musa ?–1332, ruler of Mali, 1307–1332 (p. 119).

Mansur, Abu Jafar al c. 712–775, Abbasid caliph who built Baghdad, 754–775 (p. 86).

Mary I 1516–1558, English queen, 1553–1558, daughter of Henry VIII's first wife (p. 459).

Mary II 1662–1694, English queen, 1689–1694, became queen during Glorious Revolution (p. 462).

Mehmed II, Mehmed the Conqueror 1432–1481, Ottoman Sultan, 1451–1481 (p. 172).

Michelangelo Buonarroti *(BWAN nahr raw tih)* 1475–1564, Italian artist (p. 322).

Moctezuma c. 1480–1520, Aztec emperor (p. 437).

Montesquieu, Charles *(MAHN teh skyoo)* 1689–1755, French lawyer and political philosopher (p. 479).

More, Thomas 1478–1535, English statesman and author (p. 332).

Muawiya *(mu AH wih ya)* ?–680, Umayyad caliph, 661–680 (p. 67).

Muhammad 570–632, prophet of Islam, messenger of Allah (p. 58).

Mwene Mutapa c. 1400s, king of Monomutapa in Africa (p. 148).

N

Newton, Isaac 1642–1727, English scientist, astronomer, and mathematician (p. 356).

O

Oda, Nobunaga 1534–1582, general who unified Japan (p. 238).

Odoacer c. 434–493, barbarian ruler of Italy, 476–493 (p. 256).

Ogodei *(ahg ah DY)* 1185–1241, Mongol leader, 1229–1241 (p. 166).

Pronunciation Key

This chart presents the pronunciation key used in this Glossary. For a key to the phonetic respellings used to indicate pronunciation in the text of the chapters, see page 539.

Spellings	Symbol	Spellings	Symbol	Spellings	Symbol
pat	ă	kick, cat, pique	k	thin	th
pay	ā	lid, needle	l	this	*th*
care	âr	mum	m	cut	ŭ
father	ä	no, sudden	n	urge, term, firm,	ûr
bib	b	thing	ng	word, heard	
church	ch	pot, horrid	ŏ	valve	v
deed, milled	d	toe	ō	with	w
pet	ĕ	caught, paw, for	ô	yes	y
bee	ē	noise	oi	zebra, xylem	z
life, phase, rough	f	took	o͝o	vision, pleasure,	zh
gag	g	boot	o͞o	garage	
hat	h	out	ou	about, item, edible,	ə
which	hw	pop	p	gallop, circus	
pit	ĭ	roar	r	butter	ər
pie, by	ī	sauce	s		
pier	îr	ship, dish	sh	Primary stress ´	
judge	j	tight, stopped	t	Secondary stress ´	

A

absolute monarch (ăb´sə-lo͞ot´ mŏn´ərk´) a ruler who has no restrictions of any kind on his or her power (p. 454).

adobe (ə-dō´bē) bricks formed of mud mixed with straw (p. 415).

Age of Enlightenment (āj ŭv ĕn-līt´n-mənt) a movement in Europe during the 1700s that critically analyzed ideas and institutions, using human reason (p. 477).

agricultural revolution (ăg-rĭ-kŭl´chər-əl rĕv´ə-lo͞o´shən) a series of agricultural developments in Europe during the 1700s that improved both farming methods and the yield of the land (p. 490).

alliance (ə-lī´əns) a pact or union between states in a common cause (p. 424).

altiplano (äl´tĭ-plä´nō) the land on a high, flat plateau in South America (p. 412).

ancestor worship (ăn´sĕs´tər wûr´shĭp) honor and reverence paid to one's deceased relatives, based on the belief that their spirits live on and can influence the gods in one's favor (p. 126).

archaeology (är´kē-ŏl´ə-jē) the recovery and study of physical remains from past human life and culture (p. 17).

aristocrat (ə-rĭs´tə-krăt´) a member of a privileged class having inherited wealth and high social position (p. 204).

B

balance of trade (băl´əns ŭv trād) the difference in value between the total imports and total exports of a nation (p. 370).

barbarian (bär-bâr´ē-ən) in the ancient Roman Empire, people living along the empire's borders; a person considered by another group to have a primitive culture (p. 29).

Buddhism (bo͞o´dĭz´əm) a religion based on the teachings of Siddhartha Gautama; Buddhism stresses that suffering is a basic part of life and that life is a cycle of death and rebirth and that suffering can be overcome (p. 194).

bullion (bo͞ol´yən) gold or silver in the form of bars or ingots of a specific weight (p. 370).

bureaucracy (byo͝o-rŏk´rə-sē) a type of organization structured like a pyramid, with one person at the top and many at the bottom; workers at each level supervise those below them (p. 82).

bushido (bo͞osh´ĭ-dō) a Japanese code of ethics involving courage, loyalty, and commitment to military life; "the way of the warrior" (p. 273).

C

caliph (kā´lĭf) the civil and religious ruler of a Muslim state (p. 66).

calligraphy (kə-lĭg´rə-fē) the art of fine handwriting, such as that practiced in Muslim art and writing (p. 88).

calpulli (kăl-pōō´lē) an Aztec settlement in which families of different social classes lived and shared the land (p. 425).

capital (kăp´ĭ-tl) wealth in the form of money or property used for the production of more wealth (p. 375).

capitalist (kăp´ĭ-tl-ĭst) an investor of money, or capital, in business (p. 493).

caravan (kăr´ə-văn´) a single file of pack animals journeying together to transport goods (p. 11).

caravel (kăr´ə-vĕl´) a swift, maneuverable sailing ship used for exploration by the Spanish and the Portuguese in the 1500s and 1600s (p. 373).

charter (chär´tər) a document issued by a monarch or other authority, creating a public or private corporation with special rights (p. 468).

checks and balances (chĕks ənd băl´əns-əz) the system of maintaining a balance of power between various branches of a government (p. 498).

chinampa (chĭ-năm´pə) narrow strips of land about 300 feet long and 30 feet wide built in swampy land and used for farming in Central America, particularly by the Aztec (p. 423).

chivalry (shĭv´əl-rē) qualities such as honor, courtesy, loyalty, and fair treatment of the weak, idealized by knights in the Middle Ages (p. 273).

circumnavigation (sûr´kəm-năv´ĭ-gā´shən) the act of sailing around the world (p. 380).

city-state (sĭtē-stāt´) an independent state made up of a city and the territory that surrounds it (p. 143).

civil war (sĭv´əl wôr) a war between factions or regions within a country (p. 438).

clan (klăn) a group of families who claim descent from a common ancestor (p. 163).

classic (klăs´ĭk) a work of art or literature from ancient Greece or Rome; something considered to be of the highest rank or excellence (p. 291).

clergy (klûr´jē) the group of people who have been ordained for religious service (p. 283).

codex (kō´dĕks´) a manuscript volume; record books kept by early Central American peoples such as the Maya and Aztec (p. 409).

colony (kŏl´ə-nē) a settlement in a distant land whose citizens keep close ties to their parent country (p. 375).

commerce (kŏm´ərs) trade, or the buying and selling of goods, on a large scale (p. 45).

commonwealth (kŏm´ən-wĕlth´) a nation governed by the people (p. 461).

Confucianism (kən-fyōō´shən-ĭz´əm) a set of beliefs, based on the teachings of Confucius, that focused on proper conduct, respect for elders, scholarship, and government service (p. 194).

conquistador (kŏng-kē´stə-dôr´) the Spanish term for conqueror used in reference to Spaniards who came to the New World in the 1500s in search of wealth (p. 437).

constitutional monarchy (kŏn´stĭ-tōō´shə-nəl mŏn´ər-kē) a monarchy in which the powers of the ruler are restricted to those granted under the constitution and the laws of the nation (p. 463).

contract (kŏn´trăckt´) an agreement between two or more parties, particularly one that is written and enforceable by law (p. 479).

council (koun´səl) an assembly called to help pick the next Muslim caliph (p. 67); a series of meetings of Roman Catholic Church leaders in the 1400s dealing with issues of church law and faith (p. 340).

Counter Reformation (koun´tər ref´ər-ma´shən) the reform movement within the Roman Catholic Church whose goals were to abolish abuses and reaffirm traditional beliefs (p. 352).

courtier (kôr´tē-ər) a person who takes part in the highly refined social life of a court (p. 228).

crop rotation (krŏp rō-tā´shən) the planting of crops such as turnips, wheat, and clover in alternate years to keep soil fertile (p. 491).

crusade (krōō-sād´) any of the military expeditions undertaken by European Christians from c. 1100 to c. 1400 to win the Holy Land from the Muslims (p. 296).

currency (kûr´ən-sē) any form of money being used as a medium of exchange (p. 150, 206).

D

daimyo (dīm´yō´) the lord of a large agricultural estate in feudal Japan who supported the shogun (p. 232).

Daoism (dou´ĭz´əm) a belief system based on the teachings of Laozi; Daoists emphasis living in harmony with nature and being content with one's life (p. 197).

delta (dĕl´tə) a triangle-shaped landform of mud and silt deposited at a river's mouth (p. 110).

denomination (dĭ-nŏm´ə-nā´shən) a religious body consisting of a group of congregations having the same faith (p. 234).

despot (dĕs´pət) a ruler who holds absolute power and uses it abusively (p. 212).

dissent (dĭ-sĕnt´) to disagree, especially with the accepted doctrine of an established religion (p. 82).

divan (dĭ-văn´) a governing council in a Muslim country, especially the Ottoman Imperial Council (p. 173).

divine right (dĭ-vīn´ rīt) the right of a monarch to rule, based on the belief that this right comes directly from God and that the monarch is responsible only to God (p. 454).

diviner (dĭ-vīn´ər) a person who is believed to communicate with the spirit world and to help other people interact with their gods (p. 126).

dowry (dou´rē) money, land, servants, or any other valuable property given by a bride's family to her husband at marriage (p. 328).

dynasty (dī´nə-stē) a succession of rulers from the same family or line (p. 32).

E

electronic communication (ĭ-lĕk-trŏn´ĭk kə-myo͞o´ nĭ- kā´shən) communication devices, such as the Internet, fax, telephone, television, and computer that have reduced the time necessary for transmitting information (p. 7).

elite (ĭ-lēt´) a small, privileged group at the top of a society (p. 401).

emir (ĭ-mîr´) a prince, chieftain, or governor, especially in the Middle East (p. 82).

empire (ĕm´pīr´) a political unit often made up of a number of territories, states, or nations, ruled by a single supreme authority (p. 78).

enclosure (ĕn-klō´zhər) the fencing in of common land to form larger estates in England during the 1700s (p. 491).

encomienda system (ĕn-kō´mē-ĕn´də sĭs´təm) a system in which New World inhabitants were granted to Spanish colonists, who were responsible for supervising their work and instructing the inhabitants in the teachings of Roman Catholicism (p. 467).

enlightened despot (ĕn-līt´nd dĕs´pət) a European ruler in the 1700s with absolute power who tried to support Enlightenment ideals such as tolerance and freedom (p. 480).

excommunication (ĕks´kə-myo͞o´nĭ-kā´shən) the act that deprives someone of membership in the church (p. 285).

extinct (ĭk-stĭngkt´) no longer existing or living (p. 398).

F

faction (făk´shən) a group of persons forming a minority in disagreement with the larger group (p. 91).

feudalism (fyo͞od´l-ĭz´əm) a political and economic system in which large landholders or lords gave protection to people in return for their service to the landholder (p. 261).

fief (fēf) a large feudal estate, particularly in medieval Europe (p. 261).

G

ghazi (gä´zē) a Muslim warrior who has fought to expand the frontiers of the Muslim state (p. 171).

grand vizier (grănd vĭ-zîr´) the senior advisor or prime minister who advises the sultan on state matters (p. 172).

griot (grē´ō) a West African storyteller (p. 118).

guild (gĭld) an association of tradespeople made up of merchants, craftspeople, or artisans, particularly in the Middle Ages (p. 269).

H

haiku (hī´ko͞o) an unrhymed Japanese poem consisting of three lines with five, seven, and five syllables, respectively (p. 241).

harem (hâr´əm) literally, sanctuary or sacred place; the women or the domestic quarters of a Muslim household (p. 173).

heretic (hĕr´ĭ-tĭk) a person who has controversial opinions, especially one who publicly disagrees with the accepted beliefs of the Roman Catholic Church (p. 313).

hierarchy (hī´ə-rär´kē) a group of people organized or classified by rank and authority (p. 261).

hieroglyph (hī´ər-ə-glĭf´) a system of writing that uses picture symbols for concepts, objects, or words (p. 403).

history (hĭs´tə-rē) a record of past human events; the study of the past, including explanations of the events (p. 17).

homage (hom´ĭj) an expression of public honor or respect; in feudalism, the ceremonial recognition of allegiance to a lord shown by a vassal (p. 263).

humanism (hyo͞o´mə-nĭz´əm) a doctrine or attitude that is concerned primarily with human beings and their values, capacities, and achievements (p. 319).

hunter-gatherer (hŭn´tər găth´ər-ər) early people who obtained their food by hunting wild animals and gathering wild plants, roots, nuts, and berries (p. 397).

hypothesis (hī-poth´ĭ-sĭs) an assumption that accounts for a set of facts and that can be tested by investigation (p. 355).

I

icon (ī´kŏn´) a picture or representation of a sacred Christian person, itself regarded as sacred (p. 292).

idol (īd´l) an image used as an object of worship (p. 55).

immigrant (ĭm´ĭ-grənt) a person who leaves one country to settle permanently in another country (p. 500).

individualism (ĭn´də-vĭj´o͞o-ə-lĭz´əm) personal independence; the idea that every person should be free to develop and pursue his or her own goals (p. 315).

indulgence (ĭn-dŭl´jəns) certificates, issued by the pope, which were said to reduce or cancel punishment for a person's sins (p. 340).

industrial revolution (ĭn-dŭs´trē-əl rĕv´ə-lo͞o´shən) major improvements in industry, especially those in Europe during the 18th century (p. 492).

infidel (ĭn´fĭ-dəl) one who is an unbeliever in Christianity (p. 296).

Inquisition (ĭn´kwĭ-zĭsh´ən) a Roman Catholic Church court revived during the Counter Reformation for the purpose of trying, convicting, and punishing heretics (p. 352).

Islam (ĭs-läm´) a religion based on the teachings of the prophet Muhammad that believes in one god, Allah; the laws of Islam are found in the Qur'an and the Sunna (p. 60).

isolation (ī´sə-lā´shən) the condition of being separated from a group (p. 223).

J

janissary (jăn´ĭ-sĕr´ē) an enslaved soldier in the elite Ottoman infantry or government service (p. 173).

K

khan (kän) a Mongol ruler (p. 165).

kinship (kĭn´shĭp´) the relationship among family members (p. 127).

knight (nīt) an armed, mounted soldier of the feudal period who gives military service to a lord (p. 261).

L

lateen sail (lə-tēn´ sāl) a triangular sail (p. 12).

legacy (lĕg´ə-sē) something handed down from an ancestor; something from the past (p. 98).

literacy (lĭt´ər-ə-sē) the ability to read and write (p. 291).

M

magnetic compass (măg-nĕt´ĭk kŭm´pəs) a device used to determine geographical direction, using a magnetic needle that is free to pivot until aligned with the magnetic field of the earth (p. 12).

malaria (mə-lâr´ē-ə) a tropical disease carried by the anopheles mosquito and characterized by chills, fever, and sweating (p. 148).

mandate (măn´dāt´) a command or instruction from an authority; an order to govern (p. 204).

manor (măn´ər) the castle and estate of a feudal lord (p. 266).

matrilineal (măt´rə-lĭn´ē-əl) relating to the system of tracing descent through the females of a family (p. 117).

mercantilism (mûr´kən-tē-lĭz´əm) a European economic system based on establishing colonies as a source of raw materials and as the market for goods from the ruling country (p. 467).

mercenary (mûr´sə-nèr´ē) a professional soldier who is hired by a foreign country (p. 318).

meritocracy (mĕr´ĭ-tŏk´rə-sē) a system in which people are chosen for jobs and promoted on the basis of their performance (p. 204).

migrate (mī´grāt´) to move from one area or country to another and settle there (p. 137).

millet (mĭ´lā) a partially self-governing group of non-Muslims in the Ottoman Empire; the most common millets were Armenian, Greek Orthodox, and Jewish (p. 174).

missionary (mĭsh´ə-nèr´ē) a person sent to a foreign country to do religious or charitable work (p. 152).

monarchy (mŏn´ər-kē) a strong central government ruled by a king or queen (p. 312).

monastery (mŏn´ə-stĕr´ē) a place in which a community of religious people, particularly monks, lives (p. 257).

money economy (mŭn´ē ĭ-kŏn´ə-mē) an economy in which cash is the most common item exchanged for goods (p. 206).

monopoly (mə-nŏp´ə-lē) the total control by one group of the means of producing a service (p. 368).

monotheism (mŏn´ə-thē-ĭz´əm) the belief that there is only one God (p. 59).

monsoon (mŏn-sōōn´) a wind system that switches direction seasonally and brings dry and wet seasons, especially the Asiatic monsoon that brings wet and dry seasons to India and southern Asia (p. 141).

mosaic (mō-zā´ĭk) a picture or design made from small colored pieces of glass or quartz embedded in plaster (p. 43).

mosque (mŏsk) a Muslim house of worship (p. 60).

Muslim (mŭz´ləm) a believer in Islam (p. 60).

N

natural right (năch´ər-əl rīt) one of the rights believed by many to be guaranteed to all people by nature, including life, liberty, and the right to own property (p. 479).

nomad (nō´măd´) a member of a group that moves from place to place following food, water, and grazing land for their herds (p. 53).

O

oasis (ō-ā´sĭs) a small area in the desert watered by springs and wells (p. 53).

oath of fealty (ōth ŭv fē´əl-tē) a feudal oath of loyalty sworn to a lord in exchange for an award of land (p. 261).

oral tradition (ôr´əl trə-dĭsh´ən) the legends, myths, and beliefs that a culture passes from generation to generation by word of mouth (p. 148).

P

pamphlet (păm´flĭt) an unbound published work such as an essay, usually on a current topic (p. 345).

parliament (pär´lə-mənt) a national representative body having the highest lawmaking powers within the state, particularly in England (p. 458).

patriarch (pā´trē-ärk´) the male leader of a family or tribe; in the Byzantine Empire, the bishop of Constantinople (p. 292).

patrician (pə-trĭsh´ən) a member of the highest class of society in Italian city-states during the Renaissance; an aristocrat (p. 327).

patrilineal (păt´rə-lĭn´ē-əl) relating to the system of tracing descent through the males of a family (p. 117).

patron (pā´trən) a person who financially supports scholars or artists (p. 327).

philosophe (fē´lə-zôf´) any of the leading philosophical, political, and social writers of the French Enlightenment of the 1700s from either the aristocracy or the middle class (p. 477).

pilgrimage (pĭl´grə-mĭj) a journey to a sacred place or shrine (p. 57).

plague (plāg) a highly infectious, usually fatal, epidemic disease (p. 310).

plantation (plăn-tā´shən) a large farm where crops are grown (p. 152).

plateau (plă-tō´) a raised and relatively flat area of land (p. 146).

predestination (prē-dĕs´tə-nā´shən) the belief that God has determined all things in advance, including the salvation of souls (p. 350).

prehistory (prē-hĭs´tə-rē) history that took place before the development of writing (p. 17).

primary source (prī´mĕr´ē sôrs) a source for historical study that was written by someone who participated in or observed the event being recorded (p. 17).

prime minister (prím mǐn´ĭ-stər) the chief government official appointed by a ruler (p. 453).

Protestant (prŏt´ĭ-stənt) a reformer who protested against the abuses of the Catholic church in the 1500s; a member of a church descended from those that seceded from the Roman Catholic Church during the 1500s (p. 344).

province (prŏv´ĭns) in the ancient Roman Empire, any of the lands outside Italy conquered and ruled by the Romans (p. 27).

Q

Qur'an (kə-răn´) the sacred book of Islam that is believed to contain the revelations made to Muhammad by Allah (p. 58).

R

realism (rē´ə-lĭz´əm) an artistic style dating from the Renaissance that attempts to visually represent people and objects as they exist naturally (p. 322).

reason (rē´zən) the capacity for logical thought (p. 476).

Reformation (rĕf´ər-mā´shən) the reform movement of the 1500s that resulted in the separation of the Protestant churches from the Roman Catholic Church (p. 344).

regent (rē´jənt) a person who rules for a monarch during periods of illness or absence, or during the monarch's extreme youth (p. 228).

Renaissance (rĕn´ĭ-säns´) the revival of attention to classical Greek and Roman art, literature, and learning that originated in Italy in the 14th century and later spread through Europe (p. 317).

republic (rĭ-pŭb´lĭk) a political order whose head of state is not a monarch and in which supreme power lies in a body of elected citizens (p. 317).

S

Sahel (sə-hāl´) a strip of dry grasslands on the southern border of the Sahara; also known as "the shore of the desert" (p. 109).

salary (săl´ə-rē) a fixed payment for services paid on a regular basis (p. 181).

salvation (săl-vā´shən) the deliverance of the soul from the penalties of sin (p. 285).

samurai (săm´ə-rī´) the feudal military aristocracy of Japan, from the term meaning "those who serve" (p. 232).

satellite (săt´ə-līt´) a relatively small object orbiting a planet or moon; a manufactured object orbiting the earth, often used to transmit information (p. 7).

savanna (sə-văn´ə) a region of grasslands containing scattered trees and vegetation (p. 109).

schism (sĭz´əm) a separation or division into factions, especially a formal separation within a Christian church (p. 293).

scientific method (sī´ən-tĭf´ĭk mĕth´əd) a series of logical steps formulated by Francis Bacon and used in scientific research that stressed observation and experimentation (p. 355).

Scientific Revolution (sī´ən-tĭf´ĭk rĕv´ə-lōō´shən) the era of scientific thought in Europe during which careful observation of the natural world was made, and accepted beliefs were questioned (p. 354).

secondary source (sĕk´ən-dĕr´ē sôrs) a source for historical study that was written after the event it describes, usually with the aid of a primary source (p. 17).

secular (sĕk´yə-lər) worldly, rather than religious, in nature (p. 332).

sedentary (sĕd´n-tĕr´ē) characterized by remaining in one place and not migrating (p. 398).

serf (sûrf) a member of the lowest feudal class, bound to the land and whoever owned the land (p. 264).

Shiite (shē´īt´) a member of the branch of Islam that supports the descendants of Muhammad as his rightful successors (p. 67).

Shinto (shĭn´tō) a Japanese religion whose followers believe that all things in the natural world are filled with divine spirits (p. 225).

shogun (shō´gən) a line of military leaders who ruled Japan under the nominal leadership of the emperor until 1868 (p. 232).

stele (stē´lē) an upright stone column with inscribed hieroglyphs used as a monument, particularly by early peoples of Central America (p. 407).

steppe (stĕp) a vast semiarid grass-covered plain, usually lightly wooded, as found in southeastern Europe and Siberia (p. 162).

sternpost rudder (stûrn´pōst´ rŭd´ər) a paddlelike device under a ship and connected to a handle on deck, for steering sailing ships (p. 12).

stirrup (stûr´əp) a loop or ring hung from either side of a horse's saddle to support the rider's foot in riding and mounting (p. 11).

succession (sək-sĕsh´ən) the sequence in which one person after another succeeds to a title, throne, or estate (p. 238).

sultan (sŭl´tən) the ruler of a Muslim country, especially the former Ottoman Empire (p. 172).

Sunna (soon´ə) traditional Islamic law observed by orthodox Muslims and based on the teaching of Muhammad (p. 61).

Sunni (soon´ē) the branch of Islam that follows orthodox tradition and accepts the validity of the first four caliphs elected as successors to Muhammad (p. 68).

T

terrace farming (tĕr´ĭs fär´mĭng) the building of raised banks of earth on steep land for farming (p. 433).

tithe (tīth) a tenth of one's income contributed voluntarily to a church (p. 285).

tribe (trīb) any system of social organization made up of villages, bands, or other groups with a common ancestry, language, culture, and name (p. 55).

tribute (trĭb´yoot) a kind of tax paid in goods or services to the ruling government (p. 425).

U

university (yoo´nə-vûr´sĭ-tē) an institution of higher learning with teaching and research facilities as well as graduate and professional schools (p. 287).

V

vassal (văs´əl) a person who receives land and protection from a feudal lord in return for loyalty to that lord (p. 261).

vertical economy (vûr´tĭ-kəl ĭ-kŏn´ə-mē) the growing of crops according to the altitude of the land, particularly in South America (p. 433).

Acknowledgments *(continued from page 558)*

442: © Merrell Wood / TIB (l); © Susan Malis / PHOTRI (r). **443**: Biblioteca Nacional, Madrid. **448–49**: The Granger Collection. **450**: Museu Nacional de Arte Antiga, Lisbon, MH (l); Bermuda News Service (r). **451**: Galleria Palatina, Florence / AR (t); Private Collection / NB (bl); The Metropolitan Museum of Art (r). **452**: Victoria & Albert Museum / Bridgeman Art Library. **453**: Bibliotheque Publique et Universitaire, Geneva. **454**: National Gallery, London / AR (t); The Mansell Collection (b). **455**: Comstock, Inc. (t); AR (b). **456**: Gianni Dagli Orti / Corbis. **458**: British Library. **459**: Private Collection / NB (t); Her Majesty's Stationery Office, England (b). **460**: National Maritime Museum, Greenwich, England (t); Victoria & Albert Museum (b). **461**: National Museum of Scotland (t); The Royal Collection (b). **462**: AR (l); Private Collection (lc); The Granger Collection (rc); The National Portrait Gallery, London (r). **463**: The National Portrait Gallery, London (l, rc, r); © Collection of The New-York Historical Society (lc). **464**: New York Public Library, Rare Books Division. **465**: RJB. **467**: The Folger Shakespeare Library (t); RJB (b). **468**: BM / Bridgeman Art Library / AR (l); The Brooklyn Museum (r). **469**: RJB.

471: © Willinger / FPG International. **474**: © Robert Descharnes, Les Delices, Geneva (l); Musee Carnavalet, Paris (r). **475**: © H. Andrew Johnson, Thomas Jefferson Memorial Foundation, Inc. (l); SCALA / AR (r). **476**: BM / Bridgeman Art Library / AR. **477**: Trinity College, Cambridge, England (t); The Granger Collection (b). **478**: Giraudon / AR (t); The Cleveland Museum of Art (b). **479**: Corbis-Bettmann. **480**: Biblioteca Nacional, Madrid. **482**: The Metropolitan Museum of Art, Gift of William H. Huntington, 1883. **483**: Musee Carnavalet, Paris, Giraudon / AR. **485**: Louvre / NB. **490**: AR. **491**: The Newberry Library, Chicago. **492**: Smithsonian Institution. **493**: LPW **494**: The Newberry Library, Chicago (t); © Eddie Hironaka / TIB (b). **495**: © Stephen Wilkes / TIB. **496**: RJB. **497**: © PHOTRI. **498**: © Don Carl Steffan / Photo Researchers, Inc. (tl); © Bill Ross / Westlight (tr); © Craig Aurness / Westlight (c); The National Archives (b). **499**: New York Public Library / NB. **500**: © Pete Turner / TIB. **503**: AR (l); SCALA / AR (r).
Picture Research Assistance by Carousel Research, Inc., Meyers Photo-Art, and Jim Lillie.

Italic numbers refer to pages on which illustrations appear.

Text *(continued from page iv)*

ii Excerpt from December 30, 1941, speech by Winston Churchill to the Canadian Senate and the House of Commons. Copyright by The Estate of Sir Winston Churchill. Reprinted by permission of Curtis Brown Ltd. on behalf of The Estate of Sir Winston Churchill. **iv** The material in the Minipedia is reprinted from *The World Book Encyclopedia* with the expressed permission of the publisher. Copyright ©1998 by World Book, Inc. **10** From *Parthian Stations of Isidore of Charax* translated by Wilfred H. Schoff, Philadelphia: Commercial Museum, 1914. **13** From *Journals of Hsuan-Tsang*, in *Chinese Accounts of India* by Samuel Beal, Calcutta, India: S. Gupta, 1958. **13** From *The Adventures of Ibn Battuta* by Ross Dunn, Berkeley: University of California Press, 1986. **19** Aztec poem translated by Miguel Leon-Portilla from *Broken Spears: The Aztec Account of the Conquest of Mexico,* Boston: Beacon Press, 1962. **19** From *The Conquest of New Spain* by Bernal Díaz, translated by J. M. Cohen, Baltimore, Maryland: Penguin Books, 1963. **26** From letter by Cyprian, Bishop of Carthage, in *Barbarian Europe* by Gerald Simons, New York: Time-Life Books, 1968. **38** Excerpt from "The King's Adviser" from *Kalilah and Dimnah* translated and adapted by Hassan Tehranchian. Copyright ©1985 by Hassan Tehranchian. Reprinted by permission of the author. **74–75** "The Cadi and the Fly" by Al-Jahiz, translated by Charles Pellat from *The Life and Works of Al-Jahiz.* Copyright ©1969 by the University of California Press. Reprinted by permission of International Thomson Publishing Services Ltd. **75–76** "The Disadvantages of Parchment" by Al-Jahiz, translated by Charles Pellat from *The Life and Works of Al-Jahiz.* Copyright ©1969 by the University of California Press. Reprinted by permission of International Thomson Publishing Services Ltd. **76–77** "Good Deeds at Random," "The Spinning Waterwheel" and "The Fountain" translated by James A. Bellamy and Patricia Owen Steiner from *Ibn Sa'id Al-Maghribi: Banners of the Champions, An Anthology of Medieval Arabic Poetry from Andalusia and Beyond.* Copyright ©1989 by James A. Bellamy and Patricia Owen Steiner. Reprinted by permission of Hispanic Seminary of Medieval Studies. **84** From *A Source Book in Geography*, edited by George Kish, Cambridge, Massachusetts: Harvard University Press, 1978. **89** "You Departed From My Sight" from *Lyrics from Arabia* edited and translated by Ghazi A. Algosaibi. Copyright ©1983 by Ghazi A. Algosaibi. Reprinted by permission of Three Continents Press. **90** From "Text 3: The Autobiography" by Avicenna, in *Avicenna and the Aristotelian Tradition*, Leiden, The Netherlands: E.J. Brill, 1988. **101** From *Readers' Guide to Periodical Literature,* August 1997, Vol. 97, #6, pp. 408 and 526. Copyright ©1997 by the H.W. Wilson Company. Reprinted by permission of the publisher. **115** From *Book of the Roads and Kingdoms*, in *The Story of Africa* by Basil Davidson, London: Mitchell Beazley, 1984. **118** From a tale recorded by D.T. Niane of Mali, in *History of African Civilization* by E. Jefferson Murphy, New York: Thomas Y. Crowell Co., 1972. **125** From *Things Fall Apart* by Chinua Achebe, New York: Ballantine Books, 1959. **128** "The Cow-Tail Switch" from *The Cow-Tail Switch and Other West African Stories* by Harold Courlander and George Herzog. Copyright 1947, ©1975 by Harold Courlander. Reprinted by permission of Henry Holt and Company, Inc. **141** Excerpt from "The Periplus of the Erythraean Sea" from *The East African Coast* by G.S.P. Freeman-Grenville. Copyright ©1962 by Oxford University Press. Reprinted by permission of the author. **144** From a chronicler's observation of the destruction of Mombasa, in *The Story of Africa* by Basil Davidson, London: Mitchell Beazley, 1984. **144** "He Who Wants to String Pearls" from *Four Centuries of Swahili Verse* edited by Jan Knappert. Copyright ©1979 by Jan Knappert. Reprinted by permission of Heinemann Educational Books Ltd. **148** From annals by Joãs de Barros, in *Introduction to African Civilizations* by John G. Jackson, New York: University Books, 1970. **153** From letter by Affonso of Congo to King John of Portugal, in *The African Past* by Basil Davidson, Boston: Little, Brown and Co., 1964. **154** From letter by Affonso of Congo to King John of Portugal, in *The Kingdom of Kongo* by Anne Hilton, Oxford: Clarendon Press, 1985. **162** From a history of Ibn al-Athir, in *A Literary History of Persia, Vol. 2* by Edward G. Browne, Cambridge University Press, 1902. **170** From *Histoire des Mongols* by Rashid ad-Din, in *The Empire of the Steppes* by Rene Grousset, translated by Naomi Walford, New Brunswick, New Jersey: Rutgers University Press, 1970. **172** From Mehmed quotation regarding legalization of fratricide (1460), in *A History of the World* by Stanley Chodorow, New York: Harcourt Brace Jovanovich, 1986. **175** From historical annals (1453) by Kritovoulos, in *The Global Experience*, edited by Philip F. Riley, Englewood Cliffs, New Jersey: Prentice-Hall, 1987. **176** From 1538 inscription, in *The World* by Geoffrey Parker, New York: Harper & Row. **176** "Elegy of Suleiman" by Baki from *Istanbul and the Civilization of the Empire* by Bernard Lewis. Copyright ©1963 by the University of Oklahoma Press. Reprinted by permission of the University of Oklahoma Press. **178** From Chronicler of Mahmud, in *A Concise History of India* by Francis Watson, New York: Charles Scribner's Sons, 1975. **178** From *The Book of Kings* by Firdawsi, in *A History of the World* by Stanley Chodorow, New York: Harcourt Brace Jovanovich, 1986. **192** Quote by Ge Hong from *Sex in History,* revised and updated by Reay Tannahill, Chelsea, Michigan: Scarborough House, 1980, 1992. **195** "On Compulsive Urges" and "Twin Verses" from *The Dhammapada* translated by Eknath Easwaran. Copyright ©1986 by the Blue Mountain Center of Meditation. Reprinted by permission of Nilgiri Press, Petaluma, CA. **198** From *The Great Wall of China* by Robert Silverberg, Philadelphia: Chilton Books, 1965. **200** "Written on a Cold Evening," "In the Gorge: We Encounter Wind," "Evening Lake Scenes," "Rain and Cold" and "Night Rain at Kuang-k" by Yang Wan-Li, translated by Jonathan Chaves from *Heaven My Blanket, Earth My Pillow.* Copyright ©1976 by John Weatherhill. Reprinted by permission of Charles Tuttle, Tokyo. **202** "Quiet Night Thoughts" from *China's Imperial Past* by Charles O. Hucker. Copyright ©1975 by the Board of Trustees of the Leland Stanford Junior University. Reprinted with the permission of the publishers, Stanford University Press. **203** From *Introduction to Painting* by Wang Wei, in *Sources of Chinese Tradition* by Wm. Theodore de Bary, New York: Columbia University Press, 1960. **206** From *Continuation of the Comprehensive Mirror for Aiding Government*, in *The Pattern of the Chinese Past* by Mark Elvin, London: Eyre Methuen, 1973. **208** From a Chinese sailor's report (1119), in *The History of Invention* by Trevor I. Williams, New York: Facts on File, 1987. **208** From *The Pattern of the Chinese Past* by Mark Elvin, London: Eyre Methuen, 1973. **208** From the *Tearful Records of the Battle of Qizhou* (1221) in *The History of Invention* by Trevor I. Williams, New York: Facts on File, 1987. **209** "Kubilai Khan" from *The Travels of Marco Polo* translated by Ronald Latham. Copyright ©1958 by Ronald Latham. Reprinted by permission of Penguin Books Ltd. **226** "Here I Lie on Straw" from *Anthology of Japanese Literature* edited by Donald Keene. Copyright ©1955 by Grove Press. Reprinted by permission of Grove Weidenfeld. **228** "This Perfectly Still" from *Anthology of Japanese Literature* edited by Donald Keene. Copyright ©1955 by Grove Press. Reprinted by permission of Grove Weidenfeld. **227, 229** From *The Diary of Murasaki Shikibu*, in *Anthology of Japanese Literature*, edited by Donald Keene, New York: Grove Press, 1955. **241** "Old Pond" from *Introduction to Haiku* by Harold G. Henderson. Copyright ©1958 by Harold G. Henderson. Used by permission of Doubleday, a division of Bantam, Doubleday, Dell Publishing Group, Inc. **250** "The Story of Roland" from *Charlemagne and His Knights* by Katharine Pyle. Copyright 1932 by J.B. Lippincott Company. Reprinted by permission of HarperCollins Children's Books. **287** "The Canticle of Brother Sun" from *Saint Francis of Assisi* by Lawrence Cunningham, San Francisco: HarperCollins, 1981. **297** From *Memoirs* by Anna Comnena, in *The Crusades*, edited by Régine Pernoud, New York: G.P. Putnam's Sons, 1962. **311** Quotation from Sienese chronicler Agnolo di Tura Del Grasso, in *The Oxford Illustrated History of Medieval Europe*, edited by George Holmes, New York: Oxford University Press, 1988. **328** Quote by Louise Labé from *Not in God's Image* edited by Julia O'Faolain and Lauro Martines, New York: Harper & Row, 1973. **341** "The Book of Margery Kempe" from *The Medieval Mystics of England* edited by Eric Colledge. Copyright ©1961 by Charles Scribner's Sons, renewed 1989. Reprinted with the permission of Scribner, a division of Simon & Schuster. **369** From *Bartolomé de Las Casas*, translated and edited by George Sanderlin, New York: Knopf, 1971. **384** "The Audience" from *Columbus Sails* by C. Walter Hodges. Copyright 1939 by Coward-McCann, Inc., copyright renewed ©1967 by C. Walter Hodges. Reprinted by permission of Coward-McCann, Inc., a division of Penguin Putnam Inc. **422** From *The Ancient American Civilizations* by Friedrich Katz, translated by K.M. Lois Simpson, New York: Praeger, 1969. **428** From *Pre-Columbian Literatures of Mexico* by Miguel Leon-Portilla. Copyright ©1969 by the University of Oklahoma Press. Reprinted by permission of the University of Oklahoma Press. **437** From *Pre-Columbian Literatures of Mexico* by Miguel Leon-Portilla, Norman, Oklahoma: University of Oklahoma Press, 1969. **442** Excerpt from *Everyday Life of the Aztecs* by Warwick Bray. Copyright ©1968 by Warwick Bray. Reprinted by permission of B.T. Batsford Ltd. **444** "The Legend of the Lake" from *Warriors, Gods and Spirits from Central & Southern American Mythology* by Douglas Gifford. Copyright ©1983 by Eurobook Limited. Reprinted by permission of Eurobook Limited. **486** Excerpt from "To the Assembly for Protection" from *The Journal of Madame Royale* by Elizabeth Powers. Copyright ©1976 by Elizabeth Powers. Reprinted by permission of Walker and Company. **494** From *Victorian People and Ideas* by Richard D. Altick, New York: Norton, Publisher, 1973. **543** Pronunciation key copyright ©1985 by Houghton Mifflin Company. Adapted and reprinted by permission from *The American Heritage Dictionary,* Second College Edition.

Illustrations

Literature border design by **Peggy Skycraft**. **Ligature** 22, 33, 132, 156, 163, 188, 235, 267 (tr), 348, 357, 360, 390, 418, 472, 492, 501. **Precision Graphics** 12, 30, 68, 70, 84, 153, 205, 206-7, 229, 238-39, 244, 265, 304, 350, 379, 399, 441, 462-63, 465, 498. **Brian Battles** 151, 346. **John T. Burgoyne** 14, 298. **Susan David** 12, 396. **Ebet Dudley** 406, 423. **Simon Galkin** 261, 265. **Dale Glasgow** 163. **Henry Iken** 410. **Phil Jones** 184, **Guy Kingsbery** 6. **Al Lorenz** 455. **Matthew Pippin** 262. **Frederick Porter** 91. **Joseph Scrofani** 331, 373. **Scott Snow** 61,111. **Gary Torissi** 534-35. **Jean & Mou-Sien Tsen** 232. **Richard Waldrep** 233. **Brent Watkinson** 484. **Oliver Yourke** 282-83. **Other: 129** From *The Cow-Tail Switch and Other West African Stories.* Copyright © 1947, 1975 by Harold Courlander. Illustration by Madye Lee Chastian. Reprinted by permission of Henry Holt and Company, Inc. **407** By Michael Goodman, from :Maya Writing" by David Stuart and Stephen D. Houston. Copyright © August 1989 by *Scientific American*, Inc. All rights reserved. **408** From *Atlas of Ancient Americas*. Copyright © Equinox, Oxford (t, r). **409** From *Atlas of Ancient Americas*. Copyright © Equinox, Oxford. (t, r).

Maps

© GeoSystems Global Corporation G15 (tl), 518–533. **GeoSystems Global Corporation** G1, G2, G5, G11, G14. **Mapping Specialists** G3, G8 G9, G12, 5, 8, 9 (b), 13, 27, 36–37, 53, 67, 80–81, 85, 97, 109, 121, 137, 140, 142, 146, 150, 167, 171, 179, 183, 193, 204, 216, 217, 219, 224, 230, 257, 260, 290, 296, 299, 311, 317, 330, 347, 352, 366, 374, 378, 382–893, 397, 398, 401, 405, 412 (b, r), 423, 430, 436, 465, 470, 481. **Precision Graphics** G 6, G 7, 9 (t). **XNR Productions** 87. **Edward Parker** G 10. **Gary Torissi** G15 (r). **Other: 10** Based on Parthian Stations by Isidore of Charax, commentary by Wilfred H. Schoff, Philadelphia Commercial Museum, 1914.

Photographs

AR: Art Resource, New York; **BM:** British Museum; **LPW:** Laurie Platt Winfrey, Inc.; **MH:** Michael Holford; **NB:** Newsweek Books; **RHPL:** Robert Harding Picture Library, London; **RJB:** Ralph J. Brunke; **TIB:** The Image Bank

Front Cover: Peter Bosey. **Back Cover**: Bibliotheque Nationale, Paris. **ii:** The Water Margin, Chen Hongshou (t); LPW (b). **iii:** AR (l); SCALA / AR (r). **v:** The Water Margin, Chen Hongshou. **vi:** Cameramann International, Ltd. (b). **vii:** BM, MH (t); Private Collection / NB (b). **viii:** © Justin Kerr (bl); Accademia, Florence, SCALA / AR (br). **ix:** Zaire, Western Kasai Province, Mweka Zone, Kuba Peoples, Mukenga mask, Laura T. Magnuson Fund Income, X-Hautelet Collection 1982.1504...Photo by Robert Hashimoto, © 1989 The Art Institute of Chicago, All Rights Reserved(t); Ontario Science Museum (b). **x:** Musee de l'Institute d'Afrique Noire, Giraudon / AR (t); **G1:** BP/NRSC/Science Photo Library / Photo Researchers. **xvii–1:** SCALA / AR. **2:** © Michael O'Neil, Inc. **2–3:** New York Public Library, Rare Books Division. **3** Mark Gibson/Corbis (t); Ancient Art & Architecture Collection (b). **4:** RJB. **6:** © Dave Bartruff / FPG International. **7:** © PHOTRI, MGA (t); © Ferdinando Scianna / Magnum Photos (b); © NASA / Westlight (r). **11:** Yann Arthus-Bertrand/Corbis. **13:** Tokyo National Museum, Wan-go H.C. Weng. **15:** The Dean and

Chapter of Hereford Cathedral. **16**: BM / NB. **17**: RJB (tr, br); © Comstock, Inc. (cr); © Heinz Plenge / RHPL (bl). **18** Bodleian Library MS. Arch. Seld.A.1 Fol.47 Recto. **19** The Granger Collection. **20**: © Arthur Tress / Photo Researchers, Inc. **20–21**: RJB. **21**: Center of American Archaeology (t); Museum of the American Indian (r). **24**: AR (tl); © Ronald Sheridan / AR (cl); SuperStock (bl); SCALA / AR (r). **25**: Louvre / NB (t); SCALA / AR (b). **26**: AR. **27**: AR. **28**: © George Gersten. **29**: Landesmuseum, Trier, Germany (t); Rheinisches Landesmuseum, Bonn (c); © Werner Forman Archive (b). **31**: Bibliotheque Nationale, Paris. **32**: The Metropolitan Museum of Art. **33**: SEF, Turin / AR (t); AR (c); Isabella Stewart Gardner Museum, Boston / AR (b). **34**: Bibliotheque Nationale, Giraudon / AR. **36**: Royal Ontario Museum, Toronto / Wan-go H. C. Weng (l, r). **37**: Royal Ontario Museum, Toronto / Wan-go H. C. Weng. **42**: Byzantium, Time-Life Books, © Time Inc. **43**: SCALA / AR (tl); AR (tr); Dumbarton Oaks, Washington, D.C. (br). **44**: SCALA / AR (tl); RJB (tr, cr, bl, br); J. Claire Deane, J. Paul Getty Museum (cl, bc). **45**: © Werner Dieterich / TIB (t); Bibliotheque Nationale, Paris (b). **48–49**: © Roger Wood. **50**: RJB (l); © Trip/Trip Photo Library (r). **51**: The Metropolitan Museum of Art (l); © Steve Northrup/Black Star/PNI (tr); Ancient Art & Architecture Collection (br). **52**: © Wolfgang Kaehler. **54**: Michael Nicholson/Corbis (t); Peter Fraenkel (b). **55**: RHPL. **56**: © John Donat (t); RJB (b). **57**: AR. **58**: © Trip/Trip Photo Library. **59**: © Ilene Perlman / Stock Boston. **60**: The Metropolitan Museum of Art / NB. **61**: © Roger Wood. **62**: © Camerapix. **63**: © Mehmet Biber / Photo Researchers, Inc. **64**: Jalil Bounhar/AP Photo. **65**: © Fred M. Donner. **66**: The Chester Beatty Library, Dublin. **68**: © Roger Wood. **72**: Ancient Art & Architecture Collection (l); © Roger Wood (r). **73**: SCALA/AR, NY (t); © Marc Romanelli / TIB (c); Museo del Ejeroito Espada de Boabdil (r). **76–77**: RJB. **79**: © G. Champlong / TIB. **83**: American Numismatic Society. **86**: SuperStock. **88**: Bibliotheque Nationale, Paris (t); © P. Breidenbach (b). **89** RJB. **90**: Princeton University (l); RJB (tr, cr); Topkapi Museum, Istanbul / AR, NY (b). **92**: Freer Gallery of Art. **93**: Private Collection, MH (t). **95**: © Marc Romanelli / TIB. **96**: © Joachim Messerschmidt / Westlight. **97**: RJB (tr, bl, br); Stuart Cohen / Comstock, Inc. (cl); SuperStock (cr). **98**: Reunion des Musees Nationaux, Paris. **100**: Royal Chapel, Granada. **104–05**: © Huet, Hoa-Qui. **106**: Gift of Mr. and Mrs. Raymond J. Weilgus by exchange, 1988.22...profile. Photograph by Alan Newman © 1989 The Art Institute of Chicago, All Rights Reserved (l); © Victor Engelbert (r). **107**: Comstock, Inc. (t); African and Oceanic Catalogue / AR (c); RJB (bl). **108**: © T. Hopker / Woodfin Camp & Associates (l); Michael Kirtley (r). **110**: Nigerian Museum, Lagos. **111**: © M. & A. Kirtley, ANA. **112**: © Victor Englebert. **113**: Arthur Tress. **114**: RJB (tl, br); Musee de l'Institute d'Afrique Noire, Giraudon / AR (tr); © Cyril Isy-Schwart / TIB (c); © Giorgio Gualco / Bruce Coleman, Inc. (bl). **115**: © P. Breidenbach (l, r); Smithsonian Institution, Museum of African Art / AR (b). **116**: M. & A. Kirtley, ANA (l); Eugene Gordon / Photo Researchers, Inc. (r). **118**: Michael Kirtley. **119**: RJB (t); Bibliotheque Nationale, Paris (b). **120**: Bibliotheque Nationale, Paris. **121**: Bibliotheque Nationale, Paris. **122**: SuperStock. **123**: Mike Dye, *The White Men*, Julia Blackburn, Orbis Publishing, London, © 1979, RJB (t); Nelson Gallery-Atkins Museum (Nelson Fund), Kansas City (b). **124**: Jason Laure / Woodfin Camp & Associates. **125**: © Marc & Evelyne Bernheim / Woodfin Camp & Associates (tr); Garfield Park Conservatory, Chicago, RJB (tl); AR (b). **126**: P. Breidenbach. **127**: Charles & Josette Lenars/Corbis. **134**: BM, Bridgeman Art Library (l); © Leonard Lee Rue III / Bruce Coleman, Inc. (r). **135**: © Rod Allin / Tom Stack & Associates (l); © Don Carl Steffen / Photo Researchers, Inc. (r). **136**: © Bruce Coleman, Inc. **141**: © Owen Franken / Stock Boston. **142**: Werner Forman Archive. **143**: Werner Forman Archive. **144**: Hutchison Library. **145**: © Sue Dorfman / Stock Boston (t); © Norman Meyers / Bruce Coleman, Inc. (b). **147**: © Jason Laure. **148**: Centers for Disease Control (t); National Archives of Zimbabwe (b). **149**: © Eric Axelson. **150**: Zaire, Kasai Provine, Mweka, Kuba People, Mask of a Mythic Royal Ancestor (Ngaang A Cyeem), late 19th-early 20th Century, Restricted Gift of the American Hospital Supply Corp., The Evanston Associates of the Women's Board in honor of Mr. Wilbur Tuggle, et al., and the A.O.A. Purchase Fund, 1982.1505. © 1989 The Art Institute of Chicago, All Rights Reserved (l); American Museum of Natural History (r). **152**: BM, MH. **153**: BM. **154**: © The Pierpont Morgan Library, 1990 (l); The Newberry Library, Chicago (r). **155**: New York Public Library, Map Division (t); Zaire, Western Kasai Province, Mweka Zone, Kuba Peoples, Mukenga mask, Laura T. Magnuson Fund Income, X-Hautelet Collection 1982.1504...Photo by Robert Hashimoto, © 1989 The Art Institute of Chicago, All Rights Reserved (b). **158–59**: Wan-go H. C. Weng. **160**: The Metropolitan Museum of Art (l); Bibliotheque Nationale, Paris (r). **160–61**: Topkapi Museum, Istanbul. **161**: Topkapi Museum, Istanbul, NB (t); Victoria & Albert Museum, London (b). **162**: Topkapi Museum, Istanbul. **163**: PHOTRI, MGA. **164–65**: Topkapi Museum, Istanbul. **165**: Topkapi Museum, Istanbul. **168**: John Massey Stewart (l); © P. Breidenbach (r). **169**: Bham Museum of Art (l); Collection of the National Palace Museum, Taiwan, Republic of China. **170**: e.t. archive. **172**: © Ara Guler / Magnum Photos (l); FPG International (r). **173**: AR (t). **174**: University Library, Instanbul (b); The Jewish National and University Library (tl). **175**: Topkapi Museum, Istanbul. **176**: Topkapi Museum, Istanbul (l, c); Topkapi Palace, Istanbul, Giraudon / AR (r). **178**: © Roger Wood. **180**: Victoria & Albert Museum, London (l); BM, MH (r). **180–81**: © Roger Wood. **181**: Victoria & Albert Museum, London, NB. **182**: © Helen Marcus / Photo Researchers, Inc. (l); Victoria & Albert Museum, London (r). **184**: Kenneth Crossman (tl); RJB (tr, bl); Archaeological Survey of India, Government of India, RJB (c, cr). **185** Prince of Wales Museum / AR. **187**: © Pramod Chandra. **189**: © Pramod Chandra. **190**: Seattle Museum, LPW (l); National palace Museum, Taiwan, Republic of China (r); © Charles Liu, Westmont, Illinois (t). **191**: AR (t); © Guido Alberto Rossi / TIB (b). **192**: Asian Art & Archaeology, Inc./Corbis. **193**: RJB. **194**: BM. **195**: © Private Collection, LPW **196**: SuperStock. **197**: Wan-go H. C. Weng. **198**: © Harald Sund / TIB (t); National Numismatic Society, Smithsonian Institution (bl, bc). **199**: Xi'an Visual Art Company, China (l); © Photo R. M. N., Paris (r). **202**: Wan-go H. C. Weng; National Palace Museum, Taipei. **203**: Wan-go H.C. Weng (t); RJB (b). **206**: National Maritime Museum, Greenwich, London (bl); Freer Gallery of Art (br); National Numismatic Society, Smithsonian Institution (t). **207**: Ontario Science Museum (t); Bibliotheque Nationale, Paris (b). **208**: RJB (t); Wan-go H. C. Weng (cr). **209**: Biblioteca Nacional, Madrid. **210** Private Collection. **211**: AR. **212**: © George Holton / Photo Researchers, Inc. **213**: © Edward Bower / TIB (l); From *The Western Sea Cruises of Eunuch San Pao*, by L. O. Mou-teng, 1597 (tr); RJB (c); AR (cr); © K. Wothe / TIB (bl); Chait Galleries, New York (br). **214**: Wan-go H.C. Weng. **215**: Wan-go H. C. Weng. **217**: SuperStock. **220** © P. & G. Bowater / TIB (l); RJB (r). **221**: LPW (t); Shashinka Photo (b); © Martha Cooper Guthrie / AR (r). **222**: The Museum of Fine Arts, Boston. **233**: © PHOTRI, MGA. **224**: Shashinka Photo Library. **225**: © Norma Morrison / PHOTRI (t); Shashinka Photo Library (b). **226**: © Paul Hurd/Tony Stone Images (t); Cameramann International, Ltd. (b). **227**: Shashinka Photo Library. **228**: LPW **229**: AR. **231**: Shashinka Photo Library. **234**: Shashinka Photo Library (t); Japanese, Panel from Amida Triad, hanging scroll, Kamakura period, 13th century, Gift of Katte S. Buckingham, 1929.856...,©1989 The Art Institute of Chicago, All Rights Reserved (b). **235**: © Urasenke Tea Ceremony Society (l, cl); © Thomas Haar / Shashinka Photo Library (cr); © Norma Morrison / PHOTRI (r). **236**: © Mike Yamashita / Westlight (t); Werner Forman Archive (r); SuperStock (b). **237**: BM, MH. **238**: © P. Breidenbach (c); © Michael J. Howell / Stock Boston (b). **238–39**: Asian Art Museum of San Francisco. **240**: Shashinka Photo. **241**: © Bernard G. Silberstein / SuperStock (t); LPW (b). **243**: AR. **246–47**: Bibliotheque Nationale, Paris / NB. **248**: History Museum, Stockholm, Giraudon / AR (t); © F.H.C. Birch / Sonia Halliday Photographs (b). **249**: Victoria & Albert Museum / MH (l); Private Collection, MH (c); Werner Forman Archive (r). **254**: Cathedral Treasury, Aachen. **256**: Trustees of the BM. **257**: Walters Art Gallery. **258**: Cathedral Treasury, Aachen / AR. **259**: AKG London. **263**: BM, MH. **264**: Musee Conde, Chantilly, France / AR. **265**: AR. **266**: Musee Conde, Chantilly, France, NB. **267**: RJB (b); AR (c). **268**: AR (t); Hotel Lunaret, Montpellier, France, Giraudon / AR (b). **269**: Ecole des Beaux Arts, Paris, Giraudon / AR (t); Ronald Sheridan (b). **270**: AR. **271**: Trustees of the BM (t); The Granger Collection (b). **272**: City of Bayeux / AR. **273**: LPW **274**: © Alain Choisnet / TIB. **275**: RJB. **276**: Joel Sackett / Michael O'Mara Books, Ltd. (c); RJB (b). **276–77**: RJB. **277**: RJB. **280**: British Library, Bridgeman Art Library (l); Art History Museum, Vienna / NB (r). **280–81**: © N. DeVore III / Bruce Coleman, Inc. **281**: St. Mark's Venice / AR. **282**: BM. **283**: SuperStock. **284**: Treasury, Manza / AR (b); Gianni Dagli Orti/Corbis (t). **285**: AR (t); Her Majesty's Stationery Office, England (b). **286**: Goya Museum, Castres, France, Giraudon / AR (tl); Bibliotheque Arsenal, Paris, Giraudon / AR (c); Musee Condee, Chantilly, France, Giraudon / AR (b, tr). **287**: SCALA / AR. **288**: Musee des Beaux-Arts, Angers, France, Giraudon / AR (l); © Raphael Gailarde / Gamma-Liaison (r). **289**: © Michael Yamashita / Westlight (l); St. Mark's Treasury, Venice, Giraudon / AR (r). **291**: © Ara Juler / NB. **292**: © Nathan Benn / Stock Boston. **293**: RJB. **294**: The Metropolitan Museum of Art. **295**: Bibliotheque Nationale, Paris. **297**: La Reunion des Musees Nationaux, Cluny, France (t); Gian Berto Vanni, AR (b). **299**: BM / Bridgeman Art Library. **300**: Bibliotheque Nationale, Paris. **301**: Staatliche Museen zu Berlin, Preussischer Kulturbesitz, Museum fur Islamische Kunst. **302**: LPW **306–07**: SCALA / AR. **308**: National Museum, Florence / AR (l); SCALA / AR (r). **309**: SCALA / AR (t); RJB (b); AR (r). **310**: Campo Santo, Pisa / AR. **311**: RJB. **312**: AR (t, c); SCALA / AR; © R. Kord, H. Armstrong Roberts, Inc. (b). **313**: Giraudon / AR. **314**: Louvre / AR. **316**: Victoria & Albert Museum / Bridgeman Art Library (l, r); AR (b). **317**: SCALA / AR. **318**: © S. Georgio Schiavoni, Venice, SCALA / AR (b); Corbis / Bettmann (t). **319**: SCALA / AR. **320**: RJB (t); AR (bl, bc). **320–321**: IBM. **321**: IBM (tl, c); RJB (tr); Leonardo da Vinci (b); AR (br); Leonardo da Vinci (bl). **322**: © Hubatka, Mauritius / Westlight. **323**: SCALA / AR. **324**: Northwestern University Library, RJB (l); IBM (r). **325**: The Cleveland Museum of Art. **326**: Musee de Cluny, Paris (t); National Gallery of Art, Index of the Americas (c); SuperStock (b). **327**: AR. **328**: The Royal Collection © 1998 Her Majesty Queen Elizabeth II. **329**: AR. **332**: Musee Conde, Chantilly, France / AR (t); SCALA / AR (b). **333**: The Folger Shakespeare Library. **335**: RJB. **336**: Isabella Stewart Gardner Museum, Boston / AR. **336–37**: Tribuna de Galileo, Museum of Physics and Natural History, Florence. **337**: Burndy Library (l); Galleria Palatina, Florence, AR (r). **338**: SEF, Turin / AR. **339**: © Peter Menzel / Stock Boston. **340**: The Folger Shakespeare Library. **341**: SCALA / AR. **342**: AR. **343**: AR (t); Lutherhalle, Wittenberg (b). **344**: Library of Congress. **345**: Worms, Museum der Stadt Andreasstift (t); Rhode Island Historical Society (b). **349**: Bibliotheque Nationale, Paris. **350**: Corbis/Bettmann. **353**: BM. **354**: Northwestern University Library, RJB. **355**: Northwestern University Library, RJB (l); RJB (c); BM, MH (r). **356**: Northwestern University Library, RJB (t); New College, Oxford (r). **358**: Northwestern University Library, RJB. **359**: © Lou Jones / TIB (tl); © Gregory Heisler / TIB (tc); © Jay Freis / TIB (tr); © Melchior DiGiacomo / TIB (cr). **362**: RJB (l); Bibliotheque Nationale, Paris (c). **363**: National Maritime Museum, MH (tr); Uffizi, Florence / RHPL (tl). **364**: New York Public Library. **364–65**: © Ernst A. Jahn / TIB. **365**: New York Public Library, Map Division. **367**: RJB (tr, bl, br); Bibliotheque Nationale, Paris (cl); © Roger Wood (cr). **368**: Navale Museum, Pegli, Italy / AR. **369**: AR. **370**: © Scott H. Zieske / Homestake Mining Company. **371**: The Granger Collection. **372**: © Ronald Sheridan (t); New York Public Library, Prints Division (b). **373**: RJB. **375**: BM, MH. **376**: RJB. **377**: © Allan Eaton / Sheridan Photo Library. **378**: Tor Eigeland © Victor Englebert. **379**: American Numismatic Society. **380**: AR. **381**: LPW **383**: Bibliotheque Nationale, Paris. **386**: Giraudon / AR. **392–93**: The Textile Museum, Washington,. **394**: © Robert W. Parvin (l); LPW (r). **395**: © M. Martin / TIB (t); LPW (c); Museum of the American Indian, Heye Foundation (bl, br). **397**: © Jeff Foott / Tom Stack & Associates (t); © Gilcrease Institute (cr, br); LPW (bl, blc, brc). **399**: RJB. **400**: © Justin Kerr. **401**: © Mike Mazzaschi / Stock Boston. **402**: © Lee Boltin. **403**: © Justin Kerr. **404**: LPW (t); F. Catherwood (b). **405**: © Andrew Holbrooke. **406**:© Antoinette Jongen (t); © G. Gallant / TIB (b). **407**: © Lee Boltin. **408**: BM, MH (l); © Lee Boltin (r). **410**: © Justin Kerr. **411**: © Joseph Devenney / TIB (t); RJB (b). **412**: David L. Brill, © National Geographic Society. **413**: SuperStock. **414**: © Lee Boltin (t); © Julian Brown / International Film Foundation (b). **415**: Museum of the American Indian, Heye Foundation (t); © Nick Saunders (b). **416**: RJB. **417**: RJB. **420**: MH, Private Collection (l); BM (r). **421**: Werner Forman Archive (tl); © George Holton / Photo Researchers, Inc. (tr); LPW (b). **422**: LPW **423**: © Justin Kerr. **424**: © George D. Dodge, Dale R. Thompson / Bruce Coleman, Inc. (t); © Lee Boltin (b). **425**: SuperStock (t); © LPW (b). **427**: LPW (t); National Museum of Copenhagen / NB (b). **428**: LPW **429**: RHPL. **431**: American Museum of Natural History (t); BM, MH (b). **432**: © Hans W. Silvester / Photo Researchers, Inc. (t); RJB (br, bl); American Museum of Natural History (bc). **433**: Comstock, Inc. (l); RHPL (r). **434**: © Francisco Hidalgo / TIB (l); NB (tr, cr, br). **435**: Museo de America, Madrid (t); © Delacorte Gallery, New York / Lee Boltin (b). **437**: Biblioteca Nacional, Madrid. **438**: Museo de America, Madrid. **439**: Biblioteca Nacional, Madrid / NB (t); LPW (b). **440**: © Loren McIntyre / Woodfin Camp & Associates (t); Gilcrease Institute / NB (r); AR (b).

—Continued on page 548.

Chapter 1

PART ONE

page 1

(36 points)

A. 1. a
2. b
3. a
4. b
5. a
6. b
7. c

page 2

8. c
9. c
10. b
11. b
12. a

(24 points)

B. 13. a
14. b
15. b
16. a

page 3

17. b
18. a
19. a
20. a

(12 points)

C. 21. telephone
22. true
23. west
24. north or south

PART TWO

(1-4, 5 points;
5, 8 points)

page 4

1. Answers could include:

a. Methods of travel were limited to foot, horseback, cart, camel, and ship.

b. Travel was very slow.

c. Ocean travel was completely controlled by weather.

d. Travelers faced severe dangers from the climate.

e. On the open sea, travelers might die from starvation or dehydration.

2. Answers should note the following:

a. Merchants used camel caravans. Some answers might note that merchants often used ships, whether they used them for their own travel or not.

b. Soldiers traveled mainly by horseback.

c. Explorers traveled long distances by sea and, therefore, needed ships. Some answers might include horses as a means of transportation since explorers on land commonly traveled this way.

3. Answers should note that European ignorance of Ptolemy's work led to a dependence on less accurate maps, such as the maps called T-O maps.

4. Answers should include an understanding that primary sources are those written by people who participated in or observed the events they describe. Historians prefer primary sources, because the people who observed or took part in events usually tell a more accurate story.

5. Answers should refer to the advantages of an expanded world view, whether that phrase is used or not. Typical answers could include such points as the following:

a. Knowledge of the world increased trade opportunities.

b. Travelers broadened their community's knowledge of the cultures and religions of other people.

---

page 1

Date _____

Chapter 1   Test

A Changing World View

PART ONE

A. Write the letter of the best answer.

_____ 1. Distances seem greater when

    a. it takes longer to cover them.
    b. they are in foreign countries.
    c. one is traveling on the ocean.

_____ 2. The Roman world view was limited because the Romans

    a. felt superior to cultures in other parts of the world.
    b. did not know about the cultures in many parts of the world.
    c. thought that nearby places were farther away than they really were.

_____ 3. People in the Roman Empire did *not* usually travel for

    a. pleasure.
    b. military invasions.
    c. trade opportunities.

_____ 4. Our world view has expanded in modern times because of

    a. the postal service.
    b. better communication and faster travel.
    c. our greater willingness to face the dangers of the unknown.

_____ 5. Before A.D. 150, the success of a sailor's voyage was almost entirely dependent on

    a. weather.
    b. financial backing.
    c. a sense of adventure.

_____ 6. Who were the first people to make horseshoes?

    a. Mongols
    b. Roman soldiers
    c. Asian merchants

_____ 7. A pilgrim was someone whose main motivation for travel was

    a. profit from trade.
    b. military conquest.
    c. religious beliefs.

---

page 2

Date _____

_____ 8. Ptolemy was a great Roman

    a. soldier.   b. explorer.   c. mapmaker.

_____ 9. For about 1,000 years, until the 1200s, technical knowledge advanced in all of the following locations *except*

    a. Chinese centers of learning.
    b. Muslim universities.
    c. western European universities.

_____ 10. Between A.D. 150 and 1500, people traveled mostly for each of the following reasons *except*

    a. trade.
    b. cultural exchange.
    c. pilgrimages.

_____ 11. Which of the following is the most important to a historian using a source?

    a. the length of the source
    b. the accuracy of the source
    c. the artistry of the source

_____ 12. About a source, historians must always ask where it was written, when it was written, why it was written, and

    a. by whom it was written.
    b. how long it took to write.
    c. on what material it was written.

B. Write the letter of the correct answer.

_____ 13. **Satellites** are often used for

    a. communication.
    b. transportation.

_____ 14. **Caravans** were most often used by

    a. explorers.
    b. merchants.

_____ 15. The **lateen sail** decreased a sailor's dependence on

    a. the force of the wind.
    b. the direction of the wind.

_____ 16. The needle of a **magnetic compass** always points toward the

    a. north.
    b. goal of the journey.

---

page 3

Date _____

_____ 17. **Archaeology** reconstructs the past mainly by studying

    a. written sources.
    b. fossils and artifacts.

_____ 18. An eyewitness account of the destruction of Montezuma would be a

    a. **primary source.**
    b. **secondary source.**

_____ 19. Most historians prefer to work with a

    a. **primary source.**
    b. **secondary source.**

_____ 20. **Prehistory** is the period of time before

    a. the development of writing.
    b. the appearance of human beings on the earth.

D. If the statement is true, write *true* on the line below it. If it is false, change the word or phrase in dark type to make the statement true.

Example: A **T-O** map shows the time differences between different locations on the earth.

    _____ time zone _____

The exact time at any place on the earth is measured from **noon**, when the sun is directly overhead.

    _____ true _____

21. Standard time zones were established about the same time as the invention of the **television**.

    _____

22. There is a time zone for each **hour of the day**.

    _____

23. In the time zone **east** of you, the time is earlier.

    _____

24. A country directly **west** of you would almost always be in the same time zone.

    _____

---

page 4

Date _____

PART TWO

Answer the following questions.

1. Describe some of the methods and dangers of travel in the Roman Empire.

    _____

2. What kinds of transportation did merchants, soldiers, and explorers use in the ancient world?

    _____

3. How did the neglect of Ptolemy's work affect the European world?

    _____

4. Why do historians prefer to use primary sources?

    _____

Answer the following question on the back or on another sheet of paper. Use complete sentences.

5. When travelers reported back to their countries with information from their travels, how were they contributing to the good of their communities?

Chapter 2

PART ONE

page 5

(30 points)

A. 1. a
2. c
3. c
4. c
5. a
6. c

page 6

7. a
8. b
9. c
10. a

(20 points)

B. 11. true
12. barbarians
13. true

page 7

14. true
15. dynasty

(24 points)

C. 16. e
17. e
18. d
19. c
20. a
21. e
22. b
23. d

PART TWO

(1-4, 5 points;
5, 6 points)

page 8

1. Answers could include:

a. The provinces provided certain products to Rome, such as wheat.

b. Trade between Rome and the provinces brought wealth to Roman citizens.

c. The provinces paid taxes.

d. Tax money from the provinces helped support the government and the army.

e. The provinces served as a buffer zone between Rome and hostile places.

Chapter 2   Test

Empires of the Ancient World

PART ONE

A. Write the letter of the best answer.

_____ 1. What sentence best describes the times of Caesar and Augustus?

    a. The empire was expanded by conquering the territory that ran along the Rhine and Danube rivers.
    b. Caesar and Augustus were weak leaders.
    c. Disunity within the empire was tolerated.

_____ 2. The Roman Empire began to suffer serious border problems when

    a. Julius Caesar was assassinated.
    b. barbarians began to trade with the Romans.
    c. barbarians migrated to the empire to escape the Huns.

_____ 3. The Roman government attempted to solve the empire's economic problems by minting new coins that

    a. were made of silver instead of gold.
    b. were smaller in size than the old coins.
    c. contained less precious metal than the old coins.

_____ 4. Diocletian tried to make it easier to govern the Roman Empire by

    a. unifying it.
    b. giving power to the barbarians.
    c. dividing the rule of the empire among four leaders.

_____ 5. Constantine established Constantinople as the capital of the Eastern Roman Empire in order to

    a. stabilize the Roman Empire as a whole.
    b. prevent civil war between east and west.
    c. expand the territory of the Eastern Empire.

_____ 6. The Western Roman Empire was finally brought to an end by

    a. Byzantine invasions.
    b. a decrease in the military budget.
    c. barbarian invasions.

_____ 7. Which of the following was *not* a source of conflict between Rome and Persia?

    a. overland trade routes
    b. borders between the empires
    c. political control of Armenia

_____ 8. The spread of Buddhism into China came as a result of contact between China and

    a. Rome.
    b. India.
    c. Persia.

_____ 9. The Nike Riots in Constantinople in 532 resulted in all of the following *except*

    a. brutal suppression of the riots.
    b. the torching of Hagia Sophia.
    c. Justinian fleeing the city.

_____ 10. The purpose of the Justinian Code was to

    a. reorganize the legal system.
    b. establish artistic standards.
    c. maintain secrecy in military communication.

B. If the statement is true, write *true* on the line below it. If it is false, change the word in dark type to make it true.

Example: Octavian, or Augustus, came to power after the assassination of **Julius Caesar.**

        true

     Augustus was the first **general** of Rome.

        emperor

11. The lands conquered by Rome were organized into **provinces**, and governors were appointed to enforce Roman law.

12. Romans referred to the Germanic peoples on the borders of the empire as **Byzantines**.

13. Constantinople's geography protected it from invaders, while its location was convenient for traders, making the city a prosperous center of **commerce**.

---

14. When Constantinople was rebuilt, Hagia Sophia was decorated with colorful **mosaics**.

15. The Sassanid **emperor** ruled Persia for about four hundred years, until Persia was conquered by Arabs.

C. Match the description with the empire or culture.

    a. Western Roman   d. Indian
    b. Eastern Roman   e. Byzantine
    c. Persian

_____ 16. Hagia Sophia was among its architectural landmarks.

_____ 17. The Empress Theodora encouraged its emperor to put down the Nike Riots.

_____ 18. Persecuted Christians were welcomed by its king.

_____ 19. Its artistic accomplishments and multicultural centers of learning led one scholar to describe it as "a great cultural sponge."

_____ 20. Barbarian invasions contributed to its collapse.

_____ 21. Its leaders subjected Jews to cruel treatment, including massacres and forcible conversions.

_____ 22. Byzantium was its capital city before it became the center of the Byzantine Empire.

_____ 23. Its scholars developed the concept of zero and discovered that the earth rotates on its axis.

PART TWO

Answer the following questions.

1. How did the provinces of the Roman Empire contribute to Rome's wealth and safety?

2. How did Persia's prosperity in trade help to enrich Persian culture?

3. How did China and India come into contact with one another? Name one way in which Indian culture influenced Chinese culture.

4. The Persian and Byzantine empires battled each other for five hundred years, but neither empire had a decisive victory. What was the effect of the ongoing struggle on both empires?

Answer the following question on the back or on another sheet of paper. Use complete sentences.

5. The Constitution guarantees Americans the right to worship as they choose. Why do you think freedom is better than forcing people, as in the Byzantine Empire, to believe a certain way? Explain.

---

2. Answers could include:

a. Trade led to exchange of ideas between the Persians and people from other places.

b. The Persians gained knowledge from other cultures.

c. They learned building techniques from the Romans.

d. They learned how to build single-sail ships from the Greeks.

e. They welcomed scholars from overseas countries to their centers of learning.

3. Answers should note China and India came into contact through traders and missionaries. Answers could include:

a. The Chinese learned about the teachings of Buddhism from the Indians.

b. Chinese art was influenced by Indian art.

4. Answers should include points similar to the following:

a. Both empires were weakened by the fighting.

b. Both empires lost strength needed to fight invaders.

5. Answers will vary but should include points similar to one or more of the following:

a. America is historically a safe place for those running from religious persecution.

b. American society is traditionally pluralistic— many ethnic, religious, and cultural groups live together.

c. A pluralistic society challenges Americans to exercise tolerance for the opinions, customs, traditions, and lifestyles of others.

d. Byzantine society was pluralistic but did not enjoy religious tolerance and hence lacked the benefits of American society.

Chapter 3

PART ONE

page 9

(30 points)

A. 1. a
2. c
3. a
4. b
5. a
6. c

page 10

(32 points)

B. 7. a
8. d
9. g
10. b
11. c
12. k
13. f
14. j

page 11

(12 points)

C. 15. c
16. b
17. c
18. a

---

page 9

Chapter 3   Test

The Roots of Islam

PART ONE

A. Write the letter of the best answer.

_____ 1. An Arabian shaikh is a

  a. tribal elder.
  b. caravan drover.
  c. priest.

_____ 2. A suq is

  a. a watering hole.
  b. a place of worship.
  c. an open-air marketplace.

_____ 3. The ancient shrine called the Ka'bah is located in the city of

  a. Mecca.
  b. Ubar.
  c. Petra.

_____ 4. When Mecca surrendered to Muhammad in 630, he

  a. expelled his enemies.
  b. forgave his enemies.
  c. started a trade center.

_____ 5. What major problem faced Muhammad's followers after his sudden death in 632?

  a. naming a successor
  b. spreading Islam
  c. protecting trade

_____ 6. In spite of their differences, all Muslims today accept each of the following *except*

  a. Muhammad as Allah's prophet.
  b. the Five Pillars of Islam.
  c. the Shiite Imam as Muhammad's successor.

---

page 10

B. Choose a vocabulary word from the list below that matches the description. You will not use all the words.

  a. Qur'an
  b. Shiites
  c. monotheism
  d. caliph
  e. idol
  f. Sunna
  g. Sunni
  h. nomad
  i. oasis
  j. tribe
  k. Muslims
  l. pilgrimage

_____ 7. the sacred book, believed by Muslims to be the written record of God's words

_____ 8. the political and military leader of a Muslim state

_____ 9. the Muslims that accept the succession of the first four caliphs

_____ 10. the Muslim followers of Ali, who accept only members of Muhammad's family as his successors

_____ 11. the belief that there is only one God

_____ 12. the name usually given to believers in Islam

_____ 13. a collection of the sources of Islamic beliefs and practices

_____ 14. close family groups, with a common language, ancestry, culture, and name

---

page 11

C. Use the following parallel timeline to help you answer the questions below.

476, Western Roman Empire ends   520, Guptas invent decimal system in India   527-565, Justinian rules Roman Empire   610-641, Heracles rules Byzantine Empire

627, Byzantine Empire defeats Persia

450   500   550   600   650

570, Muhammad born   632, Muhammad dies   661, Muawiya becomes caliph

_____ 15. A parallel timeline would be better than a single timeline if you wanted to show

  a. how long the Byzantine Empire lasted.
  b. Muhammad's age when he had his vision at Hira.
  c. what was happening in other parts of the world when Muhammad was born.

_____ 16. Muhammad was born before

  a. the Western Roman Empire ended.
  b. the Byzantine Empire defeated Persia.
  c. the Guptas invented the decimal system in India.

_____ 17. When did Muhammad die?

  a. after Muawiya became caliph
  b. while Justinian was ruling the Roman Empire
  c. while Heracles was ruling the Byzantine Empire

_____ 18. Which one of the following events belongs on the bottom half of the parallel timeline above?

  a. Muhammad's flight from Medina
  b. the end of the Gupta Empire
  c. the Tang dynasty's unification of China

---

page 12

PART TWO

Answer the following questions.

1. How did the city of Mecca develop as an important religious and trading center?

2. Why do Muslims respect Christians and Jews as "people of the book"?

3. Why is the Ka'bah sacred to Muslims?

4. Why did Muslims divide after the death of Muhammad?

Answer the following question on the back or on another sheet of paper. Use complete sentences.

5. Explain how Islam affects the everyday lives of Muslims.

PART TWO

(1-4, 4 points; 5, 6 points)

page 12

1. Answers should include some of the following points:

a. A fresh-water well had attracted people to Mecca since about A.D. 100.

b. Mecca was located at the crossroads of two important trade routes.

c. An important religious shrine was located there.

d. The Quraysh were keepers of the Ka'bah.

e. The Quraysh protected caravans going there.

2. Answers should note that the Jews' and Christians' holy book, the Bible, is considered by Muslims to be based on God's revelations. Christians and Jews are respected as "people of the book" and all their prophets are revered.

3. Answers should note that the Ka'bah is the central shrine of Islam and that the area around the Ka'bah became the first mosque.

4. Answers should include points similar to the following:

a. When Muhammad died, there was disagreement about who should be his successor.

b. A caliph was elected to act as an administrative and military leader, not as a spiritual leader.

c. The first three caliphs were not blood relatives of Muhammad.

d. Ali, Muhammad's grandson, then gained power, and his followers believed that only descendants of Muhammad could succeed him. These followers, the Shiites, wanted a more spiritual leader.

e. All other Muslims believe the elections of the first three caliphs were valid. They are called Sunnis.

5. Answers will vary but should be based on the ways the Five Pillars, the Qur'an, and the Sunna influence the lives of Muslims from birth to death. Students should note some of the moral and social standards covered by the Qur'an and the Sunna.

Chapter 4

PART ONE

page 13

(40 points)

A.
1. a
2. b
3. a
4. c
5. b
6. a

page 14

7. c
8. c

(18 points)

B.
9. c
10. g
11. f
12. a
13. d
14. e

page 15

(9 points)

C.
15. a
16. b

(8 points)

D.
17. b
18. a
19. a
20. b

PART TWO

(25 points)

page 16

1. Answers may include: introduction of i) coins and ii) the declaration that Arabic was the official language of the empire because:

a. it made commerce easier to conduct

b. it gave Muslim a sense of pride in the power of the empire

c. Coins were inscribed with quotations from the Qur'an.

d. Coins were inscribed in Arabic.

2. Answers may include:

a. Baghdad was between two major rivers—the Tigris and Euphrates.

b. Ancient trade routes from east and west passed through the city.

c. Goods loaded at the river ports sailed to and from China, India, and Africa.

d. The empire was rich in the metals used in trade.

e. Pearls and precious gems were in great demand in the Baghdad market.

f. Baghdad's economy was based on taxes and trade.

g. Business people invested in long-distance trade and credit.

3. Answers may include:

a. The Abbasids lost several trade routes.

b. The caliphs increased taxes.

c. The Abbasids lived a fancy and costly way of life.

d. The Seljuk Turks were able to conquer the weakened empire.

4. Answers could include:

a. Culture and learning were valued.

b. Poets and musicians held positions of importance.

c. Scholars traveled to Cordoba to share knowledge.

d. Muslims brought thousands of books to Spain.

e. Thousands of students studied in Cordoba.

f. Muslims and non-Muslims shared in the intellectual life of Cordoba.

5. Answers will vary but may include:

Achievements

a. breakthrough work in the sciences

b. mapping the solar system

c. developing algebra

d. writing accurate descriptions of diseases

e. performing surgery in clean hospitals that were free to the public

f. using herbal medicines

g. Avicenna's *Canon of Medicine*

It helped

a. to increase learning

b. increase prestige

---

page 13

Date _____

Chapter 4   Test

The Empire of Islam

PART ONE

A. Write the letter of the best answer.

____ 1. Muawiya established the Umayyad capital in

   a. Damascus.
   b. Baghdad.
   c. Medina.

____ 2. The Battle of Tours was important because it

   a. established the Muslim Empire.
   b. stopped the Muslims from conquering more of Europe.
   c. pushed the Muslims out of Spain.

____ 3. Under Umayyad rule, Christians and Jews were

   a. granted full religious freedom.
   b. exempt from taxes.
   c. compelled to join the military.

____ 4. All of the following contributed to the decline of the Umayyad Empire *except*

   a. a decline in tax and conquest revenues.
   b. opposition from the Abbasids and other Muslims.
   c. intolerance of minorities within the empire.

____ 5. An early Abbasid caliph moved the capital of the eastern empire to

   a. Cairo.
   b. Baghdad.
   c. Damascus.

____ 6. Muslims do not decorate their mosques with human images because they believe that

   a. only God can create images with souls.
   b. geometric designs are traditional.
   c. plant patterns are easier to create.

page 14

Date _____

____ 7. While the Abbasids ruled in the east, which forces gained control of most of Spain?

   a. the Mongols
   b. the Seljuk Turks
   c. the Umayyads

____ 8. In 1236, Cordoba fell to

   a. the Mongols.
   b. the Seljuk Turks.
   c. Christian forces.

B. In the blank, write the letter of the word that best completes the sentence. You will not use all the words.

   a. bureaucracy
   b. emir
   c. empire
   d. factions
   e. dissent
   f. legacy
   g. calligraphy

9. During the 600s, Muslim conquests and expansion unified a number of peoples and provinces into an ____.

10. The beautiful handwriting, known as ____, flourished under the Abbasids.

11. Love of learning was Cordoba's greatest ____ to cultures and civilizations of the future.

12. The Umayyads based their ____, or highly organized system of government, on the Byzantine model.

13. Over time, the Abbasids lost power to several ____ who tried to wrest control of distant parts of the empire.

14. Muawiya encouraged those he appointed to rule strictly, in order to stamp out ____ among the conquered people.

page 15

Date _____

C. Read the following paragraph and answer the questions below.

Although Cordoba flourished for many reasons, this Muslim city was particularly noted for its fine handicrafts. Silverwork and silk embroidery were among the high quality goods produced by Cordoba's artisans. Their intricate designs and fine craftsmanship created a demand for Cordoba's goods throughout Europe. However, it was for Cordoba's fine leather goods that the kingdom was truly famous. People traveled great distances to purchase handsomely tooled Cordoba leather.

____ 15. Which is the topic sentence of the paragraph above?

   a. the first sentence
   b. the second sentence
   c. the last sentence

____ 16. The main idea of the paragraph is that

   a. Cordoba was a flourishing city.
   b. Cordoba was known for its fine handicrafts.
   c. The handicrafts of Cordoba were the kingdom's only important achievement.

D. Write the letter of the best answer.

____ 17. The *Reader's Guide to Periodical Literature* provides information about how to find

   a. books.
   b. magazine articles.
   c. newspaper articles.

____ 18. Information in the *Reader's Guide* is listed according to

   a. topic.
   b. title.
   c. author.

____ 19. Suppose you are writing a report on the expansion of the Muslim empire and need basic historical information. Which of the following would be your best source?

   a. the encyclopedia
   b. a newspaper index
   c. the *Reader's Guide*

____ 20. Suppose you are writing a report on Muslim architecture and need current information on how mosques are preserved. Which of the following would be your best source?

   a. the encyclopedia
   b. the *Reader's Guide*
   c. a book of world history

page 16

Date _____

PART TWO

Answer the following questions.

1. What were two of the factors that contributed to the unity of the Ummayad Empire?

2. What were two of the factors that contributed to the importance of Baghdad as a center of trade?

3. What were two of the factors that contributed to the end of the Abbasid Empire?

4. Why was the Muslim city of Cordoba regarded as a center of culture and learning?

Answer the following question on the back or on another sheet of paper. Use complete sentences.

5. What were two achievements in learning of the Abbasid Empire? How were these helpful to their society?

Chapter 5

PART ONE

page 17

(28 points)

A. 1. a
2. a
3. c
4. c
5. c
6. a

page 18

7. a

(21 points)

B. 8. b
9. c
10. a
11. c
12. a
13. c
14. b

page 19

(12 points)

C. 15. f
16. e
17. d
18. b
19. c
20. a

(12 points)

D. 21. a
22. c
23. b

---

page 17

Date

Chapter 5   Test

West Africa

PART ONE

A. The following questions concern the time period from 5000 B.C. to A.D. 1700. For each, write the letter of the best answer.

_____ 1. In 5000 B.C., the Sahara was lush and green—as scholars have noted from studying

    a. cave paintings and dried-up riverbeds.
    b. old maps.
    c. handmade tools.

_____ 2. Many residents of the Sahara left the region between 5000 and 2500 B.C. because

    a. the climate became drier and hotter.
    b. the region was overrun by invasions.
    c. they wanted to pursue trade opportunities.

_____ 3. The terrain of the most southern part of West Africa consists of

    a. desert.
    b. scattered vegetation.
    c. grasslands and rain forests.

_____ 4. Nok people settled near the Niger to do all of the following *except*

    a. farm the rich soil.
    b. establish a river trade.
    c. work in gold mines.

_____ 5. Which of the following was *not* brought to West Africa by Arab traders?

    a. the Islamic religion
    b. a system of writing and numbers
    c. the practice of ancestor worship

_____ 6. Where did most West Africans live?

    a. on the Sahara
    b. in large trading cities
    c. in small farming villages

---

page 18

Date

_____ 7. The ideal crop for West Africa's wetter regions was

    a. rice.
    b. millet.
    c. edible roots.

B. Match the description with the empire.

    a. Ghana
    b. Mali
    c. Songhai

_____ 8. Its ruler, Mansa Musa, led a pilgrimage to Mecca.

_____ 9. Its king was worshiped as a god.

_____ 10. After falling to Askia Muhammad, it outranked Mali as a great center of trade, culture, and learning.

_____ 11. Islam became its state religion in the 1490s.

_____ 12. It was at the center of a lucrative trade route that ran from the salt mines to the gold fields.

_____ 13. Moroccan invasions ended its position as a peaceful, orderly empire.

_____ 14. In the 1300s, Arab scholars began flocking to its centers of learning.

---

page 19

Date

C. Match each term with its description.

    a. delta   d. kinship
    b. diviner   e. sahel
    c. griot   f. savanna

_____ 15. This term means "grasslands."

_____ 16. This means "shore of the desert."

_____ 17. This formed the basis of village life in West Africa.

_____ 18. A villager would go to this person to communicate with spirits.

_____ 19. A villager would go to this person to hear a tale of Africa's history.

_____ 20. The ancient city of Jenne-jeno was built on this kind of landform.

D. Read the African proverbs below to help you answer the questions that follow.

I. *Cross the river in a crowd and the crocodile won't eat you.*

II. *No one tests the depth of a river with both feet.*

_____ 21. Which of our own proverbs agrees most with the first African one above?

    a. There is safety in numbers.
    b. Don't cry over spilled milk.
    c. While in Rome, do as the Romans do.

_____ 22. What shows that the first African proverb above comes from a culture different from that of a large American city?

    a. the river
    b. the crowd
    c. the crocodile

_____ 23. The second African proverb above advises people to be

    a. brave.
    b. cautious.
    c. studious.

---

page 20

Date

PART TWO

Answer the following questions.

1. Explain one way the Nok people used iron to improve their lives.

2. What made Ghana's location ideal for trade?

3. How did Islam affect trade in West Africa? Why did it have this effect?

4. What was the central duty of a village chief in West Africa? Why was this duty important?

Answer the following question on the back or on another sheet of paper. Use complete sentences.

5. What happened when a Songhai ruler was intolerant of Muslims? What does this imply about the political importance of the civil right of religious freedom? How do present-day Americans feel about this civil right? Do you think it is an important right? Explain.

PART TWO

(1-4, 5 points; 5, 7 points)

page 20

1. Answers could include either of the following:

a. They used longer-lasting iron points on their spears, which helped them in hunting.

b. They used iron tools for farming, which were superior to stone tools.

2. Answers should note that Ghana was situated between salt mines and gold mines, both of which were of great value. The best answers will mention the tax that Ghana imposed on trade of these products.

3. Answers should show an understanding that conversion to Islam benefited trade. Support should include reference to the fact that Islam stressed the "brotherhood of all believers," which encouraged trust and peaceful trade among its people.

4. Answers should discuss the chief's function in keeping order and refer to the villagers' need to rely on each other for survival.

5. Answers should reflect the knowledge that this ruler was overthrown by Muslim groups who joined together against him. The implication is that it is politically wise to allow this civil right.

In reference to modern-day America, answers should show an understanding that most Americans support the idea of religious freedom. Answers may vary regarding the students' own attitudes about this right but should indicate a thoughtful analysis of its value.

Chapter 6

PART ONE

page 21

(15 points)

A. 1. b
2. a
3. c

(24 points)

B. 4. b
5. a
6. c
7. a
8. a

page 22

9. c

(18 points)

C. 10. b
11. h
12. e
13. f
14. a
15. i

page 23

(15 points)

D. 16. 4,000 feet above sea level
17. 3,500 feet below sea level
18. west coast
19. Mt. August
20. Answer should approximate 250 feet above sea level

PART TWO

(1–4, 5 points; 5, 8 points)

page 24

1. Answers should recognize that the monsoons are winds that alternate twice yearly between blowing from Arabia/India to East Africa and blowing from East Africa to Arabia/India. Exceptional answers will mention that in the winter the monsoon blows from the northeast and in the summer from the southwest.
Arab traders scheduled their voyages to take advantage of the monsoons, and thus visited East Africa once a year.

2. Answers should note:
a. decades of drought or poor crops
b. people moved away in search of better land.

3. Answers may give any two of the following effects:
a. the loss of control over port cities
b. an increase in slavery
c. war among African states or clans, encouraged by the Portuguese
d. knowledge of Christianity, baptism, etc.
e. European clothing, furniture, etc.
f. European weapons
g. education

4. Answers may give any two of the following reasons:
a. by studying artifacts
b. by studying ruins, such as the Great Zimbabwe
c. by studying accounts of European or Arabic visitors
d. by studying African languages
e. by studying the oral tradition

5. Answers should note that the family was the basic social and political unit in African society. Families and clans formed villages through blood relationship. In African society, kinship determines position in the family and even in African society. This is because the family reflects the customs and traditions of a society. Americans also may have close families but their social position may rest more on education and employment than on their family.

Date _____

Chapter 6   Test

Central and Southern Africa

PART ONE

A. Match each description with the correct location.

a. Congo Basin
b. Great Rift Valley
c. eastern savanna

_____ 1. good grazing, with few disease-carrying insects and plenty of water

_____ 2. rain forest, excellent river transportation, and fishing industry

_____ 3. good for growing crops, such as yams, rice, and sugar cane

B. Write the letter of the best answer.

_____ 4. The proto-Bantu speaking people migrated in search of each of the following *except*

a. good grazing lands.
b. desert oases.
c. better travel routes.

_____ 5. People became infected with sleeping sickness as a result of

a. bites from tsetse flies.
b. poor nutrition.
c. unemployment.

_____ 6. From exchanges with other groups, Bantu-speaking people learned to

a. herd cattle.
b. hunt fish and game.
c. adapt to new customs and traditions.

_____ 7. The primary social and political unit of Bantu-speaking people was the

a. family.
b. government.
c. village.

_____ 8. Swahili language and culture was the result of the

a. blending of Bantu and Arab languages and culture.
b. interaction between different African groups.
c. trade between Africans and Europeans.

Date _____

_____ 9. The gold of Zimbabwe was mostly mined by

a. men.
b. women.
c. women and children.

C. Match each term with its description. You will not use all the terms.

a. migrate
b. ethnolinguistics
c. currency
d. oral tradition
e. plantation
f. plateau
g. monsoon
h. missionary
i. malaria

_____ 10. the gathering of information about various peoples through the study of their languages

_____ 11. a person sent to a foreign country to do religious or charitable work

_____ 12. a large farm where crops are grown

_____ 13. a raised and relatively flat area of land

_____ 14. to move from one area or country to another and settle there

_____ 15. a mosquito-transmitted disease characterized by chills, fever, and sweating

---

Date _____

D. Using this vertical profile of the southern tip of the imaginary continent of Annualia, answer the questions below. Note that each landform is marked by a letter of the alphabet.

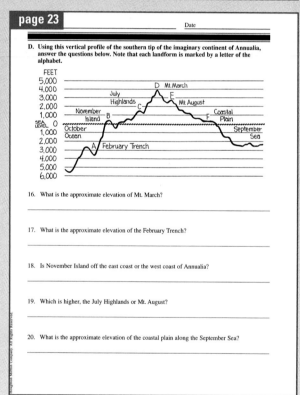

16. What is the approximate elevation of Mt. March?

17. What is the approximate elevation of the February Trench?

18. Is November Island off the east coast or the west coast of Annualia?

19. Which is higher, the July Highlands or Mt. August?

20. What is the approximate elevation of the coastal plain along the September Sea?

Date _____

PART TWO

Answer the following questions.

1. What are the monsoons? How did Arab merchants use them in trading with East Africa? What was the impact of this exchange?

2. What is believed to have led to the decline of Great Zimbabwe?

3. What were two effects, for African peoples, of trade with Portugal?

4. What are two ways in which scholars know about the early history of African peoples?

Answer the following question on the back or on another sheet of paper. Use complete sentences.

5. What was the role of the family in African society? Does the family play a similar role in American society? Give an example to support your answer.

Chapter 7

PART ONE

page 25

(24 points)

A. 1. a
2. a
3. a
4. b
5. c
6. c
7. c
8. c

page 26

(21 points)

B. 9. a
10. a
11. c
12. b
13. a
14. c
15. b

(18 points)

C. 16. true
17. true
18. vizier

page 27

19. divan
20. janissary
21. true

(12 points)

D. 22. N
23. Y
24. Y
25. Y

PART TWO

(25 points)

page 28

1. Answers could include:

a. All Mongols were taught to ride horses at an early age.

b. Horses helped Mongols to travel quickly.

c. Horses made it possible for Mongols to travel long distances without tiring.

d. Mongol soldiers had extra horses to carry food and water.

e. Horses contributed to Mongols' superiority as warriors.

2. Answers could include:

a. The Mongols promoted trade in the empire and protected trade along the Silk Road.

b. They encouraged travel in the empire, which led to the exchange of ideas and the spread of technology.

c. They were tolerant of religions that were different from their own.

3. Answers could include:

a. Non-Muslims in the Ottoman empire were taxed at a higher rate.

b. Non-Muslims were not forced to convert to Islam.

c. They were organized into partially self-ruling groups called millets.

d. Suleiman changed old legal codes to insure that non-Muslims were treated fairly.

4. Answers could include:

a. Akbar expanded the Mughal empire greatly.

b. He set up a civil service program where employment was based on qualifications, not religion.

c. He showed tolerance for Hindus by stopping the destruction of Hindu temples and the conversion of Hindus to Islam.

d. He reformed the tax system, abolishing the tax on non-Muslims.

e. He made his court a center of culture.

5. Answers will vary but should include points similar to the following regarding establishing an empire:

a. military aggressiveness

b. willingness to kill and to destroy what stands in the way.

Answers regarding governing an empire well could include:

a. strong administrative skills

b. willingness to compromise with people who don't share your point of view

---

page 25

Date _____

Chapter 7   Test

Three Empires

PART ONE

A. Write the letter of the best answer.

_____ 1. An important factor in the establishment of the Mongol Empire was the Mongols'
   a. military skill.
   b. religious tolerance.
   c. method of governing.

_____ 2. Which of the following is *not* a way in which Genghis Khan improved the Mongol army?
   a. by increasing soldiers' salaries
   b. by creating communication signals
   c. by creating a clear chain of command

_____ 3. The Mongol Empire reached its height under the rule of
   a. Ogadei.   b. Kublai Khan.   c. Genghis Khan.

_____ 4. The Arabic word *harem* means
   a. servants' quarters.   b. sacred place.   c. public place.

_____ 5. Who was the emperor, known as The Magnificent or The Lawgiver, under whom the Ottoman Empire reached its height?
   a. Selim   b. Mehmed   c. Suleiman

_____ 6. Which one of India's geographical regions was composed of rich farmland?
   a. the Himalayas in the north
   b. the Deccan, or southern, plateau
   c. the valleys of the Brahmaputra, Ganges, and Indus rivers

_____ 7. Akbar unified the Mughal Empire by
   a. imposing a tax on all non-Muslims.
   b. prohibiting the building of Hindu temples.
   c. developing his own state religion.

_____ 8. Shah Jahan
   a. forbade military campaigns.
   b. disliked art and architecture.
   c. broke with Akbar's religious policies.

---

page 26

Date _____

B. Match the description with the empire.

   a. Mongol Empire   b. Ottoman Empire   c. Mughal Empire

_____ 9. Their postal system helped communication and trade.

_____ 10. Many religions existed because the leaders believed that there was truth in all religions.

_____ 11. The Taj Mahal was among its architectural achievements.

_____ 12. The Byzantine capital of Constantinople fell to its army in 1453.

_____ 13. Its leaders were good conquerors but lacked skills in governing. As a result, the empire began to break apart, and it had lost its power by the middle of the 15th century.

_____ 14. It grew weak as a result of rebellions. By the early years of the 18th century, it no longer existed.

_____ 15. Jews were welcomed and allowed to hold high positions.

C. If the statement is true, write *true* on the line below it. If it is false, change the word in dark type to make the statement true.

Example: The wide, treeless plains of central Asia are called **steppes**.

_____ true _____

The sultan was the ruler of the **Mongol** Empire.

_____ Ottoman _____

16. In Mongol society, patrilineal groups known as **clans** banded together to form a tribe.

_____

17. In 1206, Temujin was elected to the position of **khan**, or leader of the Mongols.

_____

18. The grand **ghazi** advised the ruler of the Ottoman Empire on matters of state.

_____

---

page 27

Date _____

19. The **millet** was the governing council of the Ottoman Empire.

_____

20. A **divan** was a highly disciplined soldier in the Ottoman Empire's elite infantry corps.

_____

21. During the reign of Akbar, the government service workers of the Mughal Empire received a **salary**, or fixed payment for their work.

_____

D. The following design is from a brass pitcher made in Iraq in the early 1200s.

Write *Y* if the statement describes something that you can tell about the culture by looking at the design. Write *N* if it does not.

_____ 22. Islam was the official religion.

_____ 23. Camels were used for transportation.

_____ 24. The couple on the camel are probably related.

_____ 25. Decorative art was an important part of the culture.

---

page 28

Date _____

PART TWO

Answer the following questions.

1. What role did horses play in the establishment of the Mongol Empire?

2. What were two positive effects of the Mongol Empire?

3. How were non-Muslim people treated in the Ottoman Empire?

4. Why is Akbar considered the greatest of the Mughal emperors?

Answer the following question on the back or on another sheet of paper. Use complete sentences.

5. How are the leadership qualities that are needed to establish an empire different from those that are needed to govern it well?

Chapter 8

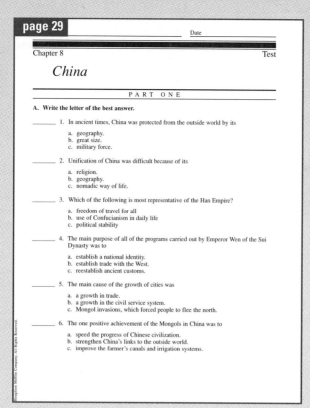

PART ONE

page 29

(24 points)

A. 1. a
    2. b
    3. c
    4. a
    5. a
    6. b

page 30

    7. c
    8. c

(24 points)

B. 9. yes
    10. no
    11. yes
    12. yes
    13. no
    14. yes
    15. yes
    16. yes

(15 points)

C. 17. f
    18. b
    19. g
    20. h
    21. d

page 31

(12 points)

D. 22. b
    23. c
    24. c

PART TWO

(25 points)

page 32

1. Answers should note that the unrest of the times caused many to seek the escape from suffering that was promised by Buddhism.

2. Answers should note that the aristocracy lost power under the new civil service system.

3. Answers should note that they were built to allow government officials to travel throughout the empire.

   As regards an additional benefit, answers could note either of the following:

   a. They promoted trade.

   b. They allowed the spread of ideas.

4. Answers should note that, at first, Ming emperors increased contact with the West. After concluding that Western people were inferior to Chinese people, they severely restricted trade.

5. Answers should note that the Chinese instituted a civil service system that eventually became a meritocracy, although that word need not be used. Answers should indicate an appreciation for the efficiency and fairness that are encouraged by such a system.

---

page 29

Date _____

Chapter 8   Test

China

PART ONE

A. Write the letter of the best answer.

_____ 1. In ancient times, China was protected from the outside world by its

    a. geography.
    b. great size.
    c. military force.

_____ 2. Unification of China was difficult because of its

    a. religion.
    b. geography.
    c. nomadic way of life.

_____ 3. Which of the following is most representative of the Han Empire?

    a. freedom of travel for all
    b. use of Confucianism in daily life
    c. political stability

_____ 4. The main purpose of all of the programs carried out by Emperor Wen of the Sui Dynasty was to

    a. establish a national identity.
    b. establish trade with the West.
    c. reestablish ancient customs.

_____ 5. The main cause of the growth of cities was

    a. a growth in trade.
    b. a growth in the civil service system.
    c. Mongol invasions, which forced people to flee the north.

_____ 6. The one positive achievement of the Mongols in China was to

    a. speed the progress of Chinese civilization.
    b. strengthen China's links to the outside world.
    c. improve the farmer's canals and irrigation systems.

---

page 30

Date _____

_____ 7. Which of the following is *not* something that Emperor Taizu and other Ming rulers did after ridding China of the Mongols?

    a. abolish slavery
    b. help the landless
    c. increase personal freedom

_____ 8. After conquering the Chinese, the Manchus adopted

    a. the tribal traditions of the Mongols.
    b. the military system of the Chinese.
    c. the civil service of the Ming.

B. Write *yes* if the statement describes a main accomplishment of the Tang and Song dynasties. Write *no* if it does not.

_____ 9. Artists excelled in the areas of poetry and painting.

_____ 10. Population growth declined.

_____ 11. Painters tried to represent the spirit, or essence, of the subject.

_____ 12. New roads and waterways spurred trade.

_____ 13. Farm production slowed down.

_____ 14. Civil servants were promoted on merit rather than connections.

_____ 15. The development of a paper currency led to a money economy.

_____ 16. The invention of printing hastened the spread of knowledge.

C. Match each description with the correct term.

    a. aristocrat   e. Daoism
    b. Buddhism   f. despot
    c. Confucianism g. mandate
    d. currency   h. meritocracy

_____ 17. a ruler who has absolute power

_____ 18. a religion that is based on the teachings of the "Enlightened One" and promises escape from suffering

_____ 19. Chinese belief that this gave an emperor the right to govern

_____ 20. a system that favors efficiency

_____ 21. not as heavy as copper and, therefore, easier to use in trade

---

page 31

Date _____

D. Write the letter of the best answer.

_____ 22. What is the most common purpose for comparing two or more maps of the same area?

    a. to check the accuracy of each map
    b. to find information no one map can supply alone
    c. to better understand the meaning of the legend on a given map

_____ 23. Which of the following is *not* a question you could answer with a land-use map?

    a. How far from the sea are the major agricultural areas?
    b. Is a particular area more agricultural or more industrial?
    c. How deep and wide are the canals that link agricultural and industrial areas?

Use the two maps below to answer the question that follows.

Elevation
Dark areas indicate land that is more than 1250 feet above sea level.

Population
Dark areas indicate where most of the people in China lived during the Han dynasty.

NORTH

_____ 24. For which of the following questions would you need to use both maps to find an answer?

    a. Which mountainous areas are near the sea?
    b. Where was most of China's population during the Han Dynasty?
    c. How did elevation affect population distribution during the Han Dynasty?

---

page 32

Date _____

PART TWO

Answer the following questions.

1. After the fall of the Han Dynasty, why did the Chinese turn away from Confucianism in favor of Buddhism?

2. How did the position of the aristocracy change during the Tang and Song dynasties?

3. What was the main reason that the Tang and Song governments built an extensive system of roads and waterways? Discuss other results of these improvements.

4. In what ways did the Ming emperors affect trade and other contacts with overseas countries?

Answer the following question on the back or on another sheet of paper. Use complete sentences.

5. How did changes in the Chinese civil service system affect the efficiency of the government? Does the system that was set up have then value in today's world? Explain.

Chapter 9

PART ONE

(52 points)

A. 1. a
2. c
3. b
4. c
5. a
6. c
7. b

page 34

8. b
9. a
10. c
11. c
12. b
13. a

(18 points)

B. 14. a

page 35

15. c
16. a
17. c
18. a
19. b

(6 points)

C. 20. b
21. a

PART TWO

(1-4, 5 points;
5, 6 points)

page 36

1. Answers should mention any two of the following:
   a. source of food
   b. transportation
   c. protection from invasion
   d. protection from outside influence

page 33

Chapter 9   Test

Japan

PART ONE

A. **Write the letter of the best answer.**

_____ 1. Japan's greatest natural resource is
   a. the sea.
   b. minerals.
   c. farmland.

_____ 2. Japan's first people were
   a. farmers.
   b. warriors.
   c. hunters and gatherers.

_____ 3. Buddhism spread to Japan by way of
   a. Cambodia and China.
   b. Korea and China.
   c. Russia and China.

_____ 4. The Taika Reforms
   a. weakened the emperor.
   b. helped the poor farmers.
   c. reduced the power of the clans.

_____ 5. The Japanese court at Kyoto was known for its
   a. refinement.
   b. warlike ways.
   c. devotion to religion.

_____ 6. Over time, the emperor lost power to the
   a. courtiers.
   b. religious leaders.
   c. Fujiwara clan.

_____ 7. Which of the following elements of Japanese culture was *not* originally borrowed from China?
   a. Buddhism
   b. Noh drama
   c. the writing system

page 34

_____ 8. Which of the following is the most common subject matter in Japanese art?
   a. war
   b. nature
   c. human beauty

_____ 9. Zen Buddhism appealed to the samurai because of its
   a. stress on personal discipline.
   b. emphasis on the happiness of the group.
   c. admiration of philosophy and book learning.

_____ 10. Which of the following ranks the shogunate social system correctly from low to high?
   a. samurai, merchants, artisans, peasants
   b. merchants, samurai, artisans, peasants
   c. samurai, artisans, peasants, merchants

_____ 11. Which religion was banned by the Tokugawa shogunate?
   a. Shinto
   b. Buddhism
   c. Christianity

_____ 12. Which of the following describes Japan between the early 1600s and the mid-1800s?
   a. It increased its world trade.
   b. It protected itself from western influence.
   c. It underwent sweeping social and political change.

_____ 13. Vietnam was valued by China because of its
   a. trading and sailing traditions.
   b. Hindu influences.
   c. interest in Chinese history.

B. **Write the letter of the best answer.**

_____ 14. Which of the following contributed most to Japan's **isolation**?
   a. the sea
   b. the Shinto religion
   c. Japan's mountainous terrain

page 35

_____ 15. A **regent's** role in the government was as
   a. an adviser to the emperor.
   b. a warrior for the emperor.
   c. a representative of the emperor.

_____ 16. The **Shinto** religion is centered on
   a. nature.
   b. happiness in the afterlife.
   c. the search for enlightenment.

_____ 17. A Japanese **courtier** would have been most familiar with
   a. fighting in battles.
   b. studying in a monastery.
   c. writing poetry for a contest.

_____ 18. A **shogun** was always
   a. a warrior.
   b. highly cultured.
   c. a supporter of Buddhism.

_____ 19. A Japanese **haiku** is a form of
   a. drama.
   b. poetry.
   c. gardening.

C. **Read the following excerpt from Lady Murasaki's diary in the box below and answer the questions that follow.**

> When my elder brother Shikubu no Jo was a boy, he was taught to read the Chinese classics. I listened, sitting beside him, and learned wonderfully fast, though he was sometimes slow and forgot. Father, who was devoted to study, regretted that I had not been a son.

_____ 20. What assumption can be made about the writer's brother?
   a. He disliked his sister.
   b. He was treated differently than his sister.
   c. His sister loved him.

_____ 21. What assumption can be made about the writer?
   a. She valued learning.
   b. She loved her father.
   c. Her father believed in educating girls.

page 36

PART TWO

Answer the following questions.

1. Name two ways that the sea has been important to Japan.

2. What qualities were valued in court life? How did this affect the development of the arts in Japan?

3. Besides the samurai, describe one way in which the influence of Zen Buddhism was seen in Japanese life.

4. Why did the Khmer build Angkor Wat? Why was it later abandoned?

Answer the following question on the back or on another sheet of paper. Use complete sentences.

5. How did the isolation of the imperial court affect life in Japan? In what ways does the nature of American society or government guard against such isolation for American government leaders?

CHAPTER TESTS: CHAPTERS 9 & 10

2. Answers should refer to such qualities as refinement, delicacy, and taste, and note that the importance of art and learning caused the arts to flourish.

3. Answers could make a general reference to the emphasis on process (or, way of performing activities) in Japanese arts and ceremonies or an emphasis on physical and mental training, or could name specifics, for example:
   a. Noh drama
   b. Japanese rock gardens
   c. the tea ceremony

4. Answers should note that the Khmer lived in a Hindu-influenced region. They built Angkor Wat as a great temple complex in honor of their god-king. When the Khmer people rebelled against their god-kings, they turned to a type of Buddhism that emphasized poverty and simplicity. By the early 1400s, Angkor Wat—which stood for the older beliefs—had been abandoned.

5. Answers should note that the isolation of the imperial court kept the emperor from seeing what was happening and what was needed in the provinces. The provincial nobles took this opportunity to attempt to run their regions in their own ways. As a result, power struggles developed among provincial nobles and made Japan a dangerous place to live.

Regarding present-day America, answers might include:
   a. media exposure
   b. the need to campaign for votes
   c. advances in electronic communication
   d. advances in travel
   e. the system of checks and balances

567

Chapter 10

page 37

(21 points)

A. 1. a
2. b
3. a
4. b
5. c
6. a
7. c

page 38

(14 points)

B. 8. a
9. c
10. e
11. d
12. f
13. h
14. g

(14 points)

C. 15. B
16. J
17. E
18. B
19. J
20. B
21. E

D. (18 points)
22. a

page 39

23. a
24. a
25. c
26. a
27. c

(6 points)

E. 28. b
29. a

Chapter 10   Test

Feudal Europe and Japan

P A R T   O N E

A. Write the letter of the best answer.

_____ 1. Which of the following was *not* something that Charlemagne accomplished during his reign?

    a. conquering the Vikings
    b. strengthening the church
    c. increasing learning in his empire

_____ 2. The main reason that the feudal system developed was to provide people with

    a. jobs.
    b. protection.
    c. a strong central government.

_____ 3. Which quality was *most* important in feudalism?

    a. loyalty
    b. bravery
    c. courtesy

_____ 4. *The Great Domesday Book* contained information about English

    a. laws.
    b. land ownership.
    c. religious ceremonies.

_____ 5. Life in a castle during the Middle Ages was

    a. lonely.
    b. refined.
    c. uncomfortable.

_____ 6. Which activity was *most* important to the growth of towns in the Middle Ages?

    a. trade
    b. education
    c. military conquest

_____ 7. During the Middle Ages, a monastery was *most* like a

    a. medieval town.
    b. modern church building.
    c. self-contained community.

B. Match each description with the correct person. You will not use every name.

    a. Clovis
    b. Alcuin
    c. Charlemagne
    d. Alfred the Great
    e. Charles Martel
    f. William the Conqueror
    g. Hildegard of Bingen
    h. Rashi

_____ 8. expanded the kingdom of the Franks and led them into Christianity

_____ 9. was crowned emperor by the pope

_____ 10. defeated Muslim invaders in France in 1732

_____ 11. defended England against Viking invaders

_____ 12. led the Normans who defeated the English Saxons at the Battle of Hastings

_____ 13. important Jewish scholar of the Torah and the Talmud

_____ 14. accomplished musician, physician, author, and founder of convents

C. Write *E* if a statement is true of European feudalism. Write *J* if it is true of Japanese feudalism. Write *B* if it is true of both.

_____ 15. The system had a specially trained warrior class.

_____ 16. Members of the warrior class often became government administrators.

_____ 17. Changes in military technology contributed to its decline.

_____ 18. The warrior class rode on horseback and wore a type of armor.

_____ 19. Its feudal arrangement lasted longest, until the mid-1800s.

_____ 20. The warriors' code of conduct emphasized loyalty and honorable behavior.

_____ 21. The religion associated with the system was Christianity.

D. Write the letter of the best answer.

_____ 22. Which of the following was *not* a **vassal** in the feudal system?

    a. a king
    b. a lord
    c. a knight

_____ 23. A person who swore an **oath of fealty** promised to be

    a. loyal to his lord.
    b. a faithful Christian.
    c. a good example to the lower classes.

_____ 24. Most **serfs** made their livings as

    a. farmers.
    b. soldiers.
    c. merchants.

_____ 25. Which of the following was most likely to be a member of a **guild**?

    a. a priest
    b. a knight
    c. a blacksmith

_____ 26. **Chivalry** was a set of rules that controlled the behavior of

    a. knights.
    b. peasants.
    c. craftspeople.

_____ 27. A **hierarchy** is a group of people classified by

    a. employment.
    b. ability.
    c. rank and authority.

E. Write the letter of the best answer.

_____ 28. Which of the following is true of a town's trade guild of weavers during the Middle Ages?

    a. All weavers in that town were members.
    b. Before joining the guild, a weaver had to be trained for years.
    c. The most expert weavers in the guild were called journeymen weavers.

_____ 29. Many Jews lived in medieval towns because they were not allowed to

    a. own land and join guilds.
    b. become bankers.
    c. form import and export companies.

P A R T   T W O

Answer the following questions.

1. What important changes took place during Charlemagne's rule? What happened to Europe after his death?

2. How did the feudal arrangement begin in England?

3. What did knights contribute to feudal society?

4. What led to the growth of towns in the 1000s? How did towns contribute to the decline of feudalism in Europe?

Answer the following question on the back or on another sheet of paper. Use complete sentences.

5. How was a guild in the Middle Ages like the modern American political system of democracy? How was it different?

(1-4, 5 points;
5, 7 points)

page 40

1. Answers should make the following points: Charlemagne:

a. strengthened the church and educated the clergy.

b. brought learning to the empire by having scholars copy old manuscripts by hand.

c. allowed Jews more freedom.

After Charlemagne:

a. Europe broke up into smaller kingdoms.

b. The Vikings plundered parts of Europe.

2. Answers should note that William the Conqueror introduced the feudal arrangement to England as a way of keeping control over the area.

3. Answers should note the role knights played in protecting their lord's land and people.

4. Answers should note that the growth of trade led to the growth of towns, which provided broader horizons and an alternative way of life to feudalism.

5. Answers could include:

a. Similarities: Both involve groups of people who work together for common goals; both involve the need to abide by group decisions.

b. Differences: Guild members had to apply for membership; many people were excluded from guild membership; people were excluded from guild membership on the basis of religion.

Chapter 11

PART ONE

page 41

(28 points)

A. 1. a
2. c
3. b
4. c
5. a
6. a
7. a

page 42

(21 points)

B. 8. g
9. h
10. a
11. e
12. c
13. d
14. j

(20 points)

C. 15. yes
16. no
17. yes
18. yes
19. yes
20. no
21. yes
22. no
23. yes
24. yes

page 43

(6 points)

D. 25. b
26. a

PART TWO

(25 points)

page 44

1. Answers may include:

a. Several new orders, or religious communities, were formed to bring Christianity directly to the people.

b. Some Christians were drawn to a simpler way of life.

c. Universities replaced monasteries as popular centers of learning.

d. The new learning, much sparked by the flow of knowledge from the Muslim world, challenged the intellectual authority of the church.

Chapter 11   Test

Europe: Rule, Religion, and Conflict

PART ONE

A. Write the letter of the best answer.

_____ 1. Which of the following choices ranks church officials correctly from low to high?

    a. parish priest, bishop, pope
    b. pope, bishop, parish priest
    c. bishop, parish priest, pope

_____ 2. What was the role of an abbess?

    a. spiritual adviser to the nuns in the convent
    b. a nun pledged to a life of poverty and good works
    c. all of the above

_____ 3. Pope Gregory VII wanted to free the church from the control of kings and nobles so that the

    a. clergy could serve the monarchy.
    b. monarchy would be subject to the pope.
    c. nobles would join the Crusades.

_____ 4. In the year 1000, the two centers of Christianity were

    a. Rome (West) and Jerusalem (East).
    b. Rome (East) and Constantinople (West).
    c. Rome (West) and Constantinople (East).

_____ 5. The main source of the wealth of the Byzantine Empire was

    a. trade.
    b. agriculture.
    c. conquest of neighboring countries.

_____ 6. In 1071 the Byzantine Empire was invaded by

    a. Seljuk Turks.
    b. Pope Urban II.
    c. Charlemagne.

_____ 7. Jerusalem is a holy city for

    a. Jews, Christians, and Muslims.
    b. Christians and Jews.
    c. Jews and Muslims.

B. Match each term with its description. You will not use all the terms.

    a. excommunication   e. salvation   i. schism
    b. icon   f. tithe   j. universities
    c. infidel   g. crusade
    d. literacy   h. clergy

_____ 8. Christian military expedition to regain the Holy Land from the Muslims

_____ 9. group of people who have been ordained for religious leadership

_____ 10. act that deprives someone of membership in a church

_____ 11. deliverance of the soul from the penalties of sin

_____ 12. an unbeliever in respect to Christianity or Islam

_____ 13. the ability to read and write

_____ 14. replaced church institutions as centers of learning

C. Write _yes_ if the statement describes a main effect of the Crusades. Write _no_ if it does not.

_____ 15. Arabic love poetry and music influenced European artists.

_____ 16. Under the code of chivalry, women received the benefits of equal education and employment.

_____ 17. Battles with Muslim armies advanced European knowledge of military technology.

_____ 18. Many powerful European families lost their lands to the monarchs.

_____ 19. Constantinople, the jewel of the Byzantine Empire, was ravaged.

_____ 20. Muslims learned to make better luxury goods from European teachers.

_____ 21. Bringing back stories of the wonders of the Muslim world made many Europeans more open-minded.

_____ 22. The church decided to give up its attempts to spread Christianity around the world.

_____ 23. On their way to the Holy Land, Crusaders killed many Jews and plundered their towns.

_____ 24. Jerusalem remained in Muslim hands.

D. Look at the map below and answer the questions that follow.

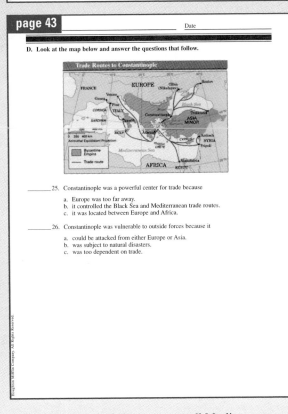

Trade Routes to Constantinople

_____ 25. Constantinople was a powerful center for trade because

    a. Europe was too far away.
    b. it controlled the Black Sea and Mediterranean trade routes.
    c. it was located between Europe and Africa.

_____ 26. Constantinople was vulnerable to outside forces because it

    a. could be attacked from either Europe or Asia.
    b. was subject to natural disasters.
    c. was too dependent on trade.

PART TWO

Answer the following questions.

1. How did the role of the church in medieval society change by the late Middle Ages?

_____

2. What are two differences between the Eastern and Western churches? Explain your answer.

_____

3. Muslim forces recaptured Jerusalem under Saladin in 1187. Name two reasons for Saladin's victory.

_____

4. Give an example that supports this statement: The Byzantine Empire valued learning.

_____

Answer the following question on the back or on another sheet of paper. Use complete sentences.

5. Under the code of chivalry, a knight viewed women as "holy, pure, and good." Do you think that women in America today would agree with this view? Why or why not?

---

2. Answers could include two of the following:

a. architecture: Gothic cathedrals in the West, plain exteriors with rounded domes in the East

b. tolerance of dissent: the Eastern church tolerated more discussion and debate about doctrine

c. language: Latin was used in the West, the vernacular in the East

3. Answers may include:

a. Saladin united the many small Muslim groups surrounding the crusader states.

b. The crusader army was exhausted.

c. The spirit of the crusades had been lost. Religious zeal was replaced by a hunger for wealth.

The best answers may note that the crusades failed because they did not finally achieve the goal of freeing Jerusalem from Muslim control.

4. Answers should mention one of the following:

a. Both the church and the government operated schools and libraries.

b. There was a higher rate of literacy in the East than in the West.

c. The most magnificent church in Constantinople was named Hagia Sophia ("Holy Wisdom")

d. Merchants' sons were educated, not just clergy.

5. In general, answers will mention that the code of chivalry gave medieval women little choice in how society viewed them. Today, thanks to pioneers in the women's rights areas, women are working as airline pilots, firefighters, lawyers and doctors. Women are in the U.S. Senate. Two women, O'Connor and Ginsburg, became Supreme Court justices. The best answers will mention that women still earn less than men for the same jobs.

Chapter 12

PART ONE

page 45

(36 points)

A. 1. b
   2. a
   3. c
   4. a
   5. c
   6. a
   7. c
   8. a
   9. c

page 46

   10. c
   11. b
   12. a

(8 points)

B. 13. no
   14. yes
   15. yes
   16. no
   17. no
   18. yes
   19. no
   20. no

(20 points)

C. 21. true

page 47

   22. rebirth (or revival, or any word or phrase that expresses this idea)
   23. upper
   24. money
   25. true

(9 points)

D. 26. a
   27. b
   28. c

PART TWO

(1-4, 5 points; 5, 7 points)

page 48

1. Answers should cover most of the following points:
a. After the plague the demand for labor was greater than the supply, so peasants demanded better wages and lower rents in return for their work.
b. Landlords resisted peasants' demands, provoking many peasants to revolt or move to towns out of the landlords' control.
c. The feudal arrangement was weakened because loyalty to the landlord no longer governed peasants' behavior.

2. Answers should center around either the idea of realism or the fact that Renaissance artists broadened the subjects of their art beyond religious subjects.

3. Answers should describe the three-tiered class system and should include: the lowest rung—farmers (or peasants); middle (or sometimes upper) class—merchants; upper class—nobility (or patricians). Answers should note that Jews were not allowed to be part of Italian Renaissance society. At the same time, Jews formed their own thriving artistic and social communities within the ghettos in which they were compelled to live.

4. Answers should note the spread of ideas through either travel (which spread the ideas through people's ability to learn from example) or printed material (which spread the ideas through people's ability to read about them).

5. Affirmative and negative answers are equally acceptable, but should give specific reasons supporting their positions. The best affirmative answers will probably assert that the government has a responsibility to improve the quality of life for its citizens; negative responses will probably say that the government should focus on other priorities, such as housing the homeless or feeding the hungry.

---

page 45

Date _____

Chapter 12   Test

The Renaissance

PART ONE

A. Write the letter of the best answer.

_____ 1. People became infected with the Great Plague as a result of
  a. drinking dirty water.
  b. being bitten by fleas.
  c. using imported products.

_____ 2. Between the 1100s and the 1300s, power in western Europe began to shift from
  a. nobles to kings.   b. kings to nobles.   c. nobles to church leaders.

_____ 3. The Hundred Years' War was fought between
  a. France and Italy.   b. England and Italy.   c. England and France.

_____ 4. Which of the following was *not* a way in which warfare changed during the Hundred Years' War?
  a. Fewer soldiers were needed.
  b. Armies of paid soldiers were used.
  c. Weapons gave foot soldiers an advantage over knights.

_____ 5. What reason did Joan of Arc's enemies give for killing her?
  a. She had led soldiers against them.
  b. She, as a peasant, had advised a king.
  c. She had stated unacceptable religious beliefs.

_____ 6. Around the time of the Renaissance, which country was the leader in trade?
  a. Italy   b. France   c. England

_____ 7. The growth of trade and towns increased people's belief in the value of
  a. religion.   b. feudalism.   c. individual goals.

_____ 8. Which country did *not* have a strong central government during the late Middle Ages?
  a. Italy   b. France   c. England

_____ 9. How did the Renaissance affect the lives of workers in Italy?
  a. Their lives changed for the better.
  b. Their lives changed for the worse.
  c. Their lives did not change very much.

---

page 46

Date _____

_____ 10. Which of the following was most able to move up in society in Renaissance Italy?
  a. a farmer   b. a Jew   c. a merchant

_____ 11. The center of life for nobles in Renaissance Italy was
  a. the church.   b. the family.   c. the marketplace.

_____ 12. Which of the following is *not* a true statement about the Renaissance in northern Europe?
  a. In northern Europe, art and learning had little importance.
  b. In northern Europe, the role of the church was important.
  c. In northern Europe, the royal courts were the centers of Renaissance learning.

B. Write *yes* if the statement reflects a view held by Italian Renaissance scholars. Write *no* if it does not.

_____ 13. Earthly life is unimportant; only eternal life in heaven really matters.

_____ 14. Art is an important part of life.

_____ 15. People of wealth should use some of their money for the public good.

_____ 16. People should specialize in one area of study.

_____ 17. Art should show life the way it should be rather than the way it is.

_____ 18. People can improve themselves through study and thought.

_____ 19. Everyone, rich or poor, should have an equal voice in government.

_____ 20. Women should be considered as equal to men in all areas of life.

C. If the statement is true, write *true* on the line below it. If it is false, change the word in dark type to make the statement true.

Example: Paid soldiers, called **mercenaries,** protected many Italian city-states.

_____ true _____

The plague was a **famine** that swept through Europe.

_____ disease _____

21. A government headed by a king or queen is called a **monarchy.**

_____

---

page 47

Date _____

22. The name *Renaissance* comes from a Latin word that means **culture.**

_____

23. A patrician was a member of the Italian **middle** class.

_____

24. Patrons were people who donated their **talent** to advance scholarship and the arts.

_____

25. A **dowry** was the property of a family provided when a young woman married.

_____

D. A dredge is a vessel equipped for excavating mud, sand, gravel, and other deposits from bodies of water. By the early seventeenth century, bucket dredges were in use in the Netherlands. Use the technical drawing of a bucket dredge below to write the letter of the best answer for the questions that follow.

_____ 26. What is the area labeled "2" probably used for?
  a. storing the mud or other deposits brought up from the bottom
  b. bringing up mud or other deposits from a body of water
  c. measuring tides

_____ 27. A vessel using a bucket dredge would probably *not* be used for
  a. developing deeper canals or harbors.
  b. deep-sea diving.
  c. constructing dams or dikes.

_____ 28. A technical drawing would be *least* likely to help someone figure out
  a. how the object works.
  b. how to build the object.
  c. how much the object will cost.

---

page 48

Date _____

PART TWO

Answer the following questions.

1. How did the plague lead to conflict between peasants and landlords? How did this conflict weaken feudal arrangements?

2. Describe one way in which Renaissance art was different from art produced in medieval times.

3. Who made up the different social classes in Renaissance Italy? What part did Jews play in this society?

4. Renaissance ideas spread to northern Europe in two major ways. What is one of the ways and how did it spread these ideas?

Answer the following question on the back or on another sheet of paper. Use complete sentences.

5. During the Renaissance, rulers were often patrons of the arts. Do you think the United States government should support artists (painters, actors, writers, dancers, and so on)? Why or why not?

Chapter 13

PART ONE

page 49

(27 points)

A. 1. b
2. a
3. a
4. b
5. a
6. c
7. b

page 50

8. c
9. c

(21 points)

B. 10. a
11. g
12. c
13. e
14. f
15. d
16. b

(12 points)

C. 17. a
18. b

page 51

19. b
20. a

(9 points)

D. 21. d
22. a
23. c

(6 points)

E. 24. a
25. b

PART TWO

(25 points)

page 52

1. Answers should note that Luther's concept of attaining salvation through faith instead of good works was significantly different from the approach taken to this issue in the Catholic church, and that it caused problems because faith is not something that can be bought or sold as were indulgences people purchased to receive forgiveness.

2. Answers may include the following points:

a. Many people wanted a simpler relationship with God.

b. Printed pamphlet spread the message of reform.

c. Peasants liked the message of egalitarianism.

d. European princes liked Luther's belief that the church should not own property.

e. Many princes liked the challenge of papal authority.

f. Making the Bible accessible to people reduced the power of the priests, who were able to read Latin while most people could not. This threatened the church's authority by allowing people to interpret the Bible for themselves.

3. Answers may include the following:

a. reforms against corruption

b. uphold traditional Catholic beliefs

c. founding new religious groups

d. educational and missionary work

e. halt the spread of Protestantism

f. establish the *Index of Prohibited Books*

4. Answers should note that technological advances made it possible for people to examine ideas and observe the world rather than having to have things explained and interpreted for them.

5. Answers should recognize the potential problems that exist when church and state are not separated. Answers may vary in terms of the importance of this separation today, but should show a thoughtful approach to this issue and note that ties between church and state are a threat to freedom of religion, which is a basic value in American society.

---

page 49

Date _____

Chapter 13   Test

Reformation and the Scientific Revolution

PART ONE

A. Write the letter of the best answer.

_____ 1. The Great Schism of the late 1300s was provoked by

   a. Protestants and Catholics.
   b. warring Catholic factions and rival popes.
   c. French and Italian monarchs.

_____ 2. Between 1100 and the late 1400s, the Catholic Church became *less*

   a. spiritual.   b. powerful.   c. wealthy.

_____ 3. Mystics, like Margery Kempe and Catherine of Siena, believed that

   a. a person could experience God directly in their hearts.
   b. only women could experience God.
   c. there was only one way to experience God.

_____ 4. Which of the following was *not* used to spread Martin Luther's ideas?

   a. essays
   b. papal bulls
   c. *Ninety-Five Theses*

_____ 5. Luther's reactions to the Peasants' War gained him support from

   a. princes.   b. peasants.   c. social reformers.

_____ 6. The Peace of Augsburg that ended the war between Catholic and Protestant German princes resulted in

   a. freedom of religion in Germany.
   b. Protestantism becoming the German national religion.
   c. a division of Germany into regions based on religion.

_____ 7. One result of the closing of the convents was that

   a. the clergy got married.
   b. women lost the safety of all-female communities.
   c. girls were educated as well as boys.

page 50

Date _____

_____ 8. The Church of England, or Anglican Church,

   a. became more like Lutheranism.
   b. recognized the pope's authority.
   c. broke away from the pope in favor of the English monarch.

_____ 9. Before the Scientific Revolution, people's ideas about science were based mostly on

   a. the Bible.
   b. guesswork.
   c. traditional works and theories.

B. Match each description with the correct person.

   a. Bacon   e. Ptolemy
   b. Copernicus   f. Vesalius
   c. Galileo   g. Kepler
   d. Newton

_____ 10. invented a method of organizing and formulating scientific research

_____ 11. proved that the planets' orbits were oval

_____ 12. tested the theory that heavier objects fall faster than lighter ones

_____ 13. an Egyptian astronomer who believed that the earth was the center of the universe

_____ 14. a physician whose study of the human body increased knowledge of anatomy

_____ 15. developed the theory that the same force that makes apples fall keeps planets in their orbits

_____ 16. first published the theory that the sun was at the center of the universe

C. Write the letter of the best answer.

_____ 17. People bought **indulgences** to avoid

   a. punishment from God.
   b. temptations to behave sinfully.
   c. excommunication from church leaders.

_____ 18. The central idea in **predestination** is that the individual believer

   a. has to try very hard to be saved.
   b. cannot affect his or her salvation.
   c. can communicate with God without help from others.

page 51

Date _____

_____ 19. The Catholic Church's main purpose in reviving the **inquisition** was to

   a. reform the church.
   b. stop Protestantism.
   c. debate religious issues.

_____ 20. **Pamphlets** were used to spread ideas because they were

   a. unbound and easily circulated.
   b. unavailable before the invention of the printing press.
   c. authorized by the church.

D. Write the letter of the text organization pattern that would most likely be used to answer each question.

   a. cause-and-effect
   b. chronological
   c. spatial
   d. compare-contrast

_____ 21. What is alike and different about the new religions established during the Reformation?

_____ 22. How did the Great Schism weaken the Catholic Church?

_____ 23. According to Ptolemy, what arrangement did the earth, the other planets, and the sun have in the universe?

E. Write the letter of the best answer.

_____ 24. A **hypothesis** is

   a. an assumption that can be tested by investigation.
   b. a method of studying the natural world.
   c. a collection of scientific data.

_____ 25. Which of the following can *best* be tested by forming a hypothesis?

   a. Galileo was born in 1642.
   b. What caused the Counter-Reformation?
   c. Henry VIII founded the Church of England.

page 52

Date _____

PART TWO

Answer the following questions.

1. How did Martin Luther's teachings conflict with the doctrine and practices of the Catholic Church?

2. Give two reasons for the success of the Protestant Reformation.

3. What were the goals of the Counter Reformation?

4. How did technological advances made between 1450 and 1700, such as the printing press and improved microscopes, encourage people to think for themselves?

Answer the following question on the back or on another sheet of paper. Use complete sentences.

5. At the time of the Reformation, the church had a great deal of political power as well as the power to try and execute people for heresy. Do you think the United States is wise to separate church and state? Explain. How would ties between church and state affect religious freedom in this country?

Chapter 14

PART ONE

page 53

(24 points)

A. 1. d
2. d
3. d
4. b
5. b
6. a

page 54

(32 points)

B. 7. a
8. e
9. c
10. b
11. d
12. g
13. f
14. h

(10 points)

C. 15. true
16. trade

page 55

17. true
18. colonies
19. completely, all, etc.

(9 points)

D. 20. a
21. a
22. b

PART TWO

(25 points)

page 56

1. Answers could include:

a. Portugal wanted to find its own gold markets in Africa in order to buy gold at cheaper prices.

b. Previously, it had to buy gold from North African traders who charged high prices.

c. Portugal needed more gold to pay off its trade debt.

2. Answers may include:

a. find personal riches.

b. find adventure.

c. spread Christianity.

d. seeking personal riches only.

e. seeking slaves

f. make the mother country stronger.

---

page 53

Date

Chapter 14   Test

The Age of Exploration

PART ONE

A. Write the letter of the best answer.

_____ 1. Which of the following was *not* a major goal of exploration during the 1400s?
   a. spreading Christianity
   b. making a profit by trading
   c. finding new sources of gold
   d. learning how people in other countries lived

_____ 2. In the 1400s, the country that *most* threatened Italy's domination of European trade with the East was
   a. Spain.
   b. France.
   c. England.
   d. Portugal.

_____ 3. The main reason that European nations sought a sea route to the East was
   a. to find a new world.
   b. to gain military allies.
   c. to improve map knowledge.
   d. to make trade more profitable.

_____ 4. The area that Europeans colonized first was
   a. Central America.
   b. the islands off West Africa.
   c. the islands in the Caribbean Sea.
   d. the northeastern coast of North America.

_____ 5. The major reason why no ship went south of Cape Bojador before 1434 was
   a. lack of money.
   b. fear of the unknown.
   c. lack of interest in the area.
   d. attacks by hostile Canary Islanders.

_____ 6. The first Europeans to explore North America were the
   a. Vikings.
   b. English.
   c. Spanish.
   d. Portuguese.

---

page 54

Date

B. Match the person with his achievement.

  a. Vasco da Gama   e. Prince Henry of Portugal
  b. Marco Polo   f. Vasco de Balboa
  c. Ptolemy   g. John Cabot
  d. Prester John   h. Ferdinand Magellan

_____ 7. He was the first European to sail around Africa to India.

_____ 8. He set up a center in Sagres where people studied navigation and exploration.

_____ 9. In A.D. 150, he made a map of the world that was brought to Florence in 1400.

_____ 10. Stories of his travels to China in the 1200s helped interest people in exploration.

_____ 11. According to legend, he ruled a Christian kingdom in Africa.

_____ 12. He was an Italian voyager who explored the coast of North America for England.

_____ 13. He was the first European to see the Pacific Ocean.

_____ 14. He was the commander of the first fleet to said around the world.

C. If the statement is true, write *true* on the line below it. If it is false, change the word in dark type to make the statement true.

Example: Jesuit missionaries worked in **China** during the 1600s.

      _____true_____

European **imports** included wool, timber, and guns.

      _____exports_____

15. For many years Venice had a **monopoly**, or complete control, over the spice trade with the East.

_____

16. The difference between the value of the goods a country sells to other countries and the value of the goods it buys from other countries is called the balance of **power**.

_____

---

page 55

Date

17. Gold that has been melted down and then molded into bars of specific weights is called **bullion**.

_____

18. Countries established **missions**, or settlements of their own citizens, in the lands they explored.

_____

19. A voyage of circumnavigation is a journey **halfway** around the earth.

_____

D. Imagine that you are the captain of a sailing ship planning a voyage from the island of Cuba to Lisbon, Portugal. Use the map below to help you answer the questions.

_____ 20. The map would help you to determine
   a. the best route for the journey.
   b. the best season for the journey.
   c. the weather you would encounter on the journey.

_____ 21. The journey would take less time if you chose to sail with the
   a. Gulf Stream.
   b. Labrador Current.
   c. North Equatorial Current.

_____ 22. You would eventually need to sail out of the current used for the first part of the journey because
   a. it would carry you too far south.
   b. it would carry you too far north.
   c. it wouldn't carry you far enough.

---

page 56

Date

PART TWO

Answer the following questions.

1. In 1419, why did Portugal begin exploration of the west coast of Africa?

2. Consider the goals of European colonization. What might have been the possible effects of those goals on European settlers who ran plantations in the colonies?

3. How were maps developed at Sagres superior to the T-O maps and portolan charts?

4. How was Columbus's first voyage a success? How was it a failure?

Answer the following question on the back or on another sheet of paper. Use complete sentences.

5. What person do you think was most responsible for the advancements made in navigation during the 1400s and 1500s? Explain your choice.

---

g. increase the reputation and influence of the mother country.

h. improve the mother country's knowledge about the world.

3. Answers should note points similar to the following about the maps developed at Sagres:

a. They were more accurate.

b. They were based on detailed accounts kept by sailors.

c. Travelers and scholars provided important information for the creation of the maps.

d. They were made by the skillful mapmakers at Sagres.

4. Answers should include points similar to the following about the success of Columbus's first voyage:

a. The ships were not lost at sea as many feared they would be.

b. It resulted in the discovery of land not previously known to Europeans.

c. Columbus claimed the land for Spain.

Answers should include points similar to the following about how his first voyage was a failure:

a. He did not discover a sea route to the East.

b. He believed that the place his ships landed was India.

5. Answers will vary. Possible responses include:

a. Prince Henry was most responsible because he established a center for the study of navigation.

b. Marco Polo was most responsible because the accounts of his travels increased interest in exploration.

c. Ptolemy was most responsible because the discovery of his map provided an accurate map of the world.

d. Gil Eanes was most responsible because he broke the "barrier of fear" when he sailed around Cape Bojador.

Chapter 15

PART ONE

page 57

(27 points)

A. 1. a
2. c
3. a
4. b
5. c
6. c
7. c

page 58

8. a
9. b

(14 points)

B. 10. T
11. M
12. T
13. T
14. B
15. B
16. M

(21 points)

C. 17. a
18. c
19. c

page 59

20. a
21. c
22. c
23. b

(8 points)

D. 24. b
25. a
26. b
27. a

---

page 57

Date

Chapter 15   Test

Early American Civilizations

PART ONE

A. Write the letter of the best answer.

_____ 1. People first came to North America from

     a. Asia.
     b. Europe.
     c. South America.

_____ 2. Early Americans learned how to

     a. grow corn and build durable homes.
     b. domesticate wild animals for food, wool, and transportation.
     c. do all of the above.

_____ 3. Villages probably developed because people learned how to

     a. farm.
     b. track animals.
     c. make tools with sharp points.

_____ 4. Archaeological evidence suggests that Olmec society was

     a. based on social equality.
     b. divided into distinct social levels.
     c. governed by priests.

_____ 5. The Olmec developed their own calendar to

     a. keep track of religious holidays.
     b. register birthdays and deaths.
     c. record sowing and harvesting times.

_____ 6. Archaeologists believe that the Olmec were destroyed by enemies who fought with them for

     a. farmland.
     b. religious reasons.
     c. trade goods and trade routes.

_____ 7. Mayan cities were built around

     a. plazas.
     b. palaces.
     c. religious centers.

page 58

Date

_____ 8. Which farming technique was *not* used by the Maya?

     a. burning off vegetation to clear forested areas
     b. building raised fields for better drainage
     c. building irrigation canals to carry water to dry fields

_____ 9. Which of the following was an achievement of the Mayan civilization but *not* the Olmec?

     a. had a calendar
     b. built pyramids
     c. used a writing system

B. Write *T* if the statement is true of the Tiwanakans. Write *M* if it is true of the Moche. Write *B* if it is true of both.

_____ 10. occupied a high, cold plateau

_____ 11. used mud to build aqueducts to carry river water to their fields

_____ 12. dug canals to irrigate large raised beds of soil

_____ 13. were found in Peru, Bolivia, and Chile

_____ 14. common people did the hard labor, such as farming and building

_____ 15. eventually abandoned their major city

_____ 16. were found along the desert coast of Northern Peru

C. Write the letter of the best answer.

_____ 17. Whose way of life is most **sedentary**?

     a. a farmer's
     b. a trader's
     c. a hunter-gatherer's

_____ 18. Who would be considered a member of the **elite** in Olmec society?

     a. a farmer
     b. a trader
     c. a priest-king

_____ 19. The **steles** that archaeologists study to find out about the Maya are

     a. tombs.
     b. pyramids.
     c. stone columns.

page 59

Date

_____ 20. Which kind of land is an **altiplano**?

     a. a high, flat plateau
     b. a low, swampy jungle
     c. a steep, terraced hillside

_____ 21. **Adobe** is a building material made of

     a. gravel.   b. limestone.   c. mud and straw.

_____ 22. The **hieroglyphs** that archeologists study are a form of

     a. jewelry.   b. pottery.   c. picture-writing.

_____ 23. A **codex** is a Mayan

     a. calendar.
     b. record book.
     c. astronomical chart.

D. Write the letter of the correct answer.

_____ 24. Which should you do first when doing research for a report?

     a. Make note cards.
     b. Think of questions your report should answer.

_____ 25. What should each of your note cards contain?

     a. information about one subtopic
     b. all the information from one source book

Suppose you are doing a report on the Olmec. Read the paragraph below. Then write the letter of the best answer.

The Olmec had as many as 15 gods, but the jaguar-man was probably the most important god. It represented the mystery of life and death. The Olmec made small jade sculptures of jaguars and other images of gods to use in their religious rituals.

_____ 26. Which research question does this passage answer?

     a. Who were the Olmec?
     b. Who was the main Olmec god?
     c. What was the role of an Olmec priest?

_____ 27. Under what subtopic would you put information from this paragraph?

     a. Olmec religion
     b. Olmec sculpture
     c. Olmec civilization

page 60

Date

PART TWO

Answer the following questions.

1. How and why did people first come to the Americas?

2. Name two things hunter-gatherers noticed that helped them become farmers.

3. Describe two cultural achievements of the Maya.

4. The Tiwanakans and the Moche both lived in challenging environments. Tell one way that the farmers of each group adapted to the land.

Answer the following question on the back or on another sheet of paper. Use complete sentences.

5. Explain why you agree or disagree with this statement: Because America is a democracy, there is no elite group in our society.

PART TWO

(30 points)

page 60

1. Answers should note that people followed the large animals they hunted across a land bridge.

2. Answers should mention any two of the following:

a. Many food plants grew in the same place year after year.

b. Plants sprouted from discarded seeds.

c. Plants grew best in open, sunny areas.

3. Answers may include two of the following:

a. a number system

b. a writing system of hieroglyphs

c. two calendars to record and plan their years.

d. astronomical charts and tables

e. created the basis for our decimal system

f. codices enabling scholars to learn about their culture

g. magnificent architecture

h. fine jade, gold, and shell jewelery

i. accomplished weavers

4. Answers should include one of the following for each group:

a. Tiwanakans: channeled lake water to their fields; built raised soil beds surrounded by irrigation canals; grew crops suited to the environment

b. Moche: built aqueducts to carry river water to their fields; built terraced farms on mountain slopes; grew crops suited to the environment

5. Although any well-reasoned answer should be given credit, most students will probably disagree with this statement, pointing out that people who have money, power and/or high visibility, such as government officials, business leaders, and popular entertainers, do constitute an elite. The best answers will note that in our society, it is sometimes possible for people to move in and out of the elite by their own efforts and talents.

Chapter 16

PART ONE

page 61
(24 points)
A. 1. c
   2. a
   3. b
   4. c
   5. c
   6. c

(24 points)
B. 7. A
   8. I
   9. B

page 62
   10. B
   11. I
   12. A
   13. A
   14. B
   15. I
   16. I
   17. I
   18. I

(10 points)
C. 19. b
   20. a
   21. b
   22. a
   23. a

page 63
(12 points)
D. 24. c
   25. f
   26. e
   27. a
   28. d
   29. b

(4 points)
E. 30. c
   31. d

PART TWO

(1-4, 5 points; 5, 6 points)

page 64

1. Answers could include:
a. They made huts out of reeds and mud.
b. They used birds and fish for food.
c. They learned new farming techniques.
d. They made floating gardens with canals.
e. They traveled in the canals by boat.
f. They traded with people in the areas nearby.

2. The classes in Aztec society were nobles, commoners, serfs, and slaves.
The lower classes supported the upper classes by:
a. paying tribute
b. giving goods and services
c. giving a portion of their crops and crafts
d. working on government projects.

3. Answers may include:
a. They did a good job of organizing agriculture.
b. They sent administrators to evaluate resources.
c. They grew crops and raised livestock.
d. They grew crops in the valleys and raised livestock at the higher altitudes.
e. They practiced terrace farming.
f. They built irrigation canals.
g. They stored surplus food and kept records.

4. Answers could include:
a. Both the Aztec and Inca Empires were suffering from civil war.
b. Some of the subject tribes were rebelling against the Aztec rulers.
c. The Aztec were fighting in many areas at once.
d. The cost of fighting wars was very high.
e. The Aztec rulers demanded more tribute.
f. The Aztec suffered a famine.
g. After the death of the Inca ruler, the empire was split in two.

5. Some students will suggest:
a. The Inca forced subject people to speak the Inca language and practice the Inca religion. But the Inca rarely went hungry. Some students will suggest:
b. The Aztec forced its conquered people to pay so much tribute that they lived on the brink of starvation. But, they allowed people to keep their own customs.

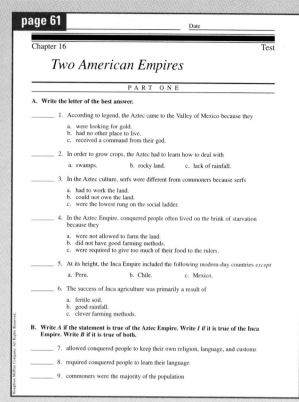

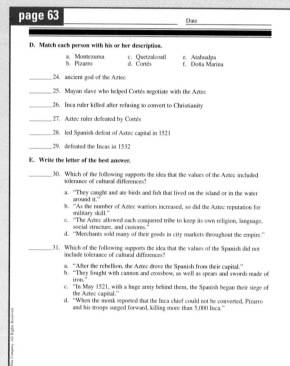

Chapter 17

PART ONE

page 65

(28 points)

A. 1. a
2. b
3. a
4. a
5. a
6. c

page 66

7. b

(12 points)

B. 8. c
9. a
10. d
11. b
12. e

(15 points)

C. 13. h
14. b
15. c
16. d
17. e

page 67

(15 points)

D. 18. b
19. c
20. b

PART TWO

(30 points)

page 68

1. Answers should include: Versailles was useful to Louis XIV because it allowed him to house many nobles and thereby keep his eye on them. And, when the nobles lived at Versailles, they were out of touch with the peasants, on whose welfare France's wealth was based.

2. Answers may list any two of the following achievements: Elizabeth:

   a. reigned for 45 years.

   b. encouraged great works of literature.

   c. made the Church of England the state religion.

   d. reduced religious persecution; did not outlaw Catholicism.

   e. beat Spanish Armada.

---

page 65

Date _____

Chapter 17   Test

European Rule and Expansion

PART ONE

A. Write the letter of the best answer.

_____ 1. The Huguenots in France were
   a. Protestants.
   b. peasant farmers.
   c. a council of advisers to the king.

_____ 2. Cardinal Richelieu wanted to
   a. ensure the power of the nobility.
   b. strengthen the monarchy and the power of France.
   c. force the Huguenots to convert to Catholicism.

_____ 3. French king Louis XIV threw out the
   a. Huguenots.
   b. nobles.
   c. Catholic Church.

_____ 4. From the mid-1500s to the mid-1600s, English monarchs consistently had trouble with Parliament about
   a. taxes.
   b. religion.
   c. war with Spain.

_____ 5. In the English Civil War, the supporters of King Charles I fought against those who supported
   a. Parliament.
   b. King Charles II.
   c. the nobles and the clergy.

_____ 6. William and Mary became the rulers of England as part of the
   a. Restoration.
   b. English Civil War.
   c. Glorious Revolution.

---

page 66

Date _____

_____ 7. In the late 1400s, Portuguese navigators sailed around the southern tip of Africa in order to
   a. bring civilization to African natives.
   b. find a new trade route to the East Indies.
   c. claim the glory of discovery for their country.

B. Match each person with his or her description.
   a. King Charles IX of France   d. Queen Elizabeth I of England
   b. King Henry IV of France   e. Oliver Cromwell
   c. Queen Mary I of England

_____ 8. bears the nickname "Bloody" for persecuting non-Catholics

_____ 9. plotted against Protestants, hundreds of whom died in the St. Bartholomew's Day Massacre

_____ 10. risked invasion by Catholic Spain in order to support Dutch Protestants

_____ 11. changed religions three times and ended up a Catholic ruler

_____ 12. led an English Parliament dominated by Puritans

C. Write the letter of the best answer. You will not use all the choices.
   a. absolute monarch   e. Parliament
   b. constitutional monarchy   f. prime minister
   c. encomienda system   g. divine right
   d. mercantilism   h. commonwealth

_____ 13. a nation governed by the people

_____ 14. a monarchy in which the powers of the ruler are restricted to those granted under the constitution and laws of the nation

_____ 15. an arrangement that gave Spanish officials some land and the right to enslave and forcibly convert the people who lived on that land

_____ 16. an economic system based on founding colonies as a source of raw materials and as a market for the colonizer's goods

_____ 17. a national representative body having the highest lawmaking powers within the state

---

page 67

Date _____

D. Read the following excerpt from the textbook. Use the excerpt and your knowledge of predicting consequences to answer the questions that follow.

> The English finally defeated the French in 1763. As a result, the American colonies felt less dependent militarily on the English, who had been protecting them from the French and the Indians. Now, the American colonists began to question the rules of mercantilism which limited their rights to trade and manufacture.

_____ 18. Which of the following statements would make the best prediction of the consequences of the above information?
   a. Indians will get better treatment in the colonies.
   b. The American colonies will demand more independence from England.
   c. The English will offer independence to the colonies.

_____ 19. Which of the following is usually the best information to use in predicting what people will do in a particular situation?
   a. what they say they will do
   b. what they have done before in similar situations
   c. what others of their race or religion do in similar situations

_____ 20. Which of the following statements is a stereotype?
   a. Louis XIV forced about 200,000 Huguenots into exile.
   b. All Huguenots were disloyal to the king.
   c. Louis XIV often favored Catholics over Protestants.

---

page 68

Date _____

PART TWO

Answer the following questions.

1. Why was the palace at Versailles useful to the king? Was it harmful to France in any way? If so, how?

2. What were two achievements of Queen Elizabeth I of England?

3. Why did the English reject King James II and ask his daughter Mary to be their ruler instead?

4. How did Cromwell rule England and what was his power base?

Answer the following question on the back or on another sheet of paper. Use complete sentences.

5. List one way in which the English Bill of Rights limited the power of the monarch. How is this related to modern American government?

---

3. Answers should note that James II was a Catholic and Mary was a Protestant. Answers may include:

   a. The English feared that James II would try to establish Catholicism as the state religion.

   b. James appointed Catholics to public office.

   c. He stationed soldiers near London.

   d. James's Catholic wife had a male heir to the throne.

4. Answers may list any of the following concerning Cromwell's rule:

   a. military dictatorship

   b. imposed Puritan values

   c. limited freedom of the press

   d. enforced strict moral standards

   e. prohibited gambling, dancing, and theater

   Cromwell's power base:

   a. the military

   b. a government he headed called the Protectorate

5. Answers may list any of the following provisions:

   a. monarch: could appoint only persons acceptable to a majority of Parliament; modern America: Senate approves high-level presidential appointments

   b. monarch: could not keep an army in peacetime; modern America: army is in existence at all times

   c. monarch could not suspend any laws without the consent of Parliament; modern America: the president can temporarily suspend some laws, must eventually gain the support of Congress

   d. Parliament was required to meet regularly. In modern America— Congress is in session at regular intervals.

   e. A Catholic could no longer become monarch; modern America: no religious restriction on the presidency

Chapter 18

PART ONE

page 69

(25 points)

A. 1. d
2. d
3. a
4. a
5. d

page 70

(20 points)

B. 6. f
7. c
8. e
9. b
10. h

(12 points)

C. 11. c
12. b
13. a
14. c

page 71

(12 points)

D. 15. c
16. c
17. a

---

page 69

Date

Chapter 18   Test

The Enlightenment

PART ONE

A. Write the letter of the best answer.

_____ 1. Enlightenment thinkers believed that the key to changing the world was

    a. force.
    b. optimism.
    c. tolerance.
    d. logical thought.

_____ 2. How did the French government and the pope respond to the *Encyclopédie*?

    a. They ignored it.
    b. They encouraged its publication.
    c. They contributed their thoughts to it.
    d. They tried to keep people from reading it.

_____ 3. Why was it difficult for monarchs who agreed with Enlightenment ideals to fulfill those ideals?

    a. The nobility resisted the loss of their favored positions.
    b. Their efforts were not taken seriously by their subjects.
    c. They did not have examples of enlightened government to follow.
    d. They did not understand the basic ideas of the Enlightenment thinkers.

_____ 4. The main cause of the French Revolution was anger over

    a. unfair taxes.
    b. food shortages.
    c. prison conditions.
    d. religious intolerance.

_____ 5. Which of the following did *not* contribute to the growth of industry in the late 1700s?

    a. new inventions
    b. industrial competition
    c. the availability of more workers
    d. traditional manufacturing methods

---

page 70

Date

B. Match each person with his or her description. You will not use all of the choices.

    a. Marie Antoinette   e. Mary Wollstonecraft
    b. Voltaire   f. Denis Diderot
    c. John Locke   g. Olyme de Gougese
    d. Jean-Jacques Rousseau   h. Moses Mendelssohn

_____ 6. published the first *Encyclopédie*

_____ 7. wrote that government was a contract between the people and their ruler

_____ 8. British writer who called for equal rights for women

_____ 9. used the pen to fight against censorship and individual freedom

_____ 10. sparked a reform movement within Judaism

C. Write the letter of the best answer.

_____ 11. The term **natural rights**, as used by Locke and the Enlightenment thinkers, refers to the idea that

    a. doing what is right comes naturally to people.
    b. the world of nature works in a fair and moral way.
    c. all people are born with certain rights that do not have to be earned.

_____ 12. The Enlightenment **philosophes** were people whose main interest was

    a. studying ancient civilizations.
    b. using ideas to improve the world.
    c. increasing people's respect for the law.

_____ 13. The practice of **enclosing** farm land was harmful to

    a. peasants.
    b. landowners.
    c. farm productivity.

_____ 14. The **checks and balances** system maintained a

    a. power base for the monarchy.
    b. banking resource for the colonists.
    c. balance of power between various branches of a government.

---

page 71

Date

D. Read the following excerpt from a letter from Thomas Jefferson to his daughter Martha. Use the excerpt and your knowledge of primary sources to answer the questions that follow.

> The conviction that you would be more improved in the situation I have placed you than if still with me has solaced [comforted] me on my parting with you, which my love for you has rendered [made] a difficult thing.
>
> With respect to the distribution of your time the following is what I should approve:
>
> from 8 to 10 o'clock practice music.
> from 10 to 1 dance one day and draw another.
> from 1 to 3 draw on the day you dance, and write a letter the next day.
> from 3 to 4 read French.
> from 4 to 5 exercise yourself in music.
> from 5 till bedtime read English, write &c. [etc.]
>
> I expect you will write to me by every post. Inform me what books you read, what tunes you learn, and inclose me your best copy of every lesson in drawing…

_____ 15. Which of the following is *not* something you can tell about Jefferson by reading this excerpt?

    a. He loved his daughter.
    b. He was somewhat bossy to his daughter.
    c. He was afraid that his daughter would disappoint him.

_____ 16. Which of the following is *not* an example of a primary source for a report on Thomas Jefferson?

    a. Jefferson's autobiography
    b. a letter from John Adams to Jefferson
    c. a book about Jefferson by a history professor at the University of Oregon

_____ 17. Which of the following is a good way to use primary sources?

    a. Use quotations from them.
    b. Use just one source for one report.
    c. Complete your report before looking for primary source materials.

---

page 72

Date

PART TWO

Answer the following questions.

1. How did Enlightenment philosophers view the individual and his or her importance in the world?

2. What are two things that the Enlightenment philosophers thought should be improved in society?

3. What is one clue contained in the Declaration of Independence that indicates that the American colonists were influenced by Enlightenment ideals?

4. How did the industrial revolution change people's lives?

Answer the following question on the back or on another sheet of paper. Use complete sentences.

5. How close do you think present-day American society comes to realizing the goals of the Enlightenment thinkers? Do you think people today should try to come closer to those goals? Explain.

PART TWO

(1-4, 6 points; 5, 7 points)

page 72

1. Answers should note that Enlightenment thinkers viewed the individual as quite important. Answers could refer to the dignity and potential of the individual and the belief that more power should be held by the individual.

2. Answers could include any two of the following:

a. limits on the government's power

b. the rights of the individual

c. freedom from censorship

d. religious freedom

e. tolerance

Other answers are acceptable if they are in agreement with basic ideals of the Enlightenment.

3. Students could note any of the following ideas:

a. people have certain inalienable rights

b. people have the right to freedom of speech and belief

c. people have the right to establish a government

d. government is "of the people, by the people, and for the people."

Other ideas from the Declaration are acceptable.

4. Answers could include the following:

a. More people worked in factories.

b. People's jobs were monotonous and dangerous.

c. Cities grew and pollution increased.

d. More manufactured goods were available.

5. Answers will vary but should note at least one way that present-day America reflects Enlightenment ideals. Most answers about whether people should still work to come closer to these ideals will indicate that they should. Support will vary but likely areas of concern include racial intolerance and poverty.